Collins German Dictionary

HarperCollins Publishers
Westerhill Road
Bishopbriggs
Glasgow
G64 2QT
Great Britain

Sixth Edition 2009

Reprint 10 9 8 7 6 5 4 3 2 1 0

ISBN 978-0-00-733150-5

Collins® is a registered trademark of HarperCollins Publishers Limited

www.collinslanguage.com

A catalogue record for this book is available from the British Library

Art Direction by Mark Thomson
Designed by Wolfgang Homola
Typeset by Davidson Publishing Solutions, Glasgow

Printed in India by Gopsons Papers Ltd

Acknowledgements
We would like to thank those authors and publishers who kindly gave permission for copyright material to be used in the Collins Word Web. We would also like to thank Times Newspapers Ltd for providing valuable data.

EDITORIAL MANAGEMENT
Gaëlle Amiot-Cadey

EDITORIAL COORDINATION
Susie Beattie

EDITORS
Horst Kopleck, Veronika Schnorr, Christine Bahr, Elizabeth Morris, Philip Mann, Martin Crellin, Elspeth Anderson, Carol McCann

CONCEPT DEVELOPMENT
Michela Clari
Ray Carrick

TECHNICAL SUPPORT
Thomas Callan

SERIES EDITOR
Rob Scriven

These help you choose the translation you want because they show how the translation they follow can be used.

5 Use the phrases given at the entry *'hard'* to help you translate: *'This bread is hard'*.

Words often have more than one meaning and more than one translation, for example, a **pool** can be a puddle, a pond or a swimming pool; **pool** can also be a game. When you are translating from English into German, be careful to choose the German word that has the particular meaning you want. The dictionary offers you a lot of help with this. Look at the following entry:

pool NOUN
1 die Pfütze *(puddle)*
2 der Teich (PL die Teiche) *(pond)*
3 das Schwimmbecken (PL die Schwimmbecken) *(for swimming)*
4 das Poolbillard *(game)*
□ Shall we have a game of pool? Sollen wir eine Partie Poolbillard spielen?
■ **the pools** *(football)* das Toto □ to do the pools Toto spielen

The underlining points out all the main translations, the numbers tell you that there is more than one possible translation and the words in brackets in *italics* help you choose which translation you want.

6 How would you translate '*I like playing pool*'?

Never take the first translation you see without looking at the others. Always look to see if there is more than one translation underlined.

Phrases in **bold type** preceded by a blue or black square / are phrases which are particularly common or important. Sometimes these phrases have a completely different translation from the main translation; sometimes the translation is the same. For example:

cancer NOUN
der Krebs (GEN des Krebses)
□ He's got cancer. Er hat Krebs.
■ **I'm Cancer.** Ich bin Krebs.

abgemacht ADJECTIVE
agreed
□ Wir trafen uns zur abgemachten Zeit. We met at the agreed time.
■ **Abgemacht!** OK!

When you look up a word, make sure you look beyond the main translations to see if the entry includes any **bold phrases**.

7 **Look up 'fahren' to help you translate the sentence 'Ich werde morgen mit dem Zug fahren'.**

Making use of the phrases in the dictionary

Sometimes when you look up a word you will find not only the word, but the exact phrase you want. For example, you might want to say '*What's the date today?*' Look up **date** and you will find the exact phrase and its translation.

Sometimes you have to adapt what you find in the dictionary. If you want to say '*I play darts*' and look up **dart** you will find:

dart NOUN
der Pfeil (PL die Pfeile)
■ **to play darts** Darts spielen

You have to substitute **ich spiele** for the infinitive form **spielen**. You will often have to adapt the infinitive in this way, adding the correct ending to the verb for **ich**, **du**, **er** etc and choosing the present, future or past form. For help with this, look at the German verb tables. On the **German-English** side of the dictionary, you will notice that verbs are followed by a number in square brackets, which correspond to verb tables on pages 22–38 in the middle section of this dictionary. **Spielen** is a regular verb so it follows the same pattern as verb number [48] **machen**, which is set out in full on page 34.

8 **How would you say *'We played football'*?**

Phrases containing nouns and adjectives also need to be adapted. You may need to make the noun genitive, plural or dative plural, or the adjective feminine, neuter or plural. Remember that some nouns have irregular genitive or plural forms and that this information is shown in the entry.

9 How would you say *'The red flowers are beautiful'*?

Don't overuse the dictionary

It takes time to look up words so try to avoid using the dictionary unnecessarily, especially in exams. Think carefully about what you want to say and see if you can put it another way, using the words you already know. To rephrase things you can:

> Use a word with a similar meaning. This is particularly easy with adjectives, as there are a lot of words which mean *good*, *bad*, *big* etc and you're sure to know at least one.

> Use negatives: if the cake you made was a total disaster, you could just say that it wasn't very good.

> Use particular examples instead of general terms. If you are asked to describe the sports *'facilities'* in your area, and time is short, you could say something like *'In our town there is a swimming pool and a football ground'*.

10 How could you say *'The Black Forest is huge'* without looking up the word *'huge'*?

You can also guess the meaning of a German word by using others to give you a clue. If you see the sentence *'ich lese ein gutes Buch'*, you may not know the meaning of the word **lese**, but you know it's a verb because it's preceded by **ich**. Therefore it must be something you can do to a book: **read.** So the translation is: *I'm reading a good book.*

11 Try NOT to use your dictionary to work out the meaning of the sentence 'Das Mädchen schreibt ihrer Brieffreundin einen Brief auf Deutsch'.

Parts of Speech

If you look up the word **flat**, you will see that there are two entries for this word as it can be a noun or an adjective. It helps to choose correctly between the entries if you know how to recognize these different types of words.

Nouns

Nouns often appear with words like *a, the, this, that, my, your* and *his*. They can be singular (abbreviated to SING in the dictionary):

his ***dog*** *her* ***cat*** *a* ***street***

or plural (abbreviated to PL in the dictionary):

the ***facts*** *those* ***people*** *his* ***shoes*** *our* ***holidays***

They can be the subject of a verb:

Vegetables *are good for you*

or the object of a verb:

I play ***tennis***

I bought my mother a box of chocolates.

12 **Which three words in this sentence are nouns?**

13 **Which of the nouns is plural?**

German nouns all start with a capital letter and can be either masculine, feminine or neuter (abbreviated to MASC, FEM or NEUT in the dictionary).

Masculine nouns are shown by **der**:

der *Hund* ***der*** *Zug* ***der*** *Arm*

Feminine nouns are shown by **die**:

die *Katze* ***die*** *Milch* ***die*** *Tür*

Neuter nouns are shown by **das**:

das *Auto* ***das*** *Kind* ***das*** *Sofa*

The plural form of **der**, **die** and **das** is **die**. The plural of most feminine German nouns is made by adding **en** or **n**:

die *Katze**n***   ***die*** *Tür**en***   ***die*** *Famili**en***

Many German nouns, however, do not add **en** or **n** in the plural, so the plural of these nouns is shown in the entry:

die Hunde   ***die Häuser***   ***die Autos***   ***die Wagen***   ***die Mütter***

In German **der**, **die** and **das** (and also **ein** and **eine**) may change when the noun they precede is used in another case, for example in the accusative, genitive or dative case (abbreviated to ACC, GEN and DAT in the dictionary). It is important to learn when you should use each case in German.

The **nominative** case is used to show the subject of a sentence – ***the dog*** is chasing the cat. All German nouns are shown in the nominative case in the dictionary:

Ich *esse ein Eis.*   ***Die Katze*** *schläft.*   ***Der Ball*** *ist im Garten.*

The **accusative** case is used to show the direct object of a sentence – I love ***chocolate*** – and after certain prepositions e.g. **durch**, **ohne**:

*Ich sehe **den Hund**.*   *Sie liebt **mich**.*   *Wir gingen durch **den Wald**.*

The **genitive** case is used to show that something belongs to somebody – my ***father's*** hat – and after certain prepositions e.g. **wegen**:

*das Auto **des Mannes***

*der Hund **meiner Mutter***

*wegen **des** schlechten **Wetters***

The **dative** case is used to show the indirect object of a sentence – she told ***me*** the news – and after certain prepositions e.g. **mit**, **aus**:

*Ich gebe **dem Lehrer** das Heft.*

*Er schreibt **mir** einen Brief.*

*Sie spielen mit **dem Ball**.*

The rules for the changes to **der**, **die**, **das**, **ein** and **eine** are shown here:

	MASC SING	FEM SING	NEUT SING	PL
NOM	der	die	das	die
ACC	den	die	das	die
GEN	des	der	des	der
DAT	dem	der	dem	den

	MASC SING	FEM SING	NEUT SING
NOM	ein	eine	ein
ACC	einen	eine	ein
GEN	eines	einer	eines
DAT	einem	einer	einem

Masculine and neuter singular German nouns usually add **-es** or **-s** when they are used in the genitive case:
des *Vater****s*** ***des*** *Hund****es*** ***des*** *Auto****s***

Feminine and plural German nouns do not change in the genitive:
der Mutter ***der Tür*** ***der Katzen*** ***der Männer***

Sometimes the genitive form is irregular, and this is shown in the entry:
des Jazz ***des Herrn*** ***des Abiturienten***

An **n** is added to the plural form of German nouns in the dative case, unless the plural form already ends in **-n**:
den *Kinder****n*** ***den*** *Häuser****n*** ***den*** *Katze****n*** ***den*** *Lehrerinne****n***

Ich gebe meinem Bruder ein Buch.

14 Which two words in the sentence are nouns – are they singular or plural?
15 What is the genitive form of 'Bruder'?
16 Use your dictionary to find the plural form of 'Buch'. Then work out the dative plural form.

Pronouns

Words like *I, me, you, he, she, him, her* and *they* are pronouns. They can be used instead of nouns. You can refer to a person as *he* or *she* or to a thing as *it.*

I showed her the new computer.

17 Which words are pronouns in this sentence?

Adjectives

Flat can be an adjective as well as a noun. Adjectives describe nouns: your tyre can be **flat**, you can have a pair of **flat** shoes.

I'm afraid of the dark.
The girl has dark hair.

18 In which sentence is '*dark*' an adjective?

German adjectives can be masculine, feminine or neuter, singular or plural. The ending of the adjective may also change depending on whether the noun is preceded by **ein**, **eine** etc or by **der**, **die** or **das**:

*der **kleine** Hund*	*ein **kleines** Kind*
***kleine** Kinder*	*die **kleinen** Katzen*

Adjectives are also affected by the case i.e. **nominative**, **accusative** etc of the noun they describe:

*des **kleinen** Hundes*	*der **kleinen** Katze*
*einem **kleinen** Mädchen*	*den **kleinen** Kindern*

The endings of German adjectives follow the rules shown here:

	MASC SING(DER)	FEM SING(DIE)	NEUT SING(DAS)	PL(DIE)
NOM	kleine	kleine	kleine	kleinen
ACC	kleinen	kleine	kleine	kleinen
GEN	kleinen	kleinen	kleinen	kleinen
DAT	kleinen	kleinen	kleinen	kleinen

	MASC SING(EIN)	FEM SING(EINE)	NEUT SING(EIN)	PL
NOM	kleiner	kleine	kleines	kleine
ACC	kleinen	kleine	kleines	kleine
GEN	kleinen	kleinen	kleinen	kleiner
DAT	kleinen	kleinen	kleinen	kleinen

Only the basic form of the adjective is shown in the dictionary. So, if you want to find out what kind of girls **die schönen Mädchen** are, look under **schön**.

Some adjectives, called **invariable adjectives**, don't change whether they are masculine, feminine, neuter or plural or describing a noun in a different case. This is shown in the dictionary:

pink ADJECTIVE
rosa
LANGUAGE TIP **rosa** is invariable.
□ a pink shirt ein rosa Hemd

19 What is the feminine accusative singular form of 'schwarz'?
20 What is the basic form of the adjective in the sentence 'Peter ist ein braves Kind'?

Verbs

She's going to record the programme for me.
His time in the race was a new world record.

Record is a verb in the first sentence, and a noun in the second.

One way to recognize a verb is that it frequently comes with a pronoun such as **I**, **you** or **she**, or with somebody's name. Verbs can relate to the present, the past or the future. They have a number of different forms to show this: **I'm going** (present), **he will go** (future), and **Nicola went** (past). Often verbs appear with **to**: **they promised to go**. This basic form of the verb is called the infinitive.

In this dictionary verbs are preceded by 'to', so you can identify them at a glance. No matter which of the four previous examples you want to translate, you should look up 'to **go**', not '**going**' or '**went**'. If you want to translate 'I **thought**', look up to '**think**'.

21 What would you look up to translate the verbs in these phrases?
*I **came** she**'s crying** they**'ve done** it he**'s** out*

Verbs have different endings in German, depending on whether you are talking about **ich**, **du**, **wir** etc: **ich mache**, **du machst**, **wir machen** etc. They also have different forms for the present, past (imperfect and perfect tenses), future etc: **wir machen** (*we do* = present), **wir machten** (*we did* = imperfect), **wir haben gemacht** (*we have done* = perfect), **wir werden machen** (*we will do* = future). **machen** is the infinitive and is the form that appears in the dictionary.

Sometimes the verb changes completely between the infinitive form and the **ich**, **du**, **er** etc form. For example, *to give* is **geben**, but *he gives* is **er gibt**, and **ich bin gegangen** comes from the verb **gehen** (*to go*).

On pages 28-38 of the dictionary, you will find tables of the most important forms of German verbs. And on pages 22-27 you will find a list of the most important forms of other German irregular verbs. Any irregular forms of verbs are also shown in the entry.

to **bowl** VERB
▷ *see also* **bowl** NOUN
werfen (PRESENT wirft, IMPERFECT warf, PERFECT hat geworfen) *(in cricket)*

heben (IMPERFECT **hob**, PERFECT **hat gehoben**)
VERB
to lift

22 Look up the dictionary to find the imperfect and perfect tenses of 'laufen'.

Adverbs

An adverb is a word which describes a verb or an adjective:
*Write **soon**.* *Check your work **carefully**.* *The film was **very** good.*

In the sentence '*The swimming pool is open daily*', **daily** is an adverb describing the adjective **open**. In the phrase '*my daily routine*', **daily** is an adjective describing the noun **routine**. We use the same word in English for both adjective and adverb forms, and the same word is used in German too. In many cases the same German word is used to translate an adjective and an adverb in English. Sometimes, however, the translations are different and you will need to know the difference between an adjective and an adverb to be able to choose the correct German translation.

Take the sentence *'The menu changes daily'*.

23 Is '*daily*' an adverb or an adjective here?

Prepositions

Prepositions are words like **for**, **with** and **across**, which are followed by nouns or pronouns:

*I've got a present **for** David.* *Come **with** me.* *He ran **across** the road.*

In German, all prepositions are followed by nouns or pronouns in a certain case, for example, **mit** is followed by nouns or pronouns in the dative case. The case which follows a preposition is shown in the entry:

ab PREPOSITION, ADVERB

LANGUAGE TIP The preposition **ab** takes the dative.

1 from

□ Kinder ab zwölf Jahren children from the age of twelve □ ab morgen from tomorrow

2 off

□ Die Straße geht nach links ab. The road goes off to the left. □ Der Knopf ist ab. The button has come off. □ Ab nach Hause! Off you go home!

■ **ab sofort** as of now

■ **ab und zu** now and then

above PREPOSITION, ADVERB

über

□ above forty degrees über vierzig Grad

LANGUAGE TIP Use the accusative to express movement or a change of place. Use the dative when there is no change of place.

□ He put his hands above his head. Er hielt die Hände über den Kopf. □ It's in the cupboard above the sink. Es ist im Schrank über der Spüle.

■ **the flat above** die Wohnung darüber

■ **mentioned above** oben erwähnt

■ **above all** vor allem

The party's over.

The shop's just over the road.

24 Which sentence shows a preposition followed by a noun?

25 What case does the preposition 'durch' take?

26 Use your dictionary to help you translate '*He is going into the garden*'.

Answers

1 the German side
2 on page 109
3 **Brötchen** comes first
4 the first (ADJECTIVE) entry
5 **Dieses Brot ist hart.**
6 **Ich spiele gern Poolbillard.**
7 **I'm going by train tomorrow.**
8 **Wir spielten Fußball.**
9 **Die roten Blumen sind schön.**
10 **Der Schwarzwald ist sehr groß.**
11 **The girl is writing a letter to her pen friend in German.**
12 **mother**, **box** and **chocolates** are nouns
13 **chocolates** is plural
14 **Bruder** and **Buch** are nouns – they are both singular
15 **Bruders**
16 **Bücher** – **Büchern** is the dative plural form
17 **I** and **her** are pronouns
18 in the second sentence
19 **schwarze**
20 **brav**
21 to **come**, to **cry**, to **do**, to **be**
22 the imperfect tense is **lief**, the perfect tense is **ist gelaufen**
23 **daily** is an adverb
24 the second sentence
25 **durch** takes the accusative case
26 **Er geht in den Garten.**

Aa

der **Aal** (PL die **Aale**) NOUN
eel

ab PREPOSITION, ADVERB

LANGUAGE TIP The preposition **ab** takes the dative.

1 from
□ Kinder ab zwölf Jahren children from the age of twelve □ ab morgen from tomorrow

2 off
□ Die Straße geht nach links ab. The road goes off to the left. □ Der Knopf ist ab. The button has come off. □ Ab nach Hause! Off you go home!
■ **ab sofort** as of now
■ **ab und zu** now and then

abbiegen (IMPERFECT **bog ab**, PERFECT **ist abgebogen**) VERB

1 to turn off
□ Sie bog an der Kreuzung nach links ab. At the crossroads she turned off to the left.

2 to bend
□ Die Hauptstraße biegt nach rechts ab. The main road bends to the right.

die **Abbildung** NOUN
illustration

abbrechen (PRESENT **bricht ab**, IMPERFECT **brach ab**, PERFECT **hat abgebrochen**) VERB [11]

1 to break off
□ Sie brach einen blühenden Zweig ab. She broke off a flowering branch.

2 to pull down
□ Das alte Gebäude muss abgebrochen werden. The old building will have to be pulled down.

3 to stop
□ Es ist schon spät, wir sollten abbrechen. It's late now; we ought to stop.

4 to abort
□ Das dauert zu lang, du solltest das Programm abbrechen. It's taking too long; you should abort the program.

abbuchen (PERFECT **hat abgebucht**) VERB [4]
to debit
□ Der Betrag wird von Ihrem Konto abgebucht. The amount will be debited from your account.

der **Abend** (PL die **Abende**) NOUN
evening
□ Sie macht jeden Abend einen Spaziergang. She goes for a walk every evening. □ guten Abend good evening
■ **zu Abend essen** to have dinner
■ **heute Abend** this evening

das **Abendbrot** NOUN
supper

das **Abendessen** (PL die **Abendessen**) NOUN
dinner
□ Zum Abendessen gibt es Spaghetti. There's spaghetti for dinner.

abends ADVERB
in the evening

das **Abenteuer** (PL die **Abenteuer**) NOUN
adventure

aber CONJUNCTION, ADVERB

1 but
□ Er wollte mit uns mitkommen, aber seine Eltern haben es nicht erlaubt. He wanted to come with us, but his parents wouldn't let him.

2 however
□ Ich möchte nach Ägypten reisen. Ich habe aber kein Geld. I'd like to go to Egypt. However, I haven't got any money.
■ **Das ist aber schön!** That's really nice.
■ **Nun ist aber Schluss!** Now that's enough!

abfahren (PRESENT **fährt ab**, IMPERFECT **fuhr ab**, PERFECT **ist abgefahren**) VERB [21]
to leave
□ Wir fahren morgen sehr früh ab. We're leaving very early tomorrow. □ Wann fährt dein Zug ab? When does your train leave?

die **Abfahrt** NOUN
departure

der **Abfall** (PL die **Abfälle**) NOUN
rubbish

der **Abfalleimer** (PL die **Abfalleimer**) NOUN
rubbish bin

abfällig ADJECTIVE
disparaging

abfliegen (IMPERFECT **flog ab**, PERFECT **ist abgeflogen**) VERB [25]
to take off
□ Die Maschine ist mit Verspätung abgeflogen. The plane was late taking off.
■ **Um wie viel Uhr fliegt ihr ab?** What time does your plane leave?

der **Abflug** (PL die **Abflüge**) NOUN
1 departure
□ Wir müssen eine Stunde vor Abflug am Flughafen sein. We have to be at the airport one hour before departure.
2 takeoff
□ Die Maschine stürzte kurz nach dem Abflug ab. The plane crashed shortly after takeoff.

abfragen (PERFECT **hat abgefragt**) VERB [4]
1 to test orally
□ die Vokabeln abfragen to give an oral vocabulary test
2 to call up
□ Sie können die Abfahrtszeiten am Computer abfragen. You can call up departure times on the computer.

das **Abführmittel** (PL die **Abführmittel**) NOUN
laxative

das **Abgas** (GEN des **Abgases**, PL die **Abgase**) NOUN
exhaust fumes

abgeben (PRESENT **gibt ab**, IMPERFECT **gab ab**, PERFECT **hat abgegeben**) VERB [28]
1 to hand in
□ Die Klassenarbeiten müssen am Ende der Stunde abgegeben werden. Tests must be handed in at the end of the lesson.
2 to pass
□ Er gab den Ball an den Mittelstürmer ab. He passed the ball to the centre-forward.
■ **sich mit jemandem abgeben** to associate with somebody
■ **sich mit etwas abgeben** to bother with something □ Mit solch dummen Fragen will ich mich nicht abgeben. I don't want to bother with such stupid questions.
■ **jemandem etwas abgeben** to let somebody have something

abgelegen ADJECTIVE
remote

abgemacht ADJECTIVE
agreed
□ Wir trafen uns zur abgemachten Zeit. We met at the agreed time.
■ **Abgemacht!** OK!

abgesehen ADJECTIVE
■ **es auf jemanden abgesehen haben** to be out to get somebody
■ **es auf etwas abgesehen haben** to be after something
■ **abgesehen von ...** apart from ...
□ Abgesehen von ein paar Fehlern war der Aufsatz sehr gut. The essay was very good, apart from a few mistakes.

abgewöhnen (PERFECT **hat abgewöhnt**) VERB [38]
■ **sich etwas abgewöhnen** to give something up □ Ich will mir das Rauchen abgewöhnen. I want to give up smoking.

der **Abhang** (PL die **Abhänge**) NOUN
slope

abhängen (1) (PERFECT **hat abgehängt**) VERB [4]
1 to take down
□ Weil ihr das Bild nicht mehr gefiel, hängte sie es ab. She took the picture down because she didn't like it any more.
2 to unhitch
□ Er hängte den Wohnwagen ab, bevor er in die Stadt fuhr. He unhitched the caravan before he drove into town.
3 to shake off
□ Den Räubern gelang es, die Polizei abzuhängen. The robbers managed to shake off the police.

abhängen (2) (IMPERFECT **hing ab**, PERFECT **hat abgehangen**) VERB [35]
■ **von jemandem abhängen** to depend on somebody
■ **von etwas abhängen** to depend on something □ Es hängt vom Wetter ab. It depends on the weather.

abhängig ADJECTIVE
■ **abhängig von** dependent on

abheben (IMPERFECT **hob ab**, PERFECT **hat abgehoben**) VERB
1 to answer
□ Es scheint niemand zu Hause zu sein, es hebt nämlich keiner ab. There doesn't seem to be anyone at home as nobody's answering the phone.
2 to withdraw
□ Ich muss Geld vom Sparbuch abheben. I'll have to withdraw some money from my savings account.
3 to take off
□ Wir sahen zu, wie das Flugzeug abhob. We watched the plane take off.
4 to lift off
□ Die Rakete hob senkrecht ab. The rocket lifted off vertically.
■ **sich von etwas abheben** to stand out against something □ Das Muster hebt sich gut vom Hintergrund ab. The pattern stands out well against this background.

abholen (PERFECT **hat abgeholt**) VERB [4]
1 to collect
□ Der Müll wird einmal in der Woche abgeholt. Rubbish is collected once a week.
2 to pick up
□ Ich hole dich um sieben ab. I'll pick you up at seven.

das **Abitur** NOUN
A levels

der **Abiturient** (GEN des **Abiturienten**, PL die **Abiturienten**) NOUN
A level student

die **Abiturientin** NOUN
A level student

abkürzen (PERFECT **hat abgekürzt**) VERB [36]
to abbreviate
□ Man kann 'bitte wenden' mit b. w. abkürzen. You can abbreviate 'please turn over' to PTO.
■ **den Weg abkürzen** to take a short cut

die **Abkürzung** NOUN
1 abbreviation
□ Die Abkürzung für Europäische Union ist EU. The abbreviation for European Union is EU.
2 short cut
□ Wir haben eine Abkürzung genommen. We took a short cut.

abladen (PRESENT **lädt ab**, IMPERFECT **lud ab**, PERFECT **hat abgeladen**) VERB
to unload

ablaufen (PRESENT **läuft ab**, IMPERFECT **lief ab**, PERFECT **ist abgelaufen**) VERB [43]
1 to expire
□ Ihr Pass ist leider abgelaufen. Unfortunately, your passport has expired.
2 to drain away
□ Der Abfluss ist verstopft, und deshalb läuft das Wasser nicht ab. The waste pipe is blocked, and that's why the water won't drain away.

ablehnen (PERFECT **hat abgelehnt**) VERB [4]
1 to turn down
□ Sie hat das Amt der Klassensprecherin abgelehnt. She turned down being class representative. □ Mein Antrag auf ein Stipendium wurde abgelehnt. My application for a grant was turned down.
2 to disapprove of
□ Ich lehne eine solche Arbeitseinstellung ab. I disapprove of such an attitude to work.

ablenken (PERFECT **hat abgelenkt**) VERB [4]
to distract
□ Lenk ihn nicht von seiner Arbeit ab. Don't distract him from his work.
■ **vom Thema ablenken** to change the subject

abliefern (PERFECT **hat abgeliefert**) VERB [88]
1 to drop off
□ Wir haben die Kinder wieder wohlbehalten zu Hause abgeliefert. We dropped the children off at home safe and sound.
2 to hand in
□ Bis wann musst du das Referat abliefern? When do you have to hand your assignment in by?
■ **etwas bei jemandem abliefern** to take something to somebody □ Wir haben die gefundene Uhr beim Fundbüro abgeliefert. We took the watch we found to the lost property office.

abmachen (PERFECT **hat abgemacht**) VERB [4]
1 to take off
□ Weißt du, wie man den Deckel abmacht? Do you know how to take the lid off?
2 to agree
□ Wir haben abgemacht, dass wir uns um sieben Uhr treffen. We agreed to meet at seven.
3 to sort out
□ Ihr solltet das untereinander abmachen, wer heute aufräumt. Sort out amongst yourselves who's going to clear up today.

die **Abmachung** NOUN
agreement

die **Abnahme** NOUN
decrease
□ eine weitere Abnahme der Teilnehmerzahlen a further decrease in attendance

abnehmen (PRESENT **nimmt ab**, IMPERFECT **nahm ab**, PERFECT **hat abgenommen**) VERB [52]
1 to remove
□ Bei diesem Auto kann man das Verdeck abnehmen. You can remove the hood on this car.
■ **Als das Telefon klingelte, nahm sie ab.** When the telephone rang, she answered it.
■ **jemandem etwas abnehmen** to take something away from somebody □ Ihr wurde der Führerschein abgenommen. They took away her driving licence.
2 to decrease
□ Die Zahl der Teilnehmer hat stark abgenommen. The number of participants has decreased dramatically.
3 to lose weight
□ Ich muss dringend abnehmen. I really must lose weight. □ Ich habe schon zwei Kilo abgenommen. I've already lost two kilos.
4 to buy
□ Wenn Sie mehr als zehn Stück abnehmen, bekommen Sie einen Rabatt. If you buy more than ten you get a discount. □ Hat sie dir diese Geschichte wirklich abgenommen? Did she really buy that story?

das **Abonnement** (PL die **Abonnements**) NOUN
subscription

abonnieren (PERFECT **hat abonniert**) VERB [76]
to subscribe to

abräumen (PERFECT **hat abgeräumt**) VERB [4]
to clear away
□ Sie räumte die Teller ab. She cleared away the plates.
■ **den Tisch abräumen** to clear the table

abreagieren (PERFECT **hat abreagiert**) VERB [4]
■ **etwas an jemandem abreagieren** to take something out on somebody
■ **sich abreagieren** to calm down

die **Abreise** NOUN
departure

abreisen (PERFECT **ist abgereist**) VERB [4]
to leave

Abs. ABBREVIATION (= *Absender*)
sender

die **Absage** NOUN
refusal

absagen (PERFECT **hat abgesagt**) VERB [4]
1 to call off
□ Die Vorstellung wurde abgesagt, weil ein Schauspieler krank war. The performance was called off because one of the actors was ill.
2 to turn down
□ eine Einladung absagen to turn down an invitation

der **Absatz** (GEN des **Absatzes**, PL die **Absätze**) NOUN
1 heel
□ Die Absätze von deinen Schuhen sind ganz schief. The heels of your shoes are worn down.
2 paragraph
□ Hier solltest du einen Absatz machen. You need to start a new paragraph here.
3 sales
□ Der Absatz an elektrischen Geräten ist gestiegen. Sales of electrical appliances have risen.

abschaffen (PERFECT **hat abgeschafft**) VERB [4]
1 to abolish
□ Wann wurde in Deutschland die Todesstrafe abgeschafft? When was the death sentence abolished in Germany?
2 to get rid of
□ Ich werde mein Auto abschaffen. I'm going to get rid of my car.

abscheulich ADJECTIVE
abominable

abschicken (PERFECT **hat abgeschickt**) VERB [4]
to send off

der **Abschied** (PL die **Abschiede**) NOUN
parting
■ **von jemandem Abschied nehmen** to say goodbye to somebody

der **Abschleppdienst** (PL die **Abschleppdienste**) NOUN
breakdown service

abschleppen (PERFECT **hat abgeschleppt**) VERB [4]
to tow
□ ein Auto abschleppen to tow a car
■ **jemanden abschleppen** to pick somebody up □ Paul hat auf der Party versucht, Petra abzuschleppen. Paul tried to pick Petra up at the party.

abschließen (IMPERFECT **schloss ab**, PERFECT **hat abgeschlossen**) VERB
1 to lock
□ Ich schließe meinen Schreibtisch immer ab. I always lock my desk.
2 to conclude
□ einen Vertrag abschließen to conclude a contract

abschließend ADJECTIVE, ADVERB
in conclusion
□ Abschließend möchte ich noch Folgendes sagen: ... In conclusion I would like to say this: ...

die **Abschlussprüfung** NOUN
final exam

abschneiden (IMPERFECT **schnitt ab**, PERFECT **hat abgeschnitten**) VERB [60]
1 to cut
□ Kannst du mir bitte eine Scheibe Brot abschneiden? Can you cut me a slice of bread, please?
2 to do
□ Sie hat in der Prüfung sehr gut abgeschnitten. She did very well in the exam.

abschrecken (PERFECT **hat abgeschreckt**) VERB [4]
to deter
□ Diese Maßnahmen sollen Jugendliche davon abschrecken, Drogen zu nehmen. These measures are intended to deter young people from taking drugs.

abschreiben (IMPERFECT **schrieb ab**, PERFECT **hat abgeschrieben**) VERB [61]
to copy
□ Er wurde dabei erwischt, wie er von seinem Nachbarn abgeschrieben hat. He was caught copying from his neighbour. □ Schreibt diesen Satz bitte in eure Hefte ab. Please copy this sentence into your exercise books.

absehbar ADJECTIVE
foreseeable
□ in absehbarer Zeit in the foreseeable future
■ **Das Ende ist absehbar.** The end is in sight.

abseits ADVERB
apart
□ Sie stand etwas abseits von den anderen. She was standing somewhat apart from the others.

der **Absender** (PL die **Absender**) NOUN
sender

absetzen (PERFECT **hat abgesetzt**) VERB [36]
1 to drop off
□ Ich setze dich am Bahnhof ab. I'll drop you off at the station.
2 to take off
□ Willst du nicht deinen Motorradhelm absetzen? Don't you want to take your helmet off?
3 to drop
□ Dieser Sprachkurs musste vom Programm abgesetzt werden. This language course has had to be dropped from the syllabus.
■ **die Pille absetzen** to stop taking the pill

die **Absicht** NOUN
intention

□ Das war nicht meine Absicht. That was not my intention.

■ **mit Absicht** on purpose

absichtlich ADJECTIVE, ADVERB
deliberate
□ eine absichtliche Beleidigung a deliberate insult
■ **etwas absichtlich tun** to do something deliberately

absolut ADJECTIVE, ADVERB
absolute
■ **Das ist absolut unmöglich.** That's absolutely impossible.
■ **Ich habe absolut keine Lust.** I really don't feel like it.

abspülen (PERFECT **hat abgespült**) VERB [4]
to rinse
□ Er spülte die Teller ab. He rinsed the plates.
■ **Geschirr abspülen** to wash up

der **Abstand** (PL die **Abstände**) NOUN
distance
□ Abstand halten to keep one's distance

abstellen (PERFECT **hat abgestellt**) VERB [4]
1 to put down
□ Der Koffer ist so schwer, ich muss ihn kurz abstellen. The case is so heavy that I'll have to put it down for a moment.
2 to park
□ Wir haben das Auto am Stadtrand abgestellt. We parked the car on the outskirts of town.
3 to switch off
□ Kannst du bitte das Radio abstellen? Can you switch the radio off, please?

die **Abstimmung** NOUN
vote

abstreiten (IMPERFECT **stritt ab**, PERFECT **hat abgestritten**) VERB
to deny

abstürzen (PERFECT **ist abgestürzt**) VERB [36]
1 to fall
□ Mathis ist beim Klettern abgestürzt. Mathis fell while climbing.
2 to crash
□ Die Maschine ist kurz nach dem Start abgestürzt. The plane crashed shortly after takeoff.

das **Abteil** (PL die **Abteile**) NOUN
compartment

die **Abteilung** NOUN
1 department
□ Sie wurde in eine andere Abteilung versetzt. She was transferred to another department.
2 ward
□ In welcher Abteilung liegt Mathis? Which ward is Mathis in?

die **Abtreibung** NOUN
abortion

abtrocknen (PERFECT **hat abgetrocknet**) VERB [53]
to dry

abwärts ADVERB
down

der **Abwasch** NOUN
washing-up
□ den Abwasch machen to do the washing-up

abwaschen (PRESENT **wäscht ab**, IMPERFECT **wusch ab**, PERFECT **hat abgewaschen**) VERB [89]
1 to wash
□ Wer muss heute das Geschirr abwaschen? Who's turn is it to wash the dishes today?
2 to wash off
□ Wasch dir mal die Soße vom Gesicht ab! Wash that gravy off your face.

das **Abwasser** (PL die **Abwässer**) NOUN
sewage

die **Abwechslung** NOUN
change
□ zur Abwechslung for a change

abwerten (PERFECT **hat abgewertet**) VERB [2]
to devalue

abwertend ADJECTIVE, ADVERB
derogatory
□ sich abwertend über etwas äußern to talk in a derogatory way about something

abwesend ADJECTIVE
absent

die **Abwesenheit** NOUN
absence

abwischen (PERFECT **hat abgewischt**) VERB [4]
to wipe
□ Er wischte die Tafel ab. He wiped the board.

abzählen (PERFECT **hat abgezählt**) VERB [4]
to count

das **Abzeichen** (PL die **Abzeichen**) NOUN
badge

abziehen (IMPERFECT **zog ab**, PERFECT **hat/ist abgezogen**) VERB [96]

LANGUAGE TIP For the perfect tense use **haben** when the verb has an object and **sein** when there is no object.

1 to take out
□ Er zog den Zündschlüssel ab. He took out the ignition key.
2 to withdraw
□ Sie haben ihre Truppen aus der Stadt abgezogen. They have withdrawn their troops from the town.
3 to deduct
□ Die Steuer wird vom Gehalt abgezogen. Tax is deducted from earnings.
■ **Er ist beleidigt abgezogen.** He went away in a huff.

abzüglich PREPOSITION

LANGUAGE TIP The preposition **abzüglich** takes the genitive.

less
□ das Gehalt abzüglich der Steuern earnings less tax

die **Achsel** NOUN
shoulder

acht NUMBER
▷ *see also* **die Acht** NOUN
eight
■ **acht Tage** a week

die **Acht** NOUN
▷ *see also* **acht** NUMBER
eight
□ Schreibe eine Acht. Write the figure eight.
■ **sich in Acht nehmen** to beware
□ Du solltest dich vor ihr in Acht nehmen! You should beware of her.
■ **etwas außer Acht lassen** to disregard something
■ **Acht geben** ▷ *see* **achtgeben**

achte ADJECTIVE
eighth
□ Sie wiederholte den Satz ein achtes Mal. She repeated the sentence for an eighth time.
□ Er kam als Achter. He was the eighth to arrive.

achten VERB [2]
to respect
□ Ich achte deine Meinung. I respect your opinion. □ Sie ist sehr geachtet. She's highly respected.
■ **auf etwas achten** to pay attention to something □ Du solltest auf die Verkehrsschilder achten. You should pay attention to the road signs.
■ **auf jemanden achten** to take notice of somebody □ Achte nicht auf ihn! Don't take any notice of him!

die **Achterbahn** NOUN
roller coaster

achtgeben (PRESENT **gibt acht**, IMPERFECT **gab acht**, PERFECT **hat achtgegeben**) VERB [28]
to pay attention
□ Du solltest etwas mehr auf die Rechtschreibung achtgeben! You should pay a bit more attention to spelling.
■ **auf jemanden achtgeben** to keep an eye on somebody □ Würden Sie mal bitte auf meinen Sohn achtgeben? Would you keep an eye on my son for a minute, please?
■ **Gib acht!** Look out!

achtmal ADVERB
eight times

die **Achtung** NOUN
respect
□ Ich habe große Achtung vor ihr. I've great respect for her.
■ **Achtung!** Look out!
■ **Achtung Stufe!** Mind the step.
■ **Achtung, Achtung, hier eine Durchsage!** Your attention, please. Here is an announcement.
■ **Alle Achtung!** Well done!

achtzehn NUMBER
eighteen

achtzig NUMBER
eighty

der **Acker** (PL die **Äcker**) NOUN
field

addieren (PERFECT **hat addiert**) VERB [76]
to add

der **Adel** NOUN
nobility

die **Ader** NOUN
vein

das **Adjektiv** (PL die **Adjektive**) NOUN
adjective

der **Adler** (PL die **Adler**) NOUN
eagle

adlig ADJECTIVE
noble

adoptieren (PERFECT **hat adoptiert**) VERB [76]
to adopt

die **Adoption** NOUN
adoption

die **Adoptiveltern** PL NOUN
adoptive parents

das **Adoptivkind** (PL die **Adoptivkinder**) NOUN
adopted child

die **Adresse** NOUN
address

adressieren (PERFECT **hat adressiert**) VERB [76]
to address
□ An wen soll ich den Brief adressieren? To whom should I address the letter?

der **Advent** NOUN
Advent

der **Adventskalender** (PL die **Adventskalender**) NOUN
Advent calendar

der **Adventskranz** (PL die **Adventskränze**) NOUN
Advent wreath

das **Adverb** (PL die **Adverbien**) NOUN
adverb

der **Affe** (GEN des **Affen**, PL die **Affen**) NOUN
monkey

Afrika NEUT NOUN
Africa
■ **aus Afrika** from Africa
■ **nach Afrika** to Africa

der **Afrikaner** (PL die **Afrikaner**) NOUN
African

die **Afrikanerin** NOUN
African

afrikanisch ADJECTIVE
African

Ägypten NEUT NOUN
Egypt
□ nach Ägypten to Egypt

der **Ägypter** (PL die **Ägypter**) NOUN
Egyptian

die **Ägypterin** NOUN
Egyptian

ägyptisch ADJECTIVE
Egyptian

ähneln VERB [34]
■ **jemandem ähneln** to resemble somebody
□ Sie ähnelt ihrer Mutter. She resembles her mother.
■ **Sie ähneln sich.** They are alike.

ahnen VERB [38]
1 to know
□ Ich habe geahnt, dass er nicht kommen würde. I knew he wouldn't come.
□ Das konnte ich doch nicht ahnen! How was I supposed to know that?
2 to sense
□ Das Tier hat die Gefahr geahnt und ist schnell verschwunden. The animal sensed the danger and quickly disappeared.

ähnlich ADJECTIVE
similar
□ Unsere Kleider sind sehr ähnlich. Our dresses are very similar.
■ **Sein Auto sieht ähnlich aus wie meines.** His car looks like mine.
■ **Er ist seinem Vater sehr ähnlich.** He's very like his father.
■ **Das sieht ihr ähnlich!** That's typical of her.

die **Ähnlichkeit** NOUN
similarity

die **Ahnung** NOUN
1 idea
□ Ich habe keine Ahnung, ob er kommt. I've no idea whether he's coming.
■ **Er hat von Computern keine Ahnung.** He doesn't know the first thing about computers.
2 hunch
□ Er hatte eine Ahnung, dass etwas Schlimmes geschehen würde. He had a hunch that something terrible would happen.

ahnungslos ADJECTIVE
unsuspecting

das **Aids** (GEN des **Aids**) NOUN
AIDS *(= Acquired Immune Deficiency Syndrome)*
□ Gerd ist an Aids gestorben. Gerd died of AIDS.

der **Akademiker** (PL die **Akademiker**) NOUN
university graduate

die **Akademikerin** NOUN
university graduate

akademisch ADJECTIVE
academic

der **Akkusativ** (PL die **Akkusative**) NOUN
accusative

die **Akne** NOUN
acne
□ Sie hat Akne. She's got acne.

die **Akte** NOUN
file
■ **etwas zu den Akten legen** to file something away

die **Aktentasche** NOUN
briefcase

die **Aktie** NOUN
share
□ in Aktien investieren to invest in shares

die **Aktion** NOUN
1 campaign
□ eine Aktion für den Frieden a campaign for peace
2 operation
□ Wir alle nahmen an der Aktion teil. We all took part in the operation.
■ **in Aktion treten** to go into action
LANGUAGE TIP Word for word, **in Aktion treten** means 'to step into action'.
□ In solchen Fällen tritt die Feuerwehr in Aktion. In cases like these, the fire brigade goes into action.

aktiv ADJECTIVE
active

die **Aktivität** NOUN
activity

aktuell ADJECTIVE
1 topical
□ ein aktuelles Thema a topical issue
2 up-to-date
□ ein aktueller Fahrplan an up-to-date timetable

der **Akzent** (PL die **Akzente**) NOUN
1 accent
□ Sie spricht mit einem amerikanischen Akzent. She speaks with an American accent.
2 emphasis
□ Der Akzent liegt auf Benutzerfreundlichkeit. The emphasis is on user-friendliness.

albern ADJECTIVE
silly
■ **sich albern benehmen** to act silly

der **Albtraum** (PL die **Albträume**) NOUN
nightmare

das **Album** (PL die **Alben**) NOUN
album

die **Algebra** NOUN
algebra

der **Alkohol** NOUN
alcohol

alkoholfrei ADJECTIVE
nonalcoholic

der **Alkoholiker** (PL die **Alkoholiker**) NOUN
alcoholic

die **Alkoholikerin** NOUN
alcoholic

alkoholisch ADJECTIVE
alcoholic

das **All** NOUN
space
□ Sie haben eine Rakete ins All geschossen. They've sent a rocket into space.

alle ADJECTIVE, PRONOUN
▷ *see also* **alles** PRONOUN

1 all the
□ Alle Schüler sollten kommen. All the pupils should come.
2 all
□ Nicht alle Afrikaner sind schwarz. Not all Africans are black.
3 all of them
□ Wir haben alle gesehen. We saw all of them.
■ **Sie kamen alle.** They all came.
■ **wir alle** all of us
■ **Ich habe alle beide eingeladen.** I've invited both of them.
4 every
□ alle vier Jahre every four years □ alle fünf Meter every five metres
■ **Die Milch ist alle.** The milk's all gone.
■ **etwas alle machen** to finish something up

die **Allee** (PL die **Alleen**) NOUN
avenue

allein ADJECTIVE, ADVERB, CONJUNCTION
1 alone
□ Sie lebt allein. She lives alone. □ Du allein kannst das entscheiden. You alone can decide.
2 on one's own
□ Sie hat das ganz allein geschrieben. She wrote that all on her own. □ Seit ich allein bin, habe ich mehr Zeit. Since I've been on my own, I've had more time.
■ **Er fühlt sich allein.** He feels lonely.
■ **nicht allein** not only

alleinstehend ADJECTIVE
single

LANGUAGE TIP Word for word, **alleinstehend** means 'standing alone'.

allerbeste ADJECTIVE
very best
□ Felix ist mein allerbester Schüler. Felix is my very best pupil.

allerdings ADVERB
1 though
□ Der Urlaub war schön, allerdings etwas kurz. The holiday was nice, though it was rather short.
2 certainly
□ Das ist allerdings schwierig. That's certainly difficult.

die **Allergie** NOUN
allergy

allergisch ADJECTIVE
allergic
□ Sie ist allergisch gegen Katzen. She's allergic to cats.

das **Allerheiligen** NOUN
All Saints' Day

DID YOU KNOW...?
Allerheiligen (November 1st) is a public holiday in those parts of Germany where most of the population are Roman Catholics.

allerlei ADJECTIVE
all sorts of
□ allerlei Sachen all sorts of things

allerletzte ADJECTIVE
very last
□ zum allerletzten Mal for the very last time

alles PRONOUN
▷ *see also* **alle** ADJECTIVE, PRONOUN
everything
□ Sie haben alles aufgegessen. They've eaten everything up.
■ **alles, was er sagt** everything he says
■ **alles in Allem** all in all
■ **Alles Gute!** All the best!

allgemein ADJECTIVE
general
■ **im Allgemeinen** in general

allmählich ADJECTIVE, ADVERB
1 gradual
□ eine allmähliche Besserung a gradual improvement
2 gradually
□ Es wird allmählich wärmer. It's gradually getting warmer.
■ **Allmählich solltest du das wissen.** You should know that by now.

der **Alltag** NOUN
everyday life

allzu ADVERB
all too
□ allzu oft all too often
■ **allzu viel** far too much

die **Alm** NOUN
alpine pasture

die **Alpen** PL NOUN
Alps

das **Alphabet** (PL die **Alphabete**) NOUN
alphabet

alphabetisch ADJECTIVE
alphabetical
□ alphabetisch geordnet arranged in alphabetical order

der **Alptraum** (PL die **Alpträume**) NOUN
nightmare

als CONJUNCTION
1 when
□ Als ich ein Kind war ... When I was a child ...
2 as
□ Sie kam, als ich gerade gehen wollte. She arrived as I was about to leave. □ Ich als Lehrerin weiß, ... As a teacher, I know ...
■ **gerade, als ...** just as ...
■ **als ob** as if □ Er tat, als ob er nichts bemerkt hätte. He acted as if he hadn't noticed anything.
3 than
□ Sie ist älter als ich. She's older than me.
□ Ich kam später als er. I came later than he did.
■ **lieber als ...** rather than ... □ Ich mag Süßes lieber als Salziges. I like sweet things rather than savoury things.
■ **nichts als Ärger** nothing but trouble

also ADVERB, CONJUNCTION, EXCLAMATION
1 then
□ Was sollen wir also tun? What shall we do, then? □ Du willst also nicht mit. You don't want to come along, then. □ Du hast es also gewusst. You did know then.
2 so
□ Es war schon spät, also bin ich nach Hause gegangen. It had got late, so I went home.
3 well
□ Also ich gehe jetzt! Well, I'm off now.
□ Also, Sie fahren immer geradeaus ... Well, keep going straight on ...
■ **Also gut!** Okay then.
■ **Also, so was!** Well really!
■ **Na also!** There you are then!

LANGUAGE TIP Be careful! The German word **also** does not mean **also**.

alt ADJECTIVE
old
□ Wie alt bist du? How old are you?
□ Felix ist zehn Jahre alt. Felix is ten years old.
□ Sein Auto ist älter als unseres. His car is older than ours.
■ **meine ältere Schwester** my elder sister
■ **alles beim Alten lassen** to leave everything as it was

der **Altar** (PL die **Altäre**) NOUN
altar

das **Alter** (PL die **Alter**) NOUN
1 age
□ In deinem Alter sollte man das wissen. You ought to know that at your age.
2 old age
□ Im Alter sind die Menschen oft einsam. People are often lonely in old age.
■ **im Alter von** at the age of

das **Altglas** (GEN des **Altglases**) NOUN
used glass

der **Altglascontainer** (PL die **Altglascontainer**) NOUN
bottle bank

altmodisch ADJECTIVE
old-fashioned

das **Altpapier** NOUN
waste paper

die **Altstadt** (PL die **Altstädte**) NOUN
old town

die **Alufolie** NOUN
tinfoil

das **Aluminium** NOUN
aluminium

am = an dem
■ **am fünften März** on the fifth of March
■ **am höchsten** the highest
■ **am schönsten** the most beautiful

die **Ameise** NOUN
ant

Amerika NEUT NOUN
America
■ **aus Amerika** from America
■ **in Amerika** in America
■ **nach Amerika** to America

der **Amerikaner** (PL die **Amerikaner**) NOUN
American

die **Amerikanerin** NOUN
American

amerikanisch ADJECTIVE
American

die **Ampel** NOUN
traffic lights
□ Die Ampel ist grün. The traffic lights are at green.

die **Amsel** NOUN
blackbird

das **Amt** (PL die **Ämter**) NOUN
office
□ Welches Amt ist für Kindergeld zuständig? Which office deals with child benefit?

amtlich ADJECTIVE
official

amüsant ADJECTIVE
amusing

amüsieren (PERFECT **hat amüsiert**) VERB [76]
to amuse
□ Diese Geschichte hat uns sehr amüsiert. The story amused us very much.
■ **sich amüsieren** to enjoy oneself □ Wir haben uns blendend amüsiert. We enjoyed ourselves immensely.

an PREPOSITION, ADVERB
▷ *see also* **am**

LANGUAGE TIP Use the accusative to express movement or a change of place. Use the dative when there is no change of place.

1 on
□ Das Wort stand an der Tafel. The word was written on the blackboard. □ Der Lehrer schrieb das Wort an die Tafel. The teacher wrote the word on the blackboard. □ Köln liegt am Rhein. Cologne is on the Rhine.
□ Christoph hat am neunten November Geburtstag. Christoph's birthday is on the ninth of November. □ an diesem Tag on this day
2 to
□ Er ging ans Fenster. He went to the window. □ Wir waren gestern am Meer. We went to the seaside yesterday. □ Wir wollen morgen ans Meer fahren. We want to go to the seaside tomorrow. □ Ich habe einen Brief an meine Mutter geschrieben. I've written a letter to my mother.
■ **eine Frage an dich** a question for you
■ **an diesem Ort** in this place
■ **unten am Fluss** down by the river
3 by
□ Ihr Haus liegt an der Autobahn. Their house is by the motorway.
■ **an Ostern** at Easter

■ **an etwas denken** to think of something
■ **reich an Nährstoffen** rich in nutrients
■ **an etwas sterben** to die of something
■ **an und für sich** actually □ Das ist an und für sich ganz einfach. Actually, it's quite simple.
■ **an die hundert** about a hundred
■ **von heute an** from today onwards
■ **Das Licht ist an.** The light's on.
■ **ohne etwas an** with nothing on

die **Ananas** (PL die **Ananas**) NOUN
pineapple

anbauen (PERFECT **hat angebaut**) VERB [4]
1 to build on
□ eine Garage ans Haus anbauen to build a garage onto the house
2 to cultivate
□ Reis anbauen to cultivate rice

anbei ADVERB
enclosed

anbieten (IMPERFECT **bot an**, PERFECT **hat angeboten**) VERB [8]
to offer
□ Ich bot ihr eine Tasse Kaffee an. I offered her a cup of coffee.
■ **anbieten, etwas zu tun** to volunteer to do something □ Er hat angeboten, mir beim Umzug zu helfen. He volunteered to help me move house.

der **Anblick** (PL die **Anblicke**) NOUN
sight

anbrechen (PRESENT **bricht an**, IMPERFECT **brach an**, PERFECT **ist/hat angebrochen**) VERB [11]

LANGUAGE TIP For the perfect tense use **haben** when the verb has an object and **sein** when there is no object.

1 to break into
□ Für den Kauf müsste ich meine Ersparnisse anbrechen. To buy it, I'd have to break into my savings.
2 to break
□ wenn der Tag anbricht when day breaks
3 to dawn
□ Ein neues Zeitalter ist angebrochen. A new age has dawned.

anbrennen (IMPERFECT **brannte an**, PERFECT **ist angebrannt**) VERB [12]
to burn
□ Der Kuchen ist angebrannt. The cake's burnt.

andauernd ADJECTIVE, ADVERB
1 continual
□ diese andauernden Unterbrechungen these continual interruptions
2 constantly
□ Er stört andauernd. He's constantly interrupting.

das **Andenken** (PL die **Andenken**) NOUN
1 memory
□ Zum Andenken an eine schöne Zeit. In memory of a wonderful time.
2 souvenir
□ Ich habe mir aus dem Urlaub einige Andenken mitgebracht. I brought a few souvenirs back from my holiday.

andere ADJECTIVE, PRONOUN
1 other
□ Nein, nicht dieses Buch, gib mir bitte das andere. No, not that book, please give me the other one.
2 different
□ Er hat jetzt eine andere Freundin. He's got a different girlfriend now.
3 another
□ ein anderes Mal another time □ Wir werden das an einem anderen Tag machen. We'll do that another day.
■ **kein anderer** nobody else
■ **die anderen** the others □ Martin ist noch da, die anderen sind schon gegangen. Martin's still here, the others have already left.
■ **etwas anderes** something else □ von etwas anderem sprechen to talk about something else

andererseits ADVERB
on the other hand
□ Einerseits ..., andererseits ... On the one hand ..., on the other hand ...

andermal ADVERB
■ **ein andermal** some other time

ändern VERB [88]
to alter
□ Ich habe das Kleid ändern lassen. I've had the dress altered.
■ **sich ändern** to change □ Sie hat sich in letzter Zeit sehr geändert. She's changed a lot recently. □ Wenn sich die Lage nicht ändert ... If the situation doesn't change ...

anders ADVERB
differently
□ So geht das nicht, du musst das anders machen. Not like that – you have to do it differently.
■ **anders als** different from □ Sie ist ganz anders als ihr Bruder. She's quite different from her brother. □ Sie hat das anders als ich übersetzt. She translated it differently from me.
■ **Wer anders?** Who else?
■ **jemand anders** somebody else
■ **irgendwo anders** somewhere else
■ **anders aussehen** to look different

anderthalb ADJECTIVE
one and a half

die **Änderung** NOUN
alteration

andeuten (PERFECT **hat angedeutet**) VERB [2]
to hint
□ Sie hat angedeutet, dass sie weiß, wer es war. She's hinted that she knows who it was.

die **Andeutung** NOUN
hint

□ Sie hat eine Andeutung gemacht, dass sie es weiß. She hinted that she knew.

anerkennend ADJECTIVE, ADVERB
appreciative

die **Anerkennung** NOUN
1 appreciation
□ Ihre Leistung fand nicht die entsprechende Anerkennung. Her work didn't get the appreciation it deserved.
2 recognition
□ Dieser neue Staat hofft auf Anerkennung durch die Bundesrepublik. This new country is hoping for recognition by the Federal Republic.

anfahren (PRESENT **fährt an**, IMPERFECT **fuhr an**, PERFECT **hat/ist angefahren**) VERB [21]
1 to hit
□ Er hat einen Fußgänger angefahren. He hit a pedestrian.
2 to start up
□ beim Anfahren when starting up

der **Anfall** (PL die **Anfälle**) NOUN
fit
□ Sie hatte einen epileptischen Anfall. She had an epileptic fit. □ Wenn er das erfährt, bekommt er einen Anfall. If he finds out, he'll have a fit.

der **Anfang** (PL die **Anfänge**) NOUN
beginning
□ von Anfang an right from the beginning □ am Anfang at the beginning □ Anfang Mai at the beginning of May
■ **zu Anfang** first

anfangen (PRESENT **fängt an**, IMPERFECT **fing an**, PERFECT **hat angefangen**) VERB [23]
1 to begin
□ Es fängt an zu regnen. It's beginning to rain.
2 to start
□ Der Film hat schon angefangen. The film's already started. □ Hast du den Aufsatz schon angefangen? Have you already started your essay?
■ **Damit kann ich nichts anfangen.** It doesn't mean anything to me.
■ **Das fängt ja gut an!** That's a good start!

der **Anfänger** (PL die **Anfänger**) NOUN
beginner

anfassen (PERFECT **hat angefasst**) VERB [31]
1 to touch
□ Fass den Hund besser nicht an! You'd better not touch the dog.
2 to treat
□ Du solltest die Kinder nicht immer so rau anfassen! You shouldn't treat the children so roughly.
■ **mit anfassen** to lend a hand □ Kannst du mal mit anfassen, den Schrank wegzuschieben? Can you lend a hand shifting this cupboard to one side?
■ **sich anfassen** to feel □ Samt fühlt sich weich an. Velvet feels soft.

sich **anfreunden** (PERFECT **hat sich angefreundet**) VERB [4]
1 to make friends
□ Ich habe mich in den Ferien mit einer Engländerin angefreundet. I made friends with an English girl during the holidays.
2 to become friends
□ Die beiden haben sich angefreundet. The two of them have become friends.

anfühlen (PERFECT **hat angefühlt**) VERB [4]
to feel
□ Fühl mal meine Stirn an, ich glaube, ich habe Fieber. Feel my forehead, I think I've got a temperature. □ Der Stoff fühlt sich weich an. The material feels soft.

die **Angabe** NOUN
1 information
□ Die Angaben waren falsch. The information was wrong.
2 serve *(tennis)*
□ Wer hat Angabe? Whose serve is it?
■ **Das ist doch alles nur Angabe!** That's nothing but show.

angeben (PRESENT **gibt an**, IMPERFECT **gab an**, PERFECT **hat angegeben**) VERB [28]
1 to give
□ Geben Sie bitte Ihre Personalien an. Please give your personal details.
2 to state
□ Sie hat angegeben, dass sie zu dem Zeitpunkt zu Hause war. She stated that she was at home at the time.
3 to indicate
□ Alle Raststätten sind auf der Karte angegeben. All service areas are indicated on the map.
4 to show off
□ Glaub ihm kein Wort, er gibt nur an. Don't believe a word he says – he's just showing off.

der **Angeber** (PL die **Angeber**) NOUN
show-off

angeblich ADJECTIVE, ADVERB
1 alleged
□ Sie ist die angebliche Täterin. She's the alleged culprit.
2 allegedly
□ Angeblich hat sie es getan. Allegedly, she did it.

das **Angebot** (PL die **Angebote**) NOUN
offer
□ Ich nehme dein Angebot an. I accept your offer.
■ **ein Angebot an etwas** a selection of something □ Das Kaufhaus hat ein großes Angebot an Kleidern. The department store has a large selection of dresses.
■ **Angebot und Nachfrage** supply and demand

angehen (IMPERFECT **ging an**, PERFECT **hat/ist angegangen**) VERB [29]

LANGUAGE TIP For the perfect tense use **haben** when the verb has an object and **sein** when there is no object.

1 to concern

□ Diese Angelegenheit geht mich nichts an. This matter doesn't concern me.

■ **Was geht dich das an?** What business is it of yours?

2 to tackle

□ Ich weiß noch nicht so richtig, wie ich das Thema angehen soll. I'm not really sure how to tackle the subject.

3 to go on

□ Das Licht ging an. The light went on.

■ **was ... angeht** as regards ... □ Was die Ferien angeht, haben wir noch nichts entschieden. As regards the holidays, we still haven't decided anything.

der/die **Angehörige** (GEN des/der **Angehörigen**, PL die **Angehörigen**) NOUN

relative

□ Er ist ein Angehöriger von mir. He's a relative of mine.

die **Angel** NOUN

1 fishing rod

2 hinge *(of door)*

LANGUAGE TIP Be careful! The German word **Angel** does not mean **angel**.

die **Angelegenheit** NOUN

1 matter

□ Ich werde diese Angelegenheit prüfen. I'll look into the matter.

2 affair

□ Das ist meine Angelegenheit. That's my affair.

angeln VERB [34]

1 to catch

□ Er hat eine große Forelle geangelt. He caught a large trout.

2 to fish

□ Sonntags geht Alex immer angeln. Alex always goes fishing on Sundays.

angenehm ADJECTIVE, ADVERB

pleasant

■ **Angenehm!** Pleased to meet you.

angesehen ADJECTIVE

respected

der/die **Angestellte** (GEN des/der **Angestellten**, PL die **Angestellten**) NOUN

employee

□ Er ist nur ein kleiner Angestellter. He's just a lowly employee.

angewiesen ADJECTIVE

■ **auf jemanden angewiesen sein** to be dependent on somebody

■ **auf etwas angewiesen sein** to be dependent on something

angewöhnen (PERFECT **hat angewöhnt**) VERB [38]

■ **jemandem etwas angewöhnen** to teach somebody something □ Sie sollten Ihrem Sohn bessere Manieren angewöhnen. You ought to teach your son better manners.

■ **sich etwas angewöhnen** to get into the habit of doing something □ Ich habe es mir angewöhnt, jeden Morgen um sieben Uhr aufzustehen. I've got into the habit of getting up at seven every morning.

die **Angewohnheit** NOUN

habit

□ Das ist so eine Angewohnheit von ihr. That's a habit of hers.

angreifen (IMPERFECT **griff an**, PERFECT **hat angegriffen**) VERB

1 to attack

□ Ich wurde von einem Hund angegriffen. I was attacked by a dog.

2 to criticize

□ Sie wurde wegen dieser Aussage von ihren Freunden angegriffen. She was criticized by her friends for what she said.

der **Angriff** (PL die **Angriffe**) NOUN

attack

■ **etwas in Angriff nehmen** to make a start on something

die **Angst** (PL die **Ängste**) NOUN

fear

■ **vor jemandem Angst haben** to be afraid of somebody

■ **vor etwas Angst haben** to be afraid of something

■ **Ich habe Angst vor der Prüfung.** I'm worried about the exam.

■ **Angst um jemanden haben** to be worried about somebody

■ **jemandem Angst machen** to scare somebody

ängstlich ADJECTIVE, ADVERB

1 scared

□ Nun sei doch nicht so ängstlich, der Hund tut dir nichts! There's no need to be scared, the dog won't harm you.

2 anxious

□ 'Wird er wieder gesund?', fragte sie ängstlich. 'Will he get well again?', she asked anxiously.

anhaben (PRESENT **hat an**, IMPERFECT **hatte an**, PERFECT **hat angehabt**) VERB [32]

to have on

□ Sie hatte heute das rote Kleid an. She had her red dress on today.

■ **jemandem nichts anhaben können** to have nothing on somebody □ Ich bin unschuldig, die Polizei kann mir nichts anhaben. I'm innocent, the police have got nothing on me.

anhalten (PRESENT **hält an**, IMPERFECT **hielt an**, PERFECT **hat angehalten**) VERB [33]

1 to stop

□ Können wir bitte anhalten, mir ist schlecht. Can we stop please? I feel sick. □ Kannst du bitte das Auto anhalten? Can you stop the car please?

2 to last
□ Das wird nicht lange anhalten. It won't last long.
■ **die Luft anhalten** to hold one's breath

der **Anhalter** (PL die **Anhalter**) NOUN
hitchhiker
■ **per Anhalter fahren** to hitchhike

anhand PREPOSITION
LANGUAGE TIP The preposition **anhand** takes the genitive.
with the help of
□ Wir werden das anhand der Unterlagen prüfen. We'll check that with the help of the documents.

der **Anhang** (PL die **Anhänge**) NOUN
appendix

der **Anhänger** (PL die **Anhänger**) NOUN
1 supporter
□ Er ist Anhänger von Schalke. He's a Schalke supporter.
2 trailer *(on car)*
3 label
□ Mach einen Anhänger mit deinem Namen und deiner Adresse an deinen Koffer. Put a label with your name and address on your case.
4 pendant
□ Sie trug eine Kette mit Anhänger. She was wearing a chain with a pendant.

die **Anhängerin** NOUN
supporter
□ Sie ist Anhängerin von Schalke. She's a Schalke supporter.

anhören (PERFECT **hat angehört**) VERB [4]
to listen to
□ Wir haben CDs angehört. We listened to CDs.
■ **jemandem etwas anhören** to hear something in somebody's voice □ Man hat ihr ihre Aufregung angehört. You could hear the excitement in her voice.
■ **sich anhören** to sound □ Der Vorschlag hört sich gut an. That sounds a good suggestion.

der **Anker** (PL die **Anker**) NOUN
anchor

die **Ankleidekabine** NOUN
changing cubicle

anklicken (PERFECT **hat angeklickt**) VERB [4]
to click on *(computer)*
□ ein Icon anklicken to click on an icon

ankommen (IMPERFECT **kam an**, PERFECT **ist angekommen**) VERB [40]
to arrive
□ Wir kommen morgen Nachmittag an. We'll arrive tomorrow afternoon. □ Ist der Brief schon angekommen? Has the letter arrived yet?
■ **bei jemandem gut ankommen** to go down well with somebody □ Das Stück ist bei den Zuschauern gut angekommen. The play went down well with the audience.
■ **bei jemandem schlecht ankommen** to go down badly with somebody □ Der Witz ist offensichtlich schlecht angekommen. The joke clearly went down badly.
■ **es kommt darauf an** it depends □ Es kommt darauf an, wie das Wetter ist. It depends what the weather's like.
■ **wenn es darauf ankommt ...** when it really matters ...
■ **es darauf ankommen lassen** to wait and see

ankreuzen (PERFECT **hat angekreuzt**) VERB [36]
to mark with a cross

ankündigen (PERFECT **hat angekündigt**) VERB [4]
to announce

die **Ankunft** (PL die **Ankünfte**) NOUN
arrival

die **Anlage** NOUN
1 gardens
□ Wir sind in der Anlage spazieren gegangen. We went for a walk in the gardens.
2 plant
□ Das ist eine neuartige Anlage zum Recycling von Kunststoff. That's a new plastics recycling plant.
3 investment
□ Wir raten zu einer Anlage in Immobilien. We would advise investment in real estate.

der **Anlass** (GEN des **Anlasses**, PL die **Anlässe**) NOUN
occasion
□ ein festlicher Anlass a festive occasion
■ **ein Anlass zu etwas** cause for something □ Das ist ein Anlass zum Feiern. That's cause for celebration.
■ **aus Anlass** on the occasion of □ Aus Anlass ihres fünfzigsten Geburtstags ... On the occasion of her fiftieth birthday ...
■ **Anlass zu etwas geben** to give cause for something □ Ihr Sohn gibt keinen Anlass zu Klagen. Your son doesn't give cause for complaint.

der **Anlasser** (PL die **Anlasser**) NOUN
starter *(of car)*

die **Anleitung** NOUN
instructions

der **Anlieger** (PL die **Anlieger**) NOUN
resident
□ 'Anlieger frei' 'residents only'

anmachen (PERFECT **hat angemacht**) VERB [4]
1 to put on
□ Mach bitte das Licht an. Please put the light on.
2 to light
□ Wir haben ein Feuer angemacht. We lit a fire.

3 to dress
□ Sie macht den Salat immer mit Zitrone an. She always dresses her salads with lemon.
4 to chat up
□ Ich glaube, der Typ versucht, dich anzumachen. I think that bloke is trying to chat you up.

anmelden (PERFECT **hat angemeldet**) VERB [54]
1 to announce
□ Sie hat für morgen ihren Besuch angemeldet. She's announced that she'll visit us tomorrow.
■ **jemanden anmelden 1** to make an appointment for somebody □ Er hat seinen Sohn für morgen beim Zahnarzt angemeldet. He's made a dental appointment for his son for tomorrow. **2** to put somebody's name down □ Habt ihr Max schon im Gymnasium angemeldet? Have you already put Max's name down for grammar school?
■ **sich anmelden 1** to make an appointment □ Ich muss mich beim Zahnarzt anmelden. I must make an appointment with the dentist. **2** to put one's name down □ Sie hat sich für einen Judokurs angemeldet. She's put her name down for a judo course.
2 to report
□ Alle Besucher müssen sich beim Pförtner anmelden. All visitors must report to the gatehouse.
3 to register
□ Haben Sie sich schon beim Einwohnermeldeamt angemeldet? Have you already registered with the residents' registration office?

DID YOU KNOW...?
Anyone moving to a new address in Germany is required by law to register (**sich anmelden**) at the residents' registration office (**Einwohnermeldeamt**).

die **Anmeldung** NOUN
registration
□ Schluss für Anmeldungen ist der erste Mai. The deadline for registrations is the first of May.

annehmen (PRESENT **nimmt an**, IMPERFECT **nahm an**, PERFECT **hat angenommen**) VERB [1]
1 to accept
□ Sie wollte das Geschenk nicht annehmen. She didn't want to accept the present.
□ Danke für die Einladung, ich nehme gerne an. Thank you for the invitation, which I'm happy to accept.
2 to take
□ Er hat den Namen seiner Frau angenommen. He took his wife's name.
■ **ein Kind annehmen** to adopt a child
3 to believe
□ Die Polizei nimmt an, dass er der Täter war. The police believe he did it.
4 to suppose
□ Nehmen wir einmal an, es wäre so. Let's suppose that was the case.
■ **angenommen ...** supposing ...
□ Angenommen, er kommt nicht. Supposing he doesn't come.

anordnen (PERFECT **hat angeordnet**) VERB [53]
1 to arrange
□ Er ordnete die Blumen zu einem hübschen Gesteck an. He arranged the flowers into a pretty bouquet.
2 to order
□ Wer hat das angeordnet? Who ordered that?

anprobieren (PERFECT **hat anprobiert**) VERB [76]
to try on

die **Anrede** NOUN
form of address
□ Für verheiratete und unverheiratete Frauen benutzt man die Anrede 'Frau'. 'Frau' is the form of address used for married and unmarried women.

der **Anruf** (PL die **Anrufe**) NOUN
phone call

der **Anrufbeantworter** (PL die **Anrufbeantworte**) NOUN
answering machine

anrufen (IMPERFECT **rief an**, PERFECT **hat angerufen**) VERB [56]
to phone
□ Hat jemand angerufen? Did anyone phone?
□ Ich muss mal eben meine Eltern anrufen. I must just phone my parents.

ans = **an das**

anschalten (PERFECT **hat angeschaltet**) VERB [2]
to switch on

anschauen (PERFECT **hat angeschaut**) VERB [4]
1 to look at
□ Schau mich an! Look at me. □ Willst du dir mal die Fotos anschauen? Do you want to look at the photos?
2 to see
□ Den Film will ich mir unbedingt anschauen. I must go and see that film.

anscheinend ADVERB
apparently

der **Anschlag** (PL die **Anschläge**) NOUN
1 notice
□ Sie machte einen Anschlag am Schwarzen Brett. She put a notice on the notice board.
2 attack
□ Es gab einen Anschlag auf den Präsidenten. There's been an attack on the President.

anschließen (IMPERFECT **schloss an**, PERFECT **hat angeschlossen**) VERB
to connect
□ Das Telefon ist noch nicht angeschlossen. The telephone hasn't been connected yet.

■ **sich jemandem anschließen** to join somebody □ Wir gehen ins Kino, willst du dich uns nicht anschließen? We're going to the cinema. Won't you join us?
■ **Ich schließe mich dieser Meinung an.** I endorse this view.

anschließend ADJECTIVE, ADVERB
1 subsequent
□ die daran anschließende Diskussion the subsequent discussion
2 adjacent
□ das anschließende Grundstück the adjacent plot of land
3 afterwards
□ Wir waren essen, und anschließend sind wir ins Kino gegangen. We had a meal and afterwards went to the cinema.

der **Anschluss** (GEN des **Anschlusses**, PL die **Anschlüsse**) NOUN
connection
□ Sie haben Anschluss an einen Zug nach Paris. You have a connection with a train to Paris.
■ **im Anschluss an** following □ Im Anschluss an die Ansprache findet ein Empfang statt. Following the speech there will be a reception.
■ **Anschluss finden** to make friends

LANGUAGE TIP Word for word, **Anschluss finden** means 'to find a connection'.

□ Sie hat in der neuen Klasse schnell Anschluss gefunden. She quickly made friends in her new class.

sich **anschnallen** (PERFECT **hat sich angeschnallt**) VERB [4]
to fasten one's seat belt

die **Anschrift** NOUN
address

ansehen (PRESENT **sieht an**, IMPERFECT **sah an**, PERFECT **hat angesehen**) VERB [64]
▹ *see also* **das Ansehen** NOUN
1 to look at
□ Sieh mich an! Look at me. □ Willst du dir mal die Fotos ansehen? Do you want to look at the photos?
2 to see
□ Den Film will ich mir unbedingt ansehen. I must go and see that film. □ Man hat ihr ihre Enttäuschung angesehen. You could see the disappointment in her face.
3 to regard
□ Sie wird als eine Expertin auf diesem Gebiet angesehen. She's regarded as an expert in this field.
■ **Sieh mal einer an!** Well, fancy that!

das **Ansehen** NOUN
▹ *see also* **ansehen** VERB
1 respect
□ Sie genießt großes Ansehen bei ihren Kollegen. She enjoys great respect among her colleagues.
2 reputation
□ Ein solches Benehmen könnte unserem Ansehen schaden. Behaviour like that could damage our reputation.

die **Ansicht** NOUN
view
□ eine Postkarte mit der Ansicht des Matterhorns a postcard with a view of the Matterhorn □ Wenn Sie meine Ansicht in dieser Sache hören wollen ... If you want to hear my view on this business ... □ meiner Ansicht nach in my view
■ **zur Ansicht** on approval

die **Ansichtskarte** NOUN
picture postcard

ansprechen (PRESENT **spricht an**, IMPERFECT **sprach an**, PERFECT **hat angesprochen**) VERB [70]
1 to approach
□ Mich hat ein wildfremder Mann angesprochen. I was approached by a complete stranger.
2 to appeal to
□ Diese Art von Malerei spricht mich nicht an. This style of painting doesn't appeal to me.
3 to ask
□ Ich werde Herrn Arnold ansprechen, ob er uns vielleicht hilft. I'll ask Mr Arnold if he'll maybe help us.
4 to mention
□ Sie hat dieses Problem bis jetzt noch nicht angesprochen. She hasn't mentioned this problem yet.
■ **auf etwas ansprechen** to respond to something □ Der Patient spricht auf die Medikamente nicht an. The patient isn't responding to the drugs.

der **Anspruch** (PL die **Ansprüche**) NOUN
demand
□ Sie war den Ansprüchen ihres Berufs nicht gewachsen. She wasn't up to the demands of her job.
■ **hohe Ansprüche haben** to demand a lot
■ **hohe Ansprüche an jemanden stellen** to demand a lot of somebody
■ **Anspruch auf etwas haben** to be entitled to something □ Ich habe Anspruch auf eine Erklärung. I'm entitled to an explanation.
■ **etwas in Anspruch nehmen** to take advantage of something □ Wir sollten dieses Angebot in Anspruch nehmen. We should take advantage of this offer.
■ **Ihr Beruf nimmt sie sehr in Anspruch.** Her job's very demanding.

anständig ADJECTIVE
decent
□ ein anständiges Essen a decent meal
■ **sich anständig benehmen** to behave oneself

anstatt PREPOSITION, CONJUNCTION

LANGUAGE TIP The preposition **anstatt** takes the genitive.

instead of

□ Sie kam anstatt ihres Bruders. She came instead of her brother.

anstecken (PERFECT **hat angesteckt**) VERB [4]

■ **Er hat die halbe Klasse mit seiner Grippe angesteckt.** He gave half the class his flu.

■ **Lachen steckt an.** Laughter is infectious.

■ **sich anstecken** to catch something □ Pass auf, dass du dich nicht ansteckst. Be careful you don't catch anything. □ Ich habe mich bei ihm angesteckt. I caught it from him.

ansteckend ADJECTIVE

infectious

□ eine ansteckende Krankheit an infectious disease

anstelle PREPOSITION

LANGUAGE TIP The preposition **anstelle** takes the genitive.

instead of

□ Anstelle der Mutter hat seine Tante unterschrieben. His aunt has signed instead of his mother. □ Pralinen anstelle von Blumen chocolates instead of flowers

anstellen (PERFECT **hat angestellt**) VERB [4]

1 to turn on

□ Kannst du mal bitte den Fernseher anstellen? Can you turn the television on, please?

2 to employ

□ Sie ist bei einem Versandhaus angestellt. She's employed by a mail-order company.

3 to do

□ Wie soll ich es bloß anstellen, dass er es erlaubt? What can I do to get him to allow it? □ Was stellen wir denn heute Nachmittag an? What shall we do this afternoon?

4 to be up to

□ Was hat der Lümmel denn schon wieder angestellt? What has that rascal been up to this time?

■ **sich anstellen** **1** to queue □ Musstet ihr euch für die Karten lange anstellen? Did you have to queue for long for the tickets? **2** to act □ Sie hat sich wirklich dumm angestellt. She acted really stupidly.

■ **Stell dich nicht so an.** Don't make such a fuss.

anstrengen (PERFECT **hat angestrengt**) VERB [4]

■ **Die Reise hat mich sehr angestrengt.** The journey took a lot out of me.

■ **Streng deinen Kopf an!** Use your head!

■ **sich anstrengen** to make an effort

anstrengend ADJECTIVE

tiring

die **Anstrengung** NOUN

effort

die **Antarktis** NOUN

the Antarctic

□ in der Antarktis in the Antarctic

der **Anteil** (PL die **Anteile**) NOUN

share

□ Ich möchte meinen Anteil am Gewinn haben. I would like to have my share of the profit.

■ **Anteil nehmen an** to sympathize with □ Ich nehme Anteil an deinem Pech. I sympathize with you in your bad luck.

die **Antenne** NOUN

aerial

antiautoritär ADJECTIVE

anti-authoritarian

das **Antibiotikum** (PL die **Antibiotika**) NOUN

antibiotic

antik ADJECTIVE

antique

die **Antiquitäten** FEM PL NOUN

antiques

der **Antrag** (PL die **Anträge**) NOUN

1 application

□ Sie stellte einen Antrag auf Arbeitslosenunterstützung. She put in an application for unemployment benefit.

2 motion

□ der Antrag der Opposition the motion put by the opposition

antun (IMPERFECT **tat an**, PERFECT **hat angetan**) VERB [81]

■ **jemandem etwas antun** to do something to somebody □ Das kannst du deinen Eltern nicht antun! You can't do that to your parents.

■ **jemandem ein Unrecht antun** to wrong somebody □ Uns ist ein großes Unrecht angetan worden. We've been cruelly wronged.

■ **sich Zwang antun** to force oneself □ Tu dir keinen Zwang an! Don't force yourself!

■ **sich etwas antun** to kill oneself □ Wenn ich durchfalle, dann tue ich mir was an. If I fail, I'll kill myself.

die **Antwort** NOUN

answer

□ jemandem eine Antwort geben to give somebody an answer

antworten VERB [2]

to answer

□ Antworte bitte! Please answer.

■ **auf etwas antworten** to answer something □ Sie konnte auf diese Frage nicht antworten. She couldn't answer the question.

■ **jemandem antworten** to answer somebody □ Wo warst du? Antworte mir gefälligst! Where have you been? Answer me, will you!

der **Anwalt** (PL die **Anwälte**) NOUN
lawyer

die **Anwältin** NOUN
lawyer

die **Anweisung** NOUN
instruction
□ Folgen Sie bitte den Anweisungen Ihres Führers. Please follow your guide's instructions. □ Anweisung haben, etwas zu tun to have instructions to do something

anwenden (IMPERFECT **wendete** *or* **wandte an**, PERFECT **hat angewendet** *or* **angewandt**) VERB
1 to use
□ Welche Software wenden Sie an? What software do you use?
□ Gewalt anwenden to use violence
2 to apply *(law, rule)*

anwesend ADJECTIVE
present

die **Anwesenheit** NOUN
presence

die **Anzahl** NOUN
number
□ je nach Anzahl der Teilnehmer according to the number of participants □ eine große Anzahl an Fehlern a large number of mistakes

anzahlen (PERFECT **hat angezahlt**) VERB [4]
■ **fünfzig Euro anzahlen** to pay fifty euros deposit
■ **ein Auto anzahlen** to put down a deposit on a car

die **Anzahlung** NOUN
deposit
□ eine Anzahlung leisten to pay a deposit

das **Anzeichen** (PL die **Anzeichen**) NOUN
sign

die **Anzeige** NOUN
advertisement
□ Ich habe ihn über eine Anzeige kennengelernt. I met him through an advertisement.
■ **Anzeige gegen jemanden erstatten** to report somebody to the police
■ **Ich möchte Anzeige wegen Diebstahls erstatten.** I wish to report a theft.

anzeigen (PERFECT **hat angezeigt**) VERB [4]
1 to show
□ Der Tachometer zeigt die Geschwindigkeit an. The speedometer shows the speed.
2 to report
□ Ich werde Sie wegen Ruhestörung anzeigen! I'll report you for breach of the peace. □ Ich habe einen Diebstahl anzuzeigen. I wish to report a theft.

anziehen (IMPERFECT **zog an**, PERFECT **hat angezogen**) VERB [96]
1 to put on
□ Ich muss mir nur noch die Schuhe anziehen. I just have to put my shoes on.
2 to dress
□ Kannst du bitte die Kinder anziehen? Can you dress the children, please? □ Er war sehr schick angezogen. He was dressed very elegantly.
3 to attract
□ Der Zoo zieht viele Besucher an. The zoo attracts a lot of visitors.
■ **sich von jemandem angezogen fühlen** to feel attracted to somebody
4 to tighten *(screw)*
■ **sich anziehen** to get dressed

der **Anzug** (PL die **Anzüge**) NOUN
suit

anzünden (PERFECT **hat angezündet**) VERB [54]
to light
□ Ich habe mir eine Zigarette angezündet. I lit a cigarette.

der **Apfel** (PL die **Äpfel**) NOUN
apple

das **Apfelmus** (GEN des **Apfelmuses**) NOUN
apple purée

der **Apfelsaft** (PL die **Apfelsäfte**) NOUN
apple juice

die **Apfelsine** NOUN
orange

die **Apfeltasche** NOUN
apple turnover

die **Apotheke** NOUN
chemist's
□ in der Apotheke at the chemist's

der **Apotheker** (PL die **Apotheker**) NOUN
pharmacist
□ Er ist Apotheker. He's a pharmacist.

der **Apparat** (PL die **Apparate**) NOUN
1 gadget
□ Mit diesem Apparat kann man Dosen zerkleinern. You can crush tins with this gadget.
2 camera
3 telephone
□ Wer war am Apparat? Who was on the telephone?
■ **Am Apparat!** Speaking!
4 set

das **Appartement** (PL die **Appartements**) NOUN
flat

der **Appetit** NOUN
appetite
■ **Ich habe keinen Appetit.** I'm not hungry.

LANGUAGE TIP Word for word, **Ich habe keinen Appetit** means 'I don't have an appetite'.

■ **Guten Appetit!** Enjoy your meal!

LANGUAGE TIP Word for word, **Guten Appetit!** means 'Good appetite!'.

die **Aprikose** NOUN
apricot

der **April** (GEN des **April** *or* **Aprils**, PL die **Aprile**) NOUN
April
□ im April in April □ am dritten April on the third of April □ Ulm, den 3. April 2007 Ulm, 3 April 2007 □ Heute ist der dritte April. Today is the third of April.
■ **April, April!** April Fool!

der **Araber** (PL die **Araber**) NOUN
Arab

die **Araberin** NOUN
Arab

arabisch ADJECTIVE
■ **arabische Länder** Arab countries
■ **die arabische Sprache** Arabic

die **Arbeit** NOUN
1 job
□ Das ist eine sehr anstrengende Arbeit. That's a very tiring job. □ Er sucht eine Arbeit auf dem Bau. He's looking for a job on a building site.
2 work
□ Ich habe im Moment viel Arbeit. I've got a lot of work at the moment. □ Sie hat keine Arbeit. She's out of work. □ Das war eine Arbeit! That was hard work.
3 dissertation
□ Sie schreibt eine Arbeit über englische Ortsnamen. She's writing a dissertation on English place names.
4 test
□ Ich habe in der Arbeit eine Fünf geschrieben. I got an 'E' in the test.
□ Morgen schreiben wir in Mathe eine Arbeit. We've got a maths test tomorrow.
■ **in Arbeit sein** to be in hand □ Ihre Reparatur ist in Arbeit. Your repair work is in hand.

arbeiten VERB [2]
to work
□ Sie arbeitet hart. She works hard.
□ Er arbeitet als Elektriker bei der Firma Müller. He works as an electrician for Müller's. □ Seine Nieren arbeiten nicht richtig. His kidneys don't work properly.
■ **sich durch etwas arbeiten** to work one's way through something

der **Arbeiter** (PL die **Arbeiter**) NOUN
worker

die **Arbeiterin** NOUN
worker

der **Arbeitgeber** (PL die **Arbeitgeber**) NOUN
employer

der **Arbeitnehmer** (PL die **Arbeitnehmer**) NOUN
employee
□ Als Arbeitnehmer hat man gewisse Rechte. As an employee you have certain rights.

das **Arbeitsamt** (PL die **Arbeitsämter**) NOUN
job centre

die **Arbeitsbedingungen** PL NOUN
working conditions

die **Arbeitserlaubnis** (PL die **Arbeitserlaubnisse**) NOUN
work permit

arbeitslos ADJECTIVE
unemployed

der/die **Arbeitslose** (GEN des/der **Arbeitslosen**, PL die **Arbeitslosen**) NOUN
unemployed person
□ Ein Arbeitsloser hat die Stelle bekommen. An unemployed person got the job.
■ **die Arbeitslosen** the unemployed

die **Arbeitslosigkeit** NOUN
unemployment

der **Arbeitsort** (PL die **Arbeitsorte**) NOUN
place of work

der **Arbeitsplatz** (GEN des **Arbeitsplatzes**, PL die **Arbeitsplätze**) NOUN
1 job
□ Suchen Sie einen neuen Arbeitsplatz? Are you looking for a new job?
2 desk
□ Frau Marr ist im Moment nicht an ihrem Arbeitsplatz. Ms Marr isn't at her desk at the moment.

die **Arbeitszeit** NOUN
working hours
■ **gleitende Arbeitszeit** flexitime

LANGUAGE TIP Word for word, **gleitende Arbeitszeit** means 'gliding working hours'.

das **Arbeitszimmer** (PL die **Arbeitszimmer**) NOUN
study

der **Architekt** (GEN des **Architekten**, PL die **Architekten**) NOUN
architect
□ Er ist Architekt. He's an architect.

die **Architektur** NOUN
architecture

Argentinien NEUT NOUN
Argentina
□ nach Argentinien to Argentina

der **Ärger** NOUN
1 anger
□ Er hat seinen Ärger über die Verspätung an mir ausgelassen. He took out his anger at the delay on me.
2 trouble
□ Wenn du das machst, bekommst du Ärger. If you do that, you'll get into trouble.
■ **Ärger mit etwas haben** to have trouble with something □ Hast du wieder Ärger mit deinem Computer? Are you having trouble with your computer again?

ärgerlich ADJECTIVE
1 annoying
□ Diese dauernden Störungen sind sehr ärgerlich. These constant interruptions are very annoying.
2 angry

□ Ich bin auf ihn ärgerlich. I'm angry with him. □ Er ist über die Verzögerung ärgerlich. He's angry at the delay.
■ **jemanden ärgerlich machen** to annoy somebody

ärgern VERB [88]
to annoy
□ Du sollst deine Schwester nicht immer ärgern! Don't keep annoying your sister.
■ **sich ärgern** to be annoyed □ Ich habe mich über diesen Fehler sehr geärgert. I was very annoyed about that mistake.

die **Arktis** NOUN
the Arctic
□ in der Arktis in the Arctic

der **Arm** (PL die **Arme**) NOUN
▷ *see also* **arm** ADJECTIVE
arm
■ **jemanden auf den Arm nehmen** to pull somebody's leg □ Du willst mich wohl auf den Arm nehmen? You're pulling my leg.

arm ADJECTIVE
▷ *see also* **der Arm** NOUN
poor
□ Er ist ärmer als ich. He's poorer than me.

das **Armband** (PL die **Armbänder**) NOUN
bracelet

die **Armbanduhr** NOUN
wristwatch

die **Armee** NOUN
army

der **Ärmel** (PL die **Ärmel**) NOUN
sleeve

der **Ärmelkanal** NOUN
the English Channel

die **Armut** NOUN
poverty

arrangieren (PERFECT **hat arrangiert**) VERB [76]
to arrange
□ Sie hat ein Treffen der beiden arrangiert. She arranged for them both to meet.

die **Art** (PL die **Arten**) NOUN
1 way
□ Ich mache das auf meine Art. I do that my way.
2 kind
□ Ich mag diese Art Obst nicht. I don't like this kind of fruit. □ Häuser aller Art all kinds of houses
3 species
□ Diese Art ist vom Aussterben bedroht. This species is in danger of extinction.
■ **Es ist nicht seine Art, das zu tun.** It's not like him to do that.

der **Artikel** (PL die **Artikel**) NOUN
article

die **Arznei** NOUN
medicine

das **Arzneimittel** (PL die **Arzneimittel**) NOUN
drug

der **Arzt** (PL die **Ärzte**) NOUN
doctor
□ Helmut ist Arzt. Helmut's a doctor.

die **Ärztin** NOUN
doctor
□ Jutta ist Ärztin. Jutta's a doctor.

ärztlich ADJECTIVE
medical
■ **Die Wunde muss ärztlich behandelt werden.** The wound will have to be treated by a doctor.

das **As** NOUN ▷ *see* **Ass**

die **Asche** NOUN (PL die **Aschen**
ash

der **Aschenbecher** (PL die **Aschenbecher**) NOUN
ashtray

der **Aschermittwoch** NOUN
Ash Wednesday
□ am Aschermittwoch on Ash Wednesday

der **Asiat** (GEN des **Asiaten**, PL die **Asiaten**) NOUN
Asian

die **Asiatin** NOUN
Asian

asiatisch ADJECTIVE
Asian

Asien NEUT NOUN
Asia
■ **aus Asien** from Asia
■ **nach Asien** to Asia

aß VERB ▷ *see* **essen**

das **Ass** (GEN des **Asses**, PL die **Asse**) NOUN
ace
□ das Herzass the ace of hearts

der **Assistent** (GEN des **Assistenten**, PL die **Assistenten**) NOUN
assistant

die **Assistentin** NOUN
assistant

der **Ast** (PL die **Äste**) NOUN
branch

das **Asthma** NOUN
asthma
□ Sie hat Asthma. She's got asthma.

die **Astrologie** NOUN
astrology

der **Astronaut** (GEN des **Astronauten**, PL die **Astronauten**) NOUN
astronaut
□ Er ist Astronaut. He's an astronaut.

die **Astronomie** NOUN
astronomy

das **Asyl** (PL die **Asyle**) NOUN
asylum
□ um Asyl bitten to ask for asylum
■ **ein Obdachlosenasyl** a hostel for the homeless

der **Asylbewerber** (PL die **Asylbewerber**) NOUN
asylum-seeker

German-English

a

die **Asylbewerberin** NOUN
asylum-seeker

der **Atem** NOUN
breath
□ außer Atem out of breath

atemlos ADJECTIVE
breathless

der **Atlantik** NOUN
the Atlantic
□ eine Insel im Atlantik an island in the Atlantic

der **Atlas** (GEN des **Atlasses**, PL die **Atlasse** *or* **Atlanten**) NOUN
atlas

atmen VERB [3]
to breathe

die **Atmosphäre** NOUN
atmosphere

das **Atom** (PL die **Atome**) NOUN
atom

die **Atombombe** NOUN
atom bomb

die **Atomwaffen** FEM PL NOUN
atomic weapons

atomwaffenfrei ADJECTIVE
nuclear-free

attraktiv ADJECTIVE
attractive
□ attraktiv aussehen to look attractive

ätzend ADJECTIVE
1 rubbish
□ Die Musik ist ätzend. The music's rubbish.
2 corrosive
3 caustic

auch ADVERB
1 also
□ Gummienten verkaufen wir auch. We also sell rubber ducks.
2 too
□ Das ist auch schön. That's nice, too.
□ Ich auch. Me too.
■ **Ich auch nicht.** Me neither.
■ **auch nicht** not ... either □ Nein, das Kleid gefällt mir auch nicht. No, I don't like that dress either.
■ **Auch das noch!** That's all we needed!
3 even
□ Auch wenn das Wetter schlecht ist. Even if the weather's bad. □ ohne auch nur zu fragen without even asking
■ **wer auch** whoever □ Wer das auch gesagt hat, ich glaube es nicht. I don't believe it, whoever said it.
■ **was auch** whatever □ Was du auch sagst, ich finde es schön. Whatever you say, I think it's nice.
■ **wie dem auch sei** be that as it may
□ Wie dem auch sei, ich gehe jetzt trotzdem. Be that as it may, I'm still going.
■ **wie sehr er sich auch bemühte** however much he tried

auf PREPOSITION, ADVERB
1 on

LANGUAGE TIP Use the accusative to express movement or a change of place. Use the dative when there is no change of place.

□ Stell die Suppe bitte auf den Tisch. Please put the soup on the table. □ Die Suppe steht auf dem Tisch. The soup's on the table.
■ **auf dem Land** in the country
■ **auf der ganzen Welt** in the whole world
■ **auf Deutsch** in German
■ **bis auf ihn** except for him
■ **auf einmal** at once
■ **auf seinen Vorschlag hin** at his suggestion
2 open
□ Das Fenster ist auf. The window's open.
□ Die Geschäfte sind am Sonntag nicht auf. The shops aren't open on Sunday.
3 up
□ Ist er schon auf? Is he up yet? □ Ich bin schon seit sieben Uhr auf. I've been up since seven.
■ **auf und ab** up and down
■ **auf und davon** up and away

aufatmen (PERFECT **hat aufgeatmet**) VERB [4]
to heave a sigh of relief

aufbauen (PERFECT **hat aufgebaut**) VERB [4]
to build up

aufbekommen (IMPERFECT **bekam auf**, PERFECT **hat aufbekommen**) VERB [40]
1 to get open
□ Ich bekomme das Fenster nicht auf. I can't get the window open.
2 to be given homework
□ Wir haben heute nichts aufbekommen. We weren't given any homework today.

aufbewahren (PERFECT **hat aufbewahrt**) VERB [38]
to keep
□ Sie bewahrt ihre Ersparnisse in einer Blechdose auf. She keeps her savings in a tin.

aufblasen (PRESENT **bläst auf**, IMPERFECT **blies auf**, PERFECT **hat aufgeblasen**) VERB
to inflate

aufbleiben (IMPERFECT **blieb auf**, PERFECT **ist aufgeblieben**) VERB [10]
1 to stay open
□ Heute bleiben die Geschäfte länger auf. The shops stay open longer today.
2 to stay up
□ Heute dürft ihr ausnahmsweise länger aufbleiben. Today you can stay up late for once.

aufbrechen (PRESENT **bricht auf**, IMPERFECT **brach auf**, PERFECT **hat/ist aufgebrochen**) VERB [11]

LANGUAGE TIP For the perfect tense use **haben** when the verb has an object and **sein** when there is no object.

1 to break open
□ Die Diebe haben den Safe aufgebrochen. The thieves broke the safe open.
2 to open up
□ Die Wunde ist wieder aufgebrochen. The wound has opened up again.
3 to set off
□ Wann seid ihr aufgebrochen? When did you set off?

aufbringen (IMPERFECT **brachte auf**, PERFECT **hat aufgebracht**) VERB [13]
1 to open
□ Ich bringe das Konservenglas nicht auf. I can't open the jar.
2 to raise
□ Wie soll ich nur das Geld für die Reparatur aufbringen? However am I going raise the money for the repairs?
■ **Verständnis für etwas aufbringen** to be able to understand something

aufeinander ADVERB
on top of each other
□ Leg die Handtücher aufeinander. Put the towels on top of each other.
■ **aufeinander schießen** to shoot at one another
■ **aufeinander vertrauen** to trust each other

der **Aufenthalt** (PL die **Aufenthalte**) NOUN
1 stay
□ Während unseres Aufenthalts in London ... During our stay in London ...
2 stop
□ Der Zug hat fünf Minuten Aufenthalt in Ulm. The train has a five-minute stop in Ulm.

aufessen (PRESENT **isst auf**, IMPERFECT **aß auf**, PERFECT **hat aufgegessen**) VERB [20]
to eat up

auffallen (PRESENT **fällt auf**, IMPERFECT **fiel auf**, PERFECT **ist aufgefallen**) VERB [22]
to be conspicuous
■ **jemandem auffallen** to strike somebody
□ Es fiel mir auf, dass sie sich recht seltsam benahm. It struck me that she was behaving rather strangely.

auffällig ADJECTIVE
conspicuous
■ **auffällig gekleidet sein** to be dressed strikingly

auffangen (PRESENT **fängt auf**, IMPERFECT **fing auf**, PERFECT **hat aufgefangen**) VERB [23]
to catch

aufführen (PERFECT **hat aufgeführt**) VERB [4]
1 to perform
□ ein Stück aufführen to perform a play
2 to list
□ Alle Fachausdrucke sind im Anhang aufgeführt. All technical terms are listed in the appendix.
■ **sich aufführen** to behave

die **Aufführung** NOUN
performance

die **Aufgabe** NOUN
1 task
□ Vier Kinder zu erziehen ist eine schwierige Aufgabe. Bringing up four children is a difficult task.
2 question
□ Ich konnte die zweite Aufgabe in der Mathearbeit nicht lösen. I couldn't solve the second question in the maths test.
3 homework
□ Hast du deine Aufgaben schon gemacht? Have you done your homework yet?

aufgeben (PRESENT **gibt auf**, IMPERFECT **gab auf**, PERFECT **hat aufgegeben**) VERB [28]
1 to give up
□ Du solltest das Rauchen aufgeben. You should give up smoking.
2 to post
□ Ich habe das Paket an dich vor drei Tagen aufgegeben. I posted the parcel to you three days ago.
3 to check in
□ Du kannst den Koffer ja vor der Reise aufgeben. You can check in your suitcase before you travel.
■ **eine Anzeige aufgeben** to place an advertisement
■ **Ich gebe auf!** I give up.

aufgehen (IMPERFECT **ging auf**, PERFECT **ist aufgegangen**) VERB [29]
1 to rise
□ Der Mond ist aufgegangen. The moon has risen.
2 to open
□ Die Tür ging auf, und Christoph kam herein. The door opened and Christoph came in.
■ **Zwanzig durch sechs geht nicht auf.** Six into twenty doesn't go.

aufgeregt ADJECTIVE
excited

aufgrund PREPOSITION
LANGUAGE TIP The preposition **aufgrund** takes the genitive.
1 because of
□ Das Spiel ist aufgrund des schlechten Wetters ausgefallen. The game was cancelled because of the bad weather.
2 on the basis of
□ Sie wurde aufgrund von Indizien überführt. She was convicted on the basis of circumstantial evidence.

aufhaben (PRESENT **hat auf**, IMPERFECT **hatte auf**, PERFECT **hat aufgehabt**) VERB [32]
1 to have on
□ Sie hatte einen roten Hut auf. She had a red hat on.
2 to have homework to do
□ Wir haben heute in Englisch nichts auf.

We haven't got any English homework to do today.

aufhalten (PRESENT **hält auf**, IMPERFECT **hielt auf**, PERFECT **hat aufgehalten**) VERB [33]

1 to detain
□ Ich möchte dich nicht aufhalten. I don't want to detain you.

2 to check
□ Wie kann die Vergrößerung des Ozonlochs aufgehalten werden? How can the growth of the ozone hole be checked?

3 to hold open
□ Kannst du mir bitte die Tür aufhalten? Can you hold the door open for me, please?
■ **Sie hielt die Hand auf.** She held out her hand.
■ **sich aufhalten** 1 to live □ Sie hat sich lange im Ausland aufgehalten. She lived abroad for a long time. 2 to stay □ Ich möchte mich nicht lange aufhalten. I don't want to stay long.
■ **sich mit etwas aufhalten** to waste time over something □ Mit solchen Kinderspielen halte ich mich doch nicht auf. I'm not wasting my time over such childish games.

aufhängen (PERFECT **hat aufgehängt**) VERB [35]

to hang up *(washing)*
■ **sich aufhängen** to hang oneself □ Er hat gedroht, sich aufzuhängen. He's threatened to hang himself.

aufheben (IMPERFECT **hob auf**, PERFECT **hat aufgehoben**) VERB

1 to pick up
□ Sie hob das Heft, das auf den Boden gefallen war, auf. She picked up the exercise book which had fallen on the floor.

2 to keep
□ Sie hat alle seine Briefe aufgehoben. She's kept all his letters.
■ **gut aufgehoben sein** to be well looked after □ Unsere Tochter ist bei ihrer Oma gut aufgehoben. Our daughter's being well looked after at her granny's.

aufhören (PERFECT **hat aufgehört**) VERB [4]

to stop
□ Der Regen hat aufgehört. The rain's stopped.
■ **aufhören, etwas zu tun** to stop doing something □ Hör endlich auf, dich dauernd zu beklagen. Will you stop complaining all the time!

der **Aufkleber** (PL die **Aufkleber**) NOUN

sticker

auflassen (PRESENT **lässt auf**, IMPERFECT **ließ auf**, PERFECT **hat aufgelassen**) VERB [42]

1 to leave open
□ Lass bitte das Fenster auf. Please leave the window open.

2 to keep on
□ Kann ich meine Mütze auflassen? Can I keep my hat on?

auflegen (PERFECT **hat aufgelegt**) VERB [4]

to hang up
□ Sie hat einfach aufgelegt. She simply hung up.

auflesen (PRESENT **liest auf**, IMPERFECT **las auf**, PERFECT **hat aufgelesen**) VERB [45]

to pick up
□ etwas von der Straße auflesen to pick something up off the street

auflösen (PERFECT **hat aufgelöst**) VERB [4]

1 to dissolve
□ Du solltest die Tablette in Wasser auflösen. You should dissolve the tablet in water.

2 to break up
□ Die Polizei hat die Demonstration aufgelöst. The police broke up the demonstration.
■ **sich auflösen** to dissolve □ Der Zucker hatte sich schnell im Tee aufgelöst. The sugar had quickly dissolved in the tea.
■ **wenn sich der Nebel aufgelöst hat** when the fog has lifted
■ **in Tränen aufgelöst sein** to be in tears

aufmachen (PERFECT **hat aufgemacht**) VERB [4]

1 to open
□ Kannst du bitte die Tür aufmachen? Can you open the door, please? □ Wann machen die Geschäfte auf? When do the shops open?

2 to undo
□ Ich schaffe es nicht, den Reißverschluss aufzumachen. I can't undo the zip.
■ **sich aufmachen** to set out □ Wir machten uns nach London auf. We set out for London.

aufmerksam ADJECTIVE

attentive
■ **jemanden auf etwas aufmerksam machen** to point something out to somebody □ Ich habe ihn auf das Schloss aufmerksam gemacht. I pointed the castle out to him.

die **Aufmerksamkeit** NOUN

attention
□ Darf ich um Ihre Aufmerksamkeit bitten! May I have your attention?
■ **Wir sollten ihnen eine kleine Aufmerksamkeit mitbringen.** We ought to take them a little something.

die **Aufnahme** NOUN

1 welcome
□ Wir fanden eine sehr freundliche Aufnahme in unserer Partnerstadt. We were given a very friendly welcome in our twin town.

2 recording
□ Wir haben uns die Aufnahme des Konzerts angehört. We listened to a recording of the concert.

3 photograph
□ Möchtest du die Aufnahmen sehen, die ich in den Ferien gemacht habe? Would you like to see the photographs I took on holiday?

die **Aufnahmeprüfung** NOUN
entrance test

aufnehmen (PRESENT **nimmt auf**, IMPERFECT **nahm auf**, PERFECT **hat aufgenommen**) VERB [52]
1 to take
□ Wie hat sie die Nachricht aufgenommen? How did she take the news?
2 to record
□ eine Sendung aufnehmen to record a programme
3 to photograph
□ Diesen tollen Sonnenuntergang muss ich aufnehmen. I must photograph this wonderful sunset.
4 to admit
□ Was muss man tun, um in den Tennisklub aufgenommen zu werden? What do you have to do to be admitted to the tennis club?
■ **es mit jemandem aufnehmen können** to be able to compete with somebody

aufpassen (PERFECT **hat aufgepasst**) VERB [31]
to pay attention
□ Ich habe heute im Unterricht nicht aufgepasst. I didn't pay attention in class today.
■ **auf jemanden aufpassen** to look after somebody □ Ich muss auf meinen kleinen Bruder aufpassen. I have to look after my little brother.
■ **auf etwas aufpassen** to look after something □ Kannst du mal eben auf meinen Koffer aufpassen? Can you look after my suitcase for a moment?
■ **Aufgepasst!** Look out!

aufpumpen (PERFECT **hat aufgepumpt**) VERB [4]
to pump up

aufräumen (PERFECT **hat aufgeräumt**) VERB [4]
to tidy up
□ Ich darf erst raus, wenn ich mein Zimmer aufgeräumt habe. I can't go out until I've tidied up my room.

aufrecht ADJECTIVE
upright

aufrechterhalten (PRESENT **erhält aufrecht**, IMPERFECT **erhielt aufrecht**, PERFECT **hat aufrechterhalten**) VERB [33]
to maintain

aufregen (PERFECT **hat aufgeregt**) VERB [4]
to excite
■ **sich aufregen** to get excited

aufregend ADJECTIVE
exciting

aufs = **auf das**

der **Aufsatz** (GEN des **Aufsatzes**, PL die **Aufsätze**) NOUN
essay
□ Wir haben heute in Deutsch einen Aufsatz geschrieben. We wrote an essay in today's German lesson.

aufschieben (IMPERFECT **schob auf**, PERFECT **hat aufgeschoben**) VERB
1 to push open
□ Man kann diese Tür aufschieben. You can push this door open.
2 to put off
□ Wir haben unsere Abreise noch einmal aufgeschoben. We put off our departure once again.

aufschlagen (PRESENT **schlägt auf**, IMPERFECT **schlug auf**, PERFECT **hat aufgeschlagen**) VERB [59]
1 to open
□ ein Buch aufschlagen to open a book
□ Schlagt Seite 111 auf. Open your books at page 111.
2 to pitch
□ Sie schlugen ihre Zelte auf. They pitched their tents.
3 to go up *(prices)*
□ Butter ist wieder aufgeschlagen. The price of butter has gone up again.
4 to serve *(tennis)*
□ Du schlägst auf. It's your turn to serve.

aufschließen (IMPERFECT **schloss auf**, PERFECT **hat aufgeschlossen**) VERB
to unlock
□ Schließ bitte die Tür auf! Please unlock the door. □ Sie schloss auf und ging hinein. She unlocked the door and went in.

aufschlussreich ADJECTIVE
informative

der **Aufschnitt** (PL die **Aufschnitte**) NOUN
cold meat

aufschreiben (IMPERFECT **schrieb auf**, PERFECT **hat aufgeschrieben**) VERB [61]
to write down

das **Aufsehen** NOUN
▷ *see also* **aufsehen** VERB
stir
□ Ihre Kleidung hat Aufsehen erregt. Her outfit caused a stir.

aufsehenerregend ADJECTIVE
sensational

auf sein VERB [65] ▷ *see* **auf**

aufsetzen (PERFECT **hat aufgesetzt**) VERB [36]
to put on
□ Setz dir eine Mütze auf! Put a hat on.
■ **Ich setze das Teewasser auf.** I'll put the kettle on.
■ **sich aufsetzen** to sit up □ Der Patient setzte sich auf. The patient sat up.

die **Aufsicht** NOUN
supervision
■ **die Aufsicht haben** to be in charge

aufstehen (IMPERFECT **stand auf**, PERFECT **ist/hat aufgestanden**) VERB [72]
LANGUAGE TIP Use **sein** for 'to get up' and **haben** for 'to be open'.
1 to get up

□ Wann bist du heute Morgen aufgestanden? When did you get up this morning?
□ Sie stand auf und ging. She got up and left.

2 to be open
□ Die Tür hat aufgestanden, also ging ich hinein. The door was open, so I went in.

aufstellen (PERFECT **hat aufgestellt**) VERB [4]

1 to pitch
□ Wir haben unser Zelt am Waldrand aufgestellt. We pitched our tent at the edge of the woods.

2 to stand up
□ Der Sonnenschirm ist umgefallen, ich muss ihn wieder aufstellen. The sunshade has fallen over. I'll have to stand it up again.

3 to set up
□ Sie stellte die Schachfiguren auf. She set up the chess pieces.
■ **eine Liste aufstellen** to draw up a list
■ **einen Rekord aufstellen** to set a record
■ **jemanden für ein Spiel aufstellen** to pick somebody for a game
■ **sich aufstellen** to line up □ Stellt euch bitte in Zweierreihen auf! Please line up in twos.

auftauchen (PERFECT **ist aufgetaucht**) VERB [4]
to appear

auftauen (PERFECT **hat/ist aufgetaut**) VERB [4]

LANGUAGE TIP For the perfect tense use **haben** when the verb has an object and **sein** when there is no object.

1 to thaw
□ Der Schnee taute auf. The snow thawed.

2 to defrost
□ Ich habe die Pizza im Mikrowellenherd aufgetaut. I've defrosted the pizza in the microwave.

aufteilen (PERFECT **hat aufgeteilt**) VERB [4]
to divide up
□ Wir wurden in drei Gruppen aufgeteilt. We were divided up into three groups.

der **Auftrag** (PL die **Aufträge**) NOUN
orders
□ Ich habe den Auftrag, Sie davon zu unterrichten, dass... I have orders to inform you that ...
■ **im Auftrag von** on behalf of □ Ich komme im Auftrag der Firma Haehnle & Co. I'm here on behalf of Haehnle and Co.

auftreten (PRESENT **tritt auf**, IMPERFECT **trat auf**, PERFECT **ist aufgetreten**) VERB [79]

1 to appear
□ Dieser Schauspieler tritt erst im dritten Akt auf. This actor doesn't appear until the third act.

2 to occur
□ Sollten Probleme auftreten, wende dich an uns. If any problems occur, get in touch with us.

3 to behave
□ Er ist ziemlich unbeliebt, weil er immer so überheblich auftritt. He's quite unpopular because he always behaves so arrogantly.

aufwachen (PERFECT **ist aufgewacht**) VERB [4]
to wake up

aufwachsen (PRESENT **wächst auf**, IMPERFECT **wuchs auf**, PERFECT **ist aufgewachsen**) VERB [87]
to grow up

aufwecken (PERFECT **hat aufgeweckt**) VERB [4]
to wake up

aufzählen (PERFECT **hat aufgezählt**) VERB [4]
to list

der **Aufzug** (PL die **Aufzüge**) NOUN
lift
□ Wir sind mit dem Aufzug nach oben gefahren. We went up in the lift.

das **Auge** (PL die **Augen**) NOUN
eye
□ Sie hat dunkle Augen. She's got dark eyes.
■ **unter vier Augen** in private

der **Augenblick** (PL die **Augenblicke**) NOUN
moment
■ **im Augenblick** at the moment

die **Augenbraue** NOUN
eyebrow

der **August** (GEN des **Augustes** *or* **August**, PL die **Auguste**) NOUN
August
□ im August in August □ am fünften August on 5 August □ Ulm, den 5. August 2008 Ulm, 5 August 2008 □ Heute ist der fünfte August. Today is the fifth of August.

die **Aula** (PL die **Aulen**) NOUN
assembly hall

aus PREPOSITION, ADVERB

LANGUAGE TIP The preposition **aus** takes the dative.

1 out of
□ Sie nahm ein Bonbon aus der Tüte. She took a sweet out of the bag. □ aus dem Fenster out of the window

2 from
□ Wenn er aus der Schule kommt, ist er immer sehr müde. When he comes home from school he's always very tired.
□ Ich komme aus Deutschland. I come from Germany. □ Er ist aus Berlin. He's from Berlin.

3 made of
□ Die Vase ist aus Porzellan. The vase is made of china.
■ **aus Erfahrung** from experience
■ **aus Spaß** for fun
■ **aus Freundschaft** out of a sense of friendship

4 finished
□ wenn das Kino aus ist when the film's

finished □ Komm sofort nach Hause, wenn die Schule aus ist. Come straight home when school has finished.

■ **Wann ist die Schule aus?** When does school finish?

5 off

□ Der Fernseher ist aus. The television's off.

■ **Licht aus!** Lights out!

■ **Sie können meinen Mann nicht sprechen, er ist aus.** You can't speak to my husband. He's out.

■ **von sich aus** of one's own accord

■ **von ihm aus** as far as he's concerned

ausatmen (PERFECT **hat ausgeatmet**) VERB [2]
to breathe out

ausbeuten (PERFECT **hat ausgebeutet**) VERB [2]
to exploit

ausbilden (PERFECT **hat ausgebildet**) VERB [54]
to train

□ Er bildet Lehrlinge aus. He trains apprentices. □ Sie ist ausgebildete Krankenschwester. She's a qualified nurse.

die **Ausbildung** NOUN
training

□ eine solide Ausbildung a decent training

der **Ausbildungsplatz** (GEN des **Ausbildungsplatzes**, PL die **Ausbildungsplätze**) NOUN
training job

die **Ausdauer** NOUN
stamina

ausdenken (IMPERFECT **dachte aus**, PERFECT **hat ausgedacht**) VERB [14]

■ **sich etwas ausdenken** to think something up □ Da hast du dir aber was Witziges ausgedacht. You've certainly thought up something imaginative.

der **Ausdruck (1)** (PL die **Ausdrücke**) NOUN
expression

□ Sie hat in der Schule ein paar schlimme Ausdrücke gelernt. She's learned a few nasty expressions at school. □ Als Ausdruck meiner Dankbarkeit habe ich ihr Blumen geschenkt. I gave her flowers as an expression of my gratitude. □ Ich kann am Ausdruck in deinem Gesicht sehen, dass dir das nicht passt. I can see by your expression that it doesn't suit you.

der **Ausdruck (2)** (PL die **Ausdrucke**) NOUN
printout

□ Kannst du mir von der Datei einen Ausdruck machen? Can you do me a printout of the file?

ausdrucken (PERFECT **hat ausgedruckt**) VERB [4]
to print out

□ Soll ich dir die Namen ausdrucken? Shall I print out the names for you?

ausdrücken (PERFECT **hat ausgedrückt**) VERB [4]
to express

□ Ich weiß nicht, wie man das auf Englisch ausdrückt. I don't know how to express it in English.

ausdrücklich ADJECTIVE
explicit

□ Sie hat dir das ausdrücklich verboten. She explicitly forbade you to do it.

auseinander ADVERB
apart

□ weit auseinander far apart

auseinanderhalten (PRESENT **hält auseinander**, IMPERFECT **hielt auseinander**, PERFECT **hat auseinandergehalten**) VERB [33]
to distinguish

auseinandernehmen (PRESENT **nimmt auseinander**, IMPERFECT **nahm auseinander**, PERFECT **hat auseinandergenommen**) VERB [52]
to take to pieces

die **Ausfahrt** NOUN
exit

□ Wir müssen an der nächsten Ausfahrt raus. We have to take the next exit.

ausfallen (PRESENT **fällt aus**, IMPERFECT **fiel aus**, PERFECT **ist ausgefallen**) VERB [22]

1 to be cancelled

□ Der Sportunterricht fällt heute aus. PE has been cancelled today.

2 to break down

□ Die Heizung ist mal wieder ausgefallen. The heating has broken down again.

■ **Wenn der Strom ausfällt, ...** If there's a power cut ...

■ **Die Arbeit ist sehr schlecht ausgefallen.** The results of the test were awful.

3 to fall out

□ Ihm sind die Haare ausgefallen, als er noch ziemlich jung war. His hair fell out when he was still quite young.

der **Ausflug** (PL die **Ausflüge**) NOUN
outing

□ einen Ausflug machen to go on an outing

ausfragen (PERFECT **hat ausgefragt**) VERB [4]
to question

die **Ausfuhr** NOUN
export

ausführen (PERFECT **hat ausgeführt**) VERB [4]

1 to carry out

□ Sie hat ihren Plan ausgeführt. She carried out her plan.

2 to export

□ Waren ausführen to export goods

■ **jemanden ausführen** to take somebody out □ Er hat mich zum Essen ausgeführt. He took me out for a meal.

■ **einen Hund ausführen** to take a dog for a walk

ausführlich ADJECTIVE, ADVERB

1 detailed

□ ein ausführlicher Bericht a detailed report

2 in detail
□ Sie hat mir ausführlich erzählt, wie es in den Ferien war. She told me in detail what her holidays were like.

ausfüllen (PERFECT **hat ausgefüllt**) VERB [4]
to fill in
□ Füllt bitte die Lücken im Text aus. Please fill in the gaps in the text. □ Hast du den Antrag schon ausgefüllt? Have you filled in the application form yet?

die **Ausgabe** NOUN
1 expenditure
□ Wir hatten in der letzten Zeit viele Ausgaben. We've had a lot of expenditure recently.
2 edition
□ Sie hat eine sehr alte Ausgabe von Goethes Werken. She's got a very old edition of Goethe's works.
3 issue
□ Ich habe das in der letzten Ausgabe meines Computermagazins gelesen. I read it in the last issue of my computer magazine.

der **Ausgang** (PL die **Ausgänge**) NOUN
1 exit
□ Ich warte dann am Ausgang auf euch. I'll wait for you at the exit, then.
■ **'Kein Ausgang'** 'No exit'
2 ending
□ Der Film hat einen sehr traurigen Ausgang. The film has a very sad ending.
3 result
□ Welchen Ausgang hatte das Spiel? What was the result of the match?

ausgeben (PRESENT **gibt aus**, IMPERFECT **gab aus**, PERFECT **hat ausgegeben**) VERB [28]
1 to spend
□ Wir haben auf dem Volksfest hundert Euro ausgegeben. We spent a hundred euros at the fair.
2 to distribute
□ Du musst dich da vorn anstellen, da werden die Karten ausgegeben. You have to queue at the front there: that's where the tickets are being distributed.
■ **einen ausgeben** to stand a round □ Ich habe heute Geburtstag, darum gebe ich einen aus. It's my birthday today, so I'm standing a round.
■ **sich für jemanden ausgeben** to pass oneself off as somebody □ Sie hat sich für meine Schwester ausgegeben. She passed herself off as my sister.
■ **sich als etwas ausgeben** to pretend to be something □ Er hat sich als Computerfachmann ausgegeben. He pretended to be a computer expert.

ausgehen (IMPERFECT **ging aus**, PERFECT **ist ausgegangen**) VERB [29]
1 to go out
□ Sollen wir heute Abend ausgehen? Shall we go out this evening? □ Fritz will mit dir ausgehen. Fritz wants to go out with you. □ Plötzlich ging das Licht aus. Suddenly the light went out.
2 to run out
□ Wir sollten tanken, bevor das Benzin ausgeht. We ought to fill up before we run out of petrol. □ Mir ging das Benzin aus. I ran out of petrol.
■ **Wie ist das Spiel ausgegangen?** How did the game end?
■ **schlecht ausgehen** to turn out badly
■ **wir können davon ausgehen, dass ...** we can assume that ...

ausgelassen ADJECTIVE
exuberant

ausgenommen CONJUNCTION
except
□ Alle kamen, ausgenommen Günter. Everyone came except Günter. □ Anwesende sind ausgenommen. Present company excepted.

ausgerechnet ADVERB
■ **ausgerechnet heute** today of all days
■ **ausgerechnet du** you of all people

ausgeschlossen ADJECTIVE
impossible
□ Ich halte das für ausgeschlossen. I think that's impossible.

ausgezeichnet ADJECTIVE, ADVERB
1 excellent
□ Werner ist ein ausgezeichneter Koch. Werner's an excellent cook.
2 excellently
□ Sie hat es ausgezeichnet gemacht. She did it excellently.

ausgiebig ADJECTIVE
substantial
□ Das Frühstück war sehr ausgiebig. Breakfast was very substantial.
■ **ausgiebig schlafen** to have a good sleep
■ **sich ausgiebig erholen** to have a good long rest

aushalten (PRESENT **hält aus**, IMPERFECT **hielt aus**, PERFECT **hat ausgehalten**) VERB [33]
■ **Ich halte diese Hitze nicht aus!** I can't stand this heat.
■ **Das ist nicht zum Aushalten.** It's unbearable.

sich **auskennen** (IMPERFECT **kannte sich aus**, PERFECT **hat sich ausgekannt**) VERB [39]
1 to know about
□ Sie kennt sich mit Kindern gut aus. She knows a lot about children.
2 to know one's way around
□ Er kennt sich in Stuttgart aus. He knows his way around Stuttgart.

auskommen (IMPERFECT **kam aus**, PERFECT **ist ausgekommen**) VERB [40]
■ **mit jemandem auskommen** to get on with somebody □ Ich komme mit meinen Eltern gut aus. I get on well with my parents.

■ **mit etwas auskommen** to manage on something □ Ich muss mit hundert Euro in der Woche auskommen. I have to manage on a hundred euros a week.

die **Auskunft** (PL die **Auskünfte**) NOUN
1 information
□ Nähere Auskunft erhalten Sie unter der folgenden Nummer. For further information ring the following number.
2 information office
□ Fragen Sie bei der Auskunft, wann der nächste Zug nach Bremen geht. Ask at the information office when the next train leaves for Bremen.
■ **Telefonauskunft** directory inquiries
□ Ruf doch die Auskunft an! Ring directory inquiries.

auslachen (PERFECT **hat ausgelacht**) VERB [4]
to laugh at
□ Sie hat mich nur ausgelacht. She just laughed at me.

das **Ausland** NOUN
■ **im Ausland** abroad □ Er lebt im Ausland. He lives abroad.
■ **ins Ausland** abroad □ Nach dem Examen möchte sie ins Ausland gehen. After the exams she wants to go abroad.

der **Ausländer** (PL die **Ausländer**) NOUN
foreigner
□ Ihr Mann ist Ausländer. Her husband's a foreigner.

die **Ausländerin** NOUN
foreigner
□ Seine Frau ist Ausländerin. His wife's a foreigner.

ausländisch ADJECTIVE
foreign

das **Auslandsgespräch** (PL die **Auslandsgespräche**) NOUN
international call

auslassen (PRESENT **lässt aus**, IMPERFECT **ließ aus**, PERFECT **hat ausgelassen**) VERB [42]
1 to leave out
□ Die nächste Übung können wir auslassen. We can leave out the next exercise.
■ **Ich lasse heute das Mittagessen aus.** I'm skipping lunch today.
2 to leave off
□ Heute lass ich den Fernseher aus. I'm leaving the television off today. □ Bei der Hitze kannst du die Jacke auslassen. You can leave your jacket off in this heat.
■ **seine Wut an jemandem auslassen** to take one's anger out on somebody

ausleeren (PERFECT **hat ausgeleert**) VERB [4]
to empty

ausleihen (IMPERFECT **lieh aus**, PERFECT **hat ausgeliehen**) VERB
to lend
□ Kannst du mir dein Moped ausleihen? Can you lend me your moped?
■ **sich etwas ausleihen** to borrow something □ Ich habe mir das Wörterbuch meines Bruders ausgeliehen. I've borrowed my brother's dictionary.

ausloggen (PERFECT **hat ausgeloggt**) VERB [4]
to log off *(computer)*

ausmachen (PERFECT **hat ausgemacht**) VERB [48]
1 to turn off
□ Mach bitte das Radio aus, die Musik stört mich. Please turn the radio off. The music's disturbing me.
■ **das Licht ausmachen** to switch off the light
2 to put out
□ Du solltest deine Zigarette ausmachen, bevor du hineingehst. You should put your cigarette out before you go in.
3 to arrange
□ Habt ihr schon einen Termin für das Fest ausgemacht? Have you arranged a date for the party yet? □ Ich habe mit ihr ausgemacht, dass wir uns um fünf Uhr treffen. I've arranged to meet her at five.
4 to settle
□ Macht das unter euch aus. Settle the matter between you.
5 to mind
□ Es macht mir nichts aus, wenn ich allein gehen muss. I don't mind having to go alone. □ Macht es Ihnen etwas aus, wenn ...? Would you mind if ...?

die **Ausnahme** NOUN
exception

ausnahmsweise ADVERB
for once

ausnützen (PERFECT **hat ausgenützt**) VERB [4]
to use

auspacken (PERFECT **hat ausgepackt**) VERB [4]
to unpack

ausprobieren (PERFECT **hat ausprobiert**) VERB [4]
to try out

der **Auspuff** (PL die **Auspuffe**) NOUN
exhaust

ausrechnen (PERFECT **hat ausgerechnet**) VERB [4]
to calculate

die **Ausrede** NOUN
excuse

ausreichend ADJECTIVE
1 sufficient
□ ausreichend Geld sufficient money
2 adequate

DID YOU KNOW...?
German marks range from one (**sehr gut**) to six (**ungenügend**).

die **Ausreise** NOUN
departure
■ **bei der Ausreise** when leaving the country

German-English

a

ausrichten (PERFECT **hat ausgerichtet**) VERB [4]
1 to tell
□ Ich werde es ihm ausrichten. I'll tell him.
■ **Richte bitte an deine Eltern schöne Grüße aus.** Please give my regards to your parents.
2 to gear to
□ Wir müssen unser Veranstaltungsangebot mehr auf Jugendliche ausrichten. We must gear our events more to young people.

ausrufen (IMPERFECT **rief aus**, PERFECT **hat ausgerufen**) VERB [56]
to cry out
■ **jemanden ausrufen lassen** to page somebody

das **Ausrufezeichen** (PL die **Ausrufezeichen**) NOUN
exclamation mark

sich **ausruhen** (PERFECT **hat sich ausgeruht**) VERB [4]
to rest

ausrüsten (PERFECT **hat ausgerüstet**) VERB [4]
to equip

die **Ausrüstung** NOUN
equipment

ausschalten (PERFECT **hat ausgeschaltet**) VERB [2]
to switch off

ausschlafen (PRESENT **schläft aus**, IMPERFECT **schlief aus**, PERFECT **hat ausgeschlafen**) VERB [58]
to have a good sleep
■ **Morgen kann ich ausschlafen.** I can have a lie-in tomorrow.
■ **Ich bin nicht ausgeschlafen.** I didn't get enough sleep.

ausschließlich ADVERB, PREPOSITION
1 exclusively
□ Der Schulhof ist ausschließlich für Schüler dieser Schule. The school yard is exclusively for pupils of this school.
2 except
□ Wir haben jeden Tag geöffnet ausschließlich Sonntag. We're open every day except Sunday.

ausschneiden (IMPERFECT **schnitt aus**, PERFECT **hat ausgeschnitten**) VERB [60]
to cut out

aussehen (PRESENT **sieht aus**, IMPERFECT **sah aus**, PERFECT **hat ausgesehen**) VERB [64]
▷ *see also* **das Aussehen** NOUN
to look
□ Sie sieht sehr hübsch aus. She looks very pretty. □ Wie siehst du denn aus? What do you look like! □ Es sieht nach Regen aus. It looks like rain. □ Es sieht schlecht aus. Things look bad.

das **Aussehen** NOUN
▷ *see also* **aussehen** VERB
appearance

aus sein VERB [65] ▷ *see* **aus**

außen ADVERB
on the outside
□ Außen ist es rot. It's red on the outside.

die **Außenpolitik** NOUN
foreign policy

der **Außenseiter** (PL die **Außenseiter**) NOUN
outsider

außer PREPOSITION, CONJUNCTION
LANGUAGE TIP The preposition **außer** takes the dative.
1 apart from
□ Außer dir haben das alle verstanden. Everyone has understood apart from you. □ Wer war noch da außer Horst? Apart from Horst, who was there?
■ **außer Haus** out □ Er ist heute den ganzen Tag außer Haus. He's out all day today.
■ **außer Landes** abroad
■ **außer Gefahr** out of danger
■ **außer Betrieb** out of order
■ **außer sich sein** to be beside oneself
□ Sie war außer sich vor Wut. She was beside herself with rage.
2 if ... not
□ Wir machen morgen ein Picknick, außer es regnet. We're having a picnic tomorrow if it doesn't rain.

außerdem CONJUNCTION
in addition

äußere ADJECTIVE
1 outer
□ Sie bildeten einen äußeren und einen inneren Kreis. They formed an outer and an inner circle.
2 external
□ Nur zur äußeren Anwendung. For external use only.

außergewöhnlich ADJECTIVE
unusual

außerhalb PREPOSITION, ADVERB
LANGUAGE TIP The preposition **außerhalb** takes the genitive.
1 outside
□ Es liegt außerhalb der Stadt. It's outside the town.
2 out of town
□ Sie wohnt nicht in Ulm, sondern ziemlich weit außerhalb. She doesn't live in Ulm, but quite a way out of town.
■ **außerhalb der Saison** out of season

äußern VERB [88]
to express
□ Sie hat den Wunsch geäußert, allein in die Ferien fahren zu dürfen. She's expressed the wish to be allowed to go on holiday alone.
■ **eine Meinung äußern** to give an opinion
□ Willst du nicht auch deine Meinung äußern? Don't you want to give your opinion, too?
■ **sich äußern** to comment □ Sie wollte sich

zu dem Vorwurf nicht äußern. She didn't wish to comment on the accusation.

außerordentlich ADJECTIVE, ADVERB
exceptional
□ Sie hat eine außerordentliche Begabung. She's exceptionally gifted. □ Sie ist außerordentlich intelligent. She's exceptionally intelligent.

äußerst ADVERB
▷ *see also* **äußerste** ADJECTIVE
extremely

äußerste ADJECTIVE
▷ *see also* **äußerst** ADVERB
utmost
□ Diese Sache ist von äußerster Wichtigkeit. This matter is of the utmost importance.

die **Äußerung** NOUN
remark

die **Aussicht** NOUN
1 view
□ Vom Hotel aus hat man eine schöne Aussicht aufs Meer. You have a wonderful view of the sea from the hotel.
2 prospect
□ Die Aussicht auf diese Stelle hat ihr neuen Mut gegeben. The prospect of this job gave her new hope. □ Das sind ja schöne Aussichten! What a prospect!
■ **etwas in Aussicht haben** to have the prospect of something □ Sie hat eine Stelle bei Collins in Aussicht. She has the prospect of a job with Collins.

ausspannen (PERFECT **hat ausgespannt**) VERB [4]
to relax

die **Aussprache** NOUN
1 pronunciation
□ Die Aussprache der Wörter ist mit phonetischen Zeichen angegeben. The pronunciation of the words is shown by phonetic symbols.
2 frank discussion
□ Ich hatte gestern eine lange Aussprache mit ihm. I had a long, frank discussion with him yesterday.

aussprechen (PRESENT **spricht aus**, IMPERFECT **sprach aus**, PERFECT **hat ausgesprochen**) VERB [70]
to pronounce
□ Wie spricht man dieses Wort aus? How do you pronounce this word?
■ **sich mit jemandem aussprechen** to talk things out with somebody □ Meinst du nicht, wir sollten uns einmal aussprechen? Don't you think we ought to talk things out?
■ **sich gegen etwas aussprechen** to speak out against something □ Die Mehrheit hat sich gegen eine Klassenfahrt nach Helgoland ausgesprochen. The majority spoke out against a school trip to Heligoland.
■ **sich für etwas aussprechen** to speak out in favour of something □ Die Lehrer haben sich für eine Verlängerung der Pausenzeiten ausgesprochen. The teachers spoke out in favour of longer breaks.
■ **Lass ihn doch aussprechen!** Let him finish.

aussteigen (IMPERFECT **stieg aus**, PERFECT **ist ausgestiegen**) VERB [74]
to get off
□ Ich sah, wie sie aus der Straßenbahn ausstieg. I saw her get off the tram.

ausstellen (PERFECT **hat ausgestellt**) VERB [4]
1 to exhibit
□ Im Museum werden zurzeit Bilder von Chagall ausgestellt. Pictures by Chagall are currently being exhibited in the museum.
2 to be on display
□ Im Schaufenster war exotisches Obst ausgestellt. Exotic fruit was on display in the window.
3 to switch off
□ Die Heizung wird im Mai ausgestellt. The heating's switched off in May.
4 to write
□ Die Lehrerin hat ihm ein gutes Zeugnis ausgestellt. The teacher wrote him a good report.
5 to issue
□ Auf welchem Amt werden Pässe ausgestellt? Which office issues passports?

die **Ausstellung** NOUN
exhibition

aussterben (PRESENT **stirbt aus**, IMPERFECT **starb aus**, PERFECT **ist ausgestorben**) VERB [75]
to die out

der **Ausstieg** NOUN
1 exit
□ Der Ausstieg ist hinten. The exit is at the back.
2 abandonment
□ der Ausstieg aus der Atomenergie abandonment of nuclear energy

aussuchen (PERFECT **hat ausgesucht**) VERB [4]
to choose
□ Such dir ein Eis aus. Choose yourself an ice cream.

der **Austausch** (GEN des **Austausches**) NOUN
exchange
□ ein Schüleraustausch a school exchange

austauschen (PERFECT **hat ausgetauscht**) VERB [4]
1 to replace
□ Ich habe die Festplatte ausgetauscht. I've replaced the hard disk.
2 to substitute
□ Der Mittelstürmer wurde ausgetauscht. The centre-forward was substituted.

austeilen (PERFECT **hat ausgeteilt**) VERB [4]
to give out

austragen (PRESENT **trägt aus**, IMPERFECT **trug aus**, PERFECT **hat ausgetragen**) VERB [77]
1 to deliver
□ Morgens trägt er immer die Post aus. In the morning he always delivers the post.
2 to hold
□ Der Wettkampf wird im Olympiastadion ausgetragen. The competition will be held in the Olympic stadium.

Australien NEUT NOUN
Australia
■ **aus Australien** from Australia
■ **in Australien** in Australia
■ **nach Australien** to Australia

der **Australier** (PL die **Australier**) NOUN
Australian

die **Australierin** NOUN
Australian

australisch ADJECTIVE
Australian

austreten (PRESENT **tritt aus**, IMPERFECT **trat aus**, PERFECT **ist ausgetreten**) VERB [79]
■ **aus etwas austreten** to leave something
□ Sie ist aus dem Verein ausgetreten. She's left the club.
■ **Ich muss mal austreten.** I need to go to the loo.

austrinken (IMPERFECT **trank aus**, PERFECT **hat ausgetrunken**) VERB [80]
1 to drink up
□ Er trank aus und ging. He drank up and left.
2 to finish
□ Lass mich noch schnell meinen Saft austrinken. Let me just quickly finish my juice.

der **Ausverkauf** (PL die **Ausverkäufe**) NOUN
clearance sale

ausverkauft ADJECTIVE
1 sold out
□ Die Vorstellung ist leider ausverkauft. The performance is sold out, I'm afraid.
2 full
□ Das Kino war ausverkauft. The cinema was full.

die **Auswahl** NOUN
selection
□ Sie haben eine große Auswahl an Schuhen. They have a large selection of shoes.

auswählen (PERFECT **hat ausgewählt**) VERB [4]
to select

auswandern (PERFECT **ist ausgewandert**) VERB [88]
to emigrate
□ Sie sind nach Australien ausgewandert. They emigrated to Australia.

auswärts ADVERB
1 in another town
□ Sie wohnt in Calw, arbeitet aber auswärts. She lives in Calw but works in another town.
2 away
□ Unsere Mannschaft spielt nächste Woche auswärts. Our team's playing away next week.
■ **auswärts essen** to eat out

das **Auswärtsspiel** (PL die **Auswärtsspiele**) NOUN
away game

der **Ausweg** (PL die **Auswege**) NOUN
way out

der **Ausweis** (PL die **Ausweise**) NOUN
1 identity card
□ Der Polizist wollte meinen Ausweis sehen. The policeman wanted to see my identity card.
2 card
□ Wenn du Schüler bist und deinen Ausweis zeigst, bekommst du Ermäßigung. If you're a student and show them your card, you get a reduction.

auswendig ADVERB
by heart
□ etwas auswendig lernen to learn something by heart

auswerten (PERFECT **hat ausgewertet**) VERB [4]
to evaluate

ausziehen (IMPERFECT **zog aus**, PERFECT **hat/ist ausgezogen**) VERB [96]

LANGUAGE TIP For the perfect tense use **haben** when the verb has an object and **sein** when there is no object.

1 to take off
□ Sie hat ihren Mantel nicht ausgezogen. She didn't take off her coat.
2 to undress
□ Kannst du bitte die Kinder ausziehen und ins Bett bringen? Can you undress the children and put them to bed, please?
■ **sich ausziehen** to undress □ Haben die Kinder sich schon ausgezogen? Have the children undressed yet?
3 to move out
□ Meine Nachbarn sind letzte Woche ausgezogen. My neighbours moved out last week.

der/die **Auszubildende** (GEN des/der **Auszubildenden**, PL die **Auszubildenden**) NOUN
trainee

das **Auto** (PL die **Autos**) NOUN
car
■ **Auto fahren** to drive

die **Autobahn** NOUN
motorway

das **Autobahnkreuz** (GEN des **Autobahnkreuzes**, PL die **Autobahnkreuze**) NOUN
motorway intersection

der **Autobus** (GEN des **Autobusses**, PL die **Autobusse**) NOUN
bus

der **Autofahrer** (PL die **Autofahrer**) NOUN
motorist

das **Autogramm** (PL die **Autogramme**) NOUN
autograph

das **Autokennzeichen** (PL die **Autokennzeichen**) NOUN
registration number

der **Automat** (GEN des **Automaten**, PL die **Automaten**) NOUN
machine

automatisch ADJECTIVE
automatic
□ Die Türen schließen automatisch.
The doors close automatically.

der **Autor** (PL die **Autoren**) NOUN
author

das **Autoradio** (PL die **Autoradios**) NOUN
car radio

das **Autorennen** (PL die **Autorennen**) NOUN
motor racing

die **Autorin** NOUN
author

autoritär ADJECTIVE
authoritarian

die **Autorität** NOUN
authority

der **Autounfall** (PL die **Autounfälle**) NOUN
car accident

die **Axt** (PL die **Äxte**) NOUN
axe

Bb

das Baby (PL die **Babys**) NOUN
baby

babysitten (PERFECT **hat gebabysittet**) VERB [2]
to babysit

der Babysitter (PL die **Babysitter**) NOUN
babysitter

die Babysitterin NOUN
babysitter

der Bach (PL die **Bäche**) NOUN
stream

die Backe NOUN
cheek

backen (PRESENT **bäckt**, IMPERFECT **backte** *or* **buk**, PERFECT **hat gebacken**) VERB
to bake

der Bäcker (PL die **Bäcker**) NOUN
baker
□ beim Bäcker at the baker's □ zum Bäcker to the baker's

die Bäckerei NOUN
baker's

der Backofen (PL die **Backöfen**) NOUN
oven

das Bad (PL die **Bäder**) NOUN
bath
■ **ein Bad im Meer** a swim in the sea

der Badeanzug (PL die **Badeanzüge**) NOUN
bathing suit

die Badehose NOUN
swimming trunks

die Bademütze NOUN
bathing cap

baden VERB [54]
to have a bath
■ **jemanden baden** to bath somebody
□ Das Baby muss noch gebadet werden. The baby still has to be bathed.
■ **sich baden** to have a bath

Baden-Württemberg NEUT NOUN
Baden-Württemberg

> **DID YOU KNOW...?**
> **Baden-Württemberg** is one of the 16 **Länder**. Its capital is Stuttgart. Baden-Württemberg is home to the cuckoo clock and to Mercedes-Benz and Porsche.

der Badeort NOUN
spa

das Badetuch (PL die **Badetücher**) NOUN
bath towel

die Badewanne NOUN
bath *(tub)*

das Badezimmer (PL die **Badezimmer**) NOUN
bathroom

die Bahn (PL die **Bahnen**) NOUN
1 railway
□ Er arbeitet bei der Bahn. He works for the railway.
■ **mit der Bahn fahren** to go by train
2 tram
3 lane
□ Die Schwimmerin auf Bahn drei liegt in Führung. The swimmer in lane three is in the lead.
■ **auf die schiefe Bahn geraten** to go off the rails

die Bahnfahrt NOUN
railway journey

der Bahnhof (PL die **Bahnhöfe**) NOUN
station
□ auf dem Bahnhof at the station

die Bahnhofshalle NOUN
station concourse

der Bahnsteig (PL die **Bahnsteige**) NOUN
platform

der Bahnübergang (PL die **Bahnübergänge**) NOUN
level crossing

bald ADVERB
1 soon
□ Es wird bald Frühling. It'll soon be spring.
■ **Bis bald!** See you later.
2 almost
□ Ich hätte bald was gesagt. I almost said something.
■ **Wird's bald!** Get a move on!

der Balkan NOUN
Balkans
■ **auf dem Balkan** in the Balkans

der Balken (PL die **Balken**) NOUN
beam

der Balkon (PL die **Balkons** *or* **Balkone**) NOUN
balcony

der Ball (PL die **Bälle**) NOUN
ball

□ Die Kinder spielen mit dem Ball. The children are playing with the ball.
□ Mit wem kommst du zum Ball? Who are you going to the ball with?

das **Ballett** (PL die **Ballette**) NOUN
ballet

der **Ballon** (PL die **Ballons** *or* **Ballone**) NOUN
balloon

der **Bambus** (GEN des **Bambusses**, PL die **Bambusse**) NOUN
bamboo

die **Banane** NOUN
banana

der **Band** (PL die **Bände**) NOUN
▷ *see also* **die Band** NOUN, **das Band** NOUN
volume
□ ein Lexikon in fünf Bänden an encyclopedia in five volumes

die **Band** (PL die **Bands**) NOUN
▷ *see also* **der Band** NOUN, **das Band** NOUN
band
□ Er spielt Gitarre in einer Band. He plays the guitar in a band.

das **Band** (PL die **Bänder**) NOUN
▷ *see also* **der Band** NOUN, **die Band** NOUN
1 ribbon
□ Sie hatte ein rotes Band im Haar. She had a red ribbon in her hair.
2 production line
□ Mein Vater arbeitet am Band. My father works on the production line.
3 tape
□ Ich habe diesen Song auf Band. I've got this song on tape.
■ **am laufenden Band** nonstop

band VERB ▷ *see* **binden**

die **Bank (1)** (PL die **Bänke**) NOUN
bench
□ Sie saß auf einer Bank im Park. She was sitting on a park bench.

die **Bank (2)** (PL die **Banken**) NOUN
bank
□ Ich muss Geld von der Bank holen. I'll have to get money from the bank.

der **Bankkonto** (PL die **Bankkonten**) NOUN
bank account

die **Bankleitzahl** NOUN
bank sort code

die **Banknote** NOUN
banknote

bankrott ADJECTIVE
bankrupt
□ Die Firma ist bankrott. The firm is bankrupt.
■ **Bankrott machen** to go bankrupt

die **Bar** (PL die **Bars**) NOUN
▷ *see also* **bar** ADJECTIVE
bar

bar ADJECTIVE
▷ *see also* **die Bar** NOUN
■ **bares Geld** cash
■ **etwas bar bezahlen** to pay cash for something

der **Bär** (GEN des **Bären**, PL die **Bären**) NOUN
bear

barfuß ADJECTIVE
barefoot

das **Bargeld** NOUN
cash

der **Barren** (PL die **Barren**) NOUN
parallel bars

der **Bart** (PL die **Bärte**) NOUN
beard

bärtig ADJECTIVE
bearded

Basel NEUT NOUN
Basle
■ **nach Basel** to Basle

die **Basis** (PL die **Basen**) NOUN
basis

der **Bass** (GEN des **Basses**, PL die **Bässe**) NOUN
bass

basteln VERB [34]
to make things
□ Ich bastle gern. I like making things.
■ **etwas basteln** to make something □ Ich habe einen Untersetzer gebastelt. I've made a coaster.

bat VERB ▷ *see* **bitten**

die **Batterie** NOUN
battery

der **Bau** (PL die **Bauten**) NOUN
1 construction
□ Das Haus ist noch im Bau befindlich. The house is still under construction.
2 building
□ In New York gibt es viele beeindruckende Bauten. There are many impressive buildings in New York.
3 building site
□ In den Ferien arbeitet er auf dem Bau. He works on a building site in the holidays.

der **Bauarbeiter** (PL die **Bauarbeiter**) NOUN
building worker

der **Bauch** (PL die **Bäuche**) NOUN
stomach
□ Mir tut der Bauch weh. My stomach's sore.

der **Bauchnabel** (PL die **Bauchnabel**) NOUN
belly button

die **Bauchschmerzen** MASC PL NOUN
stomachache

bauen VERB [38]
to build
□ Meine Eltern haben das Haus gebaut, in dem wir wohnen. My parents built the house we live in.

der **Bauer** (GEN des **Bauern**, PL die **Bauern**) NOUN
1 farmer
□ Friedas Vater ist Bauer. Frieda's father is a farmer.

2 pawn
□ Sie zog mit dem Bauer. She moved the pawn.

die **Bäuerin** NOUN
1 farmer
□ Sie möchte Bäuerin werden. She would like to be a farmer.
2 farmer's wife

der **Bauernhof** (PL die **Bauernhöfe**) NOUN
farm

baufällig ADJECTIVE
dilapidated

der **Baum** (PL die **Bäume**) NOUN
tree

die **Baumwolle** NOUN
cotton
□ eine Tischdecke aus Baumwolle a cotton tablecloth

die **Baustelle** NOUN
building site

die **Bauten** PL NOUN ▷ *see* Bau

der **Bayer** (GEN des **Bayern**, PL die **Bayern**) NOUN
Bavarian

die **Bayerin** NOUN
Bavarian

Bayern NEUT NOUN
Bavaria

DID YOU KNOW...?
Bayern is one of the 16 **Länder**. Its capital is München (Munich). Bavaria has the longest political tradition of any of the Länder, and since 1945 has developed into an important industrial region.

bayrisch ADJECTIVE
Bavarian

beabsichtigen (PERFECT **hat beabsichtigt**) VERB [7]
to intend
□ Ich beabsichtige, ins Ausland zu fahren. I intend to go abroad.

beachten (PERFECT **hat beachtet**) VERB [2]
1 to pay attention to
□ Beachte ihn nicht! Don't pay any attention to him. □ Du solltest den Hinweis auf der Packung beachten. You should pay attention to the instructions on the packet.
2 to obey
□ Man muss die Verkehrsregeln beachten. You have to obey the traffic regulations.
3 to observe
□ Sie hat die Vorfahrt nicht beachtet. She didn't observe the right of way.

beachtlich ADJECTIVE
considerable

der **Beamte** (GEN des **Beamten**, PL die **Beamten**) NOUN
1 official
□ Der Beamte stempelte meinen Pass ab. The official stamped my passport.
2 civil servant

DID YOU KNOW...?
In Germany, traditionally all public employees are civil servants. They enjoy many privileges.

□ Deutsche Lehrer sind Beamte. German teachers are civil servants.

die **Beamtin** NOUN
civil servant
□ Meine Mutter ist Beamtin. My mother's a civil servant.

beantragen (PERFECT **hat beantragt**) VERB [7]
to apply for

beantworten (PERFECT **hat beantwortet**) VERB [2]
to answer

bearbeiten (PERFECT **hat bearbeitet**) VERB [2]
1 to deal with
□ Welches Thema hat sie in ihrer Diplomarbeit bearbeitet? What subject did she deal with in her dissertation?
2 to process
□ Wir haben Ihren Antrag noch nicht bearbeitet. We haven't processed your application yet.
3 to treat
□ Sie hat den Fleck mit Fleckenmittel bearbeitet. She treated the stain with stain remover.
■ **jemanden bearbeiten** to work on somebody □ Ich werde meine Mutter bearbeiten, dass sie mich gehen lässt. I'll work on my mother and get her to let me go.

der **Becher** (PL die **Becher**) NOUN
1 mug
□ Auf ihrem Schreibtisch stand ein Becher mit Kaffee. There was a mug of coffee on her desk.
2 carton
3 tub

das **Becken** (PL die **Becken**) NOUN
1 sink
□ Er ließ Wasser ins Becken laufen. He ran water into the sink.
2 pool
■ **ein breites Becken** broad hips

sich **bedanken** (PERFECT **hat sich bedankt**) VERB [7]
to say thank you
□ Hast du dich auch bedankt? Did you say thank you?
■ **sich bei jemandem bedanken** to say thank you to somebody

der **Bedarf** NOUN
demand
□ je nach Bedarf according to demand
■ **bei Bedarf** if necessary
■ **Bedarf an etwas haben** to be in need of something □ Wir haben Bedarf an Aushilfskräften. We're in need of temporary workers.

bedauerlich ADJECTIVE
regrettable

bedauern (PERFECT **hat bedauert**) VERB [88]
1 to be sorry for
□ Wir bedauern es sehr, dass wir nicht kommen können. We're very sorry that we can't come.
■ **Ich bedaure!** I'm sorry!
■ **Ich bedaure kein Wort.** I don't regret a single word!
2 to pity
□ Ich bedaure dich wirklich! I really pity you!

die **Bedenken** NEUT PL NOUN
doubts
□ Ich habe Bedenken, ob das klappt. I have my doubts as to whether it'll work.
■ **Hast du keine Bedenken, wenn du deine Eltern so anlügst?** Don't you feel bad about lying to your parents like that?

bedenklich ADJECTIVE
1 dubious
□ Das sind sehr bedenkliche Methoden. These are very dubious methods.
2 dangerous
□ Die Lage ist bedenklich. The situation is dangerous.
■ **Ihr Gesundheitszustand ist bedenklich.** Her state of health is giving cause for concern.

bedeuten (PERFECT **hat bedeutet**) VERB [2]
to mean
□ Was bedeutet dieser Ausdruck? What does this expression mean? □ Was hat das zu bedeuten? What's that supposed to mean? □ Er bedeutet mir sehr viel. He means a lot to me.

bedeutend ADJECTIVE
1 important
□ Er ist ein bedeutender Wissenschaftler. He's an important scientist.
2 considerable
□ Sie haben eine bedeutende Summe dafür bezahlt. They paid a considerable sum for it.
■ **bedeutend besser** considerably better
■ **bedeutend schlechter** considerably worse

die **Bedeutung** NOUN
1 meaning
□ die Bedeutung eines Worts the meaning of a word
2 importance
□ eine Erfindung von großer Bedeutung an invention of great importance

bedienen (PERFECT **hat bedient**) VERB [7]
1 to serve
□ Wir wurden sehr schnell bedient. We were served very quickly.
2 to operate
□ Er bedient die Druckmaschine. He operates the printing press.
■ **sich bedienen** to help oneself
□ Bitte bedien dich! Please help yourself.

die **Bedienung** NOUN
1 service
□ In diesem Geschäft ist die Bedienung schlecht. The service is very poor in this shop.
2 waiter
waitress
□ Wir haben bei der Bedienung ein Bier bestellt. We ordered a beer from the waitress.
3 shop assistant
□ Die Bedienung im Kaufhaus war äußerst unfreundlich. The shop assistant in the department store was extremely unfriendly.
4 service charge
□ Die Bedienung ist im Preis enthalten. The service charge is included in the price.

die **Bedingung** NOUN
condition
□ unter der Bedingung, dass ... on condition that ...

bedrohen (PERFECT **hat bedroht**) VERB [7]
to threaten

das **Bedürfnis** (GEN des **Bedürfnisses**, PL die **Bedürfnisse**) NOUN
need

das **Beefsteak** (PL die **Beefsteaks**) NOUN
steak
■ **deutsches Beefsteak** hamburger

sich **beeilen** (PERFECT **hat sich beeilt**) VERB [7]
to hurry

beeindrucken (PERFECT **hat beeindruckt**) VERB [7]
to impress

beeindruckend ADJECTIVE
impressive

beeinflussen (PRESENT **beeinflusst**, IMPERFECT **beeinflusste**, PERFECT **hat beeinflusst**) VERB [7]
to influence

beenden (PERFECT **hat beendet**) VERB [54]
to end

die **Beerdigung** NOUN
funeral

die **Beere** NOUN
1 berry
2 grape

der **Befehl** (PL die **Befehle**) NOUN
command

befehlen (PRESENT **befiehlt**, IMPERFECT **befahl**, PERFECT **hat befohlen**) VERB
1 to order
□ Der General hat den Rückzug befohlen. The general ordered his men to retreat.
2 to give orders
□ Du hast hier nicht zu befehlen! You're not the one who gives the orders here!
■ **jemandem etwas befehlen** to order somebody to do something

befestigen (PERFECT **hat befestigt**) VERB [7]
to fix
□ Die Regalbretter sind mit Schrauben an der Wand befestigt. The shelves are fixed to the wall with screws.

sich **befinden** (IMPERFECT **befand sich**, PERFECT **hat sich befunden**) VERB [24]
to be

□ Er befindet sich zurzeit im Ausland. He's abroad at the moment.

befolgen (PERFECT **hat befolgt**) VERB [7]
to obey

befördern (PERFECT **hat befördert**) VERB [88]
1 to carry
□ Die städtischen Busse befördern täglich viele Menschen. The municipal buses carry many people every day.
2 to promote
□ Sie ist zur Abteilungsleiterin befördert worden. She's been promoted to head of department.

die **Beförderung** NOUN
1 transport
□ Das Rote Kreuz übernimmt die Beförderung der Hilfsgüter. The Red Cross undertakes the transport of emergency supplies.
2 promotion
□ Bei einer Beförderung bekommt man auch mehr Geld. Promotion also means more money.

befragen (PERFECT **hat befragt**) VERB [7]
to question

befreien (PERFECT **hat befreit**) VERB [7]
1 to set free
□ Die Geiseln sind noch nicht befreit. The hostages haven't been set free yet.
2 to exempt
□ Sie ist vom Sportunterricht befreit. She's exempt from PE lessons.

befreundet ADJECTIVE
■ **mit jemandem befreundet sein** to be friends with somebody □ Ich bin mit Petra seit Jahren befreundet. I've been friends with Petra for years.

befriedigen (PERFECT **hat befriedigt**) VERB [7]
to satisfy

befriedigend ADJECTIVE
satisfactory

DID YOU KNOW...?
German marks range from one (**sehr gut**) to six (**ungenügend**).

befristet ADJECTIVE
limited

befürchten (PERFECT **hat befürchtet**) VERB [2]
to fear

befürworten (PERFECT **hat befürwortet**) VERB [2]
to support

begabt ADJECTIVE
talented

die **Begabung** NOUN
talent

begann VERB ▷ *see* **beginnen**

begegnen (PERFECT **ist begegnet**) VERB [53]
■ **jemandem begegnen** to meet somebody
□ Ich bin ihr heute schon einmal begegnet. I've met her once today already. □ Wir sind uns das erste Mal in London begegnet. The first time we met was in London.
□ Eine solche Frechheit ist mir noch nie begegnet. I've never met such cheek.

die **Begegnung** NOUN
meeting

begehen (IMPERFECT **beging**, PERFECT **hat begangen**) VERB [29]
to commit
□ Er hat einen Mord begangen. He committed a murder.

begehren (PERFECT **hat begehrt**) VERB [7]
to desire

begehrt ADJECTIVE
1 in demand
2 eligible

begeistern (PERFECT **hat begeistert**) VERB [88]
to thrill
□ Der Film hat mich begeistert. I was thrilled with the film.
■ **sich für etwas begeistern** to get enthusiastic about something

begeistert ADJECTIVE
enthusiastic

begießen (IMPERFECT **begoss**, PERFECT **hat begossen**) VERB
to water
□ Sie begoss ihre Rosen. She watered her roses.
■ **das muss begossen werden!** that calls for a drink!

der **Beginn** NOUN
beginning
□ zu Beginn at the beginning

beginnen (IMPERFECT **begann**, PERFECT **hat begonnen**) VERB [5]
to start

begleiten (PERFECT **hat begleitet**) VERB [2]
to accompany
□ Er hat mich zum Ball begleitet. He accompanied me to the ball.

beglückwünschen (PERFECT **hat beglückwünscht**) VERB [7]
to congratulate
□ Alle meine Freunde haben mich zur bestandenen Prüfung beglückwünscht. All my friends congratulated me on passing the exam.

begonnen VERB ▷ *see* **beginnen**

begraben (PRESENT **begräbt**, IMPERFECT **begrub**, PERFECT **hat begraben**) VERB
to bury

begreifen (IMPERFECT **begriff**, PERFECT **hat begriffen**) VERB
to understand

der **Begriff** (PL die **Begriffe**) NOUN
term
□ Das ist ein Begriff aus der Architektur. That is an architectural term.
■ **im Begriff sein, etwas zu tun** to be about to do something □ Ich war im Begriff zu gehen. I was about to go.
■ **schwer von Begriff** slow on the uptake
■ **sich einen Begriff von etwas machen**

to imagine something □ Du machst dir keinen Begriff, wie schwierig das war. You can't imagine how difficult it was.

begründen (PERFECT **hat begründet**) VERB [54]
to justify

die **Begründung** NOUN
justification

begrüßen (PERFECT **hat begrüßt**) VERB [31]
to welcome
□ Ich begrüße diese Änderung sehr. I very much welcome this change.
■ **herzlich begrüßt werden** to receive a warm welcome

die **Begrüßung** NOUN
welcome

behaglich ADJECTIVE
cosy

behalten (PRESENT **behält**, IMPERFECT **behielt**, PERFECT **hat behalten**) VERB [33]
1 to keep
□ Kann ich das Buch noch ein paar Tage behalten? Can I keep the book for another couple of days?
2 to remember
□ Ich kann mir ihren Namen nie behalten. I can never remember her name.

der **Behälter** (PL die **Behälter**) NOUN
container

behandeln (PERFECT **hat behandelt**) VERB [34]
1 to treat
□ Wir wurden sehr freundlich behandelt. We were treated in a very friendly manner. □ Die Wunde muss behandelt werden. The wound will have to be treated. □ Welcher Arzt behandelt Sie? Which doctor is treating you?
2 to deal with
□ Der Film behandelt das Thema Jugendkriminalität. The film deals with the subject of juvenile delinquency.

die **Behandlung** NOUN
treatment

behaupten (PERFECT **hat behauptet**) VERB [2]
to claim

beherrschen (PERFECT **hat beherrscht**) VERB [7]
1 to master
□ Ich beherrsche diese Technik noch nicht. I haven't mastered this technique yet.
2 to control
□ Er konnte seine Wut nicht mehr beherrschen. He couldn't control his anger any longer.
■ **sich beherrschen** to control oneself

behilflich ADJECTIVE
helpful
■ **jemandem bei etwas behilflich sein** to help somebody with something

behindern (PERFECT **hat behindert**) VERB [88]
to hinder

behindert ADJECTIVE
disabled

der/die **Behinderte** (GEN des/der **Behinderten**, PL die **Behinderten**) NOUN
disabled person
■ **die Behinderten** the disabled

die **Behinderung** NOUN
1 obstruction
□ Das Fahrzeug stellt eine Behinderung des Verkehrs dar. The vehicle is an obstruction to traffic.
2 handicap
□ Sie hat gelernt, mit ihrer Behinderung zu leben. She's learned to live with her handicap.

die **Behörde** NOUN
authorities

bei PREPOSITION
LANGUAGE TIP The preposition **bei** takes the dative.
1 near
□ Unser Haus ist beim Bahnhof. Our house is near the station. □ bei München near Munich
2 at
□ Felix ist zurzeit bei seiner Großmutter. Felix is at his grandmother's at the moment. □ Wenn man bei fremden Leuten zu Besuch ist ... When you're at other people's houses ... □ beim Friseur at the hairdresser's □ bei Nacht at night □ bei uns at our place
3 with
□ bei seinen Eltern wohnen to live with one's parents □ Wenn du bei mir bist, habe ich keine Angst. When you're with me, I'm not afraid.
■ **Ich habe kein Geld bei mir.** I don't have any money on me.
■ **bei einer Firma arbeiten** to work for a firm □ Sie arbeitet bei der Post. She works for the post office.
■ **beim Militär** in the army
4 on
□ bei meiner Ankunft on my arrival
□ bei der Abreise on departure
5 during
□ beim Abendessen during dinner
■ **beim Fahren** while driving
■ **bei solcher Hitze** in such heat
■ **bei Nebel** in fog
■ **bei Regen** if it rains

beibringen (IMPERFECT **brachte bei**, PERFECT **hat beigebracht**) VERB [13]
■ **jemandem etwas beibringen** to teach somebody something □ Sie hat mir Schwimmen beigebracht. She taught me to swim.

beide ADJECTIVE, PRONOUN
▷ *see also* **beides** PRONOUN
both
□ Ich habe beide Bücher gelesen. I've read both books. □ Ich will beide. I want both of them. □ jeder der beiden both of them
□ Meine Eltern haben das beide verboten. Both my parents have forbidden it.
■ **meine beiden Brüder** both my brothers

■ **die ersten beiden** the first two
■ **wir beide** we two
■ **einer von beiden** one of the two

beides PRONOUN
▷ *see also* **beide** ADJECTIVE
both
□ Ich möchte beides. I want both of them.
□ Beides ist schön. Both of them are lovely.
■ **alles beides** both of them

beieinander ADVERB
together

der **Beifall** NOUN
applause
■ **Beifall spenden** to applaud

beige ADJECTIVE
beige

das **Beil** (PL die **Beile**) NOUN
axe

die **Beilage** NOUN
1 supplement
□ eine Beilage zur Samstagszeitung a supplement in Saturday's paper
2 side dish

beilegen (PERFECT **hat beigelegt**) VERB [4]
1 to enclose
□ Ich lege einen Scheck bei. I enclose a cheque.
2 to settle
□ Der Streit war schnell beigelegt. The argument was quickly settled.

das **Beileid** NOUN
sympathy
□ Wir haben ihr unser Beileid ausgesprochen. We offered her our sympathy.
■ **herzliches Beileid** deepest sympathy

beiliegend ADVERB
enclosed

beim = **bei dem**

das **Bein** (PL die **Beine**) NOUN
leg

beinahe ADVERB
almost

beisammen ADVERB
together

beiseite ADVERB
to one side
□ Sie schob ihren Teller beiseite. She pushed her plate to one side.

beiseitelegen VERB [4]
to put by
□ Ich habe ein paar Hundert Euro beiseitegelegt. I've got a few hundred euros put by.

beiseitelassen (PRESENT **lässt beiseite**, IMPERFECT **ließ beiseite**, PERFECT **hat beiseitegelassen**) VERB [42]
to leave
□ Diese Frage sollten wir im Moment beiseitelassen. We should leave this question for the moment.

beiseiteschaffen VERB [4]
to put by
□ Er hat sehr viel Geld beiseitegeschafft. He's put a lot of money by.

das **Beispiel** (PL die **Beispiele**) NOUN
example
■ **sich an jemandem ein Beispiel nehmen** to take a leaf out of somebody's book □ Du solltest dir an deinem Bruder ein Beispiel nehmen. You should take a leaf out of your brother's book.
■ **zum Beispiel** for example

beispielsweise ADVERB
for example

beißen (IMPERFECT **biss**, PERFECT **hat gebissen**) VERB [6]
1 to bite
□ Mein Hund beißt nicht. My dog doesn't bite.
□ Sie biss in den Apfel. She bit into the apple.
2 to burn
□ Der Rauch beißt mich in den Augen. The smoke's burning my eyes.
■ **sich beißen** to clash □ Rosa beißt sich mit Orange. Pink clashes with orange.

der **Beitrag** (PL die **Beiträge**) NOUN
1 contribution
□ einen Beitrag zu etwas leisten to make a contribution to something
■ **Beiträge für die Zeitung** articles for the newspaper
2 membership fee
□ Der Beitrag für den Klub wird am Monatsanfang fällig. Membership fees for the club are due at the beginning of the month.
3 premium
□ die Beiträge zur Krankenversicherung the health insurance premiums

beitragen (PRESENT **trägt bei**, IMPERFECT **trug bei**, PERFECT **hat beigetragen**) VERB [77]
■ **zu etwas beitragen** to contribute to something □ Er trägt selten etwas zum Unterricht bei. He seldom contributes anything to the lesson.

bekämpfen (PERFECT **hat bekämpft**) VERB [7]
to fight
□ ein Feuer bekämpfen to fight a fire
■ **sich bekämpfen** to fight □ Diese beiden Parteien bekämpfen sich seit Jahren. These two parties have been fighting for years.

bekannt ADJECTIVE
1 well-known
□ Sie ist eine bekannte Schauspielerin. She's a well-known actress.
2 familiar
□ Bekannte Wörter brauche ich nicht nachzuschlagen. I don't have to look up familiar words. □ Sie kommt mir bekannt vor. She seems familiar. □ Das kommt mir bekannt vor. That sounds familiar.
■ **mit jemandem bekannt sein** to know somebody □ Wir sind seit Jahren mit den Bauers bekannt. We've known the Bauers for years.

■ **für etwas bekannt sein** to be known for something □ Sie ist für ihren Witz bekannt. She's known for her humour.
■ **Das ist mir bekannt.** I know that.
■ **etwas bekannt geben** to announce something publicly
■ **etwas bekannt machen** to announce something

der/die **Bekannte** (GEN des/der **Bekannten**, PL die **Bekannten**) NOUN
1 friend
□ Ein Bekannter von mir hat mir das erzählt. A friend of mine told me.
2 acquaintance
□ Sie hat viele Bekannte, aber wenig Freunde. She has a lot of acquaintances but few friends.

bekanntgeben VERB [28] ▷ *see* **bekannt**

bekanntlich ADVERB
as you know
□ Rauchen macht bekanntlich süchtig. As you know, smoking is addictive.

bekanntmachen VERB [48] ▷ *see* **bekannt**

sich **beklagen** (PERFECT **hat sich beklagt**) VERB [7]
to complain
□ Die Schüler haben sich darüber beklagt, dass sie Hausaufgaben aufbekommen haben. The pupils complained about being given homework.

die **Bekleidung** NOUN
clothing

bekommen (IMPERFECT **bekam**, PERFECT **hat bekommen**) VERB [40]
1 to get
□ Was hast du zum Geburtstag bekommen? What did you get for your birthday? □ Sie hat in Englisch eine schlechte Note bekommen. She got bad marks in English. □ Wir haben nichts zu essen bekommen. We didn't get anything to eat.
■ **Hunger bekommen** to feel hungry
■ **Durst bekommen** to feel thirsty
■ **Angst bekommen** to become afraid
■ **ein Kind bekommen** to have a baby
□ Unsere Deutschlehrerin bekommt ein Kind. Our German teacher's having a baby.
2 to catch
□ Ich habe den letzten Bus gerade noch bekommen. I just caught the last bus.
■ **Das fette Essen ist ihm nicht bekommen.** The fatty food didn't agree with him.
■ **Was bekommen Sie?** What would you like?
■ **Bekommen Sie schon?** Are you being served?
■ **Was bekommen Sie dafür?** How much do I owe you?

LANGUAGE TIP Be careful! **bekommen** does not mean **to become**.

belasten (PERFECT **hat belastet**) VERB [2]
1 to burden
□ Ich möchte dich nicht mit meinen Problemen belasten. I don't want to burden you with my problems.
2 to load
□ Der Aufzug darf mit maximal zehn Personen belastet werden. The lift's maximum load is ten people.
3 to pollute
□ Unsere Umwelt ist mit zu vielen Schadstoffen belastet. The environment is polluted by too many harmful substances.
4 to debit
□ Wir werden Ihr Konto mit diesem Betrag belasten. We will debit this amount from your account.
5 to incriminate
□ Die Zeugin hat den Angeklagten belastet. The witness incriminated the accused.

belästigen (PERFECT **hat belästigt**) VERB [7]
to pester
■ **jemanden sexuell belästigen** to sexually harass somebody

belegt ADJECTIVE
■ **ein belegtes Brot** an open sandwich
■ **Es ist belegt.** It's engaged. □ Die Nummer ist belegt. The number's engaged.

beleidigen (PERFECT **hat beleidigt**) VERB [7]
to insult

die **Beleidigung** NOUN
insult

Belgien NEUT NOUN
Belgium
■ **aus Belgien** from Belgium
■ **in Belgien** in Belgium
■ **nach Belgien** to Belgium

der **Belgier** (PL die **Belgier**) NOUN
Belgian

die **Belgierin** NOUN
Belgian

belgisch ADJECTIVE
Belgian

beliebig ADJECTIVE, ADVERB
1 any you like
□ in beliebiger Reihenfolge in any order you like □ eine beliebige Anzahl any number you like
2 as you like
□ beliebig oft as often as you like □ beliebig viel as much as you like □ beliebig viele as many as you like

beliebt ADJECTIVE
popular
□ sich bei jemandem beliebt machen to make oneself popular with somebody

die **Beliebtheit** NOUN
popularity

bellen VERB [38]
to bark

belohnen (PERFECT **hat belohnt**) VERB [7]
to reward

die **Belohnung** NOUN
reward
□ zur Belohnung as a reward

belügen (IMPERFECT **belog**, PERFECT **hat belogen**) VERB [47]
to lie to

belustigen (PERFECT **hat belustigt**) VERB [7]
to amuse

bemerken (PERFECT **hat bemerkt**) VERB [7]
to notice
□ Ich habe keine Änderung bemerkt. I haven't noticed any change.

die **Bemerkung** NOUN
remark

bemitleiden (PERFECT **hat bemitleidet**) VERB [7]
to pity

sich **bemühen** (PERFECT **hat sich bemüht**) VERB [7]
to make an effort
□ Er hat sich bemüht, höflich zu bleiben. He made an effort to remain polite.
■ **Bemühen Sie sich nicht.** Don't trouble yourself.
■ **sich um eine neue Arbeit bemühen** to try and find a new job
■ **Ich werde mich bemühen!** I'll do my best!

benachrichtigen (PERFECT **hat benachrichtigt**) VERB [7]
to inform

die **Benachrichtigung** NOUN
notification

benachteiligt ADJECTIVE
disadvantaged

sich **benehmen** (PRESENT **benimmt sich**, IMPERFECT **benahm sich**, PERFECT **hat sich benommen**) VERB [52]
▷ *see also* **das Benehmen** NOUN
to behave
□ sich anständig benehmen to behave properly □ Sie haben sich furchtbar benommen. They behaved terribly.
□ Benimm dich! Behave yourself!

das **Benehmen** NOUN
▷ *see also* **sich benehmen** VERB
behaviour

beneiden (PERFECT **hat beneidet**) VERB [54]
to envy
□ Er ist nicht zu beneiden. I don't envy him.
■ **jemanden um etwas beneiden** to envy somebody something □ Ich beneide dich um deine schöne Wohnung. I envy you your lovely flat.

beneidenswert ADJECTIVE
enviable
■ **Sie ist beneidenswert reich.** She's enviably rich.

benoten (PERFECT **hat benotet**) VERB [2]
to mark

benutzen (PERFECT **hat benutzt**) VERB [36]
to use

der **Benutzer** (PL die **Benutzer**) NOUN
user

benutzerfreundlich ADJECTIVE
user-friendly

die **Benutzung** NOUN
use

das **Benzin** NOUN
petrol

beobachten (PERFECT **hat beobachtet**) VERB [2]
to observe

bequem ADJECTIVE
1 comfortable
□ ein bequemer Stuhl a comfortable chair
■ **eine bequeme Ausrede** a convenient excuse
2 lazy
□ Er ist zu bequem, sich selbst etwas zu kochen. He's too lazy to cook himself something.

beraten (PRESENT **berät**, IMPERFECT **beriet**, PERFECT **hat beraten**) VERB
1 to give advice
□ Der Mann vom Arbeitsamt hat mich gut beraten. The man at the job centre gave me good advice.
■ **Lassen Sie sich von Ihrem Arzt beraten.** Consult your doctor.
2 to discuss
□ Wir müssen das weitere Vorgehen beraten. We have to discuss further action.
■ **gut beraten sein** to be well advised
■ **schlecht beraten sein** to be ill advised

berauben (PERFECT **hat beraubt**) VERB [7]
to rob

berechnen (PERFECT **hat berechnet**) VERB [53]
to charge
□ Was berechnen Sie für eine Beratung? What do you charge for a consultation?

bereit ADJECTIVE
ready
□ Wir sind bereit abzufahren. We're ready to leave. □ Das Essen ist bereit. Dinner's ready.
■ **bereit sein, etwas zu tun** to be prepared to do something □ Ich bin nicht bereit, noch länger zu warten. I'm not prepared to wait any longer.
■ **etwas bereit haben** to have something ready □ Sie hat immer eine Ausrede bereit. She always has an excuse ready.

bereiten (PERFECT **hat bereitet**) VERB [2]
to cause
□ Das hat mir einige Schwierigkeiten bereitet. That caused me some problems.
■ **Die Kinder bereiten mir sehr viel Freude.** The children give me a great deal of pleasure.

bereits ADVERB
already

bereuen (PERFECT **hat bereut**) VERB [7]
to regret

der **Berg** (PL die **Berge**) NOUN
1 mountain
□ Im Winter fahren wir in die Berge zum Skifahren. In winter we go skiing in the mountains.
2 hill
□ Hinter unserem Haus ist ein kleiner Berg. There's a small hill behind our house.

der **Bergbau** NOUN
mining

das **Bergsteigen** NOUN
mountaineering
□ Bergsteigen ist ihr Hobby. Her hobby's mountaineering. □ Sie ist beim Bergsteigen verunglückt. She had a mountaineering accident.

der **Bergsteiger** (PL die **Bergsteiger**) NOUN
mountaineer

die **Bergwacht** NOUN
mountain rescue service

das **Bergwerk** (PL die **Bergwerke**) NOUN
mine

der **Bericht** (PL die **Berichte**) NOUN
report

berichten (PERFECT **hat berichtet**) VERB [2]
to report
□ Die Zeitungen haben nichts über diesen Zwischenfall berichtet. The newspapers didn't report anything about this incident.

Berlin NEUT NOUN
Berlin

DID YOU KNOW...?
Berlin is one of the 16 **Länder**. It is a 'city-state' like Bremen and Hamburg. From 1963 to 1989 it was divided by the Berlin Wall. Now it is again the German capital.

berücksichtigen (PERFECT **hat berücksichtigt**) VERB [7]
to bear in mind

der **Beruf** (PL die **Berufe**) NOUN
occupation
□ Welchen Beruf hat dein Vater? What's your father's occupation?
■ **Sie ist Lehrerin von Beruf.** She's a teacher by profession.

beruflich ADJECTIVE
professional
■ **beruflich unterwegs sein** to be away on business

der **Berufsberater** (PL die **Berufsberater**) NOUN
careers adviser

die **Berufsschule** NOUN
technical college

berufstätig ADJECTIVE
working
□ Seit wann ist deine Mutter wieder berufstätig? When did your mother start working again?

der **Berufsverkehr** NOUN
rush-hour traffic

beruhigen (PERFECT **hat beruhigt**) VERB [18]
to calm down
□ Dem Lehrer gelang es nicht, die Klasse zu beruhigen. The teacher didn't manage to calm the class down. □ Beruhige dich doch! Calm down!
■ **sich beruhigen** to calm down □ Die Lage hat sich beruhigt. Things have calmed down.

das **Beruhigungsmittel** (PL die **Beruhigungsmittel**) NOUN
tranquillizer

berühmt ADJECTIVE
famous

berühren (PERFECT **hat berührt**) VERB [18]
1 to touch
□ Er berührte meinen Arm. He touched my arm.
2 to affect
□ Die Armut der Menschen hat mich sehr berührt. The poverty of the people affected me deeply.
3 to touch on
□ Ich kann diese Frage heute nur berühren. I can only touch on this question today.
■ **sich berühren** to touch □ Die beiden Drähte berührten sich. The two wires touched.

die **Berührung** NOUN
contact
□ mit etwas in Berührung kommen to come into contact with something

beschädigen (PERFECT **hat beschädigt**) VERB [7]
to damage

beschaffen (PERFECT **hat beschafft**) VERB [7]
to get
□ Ich muss mir ein Visum beschaffen. I have to get a visa. □ Können Sie mir nicht einen Job beschaffen? Can't you get me a job?

beschäftigen (PERFECT **hat beschäftigt**) VERB [18]
1 to occupy
□ Kannst du nicht irgendwie die Kinder beschäftigen? Can't you occupy the children somehow? □ Diese Frage beschäftigt mich seit Langem. This question has been occupying me for a long time.
2 to employ
□ Unsere Firma beschäftigt zweihundert Leute. Our company employs two hundred people.
■ **sich beschäftigen** to occupy oneself
□ Sebastian hat Mühe, sich allein zu beschäftigen. Sebastian has difficulty occupying himself.
■ **sich beschäftigen mit** to deal with
□ Der Artikel beschäftigt sich mit Jugendarbeitslosigkeit. The article deals with youth unemployment.

German-English

b

beschäftigt ADJECTIVE
busy

die **Beschäftigung** NOUN
work
□ Er sucht eine Beschäftigung. He's looking for work.
■ **Sie ist zurzeit ohne Beschäftigung.** She is unemployed at the moment.

der **Bescheid** (PL die **Bescheide**) NOUN
information
□ Ich warte auf den Bescheid des Konsulats. I'm waiting for information from the consulate.
■ **Bescheid wissen** to know □ Weiß deine Mutter Bescheid, dass du hier bist? Does your mother know that you're here? □ Ich weiß Bescheid. I know.
■ **über etwas Bescheid wissen** to know a lot about something □ Sie weiß über Grammatik gut Bescheid. She knows a lot about grammar.
■ **jemandem Bescheid sagen** to let somebody know

bescheiden ADJECTIVE
modest

die **Bescheinigung** NOUN
certificate
□ Du brauchst eine Bescheinigung über die Teilnahme am Kurs. You need a certificate showing that you attended the course. □ eine Bescheinigung des Arztes a doctor's certificate

die **Bescherung** NOUN
giving out of Christmas presents
■ **Da haben wir die Bescherung!** What did I tell you!

beschimpfen (PERFECT **hat beschimpft**) VERB [18]
to swear at

beschleunigen (PERFECT **hat beschleunigt**) VERB [7]
1 to increase
□ Wir müssen das Arbeitstempo beschleunigen. We have to increase our work rate.
2 to accelerate
□ Das Auto vor mir beschleunigte. The car in front of me accelerated.

beschließen (IMPERFECT **beschloss**, PERFECT **hat beschlossen**) VERB
to decide
□ Wir haben beschlossen, nach Spanien zu fahren. We decided to go to Spain.

der **Beschluss** (GEN des **Beschlusses**, PL die **Beschlüsse**) NOUN
decision

beschränken (PERFECT **hat beschränkt**) VERB [18]
to limit
□ Wir müssen unsere Ausgaben beschränken. We have to limit our spending.
■ **sich auf etwas beschränken** to restrict oneself to something □ Ich werde mich auf ein paar Worte beschränken. I'll restrict myself to a few words.

beschränkt ADJECTIVE
1 limited
□ Diese Regel hat nur beschränkte Gültigkeit. This regulation only has limited validity.
2 stupid
□ Wie kann man nur so beschränkt sein? How can anyone be so stupid?

beschreiben (IMPERFECT **beschrieb**, PERFECT **hat beschrieben**) VERB [61]
to describe
□ Können Sie den Täter beschreiben? Can you describe the culprit?

die **Beschreibung** NOUN
description

beschützen (PERFECT **hat beschützt**) VERB [7]
to protect
□ Ich möchte euch vor diesen Gefahren beschützen. I want to protect you from these dangers.

die **Beschwerde** NOUN
complaint
□ Wenn Sie eine Beschwerde haben, dann wenden Sie sich an den Geschäftsführer. If you have a complaint, then please contact the manager.
■ **Beschwerden** trouble □ Mein Knie macht mir immer noch Beschwerden. My knee's still giving me trouble.

sich **beschweren** (PERFECT **hat beschwert**) VERB [18]
to complain
□ Deine Lehrerin hat sich über dich beschwert. Your teacher has complained about you.

beseitigen (PERFECT **hat beseitigt**) VERB [7]
to remove

der **Besen** (PL die **Besen**) NOUN
broom

besetzen (PERFECT **hat besetzt**) VERB [7]
1 to occupy
□ Napoleons Truppen haben weite Teile Deutschlands besetzt. Napoleon's troops occupied large areas of Germany.
2 to fill
□ Der Posten soll mit einer Frau besetzt werden. The position is to be filled by a woman. □ Die Stelle ist noch nicht besetzt. The position hasn't been filled yet.

besetzt ADJECTIVE
1 full
□ Der Zug war voll besetzt. The train was full.
2 engaged
□ Es ist besetzt. It's engaged.
3 taken
□ Ist der Platz hier besetzt? Is this seat taken?

besichtigen (PERFECT **hat besichtigt**) VERB [18]
to visit

die **Besichtigung** NOUN
visit

besitzen (IMPERFECT **besaß**, PERFECT **hat besessen**) VERB [68]
1 to own
□ Sie besitzen ein Haus am Meer. They own a house by the seaside.
2 to have
□ Sie besitzt das Talent, sich mit allen zu zerstreiten. She has the talent of quarrelling with everyone.

der **Besitzer** (PL die **Besitzer**) NOUN
owner

besoffen ADJECTIVE
plastered

besondere ADJECTIVE
special
□ Das sind besondere Umstände. Those are special circumstances.
■ **keine besonderen Kennzeichen** no distinguishing features

die **Besonderheit** NOUN
peculiarity

besonders ADVERB
particularly
□ Es hat mir nicht besonders gefallen. I didn't particularly like it.

besorgen (PERFECT **hat besorgt**) VERB [18]
to get
□ Kannst du mir nicht einen Ferienjob besorgen? Can't you get me a holiday job?
□ Soll ich dir ein Taxi besorgen? Shall I get you a taxi? □ Ich muss Milch und Eier besorgen. I'll have to get milk and eggs.

besorgt ADJECTIVE
worried
□ Sie ist sehr besorgt um dich. She's very worried about you.

besprechen (PRESENT **bespricht**, IMPERFECT **besprach**, PERFECT **hat besprochen**) VERB [70]
to discuss
□ Das muss ich mit deiner Mutter besprechen. I'll have to discuss it with your mother.

die **Besprechung** NOUN
1 meeting
□ Frau Airlie ist in einer Besprechung. Ms Airlie is in a meeting.
2 review
□ Hast du die Besprechung dieses Films gelesen? Have you read the review of this film?

besser ADJECTIVE, ADVERB
better
□ eine bessere Note a better mark
□ Du gehst jetzt besser nach Hause. You'd better go home now.
■ **Es geht ihm besser.** He's feeling better.
■ **je schneller, desto besser** the quicker the better

sich **bessern** VERB [88]
to improve
□ Das Wetter hat sich gebessert. The weather's improved.

die **Besserung** NOUN
improvement
■ **Gute Besserung!** Get well soon!

der **Bestandteil** (PL die **Bestandteile**) NOUN
1 component
□ Hier werden die einzelnen Bestandteile der Maschine zusammengesetzt. The individual components of the machine are assembled here.
2 ingredient
□ Die Bestandteile sind in Gramm angegeben. The ingredients are given in grams.
■ **sich in seine Bestandteile auflösen** to fall to pieces

bestätigen (PERFECT **hat bestätigt**) VERB [18]
1 to confirm
□ Ich kann bestätigen, dass sie die Wahrheit gesagt hat. I can confirm that she told the truth.
2 to acknowledge
□ Hiermit bestätigen wir den Erhalt Ihres Briefes. We hereby acknowledge receipt of your letter.
■ **sich bestätigen** to prove to be true
□ Mein Verdacht hat sich bestätigt. My suspicion proved to be true.

beste ADJECTIVE
best
□ Sie ist die beste Schülerin der Klasse. She's the best pupil in the class. □ So ist es am besten. It's best that way.
■ **Am besten gehst du gleich.** You'd better go at once.
■ **jemanden zum Besten haben** to pull somebody's leg
■ **einen Witz zum Besten geben** to tell a joke
■ **Es ist nur zu deinem Besten.** It's for your own good.

bestechen (PRESENT **besticht**, IMPERFECT **bestach**, PERFECT **hat bestochen**) VERB
to bribe

die **Bestechung** NOUN
bribery

das **Besteck** (PL die **Bestecke**) NOUN
cutlery

bestehen (IMPERFECT **bestand**, PERFECT **hat bestanden**) VERB [72]
1 to be
□ Es besteht die Möglichkeit, einen Sprachkurs zu belegen. There's the chance of registering for a language course.
□ Es besteht keine Hoffnung mehr, sie jemals wiederzusehen. There's no more hope of ever seeing her again.

2 to exist
□ Die Firma besteht seit hundert Jahren. The firm has existed for a hundred years.
■ **etwas bestehen** to pass something
□ Ich hoffe, dass ich die Prüfung bestehe. I hope I pass the exam.
■ **auf etwas bestehen** to insist on something □ Wir bestehen auf sofortiger Bezahlung. We insist on immediate payment.
■ **bestehen aus** to consist of □ Eine Fußballmannschaft besteht aus elf Spielern. A football team consists of eleven players.

bestehlen (PRESENT **bestiehlt**, IMPERFECT **bestahl**, PERFECT **hat bestohlen**) VERB [73]
■ **jemanden bestehlen** to rob somebody

bestellen (PERFECT **hat bestellt**) VERB [7]
1 to order
□ Ich habe im Versandhaus ein Kleid bestellt. I've ordered a dress from a mail-order company. □ Haben Sie schon bestellt? Have you ordered yet? □ Wir sollten ein Taxi bestellen. We should order a taxi.
2 to reserve
□ Ich habe einen Tisch beim Chinesen bestellt. I've reserved a table at the Chinese restaurant.
3 to send for
□ Der Direktor hat mich zu sich bestellt. The headmaster sent for me.
■ **Bestell deiner Mutter schöne Grüße.** Give my regards to your mother.
■ **Soll ich ihr etwas von dir bestellen?** Shall I give her a message from you?

die **Bestellung** NOUN
order
■ **auf Bestellung** to order

bestenfalls ADVERB
at best

bestens ADVERB
very well
□ Die Geschäfte gehen bestens. Business is going very well.

bestimmen (PERFECT **hat bestimmt**) VERB [7]
to decide
□ Du kannst bestimmen, wer mitkommen soll. You can decide who's coming.
□ Wer bestimmt hier, was gemacht werden muss? Who decides what has to be done?
■ **Du hast hier nichts zu bestimmen!** You're not the one who decides here!
■ **für jemanden bestimmt sein** to be meant for somebody □ Diese Bemerkung war für mich bestimmt. This comment was meant for me.
■ **für etwas bestimmt sein** to be intended for something □ Dieses Geld ist für die Anschaffung von Computern bestimmt. This money's intended for the purchase of computers.

bestimmt ADJECTIVE, ADVERB
1 certain
□ Wir treffen uns immer zu einer bestimmten Zeit. We always meet at a certain time.
□ Die Teilnehmer sollten eine bestimmte Anzahl nicht überschreiten. The participants shouldn't exceed a certain number.
2 particular
□ Ich suche ein ganz bestimmtes Buch. I'm looking for a particular book.
■ **Suchen Sie etwas Bestimmtes?** Are you looking for something in particular?
■ **der bestimmte Artikel** the definite article
■ **Ich habe ihn bestimmt gesehen.** I'm sure I've seen him.
■ **Das hat er bestimmt nicht so gemeint.** I'm sure that's not how he meant it.
■ **Das hat sie bestimmt vergessen.** She's bound to have forgotten.

bestrafen (PERFECT **hat bestraft**) VERB [7]
to punish

der **Besuch** (PL die **Besuche**) NOUN
1 visit
□ Deutschland bereitet sich auf den Besuch der Königin vor. Germany's preparing for the Queen's visit. □ bei unserem Besuch in London during our visit to London
■ **Der Schulbesuch ist Pflicht.** School attendance is compulsory.
2 visitor
□ Ist euer Besuch noch da? Is your visitor still there? □ Besuch haben to have visitors
■ **bei jemandem einen Besuch machen** to pay somebody a visit
■ **bei jemandem zu Besuch sein** to be visiting somebody
■ **zu Besuch kommen** to be visiting
□ Nächste Woche kommt Onja zu Besuch. Onja's visiting us next week.

besuchen (PERFECT **hat besucht**) VERB [7]
1 to visit
□ Hast du schon das Planetarium besucht? Have you visited the planetarium yet?
■ **Besuch uns mal wieder!** Come again!
2 to attend
□ Sie besucht das Gymnasium. She attends grammar school. □ Der Vortrag war sehr gut besucht. The lecture was very well-attended.
■ **Wir haben ein Konzert besucht.** We went to a concert.

der **Besucher** (PL die **Besucher**) NOUN
visitor

betätigen (PERFECT **hat betätigt**) VERB [7]
■ **die Hupe betätigen** to sound the horn
■ **einen Schalter betätigen** to press a switch
■ **die Bremse betätigen** to apply the brakes
■ **Du solltest dich sportlich betätigen.** You should do some sport.

die **Bete** NOUN
■ **Rote Bete** beetroot

beteiligen (PERFECT **hat beteiligt**) VERB [7]
■ **sich an etwas beteiligen** to take part in something □ Franz beteiligte sich nicht an

der Diskussion. Franz didn't take part in the discussion.
■ **Alle werden am Gewinn beteiligt.** Everyone will share in the winnings.

beten VERB [2]
to pray

der **Beton** (PL die **Betons**) NOUN
concrete

betonen (PERFECT **hat betont**) VERB [7]
to stress

die **Betonung** NOUN
stress
□ Wo liegt die Betonung bei diesem Wort? Where's the stress in this word?

beträchtlich ADJECTIVE, ADVERB
1 considerable
□ eine beträchtliche Summe a considerable amount
2 considerably
□ Es hat beträchtlich länger gedauert. It took considerably longer.

der **Betrag** (PL die **Beträge**) NOUN
amount

betragen (PRESENT **beträgt**, IMPERFECT **betrug**, PERFECT **hat betragen**) VERB [77]
▷ *see also* **das Betragen** NOUN
to come to
□ Die Reparatur betrug dreihundert Euro. The repair came to three hundred euros.
■ **sich betragen** to behave □ Ich hoffe, die Kinder haben sich ordentlich betragen. I hope the children behaved well.

das **Betragen** NOUN
▷ *see also* **betragen** VERB
behaviour
□ Ich werde mich über dein schlechtes Betragen beschweren. I'm going to complain about your bad behaviour.

betreffen (PRESENT **betrifft**, IMPERFECT **betraf**, PERFECT **hat betroffen**) VERB [78]
to concern
■ **was mich betrifft** as far as I'm concerned

betreten (PRESENT **betritt**, IMPERFECT **betrat**, PERFECT **hat betreten**) VERB [79]
to enter
□ Sie klopfte, bevor sie das Zimmer betrat. She knocked before entering the room.
■ **'Betreten verboten'** 'Keep out'

der **Betrieb** (PL die **Betriebe**) NOUN
1 firm
□ Unser Betrieb beschäftigt dreihundert Menschen. Our firm employs three hundred people.
2 operation
□ Die Maschine ist jetzt in Betrieb. The machine is now in operation.
■ **In der Stadt war heute viel Betrieb.** It was really busy in town today.
■ **außer Betrieb sein** to be out of order
□ Der Fahrstuhl ist außer Betrieb. The lift's out of order.

sich **betrinken** (IMPERFECT **betrank sich**, PERFECT **hat sich betrunken**) VERB [80]
to get drunk

betroffen ADJECTIVE
1 full of concern
□ Sie machte ein betroffenes Gesicht. Her face was full of concern.
2 affected
□ von etwas betroffen sein to be affected by something □ Wir sind über diese Nachricht zutiefst betroffen. We are deeply affected by the news.

betrügen (IMPERFECT **betrog**, PERFECT **hat betrogen**) VERB
1 to cheat
□ Der Händler hat dich betrogen. The dealer's cheated you.
2 to defraud
□ Er hat seinen Arbeitgeber um Millionen betrogen. He defrauded his employer of millions.
3 to be unfaithful to
□ Hast du deine Freundin schon mal betrogen? Have you ever been unfaithful to your girlfriend?

betrunken ADJECTIVE
drunk

das **Bett** (PL die **Betten**) NOUN
bed
□ ins Bett gehen to go to bed □ das Bett machen to make the bed

die **Bettdecke** NOUN
blanket

betteln VERB [34]
to beg

das **Bettlaken** (PL die **Bettlaken**) NOUN
sheet

der **Bettler** (PL die **Bettler**) NOUN
beggar

das **Betttuch** (PL die **Betttücher**) NOUN
sheet

die **Bettwäsche** NOUN
bed linen

das **Bettzeug** NOUN
bedding

beugen VERB [38]
to bend
□ Ich kann den Arm nicht beugen. I can't bend my arm.
■ **sich beugen** to bow □ Ich beuge mich der Mehrheit. I bow to the majority.

die **Beule** NOUN
1 bump
□ eine Beule am Kopf a bump on the head
2 dent
□ Das Auto hat eine Beule. The car has a dent in it.

beunruhigen (PERFECT **hat beunruhigt**) VERB [7]
to alarm

beurteilen (PERFECT **hat beurteilt**) VERB [7]
to judge
□ Ich beurteile die Leute nicht nach ihrem Aussehen. I don't judge people on their appearance.

der **Beutel** (PL die **Beutel**) NOUN
1 bag
□ Sie tat die Einkäufe in den Beutel. She put the shopping in the bag.
2 purse
□ Er nahm einen Euro aus dem Beutel. He took a euro from the purse.

die **Bevölkerung** NOUN
population

bevor CONJUNCTION
before
□ Sie war gegangen, bevor ich es ihr sagen konnte. She left before I could tell her.

bevorstehen (IMPERFECT **stand bevor**, PERFECT **hat bevorgestanden**) VERB [72]
to be imminent
□ Die Prüfung steht bevor. The exam's imminent.
■ **jemandem bevorstehen** to be in store for somebody □ Da steht uns ja einiger Ärger bevor. There's trouble in store for us.

bevorzugen (PERFECT **hat bevorzugt**) VERB [7]
to prefer

sich **bewähren** (PERFECT **hat sich bewährt**) VERB [7]
to prove oneself
□ Er hat sich als mein Freund bewährt. He proved himself to be my friend.
□ Diese Methode hat sich bewährt. This method has proved itself.

bewährt ADJECTIVE
tried and tested
□ Das ist eine bewährte Methode. That's a tried and tested method.
■ **Sie ist eine bewährte Mitarbeiterin.** She's a reliable colleague.

bewegen (PERFECT **hat bewegt**) VERB [7]
to move
■ **sich bewegen** to move
■ **jemanden zu etwas bewegen** to persuade somebody to do something

beweglich ADJECTIVE
1 movable
□ Die Puppe hat bewegliche Beine. The doll has movable legs.
2 agile
□ Sie ist trotz ihres Alters noch sehr beweglich. She's still very agile despite her age.

bewegt ADJECTIVE
1 eventful
□ Sie hatte ein bewegtes Leben. She had an eventful life.
2 touched
□ Wir waren von seinen Worten sehr bewegt. We were very touched by his words.

die **Bewegung** NOUN
1 movement
□ Mir fällt jede Bewegung schwer. Every movement is difficult for me.
2 motion
□ Er setzte das Fahrzeug in Bewegung. He set the vehicle in motion.
3 exercise
□ Du brauchst mehr Bewegung. You need more exercise.

der **Beweis** (PL die **Beweise**) NOUN
1 proof
□ Die Polizei hat keine Beweise. The police don't have any proof.
2 sign
□ als Beweis meiner Freundschaft as a sign of my friendship

beweisen (IMPERFECT **bewies**, PERFECT **hat bewiesen**) VERB
1 to prove
□ Ich kann nicht beweisen, dass sie das gesagt hat. I can't prove that she said it.
□ Die Polizei kann nichts beweisen. The police can't prove anything.
2 to show
□ Er hat sehr viel Mut bewiesen. He showed great courage.

sich **bewerben** (PRESENT **bewirbt sich**, IMPERFECT **bewarb sich**, PERFECT **hat sich beworben**) VERB [90]
to apply
□ Es haben sich dreißig Kandidaten beworben. Thirty candidates have applied.
□ Sie hat sich bei Siemens um einen Ausbildungsplatz beworben. She applied to Siemens for an apprenticeship.

der **Bewerber** (PL die **Bewerber**) NOUN
applicant

die **Bewerbung** NOUN
application

bewerten (PERFECT **hat bewertet**) VERB [2]
to assess
□ Der Lehrer hat unsere Aufsätze zu bewerten. The teacher has to assess our essays.

bewirken (PERFECT **hat bewirkt**) VERB [7]
1 to bring about
□ Dieses Medikament wird eine schnelle Besserung bewirken. This medicine will bring about a rapid improvement.
2 to achieve
□ Meine Bitte hat nichts bewirkt. My request didn't achieve anything.
■ **Ich konnte bei ihm nichts bewirken.** I couldn't get anywhere with him.

bewohnen (PERFECT **hat bewohnt**) VERB [7]
to live in
□ Das Haus wird von drei Familien bewohnt. Three families live in the house.

der **Bewohner** (PL die **Bewohner**) NOUN
1 inhabitant

◻ die Bewohner des Landes the inhabitants of the country
2 resident
◻ die Bewohner des Hauses the residents of the house

bewölkt ADJECTIVE
cloudy

die **Bewölkung** NOUN
clouds

bewundern (PERFECT **hat bewundert**) VERB [88]
to admire

die **Bewunderung** NOUN
admiration

bewusst ADJECTIVE
1 conscious
◻ umweltbewusst environmentally conscious
2 deliberate
◻ Er hat ganz bewusst gelogen. He lied quite deliberately.
▪ **sich einer Sache bewusst sein** to be aware of something ◻ Ich bin mir der Konsequenzen bewusst. I'm aware of the consequences.
▪ **Ihr wurde plötzlich bewusst, dass ...** She suddenly realized that ...

bewusstlos ADJECTIVE
unconscious
▪ **bewusstlos werden** to lose consciousness

die **Bewusstlosigkeit** NOUN
unconsciousness

das **Bewusstsein** NOUN
consciousness
▪ **bei Bewusstsein** conscious

bezahlen (PERFECT **hat bezahlt**) VERB [7]
to pay
◻ Er bezahlte die Rechnung. He paid the bill.

die **Bezahlung** NOUN
payment

bezeichnen (PERFECT **hat bezeichnet**) VERB [53]
1 to mark
◻ Bezeichnen Sie die Stelle mit einem Kreuz. Mark the spot with a cross.
2 to call
◻ Sie hat mich als Lügnerin bezeichnet. She called me a liar.

bezeichnend ADJECTIVE
typical
◻ Das ist bezeichnend für sie! That's typical of her!

beziehen (IMPERFECT **bezog**, PERFECT **hat bezogen**) VERB [96]
1 to cover
◻ Sie beschloss, alle Kissen zu beziehen. She decided to cover all the cushions.
▪ **das Bett beziehen** to change the bed
2 to move into
◻ Wann könnt ihr euer neues Haus beziehen? When can you move into your new house?
3 to get
◻ Wir beziehen unsere Kartoffeln direkt vom Bauern. We get our potatoes straight from the farm. ◻ Sie beziehen Arbeitslosenhilfe. They get unemployment benefit.
4 to subscribe to
◻ Ich beziehe eine Tageszeitung. I subscribe to a daily newspaper.
▪ **sich beziehen** to cloud over ◻ Der Himmel bezieht sich. It's clouding over.
▪ **sich auf etwas beziehen** to refer to something ◻ Sein Beispiel bezog sich auf das Tierreich. His example referred to the animal kingdom.

die **Beziehung** NOUN
1 relationship
◻ Er hat eine Beziehung mit einer verheirateten Frau. He has a relationship with a married woman.
2 relations
◻ unsere Beziehungen zu dieser Firma our relations with this company ◻ diplomatische Beziehungen diplomatic relations
3 connection
◻ Es besteht eine Beziehung zwischen den beiden Straftaten. There's a connection between the two crimes.
▪ **in dieser Beziehung** in this respect
▪ **Beziehungen haben** to have contacts
◻ Er kann bestimmt etwas für dich tun, er hat schließlich Beziehungen. I'm sure he can do something for you, he has contacts.
▪ **eine Beziehung zu etwas haben** to be able to relate to something ◻ Ich habe keine Beziehung zu moderner Kunst. I can't relate to modern art.

der **Bezirk** (PL die **Bezirke**) NOUN
district

der **Bezug** (PL die **Bezüge**) NOUN
cover
◻ Das Sofa hatte einen bunten Bezug. The sofa had a brightly-coloured cover.
▪ **in Bezug auf** regarding ◻ in Bezug auf Kinder regarding children
▪ **Bezug nehmen auf** to refer to

bezüglich PREPOSITION
LANGUAGE TIP The preposition **bezüglich** takes the genitive.
with reference to
◻ Bezüglich Ihrer Anfrage können wir Ihnen mitteilen ... With reference to your inquiry we can inform you that ...

bezweifeln (PERFECT **hat bezweifelt**) VERB [34]
to doubt
◻ Ich bezweifle das. I doubt it.

der **BH** (PL die **BHs**) NOUN (*= Büstenhalter*)
bra

die **Bibel** NOUN
Bible

die **Bibliothek** (PL die **Bibliotheken**) NOUN
library

biegen (IMPERFECT **bog**, PERFECT **hat gebogen**) VERB
1 to bend
□ Sie bog den Draht zur Seite. She bent the wire to one side.
2 to turn
□ Du musst an der Ampel rechts in die Seitenstraße biegen. You have to turn right at the lights, into the side street.
■ **sich biegen** to bend □ Die Bäume bogen sich im Wind. The trees were bending in the wind.

die **Biene** NOUN
bee

das **Bier** (PL die **Biere** *or* **Bier**) NOUN
beer
□ Zwei Bier, bitte! Two beers, please!

der **Bierkeller** (PL die **Bierkeller**) NOUN
beer cellar

bieten (IMPERFECT **bot**, PERFECT **hat geboten**) VERB [8]
1 to offer
□ Dieser Job bietet mir die Möglichkeit, meine Englischkenntnisse anzuwenden. This job offers me the chance to use my knowledge of English.
2 to bid
□ Sie hat zweihundert Euro für den Stuhl geboten. She bid two hundred euros for the chair. □ Wer bietet mehr? Any more bids?
■ **sobald sich die Gelegenheit bietet** as soon as the opportunity arises
■ **sich etwas bieten lassen** to put up with something □ Eine solche Frechheit lasse ich mir nicht bieten. I won't put up with such cheek.

das **Bild** (PL die **Bilder**) NOUN
1 picture
□ ein Bild von Picasso a picture by Picasso
■ **ein Bild der Verwüstung** a scene of destruction
2 photo
□ Hast du ein Bild von deinem Freund? Have you got a photo of your boyfriend?

bilden VERB [54]
1 to form
□ Bildet einen Kreis. Form a circle.
□ Wie wird der Plural dieses Worts gebildet? How do you form the plural of this word?
2 to set up
□ Sie haben einen Ausschuss gebildet. They set up a committee.
■ **sich eine Meinung bilden** to form an opinion □ In dieser Frage habe ich mir noch keine Meinung gebildet. I haven't formed an opinion on this question yet.
■ **sich bilden 1** to form □ Am Himmel bildeten sich dunkle Wolken. Dark clouds formed in the sky. **2** to educate oneself □ Sie macht Kurse, um sich zu bilden. She attends courses in order to educate herself.

der **Bildschirm** (PL die **Bildschirme**) NOUN
screen

der **Bildschirmschoner** (PL die **Bildschirmschoner**) NOUN
screen saver

die **Bildung** NOUN
1 education
□ Sie hat eine gute Bildung. She has a good education.
2 formation
□ Die Bildung des Plurals im Englischen ist ziemlich regelmäßig. The formation of the plural in English is quite regular. □ die Bildung der Regierung the formation of the government

billig ADJECTIVE
cheap

der **Billigflieger** (PL die **Billigflieger**) NOUN
low-cost airline

der **Billigjob** (PL die **Billigjobs**) NOUN
low-paid job

die **Binde** NOUN
1 bandage
□ eine elastische Binde an elastic bandage
2 sanitary towel
□ Sie benützt lieber Binden als Tampons. She prefers sanitary towels to tampons.

binden (IMPERFECT **band**, PERFECT **hat gebunden**) VERB
to tie
□ Die Tomaten werden an einen Stock gebunden. The tomatoes are tied to a cane.
□ Sie band die Haare zu einem Pferdeschwanz. She tied her hair back into a ponytail.
■ **ein Buch binden** to bind a book
■ **sich binden** to get involved □ Sie möchte sich in ihrem Alter noch nicht binden. She doesn't want to get involved at her age.

der **Bindfaden** (PL die **Bindfäden**) NOUN
string

die **Bindung** NOUN
1 tie
□ Meine emotionale Bindung an meine Eltern ... My emotional ties to my parents ...
2 bindings
□ Bei einem Sturz müsste die Bindung aufgehen. When you fall the bindings should come open.

Bio- PREFIX
organic
□ Biomüll organic waste

die **Biologie** NOUN
biology

biologisch ADJECTIVE
biological

die **Birke** NOUN
birch

die **Birne** NOUN
1 pear
□ Zum Nachtisch gab es Birnen mit Schokoladensoße. There were pears with chocolate sauce for dessert.
2 bulb
□ Die Lampe funktioniert nicht, weil die Birne kaputt ist. The lamp isn't working because the bulb's gone.

bis PREPOSITION, CONJUNCTION

LANGUAGE TIP The preposition **bis** takes the accusative.

1 until
□ Sie bleibt bis Ende August in England. She's staying in England until the end of August.
□ Du hast bis Montag Zeit. You have until Monday. □ bis es dunkel wird until it gets dark
■ **bis auf weiteres** until further notice
2 by
□ Das Referat muss bis nächsten Montag fertig sein. The assignment must be finished by next Monday.
■ **bis in die Nacht** into the night
■ **bis bald** see you later
■ **bis gleich** see you soon
3 as far as
□ Ich fahre bis Köln. I'm going as far as Cologne.
■ **bis hierher** this far
■ **von ... bis ...** from ... to ... □ von Köln bis Bonn from Cologne to Bonn □ von Anfang Mai bis Ende Juni from the beginning of May to the end of June
4 up to
□ Kinder bis drei fahren umsonst. Children up to three travel free. □ bis zu dreißig Grad up to thirty degrees
■ **zehn bis zwanzig** ten to twenty
■ **bis zu** up to □ Ich kann bis zu drei Personen mitnehmen. I can take up to three people.
■ **bis auf** apart from □ Bis auf Jan sind alle mitgekommen. Everybody came along apart from Jan.

bisher ADVERB
up to now

bisherig ADJECTIVE
previous

der **Biss** (GEN des **Bisses**, PL die **Bisse**) NOUN
bite

biss VERB ▷ *see* **beißen**

bisschen ADJECTIVE, ADVERB
bit
□ ein bisschen a bit

bissig ADJECTIVE
1 vicious
■ **Vorsicht, bissiger Hund!** Beware of the dog!
2 cutting
□ Er machte eine bissige Bemerkung. He made a cutting remark.

bist VERB ▷ *see* **sein**

das **Bit** (PL die **Bits**) NOUN
bit
□ Bits und Bytes bits and bytes

die **Bitte** NOUN
▷ *see also* **bitte** EXCLAMATION
request
□ Ich habe eine Bitte. I have a request.
□ auf seine Bitte hin at his request

bitte EXCLAMATION
▷ *see also* **die Bitte** NOUN
1 please
□ Kann ich bitte noch etwas Saft haben? Can I have some more juice, please?
□ Darf ich? — Aber bitte! May I? — Please do.
■ **Wie bitte?** Pardon?
■ **Hier bitte!** Here you are.
■ **Bitte warten.** Please hold the line. *(phone)*
2 don't mention it
□ Vielen Dank für die Hilfe! — Bitte! Many thanks for your help! — Don't mention it!
■ **Bitte schön!** It was a pleasure.
■ **Bitte sehr!** You're welcome.

bitten (IMPERFECT **bat**, PERFECT **hat gebeten**) VERB [9]
■ **jemanden um etwas bitten** to ask somebody for something

bitter ADJECTIVE
bitter

blamieren (PERFECT **hat blamiert**) VERB [76]
■ **sich blamieren** to make a fool of oneself
■ **jemanden blamieren** to let somebody down

die **Blase** NOUN
1 bubble
□ Die Blase platzte. The bubble burst.
2 blister
□ Ich habe Blasen an den Füßen. I've got blisters on my feet.
3 bladder
□ Sie hat eine schwache Blase. She has a weak bladder.

blasen (PRESENT **bläst**, IMPERFECT **blies**, PERFECT **hat geblasen**) VERB
to blow

das **Blasinstrument** (PL die **Blasinstrumente**) NOUN
wind instrument

die **Blaskapelle** NOUN
brass band

die **Blasmusik** NOUN
brass band music

blass ADJECTIVE
pale
□ Als sie das hörte, wurde sie blass. When she heard that, she turned pale.

das **Blatt** (PL die **Blätter**) NOUN
1 leaf
□ Im Herbst fallen die Blätter von den Bäumen. In autumn, the leaves fall from the trees.

German-English

b

2 sheet
□ ein Blatt Papier a sheet of paper
3 newspaper
□ In welchem Blatt hast du die Anzeige aufgegeben? Which newspaper did you place the advertisement in?

blau ADJECTIVE
1 blue
□ Er hat blaue Augen. He has blue eyes.
2 sloshed
□ Gestern Abend warst du ganz schön blau. You were absolutely sloshed yesterday evening.
■ **ein blaues Auge** a black eye
LANGUAGE TIP Word for word, **ein blaues Auge** means 'a blue eye'.
■ **ein blauer Fleck** a bruise
LANGUAGE TIP Word for word, **ein blauer Fleck** means 'a blue spot'.
■ **eine Fahrt ins Blaue** a mystery tour

das **Blech** (PL die **Bleche**) NOUN
1 sheet metal
2 baking tray

das **Blei** NOUN
lead

bleiben (IMPERFECT **blieb**, PERFECT **ist geblieben**) VERB [10]
1 to stay
□ Wie lange bleiben Sie hier? How long are you staying here? □ Hoffentlich bleibt das Wetter schön. I hope the weather will stay fine.
■ **bei etwas bleiben** to stick to something
□ Ich bleibe bei meiner Meinung. I'm sticking to my opinion.
2 to be left
□ Vom Kuchen war nur noch ein Stück für mich geblieben. There was only one piece of cake left for me.
■ **Bleibt es bei morgen zehn Uhr?** Is ten o'clock tomorrow morning still on?
■ **Wo bleibt sie denn?** Where's she got to?

bleich ADJECTIVE
pale
□ Als er das hörte, wurde er bleich. When he heard that, he turned pale.

bleifrei ADJECTIVE
unleaded

der **Bleistift** (PL die **Bleistifte**) NOUN
pencil

blendend ADJECTIVE
marvellous
□ Du siehst blendend aus. You look marvellous.
■ **sich blendend amüsieren** to have a wonderful time
■ **Mir geht's blendend.** I'm feeling great.

der **Blick** (PL die **Blicke**) NOUN
1 glance
□ Ich habe mit einem Blick gesehen, dass das nicht gut gehen kann. I saw at a glance that it couldn't work.
■ **Er warf einen Blick auf die Uhr.** He glanced at the clock.
2 look
□ Sie warf mir einen verzweifelten Blick zu. She gave me a desperate look.
3 view
□ Das Zimmer hat einen herrlichen Blick auf die Berge. The room has a wonderful view of the mountains.
■ **auf den ersten Blick** at first glance

blicken VERB [48]
to look
□ Sie blickte zur Seite. She looked to one side.
■ **sich blicken lassen** to show one's face
□ Er hat sich hier nie wieder blicken lassen. He's never shown his face here again.
■ **Das lässt tief blicken!** That's very revealing!

blieb VERB ▷ *see* **bleiben**

blind ADJECTIVE
1 blind
□ Er ist auf einem Auge blind. He's blind in one eye.
2 tarnished
□ Der Spiegel war blind geworden. The mirror had become tarnished.
■ **ein blinder Passagier** a stowaway
LANGUAGE TIP Word for word, **ein blinder Passagier** means 'a blind passenger'.

der **Blinddarm** (PL die **Blinddärme**) NOUN
appendix
□ Er wurde am Blinddarm operiert. He had his appendix out.

blinzeln VERB [88]
to blink

der **Blitz** (PL die **Blitze**) NOUN
lightning
□ Der Blitz schlug in den Baum ein. The tree was struck by lightning.

blitzen VERB [36]
■ **Es blitzt.** There's a flash of lightning.

das **Blitzlicht** (PL die **Blitzlichter**) NOUN
flashlight

der **Block** (PL die **Blöcke**) NOUN
1 block
□ Unsere Nachbarn aus dem nächsten Block haben uns gestern besucht. Our neighbours from the next block visited us yesterday.
2 pad
□ Er riss ein Blatt vom Block und fing an zu schreiben. He tore a sheet from the pad and began to write.

die **Blockflöte** NOUN
recorder

blöd ADJECTIVE
stupid
□ Du bist blöd! You're stupid!
■ **blöd fragen** to ask stupid questions □ Wer blöd fragt, bekommt auch eine blöde

Antwort. If you ask a stupid question, then you get a stupid answer.

der **Blödsinn** NOUN
nonsense

blond ADJECTIVE
1 blond
□ Er hat blonde Haare. He has blond hair.
2 blonde
□ Meine Schwester ist blond. My sister's blonde. □ Sie hat ihre Haare blond gefärbt. She dyed her hair blonde.

bloß ADVERB, ADJECTIVE
only
□ Er hat bloß einen Fehler gemacht. He only made one mistake. □ Wenn das bloß schon fertig wäre! If only it was finished.
■ **Lass das bloß!** Don't do that!
■ **Wie ist das bloß passiert?** How on earth did that happen?
■ **Wo ist er bloß?** Where's he got to?
■ **mit bloßem Auge** with the naked eye
■ **der bloße Gedanke** the very thought
■ **bloßer Neid** sheer envy

blühen VERB [38]
to be in bloom
□ Zurzeit blüht der Flieder. The lilac's in bloom at the moment.

die **Blume** NOUN
flower
□ Sie hat mir einen Strauß Blumen mitgebracht. She brought me a bunch of flowers.

das **Blumenbeet** (PL die **Blumenbeete**) NOUN
flowerbed

der **Blumenkohl** (PL die **Blumenkohle**) NOUN
cauliflower

die **Bluse** NOUN
blouse

das **Blut** NOUN
blood

der **Blutdruck** NOUN
blood pressure

die **Blüte** NOUN
blossom

bluten VERB [2]
to bleed
□ Meine Nase blutet. My nose is bleeding.

die **Blutprobe** NOUN
blood test

die **Blutvergiftung** NOUN
blood poisoning

der **Bock** NOUN
■ **Bock haben, etwas zu tun** to fancy doing something □ Ich habe heute überhaupt keinen Bock auf die Schule. I don't fancy school today at all.

die **Bockwurst** NOUN (PL die **Bockwürste**
frankfurter

der **Boden** (PL die **Böden**) NOUN
1 soil
□ Der Boden ist in dieser Gegend sehr fruchtbar. The soil in this area is very fertile. □ auf deutschem Boden on German soil
2 floor
□ Wir haben auf dem Boden gesessen. We sat on the floor.
3 bottom
□ Das Schiff sank auf den Boden des Meers. The ship sank to the bottom of the sea. □ Das Fass hat einen hölzernen Boden. The barrel has a wooden bottom.
4 attic
□ Wir haben die alten Möbel auf den Boden gebracht. We put the old furniture into the attic.

die **Bodenschätze** MASC PL NOUN
mineral resources

der **Bodensee** NOUN
Lake Constance
□ eine Stadt am Bodensee a town on Lake Constance

die **Bohne** NOUN
bean

bohren VERB [38]
1 to bore
□ Sie bohrte ein Loch in das Brett. She bored a hole in the shelf.
■ **Der Zahnarzt musste nicht bohren.** The dentist didn't have to drill.
2 to drill
□ In der Nordsee wird nach Erdöl gebohrt. They're drilling for oil in the North Sea.
■ **in der Nase bohren** to pick one's nose

der **Bohrer** (PL die **Bohrer**) NOUN
drill

die **Bohrmaschine** NOUN
drill

die **Bombe** NOUN
bomb

der **Bonbon** (PL die **Bonbons**) NOUN
sweet

das **Boot** (PL die **Boote**) NOUN
boat

der **Bord** NOUN
▷ *see also* **das Bord** NOUN
■ **an Bord** on board

das **Bord** (PL die **Borde**) NOUN
▷ *see also* **der Bord** NOUN
shelf
□ Er brachte über dem Schreibtisch ein Bord für seine Bücher an. He put up a shelf over his desk for his books.

borgen VERB [38]
to borrow
□ Das gehört nicht mir, das habe ich mir geborgt. That doesn't belong to me, I borrowed it.
■ **jemandem etwas borgen** to lend somebody something □ Meine Schwester hat

mir ihr Rennrad geborgt. My sister lent me her racing bike.

die **Börse** NOUN

1 purse

□ Sie nahm zehn Euro aus ihrer Börse. She took ten euros out of her purse.

2 stock exchange

□ Diese Aktien werden an der Börse gehandelt. These shares are traded on the stock exchange.

böse ADJECTIVE

1 bad

□ Er ist ein böser Mensch. He's a bad man. □ Die Kinder waren böse. The children were bad. □ Sie hat eine böse Erkältung. She has a bad cold. □ Er hat sich böse verletzt. He's injured himself badly.

2 angry

□ Ich habe ihm einen bösen Brief geschrieben. I wrote him an angry letter.

■ **böse werden** to get angry □ Wenn du das noch einmal tust, werde ich böse. If you do that again, I'll get angry. □ Bist du mir noch böse? Are you still angry with me?

■ **auf jemanden böse sein** to be angry with somebody □ Ich bin böse auf Martin, weil er nicht gekommen ist. I'm angry with Martin because he didn't come.

■ **eine böse Überraschung** a nasty shock

■ **Mit ihm sieht es böse aus.** It doesn't look too good for him.

Bosnien NEUT NOUN

Bosnia

bot VERB ▷ *see* **bieten**

die **Botschaft** NOUN

1 message

□ Kannst du ihm eine Botschaft übermitteln? Can you give him a message?

2 embassy

□ Sie müssen das Visum auf der Botschaft beantragen. You have to apply to the embassy for a visa.

boxen VERB [48]

to box

der **Boxer** (PL die **Boxer**) NOUN

boxer

brach VERB ▷ *see* **brechen**

brachte VERB ▷ *see* **bringen**

der **Brand** (PL die **Brände**) NOUN

fire

Brandenburg NEUT NOUN

Brandenburg

> **DID YOU KNOW...?**
> **Brandenburg** is one of the 16 **Länder**. Its capital is Potsdam, which is famous as Frederick the Great's residence. Agriculture and forestry are still important parts of the economy.

Brasilien NEUT NOUN

Brazil

■ **aus Brasilien** from Brazil

■ **nach Brasilien** to Brazil

braten (PRESENT **brät**, IMPERFECT **briet**, PERFECT **hat gebraten**) VERB

▷ *see also* **der Braten** NOUN

1 to roast

□ Wir haben das Hähnchen im Backofen gebraten. We roasted the chicken in the oven.

2 to fry

□ Sie briet die Kartoffeln in der Pfanne. She fried the potatoes in the frying pan.

der **Braten** (PL die **Braten**) NOUN

▷ *see also* **braten** VERB

roast

das **Brathähnchen** NOUN (PL die **Brathähnchen**

roast chicken

die **Bratkartoffeln** FEM PL NOUN

fried potatoes

die **Bratpfanne** NOUN

frying pan

die **Bratwurst** (PL die **Bratwürste**) NOUN

fried sausage

der **Brauch** (PL die **Bräuche**) NOUN

custom

brauchbar ADJECTIVE

1 usable

□ Dieses alte Gerät ist nicht mehr brauchbar. The old appliance is no longer usable.

2 capable

□ Sie ist eine sehr brauchbare Mitarbeiterin. She's a very capable colleague.

brauchen VERB [48]

1 to need

□ Wir brauchen noch Brot und Butter. We still need bread and butter. □ Dazu brauche ich mindestens zwei Tage. I'll need at least two days.

2 to have to

□ Du brauchst heute nicht kommen. You don't have to come today. □ Du brauchst nur Bescheid zu sagen, dann helfe ich dir. You only have to let me know and I'll help you.

■ **Das kann ich gut brauchen.** I could really do with that.

die **Brauerei** NOUN

brewery

braun ADJECTIVE

1 brown

□ Sie hat braune Haare und braune Augen. She has brown hair and brown eyes.

2 tanned

□ Wir kamen ganz braun aus den Ferien zurück. We came back all tanned from our holidays.

die **Braut** (PL die **Bräute**) NOUN

bride

der **Bräutigam** (PL die **Bräutigame**) NOUN

bridegroom

das **Brautpaar** (PL die **Brautpaare**) NOUN
bride and groom

brav ADJECTIVE
good
□ Die Kinder waren brav. The children were good.
■ **Er ist ganz brav ins Bett gegangen.** He went to bed as good as gold.

LANGUAGE TIP Be careful! **brav** does not mean **brave**.

bravo! EXCLAMATION
well done!

die **BRD** NOUN *(= Bundesrepublik Deutschland)*
Federal Republic of Germany

brechen (PRESENT **bricht**, IMPERFECT **brach**, PERFECT **hat/ist gebrochen**) VERB [11]

LANGUAGE TIP For the perfect tense use **haben** when the verb has an object and **sein** when there is no object. Use **haben** for 'to vomit'.

1 to break
□ Der Zweig ist gebrochen. The branch broke. □ Ich habe den Stock in zwei Teile gebrochen. I broke the stick in two. □ Ich habe mir den rechten Arm gebrochen. I've broken my right arm. □ Sie hat ihr Versprechen gebrochen. She broke her promise. □ einen Rekord brechen to break a record
2 to vomit
□ Ihm wurde schlecht, und er musste brechen. He felt ill and had to vomit.

breit ADJECTIVE
wide
□ Das ist ein breiter Fluss. That's a wide river. □ Das Brett ist fünfzehn Zentimeter breit. The plank is fifteen centimetres wide.

der **Breitbandanschluss** (PL die **Breitbandanschlüsse**) NOUN
broadband connection

die **Breite** NOUN
width
□ die Breite des Tisches the width of the table

Bremen NEUT NOUN
Bremen

DID YOU KNOW...?
The 'Free Hanseatic City of Bremen' is one of the 16 **Länder**. It is a 'city-state' like Berlin and Hamburg, and is made up of the cities Bremen and Bremerhaven. It is the smallest **Land**, but the second-oldest city-republic in the world.

die **Bremse** NOUN
1 brake
□ Sie trat auf die Bremsen. She stepped on the brakes.
2 horsefly
□ Wir sind von Bremsen gestochen worden. We were bitten by horseflies.

bremsen VERB [36]
to brake
□ Als er das Kind sah, bremste er. When he saw the child, he braked.
■ **Sie versuchte, das Auto zu bremsen.** She tried to stop the car.
■ **Sie ist nicht zu bremsen.** There's no stopping her.

brennen (IMPERFECT **brannte**, PERFECT **hat gebrannt**) VERB [12]
1 to burn
□ Das Holz ist zu nass, es brennt nicht. The wood's too wet, it won't burn. □ Im Wohnzimmer brennt Licht. There's a light burning in the living room. □ Der Schnaps brennt auf der Zunge. The schnapps burns your tongue. □ ein Loch in etwas brennen to burn a hole in something
2 to be on fire
□ Das Haus brannte. The house was on fire.
■ **sich brennen** to burn oneself □ Ich habe mich an der heißen Platte gebrannt. I've burned myself on the hot plate.
■ **darauf brennen, etwas zu tun** to be dying to do something □ Ich brenne darauf, deinen Freund kennenzulernen. I'm dying to meet your boyfriend.

die **Brennnessel** NOUN
stinging nettle

der **Brennstoff** (PL die **Brennstoffe**) NOUN
fuel

das **Brett** (PL die **Bretter**) NOUN
1 board
□ Die Hütte bestand aus ein paar zusammengenagelten Brettern. The hut consisted of a few boards nailed together. □ Sie stellte die Schachfiguren aufs Brett. She set up the chessmen on the board.
2 shelf
□ Die Gewürze stehen auf einem Brett über dem Herd. The spices are on a shelf above the cooker.
■ **das Schwarze Brett** the notice board

LANGUAGE TIP Word for word, **das Schwarze Brett** means 'the black board'.

■ **Ich hatte ein Brett vor dem Kopf.** My mind went blank.

die **Brezel** NOUN
pretzel

bricht VERB ▷ *see* **brechen**

der **Brief** (PL die **Briefe**) NOUN
letter

der **Brieffreund** (PL die **Brieffreunde**) NOUN
pen friend

die **Brieffreundin** NOUN
pen friend

der **Briefkasten** (PL die **Briefkästen**) NOUN
1 letterbox
2 postbox

die **Briefmarke** NOUN
stamp

die **Brieftasche** NOUN
wallet

der **Briefträger** (PL die **Briefträger**) NOUN
postman
□ Günter ist Briefträger. Günter's a postman.

die **Briefträgerin** NOUN
postwoman
□ Meine Tante ist Briefträgerin. My aunt's a postwoman.

der **Briefumschlag** (PL die **Briefumschläge**) NOUN
envelope

briet VERB ▷ *see* **braten**

die **Brille** NOUN
1 glasses
□ Lesley trägt eine Brille. Lesley wears glasses. □ eine Brille a pair of glasses
2 goggles
□ Beim Schweißen sollte man eine Brille tragen. You should wear goggles when welding.
3 toilet seat
□ Ich hasse es, wenn Männer die Brille oben lassen. I hate it when men leave the seat up.

bringen (IMPERFECT **brachte**, PERFECT **hat gebracht**) VERB [13]
1 to bring
□ Unsere Gäste haben uns einen schönen Blumenstrauß gebracht. Our guests have brought us a lovely bunch of flowers. □ Kann ich meine Schwester mit zur Party bringen? Can I bring my sister to the party?
2 to take
□ Meine Freunde haben mich zum Flughafen gebracht. My friends took me to the airport. □ jemanden nach Hause bringen to take somebody home
3 to bring in
□ Diese Anlage bringt fünf Prozent Zinsen. This investment brings in five per cent interest.
4 to publish
□ Alle Zeitungen brachten diese Geschichte auf der ersten Seite. All the newspapers published this story on the first page.
5 to be on
□ Sieh mal in der Zeitung nach, was das Theater bringt. Look in the paper to see what's on at the theatre.
■ **jemanden zu etwas bringen** to make somebody do something □ Sie hat mich zum Lachen gebracht. She made me laugh. □ Du bringst mich noch zur Verzweiflung. You make me despair.
■ **jemanden dazu bringen, etwas zu tun** to get somebody to do something □ Wie hast du deine Eltern dazu gebracht, dass sie das erlaubt haben? How did you get your parents to let you do that?
■ **es über sich bringen, etwas zu tun** to bring oneself to do something □ Ich habe es nicht über mich gebracht, ihr das zu sagen. I couldn't bring myself to tell her.
■ **jemanden um etwas bringen** to cheat somebody out of something □ Der Betrüger hat die alte Frau um ihre ganzen Ersparnisse gebracht. The swindler cheated the old lady out of all her savings.
■ **jemanden in Gefahr bringen** to put somebody in danger
■ **Unser Computer bringt's nicht.** Our computer's rubbish.
■ **Das bringt nichts!** That's no use!

der **Brite** (GEN des **Briten**, PL die **Briten**) NOUN
Briton
■ **die Briten** the British

die **Britin** NOUN
Briton

britisch ADJECTIVE
British

die **Brombeere** NOUN
blackberry

die **Broschüre** NOUN
brochure

das **Brot** (PL die **Brote**) NOUN
1 bread
□ Haben wir noch Brot im Haus? Do we still have some bread in the house?
2 loaf
□ Kannst du für die Party drei Brote holen? Can you get three loaves for the party?

das **Brötchen** (PL die **Brötchen**) NOUN
roll

browsen (PERFECT **hat gebrowst**) VERB [38]
to browse

der **Browser** (PL die **Browser**) NOUN
web browser

der **Bruch** (PL die **Brüche**) NOUN
1 fracture
□ Sie wurde mit einem Bruch ins Krankenhaus eingeliefert. She was taken to hospital with a fracture.
■ **zu Bruch gehen** to get broken
□ Die ganzen Teller sind zu Bruch gegangen. All the plates got broken.
2 hernia
□ Trag das nicht allein, du hebst dir sonst einen Bruch! Don't carry that on your own, you'll give yourself a hernia!
3 fraction
□ Das Rechnen mit Brüchen haben wir noch nicht gelernt. We haven't learned fractions yet.

die **Brücke** NOUN
bridge

der **Bruder** (PL die **Brüder**) NOUN
brother

brüllen VERB [38]
to roar
□ Der Löwe brüllte. The lion roared.
■ **Er brüllte vor Schmerz.** He screamed with pain.

brummen VERB [38]
1 to growl
□ Der Bär brummte. The bear growled.
2 to buzz
□ Eine dicke Fliege brummte durchs Zimmer. A huge fly buzzed around the room.
■ **etwas brummen** to mumble something
□ Er hat irgendetwas Unfreundliches gebrummt. He mumbled something unfriendly.

der **Brunnen** (PL die **Brunnen**) NOUN
1 fountain
□ Am Marktplatz steht ein Brunnen. There's a fountain in the market square.
2 well
□ Wasser aus dem Brunnen water from the well

die **Brust** (PL die **Brüste**) NOUN
breast
□ Sie hat kleine Brüste. She has small breasts.

das **Brustschwimmen** NOUN
breaststroke

brutal ADJECTIVE
brutal

die **Brutalität** NOUN
brutality

brutto ADVERB
gross

das **Buch** (PL die **Bücher**) NOUN
book

die **Buche** NOUN
beech tree

buchen VERB [48]
to book
□ Wir haben eine Reise nach Kreta gebucht. We've booked a trip to Crete.

die **Bücherei** NOUN
library

das **Bücherregal** (PL die **Bücherregale**) NOUN
bookcase

der **Buchhalter** (PL die **Buchhalter**) NOUN
accountant

die **Buchhandlung** NOUN
bookshop

der **Buchladen** (PL die **Buchläden**) NOUN
bookshop

die **Büchse** NOUN
tin
□ Sie bewahrt den Tee in einer Büchse auf. She keeps her tea in a tin.

der **Büchsenöffner** (PL die **Büchsenöffner**) NOUN
tin opener

der **Buchstabe** (GEN des **Buchstabens**, PL die **Buchstaben**) NOUN
letter of the alphabet

buchstabieren (PERFECT **hat buchstabiert**) VERB [76]
to spell

buchstäblich ADVERB
literally
□ Sie kam buchstäblich in der letzten Minute. She arrived at literally the last minute.

sich **bücken** VERB [48]
to bend down

die **Bude** NOUN
stall
□ die Buden auf dem Jahrmarkt the stalls at the fair
■ **Kommt ihr noch mit auf meine Bude?** Do you want to come back to my place?

das **Büfett** (PL die **Büfetts**) NOUN
sideboard
■ **kaltes Büfett** cold buffet

der **Bügel** (PL die **Bügel**) NOUN
hanger

das **Bügeleisen** (PL die **Bügeleisen**) NOUN
iron
□ Ich habe mir die Hand am Bügeleisen verbrannt. I burnt my hand on the iron.

bügeln VERB [34]
to iron

die **Bühne** NOUN
stage
□ auf der Bühne stehen to be on stage

buk VERB ▷ *see* **backen**

Bulgarien NEUT NOUN
Bulgaria
■ **aus Bulgarien** from Bulgaria
■ **nach Bulgarien** to Bulgaria

der **Bummel** (PL die **Bummel**) NOUN
stroll
□ Wir machten einen Bummel an der Donau entlang. We went for a stroll along the Danube.

bummeln VERB [88]

> LANGUAGE TIP Use **sein** to form the perfect tense for 'to stroll' and **haben** for 'to dawdle'.

1 to stroll
□ Wir sind durch die Stadt gebummelt. We strolled through the town.
2 to dawdle
□ Heute hast du auf dem Heimweg aber gebummelt. You've really been dawdling on your way home today.

der **Bund** (PL die **Bünde**) NOUN
1 association
□ Die Bauern schlossen sich zu einem Bund zusammen. The farmers formed an association.
■ **Bund und Länder** the Federal Government and the Länder
2 waistband
□ Die Hose ist am Bund zu eng. The trousers are too tight at the waistband.

Bundes- PREFIX
Federal

der **Bundeskanzler** (PL die **Bundeskanzler**) NOUN
Federal Chancellor

das **Bundesland** (PL die **Bundesländer**) NOUN
state

die **Bundesliga** NOUN
Premier League

der **Bundesrat** NOUN
upper chamber of the German Parliament

> **DID YOU KNOW...?**
> The **Bundesrat** is not directly elected, but is made up of representatives of the 16 **Länder**. In many cases, **Bundesrat** approval is required before laws (particularly amendments to the constitution) can be passed.

die **Bundesregierung** NOUN
Federal government

die **Bundesrepublik** NOUN
Federal Republic
□ die Bundesrepublik Deutschland the Federal Republic of Germany

die **Bundesstraße** NOUN
federal road

der **Bundestag** NOUN
German Parliament

> **DID YOU KNOW...?**
> The **Bundestag** is the German parliamentary assembly, elected every four years.

die **Bundeswehr** NOUN
German Armed Forces

> **DID YOU KNOW...?**
> The **Bundeswehr** is based on conscription for men, but there are also career servicemen. The basic period of military service is 9 months.

bunt ADJECTIVE
1 brightly-coloured
□ Sie hatte ein buntes Kleid an. She was wearing a brightly-coloured dress.
2 mixed
□ Unsere Klasse ist ein buntes Häufchen. Our class is a mixed bunch.
■ **Mir wird es zu bunt.** It's getting too much for me.

> **LANGUAGE TIP** Word for word, **Mir wird es zu bunt** means 'It's getting too colourful for me'.

der **Buntstift** (PL die **Buntstifte**) NOUN
coloured pencil

die **Burg** (PL die **Burgen**) NOUN
castle

der **Bürger** (PL die **Bürger**) NOUN
citizen

bürgerlich ADJECTIVE
1 civil
□ bürgerliche Rechte civil rights
2 middle-class
□ eine gute bürgerliche Familie a good middle-class family

der **Bürgermeister** (PL die **Bürgermeister**) NOUN
mayor

der **Bürgersteig** (PL die **Bürgersteige**) NOUN
pavement

das **Büro** (PL die **Büros**) NOUN
office

die **Büroklammer** NOUN
paper clip

die **Bürste** NOUN
brush

bürsten (PERFECT **hat gebürstet**) VERB [2]
to brush

der **Bus** (GEN des **Busses**, PL die **Busse**) NOUN
bus
□ mit dem Bus fahren to go by bus

der **Busbahnhof** (PL die **Busbahnhöfe**) NOUN
bus station

der **Busch** (PL die **Büsche**) NOUN
bush

der **Busen** (PL die **Busen**) NOUN
bosom

der **Busfahrer** (PL die **Busfahrer**) NOUN
bus driver

die **Bushaltestelle** NOUN
bus stop

die **Buslinie** NOUN
bus route

das **Bußgeld** (PL die **Bußgelder**) NOUN
fine

der **Büstenhalter** (PL die **Büstenhalter**) NOUN
bra

die **Butter** NOUN
butter

das **Butterbrot** (PL die **Butterbrote**) NOUN
bread and butter

bzw. ABBREVIATION *(= beziehungsweise)*
or

Cc

ca. ABBREVIATION *(= circa)*
approx.

das **Café** (PL die **Cafés**) NOUN
café
□ Sonntags gehen wir immer ins Café. On Sundays we always go to a café.

die **Cafeteria** (PL die **Cafeterias**) NOUN
cafeteria

das **Callcenter** (PL die **Callcenter**) NOUN
call centre

campen VERB [38]
to camp

der **Campingplatz** (GEN des **Campingplatzes**, PL die **Campingplätze**) NOUN
campsite

die **CD** (PL die **CDs**) NOUN
CD

die **CD-ROM** (PL die **CD-ROMs**) NOUN
CD-ROM

der **CD-Spieler** (PL die **CD-Spieler**) NOUN
CD player

das **Cello** (PL die **Cellos** *or* **Celli**) NOUN
cello
□ Ich spiele Cello. I play the cello.

der **Cent** (PL die **Cents**) NOUN
cent

der **Champignon** (PL die **Champignons**) NOUN
button mushroom

die **Chance** NOUN
chance

das **Chaos** (GEN des **Chaos**) NOUN
chaos

chaotisch ADJECTIVE
chaotic

der **Charakter** (PL die **Charakter**) NOUN
character

charmant ADJECTIVE
charming

der **Charterflug** (PL die **Charterflüge**) NOUN
charter flight

der **Chat** (PL die **Chats**) NOUN
chat *(Internet)*

der **Chatroom** (PL die **Chatrooms**) NOUN
chat room

chatten VERB [2]
to chat
□ Wir haben im Internet gechattet. We chatted on the Net.

der **Chef** (PL die **Chefs**) NOUN
1 head
□ Er ist Chef einer großen Firma. He's the head of a large company.
2 boss
□ Da muss ich den Chef fragen. I'll have to ask my boss.

die **Chefin** NOUN
boss

die **Chemie** NOUN
chemistry

der **Chemiker** (PL die **Chemiker**) NOUN
industrial chemist

chemisch ADJECTIVE
chemical
■ **chemische Reinigung** dry cleaning

der **Chicorée** NOUN
chicory

Chile NEUT NOUN
Chile
■ **aus Chile** from Chile
■ **nach Chile** to Chile

China NEUT NOUN
China
■ **aus China** from China
■ **nach China** to China

der **Chinese** (GEN des **Chinesen**, PL die **Chinesen**) NOUN
Chinese
■ **die Chinesen** the Chinese

die **Chinesin** NOUN
Chinese

chinesisch ADJECTIVE
Chinese

die **Chips** PL NOUN
crisps

LANGUAGE TIP Be careful! The German word **Chips** does not mean **chips**.

der **Chirurg** (GEN des **Chirurgen**, PL die **Chirurgen**) NOUN
surgeon

die **Chirurgie** NOUN
surgery

das **Chlor** NOUN
chlorine

der **Chor** (PL die **Chöre**) NOUN
choir

□ Sie singt im Chor. She sings in a choir.
der **Christ** (GEN des **Christen**, PL die **Christen**) NOUN
Christian
□ Er ist Christ. He's a Christian.
die **Christin** NOUN
Christian
□ Sie ist Christin. She's a Christian.
christlich ADJECTIVE
Christian
circa ADVERB
approximately
cm ABBREVIATION *(= Zentimeter)*
cm
die **Cola** (PL die **Colas**) NOUN
Coke®
der **Computer** (PL die **Computer**) NOUN
computer
die **Computeranlage** NOUN
computer system
das **Computerspiel** (PL die **Computerspiele**) NOUN
computer game
cool ADJECTIVE
cool
der **Cousin** (PL die **Cousins**) NOUN
cousin
die **Cousine** NOUN
cousin
die **Creme** (PL die **Cremes**) NOUN
1 cream
□ eine Handcreme a hand cream
2 polish
□ Hast du schwarze Schuhcreme? Do you have any black shoe polish?
3 mousse
□ eine Zitronencreme a lemon mousse
der **Curry** NOUN
curry powder
die **Currywurst** NOUN (PL die **Currywürste**
curried sausage

Dd

da ADVERB, CONJUNCTION
1 there
□ Da ist es schön. It's beautiful there.
□ da draußen out there □ Da haben wir Glück gehabt. We were lucky there.
■ **da sein** to be there
2 here
□ Da liegt meine Brille ja. Here are my glasses. □ Da bin ich. Here I am.
■ **Ist noch Milch da?** Is there any milk left?
3 since
□ Da du gerade hier bist ... Since you're here ...

dabei ADVERB
■ **nahe dabei** close by □ Er stand nahe dabei. He was standing close by.
■ **Sie hatten ihren Hund dabei.** They had their dog with them.
■ **Was ist schon dabei?** What of it?
■ **es ist doch nichts dabei, wenn ...** it doesn't matter if ...
■ **Bleiben wir dabei.** Let's leave it at that.
■ **Es bleibt dabei.** That's settled.
■ **dabei sein** to be there □ Ich bin dabei gewesen. I was there.
■ **Er war gerade dabei, zu gehen.** He was just about to leave.

das **Dach** (PL die **Dächer**) NOUN
roof

der **Dachboden** (PL die **Dachböden**) NOUN
attic

dachte VERB ▷ *see* **denken**

der **Dackel** (PL die **Dackel**) NOUN
dachshund

dadurch ADVERB, CONJUNCTION
1 through it
□ Er muss dadurch gekrochen sein. He must have crawled through it.
2 that's why
□ Dadurch habe ich mich verspätet. That's why I was late.
3 as a result
□ Der Zug hatte Verspätung, dadurch haben wir unseren Anschluss verpasst. The train was late, and as a result we missed our connection.
■ **dadurch, dass** because □ Dadurch, dass sie kein Englisch kann ... Because she doesn't speak any English ...

dafür ADVERB
1 for it
□ Was hast du dafür bezahlt? How much did you pay for it? □ Was bekomme ich dafür? What will I get for it?
■ **Er ist bekannt dafür.** He's well-known for that.
2 instead
□ Wenn du nicht mit ins Schwimmbad kannst, dann komm dafür doch mit ins Kino. If you can't come with us to the swimming pool, then come along to the cinema instead.
■ **Er kann nichts dafür.** He can't help it.

dagegen ADVERB, CONJUNCTION
1 against it
□ Was hast du dagegen? What have you got against it? □ Ich war dagegen. I was against it.
■ **Ich habe nichts dagegen.** I don't mind.
■ **Dagegen kann man nichts tun.** You can't do anything about it.
2 into it
□ Er sah den Baum nicht und rannte dagegen. He didn't see the tree and ran into it.
3 for it
□ Das ist jetzt mein Ball, ich habe meine Murmeln dagegen getauscht. This is my ball now - I swapped my marbles for it.
4 by comparison
□ Dagegen ist unser Haus klein. Our house is small by comparison.
5 however
□ Sie wollte gehen, er dagegen wollte bleiben. She wanted to leave, however he wanted to stay.

daheim ADVERB
at home

daher ADVERB, CONJUNCTION
1 from there
□ Daher komme ich gerade. I've just come from there.
2 that's where
□ Das war ein schwerer Unfall; daher hat er sein kaputtes Bein. It was a serious accident - that's where he got his bad leg.
3 that's why
□ Sie war krank und konnte daher nicht mitkommen. She was ill, and that's why she couldn't come.

dahin ADVERB
there
□ Dahin gehe ich jetzt. I'm going there now.

dahinten ADVERB
over there

dahinter ADVERB
behind it
□ Er versteckte sich dahinter. He hid behind it.

dahinterkommen (IMPERFECT **kam dahinter**, PERFECT **ist dahintergekommen**) VERB [40]
to find out
□ Meine Mutter ist dahintergekommen, dass ich gestern nicht bei dir war. My mother has found out that I wasn't at your place yesterday.

damals ADVERB
in those days

die **Dame** NOUN
1 lady
2 queen *(chess, cards)*
3 draughts
□ Dame ist mein Lieblingsspiel. Draughts is my favourite game.

damit ADVERB, CONJUNCTION
1 with it
□ Wisch damit den Tisch ab. Wipe the table with it.
2 by that
□ Was meint er damit? What does he mean by that?
■ **Was willst du damit sagen?** What are you getting at?
■ **Genug damit!** That's enough of that!
■ **Damit eilt es nicht.** There's no hurry.
3 so that
□ Ich sage dir das, damit du das weißt. I'm telling you so that you know.

der **Dampf** NOUN
steam

der **Dampfer** (PL die **Dampfer**) NOUN
steamer
□ mit dem Dampfer fahren to go by steamer
■ **Du bist auf dem falschen Dampfer.** You've got the wrong idea.

LANGUAGE TIP Word for word, **Du bist auf dem falschen Dampfer** means 'You're on the wrong steamer'.

danach ADVERB
1 afterwards
□ Ich habe etwas getrunken, und danach fühlte ich mich besser. I had something to drink and afterwards felt much better.
2 accordingly
□ Verhalte dich bitte danach. Please behave accordingly.

der **Däne** (GEN des **Dänen**, PL die **Dänen**) NOUN
Dane

Dänemark NEUT NOUN
Denmark
■ **aus Dänemark** from Denmark
■ **nach Dänemark** to Denmark

die **Dänin** NOUN
Dane

dänisch ADJECTIVE
Danish

der **Dank** NOUN
▷ *see also* **dank** PREPOSITION
thanks
□ Unser Dank gilt vor allem Herrn Morris. Our thanks to Mr Morris in particular.
■ **Vielen Dank!** Many thanks.

dank PREPOSITION
▷ *see also* **der Dank** NOUN

LANGUAGE TIP **dank** takes the genitive or dative.

thanks to
□ Dank meiner Schwester habe ich noch rechtzeitig davon erfahren. Thanks to my sister I found out about it in time.

dankbar ADJECTIVE
grateful
□ Ich bin dir sehr dankbar. I'm very grateful to you.
■ **eine dankbare Aufgabe** a rewarding task

danke EXCLAMATION
thank you
■ **Danke sehr!** Thank you.
■ **Danke schön!** Thank you very much.
■ **Nein, danke!** No, thanks.

danken VERB [38]
to thank
□ Ich möchte dir dafür danken. I'd like to thank you for that.
■ **nichts zu danken!** don't mention it!

dann ADVERB
then
■ **dann und wann** now and then

daran ADVERB
1 on it
□ ein Päckchen mit einem Zettel daran a parcel with a label on it
2 of it
□ Er ist daran gestorben. He died of it. □ Ich habe nicht daran gedacht. I didn't think of it.
■ **Es liegt daran, dass ...** This is because ...
■ **das Beste daran** the best thing about it
■ **Ich war nahe daran, zu gehen.** I was on the point of going.

darauf ADVERB
1 on it
□ Nimm einen Untersetzer und stelle den Topf darauf. Take a mat and put the pan on it.
2 afterwards
□ kurz darauf shortly afterwards
■ **die Tage darauf** the following days
■ **am Tag darauf** the next day
■ **Er ging darauf zu.** He walked towards it.
■ **es kommt ganz darauf an, ob ...** it all depends whether ...

daraus ADVERB
1 out of it
□ Sie nahm einen Keks daraus. She took a biscuit out of it.
2 of it
□ Was ist daraus geworden? What became of it?
■ **daraus geht hervor, dass ...** this means that ...

darf VERB ▷ *see* **dürfen**

darin ADVERB
in it
□ eine Dose mit Keksen darin a tin with biscuits in it
■ **Darin sehe ich kein Problem.** I don't see any problem there.

der **Darm** (PL die **Därme**) NOUN
intestine

darstellen (PERFECT **hat dargestellt**) VERB [4]
to portray
□ etwas in einem günstigen Licht darstellen to portray something in a good light

darüber ADVERB
1 over it
□ ein Tisch mit einer Lampe darüber a table with a light over it □ Da war eine Brücke, wir sind aber nicht darüber gefahren. There was a bridge, but we didn't drive over it.
2 about it
□ Wir haben darüber gesprochen. We talked about it. □ Denk mal darüber nach. Think about it.
3 more
□ Sie verdient fünftausend oder vielleicht sogar darüber. She earns five thousand or maybe even more.

darum ADVERB, CONJUNCTION
1 round it
□ Sie machte ein rotes Band darum. She put a red ribbon round it.
■ **es geht darum, dass ...** the important thing is to ...
■ **er würde viel darum geben, wenn ...** he would give a lot to ...
2 that's why
□ Darum bin ich nicht gekommen. That's why I didn't come.
■ **Ich tue es darum, weil ...** I'm doing it because ...

darunter ADVERB
1 under it
□ Der Topf ist heiß, leg einen Untersetzer darunter. The pot's hot, put a mat under it.
■ **ein Stockwerk darunter** one floor below
2 less
□ Er verdient nur dreitausend Euro oder vielleicht sogar darunter. He earns only three thousand euros or maybe even less.
■ **Was verstehst du darunter?** What do you understand by that?

das ARTICLE, PRONOUN

LANGUAGE TIP **das** is the definite neuter article.

1 the
□ das Auto the car
■ **das Leben** life
■ **Er hat sich das Knie verletzt.** He's hurt his knee.
2 who
□ das Kind, das dir das gesagt hat the child who told you
■ **das Kind, das du gesehen hast** the child you saw
3 which
□ das Fahrrad, das du da siehst the bike which you can see over there
■ **das mit dem roten Sattel** the one with the red saddle
4 that
□ Das habe ich nicht gehört. I didn't hear that.
■ **das da** that one

dasein VERB ▷ *see* **da**

dass CONJUNCTION
that
□ Ich bin böse, dass er nicht gekommen ist. I'm annoyed that he didn't come. □ Ich weiß, dass du besser in Mathe bist als ich. I know you're better at maths than me.

dasselbe PRONOUN
the same
□ dasselbe Kind the same child

dastehen (IMPERFECT **stand da**, PERFECT **hat dagestanden**) VERB [72]
to stand there

die **Datei** NOUN
file

die **Daten** NEUT PL NOUN
data

die **Datenbank** (PL die **Datenbanken**) NOUN
data base

die **Datenverarbeitung** NOUN
data processing

der **Dativ** (PL die **Dative**) NOUN
dative

das **Datum** (PL die **Daten**) NOUN
date

die **Dauer** NOUN
1 duration
□ für die Dauer meines Aufenthalts for the duration of my stay
2 length
□ die Dauer einer Reise the length of a journey □ die Dauer eines Anrufs the length of a call
■ **von Dauer sein** to be permanent
■ **Ihr Glück war nur von kurzer Dauer.** Their happiness was only short-lived.
■ **auf die Dauer 1** in the long run □ Auf die Dauer wird ihm das langweilig werden. He'll get bored with it in the long run.
2 indefinitely □ Auf die Dauer geht das aber

nicht. That can't go on indefinitely.

dauern VERB [88]
to last
□ Der Krieg hat zehn Jahre gedauert. The war lasted ten years.
■ **lange dauern** to take a long time
□ Das hat lange gedauert. That took a long time. □ Es hat sehr lang gedauert, bis er ... It took him a long time to ...
■ **Wie lange dauert das denn noch?** How much longer is this going to take?

dauernd ADJECTIVE, ADVERB
constant
□ Ich konnte sein dauerndes Stöhnen nicht ertragen. I couldn't stand his constant moaning.
■ **Musst du mich dauernd stören?** Do you have to constantly interrupt me?

die **Dauerwelle** NOUN
perm

der **Daumen** (PL die **Daumen**) NOUN
thumb
■ **Ich drücke dir die Daumen.** I'll keep my fingers crossed for you.

davon ADVERB
1 of them
□ Sie nahm zwei davon. She took two of them.
■ **Sie nahm hundert Gramm davon.** She took a hundred grams.
2 away
□ Er lief davon. He ran away.
3 from it
□ Sie hat den Knopf davon abgetrennt. She removed the button from it.
■ **Sie bekommt Kopfschmerzen davon.** It gives her a headache.
■ **davon abgesehen** apart from that
4 about it
□ davon sprechen to talk about it □ Sie weiß nichts davon. She doesn't know anything about it.
■ **Was habe ich davon?** What's the point?
■ **Das kommt davon!** That's what you get.

davonkommen (IMPERFECT **kam davon**, PERFECT **ist davongekommen**) VERB [40]
to escape
□ Wir sind noch einmal davongekommen. We've had a lucky escape.

davor ADVERB
1 in front of it
□ Ich stellte mich davor. I stood in front of it.
2 first
□ Du solltest davor aber noch zum Friseur. You ought to go to the hairdresser's first.
■ **Ich habe dich davor gewarnt.** I warned you about it.

dazu ADVERB
with it
□ Was sollen wir dazu trinken? What shall we drink with it?
■ **ein Beispiel dazu** an example of this
■ **seine Gedanken dazu** his thoughts on this
■ **dazu fähig sein** to be capable of it
■ **und dazu noch** and in addition

dazwischen ADVERB
1 in between
□ Wir können dazwischen ja eine Pause machen. We can have a break in between.
2 between them
□ Siehst du die beiden Pfosten, stell dich dazwischen. You see the two posts? Go and stand between them. □ der Unterschied dazwischen the difference between them

dazwischenkommen (IMPERFECT **kam dazwischen**, PERFECT **ist dazwischengekommen**) VERB [40]
■ **Es ist etwas dazwischengekommen.** Something's cropped up.

LANGUAGE TIP Word for word, **Es ist etwas dazwischengekommen** means 'Something's come in-between'.

die **DDR** (GEN der **DDR**) NOUN (= *Deutsche Demokratische Republik*)
GDR
□ die ehemalige DDR the former GDR

die **Decke** NOUN
1 ceiling
□ Wir haben die Decke des Kinderzimmers gestrichen. We've painted the ceiling of the children's room.
2 blanket
□ eine Wolldecke a woollen blanket
■ **eine Tischdecke** a tablecloth

der **Deckel** (PL die **Deckel**) NOUN
lid

decken VERB [38]
to cover
□ Er deckte die Hand über seine Augen. He covered his eyes with his hand.
■ **den Tisch decken** to lay the table

dehnen VERB [38]
to stretch
□ Er dehnte sich und gähnte. He stretched and yawned.

dein ADJECTIVE
1 your
□ Dein Englischlehrer ist nett. Your English teacher's nice. □ Hat deine Mutter das erlaubt? Did your mother let you? □ Ist das dein Buch? Is that your book? □ Wo sind deine Eltern? Where are your parents?
2 yours
□ Der Bleistift hier, ist das deiner? Is this pencil yours? □ Meine Mutter heißt Ulla, wie heißt deine? My mother's called Ulla, what's yours called? □ Mein Fahrrad ist kaputt, kann ich deins benutzen? My bike's broken, can I use yours?

deinetwegen ADVERB
1 for your sake

□ Ich habe deinetwegen darauf verzichtet. I did without for your sake.
2 on your account
□ Er hat sich deinetwegen aufgeregt. He got upset on your account.

deklinieren (PERFECT **hat dekliniert**) VERB [76]
to decline

der **Delphin** (PL die **Delphine**) NOUN
dolphin

dem ARTICLE

LANGUAGE TIP **dem** is the dative of **der** and **das**.

the
□ auf dem Tisch on the table
■ **Gib es dem Mann.** Give it to the man.
■ **der Mann, dem ich es gegeben habe** the man I gave it to

demnächst ADVERB
shortly

die **Demokratie** NOUN
democracy

demokratisch ADJECTIVE
democratic

die **Demonstration** NOUN
demonstration

demonstrieren (PERFECT **hat demonstriert**) VERB [76]
to demonstrate

den ARTICLE

LANGUAGE TIP **den** is the accusative of **der**.

the
□ Ich sehe den Mann. I can see the man.
□ durch den Wald through the wood
■ **Er hat sich den Fuß verletzt.** He's hurt his foot.
■ **der Mann, den ich gesehen habe** the man I saw

denen PRONOUN

LANGUAGE TIP **denen** is the dative of **die** (plural).

1 whom
■ **die Leute, denen ich die Bücher gegeben habe** the people I gave the books to
■ **die Leute, denen ich helfen wollte** the people I wanted to help
2 which
□ Probleme, denen wir nicht gewachsen sind problems which we can't cope with

denkbar ADJECTIVE
conceivable

denken (IMPERFECT **dachte**, PERFECT **hat gedacht**) VERB [14]
to think

das **Denkmal** (PL die **Denkmäler**) NOUN
monument

denn CONJUNCTION, ADVERB
1 because
□ Ich habe sie nicht gesehen, denn sie war schon weg. I didn't see her because she had already left.
2 than
□ besser denn je better than ever
■ **es sei denn ...** unless ...
■ **Warum denn?** But why?

dennoch CONJUNCTION
nevertheless

der ARTICLE, PRONOUN

LANGUAGE TIP **der** is the definite masculine article and genitive and dative of **die**.

1 the
□ der Mann the man
■ **der Tod** death
■ **das Auto der Frau** the woman's car
■ **Gib es der Frau.** Give it to the woman.
2 who
□ der, der dir das gesagt hat the person who told you that
■ **die Frau, der ich es gegeben habe** the woman I gave it to
3 which
□ der Computer, der mir gehört the computer which belongs to me
■ **der mit der Brille** the one with glasses
■ **der da** that one

derselbe PRONOUN
the same
□ derselbe Mann the same man

deshalb ADVERB
that's why

dessen PRONOUN

LANGUAGE TIP **dessen** is the genitive of **der** and **das**.

whose
□ mein Freund, dessen Schwester krank ist my friend whose sister is ill

desto ADVERB
all the
□ desto besser all the better
■ **je ... desto ...** the ... the ... □ Je mehr er sagte, desto wütender wurde sie. The more he said, the angrier she became. □ je eher, desto besser the earlier the better

deswegen CONJUNCTION
that's why
□ Hat er deswegen so geschimpft? Is that why he was so mad?
■ **Es ist spät, deswegen gehen wir jetzt.** It's late, so we're leaving.
■ **Ich sage das deswegen, weil ...** The reason I'm saying this is that ...

deutlich ADJECTIVE, ADVERB
1 clear
□ mit klarer Stimme in a clear voice
2 clearly
□ Drück dich bitte deutlicher aus. Please speak more clearly. □ Es war deutlich zu sehen. It was clearly visible.

■ **ein deutlicher Unterschied** a distinct difference

das **Deutsch** (GEN des **Deutschen**) NOUN
▷ *see also* **deutsch** ADJECTIVE
German
□ Er lernt Deutsch in der Schule. He's learning German at school.
■ **auf Deutsch** in German

deutsch ADJECTIVE
▷ *see also* **das Deutsch** NOUN
German

der/die **Deutsche** (GEN des/der **Deutschen**, PL die **Deutschen**) NOUN
German
■ **Ich bin Deutscher.** I'm German.

Deutschland NEUT NOUN
Germany
■ **aus Deutschland** from Germany
■ **in Deutschland** in Germany
■ **nach Deutschland** to Germany

der **Dezember** (GEN des **Dezember** *or* **Dezembers**, PL die **Dezember**) NOUN
December
□ im Dezember in December □ am vierten Dezember on the fourth of December □ Ulm, den 5. Dezember 2007 Ulm, 5 December 2007 □ Heute ist der sechste Dezember. Today is the sixth of December.

d. h. ABBREVIATION *(= das heißt)*
i.e.

das **Dia** (PL die **Dias**) NOUN
slide

diagonal ADJECTIVE
diagonal

der **Dialekt** (PL die **Dialekte**) NOUN
dialect

der **Diamant** (GEN des **Diamanten**, PL die **Diamanten**) NOUN
diamond

die **Diät** NOUN
diet
□ Sie muss Diät halten. She has to stick to a strict diet.

dich PRONOUN
1 you
□ Ich habe dich gesehen. I saw you.
2 yourself
□ Sieh dich mal im Spiegel an. Look at yourself in the mirror.

dicht ADJECTIVE, ADVERB
1 dense
□ dichte Wälder dense woods
2 thick
□ dichter Nebel thick fog
3 watertight
□ Ist der Behälter dicht? Is the container watertight?
■ **Die Gasleitung war nicht dicht.** There was a leak in the gas pipe.
■ **dichter Verkehr** heavy traffic
■ **dicht an** close to □ Geh nicht zu dicht ans Feuer. Don't go too close to the fire.

der **Dichter** (PL die **Dichter**) NOUN
poet

dick ADJECTIVE
1 thick
□ Das Brett ist drei Zentimeter dick. The plank's three centimetres thick.
2 fat
□ Ich bin zu dick. I'm too fat.

der **Dickkopf** (PL die **Dickköpfe**) NOUN
■ **einen Dickkopf haben** to be stubborn
LANGUAGE TIP Word for word, **einen Dickkopf haben** means 'to have a thick head'.

die **Dickmilch** NOUN
soured milk

die ARTICLE, PRONOUN
LANGUAGE TIP **die** is the definite feminine article and the definite article plural.
1 the
□ die Frau the woman □ die Kinder the children
■ **die Liebe** love
■ **Er hat sich die Hand verletzt.** He's hurt his hand.
2 who
□ die, die dir das gesagt hat the person who told you that
■ **die Frau, die du gesehen hast** the woman you saw
3 which
□ die Uhr, die mir gehört the watch which belongs to me
■ **die mit der Brille** the one with glasses
■ **die da** that one

der **Dieb** (PL die **Diebe**) NOUN
thief

der **Diebstahl** (PL die **Diebstähle**) NOUN
theft

die **Diele** NOUN
hall
□ Sie stand vor dem Spiegel in der Diele. She stood in front of the mirror in the hall.

dienen (PERFECT **hat gedient**) VERB [38]
to serve
□ Es dient einem guten Zweck. It serves a useful purpose.
■ **womit kann ich Ihnen dienen?** what can I do for you?

der **Dienst** (PL die **Dienste**) NOUN
service
■ **Dienst haben** to be on duty

der **Dienstag** (PL die **Dienstage**) NOUN
Tuesday
□ am Dienstag on Tuesday

dienstags ADVERB
on Tuesdays

dies PRONOUN
1 this

□ Dies ist unser Haus. This is our house.
2 these
□ Dies sind meine Bücher. These are my books.

diese PRONOUN
1 this
□ Dieses Kleid gefällt mir besonders gut. I particularly like this dress.
2 these
□ diese Bücher these books
3 this one
□ Ich möchte diesen hier. I'd like this one.
4 these ones
□ Ich suche ein Paar Sandalen, kann ich diese anprobieren? I'm looking for a pair of sandals, can I try these ones on?

der **Diesel** NOUN
diesel

dieselbe PRONOUN
the same
□ dieselbe Frau the same woman

diesmal ADVERB
this time

digital ADJECTIVE
digital
□ die digitale Revolution the digital revolution

das **Digitalfernsehen** NOUN
digital television

das **Diktat** (PL die **Diktate**) NOUN
dictation

diktieren (PERFECT **hat diktiert**) VERB [76]
to dictate

das **Ding** (PL die **Dinge**) NOUN
thing

das **Diplom** (PL die **Diplome**) NOUN
diploma

die **Diplomatie** NOUN
diplomacy

diplomatisch ADJECTIVE
diplomatic

dir PRONOUN
LANGUAGE TIP **dir** is the dative of **du**.
1 you
□ Ich habe es dir doch gesagt. I told you so.
2 to you
□ Ich habe es dir gestern gegeben. I gave it to you yesterday.

direkt ADJECTIVE
direct
□ Der Flug geht direkt. It's a direct flight.

der **Direktor** (PL die **Direktoren**) NOUN
1 director
□ der Direktor der Firma the director of the company
2 headmaster
□ Mein Bruder musste gestern zum Direktor. My brother was sent to the headmaster yesterday.

die **Disco** (PL die **Discos**) NOUN
disco

die **Diskette** NOUN
diskette

die **Diskothek** NOUN
disco

die **Diskussion** NOUN
discussion
■ **zur Diskussion stehen** to be under discussion

das **Diskuswerfen** NOUN
throwing the discus

diskutieren (PERFECT **hat diskutiert**) VERB [76]
to discuss
□ Wir haben über Politik diskutiert. We discussed politics.

doch ADVERB, CONJUNCTION
1 after all
□ Sie ist doch noch gekommen. She came after all.
2 anyway
□ Du machst ja doch, was du willst. You do what you want anyway.
3 but
□ Ich habe ihn eingeladen, doch er hatte keine Lust. I invited him, but he didn't feel like it. □ Sie ist doch noch so jung. But she's still so young.
4 yes
LANGUAGE TIP **doch** is used to contradict a negative statement.
□ Du magst doch keine Süßigkeiten. - Doch! You don't like sweets. - Yes I do. □ Das ist nicht wahr. - Doch! That's not true. - Yes it is!
■ **Komm doch.** Do come.
■ **Lass ihn doch.** Just leave him.

der **Doktor** (PL die **Doktoren**) NOUN
doctor
□ Er ist Doktor der Philosophie. He's a doctor of philosophy.

das **Dokument** NOUN
document

der **Dokumentarfilm** (PL die **Dokumentarfilme**) NOUN
documentary

dolmetschen VERB [48]
to interpret

der **Dolmetscher** (PL die **Dolmetscher**) NOUN
interpreter

der **Dom** (PL die **Dome**) NOUN
cathedral

die **Donau** NOUN
Danube

der **Donner** (PL die **Donner**) NOUN
thunder

donnern VERB [88]
to thunder
□ Es donnerte. It was thundering.

der **Donnerstag** (PL die **Donnerstage**) NOUN
Thursday
□ am Donnerstag on Thursday

donnerstags ADVERB
on Thursdays

doof ADJECTIVE
thick

das **Doppelbett** (PL die **Doppelbetten**) NOUN
double bed

die **Doppelfenster** NEUT PL NOUN
double glazing

das **Doppelhaus** (GEN des **Doppelhauses**, PL die **Doppelhäuser**) NOUN
semidetached house

der **Doppelpunkt** (PL die **Doppelpunkte**) NOUN
colon

die **Doppelstunde** NOUN
double period

doppelt ADJECTIVE
1 double
□ die doppelte Menge double the amount
2 twice the
□ der doppelte Preis twice the price □ die doppelte Geschwindigkeit twice the speed
■ **doppelt so viel** twice as much
■ **in doppelter Ausführung** in duplicate

das **Doppelzimmer** (PL die **Doppelzimmer**) NOUN
double room

das **Dorf** (PL die **Dörfer**) NOUN
village

dort ADVERB
there
■ **dort drüben** over there

dorther ADVERB
from there

dorthin ADVERB
there
□ Wir gehen jetzt dorthin. We're going there now.

die **Dose** NOUN
tin

der **Dosenöffner** (PL die **Dosenöffner**) NOUN
tin opener

der **Dotter** (PL die **Dotter**) NOUN
yolk

das **Drachenfliegen** NOUN
hang-gliding
□ Er ist beim Drachenfliegen verunglückt. He had a hang-gliding accident.

der **Draht** (PL die **Drähte**) NOUN
wire
■ **auf Draht sein** to be on the ball

das **Drama** (PL die **Dramen**) NOUN
drama

dran ADVERB
■ **Jetzt bin ich dran!** It's my turn now.
■ **Wer ist dran?** Whose turn is it?
■ **gut dran sein** to be well-off
■ **schlecht dran sein** to be in a bad way

drauf ADVERB ▷ *see* **darauf**

draußen ADVERB
outside

der **Dreck** NOUN
dirt

dreckig ADJECTIVE
dirty
□ Mach deine Kleider nicht dreckig. Don't get your clothes dirty.

drehen VERB [38]
to turn
□ Dreh mal deinen Kopf zur Seite. Turn your head to one side. □ Du musst an dem Rad drehen. You have to turn the wheel.
■ **eine Zigarette drehen** to roll a cigarette
■ **einen Film drehen** to shoot a film
■ **sich drehen** to turn □ Das Rad drehte sich schnell. The wheel was turning fast.
■ **es dreht sich um ...** it's about ...

drei NUMBER
▷ *see also* **die Drei** NOUN
three

die **Drei** NOUN
▷ *see also* **drei** NUMBER
1 three
2 satisfactory

DID YOU KNOW...?
German marks range from one (**sehr gut**) to six (**ungenügend**).

das **Dreieck** (PL die **Dreiecke**) NOUN
triangle

dreieckig ADJECTIVE
triangular

dreihundert NUMBER
three hundred

dreimal ADVERB
three times

dreißig NUMBER
thirty

dreiviertel NUMBER
three-quarters

die **Dreiviertelstunde** NOUN
three-quarters of an hour
□ Eine Dreiviertelstunde war vergangen. Three-quarters of an hour had passed.

dreizehn NUMBER
thirteen

drin ADVERB ▷ *see* **darin**

dringend ADJECTIVE
urgent

drinnen ADVERB
inside

dritte ADJECTIVE
third
□ Sie nahm beim dritten Klingeln ab. She answered on the third ring. □ Er kam als Dritter. He was the third to arrive.
■ **die Dritte Welt** the Third World
■ **das Dritte Reich** the Third Reich

das **Drittel** (PL die **Drittel**) NOUN
third

drittens ADVERB
thirdly

die **Droge** NOUN
drug

drogenabhängig ADJECTIVE
addicted to drugs

die **Drogerie** NOUN
chemist's shop

der **Drogist** (GEN des **Drogisten**, PL die **Drogisten**) NOUN
pharmacist

die **Drogistin** NOUN
pharmacist

drohen VERB [38]
to threaten
□ jemandem drohen to threaten somebody

drüben ADVERB
over there

der **Druck** (PL die **Drucke**) NOUN
1 pressure
□ Der Behälter muss viel Druck aushalten. The container has to withstand a lot of pressure.
■ **jemanden unter Druck setzen** to put pressure on somebody
2 printing
□ der Druck eines Buches the printing of a book
3 print
□ An der Wand hingen Drucke. There were prints on the wall.

drücken VERB [38]
1 to press
□ Er drückte auf den Knopf. He pressed the button.
■ **Sie drückte ihm die Hand.** She squeezed his hand.
2 to pinch
□ Meine Schuhe drücken. My shoes pinch.
■ **sich vor etwas drücken** to get out of something □ Du willst dich bloß wieder vor dem Abwasch drücken. You just want to get out of washing up again.

der **Drucker** (PL die **Drucker**) NOUN
printer

die **Drucksache** NOUN
printed matter

die **Drüse** NOUN
gland

der **Dschungel** (PL die **Dschungel**) NOUN
jungle

du PRONOUN
you
□ Hast du das gesehen? Did you see that?
■ **du sagen** to use the 'du' form of address

DID YOU KNOW...?
The familiar form of address **du** (plural **ihr**) is used when addressing family members, friends, children under 16 and pets.

sich **ducken** VERB [48]
to duck

der **Dudelsack** (PL die **Dudelsäcke**) NOUN
bagpipes
□ Er spielt Dudelsack. He plays the bagpipes.

der **Duft** (PL die **Düfte**) NOUN
scent

duften VERB [2]
to smell
□ Hier duftet es nach Kaffee. It smells of coffee here.

dumm ADJECTIVE
1 stupid
□ Das ist die dümmste Ausrede, die ich je gehört habe. That's the stupidest excuse I've ever heard.
2 bad
□ Es ist wirklich zu dumm, dass du nicht gekommen bist. It's really too bad that you didn't come.
■ **der Dumme sein** to draw the short straw

dummerweise ADVERB
stupidly

die **Dummheit** NOUN
1 stupidity
□ Deine Dummheit ist wirklich grenzenlos. Your stupidity really knows no bounds.
2 stupid mistake
□ Es war eine Dummheit, ihr das zu erzählen. It was a stupid mistake telling her that.
■ **Dummheiten machen** to do something stupid □ Macht bloß keine Dummheiten! Don't do anything stupid.

der **Dummkopf** (PL die **Dummköpfe**) NOUN
idiot

dunkel ADJECTIVE
dark
□ Im Zimmer war es dunkel. It was dark in the room.
■ **eine dunkle Stimme** a deep voice
■ **eine dunkle Ahnung** a vague idea
■ **dunkle Gestalten** sinister figures
■ **dunkle Geschäfte** shady dealings
■ **im Dunkeln tappen** to grope about in the dark
■ **ein Dunkles** a dark beer

die **Dunkelheit** NOUN
dark
□ Er hat Angst vor der Dunkelheit. He's afraid of the dark.

dünn ADJECTIVE
thin

der **Dunst** (PL die **Dünste**) NOUN
haze

durch PREPOSITION, ADVERB
LANGUAGE TIP The preposition **durch** takes the accusative.
1 through
□ durch den Wald through the wood
□ Ich habe die Stelle durch meinen Onkel bekommen. I got the job through my uncle.
□ durch seine Bemühungen through his efforts

German-English

d

2 throughout
□ die ganze Nacht durch throughout the night □ den Sommer durch throughout the summer
3 owing to
□ Durch die Verspätung haben wir den Anschluss verpasst. Owing to the delay we missed our connection.
■ **Tod durch Herzschlag** death from a heart attack
■ **durch die Post** by post
■ **durch und durch** completely □ Wir waren durch und durch nass. We were completely soaked.

durcharbeiten (PERFECT **hat durchgearbeitet**) VERB [15]
to work without a break

durchblicken (PERFECT **hat durchgeblickt**) VERB [15]
to understand
■ **Bei Computern blickt Tobias durch.** Tobias knows his stuff with computers.
■ **etwas durchblicken lassen** to hint at something

durchdrehen (PERFECT **ist durchgedreht**) VERB [15]
to crack up

durcheinander ADVERB
▷ *see also* **das Durcheinander** NOUN
1 in a mess
□ Warum ist dein Zimmer so durcheinander? Why is your room in such a mess?
2 confused
□ Ich war völlig durcheinander. I was completely confused.
■ **Du bringst mich ganz durcheinander.** You completely confuse me.

das **Durcheinander** NOUN
▷ *see also* **durcheinander** ADVERB
mess
□ In ihrem Zimmer war ein völliges Durcheinander. Her room was in a complete mess.

durchfahren (PRESENT **fährt durch**, IMPERFECT **fuhr durch**, PERFECT **ist durchgefahren**) VERB [21]
1 to drive through
□ Wir sind durch einen Tunnel durchgefahren. We drove through a tunnel.
2 to drive without a break
□ Wir sind die ganze Nacht durchgefahren. We drove all night without a break.
■ **Der Zug fährt bis Hamburg durch.** The train runs direct to Hamburg.

die **Durchfahrt** (PL die **Durchfahrten**) NOUN
way through
□ auf unserer Durchfahrt durch Frankreich on our way through France
■ **'Durchfahrt verboten'** 'no through road'

der **Durchfall** NOUN
diarrhoea

durchfallen (PRESENT **fällt durch**, IMPERFECT **fiel durch**, PERFECT **ist durchgefallen**) VERB [22]
1 to fall through
□ Die Münze ist durch dieses Gitter durchgefallen. The coin fell through this grating.
2 to fail
□ Sie ist in der Prüfung durchgefallen. She failed the exam.

durchführen (PERFECT **hat durchgeführt**) VERB [4]
to carry out

der **Durchgang** (PL die **Durchgänge**) NOUN
passageway
□ Zwischen den Häusern ist ein schmaler Durchgang. There's a narrow passageway between the houses.

durchgehen (IMPERFECT **ging durch**, PERFECT **ist durchgegangen**) VERB [29]
1 to go through
□ durch einen Tunnel durchgehen to go through a tunnel
2 to break loose
□ Das Pferd ist durchgegangen. The horse has broken loose.
■ **jemandem etwas durchgehen lassen** to let somebody get away with something
■ **ein durchgehender Zug** a through train

durchkommen (IMPERFECT **kam durch**, PERFECT **ist durchgekommen**) VERB [40]
1 to get through
□ Obwohl die Öffnung sehr schmal war, sind wir durchgekommen. Although the opening was very narrow, we got through.
2 to pass
□ Es war knapp, aber ich bin durchgekommen. It was a close shave, but I passed.
3 to pull through
□ Er war schwer verletzt, ist aber durchgekommen. He was seriously injured, but he pulled through.

durchlassen (PRESENT **lässt durch**, IMPERFECT **ließ durch**, PERFECT **hat durchgelassen**) VERB [42]
to let through
□ Der Ordner wollte uns nicht durchlassen. The steward didn't want to let us through.
■ **Der Behälter lässt Wasser durch.** The container isn't watertight.

durchlesen (PRESENT **liest durch**, IMPERFECT **las durch**, PERFECT **hat durchgelesen**) VERB [45]
to read through

durchmachen (PERFECT **hat durchgemacht**) VERB [15]
to go through
□ Sie hat viel durchgemacht in ihrem Leben. She's been through a lot in her life.
■ **die Nacht durchmachen** to make a night of it

der **Durchmesser** (PL die **Durchmesser**)
NOUN
diameter

durchnehmen (PRESENT **nimmt durch**, IMPERFECT **nahm durch**, PERFECT **hat durchgenommen**) VERB [52]
to do
□ Wir nehmen gerade Shakespeare durch. We're doing Shakespeare just now.

die **Durchreise** NOUN
journey through
□ die Durchreise durch die Schweiz the journey through Switzerland
■ **Ich bin nur auf der Durchreise.** I'm just passing through.

durchs = **durch das**

der **Durchschnitt** NOUN
average
□ über dem Durchschnitt above average
□ unter dem Durchschnitt below average
■ **im Durchschnitt** on average

durchschnittlich ADJECTIVE, ADVERB
1 average
□ Ich habe durchschnittliche Noten. My marks are average.
2 on average
□ Durchschnittlich brauche ich eine Stunde für die Hausaufgaben. On average, my homework takes me an hour.

durchsetzen (PERFECT **hat durchgesetzt**)
VERB [15]
■ **sich durchsetzen** to assert oneself
□ Er kann sich nicht durchsetzen. He doesn't know how to assert himself.
■ **Du solltest dich mehr durchsetzen.** You should be more assertive.
■ **seinen Kopf durchsetzen** to get one's way

durchsichtig ADJECTIVE
transparent

durchsuchen (PERFECT **hat durchsucht**)
VERB [18]
to search

dürfen (PRESENT **darf**, IMPERFECT **durfte**, PERFECT **hat gedurft** *or* **dürfen**) VERB [16]
to be allowed to
□ Ich darf das. I'm allowed to do that.
□ Er darf das nicht. He's not allowed to do that. □ Ich habe leider nicht gedurft. Unfortunately, I wasn't allowed.
■ **Darf ich?** May I?
■ **Darf ich ins Kino?** Can I go to the cinema?

LANGUAGE TIP The past participle **dürfen** is used when **dürfen** is a modal auxiliary.

■ **etwas tun dürfen** to be allowed to do something □ Die Kinder haben gestern länger aufbleiben dürfen. The children were allowed to stay up late yesterday.
■ **darf nicht** must not □ Das darf nicht geschehen. That must not happen.
■ **Da darf sie sich nicht wundern.** That shouldn't surprise her.
■ **Das darf nicht wahr sein!** I don't believe it!
■ **Darf ich Sie bitten, das zu tun?** Could I ask you to do that?
■ **Was darf es sein?** What can I do for you?
■ **Das dürfen Sie mir glauben.** You can take my word for it.
■ **Das dürfte genug sein.** That should be enough.
■ **Es dürfte Ihnen bekannt sein, dass ...** As you will probably know ...

der **Durst** NOUN
thirst
■ **Durst haben** to be thirsty

durstig ADJECTIVE
thirsty

die **Dusche** NOUN
shower

duschen VERB [48]
to have a shower
■ **sich duschen** to have a shower

düster ADJECTIVE
1 dark
□ Hier drin ist es so düster. It's so dark in here.
2 gloomy

das **Dutzend** (PL die **Dutzende** *or* **Dutzend**)
NOUN
dozen
□ zwei Dutzend Bücher two dozen books

duzen VERB [36]
to address sb as 'du'

DID YOU KNOW...?
The familiar form of address **du** (plural **ihr**) is used when addressing family members, friends, children under 16 and pets.

der **DVD-Player** (PL die **DVD-Player**) NOUN
DVD player

dynamisch ADJECTIVE
dynamic

der **D-Zug** (PL die **D-Züge**) NOUN
through train

Ee

die **Ebbe** NOUN
low tide
□ bei Ebbe at low tide

eben ADJECTIVE, ADVERB
1 flat
□ eine ebene Fläche a flat surface
2 just
□ Er ist eben erst gegangen. He's just gone.
3 exactly
□ Eben, das sage ich ja. That's exactly what I'm saying.
■ **eben deswegen** that's precisely why

die **Ebene** NOUN
1 plain
□ Wir sahen auf die Ebene hinunter. We looked down onto the plain.
2 level
□ Das muss auf höherer Ebene entschieden werden. That has to be decided at a higher level.

ebenfalls ADVERB
likewise

ebenso ADVERB
just as
□ Sie ist ebenso groß wie ihr Bruder. She's just as tall as her brother.

das **Echo** (PL die **Echos**) NOUN
echo

echt ADJECTIVE, ADVERB
1 real
□ echtes Gold real gold
■ **Der Geldschein ist nicht echt.** That banknote's a fake.
2 really
□ Die Party war echt gut. The party was really good.
■ **Echt?** Really?

die **Ecke** NOUN
corner
□ um die Ecke round the corner

der **Edelstein** (PL die **Edelsteine**) NOUN
precious stone

die **EDV** NOUN (*= elektronische Datenverarbeitung)*
electronic data processing

egal ADJECTIVE
all the same
□ Das ist mir egal. It's all the same to me.
■ **Das ist egal.** That makes no difference.
■ **egal, ob ...** it doesn't matter whether ...

egoistisch ADJECTIVE
selfish

die **Ehe** NOUN
▷ *see also* **ehe** CONJUNCTION
marriage

ehe CONJUNCTION
▷ *see also* **die Ehe** NOUN
before
□ Ehe ich es vergesse, ... Before I forget, ...

die **Ehefrau** NOUN
wife

ehemalig ADJECTIVE
former

der **Ehemann** (PL die **Ehemänner**) NOUN
husband

das **Ehepaar** (PL die **Ehepaare**) NOUN
married couple

eher ADVERB
sooner
□ Das hättest du eher sagen müssen. You should have said that sooner.
■ **Das kommt schon eher der Wahrheit nahe.** That's more like the truth.

die **Ehre** NOUN
honour

ehrgeizig ADJECTIVE
ambitious

ehrlich ADJECTIVE
honest

die **Ehrlichkeit** NOUN
honesty

das **Ei** (PL die **Eier**) NOUN
egg

die **Eiche** NOUN
oak

das **Eichhörnchen** (PL die **Eichhörnchen**) NOUN
squirrel

der **Eid** (PL die **Eide**) NOUN
oath
□ einen Eid schwören to swear an oath

der **Eierbecher** (PL die **Eierbecher**) NOUN
egg cup

der **Eifer** NOUN
enthusiasm

die **Eifersucht** NOUN
jealousy

eifersüchtig ADJECTIVE
jealous
□ Er ist eifersüchtig auf seine kleine Schwester. He's jealous of his little sister.

eifrig ADJECTIVE
eager

das **Eigelb** (PL die **Eigelb**) NOUN
egg yolk

eigen ADJECTIVE
own
□ meine eigene Meinung my own opinion

die **Eigenart** NOUN
peculiarity
□ Wir haben alle unsere Eigenarten. We all have our own peculiarities.

eigenartig ADJECTIVE
peculiar

die **Eigenschaft** NOUN
quality

eigensinnig ADJECTIVE
obstinate

eigentlich ADJECTIVE, ADVERB
1 actual
□ Er ist der eigentliche Besitzer. He's the actual owner.
2 actually
□ Eigentlich wollte ich heute nicht weggehen. Actually I didn't want to go out today.
■ **Eigentlich nicht.** Not really.

das **Eigentum** NOUN
property

der **Eigentümer** (PL die **Eigentümer**) NOUN
owner

sich **eignen** VERB [53]
to be suited
□ Er eignet sich nicht für diese Stelle. He's not suited to this position.

eilen VERB [38]
to be urgent
□ Das eilt nicht. It's not urgent.

eilig ADJECTIVE
urgent
□ Ich muss zuerst die eiligen Dinge erledigen. I'll have to do the urgent things first.
■ **es eilig haben** to be in a hurry

der **Eilzug** (PL die **Eilzüge**) NOUN
fast stopping train

der **Eimer** (PL die **Eimer**) NOUN
bucket

ein NUMBER, ARTICLE
▷ *see also* **eins** NUMBER, **die Eins** NOUN
1 one
□ Es war nur ein Kind da. There was only one child there. □ Ich möchte nur einen. I only want one.
2 somebody
□ Wenn einer dir das sagt, glaube es nicht. If somebody tells you that, don't believe it.
3 you
□ Da kann einem die Lust vergehen. It's enough to put you off.
4 a
□ ein Mann a man □ eine Frau a woman □ ein Kind a child
an
□ ein Ei an egg □ eine Stunde an hour

einander PRONOUN
each other

die **Einbahnstraße** NOUN
one-way street

einbilden (PERFECT **hat eingebildet**) VERB [54]
■ **sich etwas einbilden** to imagine something □ Das bildest du dir nur ein. You're imagining it.

einbrechen (PRESENT **bricht ein**, IMPERFECT **brach ein**, PERFECT **ist eingebrochen**) VERB [11]
to break in
□ Bei ihnen wurde eingebrochen. Their house has been broken into. □ Er ist in das Haus eingebrochen. He broke into the house.

der **Einbrecher** (PL die **Einbrecher**) NOUN
burglar

der **Einbruch** (PL die **Einbrüche**) NOUN
break-in
□ In dieser Gegend gibt es häufiger Einbrüche. There are a lot of break-ins in this area.
■ **bei Einbruch der Nacht** at nightfall
■ **vor Einbruch der Nacht** before nightfall

eindeutig ADJECTIVE
clear
□ eine eindeutige Antwort geben to give a clear answer

der **Eindruck** (PL die **Eindrücke**) NOUN
impression

eindrucksvoll ADJECTIVE
impressive

eine ▷ *see* **ein**

eineinhalb NUMBER
one and a half

einer ▷ *see* **ein**

einerseits ADVERB
on the one hand
□ Einerseits ..., andererseits ... On the one hand ..., on the other hand ...

eines ▷ *see* **ein**

einfach ADJECTIVE, ADVERB
1 easy
□ Das war eine einfache Frage. That was an easy question. □ Das ist nicht einfach. That isn't easy.
2 simple
□ aus dem einfachen Grund ... for the simple reason ... □ Sie leben in sehr einfachen Verhältnissen. They live very simple lives.
3 single
□ eine einfache Fahrkarte a single ticket
4 simply
□ Ich will das einfach nicht. I simply don't want it. □ Er wollte einfach nicht begreifen. He simply didn't want to understand.

die **Einfachheit** NOUN
simplicity

die **Einfahrt** NOUN
entrance

der **Einfall** (PL die **Einfälle**) NOUN
idea
□ Das war so ein Einfall von mir. It was just an idea. □ Du hast manchmal Einfälle! You do come up with strange ideas sometimes!

einfallen (PRESENT **fällt ein**, IMPERFECT **fiel ein**, PERFECT **ist eingefallen**) VERB [22]
■ **jemandem einfallen** to occur to somebody □ Mir ist das Wort nicht eingefallen. The word didn't occur to me.
■ **Das fällt mir gar nicht ein.** I wouldn't dream of it.
■ **sich etwas einfallen lassen** to come up with a good idea □ Meine Freunde haben sich zu meinem Geburtstag etwas Tolles einfallen lassen. My friends came up with a really great idea for my birthday.

das **Einfamilienhaus** (GEN des **Einfamilienhauses**, PL die **Einfamilienhäuser**) NOUN
detached family house

einfarbig ADJECTIVE
plain

der **Einfluss** (GEN des **Einflusses**, PL die **Einflüsse**) NOUN
influence
□ Er hat einen schlechten Einfluss auf dich. He has a bad influence on you.

einfrieren (IMPERFECT **fror ein**, PERFECT **hat/ist eingefroren**) VERB

LANGUAGE TIP For the perfect tense use **haben** when the verb has an object and **sein** when there is no object.

to freeze
□ Wir haben die Reste eingefroren. We've frozen the left-overs. □ Die Leitung ist eingefroren. The pipe has frozen.

die **Einfuhr** NOUN
import

die **Eingabe** NOUN
input
□ die Eingabe von Daten data input

der **Eingang** (PL die **Eingänge**) NOUN
entrance

eingeben (PRESENT **gibt ein**, IMPERFECT **gab ein**, PERFECT **hat eingegeben**) VERB [28]
to enter
□ Beate hat den Text in den Computer eingegeben. Beate entered the text into the computer.

eingebildet ADJECTIVE
conceited
□ Sie ist furchtbar eingebildet. She's terribly conceited.
■ **Ihre Krankheit ist nur eingebildet.** Her illness is all in the imagination.

eingehen (IMPERFECT **ging ein**, PERFECT **ist eingegangen**) VERB [29]
1 to die
□ Mir ist schon wieder eine Pflanze eingegangen. Another of my plants has died.
2 to shrink
□ Der Pulli ist in der Wäsche eingegangen. The pullover shrank in the wash.
■ **auf etwas eingehen** to comment on something □ Er ist auf meinen Vorschlag nicht eingegangen. He didn't comment on my suggestion.

eingenommen ADJECTIVE
■ **eingenommen von** taken with □ Ich war sofort von dem Plan eingenommen. I was immediately taken with the plan.

eingeschrieben ADJECTIVE
registered
□ ein eingeschriebener Brief a registered letter

eingestellt ADJECTIVE
■ **auf etwas eingestellt sein** to be prepared for something □ Ich war nicht auf Ihren Besuch eingestellt. I wasn't prepared for your visit.

eingießen (IMPERFECT **goss ein**, PERFECT **hat eingegossen**) VERB
to pour
□ Darf ich Ihnen noch Kaffee eingießen? Can I pour you some more coffee?

sich **eingewöhnen** (PERFECT **hat sich eingewöhnt**) VERB [7]
■ **sich eingewöhnen in** to settle down in □ Sie hat sich gut in der neuen Schule eingewöhnt. She's settled down very well in her new school.

eingreifen (IMPERFECT **griff ein**, PERFECT **hat eingegriffen**) VERB
to intervene

der/die **Einheimische** (GEN des/der **Einheimischen**, PL die **Einheimischen**) NOUN
local
□ Wir sollten einen Einheimischen fragen. We should ask a local.

einholen (PERFECT **hat eingeholt**) VERB [4]
1 to catch up with
□ Wir werden euch sicher bald einholen. We'll soon catch up with you.
2 to make up
□ Wir haben die Verspätung nicht mehr eingeholt. We didn't make up the delay.

einhundert NUMBER
a hundred

einig ADJECTIVE
■ **sich einig sein** to be in agreement
■ **einig werden** to reach an agreement

einige ADJECTIVE, PRONOUN
1 some
□ einige Bücher some books □ einige von uns some of us
■ **einiges** quite a lot of things □ Wir haben einiges gesehen. We saw quite a lot of things.

2 several
□ Wir sind dort einige Tage geblieben. We stayed there several days. □ Bei dem Konzert sind einige früher gegangen. Several people left the concert early.

sich **einigen** VERB [38]
to agree
□ Wir haben uns auf diesen Termin geeinigt. We agreed on this date.

einigermaßen ADVERB
1 somewhat
□ Ich war einigermaßen erstaunt. I was somewhat surprised.
2 reasonably
□ Diesmal hast du dich wenigstens einigermaßen angestrengt. At least this time you've tried reasonably hard. □ Das Wetter war einigermaßen trocken. The weather was reasonably dry.

die **Einigung** NOUN
agreement

der **Einkauf** (PL die **Einkäufe**) NOUN
purchase
■ **Einkäufe machen** to go shopping

einkaufen (PERFECT **hat eingekauft**) VERB [4]
1 to buy
□ Wir müssen Brot einkaufen. We'll have to buy bread.
2 to shop
□ Wir kaufen meist samstags ein. We usually shop on Saturdays.
■ **einkaufen gehen** to go shopping

der **Einkaufsbummel** (PL die **Einkaufsbummel**) NOUN
shopping spree

die **Einkaufsliste** NOUN
shopping list

der **Einkaufswagen** (PL die **Einkaufswagen**) NOUN
shopping trolley

das **Einkaufszentrum** (PL die **Einkaufszentren**) NOUN
shopping centre

der **Einkaufszettel** (PL die **Einkaufszettel**) NOUN
shopping list

einklammern (PERFECT **hat eingeklammert**) VERB [4]
to put in brackets

das **Einkommen** (PL die **Einkommen**) NOUN
income

einladen (PRESENT **lädt ein**, IMPERFECT **lud ein**, PERFECT **hat eingeladen**) VERB
1 to invite
□ Sie hat mich zu ihrer Party eingeladen. She's invited me to her party.
■ **jemanden ins Kino einladen** to take somebody to the cinema
■ **Ich lade dich ein.** I'll treat you.
2 to load
□ Kannst du bitte die Koffer ins Auto einladen? Can you load the cases into the car, please?

die **Einladung** NOUN
invitation

einlaufen (PRESENT **läuft ein**, IMPERFECT **lief ein**, PERFECT **ist eingelaufen**) VERB [43]
1 to come in
□ Das Schiff läuft in den Hafen ein. The ship is coming into the harbour.
2 to shrink
□ Mein Pullover ist eingelaufen. My jumper has shrunk.

sich **einleben** (PERFECT **hat sich eingelebt**) VERB [4]
to settle down
□ Wir haben uns in unserer neuen Schule gut eingelebt. We've settled down well in our new school.

die **Einleitung** NOUN
introduction

einleuchten (PERFECT **hat eingeleuchtet**) VERB [4]
■ **jemandem einleuchten** to make sense to somebody □ Das leuchtet mir nicht ein. That doesn't make sense to me.

einleuchtend ADJECTIVE
clear

einloggen (PERFECT **hat eingeloggt**) VERB [4]
to log on *(computer)*

einlösen VERB [4]
to cash
□ Kann ich diesen Scheck einlösen? Can I cash this cheque?
■ **ein Versprechen einlösen** to keep a promise

einmal ADVERB
1 once
□ Wenn du das erst einmal begriffen hast ... Once you've understood it ...
■ **Es war einmal ...** Once upon a time there was ...
■ **noch einmal** once more
■ **auf einmal** all at once □ Auf einmal waren alle weg. All at once they were all gone.
2 one day
□ Das wirst du schon einmal begreifen. You'll understand it one day.
■ **Nehmen wir einmal an: ...** Let's just suppose: ...
■ **nicht einmal** not even

einmalig ADJECTIVE
1 unique
□ Das ist eine einmalige Gelegenheit. This is a unique opportunity.
2 single
□ Das erfordert nur eine einmalige Überprüfung. That requires only a single check.
3 fantastic
□ Das war eine einmalige Party. That was a fantastic party.

sich **einmischen** (PERFECT **hat sich eingemischt**) VERB [4]
to interfere
□ Ich will mich nicht in deine Angelegenheiten einmischen. I don't want to interfere in your affairs.

einpacken (PERFECT **hat eingepackt**) VERB [4]
to pack
□ Hast du deine Zahnbürste eingepackt? Have you packed your toothbrush?

einplanen (PERFECT **hat eingeplant**) VERB [4]
to plan for

einreichen (PERFECT **hat eingereicht**) VERB [4]
to hand in

die **Einreise** NOUN
entry
■ **bei der Einreise** when entering the country

einreisen (PERFECT **ist eingereist**) VERB [4]
■ **in ein Land einreisen** to enter a country

einrichten (PERFECT **hat eingerichtet**) VERB [2]
1 to furnish
□ Sie haben ihr Haus antik eingerichtet. They've furnished their house with antiques.
2 to set up
□ Die Stadt hat eine Beratungsstelle eingerichtet. The town has set up an advice bureau.
■ **sich auf etwas einrichten** to prepare for something □ Wir hatten uns auf mehr Besucher eingerichtet. We had prepared for more visitors.

die **Einrichtung** NOUN
1 furnishings
□ Die moderne Einrichtung gefiel mir gut. I liked the modern furnishings.
2 facility
□ städtische Einrichtungen municipal facilities

einrosten (PERFECT **ist eingerostet**) VERB [4]
to get rusty

die **Eins** (PL die **Einsen**) NOUN
▷ *see also* **eins** NUMBER
1 one
2 very good

DID YOU KNOW...?
German marks range from one (**sehr gut**) to six (**ungenügend**).

eins NUMBER
▷ *see also* **die Eins** NOUN, **ein** NUMBER, ARTICLE
one
□ Ich habe nur eins bekommen. I only got one.
■ **Es ist mir alles eins.** It's all the same to me.

einsam ADJECTIVE
1 lonely
□ Ich fühle mich einsam. I'm feeling lonely.
2 remote
□ eine einsame Gegend a remote area

einsammeln (PERFECT **hat eingesammelt**) VERB [4]
to collect

einschalten (PERFECT **hat eingeschaltet**) VERB [2]
to switch on
□ Schalt mal das Radio ein. Switch the radio on.

einschl. ABBREVIATION *(= einschließlich)*

einschlafen (PRESENT **schläft ein**, IMPERFECT **schlief ein**, PERFECT **ist eingeschlafen**) VERB [58]
to fall asleep

einschließen (IMPERFECT **schloss ein**, PERFECT **hat eingeschlossen**) VERB
1 to lock in
□ Sie hat mich im Badezimmer eingeschlossen. She locked me in the bathroom.
2 to lock away
□ Du solltest die Wertsachen einschließen. You should lock away the valuables.
3 to include
□ Der Preis schließt die Verpflegung ein. The price includes all meals.
■ **sich einschließen** to lock oneself in □ Sie hat sich in ihrem Zimmer eingeschlossen. She locked herself in her room.

einschließlich ADVERB, PREPOSITION

LANGUAGE TIP The preposition **einschließlich** takes the genitive.

1 inclusive
□ Wir sind vom zehnten bis einschließlich fünfzehnten Juni weg. We're away from the tenth to the fifteenth of June inclusive.
2 including
□ Das macht zwanzig Euro einschließlich Bedienung. That's twenty euros including service.

einschränken (PERFECT **hat eingeschränkt**) VERB [4]
1 to restrict
□ Dadurch wurde unsere Freiheit eingeschränkt. This restricted our freedom.
2 to reduce
□ Wir müssen die Kosten einschränken. We'll have to reduce costs.
■ **sich einschränken** to cut down

sich **einschreiben** (IMPERFECT **schrieb sich ein**, PERFECT **hat sich eingeschrieben**) VERB [61]
▷ *see also* **das Einschreiben** NOUN
1 to register
□ Hast du dich für den Kurs eingeschrieben? Have you registered for the course?
2 to enrol
□ sich an der Universität einschreiben to enrol at university

das **Einschreiben** (PL die **Einschreiben**) NOUN
▷ *see also* **einschreiben** VERB
recorded delivery

einschüchtern (PERFECT **hat eingeschüchtert**) VERB [88]
to intimidate

einsehen (PRESENT **sieht ein**, IMPERFECT **sah ein**,

PERFECT **hat eingesehen**) VERB [64]
to see
□ Siehst du das nicht ein? Don't you see that?

einseitig ADJECTIVE
one-sided

einsenden (IMPERFECT **sendete ein** *or* **sandte ein**, PERFECT **hat eingesendet** *or* **hat eingesandt**) VERB
to send in

einsetzen (PERFECT **hat eingesetzt**) VERB [36]
1 to put in
□ Setzt das richtige Wort ein. Put in the correct word.
2 to bet
□ Wie viel Geld hast du eingesetzt? How much money did you bet?
3 to use
□ An den Schulen werden immer mehr Computer eingesetzt. More and more computers are being used in schools.
4 to set in
□ Wenn der Winter einsetzt ... When winter sets in ...
■ **sich einsetzen** to work hard □ Du solltest dich in der Schule etwas mehr einsetzen. You should work harder at school.
■ **sich für jemanden einsetzen** to support somebody

die **Einsicht** NOUN
■ **zu der Einsicht kommen, dass ...** to come to the conclusion that ...

einsilbig ADJECTIVE
1 monosyllabic
□ ein einsilbiges Wort a monosyllabic word
2 uncommunicative
□ Er war sehr einsilbig. He was very uncommunicative.

einsperren (PERFECT **hat eingesperrt**) VERB [4]
to lock up

einsprachig ADJECTIVE
monolingual

der **Einspruch** (PL die **Einsprüche**) NOUN
objection

einsteigen (IMPERFECT **stieg ein**, PERFECT **ist eingestiegen**) VERB [74]
1 to get on
□ Wir sind in den Bus eingestiegen. We got on the bus.
■ **Bitte einsteigen!** All aboard!
2 to climb in
□ Wir sind durchs Kellerfenster ins Haus eingestiegen. We climbed into the house through the cellar window.

einstellen (PERFECT **hat eingestellt**) VERB [4]
1 to adjust
□ den Spiegel einstellen to adjust the mirror
■ **eine Kamera einstellen** to focus a camera
2 to tune in to
□ Welchen Sender hast du da eingestellt? Which station have you tuned in to?
3 to stop
□ Sie haben die Produktion eingestellt. They've stopped production.
4 to employ
□ Sie wurde als Sekretärin eingestellt. She was employed as a secretary.
■ **sich auf etwas einstellen** to prepare oneself for something □ Stell dich besser auf eine lange Warterei ein. You'd better prepare yourself for a long wait.

die **Einstellung** NOUN
attitude
□ Ich mag deine Einstellung nicht. I don't like your attitude.

der **Einstieg** NOUN
entrance
□ Der Einstieg ist vorn. The entrance is at the front.

einstimmen (PERFECT **hat eingestimmt**) VERB [4]
to join in
□ Alle stimmten in das Lied ein. Everyone joined in the singing.
■ **sich auf etwas einstimmen** to get oneself in the right mood for something

eintägig ADJECTIVE
one-day

eintausend NUMBER
a thousand

eintönig ADJECTIVE
monotonous

der **Eintopf** (PL die **Eintöpfe**) NOUN
stew

der **Eintrag** (PL die **Einträge**) NOUN
entry
□ ein Eintrag im Wörterbuch a dictionary entry

eintragen (PRESENT **trägt ein**, IMPERFECT **trug ein**, PERFECT **hat eingetragen**) VERB [77]
to write
□ Tragt die Vokabeln in euer Heft ein. Write the vocabulary in your exercise book.
■ **sich eintragen** to put one's name down
□ Hast du dich schon in die Liste eingetragen? Have you put your name down on the list yet?

einträglich ADJECTIVE
profitable

eintreffen (PRESENT **trifft ein**, IMPERFECT **traf ein**, PERFECT **ist eingetroffen**) VERB [78]
1 to arrive
□ Sobald die Gäste eintreffen ... As soon as the guests arrive ...
2 to come true
□ Die Prophezeiung ist tatsächlich eingetroffen. The prophecy actually came true.

eintreten (PRESENT **tritt ein**, IMPERFECT **trat ein**, PERFECT **ist eingetreten**) VERB [79]
■ **eintreten in 1** to enter □ Er ist ins Zimmer eingetreten. He entered the room. **2** to join
□ Wann bist du in den Tennisklub eingetreten? When did you join the tennis club?

German-English

e

■ **Es ist eine Verzögerung eingetreten.** There has been a delay.

der **Eintritt** (PL die **Eintritte**) NOUN
admission
□ Wie viel kostet der Eintritt? How much does the admission cost?
■ **'Eintritt frei'** 'Admission free'

das **Eintrittsgeld** (PL die **Eintrittsgelder**) NOUN
admission charge

die **Eintrittskarte** NOUN
admission ticket

einverstanden ADJECTIVE
■ **einverstanden sein** to agree □ Bist du mit dem Vorschlag einverstanden? Do you agree to the suggestion?
■ **Einverstanden!** Okay!

der **Einwanderer** (PL die **Einwanderer**) NOUN
immigrant

einwandern (PERFECT **ist eingewandert**) VERB [88]
to immigrate

die **Einwegflasche** NOUN
nonreturnable bottle

einweihen (PERFECT **hat eingeweiht**) VERB [4]
to open
□ Morgen wird die neue Brücke eingeweiht. The new bridge is being opened tomorrow.
■ **jemanden in etwas einweihen** to initiate somebody into something □ Wir haben die Neue in unseren Klub eingeweiht. We've initiated the newcomer into our club.
■ **jemanden in ein Geheimnis einweihen** to let somebody in on a secret

einwerfen (PRESENT **wirft ein**, IMPERFECT **warf ein**, PERFECT **hat eingeworfen**) VERB [92]
to smash
□ Ich habe eine Scheibe eingeworfen. I've smashed a pane.
■ **einen Brief einwerfen** to post a letter
■ **Geld einwerfen** to insert money

der **Einwohner** (PL die **Einwohner**) NOUN
inhabitant

das **Einwohnermeldeamt** (PL die **Einwohnermeldeämter**) NOUN
registration office

DID YOU KNOW...?
Anyone moving to a new address in Germany is required by law to register (**sich anmelden**) at the residents' registration office (**Einwohnermeldeamt**).

der **Einwurf** (PL die **Einwürfe**) NOUN
1 slot
□ Sie steckte den Brief in den Einwurf. She put the letter through the slot.
2 throw-in *(sport)*
□ Der Schiedsrichter gab einen Einwurf. The referee gave a throw-in.

die **Einzahl** NOUN
singular

einzahlen (PERFECT **hat eingezahlt**) VERB [4]
to pay

das **Einzelbett** (PL die **Einzelbetten**) NOUN
single bed

der **Einzelfahrschein** (PL die **Einzelfahrscheine**) NOUN
single ticket

die **Einzelheit** NOUN
detail

das **Einzelkind** (PL die **Einzelkinder**) NOUN
only child

einzeln ADJECTIVE, ADVERB
1 single
□ Jeder einzelne Schüler wurde befragt. Every single pupil was asked.
2 odd
□ Ich habe ein paar einzelne Socken. I've got a couple of odd socks.
3 one at a time
□ Bitte einzeln eintreten. Please come in one at a time.
■ **einzeln angeben** to specify
■ **der Einzelne** the individual
■ **ins Einzelne gehen** to go into details

das **Einzelteil** (PL die **Einzelteile**) NOUN
component

das **Einzelzimmer** (PL die **Einzelzimmer**) NOUN
single room

einziehen (IMPERFECT **zog ein**, PERFECT **ist/hat eingezogen**) VERB [96]

LANGUAGE TIP For the perfect tense use **haben** when the verb has an object and **sein** when there is no object.

1 to retract
■ **den Kopf einziehen** to duck one's head
2 to collect
3 to move in
□ Wann sind die neuen Nachbarn eingezogen? When did the new neighbours move in?

einzig ADJECTIVE
only
□ Er ist unser einziges Kind. He's our only child.
■ **das Einzige** the only thing
■ **der Einzige** the only one

einzigartig ADJECTIVE
unique

das **Eis** (PL die **Eis**) NOUN
1 ice
□ Es war Eis auf dem See. There was ice on the lake.
2 ice cream
□ Möchtest du ein Eis? Would you like an ice cream?

der **Eisbär** (GEN des **Eisbären**, PL die **Eisbären**) NOUN
polar bear

der **Eisberg** (PL die **Eisberge**) NOUN
iceberg

das Eisen (PL die **Eisen**) NOUN
iron
□ Die Brücke ist aus Eisen. The bridge is made of iron.

die Eisenbahn NOUN
railway

eisern ADJECTIVE
iron
□ eine eiserne Stange an iron rod
■ **die eiserne Reserve** emergency reserves

das Eishockey NOUN
ice hockey

eisig ADJECTIVE
icy

eiskalt ADJECTIVE
1 ice-cold
□ ein eiskaltes Getränk an ice-cold drink
2 icy cold
□ In diesem Zimmer ist es eiskalt. This room's icy cold.

der Eiswürfel (PL die **Eiswürfel**) NOUN
ice cube

eitel ADJECTIVE
vain

der Eiter NOUN
pus

das Eiweiß (PL die **Eiweiße**) NOUN
1 egg white
□ Das Eiweiß zu Schnee schlagen. Whisk the egg whites until stiff.
2 protein
□ eine eiweißreiche Diät a diet rich in protein

der Ekel NOUN
disgust

ekelhaft ADJECTIVE
disgusting

sich ekeln VERB [34]
to disgust
■ **sich vor etwas ekeln** to find something disgusting □ Ich ekle mich vor diesem Dreck. I find this dirt disgusting.

der Elch (PL die **Elche**) NOUN
elk

der Elefant (GEN des **Elefanten**, PL die **Elefanten**) NOUN
elephant

elegant ADJECTIVE
elegant

der Elektriker (PL die **Elektriker**) NOUN
electrician

elektrisch ADJECTIVE
electric

die Elektrizität NOUN
electricity

das Elektrogerät NOUN
electrical appliance

der Elektroherd (PL die **Elektroherde**) NOUN
electric cooker

die Elektronik NOUN
electronics
□ Er studiert Elektronik. He's studying electronics. □ Die Elektronik am Auto ist kaputt. There's something wrong with the electronics in the car.

elektronisch ADJECTIVE
electronic
□ elektronische Post electronic mail
□ elektronischer Briefkasten electronic mailbox

das Element (PL die **Elemente**) NOUN
element

das Elend NOUN
▷ *see also* **elend** ADJECTIVE
misery

elend ADJECTIVE
▷ *see also* **das Elend** NOUN
miserable
□ Ich fühle mich so elend. I feel so miserable.

elf NUMBER
eleven
□ Sie ist elf. She's eleven.

der Elfmeter (PL die **Elfmeter**) NOUN
penalty

LANGUAGE TIP Word for word, **Elfmeter** means 'eleven metres'.

□ einen Elfmeter schießen to take a penalty

der Ellbogen (PL die **Ellbogen**) NOUN
elbow

die Eltern PL NOUN
parents

der Elternteil (PL die **Elternteile**) NOUN
parent
□ beide Elternteile both parents

die E-Mail (PL die **E-Mails**) NOUN
email
□ Meine E-Mail-Adresse ist ... My email address is ...

das Emoticon (PL die **Emoticons**) NOUN
smiley

der Empfang (PL die **Empfänge**) NOUN
1 reception
□ Wart ihr auch bei dem Empfang? Were you at the reception too?
2 receipt
□ Bitte bestätigen Sie den Empfang der Ware. Please acknowledge receipt of the goods.
■ **in Empfang nehmen** to receive

empfangen (PRESENT **empfängt**, IMPERFECT **empfing**, PERFECT **hat empfangen**) VERB [23]
to receive

der Empfänger (PL die **Empfänger**) NOUN
receiver

empfänglich ADJECTIVE
susceptible
□ Sie ist für Schmeicheleien sehr empfänglich. She's very susceptible to flattery.

die Empfängnisverhütung NOUN
contraception

empfehlen (PRESENT **empfiehlt**, IMPERFECT **empfahl**, PERFECT **hat empfohlen**) VERB [17]
to recommend

□ Dieses Restaurant ist zu empfehlen. This restaurant is to be recommended.

empfinden (IMPERFECT **empfand**, PERFECT **hat empfunden**) VERB [24]
to feel
□ Ich empfinde nichts für sie. I don't feel anything for her.

empfindlich ADJECTIVE
1 sensitive
□ Er ist ein sehr empfindlicher Mensch. He's very sensitive.
2 touchy
□ Sie ist schrecklich empfindlich. She's terribly touchy.

empfohlen VERB ▷ *see* **empfehlen**

das **Ende** (PL die **Enden**) NOUN
end
■ **am Ende** 1 at the end □ am Ende des Zuges at the end of the train 2 in the end
□ Am Ende ist er dann doch mitgekommen. He came in the end.
■ **zu Ende gehen** to come to an end
■ **zu Ende sein** to be finished
■ **Ende Dezember** at the end of December

enden VERB [54]
to end

endgültig ADJECTIVE
definite

endlich ADVERB
finally
□ Ich bin endlich fertig. I've finally finished.
□ Hast du das endlich begriffen? Have you finally understood it?
■ **Endlich!** At last!
■ **Komm endlich!** Come on!

endlos ADJECTIVE
endless

das **Endspiel** (PL die **Endspiele**) NOUN
final

die **Endstation** NOUN
terminus

die **Endung** NOUN
ending

die **Energie** NOUN
energy
□ seine ganze Energie für etwas einsetzen to devote all one's energies to something

energisch ADJECTIVE
energetic

eng ADJECTIVE
1 narrow
□ ein enger Durchgang a narrow passageway
2 tight
□ Die Hose ist mir zu eng. The trousers are too tight for me.
3 close
□ Wir sind eng befreundet. We are close friends.

die **Enge** NOUN
narrowness
■ **jemanden in die Enge treiben** to drive somebody into a corner

der **Engel** (PL die **Engel**) NOUN
angel

England NEUT NOUN
England
■ **aus England** from England
■ **in England** in England
■ **nach England** to England

der **Engländer** (PL die **Engländer**) NOUN
Englishman
■ **Er ist Engländer.** He's English.
■ **die Engländer** the English

die **Engländerin** NOUN
Englishwoman
■ **Sie ist Engländerin.** She's English.

das **Englisch** (GEN des **Englischen**) NOUN
▷ *see also* **englisch** ADJECTIVE
English
□ Er lernt Englisch in der Schule. He's learning English at school.

englisch ADJECTIVE
English

der **Engpass** (GEN des **Engpasses**, PL die **Engpässe**) NOUN
bottleneck

der **Enkel** (PL die **Enkel**) NOUN
grandson
■ **alle ihre Enkel** all her grandchildren

die **Enkelin** NOUN
granddaughter

das **Enkelkind** (PL die **Enkelkinder**) NOUN
grandchild

enorm ADJECTIVE
enormous
□ Er verdient enorm viel Geld. He earns an enormous amount of money.

entdecken (PERFECT **hat entdeckt**) VERB [18]
to discover

die **Ente** NOUN
duck

entfernen (PERFECT **hat entfernt**) VERB [18]
to remove

entfernt ADJECTIVE
distant
□ ein entfernter Verwandter a distant relative
■ **weit entfernt** far away
■ **weit davon entfernt sein, etwas zu tun** to be far from doing something
■ **nicht im Entferntesten** not in the slightest

die **Entfernung** NOUN
distance

entführen (PERFECT **hat entführt**) VERB [18]
to kidnap

entgegen PREPOSITION
LANGUAGE TIP **entgegen** takes the dative.
contrary to
□ entgegen meinen Anweisungen contrary to my instructions

entgegenkommen (IMPERFECT **kam entgegen**, PERFECT **ist entgegengekommen**) VERB [40]
1 to come towards
□ Uns kam ein Lastwagen entgegen. A lorry came towards us.
2 to meet half way
□ Ich werde Ihnen entgegenkommen, sagen wir zwanzig Euro. I'll meet you half way, let's say twenty euros.

entgegenkommend ADJECTIVE
obliging

entgehen (IMPERFECT **entging**, PERFECT **ist entgangen**) VERB [29]
■ **jemandem entgehen** to escape somebody's attention □ Dieser Fehler ist mir entgangen. That mistake escaped my attention.
■ **sich etwas entgehen lassen** to miss something □ Das Konzert will ich mir nicht entgehen lassen. I'm not going to miss the concert.

enthalten (PRESENT **enthält**, IMPERFECT **enthielt**, PERFECT **hat enthalten**) VERB [33]
to contain
□ Dieses Fass enthält radioaktiven Müll. This drum contains radioactive waste.
■ **sich enthalten** to abstain □ Sie hat sich bei der Abstimmung enthalten. She abstained from voting.

entkommen (IMPERFECT **entkam**, PERFECT **ist entkommen**) VERB [40]
to escape

entlang PREPOSITION
LANGUAGE TIP **entlang** takes the accusative or the dative.
along
□ Entlang der Mauer wuchs Efeu. Ivy was growing along the wall. □ Wir gingen den Fluss entlang. We walked along the river.

entlassen (PRESENT **entlässt**, IMPERFECT **entließ**, PERFECT **hat entlassen**) VERB [42]
1 to release
□ Er wurde aus dem Gefängnis entlassen. He was released from prison.
2 to make redundant
□ 500 Arbeiter mussten entlassen werden. 500 workers had to be made redundant.

entrüstet ADJECTIVE
outraged

entschädigen (PERFECT **hat entschädigt**) VERB [18]
to compensate
□ jemanden für etwas entschädigen to compensate somebody for something

entscheiden (IMPERFECT **entschied**, PERFECT **hat entschieden**) VERB
to decide
■ **sich entscheiden** to make up one's mind

entscheidend ADJECTIVE
decisive

die **Entscheidung** NOUN
decision

entschieden ADJECTIVE
1 decided
□ Es ist entschieden, wir fahren nach Rom. It's been decided that we're going to Rome.
2 resolute
□ ein sehr entschiedener Mensch a very resolute person

sich **entschließen** (IMPERFECT **entschloss sich**, PERFECT **hat sich entschlossen**) VERB
to decide

entschlossen ADJECTIVE
determined

der **Entschluss** (GEN des **Entschlusses**, PL die **Entschlüsse**) NOUN
decision

entschuldigen (PERFECT **hat entschuldigt**) VERB [18]
1 to excuse
□ Entschuldige bitte die Verspätung. Please excuse the delay.
2 to apologize
□ Du solltest dich besser bei ihm entschuldigen. You'd better apologize to him.

die **Entschuldigung** NOUN
1 apology
□ Hat er deine Entschuldigung angenommen? Did he accept your apology?
■ **jemanden um Entschuldigung bitten** to apologize to somebody
2 excuse
□ Krankheit ist keine Entschuldigung. Illness is no excuse.
■ **Entschuldigung!** Sorry.
■ **Entschuldigung ...** Excuse me ...
□ Entschuldigung, können Sie mir sagen, wie spät es ist? Excuse me, could you tell me what time it is?

entsetzlich ADJECTIVE
dreadful

entsetzt ADJECTIVE, ADVERB
horrified

die **Entsorgung** NOUN
waste disposal

sich **entspannen** (PERFECT **hat sich entspannt**) VERB [18]
1 to relax
□ Entspann dich! Relax!
2 to ease
□ Die Lage hat sich entspannt. The situation has eased.

entsprechen (PRESENT **entspricht**, IMPERFECT **entsprach**, PERFECT **hat entsprochen**) VERB [70]
1 to meet
□ Sie hat den Anforderungen nicht entsprochen. She didn't meet the requirements.
2 to comply with
□ Dieses Gerät entspricht nicht den Normen.

This appliance doesn't comply with the standards.

entsprechend ADJECTIVE, ADVERB
1 appropriate
□ Die entsprechende Antwort ankreuzen. Tick the appropriate answer.
2 accordingly
□ Benimm dich entsprechend. Behave accordingly.

enttäuschen (PERFECT **hat enttäuscht**) VERB [18]
to disappoint

enttäuschend ADJECTIVE
disappointing

die **Enttäuschung** NOUN
disappointment

entweder CONJUNCTION
either
■ **entweder ... oder ...** either ... or ...

entwerten VERB [18]
to cancel
□ Du musst die Fahrkarte erst entwerten. You have to cancel your ticket first.

der **Entwerter** (PL die **Entwerter**) NOUN
ticket stamping machine

DID YOU KNOW...?
When you travel by train or tram (and sometimes by bus) you have to stamp your ticket in an **Entwerter**. The machines are either on the platforms or inside the vehicles.

entwickeln (PERFECT **hat entwickelt**) VERB [34]
1 to develop
□ Fähigkeiten entwickeln to develop skills
□ einen Film entwickeln to develop a film
2 to show
□ Sie hat eine enorme Energie entwickelt. She showed terrific energy.
■ **sich entwickeln** to develop □ Das Geschäft entwickelt sich gut. The business is developing well.

die **Entwicklung** NOUN
development

die **Entwicklungshilfe** NOUN
development aid

das **Entwicklungsland** (PL die **Entwicklungsländer**) NOUN
developing country

sich **entzünden** (PERFECT **hat sich entzündet**) VERB [18]
to become inflamed
□ Die Wunde hat sich entzündet. The wound has become inflamed.

die **Entzündung** NOUN
inflammation

entzwei ADVERB
broken
□ Die Vase ist entzwei. The vase is broken.

der **Enzian** (PL die **Enziane**) NOUN
gentian

er PRONOUN
1 he
□ Er ist größer als ich. He's taller than me.
2 it
□ Schöner Ring, ist er neu? Lovely ring, is it new?
3 him
□ Er ist es. It's him. □ Er war es nicht, ich war's. It wasn't him, it was me.

erben VERB [38]
to inherit

erbrechen (PRESENT **erbricht**, IMPERFECT **erbrach**, PERFECT **hat erbrochen**) VERB [11]
to vomit

die **Erbschaft** NOUN
inheritance

die **Erbse** NOUN
pea

das **Erdbeben** (PL die **Erdbeben**) NOUN
earthquake

die **Erdbeere** NOUN
strawberry

die **Erde** NOUN
earth
■ **zu ebener Erde** at ground level
■ **auf der ganzen Erde** all over the world

das **Erdgas** (GEN des **Erdgases**) NOUN
natural gas

das **Erdgeschoss** (GEN des **Erdgeschosses**, PL die **Erdgeschosse**) NOUN
ground floor
□ im Erdgeschoss on the ground floor

die **Erdkunde** NOUN
geography

die **Erdnuss** (PL die **Erdnüsse**) NOUN
peanut

das **Erdöl** NOUN
mineral oil

sich **ereignen** (PERFECT **hat sich ereignet**) VERB [53]
to happen

das **Ereignis** (GEN des **Ereignisses**, PL die **Ereignisse**) NOUN
event

erfahren (PRESENT **erfährt**, IMPERFECT **erfuhr**, PERFECT **hat erfahren**) VERB [21]
▷ *see also* **erfahren** ADJECTIVE
1 to hear
□ Ich habe erfahren, dass du heiraten willst. I've heard that you want to get married.
2 to experience
□ Sie hat im Leben viel Gutes erfahren. She's experienced a lot of good things in her life.

erfahren ADJECTIVE
▷ *see also* **erfahren** VERB
experienced
□ Er ist ein erfahrener Lehrer. He's an experienced teacher.

die **Erfahrung** NOUN
experience

erfassen (PERFECT **hat erfasst**) VERB [31]
1 to understand
□ Ich habe den Text noch nicht erfasst. I haven't understood the text yet.
2 to register
□ Alle Aidsfälle werden erfasst. All AIDS cases are registered.

erfinden (IMPERFECT **erfand**, PERFECT **hat erfunden**) VERB [24]
to invent

der **Erfinder** (PL die **Erfinder**) NOUN
inventor

erfinderisch ADJECTIVE
inventive

die **Erfindung** NOUN
invention

der **Erfolg** (PL die **Erfolge**) NOUN
success
■ **Erfolg versprechend** promising
■ **Viel Erfolg!** Good luck!

erfolglos ADJECTIVE
unsuccessful

erfolgreich ADJECTIVE
successful

erfolgversprechend ADJECTIVE ▷ *see* **Erfolg**

erforderlich ADJECTIVE
necessary

erfreulicherweise ADVERB
happily

erfreut ADJECTIVE
pleased
□ Über mein gutes Zeugnis war ich sehr erfreut. I was very pleased with my good report.

erfrieren (IMPERFECT **erfror**, PERFECT **ist erfroren**) VERB
to freeze to death
□ Er ist erfroren. He froze to death.
■ **Die Pflanze ist erfroren.** The plant was killed by frost.

die **Erfrischung** NOUN
refreshment

erfüllen (PERFECT **hat erfüllt**) VERB [7]
to fulfil
□ Er hat ihr den Wunsch erfüllt. He fulfilled her wish.
■ **sich erfüllen** to come true
□ Die Prophezeiung hat sich erfüllt. The prophecy came true.

ergänzen (PERFECT **hat ergänzt**) VERB [36]
to complete
□ Ergänzt den Satz. Complete the sentence.
■ **sich ergänzen** to complement one another

das **Ergebnis** (GEN des **Ergebnisses**, PL die **Ergebnisse**) NOUN
result

ergreifen (IMPERFECT **ergriff**, PERFECT **hat ergriffen**) VERB
1 to seize
□ Er ergriff meine Hand. He seized my hand.
□ die Gelegenheit ergreifen to seize the opportunity
■ **einen Beruf ergreifen** to take up a profession
■ **Maßnahmen gegen etwas ergreifen** to take measures against something
2 to move
□ Ihr Schicksal hat uns sehr ergriffen. Her fate moved us deeply.

ergreifend ADJECTIVE
moving

ergriffen ADJECTIVE
deeply moved

erhalten (PRESENT **erhält**, IMPERFECT **erhielt**, PERFECT **hat erhalten**) VERB [33]
1 to receive
□ Sie hat den ersten Preis erhalten. She received first prize.
2 to preserve
□ Das Gebäude sollte erhalten werden. The building should be preserved.
■ **gut erhalten** in good condition

LANGUAGE TIP Word for word, **gut erhalten** means 'well preserved'.

erhältlich ADJECTIVE
obtainable

erheitern (PERFECT **hat erheitert**) VERB [88]
to amuse

erhitzen (PERFECT **hat erhitzt**) VERB [7]
to heat

sich **erholen** (PERFECT **hat sich erholt**) VERB [19]
1 to recover
□ Der Patient muss sich nach der Operation erholen. The patient needs to recover after the operation.
2 to have a rest
□ Wir haben uns in den Ferien gut erholt. We had a good rest when we were on holiday.

erholsam ADJECTIVE
restful

die **Erholung** NOUN
rest
□ Wir fahren zur Erholung ans Meer. We're going to the sea for a rest.

erinnern (PERFECT **hat erinnert**) VERB [88]
■ **erinnern an** to remind of □ Du erinnerst mich an meine Schwester. You remind me of my sister. □ Erinnere mich bitte daran, dass wir noch Butter kaufen müssen. Remind me that we still have to buy butter.
■ **sich erinnern** to remember □ Ich kann mich nicht erinnern. I can't remember.
□ Erinnerst du dich noch an unser Abenteuer in Erlangen? Can you still remember our adventure in Erlangen?

die **Erinnerung** NOUN
1 memory
□ Wir haben Erinnerungen ausgetauscht. We swapped memories.

German-English

2 souvenir
□ eine Erinnerung an meinen Russlandaufenthalt a souvenir of my stay in Russia

erkältet ADJECTIVE
■ **erkältet sein** to have a cold

die **Erkältung** NOUN
cold

erkennbar ADJECTIVE
recognizable

erkennen (IMPERFECT **erkannte**, PERFECT **hat erkannt**) VERB [39]
1 to recognize
□ Ich hätte dich fast nicht erkannt. I would hardly have recognized you.
2 to see
□ Jetzt erkenne ich, dass das ein Fehler war. I see now that it was a mistake.

erklären (PERFECT **hat erklärt**) VERB [19]
to explain

die **Erklärung** NOUN
explanation
■ **eine Liebeserklärung** a declaration of love

sich **erkundigen** (PERFECT **hat sich erkundigt**) VERB [19]
■ **sich erkundigen nach** to inquire about
□ Wir sollten uns nach den Abfahrtszeiten erkundigen. We should inquire about departure times.
■ **Er hat sich nach dir erkundigt.** He was asking about you.

erlauben (PERFECT **hat erlaubt**) VERB [19]
■ **jemandem etwas erlauben** to allow somebody to do something □ Mein Vater hat mir erlaubt auszugehen. My father allowed me to go out.
■ **sich etwas erlauben** to allow oneself something □ Ich erlaube mir jetzt ein Bier. Now I'm going to allow myself a beer.
■ **Was erlaubst du dir denn eigentlich?** How dare you!

die **Erlaubnis** (PL die **Erlaubnisse**) NOUN
permission

erleben (PERFECT **hat erlebt**) VERB [19]
1 to experience
□ Eine solche Frechheit habe ich selten erlebt. I've seldom experienced such cheek.
■ **Wir haben in den Ferien viel Schönes erlebt.** We had a lovely time on holiday.
■ **Sie hat viel Schlimmes erlebt.** She's had a lot of bad experiences.
2 to live through
□ Mein Opa hat den Zweiten Weltkrieg erlebt. My grandpa lived through the Second World War.
3 to live to see
□ Ich möchte die Geburt deines Kindes noch erleben. I would like to live to see the birth of your child.

das **Erlebnis** (GEN des **Erlebnisses**, PL die **Erlebnisse**) NOUN
experience

erledigen (PERFECT **hat erledigt**) VERB [19]
1 to see to
□ Ich habe heute noch viel zu erledigen. I've a lot to see to today.
2 to do
□ Hast du deine Hausaufgaben schon erledigt? Have you done your homework already?
3 to wear out
□ Die Wanderung hat mich ziemlich erledigt. The hike's really worn me out.

die **Erleichterung** NOUN
relief
□ Das war eine Erleichterung! That was a relief!

der **Erlös** (GEN des **Erlöses**, PL die **Erlöse**) NOUN
proceeds
□ Der Erlös kommt Kindern in Rumänien zugute. The proceeds will go to children in Romania.

erlösen (PERFECT **hat erlöst**) VERB [7]
to save
□ Sie erlöste ihn aus einer gefährlichen Lage. She saved him from a dangerous situation.

die **Ermahnung** NOUN
admonition

die **Ermäßigung** NOUN
reduction

ermöglichen (PERFECT **hat ermöglicht**) VERB [7]
■ **jemandem etwas ermöglichen** to make something possible for somebody

ermorden (PERFECT **hat ermordet**) VERB [53]
to murder

ermüdend ADJECTIVE
tiring

ermutigen (PERFECT **hat ermutigt**) VERB [7]
to encourage

ernähren (PERFECT **hat ernährt**) VERB [19]
to support
□ Er hat eine Familie zu ernähren. He has a family to support.
■ **sich von etwas ernähren** to live on something □ Sie ernähren sich hauptsächlich von Reis. They live mainly on rice.

ernennen (IMPERFECT **ernannte**, PERFECT **hat ernannt**) VERB
to appoint

erneuern (PERFECT **hat erneuert**) VERB [88]
to renew

ernst ADJECTIVE
▷ *see also* **der Ernst** NOUN
serious

der **Ernst** NOUN
▷ *see also* **ernst** ADJECTIVE
seriousness
■ **Das ist mein Ernst.** I'm quite serious.
■ **im Ernst** in earnest

ernsthaft ADJECTIVE
serious
□ ein ernsthaftes Gespräch a serious talk
□ Glaubst du das ernsthaft? Do you seriously believe that?

ernstlich ADJECTIVE, ADVERB
serious
■ **ernstlich besorgt** seriously concerned

die **Ernte** NOUN
harvest

ernten VERB [2]
to harvest
□ Es ist Zeit, die Kirschen zu ernten. It's time to harvest the cherries.
■ **Lob ernten** to earn praise

erobern (PERFECT **hat erobert**) VERB [88]
to conquer

erotisch ADJECTIVE
erotic

erpressen (PERFECT **hat erpresst**) VERB [7]
1 to blackmail
□ Du willst mich wohl erpressen? Are you trying to blackmail me?
2 to extort
□ Er hat von ihm Geld erpresst. He extorted money from him.

erraten (PRESENT **errät**, IMPERFECT **erriet**, PERFECT **hat erraten**) VERB
to guess

die **Erregung** NOUN
excitement

erreichen (PERFECT **hat erreicht**) VERB [19]
1 to reach
□ Wir haben Hamburg am späten Nachmittag erreicht. We reached Hamburg in the late afternoon.
2 to catch
□ Wir haben den Zug nicht mehr erreicht. We didn't manage to catch the train.
3 to achieve
□ seinen Zweck erreichen to achieve one's purpose □ Was willst du damit erreichen? What do you aim to achieve by this?
■ **So erreichst du bei mir gar nichts.** You won't get anywhere with me by doing that.

das **Ersatzteil** (PL die **Ersatzteile**) NOUN
spare part

erschaffen (IMPERFECT **erschuf**, PERFECT **hat erschaffen**) VERB
to create

erscheinen (IMPERFECT **erschien**, PERFECT **ist erschienen**) VERB [57]
to appear

erschießen (IMPERFECT **erschoss**, PERFECT **hat erschossen**) VERB
to shoot dead

erschöpft ADJECTIVE
exhausted

die **Erschöpfung** NOUN
exhaustion

erschrecken (1) (PERFECT **hat erschreckt**) VERB [19]
to frighten
□ Hast du mich erschreckt! You really frightened me!

erschrecken (2) (PRESENT **erschrickt**, IMPERFECT **erschrak**, PERFECT **ist erschrocken**) VERB
to be frightened
□ Ich bin furchtbar erschrocken, als plötzlich das Licht ausging. I was terribly frightened when the light suddenly went out.

erschreckend ADJECTIVE
alarming

erschrocken ADJECTIVE
frightened

ersetzen (PERFECT **hat ersetzt**) VERB [36]
to replace
□ Du musst die Vase ersetzen. You'll have to replace that vase.
■ **jemandem die Unkosten ersetzen** to pay somebody's expenses

die **Ersparnisse** FEM PL NOUN
savings

erst ADVERB
1 first
□ Erst will ich wissen, was das kostet. First I want to know what it costs. □ Mach erst mal die Arbeit fertig. Finish your work first.
■ **Wenn du das erst mal hinter dir hast, ...** Once you've got that behind you, ...
2 only
□ Das ist erst gestern passiert. That happened only yesterday. □ Er ist gerade erst angekommen. He's only just arrived.
3 not until
□ Er hat es erst gemacht, als ich es ihm befohlen habe. He didn't do it until I told him. □ erst morgen not until tomorrow □ erst um 5 Uhr not until 5 o'clock

erstaunlich ADJECTIVE
astonishing

erstaunt ADJECTIVE
astonished

erste ADJECTIVE
first
□ Ich habe gerade mein erstes Auto gekauft. I've just bought my first car. □ Er kam als Erster. He was the first to arrive.
■ **Erste Hilfe** first aid

erstechen (PRESENT **ersticht**, IMPERFECT **erstach**, PERFECT **hat erstochen**) VERB
to stab to death

erstens ADVERB
firstly

ersticken (PERFECT **ist erstickt**) VERB [19]
1 to suffocate
□ Ich bin fast erstickt. I almost suffocated.
2 to smother
□ Er versuchte, die Flammen zu ersticken. He tried to smother the flames.

■ **in Arbeit ersticken** to be snowed under with work

erstklassig ADJECTIVE
first-class

erstmals ADVERB
for the first time

ertragen (PRESENT **erträgt**, IMPERFECT **ertrug**, PERFECT **hat ertragen**) VERB [77]
to stand
□ Ich kann die Schmerzen kaum ertragen. I can hardly stand the pain. □ Sie erträgt es nicht, wenn man ihr widerspricht. She can't stand being contradicted.

erträglich ADJECTIVE
bearable

ertrinken (IMPERFECT **ertrank**, PERFECT **ist ertrunken**) VERB [80]
to drown

erwachsen ADJECTIVE
grown-up

der/die **Erwachsene** (GEN des/der **Erwachsenen**, PL die **Erwachsenen**) NOUN
adult
□ Erwachsene können das nicht verstehen. Adults can't understand that.

erwähnen (PERFECT **hat erwähnt**) VERB [19]
to mention

erwarten (PERFECT **hat erwartet**) VERB [2]
to expect
□ Er erwartet zu viel von uns. He's expecting too much of us.
■ **Wir können es kaum erwarten, dass die Ferien beginnen.** We can hardly wait for the holidays to begin.

erweisen (IMPERFECT **erwies**, PERFECT **hat erwiesen**) VERB
■ **sich erweisen als** to prove to be
□ Er erwies sich als guter Schüler. He proved to be a good pupil.

erwerben (PRESENT **erwirbt**, IMPERFECT **erwarb**, PERFECT **hat erworben**) VERB [90]
to acquire

das **Erz** (GEN des **Erzes**, PL die **Erze**) NOUN
ore

erzählen (PERFECT **hat erzählt**) VERB [19]
to tell

die **Erzählung** NOUN
story

erzeugen (PERFECT **hat erzeugt**) VERB [19]
1 to produce
□ In dieser Gegend wird Wein erzeugt. Wine is produced in this region.
2 to generate
□ Strom erzeugen to generate electricity

das **Erzeugnis** (GEN des **Erzeugnisses**, PL die **Erzeugnisse**) NOUN
produce
□ ausländische Erzeugnisse foreign produce

erziehen (IMPERFECT **erzog**, PERFECT **hat erzogen**) VERB [96]
to bring up
□ Sie hat fünf Kinder erzogen. She brought up five children. □ Sie sollte ihre Kinder zu etwas mehr Höflichkeit erziehen. She should bring her children up to be more polite.

die **Erziehung** NOUN
education

es PRONOUN
it
□ Es ist rot. It's red. □ Ich habe es nicht gesehen. I didn't see it. □ Es schneit. It's snowing.

der **Esel** (PL die **Esel**) NOUN
donkey

essbar ADJECTIVE
edible

essen (PRESENT **isst**, IMPERFECT **aß**, PERFECT **hat gegessen**) VERB [20]
▷ *see also* **das Essen** NOUN
to eat

das **Essen** (PL die **Essen**) NOUN
▷ *see also* **essen** VERB
1 meal
□ Komm doch am Freitag zum Essen. Why don't you come for a meal on Friday?.
2 food
□ Das Essen war lecker. The food was delicious.

der **Essig** (PL die **Essige**) NOUN
vinegar

das **Esszimmer** (PL die **Esszimmer**) NOUN
dining room

die **Etage** NOUN
floor
□ Wir wohnen in der dritten Etage. We live on the third floor.

die **Etagenbetten** NEUT PL NOUN
bunk beds

das **E-Ticket** (PL die **E-Tickets**) NOUN
e-ticket

das **Etikett** (PL die **Etikette** *or* **Etiketten**) NOUN
label
□ Lies mal, was auf dem Etikett steht. Read what's on the label.

etliche PL PRONOUN
quite a few
□ etliche Leute quite a few people

das **Etui** (PL die **Etuis**) NOUN
case
□ ein Brillenetui a glasses case

etwa ADVERB
1 about
□ Es waren etwa zwanzig. There were about twenty.
2 for instance
□ Leute wie etwa Jochen wissen das eben nicht. People like Jochen, for instance, just don't know that.
■ **Soll das etwa heißen, dass ...** Is that supposed to mean that ...

■ Du willst doch nicht etwa schon gehen. You're not going already, are you?

etwaig ADJECTIVE
possible

etwas PRONOUN, ADVERB
1 something
□ Wir sollten ihr etwas schenken. We should give her something.
2 anything
□ Hast du nicht etwas gehört? Haven't you heard anything?
3 a little
□ Wir sollten uns etwas ausruhen. We should have a little rest. □ Nur etwas Milch bitte. Just a little milk, please.

die **EU** NOUN *(= Europäische Union)*
EU *(= European Union)*

euch PRONOUN
LANGUAGE TIP **euch** is the accusative and dative of **ihr**.
1 you
□ Ich habe euch gesehen. I saw you.
□ Ich komme mit euch. I'll come with you.
2 yourselves
□ Seht euch mal im Spiegel an. Look at yourselves in the mirror.
3 to you
□ Sie hat es euch gegeben. She gave it to you.

euer PRONOUN, ADJECTIVE
1 your
□ Euer Deutschlehrer ist nett. Your German teacher is nice. □ Wenn das eure Mutter erlaubt. If your mother lets you. □ Ist das euer Haus? Is that your house?
2 yours
□ Das ist nicht unser Computer, das ist eurer. That's not our computer, that's yours.
□ Unsere Mutter heißt Ulla, wie heißt eure? Our mother's called Ulla, what's yours called?
□ Wenn es in unserem Haus nicht geht, feiern wir in eurem. If it's not OK in our house, then we'll celebrate in yours.

die **Eule** NOUN
owl

eure ▷ *see* **euer**

eures ▷ *see* **euer**

euretwegen ADVERB
1 for your sakes
□ Wir sind euretwegen nicht in Urlaub gefahren. We didn't go on holiday for your sakes.
2 on your account
□ Er hat sich euretwegen aufgeregt. He got upset on your account.

der **Euro** (PL die **Euros**) NOUN
euro
□ Das kostet fünf Euro. It costs five euros.

Europa NEUT NOUN
Europe
■ aus Europa from Europe
■ in Europa in Europe
■ nach Europa to Europe

der **Europäer** (PL die **Europäer**) NOUN
European

die **Europäerin** NOUN
European

europäisch ADJECTIVE
European

e. V. ABBREVIATION *(= eingetragener Verein)*
registered society

evangelisch ADJECTIVE
Protestant

eventuell ADVERB, ADJECTIVE
perhaps
□ Eventuell komme ich später nach. Perhaps I'll come on later.
■ Eventuelle Fragen wird mein Kollege gerne beantworten. My colleague will be pleased to answer any questions you may have.
LANGUAGE TIP Be careful! **eventuell** does not mean **eventual**.

ewig ADJECTIVE
eternal

die **Ewigkeit** NOUN
eternity

das **Examen** (PL die **Examen**) NOUN
exam

explodieren (PERFECT **ist explodiert**) VERB [76]
to explode

die **Explosion** NOUN
explosion

exportieren (PERFECT **hat exportiert**) VERB [76]
to export

extra ADVERB, ADJECTIVE
1 separately
□ Schicke die Diskette lieber extra. It'd be better to send the diskette separately.
2 specially
□ Das wurde extra für sie angefertigt. That was made specially for her. □ Ich bin extra wegen dir gekommen. I came specially because of you.
3 on purpose
□ Das hat er extra gemacht. He did that on purpose.
4 extra
□ Ich habe das extra schnell gemacht. I did it extra quickly. □ Das sind extra starke Pfefferminzbonbons. These are extra strong peppermints.

extrem ADJECTIVE
extreme

German-English

e

Ff

die **Fabrik** NOUN
factory
LANGUAGE TIP Be careful! **Fabrik** does not mean **fabric**.

der **Fabrikarbeiter** (PL die **Fabrikarbeiter**) NOUN
factory worker

die **Fabrikarbeiterin** NOUN
factory worker

das **Fach** (PL die **Fächer**) NOUN
1 shelf
□ Das ist mein Fach im Schrank. This is my shelf in the cupboard.
2 pigeonhole
□ Jeder Lehrer hat im Lehrerzimmer ein Fach. Every teacher has a pigeonhole in the staff room.
3 subject
□ In welchem Fach bist du am besten? What subject are you best at?

der **Facharzt** (GEN des **Facharztes**, PL die **Fachärzte**) NOUN
specialist *(doctor)*

die **Fachärztin** NOUN
specialist *(doctor)*

der **Fachausdruck** (PL die **Fachausdrücke**) NOUN
technical term

die **Fachfrau** NOUN
expert

die **Fachhochschule** NOUN
college

die **Fachschule** NOUN
technical college

der **Fachmann** (PL die **Fachleute**) NOUN
expert

die **Fackel** NOUN
torch

der **Faden** (PL die **Fäden**) NOUN
thread

fähig ADJECTIVE
capable
□ Sie ist eine sehr fähige Lehrerin. She's a very capable teacher.
■ **fähig sein, etwas zu tun** to be capable of doing something □ Bist du fähig, diesen Text zu übersetzen? Are you capable of translating this text?

die **Fähigkeit** NOUN
ability

die **Fahne** NOUN
flag
■ **eine Fahne haben** to stink of booze

der **Fahrausweis** (GEN des **Fahrausweises**, PL die **Fahrausweise**) NOUN
ticket
□ Die Fahrausweise, bitte. Tickets, please.

die **Fahrbahn** NOUN
carriageway

die **Fähre** NOUN
ferry

fahren (PRESENT **fährt**, IMPERFECT **fuhr**, PERFECT **ist/hat gefahren**) VERB [21]
LANGUAGE TIP For the perfect tense use **haben** when the verb has an object and **sein** when there is no object.
1 to drive
□ Er hat mich nach Hause gefahren. He drove me home. □ Er ist sehr schnell gefahren. He drove very fast.
■ **ein Rennen fahren** to drive in a race
2 to go
□ Der Intercity fährt stündlich. The Intercity train goes every hour.
3 to leave
□ Wann seid ihr gefahren? When did you leave?
4 to sail
□ Das Schiff fährt nach Amerika. The ship's sailing to America. □ Wir sind mit dem Schiff nach Amerika gefahren. We sailed to America.
■ **Rad fahren** to cycle □ Früher bin ich viel Rad gefahren. I used to cycle a lot.
■ **mit dem Auto fahren** to go by car
■ **mit dem Zug fahren** to go by train
□ Seid ihr mit dem Zug gefahren? Did you go by train?

der **Fahrer** (PL die **Fahrer**) NOUN
driver

die **Fahrerin** NOUN
driver

der **Fahrgast** (PL die **Fahrgäste**) NOUN
passenger

das **Fahrgeld** (PL die **Fahrgelder**) NOUN
fare
□ Bitte das Fahrgeld abgezählt bereithalten. Please have exact fare ready.

die **Fahrkarte** NOUN
ticket
□ Die Fahrkarten, bitte. Tickets, please.

der **Fahrkartenautomat** (GEN des **Fahrkartenautomaten**, PL die **Fahrkartenautomaten**) NOUN
ticket machine

der **Fahrkartenschalter** (PL die **Fahrkartenschalter**) NOUN
ticket office

fahrlässig ADJECTIVE
negligent

der **Fahrlehrer** (PL die **Fahrlehrer**) NOUN
driving instructor

der **Fahrplan** (PL die **Fahrpläne**) NOUN
timetable

fahrplanmäßig ADJECTIVE
scheduled

der **Fahrpreis** (GEN des **Fahrpreises**, PL die **Fahrpreise**) NOUN
fare

die **Fahrprüfung** NOUN
driving test

das **Fahrrad** (PL die **Fahrräder**) NOUN
bicycle

der **Fahrradweg** (PL die **Fahrradwege**) NOUN
cycle lane

der **Fahrschein** (PL die **Fahrscheine**) NOUN
ticket
□ Die Fahrscheine, bitte. Tickets, please.

der **Fahrscheinentwerter** (PL die **Fahrscheinentwerter**) NOUN
ticket stamping machine

DID YOU KNOW...?
When you travel by train or tram (and sometimes by bus) you have to stamp your ticket in a **Fahrscheinentwerter**. The machines are either on the platforms or inside the vehicles.

die **Fahrschule** NOUN
driving school

der **Fahrstuhl** (PL die **Fahrstühle**) NOUN
lift

die **Fahrt** NOUN
1 journey
□ Die Fahrt nach Hamburg war lang. It was a long journey to Hamburg.
2 trip
□ Am Wochenende haben wir eine Fahrt in den Schwarzwald gemacht. We went on a trip to the Black Forest at the weekend.
■ **Gute Fahrt!** Have a good journey.

die **Fahrtkosten** PL NOUN
travelling expenses

das **Fahrzeug** (PL die **Fahrzeuge**) NOUN
vehicle

fair ADJECTIVE
fair
□ Das ist nicht fair! That's not fair!

der **Faktor** (PL die **Faktoren**) NOUN
factor

die **Fakultät** NOUN
faculty

der **Falke** (GEN des **Falken**, PL die **Falken**) NOUN
falcon

der **Fall** (PL die **Fälle**) NOUN
case
□ Die Polizei untersucht den Fall. The police are investigating the case. □ In diesem Fall mache ich eine Ausnahme. I'll make an exception in this case. □ Welcher Fall steht nach 'außer'? Which case does 'außer' take?
■ **auf jeden Fall** definitely □ Ich komme auf jeden Fall. I'll definitely come.
■ **für alle Fälle** just in case □ Nimm für alle Fälle einen Schirm mit. Take an umbrella, just in case.
■ **Auf keinen Fall!** No way!

die **Falle** NOUN
trap

fallen (PRESENT **fällt**, IMPERFECT **fiel**, PERFECT **ist gefallen**) VERB [22]
to fall
■ **etwas fallen lassen** 1 to drop something □ Lass es nicht fallen! Don't drop it! 2 to abandon something □ Wir haben die Idee, in Frankreich Ferien zu machen, wieder fallen lassen. We've abandoned the idea of spending our holidays in France.
■ **eine Bemerkung fallen lassen** to make a remark

fällen VERB [38]
■ **einen Baum fällen** to fell a tree
■ **ein Urteil fällen** to pronounce judgement

fallenlassen VERB [42] ▷ *see* **fallen**

fällig ADJECTIVE
due

falls ADVERB
if

der **Fallschirm** (PL die **Fallschirme**) NOUN
parachute

falsch ADJECTIVE
1 wrong
□ Die Antwort war falsch. The answer was wrong.
■ **jemanden falsch verstehen** to get somebody wrong
2 false
□ falsche Zähne false teeth

fälschen VERB [38]
to forge

die **Fälschung** NOUN
forgery

die **Falte** NOUN
1 fold
□ eine Falte im Papier a fold in the paper
2 crease
□ Die Hose ist voller Falten. The trousers are all creased.

3 wrinkle
□ Ihr Gesicht ist voller Falten. Her face is all wrinkled.
4 pleat
□ eine Rockfalte a pleat in a skirt

falten VERB [2]
to fold

faltig ADJECTIVE
1 wrinkled
□ Er hat ein faltiges Gesicht. He's got a wrinkled face.
2 creased
□ Deine Hose ist ganz faltig. Your trousers are all creased.

die **Familie** NOUN
family

der **Familienname** (GEN des **Familiennamens**, PL die **Familiennamen**) NOUN
surname

der **Familienstand** (PL die **Familienstände**) NOUN
marital status

der **Fan** (PL die **Fans**) NOUN
fan
□ Sie ist ein Fan von Sting. She's a Sting fan.

fand VERB ▷ *see* **finden**

fangen (PRESENT **fängt**, IMPERFECT **fing**, PERFECT **hat gefangen**) VERB [23]
to catch

die **Fantasie** NOUN
imagination

fantasielos ADJECTIVE
unimaginative

fantasieren (PERFECT **hat fantasiert**) VERB [76]
to fantasize
□ Er fantasierte von einem Lottogewinn. He fantasized about a win on the lottery.

fantasievoll ADJECTIVE
imaginative

fantastisch ADJECTIVE
fantastic

die **Farbe** NOUN
1 colour
□ Rosa ist Beates Lieblingsfarbe. Pink is Beate's favourite colour.
2 paint
□ Hast du Farben, ich möchte was malen? I'd like to do some painting, have you got any paints?

farbecht ADJECTIVE
colourfast

färben VERB [38]
to dye
□ Sie hat ihre Haare gefärbt. She's dyed her hair.

farbenblind ADJECTIVE
colour-blind

das **Farbfernsehen** NOUN
colour television

der **Farbfilm** (PL die **Farbfilme**) NOUN
colour film

das **Farbfoto** (PL die **Farbfotos**) NOUN
colour photograph

farbig ADJECTIVE
coloured

farblos ADJECTIVE
colourless

der **Farbstift** (PL die **Farbstifte**) NOUN
coloured pencil

der **Farbstoff** (PL die **Farbstoffe**) NOUN
dye

der **Farbton** (PL die **Farbtöne**) NOUN
shade

der **Fasan** (PL die **Fasane** *or* **Fasanen**) NOUN
pheasant

der **Fasching** (PL die **Faschinge**) NOUN
carnival

DID YOU KNOW...?
The German carnival season lasts from 11 November to Shrove Tuesday but most events, fancy-dress processions and parties take place in the week leading up to Ash Wednesday.

der **Faschingsdienstag** NOUN
Shrove Tuesday

die **Faser** NOUN
fibre

das **Fass** (GEN des **Fasses**, PL die **Fässer**) NOUN
barrel
□ ein Weinfass a wine barrel
■ **ein Ölfass** an oil drum
■ **Bier vom Fass** draught beer

fassen (PERFECT **hat gefasst**) VERB [31]
1 to grasp
□ Er fasste mich am Arm. He grasped my arm.
2 to hold
□ Der Behälter fasst zwanzig Liter. The container holds twenty litres.
3 to understand
□ Ich kann es nicht fassen, dass du das noch immer nicht gemacht hast. I can't understand why you still haven't done it.
■ **nicht zu fassen** unbelievable
■ **sich fassen** to calm down

die **Fassung** NOUN
1 composure
□ Sie hat die Fassung verloren. She lost her composure.
■ **jemanden aus der Fassung bringen** to upset somebody
2 version
□ der Text in einer neuen Fassung the text in a new version

fassungslos ADJECTIVE
speechless

fast ADVERB
almost

LANGUAGE TIP Be careful! The German word **fast** does not mean **fast**.

fasten VERB [2]

to fast

die **Fastenzeit** NOUN
Lent

die **Fastnacht** NOUN
carnival

DID YOU KNOW...?
The German carnival season lasts from 11 November to Shrove Tuesday but most events, fancy-dress processions and parties take place in the week leading up to Ash Wednesday.

faul ADJECTIVE
1 rotten
□ Der Apfel ist faul. The apple's rotten.
2 lazy
□ Er ist der faulste Schüler. He's our laziest pupil.
■ **eine faule Ausrede** a lame excuse
■ **Daran ist etwas faul.** There's something fishy about it.

faulen VERB [38]
to rot

faulenzen VERB [36]
to laze about

die **Faust** (PL die **Fäuste**) NOUN
fist
■ **auf eigene Faust** off one's own bat

faxen VERB [36]
to fax
□ jemandem etwas faxen to fax something to somebody

der **FCKW** NOUN
(= Fluorchlorkohlenwasserstoff)
CFC *(= chlorofluorocarbon)*

der **Februar** (GEN des **Februar** *or* **Februars**, PL die **Februare**) NOUN
February
□ im Februar in February □ am dritten Februar on the third of February □ Bonn, den 3. Februar 2009 Bonn, 3 February 2009
□ Heute ist der zweite Februar. Today is the second of February.

fechten (PRESENT **ficht**, IMPERFECT **focht**, PERFECT **hat gefochten**) VERB
to fence

die **Feder** NOUN
1 feather
□ Er hatte eine Feder am Hut. He had a feather in his hat.
2 spring
□ Die Federn des Betts sind ausgeleiert. The bed springs have worn out.

das **Federbett** (PL die **Federbetten**) NOUN
continental quilt

die **Fee** NOUN
fairy

fegen VERB [38]
to sweep

fehl ADJECTIVE
■ **fehl am Platz** out of place

fehlen VERB [38]
1 to be absent
□ Er hat gestern in der Schule gefehlt. He was absent from school yesterday.
2 to be missing
□ Da fehlt ein Knopf. There's a button missing. □ Wer fehlt? Is anyone missing?
■ **Mir fehlt das nötige Geld.** I haven't got the money.
■ **Du fehlst mir.** I miss you.
■ **Was fehlt ihm?** What's wrong with him?

der **Fehler** (PL die **Fehler**) NOUN
1 mistake
□ Wie viele Fehler hast du gemacht? How many mistakes did you make?
2 fault
□ Sein einziger Fehler ist, dass er den Mund nicht halten kann. His only fault is that he can't keep his mouth shut.

die **Feier** NOUN
celebration

der **Feierabend** (PL die **Feierabende**) NOUN
clocking-off time
■ **Feierabend machen** to clock off
■ **Wann hat dein Vater Feierabend?** When does your father finish work?

feierlich ADJECTIVE
solemn

die **Feierlichkeit** NOUN
festivity

feiern VERB [88]
to celebrate

der **Feiertag** (PL die **Feiertage**) NOUN
holiday
□ ein öffentlicher Feiertag a public holiday

feige ADJECTIVE
▷ *see also* **die Feige** NOUN
cowardly

die **Feige** NOUN
▷ *see also* **feige** ADJECTIVE
fig

der **Feigling** (PL die **Feiglinge**) NOUN
coward

die **Feile** NOUN
file
□ eine Nagelfeile a nailfile

feilschen VERB [38]
to haggle

fein ADJECTIVE
1 fine
□ feiner Sand fine sand
2 refined
□ feine Leute refined people
■ **Fein!** Great!

der **Feind** (PL die **Feinde**) NOUN
enemy

feindlich ADJECTIVE
hostile

die **Feindschaft** NOUN
hostility

das **Feld** (PL die **Felder**) NOUN
1 field
□ Auf diesem Feld wächst Hafer. There are oats growing in this field.
2 pitch
□ ein Fußballfeld a football pitch
3 square
□ Er rückte mit seinem Bauern ein Feld vor. He moved his pawn forward one square.

der **Fels** (GEN des **Felsen**, PL die **Felsen**) NOUN
rock
■ **die weißen Felsen von Dover** the white cliffs of Dover

feminin ADJECTIVE
feminine

das **Fenster** (PL die **Fenster**) NOUN
window

der **Fensterladen** (PL die **Fensterläden**) NOUN
shutter

die **Fensterscheibe** NOUN
windowpane

die **Ferien** PL NOUN
holidays
■ **Ferien haben** to be on holiday

der **Ferienjob** (PL die **Ferienjobs**) NOUN
holiday job

der **Ferienkurs** (GEN des **Ferienkurses**, PL die **Ferienkurse**) NOUN
vacation course

das **Ferienlager** (PL die **Ferienlager**) NOUN
holiday camp

fern ADJECTIVE, ADVERB
distant
□ in ferner Zukunft in the distant future
■ **fern von hier** a long way from here
■ **der Ferne Osten** the Far East

die **Fernbedienung** NOUN
remote control

das **Ferngespräch** (PL die **Ferngespräche**) NOUN
long-distance call

das **Fernglas** (GEN des **Fernglases**, PL die **Ferngläser**) NOUN
binoculars
□ ein Fernglas a pair of binoculars

der **Fernsehapparat** (PL die **Fernsehapparate**) NOUN
television set

das **Fernsehen** NOUN
▷ *see also* **fernsehen** VERB
television
□ im Fernsehen on television

fernsehen (PRESENT **sieht fern**, IMPERFECT **sah fern**, PERFECT **hat ferngesehen**) VERB [64]
▷ *see also* **das Fernsehen** NOUN
to watch television

der **Fernseher** (PL die **Fernseher**) NOUN
television set

der **Fernsehfilm** (PL die **Fernsehfilme**) NOUN
TV film

die **Fernsehsendung** NOUN
TV programme

die **Fernsehserie** NOUN
TV series

der **Fernsprecher** (PL die **Fernsprecher**) NOUN
telephone

die **Fernsteuerung** NOUN
remote control

die **Ferse** NOUN
heel
□ Ich habe eine Blase an der Ferse. I've got a blister on my heel.

fertig ADJECTIVE
1 ready
□ Das Essen ist fertig. Dinner's ready.
2 finished
□ Der Aufsatz ist fertig. The essay's finished.
□ Bist du mit deinen Hausaufgaben fertig? Have you finished your homework?
■ **etwas fertig machen** to finish something
□ Ich muss noch die Matheaufgaben fertig machen. I've just got to finish my maths homework.
■ **sich fertig machen** to get ready

fertigbringen (IMPERFECT **brachte fertig**, PERFECT **hat fertiggebracht**) VERB [13]
■ **es fertigbringen, etwas zu tun** to bring oneself to do something □ Ich bringe es nicht fertig, ihr das zu sagen. I can't bring myself to tell her.

das **Fertiggericht** (PL die **Fertiggerichte**) NOUN
ready meal

fertigmachen VERB [48]
■ **jemanden fertigmachen 1** to wear somebody out □ Die Radtour hat mich fertiggemacht. The cycling trip wore me out. **2** to tear somebody off a strip □ Meine Englischlehrerin hat mich heute fertiggemacht. My English teacher tore me off a strip today.

fesselnd ADJECTIVE
captivating

das **Fest** (PL die **Feste**) NOUN
▷ *see also* **fest** ADJECTIVE
1 party
□ Fritz macht am Samstag ein Fest. Fritz is having a party on Saturday.
2 festival
□ das Backnanger Straßenfest the Backnang Street Festival
■ **Frohes Fest!** Happy Christmas!

fest ADJECTIVE, ADVERB
▷ *see also* **das Fest** NOUN
firm
□ Er hielt sie mit festem Griff. He had a firm grip of her. □ Er hat einen festen Händedruck. He has a firm handshake.
■ **ein festes Einkommen** a regular income

■ **fest schlafen** to sleep soundly
■ **feste Nahrung** solids

festhalten (PRESENT **hält fest**, IMPERFECT **hielt fest**, PERFECT **hat festgehalten**) VERB [33]
to keep hold of
□ Du musst das Steuer festhalten. You must keep hold of the wheel.
■ **sich festhalten an** to hold on to □ Sie hielt sich am Geländer fest. She held on to the banister.

die **Festigkeit** NOUN
strength

festlegen (PERFECT **hat festgelegt**) VERB [4]
to fix
□ einen Termin festlegen to fix a date
■ **sich festlegen** to commit oneself

festlich ADJECTIVE
festive

festmachen (PERFECT **hat festgemacht**) VERB [48]
1 to fix
□ Habt ihr den Termin schon festgemacht? Have you fixed the date yet?
2 to moor
□ Wir haben das Boot im Hafen festgemacht. We moored the boat in the harbour.

die **Festnahme** NOUN
arrest

festnehmen (PRESENT **nimmt fest**, IMPERFECT **nahm fest**, PERFECT **hat festgenommen**) VERB [52]
to arrest

die **Festplatte** NOUN
hard disk

die **Festspiele** NEUT PL NOUN
festival

feststehen (IMPERFECT **stand fest**, PERFECT **hat festgestanden**) VERB [72]
to be certain
□ So viel steht fest: ... This much is certain: ...

feststellen (PERFECT **hat festgestellt**) VERB [4]
1 to establish
□ Wir konnten nicht feststellen, wer das geschrieben hatte. We couldn't establish who'd written it.
2 to see
□ Ich stelle fest, dass du schon wieder nicht aufgepasst hast. I see that you haven't been paying attention again.
3 to detect
□ Wir haben da einen Fehler festgestellt. We've detected an error.

der **Festtag** NOUN
special day

das **Fett** (PL die **Fette**) NOUN
▷ *see also* **fett** ADJECTIVE
fat

fett ADJECTIVE
▷ *see also* **das Fett** NOUN
fat
□ Er ist zu fett. He's too fat.
■ **fettes Essen** greasy food
■ **fette Schrift** bold type

fettarm ADJECTIVE
low-fat

fettig ADJECTIVE
greasy

der **Fetzen** (PL die **Fetzen**) NOUN
scrap
□ ein Fetzen Papier a scrap of paper

feucht ADJECTIVE
1 damp
□ etwas mit einem feuchten Tuch abwischen to wipe something with a damp cloth
2 humid
□ Das Klima ist sehr feucht. The climate's very humid.

die **Feuchtigkeit** NOUN
1 moisture
□ Salz zieht Feuchtigkeit an. Salt attracts moisture.
2 humidity
□ hohe Luftfeuchtigkeit high humidity

das **Feuer** (PL die **Feuer**) NOUN
fire

der **Feuerlöscher** (PL die **Feuerlöscher**) NOUN
fire extinguisher

die **Feuerwehr** (PL die **Feuerwehren**) NOUN
fire brigade

das **Feuerwehrauto** (PL die **Feuerwehrautos**) NOUN
fire engine

der **Feuerwehrmann** (PL die **Feuerwehrleute** *or* **Feuerwehrmänner**) NOUN
fireman

das **Feuerwerk** (PL die **Feuerwerke**) NOUN
fireworks
□ Wir waren beim Feuerwerk. We went to the fireworks.

das **Feuerzeug** (PL die **Feuerzeuge**) NOUN
lighter

das **Fieber** (PL die **Fieber**) NOUN
1 fever
□ Das Fieber wird sich in ein paar Tagen senken. The fever will pass in a couple of days.
2 temperature
□ Hast du Fieber? Have you got a temperature?

fiel VERB ▷ *see* **fallen**

fies ADJECTIVE
nasty

die **Figur** NOUN
figure
□ Sie hat eine gute Figur. She's got a good figure.
■ **eine Schachfigur** a chessman

die **Filiale** NOUN
branch

der **Film** (PL die **Filme**) NOUN
film

filmen VERB [38]
to film

der **Filter** (PL die **Filter**) NOUN
filter

der **Filzstift** (PL die **Filzstifte**) NOUN
felt-tip pen

das **Finanzamt** (PL die **Finanzämter**) NOUN
Inland Revenue Office

finanziell ADJECTIVE
financial

finanzieren (PERFECT **hat finanziert**) VERB [76]
to finance

finden (IMPERFECT **fand**, PERFECT **hat gefunden**) VERB [24]
1 to find
□ Hast du deinen Radiergummi gefunden? Have you found your rubber?
2 to think
□ Ich finde, er sieht gut aus. I think he's good-looking. □ Ich finde sie nicht attraktiv. I don't think she's attractive.
■ **Ich finde nichts dabei, wenn ...** I don't see what's wrong with ... □ Ich finde nichts dabei, wenn man mal einen Tag faulenzt. I don't see what's wrong with lazing about for one day.
■ **Das wird sich finden.** Things will work out.

fing VERB ▷ *see* **fangen**

der **Finger** (PL die **Finger**) NOUN
finger

der **Fingerabdruck** (PL die **Fingerabdrücke**) NOUN
fingerprint
■ **genetische Fingerabdrücke** genetic fingerprinting

der **Fingernagel** (PL die **Fingernägel**) NOUN
fingernail

der **Finne** (GEN des **Finnen**, PL die **Finnen**) NOUN
Finn

die **Finnin** NOUN
Finn

finnisch ADJECTIVE
Finnish

Finnland NEUT NOUN
Finland
■ **aus Finnland** from Finland
■ **nach Finnland** to Finland

finster ADJECTIVE
1 dark
□ Hier ist es aber finster. It's dark in here.
2 sinister
□ finstere Gestalten sinister figures
■ **ein finsteres Gesicht** a grim face

die **Finsternis** NOUN
darkness

die **Firma** (PL die **Firmen**) NOUN
firm

der **Fisch** (PL die **Fische**) NOUN
fish
□ Ich habe fünf Fische. I've got five fish.
■ **Fische** Pisces □ Adelheid ist Fisch. Adelheid's Pisces.

fischen VERB [48]
to fish
□ Sonntags geht Alex immer fischen. Alex always goes fishing on Sundays.

der **Fischer** (PL die **Fischer**) NOUN
fisherman

die **Fischerei** NOUN
fishing

fit ADJECTIVE
fit
□ Ich halte mich mit Schwimmen fit. I keep fit by swimming.

fix ADJECTIVE
■ **fix und fertig 1** finished □ Alles war fix und fertig. Everything was finished. **2** all in □ Ich bin fix und fertig. I'm all in.

der **Fixer** (PL die **Fixer**) NOUN
junkie

flach ADJECTIVE
1 flat
□ Norddeutschland ist flach. North Germany's flat.
2 shallow
□ Ich brauche eine flache Schale. I need a shallow bowl.

der **Flachbildschirm** (PL die **Flachbildschirme**) NOUN
flat screen
□ ein Fernseher mit Flachbildschirm a flatscreen TV

die **Fläche** NOUN
area
□ eine Fläche von hundert Quadratkilometern an area of a hundred square kilometres

das **Flachland** NOUN
lowland

flackern VERB [88]
to flicker

die **Flagge** NOUN
flag

die **Flamme** NOUN
flame

die **Flasche** NOUN
bottle
□ eine Flasche Mineralwasser a bottle of mineral water

der **Flaschenöffner** (PL die **Flaschenöffner**) NOUN
bottle-opener

flauschig ADJECTIVE
fluffy

der **Fleck** (PL die **Flecke**) NOUN
1 stain
□ Der Wein hat einen Fleck auf dem Teppich gemacht. The wine left a stain on the carpet.
2 spot
□ Das ist ein hübscher Fleck. This is a

beautiful spot.

das **Fleckenmittel** (PL die **Fleckenmittel**) NOUN
stain remover

fleckig ADJECTIVE
1 spotted
□ Ein Dalmatiner hat ein fleckiges Fell. A Dalmatian has a spotted coat.
2 stained
□ Die Tischdecke ist ganz fleckig. The tablecloth's all stained.

die **Fledermaus** (PL die **Fledermäuse**) NOUN
bat

das **Fleisch** NOUN
meat
□ Ich esse kein Fleisch. I don't eat meat.

der **Fleischer** (PL die **Fleischer**) NOUN
butcher

die **Fleischerei** NOUN
butcher's

der **Fleiß** (GEN des **Fleißes**) NOUN
hard work
□ Mit etwas Fleiß könntest du deine Noten verbessern. With a bit of hard work you could improve your marks.

fleißig ADJECTIVE
hard-working
□ Silke ist eine fleißige Schülerin. Silke's a hard-working pupil.
■ **Ich war heute schon fleißig.** I've already done quite a bit of work today.

flexibel ADJECTIVE
flexible

flicken VERB [48]
to mend

die **Fliege** NOUN
1 fly
□ Er tut keiner Fliege etwas zuleide. He wouldn't hurt a fly.
2 bow tie
□ Er trug eine Fliege. He was wearing a bow tie.

fliegen (IMPERFECT **flog**, PERFECT **ist geflogen**) VERB [25]
to fly

fliehen (IMPERFECT **floh**, PERFECT **ist geflohen**) VERB [26]
to flee

die **Fliese** NOUN
tile

das **Fließband** (PL die **Fließbänder**) NOUN
assembly line

fließen (IMPERFECT **floss**, PERFECT **ist geflossen**) VERB [27]
to flow

fließend ADJECTIVE, ADVERB
1 running
□ fließendes Wasser running water
2 fluent
□ Sie spricht fließend Englisch. She is fluent in English.

flink ADJECTIVE
nimble

die **Flitterwochen** FEM PL NOUN
honeymoon

flitzen (PERFECT **ist geflitzt**) VERB [48]
to dash

die **Flocke** NOUN
flake
□ eine Schneeflocke a snowflake

flog VERB ▷ *see* **fliegen**

der **Floh** (PL die **Flöhe**) NOUN
flea

der **Flohmarkt** (PL die **Flohmärkte**) NOUN
flea market

floss VERB ▷ *see* **fließen**

die **Flosse** NOUN
1 fin
□ die Flosse eines Hais a shark's fin
2 flipper
□ Er hat seine Flossen mit ins Schwimmbad genommen. He took his flippers with him to the swimming baths.

die **Flöte** NOUN
1 flute
□ Cordula spielt Flöte. Cordula plays the flute.
2 recorder
□ Phil spielt Flöte. Phil plays the recorder.

fluchen VERB [38]
to curse

flüchtig ADJECTIVE
at large
□ Der Einbrecher ist noch flüchtig. The burglar's still at large.
■ **jemanden nur flüchtig kennen** to know somebody only superficially

der **Flüchtling** (PL die **Flüchtlinge**) NOUN
refugee

der **Flug** (PL die **Flüge**) NOUN
flight
□ Der Flug nach Atlanta ist verspätet. The flight to Atlanta's been delayed.

das **Flugblatt** (PL die **Flugblätter**) NOUN
leaflet

der **Flügel** (PL die **Flügel**) NOUN
1 wing
□ die Flügel des Adlers the eagle's wings
2 grand piano
□ Im Musikzimmer steht ein Flügel. There's a grand piano in the music room.

der **Fluggast** (PL die **Fluggäste**) NOUN
airline passenger

die **Fluggesellschaft** NOUN
airline

der **Flughafen** (PL die **Flughäfen**) NOUN
airport

der **Fluglotse** (GEN des **Fluglotsen**, PL die **Fluglotsen**) NOUN
air traffic controller

der **Flugplan** (PL die **Flugpläne**) NOUN
flight schedule

der **Flugplatz** (GEN des **Flugplatzes**, PL die **Flugplätze**) NOUN
1 airport
□ Wir bringen dich zum Flugplatz. We'll take you to the airport.
2 airfield
□ Dieser Flugplatz ist nur für Privatflugzeuge. This airfield is only for private planes.

der **Flugschein** (PL die **Flugscheine**) NOUN
plane ticket

das **Flugticket** (PL die **Flugtickets**) NOUN
plane ticket

das **Flugzeug** (PL die **Flugzeuge**) NOUN
aeroplane

die **Flugzeugentführung** NOUN
hijacking

das **Fluor** NOUN
fluorine

der **Flur** (PL die **Flure**) NOUN
corridor

LANGUAGE TIP Be careful! **Flur** does not mean **floor**.

der **Fluss** (GEN des **Flusses**, PL die **Flüsse**) NOUN
river

das **Flüsschen** (PL die **Flüsschen**) NOUN
little river

flüssig ADJECTIVE
liquid

die **Flüssigkeit** NOUN
liquid

flüstern VERB [88]
to whisper

die **Flut** (PL die **Fluten**) NOUN
1 flood
□ Wir haben eine Flut von Briefen bekommen. We received a flood of letters.
2 high tide
□ Das Schiff läuft bei Flut aus. The ship sails at high tide.

das **Flutlicht** (PL die **Flutlichter**) NOUN
floodlight

der **Föhn** (PL die **Föhne**) NOUN
hair dryer

föhnen VERB [38]
to blow-dry

die **Folge** NOUN
1 result
□ Er starb an den Folgen des Unfalls. He died as a result of the accident.
■ **etwas zur Folge haben** to result in something □ Deine Faulheit wird schlechte Noten zur Folge haben. Your laziness will result in bad marks.
■ **Folgen haben** to have consequences
□ Das wird schlimme Folgen haben. That'll have serious consequences.
2 episode
□ Hast du die letzte Folge der 'Lindenstraße' gesehen? Did you see the latest episode of 'Lindenstraße'?
■ **ein Roman in Folgen** a serialized novel

folgen (PERFECT **ist gefolgt**) VERB [38]
to follow
□ Uns ist ein grünes Auto gefolgt. We were followed by a green car. □ Folgen Sie dem Wagen da. Follow that car. □ Ich konnte ihm nicht folgen. I couldn't follow what he was saying.
■ **Meine Kinder folgen nicht immer.** My children don't always do what they're told.

folgend ADJECTIVE
following

die **Folgerung** NOUN
conclusion

folglich ADVERB
consequently

folgsam ADJECTIVE
obedient

die **Folie** NOUN
foil

foltern VERB [88]
to torture

der **Fön®** (PL die **Föne**) NOUN
hair dryer

fordern VERB [88]
to demand

die **Forderung** NOUN
demand

die **Forelle** NOUN
trout
□ drei Forellen three trout

die **Form** NOUN
1 shape
□ Das Auto hat eine elegante Form. The car has an elegant shape.
2 mould
□ Das Metall wird in eine Form gegossen. The metal is poured into a mould.
3 baking tin

das **Format** (PL die **Formate**) NOUN
format

formatieren (PERFECT **hat formatiert**) VERB [76]
to format

die **Formel** NOUN
formula

formen VERB [38]
to form

förmlich ADJECTIVE
formal

das **Formular** (PL die **Formulare**) NOUN
form
□ ein Formular ausfüllen to fill in a form

formulieren (PERFECT **hat formuliert**) VERB [76]
to formulate

der **Forscher** (PL die **Forscher**) NOUN
1 research scientist
□ Die Forscher haben noch keinen Impfstoff gegen Aids entwickelt. Research scientists have still not developed an AIDS vaccine.

2 explorer
□ Ein Gruppe von Forschern ist im Amazonasgebiet verschollen. A group of explorers is missing in the Amazon region.

die **Forschung** NOUN
research

fort ADVERB
gone
□ Mein Geldbeutel ist fort. My purse is gone.
■ **und so fort** and so on
■ **in einem fort** on and on
■ **Fort mit dir!** Away with you!

sich **fortbewegen** (PERFECT **hat sich fortbewegt**) VERB [4]
to move

fortbleiben (IMPERFECT **blieb fort**, PERFECT **ist fortgeblieben**) VERB [10]
to stay away

fortfahren (PRESENT **fährt fort**, IMPERFECT **fuhr fort**, PERFECT **ist fortgefahren**) VERB [21]
1 to leave
□ Sie sind gestern fortgefahren. They left yesterday.
2 to continue
□ Er fuhr in seiner Rede fort. He continued with his speech.

fortgeschritten ADJECTIVE
advanced

der **Fortschritt** (PL die **Fortschritte**) NOUN
progress
□ Fortschritte machen to make progress

fortschrittlich ADJECTIVE
progressive

fortsetzen (PERFECT **hat fortgesetzt**) VERB [15]
to continue

die **Fortsetzung** NOUN
1 continuation
□ die Fortsetzung des Krieges the continuation of the war
2 sequel
□ Hast du die Fortsetzung gelesen? Have you read the sequel?
■ **Fortsetzung folgt** to be continued

das **Foto** (PL die **Fotos**) NOUN
photo

der **Fotoapparat** (PL die **Fotoapparate**) NOUN
camera

der **Fotograf** (GEN des **Fotografen**, PL die **Fotografen**) NOUN
photographer

LANGUAGE TIP Be careful! **Fotograf** does not mean **photograph**.

die **Fotografie** NOUN
1 photography
□ Die Fotografie ist sein Hobby. His hobby is photography.
2 photograph
□ Ich habe eine Fotografie davon gesehen. I've seen a photograph of it.

fotografieren (PERFECT **hat fotografiert**) VERB [76]
1 to take a photo of
□ Kannst du uns mal fotografieren? Can you take a photo of us?
2 to take photographs
□ Ich fotografiere in den Ferien nie. I never take photographs on holiday.

das **Fotohandy** (PL die **Fotohandys**) NOUN
camera phone

die **Fotokopie** NOUN
photocopy

Fr. ABBREVIATION *(= Frau)*
1 Mrs
2 Ms

die **Fracht** NOUN
freight
□ Frachtkosten freight charges

die **Frage** NOUN
question
□ Könntest du bitte meine Frage beantworten? Could you please answer my question? □ jemandem eine Frage stellen to ask somebody a question
■ **in Frage kommen/stellen** ▷ *see* **infrage**

der **Fragebogen** (PL die **Fragebogen**) NOUN
questionnaire

fragen VERB [38]
to ask
□ Kann ich dich was fragen? Can I ask you something?

das **Fragezeichen** (PL die **Fragezeichen**) NOUN
question mark

fraglich ADJECTIVE
doubtful
□ Es ist sehr fraglich, ob wir kommen können. It's very doubtful whether we can come.

der **Franken** (PL die **Franken**) NOUN
franc
□ Er bezahlte 50 Franken. He paid 50 francs.
■ **der Schweizer Franken** the Swiss franc

frankieren (PERFECT **hat frankiert**) VERB [76]
■ **einen Brief frankieren** to put a stamp on a letter
■ **ein frankierter Briefumschlag** a stamped self-addressed envelope

Frankreich NEUT NOUN
France
■ **aus Frankreich** from France
■ **in Frankreich** in France
■ **nach Frankreich** to France

der **Franzose** (GEN des **Franzosen**, PL die **Franzosen**) NOUN
Frenchman
■ **Er ist Franzose.** He's French.
■ **die Franzosen** the French

die **Französin** NOUN
Frenchwoman
■ **Sie ist Französin.** She's French.

German-English

f

das **Französisch** (GEN des **Französischen**) NOUN
▷ *see also* **französisch** ADJECTIVE
French
□ Er lernt Französisch in der Schule. He's learning French at school.

französisch ADJECTIVE
▷ *see also* **das Französisch** NOUN
French

fraß VERB ▷ *see* **fressen**

die **Frau** NOUN
1 woman
□ Sie ist eine nette Frau. She's a nice woman.
2 wife
□ Herr Arnold ist mit seiner Frau gekommen. Mr Arnold came with his wife.
■ **Sehr geehrte Frau Braun** 1 Dear Mrs Braun 2 Dear Ms Braun

DID YOU KNOW...?
Generally **Frau** is used to address all women whether married or not.

■ **Frau Doktor** Doctor

der **Frauenarzt** (GEN des **Frauenarztes**, PL die **Frauenärzte**) NOUN
gynaecologist

das **Fräulein** (PL die **Fräulein**) NOUN
Miss
□ Liebes Fräulein Dümmler Dear Miss Dümmler

DID YOU KNOW...?
Fräulein is hardly ever used nowadays and **Frau** is used instead to address all women whether married or not.

frech ADJECTIVE
cheeky

die **Frechheit** NOUN
cheek

frei ADJECTIVE
free
■ **Ist der Platz hier frei?** Is this seat taken?
■ **Soll ich einen Platz für dich frei halten?** Shall I keep a seat for you?
■ **'Einfahrt frei halten'** 'Keep clear'
■ **Wir haben im Moment keine freien Stellen.** We haven't got any vacancies at the moment.
■ **ein freier Mitarbeiter** a freelancer
■ **im Freien** in the open air

das **Freibad** (PL die **Freibäder**) NOUN
open-air swimming pool
□ Im Sommer gehe ich gern ins Freibad. I like going to the open-air swimming pool in the summer.

freigebig ADJECTIVE
generous

freihalten VERB [33] ▷ *see* **frei**

die **Freiheit** NOUN
1 freedom
2 liberty
□ sich Freiheiten herausnehmen to take liberties

freilassen (PRESENT **lässt frei**, IMPERFECT **ließ frei**, PERFECT **hat freigelassen**) VERB [42]
to free

der **Freitag** (PL die **Freitage**) NOUN
Friday
□ am Freitag on Friday

freitags ADVERB
on Fridays

freiwillig ADJECTIVE
voluntary

die **Freizeit** NOUN
spare time
□ Was machst du in deiner Freizeit? What do you do in your spare time?

die **Freizeitbeschäftigung** NOUN
leisure activity

fremd ADJECTIVE
1 strange
□ eine fremde Umgebung strange surroundings
2 foreign
□ fremde Länder und Sprachen foreign countries and languages
■ **Ich bin in London fremd.** I'm a stranger to London.

der **Fremdenverkehr** NOUN
tourism

das **Fremdenzimmer** (PL die **Fremdenzimmer**) NOUN
guest room

die **Fremdsprache** NOUN
foreign language

das **Fremdwort** (PL die **Fremdwörter**) NOUN
foreign word

fressen (PRESENT **frisst**, IMPERFECT **fraß**, PERFECT **hat gefressen**) VERB
to eat
□ Er frisst wie ein Schwein. He eats like a pig.

die **Freude** NOUN
1 joy
□ Welche Freude! What joy!
2 delight
□ Zu meiner Freude hatten wir gestern keine Schule. To my delight we didn't have any school yesterday.
■ **Er hat viel Freude an seinem Mountainbike.** He's delighted with his mountain bike.
■ **Das wird den Kindern Freude machen.** That'll please the children.
■ **Ich wollte dir eine Freude machen.** I wanted to make you happy.

freuen VERB [38]
■ **sich freuen** to be glad □ Ich freue mich, dass du gekommen bist. I'm glad you've come.
■ **sich auf etwas freuen** to look forward to something □ Wir freuen uns darauf, euch zu sehen. We're looking forward to seeing you.
■ **sich über etwas freuen** to be pleased with something □ Sie hat sich sehr über das Geschenk gefreut. She was very pleased with

the present.
■ **Dein Brief hat mich sehr gefreut.** Your letter made me very happy.
■ **Freut mich!** Pleased to meet you.

der **Freund** (PL die **Freunde**) NOUN
1 friend
□ Alle meine Freunde waren da. All my friends were there.
2 boyfriend
□ Hast du einen Freund? Have you got a boyfriend?

die **Freundin** NOUN
1 friend
□ Wiltrud kommt mit ihrer Freundin. Wiltrud's coming with her friend.
2 girlfriend
□ Tobias hat keine Freundin. Tobias hasn't got a girlfriend.

freundlich ADJECTIVE
1 friendly
□ Die Leute waren sehr freundlich. The people were very friendly.
□ ein freundliches Lächeln a friendly smile
2 kind
□ Das ist sehr freundlich von Ihnen. That's very kind of you.

freundlicherweise ADVERB
kindly
□ Er hat uns freundlicherweise geholfen. He kindly helped us.

die **Freundlichkeit** NOUN
friendliness

die **Freundschaft** NOUN
friendship

der **Frieden** (PL die **Frieden**) NOUN
peace
■ **im Frieden** in peacetime

der **Friedhof** (PL die **Friedhöfe**) NOUN
cemetery

friedlich ADJECTIVE
peaceful

frieren (IMPERFECT **fror**, PERFECT **hat gefroren**) VERB
to freeze
□ Ich friere. I'm freezing.
■ **Es friert mich.** I'm freezing.
■ **Letzte Nacht hat es gefroren.** It was frosty last night.

die **Frikadelle** NOUN
rissole

frisch ADJECTIVE
fresh
□ frische Milch fresh milk □ ein frischer Wind a fresh wind □ Nimm ein frisches Blatt. Take a fresh sheet of paper.
■ **Frisch gestrichen!** Wet paint!
■ **sich frisch machen** to freshen oneself up

der **Friseur** (PL die **Friseure**) NOUN
hairdresser

die **Friseuse** NOUN
hairdresser

frisieren (PERFECT **hat frisiert**) VERB [76]
■ **jemanden frisieren** to do somebody's hair
■ **sich frisieren** to do one's hair
□ Sie frisierte sich vor dem Spiegel. She did her hair in front of the mirror.

frisst VERB ▷ *see* **fressen**

die **Frist** NOUN
deadline
□ eine Frist einhalten to meet a deadline

die **Frisur** NOUN
hairdo

Frl. ABBREVIATION (= *Fräulein*)
Miss

froh ADJECTIVE
happy
□ frohe Gesichter happy faces
■ **Ich bin froh, dass ...** I'm glad that ...

fröhlich ADJECTIVE
cheerful

die **Fröhlichkeit** NOUN
cheerfulness

fromm ADJECTIVE
devout

fror VERB ▷ *see* **frieren**

der **Frosch** (PL die **Frösche**) NOUN
frog

der **Frost** (PL die **Fröste**) NOUN
frost
□ ein strenger Frost a hard frost

frösteln VERB [88]
to shiver

die **Frucht** (PL die **Früchte**) NOUN
fruit

fruchtbar ADJECTIVE
1 fruitful
□ ein fruchtbares Gespräch a fruitful conversation
2 fertile
□ fruchtbarer Boden fertile soil

der **Fruchtsaft** (PL die **Fruchtsäfte**) NOUN
fruit juice

früh ADJECTIVE, ADVERB
early
□ Komm lieber etwas früher. It's better if you come a bit earlier.
■ **heute früh** this morning

früher ADJECTIVE, ADVERB
1 former
□ eine frühere Schülerin unserer Schule a former pupil of our school
2 once
□ Hier stand früher ein Haus. A house once stood here.
■ **Früher war das anders.** That used to be different.

frühestens ADVERB
at the earliest

das **Frühjahr** (PL die **Frühjahre**) NOUN
spring
□ im Frühjahr in spring

der Frühling (PL die **Frühlinge**) NOUN
spring
□ im Frühling in spring

das Frühstück NOUN
breakfast

frühstücken VERB [38]
to have breakfast

frustrieren (PERFECT **hat frustriert**) VERB [76]
to frustrate

der Fuchs (GEN des **Fuchses**, PL die **Füchse**) NOUN
fox

fügen VERB [38]
to join
□ Er fügte ein Teil an ein anderes. He joined one piece to another.
■ **sich fügen** to be obedient

fühlen VERB [38]
to feel
□ Fühl mal, wie weich das ist. Feel how soft it is. □ Ich fühle mich wohl. I feel fine.

fuhr VERB ▷ *see* **fahren**

führen VERB [38]
1 to lead
□ Sie führte uns nach draußen. She led us outside.
■ **ein Geschäft führen** to run a business
2 to be winning
□ Welche Mannschaft führt? Which team's winning?

der Führer (PL die **Führer**) NOUN
1 leader
□ der Parteiführer the party leader
2 guide
□ Unser Führer zeigte uns alle Sehenswürdigkeiten. Our guide showed us all the sights.
3 guidebook
□ Hast du einen Führer von Rom? Have you got a guidebook of Rome?

der Führerschein (PL die **Führerscheine**) NOUN
driving licence
■ **den Führerschein machen** to take one's driving test

die Führung NOUN
1 lead
□ Unsere Mannschaft liegt in Führung. Our team is in the lead.
2 leadership
□ Er übernahm die Führung der Partei. He took over the leadership of the party.
3 management
□ Das Geschäft hat unter neuer Führung wiedereröffnet. The business has reopened under new management.
4 guided tour
□ Führungen durchs Museum finden stündlich statt. There are guided tours of the museum every hour.

füllen VERB [38]
1 to fill
□ Sie füllte das Glas bis zum Rand. She filled the glass to the brim.
2 to stuff
□ Heute gibt es gefüllte Paprika. We're having stuffed peppers today.

der Füller (PL die **Füller**) NOUN
fountain pen

die Füllung NOUN
filling

das Fundament (PL die **Fundamente**) NOUN
foundations

das Fundbüro (PL die **Fundbüros**) NOUN
lost property office

fundiert ADJECTIVE
sound
□ fundierte Englischkenntnisse a sound knowledge of English

fünf NUMBER
▷ *see also* **die Fünf** NOUN
five

die Fünf NOUN
▷ *see also* **fünf** NUMBER
1 five
2 poor

> **DID YOU KNOW...?**
> German marks range from one (**sehr gut**) to six (**ungenügend**).

fünfte ADJECTIVE
fifth
□ Ich erkläre dir das jetzt zum fünften Mal. This is the fifth time I've explained this to you.
□ Er kam als Fünfter. He was the fifth to arrive.

fünfzehn NUMBER
fifteen

fünfzig NUMBER
fifty

der Funke (GEN des **Funkens**, PL die **Funken**) NOUN
spark

funkeln VERB [88]
to sparkle

das Funkgerät (PL die **Funkgeräte**) NOUN
radio set

das Funkloch (PL die **Funklöcher**) NOUN
dead spot *(mobile phone)*

die Funktion NOUN
function

funktionieren (PERFECT **hat funktioniert**) VERB [76]
to work

die Funktionstaste NOUN
function key

für PREPOSITION

> **LANGUAGE TIP** The preposition **für** takes the accusative.

for
□ Das ist für dich. This is for you.

■ **was für** what kind of □ Was für ein Fahrrad hast du? What kind of bike have you got?
■ **das Für und Wider** the pros and cons

LANGUAGE TIP Word for word, **das Für und Wider** means 'the for and against'.

die **Furcht** NOUN
fear

furchtbar ADJECTIVE
terrible

fürchten VERB [2]
to be afraid
□ Ich fürchte mich vor diesem Mann. I'm afraid of that man.

fürchterlich ADJECTIVE
awful

füreinander ADVERB
for each other

fürs = **für das**

der **Fuß** (GEN des **Fußes**, PL die **Füße**) NOUN
1 foot
□ Mir tun die Füße weh. My feet hurt.
2 leg
□ Der Tisch hat vier Füße. The table's got four legs.
■ **zu Fuß** on foot

der **Fußball** (PL die **Fußbälle**) NOUN
football

der **Fußballplatz** (GEN des **Fußballplatzes**, PL die **Fußballplätze**) NOUN
football pitch

das **Fußballspiel** (PL die **Fußballspiele**) NOUN
football match

der **Fußballspieler** (PL die **Fußballspieler**) NOUN
footballer

der **Fußboden** (PL die **Fußböden**) NOUN
floor

der **Fußgänger** (PL die **Fußgänger**) NOUN
pedestrian

die **Fußgängerzone** NOUN
pedestrian precinct

der **Fußweg** (PL die **Fußwege**) NOUN
footpath

das **Futter** (PL die **Futter**) NOUN
1 feed
□ BSE entstand durch verseuchtes Futter. BSE was the result of contaminated feed.
2 food
□ Hast du Futter für die Katze gekauft? Have you bought cat food?
3 lining
□ Der Mantel hat ein Futter aus Pelz. The coat has a fur lining.

füttern VERB [88]
1 to feed
□ Kannst du bitte das Baby füttern? Can you feed the baby, please?
2 to line
□ Der Mantel ist gefüttert. The coat's lined.

das **Futur** (PL die **Future**) NOUN
future

Gg

g ABBREVIATION *(= Gramm)*
g

gab VERB ▷ *see* **geben**

die **Gabel** NOUN
fork

gähnen VERB [38]
to yawn

die **Galerie** NOUN
gallery

gammeln VERB [88]
to bum around

der **Gang** (PL die **Gänge**) NOUN
1 corridor
□ Häng deinen Mantel im Gang auf. Hang your coat up in the corridor.
2 aisle
□ Ich hätte gern einen Platz am Gang. I'd like an aisle seat.
3 gear
□ Mein Fahrrad hat zehn Gänge. My bike has ten gears.
4 course
□ Das war erst der zweite Gang, und ich bin schon satt. That was only that second course and I'm full already. □ der Gang der Dinge the course of events
■ **etwas in Gang bringen** to get something off the ground □ Sie hat das Projekt in Gang gebracht. She got the project off the ground.

die **Gans** (PL die **Gänse**) NOUN
goose

das **Gänseblümchen** (PL die **Gänseblümchen**) NOUN
daisy

die **Gänsehaut** NOUN
goose pimples

ganz ADJECTIVE, ADVERB
1 whole
□ die ganze Welt the whole world
□ ganz Europa the whole of Europe
■ **sein ganzes Geld** all his money
2 quite
□ ganz gut quite good
■ **ganz und gar nicht** not at all
■ **Es sieht ganz so aus.** It really looks like it.

ganztags ADVERB
full time
□ ganztags arbeiten to work full time

die **Ganztagsschule** NOUN
all-day school

die **Ganztagsstelle** NOUN
full-time job

gar ADJECTIVE, ADVERB
done
□ Die Kartoffeln sind gar. The potatoes are done.
■ **gar nicht** not at all □ Sie hat sich gar nicht gefreut. She was not at all pleased.
□ gar nicht schlecht not bad at all
■ **gar nichts** nothing at all □ Ich habe gar nichts zu tun. I have nothing at all to do.
□ Ich habe gar nichts verstanden. I didn't understand anything at all.
■ **gar niemand** nobody at all □ Es war gar niemand da. There was nobody there at all.

die **Garage** NOUN
garage *(for parking)*

garantieren (PERFECT **hat garantiert**) VERB [76]
to guarantee
■ **Er kommt garantiert.** He's sure to come.

die **Garderobe** NOUN
cloakroom
□ Ich habe meinen Mantel an der Garderobe abgegeben. I left my coat in the cloakroom.

die **Gardine** NOUN
curtain
□ die Gardinen zuziehen to shut the curtains

der **Garten** (PL die **Gärten**) NOUN
garden

das **Gas** (GEN des **Gases**, PL die **Gase**) NOUN
gas
□ Wir kochen mit Gas. We cook with gas.
■ **Gas geben** to accelerate

der **Gasherd** (PL die **Gasherde**) NOUN
gas cooker

das **Gaspedal** (PL die **Gaspedale**) NOUN
accelerator

die **Gasse** NOUN
lane
□ die schmalen Gassen der Altstadt the narrow lanes of the old town

der **Gast** (PL die **Gäste**) NOUN
guest
□ Wir haben Gäste aus England. We've got guests from England.
■ **bei jemandem zu Gast sein** to be somebody's guest

das **Gästehaus** (GEN des **Gästehauses**, PL die **Gästehäuser**) NOUN
guest house

gastfreundlich ADJECTIVE
hospitable

die **Gastfreundschaft** NOUN
hospitality

der **Gastgeber** (PL die **Gastgeber**) NOUN
host

die **Gastgeberin** NOUN
hostess

das **Gasthaus** (GEN des **Gasthauses**, PL die **Gasthäuser**) NOUN
inn

der **Gasthof** (PL die **Gasthöfe**) NOUN
inn

die **Gaststätte** NOUN
pub

DID YOU KNOW...?
In Germany there's practically no difference between pubs and restaurants. You can eat or drink in a **Gaststätte**, families are welcome and the opening hours are flexible.

das **Gebäck** (PL die **Gebäcke**) NOUN
pastry
□ Kuchen und Gebäck cakes and pastries

gebären (PRESENT **gebiert**, IMPERFECT **gebar**, PERFECT **hat geboren**) VERB
to give birth to

das **Gebäude** (PL die **Gebäude**) NOUN
building

geben (PRESENT **gibt**, IMPERFECT **gab**, PERFECT **hat gegeben**) VERB [28]
to give
□ Gib ihm bitte das Geld. Please give him the money. □ Kannst du dieses Buch bitte deiner Mutter geben. Could you give this book to your mother, please.
■ **Karten geben** to deal

LANGUAGE TIP Word for word, **Karten geben** means 'to give cards'.

■ **es gibt** there is □ Hier gibt es ein schönes Freibad. There's a lovely open-air pool here. □ In Stuttgart gibt es viele Parks. There are many parks in Stuttgart. □ Wenn wir zu spät kommen, gibt es Ärger. There will be trouble if we arrive late.
■ **Was gibt's?** What's up?
■ **Was gibt es im Kino?** What's on at the cinema?
■ **sich geschlagen geben** to admit defeat
■ **Das wird sich schon geben.** That'll sort itself out.

das **Gebet** (PL die **Gebete**) NOUN
prayer

gebeten VERB ▷ *see* **bitten**

das **Gebiet** (PL die **Gebiete**) NOUN
1 area
□ ein bewaldetes Gebiet a wooded area
2 field
□ Er ist Experte auf diesem Gebiet. He's an expert in this field.

gebildet ADJECTIVE
cultured

das **Gebirge** (PL die **Gebirge**) NOUN
mountain chain
□ Die Alpen sind ein großes Gebirge. The Alps are a large mountain chain.
■ **ins Gebirge fahren** to go to the mountains

das **Gebiss** (GEN des **Gebisses**, PL die **Gebisse**) NOUN
1 teeth
□ Sie hat ein gesundes Gebiss. She's got healthy teeth.
2 dentures
□ Opas Gebiss lag auf dem Tisch. Grandpa's dentures were lying on the table.

gebissen VERB ▷ *see* **beißen**

geblieben VERB ▷ *see* **bleiben**

geboren VERB ▷ *see* **gebären**

geboren ADJECTIVE
1 born
□ Wann bist du geboren? When were you born?
2 née
□ Frau Dümmler, geborene Schnorr Mrs Dümmler, née Schnorr

geboten VERB ▷ *see* **bieten**

gebracht VERB ▷ *see* **bringen**

gebraten ADJECTIVE
fried

gebrauchen (PERFECT **hat gebraucht**) VERB [48]
to use

die **Gebrauchsanweisung** NOUN
directions for use
□ Wo ist die Gebrauchsanweisung? Where are the directions for use?

gebraucht ADJECTIVE
used

der **Gebrauchtwagen** (PL die **Gebrauchtwagen**) NOUN
second-hand car

gebrochen VERB ▷ *see* **brechen**

die **Gebühr** NOUN
fee

die **Gebühreneinheit** NOUN
unit *(telephone)*

gebührenpflichtig ADJECTIVE
subject to a charge
■ **eine gebührenpflichtige Verwarnung** a fine

gebunden VERB ▷ *see* **binden**

die **Geburt** NOUN
birth
□ bei der Geburt at the birth

gebürtig ADJECTIVE
native of
□ ein gebürtiger Schweizer a native of Switzerland

das **Geburtsdatum** (PL die **Geburtsdaten**) NOUN
date of birth

der **Geburtsort** (PL die **Geburtsorte**) NOUN
birthplace

der **Geburtstag** (PL die **Geburtstage**) NOUN
birthday
□ Herzlichen Glückwunsch zum Geburtstag! Happy Birthday!

das **Gebüsch** (PL die **Gebüsche**) NOUN
bushes

gedacht VERB ▷ *see* **denken**

das **Gedächtnis** (GEN des **Gedächtnisses**, PL die **Gedächtnisse**) NOUN
memory
□ Ich habe ein schlechtes Gedächtnis. I've got a bad memory.

der **Gedanke** (GEN des **Gedankens**, PL die **Gedanken**) NOUN
thought
■ **sich über etwas Gedanken machen** to think about something □ Ich habe mir Gedanken über das gemacht, was du gesagt hast. I've thought about what you said.

der **Gedankenstrich** (PL die **Gedankenstriche**) NOUN
dash

gedeihen (IMPERFECT **gedieh**, PERFECT **ist gediehen**) VERB
to thrive

das **Gedenken** NOUN
■ **zum Gedenken an jemanden** in memory of somebody

das **Gedicht** (PL die **Gedichte**) NOUN
poem

das **Gedränge** NOUN
crush
□ Vor der Kinokasse herrschte großes Gedränge. There was a huge crush at the cinema box office.

die **Geduld** NOUN
patience

sich **gedulden** (PERFECT **hat sich geduldet**) VERB [7]
to be patient

geduldig ADJECTIVE
patient

gedurft VERB ▷ *see* **dürfen**

geehrt ADJECTIVE
■ **Sehr geehrter Herr Butterfeld** Dear Mr Butterfeld

geeignet ADJECTIVE
suitable

die **Gefahr** NOUN
1 danger
□ in Gefahr schweben to be in danger
2 risk
□ Gefahr laufen, etwas zu tun to run the risk of doing something □ auf eigene Gefahr at one's own risk

gefährden (PERFECT **hat gefährdet**) VERB [7]
to endanger

gefährlich ADJECTIVE
dangerous

das **Gefälle** (PL die **Gefälle**) NOUN
gradient

gefallen (1) VERB [22] ▷ *see* **fallen**

gefallen (2) (PRESENT **gefällt**, IMPERFECT **gefiel**, PERFECT **hat gefallen**) VERB [22]
▷ *see also* **der Gefallen** NOUN
to like
□ Es gefällt mir. I like it. □ Das Geschenk hat ihr gefallen. She liked the present. □ Er gefällt mir. I like him. □ Das gefällt mir an ihm. That's one thing I like about him.
■ **sich etwas gefallen lassen** to put up with something □ Eine solche Frechheit lasse ich mir nicht gefallen. I'm not putting up with cheek like that.

der **Gefallen** (PL die **Gefallen**) NOUN
▷ *see also* **gefallen** VERB
favour
□ Könntest du mir einen Gefallen tun? Could you do me a favour?

gefangen VERB ▷ *see* **fangen**
■ **jemanden gefangen nehmen** to take somebody prisoner

der/die **Gefangene** (GEN des/der **Gefangenen**, PL die **Gefangenen**) NOUN
prisoner
□ Ein Gefangener ist geflohen. A prisoner has escaped.

gefangennehmen VERB [52] ▷ *see* **gefangen**

die **Gefangenschaft** NOUN
captivity

das **Gefängnis** (GEN des **Gefängnisses**, PL die **Gefängnisse**) NOUN
prison

die **Gefängnisstrafe** NOUN
prison sentence

das **Gefäß** (GEN des **Gefäßes**, PL die **Gefäße**) NOUN
container

gefasst ADJECTIVE
composed
□ Sie war sehr gefasst. She was very composed.
■ **auf etwas gefasst sein** to be prepared for something □ Ich war schon aufs Schlimmste gefasst. I was prepared for the worst.

geflogen VERB ▷ *see* **fliegen**

geflossen VERB ▷ *see* **fließen**

das **Geflügel** NOUN
poultry

gefragt ADJECTIVE
in demand
□ Er ist ein sehr gefragter Künstler. He's an artist very much in demand. □ Handwerker sind sehr gefragt. Tradesmen are in great demand.

gefräßig ADJECTIVE
greedy

das **Gefrierfach** (PL die **Gefrierfächer**) NOUN
icebox

die **Gefriertruhe** NOUN
deep-freeze

gefroren ADJECTIVE
frozen

das **Gefühl** (PL die **Gefühle**) NOUN
feeling
□ Sie hat ein Gefühl für Kunst. She's got a feeling for art.
■ **etwas im Gefühl haben** to have a feel for something

gefüllt ADJECTIVE
stuffed
□ gefüllte Auberginen stuffed aubergines

gefunden VERB ▷ *see* **finden**

gegangen VERB ▷ *see* **gehen**

gegeben VERB ▷ *see* **geben**

gegen PREPOSITION

LANGUAGE TIP The preposition **gegen** takes the accusative.

1 against
□ Ich bin gegen diese Idee. I'm against this idea. □ nichts gegen jemanden haben to have nothing against somebody
■ **ein Mittel gegen Schnupfen** something for colds
■ **Maske gegen Botha** Maske versus Botha

2 towards
□ gegen Osten towards the east
□ gegen Abend towards evening
■ **gegen einen Baum fahren** to drive into a tree

3 round about
□ gegen drei Uhr round about three o'clock

die **Gegend** NOUN
area
□ die Gegend um Ulm the area around Ulm

das **Gegenmittel** (PL die **Gegenmittel**) NOUN
antidote

der **Gegensatz** (GEN des **Gegensatzes**, PL die **Gegensätze**) NOUN
contrast
■ **Im Gegensatz zu mir ist er gut in Mathe.** Unlike me, he's good at maths.

gegenseitig ADJECTIVE
mutual
□ gegenseitiges Vertrauen mutual trust
■ **sich gegenseitig helfen** to help each other

der **Gegenstand** (PL die **Gegenstände**) NOUN
object

das **Gegenteil** NOUN
opposite
□ Das ist das Gegenteil von schön. That's the opposite of lovely.
■ **im Gegenteil** on the contrary

gegenüber PREPOSITION, ADVERB

LANGUAGE TIP The preposition **gegenüber** takes the dative.

1 opposite
□ Die Apotheke ist gegenüber. The chemist's is opposite. □ Er saß mir gegenüber. He sat opposite me.

2 towards
□ Sie waren mir gegenüber sehr freundlich. They were very friendly towards me.

der **Gegenverkehr** NOUN
oncoming traffic

die **Gegenwart** NOUN
present
□ in der Gegenwart leben to live in the present

gegessen VERB ▷ *see* **essen**

der **Gegner** (PL die **Gegner**) NOUN
opponent

gegrillt ADJECTIVE
grilled

das **Gehackte** (GEN des **Gehackten**) NOUN
mince
□ Ein Kilo Gehacktes, bitte. A kilo of mince, please.

das **Gehalt** (PL die **Gehälter**) NOUN
salary
□ Er verdient ein gutes Gehalt. He earns a good salary.

gehässig ADJECTIVE
spiteful

geheim ADJECTIVE
secret
□ geheim halten to keep secret

das **Geheimnis** (GEN des **Geheimnisses**, PL die **Geheimnisse**) NOUN

1 secret
□ Kannst du ein Geheimnis behalten? Can you keep a secret?

2 mystery
□ die Geheimnisse der Erde the Earth's mysteries

geheimnisvoll ADJECTIVE
mysterious

die **Geheimnummer** NOUN
ex-directory number
□ Wir haben eine Geheimnummer. We're ex-directory.

gehen (IMPERFECT **ging**, PERFECT **ist gegangen**) VERB [29]

1 to go
□ Wir gehen jetzt. We're going now.
□ schwimmen gehen to go swimming

2 to walk
□ Sollen wir gehen oder den Bus nehmen? Shall we walk or go by bus?
■ **Wie geht es dir?** How are you?
■ **Wie geht's?** How are things?
■ **Mir geht's gut.** I'm fine.
■ **Ihm geht's gut.** He's fine.
■ **Es geht.** Not bad.
■ **Geht das?** Is that possible?
■ **Geht's noch?** Can you manage?
■ **Das geht nicht.** That's not on.
■ **um etwas gehen** to be about something

□ In dem Film geht es um einen Bankraub. The film's about a bank robbery.
■ **Hier geht es um sehr viel Geld.** There's a lot of money at stake here.

der **Gehilfe** (GEN des **Gehilfen**, PL die **Gehilfen**) NOUN
assistant

das **Gehirn** (PL die **Gehirne**) NOUN
brain

die **Gehirnerschütterung** NOUN
concussion

gehoben VERB ▷ *see* **heben**

geholfen VERB ▷ *see* **helfen**

gehorchen (PERFECT **hat gehorcht**) VERB [48]
to obey
□ Du solltest deinem Vater gehorchen. You should obey your father. □ Ein Hund sollte lernen zu gehorchen. A dog should learn to obey.

gehören (PERFECT **hat gehört**) VERB [38]
■ **jemandem gehören** to belong to somebody □ Dieses Buch gehört mir. This book belongs to me.
■ **Das gehört sich einfach nicht.** That just isn't done.

gehorsam ADJECTIVE
▷ *see also* **der Gehorsam** NOUN
obedient

der **Gehorsam** NOUN
▷ *see also* **gehorsam** ADJECTIVE
obedience

der **Gehweg** (PL die **Gehwege**) NOUN
pavement

der **Geier** (PL die **Geier**) NOUN
vulture

die **Geige** NOUN
violin
□ Wiltrud spielt Geige. Wiltrud plays the violin.

geil ADJECTIVE
1 horny
□ Wenn er das sieht, wird er geil. When he sees that, he'll get horny.
2 cool
□ Das war eine geile Party. That was a cool party. □ ein geiler Song a cool song

die **Geisel** NOUN
hostage

der **Geist** (PL die **Geister**) NOUN
1 ghost
2 mind
□ Er hat einen regen Geist. He has a lively mind.
■ **Seine Rede sprühte vor Geist.** His speech was very witty.

geisteskrank ADJECTIVE
mentally ill

die **Geisteskrankheit** NOUN
mental illness

geistig ADJECTIVE
intellectual
□ ihre geistigen Fähigkeiten her intellectual capabilities
■ **geistige Getränke** alcoholic drinks
■ **geistig behindert** mentally handicapped

der **Geiz** (GEN des **Geizes**) NOUN
meanness

der **Geizhals** (GEN des **Geizhalses**, PL die **Geizhälse**) NOUN
miser

geizig ADJECTIVE
mean

gekannt VERB ▷ *see* **kennen**

gekonnt VERB ▷ *see* **können**

gekonnt ADJECTIVE
skilful

das **Gel** (PL die **Gele**) NOUN
gel

das **Gelächter** NOUN
laughter

geladen VERB ▷ *see* **laden**

geladen ADJECTIVE
1 loaded
□ eine geladene Waffe a loaded weapon
2 invited
□ geladene Gäste invited guests
■ **geladen sein** to be furious □ Meine Mutter war geladen. My mother was furious.

gelähmt ADJECTIVE
paralysed

das **Gelände** (PL die **Gelände**) NOUN
1 grounds
□ auf dem Gelände der Schule on the school grounds
2 terrain
□ unwegsames Gelände difficult terrain
■ **durchs Gelände fahren** to go cross-country
■ **ein Baugelände** a building site

gelangweilt ADJECTIVE
bored

gelassen VERB ▷ *see* **lassen**

gelassen ADJECTIVE
calm
□ Sie blieb gelassen. She remained calm.

geläufig ADJECTIVE
common
□ ein geläufiger Begriff a common term
■ **Das ist mir nicht geläufig.** I'm not familiar with that.

gelaunt ADJECTIVE
■ **gut gelaunt** in a good mood
■ **schlecht gelaunt** in a bad mood
■ **Wie ist er gelaunt?** What sort of mood's he in?

gelb ADJECTIVE
1 yellow
2 amber
□ Die Ampel war gelb. The traffic lights were at amber.

das **Geld** (PL die **Gelder**) NOUN
money

■ etwas zu Geld machen to sell something off

der **Geldautomat** (GEN des **Geldautomaten**, PL die **Geldautomaten**) NOUN
cash dispenser

der **Geldbeutel** (PL die **Geldbeutel**) NOUN
purse

der **Geldschein** (PL die **Geldscheine**) NOUN
banknote

die **Geldstrafe** NOUN
fine

das **Geldstück** (PL die **Geldstücke**) NOUN
coin

die **Geldtasche** NOUN
wallet

der **Geldwechsel** NOUN
changing of money
□ Beim Geldwechsel muss man eine Gebühr bezahlen. There is a charge for changing money.
■ 'Geldwechsel' 'bureau de change'

gelegen VERB ▷ *see* **liegen**

die **Gelegenheit** NOUN
1 opportunity
□ Sobald ich eine Gelegenheit bekomme ... As soon as I get an opportunity ... □ bei jeder Gelegenheit at every opportunity
2 occasion
□ Bei dieser Gelegenheit trug sie das blaue Kostüm. On this occasion she wore her blue suit.

gelegentlich ADVERB
1 occasionally
□ Gelegentlich gehe ich ganz gern ins Kino. I occasionally like going to the cinema.
2 some time or other
□ Ich werde mich gelegentlich darum kümmern. I'll do it some time or other.

das **Gelenk** (PL die **Gelenke**) NOUN
joint *(in body)*

gelenkig ADJECTIVE
supple

gelernt ADJECTIVE
skilled

geliehen VERB ▷ *see* **leihen**

gelingen (IMPERFECT **gelang**, PERFECT **ist gelungen**) VERB
to succeed
□ Sein Plan ist ihm nicht gelungen. His plan didn't succeed.
■ Es ist mir gelungen, ihn zu überzeugen. I succeeded in convincing him.
■ Der Kuchen ist gelungen. The cake turned out well.

gelten (PRESENT **gilt**, IMPERFECT **galt**, PERFECT **hat gegolten**) VERB
to be valid
□ Dein Ausweis gilt nicht mehr. Your passport is no longer valid.
■ es gilt, etwas zu tun it's necessary to do something □ Es gilt, sich zu entscheiden. It's necessary to make a decision.
■ jemandem gelten to be aimed at somebody □ Diese Bemerkung hat dir gegolten. This comment was aimed at you.
■ etwas gelten lassen to accept something
■ Was gilt die Wette? What do you bet?

gelungen VERB ▷ *see* **gelingen**

gelungen ADJECTIVE
successful

das **Gemälde** (PL die **Gemälde**) NOUN
painting
□ ein Gemälde von Rembrandt a painting by Rembrandt

gemein ADJECTIVE
mean
□ Das war gemein! That was mean!
■ etwas gemein haben mit to have something in common with □ Mit solchen Leuten habe ich nichts gemein. I don't have anything in common with people like that.

gemeinsam ADJECTIVE, ADVERB
1 joint
□ gemeinsame Anstrengungen joint efforts
2 together
□ Wir sind gemeinsam zum Lehrer gegangen. We went together to the teacher. □ ein gemeinsames Abendessen dinner together
■ etwas gemeinsam haben to have something in common □ Wir haben viel gemeinsam. We've a lot in common.

gemischt ADJECTIVE
mixed

gemocht VERB ▷ *see* **mögen**

das **Gemüse** (PL die **Gemüse**) NOUN
vegetables
□ Gemüse ist gesund. Vegetables are healthy.

gemusst VERB ▷ *see* **müssen**

gemütlich ADJECTIVE
1 cosy
□ eine gemütliche Wohnung a cosy flat
■ ein gemütlicher Abend a pleasant evening
2 good-natured
□ Sie ist ein gemütlicher Mensch. She's good-natured.

das **Gen** (PL die **Gene**) NOUN
gene

genannt VERB ▷ *see* **nennen**

genau ADJECTIVE, ADVERB
1 exact
□ Ich brauche genaue Zahlen. I need exact figures.
2 accurate
□ Diese Übersetzung ist nicht sehr genau. This translation isn't very accurate.
3 exactly
□ Genau das habe ich auch gesagt. That's exactly what I said. □ Sie hatte genau dasselbe Kleid an. She was wearing exactly the same dress. □ Das ist genau anders herum. That's exactly the opposite.

■ **etwas genau nehmen** to take something seriously
■ **genau genommen** strictly speaking

die **Genauigkeit** NOUN
accuracy

genauso ADVERB
■ **genauso gut** just as good

genehmigen (PERFECT **hat genehmigt**) VERB [7]
to approve
■ **sich etwas genehmigen** to treat oneself to something □ Ich werde mir jetzt ein Eis genehmigen. I'm going to treat myself to an ice cream.

die **Genehmigung** NOUN
1 permission
□ Für den Umbau brauchen wir eine Genehmigung. We need permission for the conversion.
2 permit
□ Hier ist meine Genehmigung. Here's my permit.

die **Generation** NOUN
generation

Genf NEUT NOUN
Geneva
■ **der Genfer See** Lake Geneva

genial ADJECTIVE
brilliant

das **Genick** (PL die **Genicke**) NOUN
back of the neck
■ **sich das Genick brechen** to break one's neck

das **Genie** (PL die **Genies**) NOUN
genius

genießbar ADJECTIVE
1 edible
□ Das Essen war nicht genießbar. The meal wasn't edible.
2 drinkable
□ Probier mal, ob der Tee genießbar ist. Try the tea and see if it's drinkable.

genießen (IMPERFECT **genoss**, PERFECT **hat genossen**) VERB
to enjoy
□ Wir haben die Ferien genossen. We enjoyed our holidays.

genmanipuliert ADJECTIVE
genetically modified
□ genmanipulierte Lebensmittel genetically modified food

genommen VERB ▷ *see* **nehmen**

die **Gentechnologie** NOUN
genetic engineering

genug ADJECTIVE
enough
□ Wir haben genug Geld. We've got enough money. □ gut genug good enough

genügen (PERFECT **hat genügt**) VERB [38]
to be enough
□ Das genügt noch nicht. That isn't enough.
■ **jemandem genügen** to be enough for somebody □ Genügt dir das eine Stück? Is one piece enough for you?

genügend ADJECTIVE
sufficient

der **Genuss** (GEN des **Genusses**, PL die **Genüsse**) NOUN
1 pleasure
□ Es war ein Genuss! That was sheer pleasure!
2 consumption
□ der Genuss von Alkohol the consumption of alcohol
■ **in den Genuss von etwas kommen** to receive the benefit of something

genüsslich ADVERB
with relish

geöffnet ADJECTIVE
open

die **Geografie** NOUN
geography

die **Geometrie** NOUN
geometry

das **Gepäck** NOUN
luggage

die **Gepäckannahme** NOUN
luggage office

die **Gepäckausgabe** NOUN
baggage reclaim

gepflegt ADJECTIVE
1 well-groomed
□ gepflegte Hände well-groomed hands
2 well-kept
□ ein gepflegter Park a well-kept park

gerade ADJECTIVE, ADVERB
1 straight
□ eine gerade Strecke a straight stretch
2 upright
□ eine gerade Haltung an upright posture
■ **eine gerade Zahl** an even number
3 just
□ Du kommst gerade richtig. You've come just at the right time. □ Das ist es ja gerade! That's just it! □ Er wollte gerade aufstehen. He was just about to get up.
■ **gerade erst** only just □ Ich bin gerade erst gekommen. I've only just arrived.
■ **gerade noch** only just □ Das geht gerade noch. That's only just OK.
■ **gerade deshalb** that's exactly why
■ **gerade du** you of all people □ Warum gerade ich? Why me of all people?
■ **nicht gerade** not exactly □ Das war nicht gerade nett. That wasn't exactly nice.

geradeaus ADVERB
straight ahead

gerannt VERB ▷ *see* **rennen**

das **Gerät** (PL die **Geräte**) NOUN
1 gadget
□ ein Gerät zum Papierschneiden a gadget for cutting paper

2 appliance
□ ein Haushaltsgerät a household appliance
3 tool
□ ein Gartengerät a garden tool
4 apparatus
□ Wir haben heute an den Geräten geturnt. We did gymnastics on the apparatus today.
5 equipment
□ Geräte zum Angeln fishing equipment

geraten (PRESENT **gerät**, IMPERFECT **geriet**, PERFECT **ist geraten**) VERB
1 to thrive
□ Hier geraten die Pflanzen. Plants thrive here.
2 to turn out
□ Ihre Kinder sind alle gut geraten. All their children have turned out well. □ Der Kuchen ist mir nicht geraten. The cake hasn't turned out well.
■ **in etwas geraten** to get into something
□ Wir sind in den Stau geraten. We got into a traffic jam.
■ **in Angst geraten** to get frightened
■ **nach jemandem geraten** to take after somebody

geräuchert ADJECTIVE
smoked

das **Geräusch** (PL die **Geräusche**) NOUN
sound

gerecht ADJECTIVE
fair
□ Das ist nicht gerecht! That's not fair!

die **Gerechtigkeit** NOUN
justice

das **Gerede** NOUN
gossip
□ Das ist alles nur Gerede. That's all just gossip.

gereizt ADJECTIVE
irritable

das **Gericht** (PL die **Gerichte**) NOUN
1 court
□ Wir sehen uns vor Gericht. I'll see you in court.
2 dish
□ ein leckeres Gericht a tasty dish
■ **das Jüngste Gericht** the Last Judgement

gerieben VERB ▷ *see* **reiben**

gering ADJECTIVE
1 small
□ eine geringe Menge a small amount
2 low
□ geringe Beteiligung low participation
■ **eine geringe Zeit** a short time

geringschätzig ADJECTIVE
disparaging

geringste ADJECTIVE
least
□ Das ist meine geringste Sorge. That's the least of my worries.

geritten VERB ▷ *see* **reiten**

gern ADVERB
gladly
□ Das habe ich gern getan. I did it gladly.
■ **gern mögen** to like □ Ich mag diese Art von Musik gern. I like this kind of music.
■ **etwas gern tun** to like doing something
□ Ich schwimme gern. I like swimming.
■ **Ich hätte gern ...** I'd like ... □ Ich hätte gern ein Zitroneneis. I'd like a lemon ice cream.
■ **Ja, gern!** Yes, please.
■ **Gern geschehen!** It's a pleasure.

gernhaben (PRESENT **hat gern**, IMPERFECT **hatte gern**, PERFECT **hat gerngehabt**) VERB [32]
to like
□ Ich habe sie sehr gern. I like her a lot.

gerochen VERB ▷ *see* **riechen**

der **Geruch** (PL die **Gerüche**) NOUN
smell

das **Gerücht** (PL die **Gerüchte**) NOUN
rumour

das **Gerümpel** NOUN
junk

gesalzen VERB ▷ *see* **salzen**

gesalzen ADJECTIVE
■ **gesalzene Preise** hefty prices

LANGUAGE TIP Word for word, **gesalzene Preise** means 'salted prices'.

gesamt ADJECTIVE
whole
□ die gesamte Klasse the whole class
■ **die gesamten Kosten** the total cost
■ **gesamte Werke** complete works
■ **im Gesamten** all in all

die **Gesamtschule** NOUN
comprehensive school

DID YOU KNOW...?
Gesamtschulen are the exception rather than the rule in Germany.

gesandt VERB ▷ *see* **senden**

das **Geschäft** (PL die **Geschäfte**) NOUN
1 shop
□ In welchem Geschäft hast du das gekauft? Which shop did you buy that in?
2 business
□ Die Geschäfte gehen gut. Business is good.
3 deal
□ Ich schlage dir ein Geschäft vor. I'll make a deal with you. □ Das war ein gutes Geschäft. That was a good deal.

die **Geschäftsfrau** NOUN
businesswoman

der **Geschäftsmann** (PL die **Geschäftsmänner**) NOUN
businessman

geschehen (PRESENT **geschieht**, IMPERFECT **geschah**, PERFECT **ist geschehen**) VERB
to happen
□ Was ist geschehen? What's happened?
□ Was ist mit ihm geschehen? What's happened to him?

gescheit ADJECTIVE
clever

das **Geschenk** (PL die **Geschenke**) NOUN
present

die **Geschichte** NOUN
1 story
□ eine lustige Geschichte a funny story
2 history
□ die deutsche Geschichte German history
3 business
□ die Geschichte mit dem verschwundenen Pass the business of the missing passport

geschichtlich ADJECTIVE
historical

geschickt ADJECTIVE
skilful

geschieden VERB ▷ *see* **scheiden**

geschieden ADJECTIVE
divorced

geschienen VERB ▷ *see* **scheinen**

das **Geschirr** NOUN
crockery
□ In welchem Schrank steht das Geschirr? What cupboard is the crockery kept in?
■ **das Geschirr spülen** to do the dishes

die **Geschirrspülmaschine** NOUN
dishwasher

das **Geschirrtuch** (PL die **Geschirrtücher**) NOUN
dish cloth

das **Geschlecht** (PL die **Geschlechter**) NOUN
1 sex
□ ein Kind weiblichen Geschlechts a child of the female sex
2 gender
□ Welches Geschlecht hat dieses Substantiv? What gender is this noun?

die **Geschlechtskrankheit** NOUN
sexually transmitted disease

der **Geschlechtsverkehr** NOUN
sexual intercourse

geschlossen VERB ▷ *see* **schließen**

geschlossen ADJECTIVE
shut
■ **'Geschlossen'** 'Closed'

der **Geschmack** (PL die **Geschmäcke**) NOUN
taste
□ Das ist nicht nach meinem Geschmack. This is not to my taste.
■ **Geschmack an etwas finden** to come to like something □ Sie hat inzwischen Geschmack an dieser Art von Sport gefunden. In the meantime she's come to like this kind of sport.

geschmacklos ADJECTIVE
1 tasteless
□ Die Suppe war ziemlich geschmacklos. The soup was pretty tasteless.
2 in bad taste
□ Das war ein geschmackloser Witz. That joke was in bad taste.

geschmackvoll ADJECTIVE
tasteful

geschnitten VERB ▷ *see* **schneiden**

geschossen VERB ▷ *see* **schießen**

geschrieben VERB ▷ *see* **schreiben**

geschrien VERB ▷ *see* **schreien**

geschützt ADJECTIVE
protected

das **Geschwätz** NOUN
chatter

geschwätzig ADJECTIVE
talkative

die **Geschwindigkeit** NOUN
speed

die **Geschwindigkeitsbeschränkung** NOUN
speed limit

die **Geschwindigkeitskontrolle** NOUN
speed check

die **Geschwister** PL NOUN
brothers and sisters

geschwommen VERB ▷ *see* **schwimmen**

das **Geschwür** (PL die **Geschwüre**) NOUN
ulcer

gesellig ADJECTIVE
sociable

die **Gesellschaft** NOUN
1 society
□ die Gesellschaft verändern to change society
2 company
□ jemandem Gesellschaft leisten to keep somebody company

gesessen VERB ▷ *see* **sitzen**

das **Gesetz** (GEN des **Gesetzes**, PL die **Gesetze**) NOUN
law

gesetzlich ADJECTIVE
legal
■ **gesetzlicher Feiertag** public holiday

das **Gesicht** (PL die **Gesichter**) NOUN
face

der **Gesichtsausdruck** NOUN
expression

gespannt ADJECTIVE
1 strained
□ Die Lage im Nahen Osten ist gespannt. The situation in the Middle East is strained.
2 eager
□ gespannte Zuhörer eager listeners
■ **Ich bin gespannt, ob ...** I wonder whether ...
■ **auf etwas gespannt sein** to look forward to something □ Ich bin auf das Fest gespannt. I'm looking forward to the party.

das **Gespenst** (PL die **Gespenster**) NOUN
ghost

gesperrt ADJECTIVE
closed off

das **Gespräch** (PL die **Gespräche**) NOUN
1 conversation
□ ein langes Gespräch a long conversation

2 call
□ Frau Morris, ein Gespräch für Sie. Mrs Morris, there's a call for you.

gesprächig ADJECTIVE
talkative

gesprochen VERB ▷ *see* **sprechen**

gesprungen VERB ▷ *see* **springen**

die **Gestalt** NOUN
1 shape
□ die Gestalt der Skulptur the shape of the sculpture
■ **Gestalt annehmen** to take shape
□ Mein Referat nimmt langsam Gestalt an. My assignment is slowly taking shape.
2 figure
□ Ich konnte eine dunkle Gestalt im Garten erkennen. I could see a dark figure in the garden.
■ **in Gestalt von** in the form of

gestalten (PERFECT **hat gestaltet**) VERB [2]
to lay out
□ Wer hat euren Garten gestaltet? Who laid out your garden?
■ **Wie gestaltest du deine Freizeit?** How do you spend your spare time?

gestanden VERB ▷ *see* **stehen**

das **Geständnis** (GEN des **Geständnisses**, PL die **Geständnisse**) NOUN
confession

der **Gestank** NOUN
stench

gestatten (PERFECT **hat/ist gestattet**) VERB [2]
to allow
■ **Gestatten Sie?** May I?

gestattet ADJECTIVE
permitted
□ Das ist nicht gestattet. That is not permitted.

die **Geste** NOUN
gesture

gestehen (IMPERFECT **gestand**, PERFECT **hat gestanden**) VERB [72]
to confess

das **Gestein** (PL die **Gesteine**) NOUN
rock
□ vulkanisches Gestein volcanic rock

das **Gestell** (PL die **Gestelle**) NOUN
1 frame
□ ein Brillengestell spectacle frames
2 rack
□ ein Gestell für Weinflaschen a wine rack

gestern ADVERB
yesterday
■ **gestern Abend** yesterday evening
■ **gestern Morgen** yesterday morning

gestohlen VERB ▷ *see* **stehlen**

gestorben VERB ▷ *see* **sterben**

gestört ADJECTIVE
disturbed

gestreift ADJECTIVE
striped

gesund ADJECTIVE
healthy
■ **wieder gesund werden** to get better

die **Gesundheit** NOUN
health
■ **Gesundheit!** Bless you!

gesungen VERB ▷ *see* **singen**

getan VERB ▷ *see* **tun**

das **Getränk** (PL die **Getränke**) NOUN
drink

die **Getränkekarte** NOUN
wine list

sich **getrauen** (PERFECT **hat sich getraut**) VERB [7]
to dare
□ Sie hat sich nicht getraut hineinzugehen. She didn't dare go in.

das **Getreide** (PL die **Getreide**) NOUN
cereals

getrennt ADJECTIVE
separate

das **Getriebe** (PL die **Getriebe**) NOUN
gearbox

getrieben VERB ▷ *see* **treiben**

getroffen VERB ▷ *see* **treffen**

getrunken VERB ▷ *see* **trinken**

geübt ADJECTIVE
experienced

gewachsen VERB ▷ *see* **wachsen**

gewachsen ADJECTIVE
■ **jemandem gewachsen sein** to be a match for somebody □ Er war seinem Gegner gewachsen. He was a match for his opponent.
■ **Sie ist den Kindern nicht gewachsen.** She can't cope with the children.
■ **einer Sache gewachsen sein** to be up to something □ Meinst du, du bist dieser Aufgabe gewachsen? Do you think you're up to this job?

gewagt ADJECTIVE
risky

die **Gewalt** NOUN
1 force
□ die Gewalt des Aufpralls the force of the impact
2 power
□ die staatliche Gewalt the power of the state
3 violence
□ Gewalt gegen Kinder violence against children
■ **mit aller Gewalt** with all one's might

gewaltig ADJECTIVE
tremendous
□ eine gewaltige Menge a tremendous amount □ Sie hat sich gewaltig angestrengt. She tried tremendously hard.
■ **ein gewaltiger Irrtum** a huge mistake

gewalttätig ADJECTIVE
violent

gewann VERB ▷ *see* **gewinnen**

das **Gewässer** (PL die **Gewässer**) NOUN
waters

das **Gewebe** (PL die **Gewebe**) NOUN
1 fabric
□ ein feines Gewebe a fine fabric
2 tissue
□ Die Gewebeprobe hat ergeben, dass alles in Ordnung ist. The tissue samples showed that there's nothing wrong.

das **Gewehr** (PL die **Gewehre**) NOUN
gun

die **Gewerkschaft** NOUN
trade union

> **DID YOU KNOW...?**
> Unions in Germany are mainly organized within the **Deutscher Gewerkschaftsbund (DGB)**.

gewesen VERB ▷ *see* **sein**

das **Gewicht** (PL die **Gewichte**) NOUN
weight
□ das Gewicht meines Koffers the weight of my case

der **Gewinn** (PL die **Gewinne**) NOUN
profit
□ Wir haben dieses Jahr einen Gewinn gemacht. We've made a profit this year.
□ etwas mit Gewinn verkaufen to sell something at a profit

gewinnen (IMPERFECT **gewann**, PERFECT **hat gewonnen**) VERB [30]
to win
□ Sie hat den ersten Preis gewonnen. She won first prize.
■ **im Lotto gewinnen** to have a win on the lottery
■ **an etwas gewinnen** to gain in something
□ Die Stadt hat an Beliebtheit gewonnen. The town has gained in popularity.

der **Gewinner** (PL die **Gewinner**) NOUN
winner

gewiss ADJECTIVE, ADVERB
certain
□ Zwischen den beiden besteht eine gewisse Ähnlichkeit. There's a certain similarity between them.
■ **Das weiß ich ganz gewiss.** I'm certain about that.
■ **Das hat sie gewiss vergessen.** She must have forgotten.

das **Gewissen** (PL die **Gewissen**) NOUN
conscience

gewissenhaft ADJECTIVE
conscientious

gewissermaßen ADVERB
more or less

die **Gewissheit** NOUN
certainty

das **Gewitter** (PL die **Gewitter**) NOUN
thunderstorm

gewöhnen (PERFECT **hat gewöhnt**) VERB [75]
■ **sich an etwas gewöhnen** to get used to something □ Ich muss mich erst an die neue Rechtschreibung gewöhnen. I have to get used to the new spelling rules.
■ **jemanden an etwas gewöhnen** to teach somebody something □ Der Klassenlehrer hat versucht, seine Klasse an Disziplin zu gewöhnen. The form teacher tried to teach his class discipline.

die **Gewohnheit** NOUN
habit
□ Es ist so eine Gewohnheit von mir, morgens Kaffee zu trinken. I drink coffee in the morning. It's a habit of mine.
□ zur Gewohnheit werden to become a habit
■ **aus Gewohnheit** from habit

gewöhnlich ADJECTIVE
1 usual
□ Ich bin heute früh zu der gewöhnlichen Zeit aufgestanden. I got up at my usual time this morning. □ Ich stehe gewöhnlich um sieben Uhr auf. I usually get up at seven o'clock.
2 ordinary
□ Das sind ganz gewöhnliche Leute. They're quite ordinary people.
■ **wie gewöhnlich** as usual

gewohnt ADJECTIVE
usual
□ Mir fehlt die gewohnte Umgebung. I miss my usual surroundings.
■ **etwas gewohnt sein** to be used to something □ Ich bin es nicht gewohnt, dass man mir widerspricht. I'm not used to being contradicted.

gewonnen VERB ▷ *see* **gewinnen**

geworden VERB ▷ *see* **werden**

geworfen VERB ▷ *see* **werfen**

das **Gewürz** (GEN des **Gewürzes**, PL die **Gewürze**) NOUN
spice

gewusst VERB ▷ *see* **wissen**

die **Gezeiten** PL NOUN
tides

gezogen VERB ▷ *see* **ziehen**

gezwungen VERB ▷ *see* **zwingen**

gibt VERB ▷ *see* **geben**

die **Gier** NOUN
greed

gierig ADJECTIVE
greedy
□ gierig nach Geld greedy for money

gießen (IMPERFECT **goss**, PERFECT **hat gegossen**) VERB
to pour
□ Sie goss mir Wein ins Glas. She poured wine into my glass.
■ **die Blumen gießen** to water the flowers
■ **Es gießt in Strömen.** It's pouring.

die **Gießkanne** NOUN
watering can

das **Gift** (PL die **Gifte**) NOUN
poison

LANGUAGE TIP Be careful! The German word **Gift** does not mean **gift**.

giftig ADJECTIVE
poisonous
□ eine giftige Pflanze a poisonous plant

ging VERB ▷ *see* **gehen**

der **Gipfel** (PL die **Gipfel**) NOUN
1 peak
□ die schneebedeckten Gipfel the snow-covered peaks
2 height
□ Das ist der Gipfel der Unverschämtheit. That's the height of impudence.

die **Giraffe** NOUN
giraffe

das **Girokonto** (PL die **Girokonten**) NOUN
current account

die **Gitarre** NOUN
guitar
□ Ich spiele Gitarre. I play the guitar.

glänzen VERB [36]
to shine
□ Ihr Gesicht glänzte vor Freude. Her face shone with joy.

glänzend ADJECTIVE
1 shining
□ ein glänzendes Metall shining metal
2 brilliant
□ Das war eine glänzende Leistung. That was a brilliant achievement.

das **Glas** (GEN des **Glases**, PL die **Gläser**) NOUN
glass

die **Glasscheibe** NOUN
pane

glatt ADJECTIVE
1 smooth
□ Der Tisch hat eine glatte Oberfläche. The table has a smooth surface.
2 slippery
□ Pass auf, die Straßen sind glatt. Be careful, the streets are slippery.
■ **eine glatte Absage** a flat refusal
■ **eine glatte Lüge** a downright lie
■ **Das habe ich glatt vergessen.** It completely slipped my mind.

das **Glatteis** (GEN des **Glatteises**) NOUN
black ice
□ Bei Glatteis sollte man vorsichtig fahren. When there's black ice, you have to drive carefully.

die **Glatze** NOUN
■ **Er hat eine Glatze.** He's bald.
■ **eine Glatze bekommen** to go bald

glauben VERB [38]
1 to believe
□ Ich habe kein Wort geglaubt. I didn't believe a word.
2 to think
□ Ich glaube, wir sind hier nicht willkommen. I don't think we're welcome here.
■ **jemandem glauben** to believe somebody
□ Ich glaube dir. I believe you.
■ **an etwas glauben** to believe in something
□ Glaubst du an ein Leben nach dem Tod? Do you believe in life after death?

glaubwürdig ADJECTIVE
1 credible
□ Das ist keine besonders glaubwürdige Geschichte. That story's not particularly credible.
2 trustworthy
□ Er ist ein glaubwürdiger Mensch. He's a trustworthy person.

gleich ADJECTIVE, ADVERB
1 same
□ Wir haben das gleiche Problem. We have the same problem.
2 identical
□ Bei einem Würfel sind alle Seiten gleich. All the sides of a cube are identical.
3 the same
□ Ich behandle alle meine Kinder gleich. I treat all my children the same. □ Sie waren genau gleich angezogen. They were dressed exactly the same.
■ **gleich groß** the same size
4 equal
□ Wir wollen für die gleiche Arbeit auch die gleiche Bezahlung. We want equal pay for equal work.
5 straight away
□ Ich werde ihn gleich anrufen. I'll call him straight away.
■ **Ich bin gleich fertig.** I'll be ready in a minute.
■ **Es ist mir gleich.** It's all the same to me.
■ **Zwei mal zwei gleich vier.** Two times two equals four.
■ **gleich nach** right after □ Wir sind gleich nach dem Mittagessen abgefahren. We left right after lunch.
■ **gleich neben** right next to □ Wir wohnen gleich neben der Schule. We live right next to the school.

gleichaltrig ADJECTIVE
of the same age
□ gleichaltrige Schüler pupils of the same age
□ Sie sind gleichaltrig. They're the same age.

gleichartig ADJECTIVE
similar

die **Gleichberechtigung** NOUN
equal rights
□ die Gleichberechtigung der Frau equal rights for women

gleichen (IMPERFECT **glich**, PERFECT **hat geglichen**) VERB
■ **jemandem gleichen** to be like somebody

□ Du gleichst deinem Vater. You're like your father.
■ **einer Sache gleichen** to be like something □ Unser Haus gleicht eurem. Our house is like yours.
■ **sich gleichen** to be alike

gleichfalls ADVERB
■ **Danke gleichfalls!** The same to you.

das **Gleichgewicht** NOUN
balance

gleichgültig ADJECTIVE
1 indifferent
□ Er zeigte sich ihr gegenüber ziemlich gleichgültig. He seemed to be quite indifferent to her.
2 not important
□ Es ist doch gleichgültig, wie wir das machen. It's not important how we do it.

gleichzeitig ADVERB
at the same time
□ Ich kann doch nicht drei Dinge gleichzeitig tun. I can't do three things at the same time.

das **Gleis** (GEN des **Gleises**, PL die **Gleise**) NOUN
1 line
□ die Straßenbahngleise the tram lines
2 platform
□ Achtung auf Gleis drei. Attention on platform three.

der **Gletscher** (PL die **Gletscher**) NOUN
glacier

gliedern VERB [88]
to structure
□ Du musst deinen Aufsatz besser gliedern. You must structure your essay better.

glitzern VERB [88]
1 to glitter
□ Das Wasser glitzerte in der Sonne. The water glittered in the sun.
2 to twinkle
□ Die Sterne glitzerten. The stars twinkled.

die **Globalisierung** NOUN
globalization

die **Glocke** NOUN
bell
■ **etwas an die große Glocke hängen** to shout something from the rooftops

LANGUAGE TIP Word for word, **etwas an die große Glocke hängen** means 'to hang something from the big bell'.

das **Glück** NOUN
1 luck
□ Ein vierblättriges Kleeblatt bringt Glück. A four-leaf clover brings good luck.
■ **Glück haben** to be lucky □ Ich habe in der Prüfung viel Glück gehabt. I was very lucky in the exam.
■ **Viel Glück!** Good luck!
■ **zum Glück** fortunately
2 happiness
□ Sie strahlte vor Glück. She was beaming with happiness.

glücklich ADJECTIVE
1 happy
□ Ich bin sehr glücklich mit ihm. I'm very happy with him. □ Das waren glückliche Tage. Those were happy days.
2 lucky
□ Das war ein glücklicher Zufall. That was a lucky coincidence.

glücklicherweise ADVERB
fortunately

der **Glückwunsch** (PL die **Glückwünsche**) NOUN
congratulations
□ Herzlichen Glückwunsch zur bestandenen Prüfung. Congratulations on passing your exam.
■ **Herzlichen Glückwunsch zum Geburtstag.** Happy Birthday.

die **Glühbirne** NOUN
light bulb

GmbH ABBREVIATION (= *Gesellschaft mit beschränkter Haftung*)
limited company

das **Gold** NOUN
gold

golden ADJECTIVE
golden

der **Goldfisch** (PL die **Goldfische**) NOUN
goldfish
□ Ich habe zwei Goldfische. I've got two goldfish.

der **Golf** (PL die **Golfe**) NOUN
▷ *see also* **das Golf** NOUN
gulf
□ der Persische Golf the Persian Gulf

das **Golf** NOUN
▷ *see also* **der Golf** NOUN
golf
□ Mein Vater spielt Golf. My father plays golf.

der **Golfplatz** (GEN des **Golfplatzes**, PL die **Golfplätze**) NOUN
golf course

der **Golfstrom** NOUN
the Gulf Stream

gönnen VERB [38]
■ **sich etwas gönnen** to treat oneself to something □ Ich werde mir ein Stück Kuchen gönnen. I'm going to treat myself to a piece of cake.
■ **Sie gönnt mir meinen Erfolg nicht.** She begrudges me my success.

googeln VERB [88]
to Google®

der **Gott** (PL die **Götter**) NOUN
god
■ **Mein Gott!** For heaven's sake! □ Mein Gott, wie kann man nur so dumm sein! For heaven's sake, how can you be so stupid!
■ **Um Gottes willen!** For heaven's sake! □ Um Gottes willen, tu das bloß nicht! For

heaven's sake don't do that!
■ **Grüß Gott!** Hello!
■ **Gott sei Dank!** Thank God!

die **Göttin** NOUN
goddess

göttlich ADJECTIVE
divine

das **Grab** (PL die **Gräber**) NOUN
grave

graben (PRESENT **gräbt**, IMPERFECT **grub**, PERFECT **hat gegraben**) VERB
▷ *see also* **der Graben** NOUN
to dig

der **Graben** (PL die **Gräben**) NOUN
▷ *see also* **graben** VERB
ditch

der **Grad** (PL die **Grad**) NOUN
degree
□ dreißig Grad im Schatten thirty degrees in the shade

die **Grafikkarte** NOUN
graphics card
□ Welche Grafikkarte hast du in deinem PC? What graphics card do you have in your PC?

grafisch ADJECTIVE
graphic

das **Gramm** (PL die **Gramme** *or* **Gramm**) NOUN
gram
□ hundert Gramm Käse a hundred grams of cheese

die **Grammatik** NOUN
grammar

graphisch ADJECTIVE ▷ *see* **grafisch**

das **Gras** (GEN des **Grases**, PL die **Gräser**) NOUN
grass

grässlich ADJECTIVE
horrible

die **Gräte** NOUN
bone
□ Dieser Fisch hat zu viele Gräten. This fish has too many bones in it.

gratis ADVERB
free of charge

gratulieren (PERFECT **hat gratuliert**) VERB [76]
■ **jemandem gratulieren** to congratulate somebody □ Wir gratulierten ihr zum bestandenen Examen. We congratulated her on passing her exam.
■ **Gratuliere!** Congratulations!

grau ADJECTIVE
grey

das **Graubrot** (PL die **Graubrote**) NOUN
brown bread

der **Gräuel** (PL die **Gräuel**) NOUN
horror
□ die Gräuel des Bürgerkriegs the horrors of civil war
■ **Das ist mir ein Gräuel.** I loathe it.

grauenhaft ADJECTIVE
horrible

grauhaarig ADJECTIVE
grey-haired

grausam ADJECTIVE
cruel

die **Grausamkeit** NOUN
cruelty

greifen (IMPERFECT **griff**, PERFECT **hat gegriffen**) VERB
■ **nach etwas greifen** to reach for something □ Er griff nach meiner Hand. He reached for my hand.
■ **um sich greifen** to spread □ Das Feuer griff schnell um sich. The fire spread quickly.

grell ADJECTIVE
harsh
□ eine grelle Farbe a harsh colour
■ **ein greller Schrei** a piercing scream

die **Grenze** NOUN
1 border
□ Wir sind an der Grenze nach Frankreich kontrolliert worden. Our papers were checked at the French border.
2 boundary
□ Der Zaun ist die Grenze zum Grundstück des Nachbarn. The fence marks the boundary with our neighbour's property.
3 limit
□ die Grenzen des guten Geschmacks the limits of good taste

grenzen VERB [36]
■ **an etwas grenzen** to border on something □ Unser Grundstück grenzt an das von Schmidts. Our property borders on the Schmidt's.
■ **Das grenzt an Wahnsinn.** It verges on madness.

grenzenlos ADJECTIVE
boundless

der **Greuel** NOUN ▷ *see* **Gräuel**

der **Grieche** (GEN des **Griechen**, PL die **Griechen**) NOUN
Greek

Griechenland NEUT NOUN
Greece
■ **aus Griechenland** from Greece
■ **nach Griechenland** to Greece

die **Griechin** NOUN
Greek

griechisch ADJECTIVE
Greek

der **Grieß** (GEN des **Grießes**) NOUN
semolina

der **Griff** (PL die **Griffe**) NOUN
1 handle
□ Halte dich da an dem Griff fest. Hold on to the handle.
2 hold
□ Ich habe Judogriffe geübt. I've been practising judo holds.

griffbereit ADJECTIVE
handy

□ etwas griffbereit halten to keep something handy

der **Grill** (PL die **Grills**) NOUN
grill

grillen VERB [48]
1 to grill
□ gegrillter Fisch grilled fish
2 to have a barbecue
□ Wir wollen am Sonntag grillen. We'd like to have a barbecue on Sunday.

grinsen VERB [38]
to grin

die **Grippe** NOUN
flu

grob ADJECTIVE
1 coarse
□ grober Sand coarse sand
2 rough
□ Sei nicht so grob zu deiner Schwester. Don't be so rough with your sister.
3 serious
□ ein grober Fehler a serious mistake

groß ADJECTIVE, ADVERB
1 big
□ Das war mein größter Fehler. That was my biggest mistake. □ Sie haben ein großes Haus. They have a big house.
2 tall
□ Mein Bruder ist viel größer als ich. My brother is much taller than me.
□ Wie groß bist du? How tall are you?
3 great
□ Das war eine große Leistung. That was a great achievement. □ Er war ein großer Politiker. He was a great politician.
■ **großen Hunger haben** to be very hungry
■ **die großen Ferien** the summer holidays
■ **Er hat sich nicht groß angestrengt.** He didn't try very hard.
■ **im Großen und Ganzen** on the whole

großartig ADJECTIVE
splendid

Großbritannien NEUT NOUN
Great Britain
■ **aus Großbritannien** from Great Britain
■ **in Großbritannien** in Great Britain
■ **nach Großbritannien** to Great Britain

die **Größe** NOUN
1 size
□ Welche Schuhgröße hast du? What size shoes do you take?
2 height
□ Im Pass steht bei den Angaben zur Person auch die Größe. Your height's also included in your passport under personal details.

die **Großeltern** PL NOUN
grandparents

die **Großmutter** (PL die **Großmütter**) NOUN
grandmother

großschreiben (IMPERFECT **schrieb groß**, PERFECT **hat großgeschrieben**) VERB [61]
to write in capitals

die **Großstadt** (PL die **Großstädte**) NOUN
city

größtenteils ADVERB
for the most part

der **Großvater** (PL die **Großväter**) NOUN
grandfather

großzügig ADJECTIVE, ADVERB
generous
□ Meine Eltern sind sehr großzügig. My parents are very generous. □ Sie hat großzügig darauf verzichtet. She generously did without.

grün ADJECTIVE
green
□ Die Ampel ist grün. The traffic lights are at green.

der **Grund** (PL die **Gründe**) NOUN
1 reason
□ Nenn mir einen Grund, warum wir das nicht so machen können. Give me one reason why we can't do it like this.
■ **Aus welchem Grund ist er so böse?** Why is he so angry?
2 ground
□ Das Haus ist auf felsigem Grund gebaut. The house is built on rocky ground.
3 bottom
□ Das Schiff sank auf den Grund des Meeres. The ship sank to the bottom of the sea.
■ **im Grunde genommen** basically
■ **auf Grund** ▷ *see* **aufgrund**
■ **zu Grunde** ▷ *see* **zugrunde**

gründen VERB [54]
to found
□ Wir haben einen Fanklub gegründet. We've founded a fan club.

gründlich ADJECTIVE, ADVERB
thorough
□ eine gründliche Vorbereitung zur Prüfung thorough preparation for the exam
□ Wir haben das Haus gründlich geputzt. We cleaned the house thoroughly.
■ **Ich habe mich gründlich geirrt.** I was completely wrong.

der **Grundsatz** (GEN des **Grundsatzes**, PL die **Grundsätze**) NOUN
principle

grundsätzlich ADJECTIVE, ADVERB
1 fundamental
□ Es bleibt die grundsätzliche Frage, ob das erlaubt werden soll. The fundamental question remains: should it be allowed?
2 basically
□ Grundsätzlich bin ich ja dafür, aber ... Basically I'm in favour, but ...
3 on principle
□ Ich bin grundsätzlich gegen die Prügelstrafe. I'm against corporal punishment on principle.

die **Grundschule** NOUN
primary school
die **Grünen** PL NOUN
the Greens
grunzen VERB [36]
to grunt
die **Gruppe** NOUN
group
der **Gruselfilm** (PL die **Gruselfilme**) NOUN
horror film
gruselig ADJECTIVE
creepy
der **Gruß** (GEN des **Grußes**, PL die **Grüße**) NOUN
greeting
■ **viele Grüße** best wishes
■ **mit freundlichen Grüßen** yours sincerely
■ **Grüße an** regards to □ Grüße an deine Eltern. Regards to your parents.
grüßen VERB [31]
to say hello
□ Sie hat mich nicht gegrüßt. She didn't say hello to me.
■ **Grüß Lorna von mir.** Give Lorna my regards.
■ **Lorna läßt dich grüßen.** Lorna sends her regards.
gucken VERB [38]
to look
der **Gulasch** (PL die **Gulaschs**) NOUN
goulash
die **Gulaschsuppe** NOUN
goulash soup
gültig ADJECTIVE
valid
das **Gummi** (PL die **Gummis**) NOUN
LANGUAGE TIP You can also say **der Gummi**.
rubber
□ Die Reifen sind aus Gummi. The tyres are made of rubber.
das **Gummiband** (PL die **Gummibänder**) NOUN
elastic band
□ Sie machte ein Gummiband um das Geschenk. She put an elastic band round the present.
das **Gummibärchen** (PL die **Gummibärchen**) NOUN
jelly bear
LANGUAGE TIP Word for word, **Gummibärchen** means 'little rubber bear'.
günstig ADJECTIVE
convenient
□ Morgen wäre günstig. Tomorrow would be convenient.
■ **eine günstige Gelegenheit** a favourable opportunity
■ **Das habe ich günstig bekommen.** It was a bargain.

die **Gurke** NOUN
cucumber
□ Sie mag Gurkensalat nicht. She doesn't like cucumber salad.
■ **saure Gurke** gherkin
der **Gurt** (PL die **Gurte**) NOUN
belt
der **Gürtel** (PL die **Gürtel**) NOUN
belt
gut ADJECTIVE, ADVERB
1 good
□ Ich habe gute Noten bekommen. I got good marks. □ Sie ist ein guter Mensch. She's a good person. □ Das ist ein guter Witz. That's a good joke.
■ **In Englisch habe ich 'gut'.** I got a B in English.
DID YOU KNOW...? German marks range from one (**sehr gut**) to six (**ungenügend**).
■ **Alles Gute!** All the best.
■ **also gut** all right then □ Also gut, ich komme. All right then, I'll come.
2 well
□ Sie hat das gut gemacht. She did it well.
□ Ich kenne ihn gut. I know him well.
■ **gut schmecken** to taste good
■ **gut drei Stunden** a good three hours
■ **das kann gut sein** that may well be
■ **Gut, aber ...** OK, but ...
■ **Lass es gut sein.** That'll do.
■ **Es ist zum Glück gut gegangen.** Fortunately it came off.
■ **Mir geht's gut.** I'm fine.
■ **gut gemeint** well-meant □ ein gut gemeinter Rat a well-meant piece of advice
■ **gut tun** ▷ *see* **guttun**
die **Güter** NEUT PL NOUN
goods
gutgehen VERB [29] ▷ *see* **gut**
gutgemeint ADJECTIVE ▷ *see* **gut**
das **Guthaben** (PL die **Guthaben**) NOUN
credit
gütig ADJECTIVE
kind
gutmütig ADJECTIVE
good-natured
der **Gutschein** (PL die **Gutscheine**) NOUN
voucher
guttun (IMPERFECT **tat gut**, PERFECT **hat gutgetan**) VERB [81]
■ **jemandem guttun** to do somebody good
□ Die Pause hat mir gutgetan. The break did me good.
das **Gymnasium** (PL die **Gymnasien**) NOUN
grammar school
die **Gymnastik** NOUN
keep-fit
□ Ich mache einmal in der Woche Gymnastik. I do keep-fit once a week.

Hh

das **Haar** (PL die **Haare**) NOUN
hair
□ Sie hat dunkle Haare. She's got dark hair.
■ **um ein Haar** nearly

haben (PRESENT **hat**, IMPERFECT **hatte**, PERFECT **hat gehabt**) VERB [32]
to have
□ Ich habe einen neuen Pulli. I've got a new pullover. □ Sie hat ihn nicht gesehen. She hasn't seen him.
■ **Welches Datum haben wir heute?** What's the date today?
■ **Hunger haben** to be hungry
■ **Angst haben** to be afraid
■ **Woher hast du das?** Where did you get that from?
■ **Was hast du denn?** What's the matter with you?
■ **Ich hätte gern ...** I would like ...

das **Hackfleisch** NOUN
mince

der **Hafen** (PL die **Häfen**) NOUN
harbour

die **Hafenstadt** (PL die **Hafenstädte**) NOUN
port

der **Hafer** NOUN
oats

die **Haferflocken** FEM PL NOUN
porridge oats

haftbar ADJECTIVE
responsible
□ Eltern sind für ihre Kinder haftbar. Parents are responsible for their children.

haften VERB [2]
to stick
□ Der Klebstreifen haftet nicht. The adhesive tape isn't sticking.
■ **haften für** to be responsible for

die **Haftpflichtversicherung** NOUN
third party insurance

der **Hagel** NOUN
hail

hageln VERB [88]
■ **Es hagelt.** It's hailing.

der **Hahn** (PL die **Hähne**) NOUN
1 cock
□ Der Hahn krähte. The cock crowed.
2 tap
□ Der Hahn tropft. The tap's dripping.

das **Hähnchen** (PL die **Hähnchen**) NOUN
chicken
□ Heute gibt es Hähnchen. We're having chicken today.

der **Hai** (PL die **Haie**) NOUN
shark

der **Haken** (PL die **Haken**) NOUN
1 hook
□ Häng deinen Anorak an den Haken. Hang your anorak up on the hook.
2 catch
□ Die Sache hat einen Haken. There's a catch.

halb ADJECTIVE
half
□ ein halber Kuchen half a cake □ eine halbe Stunde half an hour
■ **halb eins** half past twelve

halbieren (PERFECT **hat halbiert**) VERB [76]
to halve

das **Halbjahr** (PL die **Halbjahre**) NOUN
six months

halbjährlich ADJECTIVE
half-yearly

die **Halbpension** NOUN
half board

halbtags ADVERB
■ **halbtags arbeiten** to work part-time

die **Halbtagsarbeit** NOUN
part-time job

half VERB ▷ *see* **helfen**

die **Hälfte** NOUN
half

die **Halle** NOUN
hall
□ eine Messehalle an exhibition hall

das **Hallenbad** (PL die **Hallenbäder**) NOUN
indoor swimming pool

hallo EXCLAMATION
hello!

der **Hals** (GEN des **Halses**, PL die **Hälse**) NOUN
1 neck
□ Ich habe einen steifen Hals. I've got a stiff neck.
2 throat
□ Mir tut der Hals weh. My throat's sore.

■ **Hals über Kopf** in a rush

die **Halskette** NOUN
necklace

die **Halsschmerzen** MASC PL NOUN
sore throat
□ Ich habe Halsschmerzen. I've got a sore throat.

das **Halstuch** (PL die **Halstücher**) NOUN
scarf

halt EXCLAMATION
stop!

haltbar ADJECTIVE
durable
□ Das ist ein sehr haltbares Material. That's a very durable material.
■ **Butter ist nur begrenzt haltbar.** Butter only keeps for a limited time.
■ **'Mindestens haltbar bis ...'** 'Best before ...'

halten (PRESENT **hält**, IMPERFECT **hielt**, PERFECT **hat gehalten**) VERB [33]
1 to hold
□ Er hielt sie an der Hand. He held her by the hand. □ Kannst du das mal halten? Can you hold that for a moment?
2 to keep
□ Obst hält nicht lange. Fruit doesn't keep long.
3 to last
□ Ihre Freundschaft hat lange gehalten. Their friendship has lasted a long time.
4 to stop
□ Der Bus hielt vor dem Rathaus. The bus stopped in front of the town hall.
■ **halten für** to regard as □ Man hält ihn für den besten Chirurgen in Deutschland. He's regarded as being the best surgeon in Germany.
■ **Ich habe sie für deine Mutter gehalten.** I took her for your mother.
■ **halten von** to think of □ Sie hält viel von dir. She thinks a lot of you. □ Ich halte nichts von dieser Methode. I don't think much of this method.
■ **sich rechts halten** to keep to the right

die **Haltestelle** NOUN
stop
□ die Haltestelle der Straßenbahn the tram stop

haltmachen VERB [48]
to stop

die **Haltung** NOUN
1 posture
□ Er hat eine aufrechte Haltung. He has an upright posture.
2 attitude
□ Ich bewundere deine Haltung in dieser Frage. I admire your attitude in this issue.

Hamburg NEUT NOUN
Hamburg

DID YOU KNOW...?
The 'Free Hanseatic City of Hamburg' is one of the 16 **Länder**. It is a 'city-state' like Bremen and Berlin, and is Germany's principal seaport.

der **Hammer** (PL die **Hämmer**) NOUN
hammer

hamstern VERB [88]
to hoard

die **Hand** (PL die **Hände**) NOUN
hand

die **Handarbeit** NOUN
1 manual work
□ Handarbeit macht ihm mehr Spaß als geistige Arbeit. He enjoys manual work more than intellectual work.
2 needlework
□ In Handarbeit hat sie eine Zwei. She got a B in needlework.

der **Handball** NOUN
handball

die **Handbremse** NOUN
handbrake

das **Handbuch** (PL die **Handbücher**) NOUN
manual

der **Händedruck** NOUN
handshake

der **Handel** NOUN
1 trade
□ der Handel mit Osteuropa trade with Eastern Europe
■ **Dieses Gerät ist überall im Handel erhältlich.** This appliance is available in all shops and retail outlets.
2 deal
□ Wir haben einen Handel abgeschlossen. We have concluded a deal.

handeln VERB [34]
1 to act
□ Wir müssen schnell handeln. We'll have to act quickly.
2 to trade
□ Er handelt mit Gebrauchtwaren. He trades in second-hand goods.
■ **mit jemandem handeln** to bargain with somebody □ Ich habe versucht, mit ihm zu handeln, aber er wollte es mir nicht billiger geben. I tried to bargain with him but he didn't want to give it to me any cheaper.
■ **es handelt sich um ...** it's about ...
□ Sie wollte mir nicht sagen, worum es sich handelt. She didn't want to tell me what it was about.
■ **handeln von** to be about □ Die Geschichte handelt von einer kranken Frau. The story's about a sick woman.

die **Handelsschule** NOUN
business school

das **Handgepäck** NOUN
hand luggage

der **Händler** (PL die **Händler**) NOUN
dealer
□ Ich habe meinen Computerhändler danach gefragt. I asked my computer dealer about it.

handlich ADJECTIVE
handy

die **Handlung** NOUN
1 act
□ Das war eine unüberlegte Handlung. That was a rash act.
2 plot
□ Ich habe die Handlung des Buches nicht genau verstanden. I didn't really understand the plot of the book.
3 shop
□ eine Eisenwarenhandlung an ironmonger's shop

die **Handschrift** NOUN
handwriting

der **Handschuh** (PL die **Handschuhe**) NOUN
glove

die **Handtasche** NOUN
handbag

das **Handtuch** (PL die **Handtücher**) NOUN
towel

das **Handy** (PL die **Handys**) NOUN
mobile phone

der **Hang** (PL die **Hänge**) NOUN
slope

hängen (1) (IMPERFECT **hängte**, PERFECT **hat gehängt**) VERB [48]
to hang
□ Sie hat die Wäsche auf die Leine gehängt. She hung her washing on the line.
□ Sie hängten den Verbrecher. They hanged the criminal.

hängen (2) (IMPERFECT **hing**, PERFECT **hat gehangen**) VERB [35]
to hang
□ An der Wand hing ein Bild von Picasso. A painting by Picasso was hanging on the wall.
■ **hängen an** to be attached to □ Sie hat sehr an ihrem Vater gehangen. She was very attached to her father.

hänseln VERB [88]
to tease

die **Hansestadt** (PL die **Hansestädte**) NOUN
Hanseatic town

DID YOU KNOW...?
The **Hanse** (Hanseatic League) was a powerful association of cities which dominated Baltic trade in the Middle Ages. Even today, Bremen, Hamburg, Lübeck, Rostock and Wismar still call themselves **Hansestädte**.

harmlos ADJECTIVE
harmless

harmonisch ADJECTIVE
harmonious

hart ADJECTIVE
hard
□ hart wie Stein as hard as stone
□ Wir haben hart gearbeitet. We worked hard.
■ **harte Worte** harsh words
■ **Das ist hart.** That's tough.
■ **ein hart gekochtes Ei** a hard-boiled egg

hartnäckig ADJECTIVE
stubborn

das **Haschisch** (GEN des **Haschisch**) NOUN
hashish

der **Hase** (GEN des **Hasen**, PL die **Hasen**) NOUN
hare

die **Haselnuss** (PL die **Haselnüsse**) NOUN
hazelnut

der **Hass** (GEN des **Hasses**) NOUN
hatred

hassen (PERFECT **hat gehasst**) VERB [31]
to hate

hässlich ADJECTIVE
1 ugly
□ Sie ist das hässlichste Mädchen der Klasse. She's the ugliest girl in the class.
2 nasty
□ Es ist hässlich, so etwas zu sagen. It's nasty to say things like that.

hast VERB ▷ *see* **haben**

hastig ADJECTIVE
hasty

hat, hatte VERB ▷ *see* **haben**

der **Haufen** (PL die **Haufen**) NOUN
heap
□ In ihrem Schlafzimmer lag ein Haufen schmutziger Wäsche. There was a heap of dirty washing lying in her bedroom.
■ **ein Haufen ...** heaps of ... □ Ich habe einen Haufen Fehler gemacht. I've made heaps of mistakes. □ Er hat einen Haufen Geld dafür bezahlt. He paid heaps of money for it. □ ein Haufen Leute heaps of people

häufen VERB [38]
■ **sich häufen 1** to accumulate □ Der Müll häufte sich in den Straßen. The rubbish accumulated in the streets. **2** to be on the increase □ Die Fälle von Asthma häufen sich. Cases of asthma are on the increase.

häufig ADJECTIVE, ADVERB
1 frequent
□ sein häufiges Fehlen his frequent absences
2 frequently
□ Er fehlt häufig. He is frequently absent.

der **Hauptbahnhof** (PL die **Hauptbahnhöfe**) NOUN
main station

hauptberuflich ADVERB
full-time
□ Er ist hauptberuflich als Gärtner tätig. He's employed full-time as a gardener.

das **Hauptfach** (PL die **Hauptfächer**) NOUN
main subject

das **Hauptgericht** (PL die **Hauptgerichte**) NOUN
main course

die **Hauptsache** NOUN
main thing
□ Hauptsache, du bist gesund. The main thing is that you're healthy.

die **Hauptsaison** (PL die **Hauptsaisons**) NOUN
high season

die **Hauptschule** NOUN
secondary school

die **Hauptstadt** (PL die **Hauptstädte**) NOUN
capital
□ Berlin ist die Hauptstadt von Deutschland. Berlin's the capital of Germany.

die **Hauptstraße** NOUN
main street

die **Hauptverkehrszeit** NOUN
rush hour

das **Hauptwort** (PL die **Hauptwörter**) NOUN
noun

das **Haus** (GEN des **Hauses**, PL die **Häuser**) NOUN
house
■ **nach Hause** home □ Ich muss jetzt nach Hause. I'll have to go home now.
■ **zu Hause** at home

die **Hausarbeit** NOUN
1 housework
□ Am Wochenende hilft mein Vater bei der Hausarbeit. My father helps with the housework at the weekend.
2 homework
□ Wir haben eine Hausarbeit zum Thema Umweltverschmutzung auf. We've got homework on the subject of pollution.

der **Hausarzt** (GEN des **Hausarztes**, PL die **Hausärzte**) NOUN
family doctor

die **Hausaufgaben** FEM PL NOUN
homework
□ Heute waren die Hausaufgaben nicht schwierig. Our homework wasn't difficult today.

die **Hausfrau** NOUN
housewife

der **Haushalt** (PL die **Haushalte**) NOUN
1 household
□ den Haushalt führen to run the household
2 budget
□ der Haushalt für 2007 the 2007 budget

der **Hausmeister** (PL die **Hausmeister**) NOUN
caretaker

die **Hausnummer** NOUN
house number

der **Hausschlüssel** (PL die **Hausschlüssel**) NOUN
front-door key

der **Hausschuh** (PL die **Hausschuhe**) NOUN
slipper

das **Haustier** (PL die **Haustiere**) NOUN
pet

die **Haustür** NOUN
front door

die **Hauswirtschaft** NOUN
home economics

die **Haut** (PL die **Häute**) NOUN
skin

Hbf. ABBREVIATION (= *Hauptbahnhof*)
central station

der **Hebel** (PL die **Hebel**) NOUN
lever

heben (IMPERFECT **hob**, PERFECT **hat gehoben**) VERB
to lift

die **Hecke** NOUN
hedge

die **Hefe** NOUN
yeast

das **Heft** (PL die **Hefte**) NOUN
1 exercise book
□ Schreibt die Verbesserung in euer Heft. Write the correction in your exercise books.
2 issue
□ Hast du noch das letzte Heft von 'Geo'? Have you got the latest issue of 'Geo'?

die **Heftklammer** NOUN
paper clip

das **Heftpflaster** (PL die **Heftpflaster**) NOUN
sticking plaster

die **Heide** NOUN
moor
□ Wir haben einen Spaziergang durch die Heide gemacht. We went for a walk over the moor.
■ **die Lüneburger Heide** Lüneburg Heath

das **Heidekraut** NOUN
heather

die **Heidelbeere** NOUN
blueberry

heilbar ADJECTIVE
curable

heilen (PERFECT **hat/ist geheilt**) VERB [38]

LANGUAGE TIP For the perfect tense use **haben** when the verb has an object and **sein** when there is no object.

1 to cure
□ Viele Arten von Krebs kann man heilen. Many kinds of cancer can be cured.
2 to heal
□ Die Wunde ist schnell geheilt. The wound healed quickly.

heilig ADJECTIVE
holy

der **Heiligabend** (PL die **Heiligabende**) NOUN
Christmas Eve

der/die **Heilige** (GEN des/der **Heiligen**, PL die **Heiligen**) NOUN
saint

□ Er ist auch kein Heiliger. He's no saint.

das **Heilmittel** (PL die **Heilmittel**) NOUN
remedy

das **Heim** (PL die **Heime**) NOUN
▷ *see also* **heim** ADVERB
home
□ ein Heim für Kinder mit Lernschwierigkeiten a home for children with learning difficulties

heim ADVERB
▷ *see also* **das Heim** NOUN
home
□ Ich muss jetzt heim. I'll have to go home now.

die **Heimat** NOUN
homeland
□ Deutschland ist meine Heimat. Germany's my homeland.

heimatlos ADJECTIVE
homeless

die **Heimfahrt** NOUN
journey home

heimgehen (IMPERFECT **ging heim**, PERFECT **ist heimgegangen**) VERB [29]
to go home

heimlich ADJECTIVE
secret
□ Er hat das heimlich gemacht. He did it secretly.

die **Heimreise** NOUN
journey home

das **Heimspiel** (PL die **Heimspiele**) NOUN
home game

der **Heimweg** (PL die **Heimwege**) NOUN
way home

das **Heimweh** NOUN
homesickness

die **Heirat** NOUN
marriage

heiraten VERB [2]
to get married
□ Sie heiraten morgen. They're getting married tomorrow.
■ **jemanden heiraten** to marry somebody

heiser ADJECTIVE
hoarse

die **Heiserkeit** NOUN
hoarseness

heiß ADJECTIVE
hot
□ Mir ist heiß. I'm hot. □ heiße Schokolade hot chocolate

heißen (IMPERFECT **hieß**, PERFECT **hat geheißen**) VERB
1 to be called
□ Er heißt Marek. He's called Marek.
2 to mean
□ Das heißt, dass wir morgen früh aufstehen müssen. That means that we'll have to get up early tomorrow.
■ **es heißt ...** it is said ...
■ **das heißt** that is to say

heiter ADJECTIVE
1 cheerful
□ Ich war in heiterer Laune. I was in a cheerful mood.
2 bright
□ Das Wetter wird heiter bis bewölkt. The weather will be cloudy with bright spells.

heizen VERB [36]
to heat

der **Heizkörper** (PL die **Heizkörper**) NOUN
radiator

die **Heizung** NOUN
heating

hektisch ADJECTIVE
hectic

der **Held** (GEN des **Helden**, PL die **Helden**) NOUN
hero

die **Heldin** NOUN
heroine

helfen (PRESENT **hilft**, IMPERFECT **half**, PERFECT **hat geholfen**) VERB [37]
to help
□ Kann ich dir helfen? Can I help you?
□ Die Tablette hat geholfen. The pill helped.
□ jemandem bei etwas helfen to help somebody with something
■ **sich zu helfen wissen** to be resourceful
□ Er weiß sich zu helfen. He's very resourceful.
■ **Es hilft nichts, du musst ...** It's no use, you'll have to ...

hell ADJECTIVE
bright
□ Hier ist es schön hell. It's nice and bright here.
■ **Sie hat einen hellen Teint.** She has a clear complexion.
■ **eine helle Farbe** a light colour
■ **ein Helles** a light beer

hellblau ADJECTIVE
light blue

hellblond ADJECTIVE
ash-blond

der **Helm** (PL die **Helme**) NOUN
helmet

das **Hemd** (PL die **Hemden**) NOUN
shirt
■ **ein Unterhemd** a vest

die **Hemmung** NOUN
inhibition
□ Er hat furchtbare Hemmungen. He has terrible inhibitions.

die **Henne** NOUN
hen

her ADVERB
ago
□ Das ist fünf Jahre her. That was five years ago.
■ **von ... her** from ... □ von England her from England □ von weit her from a long way away

■ **Wo bist du her?** Where do you come from?
■ **Komm her zu mir.** Come here.
■ **Her damit!** Hand it over!

herab ADVERB
down

herabhängen (IMPERFECT **hing herab**, PERFECT **hat herabgehangen**) VERB [35]
to hang down

herablassend ADJECTIVE
condescending

heran ADVERB
■ **Näher heran!** Come closer!

herauf ADVERB
up
□ Komm hier herauf. Come up here.

heraus ADVERB
out

herausbekommen (IMPERFECT **bekam heraus**, PERFECT **hat herausbekommen**) VERB [40]
1 to get out
□ Ich habe den Fleck nicht herausbekommen. I didn't get the stain out.
2 to find out
□ Ich muss herausbekommen, warum er das gemacht hat. I'll have to find out why he did it.

herausfordern (PERFECT **hat herausgefordert**) VERB [15]
to challenge

herauskommen (IMPERFECT **kam heraus**, PERFECT **ist herausgekommen**) VERB [40]
to come out
□ Die Maus ist aus ihrem Loch herausgekommen. The mouse came out of its hole.
■ **Dabei kommt nichts heraus.** Nothing will come of it.

herausnehmen (PRESENT **nimmt heraus**, IMPERFECT **nahm heraus**, PERFECT **hat herausgenommen**) VERB [52]
to take out
□ Sie hat das Lesezeichen aus dem Buch herausgenommen. She took the bookmark out of the book.
■ **sich etwas herausnehmen** to take liberties □ Du nimmst dir wirklich etwas zu viel heraus. You really do take far too many liberties.

sich **herausstellen** (PERFECT **hat sich herausgestellt**) VERB [15]
to turn out
□ Es stellte sich heraus, dass ... It turned out that ...

herausziehen (IMPERFECT **zog heraus**, PERFECT **hat herausgezogen**) VERB [96]
to pull out

herb ADJECTIVE
bitter
□ eine herbe Enttäuschung a bitter disappointment □ ein herber Geschmack a bitter taste

herbei ADVERB
over
□ Alle eilten herbei. Everyone hurried over.

die **Herbergseltern** PL NOUN
wardens *(in youth hostel)*

herbringen (IMPERFECT **brachte her**, PERFECT **hat hergebracht**) VERB [13]
to bring here

der **Herbst** (PL die **Herbste**) NOUN
autumn
□ im Herbst in autumn

die **Herbstferien** PL NOUN
autumn holidays

herbstlich ADJECTIVE
autumnal

der **Herd** (PL die **Herde**) NOUN
cooker
□ ein Herd mit vier Platten a cooker with four rings

die **Herde** NOUN
herd
□ eine Herde Kühe a herd of cows
■ **eine Schafherde** a flock of sheep

herein ADVERB
in
□ Noch mehr Menschen drängten herein. Even more people pushed their way in. □ Das Wasser strömte herein. The water poured in.
■ **Herein!** Come in!

hereinbitten (IMPERFECT **bat herein**, PERFECT **hat hereingebeten**) VERB [9]
to ask in

hereinfallen (PRESENT **fällt herein**, IMPERFECT **fiel herein**, PERFECT **ist hereingefallen**) VERB [22]
■ **auf etwas hereinfallen** to fall for something □ Auf einen solch plumpen Trick falle ich nicht herein. I'm not falling for an obvious trick like that. □ Sie ist auf einen Betrüger hereingefallen. She fell for a swindler.

hereinkommen (IMPERFECT **kam herein**, PERFECT **ist hereingekommen**) VERB [40]
to come in

hereinlassen (PRESENT **lässt herein**, IMPERFECT **ließ herein**, PERFECT **hat hereingelassen**) VERB [42]
to let in

hereinlegen (PERFECT **hat hereingelegt**) VERB [4]
■ **jemanden hereinlegen** to take somebody for a ride □ Er will dich bloß hereinlegen. He's just trying to take you for a ride.

hergeben (PRESENT **gibt her**, IMPERFECT **gab her**, PERFECT **hat hergegeben**) VERB [28]
to hand over
□ Gib das Buch her! Hand over the book!
■ **sich zu etwas hergeben** to lend one's name to something

hergehen (IMPERFECT **ging her**, PERFECT **ist hergegangen**) VERB [29]
■ **hinter jemandem hergehen** to follow somebody
■ **Es geht hoch her.** There are a lot of goings-on.

herhören (PERFECT **hat hergehört**) VERB [4]
to listen
□ Alle mal herhören! Listen everybody!

der **Hering** (PL die **Heringe**) NOUN
herring

herkommen (IMPERFECT **kam her**, PERFECT **ist hergekommen**) VERB [40]
to come
□ Komm mal her! Come here!

die **Herkunft** (PL die **Herkünfte**) NOUN
origin

das **Heroin** NOUN
heroin

der **Herr** (GEN des **Herrn**, PL die **Herren**) NOUN
1 gentleman
□ Er ist ein feiner Herr. He's a fine gentleman.
□ Meine Herren! Gentlemen!
2 Lord
□ Herr, gib uns Frieden! Lord, give us peace.
3 Mr
□ Herr Mosbacher Mr Mosbacher
■ **Mein Herr!** Sir!

herrlich ADJECTIVE
marvellous

herrschen VERB [48]
1 to reign
□ Wann hat Karl der Große geherrscht? When did Charlemagne reign?
2 to be
□ Hier herrschen ja schöne Zustände. This is a fine state of affairs. □ Es herrscht noch Ungewissheit, wann das gemacht werden soll. It's still uncertain when it's to be done.

herstellen (PERFECT **hat hergestellt**) VERB [4]
to manufacture

der **Hersteller** (PL die **Hersteller**) NOUN
manufacturer

die **Herstellung** NOUN
manufacture

herüber ADVERB
1 over here
□ Er kam langsam zu uns herüber. He came slowly over to us.
2 across
□ Sie versuchte, zu uns herüberzuschwimmen. She tried to swim across to us.

herum ADVERB
round
□ Mach ein rotes Band herum. Tie a red band round it.
■ **um etwas herum** round something
□ Sie gingen ums Haus herum. They went round the house.

herumführen (PERFECT **hat herumgeführt**) VERB [4]
to show around

herumgehen (IMPERFECT **ging herum**, PERFECT **ist herumgegangen**) VERB [29]
to walk about
□ Wir sind ein paar Stunden in der Stadt herumgegangen. We walked about the town for a couple of hours.
■ **um etwas herumgehen** to walk round something □ Sie ging um den Tisch herum. She walked round the table.

sich **herumsprechen** (PRESENT **spricht sich herum**, IMPERFECT **sprach sich herum**, PERFECT **hat sich herumgesprochen**) VERB [70]
to get around

herunter ADVERB
down

heruntergekommen ADJECTIVE
run-down

herunterkommen (IMPERFECT **kam herunter**, PERFECT **ist heruntergekommen**) VERB [40]
1 to come down
□ Sie ist zu uns heruntergekommen. She came down to us.
2 to become run-down
□ Das Haus ist in den letzten Jahren ziemlich heruntergekommen. The house has become rather run-down in the past few years.

herunterladen (PRESENT **lädt herunter**, IMPERFECT **lud herunter**, PERFECT **hat heruntergeladen**) VERB
to download *(computer)*
□ eine Datei herunterladen to download a file

hervorbringen (IMPERFECT **brachte hervor**, PERFECT **hat hervorgebracht**) VERB [13]
to produce

hervorragend ADJECTIVE
excellent

hervorrufen (IMPERFECT **rief hervor**, PERFECT **hat hervorgerufen**) VERB [56]
to cause

das **Herz** (GEN des **Herzens**, PL die **Herzen**) NOUN
1 heart
□ Es bricht mir fast das Herz. It almost breaks my heart.
2 hearts
□ Herz ist Trumpf. Hearts is trumps.

der **Herzinfarkt** (PL die **Herzinfarkte**) NOUN
heart attack

herzlich ADJECTIVE
warm
□ ein herzlicher Empfang a warm welcome
□ Wir wurden herzlich begrüßt. We were warmly welcomed.
■ **Herzlich willkommen in Bamberg.** Welcome to Bamberg.
■ **Herzlichen Glückwunsch!** Congratulations.

■ **Herzliche Grüße.** Best wishes.

herzlos ADJECTIVE
heartless

der **Herzschlag** (PL die **Herzschläge**) NOUN
1 heartbeat
□ bei jedem Herzschlag with every heartbeat
2 heart attack
□ Er hat einen Herzschlag bekommen. He had a heart attack.

Hessen NEUT NOUN
Hesse

DID YOU KNOW...?
Hessen is one of the 16 **Länder**. Its capital is Wiesbaden, yet its biggest city is Frankfurt am Main, which is Germany's principal financial centre and home to the Bundesbank.

das **Heu** NOUN
hay
■ **Geld wie Heu** stacks of money

heulen VERB [38]
1 to howl
□ Die Wölfe heulten. The wolves were howling.
2 to cry
□ Jetzt fang nicht gleich an zu heulen. Now don't start crying.

der **Heuschnupfen** NOUN
hay fever
□ Sie leidet an Heuschnupfen. She suffers from hay fever.

heute ADVERB
today
■ **heute Abend** this evening
■ **heute Morgen** this morning
■ **heute früh** this morning

heutig ADJECTIVE
today's
□ die heutige Jugend today's youth

heutzutage ADVERB
nowadays

die **Hexe** NOUN
witch

der **Hexenschuss** (GEN des **Hexenschusses**) NOUN
lumbago

hielt VERB ▷ *see* **halten**

hier ADVERB
here
□ hier drinnen in here
■ **Hier spricht Lisa.** This is Lisa.
■ **hier bleiben** to stay here

hierher ADVERB
here

hiesig ADJECTIVE
local
□ die hiesige Bevölkerung the local population

hieß VERB ▷ *see* **heißen**

die **Hilfe** NOUN
help
■ **Erste Hilfe** first aid
■ **Hilfe!** Help!

hilflos ADJECTIVE
helpless

hilfreich ADJECTIVE
helpful

hilfsbereit ADJECTIVE
ready to help

hilft VERB ▷ *see* **helfen**

die **Himbeere** NOUN
raspberry

der **Himmel** (PL die **Himmel**) NOUN
1 sky
□ ein wolkenloser Himmel a cloudless sky
2 heaven
□ in den Himmel kommen to go to heaven

himmelblau ADJECTIVE
sky-blue

die **Himmelsrichtung** NOUN
■ **die vier Himmelsrichtungen** the four points of the compass

himmlisch ADJECTIVE
heavenly

hin ADVERB
■ **hin und zurück** there and back
■ **hin und her** to and fro
■ **Wo ist er hin?** Where has he gone?
■ **auf meine Bitte hin** at my request

hinab ADVERB
down

hinauf ADVERB
up

hinaufsteigen (IMPERFECT **stieg hinauf**, PERFECT **ist hinaufgestiegen**) VERB [74]
to climb
□ Wir sind auf den Berg hinaufgestiegen. We climbed up the mountain.

hinaus ADVERB
out

hinausgehen (IMPERFECT **ging hinaus**, PERFECT **ist hinausgegangen**) VERB [29]
to go out
□ Sie ist kurz hinausgegangen. She's gone out for a minute.
■ **über etwas hinausgehen** to exceed something □ Das geht weit über meine Erwartungen hinaus. That far exceeds my expectations.

hinausschieben (IMPERFECT **schob hinaus**, PERFECT **hat hinausgeschoben**) VERB
to put off
□ Sie haben die Entscheidung hinausgeschoben. They put the decision off.

hinauswerfen (PRESENT **wirft hinaus**, IMPERFECT **warf hinaus**, PERFECT **hat hinausgeworfen**) VERB [92]
to throw out

hindern VERB [88]
■ **jemanden an etwas hindern** to prevent somebody from doing something
□ Ich konnte ihn nicht am Weggehen hindern.

I couldn't prevent him from going.

das **Hindernis** (GEN des **Hindernisses**, PL die **Hindernisse**) NOUN
obstacle

hinein ADVERB
in
□ Hinein mit dir! In you go!

hineingehen (IMPERFECT **ging hinein**, PERFECT **ist hineingegangen**) VERB [29]
to go in
□ Geh doch hinein. Go in.
■ **hineingehen in** to go into □ Sie traute sich nicht, ins Zimmer hineinzugehen. She didn't dare go into the room.

die **Hinfahrt** NOUN
outward journey

hinfallen (PRESENT **fällt hin**, IMPERFECT **fiel hin**, PERFECT **ist hingefallen**) VERB [22]
to fall
□ Sie stolperte und fiel hin. She stumbled and fell.

der **Hinflug** (PL die **Hinflüge**) NOUN
outward flight

hinhalten (PRESENT **hält hin**, IMPERFECT **hielt hin**, PERFECT **hat hingehalten**) VERB [33]
to hold out
□ Sie hielt ihren Teller hin. She held out her plate.
■ **jemanden hinhalten** to put somebody off

hinken VERB [38]
to limp

hinlegen (PERFECT **hat hingelegt**) VERB [4]
to put down
□ Leg das Buch dort drüben hin. Put the book down over there.
■ **sich hinlegen** to lie down

hinnehmen (PRESENT **nimmt hin**, IMPERFECT **nahm hin**, PERFECT **hat hingenommen**) VERB [52]
to put up with
□ Das kann ich nicht länger hinnehmen. I can't put up with this any longer.

die **Hinreise** NOUN
outward journey

sich **hinsetzen** (PERFECT **hat sich hingesetzt**) VERB [15]
to sit down

hinstellen (PERFECT **hat hingestellt**) VERB [4]
to put
□ Wo soll ich die Vase hinstellen? Where shall I put the vase?
■ **Er stellte sich vor den Lehrer hin.** He went and stood in front of the teacher.

hinten ADVERB
at the back
□ Er sitzt ganz hinten. He sits at the very back.

hinter PREPOSITION

LANGUAGE TIP Use the accusative to express movement or a change of place. Use the dative when there is no change of place.

1 behind
□ Stell dich hinter deine Schwester. Stand behind your sister. □ Ich saß hinter ihr. I was sitting behind her.
2 after
□ Wir hatten kurz hinter Köln eine Panne. We broke down just after Cologne.

hintere ADJECTIVE
back
□ die hinteren Reihen the back rows
■ **der hintere Reifen** the rear tyre

hintereinander ADVERB
one after the other
■ **dreimal hintereinander** three times in a row

der **Hintergrund** (PL die **Hintergründe**) NOUN
background

hinterher ADVERB
afterwards

der **Hintern** (GEN des **Hintern**, PL die **Hintern**) NOUN
bottom

das **Hinterrad** (PL die **Hinterräder**) NOUN
back wheel

hinüber ADVERB
over

hinübergehen (IMPERFECT **ging hinüber**, PERFECT **ist hinübergegangen**) VERB [29]
to go over

hinunter ADVERB
down

hinunterschlucken (PERFECT **hat hinuntergeschluckt**) VERB [4]
to swallow

der **Hinweg** (PL die **Hinwege**) NOUN
way there
□ auf dem Hinweg on the way there

der **Hinweis** (GEN des **Hinweises**, PL die **Hinweise**) NOUN
1 hint
□ Er hat mir nicht den kleinsten Hinweis gegeben, wie ich das machen soll. He didn't give me the slightest hint as to how I was supposed to do it.
2 instruction
□ Hinweise zur Bedienung operating instructions

hinweisen (IMPERFECT **wies hin**, PERFECT **hat hingewiesen**) VERB
■ **jemanden auf etwas hinweisen** to point something out to somebody □ Er wies mich darauf hin, dass ... He pointed out to me that ...

hinzufügen (PERFECT **hat hinzugefügt**) VERB [15]
to add

das **Hirn** (PL die **Hirne**) NOUN
brain

der **Hirsch** (PL die **Hirsche**) NOUN
stag

historisch ADJECTIVE
historic

die **Hitparade** NOUN
charts

die **Hitze** NOUN
heat

hitzefrei ADJECTIVE
■ **hitzefrei haben** to have time off school because of excessively hot weather

DID YOU KNOW...?
If the temperature reaches 28°C – 30°C at 10 a.m., then German children are sent home early and any afternoon lessons are cancelled.

die **Hitzewelle** NOUN
heat wave

der **Hitzschlag** (PL die **Hitzschläge**) NOUN
heatstroke

das **Hoch** (PL die **Hochs**)
▷ *see also* **hoch** ADJECTIVE NOUN
1 cheer
□ Ein Hoch auf die Gastgeber! Three cheers for the hosts!
2 area of high pressure
□ ein Hoch über dem Atlantik an area of high pressure over the Atlantic

hoch ADJECTIVE
▷ *see also* **das Hoch** NOUN
high
□ zehn Meter hoch ten metres high

LANGUAGE TIP Before a noun or after an article, use **hohe**.

□ ein hoher Zaun a high fence
■ **Das ist mir zu hoch.** That's beyond me.

LANGUAGE TIP Word for word, **Das ist mir zu hoch** means 'It's too high for me'.

hochachtungsvoll ADVERB
yours faithfully

hochbegabt ADJECTIVE
extremely talented

der **Hochdruck** NOUN
high pressure

das **Hochhaus** (GEN des **Hochhauses**, PL die **Hochhäuser**) NOUN
multistorey building

hochheben (IMPERFECT **hob hoch**, PERFECT **hat hochgehoben**) VERB
to lift up

hochnäsig ADJECTIVE
stuck-up

die **Hochsaison** (PL die **Hochsaisons**) NOUN
high season

die **Hochschule** NOUN
1 college
2 university

der **Hochsommer** (PL die **Hochsommer**) NOUN
high summer

der **Hochsprung** (PL die **Hochsprünge**) NOUN
high jump

höchst ADVERB
extremely

höchste ADJECTIVE
highest
□ Die Zugspitze ist der höchste Berg Deutschlands. The Zugspitze is the highest mountain in Germany.

höchstens ADVERB
at most

die **Höchstgeschwindigkeit** NOUN
maximum speed

höchstwahrscheinlich ADVERB
most probably

die **Hochzeit** NOUN
wedding

der **Hochzeitstag** (PL die **Hochzeitstage**) NOUN
1 wedding day
□ An ihrem Hochzeitstag trug sie ein wunderschönes Kleid. She wore a beautiful dress on her wedding day.
2 wedding anniversary
□ Morgen ist ihr zehnter Hochzeitstag. It's their tenth wedding anniversary tomorrow.

der **Hocker** (PL die **Hocker**) NOUN
stool

der **Hof** (PL die **Höfe**) NOUN
1 yard
□ Die Kinder spielen im Hof. The children are playing in the yard.
2 farm
□ Dieser Bauer hat den größten Hof im Dorf. This farmer has the largest farm in the village.

hoffen VERB [38]
to hope
□ Ich hoffe, er kommt noch. I hope he's coming.
■ **auf etwas hoffen** to hope for something
□ Wir hoffen auf besseres Wetter. We're hoping for better weather.

hoffentlich ADVERB
hopefully
□ Hoffentlich kommt er bald. Hopefully he'll come soon. □ Das passiert hoffentlich nie wieder. Hopefully that won't happen again.
■ **Hoffentlich nicht.** I hope not.

die **Hoffnung** NOUN
hope

hoffnungslos ADJECTIVE
hopeless

hoffnungsvoll ADJECTIVE
hopeful

höflich ADJECTIVE
polite

die **Höflichkeit** NOUN
politeness

hohe ADJECTIVE

LANGUAGE TIP **hohe** is the form of **hoch** used before a noun.

high
□ ein hoher Zaun a high fence

die **Höhe** NOUN
height

der **Höhepunkt** (PL die **Höhepunkte**) NOUN
climax
□ der Höhepunkt des Abends the climax of the evening

höher ADJECTIVE, ADVERB
higher

hohl ADJECTIVE
hollow

die **Höhle** NOUN
cave

holen VERB [38]
to get
□ Ich hole ihn. I'll get him.
■ **jemanden holen lassen** to send for somebody

Holland NEUT NOUN
Holland
■ **aus Holland** from Holland
■ **in Holland** in Holland
■ **nach Holland** to Holland

der **Holländer** (PL die **Holländer**) NOUN
Dutchman
■ **Er ist Holländer.** He's Dutch.
■ **die Holländer** the Dutch

die **Holländerin** NOUN
Dutchwoman
■ **Sie ist Holländerin.** She's Dutch.

holländisch ADJECTIVE
Dutch

die **Hölle** NOUN
hell

das **Holz** (GEN des **Holzes**, PL die **Hölzer**) NOUN
wood

die **Holzkohle** NOUN
charcoal

homosexuell ADJECTIVE
homosexual

der **Honig** (PL die **Honige**) NOUN
honey

die **Honigmelone** NOUN
honeydew melon

der **Hopfen** (PL die **Hopfen**) NOUN
hops

hörbar ADJECTIVE
audible

horchen VERB [48]
1 to listen
□ Er horchte auf das kleinste Geräusch. He listened for the slightest noise.
2 to eavesdrop
□ Du hast an der Tür gehorcht! You've been eavesdropping at the door!

hören VERB [38]
to hear
□ Ich höre dich nicht. I can't hear you.
■ **Musik hören** to listen to music
■ **Radio hören** to listen to the radio

der **Hörer** (PL die **Hörer**) NOUN
receiver
□ Sie hat einfach den Hörer aufgelegt. She simply put down the receiver.

der **Horizont** (PL die **Horizonte**) NOUN
horizon
□ am Horizont on the horizon

horizontal ADJECTIVE
horizontal

das **Horn** (PL die **Hörner**) NOUN
horn

der **Horror** NOUN
horror

der **Horrorfilm** (PL die **Horrorfilme**) NOUN
horror film

der **Horrorroman** (PL die **Horrorromane**) NOUN
horror novel

die **Hose** NOUN
trousers
□ eine Hose a pair of trousers

LANGUAGE TIP Be careful! The German word **Hose** does not mean **hose**.

der **Hosenanzug** (PL die **Hosenanzüge**) NOUN
trouser suit

die **Hosentasche** NOUN
trouser pocket

der **Hosenträger** (PL die **Hosenträger**) NOUN
braces

das **Hotel** (PL die **Hotels**) NOUN
hotel

Hr. ABBREVIATION *(= Herr)*
Mr

hübsch ADJECTIVE
pretty

der **Hubschrauber** (PL die **Hubschrauber**) NOUN
helicopter

das **Hufeisen** (PL die **Hufeisen**) NOUN
horseshoe

die **Hüfte** NOUN
hip

der **Hügel** (PL die **Hügel**) NOUN
hill

hügelig ADJECTIVE
hilly

das **Huhn** (PL die **Hühner**) NOUN
chicken
□ Huhn mit Reis chicken with rice

die **Hummel** NOUN
bumblebee

der **Humor** NOUN
humour
■ **Humor haben** to have a sense of humour

humorvoll ADJECTIVE
humorous

der **Hund** (PL die **Hunde**) NOUN
dog

hundemüde ADJECTIVE
dog-tired

hundert NUMBER
a hundred
der **Hunger** NOUN
hunger
■ **Hunger haben** to be hungry
hungrig ADJECTIVE
hungry
die **Hupe** NOUN
horn
□ auf die Hupe drücken to sound the horn
hupen VERB [38]
to sound the horn
hüpfen (PERFECT **ist gehüpft**) VERB [38]
to hop
der **Hürdenlauf** (GEN (PL die **Hürdenläufe**) NOUN
hurdles
der **Husten** NOUN
▷ *see also* **husten** VERB
cough
□ Sie hat Husten. She has a cough.
husten VERB [2]
▷ *see also* **der Husten** NOUN
to cough
das **Hustenbonbon** (PL die **Hustenbonbons**) NOUN
cough drop
der **Hustensaft** (PL die **Hustensäfte**) NOUN
cough mixture
der **Hut** (PL die **Hüte**) NOUN
▷ *see also* **die Hut** NOUN
hat
die **Hut** NOUN
▷ *see also* **der Hut** NOUN
■ **auf der Hut sein** to be on one's guard
hüten VERB [2]
to look after
□ Silke hütet heute Abend unsere Kinder. Silke's looking after our children this evening.
■ **ein Geheimnis hüten** to keep a secret
■ **sich hüten, etwas zu tun** to take care not to do something □ Ich werde mich hüten, ihr das zu sagen. I'll take care not to say that to her.
■ **sich hüten vor** to be on one's guard against □ Hüte dich vor ihm, er lügt. Be on your guard against him, he's a liar.
die **Hütte** NOUN
hut
hygienisch ADJECTIVE
hygienic
hysterisch ADJECTIVE
hysterical
□ Sie wurde hysterisch. She became hysterical.

ICE ABBREVIATION (*= Intercityexpress*)
Intercity Express train

ich PRONOUN
I
□ Ich weiß nicht. I don't know.
■ **Ich bin's!** It's me!

das **Icon** (PL die **Icons**) NOUN
icon *(computer)*
□ ein Icon anklicken to click on an icon

das **Ideal** (PL die **Ideale**) NOUN
▷ *see also* **ideal** ADJECTIVE
ideal

ideal ADJECTIVE
▷ *see also* **das Ideal** NOUN
ideal

die **Idee** NOUN
idea

identifizieren (PERFECT **hat identifiziert**) VERB [76]
to identify

identisch ADJECTIVE
identical

die **Ideologie** NOUN
ideology

ideologisch ADJECTIVE
ideological

der **Idiot** (GEN des **Idioten**, PL die **Idioten**) NOUN
idiot

idiotisch ADJECTIVE
idiotic

der **Igel** (PL die **Igel**) NOUN
hedgehog

ihm PRONOUN
LANGUAGE TIP **ihm** is the dative of **er** and **es**.

1 him
□ Kannst du ihm sagen, wie spät es ist? Can you tell him what the time is?

2 to him
□ Gib es ihm! Give it to him.

3 it
□ Das Meerschweinchen hat Hunger, gib ihm was zu essen. The guinea pig's hungry, give it something to eat.

ihn PRONOUN
LANGUAGE TIP **ihn** is the accusative of **er**.

him
□ Ich habe ihn gesehen. I saw him.

ihnen PRONOUN
▷ *see also* **Ihnen** PRONOUN
LANGUAGE TIP **ihnen** is the dative of **sie** (plural).

1 them
□ Ich sage es ihnen. I'll tell them.

2 to them
□ Gib es ihnen. Give it to them.

Ihnen PRONOUN
▷ *see also* **ihnen** PRONOUN
LANGUAGE TIP **Ihnen** is the dative of **Sie**.

1 you
□ Darf ich Ihnen etwas zu trinken anbieten? May I offer you something to drink?

2 to you
□ Darf ich Ihnen das geben? May I give this to you?

ihr PRONOUN
▷ *see also* **Ihr** ADJECTIVE, **ihr** ADJECTIVE

1 you
□ Habt ihr das gesehen? Did you see that?

DID YOU KNOW...?
The familiar form of address **ihr** is used when addressing family members, friends, children under 16 and pets.

□ Ihr seid es. It's you.

LANGUAGE TIP **ihr** is also the dative of **sie** (singular).

2 her
□ Kannst du ihr das bitte ausrichten? Can you please tell her? □ Er steht neben ihr. He's standing beside her.

3 to her
□ Gib es ihr. Give it to her.

ihr ADJECTIVE
▷ *see also* **Ihr** ADJECTIVE, **ihr** PRONOUN

1 her
□ Ihr Vater ist nett. Her father's nice. □ Ihre Mutter hat mir das gesagt. Her mother told me. □ Das ist ihr Fahrrad. That's her bike.

2 hers
□ Das ist nicht ihr Füller, ihrer ist schwarz. That's not her pen, hers is black. □ Meine Mutter heißt Ulla, ihre auch. My mother's called Ulla, so is hers. □ Mein Fahrrad war kaputt, also habe ich ihres genommen. My bike was broken, so I took hers.

3 their
□ Das ist ihr Lehrer. That's their teacher.
□ Ihre Englischlehrerin ist netter als unsere. Their English teacher's nicer than ours.
□ Ihr Haus liegt gleich neben unserem. Their house is right next door to ours.

4 theirs
□ Das ist nicht ihr Lehrer, ihrer heißt Herr Schulz. That's not their teacher, theirs is called Mr Schulz. □ Unsere Schule macht einen Wandertag, ihre nicht. Our school is going rambling, theirs isn't.

Ihr ADJECTIVE
▷ *see also* **ihr** ADJECTIVE, **ihr** PRONOUN

1 your
□ Ihr Vater ist nett. Your father's nice. □ Ihre Mutter hat mir das gesagt. Your mother told me. □ Ist das Ihr Fahrrad? Is that your bike?
□ Leben Ihre Eltern noch? Are your parents still alive?

2 yours
□ Das ist nicht Ihr Füller, Ihrer ist hier. That's not your pen, yours is here. □ Meine Mutter heißt Ulla, wie heißt Ihre? My mother's called Ulla, what's yours called? □ Mein Fahrrad ist kaputt, kann ich Ihres nehmen? My bike's broken, can I take yours?

ihretwegen ADVERB
▷ *see also* **Ihretwegen**

LANGUAGE TIP **ihretwegen** refers to **sie** (singular or plural).

1 for her sake
□ Ich habe ihretwegen auf den Urlaub verzichtet. I went without a holiday for her sake.

2 on her account
□ Er hat sich ihretwegen furchtbar aufgeregt. He got terribly upset on her account.

3 as far as she's concerned
□ Sie sagt, dass du ihretwegen ruhig gehen kannst. She says that as far as she's concerned you can go.

4 for their sake
□ Wir haben ihretwegen auf den Urlaub verzichtet. We went without a holiday for their sake.

5 on their account
□ Er hat sich ihretwegen furchtbar aufgeregt. He got terribly upset on their account.

6 as far as they're concerned
□ Sie sagen, dass du ihretwegen ruhig gehen kannst. They say that as far as they're concerned you can go.

Ihretwegen ADVERB
▷ *see also* **ihretwegen**

LANGUAGE TIP **Ihretwegen** refers to **Sie**.

1 for your sake
□ Ich habe Ihretwegen auf den Urlaub verzichtet. I went without a holiday for your sake.

2 on your account
□ Er hat sich Ihretwegen furchtbar aufgeregt. He got terribly upset on your account.

die **Illustrierte** (GEN der **Illustrierten**) NOUN
magazine

im = in dem

der **Imbiss** (GEN des **Imbisses**, PL die **Imbisse**) NOUN
snack

der **Imbissstand** (PL die **Imbissstände**) NOUN
hot-dog stand

die **Imbissstube** NOUN
snack bar

immatrikulieren (PERFECT **hat immatrikuliert**) VERB [76]
to register *(at university)*

immer ADVERB
always
□ Du kommst immer zu spät. You're always late.
■ **immer wieder** again and again
■ **immer noch** still
■ **immer noch nicht** still not
■ **für immer** forever
■ **immer wenn ich ...** every time I ...
■ **immer schöner** more and more beautiful
■ **immer trauriger** sadder and sadder
■ **wer auch immer** whoever
■ **was auch immer** whatever

immerhin ADVERB
at least

das **Imperfekt** (PL die **Imperfekte**) NOUN
imperfect

impfen VERB [38]
to vaccinate
□ jemanden gegen etwas impfen to vaccinate somebody against something

der **Impfstoff** (PL die **Impfstoffe**) NOUN
vaccine

die **Impfung** NOUN
vaccination

der **Import** (PL die **Importe**) NOUN
import

importieren (PERFECT **hat importiert**) VERB [76]
to import

improvisieren (PERFECT **hat improvisiert**) VERB [76]
to improvise

imstande ADJECTIVE
■ **imstande sein, etwas zu tun** to be able to do something

in PREPOSITION

LANGUAGE TIP Use the accusative to express movement or a change of place. Use the dative when there is no change of place.

1 in
□ Es ist im Schrank. It's in the cupboard.
□ Sie ist in der Stadt. She's in town.

□ Sie wurde rot im Gesicht. She went red in the face.

2 into

□ Lege es in diese Schublade. Put it into this drawer. □ Sie geht in die Stadt. She's going into town.

■ **in der Schule sein** to be at school

■ **in die Schule gehen** to go to school

■ **in diesem Jahr** this year

■ **heute in zwei Wochen** two weeks today

■ **in sein** to be in □ Inline-Skates sind jetzt in. In-line skates are in at the moment.

inbegriffen ADVERB
included

der **Inder** (PL die **Inder**) NOUN
Indian

die **Inderin** NOUN
Indian

der **Indianer** (PL die **Indianer**) NOUN
Native American

die **Indianerin** NOUN
Native American

indianisch ADJECTIVE
Native American

das **Indien** NOUN
India

■ **aus Indien** from India

■ **nach Indien** to India

indisch ADJECTIVE
Indian

die **Industrie** NOUN
industry

das **Industriegebiet** (PL die **Industriegebiete**) NOUN
industrial area

der **Infarkt** (PL die **Infarkte**) NOUN
coronary

die **Infektion** NOUN
infection

der **Infinitiv** (PL die **Infinitive**) NOUN
infinitive

infizieren (PERFECT **hat infiziert**) VERB [76]
to infect

□ Sie hat ihren Bruder infiziert. She infected her brother.

■ **sich bei jemandem infizieren** to catch something from somebody

die **Inflation** NOUN
inflation

infolge PREPOSITION

LANGUAGE TIP The preposition **infolge** takes the genitive.

as a result of

infolgedessen ADVERB
consequently

die **Informatik** NOUN
computer science

der **Informatiker** (PL die **Informatiker**) NOUN
computer scientist

die **Information** NOUN
information

□ Weitere Informationen lassen wir Ihnen zukommen. We will send you further information.

informieren (PERFECT **hat informiert**) VERB [76]
to inform

■ **sich über etwas informieren** to find out about something □ Ich werde mich über die Bedingungen informieren. I'll find out about the terms.

■ **sich über jemanden informieren** to make enquiries about somebody □ Ich habe mich über ihn informiert. I've made enquiries about him.

infrage ADVERB

■ **etwas infrage stellen** to question something

■ **nicht infrage kommen** to be out of the question

der **Ingenieur** (PL die **Ingenieure**) NOUN
engineer

die **Ingenieurschule** NOUN
school of engineering

der **Ingwer** NOUN
ginger

der **Inhaber** (PL die **Inhaber**) NOUN
owner

□ Wir müssen den Inhaber des Hauses fragen, ob das geht. We'll have to ask the owner of the house if it's all right.

■ **der Inhaber einer Lizenz** the licence holder

der **Inhalt** (PL die **Inhalte**) NOUN

1 contents

□ Der Inhalt der Flasche war grün. The contents of the bottle were green.

2 content

□ Fasse den Inhalt dieser Geschichte zusammen. Summarize the content of this story.

3 volume

□ Berechne den Inhalt des Würfels. Calculate the volume of the cube.

die **Inhaltsangabe** NOUN
summary

das **Inhaltsverzeichnis** (GEN des **Inhaltsverzeichnisses**, PL die **Inhaltsverzeichnisse**) NOUN
table of contents

inkl. ABBREVIATION (= *inklusive*)
incl.

inklusive PREPOSITION, ADVERB

LANGUAGE TIP The preposition **inklusive** takes the genitive.

1 inclusive of

□ ein Computer inklusive Bildschirm a computer inclusive of monitor

2 included

□ Die Bedienung ist inklusive. Service is included.

das **Inland** NOUN
■ **im In- und Ausland** at home and abroad

innen ADVERB
inside

die **Innenpolitik** NOUN
domestic policy

innenpolitisch ADJECTIVE
internal

die **Innenstadt** (PL die **Innenstädte**) NOUN
town centre

innere ADJECTIVE
internal
□ innere Blutungen internal bleeding
□ die inneren Angelegenheiten des Landes the internal matters of the country

innerhalb ADVERB, PREPOSITION
LANGUAGE TIP The preposition **innerhalb** takes the genitive.
1 within
□ Das muss innerhalb von zwei Tagen gemacht werden. That must be done within two days.
2 during
□ Der Bus fährt nur innerhalb der Woche, nicht an Wochenenden. The bus only runs during the week, not at the weekend.

inoffiziell ADJECTIVE
unofficial

ins = **in das**

insbesondere ADVERB
particularly

die **Inschrift** NOUN
inscription

das **Insekt** (PL die **Insekten**) NOUN
insect

die **Insel** NOUN
island

insgesamt ADVERB
in all
□ Er hat insgesamt drei Fahrräder. He has three bikes in all. □ Insgesamt waren dreihundert Leute gekommen. In all, three hundred people came.

der **Instinkt** (PL die **Instinkte**) NOUN
instinct

das **Instrument** (PL die **Instrumente**) NOUN
instrument

intellektuell ADJECTIVE
intellectual

intelligent ADJECTIVE
intelligent

die **Intelligenz** NOUN
intelligence

intensiv ADJECTIVE
intensive

der **Intercityexpress** (GEN des **Intercityexpresses**, PL die **Intercityexpresse**) NOUN
Intercity Express train

der **Intercityzug** (PL die **Intercityzüge**) NOUN
Intercity train

interessant ADJECTIVE
interesting

das **Interesse** (PL die **Interessen**) NOUN
interest
■ **Interesse haben an** to be interested in
□ Hast du Interesse an einem gebrauchten Notebook? Are you interested in a used notebook? □ Manfred scheint Interesse an dir zu haben. Manfred seems to be interested in you.

interessieren (PERFECT **hat interessiert**) VERB [76]
to interest
□ Es interessiert mich, was du in den Ferien erlebt hast. I'm interested to know what you did in your holidays.
■ **sich interessieren für** to be interested in
□ Ich interessiere mich für Kunst. I'm interested in art.

das **Internat** (PL die **Internate**) NOUN
boarding school

international ADJECTIVE
international

das **Internet** NOUN
internet

der **Internet-Anbieter** (PL die **Internet-Anbieter**) NOUN
Internet Service Provider

der **Internetbenutzer** (PL die **Internetbenutzer**) NOUN
internet user

das **Internet-Café** (PL die **Internet-Cafés**) NOUN
internet café

die **Internetseite** (PL die **Internetseiten**) NOUN
web page

interpretieren (PERFECT **hat interpretiert**) VERB [76]
to interpret

intransitiv ADJECTIVE
intransitive

inwiefern ADVERB
how far
□ Ich weiß nicht, inwiefern das stimmt. I don't know how far that's right.

inzwischen ADVERB
meanwhile

der **Irak** NOUN
Iraq
■ **aus dem Irak** from Iraq
■ **im Irak** in Iraq
■ **in den Irak** to Iraq

irakisch ADJECTIVE
Iraqi

der **Iran** NOUN
Iran
■ **aus dem Iran** from Iran
■ **im Iran** in Iran
■ **in den Iran** to Iran

iranisch ADJECTIVE
Iranian

der **Ire** (GEN des **Iren**, PL die **Iren**) NOUN
Irishman
■ **die Iren** the Irish

irgend ADVERB
at all
□ Komm, wenn es irgend geht. Come if it's at all possible.

irgendein ADJECTIVE
1 some
□ Irgendein Mann hat mir das gesagt. Some man told me. □ Irgendeine Ausrede wird dir schon einfallen. You'll think of some excuse.
2 any
□ Ich will nicht irgendeinen Computer. I don't just want any computer. □ Gibt es nicht irgendeine Möglichkeit? Isn't there any chance?
□ Welchen Kuli willst du? — Irgendeinen. Which pen do you want? — Any one.

irgendetwas PRONOUN
1 something
□ irgendetwas Schönes something nice
2 anything
□ Hast du irgendetwas gehört? Did you hear anything?

irgendjemand PRONOUN
1 somebody
□ Das hat mir irgendjemand gesagt. Somebody told me.
2 anybody
□ Hast du irgendjemanden gesehen? Did you see anybody?

irgendwann ADVERB
sometime

irgendwas PRONOUN
1 something
□ Er murmelte irgendwas. He murmured something.
2 anything
□ Was soll ich anziehen? — Irgendwas. What shall I wear? — Anything.

irgendwie ADVERB
somehow

irgendwo ADVERB
somewhere

die **Irin** NOUN
Irishwoman

irisch ADJECTIVE
Irish

Irland NEUT NOUN
Ireland
■ **aus Irland** from Ireland
■ **in Irland** in Ireland
■ **nach Irland** to Ireland

die **Ironie** NOUN
irony

ironisch ADJECTIVE
ironic
□ Das war ironisch gemeint. That was meant to be ironic.

irre ADJECTIVE, ADVERB
1 mad
□ Wer ist denn auf diese irre Idee gekommen? Who thought up this mad idea?
2 fantastic
□ Das war ein irres Konzert. That was a fantastic concert.
3 incredibly
□ Er ist irre schnell gefahren. He drove incredibly fast. □ Die Party war irre gut. The party was incredibly good.

irreführen (PERFECT **hat irregeführt**) VERB [4]
to mislead

irren VERB [38]

LANGUAGE TIP Use **haben** to form the perfect tense for 'to be mistaken' but **sein** for 'to wander about'.

■ **sich irren** to be mistaken □ Du hast dich geirrt. You were mistaken.
to wander about
□ Sie ist durch die Straßen geirrt. She wandered about the streets.

der **Irrtum** (PL die **Irrtümer**) NOUN
mistake

der **Islam** NOUN
Islam

Island NEUT NOUN
Iceland
■ **nach Island** to Iceland

Israel NEUT NOUN
Israel
■ **aus Israel** from Israel
■ **nach Israel** to Israel

der/die **Israeli** (PL die **Israelis**) NOUN
Israeli
□ Sie ist mit einem Israeli verheiratet. He is married to an Israeli.

israelisch ADJECTIVE
Israeli

isst VERB ▷ *see* **essen**

ist VERB ▷ *see* **sein**

Italien NEUT NOUN
Italy
■ **aus Italien** from Italy
■ **in Italien** in Italy
■ **nach Italien** to Italy

der **Italiener** (PL die **Italiener**) NOUN
Italian

die **Italienerin** NOUN
Italian

italienisch ADJECTIVE
Italian

German-English

Jj

ja ADVERB

1 yes

□ Hast du das gesehen? — Ja. Did you see that? — Yes, I did.

■ **Ich glaube ja.** I think so.

2 really?

□ Ich habe mir ein neues Auto gekauft. — Ach ja? I've bought a new car. — Really?

■ **Du kommst, ja?** You're coming, aren't you?

■ **Sei ja vorsichtig!** Do be careful.

■ **Sie wissen ja, dass ...** As you know, ...

■ **Tu das ja nicht!** Don't you dare do that!

■ **Ich habe es ja gewusst.** I just knew it.

■ **ja, also ...** well ... □ Ja, also wenn ihr alle geht, dann gehe ich mit. Well, if you're all going, then I'm going too.

die **Jacht** NOUN

yacht

die **Jacke** NOUN

1 jacket

□ Sie trug einen blauen Rock und eine schwarze Jacke. She was wearing a blue skirt and a black jacket.

2 cardigan

□ Wenn es dir kalt ist, solltest du eine Jacke anziehen. If you're cold, you should put on a cardigan.

das **Jackett** (PL die **Jacketts**) NOUN

jacket

die **Jagd** (PL die **Jagden**) NOUN

1 hunt

□ Er fiel während der Jagd vom Pferd. He fell off his horse during the hunt.

2 hunting

□ Alan geht oft zur Jagd. Alan often goes hunting.

jagen VERB [38]

LANGUAGE TIP Use **haben** to form the perfect tense for 'to hunt' or 'to chase' but **sein** for 'to race'.

1 to hunt

□ Sonntags geht er jagen. He goes hunting on Sundays. □ Er hat in Afrika Löwen gejagt. He hunted lions in Africa. □ Meine Katze jagt Mäuse. My cat hunts mice.

2 to chase

□ Die Polizei hat die Bankräuber gejagt, aber nicht eingeholt. The police chased the bank robbers but didn't catch them.

3 to race

□ Wir sind mit ihr ins Krankenhaus gejagt. We raced with her to the hospital.

■ **Damit kann man mich jagen.** I can't stand that.

das **Jahr** (PL die **Jahre**) NOUN

year

□ Ich bin vierzehn Jahre alt. I'm fourteen years old.

■ **die Neunzigerjahre** the nineties

die **Jahreszeit** NOUN

season

■ **zu jeder Jahreszeit** throughout the year

□ Man bekommt inzwischen zu jeder Jahreszeit Erdbeeren. You can now get strawberries throughout the year.

der **Jahrgang** (PL die **Jahrgänge**) NOUN

year

□ Sie ist mein Jahrgang. She was born in the same year as me. □ Welcher Jahrgang bist du? In which year were you born?

das **Jahrhundert** (PL die **Jahrhunderte**) NOUN

century

jährlich ADJECTIVE, ADVERB

yearly

der **Jahrmarkt** (PL die **Jahrmärkte**) NOUN

funfair

das **Jahrtausend** (PL die **Jahrtausende**) NOUN

millennium

jähzornig ADJECTIVE

hot-tempered

die **Jalousie** NOUN

Venetian blind

der **Jammer** NOUN

misery

■ **Es ist ein Jammer, dass ...** It's a crying shame that ...

jammern VERB [88]

to whine

□ Hör auf zu jammern! Stop whining.

der **Januar** (GEN des **Januar** *or* **Januars**, PL die **Januare**) NOUN

January

□ im Januar in January □ am dritten Januar

j

on the third of January □ Ulm, den 3. Januar 2008 Ulm, 3 January 2008 □ Heute ist der dritte Januar. Today is the third of January.

Japan NEUT NOUN
Japan
■ **aus Japan** from Japan
■ **nach Japan** to Japan

der **Japaner** (PL die **Japaner**) NOUN
Japanese

die **Japanerin** NOUN
Japanese

japanisch ADJECTIVE
Japanese

jaulen VERB [38]
to howl

jawohl ADVERB
yes

je ADVERB, CONJUNCTION
1 ever
□ Warst du je in Italien? Have you ever been to Italy? □ Hast du so was je gesehen? Did you ever see anything like it?
□ besser denn je better than ever
2 each
□ Wir haben je zwei Stück bekommen. We got two pieces each. □ Sie zahlten je zehn Euro. They paid ten euros each.
■ **je nach** depending on □ Je nach Größe sind sie verschieden teuer. Prices vary depending on size.
■ **je nachdem** it depends □ Wir kommen vielleicht etwas später, je nachdem, wie lange wir unterwegs sind. We'll perhaps be a little late, it depends how long we take to get there.
■ **je nachdem, ob ...** depending on whether ... □ Wir kommen vielleicht mit den Kindern, je nachdem ob sie Lust haben. We'll come with the children depending on whether they feel like it or not.
■ **je ... umso ...** the ... the ... □ Je schneller er fuhr, umso mehr Angst hatte sie. The faster he drove, the more frightened she was.
■ **je eher, desto besser** the sooner the better

die **Jeans** (PL die **Jeans**) NOUN
jeans
■ **eine Jeans** a pair of jeans □ Ich habe mir eine neue Jeans gekauft. I've bought myself a new pair of jeans.

jede ADJECTIVE, PRONOUN
1 every
□ Jeder Schüler bekommt ein Zeugnis. Every pupil receives a report. □ Ich besuche sie jede Woche. I visit her every week.
□ Er gab jedem Mädchen ein Bonbon. He gave every girl a sweet.
■ **jeder** everybody □ Jeder weiß, dass das nicht erlaubt ist. Everybody knows that that's not allowed.
2 each
□ Jeder von euch bekommt ein Stück. Each of you will get a piece. □ Jede seiner Freundinnen war anders. Each of his girlfriends was different. □ Jedes der Kinder hat mir etwas geschenkt. Each child gave me something.
■ **jedes Mal** every time

jedenfalls ADVERB
in any case

jederzeit ADVERB
at any time

jedoch ADVERB
however

jemals ADVERB
ever

jemand PRONOUN
1 somebody
□ Jemand hat mir gesagt, dass du krank bist. Somebody told me that you were ill.
2 anybody
□ War jemand zu Hause? Was anybody at home?

jene PRONOUN
1 that
□ in jener Zeit at that time
2 those
□ in jenen Tagen in those days

jetzt ADVERB
now
□ Sie ist jetzt in der Schweiz. She's in Switzerland now.

jeweils ADVERB
■ **jeweils zwei zusammen** two at a time
■ **zu jeweils fünf Euro** at five euros each

der **Job** (PL die **Jobs**) NOUN
job

das **Jod** NOUN
iodine

jodeln VERB [88]
to yodel

joggen VERB [48]

> LANGUAGE TIP Use **haben** for the perfect tense when you describe the activity and **sein** when you describe the motion.

to jog
□ Früher habe ich oft gejoggt. I used to jog a lot. □ Wir sind durch den Wald gejoggt. We jogged through the woods.

das **Jogging** NOUN
jogging

der **Jogginganzug** (PL die **Jogginganzüge**) NOUN
tracksuit

der **Joghurt** (PL die **Joghurts**) NOUN
yogurt

der **Jogurt** (PL die **Jogurts**) NOUN ▷ *see* **Joghurt**

die **Johannisbeere** NOUN
redcurrant
□ Johannisbeeren sind mir zu sauer. Redcurrants are too sour for me.
■ **Schwarze Johannisbeere** blackcurrant

der **Journalist** (GEN des **Journalisten**, PL die **Journalisten**) NOUN
journalist

jubeln VERB [34]
to rejoice

das **Jubiläum** (PL die **Jubiläen**) NOUN
anniversary
□ Nächstes Jahr feiert unsere Schule ihr zwanzigjähriges Jubiläum. Our school's celebrating its twentieth anniversary next year.

jucken VERB [38]
to be itchy
□ Meine Nase juckt. My nose is itchy.
□ Es juckt mich am Arm. My arm's itchy.

der **Jude** (GEN des **Juden**, PL die **Juden**) NOUN
Jew

die **Jüdin** NOUN
Jew

jüdisch ADJECTIVE
Jewish

die **Jugend** NOUN
youth
□ In meiner Jugend habe ich Fußball gespielt. I used to play football in my youth. □ die Jugend von heute the youth of today

die **Jugendherberge** NOUN
youth hostel

der **Jugendklub** (PL die **Jugendklubs**) NOUN
youth club

jugendlich ADJECTIVE
youthful
□ Er hat ein jugendliches Gesicht. He has a youthful face. □ Sie sieht sehr jugendlich aus. She looks very youthful.

der/die **Jugendliche** (GEN des/der **Jugendlichen**, PL die **Jugendlichen**) NOUN
teenager
□ Ich habe einen Jugendlichen dabei beobachtet, wie er die Wand besprüht hat. I watched a teenager spray the wall.

das **Jugendzentrum** (PL die **Jugendzentren**) NOUN
youth centre

der **Juli** (GEN des **Juli** *or* **Julis**, PL die **Julis**) NOUN
July
□ im Juli in July □ am dritten Juli on the third of July □ Ulm, den 3. Juli 2008 Ulm, 3 July 2008 □ Heute ist der dritte Juli. Today is the third of July.

jung ADJECTIVE
young
□ Er ist drei Jahre jünger als ich. He's three years younger than me.

der **Junge** (GEN des **Jungen**, PL die **Jungen**) NOUN
▷ *see also* **das Junge** NOUN
boy
□ In unserer Klasse gibt es zehn Jungen und fünfzehn Mädchen. There are ten boys and fifteen girls in our class.

das **Junge** (GEN des **Jungen**, PL die **Jungen**) NOUN
▷ *see also* **der Junge** NOUN
young animal
■ **eine Löwin mit ihren Jungen** a lioness with her young

die **Jungfrau** NOUN
1 virgin
2 Virgo
□ Veronika ist Jungfrau. Veronika's Virgo.

jüngste ADJECTIVE
1 youngest
□ Er ist der jüngste Schüler der Klasse. He's the youngest pupil in the class.
2 latest
□ die jüngsten Entwicklungen the latest developments

der **Juni** (GEN des **Juni** *or* **Junis**, PL die **Junis**) NOUN
June
□ im Juni in June □ am fünfzehnten Juni on the fifteenth of June □ Ulm, den 3. Juni 2009 Ulm, 3 June 2009 □ Heute ist der dritte Juni. Today is the third of June.

der **Juwelier** (PL die **Juweliere**) NOUN
jeweller

Kk

das **Kabel** (PL die **Kabel**) NOUN
1 wire
□ Das Kabel des Telefons ist zu kurz. The telephone wire is too short.
2 cable
□ Das Kabel der Seilbahn muss regelmäßig überprüft werden. The cable on the cable car has to be checked regularly.

das **Kabelfernsehen** NOUN
cable television

die **Kabine** NOUN
1 cabin
□ Wir hatten zu zweit eine Kabine auf dem Schiff. The two of us shared a cabin on the ship.
2 cubicle
□ Sie können das Kleid dort hinten in der Kabine anprobieren. You can try the dress on in the cubicle over there.

der **Käfer** (PL die **Käfer**) NOUN
beetle

der **Kaffee** (PL die **Kaffees** *or* **Kaffee**) NOUN
coffee
□ Herr Ober, zwei Kaffee bitte. Two coffees please, waiter.

die **Kaffeekanne** NOUN
coffeepot

die **Kaffeepause** NOUN
coffee break
□ Wir machten Kaffeepause. We had a coffee break.

der **Käfig** (PL die **Käfige**) NOUN
cage

kahl ADJECTIVE
bald
□ sein kahler Kopf his bald head
■ **die kahlen Bäume im Winter** the bare trees in winter
■ **kahl geschoren** shaven

der **Kakao** (PL die **Kakaos** *or* **Kakao**) NOUN
cocoa
□ Herr Ober, zwei Kakao bitte. Two cups of cocoa please, waiter.

das **Kalb** (PL die **Kälber**) NOUN
calf *(animal)*

das **Kalbfleisch** NOUN
veal

der **Kalender** (PL die **Kalender**) NOUN
1 calendar
□ An der Wand hing ein Kalender mit Bildern von Picasso. A calendar with pictures by Picasso was hanging on the wall.
2 diary
□ Sie holte ihren Kalender aus der Tasche. She got her diary out of her bag.

die **Kalorie** NOUN
calorie

kalorienarm ADJECTIVE
low in calories

kalt ADJECTIVE
cold
□ Heute ist es kälter als gestern. It's colder today than yesterday. □ Mir ist kalt. I'm cold.
■ **etwas kalt stellen** to chill something
□ Du solltest den Weißwein kalt stellen. You should chill the white wine.

die **Kälte** NOUN
1 cold
□ Bei dieser Kälte gehe ich nicht raus. I'm not going out in this cold.
2 coldness
□ Die Kälte des Wassers hat uns vom Baden abgehalten. The coldness of the water stopped us from bathing.

kam VERB ▷ *see* **kommen**

das **Kamel** (PL die **Kamele**) NOUN
camel

die **Kamera** (PL die **Kameras**) NOUN
camera

der **Kamerad** (GEN des **Kameraden**, PL die **Kameraden**) NOUN
friend

der **Kamin** (PL die **Kamine**) NOUN
open fire
■ **Wir saßen am Kamin.** We sat by the fire.

der **Kamm** (PL die **Kämme**) NOUN
comb

kämmen VERB [38]
to comb
□ Sie kann es nicht leiden, wenn man sie kämmt. She can't stand having her hair combed. □ Ich muss meiner kleinen Schwester die Haare kämmen. I have to comb my little sister's hair.
■ **sich kämmen** to comb one's hair

der **Kampf** (PL die **Kämpfe**) NOUN

1 fight
□ der Kampf zwischen Tyson und Bruno the fight between Tyson and Bruno
2 contest
□ Dieses Jahr findet der Kampf um den Pokal in Großbritannien statt. The contest for the cup is taking place in Great Britain this year.
3 struggle
□ Ich habe die Prüfung geschafft, aber es war ein Kampf. I passed the exam but it was a struggle.

kämpfen VERB [38]
to fight

Kanada NEUT NOUN
Canada
■ **aus Kanada** from Canada
■ **in Kanada** in Canada
■ **nach Kanada** to Canada

der **Kanadier** (PL die **Kanadier**) NOUN
Canadian

die **Kanadierin** NOUN
Canadian

kanadisch ADJECTIVE
Canadian

der **Kanal** (PL die **Kanäle**) NOUN
1 canal
□ Diese beiden Flüsse sind durch einen Kanal verbunden. These two rivers are connected by a canal.
2 drain

die **Kanalinseln** FEM PL NOUN
the Channel Islands

der **Kanaltunnel** (PL die **Kanaltunnel**) NOUN
Channel Tunnel

der **Kanarienvogel** (PL die **Kanarienvögel**) NOUN
canary

der **Kandidat** (GEN des **Kandidaten**, PL die **Kandidaten**) NOUN
candidate

das **Känguru** (PL die **Kängurus**) NOUN
kangaroo

das **Kaninchen** (PL die **Kaninchen**) NOUN
rabbit

der **Kanister** (PL die **Kanister**) NOUN
can
□ ein Benzinkanister a petrol can

kann VERB ▷ *see* **können**

das **Kännchen** (PL die **Kännchen**) NOUN
pot
□ ein Kännchen Kaffee a pot of coffee
■ **ein Kännchen mit Milch** a jug of milk

die **Kanne** NOUN
1 pot *(for coffee)*
2 churn *(for milk)*
3 watering can

die **Kante** NOUN
edge

die **Kantine** NOUN
canteen
□ Mittags isst sie in der Kantine. She eats in the canteen at lunchtime.

das **Kanu** (PL die **Kanus**) NOUN
canoe
■ **Kanu fahren** to go canoeing

der **Kanzler** (PL die **Kanzler**) NOUN
chancellor

kapieren (PERFECT **hat kapiert**) VERB [76]
to understand
□ Ich habe heute in Mathe nichts kapiert. I didn't understand anything in maths today.
□ Hast du das endlich kapiert? Have you finally understood?

das **Kapital** NOUN
capital *(money)*

der **Kapitän** (PL die **Kapitäne**) NOUN
captain

das **Kapitel** (PL die **Kapitel**) NOUN
chapter

die **Kappe** NOUN
cap

kaputt ADJECTIVE
▷ *see also* **kaputtmachen** VERB
1 broken
□ Mein Computer ist kaputt. My computer's broken.
■ **Am Auto ist etwas kaputt.** There's something wrong with the car.
■ **kaputt machen** to break □ Mach mir bloß mein Fahrrad nicht kaputt! Don't you dare break my bike! □ Sie hat den Teller kaputt gemacht. She's broken the plate.
2 knackered
□ Ich bin von der Wanderung total kaputt. I'm completely knackered after the walk.

kaputtgehen (IMPERFECT **ging kaputt**, PERFECT **ist kaputtgegangen**) VERB [29]
1 to break
□ Mein Computer ist gestern kaputtgegangen. My computer broke yesterday.
2 to wear out *(material)*
3 to die *(plant)*
4 to break up *(relationship)*

kaputtmachen (PERFECT **hat kaputtgemacht**) VERB [48]
▷ *see also* **kaputt** ADJECTIVE
to wear out
□ Die viele Arbeit macht mich noch kaputt. All this work is wearing me out.
■ **sich kaputtmachen** to wear oneself out
□ Du solltest mal Ferien machen, du machst dich ja kaputt. You should take a holiday, you're wearing yourself out.

die **Kapuze** NOUN
hood
□ ein Anorak mit Kapuze an anorak with a hood

der **Karfreitag** NOUN
Good Friday

die **Karibik** NOUN
the Caribbean
□ Wir fahren in die Karibik. We're going to the Caribbean. □ Wir machen in der Karibik Ferien. We're spending our holidays in the Caribbean.

kariert ADJECTIVE
1 checked
□ Sie hatte ein kariertes Kleid an. She was wearing a checked dress.
2 squared
□ Für Mathe brauchst du ein Heft mit kariertem Papier. You need an exercise book with squared paper for maths.

die **Karies** NOUN
tooth decay
□ Sie hat Karies. She has tooth decay.

der **Karneval** (PL die **Karnevale** *or* **Karnevals**) NOUN
carnival

DID YOU KNOW...?
The German carnival season lasts from 11 November to Shrove Tuesday but most events, fancy-dress processions and parties take place in the week leading up to Ash Wednesday.

das **Karo** (PL die **Karos**) NOUN
1 square
□ Das Muster bestand aus kleinen Karos. The pattern was made up of little squares.
2 diamonds
□ Karo ist Trumpf. Diamonds is trumps.

die **Karotte** NOUN
carrot

die **Karriere** NOUN
career
■ **Karriere machen** to get on □ Es ist schwer für Frauen, in der Politik Karriere zu machen. It's hard for women to get on in politics.

die **Karte** NOUN
1 card
□ Sie hat uns aus dem Urlaub eine Karte geschickt. She sent us a card from her holiday. □ Ich weiß nicht, welche Karte ich ausspielen soll. I don't know which card I should play.
■ **die Gelbe Karte** the yellow card
■ **die Rote Karte** the red card
2 map
□ Sieh mal auf der Karte nach, wie weit wir noch fahren müssen. Look on the map to see how far we still have to go.
3 menu
□ Der Ober brachte uns die Karte. The waiter brought us the menu.
4 ticket
□ Kannst du Karten fürs Konzert besorgen? Can you get us tickets for the concert? □ Ich fahre morgen nach Bonn, die Karte habe ich schon gekauft. I'm going to Bonn tomorrow, I've already bought my ticket.
■ **alles auf eine Karte setzen** to put all one's eggs in one basket

LANGUAGE TIP Word for word, **alles auf eine Karte setzen** means 'to bet everything on one card'.

das **Kartenspiel** (PL die **Kartenspiele**) NOUN
1 card game
□ Ich habe ein neues Kartenspiel gelernt. I've learned a new card game.
2 pack of cards
□ Hast du ein Kartenspiel da? Have you got a pack of cards?

die **Kartoffel** NOUN
potato

der **Kartoffelbrei** NOUN
mashed potatoes

der **Kartoffelsalat** (PL die **Kartoffelsalate**) NOUN
potato salad

der **Karton** (PL die **Kartons**) NOUN
1 cardboard
□ Wir haben das Bild auf Karton aufgezogen. We mounted the picture on cardboard.
2 cardboard box
□ Sie packte die Bücher in einen Karton. She packed the books in a cardboard box.

das **Karussell** (PL die **Karussells**) NOUN
roundabout
□ Ich möchte Karussell fahren. I'd like to go on the roundabout.

der **Käse** (PL die **Käse**) NOUN
cheese

der **Käsekuchen** (PL die **Käsekuchen**) NOUN
cheesecake

die **Kaserne** NOUN
barracks
□ In unserer Nähe gibt es eine Kaserne. There's a barracks near us.

die **Kasse** NOUN
1 till
□ Die meisten Geschäfte haben elektronische Kassen. Most shops have an electronic till.
2 checkout
□ an der Kasse at the checkout □ Es war nur eine von fünf Kassen besetzt. Only one of the five checkouts was open.
3 box office
□ Sie können Ihre Karten telefonisch vorbestellen und an der Kasse abholen. You may order your tickets in advance and collect them from the box office.
4 ticket office
□ Karten fürs Fußballspiel bekommen Sie auch an der Kasse des Stadions. You can also get tickets for the football match at the ticket office in the stadium.
5 cash box
□ Alle Barbeträge bewahren wir in dieser Kasse auf. We keep all the cash in this cash box.
6 health insurance
□ Bei welcher Kasse sind Sie versichert?

What health insurance have you got?

DID YOU KNOW...?
In Germany one can choose between different health insurance schemes. There is no 'National Health Service'.

■ **gut bei Kasse sein** to be in the money

der **Kassenzettel** (PL die **Kassenzettel**) NOUN
receipt

die **Kassette** NOUN
1 tape
□ Diesen Song habe ich auf Kassette. I've got this song on tape.
□ eine Videokassette a video tape
2 small box
□ Sie bewahrt ihren Schmuck in einer Kassette auf. She keeps her jewellery in a small box.

kassieren (PERFECT **hat kassiert**) VERB [76]
to take
□ Die Polizei hat seinen Führerschein kassiert. The police took his driving licence.
■ **Der Parkwächter hat zehn Euro Parkgebühren kassiert.** The parking attendant charged us ten euros to park the car.
■ **Darf ich kassieren?** Would you like to pay now?

der **Kassierer** (PL die **Kassierer**) NOUN
cashier

die **Kastanie** NOUN
1 chestnut
2 chestnut tree

der **Kasten** (PL die **Kästen**) NOUN
1 box
□ Er warf den Brief in den Kasten. He put the letter in the box.
2 case
□ Sie legte die Geige zurück in den Kasten. She put the violin back in its case.
■ **ein Kasten Bier** a crate of beer

der **Katalog** (PL die **Kataloge**) NOUN
catalogue

der **Katalysator** (PL die **Katalysatoren**) NOUN
catalytic converter
□ ein Auto mit Katalysator a car with catalytic converter

katastrophal ADJECTIVE, ADVERB
catastrophic
■ **katastrophal schlecht** appallingly bad

die **Katastrophe** NOUN
disaster

die **Kategorie** NOUN
category

der **Kater** (PL die **Kater**) NOUN
1 tomcat
□ Wir haben einen Kater und eine Katze. We have a tomcat and a female cat.
2 hangover
□ Nach der Party hatte ich einen furchtbaren Kater. I had a terrible hangover after the party.

die **Kathedrale** NOUN
cathedral

katholisch ADJECTIVE
Catholic

die **Katze** NOUN
cat
■ **für die Katz** for nothing

kauen VERB [38]
to chew

der **Kauf** (PL die **Käufe**) NOUN
purchase
□ der Kauf eines Autos the purchase of a car
■ **ein guter Kauf** a bargain

kaufen VERB [38]
to buy

der **Käufer** (PL die **Käufer**) NOUN
buyer

die **Kauffrau** NOUN
businesswoman

das **Kaufhaus** (GEN des **Kaufhauses**, PL die **Kaufhäuser**) NOUN
department store

der **Kaufmann** (PL die **Kaufleute**) NOUN
1 businessman
□ ein erfolgreicher Kaufmann a successful businessman
2 grocer
□ zum Kaufmann gehen to go to the grocer's

der **Kaugummi** (PL die **Kaugummis**) NOUN
chewing gum

kaum ADVERB
hardly
□ Ich habe kaum geschlafen. I hardly slept.

die **Kegelbahn** NOUN
skittle alley

kegeln VERB [88]
to play skittles

die **Kehle** NOUN
throat

der **Keil** (PL die **Keile**) NOUN
wedge

der **Keim** (PL die **Keime**) NOUN
1 shoot
□ Eine Woche nach der Aussaat zeigen sich die ersten Keime. The first shoots appear a week after sowing.
2 germ
□ Das Mittel tötete die Keime ab. The medicine killed the germs.
■ **etwas im Keim ersticken** to nip something in the bud

kein ADJECTIVE, PRONOUN

LANGUAGE TIP When combined with a noun, **kein** is used for masculine and neuter nouns, **keine** for feminine and plural nouns. On its own **keiner** is used for masculine, **keine** for feminine and plural, and **keines** or **keins** for neuter.

1 not ... any
□ Ich habe keine Geschwister. I don't have

any brothers or sisters. □ Ich will keinen Streit. I don't want any quarrelling. □ Er zeigt kein Interesse an Computern. He doesn't show any interest in computers. □ Von den Autos hat mir keines gefallen. I didn't like any of the cars.

2 no
□ Kein Tier könnte in diesem Klima überleben. No animal could survive in this climate.
■ **'Kein Zutritt'** 'No entry'
■ **Ich habe keine Lust.** I don't feel like it.
■ **Ich habe keinen Hunger.** I'm not hungry.

3 nobody
□ Alle waren eingeladen, es ist aber keiner gekommen. Everybody was invited but nobody came.
■ **Ich kenne hier keinen.** I don't know anybody here.

keinerlei ADJECTIVE
no ... whatsoever
□ Ich habe damit keinerlei Probleme. I don't have any problems with it whatsoever.

keinesfalls ADVERB
on no account

keineswegs ADVERB
by no means

der **Keks** (PL die **Kekse**) NOUN
biscuit

der **Keller** (PL die **Keller**) NOUN
cellar

der **Kellner** (PL die **Kellner**) NOUN
waiter

die **Kellnerin** NOUN
waitress

kennen (IMPERFECT **kannte**, PERFECT **hat gekannt**) VERB [39]
to know
□ Ich kenne ihn nicht. I don't know him.
□ Ich kenne London gut. I know London well.

kennenlernen VERB [4]

1 to meet
□ Sie hat ihren Freund bei einem Fußballspiel kennengelernt. She met her boyfriend at a football match.

2 to get to know
□ Ich würde ihn gern besser kennenlernen. I'd like to get to know him better.
■ **sich kennenlernen 1** to meet □ Wir haben uns auf einer Party kennengelernt. We met at a party. **2** to get to know each other □ Wir haben uns im Laufe der Zeit immer besser kennengelernt. We got to know each other better and better as time went on.

die **Kenntnis** (PL die **Kenntnisse**) NOUN
knowledge
□ Deutschkenntnisse wären von Vorteil. Knowledge of German would be an advantage.
■ **etwas zur Kenntnis nehmen** to note something
■ **jemanden in Kenntnis setzen** to inform somebody

das **Kennzeichen** (PL die **Kennzeichen**) NOUN

1 mark
□ unveränderliche Kennzeichen distinguishing marks

2 registration
□ das Auto mit dem Kennzeichen S-MJ 2714 the car with the registration S-MJ 2714

der **Kerl** (PL die **Kerle**) NOUN
bloke
■ **Sie ist ein netter Kerl.** She's a good sort.

der **Kern** (PL die **Kerne**) NOUN

1 pip
□ Klementinen haben keine Kerne. Clementines don't have any pips.

2 stone
□ der Kern der Kirsche the cherry stone

3 kernel *(of nut)*

4 nucleus

5 core
□ der Reaktorkern the reactor core
■ **Wir sollten zum Kern des Problems kommen.** We should to get to the heart of the problem.

die **Kernenergie** NOUN
nuclear energy

das **Kernkraftwerk** (PL die **Kernkraftwerke**) NOUN
nuclear power station

die **Kerze** NOUN

1 candle
□ Sie zündete eine Kerze an. She lit a candle.

2 plug
□ Bei der Inspektion werden die Kerzen erneuert. The plugs are changed while the car is being serviced.

die **Kette** NOUN
chain

keuchen VERB [48]
to pant

der **Keuchhusten** NOUN
whooping cough
□ Meine Schwester hat Keuchhusten. My sister has whooping cough.

die **Keule** NOUN

1 club
□ Er schlug ihm mit einer Keule über den Kopf. He hit him over the head with a club.

2 leg
□ Beim Hähnchen mag ich am liebsten die Keule. My favourite part of a chicken is the leg.

kg ABBREVIATION *(= Kilogramm)*
kg

kichern VERB [88]
to giggle

der **Kiefer** (PL die **Kiefer**) NOUN
▷ *see also* **die Kiefer** NOUN
jaw

die **Kiefer** NOUN
▷ *see also* **der Kiefer** NOUN
pine tree

der **Kies** NOUN
gravel

das **Kilo** (PL die **Kilos** *or* **Kilo**) NOUN
kilo
◻ Ich muss ein paar Kilos loswerden. I need to lose a couple of kilos. ◻ Ich hätte gern zwei Kilo Tomaten. Can I have two kilos of tomatoes. ◻ Ich wiege fünfzig Kilo. I weigh eight stone.

das **Kilogramm** (PL die **Kilogramme** *or* **Kilogramm**) NOUN
kilogram
◻ zwei Kilogramm Äpfel two kilograms of apples

der **Kilometer** (PL die **Kilometer**) NOUN
kilometre
◻ mit achtzig Kilometern pro Stunde at fifty miles per hour

das **Kind** (PL die **Kinder**) NOUN
child
■ **von Kind auf** from childhood
■ **ein Kind bekommen** to have a baby

der **Kindergarten** (PL die **Kindergärten**) NOUN
kindergarten

die **Kindergärtnerin** NOUN
kindergarten teacher

das **Kindergeld** NOUN
child benefit

die **Kinderkrippe** NOUN
crèche

die **Kinderlähmung** NOUN
polio
◻ Sie hatte als Kind Kinderlähmung. She had polio as a child.

kinderleicht ADJECTIVE
child's play
◻ Es war kinderleicht. It was child's play.

das **Kindermädchen** (PL die **Kindermädchen**) NOUN
nanny

der **Kinderpfleger** (PL die **Kinderpfleger**) NOUN
paediatric nurse

die **Kinderpflegerin** NOUN
paediatric nurse

die **Kindertagesstätte** NOUN
day nursery

der **Kinderwagen** (PL die **Kinderwagen**) NOUN
pram

die **Kindheit** NOUN
childhood

kindisch ADJECTIVE
childish
■ **sich kindisch benehmen** to behave childishly

das **Kinn** (PL die **Kinne**) NOUN
chin

das **Kino** (PL die **Kinos**) NOUN
cinema
◻ ins Kino gehen to go to the cinema

der **Kiosk** (PL die **Kioske**) NOUN
kiosk

die **Kirche** NOUN
church

die **Kirmes** (PL die **Kirmessen**) NOUN
funfair

die **Kirsche** NOUN
cherry

das **Kissen** (PL die **Kissen**) NOUN
1 cushion
◻ Auf dem Sofa lagen bunte Kissen. There were brightly-coloured cushions on the sofa.
2 pillow
◻ Er schläft ohne Kissen. He sleeps without a pillow.

kitschig ADJECTIVE
kitschy

kitzeln VERB [34]
to tickle

kitzlig ADJECTIVE
ticklish
◻ Ich bin kitzlig an den Füßen. My feet are ticklish. ◻ Das ist eine ganz kitzlige Angelegenheit. That's a very ticklish matter.

klagen VERB [38]
1 to wail
◻ 'Hätte ich doch nur auf dich gehört', klagte er. 'If only I had listened to you', he wailed.
2 to complain
◻ Sie klagt dauernd über ihre Kinder. She's constantly complaining about her children. ◻ Sie klagt in letzter Zeit oft über Kopfschmerzen. She's been complaining of headaches a lot recently.
3 to sue
◻ Wir werden gegen ihn klagen. We're going to sue him.
■ **Sie hat mir ihr Leid geklagt.** She poured out her sorrows to me.

die **Klammer** (PL die **Klammern**) NOUN
1 bracket
◻ Sie schrieb in Klammern eine Erklärung dazu. She wrote an explanation in brackets.
2 peg *(clothes peg)*
3 brace *(for teeth)*
◻ Viele Kinder müssen eine Klammer tragen. Many children have to wear a brace.

der **Klang** (PL die **Klänge**) NOUN
sound

die **Klappe** NOUN
1 flap
◻ Über dem Briefkasten ist eine Klappe. There's a flap over the letterbox.
2 valve
◻ Die Klappe an seinem Herzen hat ein Loch.

His heart valve has a hole in it.

3 trap

□ Er soll die Klappe halten. He should keep his trap shut.

■ **Sie hat eine große Klappe**. She's got a big mouth.

klappen VERB [48]

1 to work

□ Das kann ja nicht klappen. That won't work. □ Das Experiment hat geklappt. The experiment worked.

2 to tip

□ Sie klappte den Sitz nach oben. She tipped up the seat. □ Er klappte den Deckel der Kiste nach hinten. He tipped the lid of the chest back.

klappern VERB [88]

to rattle

klar ADJECTIVE

clear

□ Das Wasser ist sehr klar. The water is very clear. □ Ich brauche einen klaren Kopf. I need a clear head. □ eine klare Antwort a clear answer □ Mir ist nicht klar, was er eigentlich will. I'm not clear about what he really wants.

■ **sich über etwas im Klaren sein** to be clear about something □ Bist du dir über die Konsequenzen im Klaren? Are you clear about the consequences?

■ **Na klar!** Of course!

klären VERB [38]

1 to clarify

□ Wir sollten diese Frage klären. We should clarify this matter.

2 to purify

□ In dieser Anlage wird das Abwasser geklärt. The sewage is purified in this plant.

■ **sich klären** to clear itself up □ Dieses Problem hat sich inzwischen geklärt. The problem has cleared itself up in the meantime.

die **Klarheit** NOUN

1 clarity

■ **Wir brauchen in dieser Sache Klarheit.** This matter must be clarified.

2 clearness

□ die Klarheit des Wassers the clearness of the water

die **Klarinette** NOUN

clarinet

□ Oliver spielt Klarinette. Oliver plays the clarinet.

klarstellen (PERFECT **hat klargestellt**) VERB [4]

to make clear

□ Ich möchte doch mal klarstellen, dass ich das nie gesagt habe. I would like to make it quite clear that I never said that.

die **Klasse** NOUN

▷ *see also* **klasse** ADJECTIVE

class

□ Wir sind in der ersten Klasse gefahren. We travelled first class. □ Unsere Klasse fährt nach England. Our class is going to England.

■ **große Klasse sein** to be great

□ Unser Sportlehrer ist große Klasse. Our sports teacher's really great.

klasse ADJECTIVE

▷ *see also* **die Klasse** NOUN

smashing

□ Er ist ein klasse Lehrer. He's a smashing teacher.

die **Klassenarbeit** NOUN

test

> **DID YOU KNOW...?**
> The **Klassenarbeit** is the main form of assessment in German schools. Over the school year, German pupils write between 6 and 8 **Klassenarbeiten**, usually 45 minutes long, in their core subjects (generally maths, German and English).

□ Wir schreiben morgen in Englisch eine Klassenarbeit. We've got a written English test tomorrow.

das **Klassenbuch** (PL die **Klassenbücher**) NOUN

class register

die **Klassenfahrt** (PL die **Klassenfahrten**) NOUN

class trip

der **Klassenkamerad** (GEN des **Klassenkameraden**, PL die **Klassenkameraden**) NOUN

classmate

die **Klassenkameradin** NOUN

classmate

der **Klassenlehrer** (PL die **Klassenlehrer**) NOUN

class teacher

die **Klassenlehrerin** NOUN

class teacher

der **Klassensprecher** (PL die **Klassensprecher**) NOUN

class representative

die **Klassensprecherin** NOUN

class representative

das **Klassenzimmer** (PL die **Klassenzimmer**) NOUN

classroom

klassisch ADJECTIVE

classical

der **Klatsch** (GEN des **Klatsches**) NOUN

gossip

□ Hast du schon den neuesten Klatsch gehört? Have you heard the latest gossip?

klauen (PERFECT **hat geklaut**) VERB [38]

to pinch

das **Klavier** NOUN

piano

□ Bettina spielt Klavier. Bettina plays the piano.

kleben VERB [38]
to stick
□ Ich habe die zerbrochene Vase wieder geklebt. I've stuck the broken vase together again. □ Das klebt nicht. It doesn't stick.
■ **etwas an etwas kleben** to stick something on something □ Sie hat das Bild der Gruppe an ihre Wand geklebt. She stuck the picture of the band on her wall.
■ **an etwas kleben** to stick to something
□ An der Windschutzscheibe klebten lauter tote Insekten. There were lots of dead insects stuck to the windscreen.
■ **jemandem eine kleben** to thump somebody

klebrig ADJECTIVE
sticky

der **Klebstoff** (PL die **Klebstoffe**) NOUN
glue

der **Klebstreifen** (PL die **Klebstreifen**) NOUN
adhesive tape

der **Klee** NOUN
clover

das **Kleid** (PL die **Kleider**) NOUN
dress
□ Sie trug ein rotes Kleid. She was wearing a red dress.
■ **Kleider** clothes □ Er räumte seine Kleider auf. He put his clothes away.

der **Kleiderbügel** (PL die **Kleiderbügel**) NOUN
coat hanger

der **Kleiderschrank** (PL die **Kleiderschränke**) NOUN
wardrobe

die **Kleidung** NOUN
clothing

das **Kleidungsstück** (PL die **Kleidungsstücke**) NOUN
garment

klein ADJECTIVE
small
□ ein kleines Kind a small child □ ein kleiner Betrag a small amount
■ **als ich klein war** when I was little

das **Kleingeld** NOUN
small change

der **Klempner** (PL die **Klempner**) NOUN
plumber

klettern (PERFECT **ist geklettert**) VERB [88]
to climb

klicken VERB [48]
to click *(computer)*
□ mit der Maus klicken to click on the mouse

das **Klima** (PL die **Klimas**) NOUN
climate

die **Klimaanlage** NOUN
air conditioning

die **Klingel** NOUN
bell

klingeln VERB [34]
to ring
■ **Es klingelte.** The doorbell rang.

der **Klingelton** (PL die **Klingeltöne**) NOUN
ringtone *(of mobile phone)*

klingen (IMPERFECT **klang**, PERFECT **hat geklungen**) VERB
to sound
□ Das Klavier klingt verstimmt. The piano sounds out of tune. □ Der Vorschlag klingt gut. The suggestion sounds good. □ Du klingst deprimiert. You sound depressed.

die **Klinik** NOUN
clinic

die **Klinke** NOUN
handle *(of door)*

die **Klippe** NOUN
cliff

das **Klo** (PL die **Klos**) NOUN
loo

der **Klon** (PL die **Klone**) NOUN
clone

klonen VERB [38]
to clone
□ ein geklontes Schaf a cloned sheep

klopfen VERB [38]
1 to knock
□ Sie klopfte an die Tür. She knocked on the door.
■ **Es klopft.** There's somebody knocking on the door.
2 to pound
□ Mein Herz klopfte vor Aufregung. My heart was pounding with excitement.
■ **jemandem auf die Schulter klopfen** to tap somebody on the shoulder

das **Kloster** (PL die **Klöster**) NOUN
1 monastery
2 convent

der **Klub** (PL die **Klubs**) NOUN
club *(association)*

klug ADJECTIVE
intelligent

die **Klugheit** NOUN
intelligence

km ABBREVIATION *(= Kilometer)*
km

knabbern VERB [88]
to nibble
□ Sie knabberte an einem Keks. She nibbled a biscuit.

das **Knäckebrot** NOUN
crispbread

der **Knall** (PL die **Knalle**) NOUN
bang
□ Die Tür schlug mit einem lauten Knall zu. The door closed with a loud bang.

knapp ADJECTIVE
1 tight
□ Sie hatte einen sehr knappen Pulli an. She

was wearing a very tight pullover.

2 scarce
□ Benzin ist knapp. Petrol is scarce.
■ **knapp bei Kasse** short of money

3 just
□ Sie ist knapp fünfzehn Jahre alt. She has just turned fifteen. □ Wir haben knapp verloren. We only just lost.
■ **eine knappe Stunde** just under an hour
■ **knapp unter** just under □ Das kostet knapp unter tausend Euro. That costs just under a thousand euros.

kneifen (IMPERFECT **kniff**, PERFECT **hat gekniffen**) VERB

1 to pinch
□ Er hat mich in den Arm gekniffen. He pinched my arm.

2 to back out
□ Als er springen sollte, hat er gekniffen. When it was his turn to jump, he backed out.

die **Kneipe** NOUN
pub

das **Knie** (PL die **Knie**) NOUN
knee

der **Knoblauch** NOUN
garlic

der **Knöchel** (PL die **Knöchel**) NOUN

1 knuckle
□ Ich habe mir die Knöchel an der rechten Hand geschürft. I've scraped the knuckles of my right hand.

2 ankle
□ Bei dem Sprung habe ich mir den Knöchel verstaucht. I sprained my ankle when I jumped.

der **Knochen** (PL die **Knochen**) NOUN
bone

der **Knödel** (PL die **Knödel**) NOUN
dumpling

der **Knopf** (PL die **Knöpfe**) NOUN
button

der **Knoten** (PL die **Knoten**) NOUN

1 knot
□ Sie machte einen Knoten in die Schnur. She tied a knot in the string.

2 bun
□ Sie trug das Haar in einem Knoten. She wore her hair in a bun.

3 lump
□ Sie hat einen Knoten in der Brust entdeckt. She noticed a lump in her breast.

der **Knüppel** (PL die **Knüppel**) NOUN

1 cudgel
□ Die Robbenbabys werden mit Knüppeln erschlagen. The baby seals are beaten with cudgels.

2 truncheon
□ Die Polizisten gingen mit Knüppeln gegen die Demonstranten vor. The police used truncheons against the demonstrators.

3 joystick

der **Koch** (PL die **Köche**) NOUN
cook

kochen VERB [48]

1 to cook
□ Was kochst du heute? What are you cooking today? □ Ich koche gern. I like cooking.
■ **Sie kann gut kochen.** She's a good cook.

2 to boil
□ Das Wasser kocht. The water's boiling

der **Kocher** (PL die **Kocher**) NOUN
cooker

die **Köchin** NOUN
cook

der **Kochtopf** (PL die **Kochtöpfe**) NOUN
saucepan

der **Koffer** (PL die **Koffer**) NOUN
suitcase

der **Kofferraum** (PL die **Kofferräume**) NOUN
boot *(of car)*

der **Kohl** NOUN
cabbage

die **Kohle** NOUN

1 coal
□ Wir heizen mit Kohle. We use coal for heating.

2 charcoal
□ Wir brauchen noch Kohle zum Grillen. We need charcoal for the barbecue.

3 dough
■ **Ich habe keine Kohle.** I'm broke.

das **Kohlenhydrat** (PL die **Kohlenhydrate**) NOUN
carbohydrate

die **Kohlensäure** NOUN
carbon dioxide
■ **Mineralwasser mit Kohlensäure** sparkling mineral water

die **Kokosnuss** (PL die **Kokosnüsse**) NOUN
coconut

der **Kollege** (GEN des **Kollegen**, PL die **Kollegen**) NOUN
colleague

die **Kollegin** NOUN
colleague

Köln NEUT NOUN
Cologne
■ **nach Köln** to Cologne

der **Komfort** NOUN
luxury
□ ein Auto mit allem Komfort a luxury car

der **Komiker** (PL die **Komiker**) NOUN
comedian

komisch ADJECTIVE
funny
□ ein komischer Film a funny film □ ein komisches Gefühl a funny feeling

das **Komma** (PL die **Kommas**) NOUN
comma
■ **zwei Komma drei (2,3)** two point three (2.3)

kommen (IMPERFECT **kam**, PERFECT **ist gekommen**) VERB [40]

1 to come
□ Wann ist der Brief gekommen? When did the letter come? □ Kommst du auch zur Party? Are you coming to the party too?
■ **Komm gut nach Hause!** Safe journey home.

2 to get
□ Wie komme ich zum Bahnhof? How do I get to the station?
■ **unter ein Auto kommen** to be run over by a car

3 to appear
□ Es wird Frühling, die Schneeglöckchen kommen schon. Spring is coming, the snowdrops are appearing.

4 to go
□ Er ist gestern ins Krankenhaus gekommen. He went into hospital yesterday.
□ Das kommt in den Schrank. That goes in the cupboard.
■ **Mit sechs kommt man in die Schule.** You start school at six.
■ **Wer kommt zuerst?** Who's first?
■ **Jetzt kommst du an die Reihe.** It's your turn now.
■ **kommenden Sonntag** next Sunday
■ **kommen lassen** to send for □ Ich habe mir den Katalog kommen lassen. I've sent for the catalogue. □ Der Direktor hat ihn kommen lassen. The headmaster sent for him.
■ **auf etwas kommen** to think of something □ Darauf bin ich nicht gekommen. I didn't think of that.
■ **Wie kommst du auf die Idee?** What gave you that idea?
■ **Ich komme nicht auf seinen Namen.** His name escapes me.
■ **Er kommt aus Bayern.** He comes from Bavaria.
■ **Sie ist durchs Abitur gekommen.** She got through her Abitur.
■ **ums Leben kommen** to lose one's life □ Sie ist bei einem Unfall ums Leben gekommen. She lost her life in an accident.
■ **Das kommt davon!** That's what you get!
■ **zu sich kommen** to come round □ Die Patientin ist noch nicht wieder zu sich gekommen. The patient hasn't come round again yet.
■ **zu etwas kommen** **1** to get something □ Wie bist du zu dem Computer gekommen? How did you get the computer? **2** to get round to something □ Ich mache das, sobald ich dazu komme. I'll do it as soon as I get round to it.

die **Kommode** NOUN
chest of drawers

der **Kommunismus** (GEN des **Kommunismus**) NOUN
communism

die **Komödie** NOUN
comedy

kompatibel ADJECTIVE
compatible

das **Kompliment** (PL die **Komplimente**) NOUN
compliment
□ Er hat ihr zu ihrem Kuchen ein Kompliment gemacht. He complimented her on her cake.

kompliziert ADJECTIVE
complicated

der **Komponist** (GEN des **Komponisten**, PL die **Komponisten**) NOUN
composer

das **Kompott** (PL die **Kompotte**) NOUN
compote

der **Konditor** (PL die **Konditoren**) NOUN
pastry cook

die **Konditorei** NOUN
cake shop

das **Kondom** (PL die **Kondome**) NOUN
condom

der **Konflikt** (PL die **Konflikte**) NOUN
conflict

der **König** (PL die **Könige**) NOUN
king

die **Königin** NOUN
queen

königlich ADJECTIVE
royal

das **Königreich** (PL die **Königreiche**) NOUN
kingdom
■ **das Vereinigte Königreich** the United Kingdom

die **Konjugation** NOUN
conjugation

konjugieren (PERFECT **hat konjugiert**) VERB [76]
to conjugate

die **Konjunktion** NOUN
conjunction

der **Konjunktiv** (PL die **Konjunktive**) NOUN
subjunctive

die **Konkurrenz** NOUN

1 competition
□ Auf diesem Sektor ist die Konkurrenz groß. Competition is keen in this sector.

2 competitors
□ Sie ist zur Konkurrenz gegangen. She's gone over to our competitors.

können (PRESENT **kann**, IMPERFECT **konnte**, PERFECT **hat gekonnt** *or* **können**) VERB [41]
▷ *see also* **das Können** NOUN

LANGUAGE TIP The past participle **können** is used when **können** is a modal auxiliary.

1 can
□ Kannst du schwimmen? Can you swim?

□ Sie kann keine Mathematik. She can't do mathematics. □ Sie hat nicht früher kommen können. She couldn't come earlier. □ Kann ich mit? Can I come with you? □ Ich kann nicht ... I can't ...

2 to be able to

□ Morgen werde ich nicht kommen können. I won't be able to come tomorrow.

■ **Ich kann nicht mehr. 1** I can't go on. □ Ich mache jetzt Schluss, ich kann nicht mehr. I'll have to stop now, I can't go on. **2** I'm full up. □ Willst du noch ein Stück Kuchen? — Nein danke, ich kann nicht mehr. Would you like another piece of cake? — No thanks, I'm full up.

3 may

□ Kann ich gehen? May I go? □ Sie könnten recht haben. You may be right.

■ **es kann sein, dass ...** it may be that ... □ Es kann sein, dass ich etwas später komme. It may be that I'll come a little later.

■ **Ich kann nichts dafür.** It's not my fault.

■ **Das kann sein.** That's possible.

4 to know

□ Er kann viele Geschichtszahlen. He knows a lot of historical dates.

■ **Können Sie Deutsch?** Can you speak German?

das **Können** NOUN

▷ *see also* **können** VERB

ability

□ Sie hat ihr Können bewiesen. She has proved her ability.

konnte VERB ▷ *see* **können**

konservativ ADJECTIVE

conservative

die **Konserve** NOUN

tinned food

die **Konservenbüchse** NOUN

tin

der **Konsonant** (GEN des **Konsonanten**, PL die **Konsonanten**) NOUN

consonant

der **Kontakt** (PL die **Kontakte**) NOUN

contact

die **Kontaktlinsen** FEM PL NOUN

contact lenses

der **Kontinent** (PL die **Kontinente**) NOUN

continent

das **Konto** (PL die **Konten**) NOUN

account

□ Geld auf ein Konto einzahlen to pay money into an account

die **Kontrolle** NOUN

control

□ die Passkontrolle passport control □ Sie hat die Kontrolle über das Fahrzeug verloren. She lost control of the vehicle. □ etwas unter Kontrolle haben to have something under control

der **Kontrolleur** (PL die **Kontrolleure**) NOUN

inspector

kontrollieren (PERFECT **hat kontrolliert**) VERB [76]

to check

□ Kann ich bitte Ihre Fahrkarten kontrollieren? May I check your tickets please?

sich **konzentrieren** (PERFECT **hat sich konzentriert**) VERB [76]

to concentrate

□ Ich kann mich nicht konzentrieren. I can't concentrate.

das **Konzert** (PL die **Konzerte**) NOUN

1 concert

□ Wir waren gestern Abend im Konzert. We were at a concert yesterday evening.

2 concerto

□ ein Konzert für Klavier und Violine a concerto for piano and violin

der **Kopf** (PL die **Köpfe**) NOUN

head

der **Kopfhörer** (PL die **Kopfhörer**) NOUN

headphones

das **Kopfkissen** (PL die **Kopfkissen**) NOUN

pillow

der **Kopfsalat** (PL die **Kopfsalate**) NOUN

lettuce

die **Kopfschmerzen** MASC PL NOUN

headache

□ Ich habe Kopfschmerzen. I've got a headache.

die **Kopie** NOUN

copy

kopieren (PERFECT **hat kopiert**) VERB [76]

to copy

□ kopieren und einfügen to copy and paste

das **Kopiergerät** (PL die **Kopiergeräte**) NOUN

photocopier

der **Korb** (PL die **Körbe**) NOUN

basket

■ **jemandem einen Korb geben** to turn somebody down

LANGUAGE TIP Word for word, **jemandem einen Korb geben** means 'to give somebody a basket'.

der **Korken** (PL die **Korken**) NOUN

cork

der **Korkenzieher** (PL die **Korkenzieher**) NOUN

corkscrew

das **Korn** (PL die **Körner**) NOUN

corn

der **Körper** (PL die **Körper**) NOUN

body

der **Körperteil** (PL die **Körperteile**) NOUN

part of the body

korrigieren (PERFECT **hat korrigiert**) VERB [76]

to correct

die **Kosmetik** NOUN

cosmetics

kosmetisch ADJECTIVE
cosmetic

die **Kost** NOUN
1 food
□ Sie ernährt sich von gesunder Kost. She eats healthy food.
2 board
□ Für Kost und Unterkunft ist gesorgt. Board and lodging will be provided.

kostbar ADJECTIVE
precious
□ Du vergeudest meine kostbare Zeit. You're wasting my precious time.

die **Kosten** PL NOUN
▷ *see also* **kosten** VERB
1 costs
□ die Kosten tragen to bear the costs
2 expense
□ Bei vielen Kindern hat man auch viele Kosten. Lots of children mean a lot of expense.
■ **auf jemandes Kosten** at somebody's expense □ Sie ist auf Kosten der Firma zu der Konferenz gefahren. She went to the conference at the company's expense.

kosten VERB [2]
▷ *see also* **die Kosten** NOUN
1 to cost
□ Mein Fahrrad hat zweitausend Euro gekostet. My bike cost two thousand euros.
■ **Was kostet ...?** How much is ...?
2 to taste
□ Willst du die Soße mal kosten? Would you like to taste the sauce? □ Koste mal, ob das schmeckt. Taste it and see if it's good.

kostenlos ADJECTIVE
free of charge

köstlich ADJECTIVE
1 hilarious
□ Das war ein köstlicher Film. That was a hilarious film. □ ein köstlicher Witz a hilarious joke
2 delicious *(food)*
■ **sich köstlich amüsieren** to have a marvellous time

das **Kostüm** (PL die **Kostüme**) NOUN
costume
■ **ein Damenkostüm** a ladies' suit

das **Kotelett** (PL die **Koteletts**) NOUN
chop

krabbeln (PERFECT **ist gekrabbelt**) VERB [88]
to crawl

der **Krach** NOUN
1 crash
□ Die Vase fiel mit einem lauten Krach zu Boden. The vase fell on the ground with a loud crash.
2 noise
□ Unsere Nachbarn machen viel Krach. Our neighbours make a lot of noise.
3 row
□ Sie hat Krach mit ihrem Freund. She had a row with her boyfriend.

die **Kraft** (PL die **Kräfte**) NOUN
strength
□ Samson hat seine Kraft verloren. Samson lost his strength.
■ **Er hat viel Kraft.** He's very strong.
■ **mit aller Kraft** with all one's might
■ **Kinder kosten viel Kraft.** Children require a lot of energy.
■ **Sie scheint magische Kräfte zu haben.** She seems to have magic powers.
■ **Das Gesetz tritt am ersten August in Kraft.** The law comes into effect on the first of August.

das **Kraftfahrzeug** (PL die **Kraftfahrzeuge**) NOUN
motor vehicle

kräftig ADJECTIVE, ADVERB
1 strong
□ Er ist ein kräftiger Junge. He is a strong boy.
2 hard
□ ein kräftiger Schlag a hard blow □ kräftig schütteln to shake hard
■ **kräftig üben** to practise a lot □ Wenn du kräftig übst, dann schaffst du es. If you practise a lot, you'll do it.

das **Kraftwerk** (PL die **Kraftwerke**) NOUN
power station

der **Kragen** (PL die **Kragen**) NOUN
collar

die **Kralle** NOUN
1 claw
□ die Krallen der Katze the cat's claws
2 talon
□ die Krallen des Vogels the bird's talons

krank ADJECTIVE
ill
□ Ich bin krank. I'm ill. □ Ich habe eine kranke Mutter. My mother's ill.

das **Krankenhaus** (GEN des **Krankenhauses**, PL die **Krankenhäuser**) NOUN
hospital

die **Krankenkasse** NOUN
health insurance

DID YOU KNOW...?
In Germany one can choose between different health insurance schemes. There is no 'National Health Service'.

der **Krankenpfleger** (PL die **Krankenpfleger**) NOUN
male nurse

der **Krankenschein** (PL die **Krankenscheine**) NOUN
health insurance card

die **Krankenschwester** NOUN
nurse

die **Krankenversicherung** NOUN
health insurance

der **Krankenwagen** (PL die **Krankenwagen**) NOUN
ambulance

die **Krankheit** NOUN
illness

krankschreiben (IMPERFECT **schrieb krank**, PERFECT **hat krankgeschrieben**) VERB [61]
■ **jemanden krankschreiben** to give somebody a sick note □ Der Arzt hat ihn für eine Woche krankgeschrieben. The doctor gave him a sick note for a week.

kratzen VERB [36]
to scratch
■ **sich kratzen** to scratch oneself

das **Kraut** (PL die **Kräuter**) NOUN
1 herb
□ eine Salatsoße mit frischen Kräutern a salad dressing with fresh herbs
2 sauerkraut
□ Heute gibt es Würstchen mit Kraut. We're having sausages and sauerkraut today.

die **Krawatte** NOUN
tie

kreativ ADJECTIVE
creative

der **Krebs** (GEN des **Krebses**, PL die **Krebse**) NOUN
1 crab
□ Krebse bewegen sich seitlich voran. Crabs move sideways.
2 cancer
□ Sie ist an Krebs gestorben. She died of cancer.
3 Cancer
■ **Beate ist Krebs.** Beate's Cancer.

der **Kredit** (PL die **Kredite**) NOUN
credit
□ auf Kredit on credit

die **Kreditkarte** NOUN
credit card

die **Kreide** NOUN
chalk

der **Kreis** (GEN des **Kreises**, PL die **Kreise**) NOUN
1 circle
□ Stellt euch im Kreis auf. Form a circle.
□ mein Freundeskreis my circle of friends
□ im Kreis gehen to go round in circles
2 district
□ Blaubeuren liegt im Kreis Ulm. Blaubeuren is in the district of Ulm.

kreischen VERB [38]
to shriek
□ Sie kreischte laut. She shrieked loudly.

der **Kreislauf** NOUN
circulation
□ Sie hat einen labilen Kreislauf. She has bad circulation.

der **Kreisverkehr** (PL die **Kreisverkehre**) NOUN
roundabout

das **Kreuz** (GEN des **Kreuzes**, PL die **Kreuze**) NOUN
1 cross
□ Sie markierte die Stelle mit einem Kreuz. She marked the place with a cross.
2 back
□ Mir tut das Kreuz weh. My back's sore.
3 clubs
□ Kreuz ist Trumpf. Clubs is trumps.

die **Kreuzung** NOUN
1 crossroads
□ An der Kreuzung fährst du links. You go left at the crossroads.
2 cross
□ Das ist eine Kreuzung zwischen Pferd und Esel. It's a cross between a horse and a donkey.

das **Kreuzworträtsel** (PL die **Kreuzworträtsel**) NOUN
crossword puzzle

kriechen (IMPERFECT **kroch**, PERFECT **ist gekrochen**) VERB
1 to crawl
□ Das Baby kroch zur Tür. The baby crawled towards the door. □ Der Verkehr kriecht. The traffic is crawling.
2 to grovel
□ Er kriecht vor seinem Chef. He's grovelling to his boss.

der **Krieg** (PL die **Kriege**) NOUN
war

kriegen VERB [38]
to get
□ Ich kriege einen Schnupfen. I'm getting a cold.
■ **Sie kriegt ein Kind.** She's going to have a baby.

der **Krimi** (PL die **Krimis**) NOUN
thriller

der **Kriminalfilm** (PL die **Kriminalfilme**) NOUN
crime thriller

der **Kriminalroman** (PL die **Kriminalromane**) NOUN
detective story

kriminell ADJECTIVE
criminal

die **Krise** NOUN
crisis

kritisch ADJECTIVE
critical

kritisieren (PERFECT **hat kritisiert**) VERB [76]
to criticize

Kroatien NEUT NOUN
Croatia
■ **aus Kroatien** from Croatia
■ **nach Kroatien** to Croatia

die **Krone** NOUN
crown

die **Kröte** NOUN
toad

der **Krug** (PL die **Krüge**) NOUN
1 jug
□ Sie stellte einen Krug Saft auf den Tisch. She put a jug of juice on the table.
2 beer mug
□ Er trinkt sein Bier immer aus einem Krug. He always drinks his beer out of a beer mug.

krumm ADJECTIVE
■ **ein krummer Rücken** a humped back
■ **Mach nicht so einen krummen Rücken.** Don't slouch.
■ **Sitz nicht so krumm.** Sit up straight.

die **Küche** NOUN
1 kitchen
2 cooking
□ die französische Küche French cooking

der **Kuchen** (PL die **Kuchen**) NOUN
1 cake
□ ein Marmorkuchen a marble cake
2 flan
□ ein Obstkuchen a fruit flan

der **Kuckuck** (PL die **Kuckucke**) NOUN
cuckoo

die **Kuckucksuhr** NOUN
cuckoo clock

die **Kugel** NOUN
1 bullet
□ Er wurde von einer Kugel getroffen. He was hit by a bullet.
2 ball
□ Die Wahrsagerin hat eine Kugel aus Glas. The fortune teller has a crystal ball.

der **Kugelschreiber** (PL die **Kugelschreiber**) NOUN
Biro®

die **Kuh** (PL die **Kühe**) NOUN
cow

kühl ADJECTIVE
cool
□ Abends wurde es kühl. In the evenings it got cool.

der **Kühler** (PL die **Kühler**) NOUN
radiator *(in car)*

der **Kühlschrank** (PL die **Kühlschränke**) NOUN
fridge

die **Kühltruhe** NOUN
freezer

kühn ADJECTIVE
bold

der **Kuli** (PL die **Kulis**) NOUN
Biro®

die **Kultur** NOUN
1 culture
■ **Kultur haben** to be cultured
2 civilization
□ die abendländische Kultur Western civilization

der **Kulturbeutel** (PL die **Kulturbeutel**) NOUN
toilet bag

kulturell ADJECTIVE
cultural

der **Kümmel** (PL die **Kümmel**) NOUN
caraway seed

der **Kummer** NOUN
sorrow
■ **Hast du Kummer?** Have you got problems?

kümmern VERB [38]
to concern
□ Was kümmert mich seine Kritik? Why should his criticism concern me?
■ **Das kümmert mich nicht.** That doesn't worry me.
■ **sich um jemanden kümmern** to look after somebody
■ **sich um etwas kümmern** to see to something □ Kannst du dich um meine Pflanzen kümmern? Can you see to my plants? □ Ich kümmere mich darum, dass das gemacht wird. I'll see to it that it's done.

der **Kunde** (GEN des **Kunden**, PL die **Kunden**) NOUN
customer

kündigen VERB [38]
1 to hand in one's notice
□ Die Arbeit gefällt mir nicht, ich werde kündigen. I don't like the job, I'm going to hand in my notice.
■ **Der Chef hat ihr gekündigt.** The boss gave her her notice.
■ **die Wohnung kündigen** to give notice on one's flat
2 to cancel
□ Ich habe mein Abonnement gekündigt. I've cancelled my subscription.

die **Kündigung** NOUN
notice
□ Er reichte seine Kündigung ein. He handed in his notice.

die **Kundin** NOUN
customer

die **Kundschaft** NOUN
customers

die **Kunst** (PL die **Künste**) NOUN
1 art
□ Sie interessiert sich für Kunst. She's interested in art.
2 knack
□ Er beherrscht die Kunst, andere zu überzeugen. He's got the knack of persuading others.
■ **Das ist doch keine Kunst.** It's easy.

> LANGUAGE TIP Word for word, **Das ist doch keine Kunst** means 'It's not an art'.

der **Künstler** (PL die **Künstler**) NOUN
artist

die **Künstlerin** NOUN
artist

künstlerisch ADJECTIVE
artistic
□ künstlerisch begabt sein to have artistic talents

künstlich ADJECTIVE
artificial

der **Kunststoff** (PL die **Kunststoffe**) NOUN
synthetic material

das **Kunststück** (PL die **Kunststücke**) NOUN
trick

das **Kunstwerk** (PL die **Kunstwerke**) NOUN
work of art

das **Kupfer** NOUN
copper *(metal)*

die **Kupplung** NOUN
clutch
□ Bei Automatikwagen gibt es keine Kupplung. Automatic cars don't have a clutch.

die **Kur** NOUN
health cure
□ eine Kur machen to take a health cure

der **Kurs** (GEN des **Kurses**, PL die **Kurse**) NOUN
1 course
□ Ich mache einen Kurs, um Spanisch zu lernen. I'm doing a course to learn Spanish.
2 rate
□ Wie ist der Kurs des Pfunds? What's the rate for the pound?

die **Kurve** NOUN
1 bend
□ Ein Auto bog um die Kurve. A car came round the bend.
2 curve
□ die Kurve eines Schaubilds the curve on a graph

kurz ADJECTIVE
short
□ Sie hat kurze Haare. She has short hair.
□ Sie hat eine kurze Rede gehalten. She made a short speech.
■ **kurz gesagt** in short
■ **zu kurz kommen** to come off badly
■ **den Kürzeren ziehen** to get the worst of it

LANGUAGE TIP Word for word, **den Kürzeren ziehen** means 'to pull the shorter one'.

die **Kürze** NOUN
shortness

kürzen VERB [36]
1 to shorten
□ Du solltest den Aufsatz etwas kürzen. You should shorten your essay a little.
2 to cut
□ Mein Vater hat mir das Taschengeld gekürzt. My father has cut my pocket money.

die **Kurzgeschichte** NOUN
short story

kürzlich ADVERB
recently

kurzsichtig ADJECTIVE
short-sighted

die **Kusine** NOUN
cousin

der **Kuss** (GEN des **Kusses**, PL die **Küsse**) NOUN
kiss

küssen VERB [48]
to kiss
□ Sie hat mich geküsst. She kissed me.
■ **sich küssen** to kiss □ Sie küssten sich. They kissed.

die **Küste** NOUN
coast

Ll

l ABBREVIATION *(= Liter)*
l

das **Labor** (PL die **Labore** *or* **Labors**) NOUN
lab

lächeln VERB [34]
▷ *see also* **das Lächeln** NOUN
to smile

das **Lächeln** NOUN
▷ *see also* **lächeln** VERB
smile

lachen VERB [48]
to laugh

lächerlich ADJECTIVE
ridiculous

der **Lachs** (GEN des **Lachses**, PL die **Lachse**) NOUN
salmon
□ drei Lachse **three salmon**

der **Lack** (PL die **Lacke**) NOUN
1 varnish
□ Er hat das Holz mit Lack behandelt. **He treated the wood with varnish.**
2 paint
□ Der Lack an meinem Auto ist stumpf geworden. **The paint on my car has become dull.**

der **Laden** (PL die **Läden**) NOUN
▷ *see also* **laden** VERB
1 shop
□ In welchem Laden hast du das gekauft? **Which shop did you buy it in?**
2 shutter
□ Im Sommer machen wir tagsüber die Läden zu. **In summer we close the shutters during the day.**

laden (PRESENT **lädt**, IMPERFECT **lud**, PERFECT **hat geladen**) VERB
▷ *see also* **der Laden** NOUN
1 to load
□ Wir haben das Gepäck ins Auto geladen. **We loaded the luggage into the car.**
□ Das Programm wird geladen. **The program is being loaded.** □ eine Waffe laden **to load a weapon**
2 to charge
□ eine Batterie laden **to charge a battery**
3 to summon
□ Ich wurde als Zeugin geladen. **I was summoned as a witness.**

die **Ladung** NOUN
1 cargo
□ Das Flugzeug hatte zu viel Ladung an Bord. **The plane had too much cargo on board.**
2 loading
□ Ein Arbeiter ist bei der Ladung des Schiffes verunglückt. **A worker was injured while loading the ship.**
3 summons
□ Wenn Sie eine Ladung als Zeuge bekommen, müssen Sie erscheinen. **If you receive a summons to appear as a witness, you have to attend.**
4 charge
□ eine Ladung Dynamit **a charge of dynamite**

die **Lage** NOUN
1 situation
□ Die politische Lage auf dem Balkan ist brisant. **The political situation in the Balkans is explosive.**
2 layer
□ Die Torte bestand aus mehreren Lagen. **The gateau was made up of several layers.**
■ **in der Lage sein, etwas zu tun** **to be in a position to do something**

das **Lager** (PL die **Lager**) NOUN
1 camp
□ Er fährt im Sommer in ein Lager der Pfadfinder. **He's going to a scout camp in the summer.**
2 warehouse
□ Die Fabrik hat ein eigenes Lager. **The factory has its own warehouse.**
3 stockroom
□ Die Verkäuferin hat im Lager nachgesehen. **The sales assistant looked in the stockroom.**

lagern VERB [88]
1 to store
□ kühl lagern **to store in a cool place**
□ trocken lagern **to store in a dry place**
2 to lay down
□ Der Verletzte sollte auf der Seite gelagert werden. **The injured person should be laid down on his side.**
3 to camp
□ Die Indianer lagerten am Fluss. **The Indians camped by the river.**

lahm ADJECTIVE
1 lame

□ Das Pferd ist lahm. The horse is lame.
2 slow
□ Er ist furchtbar lahm. He is terribly slow.

lähmen VERB [38]
to paralyse

die **Lähmung** NOUN
paralysis

der **Laib** (PL die **Laibe**) NOUN
loaf

der **Laie** (GEN des **Laien**, PL die **Laien**) NOUN
layman

das **Laken** (PL die **Laken**) NOUN
sheet *(on bed)*

die **Lakritze** NOUN
liquorice

das **Lamm** (PL die **Lämmer**) NOUN
lamb

das **Lammfleisch** NOUN
lamb *(meat)*

die **Lampe** NOUN
lamp

das **Land** (PL die **Länder**) NOUN
1 country
□ Italien ist ein schönes Land. Italy is a beautiful country. □ Am Wochenende fahren wir aufs Land. We're going to the country at the weekend.
■ **auf dem Land** in the country
■ **an Land** on land □ Wenn wir wieder an Land sind ... When we're on land again ...
2 state
□ Die Bundesrepublik besteht aus sechzehn Ländern. The Federal Republic consists of sixteen states.

die **Landebahn** NOUN
runway

landen (PERFECT **ist gelandet**) VERB [54]
to land

die **Landeskunde** NOUN
regional and cultural studies

die **Landkarte** NOUN
map

der **Landkreis** (GEN des **Landkreises**, PL die **Landkreise**) NOUN
administrative district

DID YOU KNOW...?
The German administrative hierarchy starts with the **Stadt/Gemeinde** (town/community), and continues via the **Landkreis** (administrative district) and **Land** (federal state) to the **Bund** (federation).

ländlich ADJECTIVE
rural

die **Landschaft** NOUN
1 countryside
□ Die toskanische Landschaft ist sehr schön. The Tuscan countryside is very beautiful.
2 landscape
□ Turner hat viele Landschaften gemalt. Turner painted many landscapes.

die **Landstraße** NOUN
country road

die **Landung** NOUN
landing
□ Das Flugzeug verunglückte bei der Landung. The plane crashed on landing.

der **Landwirt** (PL die **Landwirte**) NOUN
farmer

die **Landwirtschaft** NOUN
agriculture

lang ADJECTIVE
1 long
□ Sie hat lange Haare. She has long hair.
□ Das war eine lange Rede. That was a long speech. □ Sie war länger als erwartet weg. She was away longer than expected. □ Es wird nicht lang dauern. It won't take long.
2 tall
□ Mathis ist der Längste in unserer Klasse. Mathis is the tallest in our class.

langatmig ADJECTIVE
long-winded

lange ADVERB
for a long time
□ Sie war lange krank. She was ill for a long time.
■ **lange dauern** to last a long time
■ **lange brauchen** to take a long time

die **Länge** NOUN
length
□ Sie hat die Länge und Breite des Zimmers ausgemessen. She measured the length and breadth of the room. □ die Länge eines Films the length of a film

langen VERB [38]
to be enough
□ Das Fleisch hat nicht für alle gelangt. There wasn't enough meat to go round.
□ Meinst du das Geld langt? Do you think we have enough money?
■ **Es langt mir.** I've had enough.
■ **nach etwas langen** to reach for something
□ Er langte nach dem Apfel. He reached for the apple.

die **Langeweile** NOUN
boredom

langfristig ADJECTIVE, ADVERB
long-term
□ eine langfristige Besserung a long-term improvement □ Wir müssen langfristig planen. We have to plan long-term.

der **Langlauf** NOUN
cross-country skiing
□ Sie macht gern Langlauf. She likes to go cross-country skiing.

länglich ADJECTIVE
longish

langsam ADJECTIVE, ADVERB
1 slow
2 slowly

□ langsam fahren to drive slowly
■ **Das wird langsam langweilig.** This is getting boring.

die **Langsamkeit** NOUN
slowness

der **Langschläfer** (PL die **Langschläfer**) NOUN
late riser

die **Langspielplatte** NOUN
LP

längst ADVERB
■ **Das ist längst fertig.** That was finished a long time ago.
■ **Das weiß ich längst.** I've known that for a long time.
■ **Er ist längst nicht so gescheit wie seine Schwester.** He's far from being as bright as his sister.

längste ADJECTIVE
longest
□ der längste Tag des Jahres the longest day of the year

langweilen VERB [38]
to bore
□ Langweile ich dich? Am I boring you?
■ **sich langweilen** to be bored

langweilig ADJECTIVE
boring

langwierig ADJECTIVE
lengthy

der **Lappen** (PL die **Lappen**) NOUN
rag
□ mit einem feuchten Lappen with a damp rag

der **Laptop** (PL die **Laptops**) NOUN
laptop

der **Lärm** NOUN
noise

der **Laser** (PL die **Laser**) NOUN
laser

lassen (PRESENT **lässt**, IMPERFECT **ließ**, PERFECT **gelassen** *or* **lassen**) VERB [42]
LANGUAGE TIP The past participle **lassen** is used when **lassen** is a modal auxiliary.

1 to stop
□ Du solltest das Rauchen lassen. You should stop smoking. □ Er kann das Trinken nicht lassen. He can't stop drinking. □ Sie kann's nicht lassen. She won't stop doing it.
■ **Lass das!** Stop that!

2 to leave
□ Kann ich die Kinder hier lassen? Can I leave the children here? □ jemanden allein lassen to leave somebody alone □ Wir haben das Auto zu Hause gelassen. We left the car at home. □ etwas lassen, wie es ist to leave something as it is □ Lass mal, ich mache das schon. Leave it, I'll do it.
■ **Lassen wir das!** Let's leave it.
■ **Lass mich!** Leave me alone.
■ **jemanden irgendwohin lassen** to let somebody go somewhere □ Sie lässt die Katze nicht ins Schlafzimmer. She doesn't let the cat into the bedroom. □ jemanden ins Haus lassen to let somebody into the house
■ **etwas machen lassen** to have something done □ Ich habe mir den Katalog schicken lassen. I had the catalogue sent to me. □ Sie hat sich die Haare schneiden lassen. She had her hair cut.
■ **jemanden etwas tun lassen** to let somebody do something □ Sie hat uns nicht ins Kino gehen lassen. She didn't let us go to the cinema.
■ **jemanden warten lassen** to keep somebody waiting
■ **Das lässt sich machen.** That can be done.
■ **Lass uns gehen.** Let's go.

lässig ADJECTIVE
casual

die **Last** NOUN
load
□ Er stöhnte unter der schweren Last. He groaned under the heavy load.
■ **jemandem zur Last fallen** to be a burden to somebody

lästern VERB [88]
to make nasty remarks
□ Lästert ihr schon wieder über eure Lehrerin? Are you making nasty remarks about your teacher again?

lästig ADJECTIVE
tiresome

der **Lastwagen** (PL die **Lastwagen**) NOUN
lorry

das **Latein** NOUN
Latin

Lateinamerika NEUT NOUN
Latin America

der **Lauch** (PL die **Lauche**) NOUN
leek

der **Lauf** (PL die **Läufe**) NOUN
1 run
□ Er machte einen Lauf durch den Wald. He went for a run through the forest.
2 race
□ Sie hat den Lauf über vierhundert Meter gewonnen. She won the four-hundred-metre race.
3 course
□ der Lauf des Flusses the course of the river □ im Laufe der Woche in the course of the week □ einer Sache ihren Lauf lassen to let something take its course
4 barrel
□ Er richtete den Lauf seiner Pistole auf mich. He aimed the barrel of his pistol at me.

die **Laufbahn** NOUN
career

German-English

l

laufen (PRESENT **läuft**, IMPERFECT **lief**, PERFECT **ist gelaufen**) VERB [43]
1 to run
□ Sie liefen so schnell sie konnten. They ran as fast as they could. □ Er läuft Marathon. He runs marathons.
2 to walk
□ Wir mussten nach Hause laufen. We had to walk home.

laufend ADJECTIVE, ADVERB
1 running
□ bei laufendem Motor with the engine running
2 current
□ die laufenden Ausgaben current expenses
■ **auf dem Laufenden sein** to be up to date
■ **auf dem Laufenden halten** to keep up to date
3 always
□ Musst du mich laufend stören? Do you always have to interrupt me?

der **Läufer** (PL die **Läufer**) NOUN
1 runner
□ Die Läufer standen am Start. The runners were at the start. □ Im Flur liegt ein roter Läufer. There's a red runner in the hall.
2 bishop
□ Sie zog mit dem Läufer. She moved her bishop.

die **Läuferin** NOUN
runner

die **Laufmasche** NOUN
ladder *(in tights)*

das **Laufwerk** (PL die **Laufwerke**) NOUN
disk drive
□ Die Diskette in Laufwerk A einlegen. Put the diskette in disk drive A.

die **Laune** NOUN
mood
□ Was hat sie für eine Laune? What kind of mood is she in? □ Ich habe gute Laune. I'm in a good mood. □ Ich bin deine Launen leid. I'm fed up with your bad moods.

launisch ADJECTIVE
1 temperamental
□ Sie ist ein sehr launischer Mensch. She's very temperamental.
2 bad-tempered
□ Er war heute schrecklich launisch. He was terribly bad-tempered today.

die **Laus** (PL die **Läuse**) NOUN
louse

laut ADJECTIVE, ADVERB, PREPOSITION
▷ *see also* **der Laut** NOUN
1 loud
□ Ich mag laute Musik nicht. I don't like loud music.
2 noisy
□ Hier ist es schrecklich laut. It's terribly noisy here.
3 loudly
□ Sie schrie so laut sie konnte. She screamed as loudly as she could.
■ **laut lesen** to read aloud
4 according to
□ Laut unserem Vertrag ... According to our contract ...

der **Laut** (PL die **Laute**) NOUN
▷ *see also* **laut** ADJECTIVE
sound

lauten VERB [2]
1 to go
□ Wie lautet die zweite Strophe des Lieds? How does the second verse of the song go?
2 to be
□ Das Urteil lautete auf zehn Jahre Gefängnis. The sentence was ten years' imprisonment.

läuten VERB [2]
to ring
□ Die Glocken läuten. The bells are ringing.
□ Ich habe geläutet, es hat aber niemand aufgemacht. I rang but nobody answered.

lauter ADVERB
nothing but
□ Sie hat lauter Lügen erzählt. She told nothing but lies.

die **Lautschrift** NOUN
phonetics

der **Lautsprecher** (PL die **Lautsprecher**) NOUN
loudspeaker

die **Lautstärke** NOUN
volume

lauwarm ADJECTIVE
lukewarm

die **Lawine** NOUN
avalanche

das **Leben** (PL die **Leben**) NOUN
▷ *see also* **leben** VERB
life
■ **ums Leben kommen** to lose one's life
□ Er ist bei einem Unfall ums Leben gekommen. He lost his life in an accident.

leben VERB [38]
▷ *see also* **das Leben** NOUN
to live

lebend ADJECTIVE
living

lebendig ADJECTIVE
1 alive
□ Er konnte lebendig aus den Trümmern geborgen werden. He was rescued from the ruins alive.
2 lively
□ Sie ist ein sehr lebendiges Kind. She's a very lively child.

die **Lebensgefahr** NOUN
mortal danger
□ Die Geiseln waren in Lebensgefahr. The hostages were in mortal danger.
■ **'Lebensgefahr!'** 'danger!'

lebensgefährlich ADJECTIVE
1 dangerous
□ eine lebensgefährliche Kurve a dangerous corner
2 critical
□ eine lebensgefährliche Krankheit a critical illness □ lebensgefährlich verletzt critically injured

die **Lebenshaltungskosten** PL NOUN
cost of living

lebenslänglich ADJECTIVE
for life
■ **Er hat eine lebenslängliche Gefängnisstrafe bekommen.** He received a life sentence.

der **Lebenslauf** (PL die **Lebensläufe**) NOUN
CV *(= curriculum vitae)*

die **Lebensmittel** NEUT PL NOUN
food

das **Lebensmittelgeschäft** (PL die **Lebensmittelgeschäfte**) NOUN
grocer's shop

der **Lebensstandard** NOUN
standard of living

die **Lebensversicherung** NOUN
life insurance

die **Leber** NOUN
liver

die **Leberwurst** (PL die **Leberwürste**) NOUN
liver sausage

das **Lebewesen** (PL die **Lebewesen**) NOUN
creature

lebhaft ADJECTIVE
lively

der **Lebkuchen** (PL die **Lebkuchen**) NOUN
gingerbread

lecken VERB [48]
1 to leak
□ Der Behälter leckt. The container's leaking.
2 to lick
□ Die Katze leckte sich das Fell. The cat licked its fur. □ Sie leckte am Eis. She licked her ice cream.

lecker ADJECTIVE
delicious
□ lecker schmecken to taste delicious

das **Leder** (PL die **Leder**) NOUN
leather

die **Lederhose** NOUN
leather trousers

DID YOU KNOW...?
Lederhosen are the traditional dress in South Germany and Austria.

ledig ADJECTIVE
single
□ 'Familienstand: ledig' 'Marital status: single'

leer ADJECTIVE
empty
□ eine leere Flasche an empty bottle
□ leere Drohungen empty threats
■ **ein leeres Blatt Papier** a blank sheet of paper
■ **ein leerer Blick** a vacant expression
■ **leer machen** to empty

die **Leere** NOUN
emptiness

leeren VERB [38]
to empty

legal ADJECTIVE
legal

legen VERB [38]
1 to put
□ Sie legte das Kind ins Bett. She put the child to bed. □ Leg das Besteck in die Schublade. Put the cutlery in the drawer.
□ Er legte das Buch aus der Hand. He put the book down.
2 to lay
□ Sie legten den Verletzten auf eine Decke. They laid the injured man on a blanket.
□ Sie legte ihren Mantel über den Stuhl. She laid her coat over the chair. □ ein Ei legen to lay an egg
■ **sich legen 1** to lie down □ Sie legte sich auf das Sofa. She lay down on the sofa.
□ Ich lege mich ins Bett. I'm going to lie down. **2** to drop □ Der Wind hat sich gelegt. The wind has dropped.
■ **Das wird sich legen.** That will sort itself out.

die **Lehne** NOUN
1 arm
□ Sie saß auf der Lehne des Sofas. She sat on the arm of the sofa.
2 back
□ Der Sessel hat eine hohe Lehne. The chair has a high back.

lehnen VERB [38]
to lean

der **Lehnstuhl** (PL die **Lehnstühle**) NOUN
armchair

die **Lehre** NOUN
1 apprenticeship
□ bei jemandem in die Lehre gehen to serve one's apprenticeship with somebody
2 lesson
□ Lass dir das eine Lehre sein! Let that be a lesson to you!

lehren (PERFECT **hat gelehrt**) VERB [38]
to teach

der **Lehrer** (PL die **Lehrer**) NOUN
teacher

die **Lehrerin** NOUN
teacher

das **Lehrerzimmer** (PL die **Lehrerzimmer**) NOUN
staff room

der **Lehrling** (PL die **Lehrlinge**) NOUN
apprentice

der **Lehrplan** (PL die **Lehrpläne**) NOUN
syllabus

die **Lehrstelle** NOUN
apprenticeship

die **Leiche** NOUN
corpse

leicht ADJECTIVE
1 light
□ leichtes Gepäck light luggage
2 easy
□ Die Klassenarbeit war leicht. The class test was easy.
■ **es sich leicht machen** to make things easy for oneself □ Du machst es dir wirklich zu leicht. You really make things too easy for yourself.

die **Leichtathletik** NOUN
athletics

leichtfallen VERB [22]
■ **jemandem leichtfallen** to be easy for somebody

leichtmachen VERB [48] ▷ *see* **leicht**

der **Leichtsinn** NOUN
carelessness

leichtsinnig ADJECTIVE
careless

das **Leid** NOUN
▷ *see also* **leid** ADJECTIVE
▷ *see also* **leidtun** VERB
sorrow
■ **zu Leide** ▷ *see* **zuleide**

leid ADJECTIVE
▷ *see also* **das Leid** NOUN
■ **etwas leid sein** to be tired of something
□ Ich bin deine ewigen Klagen leid. I'm tired of your constant complaining.

leiden (IMPERFECT **litt**, PERFECT **hat gelitten**) VERB [44]
to suffer
□ Sie leidet an Asthma. She suffers from asthma. □ Wir leiden unter der Hitze. We're suffering from the heat.
■ **jemanden gut leiden können** to like somebody
■ **Ich kann ihn nicht leiden.** I can't stand him.

leider ADVERB
unfortunately
□ Ich kann leider nicht kommen. Unfortunately I can't come.
■ **Ja, leider.** Yes, I'm afraid so.
■ **Leider nicht.** I'm afraid not. □ Er hat mir leider nicht geholfen. I'm afraid he didn't help me.

leidtun (IMPERFECT **tat leid**, PERFECT **hat leidgetan**) VERB [81]
■ **Es tut mir leid.** I'm sorry.
■ **Er tut mir leid.** I'm sorry for him.

leihen (IMPERFECT **lieh**, PERFECT **hat geliehen**) VERB
to lend
□ Kannst du mir fünfzig Euro leihen? Can you lend me fifty euros?
■ **sich etwas leihen** to borrow something
□ Das ist nicht mein Fahrrad, ich habe es mir von meiner Schwester geliehen. That's not my bike, I've borrowed it from my sister.

der **Leim** (PL die **Leime**) NOUN
glue

die **Leine** NOUN
1 line
□ Sie hängte die Wäsche auf die Leine. She hung the washing on the line.
2 lead
□ Hunde müssen an der Leine geführt werden. Dogs must be kept on a lead.

das **Leinen** (PL die **Leinen**) NOUN
linen

leise ADJECTIVE, ADVERB
1 quiet
□ Seid bitte leise. Please be quiet.
2 quietly
□ Sie sprach mit leiser Stimme. She spoke quietly. □ Sie kam ganz leise ins Zimmer. She came into the room very quietly.

leisten VERB [2]
1 to do
□ Du hast gute Arbeit geleistet. You've done a good job.
2 to achieve
□ Sie hat viel geleistet im Leben. She's achieved a lot in her life.
■ **jemandem Gesellschaft leisten** to keep somebody company
■ **sich etwas leisten** to treat oneself to something □ Ich leiste mir heute einen freien Tag. I'm going to treat myself to a day off today.
■ **sich etwas leisten können** to be able to afford something □ Ich kann mir keinen neuen Computer leisten. I can't afford a new computer. □ Ich kann es mir nicht leisten, schon wieder zu spät zu kommen. I can't afford to be late again.

die **Leistung** NOUN
1 performance
□ Sie haben die Leistung des Motors verbessert. They've improved the performance of the engine.
■ **schulische Leistungen** school results
2 achievement
□ eine sportliche Leistung a sporting achievement □ Das war wirklich eine Leistung! That really was an achievement.

leiten VERB [2]
1 to direct
□ Das Wasser wird durch Rohre geleitet. The water is directed through pipes.
2 to lead
□ eine Partei leiten to lead a party
3 to run
□ Wer leitet diese Firma? Who runs this company?

4 to chair
□ Wer hat die Versammlung geleitet? Who chaired the meeting?
■ **Metall leitet Strom besonders gut.** Metal is a good conductor of electricity.

der **Leiter** (PL die **Leiter**) NOUN
▷ *see also* **die Leiter** NOUN
head
□ der Leiter des Museums the head of the museum

die **Leiter** NOUN
▷ *see also* **der Leiter** NOUN
ladder
□ eine Leiter hinaufklettern to climb a ladder

die **Leitung** NOUN
1 management
□ Ihr wurde die Leitung der Abteilung übertragen. She was entrusted with the management of the department.
2 direction
□ der Jugendchor unter Leitung von ... the youth choir under the direction of ...
3 pipe
□ In unserer Straße werden neue Leitungen für Wasser und Gas verlegt. They're laying new water and gas pipes in our road.
4 cable
□ Die Leitung steht unter Strom. The cable is live.
5 line
□ Alle Leitungen waren besetzt. All the lines were busy.
■ **eine lange Leitung haben** to be slow on the uptake

die **Lektion** NOUN
lesson

die **Lektüre** NOUN
1 reading
□ Stör sie nicht bei der Lektüre. Don't disturb her while she's reading.
2 reading matter
□ Das ist die richtige Lektüre für die Ferien. That's the right reading matter for the holidays.
3 set text
□ Welche Lektüre habt ihr dieses Jahr in Englisch? What are your set texts in English this year?

LANGUAGE TIP Be careful! **Lektüre** does not mean **lecture**.

lenken VERB [38]
to steer
□ ein Fahrzeug lenken to steer a car

das **Lenkrad** (PL die **Lenkräder**) NOUN
steering wheel

lernen VERB [38]
to learn

das **Lesebuch** (PL die **Lesebücher**) NOUN
reading book

lesen (PRESENT **liest**, IMPERFECT **las**, PERFECT **hat gelesen**) VERB [45]
to read

leserlich ADJECTIVE
legible
□ eine leserliche Handschrift legible handwriting □ leserlich schreiben to write legibly

das **Lesezeichen** (PL die **Lesezeichen**) NOUN
bookmark

letzte ADJECTIVE
1 last
□ In der letzten Arbeit habe ich eine Zwei geschrieben. I got a 'B' in the last test.
□ Ich habe noch einen letzten Wunsch. I have one last wish. □ letzte Woche last week □ zum letzten Mal for the last time
■ **als Letzter** last □ Franz kam als Letzter. Franz arrived last.
2 latest
□ Laut letzten Informationen kam es zu schweren Unruhen. According to latest reports there were serious riots.

letztens ADVERB
lately

leuchten VERB [2]
to shine
□ jemandem ins Gesicht leuchten to shine a light in somebody's face

der **Leuchter** (PL die **Leuchter**) NOUN
candlestick

der **Leuchtstift** (PL die **Leuchtstifte**) NOUN
highlighter

der **Leuchtturm** (PL die **Leuchttürme**) NOUN
lighthouse

die **Leute** PL NOUN
people

das **Lexikon** (PL die **Lexika**) NOUN
encyclopedia

das **Licht** (PL die **Lichter**) NOUN
light

das **Lichtjahr** (PL die **Lichtjahre**) NOUN
light year

das **Lid** (PL die **Lider**) NOUN
eyelid

der **Lidschatten** (PL die **Lidschatten**) NOUN
eyeshadow

lieb ADJECTIVE
dear
□ Liebe Bettina Dear Bettina □ Lieber Herr Schlüter Dear Mr Schlüter
■ **Das ist lieb von dir.** That's nice of you.
■ **jemanden lieb haben** to be fond of somebody

die **Liebe** NOUN
love

lieben VERB [38]
to love

liebenswürdig ADJECTIVE
kind

die **Liebenswürdigkeit** NOUN
kindness

German-English

L

lieber ADVERB
rather
□ Ich hätte jetzt lieber einen Kaffee. I'd rather have a coffee just now. □ Ich gehe lieber nicht. I'd rather not go.
■ **Lass das lieber!** I'd leave that if I were you.
■ **etwas lieber haben** to prefer something
□ Was hast du lieber, Mathe oder Chemie? What do you prefer, maths or chemistry?

der **Liebesbrief** (PL die **Liebesbriefe**) NOUN
love letter

die **Liebesgeschichte** NOUN
love story

der **Liebeskummer** NOUN
■ **Liebeskummer haben** to be lovesick

der **Liebesroman** (PL die **Liebesromane**) NOUN
romantic novel

liebevoll ADJECTIVE
loving

liebhaben VERB [32] ▷ *see* **lieb**

der **Liebling** (PL die **Lieblinge**) NOUN
darling

Lieblings- PREFIX
favourite
□ Was ist dein Lieblingsfach? What's your favourite subject?

liebste ADJECTIVE
favourite
□ Der Winter ist meine liebste Jahreszeit. Winter is my favourite season.
■ **am liebsten** best □ Am liebsten lese ich Kriminalromane. I like detective stories best.

das **Lied** (PL die **Lieder**) NOUN
song

lief VERB ▷ *see* **laufen**

liefern VERB [88]
1 to deliver
□ Wir liefern die Möbel ins Haus. We deliver the furniture to your door.
2 to supply
□ Das Kraftwerk liefert den Strom für die ganze Gegend. The power station supplies electricity to the whole area.
■ **den Beweis liefern** to produce proof

der **Lieferwagen** (PL die **Lieferwagen**) NOUN
van

liegen (IMPERFECT **lag**, PERFECT **hat gelegen**) VERB [46]
1 to lie
□ Sie lag auf dem Bett. She lay on the bed.
□ Wir haben den ganzen Tag am Strand gelegen. We lay on the beach all day. □ Auf meinem Schreibtisch liegt eine Menge Papier. There's a lot of paper lying on my desk.
■ **Es lag viel Schnee.** There was a lot of snow.
2 to be
□ Unser Haus liegt sehr zentral. Our house is very central. □ Ulm liegt an der Donau. Ulm is on the Danube.
■ **nach Süden liegen** to face south
■ **Mir liegt viel daran.** It matters a lot to me.
■ **Mir liegt nichts daran.** It doesn't matter to me.
■ **Es liegt bei dir, ob ...** It's up to you whether ...
■ **Sprachen liegen mir nicht.** Languages are not my thing.
■ **Woran liegt es?** How come?
■ **Das liegt am Wetter.** It's because of the weather.
■ **liegen bleiben** 1 to lie in □ Morgen ist Sonntag, da kann ich liegen bleiben. It's Sunday tomorrow, so I can lie in. 2 not to get up □ Der verletzte Spieler blieb liegen. The injured player didn't get up. 3 to be left behind □ Der Schirm ist liegen geblieben. The umbrella's been left behind.
■ **etwas liegen lassen** to leave something
□ Ich muss diese Arbeit liegen lassen. I'll have to leave this job. □ Ich habe meinen Schirm liegen lassen. I've left my umbrella.

der **Liegestuhl** (PL die **Liegestühle**) NOUN
deck chair

der **Liegewagen** (PL die **Liegewagen**) NOUN
couchette

der **Lift** (PL die **Lifte** *or* **Lifts**) NOUN
lift *(elevator)*

die **Liga** (PL die **Ligen**) NOUN
league

lila ADJECTIVE
purple
□ Sie hatte einen lila Hut auf. She was wearing a purple hat.

die **Limo** (PL die **Limos**) NOUN
lemonade

die **Limonade** NOUN
lemonade

das **Lineal** (PL die **Lineale**) NOUN
ruler
□ einen Strich mit dem Lineal ziehen to draw a line with a ruler

die **Linie** NOUN
line

die **Linke** (GEN der **Linken**) NOUN
▷ *see also* **linke** ADJECTIVE
1 left
□ Zu Ihrer Linken sehen Sie das Rathaus. On your left you'll see the town hall.
2 left hand
□ Er schlug mit der Linken zu. He hit out with his left hand.

linke ADJECTIVE
▷ *see also* **die Linke** NOUN, **links** ADVERB
left
□ In Großbritannien fährt man auf der linken Seite. In Great Britain they drive on the left.
□ Mein linkes Auge tut weh. My left eye's hurting. □ Er hat sich den linken Arm gebrochen. He broke his left arm.

links ADVERB
▷ *see also* **linke** ADJECTIVE
left
□ links abbiegen to turn left
■ **links überholen** to overtake on the left
■ **Er schreibt mit links.** He writes with his left hand.
■ **Links sehen Sie das Rathaus.** On the left you'll see the town hall.
■ **links von der Kirche** to the left of the church
■ **links von mir** on my left
■ **links wählen** to vote for a left-wing party
■ **etwas mit links machen** to do something easily

der **Linkshänder** (PL die **Linkshänder**) NOUN
■ **Er ist Linkshänder.** He's left-handed.

die **Linkshänderin** NOUN
■ **Sie ist Linkshänderin.** She's left-handed.

die **Linkskurve** NOUN
left-hand bend

der **Linksverkehr** NOUN
driving on the left
□ In Großbritannien ist Linksverkehr. They drive on the left in Britain.

die **Linse** NOUN
1 lentil
□ Linsensuppe lentil soup
2 lens
□ die Linse der Kamera the camera lens

die **Lippe** NOUN
lip

der **Lippenstift** (PL die **Lippenstifte**) NOUN
lipstick

die **Liste** NOUN
list

der **Liter** (PL die **Liter**) NOUN
LANGUAGE TIP You can also say **das Liter**.
litre

die **Literatur** NOUN
literature

die **Lizenz** NOUN
licence

der **Lkw** (GEN des **Lkw** *or* **Lkws**, PL die **Lkws**) NOUN (= *Lastkraftwagen*)
lorry

das **Lob** NOUN
praise

loben VERB [38]
to praise

das **Loch** (PL die **Löcher**) NOUN
hole

locker ADJECTIVE
1 loose
□ ein lockerer Zahn a loose tooth
2 relaxed
□ eine lockere Atmosphäre a relaxed atmosphere

lockerlassen (PRESENT **lässt locker**, IMPERFECT **ließ locker**, PERFECT **hat lockergelassen**) VERB [42]
■ **nicht lockerlassen** not to let up □ Er ließ nicht locker mit seinen Fragen. He didn't let up with his questions.

lockig ADJECTIVE
curly

der **Löffel** (PL die **Löffel**) NOUN
spoon
■ **ein Löffel Zucker** a spoonful of sugar

die **Logik** NOUN
logic

logisch ADJECTIVE
logical

der **Lohn** (PL die **Löhne**) NOUN
1 wages
□ Freitags wird der Lohn ausbezahlt. The wages are paid on Fridays.
2 reward
□ Das ist jetzt der Lohn für meine Mühe! That's the reward for my efforts.

lohnen VERB [38]
■ **Das lohnt sich.** It's worth it.
LANGUAGE TIP Word for word, **Das lohnt sich** means 'It rewards itself'.

lohnend ADJECTIVE
worthwhile

die **Lohnsteuer** NOUN
income tax

das **Lokal** (PL die **Lokale**) NOUN
pub

die **Lokomotive** NOUN
locomotive

das **Lorbeerblatt** (PL die **Lorbeerblätter**) NOUN
bay leaf

das **Los** (GEN des **Loses**, PL die **Lose**) NOUN
▷ *see also* **los** ADJECTIVE
lottery ticket
□ Mein Los hat gewonnen. My lottery ticket has won.

los ADJECTIVE
▷ *see also* **das Los** NOUN
loose
□ Die Schraube ist los. The screw's loose.
■ **Dort ist viel los.** There's a lot going on there.
■ **Dort ist nichts los.** There's nothing going on there.
■ **Was ist los?** What's the matter?
■ **Los!** Go on!

losbinden (IMPERFECT **band los**, PERFECT **hat losgebunden**) VERB
to untie

löschen VERB [48]
to put out
□ ein Feuer löschen to put out a fire
□ das Licht löschen to put out the light
■ **den Durst löschen** to quench one's thirst
■ **eine Datei löschen** to delete a file

die **Löschtaste** NOUN
delete key

lose ADJECTIVE
loose
□ lose Blätter loose sheets □ etwas lose verkaufen to sell something loose
■ **ein loses Mundwerk** a big mouth

lösen VERB [38]
1 to solve
□ ein Rätsel lösen to solve a puzzle
□ ein Problem lösen to solve a problem
2 to loosen
□ Kannst du diesen Knoten lösen? Can you loosen the knot?
■ **etwas von etwas lösen** to remove something from something □ Sie löste das Etikett vom Glas. She removed the label from the jar.
■ **sich lösen 1** to come loose
□ Eine Schraube hatte sich gelöst. A screw had come loose. **2** to dissolve □ Die Tablette löst sich in Wasser. The pill dissolves in water. **3** to resolve itself □ Das Problem hat sich inzwischen gelöst. The problem has resolved itself in the meantime.
■ **eine Fahrkarte lösen** to buy a ticket

losfahren (PRESENT **fährt los**, IMPERFECT **fuhr los**, PERFECT **ist losgefahren**) VERB [21]
to leave

loslassen (PRESENT **lässt los**, IMPERFECT **ließ los**, PERFECT **hat losgelassen**) VERB [42]
to let go of

loslaufen (PRESENT **läuft los**, IMPERFECT **lief los**, PERFECT **ist losgelaufen**) VERB [43]
to run off

löslich ADJECTIVE
soluble

die **Lösung** NOUN
solution
□ Weißt du die Lösung des Rätsels? Do you know the solution to the puzzle?

das **Lotto** (PL die **Lottos**) NOUN
National Lottery

die **Lottozahlen** FEM PL NOUN
winning lottery numbers

der **Löwe** (GEN des **Löwen**, PL die **Löwen**) NOUN
1 lion
2 Leo
□ Manfred ist Löwe. Manfred's Leo.

die **Lücke** NOUN
gap

die **Luft** (PL die **Lüfte**) NOUN
air
□ Ich brauche frische Luft. I need some fresh air.
■ **in der Luft liegen** to be in the air
■ **jemanden wie Luft behandeln** to ignore somebody

LANGUAGE TIP Word for word, **jemanden wie Luft behandeln** means 'to treat somebody like air'.

der **Luftballon** (PL die **Luftballons** *or* **Luftballone**) NOUN
balloon

der **Luftdruck** NOUN
atmospheric pressure

das **Luftkissenboot** (PL die **Luftkissenboote**) NOUN
hovercraft

die **Luftmatratze** NOUN
air bed

die **Luftpost** NOUN
airmail
□ per Luftpost by airmail

die **Luftverschmutzung** NOUN
air pollution

die **Lüge** NOUN
lie

lügen (IMPERFECT **log**, PERFECT **hat gelogen**) VERB [47]
to lie
□ Ich müsste lügen, wenn ... I would be lying if ...
■ **Er lügt ständig.** He's always telling lies.

der **Lügner** (PL die **Lügner**) NOUN
liar

die **Lunge** NOUN
lung

die **Lungenentzündung** NOUN
pneumonia

die **Lupe** NOUN
magnifying glass
■ **unter die Lupe nehmen** to scrutinize

die **Lust** NOUN
■ **Lust haben, etwas zu tun** to feel like doing something □ Hast du Lust, ins Kino zu gehen? Do you feel like going to the cinema?
■ **keine Lust haben, etwas zu tun** not to feel like doing something □ Sie hatte keine Lust, mit auf die Party zu kommen. She didn't feel like coming to the party.
■ **Lust auf etwas haben** to feel like something □ Ich habe Lust auf eine kalte Limonade. I feel like some cold lemonade.

lustig ADJECTIVE
funny
□ eine lustige Geschichte a funny story

lutschen VERB [48]
to suck
□ am Daumen lutschen to suck one's thumb

der **Lutscher** (PL die **Lutscher**) NOUN
lollipop

Luxemburg NEUT NOUN
Luxembourg
■ **aus Luxemburg** from Luxembourg
■ **nach Luxemburg** to Luxembourg

der **Luxus** (GEN des **Luxus**) NOUN
luxury

Mm

m ABBREVIATION *(= Meter)*
m

machen VERB [48]
1 to do
□ Hausaufgaben machen to do one's homework □ etwas sorgfältig machen to do something carefully □ Was machst du heute Nachmittag? What are you doing this afternoon?
■ **eine Prüfung machen** to sit an exam
■ **den Führerschein machen** to take driving lessons
2 to make
□ aus Holz gemacht made of wood □ Kaffee machen to make coffee □ einen Fehler machen to make a mistake □ Krach machen to make a noise □ jemanden traurig machen to make somebody sad □ Das macht müde. It makes you tired.
■ **Schluss machen** to finish
■ **ein Foto machen** to take a photo
3 to cause
□ Das hat mir viel Mühe gemacht. This caused me a lot of trouble. □ viel Arbeit machen to cause a lot of work
■ **Das macht die Kälte.** It's the cold that does that.
4 to be
□ Drei und fünf macht acht. Three and five is eight. □ Was macht das? How much is that? □ Das macht acht Euro. That's eight euros.
■ **Was macht die Arbeit?** How's the work going?
■ **Was macht dein Bruder?** How's your brother doing?
■ **Das macht nichts.** That doesn't matter.
■ **Die Kälte macht mir nichts.** I don't mind the cold.
■ **sich machen** to come on □ Eine Zwei in Physik, du machst dich! A 'B' in physics, you're coming on.
■ **sich nichts aus etwas machen** not to be very keen on something □ Ich mache mir nichts aus Süßigkeiten. I'm not very keen on sweets.
■ **Mach's gut!** Take care!
■ **Mach schon!** Come on!

die **Macht** (PL die **Mächte**) NOUN
power

das **Mädchen** (PL die **Mädchen**) NOUN
girl

der **Mädchenname** (GEN des **Mädchennamens**, PL die **Mädchennamen**) NOUN
maiden name

mag VERB ▷ *see* **mögen**

das **Magazin** NOUN
magazine
□ Ich habe das in einem Magazin gelesen. I read it in a magazine.

der **Magen** (PL die **Magen** *or* **Mägen**) NOUN
stomach

die **Magenschmerzen** MASC PL NOUN
stomachache
□ Ich habe Magenschmerzen. I've got a stomachache.

die **Magenverstimmung** NOUN
stomach upset

mager ADJECTIVE
1 lean
□ mageres Fleisch lean meat
2 thin
□ Sie ist furchtbar mager. She's terribly thin.

der **Magnet** (GEN des **Magnets** *or* **Magneten**, PL die **Magneten**) NOUN
magnet

magnetisch ADJECTIVE
magnetic

die **Mahlzeit** NOUN
meal
□ Wir essen drei Mahlzeiten am Tag. We eat three meals a day.

der **Mai** (GEN des **Mai** *or* **Mais**, PL die **Maie**) NOUN
May
□ im Mai in May □ am sechsten Mai on 6 May □ Ulm, den 6. Mai 2006 Ulm, 6 May 2006 □ Heute ist der sechste Mai. Today is the sixth of May.
■ **der Erste Mai** May Day

mailen VERB [38] (PERFECT **hat gemailt**)
to e-mail
□ Hast du es gemailt? Did you e-mail it?

die **Mailingliste** (PL die **Mailinglisten**) NOUN
mailing list

der **Mais** (GEN des **Maises**) NOUN
maize

die **Majonäse** NOUN
mayonnaise

das **Mal** (PL die **Male**) NOUN
▷ *see also* **mal** ADVERB
1 time
□ das fünfte Mal the fifth time □ zum ersten Mal for the first time □ Wie viele Male hast du es versucht? How many times have you tried?
2 mark
□ Sie hat ein rotes Mal im Gesicht. She has a red mark on her face.

mal ADVERB
▷ *see also* **das Mal** NOUN
times
□ zwei mal fünf two times five □ Wir haben sechsmal geklingelt. We rang six times.
■ **Warst du schon mal in Paris?** Have you ever been to Paris?

malen VERB [38]
to paint

der **Maler** (PL die **Maler**) NOUN
painter

malerisch ADJECTIVE
picturesque

das **Mallorca** NOUN
Majorca
■ **nach Mallorca** to Majorca

malnehmen (PRESENT **nimmt mal**, IMPERFECT **nahm mal**, PERFECT **hat malgenommen**) VERB [52]
to multiply

das **Malz** (GEN des **Malzes**) NOUN
malt

die **Mama** (PL die **Mamas**) NOUN
mum

man PRONOUN
you
□ Man kann nie wissen. You never know.
□ Wie schreibt man das? How do you spell that?
■ **man sagt, ...** they say ...
■ **Man hat mir gesagt ...** I was told that ...

der **Manager** (PL die **Manager**) NOUN
manager

manche PRONOUN
some
□ Manche Bücher sind langweilig. Some books are boring.

manchmal ADVERB
sometimes

die **Mandarine** NOUN
mandarin orange

die **Mandel** NOUN
1 almond
□ ein Kuchen mit Nüssen und Mandeln a cake with nuts and almonds
2 tonsil
□ Sie hat entzündete Mandeln. Her tonsils are inflamed.

der **Mangel** (PL die **Mängel**) NOUN
1 lack
□ Schlafmangel lack of sleep
2 shortage
□ Der Mangel an Arbeitsplätzen führt zu immer größerer Arbeitslosigkeit. The shortage of jobs is causing rising unemployment.
3 fault
□ Das Gerät weist mehrere Mängel auf. The appliance has several faults.

mangelhaft ADJECTIVE
1 poor
□ Er hat mangelhaft bekommen. He got a poor mark.

DID YOU KNOW...?
German marks range from one (**sehr gut**) to six (**ungenügend**).

2 faulty
□ Mangelhafte Waren kann man zurückgehen lassen. You can return faulty goods.

mangels PREPOSITION

LANGUAGE TIP The preposition **mangels** takes the genitive.

for lack of
□ Er wurde mangels Beweisen freigesprochen. He was acquitted for lack of evidence.

die **Manieren** PL NOUN
manners
□ Sie hat keine Manieren. She doesn't have any manners.

der **Mann** (PL die **Männer**) NOUN
1 man
□ Es war ein Mann am Telefon. There was a man on the phone.
2 husband
□ Frau Maier kam mit ihrem Mann. Mrs Maier came with her husband.
■ **seinen Mann stehen** to hold one's own
■ **Alle Mann an Deck!** All hands on deck!

männlich ADJECTIVE
1 male
□ meine männlichen Kollegen my male colleagues
■ **eine männliche Person** a man
2 masculine
□ ein männliches Substantiv a masculine noun

die **Mannschaft** NOUN
1 team
□ die deutsche Mannschaft the German team
2 crew
□ der Kapitän und seine Mannschaft the captain and his crew

der **Mantel** (PL die **Mäntel**) NOUN
coat
□ Er hatte einen Mantel an. He was wearing a coat.

die **Mappe** NOUN
1 briefcase
2 folder

LANGUAGE TIP Be careful! **Mappe** does not mean **map**.

das **Märchen** (PL die **Märchen**) NOUN
fairy tale

die **Margarine** NOUN
margarine

die **Marine** NOUN
navy
□ Er ist bei der Marine. He's in the navy.

die **Marionette** NOUN
puppet

die **Marke** NOUN
1 brand
□ Für diese Marke sieht man in letzter Zeit viel Werbung. There's been a lot of advertising for this brand recently.
2 make
□ Welche Marke fährt dein Vater? What make of car does your father drive?
3 voucher
■ **eine Briefmarke** a postage stamp

die **Markenware** NOUN
branded goods

markieren (PERFECT **hat markiert**) VERB [76]
to mark
□ Sie hat die Stelle mit Leuchtstift markiert. She marked the place with a highlighter.

der **Markt** (PL die **Märkte**) NOUN
market

der **Marktplatz** (GEN des **Marktplatzes**, PL die **Marktplätze**) NOUN
market place

die **Marmelade** NOUN
jam
□ Erdbeermarmelade strawberry jam
■ **Orangenmarmelade** marmalade

der **Marmor** (PL die **Marmore**) NOUN
marble

der **März** (GEN des **März** *or* **Märzes**, PL die **Märze**) NOUN
March
□ im März in March □ am dritten März on the third of March □ Ulm, den 3. März 2008 Ulm, 3 March 2008 □ Heute ist der dritte März. Today is the third of March.

die **Masche** NOUN
1 mesh
□ Das Netz hatte feine Maschen. The net had a very fine mesh.
2 stitch
■ **Das ist die neueste Masche.** That's the latest thing.

die **Maschine** NOUN
1 machine
□ Werkzeug wird heutzutage von Maschinen hergestellt. Nowadays tools are manufactured by machines. □ Kannst du die schmutzige Wäsche bitte in die Maschine tun? Can you put the dirty washing in the machine?
2 engine
□ Dieses Motorrad hat eine starke Maschine. This motorbike has a powerful engine.
3 typewriter
□ Sie hat ihr Referat mit der Maschine geschrieben. She typed her assignment.
4 plane

das **Maschinengewehr** (PL die **Maschinengewehre**) NOUN
machine gun

die **Masern** PL NOUN
measles
□ Masern sind bei Erwachsenen ziemlich gefährlich. Measles is quite dangerous for adults.

die **Maske** NOUN
mask

sich **maskieren** (PERFECT **hat sich maskiert**) VERB [76]
1 to disguise oneself
□ Die Täter hatten sich maskiert. The culprits had disguised themselves.
2 to dress up
□ Als was wirst du dich maskieren? What are you dressing up as?
■ **Die Bankräuber waren maskiert.** The bank robbers were masked.

das **Maß** (GEN des **Maßes**, PL die **Maße**) NOUN
▷ *see also* **die Maß** NOUN
1 measure
□ In Deutschland werden metrische Maße verwendet. Metric measures are used in Germany.
■ **Wie sind die Maße des Zimmers?** What are the measurements of the room?
2 extent
□ Sie war zu einem hohen Maß selbst schuld. To a large extent she had only herself to blame.
■ **Maß halten** ▷ *see* **maßhalten**

die **Maß** (PL die **Maß**) NOUN
▷ *see also* **das Maß** NOUN
litre of beer

die **Massage** NOUN
massage

die **Masse** NOUN
mass

massenhaft ADJECTIVE
masses of
□ Du hast massenhaft Fehler gemacht. You've made masses of mistakes.

die **Massenmedien** NEUT PL NOUN
mass media

massieren (PERFECT **hat massiert**) VERB [76]
to massage
□ Kannst du mir bitte den Rücken massieren? Can you massage my back, please?

mäßig ADJECTIVE
moderate

die **Maßnahme** NOUN
step
□ Maßnahmen ergreifen to take steps

der **Maßstab** (PL die **Maßstäbe**) NOUN

1 standard
□ Dieses Gerät setzt neue Maßstäbe. This appliance sets new standards.
2 scale
□ In welchem Maßstab ist diese Karte? What's the scale of this map?

der **Mast** (PL die **Maste** *or* **Masten**) NOUN
1 mast
□ Am Mast hing die britische Fahne. The Union Jack was hanging from the mast.
2 pylon
□ Neben unserem Garten steht ein Hochspannungsmast. There's a high-tension pylon beside our garden.

das **Material** (PL die **Materialien**) NOUN
material
□ Aus welchem Material ist das gemacht? What material is it made of? □ Ich sammle Material für mein Referat. I'm collecting material for my assignment.

materialistisch ADJECTIVE
materialistic
□ materialistisch eingestellt sein to be materialistic

die **Mathe** NOUN
maths

die **Mathematik** NOUN
mathematics
□ Mathematik ist mein Lieblingsfach. Mathematics is my favourite subject.

mathematisch ADJECTIVE
mathematical

die **Matratze** NOUN
mattress

der **Matrose** (GEN des **Matrosen**, PL die **Matrosen**) NOUN
sailor

der **Matsch** NOUN
1 mud
□ Deine Schuhe sind voller Matsch. Your shoes are covered in mud.
2 slush

matschig ADJECTIVE
1 muddy
□ Nach dem Regen war der Weg sehr matschig. The path was very muddy after the rain.
2 slushy
□ Bei matschigem Schnee macht das Skifahren keinen Spaß. Skiing isn't fun when the snow is slushy.

matt ADJECTIVE
1 weak
□ Bei der Hitze fühle ich mich so matt. I feel so weak in this heat.
2 dull
□ Ihre Augen waren ganz matt. Her eyes were really dull.
3 matt
□ Möchten Sie die Abzüge Hochglanz oder matt? Would you like the prints glossy or matt?
4 mate
□ Schach und matt checkmate

die **Matte** NOUN
mat

die **Mauer** NOUN
wall

das **Maul** (PL die **Mäuler**) NOUN
mouth
□ Die Katze hatte einen Vogel im Maul. The cat had a bird in its mouth.
■ **Halt's Maul!** Shut your face!

der **Maulkorb** (PL die **Maulkörbe**) NOUN
muzzle

der **Maulwurf** (PL die **Maulwürfe**) NOUN
mole

der **Maurer** (PL die **Maurer**) NOUN
bricklayer

die **Maus** (PL die **Mäuse**) NOUN
mouse
□ Sie hat Angst vor Mäusen. She's afraid of mice. □ Du musst zweimal mit der Maus klicken. You have to click the mouse twice.

die **Mausefalle** NOUN
mousetrap

der **Mausklick** (PL die **Mausklicks**) NOUN
mouse click
■ **per Mausklick** by clicking the mouse

maximal ADJECTIVE, ADVERB
1 maximum
□ der maximale Betrag the maximum amount
2 at most
□ Wir können maximal eine Woche wegfahren. We can go away for a week at most.

die **Mayonnaise** NOUN
mayonnaise

der **Mechaniker** (PL die **Mechaniker**) NOUN
mechanic

mechanisch ADJECTIVE, ADVERB
1 mechanical
□ Das Gerät hat einen mechanischen Schaden. The appliance has a mechanical fault.
2 mechanically
□ etwas mechanisch tun to do something mechanically

meckern VERB [88]
to moan
□ Müsst ihr über alles meckern? Do you have to moan about everything?

das **Mecklenburg-Vorpommern** NOUN
Mecklenburg-Western Pomerania

DID YOU KNOW...?
Mecklenburg-Vorpommern is one of the 16 **Länder**. Its capital is Schwerin. It is Germany's most rural and thinly populated **Land**, and is becoming increasingly popular with tourists.

die **Medaille** NOUN
medal

die **Medien** PL NOUN
media

das **Medikament** (PL die **Medikamente**) NOUN
drug
□ verschreibungspflichtige Medikamente prescribed drugs

die **Medizin** NOUN
medicine

medizinisch ADJECTIVE
medical

das **Meer** (PL die **Meere**) NOUN
sea
□ Wir wohnen am Meer. We live by the sea.

der **Meeresspiegel** NOUN
sea level

der **Meerrettich** NOUN
horseradish

das **Meerschweinchen** (PL die **Meerschweinchen**) NOUN
guinea pig

das **Mehl** (PL die **Mehle**) NOUN
flour

mehr ADJECTIVE, ADVERB
more

mehrdeutig ADJECTIVE
ambiguous

mehrere ADJECTIVE
several

mehreres PRONOUN
several things

mehrfach ADJECTIVE, ADVERB
1 many
□ Das Gerät hat mehrfache Verwendungsmöglichkeiten. This gadget has many uses.
2 repeated
□ Es ist mir erst nach mehrfachen Versuchen gelungen. I only managed after repeated attempts. □ Ich habe mehrfach versucht, dich zu erreichen. I've tried repeatedly to get hold of you.

die **Mehrheit** NOUN
majority

mehrmalig ADJECTIVE
repeated

mehrmals ADVERB
repeatedly

die **Mehrwertsteuer** NOUN
value added tax

die **Mehrzahl** NOUN
1 majority
□ Die Mehrzahl der Schüler besitzt einen Computer. The majority of pupils have a computer.
2 plural
□ Wie heißt die Mehrzahl von 'woman'? What's the plural of 'woman'?

meiden (IMPERFECT **mied**, PERFECT **hat gemieden**) VERB
to avoid

mein ADJECTIVE, PRONOUN
1 my
□ Mein Englischlehrer ist nett. My English teacher's nice. □ Meine Mutter erlaubt es nicht. My mother won't allow it. □ Ich finde mein Buch nicht. I can't find my book.
2 mine
□ Das ist nicht mein Füller, meiner ist blau. That's not my pen, mine's blue. □ Seine Mutter heißt Anne, meine auch. His mother's called Anne, so's mine. □ Wenn dein Fahrrad kaputt ist, kannst du meins nehmen. If your bike's broken you can use mine.

meinen VERB [38]
1 to think
□ Ich meine, wir sollten jetzt gehen. I think we should go now. □ Was meint deine Mutter zu deinem Freund? What does your mother think about your boyfriend? □ Sollen wir sie zur Party einladen, was meinst du? Should we invite her to the party, what do you think?
2 to say
□ Unser Lehrer meint, wir sollten am Wochenende keine Aufgaben machen. Our teacher says that we shouldn't do any homework at the weekend.
3 to mean
□ Was meint er mit diesem Wort? What does he mean by this word? □ Ich verstehe nicht, was du meinst. I don't understand what you mean. □ So habe ich das nicht gemeint. I didn't mean it like that.
■ **Das will ich meinen!** I should think so.

meinetwegen ADVERB
1 for my sake
□ Ihr müsst meinetwegen nicht auf euren Urlaub verzichten. You don't have to do without your holiday for my sake.
2 on my account
□ Hat er sich meinetwegen so aufgeregt? Did he get so upset on my account?
3 as far as I'm concerned
□ Meinetwegen kannst du gehen. As far as I'm concerned you can go.
4 go ahead
□ Kann ich das machen? — Meinetwegen. Can I do that? — Go ahead.

die **Meinung** NOUN
opinion
□ Er hat mich nach meiner Meinung zu diesem Punkt gefragt. He asked for my opinion on this subject.
■ **meiner Meinung nach** in my opinion
□ Meiner Meinung nach sollten Kinder nicht so viel fernsehen. In my opinion children shouldn't watch so much television.
■ **Ganz meine Meinung!** I quite agree.
■ **jemandem die Meinung sagen** to give somebody a piece of one's mind

LANGUAGE TIP Be careful! **Meinung** does not mean **meaning**.

die **Meinungsumfrage** NOUN
opinion poll

meist ADVERB
usually
□ Samstags bin ich meist zu Hause. I'm usually at home on Saturdays.

meiste ADJECTIVE
most
□ Die meisten Bücher habe ich schon gelesen. I've already read most of the books. □ Hast du die Bücher alle gelesen? — Ja, die meisten. Have you read all the books? — Yes, most of them. □ Die meisten von euch kennen dieses Wort sicher. Most of you must know this word.
■ **am meisten 1** most □ Darüber hat sie sich am meisten aufgeregt. This upset her most. **2** the most □ Er hat am meisten gewonnen. He won the most.

meistens ADVERB
usually
□ Samstags bin ich meistens zu Hause. I'm usually at home on Saturdays.

der **Meister** (PL die **Meister**) NOUN
1 champion
□ Er ist deutscher Meister im Ringen. He's the German wrestling champion.
2 master craftsman
□ Der Meister bildet Lehrlinge aus. The master craftsman trains apprentices.

die **Meisterschaft** NOUN
championship
□ Wer hat die Meisterschaft gewonnen? Who won the championship?

melden (PERFECT **hat gemeldet**) VERB [54]
to report
□ Er meldete den Diebstahl bei der Polizei. He reported the theft to the police.
■ **sich melden 1** to answer *(phone)* □ Es meldet sich niemand. There's no answer. **2** to put one's hand up *(in school)*
■ **sich polizeilich melden** to register with the police

die **Melodie** NOUN
tune

die **Melone** NOUN
1 melon
2 bowler hat
□ Er trug eine Melone. He was wearing a bowler hat.

die **Menge** NOUN
1 quantity
□ etwas in großen Mengen bestellen to order a large quantity of something
2 crowd
□ Ich habe ihn in der Menge verloren. I lost him in the crowd.
■ **eine Menge** a lot of □ Du hast eine Menge Fehler gemacht. You've made a lot of mistakes. □ Hast du CDs? — Ja, eine Menge. Have you got any CDs? — Yes, lots.

der **Mensch** (GEN des **Menschen**, PL die **Menschen**) NOUN
human being
□ Es heißt, dass sich der Mensch durch die Sprache vom Tier unterscheidet. It's said that what distinguishes human beings from animals is language.
■ **Wie viele Menschen?** How many people?
■ **kein Mensch** nobody

der **Menschenverstand** NOUN
■ **gesunder Menschenverstand** common sense

die **Menschheit** NOUN
mankind

menschlich ADJECTIVE
human

das **Menü** (PL die **Menüs**) NOUN
set meal

merken VERB [38]
to notice
□ Hat sie gemerkt, dass ich gefehlt habe? Did she notice that I wasn't there? □ Ich habe den Fehler nicht gemerkt. I didn't notice the mistake.
■ **sich etwas merken** to remember something □ Dieses Wort kann ich mir nie merken. I can never remember that word.
■ **Das werd' ich mir merken!** I won't forget that in a hurry!

merkwürdig ADJECTIVE
odd
■ **sich merkwürdig benehmen** to behave strangely

die **Messe** NOUN
1 fair
□ Auf der Messe wurden die neuesten Modelle gezeigt. The latest models were shown at the fair.
2 mass
□ Sie geht jeden Sonntag zur Messe. She goes to mass every Sunday.

messen (PRESENT **misst**, IMPERFECT **maß**, PERFECT **hat gemessen**) VERB
to measure
□ Hast du die Länge gemessen? Have you measured the length?
■ **bei jemandem Fieber messen** to take somebody's temperature
■ **Mit ihm kannst du dich nicht messen.** You're no match for him.

das **Messer** (PL die **Messer**) NOUN
knife

das **Messgerät** (PL die **Messgeräte**) NOUN
gauge

das **Messing** NOUN
brass

das **Metall** (PL die **Metalle**) NOUN
metal

der **Meter** (PL die **Meter**) NOUN
metre

die **Methode** NOUN
method

der **Metzger** (PL die **Metzger**) NOUN
butcher
□ Er ist Metzger. **He's a butcher.** □ beim Metzger **at the butcher's**

die **Metzgerei** NOUN
butcher's

miauen VERB [7]
to miaow

mich PRONOUN

LANGUAGE TIP **mich** is the accusative of **ich**.

1 me
□ Er hat mich zu seiner Party eingeladen. **He's invited me to his party.**

2 myself
□ Ich sehe mich im Spiegel. **I can see myself in the mirror.**

die **Miene** NOUN
look
■ **eine finstere Miene machen** to look grim

mies ADJECTIVE
lousy
□ Mir geht's mies. **I feel lousy.**

die **Miete** NOUN
rent
■ **zur Miete wohnen** to live in rented accommodation

mieten VERB [2]
1 to rent

DID YOU KNOW...?
It is far more usual to live in rented accommodation in Germany than it is in Britain. Flats are mainly rented unfurnished.

□ Wir haben eine Ferienwohnung gemietet. **We've rented a holiday flat.**

2 to hire
□ Man kann am Flughafen ein Auto mieten. **You can hire a car at the airport.**

das **Mietshaus** (GEN des **Mietshauses**, PL die **Mietshäuser**) NOUN
block of rented flats

der **Mietvertrag** (PL die **Mietverträge**) NOUN
lease

der **Mietwagen** (PL die **Mietwagen**) NOUN
rental car

das **Mikrofon** (PL die **Mikrofone**) NOUN
microphone

das **Mikroskop** (PL die **Mikroskope**) NOUN
microscope

die **Mikrowelle** NOUN
microwave

die **Milch** NOUN
milk

mild ADJECTIVE
1 mild
□ eine milde Seife **a mild soap**
□ mildes Wetter **mild weather**

2 lenient
□ ein mildes Urteil **a lenient sentence**
□ ein milder Richter **a lenient judge**

das **Militär** NOUN
army
□ zum Militär gehen **to join the army**

militärisch ADJECTIVE
military

die **Milliarde** NOUN
billion

der **Millimeter** (PL die **Millimeter**) NOUN
millimetre

die **Million** NOUN
million

der **Millionär** (PL die **Millionäre**) NOUN
millionaire
□ Er ist Millionär. **He's a millionaire.**

die **Minderheit** NOUN
minority
□ in der Minderheit sein **to be in the minority**

minderjährig ADJECTIVE
underage
□ Sie ist noch minderjährig. **She's still underage.**

der/die **Minderjährige** (GEN des/der **Minderjährigen**, PL die **Minderjährigen**) NOUN
minor
□ Minderjährige dürfen keinen Alkohol kaufen. **Minors are not allowed to buy alcohol.**

minderwertig ADJECTIVE
inferior

das **Mindestalter** NOUN
minimum age

mindeste ADJECTIVE
■ **das Mindeste** the least □ Das ist das Mindeste, was du tun kannst. **That's the least you can do.**
■ **nicht im Mindesten** not in the least
□ Sie war nicht im Mindesten überrascht. **She wasn't in the least surprised.**
■ **zum Mindesten** at least □ Zum Mindesten hättest du ja anrufen können. **You could at least have phoned.**

mindestens ADVERB
at least

das **Mineral** (PL die **Minerale** *or* **Mineralien**) NOUN
mineral

das **Mineralwasser** (PL die **Mineralwasser**) NOUN
mineral water

der **Minister** (PL die **Minister**) NOUN
minister *(in government)*

das **Ministerium** (PL die **Ministerien**) NOUN
ministry

German-English

minus ADVERB
minus

die **Minute** NOUN
minute

mir PRONOUN
LANGUAGE TIP **mir** is the dative of **ich**.
1 me
□ Kannst du mir sagen, wie spät es ist? Can you tell me the time?
2 to me
□ Gib es mir! Give it to me.
■ **mir nichts, dir nichts** just like that
□ Sie war mir nichts, dir nichts verschwunden. She disappeared just like that.

mischen VERB [48]
to mix

die **Mischung** NOUN
mixture

miserabel ADJECTIVE
dreadful
□ Mir geht's miserabel. I feel dreadful.

missbilligen (PERFECT **hat missbilligt**) VERB [49]
to disapprove of

der **Missbrauch** NOUN
abuse

der **Misserfolg** (PL die **Misserfolge**) NOUN
failure

misshandeln (PERFECT **hat misshandelt**) VERB [88]
to ill-treat

missmutig ADJECTIVE
sullen

m

misstrauen (PERFECT **hat misstraut**) VERB [49]
▷ *see also* **das Misstrauen** NOUN
■ **jemandem misstrauen** to mistrust somebody

das **Misstrauen** NOUN
▷ *see also* **misstrauen** VERB
suspicion

misstrauisch ADJECTIVE
suspicious

das **Missverständnis** (GEN des **Missverständnisses**, PL die **Missverständnisse**) NOUN
misunderstanding

missverstehen (IMPERFECT **missverstand**, PERFECT **hat missverstanden**) VERB [72]
to misunderstand

der **Mist** NOUN
1 manure
□ Im Frühling werden die Felder mit Mist gedüngt. The fields are fertilized with manure in the spring.
2 rubbish
□ Warum isst du so einen Mist? Why do you eat such rubbish? □ Heute kommt wieder nur Mist im Fernsehen. There's nothing but rubbish on TV again today. □ Du redest Mist. You're talking rubbish.
■ **Mist!** Blast!
LANGUAGE TIP Be careful! The German word **Mist** does not mean **mist**.

die **Mistel** NOUN
mistletoe

mit PREPOSITION, ADVERB
LANGUAGE TIP The preposition **mit** takes the dative.
1 with
□ Er ist mit seiner Freundin gekommen. He came with his girlfriend. □ mit Filzstift geschrieben written with a felt-tip pen
2 by
□ mit dem Auto by car □ mit der Bahn by train □ mit dem Bus by bus
■ **mit zehn Jahren** at the age of ten
■ **Sie ist mit die Beste in ihrer Klasse.** She is one of the best in her class.
■ **Wollen Sie mit?** Do you want to come along?

der **Mitarbeiter** (PL die **Mitarbeiter**) NOUN
1 colleague
□ meine Mitarbeiter und ich my colleagues and I
2 collaborator
□ die Mitarbeiter an diesem Projekt the collaborators on this project
3 employee
□ Die Firma hat 500 Mitarbeiter. The company has 500 employees.

mitbringen (IMPERFECT **brachte mit**, PERFECT **hat mitgebracht**) VERB [13]
to bring along
□ Kann ich meine Freundin mitbringen? Can I bring my girlfriend along?

miteinander ADVERB
with each another

der **Mitesser** (PL die **Mitesser**) NOUN
blackhead

mitfahren (PRESENT **fährt mit**, IMPERFECT **fuhr mit**, PERFECT **ist mitgefahren**) VERB [21]
to come too
□ Wir fahren nach Berlin. Willst du mitfahren? We're going to Berlin. Do you want to come too?
■ **Ich fahre nicht mit.** I'm not going.
■ **Willst du mit uns im Auto mitfahren?** Do you want a lift in our car?

mitgeben (PRESENT **gibt mit**, IMPERFECT **gab mit**, PERFECT **hat mitgegeben**) VERB [28]
to give

das **Mitglied** (PL die **Mitglieder**) NOUN
member

die **Mitgliedschaft** NOUN
membership

mithelfen (PRESENT **hilft mit**, IMPERFECT **half mit**, PERFECT **hat mitgeholfen**) VERB [37]
to help

mitkommen (IMPERFECT **kam mit**, PERFECT **ist mitgekommen**) VERB [40]

1 to come along
□ Willst du nicht mitkommen? Wouldn't you like to come along?
2 to keep up
□ In Mathe komme ich nicht mit. I can't keep up in maths.

das **Mitleid** NOUN
1 sympathy
■ **Ich habe wirklich Mitleid mit dir.** I really sympathize with you.
2 pity
□ Er kennt kein Mitleid. He knows no pity.

mitmachen (PERFECT **hat mitgemacht**) VERB [48]
to join in

mitnehmen (PRESENT **nimmt mit**, IMPERFECT **nahm mit**, PERFECT **hat mitgenommen**) VERB [52]
1 to take
□ Kannst du den Brief zur Post mitnehmen? Can you take the letter to the post office?
□ Ich habe meine Freundin zur Party mitgenommen. I took my girlfriend to the party.
2 to take away
□ Die Polizei ist gekommen und hat ihn mitgenommen. The police came and took him away.
3 to affect
□ Die Scheidung ihrer Eltern hat sie sehr mitgenommen. Her parents' divorce really affected her.
■ **zum Mitnehmen** to take away

der **Mitschüler** (PL die **Mitschüler**) NOUN
schoolmate

die **Mitschülerin** NOUN
schoolmate

mitspielen VERB [4]
to join in
□ Willst du nicht mitspielen? Don't you want to join in?
■ **Wer hat bei dem Match mitgespielt?** Who played in the match?

der **Mittag** (PL die **Mittage**) NOUN
midday
□ gegen Mittag around midday
■ **zu Mittag essen** to have lunch
■ **heute Mittag** at lunchtime
■ **morgen Mittag** tomorrow lunchtime
■ **gestern Mittag** yesterday lunchtime

das **Mittagessen** (PL die **Mittagessen**) NOUN
lunch

mittags ADVERB
at lunchtime

die **Mittagspause** NOUN
lunch break

die **Mitte** NOUN
middle

mitteilen VERB [4]
■ **jemandem etwas mitteilen** to inform somebody of something

die **Mitteilung** NOUN
communication

das **Mittel** (PL die **Mittel**) NOUN
means
□ Wir werden jedes Mittel einsetzen, um die Genehmigung zu bekommen. We will use every means to gain approval. □ ein Mittel zum Zweck a means to an end
■ **ein Mittel gegen Husten** something for a cough
■ **ein Mittel gegen Flecken** a stain remover
■ **öffentliche Mittel** public funds

Mitteleuropa NEUT NOUN
Central Europe

mittelgroß ADJECTIVE
1 medium-sized
□ Bremen ist eine mittelgroße Stadt. Bremen is a medium-sized city.
2 of medium height
□ Christine ist mittelgroß. Christine is of medium height.

mittelmäßig ADJECTIVE
mediocre

das **Mittelmeer** NOUN
the Mediterranean

der **Mittelpunkt** (PL die **Mittelpunkte**) NOUN
centre

der **Mittelstürmer** (PL die **Mittelstürmer**) NOUN
centre-forward

mitten ADVERB
in the middle
□ mitten auf der Straße in the middle of the street □ mitten am Tag in the middle of the day □ mitten in der Nacht in the middle of the night

die **Mitternacht** NOUN
midnight
□ um Mitternacht at midnight

mittlere ADJECTIVE
1 middle
□ Das mittlere von den Fahrrädern ist meins. The bike in the middle is mine. □ Der mittlere Teil des Buches ist langweilig. The middle section of the book is boring.
2 average
□ Die mittleren Temperaturen liegen bei zwanzig Grad. The average temperature is twenty degrees.
■ **mittleren Alters** middle-aged □ eine Frau mittleren Alters a middle-aged woman
■ **mittlere Reife** O-levels

mittlerweile ADVERB
meanwhile

der **Mittwoch** (PL die **Mittwoche**) NOUN
Wednesday
□ am Mittwoch on Wednesday

mittwochs ADVERB
on Wednesdays

German-English

m

das **Mobbing** NOUN
workplace bullying

die **Möbel** NEUT PL NOUN
furniture

der **Möbelwagen** (PL die **Möbelwagen**) NOUN
removal van

das **Mobiltelefon** (PL die **Mobiltelefone**) NOUN
mobile phone

möblieren (PERFECT **hat möbliert**) VERB [76]
to furnish
□ Sie hat ihre Wohnung sehr geschmackvoll möbliert. She has furnished her flat very tastefully.
■ **möbliert wohnen** to live in furnished accommodation

möchte VERB ▷ *see* **mögen**

die **Mode** NOUN
fashion

das **Modell** (PL die **Modelle**) NOUN
model

modern ADJECTIVE
modern

modernisieren (PERFECT **hat modernisiert**) VERB [76]
to modernize

modisch ADJECTIVE
fashionable
□ Jane trägt sehr modische Kleidung. Jane wears very fashionable clothes.

mogeln VERB [88]
to cheat

mögen (PRESENT **mag**, IMPERFECT **mochte**, PERFECT **hat gemocht** *or* **mögen**) VERB [50]

LANGUAGE TIP The past participle **mögen** is used when **mögen** is a modal auxiliary.

to like
□ Ich mag Süßes. I like sweet things. □ Ich habe sie noch nie gemocht. I've never liked her.
■ **Ich möchte ...** I'd like ... □ Ich möchte ein Erdbeereis. I'd like a strawberry ice cream. □ Er möchte in die Stadt. He'd like to go into town. □ Möchtest du ...? Would you like ...?
■ **Ich möchte nicht, dass du ...** I wouldn't like you to ... □ Ich möchte nicht, dass du dich übergangen fühlst. I wouldn't like you to feel you were being ignored.
■ **Ich mag nicht mehr.** I've had enough.
■ **etwas tun mögen** to like to do something □ Magst du noch mit zu mir kommen? Would you like to come back to my place? □ Möchtest du etwas essen? Would you like something to eat?
■ **etwas nicht tun mögen** not to want to do something □ Sie mag nicht bleiben. She doesn't want to stay. □ Ich möchte nicht, dass du so spät nach Hause kommst. I don't want you coming home so late.

möglich ADJECTIVE
possible
□ Das ist gar nicht möglich! That's not possible.
□ so viel wie möglich as much as possible

möglicherweise ADVERB
possibly

die **Möglichkeit** NOUN
possibility
■ **nach Möglichkeit** if possible

möglichst ADVERB
as ...as possible
□ Komm möglichst bald. Come as soon as possible.

die **Möhre** NOUN
carrot

der **Moment** (PL die **Momente**) NOUN
moment
□ Wir müssen den richtigen Moment abwarten. We have to wait for the right moment.
■ **im Moment** at the moment
■ **Moment mal!** Just a moment.

momentan ADJECTIVE, ADVERB
1 momentary
□ Das ist nur eine momentane Schwäche. It's only a momentary weakness.
2 at the moment
□ Ich bin momentan sehr beschäftigt. I'm very busy at the moment.

die **Monarchie** NOUN
monarchy

der **Monat** (PL die **Monate**) NOUN
month

monatlich ADJECTIVE, ADVERB
monthly

die **Monatskarte** NOUN
monthly ticket

der **Mond** (PL die **Monde**) NOUN
moon

der **Montag** (PL die **Montage**) NOUN
Monday
□ am Montag on Monday

montags ADVERB
on Mondays

das **Moor** (PL die **Moore**) NOUN
moor

die **Moral** NOUN
1 morals
□ Sie hat keine Moral. She hasn't any morals.
2 moral
□ Und die Moral der Geschichte ist: ... And the moral of the story is: ...

moralisch ADJECTIVE
moral

der **Mord** (PL die **Morde**) NOUN
murder

der **Mörder** (PL die **Mörder**) NOUN
murderer

LANGUAGE TIP Be careful! **Mörder** does not mean **murder**.

die **Mörderin** NOUN
murderer

morgen ADVERB
▷ *see also* **der Morgen** NOUN
tomorrow
■ **morgen früh** tomorrow morning
■ **Bis morgen!** See you tomorrow!

der **Morgen** (PL die **Morgen**) NOUN
▷ *see also* **morgen** ADVERB
morning
□ Wir haben den ganzen Morgen Unterricht. We've got lessons all morning.
■ **Guten Morgen!** Good morning.

morgens ADVERB
in the morning
□ Morgens bin ich immer müde. I'm always tired in the morning.
■ **von morgens bis abends** from morning to night

morgig ADJECTIVE
tomorrow's
□ das morgige Fest tomorrow's party
■ **der morgige Tag** tomorrow

die **Mosel** NOUN
Moselle

das **Motiv** (PL die **Motive**) NOUN
motive
□ Was war sein Motiv? What was his motive?

motivieren (PERFECT **hat motiviert**) VERB [76]
to motivate

der **Motor** (PL die **Motoren**) NOUN
1 engine
□ Das Auto hat einen starken Motor. The car has a powerful engine.
2 motor
□ ein Außenbordmotor an outboard motor

das **Motorboot** (PL die **Motorboote**) NOUN
motorboat

das **Motorrad** (PL die **Motorräder**) NOUN
motorcycle

die **Möwe** NOUN
seagull

der **MP3-Spieler** (PL die **MP3-Spieler**) NOUN
MP3 player

die **Mücke** NOUN
midge

der **Mückenstich** (PL die **Mückenstiche**) NOUN
midge bite

müde ADJECTIVE
tired
□ Ich bin sehr müde. I'm very tired.

die **Müdigkeit** NOUN
tiredness

die **Mühe** NOUN
trouble
□ Das macht gar keine Mühe. That's no trouble.
■ **mit Müh und Not** with great difficulty
■ **sich Mühe geben** to go to a lot of trouble
□ Die Gastgeberin hat sich viele Mühe gegeben. The hostess went to a lot of trouble.
■ **sich mehr Mühe geben** to try harder

die **Mühle** NOUN
mill
□ In dieser Mühle wird Korn gemahlen. Corn is ground in this mill. □ Hast du eine Mühle, um den Kaffee zu mahlen? Do you have a coffee mill?

der **Müll** NOUN
refuse

die **Müllabfuhr** NOUN
1 disposal of rubbish
□ Die Gebühren für die Müllabfuhr sollen erhöht werden. The charges for the disposal of rubbish are to be increased.
2 dustmen
□ Morgen kommt die Müllabfuhr. The dustmen come tomorrow.

der **Mülleimer** (PL die **Mülleimer**) NOUN
rubbish bin

die **Mülltonne** NOUN
dustbin

multiplizieren (PERFECT **hat multipliziert**) VERB [76]
to multiply

der **Mumps** (GEN des **Mumps**) NOUN
mumps
□ Mumps ist sehr unangenehm. Mumps is very unpleasant.

München NEUT NOUN
Munich
■ **nach München** to Munich

der **Mund** (PL die **Münder**) NOUN
mouth
■ **Halt den Mund!** Shut up!

die **Mundharmonika** NOUN
mouth organ

mündlich ADJECTIVE
oral
□ eine mündliche Prüfung an oral exam

die **Munition** NOUN
ammunition

das **Münster** (PL die **Münster**) NOUN
cathedral

munter ADJECTIVE
lively

die **Münze** NOUN
coin

murmeln VERB [34]
to mumble
□ Er murmelte irgendwas vor sich hin. He mumbled something.

mürrisch ADJECTIVE
sullen

die **Muschel** NOUN
1 mussel
□ Ich esse gern Muscheln. I like mussels.
2 shell
□ Wir haben am Strand Muscheln gesammelt. We collected shells on the beach.

3 receiver
□ Du musst in die Muschel sprechen.
You have to speak into the receiver.

das **Museum** (PL die **Museen**) NOUN
museum

die **Musik** NOUN
music

musikalisch ADJECTIVE
musical
□ musikalisch begabt sein to be musically gifted

der **Musiker** (PL die **Musiker**) NOUN
musician

das **Musikinstrument** (PL die **Musikinstrumente**) NOUN
musical instrument

musizieren (PERFECT **hat musiziert**) VERB [76]
to make music

der **Muskel** (PL die **Muskeln**) NOUN
muscle

das **Müsli** (PL die **Müsli**) NOUN
muesli

müssen (PRESENT **muss**, IMPERFECT **musste**, PERFECT **hat gemusst** *or* **müssen**) VERB [51]

LANGUAGE TIP The past participle **müssen** is used when **müssen** is a modal auxiliary.

1 must
□ Ich muss es tun. I must do it.
2 to have to
□ Er hat gehen müssen. He had to go.
□ Ich musste es tun. I had to do it.
□ Er muss es nicht tun. He doesn't have to do it.
□ Muss ich? Do I have to?
■ **Muss das sein?** Is that really necessary?
■ **Es muss nicht wahr sein.** It needn't be true.
■ **Sie hätten ihn fragen müssen.** You should have asked him.
■ **Es muss geregnet haben.** It must have rained.
■ **Ich muss mal.** I need the loo.

das **Muster** (PL die **Muster**) NOUN
1 pattern
□ ein Kleid mit einem geometrischen Muster a dress with a geometric pattern
2 sample
□ Lass dir von dem Stoff doch ein Muster geben. Ask them to give you a sample of the material.

der **Mut** NOUN
courage
■ **Nur Mut!** Cheer up!
■ **jemandem Mut machen** to encourage somebody
■ **zu Mute** ▷ *see* **zumute**

mutig ADJECTIVE
courageous

die **Mutter (1)** (PL die **Mütter**) NOUN
mother
□ Meine Mutter erlaubt das nicht. My mother doesn't allow that.

die **Mutter (2)** (PL die **Muttern**) NOUN
nut
□ Hast du die Mutter zu dieser Schraube gesehen? Have you seen the nut for this bolt?

die **Muttersprache** NOUN
mother tongue

der **Muttertag** (PL die **Muttertage**) NOUN
Mother's Day

die **Mutti** (PL die **Muttis**) NOUN
mummy

die **Mütze** NOUN
cap

MwSt ABBREVIATION (= *Mehrwertsteuer*)
VAT (= *value added tax*)

Nn

na EXCLAMATION
well
□ Na, kommst du mit? Well, are you coming?
■ **Na gut.** Okay then.
■ **Na ja, ...** Well, ...

der **Nabel** (PL die **Nabel**) NOUN
navel

nach PREPOSITION, ADVERB
LANGUAGE TIP The preposition **nach** takes the dative.

1 to
□ nach Berlin to Berlin □ nach Italien to Italy
■ **nach Süden** south
■ **nach links** left
■ **nach rechts** right
■ **nach oben** up
■ **nach hinten** back

2 after
□ Ich fange nach Weihnachten damit an. I'll start on it after Christmas. □ die nächste Straße nach der Kreuzung the first street after the crossroads □ einer nach dem anderen one after the other □ Nach Ihnen! After you! □ Ihm nach! After him!

3 past
□ zehn nach drei ten past three

4 according to
□ Nach unserer Englischlehrerin wird das so geschrieben. According to our English teacher, that's how it's spelt.
■ **nach und nach** little by little
■ **nach wie vor** still

der **Nachbar** (GEN des **Nachbarn**, PL die **Nachbarn**) NOUN
neighbour

die **Nachbarin** NOUN
neighbour

die **Nachbarschaft** NOUN
neighbourhood

nachdem CONJUNCTION

1 after
□ Nachdem er gegangen war, haben wir Witze erzählt. After he left we told jokes.

2 since
□ Nachdem du sowieso zur Post gehst, könntest du mein Päckchen aufgeben? Since you're going to the post office anyway, could you post my parcel?
■ **je nachdem** it depends □ Du kommst doch auch mit? — Je nachdem. You're coming along too, aren't you? — It depends.
■ **je nachdem, ob** depending on whether □ Wir kommen mit dem Rad oder dem Auto, je nachdem, ob es regnet oder nicht. We'll be coming by bike or by car, depending on whether it rains or not.

nachdenken (IMPERFECT **dachte nach**, PERFECT **hat nachgedacht**) VERB [14]
■ **nachdenken über** to think about □ Ich habe über deine Frage nachgedacht. I've been thinking about your question.

nachdenklich ADJECTIVE
pensive

nacheinander ADVERB
one after the other

nachgeben (PRESENT **gibt nach**, IMPERFECT **gab nach**, PERFECT **hat nachgegeben**) VERB [28]

1 to give way
□ Das Brett hat nachgegeben. The plank gave way.

2 to give in
□ Ich werde nicht nachgeben. I won't give in.

nachgehen (IMPERFECT **ging nach**, PERFECT **ist nachgegangen**) VERB [29]
■ **jemandem nachgehen** to follow somebody
■ **einer Sache nachgehen** to look into something □ Wir werden Ihrer Beschwerde nachgehen. We will look into your complaint.
■ **Die Uhr geht nach.** The clock is slow.

nachgiebig ADJECTIVE
indulgent

nachher ADVERB
afterwards

die **Nachhilfestunde** NOUN
private lesson

der **Nachhilfeunterricht** NOUN
extra tuition

nachholen (PERFECT **hat nachgeholt**) VERB [4]

1 to catch up on
□ Weil er gefehlt hat, muss er jetzt viel nachholen. As he was absent, he's got a lot to catch up on.

2 to make up for
□ Wir konnten meinen Geburtstag nicht feiern, werden das aber nachholen.

We weren't able to celebrate my birthday, but we'll make up for it.
■ **eine Prüfung nachholen** to do an exam at a later date

nachkommen (IMPERFECT **kam nach**, PERFECT **ist nachgekommen**) VERB [40]
to come later
□ Wir gehen schon mal, du kannst ja später nachkommen. We'll go on and you can come later.
■ **einer Verpflichtung nachkommen** to fulfil an obligation

nachlassen (PRESENT **lässt nach**, IMPERFECT **ließ nach**, PERFECT **hat nachgelassen**) VERB [42]
1 to deteriorate
□ Seine Leistungen haben merklich nachgelassen. His marks have deteriorated considerably.
■ **Ihr Gedächtnis lässt nach.** Her memory is going.
■ **Er hat nachgelassen.** He's got worse.
2 to ease off
□ Die Schmerzen haben nachgelassen. The pain has eased off.
3 to die down
□ sobald der Sturm nachlässt as soon as the storm dies down

nachlässig ADJECTIVE
careless
■ **etwas nachlässig machen** to do something carelessly □ Sie macht ihre Hausaufgaben ziemlich nachlässig. She does her homework pretty carelessly.

nachlaufen (PRESENT **läuft nach**, IMPERFECT **lief nach**, PERFECT **ist nachgelaufen**) VERB [43]
■ **jemandem nachlaufen** to run after somebody □ Sie hat ihren Schirm vergessen, lauf ihr schnell nach. She's forgotten her umbrella. Quick, run after her.
to chase
□ Er läuft allen Mädchen nach. He chases all the girls.

nachmachen (PERFECT **hat nachgemacht**) VERB [4]
1 to copy
□ Macht alle meine Bewegungen nach. Copy all my movements.
2 to imitate
□ Sie kann unsere Mathelehrerin gut nachmachen. She's good at imitating our maths teacher.
3 to forge
□ ein Gemälde nachmachen to forge a painting
■ **Das ist nicht echt, sondern nachgemacht.** This isn't genuine, it's a fake.

der **Nachmittag** (PL die **Nachmittage**) NOUN
afternoon
□ am Nachmittag in the afternoon
■ **heute Nachmittag** this afternoon

nachmittags ADVERB
in the afternoon

der **Nachname** (GEN des **Nachnamens**, PL die **Nachnamen**) NOUN
surname
□ Wie heißt du mit Nachnamen? What's your surname?

nachprüfen (PERFECT **hat nachgeprüft**) VERB [4]
to check
□ nachprüfen, ob to check whether

die **Nachricht** NOUN
1 news
□ Wir haben noch keine Nachricht von ihr. We still haven't had any news of her.
■ **die Nachrichten** the news □ Was kommt in den Nachrichten? What's on the news?
2 message
□ Kannst du ihm eine Nachricht von mir übermitteln? Can you give him a message from me?

nachschlagen (PRESENT **schlägt nach**, IMPERFECT **schlug nach**, PERFECT **hat nachgeschlagen**) VERB [59]
to look up *(in dictionary)*

nachsehen (PRESENT **sieht nach**, IMPERFECT **sah nach**, PERFECT **hat nachgesehen**) VERB [64]
to check
□ Sieh mal nach, ob noch genügend Brot da ist. Check whether we've still got enough bread. □ Ich habe im Wörterbuch nachgesehen. I've checked in the dictionary.
□ Mein Vater sieht immer meine Englischaufgaben nach. My father always checks my English homework.
■ **jemandem etwas nachsehen** to forgive somebody something □ Den kleinen Fehler sollten wir ihm nachsehen. We ought to forgive him this little mistake.
■ **das Nachsehen haben** to come off worst

nachsenden (IMPERFECT **sendete** *or* **sandte nach**, PERFECT **hat nachgesendet** *or* **nachgesandt**) VERB
to send on
□ Ich habe ihr den Brief nachgesendet. I've sent the letter on to her.

nachsichtig ADJECTIVE
lenient

nachsitzen (IMPERFECT **saß nach**, PERFECT **hat nachgesessen**) VERB [68]
■ **nachsitzen müssen** to be kept in
□ Er musste nachsitzen, weil er seine Hausaufgaben vergessen hatte. He was kept in because he had forgotten to do his homework.

die **Nachspeise** NOUN
pudding
□ Was gibt's als Nachspeise? What's for pudding?

nächste ADJECTIVE
▷ *see also* **nahe**, **näher**

1 next
□ Wir nehmen den nächsten Zug. We'll take the next train. □ Beim nächsten Mal passt du besser auf. Be more careful next time. □ nächstes Jahr next year
■ **als Nächstes** next □ Was machen wir als Nächstes? What'll we do next?
■ **Der Nächste bitte!** Next, please!
2 nearest
□ Wo ist hier die nächste Post? Where's the nearest post office?

die **Nacht** (PL die **Nächte**) NOUN
night
■ **Gute Nacht!** Good night.

der **Nachteil** (PL die **Nachteile**) NOUN
disadvantage

das **Nachthemd** (PL die **Nachthemden**) NOUN
nightshirt

der **Nachtisch** NOUN
pudding
□ Was gibt's zum Nachtisch? What's for pudding?

der **Nachtklub** (PL die **Nachtklubs**) NOUN
night club

nachträglich ADJECTIVE, ADVERB
1 subsequent
□ eine nachträgliche Korrektur a subsequent correction
■ **nachträgliche Glückwünsche** belated best wishes
2 later
□ Nachträglich habe ich eingesehen, dass das ein Fehler war. I later realized that it was a mistake.

die **Nachtruhe** NOUN
sleep
□ Ich brauche meine Nachtruhe. I need my sleep.

nachts ADVERB
at night

der **Nacken** (PL die **Nacken**) NOUN
nape of the neck

nackt ADJECTIVE
naked
□ Er war nackt. He was naked.
■ **nackte Arme** bare arms
■ **nackte Tatsachen** plain facts

die **Nadel** NOUN
1 needle
□ Ich brauche Nadel und Faden. I need a needle and thread.
2 pin
□ Ich habe mich an der Nadel des Ansteckers gestochen. I've pricked myself on the pin of my badge.

der **Nagel** (PL die **Nägel**) NOUN
nail

die **Nagelfeile** NOUN
nailfile

der **Nagellack** (PL die **Nagellacke**) NOUN
nail varnish

nagelneu ADJECTIVE
brand-new

nagen VERB [38]
to gnaw
□ an etwas nagen to gnaw on something

nahe ADJECTIVE, ADVERB, PREPOSITION
▷ *see also* **näher, nächste** ADJECTIVE
1 near
□ in der nahen Zukunft in the near future
■ **nahe bei** near □ nahe bei der Kirche near the church
2 close
□ Der Bahnhof ist ganz nah. The station's quite close. □ nahe Verwandte close relatives □ nahe Freunde close friends □ Unser Haus ist nahe der Universität. Our house is close to the university. □ den Tränen nahe close to tears □ mit jemandem nah verwandt sein to be closely related to somebody
■ **der Nahe Osten** the Middle East
■ **Die Prüfungen rücken näher.** The exams are getting closer.
■ **nahe daran sein, etwas zu tun** to be close to doing something □ Ich war nahe daran aufzugeben. I was close to giving up.
■ **nahe liegend** ▷ *see* **naheliegend**

die **Nähe** NOUN
■ **in der Nähe** near □ Unsere Schule liegt in der Nähe des Bahnhofs. Our school is near the station. □ Ich wohne in der Nähe von Rostock. I live near Rostock.
■ **aus der Nähe** close up □ wenn man das aus der Nähe betrachtet if you look at it close up

nahelegen VERB [4]
■ **jemandem etwas nahelegen** to suggest something to somebody

naheliegend ADJECTIVE
obvious

nähen VERB [38]
to sew

näher ADJECTIVE, ADVERB
▷ *see also* **nahe, nächste**
nearer
□ Die Straßenbahnhaltestelle ist näher als die Bushaltestelle. The tram stop is nearer than the bus stop.
■ **Näheres** details □ Ich wüsste gern Näheres. I'd like to have more details.
■ **näher kommen** to get closer

sich **nähern** VERB [88]
to get closer
□ Wir näherten uns dem Bahnhof. We were approaching the station.

nahezu ADVERB
nearly

nahm VERB ▷ *see* **nehmen**

die **Nähmaschine** NOUN
sewing machine

die **Nähnadel** NOUN
needle

nahrhaft ADJECTIVE
nourishing

die **Nahrung** NOUN
food
□ feste Nahrung solid food

das **Nahrungsmittel** (PL die **Nahrungsmittel**) NOUN
foodstuffs

die **Naht** (PL die **Nähte**) NOUN
seam
□ Die Hose ist an der Naht geplatzt. The trousers have split along the seam.

der **Nahverkehr** NOUN
local traffic

der **Nahverkehrszug** (PL die **Nahverkehrszüge**) NOUN
local train

der **Name** (GEN des **Namens**, PL die **Namen**) NOUN
name
□ Mein Name ist ... My name is ...
■ **im Namen von** on behalf of

nämlich ADVERB
1 you see
□ Sie ist nämlich meine beste Freundin. You see, she's my best friend.
2 that is to say
□ Nächstes Jahr, nämlich im März ... Next year, that is to say in March ...

nannte VERB ▷ *see* **nennen**

nanu EXCLAMATION
well, well!

die **Narbe** NOUN
scar

die **Narkose** NOUN
anaesthetic

naschen VERB [48]
■ **Sie nascht gern.** She's got a sweet tooth.
■ **Wer hat von der Torte genascht?** Who's been at the cake?

die **Nase** NOUN
nose
□ Meine Nase blutet. My nose is bleeding.

das **Nasenbluten** NOUN
nosebleed
□ Ich hatte Nasenbluten. I had a nosebleed.

nass ADJECTIVE
wet
□ Nach dem Regen war die Wäsche noch nässer. After the rain, the washing was even wetter.

die **Nässe** NOUN
wetness

die **Nation** NOUN
nation

die **Nationalhymne** NOUN
national anthem

die **Nationalität** NOUN
nationality

die **Natur** NOUN
1 country
□ Wir gehen gern in der Natur spazieren. We like to go for a walk in the country.
2 constitution
□ Sie hat eine robuste Natur. She's got a strong constitution.

natürlich ADJECTIVE, ADVERB
1 natural
□ Das ist ihre natürliche Haarfarbe. That's her natural hair colour.
2 of course
□ Wir kommen natürlich. Of course we'll come. □ Sie hat das natürlich wieder vergessen. She's forgotten it again, of course.
□ Ja, natürlich! Yes, of course.

das **Naturschutzgebiet** (PL die **Naturschutzgebiete**) NOUN
nature reserve

der **Naturschutzpark** (PL die **Naturschutzparks**) NOUN
national park

die **Naturwissenschaft** NOUN
natural science

der **Naturwissenschaftler** (PL die **Naturwissenschaftler**) NOUN
scientist

der **Nebel** (PL die **Nebel**) NOUN
1 mist
2 fog

nebelig ADJECTIVE
1 misty
2 foggy

neben PREPOSITION
LANGUAGE TIP Use the accusative to express movement or a change of place. Use the dative when there is no change of place.
1 next to
□ Dein Rad steht neben meinem. Your bike's next to mine. □ Stell dein Rad neben meines. Put your bike next to mine.
2 apart from
LANGUAGE TIP **neben** takes the dative in this sense.
□ Neben den Sehenswürdigkeiten haben wir uns auch ein Theaterstück angesehen. Apart from the sights, we also saw a play.

nebenan ADVERB
next door

nebenbei ADVERB
1 at the same time
□ Ich kann nicht Hausaufgaben machen und nebenbei fernsehen. I can't do my homework and watch TV at the same time.
2 on the side
□ Sie hat nebenbei noch einen anderen Job. She has another job on the side.
■ **Sie sagte ganz nebenbei, dass sie nicht mitkommen wollte.** She mentioned quite

casually that she didn't want to come along.
■ **Nebenbei bemerkt, ...** Incidentally, ...

nebeneinander ADVERB
side by side

das **Nebenfach** (PL die **Nebenfächer**) NOUN
subsidiary subject

der **Nebenfluss** (GEN des **Nebenflusses**, PL die **Nebenflüsse**) NOUN
tributary

nebenher ADVERB
1 on the side
□ Er verdient nebenher noch Geld durch Zeitungaustragen. He also earns money on the side doing a paper round.
2 at the same time
□ Sie bügelt und sieht nebenher fern. She does the ironing and watches TV at the same time.
3 alongside
□ Wir sind mit dem Rad gefahren, der Hund lief nebenher. We rode our bikes and the dog ran alongside.

die **Nebenstraße** NOUN
side street

neblig ADJECTIVE
1 misty
2 foggy

nee ADVERB
no

der **Neffe** (GEN des **Neffen**, PL die **Neffen**) NOUN
nephew

negativ ADJECTIVE
▷ *see also* **das Negativ** NOUN
negative
□ HIV-negativ HIV-negative

das **Negativ** (PL die **Negative**) NOUN
▷ *see also* **negativ** ADJECTIVE
negative
□ Kann ich von den Bildern das Negativ haben? Can I have the negatives of these pictures?

nehmen (PRESENT **nimmt**, IMPERFECT **nahm**, PERFECT **hat genommen**) VERB [52]
to take
□ Sie nahm fünf Euro aus dem Geldbeutel. She took five euros out of her purse.
□ Wir nehmen besser den Bus in die Stadt. We'd better take the bus into town.
□ Hast du deine Medizin genommen? Have you taken your medicine? □ Nimm ihn nicht ernst! Don't take him seriously.
■ **Ich nehme ein Erdbeereis.** I'll have a strawberry ice cream.
■ **Nimm dir doch bitte!** Please help yourself.

der **Neid** NOUN
envy

neidisch ADJECTIVE
envious
□ Sie ist neidisch auf ihren Bruder. She's envious of her brother.

nein ADVERB
no
□ Hast du das gesehen? — Nein. Did you see that? — No, I didn't.
■ **Ich glaube nein.** I don't think so.

die **Nelke** NOUN
1 carnation
□ Er brachte mir einen Strauß Nelken. He brought me a bunch of carnations.
2 clove
□ Zum Glühwein braucht man Nelken. You need cloves to make mulled wine.

nennen (IMPERFECT **nannte**, PERFECT **hat genannt**) VERB
1 to call
□ Sie haben ihren Sohn Manfred genannt. They called their son Manfred. □ Die Band nennt sich 'Die Zerstörer'. The band call themselves 'The Destroyers'. □ Wie nennt man ...? What do you call ...?
2 to name
□ Kannst du mir einen Fluss in England nennen? Can you name a river in England?

das **Neonlicht** NOUN
neon light

die **Neonröhre** NOUN
strip light

der **Nerv** (PL die **Nerven**) NOUN
nerve
■ **jemandem auf die Nerven gehen** to get on somebody's nerves

der **Nervenzusammenbruch** (PL die **Nervenzusammenbrüche**) NOUN
nervous breakdown

nervös ADJECTIVE
nervous

die **Nervosität** NOUN
nervousness

das **Nest** (PL die **Nester**) NOUN
1 nest
□ Der Vogel hat ein Nest gebaut. The bird has built a nest.
2 dump
□ Wiblingen ist ein Nest. Wiblingen is a dump.

nett ADJECTIVE
1 lovely
□ Vielen Dank für den netten Abend. Thanks for a lovely evening.
2 nice
□ Wir haben uns nett unterhalten. We had a nice talk.
3 kind
□ Wären Sie vielleicht so nett, mir zu helfen? Would you be so kind as to help me?
□ Das war sehr nett von dir. That was very kind of you.

netto ADVERB
net
□ Sie verdient dreitausend Euro netto. She earns three thousand euros net.

German-English

das Netz (GEN des **Netzes**, PL die **Netze**) NOUN
1 net
□ Die Fischer werfen ihre Netze aus. The fishermen cast their nets. □ Der Ball ging ins Netz. The ball went into the net.
2 string bag
□ Sie packte die Einkäufe ins Netz. She packed her shopping into a string bag.
3 network
□ ein weitverzweigtes Netz an Rohren an extensive network of pipes □ einen Computer ans Netz anschließen to connect a computer to the network

neu ADJECTIVE
new
□ Ist der Pulli neu? Is that pullover new? □ Sie hat einen neuen Freund. She's got a new boyfriend. □ Ich bin neu hier. I'm new here.
■ **neue Sprachen** modern languages
■ **neueste** latest □ die neuesten Nachrichten the latest news
■ **seit Neuestem** recently
■ **neu schreiben** to rewrite
■ **Das ist mir neu!** That's news to me.

neuartig ADJECTIVE
new kind of
□ ein neuartiges Wörterbuch a new kind of dictionary

die Neugier NOUN
curiosity

neugierig ADJECTIVE
curious

die Neuheit NOUN
new product
□ Auf der Messe werden alle Neuheiten vorgestellt. All new products are presented at the trade fair.

die Neuigkeit NOUN
news
□ Gibt es irgendwelche Neuigkeiten? Is there any news?

das Neujahr NOUN
New Year

der Neujahrstag (PL die **Neujahrstage**) NOUN
New Year's Day

neulich ADVERB
the other day

neun NUMBER
nine

neunte ADJECTIVE
ninth
□ Heute ist der neunte Juni. Today is the ninth of June.

neunzehn NUMBER
nineteen

neunzig NUMBER
ninety

Neuseeland NEUT NOUN
New Zealand
■ **aus Neuseeland** from New Zealand
■ **nach Neuseeland** to New Zealand

der Neuseeländer (PL die **Neuseeländer**) NOUN
New Zealander

die Neuseeländerin NOUN
New Zealander

neutral ADJECTIVE
neutral

das Neutrum (PL die **Neutra** *or* **Neutren**) NOUN
neuter

nicht ADVERB
not
□ Ich bin nicht müde. I'm not tired. □ Er ist es nicht. It's not him. □ Es regnet nicht mehr. It's not raining any more.
■ **Er raucht nicht.** 1 He isn't smoking. 2 He doesn't smoke.
■ **Ich kann das nicht. — Ich auch nicht.** I can't do it. — Neither can I.
■ **Nicht!** Don't!
■ **Nicht berühren!** Do not touch!
■ **Du bist müde, nicht wahr?** You're tired, aren't you?
■ **Das ist schön, nicht wahr?** It's nice, isn't it?
■ **Was du nicht sagst!** You don't say!

die Nichte NOUN
niece

der Nichtraucher (PL die **Nichtraucher**) NOUN
nonsmoker

nichts PRONOUN
nothing
□ nichts zu verzollen nothing to declare
□ nichts Neues nothing new
■ **Ich habe nichts gesagt.** I didn't say anything.
■ **Nichts ist so wie früher.** Things aren't what they used to be.
■ **Das macht nichts.** It doesn't matter.
■ **für nichts und wieder nichts** for nothing

nicken VERB [48]
to nod

nie ADVERB
never
□ Das habe ich nie gesagt. I never said that.
□ Das werde ich nie vergessen. I'll never forget that. □ Das habe ich noch nie gehört. I've never heard that. □ Ich war noch nie in Indien. I've never been to India.
■ **nie wieder** never again □ Tu das nie wieder. Don't ever do that again.
■ **nie mehr** never again □ Sie hat nie mehr geschrieben. She never wrote to me again.
■ **nie und nimmer** no way □ Das kann nie und nimmer stimmen. There's no way that can be right.

nieder ADJECTIVE, ADVERB
1 low
□ ein niederer Rang a low rank

■ **ein niederer Beamter** a low-ranking government officer

2 base

□ niedere Instinkte base instincts

■ **Nieder mit ...!** Down with ...! □ Nieder mit dem Diktator! Down with the dictator!

niedergeschlagen ADJECTIVE

dejected

die **Niederlage** NOUN

defeat

die **Niederlande** NEUT PL NOUN

the Netherlands

■ **aus den Niederlanden** from the Netherlands

■ **in den Niederlanden** in the Netherlands

■ **in die Niederlande** to the Netherlands

der **Niederländer** (PL die **Niederländer**) NOUN

Dutchman

■ **Er ist Niederländer.** He's Dutch.

die **Niederländerin** NOUN

Dutchwoman

■ **Sie ist Niederländerin.** She's Dutch.

niederländisch ADJECTIVE

Dutch

Niedersachsen NEUT NOUN

Lower Saxony

DID YOU KNOW...?

Niedersachsen is one of the 16 **Länder**. Its capital is Hannover. Its most important industries are mining and car manufacturing (Volkswagen). The Hannover Industrial Fair is the largest in the world.

der **Niederschlag** (PL die **Niederschläge**) NOUN

precipitation

■ **heftige Niederschläge** heavy rain

■ **radioaktiver Niederschlag** radioactive fallout

niedlich ADJECTIVE

sweet

□ niedlich aussehen to look sweet

niedrig ADJECTIVE

1 low

□ Die Decke ist sehr niedrig. The ceiling is very low. □ niedrige Temperaturen low temperatures

2 shallow

□ Hier ist der Fluss niedriger. The river is shallower here.

3 base

□ niedrige Motive base motives

niemals ADVERB

never

niemand PRONOUN

1 nobody

□ Niemand hat mir Bescheid gesagt. Nobody told me.

2 not ... anybody

□ Ich habe niemanden gesehen. I haven't seen anybody. □ Sie hat mit niemandem darüber gesprochen. She hasn't mentioned it to anybody.

die **Niere** NOUN

kidney

nieseln VERB [88]

to drizzle

niesen VERB [38]

to sneeze

die **Niete** NOUN

1 stud

□ Jeans mit Nieten jeans with studs

2 blank

□ Ich habe eine Niete gezogen. I've drawn a blank.

■ **In Mathe ist er eine Niete.** He's useless at maths.

nimmt VERB ▷ *see* **nehmen**

nirgends ADVERB

1 nowhere

□ Nirgends sonst gibt es so schöne Blumen. Nowhere else will you find such beautiful flowers.

2 not ... anywhere

□ Hier gibt es nirgends ein Schwimmbad. There isn't a swimming pool anywhere here.

□ Ich habe ihn nirgends gesehen. I haven't seen him anywhere.

nirgendwo ADVERB ▷ *see* **nirgends**

das **Niveau** (PL die **Niveaus**) NOUN

level

noch ADVERB, CONJUNCTION

still

□ Ich habe noch Hunger. I'm still hungry.

□ Das kann noch passieren. That might still happen. □ Das ist noch besser. That's better still.

■ **Bleib doch noch ein bisschen!** Stay a bit longer.

■ **Das wirst du noch lernen.** You'll learn.

■ **Er wird noch kommen.** He'll come.

■ **heute noch** today

■ **noch am selben Tag** the very same day

■ **noch vor einer Woche** only a week ago

■ **Wer noch?** Who else? □ Wer war noch da? Who else was there?

■ **Was noch?** What else? □ Was will er noch? What else does he want?

■ **noch nicht** not yet □ Ich bin noch nicht fertig. I haven't finished yet.

■ **noch nie** never □ Ich war noch nie in Leeds. I've never been to Leeds.

■ **immer noch** still □ Du bist ja immer noch da! How come you're still here? □ Das Haus ist immer noch nicht fertig. The house still isn't finished.

■ **noch einmal** again

■ **noch dreimal** three more times

■ **noch einer** another one

■ **noch größer** even bigger

German-English

n

German-English

■ **Geld noch und noch** loads of money
■ **weder ... noch ...** neither ... nor ...

nochmals ADVERB
again

der **Nominativ** (PL die **Nominative**) NOUN
nominative

Nordamerika NEUT NOUN
North America

der **Norden** NOUN
north

Nordirland NEUT NOUN
Northern Ireland
■ **aus Nordirland** from Northern Ireland
■ **in Nordirland** in Northern Ireland
■ **nach Nordirland** to Northern Ireland

nördlich ADJECTIVE, PREPOSITION, ADVERB
northerly
□ Wir fuhren in nördlicher Richtung. We drove in a northerly direction.
■ **nördlich einer Sache** to the north of something □ Das Kraftwerk liegt nördlich der Stadt. The power station is to the north of the city.
■ **nördlich von** north of □ Düsseldorf liegt nördlich von Köln. Düsseldorf is north of Cologne.

der **Nordosten** NOUN
northeast

der **Nordpol** NOUN
North Pole
□ am Nordpol at the North Pole

Nordrhein-Westfalen NEUT NOUN
North Rhine-Westphalia

DID YOU KNOW...?
Nordrhein-Westfalen is one of the 16 **Länder**. Its capital is Düsseldorf. It is Germany's most densely populated state, and includes the Ruhr district.

die **Nordsee** NOUN
North Sea
□ Wir fahren an die Nordsee. We're going to the North Sea. □ Wir waren an der Nordsee. We've been to the North Sea.

der **Nordwesten** NOUN
northwest

die **Norm** NOUN
standard
□ Für die meisten technischen Geräte gibt es Normen. There are set standards for most technical equipment.

normal ADJECTIVE
normal

das **Normalbenzin** NOUN
regular petrol

normalerweise ADVERB
normally

Norwegen NEUT NOUN
Norway
■ **aus Norwegen** from Norway
■ **nach Norwegen** to Norway

der **Norweger** (PL die **Norweger**) NOUN
Norwegian

die **Norwegerin** NOUN
Norwegian

norwegisch ADJECTIVE
Norwegian

die **Not** NOUN
■ **zur Not** if necessary □ Zur Not kannst du ja später nachkommen. You can join us later if necessary.

der **Notausgang** (PL die **Notausgänge**) NOUN
emergency exit

die **Notbremse** NOUN
emergency brake

der **Notdienst** (PL die **Notdienste**) NOUN
emergency service

die **Note** NOUN
1 mark
□ Max hat gute Noten. Max has got good marks.
2 note
□ Welche Note hast du eben gespielt? What note did you just play?

der **Notfall** (PL die **Notfälle**) NOUN
emergency

notfalls ADVERB
if need be

notieren (PERFECT **hat notiert**) VERB [76]
to note down

nötig ADJECTIVE
necessary
□ wenn nötig if necessary
■ **etwas nötig haben** to need something

die **Notiz** NOUN
1 note
□ Sein Kalender ist voller Notizen. His diary is full of notes.
2 item
□ Das stand heute in einer kleinen Notiz in der Zeitung. There was a short item on it in the newspaper today.
■ **Notiz nehmen von** to take notice of
□ Er hat von mir überhaupt keine Notiz genommen. He didn't take any notice of me at all.

das **Notizbuch** (PL die **Notizbücher**) NOUN
notebook

notlanden (PERFECT **ist notgelandet**) VERB [54]
to make an emergency landing

der **Notruf** (PL die **Notrufe**) NOUN
emergency call

notwendig ADJECTIVE
necessary

der **November** (GEN des **November** *or* **Novembers**, PL die **November**) NOUN
November
□ im November in November □ am neunten November on the ninth of November

n

□ Freiburg, den 9. November 2008 Freiburg, 9 November 2008 □ Heute ist der neunte November. Today is the ninth of November.

Nr. ABBREVIATION *(= Nummer)*
No.

nüchtern ADJECTIVE
1 sober
□ Nach drei Gläsern Wein bist du nicht mehr nüchtern. After three glasses of wine you aren't sober any more. □ nüchterne Tatsachen sober facts
2 with an empty stomach
□ Kommen Sie nüchtern ins Krankenhaus. Come to the hospital with an empty stomach.
■ **auf nüchternen Magen** on an empty stomach
■ **eine Lage nüchtern betrachten** to look at a situation rationally

die **Nudel** NOUN
noodle
□ Es waren Nudeln in der Suppe. There were noodles in the soup.
■ **Nudeln** pasta □ Nudeln sind meine Lieblingsspeise. Pasta is my favourite food.

die **Null** NOUN
▷ *see also* **null** NUMBER
1 zero
□ Du musst zuerst eine Null wählen. You have to dial zero first.
2 nonentity
□ Er ist doch eine völlige Null. He's a complete nonentity.

null NUMBER
▷ *see also* **die Null** NOUN
1 nil
□ Sie haben eins zu null gespielt. They won one nil.
2 no
□ Ich hatte null Fehler. I had no mistakes.
■ **null Uhr** midnight
■ **null und nichtig** null and void

die **Nummer** NOUN
1 number
□ Ich kann seine Nummer auswendig. I know his number by heart.
2 size
□ Die Schuhe sind eine Nummer zu groß. These shoes are a size too big.

nummerieren (PERFECT **hat nummeriert**)
VERB [76]
to number

das **Nummernschild**
(PL die **Nummernschilder**) NOUN
number plate

nun ADVERB, EXCLAMATION
1 now
□ von nun an from now on
2 well
□ Nun, was gibt's Neues? Well, what's new?
■ **Das ist nun mal so.** That's the way it is.

nur ADVERB
only
□ Das hat nur zwanzig Euro gekostet. It only cost twenty euros. □ Es sind nur fünf Leute da gewesen. There were only five people there.
■ **Wo bleibt er nur?** Where on earth can he be?
■ **Was hat sie nur?** What on earth's wrong with her?

die **Nuss** (PL die **Nüsse**) NOUN
nut

der **Nutzen** NOUN
▷ *see also* **nutzen** VERB
■ **von Nutzen** useful □ Sprachkenntnisse sind immer von Nutzen. It's always useful to know a foreign language.
■ **Das ist zu deinem Nutzen.** It's for your own good.

nutzen VERB [36]
▷ *see also* **der Nutzen** NOUN
to help
□ Sprachkenntnisse können dir im Ausland viel nutzen. Knowing a language can help you a lot abroad.
■ **etwas nutzen** to make use of something
□ Du solltest die Zeit nutzen. You ought to make use of the time.
■ **Das nutzt ja doch nichts.** That's pointless.
■ **Es nutzt alles nichts, wir müssen ...** There's no getting around it, we'll have to ...

nützen VERB [36] ▷ *see* **nutzen**

nützlich ADJECTIVE
useful
□ sich nützlich machen to make oneself useful

nutzlos ADJECTIVE
useless

German-English

n

Oo

die **Oase** NOUN
oasis

ob CONJUNCTION
1 whether
□ Ich weiß nicht, ob ich kommen kann. I don't know whether I can come.
2 if
□ Sie fragt, ob du auch kommst. She wants to know if you're coming too.
■ **Ob das wohl wahr ist?** Can that be true?
■ **Und ob!** You bet!

obdachlos ADJECTIVE
homeless

oben ADVERB
on top
□ oben auf dem Schrank on top of the cupboard
■ **oben auf dem Berg** up on the mountain
■ **Die Schlafzimmer sind oben.** The bedrooms are upstairs.
■ **nach oben** up □ Der Fahrstuhl fährt nach oben. The lift is going up. □ Ich gehe nach oben in mein Zimmer. I'm going up to my room.
■ **von oben** down □ Der Fahrstuhl kommt von oben. The lift is going down. □ Bringst du mir von oben die Bettwäsche mit? Bring the bed clothes down with you.
■ **oben ohne** topless
■ **Befehl von oben** orders from above

der **Ober** (PL die **Ober**) NOUN
waiter
■ **Herr Ober!** Waiter!

obere ADJECTIVE
▷ *see also* **oberste** ADJECTIVE
upper
□ die oberen Stockwerke the upper floors
■ **die oberen Klassen** the senior classes

die **Oberfläche** NOUN
surface

das **Obergeschoss** (GEN des **Obergeschosses**, PL die **Obergeschosse**) NOUN
upper storey

der **Oberschenkel** (PL die **Oberschenkel**) NOUN
thigh

die **Oberschule** NOUN
grammar school

oberste ADJECTIVE
▷ *see also* **obere** ADJECTIVE
topmost
□ Das Buch steht auf dem obersten Regalbrett. The book is on the topmost shelf.
■ **Sie ist in der obersten Klasse.** She's in the top class.

die **Oberstufe** NOUN
upper school

das **Oberteil** (PL die **Oberteile**) NOUN
upper part

die **Oberweite** NOUN
bust measurement

obgleich CONJUNCTION
although
□ Obgleich sie müde war, blieb sie lange auf. Although she was tired, she stayed up late.

das **Objekt** (PL die **Objekte**) NOUN
object

das **Objektiv** (PL die **Objektive**) NOUN
▷ *see also* **objektiv** ADJECTIVE
lens *(of camera)*

objektiv ADJECTIVE
▷ *see also* **das Objektiv** NOUN
objective

das **Obst** NOUN
fruit

der **Obstkuchen** (PL die **Obstkuchen**) NOUN
fruit tart

obwohl CONJUNCTION
although
□ Obwohl sie müde war, blieb sie lange auf. Although she was tired, she stayed up late.

der **Ochse** (GEN des **Ochsen**, PL die **Ochsen**) NOUN
ox

öde ADJECTIVE
dull
□ eine öde Landschaft a dull landscape
■ **Diese Arbeit ist echt öde.** This job's really the pits.

oder CONJUNCTION
or
□ entweder ich oder du either me or you
■ **Das stimmt, oder?** That's right, isn't it?

der **Ofen** (PL die **Öfen**) NOUN
1 oven
□ Der Kuchen ist im Ofen. The cake's in the oven.

2 heater
■ **Mach bitte den Ofen an, mir ist kalt.** Put the fire on, I'm cold.

offen ADJECTIVE
open
□ Das Fenster ist offen. The window's open.
□ Die Banken sind bis sechzehn Uhr offen. The banks are open until four o'clock.
□ Sie ist ein sehr offener Mensch. She's a very open person.
■ **offen gesagt** to be honest
■ **Ich gebe dir eine offene Antwort.** I'll be frank with you.
■ **eine offene Stelle** a vacancy

offenbleiben (IMPERFECT **blieb offen**, PERFECT **ist offengeblieben**) VERB [10]
to remain open
□ Diese Möglichkeit bleibt uns noch offen. This option remains open to us.

offensichtlich ADJECTIVE, ADVERB
1 obvious
□ ein offensichtlicher Fehler an obvious mistake
2 obviously
□ Er ist offensichtlich nicht zufrieden. He's obviously dissatisfied.

öffentlich ADJECTIVE
public
□ öffentliche Verkehrsmittel public transport

die **Öffentlichkeit** NOUN
public
□ Die Öffentlichkeit wurde nicht informiert. The public were not informed. □ in aller Öffentlichkeit in public

offiziell ADJECTIVE
official

der **Offizier** (PL die **Offiziere**) NOUN
officer

öffnen VERB [53]
to open
□ jemandem die Tür öffnen to open the door for somebody

der **Öffner** (PL die **Öffner**) NOUN
opener

die **Öffnung** NOUN
opening

die **Öffnungszeiten** FEM PL NOUN
opening times

oft ADVERB
▷ *see also* **öfter** ADVERB
often
□ Wie oft warst du schon in London? How often have you been to London?

öfter ADVERB
▷ *see also* **oft** ADVERB
more often
□ Ich würde dich gern öfter besuchen. I would like to visit you more often.
■ **Sie war in letzter Zeit öfter krank.** She's been ill a lot recently.

öfters ADVERB
often

ohne PREPOSITION, CONJUNCTION

LANGUAGE TIP The preposition **ohne** takes the accusative.

without
□ Ich fahre ohne meine Eltern in Ferien. I'm going on holiday without my parents.
□ Ich habe das ohne Wörterbuch übersetzt. I translated it without a dictionary. □ Sie ist gegangen, ohne Bescheid zu sagen. She left without telling anyone. □ ohne zu fragen without asking
■ **Das ist nicht ohne.** It's not half bad.
■ **ohne weiteres** easily □ Das ist ohne weiteres in einer Woche zu schaffen. That can easily be done in a week.
■ **Du kannst doch nicht so ohne weiteres gehen.** You can't just leave.

ohnmächtig ADJECTIVE
■ **ohnmächtig werden** to faint
■ **Sie ist ohnmächtig.** She's fainted.

das **Ohr** (PL die **Ohren**) NOUN
ear
■ **Er hat sehr gute Ohren.** His hearing is very good.

die **Ohrenschmerzen** MASC PL NOUN
earache
□ Sie hat Ohrenschmerzen. She's got earache.

die **Ohrfeige** NOUN
slap across the face

ohrfeigen VERB [38]
■ **jemanden ohrfeigen** to slap somebody across the face

der **Ohrring** (PL die **Ohrringe**) NOUN
earring

ökologisch ADJECTIVE
ecological

der **Oktober** (GEN des **Oktober** *or* **Oktobers**, PL die **Oktober**) NOUN
October
□ im Oktober in October □ am dritten Oktober on the third of October □ Ulm, den 3. Oktober 2010 Ulm, 3 October 2010.
□ Heute ist der dritte Oktober. Today is the third of October.

das **Oktoberfest** (PL die **Oktoberfeste**) NOUN
Munich beer festival

das **Öl** (PL die **Öle**) NOUN
oil

die **Ölheizung** NOUN
oil-fired central heating

ölig ADJECTIVE
oily

oliv ADJECTIVE
olive-green

die **Olive** NOUN
olive

die **Ölsardine** NOUN
sardine

der **Ölwechsel** (PL die **Ölwechsel**) NOUN
oil change

die **Olympiade** NOUN
Olympic Games

der **Olympiasieger** (PL die **Olympiasieger**) NOUN
Olympic champion

die **Olympiasiegerin** NOUN
Olympic champion

olympisch ADJECTIVE
Olympic

die **Oma** (PL die **Omas**) NOUN
granny

das **Omelett** (PL die **Omeletts**) NOUN
omelette

der **Onkel** (PL die **Onkel**) NOUN
uncle

online ADVERB
on line

der **Opa** (PL die **Opas**) NOUN
grandpa

die **Oper** NOUN
1 opera
□ eine Oper von Verdi an opera by Verdi
2 opera house
□ Die Mailänder Oper ist berühmt. The Milan opera house is famous.

die **Operation** NOUN
operation

der **Operationssaal** (PL die **Operationssäle**) NOUN
operating theatre

die **Operette** NOUN
operetta

operieren (PERFECT **hat operiert**) VERB [76]
to operate on
□ jemanden operieren to operate on somebody
■ **Sie muss operiert werden.** She has to have an operation.
■ **Sie wurde am Auge operiert.** She had an eye operation.

das **Opfer** (PL die **Opfer**) NOUN
1 sacrifice
□ Das war ein großes Opfer für ihn. It was a great sacrifice for him.
2 victim
□ Der Unfall hat viele Opfer gefordert. The accident claimed a lot of victims.

die **Opposition** NOUN
opposition

die **Optik** NOUN
optics

der **Optiker** (PL die **Optiker**) NOUN
optician

optimal ADJECTIVE, ADVERB
optimum
□ Das ist die optimale Lösung. That's the optimum solution.
■ **Sie hat das optimal gelöst.** She solved it in the best possible way.
■ **Wir haben den Platz optimal genutzt.** We made the best possible use of the space available.

der **Optimismus** (GEN des **Optimismus**) NOUN
optimism

der **Optimist** (GEN des **Optimisten**, PL die **Optimisten**) NOUN
optimist

optimistisch ADJECTIVE
optimistic

die **Orange** NOUN
▷ *see also* **orange** ADJECTIVE
orange

orange ADJECTIVE
▷ *see also* **die Orange** NOUN
orange

der **Orangensaft** (PL die **Orangensäfte**) NOUN
orange juice

das **Orchester** (PL die **Orchester**) NOUN
orchestra

ordentlich ADJECTIVE, ADVERB
1 tidy
□ Seine Wohnung ist sehr ordentlich. His flat's very tidy. □ Ich bin ein ordentlicher Mensch. I'm a tidy person.
2 decent
□ Das sind ordentliche Leute. They're decent people. □ Das ist doch kein ordentliches Gehalt. That's not a decent wage. □ eine ordentliche Portion a decent portion
■ **Ich brauche jetzt etwas Ordentliches zu essen.** Now I need a decent meal.
3 respectable
□ Das ist eine ordentliche Leistung. That's a respectable achievement. □ Du solltest dir einen ordentlichen Beruf aussuchen. You ought to look for a respectable job.
4 neatly
□ Du solltest ordentlicher schreiben. You should write more neatly.
5 properly
□ Kannst du dich nicht ordentlich benehmen? Can't you behave properly?
■ **Es hat ordentlich geschneit.** There's been a fair bit of snow.
■ **Sie haben ihn ordentlich verprügelt.** They beat him up good and proper.

ordinär ADJECTIVE
vulgar
■ **sich ordinär ausdrücken** to use vulgar expressions

ordnen VERB [53]
to put in order

der **Ordner** (PL die **Ordner**) NOUN
file

die **Ordnung** NOUN
order
□ Ruhe und Ordnung law and order
■ **Sie liebt Ordnung.** She likes everything to be in its place.
■ **Das hat schon alles seine Ordnung.** Everything is as it should be.
■ **Ordnung machen** to tidy up □ Du solltest in deinem Zimmer Ordnung machen. You should tidy up your room.
■ **Mit meinem Auto ist etwas nicht in Ordnung.** Something's wrong with my car.
■ **etwas wieder in Ordnung bringen** to repair something □ Er hat das defekte Gerät wieder in Ordnung gebracht. He repaired the faulty appliance.
■ **Ist alles in Ordnung?** Is everything okay?
■ **In Ordnung!** Okay!

das **Organ** (PL die **Organe**) NOUN
organ
□ die inneren Organe internal organs
■ **Er hat ein lautes Organ.** He's got a loud voice.

die **Organisation** NOUN
organization

organisch ADJECTIVE
organic

organisieren (PERFECT **hat organisiert**) VERB [76]
to organize
□ Wer hat das Fest organisiert? Who organized the party?

die **Orgel** NOUN
organ
□ Sie spielt Orgel. She plays the organ.

der **Orient** NOUN
Orient

orientalisch ADJECTIVE
oriental

sich **orientieren** (PERFECT **hat sich orientiert**) VERB [76]
1 to find one's way around
□ Ich brauche einen Stadtplan, um mich besser orientieren zu können. I need a city map to be able to find my way around better.
2 to find out
□ Ich muss mich orientieren, wie das gehandhabt wird. I'll have to find out what the procedure is.

originell ADJECTIVE
original
□ ein origineller Einfall an original idea

der **Orkan** (PL die **Orkane**) NOUN
hurricane

der **Ort** (PL die **Orte**) NOUN
place
■ **an Ort und Stelle** on the spot

die **Orthografie** NOUN
spelling

örtlich ADJECTIVE
local

das **Ortsgespräch** (PL die **Ortsgespräche**) NOUN
local phone call

der **Osten** NOUN
east

das **Osterei** (PL die **Ostereier**) NOUN
Easter egg

die **Osterferien** PL NOUN
Easter holidays

das **Ostern** (PL die **Ostern**) NOUN
Easter
□ an Ostern at Easter

Österreich NEUT NOUN
Austria

DID YOU KNOW...?
Austria borders on Germany, the Czech Republic, Slovakia, Hungary, Slovenia, Italy and Switzerland. Its capital is Vienna.

■ **aus Österreich** from Austria
■ **in Österreich** in Austria
■ **nach Österreich** to Austria

der **Österreicher** (PL die **Österreicher**) NOUN
Austrian

die **Österreicherin** NOUN
Austrian

österreichisch ADJECTIVE
Austrian

DID YOU KNOW...?
People in Austria speak a dialect of German.

östlich ADJECTIVE, PREPOSITION, ADVERB
easterly
□ Wir fuhren in östlicher Richtung. We drove in an easterly direction.
■ **östlich einer Sache** to the east of something □ Das Kraftwerk liegt östlich der Stadt. The power station is to the east of the city.
■ **östlich von** east of □ Jena liegt östlich von Erfurt. Jena is east of Erfurt.

die **Ostsee** NOUN
Baltic
□ Wir fahren an die Ostsee. We're going to the Baltic. □ Wir waren an der Ostsee. We've been to the Baltic.

oval ADJECTIVE
oval

der **Ozean** (PL die **Ozeane**) NOUN
ocean

das **Ozon** NOUN
ozone

das **Ozonloch** (PL die **Ozonlöcher**) NOUN
ozone hole

die **Ozonschicht** NOUN
ozone layer

German-English

O

Pp

das **Paar** (PL die **Paare**) NOUN

1 pair

□ Ich habe ein Paar Schuhe gekauft. I've bought a pair of shoes.

2 couple

□ Sie sind ein sehr glückliches Paar. They're a very happy couple.

■ **ein paar** a few

paarmal ADVERB

■ **ein paarmal** a few times

das **Päckchen** (PL die **Päckchen**) NOUN

1 small parcel

□ Wie viel kostet ein Päckchen ins Ausland? How much does it cost to post a small parcel abroad?

2 packet

□ Sie raucht ein Päckchen pro Tag. She smokes a packet a day.

packen VERB [38]

1 to pack

□ Hast du deinen Koffer schon gepackt? Have you already packed your suitcase?

2 to grasp

□ Sie packte mich am Arm. She grasped my arm.

■ **Er hat die Prüfung nicht gepackt.** He didn't manage to get through the exam.

das **Packpapier** NOUN

brown paper

die **Packung** NOUN

1 packet

□ eine Packung Tee a packet of tea □ eine Packung Zigaretten a packet of cigarettes

2 box

□ eine Packung Pralinen a box of chocolates

das **Paket** (PL die **Pakete**) NOUN

1 packet

□ Ich habe ein Paket Waschpulver gekauft. I bought a packet of washing powder.

2 parcel

□ Die Gebühren für Pakete stehen in dieser Liste. Parcel rates are in this list.

die **Paketannahme** NOUN

parcels office

der **Palast** (PL die **Paläste**) NOUN

palace

die **Palme** NOUN

palm tree

die **Pampelmuse** NOUN

grapefruit

die **Panik** NOUN

panic

panisch ADJECTIVE

■ **panische Angst vor etwas haben** to be terrified of something

■ **panisch reagieren** to panic

die **Panne** NOUN

1 breakdown

□ Wir hatten eine Panne auf der Autobahn. We had a breakdown on the motorway.

2 slip

□ Mir ist da eine kleine Panne passiert. I made a slight slip.

der **Panzer** (PL die **Panzer**) NOUN

1 tank

□ Die Armee setzte Panzer ein. The army used tanks.

2 shell

□ der Panzer einer Schildkröte a tortoise's shell

der **Papa** (PL die **Papas**) NOUN

daddy

der **Papagei** (PL die **Papageien**) NOUN

parrot

das **Papier** (PL die **Papiere**) NOUN

paper

der **Papierkorb** (PL die **Papierkörbe**) NOUN

wastepaper basket

die **Papiertüte** NOUN

paper bag

die **Pappe** NOUN

cardboard

der **Paprika** (PL die **Paprikas**) NOUN

1 paprika

□ Ich habe das Hähnchen mit Paprika gewürzt. I've seasoned the chicken with paprika.

2 pepper

□ Heute gibt es gefüllte Paprikas. We're having stuffed peppers today.

der **Papst** (PL die **Päpste**) NOUN

pope

das **Paradies** (GEN des **Paradieses**, PL die **Paradiese**) NOUN

paradise

parallel ADJECTIVE

parallel

die **Parallele** NOUN
parallel

das **Pärchen** (PL die **Pärchen**) NOUN
couple
□ Auf der Parkbank saß ein Pärchen. There was a couple sitting on the bench in the park.

das **Parfüm** (PL die **Parfüms** *or* **Parfüme**) NOUN
perfume

der **Pariser** (PL die **Pariser**) NOUN
1 Parisian
2 condom
□ Auf den meisten Toiletten gibt es Automaten mit Parisern. Most toilets have condom machines.

die **Pariserin** NOUN
Parisian

der **Park** (PL die **Parks**) NOUN
park

die **Parkanlage** NOUN
park

parken VERB [38]
to park

das **Parkett** (PL die **Parkette** *or* **Parketts**) NOUN
stalls *(theatre)*

das **Parkhaus** (GEN des **Parkhauses**, PL die **Parkhäuser**) NOUN
multistorey car park

die **Parklücke** NOUN
parking space

der **Parkplatz** (GEN des **Parkplatzes**, PL die **Parkplätze**) NOUN
car park

die **Parkscheibe** NOUN
parking disc

der **Parkschein** NOUN
car-park ticket

die **Parkuhr** NOUN
parking meter

das **Parkverbot** (PL die **Parkverbote**) NOUN
■ **Hier ist Parkverbot.** You're not allowed to park here.

das **Parlament** (PL die **Parlamente**) NOUN
parliament

die **Partei** NOUN
party *(political)*
■ **Partei für jemanden ergreifen** to take somebody's side

parteiisch ADJECTIVE
biased

das **Parterre** (PL die **Parterres**) NOUN
1 ground floor
□ Wir wohnen im Parterre. We live on the ground floor.
2 stalls *(theatre)*

der **Partner** (PL die **Partner**) NOUN
partner

die **Partnerin** NOUN
partner

die **Partnerstadt** (PL die **Partnerstädte**) NOUN
twin town

die **Party** (PL die **Partys**) NOUN
party
□ eine Party veranstalten to have a party

der **Pass** (GEN des **Passes**, PL die **Pässe**) NOUN
1 passport
□ Für Indien brauchst du einen Pass. You need a passport for India.
2 pass
□ Im Winter ist der Pass gesperrt. The pass is closed in winter.

die **Passage** NOUN
passage
■ **eine Einkaufspassage** a shopping arcade

der **Passagier** (PL die **Passagiere**) NOUN
passenger

passen VERB [31]
1 to fit
□ Die Hose passt nicht. The trousers don't fit.
□ Es ist zu groß und passt nicht in meinen Koffer. It's too big and doesn't fit in my suitcase.
2 to suit
□ Passt dir Dienstag? Does Tuesday suit you?
□ Dieser Termin passt mir nicht. That date doesn't suit me.
■ **Es passt mir nicht, dass du so frech bist.** I don't like you being so cheeky.
■ **zu etwas passen** to go with something
□ Der Rock passt nicht zu deiner Bluse. The skirt doesn't go with your blouse.
■ **zu jemandem passen** to be right for somebody □ Er passt nicht zu dir. He's not right for you.
3 to pass
□ Auf die Frage muss ich passen. I'll have to pass on that question.

passend ADJECTIVE
1 matching
□ Ich muss jetzt dazu passende Schuhe kaufen. I now must buy some matching shoes.
2 appropriate
□ Sie hat ein paar passende Worte gesprochen. She said a few appropriate words.
3 convenient
□ Das ist nicht die passende Gelegenheit. This isn't a convenient time.

passieren (PERFECT **ist passiert**) VERB [76]
to happen
□ Was ist passiert? What happened? □ Mir ist etwas Lustiges passiert. Something funny happened to me.

das **Passiv** (PL die **Passive**) NOUN
▷ *see also* **passiv** ADJECTIVE
passive

passiv ADJECTIVE, ADVERB
▷ *see also* **das Passiv** NOUN
passive
□ passives Rauchen passive smoking
□ passiv zuschen to watch passively

das **Passivrauchen** NOUN
passive smoking

die **Passkontrolle** NOUN
passport control

das **Passwort** (PL die **Passwörter**) NOUN
password

die **Pastete** NOUN
pie *(savoury)*

der **Pate** (GEN des **Paten**, PL die **Paten**) NOUN
godfather

das **Patenkind** (PL die **Patenkinder**) NOUN
godchild

das **Patent** (PL die **Patente**) NOUN
patent

der **Patient** (GEN des **Patienten**, PL die **Patienten**) NOUN
patient

die **Patientin** NOUN
patient

die **Patin** NOUN
godmother

die **Patrone** NOUN
cartridge

pauken VERB [38]
1 to swot
□ Vor der Arbeit habe ich ziemlich gepaukt. I swotted quite a lot before the test.
2 to swot up
□ Ich muss Vokabeln pauken. I have to swot up my vocabulary.

die **Pauschalreise** NOUN
package tour

die **Pause** NOUN
1 break
□ eine Pause machen to have a break
□ die große Pause the long break
2 interval
□ In der Pause haben wir über das Stück gesprochen. We talked about the play during the interval.

der **Pazifik** NOUN
Pacific

das **Pech** NOUN
bad luck
□ Das war Pech! That was bad luck.
■ **Pech haben** to be unlucky
■ **Pech!** Hard luck!

das **Pedal** (PL die **Pedale**) NOUN
pedal

peinlich ADJECTIVE
1 embarrassing
□ eine peinliche Frage an embarrassing question
2 awkward
□ eine peinliche Angelegenheit an awkward situation
■ **Das ist mir aber peinlich.** I'm dreadfully sorry.
■ **peinlich genau** painstakingly □ Sie hat das peinlich genau überprüft. She checked it painstakingly.

die **Peitsche** NOUN
whip

die **Pelle** NOUN
skin

der **Pelz** (GEN des **Pelzes**, PL die **Pelze**) NOUN
fur

das **Pendel** (PL die **Pendel**) NOUN
pendulum

pendeln (PERFECT **ist gependelt**) VERB [34]
to commute
□ Er pendelt zwischen Tübingen und Stuttgart. He commutes between Tübingen and Stuttgart.

der **Pendelverkehr** NOUN
1 shuttle service
□ Die Fluggesellschaft hat einen Pendelverkehr zwischen Köln und Berlin eingerichtet. The airline set up a shuttle service between Cologne and Berlin.
2 commuter traffic
□ Zwischen Tübingen und Stuttgart besteht ein reger Pendelverkehr. There is heavy commuter traffic between Tübingen and Stuttgart.

der **Pendler** (PL die **Pendler**) NOUN
commuter

penetrant ADJECTIVE
1 overpowering
□ ein penetranter Geruch an overpowering smell
2 pushy
□ ein penetranter Vertreter a pushy salesman
■ **penetrant werden** to get aggressive

der **Penis** (GEN des **Penis**, PL die **Penisse**) NOUN
penis

pennen VERB [48]
to kip
□ Ich habe auf dem Fußboden gepennt. I kipped on the floor.
■ **Er pennt.** He's having a kip.

der **Penner** (PL die **Penner**) NOUN
dosser

die **Pension** NOUN
1 pension
□ Er bezieht eine ordentliche Pension. He gets a decent pension.
■ **in Pension gehen** to retire
2 guesthouse
□ Wir haben in einer Pension übernachtet. We stayed overnight in a guesthouse.

pensioniert ADJECTIVE
retired

das **Perfekt** (PL die **Perfekte**) NOUN
▷ *see also* **perfekt** ADJECTIVE
perfect

perfekt ADJECTIVE
▷ *see also* **das Perfekt** NOUN
perfect
□ ein perfektes Alibi a perfect alibi □ perfekt passen to fit perfectly

die **Periode** NOUN
period

die **Perle** NOUN
pearl

perplex ADJECTIVE
dumbfounded

die **Person** NOUN
person
■ **ich für meine Person ...** personally I ...

das **Personal** NOUN
staff
□ das Personal der Firma the staff of the company □ das Hotelpersonal the hotel staff

der **Personalausweis** (GEN des **Personalausweises**, PL die **Personalausweise**) NOUN
identity card

der **Personalchef** (PL die **Personalchefs**) NOUN
personnel manager

die **Personalien** FEM PL NOUN
particulars

das **Personalpronomen** (PL die **Personalpronomen**) NOUN
personal pronoun

der **Personenzug** (PL die **Personenzüge**) NOUN
passenger train

persönlich ADJECTIVE, ADVERB
1 personal
□ das persönliche Fürwort the personal pronoun □ persönlich werden to get personal
2 in person
□ persönlich erscheinen to appear in person
3 personally
□ jemanden persönlich kennen to know somebody personally □ Das war nicht persönlich gemeint. It wasn't meant personally.

die **Persönlichkeit** NOUN
personality

die **Perücke** NOUN
wig

der **Pessimist** (GEN des **Pessimisten**, PL die **Pessimisten**) NOUN
pessimist

pessimistisch ADJECTIVE
pessimistic

die **Pest** NOUN
plague
■ **jemanden wie die Pest hassen** to loathe somebody

die **Petersilie** NOUN
parsley

das **Petroleum** NOUN
paraffin

der **Pfad** (PL die **Pfade**) NOUN
path

der **Pfadfinder** (PL die **Pfadfinder**) NOUN
boy scout

die **Pfadfinderin** NOUN
girl guide

das **Pfand** (PL die **Pfänder**) NOUN
1 deposit
□ Auf der Flasche ist ein Pfand von siebzig Cent. There's a deposit of seventy cents on the bottle.
2 forfeit
□ Wer die Frage nicht beantworten kann, muss ein Pfand geben. Anyone who cannot answer the question must pay a forfeit.

die **Pfandflasche** NOUN
returnable bottle

die **Pfanne** NOUN
frying pan

der **Pfannkuchen** (PL die **Pfannkuchen**) NOUN
pancake

der **Pfarrer** (PL die **Pfarrer**) NOUN
parish priest

Pfd. ABBREVIATION *(= Pfund)*
pound *(weight)*

der **Pfeffer** (PL die **Pfeffer**) NOUN
pepper

das **Pfefferkorn** (PL die **Pfefferkörner**) NOUN
peppercorn

das **Pfefferminzbonbon** (PL die **Pfefferminzbonbons**) NOUN
peppermint

die **Pfefferminze** NOUN
mint

die **Pfeffermühle** NOUN
pepper mill

die **Pfeife** NOUN
1 whistle
□ die Pfeife des Schiedsrichters the referee's whistle
2 pipe
□ Mein Bruder raucht Pfeife. My brother smokes a pipe.

pfeifen (IMPERFECT **pfiff**, PERFECT **hat gepfiffen**) VERB
to whistle

der **Pfeil** (PL die **Pfeile**) NOUN
arrow

das **Pferd** (PL die **Pferde**) NOUN
horse

das **Pferderennen** (PL die **Pferderennen**) NOUN
1 race meeting
□ Er geht regelmäßig zu Pferderennen. He regularly goes to race meetings.
2 horse-racing
□ Ich interessiere mich nicht für Pferderennen. I'm not interested in horse-racing.

der **Pferdeschwanz** (GEN des **Pferdeschwanzes**, PL die **Pferdeschwänze**) NOUN
ponytail

LANGUAGE TIP Word for word, **Pferdeschwanz** means 'horse's tail'.

der **Pferdestall** (PL die **Pferdeställe**) NOUN
stable

das **Pfingsten** (GEN des **Pfingsten**, PL die **Pfingsten**) NOUN
Whitsun
□ an Pfingsten at Whitsun

der **Pfirsich** (PL die **Pfirsiche**) NOUN
peach

die **Pflanze** NOUN
plant

pflanzen VERB [36]
to plant

das **Pflaster** (PL die **Pflaster**) NOUN
1 plaster
□ Sie klebte ein Pflaster auf die Wunde. She put a plaster on the cut.
2 paving stones
□ Jemand hatte das Pflaster in der Fußgängerzone bemalt. Somebody had been painting on the paving stones in the pedestrian precinct.

die **Pflaume** NOUN
plum

die **Pflege** NOUN
1 care
□ Diese Pflanze braucht nicht viel Pflege. This plant doesn't need much care.
□ ein Mittel zur Pflege von Leder a leather-care product
2 nursing
□ Ein krankes Baby braucht viel Pflege. A sick baby needs a lot of nursing.
■ **ein Kind in Pflege geben** to have a child fostered

die **Pflegeeltern** PL NOUN
foster parents

pflegeleicht ADJECTIVE
easy-care
□ ein pflegeleichter Stoff an easy-care fabric

pflegen VERB [38]
1 to nurse
□ Sie pflegt ihre kranke Mutter. She's nursing her sick mother.
2 to look after
□ Briten pflegen ihren Rasen. The British look after their lawns.
■ **gepflegte Hände** well-cared-for hands
■ **gepflegt aussehen** to look well-groomed

der **Pfleger** (PL die **Pfleger**) NOUN
male nurse

die **Pflicht** NOUN
duty
□ Es ist deine Pflicht, dich darum zu kümmern. It's your duty to take care of it.

pflichtbewusst ADJECTIVE
conscientious

das **Pflichtfach** (PL die **Pflichtfächer**) NOUN
compulsory subject

pflücken VERB [48]
to pick
□ Wir haben Himbeeren gepflückt. We picked raspberries. □ einen Strauß pflücken to pick a bunch of flowers

der **Pförtner** (PL die **Pförtner**) NOUN
doorman

der **Pfosten** (PL die **Pfosten**) NOUN
post
□ Der Ball traf den Pfosten. The ball hit the post.

die **Pfote** NOUN
paw
□ Der Hund hat schmutzige Pfoten. The dog's paws are dirty.

pfui EXCLAMATION
ugh!

das **Pfund** (PL die **Pfunde** *or* **Pfund**) NOUN
pound
□ drei Pfund Äpfel three pounds of apples
□ dreißig britische Pfund thirty pounds sterling

pfuschen VERB [38]
to be sloppy
■ **Die Handwerker haben gepfuscht.** The craftsmen produced sloppy work.
■ **jemandem ins Handwerk pfuschen** to stick one's nose into somebody's business

die **Pfütze** NOUN
puddle

die **Phantasie** NOUN ▷ *see* **Fantasie**

phantasieren VERB ▷ *see* **fantasieren**

phantastisch ADJECTIVE ▷ *see* **fantastisch**

die **Philosophie** NOUN
philosophy

philosophisch ADJECTIVE
philosophical

phlegmatisch ADJECTIVE
lethargic

die **Phonetik** NOUN
phonetics
□ Die Phonetik steht in eckigen Klammern. Phonetics are given in square brackets.

phonetisch ADJECTIVE
phonetic

das **Photo** NOUN ▷ *see* **Foto**

die **Physik** NOUN
physics
□ Physik ist mein Lieblingsfach. Physics is my favourite subject.

der **Physiker** (PL die **Physiker**) NOUN
physicist

physisch ADJECTIVE
physical

der **Pickel** (PL die **Pickel**) NOUN
1 pimple
□ Du hast einen Pickel auf der Nase. You've got a pimple on your nose.
2 pickaxe
□ Die Arbeiter haben den Straßenbelag mit

Pickeln aufgeschlagen. The workers broke up the road surface with pickaxes.
3 ice axe
□ Die Bergsteiger hatten Seile und Pickel dabei. The mountaineers had ropes and ice axes with them.

das **Picknick** (PL die **Picknicks**) NOUN
picnic
□ Picknick machen to have a picnic

der **Piepser** (PL die **Piepser**) NOUN
bleeper

das **Pik** (PL die **Pik**) NOUN
spades
□ Pik ist Trumpf. Spades is trumps.

pikant ADJECTIVE
spicy

die **Pille** NOUN
pill
□ Sie nimmt die Pille. She's on the pill.

der **Pilot** (GEN des **Piloten**, PL die **Piloten**) NOUN
pilot

das **Pils** (GEN des **Pils**, PL die **Pils**) NOUN
Pilsner lager

der **Pilz** (GEN des **Pilzes**, PL die **Pilze**) NOUN
1 mushroom
□ eine Soße mit Pilzen a mushroom sauce
2 toadstool
□ Der Fliegenpilz ist giftig. The fly agaric is a toadstool.

pinkeln VERB [88]
to pee

der **Pinsel** (PL die **Pinsel**) NOUN
paintbrush

die **Pinzette** NOUN
tweezers
□ eine Pinzette a pair of tweezers

der **Pirat** (GEN des **Piraten**, PL die **Piraten**) NOUN
pirate

die **Piste** NOUN
1 run
□ Wir sind die blaue Piste runtergefahren. We skied down the blue run.
2 runway
□ Das Flugzeug stand auf der Piste und wartete auf die Starterlaubnis. The plane stood on the runway waiting for clearance for takeoff.

die **Pistole** NOUN
pistol

der **Pkw** (GEN des **Pkw** *or* **Pkws**, PL die **Pkws**) NOUN *(= Personenkraftwagen)*
car

plagen VERB [38]
to bother
□ Was plagt dich denn? What's bothering you?
■ **Sie muss sich in der Schule ziemlich plagen.** She finds school hard going.

das **Plakat** (PL die **Plakate**) NOUN
poster

der **Plan** (PL die **Pläne**) NOUN
1 plan
□ Unser Plan war, vor ihm da zu sein. Our plan was to arrive before him.
2 map
□ Hast du einen Plan von München? Have you got a map of Munich?

planen VERB [38]
to plan
□ Wir planen unseren nächsten Urlaub. We're planning our next holiday.
■ **einen Mord planen** to plot a murder

der **Planet** (GEN des **Planeten**, PL die **Planeten**) NOUN
planet

planmäßig ADJECTIVE
1 according to plan
□ Alles verlief planmäßig. Everything went according to plan.
2 scheduled
□ planmäßige Ankunft scheduled arrival
3 on time
□ Die Maschine ist planmäßig gelandet. The plane landed on time.

das **Plastik** NOUN
▷ *see also* **die Plastik** NOUN
plastic
□ Die meisten Spielzeuge sind heute aus Plastik. Most toys these days are made of plastic.

die **Plastik** NOUN
▷ *see also* **das Plastik** NOUN
sculpture

der **Plastikbeutel** (PL die **Plastikbeutel**) NOUN
plastic bag

die **Plastiktüte** NOUN
plastic bag

platt ADJECTIVE
flat
□ ein platter Reifen a flat tyre □ plattes Land flat country
■ **etwas platt drücken** to flatten something
■ **Ich bin platt!** I'm flabbergasted!

plattdeutsch ADJECTIVE
low German

die **Platte** NOUN
1 plate
□ Sie stellte den Topf auf die Platte. She put the saucepan on the plate.
■ **eine Platte mit Käseaufschnitt** a platter of assorted cheeses
2 record
□ Sie hat alle Platten der Beatles. She's got all the Beatles' records.

der **Plattenspieler** (PL die **Plattenspieler**) NOUN
record player

der **Platz** (GEN des **Platzes**, PL die **Plätze**) NOUN
1 place

□ Das ist ein schöner Platz zum Zelten. That's a good place to pitch a tent. □ Das Buch steht nicht an seinem Platz. The book isn't in its place. □ der erste Platz the first place
2 seat
□ Wir hatten Plätze in der ersten Reihe. We had seats in the front row. □ Ist hier noch ein Platz frei? Are all these seats taken?
■ **Platz nehmen** to take a seat
3 room
□ Das Sofa braucht zu viel Platz. The sofa takes up too much room. □ jemandem Platz machen to make room for somebody
4 square
□ Auf dem Platz vor der Kirche ist zweimal die Woche Markt. There's a market twice a week on the square in front of the church.
5 playing field
■ **Der Schiedsrichter schickte ihn vom Platz.** The referee sent him off.

das **Plätzchen** (PL die **Plätzchen**) NOUN
1 spot
□ ein hübsches Plätzchen a beautiful spot
2 biscuit
□ Zum Kaffee gab es Plätzchen. There were biscuits with the coffee.

platzen (PERFECT **ist geplatzt**) VERB [36]
1 to burst
□ Der Luftballon ist geplatzt. The balloon has burst.
2 to explode
□ In der Innenstadt ist gestern eine Bombe geplatzt. A bomb exploded in the town centre yesterday.
■ **vor Wut platzen** to be livid

die **Platzkarte** NOUN
seat reservation

plaudern VERB [88]
to chat

die **Pleite** NOUN
▷ *see also* **pleite** ADJECTIVE
1 bankruptcy
□ die Pleite einer Firma the bankruptcy of a company
■ **Pleite machen** to go bust
2 flop
□ Die Veranstaltung war eine Pleite. The event was a flop.

pleite ADJECTIVE
▷ *see also* **die Pleite** NOUN
broke
□ Ich bin total pleite. I'm stony-broke.

die **Plombe** NOUN
filling
□ Ich habe noch keine einzige Plombe. I still haven't got a single filling.

plötzlich ADJECTIVE, ADVERB
1 sudden
□ ihr plötzliches Erscheinen her sudden appearance
2 suddenly
□ Sie war plötzlich weg. Suddenly she was gone.

plump ADJECTIVE
clumsy
□ plumpe Bewegungen clumsy movements
■ **ein plumper Körper** a shapeless body
■ **eine plumpe Lüge** a blatant lie

der **Plural** (PL die **Plurale**) NOUN
plural

das **Plus** (GEN des **Plus**) NOUN
▷ *see also* **plus** ADVERB
1 plus
□ Steht vor der Zahl ein Plus oder ein Minus? Is there a plus or a minus in front of the figure?
2 profit
□ Die Firma hat dieses Jahr ein Plus gemacht. The company has made a profit this year.
3 advantage
□ Sprachkenntnisse sind immer ein Plus. Language skills are always an advantage.

plus ADVERB
▷ *see also* **das Plus** NOUN
plus

das **Plutonium** NOUN
plutonium

PLZ ABBREVIATION (= *Postleitzahl*)
postcode

der **Po** (PL die **Pos**) NOUN
bum

der **Pokal** (PL die **Pokale**) NOUN
1 cup
□ Welche Mannschaft hat den Pokal gewonnen? Which team won the cup?
2 goblet
□ Sie tranken Wein aus Pokalen. They drank wine out of goblets.

das **Pokalspiel** (PL die **Pokalspiele**) NOUN
cup tie

der **Pol** (PL die **Pole**) NOUN
pole
□ am Pol at the Pole

der **Pole** (GEN des **Polen**, PL die **Polen**) NOUN
Pole
■ **Er ist Pole.** He's Polish.

Polen NEUT NOUN
Poland
■ **aus Polen** from Poland
■ **nach Polen** to Poland

die **Police** NOUN
insurance policy

polieren (PERFECT **hat poliert**) VERB [76]
to polish

die **Polin** NOUN
Pole
■ **Sie ist Polin.** She's Polish.

die **Politik** NOUN
1 politics
□ Politik interessiert mich nicht. Politics doesn't interest me.

2 policy
□ die Politik Großbritanniens in Bezug auf Immigration Great Britain's policy on immigration

der **Politiker** (PL die **Politiker**) NOUN
politician

politisch ADJECTIVE
political

die **Polizei** NOUN
police

LANGUAGE TIP Note that **Polizei** is used with a singular verb and 'police' with a plural verb.

□ Die Polizei ist noch nicht da. The police haven't arrived yet.

der **Polizeibeamte** (GEN des **Polizeibeamten**, PL die **Polizeibeamten**) NOUN
police officer
□ Wir wurden von einem Polizeibeamten angehalten. We were stopped by a police officer.

die **Polizeibeamtin** NOUN
police officer
□ Sie ist Polizeibeamtin. She's a police officer.

polizeilich ADJECTIVE
■ **Er wird polizeilich gesucht.** The police are looking for him.

das **Polizeirevier** (PL die **Polizeireviere**) NOUN
police station

die **Polizeistunde** NOUN
closing time *(of bars)*

die **Polizeiwache** NOUN
police station

der **Polizist** (GEN des **Polizisten**, PL die **Polizisten**) NOUN
policeman
□ Dietmar ist Polizist. Dietmar's a policeman.

die **Polizistin** NOUN
policewoman
□ Ursula ist Polizistin. Ursula's a policewoman.

polnisch ADJECTIVE
Polish

die **Pommes** PL NOUN
chips
□ Pommes mit Mayonnaise chips with mayonnaise

die **Pommes frites** PL NOUN
chips
□ Würstchen mit Pommes frites sausages and chips

pompös ADJECTIVE
ostentatious

das **Pony** (PL die **Ponys**) NOUN
▷ *see also* **der Pony** NOUN
pony
□ Wir sind auf Ponys geritten. We rode ponies.

der **Pony** (PL die **Ponys**) NOUN
▷ *see also* **das Pony** NOUN
fringe
□ Sie trägt einen Pony. She's got a fringe.

der **Pop** NOUN
pop

die **Popmusik** NOUN
pop music

poppig ADJECTIVE
bright
□ poppige Farben bright colours

der **Popstar** (PL die **Popstars**) NOUN
pop star

die **Pore** NOUN
pore

die **Pornografie** NOUN
pornography

porös ADJECTIVE
porous

der **Porree** (PL die **Porrees**) NOUN
leek

das **Portemonnaie** (PL die **Portemonnaies**) NOUN
purse

der **Portier** (PL die **Portiers**) NOUN
porter

die **Portion** NOUN
portion
□ eine große Portion a big portion
□ Zwei Portionen Pommes frites, bitte. Two portions of chips, please.
■ **Dazu gehört eine ordentliche Portion Mut.** You need quite a bit of courage for that.

das **Portmonee** (PL die **Portmonees**) NOUN
purse

das **Porto** (PL die **Portos**) NOUN
postage

Portugal NEUT NOUN
Portugal
■ **aus Portugal** from Portugal
■ **nach Portugal** to Portugal

der **Portugiese** (GEN des **Portugiesen**, PL die **Portugiesen**) NOUN
Portuguese

die **Portugiesin** NOUN
Portuguese

portugiesisch ADJECTIVE
Portuguese

das **Porzellan** NOUN
1 porcelain
□ eine Figur aus Porzellan a porcelain figurine
2 china
□ Das Porzellan habe ich von meiner Oma geerbt. I inherited the china from my grandma.

die **Posaune** NOUN
trombone
□ Franz spielt Posaune. Franz plays the trombone.

positiv ADJECTIVE
positive
□ HIV-positiv HIV-positive

das **Possessivpronomen** (PL die **Possessivpronomen**) NOUN
possessive pronoun

die **Post** NOUN
1 post office
□ Bring bitte das Päckchen zur Post. Please take the parcel to the post office.
2 mail
□ Ist Post für mich gekommen? Was there any mail for me?

das **Postamt** (PL die **Postämter**) NOUN
post office

der **Posten** (PL die **Posten**) NOUN
1 post
□ Sie hat einen guten Posten als Chefsekretärin. She's got a good post as a director's secretary.
2 sentry
□ Die Armee hat vor dem Gebäude Posten aufgestellt. The army posted sentries in front of the building.
3 item
□ Dieser Posten ist nicht auf der Preisliste aufgeführt. This item doesn't appear on the price list.

das **Poster** (PL die **Poster**) NOUN
poster

das **Postfach** (PL die **Postfächer**) NOUN
post office box

die **Postkarte** NOUN
postcard

postlagernd ADVERB
poste restante

die **Postleitzahl** NOUN
postcode

postwendend ADVERB
by return of post

das **Postwertzeichen** (PL die **Postwertzeichen**) NOUN
postage stamp

die **Pracht** NOUN
splendour

prächtig ADJECTIVE, ADVERB
1 magnificent
□ ein prächtiges Haus a magnificent house
2 marvellous
□ Wir haben uns prächtig amüsiert. We had a marvellous time.

prachtvoll ADJECTIVE
splendid

das **Prädikat** (PL die **Prädikate**) NOUN
predicate
□ Subjekt und Prädikat eines Satzes subject and predicate of a sentence

prahlen VERB [38]
to brag

der **Praktikant** (GEN des **Praktikanten**, PL die **Praktikanten**) NOUN
trainee

die **Praktikantin** NOUN
trainee

das **Praktikum** (GEN des **Praktikums**, PL die **Praktika**) NOUN
practical training
□ Sie absolviert ihr Praktikum. She's doing her practical training.

praktisch ADJECTIVE
1 practical
□ ein praktischer Mensch a practical person
□ eine praktische Lösung a practical solution
□ praktische Erfahrung practical experience
2 handy
□ ein praktisches Gerät a handy gadget
■ **praktischer Arzt** general practitioner
■ **praktisch begabt sein** to be good with one's hands

die **Praline** NOUN
chocolate

die **Präposition** NOUN
preposition

das **Präsens** (GEN des **Präsens**) NOUN
present tense

das **Präservativ** (PL die **Präservative**) NOUN
condom

der **Präsident** (GEN des **Präsidenten**, PL die **Präsidenten**) NOUN
president

die **Praxis** (PL die **Praxen**) NOUN
1 practical experience
□ Ihr fehlt die Praxis. She lacks practical experience.
■ **etwas in die Praxis umsetzen** to put something into practice
2 surgery
□ Kommen Sie zur Behandlung in die Praxis. Come to the surgery for treatment.
3 practice
□ Mein Anwalt hat seine eigene Praxis aufgemacht. My solicitor has opened his own practice.

der **Preis** (GEN des **Preises**, PL die **Preise**) NOUN
1 price
□ Die Preise für Computer sind gefallen. Computer prices have fallen.
2 prize
□ Ihr Hund hat einen Preis gewonnen. Her dog's won a prize.
■ **um keinen Preis** not at any price
□ Das mache ich um keinen Preis. I won't do it at any price.

preisgünstig ADJECTIVE
inexpensive

die **Preislage** NOUN
price range

das **Preisschild** (PL die **Preisschilder**) NOUN
price tag

der **Preisträger** (PL die **Preisträger**) NOUN
prizewinner

preiswert ADJECTIVE
inexpensive

die **Prellung** NOUN
bruise

der **Premierminister** (PL die **Premierminister**) NOUN
prime minister

die **Presse** NOUN
press

pressen VERB [31]
to press

der **Priester** (PL die **Priester**) NOUN
priest

prima ADJECTIVE
super
□ Es ist ein prima Hotel. It's a super hotel.

der **Prinz** (GEN des **Prinzen**, PL die **Prinzen**) NOUN
prince

die **Prinzessin** NOUN
princess

das **Prinzip** (PL die **Prinzipien**) NOUN
principle
■ **aus Prinzip** as a matter of principle

privat ADJECTIVE
private

der **Privatpatient** (GEN des **Privatpatienten**, PL die **Privatpatienten**) NOUN
private patient

die **Privatschule** NOUN
fee-paying school

pro PREPOSITION
LANGUAGE TIP The preposition **pro** takes the accusative.
per
□ zehn Euro pro Person ten euros per person
■ **einmal pro Woche** once a week

die **Probe** NOUN
1 test
□ Wir müssen eine Probe machen, ob er geeignet ist. We need to do a test to see if he's suitable. □ Wir haben in Englisch morgen eine Probe. We've got an English test tomorrow.
2 sample
□ Die Probe wird im Labor untersucht. The sample's being examined in the laboratory.
3 rehearsal
□ die letzte Probe vor der Aufführung the final rehearsal before the performance
■ **jemanden auf die Probe stellen** to test somebody

probieren (PERFECT **hat probiert**) VERB [76]
to try
□ Probier mal eine andere Methode. Try a different method. □ Willst du mal von dem Käse probieren? Would you like to try some of the cheese?
■ **Ich werde probieren, ob ich das kann.** I'll give it a try.

das **Problem** (PL die **Probleme**) NOUN
problem
□ Kein Problem! No problem.

das **Produkt** (PL die **Produkte**) NOUN
product

die **Produktion** NOUN
1 production
□ die Produktion von Luxusautos the production of luxury cars
2 output
□ Wir müssen unsere Produktion erhöhen. We must increase our output.

produzieren (PERFECT **hat produziert**) VERB [76]
to produce

der **Professor** (PL die **Professoren**) NOUN
professor

der **Profi** (PL die **Profis**) NOUN
pro
□ Er spielt wie ein Profi. He plays like a pro.

der **Profit** (PL die **Profite**) NOUN
profit

profitieren (PERFECT **hat profitiert**) VERB [76]
to profit
□ von etwas profitieren to profit from something

das **Programm** (PL die **Programme**) NOUN
1 programme
□ das Programm des heutigen Abends this evening's programme
2 program
□ Für die Kalkulation arbeite ich mit einem anderen Programm. I've got a different program for spreadsheets.

programmieren (PERFECT **hat programmiert**) VERB [76]
to program

der **Programmierer** (PL die **Programmierer**) NOUN
programmer

das **Projekt** (PL die **Projekte**) NOUN
project

das **Promille** (PL die **Promille**) NOUN
alcohol level
□ Er hatte drei Promille. He had an alcohol level of three hundred milligrams in a hundred millilitres of blood.

das **Pronomen** (PL die **Pronomen**) NOUN
pronoun

die **Proportion** NOUN
proportion

der **Prospekt** (PL die **Prospekte**) NOUN
brochure
LANGUAGE TIP Be careful! **Prospekt** does not mean **prospect**.

prost EXCLAMATION
cheers!

die **Prostituierte** (GEN der **Prostituierten**) NOUN
prostitute

die **Prostitution** NOUN
prostitution

das **Protein** (PL die **Proteine**) NOUN
protein

German-English

der **Protest** (PL die **Proteste**) NOUN
protest

protestantisch ADJECTIVE
Protestant

protestieren (PERFECT **hat protestiert**) VERB [76]
to protest
□ Wir protestieren gegen diese Maßnahmen. We're protesting against these measures.

das **Protokoll** (PL die **Protokolle**) NOUN
1 minutes
□ Wer schreibt das Protokoll der heutigen Besprechung? Who is taking the minutes of today's meeting?
2 statement
□ Der Zeuge muss das polizeiliche Protokoll unterschreiben. The witness must sign the statement he made to the police.

protzen VERB [48]
to show off
□ Sie protzt mit ihrem neuen Mountainbike. She's showing off with her new mountain bike.

protzig ADJECTIVE
showy
□ ein protziges Auto a showy car

der **Proviant** (PL die **Proviante**) NOUN
provisions

provisorisch ADJECTIVE
provisional

provozieren (PERFECT **hat provoziert**) VERB [76]
to provoke

das **Prozent** (PL die **Prozente**) NOUN
per cent
□ zehn Prozent ten per cent

der **Prozess** (GEN des **Prozesses**, PL die **Prozesse**) NOUN
trial
□ der Prozess gegen die Terroristen the trial of the terrorists
■ **einen Prozess gewinnen** to win a case

prüfen VERB [38]
1 to test
□ Wir werden morgen in Chemie geprüft. We're having a chemistry test tomorrow.
2 to check
□ Vor der Reise sollte man den Ölstand prüfen. You should check the oil before your journey.

der **Prüfer** (PL die **Prüfer**) NOUN
examiner

die **Prüfung** NOUN
1 examination
□ Sie hat die Prüfung bestanden. She's passed the examination.
2 check
□ Bei der Prüfung der Bremsen haben wir einen Defekt festgestellt. During a check on the brakes we found a fault.

der **Prügel** (PL die **Prügel**) NOUN
stick
□ Er schlug ihn mit einem Prügel. He hit him with a stick.
■ **Prügel bekommen** to get a hiding
□ Ich habe als Kind nie Prügel bekommen. I never got a hiding as a child.
■ **Er hat von seinen Freunden Prügel bekommen.** His friends beat him up.

die **Prügelei** NOUN
fight

prügeln VERB [34]
to beat
□ Eltern sollten ihre Kinder nicht prügeln. Parents shouldn't beat their children.
■ **sich prügeln** to fight □ Ich will mich nicht mit dir prügeln. I don't want to fight you.
■ **Die beiden haben sich in der Pause geprügelt.** The two of them had a fight in the break.

die **Prügelstrafe** NOUN
corporal punishment

psychisch ADJECTIVE
psychological

der **Psychologe** (GEN des **Psychologen**, PL die **Psychologen**) NOUN
psychologist
□ Ihr Vater ist Psychologe. Her father is a psychologist.

die **Psychologie** NOUN
psychology

psychologisch ADJECTIVE
psychological

die **Pubertät** NOUN
puberty
□ während der Pubertät during puberty

das **Publikum** NOUN
audience
□ Am Ende des Stückes klatschte das Publikum. The audience clapped at the end of the play.

der **Pudding** (PL die **Puddinge** *or* **Puddings**) NOUN
blancmange

der **Puder** (PL die **Puder**) NOUN
powder

der **Pullover** (PL die **Pullover**) NOUN
pullover

der **Puls** (GEN des **Pulses**, PL die **Pulse**) NOUN
pulse
■ **jemandem den Puls fühlen** to take somebody's pulse

das **Pult** (PL die **Pulte**) NOUN
desk

das **Pulver** (PL die **Pulver**) NOUN
powder

die **Pumpe** NOUN
pump

pumpen VERB [38]
1 to pump

P

□ Das Öl wird durch die Pipeline gepumpt. The oil's pumped along the pipeline.
2 to lend
□ Kannst du mir mal deinen Walkman pumpen? Can you lend me your Walkman?
3 to borrow
□ Ich habe mir das Rad meiner Schwester gepumpt. I've borrowed my sister's bike.

der **Punkt** (PL die **Punkte**) NOUN
1 full stop
□ Am Satzende steht ein Punkt. A full stop goes at the end of a sentence.
2 point
□ In diesem Punkt gebe ich dir recht. On this point I agree with you.
3 dot
□ Das Schiff war nur noch ein kleiner Punkt am Horizont. The ship was only a small dot on the horizon. □ Sie trug ein rotes Kleid mit weißen Punkten. She was wearing a red dress with white dots.

pünktlich ADJECTIVE, ADVERB
1 punctual
□ Sie ist nicht sehr pünktlich. She's not very punctual.
2 on time
□ Der Zug kam pünktlich an. The train arrived on time.

die **Pünktlichkeit** NOUN
punctuality

die **Puppe** NOUN
doll

pur ADJECTIVE
pure
□ Das ist pures Gold. That's pure gold.
□ Das ist doch der pure Wahnsinn. But that's pure madness.
■ **etwas pur trinken** to drink something neat
■ **Whisky pur** neat whisky

die **Pute** NOUN
turkey

der **Puter** (PL die **Puter**) NOUN
turkey

putzen VERB [36]
1 to clean
□ Sie putzt jeden Samstag das Haus. She cleans the house every Saturday.
2 to wipe
□ Putz dir die Schuhe, bevor du reinkommst. Wipe your shoes before you come in.
■ **sich die Nase putzen** to blow one's nose
□ Putz dir mal die Nase! Blow your nose.
■ **sich die Zähne putzen** to brush one's teeth

die **Putzfrau** NOUN
cleaner

der **Putzmann** (PL die **Putzmänner**) NOUN
cleaner

das **Puzzle** (PL die **Puzzles**) NOUN
jigsaw

der **Pyjama** (PL die **Pyjamas**) NOUN
pyjamas
□ ein Pyjama a pair of pyjamas

die **Pyramide** NOUN
pyramid

Qq

qm ABBREVIATION *(= Quadratmeter)*
m²

das **Quadrat** (PL die **Quadrate**) NOUN
square

quadratisch ADJECTIVE
square

der **Quadratmeter** (PL die **Quadratmeter**) NOUN
square metre
□ eine Wohnung von achtzig Quadratmetern a flat of eighty square metres

die **Qual** NOUN
1 agony
□ Treppensteigen ist für sie eine Qual. Climbing the stairs is agony for her.
2 anguish
□ Die Qualen, die ich bei dieser Prüfung ausgestanden habe ... The anguish I went through in that exam ...

quälen VERB [38]
to treat cruelly
□ Tiere quälen to treat animals cruelly
■ **sich quälen** 1 to struggle □ Sie quälte sich die Treppe hinauf. She struggled up the steps. 2 to torment oneself □ Quäl dich nicht so! Don't torment yourself like that.
■ **Er muss sich in der Schule ziemlich quälen.** School's quite a trial for him.

die **Qualifikation** (PL die **Qualifikationen**) NOUN
qualification

qualifiziert ADJECTIVE
qualified

die **Qualität** NOUN
quality

die **Qualle** NOUN
jellyfish
□ zwei Quallen two jellyfish

der **Qualm** NOUN
thick smoke

qualmen VERB [38]
to smoke
□ Der Schornstein qualmt. The chimney is smoking.

die **Quantität** NOUN
quantity

der **Quark** NOUN
quark

der **Quarz** (GEN des **Quarzes**) NOUN
quartz

quasseln VERB [88]
to natter

der **Quatsch** NOUN
rubbish
□ Erzähl keinen Quatsch. Don't talk rubbish.
■ **Quatsch machen** to fool around
■ **Mach keinen Quatsch!** Don't be foolish!

quatschen VERB [48]
to natter

die **Quelle** NOUN
1 spring
□ heiße Quellen hot springs
2 source
□ aus zuverlässiger Quelle from a reliable source

quer ADVERB
1 diagonally
□ Die Streifen auf dem Stoff verlaufen quer. The stripes run diagonally across the material.
■ **quer auf dem Bett** across the bed
2 at right angles
□ Die Mannstraße verläuft quer zur Müllerstraße. Mann Street runs at right angles to Müller Street.

die **Querflöte** NOUN
flute
□ Cordula spielt Querflöte. Cordula plays the flute.

querschnittsgelähmt ADJECTIVE
paraplegic

die **Querstraße** NOUN
■ **eine Straße mit vielen Querstraßen** a road with a lot of side streets off it
■ **Biegen Sie an der zweiten Querstraße links ab.** Take the second street on the left.

quetschen VERB [48]
1 to squash
□ Pass auf, dass die Tomaten nicht gequetscht werden. Mind the tomatoes don't get squashed.
2 to cram
□ Sie quetschte das Kleid noch in ihren Koffer. She crammed the dress into her case.

■ **Ich habe mir den Finger in der Tür gequetscht.** I trapped my finger in the door.

die **Quetschung** NOUN
bruise

quitt ADJECTIVE
quits

□ Jetzt sind wir quitt. We're quits now.

die **Quittung** NOUN
receipt

□ Brauchen Sie eine Quittung? Do you need a receipt?

German-English

Rr

der **Rabatt** (PL die **Rabatte**) NOUN
discount

die **Rache** NOUN
revenge

der **Rachen** (PL die **Rachen**) NOUN
throat

rächen VERB [48]
■ **etwas rächen** to avenge something
■ **sich rächen** to take revenge
■ **Das wird sich rächen.** You'll pay for that.

das **Rad** (PL die **Räder**) NOUN
1 wheel
2 bike
□ Wir sind mit dem Rad gekommen. We came by bike.
■ **Rad fahren** to cycle

der **Radar** (PL die **Radare**) NOUN
LANGUAGE TIP You can also say **das Radar**.
radar

die **Radarkontrolle** NOUN
radar-controlled speed check

radeln (PERFECT **ist geradelt**) VERB [88]
to cycle
□ Wir sind an den Bodensee geradelt. We cycled to Lake Constance.

radfahren VERB [21] ▷ *see* **Rad**

der **Radfahrer** (PL die **Radfahrer**) NOUN
cyclist

der **Radfahrweg** (PL die **Radfahrwege**) NOUN
cycle track

der **Radiergummi** (PL die **Radiergummis**) NOUN
rubber

das **Radieschen** (PL die **Radieschen**) NOUN
radish

das **Radio** (PL die **Radios**) NOUN
radio

radioaktiv ADJECTIVE
radioactive

die **Radioaktivität** NOUN
radioactivity

das **Radrennen** (PL die **Radrennen**) NOUN
1 cycle race
□ Er hat an dem Radrennen teilgenommen. He took part in the cycle race.
2 cycle racing
□ Sie begeistert sich für Radrennen. She's a cycle racing fan.

der **Radsport** NOUN
cycling

der **Rahm** NOUN
cream

der **Rahmen** (PL die **Rahmen**) NOUN
frame
□ der Rahmen eines Bildes the frame of a picture
■ **im Rahmen des Möglichen** within the bounds of possibility

die **Rakete** NOUN
rocket

der **Rand** (PL die **Ränder**) NOUN
1 edge
□ Er stand am Rand des Schwimmbeckens. He stood on the edge of the swimming pool.
2 rim
□ der Rand der Tasse the rim of the cup
■ **eine Brille mit Goldrand** a pair of gold-rimmed glasses
3 margin
□ Lass an der Seite des Blattes einen Rand. Leave a margin at the edge of the page.
4 ring
□ In der Badewanne waren dunkle Ränder. There were dark rings in the bath tub.
5 verge
□ Die Firma steht am Rand des Bankrotts. The company's on the verge of bankruptcy.
■ **außer Rand und Band** out of control

randalieren (PERFECT **hat randaliert**) VERB [76]
to go on the rampage

der **Rang** (PL die **Ränge**) NOUN
1 rank *(military)*
□ Er steht im Rang eines Hauptmanns. He has the rank of captain.
■ **ein Mann ohne Rang und Namen** a man without any standing
2 circle *(theatre)*
□ erster Rang dress circle □ zweiter Rang upper circle

der **Rappen** (PL die **Rappen**) NOUN
rappen
□ Der Schweizer Franken hat hundert Rappen. There're one hundred rappen in a Swiss franc.

DID YOU KNOW...?
In the French-speaking part of Switzerland you talk about **centime** rather than **Rappen**.

rasch ADJECTIVE, ADVERB
quick
□ Das war rasch gemacht. That was quickly done.
■ **Ich gehe noch rasch beim Bäcker vorbei.** I'll just pop round to the baker's.

der **Rasen** (PL die **Rasen**) NOUN
▷ *see also* **rasen** VERB
lawn

rasen (PERFECT **ist gerast**) VERB [88]
▷ *see also* **der Rasen** NOUN
to race
□ Wir sind durch die engen Straßen gerast. We raced along the narrow streets.

der **Rasenmäher** (PL die **Rasenmäher**) NOUN
lawnmower

der **Rasierapparat** (PL die **Rasierapparate**) NOUN
shaver

die **Rasiercreme** (PL die **Rasiercremes**) NOUN
shaving cream

rasieren (PERFECT **hat rasiert**) VERB [76]
to shave
■ **sich rasieren** to shave

die **Rasierklinge** NOUN
razor blade

das **Rasiermesser** (PL die **Rasiermesser**) NOUN
razor

die **Rasse** NOUN
1 race
□ Rassenunruhen race riots
2 breed
□ Welche Rasse ist Ihr Hund? What breed is your dog?

der **Rassismus** (GEN des **Rassismus**) NOUN
racism

die **Rast** NOUN
rest
■ **Rast machen** to stop for a break

rasten VERB [2]
to rest

das **Rasthaus** (PL die **Rasthäuser**) NOUN
services *(motorway)*

der **Rasthof** (PL die **Rasthöfe**) NOUN
services *(motorway)*

der **Rastplatz** (GEN des **Rastplatzes**, PL die **Rastplätze**) NOUN
lay-by

die **Raststätte** NOUN
service area

die **Rasur** NOUN
shaving

der **Rat** (PL die **Ratschläge**) NOUN
advice
□ Ich habe viele Ratschläge bekommen. I've been given a lot of advice.
■ **ein Rat** a piece of advice
■ **Ich weiß keinen Rat.** I don't know what to do.
■ **zu Rate** ▷ *see* **zurate**

die **Rate** NOUN
instalment

raten (PRESENT **rät**, IMPERFECT **riet**, PERFECT **hat geraten**) VERB
to guess
□ Rat mal, wie alt ich bin. Guess how old I am.
■ **jemandem raten** to advise somebody
□ Sie hat mir geraten, einen Arzt aufzusuchen. She advised me to see a doctor.

das **Rathaus** (GEN des **Rathauses**, PL die **Rathäuser**) NOUN
town hall

die **Ration** NOUN
ration

rationalisieren (PERFECT **hat rationalisiert**) VERB [76]
to rationalize

rationell ADJECTIVE
efficient

ratlos ADJECTIVE
at a loss
□ Ich bin ratlos, was ich tun soll. I'm at a loss as to what to do.
■ **Sie sah mich ratlos an.** She gave me a helpless look.

der **Ratschlag** (PL die **Ratschläge**) NOUN
piece of advice
□ Ich habe viele Ratschläge bekommen. I've been given a lot of advice.

das **Rätsel** (PL die **Rätsel**) NOUN
1 puzzle
□ Sie löst gern Rätsel. She likes solving puzzles.
2 mystery
□ Das ist mir ein Rätsel. It's a mystery to me.

rätselhaft ADJECTIVE
mysterious
■ **Es ist mir rätselhaft ...** It's a mystery to me ...

die **Ratte** NOUN
rat

rau ADJECTIVE
1 rough
□ raue Haut rough skin
2 husky
□ eine raue Stimme a husky voice
3 sore
□ ein rauer Hals a sore throat
4 harsh
□ raues Wetter harsh weather □ ein rauer Wind a harsh wind
■ **Hier herrschen raue Sitten.** People here have rough-and-ready ways.

der **Raub** NOUN
robbery

German-English

das **Raubtier** (PL die **Raubtiere**) NOUN
predator

der **Rauch** NOUN
smoke

rauchen VERB [48]
to smoke
□ Er raucht Pfeife. He smokes a pipe.
■ **'Rauchen verboten'** 'No smoking'

der **Raucher** (PL die **Raucher**) NOUN
smoker

das **Raucherabteil** (PL die **Raucherabteile**) NOUN
smoking compartment

räuchern VERB [88]
to smoke
□ Fisch räuchern to smoke fish

rauh ADJECTIVE ▷ *see* **rau**

der **Raum** (PL die **Räume**) NOUN
1 space
□ Sie haben eine Rakete in den Raum geschossen. They launched a rocket into space. □ Raum und Zeit space and time
2 room
□ Eine Wohnung mit vier Räumen ist nicht groß genug für uns. A four-roomed flat isn't big enough for us. □ Dieses Gerät braucht wenig Raum. This appliance doesn't take up much room.
3 area
□ Im Raum Stuttgart kommt es morgen zu Gewittern. There will be thunderstorms in the Stuttgart area tomorrow.

räumen VERB [38]
1 to clear
□ Die Polizei hat das besetzte Haus geräumt. The police cleared the squat.
2 to vacate
□ Bitte räumen Sie Ihr Zimmer bis spätestens zehn Uhr. Please vacate your room by ten o'clock at the latest.
3 to clear away
□ Könnt ihr bitte das Geschirr vom Tisch räumen? Could you clear away the dishes, please?
4 to put away
□ Räum bitte deine Spielsachen in den Schrank. Please put your toys away in the cupboard.

die **Raumfähre** NOUN
space shuttle

die **Raumfahrt** NOUN
space travel

der **Rauminhalt** (PL die **Rauminhalte**) NOUN
volume

räumlich ADJECTIVE
spatial

die **Räumlichkeiten** FEM PL NOUN
premises

das **Raumschiff** (PL die **Raumschiffe**) NOUN
spaceship

der **Rausch** (PL die **Räusche**) NOUN
■ **einen Rausch haben** to be drunk
■ **seinen Rausch ausschlafen** to sleep it off

das **Rauschgift** (PL die **Rauschgifte**) NOUN
drug

der/die **Rauschgiftsüchtige** (GEN des/der **Rauschgiftsüchtigen**, PL die **Rauschgiftsüchtigen**) NOUN
drug addict
□ Gestern wurde ein Rauschgiftsüchtiger tot aufgefunden. A drug addict was found dead yesterday.

sich **räuspern** VERB [88]
to clear one's throat

reagieren (PERFECT **hat reagiert**) VERB [76]
1 to react
□ Wie hat sie auf diesen Vorwurf reagiert? How did she react to the allegation?
2 to respond
□ Die Bremsen haben nicht reagiert. The brakes didn't respond.

die **Reaktion** NOUN
reaction

reaktionär ADJECTIVE
reactionary

der **Reaktor** (PL die **Reaktoren**) NOUN
reactor

realisieren (PERFECT **hat realisiert**) VERB [76]
1 to fulfil
□ Er hat seine Träume realisiert. He's fulfilled his dreams.
2 to carry out
□ Wir sollten diese Pläne realisieren. We ought to carry out these plans.
3 to realize
□ Sie hat gar nicht realisiert, dass er schon längst weg war. She simply didn't realize that he had long since left.

realistisch ADJECTIVE
realistic

die **Realschule** NOUN
secondary school

DID YOU KNOW...?
Pupils enter **Realschule** at the age of about ten, and leave after six years. It is not as academically oriented as the **Gymnasium**.

das **Rechnen** NOUN
▷ *see also* **rechnen** VERB
arithmetic
□ Bettina ist gut im Rechnen. Bettina's good at arithmetic.

rechnen VERB [53]
▷ *see also* **das Rechnen** NOUN
to work out
□ Lass mich rechnen, wie viel das wird. Let me work out how much that's going to be.
■ **gut rechnen können** to be good at arithmetic
■ **Schneider wird zu den besten**

r

Fußballspielern gerechnet. Schneider is regarded as one of the best footballers.
■ **rechnen zu** to class as □ Man rechnet Mexico City zu den Megastädten. Mexico City is classed as one of the megacities.
■ **rechnen mit 1** to reckon with □ Mit wie vielen Besuchern können wir rechnen? How many visitors can we reckon with? **2** to reckon on □ Mit dieser Reaktion hatte ich nicht gerechnet. I hadn't reckoned on this reaction.
■ **rechnen auf** to count on □ Wir rechnen auf deine Unterstützung. We're counting on your support.

der **Rechner** (PL die **Rechner**) NOUN
1 calculator
□ Ich habe das mit meinem Rechner nachgerechnet. I've checked it with my calculator.
2 computer
□ Er hat sich für seinen Rechner einen neuen Prozessor gekauft. He's bought a new CPU for his computer.

die **Rechnung** NOUN
1 calculations
□ Meine Rechnung ergibt, dass wir noch zweihundert Euro haben. According to my calculations, we still have two hundred euros left.
2 invoice
□ Die Rechnung liegt der Sendung bei. The invoice is enclosed.

das **Recht** (PL die **Rechte**) NOUN
▷ *see also* **recht** ADJECTIVE, ADVERB
1 right
□ Es ist mein Recht, das zu erfahren. It's my right to know that. □ Ich habe ein Recht auf eine Erklärung. I've got a right to an explanation.
■ **im Recht sein** to be in the right □ Obwohl er im Recht war, hat er nachgegeben. Although he was in the right, he gave in.
■ **etwas mit Recht tun** to be right to do something □ Sie hat sich mit Recht beschwert. She was right to complain.
2 law
□ Sie wurde nach deutschem Recht zu zehn Jahren Gefängnis verurteilt. She was sentenced under German law to ten years' imprisonment.
■ **Recht sprechen** to administer justice

recht ADJECTIVE, ADVERB
▷ *see also* **das Recht** NOUN, **rechte** ADJECTIVE, **rechts** ADVERB
1 right
□ Es war nicht recht, dass du sie belogen hast. It wasn't right of you to lie to her. □ Dies ist nicht der rechte Moment, um darüber zu sprechen. This isn't the right moment to talk about it.
■ **Wenn ich dich recht verstehe ...** If I understand you correctly ...
■ **Das geschieht dir recht!** Serves you right!
2 quite
□ Das scheint recht einfach. It seems quite simple.
■ **jemandem recht sein** to be all right with somebody □ Wenn es deiner Mutter recht ist, übernachte ich gern bei euch. If it's all right with your mother, I'd like to stay the night at your place.
■ **Das ist mir recht.** That suits me.
■ **es jemandem recht machen** to please somebody □ Dir kann man es auch nie recht machen! There's no pleasing you.
■ **recht haben** to be right □ Wer hat nun recht? Who's right? □ Sie will immer recht haben. She always has to be right.
■ **jemandem recht geben** to agree with somebody □ Ich muss dir recht geben, das war nicht nett. I have to agree with you – that wasn't nice.
■ **Jetzt erst recht!** Now more than ever.

die **Rechte** (GEN der **Rechten**) NOUN
▷ *see also* **rechte** ADJECTIVE, **das Rechte** NOUN
1 right
□ Zu Ihrer Rechten sehen Sie das Rathaus. On your right you'll see the town hall.
2 right hand
□ Er schlug mit der Rechten zu. He hit out with his right hand.
3 right-wing
□ eine Partei der Rechten a right-wing party

rechte ADJECTIVE
▷ *see also* **recht** ADJECTIVE, **die Rechte** NOUN, **das Rechte** NOUN, **rechts** ADVERB
right
□ In Deutschland fährt man auf der rechten Seite. They drive on the right in Germany. □ Mein rechtes Auge tut weh. My right eye's hurting. □ Er hat sich den rechten Arm gebrochen. He broke his right arm.

das **Rechte** (GEN des **Rechten**) NOUN
▷ *see also* **die Rechte** NOUN, **rechte** ADJECTIVE
right thing
□ Pass auf, dass du das Rechte sagst. Make sure you say the right thing.

rechteckig ADJECTIVE
rectangular

rechtfertigen VERB [38]
to justify
□ Wie kannst du dein Verhalten rechtfertigen? How can you justify your behaviour?
■ **sich rechtfertigen** to justify oneself

rechtmäßig ADJECTIVE
lawful

rechts ADVERB
▷ *see also* **rechte** ADJECTIVE
right
□ rechts abbiegen to turn right
■ **rechts überholen** to overtake on the right
■ **Er schreibt mit rechts.** He writes with his right hand.

■ **Rechts sehen Sie das Rathaus.** On the right you'll see the town hall.
■ **rechts von der Kirche** to the right of the church
■ **rechts von mir** on my right
■ **rechts wählen** to vote for a right-wing party

der **Rechtsanwalt** (PL die **Rechtsanwälte**) NOUN
lawyer

die **Rechtsanwältin** NOUN
lawyer

die **Rechtschreibung** NOUN
spelling

der **Rechtshänder** (PL die **Rechtshänder**) NOUN
■ **Er ist Rechtshänder.** He's right-handed.

die **Rechtshänderin** NOUN
■ **Sie ist Rechtshänderin.** She's right-handed.

die **Rechtskurve** NOUN
right-hand bend

der **Rechtsverkehr** NOUN
driving on the right
□ In Deutschland ist Rechtsverkehr. They drive on the right in Germany.

rechtzeitig ADJECTIVE, ADVERB
in time
□ Ich bitte um rechtzeitige Benachrichtigung. Please let me know in time. □ Wir sind rechtzeitig angekommen. We arrived in time.

recyceln (PERFECT **hat recycelt**) VERB [7]
to recycle

der **Redakteur** (PL die **Redakteure**) NOUN
editor

die **Redaktion** NOUN
1 editorial staff
□ Die Redaktion hat das Manuskript abgelehnt. The editorial staff rejected the manuscript.
2 editorial office
□ Er arbeitet in unserer Redaktion. He works in our editorial office.

die **Rede** NOUN
speech
□ Er hat eine witzige Rede gehalten. He made an amusing speech.
■ **jemanden zur Rede stellen** to take somebody to task

reden VERB [54]
1 to talk
□ Wir haben über das Wetter geredet. We talked about the weather. □ Du redest Unsinn. You're talking nonsense.
2 to speak
□ Ich werde mit deiner Mutter reden. I'll speak to your mother. □ Ich rede nicht gern vor so vielen Menschen. I don't like speaking in front of so many people.
3 to say
□ Was reden die Leute über uns? What are people saying about us?

die **Redewendung** NOUN
expression

der **Redner** (PL die **Redner**) NOUN
speaker

reduzieren (PERFECT **hat reduziert**) VERB [76]
to reduce

das **Referat** (PL die **Referate**) NOUN
1 assignment
□ Ich muss in Geografie ein Referat schreiben. I have to write an assignment in geography.
2 paper
□ Sie hat ein Referat über Shakespeare gehalten. She gave a paper on Shakespeare.
3 section
□ Er ist Leiter des Referats Umweltschutz. He's head of the environmental protection section.

reflexiv ADJECTIVE
reflexive

die **Reform** NOUN
reform

das **Regal** (PL die **Regale**) NOUN
1 bookcase
□ In ihrem Regal stehen viele Krimis. There are a lot of detective stories in her bookcase.
2 rack
□ ein Regal für Weinflaschen a wine rack
3 shelf
□ Auf dem Regal standen Kräuter. There were herbs on the shelf.

die **Regel** NOUN
1 rule
□ Keine Regel ohne Ausnahme. The exception proves the rule.
2 period
□ Meine Regel ist ausgeblieben. I've missed a period.

regelmäßig ADJECTIVE, ADVERB
regular
□ in regelmäßigen Abständen at regular intervals □ Die Busse verkehren regelmäßig. The buses run regularly.

die **Regelmäßigkeit** NOUN
regularity

regeln VERB [34]
1 to direct
□ Ein Polizist regelte den Verkehr. A policeman was directing the traffic.
2 to control
□ die Lautstärke regeln to control the volume
3 to settle
□ Ich habe da noch eine Sache mit ihm zu regeln. I've still got something to settle with him.
4 to arrange
□ Wir haben das so geregelt, dass er abwäscht und ich putze. We've arranged things so that he washes the dishes and I do the cleaning.
■ **sich von selbst regeln** to take care of itself

der **Regen** (PL die **Regen**) NOUN
rain

der **Regenbogen** (PL die **Regenbogen**) NOUN
rainbow

der **Regenmantel** (PL die **Regenmäntel**) NOUN
raincoat

der **Regenschauer** (PL die **Regenschauer**) NOUN
shower

der **Regenschirm** (PL die **Regenschirme**) NOUN
umbrella

regieren (PERFECT **hat regiert**) VERB [76]
1 to govern
□ Wer regiert zurzeit Russland? Who governs Russia nowadays?
2 to reign
□ Wann hat Elisabeth die Erste regiert? When did Elizabeth the First reign?

die **Regierung** NOUN
1 government
□ die deutsche Regierung the German government
2 reign
□ England unter der Regierung von Elisabeth der Zweiten England during the reign of Elizabeth the Second

regnen VERB [53]
to rain
□ Es regnet. It's raining.

regnerisch ADJECTIVE
rainy

das **Reh** (PL die **Rehe**) NOUN
deer

reiben (IMPERFECT **rieb**, PERFECT **hat gerieben**) VERB
1 to rub
□ Warum reibst du dir die Augen? Why are you rubbing your eyes?
2 to grate
□ Er rieb Käse über die Kartoffeln. He grated cheese over the potatoes.

die **Reibung** NOUN
friction

reich ADJECTIVE
rich

reichen VERB [48]
1 to be enough
□ Der Kuchen wird nicht für alle reichen. There won't be enough cake for everybody.
2 to give
□ Sie reichte mir die Hand. She gave me her hand.
■ **jemandem etwas reichen** to pass somebody something □ Kannst du mir bitte die Butter reichen? Can you pass me the butter, please?
■ **Nur ein Salat reicht ihm nicht.** A salad won't be enough for him.
■ **Mir reicht's!** I've had enough.

reif ADJECTIVE
1 ripe
□ Die Äpfel sind noch nicht reif. The apples aren't ripe yet.
2 mature
□ Für sein Alter ist er schon sehr reif. He's very mature for his age.

der **Reifen** (PL die **Reifen**) NOUN
1 tyre
□ Mir ist ein Reifen geplatzt. I've got a burst tyre.
2 hoop
□ ein Hula-Hoop-Reifen a hula hoop

der **Reifendruck** NOUN
tyre pressure

die **Reifenpanne** NOUN
puncture

die **Reihe** NOUN
row
□ Stellt euch in einer Reihe auf. Stand in a row. □ Wir saßen in der zweiten Reihe. We sat in the second row.
■ **der Reihe nach** in turn
■ **Er ist an der Reihe.** It's his turn.
■ **an die Reihe kommen** to have one's turn

die **Reihenfolge** NOUN
order
□ alphabetische Reihenfolge alphabetical order

das **Reihenhaus** (GEN des **Reihenhauses**, PL die **Reihenhäuser**) NOUN
terraced house

rein ADJECTIVE, ADVERB
1 pure
□ Das ist reines Gold. That's pure gold.
□ reine Seide pure silk
2 clean
□ Damit wird die Wäsche rein. This will get the washing clean. □ reine Luft clean air
□ reine Haut clear skin
3 sheer
□ Das ist der reine Wahnsinn. That's sheer madness. □ Das ist das reinste Vergnügen. It's sheer pleasure.
4 purely
□ Rein technisch ist das machbar. From a purely technical point of view it's feasible.
■ **rein gar nichts** absolutely nothing
■ **etwas ins Reine schreiben** to make a fair copy of something
■ **etwas ins Reine bringen** to clear something up
5 in
□ Deckel auf und rein mit dem Müll. Off with the lid and in with the rubbish. □ Los rein mit dir, Zeit fürs Bett! Come on, in you come, it's time for bed.

der **Reinfall** (PL die **Reinfälle**) NOUN
let-down

die **Reinheit** NOUN
purity

□ die Reinheit des Biers the purity of beer
■ **Für die Reinheit Ihrer Wäsche ...** To get your washing really clean ...

reinigen VERB [38]
to clean

die **Reinigung** NOUN
1 cleaning
□ ein Mittel zur Reinigung der Polster an cleaning agent for upholstery
2 cleaner's
□ Bring bitte meine Hose in die Reinigung. Please take my trousers to the cleaner's.
■ **chemische Reinigung** 1 dry cleaning □ Bei diesem Stoff empfehlen wir eine chemische Reinigung. We recommend dry cleaning for this material. 2 dry cleaner's □ Im Einkaufszentrum gibt es auch eine chemische Reinigung. There's also a dry cleaner's in the shopping mall.

der **Reis** (GEN des **Reises**) NOUN
rice

die **Reise** NOUN
journey
□ Auf meiner letzten Reise durch Ägypten habe ich viel gesehen. I saw a lot on my last journey through Egypt.
■ **Reisen** travels □ Auf seinen Reisen hat er viel erlebt. He has experienced a lot on his travels.
■ **Gute Reise!** Have a good journey.

das **Reiseandenken** (PL die **Reiseandenken**) NOUN
souvenir

das **Reisebüro** (PL die **Reisebüros**) NOUN
travel agency

der **Reiseführer** (PL die **Reiseführer**) NOUN
1 guidebook
□ Ich habe einen Reiseführer für Griechenland gekauft. I've bought a guidebook to Greece.
2 travel guide
□ Unser Reiseführer hat uns alles erklärt. Our travel guide explained everything to us.

der **Reiseleiter** (PL die **Reiseleiter**) NOUN
courier

reisen (PERFECT **ist gereist**) VERB [36]
to travel
□ Ich reise gern. I like travelling.
■ **reisen nach** to go to □ In den Sommerferien wollen wir nach Griechenland reisen. We want to go to Greece in the summer holidays.

der/die **Reisende** (GEN des/der **Reisenden**, PL die **Reisenden**) NOUN
traveller
□ Ein Reisender hatte sich verirrt. A traveller has got lost.

der **Reisepass** (GEN des **Reisepasses**, PL die **Reisepässe**) NOUN
passport

der **Reisescheck** (PL die **Reiseschecks**) NOUN
traveller's cheque

das **Reiseziel** (PL die **Reiseziele**) NOUN
destination

reißen (IMPERFECT **riss**, PERFECT **hat/ist gerissen**) VERB

LANGUAGE TIP Use **haben** to form the perfect tense. Use **sein** to form the perfect tense for 'to break'.

1 to tear
□ Er riss ihren Brief in tausend Stücke. He tore her letter into a thousand pieces. □ Sie riss sich die Kleider vom Leib. She tore her clothes off.
2 to break
□ Das Seil ist gerissen. The rope has broken.
3 to snatch
□ Er hat mir den Geldbeutel aus der Hand gerissen. He snatched my purse from my hand.
4 to drag
□ Sie hat ihn zu Boden gerissen. She dragged him to the floor.
5 to wrench
□ Er riss das Steuer nach links. He wrenched the steering wheel to the left.
6 to tug
□ Er riss an der Leine. He tugged at the rope.
■ **Witze reißen** to crack jokes
■ **etwas an sich reißen** to seize something □ Er hat versucht, die Macht an sich zu reißen. He tried to seize power.
■ **sich um etwas reißen** to scramble for something □ Die Kinder haben sich um die Luftballons gerissen. The children scrambled for the balloons.

der **Reißverschluss** (GEN des **Reißverschlusses**, PL die **Reißverschlüsse**) NOUN
zip

reiten (IMPERFECT **ritt**, PERFECT **ist geritten**) VERB
to ride

der **Reiter** (PL die **Reiter**) NOUN
rider

die **Reitschule** NOUN
riding school

der **Reiz** (GEN des **Reizes**, PL die **Reize**) NOUN
1 charm
□ der Reiz dieser Stadt the charm of this town
2 appeal
□ der Reiz der Großstadt the appeal of the big city

reizbar ADJECTIVE
irritable

reizen VERB [36]
1 to appeal to
□ Diese Arbeit reizt mich sehr. The work greatly appeals to me. □ Es würde mich reizen, mal nach Kreta zu fahren. The idea of going to Crete appeals to me.

2 to annoy
□ Du musst den Hund nicht reizen. Don't annoy the dog.
3 to irritate
□ Der Rauch reizt die Augen. Smoke irritates the eyes.

reizend ADJECTIVE
charming

reizvoll ADJECTIVE
attractive

die **Reklame** NOUN
1 advertising
□ Im Fernsehen gibt es viel zu viel Reklame. There's far too much advertising on television.
2 advertisement
□ zehn Seiten Reklame ten pages of advertisements

der **Rekord** (PL die **Rekorde**) NOUN
record
□ Der Rekord liegt bei zehn Metern. The record is ten metres. □ einen neuen Rekord aufstellen to set a new record

der **Rektor** (PL die **Rektoren**) NOUN
1 headteacher
□ Der Rektor ist bei uns für die Stundenpläne zuständig. At our school, the headteacher's in charge of timetables.
2 vice-chancellor
□ Zu Semesterbeginn hält der Rektor eine Rede. At the beginning of term the vice-chancellor gives a speech.

das **Rektorat** (PL die **Rektorate**) NOUN
headteacher's office
□ Franz, du sollst aufs Rektorat kommen. Franz, you're to go to the headteacher's office.

relativ ADVERB
relatively
□ Das ist relativ einfach. That's relatively easy.

relaxt ADJECTIVE
relaxed

die **Religion** NOUN
religion

religiös ADJECTIVE
religious

das **Rendezvous** (GEN des **Rendezvous**, PL die **Rendezvous**) NOUN
date
□ Sie hatte gestern Abend ein Rendezvous mit Michael. She had a date with Michael last night.

das **Rennen** (PL die **Rennen**) NOUN
▷ *see also* **rennen** VERB
race
□ ein Pferderennen a horse race
□ ein Autorennen a motor race

rennen (IMPERFECT **rannte**, PERFECT **ist gerannt**) VERB [55]
▷ *see also* **das Rennen** NOUN
to run

der **Rennfahrer** (PL die **Rennfahrer**) NOUN
racing driver

das **Rennpferd** (PL die **Rennpferde**) NOUN
racehorse

der **Rennwagen** (PL die **Rennwagen**) NOUN
racing car

renovieren (PERFECT **hat renoviert**) VERB [76]
to renovate

rentabel ADJECTIVE
1 lucrative
□ eine rentable Arbeit a lucrative job
2 profitable
□ Das wäre nicht rentabel. That wouldn't be profitable.

die **Rente** NOUN
pension
■ **in Rente gehen** to retire
LANGUAGE TIP Be careful! **Rente** does not mean **rent**.

sich **rentieren** (PERFECT **hat sich rentiert**) VERB [76]
to be profitable
□ Das Geschäft rentiert sich nicht mehr. The business is no longer profitable.
■ **Das hat sich rentiert.** That was worthwhile.

der **Rentner** (PL die **Rentner**) NOUN
pensioner

die **Reparatur** NOUN
repair

die **Reparaturwerkstatt** (PL die **Reparaturwerkstätten**) NOUN
garage *(repair shop)*

reparieren (PERFECT **hat repariert**) VERB [76]
to repair

die **Reportage** NOUN
1 report
□ Ich habe eine Reportage über die Zustände in Rumänien gelesen. I read a report about conditions in Romania.
2 live commentary
□ Hast du im Radio die Reportage des Europapokalspiels gehört? Did you hear the live commentary on the European cup game on the radio?

der **Reporter** (PL die **Reporter**) NOUN
reporter

die **Republik** NOUN
republic

republikanisch ADJECTIVE
republican

das **Reservat** (PL die **Reservate**) NOUN
reservation

die **Reserve** NOUN
reserve

das **Reserverad** (PL die **Reserveräder**) NOUN
spare wheel

reservieren (PERFECT **hat reserviert**) VERB [76]
to reserve
□ Ich habe einen Tisch für heute Abend

reservieren lassen. I've reserved a table for this evening.

die **Reservierung** NOUN
reservation

der **Respekt** NOUN
respect

respektieren (PERFECT **hat respektiert**) VERB [76]
to respect

respektlos ADJECTIVE
disrespectful

respektvoll ADJECTIVE
respectful

der **Rest** (PL die **Reste**) NOUN
1 rest
□ Den Rest bezahle ich später. I'll pay the rest later. □ Die meisten sind früher gegangen, der Rest hat noch lange gefeiert. Most left early, but the rest carried on celebrating for a long time.
2 left-over
□ Heute gab's die Reste von gestern. Today we had yesterday's left-overs.
■ **die Reste** the remains □ Das sind die Reste der alten Stadtmauer. These are the remains of the old town walls.

das **Restaurant** (PL die **Restaurants**) NOUN
restaurant

restaurieren (PERFECT **hat restauriert**) VERB [76]
to restore

restlich ADJECTIVE
remaining

der **Restmüll** NOUN
non-recyclable waste

das **Resultat** (PL die **Resultate**) NOUN
result

retten VERB [2]
to rescue

der **Rettich** (PL die **Rettiche**) NOUN
radish

die **Rettung** NOUN
1 rescue
□ Alle zeigten bei der Rettung großen Mut. They all showed great courage during the rescue.
2 salvation
□ Das war meine Rettung. That was my salvation.
3 hope
□ seine letzte Rettung his last hope

das **Rettungsboot** (PL die **Rettungsboote**) NOUN
lifeboat

der **Rettungsdienst** (PL die **Rettungsdienste**) NOUN
rescue service

der **Rettungsring** (PL die **Rettungsringe**) NOUN
lifebelt

der **Rettungswagen** (PL die **Rettungswagen**) NOUN
ambulance

die **Reue** NOUN
remorse
□ Der Täter zeigt keine Reue. The culprit doesn't show any remorse.

das **Revier** (PL die **Reviere**) NOUN
1 police station
□ Der Polizist nahm ihn mit aufs Revier. The policeman took him to the police station.
2 territory
□ Das männliche Tier verteidigt sein Revier. The male animal defends his territory.

die **Revolution** NOUN
revolution
□ die Revolution von 1789 the revolution of 1789

der **Revolver** (PL die **Revolver**) NOUN
revolver

das **Rezept** (PL die **Rezepte**) NOUN
1 recipe
□ Kannst du mir mal das Rezept von deinem Käsekuchen geben? Can you give me your cheesecake recipe?
2 prescription
□ Dieses Medikament bekommt man nur auf Rezept. You can only get this medicine on prescription.

die **Rezeption** NOUN
reception

rezeptpflichtig ADJECTIVE
available only on prescription
■ **rezeptpflichtige Medikamente** prescribed drugs

der **Rhabarber** NOUN
rhubarb

der **Rhein** NOUN
Rhine

> **DID YOU KNOW...?**
> The Rhine is 1320 km long and the entire 865 km which flows through Germany is navigable, making it an important inland waterway. It flows past such important cities as Karlsruhe, Mannheim, Ludwigshafen, Mainz, Cologne, Düsseldorf and Duisburg.

Rheinland-Pfalz NEUT NOUN
Rhineland-Palatinate

> **DID YOU KNOW...?**
> **Rheinland-Pfalz** is one of the 16 **Länder**. Its capital is Mainz. It is home to the BASF chemicals giant and to Germany's biggest television network, ZDF (Channel 2).

das **Rheuma** NOUN
rheumatism
□ Meine Oma hat Rheuma. My granny's got rheumatism.

der **Rhythmus** (GEN des **Rhythmus**, PL die **Rhythmen**) NOUN
rhythm

richten VERB [2]
to point
□ Er richtete das Fernrohr zum Himmel. He pointed the telescope at the sky.
■ **eine Waffe auf jemanden richten** to aim a weapon at somebody
■ **etwas an jemanden richten** to address something to somebody □ Der Brief war an meine Eltern gerichtet. The letter was addressed to my parents.
■ **Ich richte mich ganz nach dir.** I'll do whatever you want.
■ **sich nach etwas richten 1** to conform to something □ Auch du solltest dich danach richten, wie wir das hier machen. You should conform to our way of doing things. **2** to be determined by something □ Das Angebot richtet sich nach der Nachfrage. Supply is determined by demand.

der **Richter** (PL die **Richter**) NOUN
judge

richtig ADJECTIVE, ADVERB
1 right
□ Es war nicht richtig von dir, ihn zu belügen. It wasn't right of you to lie to him. □ Das war nicht die richtige Antwort. That wasn't the right answer.
■ **Bin ich hier richtig?** Have I come to the right place?
■ **der Richtige** the right person
■ **das Richtige** the right thing
2 correctly
□ Du hast das nicht richtig geschrieben. You haven't written that correctly.
3 proper
□ Ich will ein richtiges Motorrad und kein Moped. I want a proper motorbike, not a moped.
4 really
□ Wir waren richtig froh, als es vorbei war. We were really glad when it was over.

die **Richtung** NOUN
direction
□ Wir gehen in die falsche Richtung. We are going in the wrong direction. □ in östlicher Richtung in an easterly direction

rieb VERB ▷ *see* **reiben**

riechen (IMPERFECT **roch**, PERFECT **hat gerochen**) VERB
to smell
□ Ich rieche Gas. I can smell gas. □ Das riecht gut. That smells good. □ Ich kann nichts riechen. I can't smell anything.
■ **an etwas riechen** to smell something □ Sie roch an der Rose. She smelled the rose.
■ **nach etwas riechen** to smell of something □ Hier riecht es nach Benzin. It smells of petrol here.
■ **Ich kann ihn nicht riechen.** I can't stand him.

LANGUAGE TIP Word for word, **Ich kann ihn nicht riechen** means 'I can't smell him'.

rief VERB ▷ *see* **rufen**

der **Riegel** (PL die **Riegel**) NOUN
1 bolt
□ Sie schob den Riegel vor die Tür. She bolted the door.
2 bar
□ Für unterwegs haben wir einen Schokoriegel mitgenommen. We've brought a bar of chocolate to eat on the way.

der **Riese** (GEN des **Riesen**, PL die **Riesen**) NOUN
giant

riesengroß ADJECTIVE
gigantic

riesig ADJECTIVE
huge

riet VERB ▷ *see* **raten**

das **Rind** (PL die **Rinder**) NOUN
1 ox *(male)*
2 cow *(female)*
■ **Rinder** cattle □ Seine Rinder sind im Sommer auf der Weide. His cattle spend the summer on the meadow.
3 beef
□ Wir essen kaum noch Rind. We hardly eat beef any more.

die **Rinde** NOUN
1 rind
□ Er schnitt die Rinde vom Käse ab. He cut the rind off the cheese.
2 crust
□ frisches Brot mit knuspriger Rinde fresh crusty bread
3 bark
□ Er ritzte ihren Namen in die Rinde einer Eiche. He carved her name into the bark of an oak tree.

das **Rindfleisch** NOUN
beef

der **Ring** (PL die **Ringe**) NOUN
ring

das **Ringbuch** (PL die **Ringbücher**) NOUN
ring binder

das **Ringen** NOUN
wrestling
□ Ringen ist sein Hobby. His hobby is wrestling.

der **Ringkampf** (PL die **Ringkämpfe**) NOUN
wrestling bout

ringsum ADVERB
all around
□ Wir sahen ringsum Menschen. We saw people all around. □ Er blickte ringsum. He looked all around.

die **Rippe** NOUN
rib

das **Risiko** (PL die **Risiken**) NOUN
risk

riskant ADJECTIVE
risky

riskieren (PERFECT **hat riskiert**) VERB [76]
to risk

der **Riss** (GEN des **Risses**, PL die **Risse**) NOUN
1 crack
□ Die Maus verschwand durch einen Riss in der Mauer. The mouse disappeared into a crack in the wall. □ Der trockene Boden war voller Risse. The dry soil was full of cracks.
2 tear
□ Er hatte einen Riss in der Hose. There was a tear in his trousers.

rissig ADJECTIVE
1 cracked
□ Von der Trockenheit ist die Erde rissig geworden. The soil is cracked as a result of the drought.
2 chapped
□ Vom vielen Waschen hat sie ganz rissige Hände. Her hands are all chapped from doing so much washing.

ritt VERB ▷ *see* **reiten**

der **Rivale** (GEN des **Rivalen**, PL die **Rivalen**) NOUN
rival

die **Robbe** NOUN
seal
□ ein Robbenbaby a seal pup

der **Roboter** (PL die **Roboter**) NOUN
robot

roch VERB ▷ *see* **riechen**

der **Rock** (PL die **Röcke**) NOUN
skirt

der **Roggen** NOUN
rye

roh ADJECTIVE
1 raw
□ rohes Fleisch raw meat □ Karotten esse ich am liebsten roh. I like carrots best raw.
2 callous
□ Sei nicht so roh. Don't be so callous.
3 rough
□ Er hat sie ziemlich roh mit sich gezogen. He dragged her off pretty roughly.

das **Rohr** (PL die **Rohre**) NOUN
1 pipe
□ Das Abwasser wird durch Rohre in die Kanalisation geleitet. Sewage is fed into the sewer via pipes.
2 cane
□ ein Stuhl aus Rohr a cane chair
3 reeds
□ In dem Teich wuchs Rohr. Reeds were growing in the pond.

der **Rohstoff** (PL die **Rohstoffe**) NOUN
raw material

der **Rolladen** NOUN ▷ *see* **Rollladen**

das **Rollbrett** (PL die **Rollbretter**) NOUN
skateboard

die **Rolle** NOUN
1 role
□ Der Schauspieler hat die Rolle des Königs gut gespielt. The actor was good in the role of the king. □ Die Rolle der Frau hat sich geändert. The role of women has changed.
2 castor
□ ein Stuhl mit Rollen a chair with castors
3 roll
□ eine Rolle Toilettenpapier a roll of toilet paper
4 reel
□ Sie hat den Faden von der Rolle abgewickelt. She unwound the thread from the reel.
■ **keine Rolle spielen** not to matter
□ Das Wetter spielt keine Rolle. The weather doesn't matter.
■ **eine wichtige Rolle spielen bei** to play a major role in □ Er hat bei der Planung des Abschlussfestes eine wichtige Rolle gespielt. He played a major role in organizing the end-of-term party.

rollen (PERFECT **hat/ist gerollt**) VERB [38]
LANGUAGE TIP For the perfect tense use **haben** when the verb has an object and **sein** when there is no object.
to roll
□ Sie haben den Stein den Berg hinuntergerollt. They rolled the stone down the hill. □ Der Ball ist direkt vor ein Auto gerollt. The ball rolled right in front of a car.

der **Roller** (PL die **Roller**) NOUN
scooter

der **Rollladen** (PL die **Rollläden**) NOUN
shutter

der **Rollschuh** (PL die **Rollschuhe**) NOUN
roller skate

der **Rollstuhl** (PL die **Rollstühle**) NOUN
wheelchair

die **Rolltreppe** NOUN
escalator

Rom NEUT NOUN
Rome
■ **nach Rom** to Rome

der **Roman** (PL die **Romane**) NOUN
novel

romantisch ADJECTIVE
romantic

römisch ADJECTIVE
Roman

röntgen VERB [54]
to X-ray

rosa ADJECTIVE
pink
□ Sie hatte ein rosa Kleid an. She was wearing a pink dress.

die **Rose** NOUN
rose

der **Rosenkohl** NOUN
Brussels sprouts
□ Rosenkohl ist mein Lieblingsgemüse.
Brussels sprouts are my favourite vegetable.

der **Rosenmontag** (PL die **Rosenmontage**) NOUN
Monday before Shrove Tuesday

DID YOU KNOW...?
Rosenmontag is an important day in the carnival festivities. Cities such as Cologne, Düsseldorf and Mainz traditionally have long processions with carnival floats on **Rosenmontag**.

die **Rosine** NOUN
raisin

der **Rost** (PL die **Roste**) NOUN
rust
□ An diesem Auto ist viel Rost. This car has a lot of rust on it.
■ **ein Bratrost** a grill

rosten (PERFECT **ist gerostet**) VERB [2]
to rust

rösten VERB [2]
1 to roast
□ geröstete Erdnüsse roasted peanuts
2 to toast
□ Brot rösten to toast bread
3 to grill
□ Würstchen auf dem Grill rösten to grill sausages

rostig ADJECTIVE
rusty

rot ADJECTIVE
red
□ Sein Gesicht wurde immer röter. His face got redder and redder.
■ **in den roten Zahlen** in the red
■ **das Rote Meer** the Red Sea

die **Röteln** PL NOUN
German measles
□ Röteln sind für schwangere Frauen gefährlich. German measles is dangerous for pregnant women.

rothaarig ADJECTIVE
red-haired

der **Rotkohl** NOUN
red cabbage

der **Rotwein** (PL die **Rotweine**) NOUN
red wine

die **Roulade** NOUN
beef olive

die **Route** NOUN
route

der **Routenplaner** (PL die **Routenplaner**) NOUN
route planner

der **Rowdy** (PL die **Rowdys**) NOUN
hooligan

die **Rübe** NOUN
beet
□ Der Bauer füttert die Kühe mit Rüben.
The farmer feeds his cows on beet.
■ **Gelbe Rübe** carrot
■ **Rote Rübe** beetroot

rüber ADVERB
over
□ Komm hier rüber, da siehst du besser.
Come over here, you'll get a better view.
□ Ich geh mal zu den Nachbarn rüber.
I'm just going over to our neighbours.

der **Rücken** (PL die **Rücken**) NOUN
▹ *see also* **rücken** VERB
back
□ Er schläft auf dem Rücken. He sleeps on his back.

rücken (PERFECT **ist/hat gerückt**) VERB [38]
▹ *see also* **der Rücken** NOUN

LANGUAGE TIP For the perfect tense use **haben** when the verb has an object and **sein** when there is no object.

1 to move over
□ Rück mal ein bisschen. Move over a bit.
2 to shift
□ Sie rückten den Schrank zur Seite.
They shifted the cupboard to one side.

das **Rückenmark** NOUN
spinal cord

die **Rückenschmerzen** PL NOUN
backache

das **Rückenschwimmen** NOUN
backstroke

die **Rückfahrkarte** NOUN
return ticket

die **Rückfahrt** NOUN
return journey

der **Rückflug** (PL die **Rückflüge**) NOUN
return flight

die **Rückgabe** NOUN
return

rückgängig ADJECTIVE
■ **etwas rückgängig machen** to cancel something

das **Rückgrat** (PL die **Rückgrate**) NOUN
spine

die **Rückkehr** NOUN
return
□ bei unserer Rückkehr on our return

das **Rücklicht** (PL die **Rücklichter**) NOUN
rear light

die **Rückreise** NOUN
return journey

die **Rücksicht** NOUN
consideration
■ **auf jemanden Rücksicht nehmen** to show consideration for somebody
□ Du solltest mehr Rücksicht auf deine Mitschüler nehmen. You should show more consideration for your fellow pupils.

rücksichtslos ADJECTIVE
inconsiderate

■ **ein rücksichtsloser Fahrer** a reckless driver

rücksichtsvoll ADJECTIVE
considerate

der **Rücksitz** (PL die **Rücksitze**) NOUN
back seat
□ Dieser Sportwagen hat keine Rücksitze. This sports car has no back seats.
■ **auf dem Rücksitz** in the back

der **Rückspiegel** (PL die **Rückspiegel**) NOUN
rear-view mirror

das **Rückspiel** (PL die **Rückspiele**) NOUN
return match

der **Rücktritt** (PL die **Rücktritte**) NOUN
resignation

rückwärts ADVERB
backwards
□ rückwärts zählen to count backwards

der **Rückwärtsgang** (PL die **Rückwärtsgänge**) NOUN
reverse gear

der **Rückweg** (PL die **Rückwege**) NOUN
way back

das **Ruder** (PL die **Ruder**) NOUN
1 oar
□ ein Boot mit zwei Rudern a boat with two oars
2 rudder
□ Der Steuermann steht am Ruder. The helmsman stands at the rudder.

das **Ruderboot** (PL die **Ruderboote**) NOUN
rowing boat

rudern (PERFECT **hat/ist gerudert**) VERB [88]

LANGUAGE TIP Use **haben** for the perfect tense when you describe the activity and **sein** when you describe the motion.

to row
□ Zuerst hat er gerudert, dann sie. First he rowed, then she did. □ Wir sind über den See gerudert. We rowed across the lake.

der **Ruf** (PL die **Rufe**) NOUN
1 shout
□ Wir hörten seine Rufe. We heard his shouts.
2 reputation
□ Das schadet seinem Ruf. This will damage his reputation.

rufen (IMPERFECT **rief**, PERFECT **hat gerufen**) VERB [56]
1 to call out
□ Ich habe gerufen, es hat mich aber niemand gehört. I called out, but nobody heard me.
■ **Der Patient rief nach der Schwester.** The patient called for the nurse.
2 to call
□ Wir sollten den Arzt rufen. We ought to call the doctor. □ Sie hat mir ein Taxi gerufen. She called me a taxi.
3 to shout
□ Sie rief um Hilfe. She shouted for help.

die **Rufnummer** NOUN
telephone number

die **Ruhe** NOUN
1 rest
□ Nach den anstrengenden Tagen brauche ich etwas Ruhe. After the strain of the last few days I need a rest.
2 peace
□ Jetzt kann ich in Ruhe arbeiten. Now I can work in peace.
3 peace and quiet
□ Die Kinder sind weg, ich genieße die Ruhe. The children are out and I'm enjoying the peace and quiet.
■ **in aller Ruhe** calmly
■ **jemanden aus der Ruhe bringen** to unsettle somebody □ Dieser Anruf hat mich aus der Ruhe gebracht. The phone call unsettled me.
4 silence
□ Ich bitte um etwas mehr Ruhe. I would ask you for a bit more silence.
■ **Ruhe!** Silence!
■ **jemanden in Ruhe lassen** to leave somebody alone □ Lass endlich deine Schwester in Ruhe. Will you leave your sister alone!
■ **sich zur Ruhe setzen** to retire

die **Ruhestörung** NOUN
breach of the peace

der **Ruhetag** NOUN
day off
□ einen Ruhetag einlegen to have a day off
■ **'Mittwochs Ruhetag'** 'closed on Wednesdays'

ruhig ADJECTIVE, ADVERB
1 quiet
□ Im Haus war alles ruhig. The house was completely quiet. □ Die Kinder haben ruhig gespielt. The children played quietly.
□ Seid endlich ruhig! Will you be quiet!
2 still
□ Bleib ruhig stehen, dann tut dir der Hund nichts. If you keep still the dog won't hurt you.
■ **eine ruhige Hand** a steady hand
3 calm
□ Wie kannst du so ruhig bleiben? How can you stay so calm? □ Ich bin ganz ruhig in die Prüfung gegangen. I went quite calmly into the exam.
■ **ein ruhiges Gewissen** a clear conscience
■ **Kommen Sie ruhig herein!** Come on in.

der **Ruhm** NOUN
fame

das **Rührei** (PL die **Rühreier**) NOUN
scrambled eggs

rühren VERB [38]
1 to stir
□ Sie rührte mit dem Löffel in der Soße. She stirred the sauce with the spoon.

2 to move
□ Ich kann meine Beine nicht rühren. I can't move my legs.
■ **sich rühren** to move □ Sie hatte so Angst, dass sie sich nicht rührte. She was so afraid that she didn't move.
■ **jemanden rühren** to move somebody
□ Die Armut der Kinder hat uns gerührt. The children's poverty moved us.

rührend ADJECTIVE
touching
□ eine rührende Geschichte a touching story
□ Er ist rührend naiv. He's touchingly naive.

die **Ruine** NOUN
ruin

ruinieren (PERFECT **hat ruiniert**) VERB [76]
to ruin

der **Rumäne** (GEN des **Rumänen**, PL die **Rumänen**) NOUN
Romanian

Rumänien NEUT NOUN
Romania
■ **aus Rumänien** from Romania
■ **nach Rumänien** to Romania

die **Rumänin** NOUN
Romanian

rumänisch ADJECTIVE
Romanian

der **Rummelplatz** (GEN des **Rummelplatzes**, PL die **Rummelplätze**) NOUN
fairground

rund ADJECTIVE, ADVERB
1 round
□ Sie hat ein rundes Gesicht. She's got a round face.
2 about
□ Das kostet rund hundert Euro. It costs about a hundred euros.
■ **rund um etwas** around something
□ Die Stadtmauer geht rund um die Stadt. The town walls go around the town.

die **Runde** NOUN
1 lap
□ Das Auto fuhr ein paar Runden. The car drove a few laps.
2 round
□ Diese Runde zahle ich. I'll get this round.

DID YOU KNOW...?
It isn't usual to buy rounds in Germany. Normally people just order what they want from the waiter, and pay when they leave. You can, however, buy a round (**eine Runde schmeißen**) if you're feeling generous.

3 lap
□ Er liegt in der letzten Runde in Führung. He's in the lead on the last lap.
4 party
□ Wir waren eine fröhliche Runde. We were a merry party.

die **Rundfahrt** NOUN
round trip

der **Rundfunk** NOUN
broadcasting
■ **im Rundfunk** on the radio

runter ADVERB
1 off
□ Runter vom Tisch! Get off the table!
2 down
□ Dann ging's den Berg runter. Then off we went down the mountain.

runterladen (PRESENT **lädt runter**, IMPERFECT **lud runter**, PERFECT **hat runtergeladen**) VERB
to download *(computer)*
□ eine Datei runterladen to download a file

der **Ruß** (GEN des **Rußes**) NOUN
soot

der **Russe** (GEN des **Russen**, PL die **Russen**) NOUN
Russian

der **Rüssel** (PL die **Rüssel**) NOUN
1 snout
□ der Rüssel eines Schweins a pig's snout
2 trunk
□ der Rüssel eines Elefanten an elephant's trunk

rußig ADJECTIVE
sooty

die **Russin** NOUN
Russian

russisch ADJECTIVE
Russian

Russland NEUT NOUN
Russia
■ **aus Russland** from Russia
■ **nach Russland** to Russia

die **Rüstung** NOUN
1 suit of armour
□ In der Burg standen ein paar rostige Rüstungen. There were a couple of rusty suits of armour in the castle.
2 armaments
□ Es wird viel Geld für Rüstung ausgegeben. A lot of money is spent on armaments.

die **Rutschbahn** NOUN
slide

rutschen (PERFECT **ist gerutscht**) VERB [48]
1 to slip
□ Sie ist auf dem Eis gerutscht und hingefallen. She slipped and fell on the ice.
□ Der Teller ist mir aus der Hand gerutscht. The plate slipped out of my hand.
2 to move over
□ Rutsch mal ein bisschen! Move over a bit.

Ss

der **Saal** (PL die **Säle**) NOUN
hall

das **Saarland** NOUN
Saarland

> **DID YOU KNOW...?**
> The **Saarland** is one of the 16 **Länder**. Its capital is Saarbrücken. While its coal and steel industries have been in crisis, it still has flourishing ceramics and glass industries.

die **Sache** NOUN
1 thing
□ Räum bitte deine Sachen weg. Please put your things away. □ Pack warme Sachen ein. Pack warm things. □ Was machst du denn für Sachen? The things you do!
2 matter
□ Wir sollten diese Sache ausdiskutieren. We should discuss this matter fully. □ Die Polizei wird dieser Sache nachgehen. The police will investigate this affair.
3 job
□ Es ist deine Sache, dich darum zu kümmern. It's your job to see to it.
■ **Mach keine Sachen!** Don't be silly!
■ **zur Sache** to the point □ Komm endlich zur Sache! Get to the point!

sachlich ADJECTIVE
1 objective
□ ein sehr sachlicher Bericht a very objective report □ Du solltest sachlich bleiben. Y ou should remain objective.
2 factual
□ Was er sagt, ist sachlich falsch. What he says is factually inaccurate.

sächlich ADJECTIVE
neuter

Sachsen NEUT NOUN
Saxony

> **DID YOU KNOW...?**
> **Sachsen** is one of the 16 **Länder**. Its capital is Dresden. Its largest city, Leipzig, is famous for its industrial fair and was one of the main centres of the peaceful revolt against the DDR regime.

Sachsen-Anhalt NEUT NOUN
Saxony-Anhalt

> **DID YOU KNOW...?**
> **Sachsen-Anhalt** is one of the 16 **Länder**. Its capital is Magdeburg. It has a rich cultural past: Martin Luther and Georg Friedrich Händel were born here, and the Bauhaus school of architecture was situated in Dessau.

sächsisch ADJECTIVE
Saxon

sachte ADVERB
softly

der **Sack** (PL die **Säcke**) NOUN
sack

die **Sackgasse** NOUN
cul-de-sac

der **Saft** (PL die **Säfte**) NOUN
juice

saftig ADJECTIVE
juicy

die **Säge** NOUN
saw

sagen VERB [38]
1 to say
□ Ich kann noch nicht sagen, ob ich komme. I can't say yet if I'll come. □ Habe ich etwas Falsches gesagt? Have I said something wrong? □ Wie sagt man 'danke' auf Japanisch? How do you say 'thank you' in Japanese? □ Was sagst du zu meinem Vorschlag? What do you say to my suggestion?
■ **Man sagt, dass ...** It's said that ...
2 to tell
□ Kannst du ihm bitte sagen, er soll seine Eltern anrufen. Can you tell him to call his parents. □ Ich werde es ihr sagen. I'll tell her. □ Sag ihm, er solle das nicht tun. Tell him he shouldn't do it.
■ **etwas zu jemandem sagen** to call somebody something □ Die Kinder sagen Onja zu mir. The children call me Onja.
■ **zu sagen haben** to have a say □ Du hast hier nichts zu sagen. You don't have a say in this matter.
■ **Das hat nichts zu sagen.** It doesn't mean anything.

sägen VERB [38]
to saw

sagenhaft ADJECTIVE
1 legendary
□ der sagenhafte König Artus the legendary King Arthur
2 terrific
□ Das war ein sagenhaftes Glück. That was terrific luck.

sah VERB ▷ *see* **sehen**

die **Sahne** NOUN
cream

die **Saison** (PL die **Saisons**) NOUN
season

die **Saite** NOUN
string

das **Saiteninstrument** (PL die **Saiteninstrumente**) NOUN
stringed instrument

der **Salat** (PL die **Salate**) NOUN
1 salad
□ Es gab verschiedene Salate. There were various salads.
2 lettuce
□ Am liebsten mag ich grünen Salat. I like lettuce best.

die **Salbe** NOUN
ointment

das **Salz** (GEN des **Salzes**) NOUN
salt

salzen (PERFECT **hat gesalzen**) VERB
to salt

salzig ADJECTIVE
salty

die **Salzkartoffeln** FEM PL NOUN
boiled potatoes

die **Salzstange** NOUN
pretzel stick

das **Salzwasser** NOUN
salt water

der **Samen** (PL die **Samen**) NOUN
seed
□ Hast du die Blumensamen schon ausgesät? Have you sown the flower seeds yet?

sammeln VERB [34]
1 to collect
□ Er sammelt Briefmarken. He collects stamps.
□ Sie sammeln für ein Waisenhaus. They're collecting for an orphanage. □ Altpapier wird gesammelt und wiederverwertet. Waste paper is collected and recycled.
2 to gather
□ Wir haben Pilze gesammelt. We gathered mushrooms.

die **Sammlung** NOUN
collection

der **Samstag** (PL die **Samstage**) NOUN
Saturday
□ am Samstag on Saturday

samstags ADVERB
on Saturdays

der **Samt** (PL die **Samte**) NOUN
▷ *see also* **samt** PREPOSITION
velvet

samt PREPOSITION
▷ *see also* **der Samt** NOUN

LANGUAGE TIP The preposition **samt** takes the dative.

with
□ Sie kamen samt Kindern und Hund. They came with their children and dog.

der **Sand** NOUN
sand

die **Sandale** NOUN
sandal

sandig ADJECTIVE
sandy

der **Sandkasten** (PL die **Sandkästen**) NOUN
sandpit

der **Sandstrand** (PL die **Sandstrände**) NOUN
sandy beach

sandte VERB ▷ *see* **senden**

sanft ADJECTIVE
gentle
□ etwas sanft berühren to touch something gently

sang VERB ▷ *see* **singen**

der **Sänger** (PL die **Sänger**) NOUN
singer

die **Sängerin** NOUN
singer

die **Sardine** NOUN
sardine

der **Sarg** (PL die **Särge**) NOUN
coffin

der **Sarkasmus** (GEN des **Sarkasmus**, PL die **Sarkasmen**) NOUN
sarcasm

saß VERB ▷ *see* **sitzen**

der **Satellit** (GEN des **Satelliten**, PL die **Satelliten**) NOUN
satellite

das **Satellitenfernsehen** NOUN
satellite television

satt ADJECTIVE
1 full
□ Ich bin satt. I'm full.
■ **Wir sind nicht satt geworden.** We didn't get enough to eat.
■ **sich satt essen** to eat one's fill
■ **satt machen** to be filling
■ **jemanden satt sein** to be fed up with somebody
2 rich
□ satte Farben rich colours □ ein sattes Rot a rich red

der **Sattel** (PL die **Sättel**) NOUN
saddle

der **Satz** (GEN des **Satzes**, PL die **Sätze**) NOUN
1 sentence
□ Bitte antworte mit einem ganzen Satz. Please answer in a complete sentence.

■ **ein Nebensatz** a subordinate clause
■ **ein Adverbialsatz** an adverbial clause
2 theorem
□ der Satz des Pythagoras Pythagoras' theorem
3 set
□ Becker hat den ersten Satz verloren. Becker lost the first set. □ ein Satz Schraubenschlüssel a set of screwdrivers
4 rate
□ Die Krankenversicherung hat ihre Sätze erhöht. The health insurance has increased its rates.

das **Satzzeichen** (PL die **Satzzeichen**) NOUN
punctuation mark

sauber ADJECTIVE
1 clean
□ Die Wäsche ist nicht sauber geworden. The washing hasn't come up clean.
2 fine
□ Du bist mir ein sauberer Freund! You're a fine friend!
■ **sauber machen** to clean

die **Sauberkeit** NOUN
cleanness

saubermachen VERB [48] ▷ *see* **sauber**

die **Sauce** NOUN
sauce

sauer ADJECTIVE
1 sour
□ Der Apfel ist sauer. The apple is sour.
□ Die Milch ist sauer geworden. The milk has turned sour.
2 acid
□ saurer Regen acid rain
3 cross
□ Ich bin sauer auf meine Freundin. I'm cross with my girlfriend.

die **Sauerei** NOUN
1 scandal
□ Es ist eine Sauerei, dass wir länger arbeiten müssen. It's a scandal that we have to work longer hours.
2 mess
□ Wer hat denn die Sauerei im Bad gemacht? Who made the mess in the bathroom?
3 obscenity
□ Über solche Sauereien kann ich nicht lachen. I can't laugh at such obscenities.

das **Sauerkraut** NOUN
sauerkraut *(pickled cabbage)*

der **Sauerstoff** NOUN
oxygen

saufen (PRESENT **säuft**, IMPERFECT **soff**, PERFECT **hat gesoffen**) VERB
to booze

saugen (IMPERFECT **saugte** *or* **sog**, PERFECT **hat gesaugt** *or* **gesogen**) VERB
to suck

das **Säugetier** (PL die **Säugetiere**) NOUN
mammal

der **Säugling** (PL die **Säuglinge**) NOUN
infant

die **Säule** NOUN
column

die **Sauna** (PL die **Saunas**) NOUN
sauna

die **Säure** NOUN
acid
□ Die Säure hat den Stein zerfressen. The acid has eaten away at the stone.

das **Saxofon** (PL die **Saxofone**) NOUN
saxophone
□ Er spielt Saxofon. He plays the saxophone.

die **S-Bahn** NOUN
suburban railway

die **SB-Tankstelle** NOUN
self-service petrol station

das **Schach** NOUN
chess
□ Ich kann nicht Schach spielen. I can't play chess.

das **Schachbrett** (PL die **Schachbretter**) NOUN
chessboard

die **Schachfigur** NOUN
chessman

die **Schachtel** NOUN
box

schade ADJECTIVE, EXCLAMATION
a pity
□ Es ist schade um das gute Essen. It's a pity to waste good food. □ Das ist aber schade. That's a pity.
■ **Wie schade!** What a pity! □ Wie schade, dass du nicht mitkommen kannst. What a pity you can't come.
■ **für etwas zu schade sein** to be too good for something □ Diese Decke ist doch zu schade für ein Picknick. This blanket is too good for a picnic.
■ **sich für etwas zu schade sein** to consider oneself too good for something □ Du bist dir für so eine Arbeit wohl zu schade? So you consider yourself too good for a job like that?

der **Schädel** (PL die **Schädel**) NOUN
skull

der **Schaden** (PL die **Schäden**) NOUN
▷ *see also* **schaden** VERB
1 damage
□ Der Schaden an seinem Auto war nicht so groß. The damage to his car wasn't too bad.
2 injury
□ Sie hat den Unfall ohne Schaden überstanden. She came out of the accident without injury.
3 disadvantage
□ Es soll dein Schaden nicht sein. It won't be to your disadvantage.

schaden VERB [54]
▷ *see also* **der Schaden** NOUN

■ **jemandem schaden** to harm somebody □ Ich habe den Eindruck, dass sie mir schaden will. I've got the feeling that she wants to harm me.
■ **einer Sache schaden** to damage something □ Das hat unserem Ruf geschadet. That's damaged our reputation.
■ **es kann nicht schaden ...** it can't do any harm ... □ Es kann nicht schaden, wenn du die Vokabeln noch einmal wiederholst. It can't do any harm for you to go over the vocabulary once more.

der **Schadenersatz** (GEN des **Schadenersatzes**) NOUN
compensation

schädigen (PERFECT **hat geschädigt**) VERB [38]
to damage

schädlich ADJECTIVE
harmful
□ Rauchen ist schädlich. Smoking is harmful.
□ Alkohol ist für die Leber schädlich. Alcohol is harmful to your liver.

der **Schadstoff** (PL die **Schadstoffe**) NOUN
harmful substance

das **Schaf** (PL die **Schafe**) NOUN
sheep
□ zehn Schafe ten sheep

der **Schäferhund** (PL die **Schäferhunde**) NOUN
Alsatian

schaffen (1) (IMPERFECT **schuf**, PERFECT **hat geschaffen**) VERB
to create
□ Die Regierung will neue Arbeitsplätze schaffen. The government wants to create new jobs.

schaffen (2) (IMPERFECT **schaffte**, PERFECT **hat geschafft**) VERB [48]
to manage
□ Die Übersetzung schaffe ich heute noch. I'll manage that translation today. □ Er schafft das nicht allein. He won't manage to do that on his own. □ Wir haben den Zug gerade noch geschafft. We just managed to catch the train.
■ **eine Prüfung schaffen** to pass an exam
■ **Ich bin geschafft!** I'm shattered!

der **Schal** (PL die **Schale** *or* **Schals**) NOUN
scarf

die **Schale** NOUN
1 skin
□ eine Bananenschale a banana skin
2 peel
□ die Kartoffelschalen the potato peel
□ eine Zitronenschale lemon peel
3 shell
□ Die Nussschalen nicht in den Kompost werfen. Don't throw the nutshells onto the compost heap. □ Diese Eier haben sehr dünne Schalen. These eggs have very thin shells.
4 bowl
□ Auf dem Tisch stand eine Schale mit Obst. There was a bowl of fruit on the table.

schälen VERB [38]
1 to peel
□ einen Apfel schälen to peel an apple
2 to shell
□ Nüsse schälen to shell nuts
■ **sich schälen** to peel □ Ich schäle mich auf der Nase. My nose is peeling.

der **Schall** NOUN
sound

die **Schallmauer** NOUN
sound barrier

die **Schallplatte** NOUN
record

schalten VERB [2]
1 to switch
□ den Herd auf 'aus' schalten to switch the oven to 'off'
2 to change gear
□ Du solltest schalten. You should change gear.
■ **in den vierten Gang schalten** to change into fourth
3 to catch on
□ Ich habe zu spät geschaltet. I caught on too late.

der **Schalter** (PL die **Schalter**) NOUN
1 counter
□ Zahlen Sie bitte am Schalter dort drüben. Please pay at the counter over there.
2 switch
□ Wo ist der Lichtschalter? Where is the light switch?

das **Schaltjahr** (PL die **Schaltjahre**) NOUN
leap year

sich **schämen** VERB [38]
to be ashamed
□ sich einer Sache schämen to be ashamed of something

die **Schande** NOUN
disgrace

scharf ADJECTIVE
1 sharp
□ ein scharfes Messer a sharp knife
□ eine scharfe Kurve a sharp corner
■ **ein scharfer Wind** a biting wind
2 hot
□ Indisches Essen ist schärfer als deutsches. Indian food is hotter than German food.
■ **scharfe Munition** live ammunition
■ **scharf schießen** to shoot with live ammunition
■ **scharf nachdenken** to think hard
■ **auf etwas scharf sein** to be mad about something □ Er ist ganz scharf auf Gummibärchen. He is mad about jelly bears.
■ **auf jemanden scharf sein** to fancy somebody □ Ich glaube, Manfred ist scharf auf dich. I think Manfred fancies you.

German-English

der **Schatten** (PL die **Schatten**) NOUN
1 shadow
2 shade
□ Wir saßen im Schatten. We sat in the shade.

schattig ADJECTIVE
shady

der **Schatz** (GEN des **Schatzes**, PL die **Schätze**) NOUN
1 treasure
□ der Schatz der Piraten the pirates' treasure
2 darling
□ Du bist ein Schatz! You're a darling!
□ Mein Schatz. My darling.

das **Schätzchen** (PL die **Schätzchen**) NOUN
darling

schätzen VERB [36]
1 to guess
□ Schätz mal, wie viel das gekostet hat. Guess how much that cost.
■ **Man kann sein Alter schlecht schätzen.** It's difficult to tell how old he is.
2 to value
□ Ich werde die alte Uhr schätzen lassen. I'm going to have the old clock valued.
3 to appreciate
□ Ich schätze deine Hilfe sehr. I really appreciate your help.

das **Schaubild** (PL die **Schaubilder**) NOUN
diagram

schauen VERB [38]
to look
□ Schau mal an die Tafel. Look at the board.

der **Schauer** (PL die **Schauer**) NOUN
1 shower
□ Für morgen sind Schauer angesagt. Showers are forecast for tomorrow.
2 shudder
□ Ein Schauer überlief sie. A shudder ran through her body.

die **Schaufel** NOUN
shovel

das **Schaufenster** (PL die **Schaufenster**) NOUN
shop window

der **Schaufensterbummel** (PL die **Schaufensterbummel**) NOUN
window shopping

die **Schaukel** NOUN
swing

schaukeln VERB [34]
to swing

der **Schaumgummi** NOUN
foam rubber

das **Schauspiel** NOUN
play *(theatre)*

der **Schauspieler** (PL die **Schauspieler**) NOUN
actor

die **Schauspielerin** NOUN
actress

der **Scheck** (PL die **Schecks**) NOUN
cheque

das **Scheckheft** (PL die **Scheckhefte**) NOUN
cheque book

die **Scheckkarte** NOUN
cheque card

die **Scheibe** NOUN
slice
□ Sie belegte das Brot mit mehreren Scheiben Wurst. She put several slices of cold meat on the bread.

der **Scheibenwischer** (PL die **Scheibenwischer**) NOUN
windscreen wiper

scheiden (IMPERFECT **schied**, PERFECT **hat geschieden**) VERB
■ **sich scheiden lassen** to get a divorce
■ **geschieden sein** to be divorced

die **Scheidung** NOUN
divorce

der **Schein** (PL die **Scheine**) NOUN
1 light
□ beim Schein einer Kerze by the light of a candle
2 appearance
□ Der Schein trügt. Appearances are deceptive.
3 note
□ Er hat in großen Scheinen bezahlt. He paid in large notes.
4 certificate
□ Am Ende des Semesters bekommt man einen Schein. You get a certificate at the end of the semester.
■ **etwas zum Schein tun** to pretend to do something □ Er ging zum Schein auf den Vorschlag ein. He pretended to go along with the suggestion.

scheinbar ADVERB
apparently

scheinen (IMPERFECT **schien**, PERFECT **hat geschienen**) VERB [57]
1 to shine
□ Die Sonne scheint. The sun is shining.
2 to seem
□ Sie scheint glücklich zu sein. She seems to be happy.

der **Scheinwerfer** (PL die **Scheinwerfer**) NOUN
1 headlamp
□ Die Scheinwerfer des entgegenkommenden Autos haben mich geblendet. The headlamps of the approaching car blinded me.
2 floodlight
□ Die Scheinwerfer beleuchteten das Stadion. The floodlights lit the stadium.
3 spotlight
□ Das Gemälde wird von einem Scheinwerfer angestrahlt. The painting is lit up by a spotlight.

S

die **Scheiße** NOUN
shit

scheitern (PERFECT **ist gescheitert**) VERB [88]
to fail

der **Schenkel** (PL die **Schenkel**) NOUN
thigh

schenken VERB [38]
1 to give
□ Was haben dir deine Eltern zum Geburtstag geschenkt? What did your parents give you for your birthday? □ Das habe ich geschenkt bekommen. I was given it as a present.
2 to pour
□ Sie schenkte ihm noch etwas Rotwein ins Glas. She poured some more red wine into his glass.
■ **sich etwas schenken** to skip something
□ Die Geigenstunde werde ich mir heute schenken. I'm going to skip my violin lesson today.
■ **Das ist geschenkt!** 1 That's a giveaway! 2 That's worthless!

die **Schere** NOUN
1 scissors
□ eine Schere a pair of scissors
2 shears
□ Wo ist die Schere, um die Hecke zu schneiden? Where are the shears for cutting the hedge?

der **Scherz** (GEN des **Scherzes**, PL die **Scherze**) NOUN
joke
□ Das war doch nur ein Scherz! It was only a joke.
■ **zum Scherz** for fun

scheußlich ADJECTIVE
dreadful
□ Das Wetter war scheußlich. The weather was dreadful.
■ **Das tut scheußlich weh.** It hurts dreadfully.

der **Schi** (PL die **Schi** *or* **Schier**) NOUN ▷ *see* **Ski**

die **Schicht** NOUN
1 layer
□ Auf dem Weg lag eine Schicht Sand. There was a layer of sand on the path.
2 class
□ soziale Schichten social classes
3 shift
□ Mein Vater arbeitet Schicht. My father works shifts.

schick ADJECTIVE
stylish
□ ein schicker Hosenanzug a stylish trouser suit
■ **schick angezogen** stylishly dressed

schicken VERB [48]
to send
□ Ich habe ihr ein Päckchen geschickt. I've sent her a parcel. □ Sie hat ihren Sohn zum Bäcker geschickt. She sent her son to the baker's.

das **Schicksal** NOUN
fate

schieben (IMPERFECT **schob**, PERFECT **hat geschoben**) VERB
to push
□ Wir mussten das Auto schieben. We had to push the car. □ Könnt ihr mal schieben? Could you lot push?
■ **die Schuld auf jemanden schieben** to put the blame on somebody

der **Schiedsrichter** (PL die **Schiedsrichter**) NOUN
1 referee
□ Der Schiedsrichter pfiff das Spiel an. The referee blew the whistle to start the game.
2 umpire
□ Bei einem Tennisspiel sagt der Schiedsrichter den Spielstand an. In a tennis match the umpire gives the score.

schief ADJECTIVE, ADVERB
crooked
□ Die Wände des Hauses sind schief. The walls of the house are crooked.
■ **Das Bild hängt schief.** The picture isn't hanging straight.
■ **der Schiefe Turm von Pisa** the Leaning Tower of Pisa
■ **ein schiefer Blick** a funny look
■ **Er hatte seinen Hut schief aufgesetzt.** He was wearing his hat at an angle.

schiefgehen (IMPERFECT **ging schief**, PERFECT **ist schiefgegangen**) VERB [29]
go wrong

schielen VERB [38]
to squint

schien VERB ▷ *see* **scheinen**

die **Schiene** NOUN
1 rail
□ Die Schienen sind verrostet. The rails have rusted.
2 splint
□ Sie hatte den Arm in einer Schiene. She had her arm in a splint.

schießen (IMPERFECT **schoss**, PERFECT **hat geschossen**) VERB
1 to shoot
□ Nicht schießen! Don't shoot! □ Er hat ein Kaninchen geschossen. He shot a rabbit. □ Er hat auf einen Polizisten geschossen. He shot at a policeman.
2 to kick
□ Sie schoss den Ball ins Tor. She kicked the ball into the goal.

das **Schiff** (PL die **Schiffe**) NOUN
ship

die **Schifffahrt** NOUN
shipping

der **Schikoree** NOUN
chicory

German-English

das **Schild** (PL die **Schilder**) NOUN
sign
□ Das ist eine Einbahnstraße, hast du das Schild nicht gesehen? This is a one-way street, didn't you see the sign?
■ **ein Namensschild** a nameplate

die **Schildkröte** NOUN
1 tortoise
2 turtle

der **Schimmel** (PL die **Schimmel**) NOUN
1 mould
□ Auf dem Käse ist Schimmel. There's mould on the cheese.
2 white horse
□ Sie ritt auf einem Schimmel. She rode a white horse.

schimmelig ADJECTIVE
mouldy

der **Schimpanse** (GEN des **Schimpansen**, PL die **Schimpansen**) NOUN
chimpanzee

schimpfen VERB [38]
to scold
□ Hat deine Mutter geschimpft? Did your mother scold you?
■ **auf jemanden schimpfen** to curse somebody □ Schüler schimpfen gern auf ihre Lehrer. Pupils like cursing their teachers.
■ **über etwas schimpfen** to complain about something □ Meine Kinder schimpfen über zu viel Hausaufgaben. My children complain about having too much homework.

das **Schimpfwort** (PL die **Schimpfwörter**) NOUN
term of abuse

der **Schinken** (PL die **Schinken**) NOUN
ham

der **Schirm** (PL die **Schirme**) NOUN
umbrella
□ Nimm einen Schirm mit! Take an umbrella!
■ **der Sonnenschirm** the sunshade
■ **eine Mütze mit Schirm** a peaked cap

die **Schlacht** NOUN
battle

S

schlachten VERB [2]
to slaughter

das **Schlachtfeld** (PL die **Schlachtfelder**) NOUN
battlefield

der **Schlachthof** (PL die **Schlachthöfe**) NOUN
slaughterhouse

der **Schlaf** NOUN
sleep

der **Schlafanzug** (PL die **Schlafanzüge**) NOUN
pyjamas
□ ein Schlafanzug a pair of pyjamas

schlafen (PRESENT **schläft**, IMPERFECT **schlief**, PERFECT **hat geschlafen**) VERB [58]
to sleep
□ Hast du gut geschlafen? Did you sleep well?
□ Schlaf gut! Sleep well.
■ **schlafen gehen** to go to bed

schlaff ADJECTIVE
1 exhausted
□ Nach der Gartenarbeit war ich total schlaff. I was completely exhausted after working in the garden.
2 slack
□ Das Seil ist zu schlaff. The rope is too slack.

schlaflos ADJECTIVE
sleepless

der **Schlafsaal** (PL die **Schlafsäle**) NOUN
dormitory

der **Schlafsack** (PL die **Schlafsäcke**) NOUN
sleeping bag

die **Schlaftablette** NOUN
sleeping pill

das **Schlafzimmer** (PL die **Schlafzimmer**) NOUN
bedroom

der **Schlag** (PL die **Schläge**) NOUN
1 blow
□ ein Schlag auf den Kopf a blow to the head
□ Ich bin durchgefallen, das ist ein Schlag. I've failed, that's a blow.
2 stroke
□ Mein Opa hat einen Schlag gehabt und ist gelähmt. My granddad's had a stroke and he's now paralysed.
3 shock
□ Fass nicht an den Draht, sonst bekommst du einen Schlag. Don't touch that wire, otherwise you'll get a shock.
■ **Er hat von seinem Vater Schläge bekommen.** His father gave him a hiding.
■ **mit einem Schlag** all at once

schlagen (PRESENT **schlägt**, IMPERFECT **schlug**, PERFECT **hat geschlagen**) VERB [59]
1 to beat
□ Meine Eltern haben mich noch nie geschlagen. My parents have never beaten me.
□ England hat Holland vier zu eins geschlagen. England beat Holland four one. □ Ihr Herz schlug schneller. Her heart beat faster.
■ **Sahne schlagen** to whip cream
2 to hit
□ Er schlug mit dem Hammer auf den Nagel. He hit the nail with the hammer. □ Sie schlug mit der Faust auf den Tisch. She hit the table with her fist.
■ **Er schlägt den Nagel in die Wand.** He hammers the nail into the wall.
3 to strike
□ Die Uhr schlägt zehn. The clock strikes ten.
□ Es hat eben zehn geschlagen. It's just struck ten.
■ **nach jemandem schlagen** to take after somebody □ Sie schlägt nach ihrer Mutter. She takes after her mother.

■ **sich gut schlagen** to do well □ Er hat sich in der Prüfung gut geschlagen. He did well in the exam.

der **Schlager** (PL die **Schlager**) NOUN
hit

der **Schläger** (PL die **Schläger**) NOUN
1 thug
□ Franz ist ein Schläger. Franz is a thug.
2 bat
□ Baseball und Tischtennis spielt man mit einem Schläger. You play baseball and table tennis with a bat.
3 racket
□ Für Tennis, Federball und Squash braucht man einen Schläger. You need a racket for tennis, badminton and squash.
■ **ein Golfschläger** a golf club
■ **ein Hockeyschläger** a hockey stick

die **Schlägerei** NOUN
fight

schlagfertig ADJECTIVE
quick-witted

die **Schlagsahne** NOUN
whipped cream

die **Schlagzeile** NOUN
headline

das **Schlagzeug** (PL die **Schlagzeuge**) NOUN
drums
□ Er spielt Schlagzeug. He plays the drums.
□ Am Schlagzeug: Freddy Braun. On drums: Freddy Braun.

der **Schlamm** NOUN
mud

schlampen VERB [38]
to be sloppy
□ Bei den Hausaufgaben hast du geschlampt. Your homework's sloppy.

schlampig ADJECTIVE
sloppy

die **Schlange** NOUN
1 snake
□ eine giftige Schlange a poisonous snake
2 queue
□ Vor dem Kino stand eine lange Schlange. There was a long queue outside the cinema.
■ **Schlange stehen** to queue □ Wir mussten für die Karten Schlange stehen. We had to queue for the tickets.

schlank ADJECTIVE
slim
□ Sie ist sehr schlank. She's very slim.

die **Schlankheitskur** NOUN
diet
□ eine Schlankheitskur machen to be on a diet

schlapp ADJECTIVE
worn out
□ Ich fühle mich schlapp. I feel worn out.

schlau ADJECTIVE
cunning

der **Schlauch** (PL die **Schläuche**) NOUN
1 hose
□ Er hat den Garten mit dem Schlauch gespritzt. He watered the garden with the hose.
2 inner tube
□ Ich brauche einen neuen Schlauch für mein Fahrrad. I need a new inner tube for my bike.

das **Schlauchboot** (PL die **Schlauchboote**) NOUN
rubber dinghy

schlecht ADJECTIVE, ADVERB
1 bad
□ Er ist in Mathe schlecht. He is bad at maths.
□ Meine Augen werden immer schlechter. My eyes are getting worse.
■ **ein schlechtes Gewissen** a guilty conscience
2 badly
□ Ich habe schlecht geschlafen. I slept badly.
■ **schlecht gelaunt** in a bad mood
■ **Mir ist schlecht.** I feel sick.
■ **ein schlecht bezahlter Job** a poorly paid job
■ **Ihm geht es schlecht.** He's in a bad way.

schlechtmachen VERB [48]
■ **jemanden schlechtmachen** to run somebody down □ Du solltest ihn nicht dauernd schlechtmachen. You shouldn't constantly run him down.

schleichen (IMPERFECT **schlich**, PERFECT **ist geschlichen**) VERB
to creep

die **Schleife** NOUN
1 loop
□ Der Fluss macht eine Schleife. The river makes a loop.
2 bow
□ Sie hatte eine Schleife im Haar. She had a bow in her hair.

Schleswig-Holstein NEUT NOUN
Schleswig-Holstein

DID YOU KNOW...?
Schleswig-Holstein is one of the 16 **Länder**. Its capital is Kiel. It is Germany's northernmost state, bordered by the North Sea and the Baltic, and by Denmark in the north.

schleudern (PERFECT **hat/ist geschleudert**) VERB [88]

LANGUAGE TIP For the perfect tense use **haben** when the verb has an object and **sein** when there is no object.

1 to hurl
□ Sie hat das Buch in die Ecke geschleudert. She hurled the book into the corner.
2 to spin
□ Du solltest die nasse Wäsche schleudern. You should spin the wet washing.
3 to skid
□ Das Auto ist geschleudert. The car skidded.

German-English

schlief VERB ▷ *see* **schlafen**

schließen (IMPERFECT **schloss**, PERFECT **hat geschlossen**) VERB
to shut
□ Schließ bitte das Fenster. Please shut the window. □ Wann schließen die Geschäfte? When do the shops shut? □ Sie hatte die Augen geschlossen. She had her eyes shut. □ Der Betrieb wurde geschlossen. The company was shut down.
■ **mit jemandem Freundschaft schließen** to make friends with somebody
■ **etwas aus etwas schließen** to gather something from something □ Aus dem, was er sagte, schließe ich, dass er nicht mitkommen will. I gather from what he said that he doesn't want to come.

schließlich ADVERB
finally
■ **schließlich doch** after all

schlimm ADJECTIVE
bad

schlimmer ADJECTIVE
worse

schlimmste ADJECTIVE
worst
□ mein schlimmster Feind my worst enemy

schlimmstenfalls ADVERB
at the worst

der **Schlips** NOUN
tie *(necktie)*

der **Schlitten** (PL die **Schlitten**) NOUN
sledge
□ Im Winter sind wir viel Schlitten gefahren. We went sledging a lot in the winter.

der **Schlittschuh** (PL die **Schlittschuhe**) NOUN
skate
■ **Schlittschuh laufen** to skate

der **Schlitz** (GEN des **Schlitzes**, PL die **Schlitze**) NOUN
1 slit
□ Der Rock hat hinten einen Schlitz. The skirt has a slit at the back.
2 slot
□ Du musst das Zwei-Euro-Stück in den Schlitz werfen. You have to put the two-euro coin in the slot.
3 flies
□ Der Schlitz an deiner Hose ist auf. Your flies are open.

das **Schloss** (GEN des **Schlosses**, PL die **Schlösser**) NOUN
1 lock
□ Sie steckte den Schlüssel ins Schloss. She put the key in the lock.
2 clasp
□ Kannst du mir bitte das Schloss an meiner Kette aufmachen? Can you please open the clasp of my necklace?
3 chateau
□ das Schloss in Versailles the chateau of Versailles

schloss VERB ▷ *see* **schließen**

der **Schluckauf** NOUN
hiccups
□ Er hatte einen Schluckauf. He had hiccups.

schlucken VERB [48]
to swallow

schlug VERB ▷ *see* **schlagen**

der **Schluss** (GEN des **Schlusses**, PL die **Schlüsse**) NOUN
1 end
□ am Schluss des Jahres at the end of the year
2 ending
□ Das Buch hat einen traurigen Schluss. The book has a sad ending.
3 conclusion
□ Ich habe meine Schlüsse gezogen. I've drawn my conclusions.
■ **zum Schluss** finally □ Zum Schluss haben wir noch ein Lied gesungen. Finally we sang a song.
■ **Schluss machen** to finish □ Wir sollten langsam Schluss machen. We should be finishing now.
■ **mit jemandem Schluss machen** to finish with somebody □ Warum hast du mit Manfred Schluss gemacht? Why did you finish with Manfred?

der **Schlüssel** (PL die **Schlüssel**) NOUN
key
□ Wo ist mein Fahrradschlüssel? Where's the key for my bike? □ der Schlüssel zum Erfolg the key to success

das **Schlüsselbein** (PL die **Schlüsselbeine**) NOUN
collar bone

der **Schlüsselbund** (PL die **Schlüsselbunde**) NOUN
bunch of keys

der **Schlüsselring** (PL die **Schlüsselringe**) NOUN
keyring

der **Schlussverkauf** NOUN
sales
□ Dieses Kleid habe ich im Schlussverkauf bekommen. I got this dress in the sales.

schmal ADJECTIVE
1 narrow
□ ein schmaler Durchgang a narrow passageway
2 thin
□ Sie hat ein schmales Gesicht. She has a thin face.

LANGUAGE TIP Be careful! **schmal** does not mean **small**.

schmecken VERB [48]
to taste

S

□ Wie schmeckt eine Mango? What does a mango taste like? □ Das schmeckt gut. That tastes good.
■ **Es schmeckt ihm.** He likes it.

schmeicheln VERB [38]
■ **jemandem schmeicheln** to flatter somebody

schmeißen (IMPERFECT **schmiss**, PERFECT **hat geschmissen**) VERB
to throw

schmelzen (PRESENT **schmilzt**, IMPERFECT **schmolz**, PERFECT **ist geschmolzen**) VERB
to melt
□ Das Eis ist geschmolzen. The ice has melted.

der **Schmerz** (GEN des **Schmerzes**, PL die **Schmerzen**) NOUN
1 pain
□ ein stechender Schmerz in der Seite a stabbing pain in the side
2 grief
□ Sie verbarg ihren Schmerz über diesen Verlust. She hid her grief over her loss.

schmerzen (PERFECT **hat geschmerzt**) VERB [36]
to hurt

das **Schmerzmittel** (PL die **Schmerzmittel**) NOUN
painkiller

die **Schmerztablette** NOUN
painkiller

der **Schmetterling** (PL die **Schmetterlinge**) NOUN
butterfly

die **Schminke** NOUN
make-up

schminken VERB [38]
to make up
□ Hast du dir die Augen geschminkt? Have you made up your eyes?
■ **Ich schminke mich selten.** I seldom use make-up.

der **Schmuck** NOUN
1 jewellery
□ Sie trägt selten Schmuck. She seldom wears jewellery.
2 decoration
□ bunte Kugeln als Schmuck für den Weihnachtsbaum bright baubles as Christmas tree decorations

schmücken VERB [48]
to decorate

schmuggeln VERB [34]
to smuggle

schmusen VERB [38]
to cuddle
□ Sie hat mit Felix geschmust. She cuddled Felix.

der **Schmutz** (GEN des **Schmutzes**) NOUN
dirt

schmutzig ADJECTIVE
dirty

der **Schnabel** (PL die **Schnäbel**) NOUN
beak
□ Der Schnabel der Amsel ist gelb. The blackbird's beak is yellow.

die **Schnalle** NOUN
buckle

der **Schnaps** (GEN des **Schnapses**, PL die **Schnäpse**) NOUN
schnapps

schnarchen VERB [48]
to snore

schnaufen VERB [38]
to puff

die **Schnauze** NOUN
1 nose
□ Der Hund hat eine kalte Schnauze. The dog has a cold nose.
2 gob
□ Halt die Schnauze! Shut your gob!
■ **die Schnauze von etwas voll haben** to be fed up to the back teeth of something

LANGUAGE TIP Word for word, **die Schnauze von etwas voll haben** means 'to have one's gob full of something'.

sich **schnäuzen** VERB [36]
to blow one's nose

die **Schnecke** NOUN
snail
■ **eine Nacktschnecke** a slug

LANGUAGE TIP Word for word, **eine Nacktschnecke** means 'a naked snail'.

der **Schnee** NOUN
snow
□ Heute Nacht ist viel Schnee gefallen. A lot of snow fell last night.

der **Schneeball** (PL die **Schneebälle**) NOUN
snowball

der **Schneemann** (PL die **Schneemänner**) NOUN
snowman

schneiden (IMPERFECT **schnitt**, PERFECT **hat geschnitten**) VERB [60]
to cut
□ Kannst du bitte Brot schneiden? Can you cut some bread, please? □ jemandem die Haare schneiden to cut somebody's hair □ Du solltest dir die Haare schneiden lassen. You should have your hair cut.
■ **sich schneiden 1** to cut oneself □ Ich habe mich geschnitten. I've cut myself. □ Ich habe mir in den Finger geschnitten. I've cut my finger. **2** to intersect □ Die beiden Geraden schneiden sich. The two straight lines intersect.

schneien VERB [38]
■ **Es schneit.** It's snowing.

schnell ADJECTIVE, ADVERB
1 fast

□ Sie hat ein schnelles Auto. She has a fast car. □ Sie ist schnell gefahren. She drove fast.
2 quickly
□ Ich rief schnell einen Krankenwagen. I quickly phoned for an ambulance.

die **Schnelligkeit** NOUN
speed

der **Schnellimbiss** (GEN des **Schnellimbisses**, PL die **Schnellimbisse**) NOUN
snack bar

schnellstens ADVERB
as quickly as possible

der **Schnellzug** (PL die **Schnellzüge**) NOUN
express train

sich **schneuzen** VERB [36] ▷ *see* **schnäuzen**

der **Schnitt** (PL die **Schnitte**) NOUN
1 cut
□ Der Schnitt blutet. The cut's bleeding.
□ Das Kleid hat einen eleganten Schnitt. The dress has an elegant cut.
2 average
□ Ich habe im Zeugnis einen Schnitt von drei. I've got an average of C in my report.
3 pattern
□ Hast du zu dem Rock einen Schnitt? Have you got a pattern for this skirt?

schnitt VERB ▷ *see* **schneiden**

der **Schnittlauch** NOUN
chive

die **Schnittstelle** NOUN
interface

die **Schnittwunde** NOUN
cut

das **Schnitzel** (PL die **Schnitzel**) NOUN
escalope
□ Ich bestelle mir ein Schnitzel. I'm going to order an escalope.

schnitzen VERB [48]
to carve

der **Schnorchel** (PL die **Schnorchel**) NOUN
snorkel

der **Schnuller** (PL die **Schnuller**) NOUN
dummy
□ Das Baby saugte am Schnuller. The baby sucked the dummy.

der **Schnupfen** (PL die **Schnupfen**) NOUN
cold
□ Meine Schwester hat Schnupfen. My sister has a cold.

die **Schnur** (PL die **Schnüre**) NOUN
1 string
□ Du solltest eine Schnur um das Päckchen machen. You should put string round the parcel.
2 flex
□ Die Schnur von der Lampe ist zu kurz. The flex of the lamp is too short.

der **Schnurrbart** (PL die **Schnurrbärte**) NOUN
moustache

der **Schnürsenkel** (PL die **Schnürsenkel**) NOUN
shoelace

der **Schock** (PL die **Schocks**) NOUN
shock

die **Schokolade** NOUN
chocolate
□ eine heiße Schokolade a hot chocolate

schon ADVERB
1 already
□ Ich bin schon fertig. I've already finished.
2 yet
□ Ist er schon da? Is he there yet?
■ **Warst du schon einmal da?** Have you ever been there?
■ **Ich war schon einmal da.** I've been there before.
■ **Das war schon immer so.** That's always been the case.
■ **Hast du schon gehört?** Have you heard?
■ **schon oft** often
■ **schon der Gedanke** the very thought
■ **Du wirst schon sehen.** You'll see.
■ **Das wird schon noch gut.** That'll be OK.
■ **ja schon, aber ...** yes, but ...
■ **schon möglich** possible
■ **Schon gut!** OK!
■ **Du weißt schon.** You know.
■ **Komm schon!** Come on!

schön ADJECTIVE
1 beautiful
□ Sie haben ein schönes Haus. They have a beautiful house.
2 nice
□ Es waren schöne Ferien. The holidays were nice. □ Schönes Wochenende! Have a nice weekend.
■ **sich schön machen** to make oneself look nice
■ **Schöne Grüße an deine Eltern!** Regards to your parents.
■ **ganz schön frech** pretty damn cheeky
■ **na schön** very well □ Na schön, dann geht halt spielen. Very well then, go and play.

schonend ADJECTIVE, ADVERB
gentle
□ jemandem etwas schonend beibringen to break something gently to somebody

die **Schönheit** NOUN
beauty

sich **schönmachen** VERB [48] ▷ *see* **schön**

schöpfen VERB [38]
to ladle
□ Sie schöpfte Suppe in die Teller. She ladled soup into the plates.
■ **Luft schöpfen** to get some air

die **Schöpfung** NOUN
creation

der **Schornstein** (PL die **Schornsteine**) NOUN
chimney

schoss VERB ▷ *see* **schießen**

der **Schotte** (GEN des **Schotten**, PL die **Schotten**) NOUN
Scot
■ **Er ist Schotte.** He's Scottish.

die **Schottin** NOUN
Scot
■ **Sie ist Schottin.** She's Scottish.

schottisch ADJECTIVE
Scottish

Schottland NEUT NOUN
Scotland
■ **aus Schottland** from Scotland
■ **in Schottland** in Scotland
■ **nach Schottland** to Scotland

schräg ADJECTIVE
sloping
□ Das Haus hat ein schräges Dach. The house has a sloping roof.
■ **schräg gegenüber** diagonally opposite

der **Schrägstrich** (PL die **Schrägstriche**) NOUN
slash

der **Schrank** (PL die **Schränke**) NOUN
1 cupboard
□ Der Besen ist im Schrank in der Küche. The broom's in the cupboard in the kitchen.
2 wardrobe
□ Ich räume meine Kleider in den Schrank. I'll put my clothes away in the wardrobe.

die **Schranke** NOUN
barrier

die **Schraube** NOUN
1 screw
2 bolt

der **Schraubenschlüssel** (PL die **Schraubenschlüssel**) NOUN
spanner

LANGUAGE TIP Word for word, **Schraubenschlüssel** means 'screw key'.

der **Schraubenzieher** (PL die **Schraubenzieher**) NOUN
screwdriver

der **Schreck** NOUN
fright
□ Ich habe einen furchtbaren Schreck bekommen. I got a terrible fright.

schreckhaft ADJECTIVE
jumpy

schrecklich ADJECTIVE, ADVERB
1 terrible
□ Das Wetter war schrecklich schlecht. The weather was terrible.
2 terribly
□ Das tut schrecklich weh. It hurts terribly.
□ Es tut mir schrecklich leid. I'm terribly sorry.

der **Schrei** (PL die **Schreie**) NOUN
1 scream
□ Als sie die Spinne sah, stieß sie einen Schrei aus. When she saw the spider she let out a scream.
2 shout
□ Wir hörten einen Schrei um Hilfe. We heard a shout for help.

schreiben (IMPERFECT **schrieb**, PERFECT **hat geschrieben**) VERB [61]
1 to write
□ Ich habe ihr einen Brief geschrieben. I've written her a letter. □ Wir sollten uns schreiben. We should write to each other.
2 to spell
□ Wie schreibt man seinen Namen? How do you spell his name?

die **Schreibmaschine** NOUN
typewriter

der **Schreibtisch** (PL die **Schreibtische**) NOUN
desk

die **Schreibwaren** FEM PL NOUN
stationery

das **Schreibzeug** NOUN
writing materials

schreien (IMPERFECT **schrie**, PERFECT **hat geschrien**) VERB [62]
1 to scream
□ Sie schrie vor Schmerzen. She screamed with pain.
2 to shout
□ Wir haben geschrien, du hast uns aber nicht gehört. We shouted but you didn't hear us.

der **Schreiner** (PL die **Schreiner**) NOUN
joiner

schrieb VERB ▷ *see* **schreiben**

die **Schrift** NOUN
1 writing
□ Sie hat eine schöne Schrift. She has lovely writing.
2 font
□ Welche Schrift soll ich für das Dokument nehmen? Which font should I use for the document?

schriftlich ADJECTIVE, ADVERB
written
□ eine schriftliche Entschuldigung a written apology
■ **etwas schriftlich festhalten** to put something in writing

der **Schriftsteller** (PL die **Schriftsteller**) NOUN
writer

schrill ADJECTIVE
shrill

der **Schritt** (PL die **Schritte**) NOUN
1 step
□ Er machte einen vorsichtigen Schritt nach vorn. He took a careful step forward.
2 walk
□ Ich habe dich an deinem Schritt erkannt. I recognized you by your walk.
3 pace
□ Sie ging mit schnellen Schritten nach Hause. She walked home at a brisk pace.
■ **Schritt fahren** to drive at walking pace

der **Schrott** NOUN
scrap metal

schrumpfen (PERFECT **ist geschrumpft**) VERB [38]
1 to shrink
□ Der Pulli ist in der Wäsche geschrumpft. The pullover shrank in the wash.
2 to shrivel
□ Die Äpfel sind geschrumpft. The apples have shrivelled.

die **Schublade** NOUN
drawer

schüchtern ADJECTIVE
shy

der **Schuh** (PL die **Schuhe**) NOUN
shoe

die **Schuhcreme** (PL die **Schuhcremes**) NOUN
shoe polish

die **Schuhgröße** NOUN
shoe size
□ Welche Schuhgröße hast du? What shoe size are you?

die **Schularbeiten** FEM PL NOUN
homework
□ Hast du deine Schularbeiten schon gemacht? Have you done your homework?

die **Schulaufgaben** FEM PL NOUN
homework
□ Heute haben wir keine Schulaufgaben bekommen. We didn't get any homework today.

das **Schulbuch** (PL die **Schulbücher**) NOUN
school book

die **Schuld** NOUN
▷ *see also* **schuld** ADJECTIVE
1 guilt
□ Seine Schuld konnte nicht bewiesen werden. His guilt couldn't be proved.
2 fault
□ Es war deine Schuld, dass wir zu spät kamen. It was your fault that we arrived late.
■ **jemandem Schuld geben** to blame somebody

schuld ADJECTIVE
▷ *see also* **die Schuld** NOUN
■ **an etwas schuld sein** to be to blame for something □ Du bist an der Verspätung schuld. You are to blame for the delay.
■ **Er ist schuld.** It's his fault.

die **Schulden** PL NOUN
▷ *see also* **schulden** VERB
debt
□ Ich muss noch meine Schulden bei dir bezahlen. I still have to pay off my debts to you. □ Staatsschulden national debt

schulden VERB [54]
▷ *see also* **die Schulden** NOUN
to owe
□ Was schulde ich dir? How much do I owe you?

schuldig ADJECTIVE
guilty
□ Meinst du, dass die Angeklagte schuldig ist? Do you think that the accused is guilty?
■ **jemandem etwas schuldig sein** to owe somebody something □ Was bin ich dir schuldig? How much do I owe you?

der **Schuldirektor** (PL die **Schuldirektoren**) NOUN
headmaster

die **Schuldirektorin** NOUN
headmistress

die **Schule** NOUN
school
□ in der Schule at school

der **Schüler** (PL die **Schüler**) NOUN
pupil

die **Schülerin** NOUN
pupil

die **Schulferien** PL NOUN
school holidays

schulfrei ADJECTIVE
■ **ein schulfreier Tag** a day off school
■ **Sonntag ist schulfrei.** Sunday isn't a school day.

der **Schulhof** (PL die **Schulhöfe**) NOUN
playground

das **Schuljahr** (PL die **Schuljahre**) NOUN
school year

schulpflichtig ADJECTIVE
of school age

die **Schulstunde** NOUN
period

der **Schultag** (PL die **Schultage**) NOUN
■ **mein erster Schultag** my first day at school

die **Schultasche** NOUN
school bag

die **Schulter** NOUN
shoulder

das **Schulzeugnis** (GEN des **Schulzeugnisses**, PL die **Schulzeugnisse**) NOUN
school report

die **Schürze** NOUN
apron

der **Schuss** (GEN des **Schusses**, PL die **Schüsse**) NOUN
shot
□ Wir hörten einen Schuss. We heard a shot.

die **Schüssel** NOUN
bowl

die **Schusswaffe** NOUN
firearm

der **Schuster** (PL die **Schuster**) NOUN
cobbler

der **Schutt** NOUN
rubble
□ Der Schutt von der Baustelle wird morgen weggebracht. The rubble from the building site will be removed tomorrow.
■ **Schutt abladen verboten!** No dumping!

schütteln VERB [34]
to shake
■ **sich schütteln** to shake oneself

schütten VERB [2]
1 to pour
□ Soll ich dir Saft ins Glas schütten? Shall I pour you some juice?
2 to spill
□ Pass auf, dass du den Kaffee nicht auf die Tischdecke schüttest. Be careful that you don't spill coffee on the tablecloth.
■ **Es schüttet.** It's pouring down.

der **Schutz** (GEN des **Schutzes**) NOUN
1 protection
□ Zum Schutz gegen die Sonne solltest du dich eincremen. You should put some cream on to protect against the sun.
2 shelter
□ Sie suchten Schutz in der Berghütte. They took shelter in a mountain hut.
■ **jemanden in Schutz nehmen** to stand up for somebody

der **Schütze** (GEN des **Schützen**, PL die **Schützen**) NOUN
1 marksman
□ Er ist ein guter Schütze. He's a good marksman.
2 Sagittarius
□ Martin ist Schütze. Martin's Sagittarius.

schützen VERB [36]
to protect
□ Die Pflanzen sollten vor zu großer Hitze geschützt werden. The plants should be protected from too much heat. □ Diese Creme schützt die Haut gegen Sonnenbrand. This cream protects the skin from sunburn.
■ **sich gegen etwas schützen** to protect oneself from something □ Schützen Sie sich gegen Sonnenbrand. Protect yourself from sunburn.

schwach ADJECTIVE
weak
□ Ihre Stimme wurde immer schwächer. Her voice became weaker and weaker.
■ **Das war eine schwache Leistung!** That wasn't very good.

die **Schwäche** NOUN
weakness

der **Schwächling** (PL die **Schwächlinge**) NOUN
weakling

der **Schwachsinn** NOUN
balderdash

schwachsinnig ADJECTIVE
idiotic
□ So eine schwachsinnige Idee! What an idiotic idea!

der **Schwager** (PL die **Schwäger**) NOUN
brother-in-law

die **Schwägerin** NOUN
sister-in-law

der **Schwamm** (PL die **Schwämme**) NOUN
sponge

schwamm VERB ▷ *see* **schwimmen**

schwanger ADJECTIVE
pregnant
□ Sie ist im dritten Monat schwanger. She's three months pregnant.

schwanken VERB [38]
1 to sway
□ Das Schiff schwankte. The ship swayed.
2 to stagger
□ Er schwankte und fiel dann um. He staggered and fell down.
3 to fluctuate
□ Die Temperaturen schwanken. Temperatures are fluctuating. □ Der Kurs des Pfunds schwankt. The exchange rate of the pound is fluctuating.

der **Schwanz** (GEN des **Schwanzes**, PL die **Schwänze**) NOUN
tail

schwänzen VERB [36]
to skive off
□ Ich habe heute die Turnstunde geschwänzt. I skived off PE today.

der **Schwarm** (PL die **Schwärme**) NOUN
swarm
□ ein Schwarm Fliegen a swarm of flies
■ **Er ist mein Schwarm.** I have a crush on him.

schwärmen (PERFECT **hat/ist geschwärmt**) VERB [38]
LANGUAGE TIP Use **sein** to form the perfect tense for 'to swarm'.
to swarm
□ Die Bienen sind aus dem Bienenstock geschwärmt. The bees swarmed out of the hive.
■ **schwärmen für** to have a crush on
□ Sie schwärmt für ihren Mathelehrer. She has a crush on her maths teacher.
■ **schwärmen von** to rave about
□ Er hat von dem Konzert geschwärmt. He raved about the concert.

schwarz ADJECTIVE
black
□ Der Himmel wurde immer schwärzer. The sky turned blacker and blacker.
■ **Schwarzes Brett** notice board
LANGUAGE TIP Word for word, **Schwarzes Brett** means 'black board'.
■ **ins Schwarze treffen** to hit the bull's eye

das **Schwarzbrot** (PL die **Schwarzbrote**) NOUN
brown rye bread

der/die **Schwarze** (GEN des/der **Schwarzen**, PL die **Schwarzen**) NOUN
black

schwarzfahren (PRESENT **fährt schwarz**, IMPERFECT **fuhr schwarz**, PERFECT **ist schwarzgefahren**) VERB [21]
■ **Sie fährt in der Straßenbahn immer**

schwarz. She never pays her tram fare.

schwarzsehen (PRESENT **sieht schwarz**, IMPERFECT **sah schwarz**, PERFECT **hat schwarzgesehen**) VERB [64]
to look on the black side of things
□ Sieh doch nicht immer so schwarz. Don't always look on the black side of things.

der **Schwarzwald** NOUN
Black Forest

schwarz-weiß ADJECTIVE
black and white

schwätzen VERB [48]
to chatter

der **Schwätzer** (PL die **Schwätzer**) NOUN
windbag

der **Schwede** (GEN des **Schweden**, PL die **Schweden**) NOUN
Swede
■ **Er ist Schwede.** He's Swedish.

Schweden NEUT NOUN
Sweden
■ **aus Schweden** from Sweden
■ **nach Schweden** to Sweden

die **Schwedin** NOUN
Swede

schwedisch ADJECTIVE
Swedish

schweigen (IMPERFECT **schwieg**, PERFECT **hat geschwiegen**) VERB
1 to be silent
□ Die Kinder finden es schwierig, mehr als fünf Minuten lang zu schweigen. The children find it difficult to be silent for more than five minutes.
2 to stop talking
□ Sag ihm, er soll schweigen. Tell him to stop talking.

das **Schwein** (PL die **Schweine**) NOUN
pig
■ **Schwein haben** to be really lucky
□ Da hatten wir ja noch mal Schwein. We were really lucky there.

der **Schweinebraten** (PL die **Schweinebraten**) NOUN
roast pork

das **Schweinefleisch** NOUN
pork

der **Schweiß** (GEN des **Schweißes**) NOUN
sweat

die **Schweiz** NOUN
Switzerland

> **DID YOU KNOW...?**
> Switzerland is bordered by Germany, Austria, Liechstenstein, Italy and France. Its capital is Berne and its currency the Franken. Roughly 60% of the population (mainly in the North and East) speak a German dialect. French, Italian and Rhaeto-Romanic are also spoken.

■ **aus der Schweiz** from Switzerland
■ **in der Schweiz** in Switzerland
■ **in die Schweiz** to Switzerland

der **Schweizer** (PL die **Schweizer**) NOUN
Swiss
□ die Schweizer the Swiss

die **Schweizerin** NOUN
Swiss

schweizerisch ADJECTIVE
Swiss

schwer ADJECTIVE, ADVERB
1 heavy
□ Ich habe einen schweren Koffer. I have a heavy suitcase. □ Er hat eine schwere Erkältung. He has a heavy cold.
■ **Ich habe einen schweren Kopf.** I've got a headache.

> **LANGUAGE TIP** Word for word, **Ich habe einen schweren Kopf** means 'I have a heavy head'.

2 difficult
□ Die Mathearbeit war schwer. The maths test was difficult.
■ **Er ist schwer verletzt.** He's badly injured.

schwerfallen (PRESENT **fällt schwer**, IMPERFECT **fiel schwer**, PERFECT **ist schwergefallen**) VERB [22]
■ **jemandem schwerfallen** to be difficult for somebody □ Das dürfte dir nicht schwerfallen. That shouldn't be too difficult for you.

das **Schwert** (PL die **Schwerter**) NOUN
sword

die **Schwester** NOUN
1 sister
□ Meine Schwester ist jünger als ich. My sister's younger than me.
2 nurse
□ Die Schwester hat mir eine Schmerztablette gegeben. The nurse gave me a painkiller.

die **Schwiegereltern** PL NOUN
parents-in-law

die **Schwiegermutter** (PL die **Schwiegermütter**) NOUN
mother-in-law

der **Schwiegersohn** (PL die **Schwiegersöhne**) NOUN
son-in-law

die **Schwiegertochter** (PL die **Schwiegertöchter**) NOUN
daughter-in-law

der **Schwiegervater** (PL die **Schwiegerväter**) NOUN
father-in-law

schwierig ADJECTIVE
difficult

die **Schwierigkeit** NOUN
difficulty

das **Schwimmbad** (PL die **Schwimmbäder**) NOUN
swimming pool

das **Schwimmbecken** (PL die **Schwimmbecken**) NOUN
swimming pool

schwimmen (IMPERFECT **schwamm**, PERFECT **ist geschwommen**) VERB [63]
1 to swim
□ Er kann nicht schwimmen. He can't swim.
2 to float
□ Auf dem Fluss schwammen Äste. Branches were floating on the river.

der **Schwindel** NOUN
1 dizzy spell
□ Bei hohem Fieber muss man auch mit Schwindel rechnen. If you have a high temperature, you can also expect to have dizzy spells.
2 fraud
□ Der Schwindel wurde entdeckt. The fraud was discovered.

schwindelfrei ADJECTIVE
■ **schwindelfrei sein** to have a good head for heights □ Ich bin nicht schwindelfrei. I don't have a good head for heights.

schwindeln VERB [34]
to fib

schwindlig ADJECTIVE
dizzy
■ **Mir ist schwindlig.** I feel dizzy.

schwitzen VERB [36]
to sweat

schwören (IMPERFECT **schwor**, PERFECT **hat geschworen**) VERB
to swear

schwul ADJECTIVE
gay

schwül ADJECTIVE
close

der/die **Schwule** (GEN des/der **Schwulen**, PL die **Schwulen**) NOUN
gay
□ Ich habe nichts gegen Schwule. I have nothing against gays.

der **Schwung** (PL die **Schwünge**) NOUN
swing
□ Sie setzte das Pendel in Schwung. She started the pendulum swinging.
■ **jemanden in Schwung bringen** to get somebody going

sechs NUMBER
▷ *see also* **die Sechs** NOUN
six

die **Sechs** NOUN
▷ *see also* **sechs** NUMBER
1 six
2 unsatisfactory

DID YOU KNOW...?
German marks range from one (**sehr gut**) to six (**ungenügend**).

sechste ADJECTIVE
sixth
□ Er kam als Sechster. He was the sixth to arrive.

das **Sechstel** (PL die **Sechstel**) NOUN
sixth

sechzehn NUMBER
sixteen

sechzig NUMBER
sixty

die **See** NOUN
▷ *see also* **der See** NOUN
sea
□ auf See at sea
■ **an die See fahren** to go to the seaside

der **See** (PL die **Seen**) NOUN
▷ *see also* **die See** NOUN
lake
□ der Genfer See Lake Geneva

der **Seehund** (PL die **Seehunde**) NOUN
seal

seekrank ADJECTIVE
seasick

die **Seele** NOUN
soul

seelenruhig ADVERB
calmly

das **Segel** (PL die **Segel**) NOUN
sail

das **Segelboot** (PL die **Segelboote**) NOUN
yacht

das **Segelfliegen** NOUN
gliding

das **Segelflugzeug** (PL die **Segelflugzeuge**) NOUN
glider

segeln (PERFECT **ist gesegelt**) VERB [34]
to sail

das **Segelschiff** (PL die **Segelschiffe**) NOUN
sailing ship

der **Segen** (PL die **Segen**) NOUN
blessing

sehen (PRESENT **sieht**, IMPERFECT **sah**, PERFECT **hat gesehen**) VERB [64]
1 to see
□ Hast du den Film schon gesehen? Have you seen the film yet?
■ **siehe Seite fünf** see page five
2 to look
□ Sieh mal an die Tafel. Look at the board.
■ **schlecht sehen** to have bad eyesight
□ Sie sieht schlecht. She has bad eyesight.
■ **mal sehen, ob ...** let's see if ...
□ Mal sehen, ob Post für mich gekommen ist. Let's see if there's any post for me.
■ **Kommst du mit? - Mal sehen.** Are you coming? - I'll see.

sehenswert ADJECTIVE
worth seeing

die **Sehenswürdigkeiten** FEM PL NOUN
sights

sich **sehnen** VERB [38]
■ **sich sehnen nach** to long for

German-English

die **Sehnsucht** (PL die **Sehnsüchte**) NOUN
longing

sehnsüchtig ADJECTIVE
longing

sehr ADVERB
1 very
□ Das ist sehr schön. That's very nice.
■ **sehr gut** very good

DID YOU KNOW...?
German marks range from one (**sehr gut**) to six (**ungenügend**).

2 a lot
□ Sie hat sehr geweint. She cried a lot.
■ **zu sehr** too much
■ **Sehr geehrter Herr Ahlers** Dear Mr Ahlers

die **Seide** NOUN
silk

die **Seife** NOUN
soap

die **Seifenoper** NOUN
soap opera

das **Seil** (PL die **Seile**) NOUN
1 rope
□ Sie hatten ihn mit einem Seil gefesselt. They had tied him up with a rope.
2 cable
□ das Seil des Skilifts the cable of the ski lift

die **Seilbahn** NOUN
cable car

sein (PRESENT **ist**, IMPERFECT **war**, PERFECT **ist gewesen**) VERB [65]
▷ *see also* **sein** ADJECTIVE
to be
□ Ich bin müde. I'm tired. □ Du bist doof. You're stupid. □ Er ist reich. He's rich.
□ Sie ist Lehrerin. She's a teacher.
□ Es ist kalt. It's cold. □ Wir sind Schüler am Gymnasium. We're pupils at the grammar school. □ Wir waren dort. We were there.
□ Wir sind im Schwimmbad gewesen. We've been to the swimming pool. □ Seien Sie nicht böse. Don't be angry. □ Morgen bin ich in Rom. Tomorrow I'll be in Rome.
■ **Das wäre gut.** That would be a good thing.
■ **Wenn ich Sie wäre ...** If I were you ...
■ **Das wär's.** That's it.
■ **Mir ist kalt.** I'm cold.
■ **Was ist?** What's the matter?
■ **Ist was?** Is something the matter?
■ **es sei denn, dass ...** unless ...
■ **wie dem auch sei** be that as it may
■ **Wie wäre es mit ...?** How about ...?
■ **Lass das sein!** Stop that!

sein ADJECTIVE
▷ *see also* **sein** VERB
1 his
□ Sein Deutschlehrer ist nett. His German teacher's nice. □ Seine Mutter erlaubt das nicht. His mother doesn't allow it. □ Das ist sein Buch. That's his book. □ Seine Eltern sind klasse. His parents are great. □ Das ist nicht mein Füller, das ist seiner. That's not my pen, it's his. □ Meine Mutter heißt Anne, seine auch. My mother's called Anne, so is his.
2 its
□ Der Fuchs kam aus seiner Höhle. The fox came out of its lair. □ Jedes Buch hat seinen Platz. Each book has its place.

seiner PRONOUN

LANGUAGE TIP **seiner** is the genitive of **er**.

of him
□ Wir gedenken seiner. We're thinking of him.

seinetwegen ADVERB
1 for his sake
□ Ihr müsst seinetwegen nicht auf euren Urlaub verzichten. You don't have to do without your holiday for his sake.
2 on his account
□ Hat sie sich seinetwegen so aufgeregt? Did she get so upset on his account?
3 as far as he's concerned
□ Er sagt, dass du seinetwegen gehen kannst. He says that as far as he's concerned you can go.

seit PREPOSITION, CONJUNCTION

LANGUAGE TIP The preposition **seit** takes the dative.

1 since
□ Seit er verheiratet ist, spielt er nicht mehr Fußball. He's stopped playing football since he got married. □ Seit letztem Jahr habe ich nichts mehr von ihm gehört. I haven't heard anything from him since last year.
2 for
□ Er ist seit einer Woche hier. He's been here for a week. □ seit Langem for a long time

seitdem ADVERB, CONJUNCTION
since
□ Seitdem sie im Gymnasium ist, hat sie kaum mehr Zeit. Since she's been going to grammar school, she's hardly had any time.
■ **Ich habe seitdem nichts mehr von ihr gehört.** I haven't heard from her since then.

die **Seite** NOUN
1 side
□ Die rechte Seite des Autos war beschädigt. The right side of the car was damaged.
2 page
□ Das steht auf Seite fünfzig. It's on page fifty.

der **Sekretär** NOUN
secretary

das **Sekretariat** (PL die **Sekretariate**) NOUN
secretary's office

die **Sekretärin** NOUN
secretary

der **Sekt** (PL die **Sekte**) NOUN
sparkling wine

die **Sekunde** NOUN
second
□ zehn Sekunden ten seconds

selber PRONOUN = **selbst**

selbst PRONOUN, ADVERB
1 on one's own
□ Das Kind kann sich selbst anziehen. The child can get dressed on her own.
□ Ich werde schon selbst eine Lösung finden. I'll find a solution on my own.
■ **ich selbst** I myself
■ **er selbst** he himself
■ **wir selbst** we ourselves
■ **Sie ist die Liebenswürdigkeit selbst.** She's kindness itself.
■ **Er braut sein Bier selbst.** He brews his own beer.
■ **von selbst** by itself □ Die Bombe ist von selbst losgegangen. The bomb went off by itself.
2 even
□ Selbst meine Mutter findet Oasis gut. Even my mother likes Oasis.
■ **selbst wenn** even if □ Du musst das machen, selbst wenn du keine Lust hast. You have to do it even if you don't feel like it.

selbständig ADJECTIVE ▷ *see* **selbstständig**

die **Selbstbedienung** NOUN
self-service

selbstbewusst ADJECTIVE
self-confident

der **Selbstmord** (PL die **Selbstmorde**) NOUN
suicide
□ Selbstmord begehen to commit suicide

der **Selbstmordanschlag** (PL die **Selbstmordanschläge**) NOUN
suicide attack

selbstsicher ADJECTIVE
self-assured

selbstständig ADJECTIVE
1 independent
□ Du solltest langsam selbstständiger werden. It's about time you started to become more independent. □ ein selbstständiger Staat an independent country
2 on one's own
□ Kannst du das nicht selbstständig entscheiden? Can't you decide on your own?
■ **sich selbstständig machen** to become self-employed □ Sie hat sich als Übersetzerin selbstständig gemacht. She set herself up as a self-employed translator.

die **Selbstverpflegung** NOUN
self-catering

selbstverständlich ADJECTIVE, ADVERB
1 obvious
□ Das ist für mich durchaus nicht selbstverständlich. It's not at all obvious to me.
■ **Es ist doch selbstverständlich, dass man da hilft.** It goes without saying that you should help.
■ **Ich halte das für selbstverständlich.** I take that for granted.
2 of course
□ Ich habe mich selbstverständlich sofort bedankt. Of course I said thank you immediately. □ Kommt er mit? - Selbstverständlich. Is he coming? - Of course.
□ Ich habe selbstverständlich nicht unterschrieben. Of course I didn't sign.

das **Selbstvertrauen** NOUN
self-confidence

selig ADJECTIVE
1 blissful
□ Er hatte ein seliges Lächeln auf dem Gesicht. He had a blissful smile on his face.
2 overjoyed
□ Sie war selig, als sie ihn sah. She was overjoyed to see him.

der **Sellerie** NOUN
celeriac

selten ADJECTIVE, ADVERB
1 rare
□ eine seltene Pflanze a rare plant
2 rarely
□ Wir gehen selten ins Kino. We rarely go to the cinema.

seltsam ADJECTIVE
curious

das **Semester** (PL die **Semester**) NOUN
semester

das **Seminar** (PL die **Seminare**) NOUN
seminar
□ Ich mache dieses Semester ein Seminar über Steinbeck. I'm doing a seminar on Steinbeck this semester.

die **Sendefolge** NOUN
series

senden (IMPERFECT **sendete** *or* **sandte**, PERFECT **hat gesendet** *or* **gesandt**) VERB
1 to send
□ Bitte senden Sie mir Ihren neuesten Katalog. Please send me your latest catalogue.
2 to broadcast
□ Der Spielfilm wird im dritten Programm gesendet. The film will be broadcast on Channel three. □ Wir senden bis Mitternacht. We broadcast until midnight.

die **Sendereihe** NOUN
series

die **Sendung** NOUN
1 transmission
□ Während der Sendung darf das Studio nicht betreten werden. Nobody's allowed to enter the studio during transmission.
2 programme
□ Kennst du die Sendung 'Tiere im Zoo'? Do you know the programme 'Animals in the Zoo'?

3 consignment
□ Für Sie ist eine Sendung mit Mustern angekommen. A consignment of samples has arrived for you.

der **Senf** (PL die **Senfe**) NOUN
mustard

die **Sensation** NOUN
sensation

sensibel ADJECTIVE
sensitive
□ Sie ist ein sehr sensibler Mensch. She's a very sensitive person.

LANGUAGE TIP Be careful! **sensibel** does not mean **sensible**.

sentimental ADJECTIVE
sentimental
□ Nun werd nicht sentimental! Now don't get sentimental.

der **September** NOUN
September
□ im September in September □ am elften September on the eleventh of September
□ Ulm, den 10. September 2007 Ulm, 10 September 2007 □ Heute ist der elfte September. Today is the eleventh of September.

die **Serie** NOUN
series

seriös ADJECTIVE
respectable

LANGUAGE TIP Be careful! **seriös** does not mean **serious**.

der **Server** (PL die **Server**) NOUN
server

das **Service** (GEN des **Service** *or* **Services**, PL die **Service**) NOUN
▷ *see also* **der Service** NOUN
set
□ Sie hat ein hübsches Teeservice aus Porzellan. She has a lovely china tea set.

der **Service** (GEN des **Service**, PL die **Services**) NOUN
▷ *see also* **das Service** NOUN
service
□ In dem Hotel ist der Service ausgezeichnet. The service in the hotel is excellent.

die **Serviette** NOUN
serviette

servus EXCLAMATION
1 hello!
2 goodbye!

der **Sessel** (PL die **Sessel**) NOUN
armchair

der **Sessellift** (PL die **Sessellifte**) NOUN
chairlift

setzen VERB [36]
to put
□ Sie setzte das Kind auf den Stuhl. She put the child on the chair. □ Er setzte das Glas an den Mund. He put the glass to his lips.
□ Hast du meinen Namen auf die Liste gesetzt? Have you put my name on the list?
□ ein Komma setzen to put a comma
■ **jemandem eine Frist setzen** to set somebody a deadline
■ **sich setzen** 1 to settle □ Der Kaffeesatz hat sich gesetzt. The coffee grounds have settled. 2 to sit down □ Setz dich doch! Do sit down! □ Er setzte sich aufs Sofa. He sat down on the sofa.
■ **auf etwas setzen** to bet on something
□ Er hat hundert Euro auf die Nummer zwei gesetzt. He bet a hundred euros on number two.

die **Seuche** NOUN
epidemic

seufzen VERB [36]
to sigh

sexuell ADJECTIVE
sexual

das **Shampoo** (PL die **Shampoos**) NOUN
shampoo

Sibirien NEUT NOUN
Siberia

sich PRONOUN
1 himself
□ Er redet mit sich selbst. He's talking to himself.
herself
□ Sie spricht nicht gern über sich selbst. She doesn't like to talk about herself.
□ Sie wäscht sich. She's washing herself.
□ Sie hat sich einen Pullover gekauft. She bought herself a jumper.
itself
□ Das Boot hat sich wieder aufgerichtet. The boat righted itself.
2 themselves
□ Meine Eltern haben sich ein neues Auto gekauft. My parents have bought themselves a new car. □ Sie bleiben gern unter sich. They keep themselves to themselves.
3 each other
□ Sie lieben sich. They love each other.
■ **Sie wäscht sich die Haare.** She's washing her hair.
■ **Er schneidet sich die Nägel.** He's cutting his nails.
■ **Man fragt sich, ob ...** One wonders whether ...
■ **Sie wiederholen sich.** You're repeating yourself.
■ **Haben Sie Ihren Ausweis bei sich?** Do you have your pass on you?
■ **Dieser Artikel verkauft sich gut.** This article sells well.

sicher ADJECTIVE, ADVERB
1 safe
□ Das ist ein sehr sicheres Auto. It's a very safe car.

2 certain
□ Der Termin ist noch nicht sicher. The date isn't certain yet.
■ **Ich bin nicht sicher.** I'm not sure.
3 reliable
□ eine sichere Methode a reliable method
■ **vor jemandem sicher sein** to be safe from somebody □ In einer Großstadt ist man vor Taschendieben nicht sicher. You're never safe from pickpockets in a city.
■ **vor etwas sicher sein** to be safe from something □ Bei ihr ist man vor Überraschungen nie sicher. With her you're never safe from surprises.
4 definitely
□ Sie kommt sicher nicht mehr. She's definitely not coming anymore.
■ **Er weiß das sicher schon.** I'm sure he knows that already.
■ **sicher nicht** surely not
■ **Aber sicher!** Of course!

die **Sicherheit** NOUN
safety
□ Tragen Sie einen Helm zu Ihrer eigenen Sicherheit. Wear a helmet for your own safety. □ Diese Maßnahmen dienen der Sicherheit der Fluggäste. These measures are for passenger safety.
■ **Hier sind wir in Sicherheit.** We're safe here.
■ **Ich kann nicht mit Sicherheit sagen, ob ich komme.** I can't say for sure if I'll come.

der **Sicherheitsgurt** (PL die **Sicherheitsgurte**) NOUN
seat belt

sicherlich ADVERB
certainly

sichern VERB [88]
to secure
□ Maßnahmen, die Arbeitsplätze sichern measures to secure jobs
■ **Daten sichern** to back up data □ Die Daten werden stündlich auf Band gesichert. The data are backed up onto tape every hour.
■ **jemandem etwas sichern** to secure something for somebody □ Ich habe dir einen guten Platz gesichert. I've secured a good place for you.

die **Sicherung** NOUN
1 securing
□ Maßnahmen zur Sicherung der Arbeitsplätze measures for securing jobs
2 fuse
□ Die Sicherung ist durchgebrannt. The fuse has blown.

die **Sicherungskopie** NOUN
backup copy

die **Sicht** NOUN
view
□ Wir hatten eine gute Sicht auf die Berge. We had a good view of the mountains. □ Du versperrst mir die Sicht. You're blocking my view.
■ **auf lange Sicht** on a long-term basis
■ **aus jemandes Sicht** as somebody sees it
□ Aus meiner Sicht ist das zu schaffen. As I see it, it can be done.

sichtbar ADJECTIVE
visible

Sie PRONOUN
▷ *see also* **sie** PRONOUN
you

> **DID YOU KNOW...?**
> The formal form of address **Sie** (singular and plural) is used when addressing people you don't know or your superiors. Teachers say **Sie** to children over the age of 16.

□ Möchten Sie mitkommen? Would you like to come? □ Ich kenne Sie. I know you.

sie PRONOUN
▷ *see also* **Sie** PRONOUN
1 she
□ Sie ist sehr hübsch. She's very pretty.
2 it
□ Schöne Tasche, ist sie neu? Lovely bag, is it new? □ Kann ich deine Tasche haben, oder brauchst du sie noch? Can I have your bag or do you need it?
3 her
□ Ich kenne sie nicht. I don't know her.
4 they
□ Sie sind alle gekommen. They all came.
5 them
□ Ich habe sie alle eingeladen. I've invited all of them.

das **Sieb** (PL die **Siebe**) NOUN
1 sieve
□ Wir sollten da Mehl durch ein Sieb schütten. We should rub the flour through a sieve.
2 strainer
□ Hast du ein Teesieb? Have you got a tea strainer?

sieben NUMBER
seven

siebte ADJECTIVE
seventh
□ Er kam als Siebter. He was the seventh to arrive.

siebzehn NUMBER
seventeen

siebzig NUMBER
seventy

die **Siedlung** NOUN
1 settlement
□ eine indianische Siedlung an Indian settlement
2 estate
□ Sie wohnt in unserer Siedlung. She lives on our estate.

der **Sieg** (PL die **Siege**) NOUN
victory

siegen VERB [38]
to win
□ Welche Mannschaft hat gesiegt? Which team won?

der **Sieger** (PL die **Sieger**) NOUN
winner
□ Brasilien war 1994 Sieger der Fußballweltmeisterschaft. Brazil was the winner of the 1994 World Cup.

siehe VERB ▷ *see* **sehen**

siezen VERB [36]
to address as 'Sie'

DID YOU KNOW...?
The formal form of address **Sie** (singular and plural) is used when addressing people you don't know or your superiors. Teachers say **Sie** to children over the age of 16.

die **Silbe** NOUN
syllable

das **Silber** NOUN
silver

das **Silvester** (PL die **Silvester**) NOUN
New Year's Eve

singen (IMPERFECT **sang**, PERFECT **hat gesungen**) VERB [66]
to sing

der **Singular** (PL die **Singulare**) NOUN
singular

sinken (IMPERFECT **sank**, PERFECT **ist gesunken**) VERB [67]
1 to sink
□ Das Schiff ist gesunken. The ship has sunk.
2 to fall
□ Die Preise für Computer sind gesunken. The prices of computers have fallen.

der **Sinn** (PL die **Sinne**) NOUN
1 sense
□ die fünf Sinne the five senses
2 meaning
□ Ich verstehe den Sinn dieses Satzes nicht. I don't understand the meaning of this sentence. □ Was ist der Sinn des Lebens? What's the meaning of life?
■ **Sinn für etwas haben** to have a sense of something □ Sie hat viel Sinn für Humor. She has a great sense of humour.
■ **jemandem in den Sinn kommen** to come to somebody □ Die Idee kam mir plötzlich in den Sinn. The idea suddenly came to me.
■ **Es hat keinen Sinn.** There's no point.

sinnlos ADJECTIVE
1 pointless
□ Es ist sinnlos, das zu tun. It's pointless doing that.
2 meaningless
□ Er hat sinnloses Zeug geredet. He talked meaningless rubbish.

sinnvoll ADJECTIVE
sensible
□ Das wäre eine sinnvolle Änderung. That would be a sensible change.

die **Situation** NOUN
situation

der **Sitz** (GEN des **Sitzes**, PL die **Sitze**) NOUN
seat

sitzen (IMPERFECT **saß**, PERFECT **hat gesessen**) VERB [68]
1 to sit
□ Er saß auf dem Stuhl. He was sitting on the chair.
■ **sitzen bleiben 1** to remain seated □ Bitte bleiben Sie sitzen. Please remain seated. **2** to have to repeat a year

DID YOU KNOW...?
In Germany, pupils do not automatically move up (**versetzt werden**) to the next class at the end of the school year. If their performance is not good enough, they have to repeat the school year. This is known as **sitzen bleiben**.

□ Ich habe Angst, dass ich dieses Jahr sitzen bleibe. I'm worried that I'll have to repeat this year.
2 to fit
□ Diese Hose sitzt. These trousers fit well.

der **Sitzplatz** (GEN des **Sitzplatzes**, PL die **Sitzplätze**) NOUN
seat

die **Sitzung** NOUN
meeting

der **Skandal** (PL die **Skandale**) NOUN
scandal

Skandinavien NEUT NOUN
Scandinavia
■ **aus Skandinavien** from Scandinavia
■ **nach Skandinavien** to Scandinavia

skandinavisch ADJECTIVE
Scandinavian

das **Skelett** (PL die **Skelette**) NOUN
skeleton

der **Ski** (PL die **Ski** *or* **Skier**) NOUN
ski
■ **Ski fahren** to ski

der **Skifahrer** (PL die **Skifahrer**) NOUN
skier

das **Skilaufen** NOUN
skiing

der **Skilehrer** (PL die **Skilehrer**) NOUN
ski instructor

der **Skilift** (PL die **Skilifte** *or* **Skilifts**) NOUN
ski lift

der **Skorpion** (PL die **Skorpione**) NOUN
1 scorpion
2 Scorpio
□ Sie ist Skorpion. She's Scorpio.

der **Slip** (PL die **Slips**) NOUN
pants

□ ein Slip a pair of pants

die **Slowakei** NOUN
Slovakia
■ **aus der Slowakei** from Slovakia
■ **in die Slowakei** to Slovakia

so ADVERB, CONJUNCTION, EXCLAMATION
1 so
□ Ich hatte mich so darauf gefreut. I was so looking forward to it. □ so schön so nice □ zwanzig oder so twenty or so □ und so weiter and so on
■ **so groß wie ...** as big as ...
2 so much
□ Das hat ihn so geärgert, dass ... That annoyed him so much that ...
■ **so einer wie ich** somebody like me
3 like that
□ Mach es nicht so. Don't do it like that.
■ **... oder so was** ... or something like that
■ **Na so was!** Well, well!
■ **so dass** so that
■ **So?** Really?

sobald CONJUNCTION
as soon as

das **Söckchen** (PL die **Söckchen**) NOUN
ankle sock

die **Socke** NOUN
sock

sodass CONJUNCTION
so that

das **Sofa** (PL die **Sofas**) NOUN
sofa

sofort ADVERB
immediately

sogar ADVERB
even

sogleich ADVERB
straight away

die **Sohle** NOUN
sole

der **Sohn** (PL die **Söhne**) NOUN
son

solch PRONOUN
such
□ Sie ist solch eine nette Frau. She's such a nice lady. □ eine solche Frechheit such a cheek
■ **ein solcher** a ... like that □ Ein solcher Fehler sollte nicht passieren. A mistake like that shouldn't happen. □ Eine solche Wohnung würde mir auch gefallen. I'd like a flat like that.

der **Soldat** (GEN des **Soldaten**, PL die **Soldaten**) NOUN
soldier

solide ADJECTIVE
1 solid
□ Dieser Tisch ist aus solidem Holz. This table is made of solid wood.
2 sound
□ Sie hat solide Grammatikkenntnisse. She has a sound grasp of grammar.
3 respectable
□ Wir führen ein solides Leben. We lead a respectable life. □ Er ist solide geworden. He's become respectable.

sollen (IMPERFECT **sollte**, PERFECT **hat gesollt** *or* **sollen**) VERB [69]

LANGUAGE TIP The past participle **sollen** is used when **sollen** is a modal auxiliary.

1 to be supposed to
□ Ich soll um fünf Uhr dort sein. I'm supposed to be there at five o'clock. □ Was soll das heißen? What's that supposed to mean? □ Morgen soll es schön werden. It's supposed to be nice tomorrow.
2 to have to
□ Du sollst sofort nach Hause. You have to go home immediately. □ Sie sagt, du sollst nach Hause kommen. She says that you have to come home.
■ **Sag ihm, er soll warten.** Tell him he's to wait.
3 should
□ Ich sollte meine Hausaufgaben machen. I should do my homework. □ Du hättest nicht gehen sollen. You shouldn't have gone. □ Was soll ich machen? What should I do? □ Ich hätte eigentlich nicht gesollt. I really shouldn't have. □ Das sollst du nicht. You shouldn't do that.
■ **Sie soll verheiratet sein.** She's said to be married.
■ **man sollte glauben, dass ...** you would think that ...
■ **Soll ich dir helfen?** Shall I help you?
■ **Soll ich?** Shall I?
■ **Was soll das?** What's all this?
■ **Was soll's?** What the hell!

der **Sommer** (PL die **Sommer**) NOUN
summer
□ im Sommer in summer

die **Sommerferien** PL NOUN
summer holidays

sommerlich ADJECTIVE
1 summery
□ ein sommerliches Kleid a summery dress
2 summer
□ sommerliche Kleidung summer clothes
□ sommerliches Wetter summer weather

der **Sommerschlussverkauf** (PL die **Sommerschlussverkäufe**) NOUN
summer sale

die **Sommersprossen** FEM PL NOUN
freckles

das **Sonderangebot** (PL die **Sonderangebote**) NOUN
special offer

sonderbar ADJECTIVE
strange

sondern CONJUNCTION
but
■ **nicht nur ..., sondern auch** not only ..., but also

der **Sonderpreis** NOUN
special price

der **Sonnabend** (PL die **Sonnabende**) NOUN
Saturday
□ am Sonnabend on Saturday

sonnabends ADVERB
on Saturdays

die **Sonne** NOUN
sun

sich **sonnen** VERB [38]
to sun oneself

der **Sonnenbrand** (PL die **Sonnenbrände**) NOUN
sunburn

die **Sonnenbrille** NOUN
sunglasses
□ Sie trug eine Sonnenbrille. She was wearing sunglasses.

die **Sonnencreme** (PL die **Sonnencremes**) NOUN
suntan lotion

die **Sonnenenergie** NOUN
solar power

die **Sonnenmilch** NOUN
suntan lotion

das **Sonnenöl** (PL die **Sonnenöle**) NOUN
suntan oil

der **Sonnenschein** NOUN
sunshine

der **Sonnenschirm** (PL die **Sonnenschirme**) NOUN
sunshade

der **Sonnenstich** NOUN
sunstroke

sonnig ADJECTIVE
sunny

der **Sonntag** (PL die **Sonntage**) NOUN
Sunday
□ am Sonntag on Sunday

sonntags ADVERB
on Sundays

sonst ADVERB, CONJUNCTION
1 normally
□ Was ist mit dir? Du bist doch sonst nicht so still. What's wrong with you? You're not normally so quiet. □ Die Kinder sind sonst eigentlich artiger. The children normally behave better.
2 else
□ Wer sonst? Who else? □ Was sonst? What else? □ Sonst war niemand da. Nobody else was there. □ sonst nichts nothing else
■ **sonst noch** else □ Was hast du sonst noch bekommen? What else did you get?
■ **Haben Sie sonst noch einen Wunsch?** Would you like anything else?
■ **Sonst noch etwas?** Anything else?
■ **sonst wo** somewhere else
3 otherwise
□ Ich habe etwas Kopfschmerzen, aber sonst geht's mir gut. I've got a headache, otherwise I feel fine.

sonstig ADJECTIVE
other

die **Sorge** NOUN
worry
■ **Ich mache mir Sorgen.** I'm worried.

sorgen VERB [38]
■ **für jemanden sorgen** to look after somebody
■ **für etwas sorgen** to see to something
■ **sich um jemanden sorgen** to worry about somebody

sorgfältig ADJECTIVE
careful

die **Sorte** NOUN
1 sort
□ Welche Sorte Äpfel ist das? What sort of apple is that?
2 brand
□ Welche Sorte Waschmittel verwenden Sie? What brand of detergent do you use?

sortieren (PERFECT **hat sortiert**) VERB [76]
to sort out

die **Soße** NOUN
1 sauce
□ Eis mit Himbeersoße ice cream with raspberry sauce
2 gravy
□ Schweinebraten mit Soße roast pork with gravy
3 dressing
□ Salat mit einer Joghurtsoße salad with a yoghurt dressing

das **Souvenir** (PL die **Souvenirs**) NOUN
souvenir

soviel ADVERB ▷ *see* **viel**

soviel CONJUNCTION
as far as
□ soviel ich weiß as far as I know

soweit ADVERB ▷ *see* **weit**

soweit CONJUNCTION
as far as
□ Soweit ich weiß, kann er nicht kommen. As far as I know, he can't come.

sowenig ADVERB ▷ *see* **wenig**

sowie CONJUNCTION
as soon as
□ Ich rufe an, sowie ich Bescheid weiß. I'll phone as soon as I know.

sowieso ADVERB
anyway

sowohl CONJUNCTION
■ **sowohl ... als auch** both ... and

sozial ADJECTIVE
social

die **Sozialhilfe** NOUN
social security
□ Sozialhilfe bekommen to be on social security

die **Sozialkunde** NOUN
social studies

die **Sozialversicherung** NOUN
social security

die **Sozialwissenschaften** PL NOUN
social sciences

die **Spalte** NOUN
1 crack
□ Durch die Trockenheit hatten sich tiefe Spalten gebildet. Deep cracks had formed as a result of the dry spell.
2 column
□ Der Text ist in zwei Spalten gedruckt. The text is printed in two columns.

spalten VERB [2]
to split

Spanien NEUT NOUN
Spain
■ **aus Spanien** from Spain
■ **in Spanien** in Spain
■ **nach Spanien** to Spain

der **Spanier** (PL die **Spanier**) NOUN
Spaniard
■ **Er ist Spanier.** He's Spanish.
■ **die Spanier** the Spanish

die **Spanierin** NOUN
Spaniard
■ **Sie ist Spanierin.** She's Spanish.

das **Spanisch** (GEN des **Spanischen**) NOUN
▷ *see also* **spanisch** ADJECTIVE
Spanish
□ Er lernt Spanisch in der Schule. He's learning Spanish at school.

spanisch ADJECTIVE
Spanish

spannend ADJECTIVE
exciting

die **Spannung** NOUN
1 suspense
□ ein Film voller Spannung a film full of suspense
2 tension
□ Das führte zu Spannungen zwischen den beiden Ländern. That caused tension between the two countries.

das **Sparbuch** (PL die **Sparbücher**) NOUN
savings book

sparen VERB [38]
to save
□ Wir müssen sparen. We have to save. □ Sie hat zweihundert Euro gespart. She's saved two hundred euros. □ Energie sparen to save energy □ Er spart für ein Mountainbike. He's saving for a mountain bike.
■ **sich etwas sparen 1** not to bother with something □ Den Film kannst du dir sparen. Don't bother with that film. **2** to keep something to oneself □ Spar dir deine Bemerkungen. You can keep your remarks to yourself.
■ **mit etwas sparen** to be sparing with something
■ **an etwas sparen** to economize on something □ Sie spart in letzter Zeit am Essen. She's been economizing on food recently.

LANGUAGE TIP Be careful! **sparen** does not mean **to spare**.

der **Spargel** NOUN
asparagus

die **Sparkasse** NOUN
savings bank

sparsam ADJECTIVE
1 economical
□ ein sparsames Auto an economical car
□ Wir sollten mit den Rohstoffen sparsam umgehen. We should be economical with raw materials.
2 thrifty
□ Sie ist sehr sparsam. She's very thrifty.

das **Sparschwein** (PL die **Sparschweine**) NOUN
piggy bank

der **Spaß** (GEN des **Spaßes**, PL die **Späße**) NOUN
fun
□ Wir hatten in den Ferien viel Spaß. We had great fun in the holidays.
■ **Sie versteht keinen Spaß.** She has no sense of humour.

LANGUAGE TIP Word for word, **Sie versteht keinen Spaß** means 'She doesn't understand fun'.

■ **Skifahren macht mir Spaß.** I like skiing.
■ **zum Spaß** for fun □ Ich mache den Kurs nur zum Spaß. I'm only doing the course for fun.
■ **Viel Spaß!** Have fun!

spät ADJECTIVE, ADVERB
late
□ Es wird spät. It's getting late. □ Wir kamen zu spät. We were late.
■ **Wie spät ist es?** What's the time?

später ADJECTIVE, ADVERB
later
□ Bis später! See you later!

spätestens ADVERB
at the latest

der **Spatz** (GEN des **Spatzen**, PL die **Spatzen**) NOUN
sparrow

spazieren VERB [76]
■ **spazieren fahren** to go for a drive
■ **spazieren gehen** to go for a walk

der **Spaziergang** (PL die **Spaziergänge**) NOUN
walk
□ einen Spaziergang machen to go for a walk

German–English

S

der **Speck** NOUN
bacon

das **Speerwerfen** NOUN
throwing the javelin

der **Speicher** (PL die **Speicher**) NOUN
1 loft
□ Die alten Möbel sind auf dem Speicher. The old furniture's in the loft.
2 storehouse
□ Die alten Speicher am Hafen wurden zu Wohnungen umgebaut. The old storehouses at the harbour were converted into flats.
3 memory
□ Ich will den Speicher meines Computers erweitern. I want to expand the memory of my computer.

speichern (PERFECT **hat gespeichert**) VERB [88]
1 to store
□ Energie speichern to store energy
2 to save
□ eine Datei speichern to save a file

das **Speiseeis** NOUN
ice cream

die **Speisekarte** NOUN
menu
□ Könnte ich bitte die Speisekarte haben? Could I have the menu please?

der **Speisesaal** NOUN
dining room

der **Speisewagen** (PL die **Speisewagen**) NOUN
dining car

die **Spende** NOUN
donation

spenden VERB [54]
to donate
□ Ich habe zwanzig Euro gespendet. I've donated twenty euros.
■ **Blut spenden** to give blood

LANGUAGE TIP Be careful! **spenden** does not mean **to spend**.

der **Spender** (PL die **Spender**) NOUN
donor

spendieren (PERFECT **hat spendiert**) VERB [76]
■ **jemandem etwas spendieren** to stand somebody something □ Mutti hat uns ein Eis spendiert. Mum stood us all an ice cream.

die **Sperre** NOUN
1 barrier
□ Vor dem Eingang befand sich eine Sperre. There was a barrier in front of the entrance.
2 ban
□ Er erhielt eine Sperre von drei Monaten. He got a three-month ban.

sperren (PERFECT **hat gesperrt**) VERB [38]
1 to close
□ Die Polizei hat die Straße gesperrt. The police closed the road.
2 to obstruct
□ Es ist verboten, gegnerische Spieler zu sperren. Obstructing the opposition is not allowed.
3 to lock
□ Diese Dateien sind gesperrt. These files are locked.

die **Spezialität** NOUN
speciality

der **Spiegel** (PL die **Spiegel**) NOUN
mirror
□ Er sah in den Spiegel. He looked in the mirror.

das **Spiegelbild** (PL die **Spiegelbilder**) NOUN
reflection

das **Spiegelei** (PL die **Spiegeleier**) NOUN
fried egg

das **Spiel** (PL die **Spiele**) NOUN
1 game
□ Sollen wir ein Spiel spielen? Shall we play a game? □ Hast du das Spiel England gegen Deutschland gesehen? Did you see the England-Germany game?
2 pack
□ Hast du ein Spiel Karten? Do you have a pack of cards?
■ **ein Theaterspiel** a play

spielen VERB [38]
to play
□ Die Kinder spielen im Garten. The children are playing in the garden. □ Wollen wir Tennis spielen? Shall we play tennis? □ Wer spielt den Hamlet? Who's playing Hamlet? □ Wir haben um Geld gespielt. We played for money.

spielend ADVERB
easily

der **Spieler** (PL die **Spieler**) NOUN
1 player
□ Wir brauchen noch einen dritten Spieler. We still need a third player.
2 gambler
□ Er ist ein leidenschaftlicher Spieler. He's a passionate gambler.

das **Spielfeld** (PL die **Spielfelder**) NOUN
pitch

der **Spielfilm** (PL die **Spielfilme**) NOUN
feature film

der **Spielplatz** (GEN des **Spielplatzes**, PL die **Spielplätze**) NOUN
playground

die **Spielregel** NOUN
rule
□ Ich erkläre euch die Spielregeln. I'll explain the rules of the game to you.

das **Spielzeug** (PL die **Spielzeuge**) NOUN
toy

das **Spielzimmer** (PL die **Spielzimmer**) NOUN
playroom

der **Spinat** NOUN
spinach

die **Spinne** NOUN
spider
spinnen (IMPERFECT **spann**, PERFECT **hat gesponnen**) VERB
1 to spin
□ Wolle spinnen to spin wool
2 to be crazy
□ Du spinnst wohl! You're crazy!
die **Spionage** NOUN
espionage
spionieren (PERFECT **hat spioniert**) VERB [76]
to spy
spitz ADJECTIVE
pointed
■ **ein spitzer Winkel** an acute angle
■ **eine spitze Zunge** a sharp tongue
■ **eine spitze Bemerkung** a caustic remark
spitze ADJECTIVE
great
■ **Das war spitze!** That was great!
die **Spitze** NOUN
1 point
□ Die Spitze des Bleistifts ist abgebrochen. The point of the pencil has broken off.
2 peak
□ Die Spitzen der Berge waren schneebedeckt. The peaks of the mountains were covered with snow.
3 top
□ Welche Mannschaft liegt an der Spitze? Which team is top?
4 lace
□ An ihrem Kleid war ein Kragen aus Spitze. Her dress had a lace collar.
der **Spitzer** (PL die **Spitzer**) NOUN
pencil sharpener
der **Spitzname** (GEN des **Spitznamens**, PL die **Spitznamen**) NOUN
nickname
der **Splitter** (PL die **Splitter**) NOUN
splinter
sponsern VERB [88]
to sponsor
der **Sport** NOUN
sport
die **Sportart** NOUN
sport
□ verschiedene Sportarten various sports
der **Sportler** (PL die **Sportler**) NOUN
sportsman
die **Sportlerin** NOUN
sportswoman
sportlich ADJECTIVE
sporty
□ Bettina ist sehr sportlich. Bettina is very sporty.
der **Sportplatz** (GEN des **Sportplatzes**, PL die **Sportplätze**) NOUN
sports field
der **Sportschuh** (PL die **Sportschuhe**) NOUN
trainer
der **Sportverein** (PL die **Sportvereine**) NOUN
sports club
das **Sportzentrum** (PL die **Sportzentren**) NOUN
sports centre
sprach VERB ▷ *see* **sprechen**
die **Sprache** NOUN
language
der **Sprachführer** (PL die **Sprachführer**) NOUN
phrase book
LANGUAGE TIP Word for word, **Sprachführer** means 'language guide'.
das **Sprachlabor** (PL die **Sprachlabors** *or* **Sprachlabore**) NOUN
language laboratory
sprachlich ADJECTIVE
linguistic
sprachlos ADJECTIVE
speechless
sprang VERB ▷ *see* **springen**
sprechen (PRESENT **spricht**, IMPERFECT **sprach**, PERFECT **hat gesprochen**) VERB [70]
1 to talk
□ Seid bitte ruhig, wenn ich spreche. Please be quiet, I'm talking. □ Du sprichst so leise. You talk so quietly. □ Wir haben von dir gesprochen. We were talking about you.
2 to say
□ Sie hat kein Wort gesprochen. She didn't say a word.
3 to speak
□ Ich spreche Italienisch ziemlich schlecht. I speak Italian pretty badly.
■ **jemanden sprechen** to speak to somebody □ Der Direktor will dich sprechen. The headmaster wants to speak to you.
■ **mit jemandem über etwas sprechen** to speak to somebody about something
■ **Das spricht für ihn.** That's a point in his favour.
die **Sprechstunde** NOUN
surgery *(doctor's)*
spricht VERB ▷ *see* **sprechen**
das **Sprichwort** (PL die **Sprichwörter**) NOUN
proverb
springen (IMPERFECT **sprang**, PERFECT **ist gesprungen**) VERB [71]
1 to jump
□ Er sprang über den Zaun. He jumped over the fence.
2 to crack
□ Das Glas ist gesprungen. The glass has cracked.
die **Spritze** NOUN
1 syringe
□ Die Spritze muss steril sein. The syringe has to be sterile.
2 injection

□ Der Arzt hat mir eine Spritze gegeben. The doctor gave me an injection.
3 nozzle
□ Die Spritze am Gartenschlauch ist nicht dicht. The nozzle on the garden hose leaks.

spritzen (PERFECT **hat/ist gespritzt**) VERB [36]
LANGUAGE TIP Use **haben** to form the perfect tense. Use **sein** to form the perfect tense for 'to spurt out'.
1 to spray
□ Er hat sein Fahrrad grün gespritzt. He's sprayed his bike green.
■ **den Garten spritzen** to water the garden
■ **jemanden nass spritzen** to splash somebody
2 to spurt out
□ Das Blut spritzte aus der Wunde. The blood spurted out of the wound.

der **Sprudel** (PL die **Sprudel**) NOUN
mineral water
■ **süßer Sprudel** lemonade

sprühen (PERFECT **hat/ist gesprüht**) VERB [38]
LANGUAGE TIP For the perfect tense use **haben** when the verb has an object and **sein** when there is no object. Use **haben** to form the perfect tense for 'to sparkle'.
1 to spray
□ Sie hat Haarspray auf ihre Haare gesprüht. She sprayed her hair with hairspray.
2 to fly
□ In alle Richtungen sind Funken gesprüht. Sparks flew in all directions.
3 to sparkle
□ Er hat gestern Abend vor Witz gesprüht. He was sparkling with humour yesterday evening.

der **Sprung** (PL die **Sprünge**) NOUN
1 jump
□ Das war ein weiter Sprung. That was a long jump.
2 crack
□ Die Tasse hat einen Sprung. There is a crack in the cup.

das **Sprungbrett** (PL die **Sprungbretter**) NOUN
springboard

spucken VERB [38]
to spit

die **Spüle** NOUN
kitchen sink

spülen VERB [38]
1 to rinse
□ Wollsachen muss man gut spülen. Woollens have to be rinsed well.
2 to wash up
□ Wenn du spülst, dann trockne ich ab. If you wash up I'll dry.

die **Spülmaschine** NOUN
dishwasher

das **Spülmittel** (PL die **Spülmittel**) NOUN
washing-up liquid

die **Spur** NOUN
1 track
□ Wir sahen Spuren im Sand. We saw tracks in the sand.
2 lane
□ Der Fahrer vor mir hat plötzlich die Spur gewechselt. The driver in front of me suddenly changed lane.
3 trace
□ Auf ihrem Gesicht sah man die Spuren der Anstrengung. You could see the traces of strain on her face.
■ **eine Bremsspur** skidmarks
4 trail
□ Die Polizei verfolgte seine Spur. The police followed his trail.
■ **Das Essen war eine Spur zu scharf.** The meal was a touch too spicy.

spüren VERB [38]
to feel

der **Staat** (PL die **Staaten**) NOUN
state
■ **die Vereinigten Staaten von Amerika** the United States of America

staatlich ADJECTIVE
1 state
□ staatliche Fördermittel state subsidies
□ ein staatliche Schule a state school
2 state-run
□ eine staatliche Einrichtung a state-run organization

die **Staatsangehörigkeit** NOUN
nationality

stabil ADJECTIVE
1 stable
□ Die Lage ist stabil. The situation is stable.
□ Sie ist psychisch stabil. She's mentally stable.
2 sturdy
□ stabile Möbel sturdy furniture

der **Stachel** (PL die **Stacheln**) NOUN
1 spike
□ Ich habe mir die Hose an einem Stachel aufgerissen. I've torn my trousers on a spike.
2 spine
□ Ein Igel hat Stacheln. A hedgehog has spines. □ Dieser Kaktus hat lange Stacheln. This cactus has long spines.
3 sting
□ Ich habe versucht, den Stachel der Biene herauszuziehen. I tried to take the bee sting out.

die **Stachelbeere** NOUN
gooseberry

der **Stacheldraht** (PL die **Stacheldrähte**) NOUN
barbed wire

das **Stadion** (PL die **Stadien**) NOUN
stadium

die Stadt (PL die **Städte**) NOUN
town

städtisch ADJECTIVE
municipal

der Stadtkreis (PL die **Stadtkreise**) NOUN
town borough

die Stadtmitte NOUN
town centre

der Stadtplan (PL die **Stadtpläne**) NOUN
street map

der Stadtrand (PL die **Stadtränder**) NOUN
outskirts

die Stadtrundfahrt NOUN
tour of the city

der Stadtteil (PL die **Stadtteile**) NOUN
part of town

das Stadtzentrum (PL die **Stadtzentren**) NOUN
city centre

der Stahl NOUN
steel

stahl VERB ▷ *see* **stehlen**

der Stall (PL die **Ställe**) NOUN
stable
□ Die Pferde sind im Stall. The horses are in the stable.
■ **ein Hühnerstall** a henhouse

der Stamm (PL die **Stämme**) NOUN
1 trunk
□ Der Baum hat einen dicken Stamm. The tree has a thick trunk.
2 tribe
□ Er gehört zum Stamm der Bantus. He belongs to the Bantu tribe.
3 stem
□ Die Endung wird an den Stamm des Verbs angehängt. The ending's added to the stem of the verb.

stammen VERB [38]
■ **stammen aus** to come from

der Stammgast (PL die **Stammgäste**) NOUN
regular customer

der Stammtisch (PL die **Stammtische**) NOUN
table for the regulars

DID YOU KNOW...?
In Germany it is usual for a group of friends to reserve a table in the same pub or restaurant for the same time each week.

der Stand (PL die **Stände**) NOUN
1 state
□ Was ist der Stand der Dinge? What's the state of affairs?
2 score
□ Sie sind beim Stand von eins zu eins in die Pause. The score was one all at half-time.
3 stand
□ An welchen Stand hast du den Luftballon gekauft? Which stand did you buy the balloon at?
4 level
□ Prüf mal den Ölstand. Check the oil level.
■ **zu Stande** ▷ *see* **zustande**

stand VERB ▷ *see* **stehen**

ständig ADJECTIVE
constant
□ Musst du ständig stören? Do you constantly have to interrupt?

der Standort (PL die **Standorte**) NOUN
location

der Stapel (PL die **Stapel**) NOUN
pile

starb VERB ▷ *see* **sterben**

stark ADJECTIVE
1 strong
□ Mein Bruder ist stärker als du. My brother's stronger than you.
2 heavy
□ starke Regenfälle heavy rain
■ **starke Kopfschmerzen** a splitting headache
3 great
□ Das war stark! That was great!

der Start (PL die **Starts**) NOUN
1 start
□ Es waren über hundert Läufer am Start. There were over a hundred runners at the start.
2 takeoff
□ Die Maschine war bereit zum Start. The machine was ready for takeoff.

starten VERB [2]
1 to start
□ Wann startet das Rennen? When does the race start?
2 to take off
□ Das Flugzeug startet gleich. The plane is about to take off.

statt CONJUNCTION, PREPOSITION
LANGUAGE TIP The preposition **statt** takes the genitive or the dative.
instead of
□ Statt nach Hause zu gehen, sind wir noch in die Disco. Instead of going home, we went to the disco. □ Sie kam statt ihres Bruders. She came instead of her brother.

stattfinden (IMPERFECT **fand statt**, PERFECT **hat stattgefunden**) VERB [24]
to take place

der Stau (PL die **Staus**) NOUN
traffic jam
□ Wir sind im Stau stecken geblieben. We were stuck in a traffic jam.

der Staub NOUN
dust
■ **Staub wischen** to dust

staubig ADJECTIVE
dusty

staubsaugen (PERFECT **hat staubgesaugt**) VERB [38]
to hoover

der **Staubsauger** (PL die **Staubsauger**)
NOUN
vacuum cleaner

staunen VERB [38]
to be astonished

Std. ABBREVIATION (= *Stunde*)
hr.

stechen (PRESENT **sticht**, IMPERFECT **stach**, PERFECT **hat gestochen**) VERB
1 to prick
□ Ich habe mich mit der Nadel gestochen. I've pricked myself with the needle.
2 to sting
□ Mich hat eine Biene gestochen. A bee stung me.
3 to bite
□ Reibe dich ein, damit du nicht gestochen wirst. Rub something on so that you won't be bitten.
4 to trump
□ Sie hat meine Dame gestochen. She trumped my queen.

die **Steckdose** NOUN
socket

stecken VERB [48]
1 to put
□ Sie steckte ihren Geldbeutel in die Tasche. She put her purse in her bag.
2 to insert
□ Stecken Sie die Münze in den Schlitz. Insert the coin into the slot.
3 to stick
□ Steck deinen Finger nicht in das Loch! Don't stick your finger in the hole.
4 to pin
□ Ich steckte das Abzeichen an meine Jacke. I pinned the badge onto my jacket.
5 to be stuck
□ Wir stecken im Stau. We are stuck in a traffic jam.
■ **Wo steckt sie nur?** Where on earth is she?

der **Stecker** (PL die **Stecker**) NOUN
plug

die **Stecknadel** NOUN
pin

stehen (IMPERFECT **stand**, PERFECT **hat gestanden**) VERB [72]
1 to stand
□ Es war so voll, dass wir stehen mussten. It was so full that we had to stand.
2 to be
□ Vor unserem Haus steht eine Kastanie. There's a chestnut tree in front of our house.
3 to say
□ In der Zeitung steht, dass das Wetter besser wird. It says in the newspaper that the weather will improve.
■ **zum Stehen kommen** to come to a halt
□ Der Verkehr kam zum Stehen. The traffic came to a halt.
■ **Es steht schlecht um ihn.** Things are bad for him.
■ **jemandem stehen** to suit somebody
□ Blau steht dir gut. Blue suits you.
■ **Wie steht's? 1** How are things? **2** What's the score?
■ **stehen bleiben** to stop □ Meine Uhr ist stehen geblieben. My watch has stopped.

die **Stehlampe** NOUN
standard lamp

stehlen (PRESENT **stiehlt**, IMPERFECT **stahl**, PERFECT **hat gestohlen**) VERB [73]
to steal

steif ADJECTIVE
stiff

steigen (IMPERFECT **stieg**, PERFECT **ist gestiegen**) VERB [74]
1 to rise
□ Der Ballon stieg zum Himmel. The balloon rose into the sky.
2 to climb
□ Sie ist auf die Leiter gestiegen. She climbed up the ladder.
■ **in etwas steigen** to get into something
□ Er stieg ins Auto. He got into the car.
■ **Sie stieg in den Zug.** She got on the train.
■ **auf etwas steigen** to get on something
□ Sie stieg aufs Fahrrad. She got on her bike.

die **Steigung** NOUN
incline

steil ADJECTIVE
steep

der **Stein** (PL die **Steine**) NOUN
stone

der **Steinbock** (PL die **Steinböcke**) NOUN
Capricorn
□ Er ist Steinbock. He's Capricorn.

steinig ADJECTIVE
stony

die **Stelle** NOUN
1 place
□ Ich habe mir die Stelle im Buch angestrichen. I've marked the place in the book.
■ **an dieser Stelle** here
2 job
□ Ich suche eine neue Stelle. I'm looking for a new job.
3 office
□ Bei welcher Stelle kann man einen Pass bekommen? In which office can you get a passport?
■ **An deiner Stelle würde ich das nicht tun.** I wouldn't do it if I were you.

stellen VERB [38]
1 to put
□ Ich habe die Vase auf den Tisch gestellt. I put the vase on the table.
2 to set
□ Stell deine Uhr nach meiner. Set your watch by mine.

3 to supply
□ Die Lehrbücher werden gestellt. The course books will be supplied.
■ **sich irgendwohin stellen** to stand somewhere □ Stellt euch bitte an die Wand. Please stand against the wall.
■ **sich stellen** to give oneself up □ Der Dieb hat sich gestellt. The thief gave himself up.
■ **sich dumm stellen** to pretend to be stupid

die **Stellenanzeige** NOUN
job advertisement

die **Stellung** NOUN
position
□ In welcher Stellung schläfst du? Which position do you sleep in? □ Er hat eine gute Stellung. He has a good position.
■ **zu etwas Stellung nehmen** to comment on something

der **Stellvertreter** (PL die **Stellvertreter**) NOUN
deputy

der **Stempel** (PL die **Stempel**) NOUN
stamp

stempeln VERB [34]
to stamp
■ **jemanden zum Sündenbock stempeln** to make somebody a scapegoat

sterben (PRESENT **stirbt**, IMPERFECT **starb**, PERFECT **ist gestorben**) VERB [75]
to die

die **Stereoanlage** NOUN
stereo

der **Stern** (PL die **Sterne**) NOUN
star
□ die Sterne am Himmel the stars in the sky

das **Sternzeichen** (PL die **Sternzeichen**) NOUN
star sign
□ Was ist dein Sternzeichen? What star sign are you?

das **Steuer** (PL die **Steuer**) NOUN
▷ *see also* **die Steuer** NOUN
wheel
□ Wer saß am Steuer? Who was at the wheel?

die **Steuer** NOUN
▷ *see also* **das Steuer** NOUN
tax
□ Wir müssen viel Steuern bezahlen. We have to pay a lot of tax.

das **Steuerrad** (PL die **Steuerräder**) NOUN
steering wheel

der **Stich** (PL die **Stiche**) NOUN
1 bite
□ Das Mittel schützt vor Stichen. This gives protection from bites. □ ein Mückenstich a midge bite
■ **ein Bienenstich** a bee sting
2 stab
□ Er tötete sie mit zwölf Stichen. He killed her by stabbing her twelve times.
3 stitch
□ Sie hat den Aufhänger mit ein paar Stichen angenäht. She sewed on the loop with a couple of stitches. □ Die Wunde wurde mit drei Stichen genäht. Three stitches were put in the wound.
4 trick
□ Ich habe beim letzten Spiel keinen Stich gemacht. I didn't win any tricks in the last game.
5 engraving
□ ein Kupferstich a copper engraving
■ **jemanden im Stich lassen** to leave somebody in the lurch

sticken VERB [38]
to embroider

der **Stickstoff** NOUN
nitrogen

der **Stiefel** (PL die **Stiefel**) NOUN
boot

das **Stiefkind** (PL die **Stiefkinder**) NOUN
stepchild

die **Stiefmutter** (PL die **Stiefmütter**) NOUN
stepmother

der **Stiefvater** (PL die **Stiefväter**) NOUN
stepfather

stiehlt VERB ▷ *see* **stehlen**

der **Stiel** (PL die **Stiele**) NOUN
1 handle
□ der Stiel des Besens the broom handle
2 stem
□ Er hat den Stiel der Tulpe abgeknickt. He snapped the stem off the tulip.

der **Stier** (PL die **Stiere**) NOUN
1 bull
□ Der Stier wurde getötet. The bull was killed.
2 Taurus
□ Brigitte ist Stier. Brigitte's Taurus.

der **Stift** (PL die **Stifte**) NOUN
1 peg
□ Das Brett wird mit Stiften an der Wand befestigt. The board is fixed to the wall with pegs.
2 crayon
□ Sebastian hat lauter bunte Stifte bekommen. Sebastian got lots of coloured crayons.
3 pencil
□ Schreib lieber mit Kuli als mit einem Stift. I'd rather you wrote with a Biro than a pencil.

stiften VERB [2]
■ **Sie hat eine Runde Eis gestiftet.** She bought us all an ice cream.
■ **Unruhe stiften** to cause trouble

der **Stil** (PL die **Stile**) NOUN
style

still ADJECTIVE
quiet
□ Seid mal still. Be quiet.
■ **Sie stand ganz still.** She stood quite still.

die **Stille** NOUN
quietness
■ **in aller Stille** quietly

stillhalten (PRESENT **hält still**, IMPERFECT **hielt still**, PERFECT **hat stillgehalten**) VERB [33]
to keep still

stillschweigend ADVERB
tacitly

die **Stimme** NOUN
1 voice
□ Er hat eine laute Stimme. He has a loud voice.
2 vote
□ Er bekam nur zwanzig Stimmen. He only got twenty votes.
■ **Wem hast du deine Stimme gegeben?** Who did you vote for?

stimmen VERB [38]
1 to be right
□ Die Übersetzung stimmt nicht. The translation isn't right. □ Das stimmt nicht! That's not right!
2 to tune
□ ein Instrument stimmen to tune an instrument
3 to vote
□ stimmen für to vote for □ stimmen gegen to vote against
■ **Stimmt so!** Keep the change.

die **Stimmung** NOUN
mood

stinken (IMPERFECT **stank**, PERFECT **hat gestunken**) VERB
to stink

stirbt VERB ▷ *see* **sterben**

die **Stirn** NOUN
forehead

der **Stock (1)** (PL die **Stöcke**) NOUN
stick
□ Er hat ihn mit einem Stock geschlagen. He hit him with a stick.

der **Stock (2)** (PL die **Stock** *or* **Stockwerke**) NOUN
floor
□ Wir wohnen im dritten Stock. We live on the third floor.

der **Stoff** (PL die **Stoffe**) NOUN
1 fabric
□ Das ist ein hübscher Stoff. That's a pretty fabric.
2 material
□ Ich sammle Stoff für mein Referat. I'm collecting material for my assignment.

stöhnen VERB [38]
to groan

stolpern (PERFECT **ist gestolpert**) VERB [88]
1 to stumble
□ Er ist gestolpert und gefallen. He stumbled and fell.
2 to trip
□ Er ist über einen Stein gestolpert. He tripped over a stone.

stolz ADJECTIVE
proud
□ Ich bin stolz auf dich. I'm proud of you.

stören VERB [38]
to disturb
□ Störe ich? Am I disturbing you? □ Ich will nicht länger stören. I won't disturb you any longer.
■ **Stört es dich, wenn ich rauche?** Do you mind if I smoke?
■ **Die Leitung war gestört.** It was a bad line.
■ **sich an etwas stören** to worry about something □ Stör dich nicht an der Schrift, der Inhalt ist wichtig. Don't worry about the writing, it's the content that counts.

störend ADJECTIVE
disturbing

die **Störung** NOUN
1 interruption
□ Diese dauernden Störungen regen mich auf. These constant interruptions are getting on my nerves.
2 interference
□ Es war eine Störung beim Bild. There was interference to the picture.

stoßen (PRESENT **stößt**, IMPERFECT **stieß**, PERFECT **hat gestoßen**) VERB
■ **den Kopf an etwas stoßen** to bump one's head on something □ Ich habe mir an der niedrigen Decke den Kopf gestoßen. I bumped my head on the low ceiling.
■ **sich stoßen** to bump oneself □ Sie hat einen blauen Fleck, wo sie sich gestoßen hat. She has a bruise where she bumped herself.
■ **sich an etwas stoßen** to take exception to something □ Sie hat sich an seinem schlechten Benehmen gestoßen. She took exception to his bad behaviour.
■ **an etwas stoßen** to bump into something □ Pass auf, dass du nicht an die Statue stößt. Watch out that you don't bump into the statue.
■ **auf etwas stoßen** to come across □ Heute bin ich auf dem Flohmarkt auf ein tolles Buch gestoßen. I came across a great book at the flea market today.

stottern VERB [88]
to stutter

Str. ABBREVIATION (*= Straße*)
St

die **Strafarbeit** NOUN
lines
□ Ich habe eine Strafarbeit bekommen. I got lines.

die **Strafe** NOUN
1 punishment
□ Zur Strafe müsst ihr länger bleiben. You'll be kept in after school as a punishment.

■ **eine Gefängnisstrafe** a prison sentence
2 fine
□ Er musste eine Strafe von fünfzig Euro bezahlen. He had to pay a fifty euro fine.

der **Strahl** (PL die **Strahlen**) NOUN
1 ray
□ radioaktive Strahlen radioactive rays
□ ein Sonnenstrahl a ray of sunlight
■ **ein Lichtstrahl** a beam of light
2 jet
□ ein Wasserstrahl a jet of water

strahlen VERB [38]
1 to shine
□ Die Sterne strahlten hell. The stars shone brightly.
2 to beam
□ Sie strahlte, als sie das hörte. She beamed when she heard that.

die **Strahlung** NOUN
radiation

der **Strand** (PL die **Strände**) NOUN
1 beach
□ Wir haben den ganzen Tag am Strand gelegen. We lay on the beach all day.
2 shore
□ Das wurde an den Strand gespült. That was washed up on the shore.

strapazieren (PERFECT **hat strapaziert**) VERB [76]
1 to be hard on
□ Du hast heute deinen Computer ganz schön strapaziert. You've been really hard on your computer today.
2 to wear out
□ Die Wanderung hat uns ziemlich strapaziert. The walk has really worn us out.

die **Straße** NOUN
1 street
□ In welcher Straße wohnt Thomas? Which street does Thomas live in?
2 road
□ Wir sind die Straße entlang der Küste gefahren. We drove along the coast road.

die **Straßenbahn** NOUN
tram

der **Strauß** (GEN des **Straußes**, PL die **Sträuße**) NOUN
bunch of flowers
□ Wir haben unserer Gastgeberin einen Strauß mitgebracht. We brought our hostess a bunch of flowers.

die **Strecke** NOUN
1 distance
□ Wir haben diese Strecke an einem Tag zurückgelegt. We covered this distance in one day. □ Bis zu ihm ist es noch eine ziemliche Strecke. It's still quite a distance to his place.
2 line
□ Auf der Strecke zwischen Stuttgart und Ulm gab es ein Zugunglück. There's been a train accident on the Stuttgart to Ulm line.

streicheln VERB [88]
to stroke

streichen (IMPERFECT **strich**, PERFECT **hat gestrichen**) VERB
1 to stroke
□ Sie strich über seine Haare. She stroked his hair.
2 to spread
□ Sie strich Honig aufs Brot. She spread honey on the bread.
3 to paint
□ Ich muss dringend mein Zimmer streichen. I really must paint my room.
4 to delete
□ Den zweiten Satz kannst du streichen. You can delete the second sentence.
5 to cancel
□ Der Direktor hat den Schulausflug gestrichen. The headmaster has cancelled the school trip.

das **Streichholz** (GEN des **Streichholzes**, PL die **Streichhölzer**) NOUN
match

der **Streifen** (PL die **Streifen**) NOUN
strip

der **Streik** (PL die **Streiks**) NOUN
strike

streiken VERB [38]
to go on strike
■ **Sie streiken.** They're on strike.

der **Streit** (PL die **Streite**) NOUN
argument

sich **streiten** (IMPERFECT **stritt**, PERFECT **hat gestritten**) VERB
to argue
□ Sie streiten sich ständig. They argue constantly.
■ **Darüber lässt sich streiten.** That's debatable.

streng ADJECTIVE
1 strict
□ Meine Eltern sind furchtbar streng. My parents are terribly strict.
2 severe
□ Es war ein strenger Winter. It was a severe winter. □ Das wird streng bestraft. That will be severely punished.
3 sharp
□ Wo kommt der strenge Geruch her? Where's that sharp smell coming from?

der **Stress** (GEN des **Stresses**) NOUN
stress
■ **Ich bin im Stress!** I'm stressed out.

stressen (PRESENT **stresst**, IMPERFECT **stresste**, PERFECT **hat gestresst**) VERB [48]
to put under stress

stressig ADJECTIVE
stressful

der **Strich** (PL die **Striche**) NOUN
1 line
□ Mach einen Strich unter die Spalte. Draw a line under the column.
2 stroke
□ Mit ein paar Strichen zeichnete er ein Haus. He drew a house with a couple of strokes.
■ **auf den Strich gehen** to be on the game

der **Strichkode** (PL die **Strichkodes**) NOUN
bar code

der **Strichpunkt** (PL die **Strichpunkte**) NOUN
semicolon

der **Strick** (PL die **Stricke**) NOUN
rope

stricken VERB [48]
to knit

das **Stroh** NOUN
straw

der **Strohhalm** (PL die **Strohhalme**) NOUN
drinking straw

der **Strom** (PL die **Ströme**) NOUN
1 current
□ der Wechselstrom alternating current
■ **Vorsicht, auf dem Draht ist Strom.** Be careful, the wire is live.
2 electricity
□ Sie haben den Strom abgeschaltet. They've cut off the electricity.
3 stream
□ Ein Strom von Zuschauern kam aus dem Stadion. A stream of spectators was coming out of the stadium.

die **Strömung** NOUN
current

der **Strumpf** (PL die **Strümpfe**) NOUN
stocking

die **Strumpfhose** NOUN
tights
□ eine Strumpfhose a pair of tights

LANGUAGE TIP Word for word, **eine Strumpfhose** means 'a pair of stocking trousers'.

das **Stück** (PL die **Stücke**) NOUN
1 piece
□ Sie schnitt ein Stück Käse ab. She cut off a piece of cheese.
2 play
□ Wir haben ein Stück von Brecht angesehen. We saw a play by Brecht.

das **Stückchen** (PL die **Stückchen**) NOUN
little piece

der **Student** (GEN des **Studenten**, PL die **Studenten**) NOUN
student

die **Studentin** NOUN
student

studieren (PERFECT **hat studiert**) VERB [76]
to study
□ Mein Bruder studiert Physik. My brother's studying physics.

das **Studium** (PL die **Studien**) NOUN
studies

die **Stufe** NOUN
1 step
□ Vorsicht, Stufe! Mind the step!
2 stage
□ Er hat bereits eine fortgeschrittene Stufe erreicht. He's already reached an advanced stage. □ eine Entwicklungsstufe a stage of development

der **Stuhl** (PL die **Stühle**) NOUN
chair

stumm ADJECTIVE
1 silent
□ Sie blieb stumm. She remained silent.
2 dumb
□ Sie ist von Geburt an stumm. She's been dumb from birth.

stumpf ADJECTIVE
blunt
□ Er wurde mit einem stumpfen Gegenstand am Kopf getroffen. He was hit on the head with a blunt object.
■ **ein stumpfer Winkel** an obtuse angle

die **Stunde** NOUN
1 hour
□ Ich komme in einer Stunde. I'll come in an hour.
2 lesson
□ Was haben wir in der letzten Stunde behandelt? What did we do in the last lesson?

der **Stundenplan** (PL die **Stundenpläne**) NOUN
timetable

stündlich ADJECTIVE
hourly
□ stündlich verkehren to run hourly

stur ADJECTIVE
obstinate

der **Sturm** (PL die **Stürme**) NOUN
storm

stürmen (PERFECT **ist/hat gestürmt**) VERB [38]

LANGUAGE TIP Use **sein** to form the perfect tense for 'to storm (out)'. Use **haben** to form the perfect tense for all other meanings.

to storm
□ Er ist aus dem Zimmer gestürmt. He stormed out of the room. □ Die Polizei hat das Gebäude gestürmt. The police stormed the building.
■ **Es stürmt.** There's a gale blowing.

stürmisch ADJECTIVE
stormy

der **Sturz** (GEN des **Sturzes**, PL die **Stürze**) NOUN
1 fall
□ Bei dem Sturz hat sie sich das Bein gebrochen. She broke her leg in the fall.

2 overthrow
□ Alle freuten sich über den Sturz des Diktators. Everybody was pleased about the overthrow of the dictator.

stürzen (PERFECT **hat/ist gestürzt**) VERB [36]
LANGUAGE TIP Use **sein** to form the perfect tense. Use **haben** to form the perfect tense for 'to overthrow' and for **sich stürzen**.
1 to fall
□ Sie ist vom Pferd gestürzt. She fell off a horse.
2 to rush
□ Er kam ins Zimmer gestürzt. He rushed into the room.
3 to overthrow
□ Die Regierung wurde gestürzt. The government has been overthrown.
■ **sich stürzen** to plunge □ Sie stürzte sich ins Wasser. She plunged into the water.

der **Sturzhelm** (PL die **Sturzhelme**) NOUN
crash helmet

die **Stütze** NOUN
support

das **Subjekt** (PL die **Subjekte**) NOUN
subject

das **Substantiv** (PL die **Substantive**) NOUN
noun

die **Suche** NOUN
search

suchen VERB [48]
to look for
□ Ich suche meinen Radiergummi. I'm looking for my rubber. □ Wir haben gesucht, es aber nicht gefunden. We looked for it but couldn't find it. □ Er wird von der Polizei gesucht. The police are looking for him.
■ **nach etwas suchen** to look for something
□ Wonach suchst du? What are you looking for?

die **Suchmaschine** NOUN
search engine *(Internet)*

süchtig ADJECTIVE
addicted
□ heroinsüchtig addicted to heroin

der/die **Süchtige** (GEN des/der **Süchtigen**, PL die **Süchtigen**) NOUN
addict
□ Ein Süchtiger hat uns erzählt, wie er süchtig geworden ist. An addict told us how he became addicted.

Südafrika NEUT NOUN
South Africa
■ **aus Südafrika** from South Africa
■ **nach Südafrika** to South Africa

Südamerika NEUT NOUN
South America
■ **aus Südamerika** from South America
■ **nach Südamerika** to South America

der **Süden** NOUN
south

südlich ADJECTIVE, PREPOSITION, ADVERB
southerly
□ in südlicher Richtung in a southerly direction
■ **südlich einer Sache** to the south of something □ Das Kraftwerk liegt südlich der Stadt. The power station's to south of the city.
■ **südlich von** south of □ Das liegt südlich von Rom. It is south of Rome.

der **Südosten** NOUN
southeast

der **Südpol** NOUN
South Pole
□ am Südpol at the South Pole

der **Südwesten** NOUN
southwest

die **Summe** NOUN
total

summen VERB [38]
1 to buzz
□ Die Bienen summten. The bees were buzzing.
2 to hum
□ Sie summte vor sich hin. She was humming. □ Er hat ein Lied gesummt. He hummed a song.

die **Sünde** NOUN
sin

das **Super** NOUN
four star
□ Ich tanke Super. My car takes four star.

das **Superbenzin** NOUN
four-star petrol

der **Superlativ** (PL die **Superlative**) NOUN
superlative

der **Supermarkt** (PL die **Supermärkte**) NOUN
supermarket

die **Suppe** NOUN
soup

das **Surfbrett** (PL die **Surfbretter**) NOUN
surfboard

surfen (PERFECT **hat gesurft**) VERB [38]
to surf
■ **im Internet surfen** to surf the Net

süß ADJECTIVE
sweet

die **Süßigkeit** NOUN
sweet
□ Sie isst gern Süßigkeiten. She likes eating sweets.

der **Süßstoff** (PL die **Süßstoffe**) NOUN
sweetener

die **Süßwaren** PL NOUN
confectionery

der **Süßwarenladen** (PL die **Süßwarenläden**) NOUN
sweetshop

das **Symbol** (PL die **Symbole**) NOUN
symbol

German-English

S

symmetrisch ADJECTIVE
symmetrical

die **Sympathie** NOUN
fondness
□ Ihre Sympathie für ihn ist offensichtlich.
Her fondness for him is obvious.

sympathisch ADJECTIVE
likeable
□ Er ist ein sympathischer Mensch.
He's a likeable person.
■ **Er ist mir sympathisch.** I like him.

LANGUAGE TIP Be careful! **sympathisch** does not mean **sympathetic.**

synchronisieren (PERFECT hat **synchronisiert**) VERB [76]
to dub
□ ein synchronisierter Film a dubbed film

das **Synonym** (PL die **Synonyme**) NOUN
synonym

synthetisch ADJECTIVE
synthetic

das **System** (PL die **Systeme**) NOUN
system

systematisch ADJECTIVE
systematic

die **Szene** NOUN
scene

Tt

der Tabak (PL die **Tabake**) NOUN
tobacco

die Tabelle NOUN
table

das Tablett (PL die **Tablette**) NOUN
tray

die Tablette NOUN
tablet

der Tachometer (PL die **Tachometer**) NOUN
speedometer

tadellos ADJECTIVE
faultless

die Tafel NOUN
blackboard
□ Der Lehrer schrieb das Wort an die Tafel. The teacher wrote the word on the blackboard.
■ **eine Tafel Schokolade** a bar of chocolate

der Tag (PL die **Tage**) NOUN
1 day
□ Ich war den ganzen Tag weg. I was away all day.
2 daylight
□ Wir möchten noch bei Tag ankommen. We want to arrive in daylight.
■ **an den Tag kommen** to come to light
■ **Guten Tag!** Hello!

das Tageblatt (PL die **Tageblätter**) NOUN
daily newspaper

das Tagebuch (PL die **Tagebücher**) NOUN
diary
□ ein Tagebuch führen to keep a diary

tagelang ADVERB
for days

der Tagesanbruch NOUN
dawn
□ bei Tagesanbruch at dawn

das Tagesgericht (PL die **Tagesgerichte**) NOUN
dish of the day

die Tageskarte NOUN
1 menu of the day
2 day ticket

das Tageslicht NOUN
daylight

der Tageslichtprojektor (PL die **Tageslichtprojektoren**) NOUN
overhead projector

die Tageszeit NOUN
time of day

die Tageszeitung NOUN
daily paper

täglich ADJECTIVE, ADVERB
daily

tagsüber ADVERB
during the day

die Taille NOUN
waist

der Takt (PL die **Takte**) NOUN
tact
□ Sie behandelte die Sache mit viel Takt. She showed great tact in dealing with the matter.
■ **keinen Takt haben** to be tactless
■ **den Takt angeben** to keep time □ Der Lehrer gab den Takt an. The teacher kept time.
■ **im Stundentakt** at hourly intervals

die Taktik NOUN
tactics
□ Das ist die falsche Taktik. Those are the wrong tactics.

taktisch ADJECTIVE
tactical
□ Das war taktisch unklug That was a tactical mistake.

taktlos ADJECTIVE
tactless

taktvoll ADJECTIVE
tactful

das Tal (PL die **Täler**) NOUN
valley

das Talent (PL die **Talente**) NOUN
talent

talentiert ADJECTIVE
talented

der Tampon (PL die **Tampons**) NOUN
tampon

der Tank (PL die **Tanks**) NOUN
tank

tanken VERB [38]
to get petrol
□ Wir müssen noch tanken. We still have to get petrol.

die Tankstelle NOUN
petrol station

die Tanne NOUN
fir

der **Tannenzapfen** (PL die **Tannenzapfen**) NOUN
fir cone

die **Tante** NOUN
aunt

der **Tanz** (GEN des **Tanzes**, PL die **Tänze**) NOUN
dance

tanzen VERB [36]
to dance

die **Tanzschule** NOUN
dancing school

DID YOU KNOW...?
It is very common for German boys and girls to go to a **Tanzschule** when they are about 14.

die **Tapete** NOUN
wallpaper

tapezieren (PERFECT **hat tapeziert**) VERB [76]
to wallpaper

tapfer ADJECTIVE
brave

die **Tapferkeit** NOUN
bravery

die **Tasche** NOUN
1 pocket
□ Er hatte die Hände in der Hosentasche. He had his hands in his trouser pockets.
2 bag
□ Sie kann ihre Tasche nicht finden. She can't find her bag.

das **Taschenbuch** (PL die **Taschenbücher**) NOUN
paperback

der **Taschendieb** NOUN
pickpocket

das **Taschengeld** (PL die **Taschengelder**) NOUN
pocket money

die **Taschenlampe** NOUN
torch

das **Taschenmesser** (PL die **Taschenmesser**) NOUN
penknife

der **Taschenrechner** (PL die **Taschenrechner**) NOUN
pocket calculator

das **Taschentuch** (PL die **Taschentücher**) NOUN
handkerchief

die **Tasse** NOUN
cup
□ eine Tasse Tee a cup of tea

die **Tastatur** NOUN
keyboard

die **Taste** NOUN
1 button
□ Welche Taste muss ich drücken, um die Waschmaschine anzustellen? What button do I have to press to start the washing machine?
2 key
□ Bei der Schreibmaschine und der Computertastatur gibt es eine Hochstelltaste. There's a shift key on the typewriter and the computer keyboard.

die **Tat** (PL die **Taten**) NOUN
1 deed
□ Das war eine tapfere Tat. That was a brave deed. □ eine gute Tat a good deed
2 crime
□ Der Beschuldigte hat die Tat gestanden. The accused confessed to the crime.
■ **in der Tat** indeed

tat VERB ▷ *see* **tun**

der **Täter** (PL die **Täter**) NOUN
culprit

tätig ADJECTIVE
■ **tätig sein** to work □ Er ist als Journalist tätig. He works as a journalist.

die **Tätigkeit** NOUN
1 activity
□ kriminelle Tätigkeiten criminal activities
2 occupation
□ Welche Tätigkeit übt dein Vater aus? What's your father's occupation?

tätowieren (PERFECT **hat tätowiert**) VERB [76]
to tattoo

die **Tatsache** NOUN
fact

tatsächlich ADJECTIVE, ADVERB
1 actual
□ Der tatsächliche Grund war ein anderer als der, den sie angegeben hatte. The actual reason was different from the one she gave.
2 really
□ Das hat sie tatsächlich gesagt. She really did say that. □ Er ist tatsächlich rechtzeitig gekommen. He really has come in time.

taub ADJECTIVE
deaf
□ Sie ist auf dem rechten Ohr taub. She's deaf in her right ear.

die **Taube** NOUN
1 pigeon
□ die Tauben auf dem Marktplatz the pigeons in the market square
2 dove
□ die Friedenstaube the dove of peace

taubstumm ADJECTIVE
deaf-mute

tauchen (PERFECT **hat/ist getaucht**) VERB [48]

LANGUAGE TIP Use **haben** for the perfect tense when you describe the activity and **sein** when you describe the motion.

1 to dip
□ Sie hat ihren Zeh ins Wasser getaucht. She dipped her toe into the water.
2 to dive
□ Als Kind habe ich viel getaucht. I used to dive a lot as a child. □ Er ist nach dem versunkenen Schatz getaucht. He dived in search of the sunken treasure.

tauen VERB [38]
■ **Es taut.** It's thawing.

die **Taufe** NOUN
christening

taufen VERB [38]
to christen

taugen VERB [38]
■ **nichts taugen** to be no good □ Das Programm taugt nichts. The program's no good.

tauschen VERB [48]
to exchange

täuschen VERB [48]
1 to deceive
□ Du hast mich bewusst getäuscht. You deliberately deceived me.
2 to be deceptive
□ Der äußere Anschein täuscht oft. Appearances are often deceptive.
■ **sich täuschen** to be wrong

die **Täuschung** NOUN
deception
■ **eine optische Täuschung** an optical illusion

tausend NUMBER
thousand

das **Taxi** (GEN des **Taxis**, PL die **Taxis**) NOUN
taxi

der **Taxifahrer** (PL die **Taxifahrer**) NOUN
taxi driver

der **Taxistand** (PL die **Taxistände**) NOUN
taxi rank

die **Technik** NOUN
1 technology
□ hoch entwickelte Technik advanced technology
■ **die Gentechnik** genetic engineering
2 technique
□ Sie beherrscht diese Technik des Hochsprungs noch nicht. She hasn't mastered this high-jump technique yet.

der **Techniker** (PL die **Techniker**) NOUN
technician

technisch ADJECTIVE
technical

die **Technologie** NOUN
technology

der **Tee** (PL die **Tees**) NOUN
tea
□ Tee mit Milch und Zucker tea with milk and sugar □ Tee mit Zitrone lemon tea
■ **der Kamillentee** camomile tea

der **Teebeutel** (PL die **Teebeutel**) NOUN
tea bag

die **Teekanne** NOUN
teapot

der **Teelöffel** (PL die **Teelöffel**) NOUN
teaspoon
■ **ein Teelöffel Zucker** a teaspoonful of sugar

der **Teer** NOUN
tar

der **Teich** (PL die **Teiche**) NOUN
pond

der **Teig** (PL die **Teige**) NOUN
dough

der **Teil** (PL die **Teile**) NOUN
LANGUAGE TIP You can also say **das Teil**.
1 part
□ der erste Teil des Buches the first part of the book
■ **das Ersatzteil** the spare part
2 share
□ Ich möchte meinen Teil am Gewinn. I would like my share of the profit.
3 component part
□ Er hat das Fahrrad in seine Teile zerlegt. He dismantled the bike into its component parts.
■ **zum Teil** partly

teilen VERB [38]
to divide
■ **mit jemandem teilen** to share with somebody

teilnehmen (PRESENT **nimmt teil**, IMPERFECT **nahm teil**, PERFECT **hat teilgenommen**) VERB [52]
■ **an etwas teilnehmen** to take part in something □ Du solltest am Wettbewerb teilnehmen! You ought to take part in the competition.

der **Teilnehmer** (PL die **Teilnehmer**) NOUN
participant

teils ADVERB
partly

teilweise ADVERB
in parts
□ Das Buch war teilweise sehr spannend. The book was thrilling in parts.
■ **Sie waren teilweise beschädigt.** Some of them were damaged.

die **Teilzeitarbeit** NOUN
part-time work

der **Teint** (PL die **Teints**) NOUN
complexion

das **Telefax** (GEN des **Telefax**, PL die **Telefaxe**) NOUN
fax

das **Telefon** (PL die **Telefone**) NOUN
telephone

der **Telefonanruf** (PL die **Telefonanrufe**) NOUN
telephone call

das **Telefonat** (PL die **Telefonate**) NOUN
phone call

das **Telefonbuch** (PL die **Telefonbücher**) NOUN
phone book

der **Telefonhörer** (PL die **Telefonhörer**) NOUN
receiver
□ Er nahm den Telefonhörer ab. He picked up the receiver.

telefonieren (PERFECT **hat telefoniert**) VERB [76]
to telephone

■ **Ich habe gestern mit ihr telefoniert.** I talked to her on the phone yesterday.

telefonisch ADJECTIVE
telephone
□ eine telefonische Nachricht a telephone message
■ **Sie können mich telefonisch erreichen.** You can contact me by phone.

die **Telefonkarte** NOUN
phonecard

die **Telefonnummer** NOUN
telephone number

die **Telefonzelle** NOUN
telephone box

das **Telegramm** (PL die **Telegramme**) NOUN
telegram

das **Teleskop** (PL die **Teleskope**) NOUN
telescope

der **Teller** (PL die **Teller**) NOUN
plate

das **Temperament** (PL die **Temperamente**) NOUN
■ **Sie hat ein ziemlich lebhaftes Temperament.** She's quite a vivacious person.

temperamentvoll ADJECTIVE
vivacious

die **Temperatur** NOUN
temperature

das **Tempo** (PL die **Tempos**) NOUN
1 speed
□ Er ist mit einem irren Tempo gefahren. He drove at breakneck speed.
2 rate
□ Wir müssen unser Arbeitstempo steigern. We must increase our work rate.

tendieren (PERFECT **hat tendiert**) VERB [76]
■ **zu etwas tendieren** to tend towards something

das **Tennis** (GEN des **Tennis**) NOUN
tennis

der **Tennisplatz** (GEN des **Tennisplatzes**, PL die **Tennisplätze**) NOUN
tennis court

der **Tennisschläger** (PL die **Tennisschläger**) NOUN
tennis racket

der **Tennisspieler** (PL die **Tennisspieler**) NOUN
tennis player

der **Teppich** (PL die **Teppiche**) NOUN
carpet

der **Teppichboden** (PL die **Teppichböden**) NOUN
wall-to-wall carpet

der **Termin** (PL die **Termine**) NOUN
1 date
□ Habt ihr schon einen Termin ausgemacht? Have you already arranged a date?
2 deadline
□ Ich muss den Aufsatz bis zu dem Termin fertig haben. I must have the essay finished by that deadline.
3 appointment
□ Ich habe einen Termin beim Zahnarzt. I've got an appointment with the dentist.

der **Terminkalender** (PL die **Terminkalender**) NOUN
appointments diary

die **Terrasse** NOUN
terrace

der **Terror** NOUN
terror

der **Terrorismus** (GEN des **Terrorismus**) NOUN
terrorism

der **Terrorist** (GEN des **Terroristen**, PL die **Terroristen**) NOUN
terrorist

der **Tesafilm®** NOUN
Sellotape®

der **Test** (PL die **Tests**) NOUN
test

das **Testament** (PL die **Testamente**) NOUN
will
□ sein Testament machen to make one's will

testen VERB [2]
to test

teuer ADJECTIVE
expensive

der **Teufel** (PL die **Teufel**) NOUN
devil

der **Text** (PL die **Texte**) NOUN
1 text
□ Lest den Text auf Seite zehn. Read the text on page ten.
2 lyrics
□ Kannst du mir den Text von dem Song übersetzen? Can you translate the lyrics of the song for me?

die **Textilien** FEM PL NOUN
textiles

die **Textverarbeitung** NOUN
word processing

das **Textverarbeitungssystem** (PL die **Textverarbeitungssysteme**) NOUN
word processor

das **Theater** (PL die **Theater**) NOUN
1 theatre
□ Wir gehen ins Theater. We're going to the theatre.
■ **Theater spielen** to act
2 fuss
□ Mach nicht so ein Theater! Don't make such a fuss.

das **Theaterstück** (PL die **Theaterstücke**) NOUN
play

die **Theke** NOUN
1 bar
□ Er stand an der Theke und trank ein Bier. He stood at the bar drinking a beer.
2 counter

□ Das bekommen Sie an der Käsetheke. You'll get that at the cheese counter.

das **Thema** (PL die **Themen**) NOUN
subject

theoretisch ADJECTIVE
theoretical
□ Rein theoretisch betrachtet ist das richtig. From a purely theoretical point of view, that's correct.

die **Theorie** NOUN
theory

die **Therapie** NOUN
therapy

das **Thermometer** (PL die **Thermometer**) NOUN
thermometer

die **Thermosflasche** NOUN
Thermos®

die **These** NOUN
thesis

der **Thron** (PL die **Throne**) NOUN
throne

der **Thunfisch** (PL die **Thunfische**) NOUN
tuna

das **Thüringen** NOUN
Thuringia

DID YOU KNOW...?
Thüringen is one of the 16 **Länder**. Its capital is Erfurt. With its extensive forests, it is sometimes called 'Germany's green heartland'. It is not only rural, however: the Zeiss precision engineering company is based in Jena.

ticken VERB [48]
to tick
□ Die Uhr tickte. The clock was ticking.
■ **Du tickst ja nicht richtig!** You're off your rocker!

LANGUAGE TIP Word for word, **Du tickst ja nicht richtig** means 'You're not ticking right'.

das **Tief** (PL die **Tiefs**) NOUN
▷ *see also* **tief** ADJECTIVE
depression
□ ein Tief über Norddeutschland a depression over North Germany

tief ADJECTIVE
▷ *see also* **das Tief** NOUN
1 deep
□ Wie tief ist das Wasser? How deep's the water?
2 low *(neckline, price, note)*
□ ein tief ausgeschnittenes Kleid a low-cut dress

der **Tiefdruck** NOUN
low pressure

die **Tiefe** NOUN
depth

tiefgekühlt ADJECTIVE
frozen

die **Tiefkühlkost** NOUN
frozen food

die **Tiefkühltruhe** NOUN
freezer

das **Tier** (PL die **Tiere**) NOUN
animal

der **Tierarzt** (GEN des **Tierarztes**, PL die **Tierärzte**) NOUN
vet

der **Tiergarten** (PL die **Tiergärten**) NOUN
zoo

tierisch ADJECTIVE
1 animal
□ tierische Fette animal fats
2 terrible
□ Du hast dich tierisch benommen. You behaved terribly.

der **Tierkreis** (GEN des **Tierkreises**) NOUN
zodiac

LANGUAGE TIP Word for word, **Tierkreis** means 'animal circle'.

die **Tierquälerei** NOUN
cruelty to animals

der **Tiger** (PL die **Tiger**) NOUN
tiger

die **Tinte** NOUN
ink

der **Tintenfisch** (PL die **Tintenfische**) NOUN
squid

der **Tipp** (PL die **Tipps**) NOUN
tip

tippen VERB [38]
1 to tap
□ Sie tippte leicht an die Statue. She lightly tapped the statue.
2 to type
□ Tippst du dein Referat? Are you typing your assignment?
■ **im Lotto tippen** to play the lottery
■ **Auf wen tippst du bei den Wahlen?** Who're you tipping to win the elections?

der **Tippfehler** (PL die **Tippfehler**) NOUN
typing error

Tirol NEUT NOUN
Tyrol

der **Tiroler** (PL die **Tiroler**) NOUN
Tyrolean

die **Tirolerin** NOUN
Tyrolean

der **Tisch** (PL die **Tische**) NOUN
table
□ bei Tisch at table

die **Tischdecke** NOUN
tablecloth

das **Tischtennis** NOUN
table tennis

das **Tischtuch** (PL die **Tischtücher**) NOUN
tablecloth

der **Titel** (PL die **Titel**) NOUN
title

der **Toast** (PL die **Toasts**) NOUN
toast

das **Toastbrot** (PL die **Toastbrote**) NOUN
bread for toasting

der **Toaster** (PL die **Toaster**) NOUN
toaster

toben VERB [38]
1 to rage
□ Der Sturm tobte die ganze Nacht. The storm raged all night long.
2 to go mad
□ Wenn er das erfährt, wird er toben. If he finds out he'll go mad.
3 to romp about
□ Die Kinder toben im Garten. The children are romping about in the garden.

die **Tochter** (PL die **Töchter**) NOUN
daughter

der **Tod** (PL die **Tode**) NOUN
death

todernst ADJECTIVE, ADVERB
1 grave
□ ein todernstes Gesicht a grave face
2 in deadly earnest
□ Er hat das todernst gesagt. He said it in deadly earnest.

die **Todesstrafe** NOUN
death penalty

todkrank ADJECTIVE
critically ill

tödlich ADJECTIVE
deadly
□ eine tödliche Waffe a deadly weapon
■ **ein tödlicher Unfall** a fatal accident

todmüde ADJECTIVE
exhausted

die **Toilette** NOUN
toilet

das **Toilettenpapier** NOUN
toilet paper

tolerant ADJECTIVE
tolerant

toll ADJECTIVE
terrific

die **Tollwut** NOUN
rabies

die **Tomate** NOUN
tomato

das **Tomatenmark** NOUN
tomato purée

der **Ton** (PL die **Töne**) NOUN
1 sound
□ Es war kein Ton zu hören. Not a sound could be heard.
2 note
□ Mit welchen Ton fängt das Lied an? What note does the song start on?
3 tone of voice
□ Sein Ton gefiel mir nicht. I didn't like his tone of voice.
4 shade
□ Pastelltöne sind in. Pastel shades are in.
5 stress
□ Bei Substantiven liegt der Ton meist auf der ersten Silbe. Nouns are usually stressed on the first syllable.

die **Tonne** NOUN
ton
□ Es wiegt drei Tonnen. It weighs three tons.

der **Topf** (PL die **Töpfe**) NOUN
pot

das **Tor** (PL die **Tore**) NOUN
1 gate
□ Das Tor war offen. The gate was open.
2 goal
□ Wer hat das zweite Tor geschossen? Who scored the second goal?

der **Torf** NOUN
peat

die **Torte** NOUN
1 gateau
2 flan

der **Torwart** (PL die **Torwarte**) NOUN
goalkeeper

tot ADJECTIVE
dead
■ **Er war sofort tot.** He was killed instantly.

total ADJECTIVE, ADVERB
1 complete
□ Das ist doch der totale Wahnsinn. But that's complete madness.
2 completely
□ Das ist total verrückt. That's completely mad.

totalitär ADJECTIVE
totalitarian

der **Totalschaden** (PL die **Totalschäden**) NOUN
complete write-off

der/die **Tote** (GEN des/der **Toten**, PL die **Toten**) NOUN
dead body
□ Auf der Straße lag ein Toter. There was a dead body lying in the road.
■ **die Toten begraben** to bury the dead

töten VERB [2]
to kill

sich **totlachen** (PERFECT **hat sich totgelacht**) VERB [4]
to laugh one's head off

die **Tour** (PL die **Touren**) NOUN
trip
□ auf Tour gehen to go on a trip
■ **auf vollen Touren** at full speed

der **Tourismus** (GEN des **Tourismus**) NOUN
tourism

der **Tourist** (GEN des **Touristen**, PL die **Touristen**) NOUN
tourist

die **Tournee** NOUN
tour

□ Bon Jovi auf Tournee Bon Jovi on tour □ auf Tournee gehen to go on tour

die **Tracht** NOUN
traditional costume
□ Im Schwarzwald tragen die Frauen noch Tracht. Women still wear traditional costume in the Black Forest.
■ **eine Tracht Prügel** a sound beating

die **Tradition** NOUN
tradition

traditionell ADJECTIVE
traditional

traf VERB ▷ *see* **treffen**

tragbar ADJECTIVE
portable
□ ein tragbarer Fernseher a portable TV

träge ADJECTIVE
sluggish

tragen (PRESENT **trägt**, IMPERFECT **trug**, PERFECT **hat getragen**) VERB [77]
1 to carry
□ Kannst du meinen Koffer tragen? Can you carry my case?
2 to bear
□ die Verantwortung tragen to bear responsibility
3 to wear *(clothes, glasses)*
□ Sie trug ein weißes Kleid und eine Sonnenbrille. She was wearing a white dress and sunglasses.

die **Tragetasche** NOUN
carrier bag

tragisch ADJECTIVE
tragic

die **Tragödie** NOUN
tragedy

der **Trainer** (PL die **Trainer**) NOUN
coach

trainieren (PERFECT **hat trainiert**) VERB [76]
1 to train
□ Sie trainiert täglich für den Wettkampf. She trains for the competition every day.
2 to coach
□ Wer trainiert diese Tennisspielerin? Who coaches this tennis player?
3 to practise
□ Diese Übung muss ich noch mehr trainieren. I need to practise this exercise more.

das **Training** (PL die **Trainings**) NOUN
training

der **Trainingsanzug** (PL die **Trainingsanzüge**) NOUN
track suit

trampen VERB [38]
to hitchhike

der **Tramper** (PL die **Tramper**) NOUN
hitchhiker

die **Tramperin** NOUN
hitchhiker

die **Träne** NOUN
tear
□ in Tränen ausbrechen to burst into tears

trank VERB ▷ *see* **trinken**

der **Transport** (PL die **Transporte**) NOUN
transport

transportieren (PERFECT **hat transportiert**) VERB [76]
to transport

das **Transportmittel** (PL die **Transportmittel**) NOUN
means of transport

die **Traube** NOUN
grape

trauen VERB [38]
■ **jemandem trauen** to trust somebody
■ **sich trauen** to dare □ Ich wette, du traust dich nicht! I bet you don't dare.

der **Traum** (PL die **Träume**) NOUN
dream

träumen VERB [38]
to dream
□ Ich habe von dir geträumt. I dreamt about you.

traumhaft ADJECTIVE
wonderful
□ Es waren traumhafte Ferien. It was a wonderful holiday.

traurig ADJECTIVE
sad

die **Traurigkeit** NOUN
sadness

das **Treffen** (PL die **Treffen**) NOUN
▷ *see also* **treffen** VERB
meeting

treffen (PRESENT **trifft**, IMPERFECT **traf**, PERFECT **hat getroffen**) VERB [78]
▷ *see also* **das Treffen** NOUN
1 to hit
□ Er hat die Zielscheibe getroffen. He hit the target. □ Sie wurde am Kopf getroffen. She was hit on the head.
■ **Du hast nicht getroffen.** You missed.
2 to meet
□ Ich habe ihn gestern im Supermarkt getroffen. I met him yesterday in the supermarket. □ Wir sind in London auf ihn getroffen. We met him in London.
■ **sich treffen** to meet □ Wir treffen uns am Bahnhof. We'll meet at the station.
□ Sie treffen sich einmal in der Woche. They meet once a week.
3 to affect
□ Die Bemerkung hat sie sehr getroffen. The remark affected her deeply.
■ **eine Entscheidung treffen** to make a decision
■ **Maßnahmen treffen** to take steps
■ **es traf sich, dass ...** it so happened that ...
■ **Das trifft sich gut!** How very convenient!

treffend ADJECTIVE
pertinent

der **Treffer** (PL die **Treffer**) NOUN
1 hit
□ Das Schiff musste einen Volltreffer hinnehmen. The ship took a direct hit.
2 goal
□ Klinsmann hat einen Treffer erzielt. Klinsmann scored a goal. □ Ich hatte vier Treffer im Lotto. I got four numbers in the lottery.

der **Treffpunkt** (PL die **Treffpunkte**) NOUN
meeting place

treiben (IMPERFECT **trieb**, PERFECT **hat/ist getrieben**) VERB

LANGUAGE TIP Use **haben** to form the perfect tense. Use **sein** to form the perfect tense for 'to drift'.

1 to drive
□ Sie trieben die Kühe auf das Feld. They drove the cows into the field.
■ **Sport treiben** to do sport
■ **Unsinn treiben** to fool around
■ **jemanden zu etwas treiben** to drive somebody to something □ Du treibst mich zur Verzweiflung. You drive me to despair.
■ **Sie hat uns zur Eile getrieben.** She made us hurry up.
2 to drift
□ Das Schiff ist aufs Meer getrieben. The ship drifted out to sea.

das **Treibhaus** (GEN des **Treibhauses**, PL die **Treibhäuser**) NOUN
greenhouse

der **Treibhauseffekt** NOUN
greenhouse effect

der **Treibstoff** (PL die **Treibstoffe**) NOUN
fuel

trennen VERB [38]
1 to separate
□ Er hat die beiden Raufbolde getrennt. He separated the two ruffians.
2 to make a distinction between
□ Diese beiden Begriffe muss man sauber trennen. You have to make a clear distinction between these two concepts.
3 to hyphenate
□ Wie wird dieses Wort getrennt? Where do you hyphenate this word?
■ **sich trennen** to separate □ Die beiden haben sich getrennt. The two of them have separated.
■ **Du solltest dich von ihm trennen.** You ought to leave him.
■ **sich von etwas trennen** to part with something □ Ich trenne mich ungern von dem Buch. I'm loath to part with this book.

die **Trennung** NOUN
separation

die **Treppe** NOUN
stairs

das **Treppenhaus** (GEN des **Treppenhauses**, PL die **Treppenhäuser**) NOUN
staircase

treten (PRESENT **tritt**, IMPERFECT **trat**, PERFECT **hat/ist getreten**) VERB [79]

LANGUAGE TIP For the perfect tense use **haben** when the verb has an object and **sein** when there is no object.

1 to step
□ Sie ist in die Pfütze getreten. She stepped in the puddle. □ Er trat auf die Bremse. He stepped on the brakes. □ Er trat ans Mikrofon. He stepped up to the microphone.
■ **mit jemandem in Verbindung treten** to get in touch with somebody
■ **in Erscheinung treten** to appear
2 to kick
□ Sie hat mich getreten. She kicked me. □ Sie trat nach dem Hund. She kicked the dog.
3 to tread
□ Er ist mir auf den Fuß getreten. He trod on my foot.

treu ADJECTIVE
faithful
□ Bist du mir auch treu gewesen? Have you been faithful to me?

die **Treue** NOUN
faithfulness

die **Tribüne** NOUN
1 grandstand
□ Die Fans auf der Tribüne pfiffen. The fans on the grandstand whistled.
2 platform
□ Der Redner stand auf einer Tribüne. The speaker stood on a platform.

der **Trichter** (PL die **Trichter**) NOUN
1 funnel
□ Sie hat das Öl mit einem Trichter in die Flasche gefüllt. She used a funnel to fill the bottle with oil.
2 crater
□ Das Gelände war von Bombentrichtern übersät. The area was pitted with bomb craters.

der **Trick** (PL die **Tricks**) NOUN
trick
□ Das war ein fauler Trick. That was a dirty tricks.

der **Trickfilm** (PL die **Trickfilme**) NOUN
cartoon

trieb VERB ▷ *see* **treiben**

trifft VERB ▷ *see* **treffen**

das **Trimester** (PL die **Trimester**) NOUN
term *(university)*

trinkbar ADJECTIVE
drinkable

trinken (IMPERFECT **trank**, PERFECT **hat getrunken**) VERB [80]
to drink
■ **Ich habe zu viel getrunken.** I've had too much to drink.

das **Trinkgeld** (PL die **Trinkgelder**) NOUN
tip
□ Er gab dem Taxifahrer ein großzügiges Trinkgeld. He gave the taxi driver a generous tip.

die **Trinkhalle** NOUN
refreshment kiosk

das **Trinkwasser** (PL die **Trinkwässer**) NOUN
drinking water

trocken ADJECTIVE
dry

trocknen VERB [53]
to dry

der **Trödel** NOUN
junk

der **Trödelmarkt** (PL die **Trödelmärkte**) NOUN
flea market

trödeln VERB [88]
to dawdle

die **Trommel** NOUN
drum
□ Er spielt Trommel. He plays the drums.

das **Trommelfell** (PL die **Trommelfelle**) NOUN
eardrum

trommeln VERB [34]
to drum

die **Trompete** NOUN
trumpet
□ Sie spielt Trompete. She plays the trumpet.

die **Tropen** PL NOUN
tropics

der **Tropfen** (PL die **Tropfen**) NOUN
drop

tropisch ADJECTIVE
tropical

der **Trost** NOUN
consolation

trösten VERB [2]
to console

trostlos ADJECTIVE
bleak
□ eine trostlose Landschaft a bleak landscape

der **Trostpreis** (GEN des **Trostpreises**, PL die **Trostpreise**) NOUN
consolation prize

der **Trottel** (PL die **Trottel**) NOUN
prat

der **Trotz** (GEN des **Trotzes**) NOUN
▷ *see also* **trotz** PREPOSITION
defiance
□ ihm zum Trotz in defiance of him
■ **etwas aus Trotz tun** to do something defiantly

trotz PREPOSITION
▷ *see also* **der Trotz** NOUN
LANGUAGE TIP The preposition **trotz** takes the dative or genitive.
in spite of

trotzdem ADVERB
all the same
□ Ich gehe trotzdem. I'm going all the same.

trotzig ADJECTIVE
defiant

trüb ADJECTIVE
1 dull
□ Es war ein trüber Tag. It was a dull day.
2 cloudy
□ Das Wasser war trüb. The water was cloudy.
3 gloomy
□ Die Zukunftsaussichten sind ziemlich trüb. Prospects for the future are pretty gloomy.

der **Trubel** NOUN
hurly-burly

trübsinnig ADJECTIVE
gloomy

trug VERB ▷ *see* **tragen**

trügen (IMPERFECT **trog**, PERFECT **hat getrogen**) VERB
to be deceptive
□ Der Schein trügt. Appearances are deceptive.

die **Trümmer** PL NOUN
1 wreckage
□ die Trümmer des Flugzeugs the wreckage of the aeroplane
2 ruins
□ Nach dem Bombenangriff war die Stadt voller Trümmer. After the air raid the town was in ruins.

der **Trumpf** (PL die **Trümpfe**) NOUN
trump
□ Herz ist Trumpf. Hearts is trumps.

die **Trunkenheit** NOUN
drunkenness
■ **Trunkenheit am Steuer** drink-driving
LANGUAGE TIP Word for word, **Trunkenheit am Steuer** means 'drunkenness at the steering wheel'.

die **Truppen** FEM PL NOUN
troops

der **Truthahn** (PL die **Truthähne**) NOUN
turkey

der **Tscheche** (GEN des **Tschechen**, PL die **Tschechen**) NOUN
Czech

die **Tschechin** NOUN
Czech

tschechisch ADJECTIVE
Czech

tschüs EXCLAMATION
cheerio!

das **T-Shirt** (PL die **T-Shirts**) NOUN
T-shirt

die **Tube** NOUN
tube
□ eine Tube Zahnpasta a tube of toothpaste

das **Tuch** (PL die **Tücher**) NOUN
1 cloth
□ Mit welchem Tuch soll ich abstauben?

Which cloth should I use for dusting?
2 towel
□ Nimm dir ein großes Tuch ins Schwimmbad mit. Take a large towel with you to the swimming baths.
3 scarf
□ Sie hatte ein seidenes Tuch um den Hals. She wore a silk scarf around her neck.

tüchtig ADJECTIVE
competent
□ Er ist ein sehr tüchtiger Mensch. He's a very competent person.
■ **Er nahm einen tüchtigen Schluck aus der Flasche.** He took a hefty swig from the bottle.

die **Tulpe** NOUN
tulip

tun (IMPERFECT **tat**, PERFECT **hat getan**) VERB [81]
1 to do
□ Was sollen wir jetzt tun? What shall we do now? □ Er hat den ganzen Tag nichts getan. He hasn't done anything all day. □ Was kann ich für Sie tun? What can I do for you?
2 to put
□ Sie tat die Teller in den Schrank. She put the plates in the cupboard.
3 to act
□ Tu nicht so unschuldig! Don't act so innocent.
4 to pretend
□ Sie tat, als ob sie schliefe. She pretended to be sleeping. □ Er ist nicht krank, er tut nur so. He isn't ill, he's only pretending.
■ **Der Hund tut dir bestimmt nichts.** The dog won't hurt you.
■ **Hoffentlich hast du dir bei dem Sturz nichts getan.** I hope you didn't hurt yourself when you fell.
■ **Es tut sich viel.** A lot's happening.
■ **mit etwas zu tun haben** to have something to do with something □ Seine Laune hat etwas mit seiner Krankheit zu tun. His mood has something to do with his illness.
■ **Das tut nichts zur Sache.** That's neither here nor there.

der **Tunfisch** (PL die **Tunfische**) NOUN
tuna

der **Tunnel** (PL die **Tunnel**) NOUN
tunnel

der **Tupfen** (PL die **Tupfen**) NOUN
dot

die **Tür** NOUN
door

der **Türke** (GEN des **Türken**, PL die **Türken**) NOUN
Turk

die **Türkei** NOUN
Turkey
■ **aus der Türkei** from Turkey
■ **in der Türkei** in Turkey
■ **in die Türkei** to Turkey

die **Türkin** NOUN
Turk

türkis ADJECTIVE
turquoise

türkisch ADJECTIVE
Turkish

der **Turm** (PL die **Türme**) NOUN
1 tower
□ die Türme der Burg the castle towers
2 steeple
□ Das Ulmer Münster hat den höchsten Kirchturm der Welt. Ulm Cathedral has the world's highest steeple.
3 rook
□ Er machte einen Zug mit dem Turm. He moved his rook.

das **Turnen** NOUN
▷ *see also* **turnen** VERB
1 gymnastics
□ Die Russinnen sind im Turnen gut. The Russian women are good at gymnastics.
2 physical education
□ Wir haben in der vierten Stunde Turnen. We have PE in the fourth period.

turnen VERB [38]
▷ *see also* **das Turnen** NOUN
1 to do gymnastics
□ Sie turnt nicht gern. She doesn't like doing gymnastics.
2 to perform
□ Sie hat die Kür hervorragend geturnt. She performed the free programme brilliantly.

die **Turnhalle** NOUN
gym

die **Turnhose** NOUN
gym shorts
□ eine Turnhose a pair of gym shorts

das **Turnier** (PL die **Turniere**) NOUN
tournament

der **Turnschuh** (PL die **Turnschuhe**) NOUN
trainer
□ ein Paar Turnschuhe a pair of trainers

das **Turnzeug** NOUN
gym things
□ Wo ist mein Turnzeug? Where are my gym things?

die **Tüte** NOUN
bag

der **TÜV** (PL die **TÜVs**) NOUN (= *Technischer Überwachungsverein)*
MOT
□ Mein Auto ist nicht durch den TÜV gekommen. My car failed its MOT.

der **Typ** (PL die **Typen**) NOUN
1 type
□ Er ist ein athletischer Typ. He's an athletic type.
2 bloke
□ der Typ da drüben the bloke over there

typisch ADJECTIVE
typical
□ typisch für typical of

Uu

die **U-Bahn** NOUN
underground
□ mit der U-Bahn fahren to travel by underground

die **U-Bahn-Station** NOUN
underground station

übel ADJECTIVE
bad
□ ein übler Geruch a bad smell □ eine üble Lage a bad situation □ Nicht übel! Not bad.
■ **jemandem ist übel** somebody feels sick
■ **Sie hat dir die Bemerkung übel genommen.** She was offended by your remark.

die **Übelkeit** NOUN
nausea

übelnehmen VERB [52] ▷ *see* **übel**

üben VERB [38]
to practise

über PREPOSITION, ADVERB

LANGUAGE TIP Use the accusative to express movement or a change of place. Use the dative when there is no change of place.

1 over
□ Über dem Tisch hängt eine Lampe. There's a lamp hanging over the table. □ Sie legten ein Brett über das Loch. They put a board over the hole. □ Flugzeuge dürfen nicht über dieses Gebiet fliegen. Planes are not allowed to fly over this area. □ Über Weihnachten bin ich zu Hause. I'm at home over Christmas. □ Kinder über zwölf Jahren children over twelve years of age □ Das hat über hundert Euro gekostet. It cost over a hundred euros.
2 above
□ Das Flugzeug flog hoch über der Stadt. The plane flew high above the town.
■ **den ganzen Tag über** all day long
■ **zwei Grad über null** two degrees above zero
■ **ein Scheck über zweihundert Euro** a cheque for two hundred euros
3 across
□ Er ging quer über das Feld. He went across the field.
4 via
□ nach Köln über Aachen to Cologne via Aachen □ über Satellit via satellite
5 about
□ Wir haben über das Wetter geredet. We talked about the weather.
□ ein Buch über ... a book about ...
6 through
□ Ich habe den Job über einen Freund bekommen. I got the job through a friend.
■ **über jemanden lachen** to laugh at somebody
■ **Sie liebt ihn über alles.** She loves him more than anything.
■ **über und über** over and over
■ **über kurz oder lang** sooner or later
■ **etwas über haben** to be fed up with something □ Ich habe Kartoffeln langsam über. I'm getting fed up with potatoes.

überall ADVERB
everywhere

überbieten (IMPERFECT **überbot**, PERFECT **hat überboten**) VERB [8]
to outbid
□ Er bot zweitausend Euro, aber wir haben ihn überboten. He bid two thousand euros but we outbid him.
■ **einen Rekord überbieten** to break a record
■ **sich überbieten** to excel oneself

der **Überblick** (PL die **Überblicke**) NOUN
1 view
□ Von hier aus hat man einen guten Überblick über das Gelände. You can get a good view of the area from here.
2 overview
□ ein Überblick über die unregelmäßigen Verben an overview of irregular verbs
3 overall impression
□ Ich muss mir erst mal einen Überblick verschaffen. I have to get an overall impression first.
■ **den Überblick verlieren** to lose track of things
■ **Sie hat den Überblick über ihre Arbeit verloren.** She has no idea where she is with her work.

überdenken (IMPERFECT **überdachte**, PERFECT **hat überdacht**) VERB [14]
to think over

übereifrig ADJECTIVE
overeager

übereinander ADVERB
one on top of the other
□ Sie legte die Bücher übereinander. She put one book on top of the other.
■ **übereinander sprechen** to talk about each other

überempfindlich ADJECTIVE
hypersensitive

überfahren (PRESENT **überfährt**, IMPERFECT **überfuhr**, PERFECT **hat überfahren**) VERB [21]
to run over
□ Die Katze wurde von einem Auto überfahren. The cat was run over by a car.

die **Überfahrt** NOUN
crossing

der **Überfall** (PL die **Überfälle**) NOUN
1 raid
□ ein Banküberfall a bank raid □ ein Überfall auf ein fremdes Land a raid on a foreign country
2 assault
□ Er wurde das Opfer eines Überfalls. He was the victim of an assault.

überfallen (PRESENT **überfällt**, IMPERFECT **überfiel**, PERFECT **hat überfallen**) VERB [22]
1 to attack
□ Sie ist im Park überfallen worden. She was attacked in the park.
■ **eine Bank überfallen** to raid a bank
2 to descend on
□ Am Wochenende hat mich meine Freundin mit ihren Eltern überfallen. My girlfriend and her parents descended on me at the weekend.

überfällig ADJECTIVE
overdue

überflüssig ADJECTIVE
superfluous

überfordern (PERFECT **hat überfordert**) VERB [88]
to ask too much of
□ Unser Mathelehrer überfordert uns. Our maths teacher asks too much of us.

überfüllt ADJECTIVE
1 overcrowded
□ Die Gefängnisse sind völlig überfüllt. The prisons are completely overcrowded.
2 oversubscribed
□ Der Computerkurs ist überfüllt. The computer course is oversubscribed.

der **Übergang** (PL die **Übergänge**) NOUN
1 crossing
□ ein Fußgängerübergang a pedestrian crossing
2 transition
□ der Übergang vom Sommer zum Herbst the transition from summer to autumn

übergeben (PRESENT **übergibt**, IMPERFECT **übergab**, PERFECT **hat übergeben**) VERB [28]
to hand over
□ Sie hat uns die Schlüssel übergeben. She handed the keys over to us.
■ **sich übergeben** to be sick

überhaupt ADVERB
1 at all
□ Kannst du überhaupt Auto fahren? Can you drive a car at all? □ Hast du überhaupt zugehört? Have you been listening at all? □ Ich habe überhaupt keine Lust. I don't feel like it at all.
2 in general
□ Die Engländer sind überhaupt sehr höflich. In general the English are very polite.
■ **überhaupt nicht** not at all □ Der Film hat mir überhaupt nicht gefallen. I didn't like the film at all.
■ **überhaupt nichts** nothing at all □ Was hat er gesagt? - Überhaupt nichts. What did he say? - Nothing at all. □ Er hat überhaupt nichts gesagt. He didn't say anything at all.

überheblich ADJECTIVE
arrogant

überholen (PERFECT **hat überholt**) VERB [18]
1 to overtake
□ Er hat rechts überholt. He overtook on the right.
2 to check over
□ Ich muss mein Fahrrad überholen. I have to check my bike over.

überholt ADJECTIVE
out-of-date

das **Überholverbot** (PL die **Überholverbote**) NOUN
restriction on overtaking

überhören (PERFECT **hat überhört**) VERB [18]
1 not to hear
□ Sie hat das Klingeln überhört. She didn't hear the bell.
2 to ignore
□ Deine Frechheit überhöre ich. I shall ignore your cheek.

überlassen (PRESENT **überlässt**, IMPERFECT **überließ**, PERFECT **hat überlassen**) VERB [42]
■ **jemandem etwas überlassen** to leave something up to somebody □ Ich überlasse es dir, wann du das machst. I'll leave it up to you when you do it.

überlasten (PERFECT **hat überlastet**) VERB [2]
to overload
□ Der Aufzug war überlastet. The lift was overloaded.
■ **Ich fühle mich überlastet.** I feel overworked.

überleben (PERFECT **hat überlebt**) VERB [18]
to survive

überlegen (PERFECT **hat überlegt**) VERB [82]
▷ *see also* **überlegen** ADJECTIVE
to think about
□ Ich muss mir deinen Vorschlag überlegen. I'll have to think about your suggestion.
□ Überleg doch mal. Think about it.

überlegen ADJECTIVE
▷ *see also* **überlegen** VERB
1 better
□ Er ist ihr in Englisch überlegen. He's better at English than she is.
2 convincingly
□ Unsere Mannschaft hat überlegen gewonnen. Our team won convincingly.

die **Überlieferung** NOUN
tradition

überlisten (PERFECT **hat überlistet**) VERB [2]
to outwit

überm = **über dem**

übermäßig ADJECTIVE
excessive

übermorgen ADVERB
the day after tomorrow

übernächste ADJECTIVE
next but one
□ An der übernächsten Haltestelle muss ich aussteigen. I need to get off at the next stop but one.

übernachten (PERFECT **hat übernachtet**) VERB [2]
■ **bei jemandem übernachten** to spend the night at somebody's house

die **Übernachtung** NOUN
overnight stay
■ **Übernachtung mit Frühstück** bed and breakfast

übernehmen (PRESENT **übernimmt**, IMPERFECT **übernahm**, PERFECT **hat übernommen**) VERB [52]
to take over
□ Er hat das Geschäft seines Vaters übernommen. He's taken over his father's business. □ Er hat das Amt des Klassensprechers übernommen. He took over as class representative.
■ **sich übernehmen** to take on too much

überprüfen (PERFECT **hat überprüft**) VERB [18]
to check

überqueren (PERFECT **hat überquert**) VERB [7]
to cross

überraschen (PERFECT **hat überrascht**) VERB [18]
to surprise

überrascht ADJECTIVE
surprised

die **Überraschung** NOUN
surprise

überreden (PERFECT **hat überredet**) VERB [54]
to persuade
□ Kannst du sie nicht überreden mitzukommen? Can't you persuade her to come?

übers = **über das**

überschätzen (PERFECT **hat überschätzt**) VERB [36]
to overestimate

überschlagen (PRESENT **überschlägt**, IMPERFECT **überschlug**, PERFECT **hat überschlagen**) VERB [59]
to estimate
□ Wir sollten die Kosten für das Fest überschlagen. We should estimate how much the party will cost.
■ **eine Seite überschlagen** to miss a page
■ **Das Auto hat sich überschlagen.** The car rolled over.

überschnappen (PERFECT **ist übergeschnappt**) VERB [4]
to flip one's lid
□ Du bist wohl übergeschnappt! You've flipped your lid!

die **Überschrift** NOUN
heading

der **Überschuss** (GEN des **Überschusses**, PL die **Überschüsse**) NOUN
surplus
□ ein Überschuss an a surplus of

überschütten (PERFECT **hat überschüttet**) VERB [2]
■ **jemanden mit etwas überschütten** to shower somebody with something □ Sie haben uns mit Geschenken überschüttet. They showered us with presents.

die **Überschwemmung** NOUN
flood

übersehen (PRESENT **übersieht**, IMPERFECT **übersah**, PERFECT **hat übersehen**) VERB [64]
1 to overlook
□ Sie hat ein paar Fehler übersehen. She overlooked a couple of mistakes.
2 to see
□ Wir können die Folgen noch nicht übersehen. We can't see the consequences yet.

übersetzen (PERFECT **hat übersetzt**) VERB [36]
to translate
□ Übersetzt den Text ins Englische. Translate the text into English.

der **Übersetzer** (PL die **Übersetzer**) NOUN
translator

die **Übersetzerin** NOUN
translator

die **Übersetzung** NOUN
translation
□ Das war eine schwierige Übersetzung. That was a difficult translation.

die **Übersicht** NOUN
1 view
□ Von hier aus hat man eine gute Übersicht. You get a good view from here.
2 overview
□ eine Übersicht über die unregelmäßigen Verben an overview of irregular verbs

übersichtlich ADJECTIVE
clear
□ Die Tabelle ist nicht besonders

übersichtlich. The table isn't particularly clear. □ etwas übersichtlich gestalten to arrange something clearly
■ **ein übersichtliches Gelände** open country

überspringen (IMPERFECT **übersprang**, PERFECT **hat übersprungen**) VERB [71]
1 to jump over
□ Er hat die Hürde übersprungen. He jumped over the hurdle.
2 to skip
□ Das nächste Kapitel können wir überspringen. We can skip the next chapter.

überstehen (IMPERFECT **überstand**, PERFECT **hat überstanden**) VERB [72]
1 to get over
□ Wir haben das Schlimmste überstanden. We've got over the worst.
2 to survive
□ Die Pflanze hat den Winter nicht überstanden. The plant didn't survive the winter.

übersteigen (IMPERFECT **überstieg**, PERFECT **hat überstiegen**) VERB [74]
to exceed
□ Das übersteigt unsere Erwartungen. That exceeds our expectations.

überstimmen (PERFECT **hat überstimmt**) VERB [7]
to outvote

die **Überstunden** FEM PL NOUN
overtime
□ Er macht viele Überstunden. He does a lot of overtime.

überstürzen (PERFECT **hat überstürzt**) VERB [36]
to rush
□ Du solltest nichts überstürzen. You shouldn't rush into things.
■ **sich überstürzen** to follow one another in rapid succession □ Die Ereignisse überstürzten sich. One event followed another in rapid succession.

überstürzt ADJECTIVE
1 rash
□ eine überstürzte Entscheidung a rash decision
2 in a rush
□ Sie sind überstürzt abgereist. They left in a rush.

übertragen (PRESENT **überträgt**, IMPERFECT **übertrug**, PERFECT **hat übertragen**) VERB [77]
▷ *see also* **übertragen** ADJECTIVE
1 to broadcast
□ Wir übertragen das Spiel live. We're broadcasting the game live.
2 to copy
□ Sie hat den Text in ihr Heft übertragen. She copied the text into her exercise book.
3 to transmit
□ eine Krankheit übertragen to transmit an illness
■ **Sie hat mir diese Aufgabe übertragen.** She has assigned this task to me.
■ **sich übertragen auf** to spread to □ Ihre Nervosität hat sich auf die Kinder übertragen. Her nervousness spread to the children.

übertragen ADJECTIVE
▷ *see also* **übertragen** VERB
figurative
□ die übertragene Bedeutung eines Wortes the figurative meaning of a word

übertreffen (PRESENT **übertrifft**, IMPERFECT **übertraf**, PERFECT **hat übertroffen**) VERB [78]
to surpass

übertreiben (IMPERFECT **übertrieb**, PERFECT **hat übertrieben**) VERB
to exaggerate

die **Übertreibung** NOUN
exaggeration

übertrieben ADJECTIVE
excessive

überwachen (PERFECT **hat überwacht**) VERB [18]
1 to supervise
□ Wer soll die Kinder überwachen? Who will supervise the children?
2 to keep under surveillance
□ Die Polizei überwacht ihn. The police are keeping him under surveillance.

überweisen (IMPERFECT **überwies**, PERFECT **hat überwiesen**) VERB
to transfer

überwinden (IMPERFECT **überwand**, PERFECT **hat überwunden**) VERB
to overcome
□ Jetzt haben wir alle Schwierigkeiten überwunden. Now we've overcome all difficulties.
■ **sich überwinden** to force oneself
□ Ich musste mich überwinden, das zu essen. I had to force myself to eat it.

überzeugen (PERFECT **hat überzeugt**) VERB [18]
to convince

überzeugend ADJECTIVE
convincing

die **Überzeugung** NOUN
conviction
□ Er sagte es ohne große Überzeugung. He said it without much conviction.

üblich ADJECTIVE
usual

das **U-Boot** (PL die **U-Boote**) NOUN
submarine

übrig ADJECTIVE
remaining
□ Die übrigen Gäste sind auch bald gegangen. The remaining guests left soon afterwards.
■ **Ist noch Kuchen übrig?** Is there any cake left?

■ **die übrigen** the others
■ **das Übrige** the rest
■ **im Übrigen** besides
■ **übrig bleiben** to be left
■ **übrig lassen** to leave □ Habt ihr uns etwas Kuchen übrig gelassen? Have you left us any cake?

übrigens ADVERB
by the way
□ Übrigens, du schuldest mir noch zehn Euro. By the way, you still owe me ten euros.

übrighaben (PRESENT **hat übrig**, IMPERFECT **hatte übrig**, PERFECT **hat übriggehabt**) VERB [32]
■ **für jemanden etwas übrighaben** to be fond of somebody

übriglassen VERB [42] ▷ *see* **übrig**

die **Übung** NOUN
1 practice
□ Mir fehlt die Übung. I need more practice.
□ Übung macht den Meister. Practice makes perfect.
2 exercise
□ Bitte macht jetzt Übung dreizehn. Please do exercise thirteen now.
□ eine Turnübung a gym exercise

das **Ufer** (PL die **Ufer**) NOUN
1 bank
□ Wir saßen am Ufer des Rheins. We sat on the bank of the Rhine.
2 shore
□ Treibholz, das ans Ufer gespült wurde driftwood which was washed up onto the shore

die **Uhr** NOUN
1 clock
□ Die Uhr am Bahnhof sollte richtig gehen. The station clock should be right.
2 watch
□ Er sah auf seine Uhr. He looked at his watch.
■ **Wie viel Uhr ist es?** What time is it?
■ **ein Uhr** one o'clock
■ **zwanzig Uhr** eight o'clock in the evening
■ **um fünf Uhr** at five o'clock

der **Uhrzeigersinn** NOUN
■ **im Uhrzeigersinn** clockwise
■ **entgegen dem Uhrzeigersinn** anticlockwise

die **Uhrzeit** NOUN
time

der **Ultraschall** NOUN
ultrasound

um PREPOSITION, CONJUNCTION, ADVERB
▷ *see also* **umso** CONJUNCTION
LANGUAGE TIP The preposition **um** takes the accusative.
1 round
□ Sie legte sich einen Schal um den Hals. She wrapped a scarf round her neck.
□ Wir sind um die Stadt herumgefahren. We drove round the town.
■ **um Weihnachten** around Christmas
2 at
□ um acht Uhr at eight o'clock
3 by
□ etwas um vier Zentimeter kürzen to shorten something by four centimetres
■ **um zehn Prozent teurer** ten per cent more expensive
■ **um vieles besser** better by far
4 for
□ der Kampf um den Titel the battle for the title □ um Geld spielen to play for money
■ **um ... willen** for the sake of ...
LANGUAGE TIP **um ... willen** takes the genitive.
□ um deinetwillen for your sake □ um meiner Mutter willen for my mother's sake
■ **um ... zu** in order to ...
LANGUAGE TIP **um ... zu** is used with the infinitive.
□ Ich gehe in die Schule, um etwas zu lernen. I go to school in order to learn something.
■ **zu klug, um zu ...** too clever to ...
5 about
□ um die dreißig Leute about thirty people
■ **Die zwei Stunden sind um.** The two hours are up.

umarmen (PERFECT **hat umarmt**) VERB [7]
to hug
□ Sie umarmten sich. They hugged.

umblättern (PERFECT **hat umgeblättert**) VERB [4]
to turn over

umbringen (IMPERFECT **brachte um**, PERFECT **hat umgebracht**) VERB [13]
to kill

umdrehen (PERFECT **hat umgedreht**) VERB [4]
to turn round
□ Dreh das Bild mal um. Turn the picture round.
■ **sich umdrehen** to turn round

umfallen (PRESENT **fällt um**, IMPERFECT **fiel um**, PERFECT **ist umgefallen**) VERB [22]
to fall down

der **Umfang** NOUN
1 extent
□ Der Umfang der Arbeiten war am Anfang nicht absehbar. The extent of the work couldn't be seen at the beginning.
2 circumference
□ Berechnet den Umfang des Kreises. Calculate the circumference of the circle.

die **Umfrage** NOUN
poll

der **Umgang** NOUN
■ **erfahren im Umgang mit Kindern** experienced in dealing with children
■ **der Umgang mit dem Computer** working with computers

die **Umgangssprache** NOUN
colloquial language

umgeben (PRESENT **umgibt**, IMPERFECT **umgab**, PERFECT **hat umgeben**) VERB [28]
to surround

die **Umgebung** NOUN
1 surroundings
□ ein Haus in schöner Umgebung a house in beautiful surroundings
2 environment
□ Diese Pflanze wächst am besten in sonniger Umgebung. This plant grows best in a sunny environment.

umgehen (1) (IMPERFECT **ging um**, PERFECT **ist umgegangen**) VERB [29]
LANGUAGE TIP Note that here the stress is on **um**.
■ **mit jemandem grob umgehen** to treat somebody roughly
■ **mit Geld sparsam umgehen** to be careful with one's money
■ **Sie kann nicht gut mit Geld umgehen.** She's not very good with money.

umgehen (2) (IMPERFECT **umging**, PERFECT **hat umgangen**) VERB [29]
LANGUAGE TIP Note that here the stress is on **gehen**.
to avoid
□ Dieses Problem sollten wir besser umgehen. It would be better if we could avoid this problem.

umgehend ADJECTIVE
immediate

die **Umgehungsstraße** NOUN
bypass

umgekehrt ADJECTIVE, ADVERB
1 reverse
□ in umgekehrter Reihenfolge in reverse order
■ **genau umgekehrt** exactly the opposite
2 the other way around
□ Du musst das Bild umgekehrt hängen. You'll have to hang the picture the other way round. □ Mach das doch umgekehrt, und fang hiermit an. Do it the other way round and start here.
■ **... und umgekehrt** ... and vice versa

umhauen (PERFECT **hat umgehauen**) VERB [4]
1 to bowl over
□ Die Neuigkeit wird dich umhauen. The news will bowl you over.
2 to fell
□ Sie haben die alte Eiche umgehauen. They've felled the old oak tree.

sich **umhören** (PERFECT **hat sich umgehört**) VERB [4]
to ask around

umkehren (PERFECT **hat/ist umgekehrt**) VERB [4]
LANGUAGE TIP For the perfect tense use **haben** when the verb has an object and **sein** when there is no object.
1 to turn back
□ Wir sind auf halbem Weg umgekehrt. We turned back halfway.
2 to turn round
□ Warum hast du das Bild umgekehrt? Why did you turn the picture round?
3 to turn inside out
□ Sie hat ihre Tasche umgekehrt, den Schlüssel aber nicht gefunden. She turned her bag inside out but couldn't find the key.
4 to turn upside down
□ Kehr mal den Eimer um, dann kann ich mich draufstellen. Turn the bucket upside down so that I can stand on it.

umkippen (PERFECT **hat/ist umgekippt**) VERB [4]
LANGUAGE TIP For the perfect tense use **haben** when the verb has an object and **sein** when there is no object.
1 to tip over
□ Der Stuhl ist umgekippt. The chair tipped over.
2 to overturn
□ Sie haben das Boot umgekippt. They overturned the boat.
3 to keel over
□ Wenn ich Blut sehe, kippe ich immer um. I keel over whenever I see blood.

die **Umkleidekabine** NOUN
changing cubicle

der **Umkleideraum** (PL die **Umkleideräume**) NOUN
changing room

umkommen (IMPERFECT **kam um**, PERFECT **ist umgekommen**) VERB [40]
to be killed
□ Alle Passagiere sind umgekommen. All the passengers were killed.

der **Umkreis** (GEN des **Umkreises**, PL die **Umkreise**) NOUN
neighbourhood
■ **im Umkreis von** within a radius of

der **Umlaut** (PL die **Umlaute**) NOUN
umlaut

umlegen (PERFECT **hat umgelegt**) VERB [4]
1 to put on
□ Du solltest dir eine Jacke umlegen. You should put on a jacket.
■ **die Kosten für etwas umlegen** to divide the cost of something
2 to bump off
□ Er ist von der Mafia umgelegt worden. He was bumped off by the Mafia.

umleiten (PERFECT **hat umgeleitet**) VERB [4]
to divert

die **Umleitung** NOUN
diversion

umrechnen (PERFECT **hat umgerechnet**) VERB [4]
to convert

die **Umrechnung** NOUN
conversion

der **Umrechnungskurs**
(GEN des **Umrechnungskurses**,
PL die **Umrechnungskurse**) NOUN
rate of exchange

der **Umriss** (GEN des **Umrisses**,
PL die **Umrisse**) NOUN
outline

umrühren (PERFECT **hat umgerührt**) VERB [4]
to stir

ums = um das

der **Umsatz** (GEN des **Umsatzes**,
PL die **Umsätze**) NOUN
turnover

umschalten (PERFECT **hat umgeschaltet**)
VERB [4]
to switch
□ Schalt bitte ins zweite Programm um.
Please switch over to Channel two.
■ **Die Ampel hat auf Gelb umgeschaltet.**
The traffic lights changed to amber.
■ **Wir schalten um ins Studio.** We'll now go back to the studio.

der **Umschlag** (PL die **Umschläge**) NOUN
1 cover
□ Alle meine Mathehefte haben einen schwarzen Umschlag. All my maths exercise books have a black cover.
2 jacket
□ Ich habe den Umschlag von dem Wörterbuch abgemacht. I took the jacket off the dictionary.
3 envelope
□ Sie steckte den Brief in den Umschlag.
She put the letter in the envelope.

sich **umsehen** (PRESENT **sieht sich um**,
IMPERFECT **sah sich um**, PERFECT **hat sich umgesehen**) VERB [64]
to look around
□ Als sie Schritte hörte, sah sie sich um.
When she heard steps, she looked around.
■ **sich nach etwas umsehen** to look for something □ Ich sehe mich zurzeit nach einer neuen Wohnung um. I'm looking for a new flat at the moment.

umso CONJUNCTION
so much
□ umso besser so much the better
□ umso schlimmer so much the worse
■ **Je mehr ich höre, umso weniger verstehe ich.** The more I hear the less I understand.

umsonst ADVERB
1 in vain
□ Wir haben umsonst gewartet. We waited in vain.
2 for nothing
□ Wir sind umsonst ins Museum gekommen.
We got into the museum for nothing.
3 free of charge
□ Diese Broschüre gibt es umsonst.
This brochure is free of charge.

der **Umstand** (PL die **Umstände**) NOUN
circumstance
□ unter keinen Umständen under no circumstances
■ **Wenn es keine Umstände macht.**
If it's no trouble.
■ **unter Umständen** possibly
■ **in anderen Umständen sein** to be pregnant

LANGUAGE TIP Word for word, **in anderen Umständen sein** means 'to be in different circumstances'.

umständlich ADJECTIVE
1 complicated
□ Das ist aber umständlich, wie du das machst. The way you do it is complicated.
2 long-winded
□ eine umständliche Erklärung a long-winded explanation

umsteigen (IMPERFECT **stieg um**,
PERFECT **ist umgestiegen**) VERB [74]
to change
□ Wir müssen in München umsteigen.
We have to change in Munich.

umstellen (1) (PERFECT **hat umgestellt**) VERB [4]

LANGUAGE TIP Note that here the stress is on **um**.

to move
□ Ich werde meinen Schreibtisch umstellen.
I'm going to move my desk.
■ **auf metrische Maße umstellen** to go over to the metric system
■ **sich umstellen** to adapt □ Jetzt, wo das Baby da ist, müssen wir uns umstellen.
Now that the baby's here we have to adapt.

umstellen (2) (PERFECT **hat umstellt**) VERB [7]

LANGUAGE TIP Note that here the stress is on **stellen**.

to surround
□ Die Polizei hat das Haus umstellt.
The police have surrounded the house.

umstritten ADJECTIVE
controversial
□ ein umstrittenes Thema a controversial subject

der **Umtausch** NOUN
exchange

umtauschen (PERFECT **hat umgetauscht**)
VERB [4]
to exchange

der **Umweg** (PL die **Umwege**) NOUN
detour
□ Wir haben einen Umweg gemacht.
We made a detour.

die **Umwelt** NOUN
environment

umweltfreundlich ADJECTIVE
environment-friendly

der **Umweltschützer** (PL die **Umweltschützer**) NOUN
environmentalist

die **Umweltverschmutzung** NOUN
environmental pollution

umziehen (IMPERFECT **zog um**, PERFECT **hat/ist umgezogen**) VERB [96]

LANGUAGE TIP Use **haben** to form the perfect tense. Use **sein** to form the perfect tense for 'to move'.

1 to change
□ Ich habe Carolin heute schon zweimal umgezogen. I've already changed Carolin's clothes twice today.
■ **sich umziehen** to get changed □ Wenn ich mich umgezogen habe, können wir gehen. We can go when I've got changed.

2 to move
□ Mein Freund ist nach Bremen umgezogen. My friend's moved to Bremen.

der **Umzug** (PL die **Umzüge**) NOUN
1 move
□ Alle meine Freunde haben beim Umzug geholfen. All my friends helped with the move.
2 procession
□ Zu Karneval finden überall Umzüge statt. There are processions everywhere during the Carnival.

unabhängig ADJECTIVE
independent

die **Unabhängigkeit** NOUN
independence

unangebracht ADJECTIVE
uncalled-for

unangenehm ADJECTIVE
unpleasant

die **Unannehmlichkeiten** FEM PL NOUN
trouble
□ Das gibt Unannehmlichkeiten mit dem Klassenlehrer. That'll cause trouble with the class teacher.

unanständig ADJECTIVE
improper

unartig ADJECTIVE
naughty

unaufmerksam ADJECTIVE
inattentive

unausstehlich ADJECTIVE
intolerable

unbeabsichtigt ADJECTIVE
unintentional

unbedeutend ADJECTIVE
unimportant

unbedingt ADJECTIVE, ADVERB
1 unconditional
□ Ich verlange unbedingten Gehorsam. I demand unconditional obedience.
2 really
□ Er wollte unbedingt nach Hause. He really wanted to go home. □ Den Film musst du dir unbedingt ansehen. You really have to see that film.

unbefriedigend ADJECTIVE
unsatisfactory

unbefriedigt ADJECTIVE
unsatisfied

unbegreiflich ADJECTIVE
inconceivable

unbekannt ADJECTIVE
unknown

unbeliebt ADJECTIVE
unpopular

unbequem ADJECTIVE
uncomfortable
□ Das Bett ist unbequem. The bed's uncomfortable.

unbesetzt ADJECTIVE
vacant

unbestimmt ADJECTIVE
1 indefinite
□ der unbestimmte Artikel the indefinite article
2 uncertain
□ Es ist noch unbestimmt, wann wir Ferien machen. It's still uncertain when we're going on holiday.

unbewusst ADJECTIVE
unconscious

und CONJUNCTION
and
□ und so weiter and so on
■ **Na und?** So what?

undankbar ADJECTIVE
ungrateful

undeutlich ADJECTIVE
indistinct

unehrlich ADJECTIVE
dishonest

unempfindlich ADJECTIVE
practical
□ Wir brauchen für das Sofa einen unempfindlichen Bezug. We need a practical cover for the sofa.
■ **Ich bin gegen Kälte unempfindlich.** I don't feel the cold.

unendlich ADJECTIVE
infinite

unentschieden ADJECTIVE
undecided
■ **unentschieden enden** to end in a draw

unerfahren ADJECTIVE
inexperienced

unerfreulich ADJECTIVE
unpleasant

unerträglich ADJECTIVE
unbearable
□ Die Schmerzen sind unerträglich. The pain's unbearable.

unerwünscht ADJECTIVE
undesirable

unfähig ADJECTIVE
incapable
□ zu etwas unfähig sein to be incapable of something

unfair ADJECTIVE
unfair

der **Unfall** (PL die **Unfälle**) NOUN
accident

unfreundlich ADJECTIVE
unfriendly

die **Unfreundlichkeit** NOUN
unfriendliness

der **Unfug** NOUN
1 mischief
□ Die Kinder machen dauernd Unfug. The children are always getting up to mischief.
2 nonsense
□ Red nicht so einen Unfug. Don't talk such nonsense.

der **Ungar** (GEN des **Ungarn**, PL die **Ungarn**) NOUN
Hungarian

die **Ungarin** NOUN
Hungarian

ungarisch ADJECTIVE
Hungarian

Ungarn NEUT NOUN
Hungary
■ **aus Ungarn** from Hungary
■ **nach Ungarn** to Hungary

die **Ungeduld** NOUN
impatience

ungeduldig ADJECTIVE
impatient

ungeeignet ADJECTIVE
unsuitable

ungefähr ADJECTIVE
approximate
□ Kannst du mir eine ungefähre Zeit nennen? Can you give me an approximate time?
□ um ungefähr zwei Uhr at approximately two o'clock

ungefährlich ADJECTIVE
harmless

das **Ungeheuer** (PL die **Ungeheuer**) NOUN
monster
□ das Ungeheuer von Loch Ness the Loch Ness monster

ungehörig ADJECTIVE
impertinent

ungehorsam ADJECTIVE
disobedient

ungeklärt ADJECTIVE
unsolved
□ ein ungeklärtes Rätsel an unsolved puzzle

ungelegen ADJECTIVE
inconvenient
□ Ich hoffe, ich komme nicht ungelegen. I hope I haven't come at an inconvenient time.

ungelernt ADJECTIVE
unskilled
□ ein ungelernter Arbeiter an unskilled worker

ungemütlich ADJECTIVE
1 uncomfortable
□ ein ungemütlicher Stuhl an uncomfortable chair
2 disagreeable
□ Jetzt wird er ungemütlich. Now he's going to get disagreeable.

ungenau ADJECTIVE
inaccurate

ungenießbar ADJECTIVE
1 inedible
□ Das Essen war ungenießbar. The food was inedible.
2 undrinkable
□ Diese Limonade ist ungenießbar. This lemonade's undrinkable.
3 unbearable
□ Du bist heute aber ungenießbar. You're really unbearable today.

ungenügend ADJECTIVE
1 insufficient
□ eine ungenügende Menge an insufficient amount
2 unsatisfactory

> **DID YOU KNOW...?**
> German marks range from one (**sehr gut**) to six (**ungenügend**).

ungepflegt ADJECTIVE
■ **ein ungepflegter Garten** a neglected garden
■ **ungepflegte Hände** uncared-for hands

ungerade ADJECTIVE
■ **eine ungerade Zahl** an odd number

ungerecht ADJECTIVE
unjust

die **Ungerechtigkeit** NOUN
injustice

ungern ADVERB
reluctantly

ungeschickt ADJECTIVE
clumsy

ungestört ADJECTIVE
undisturbed

ungesund ADJECTIVE
unhealthy

ungewiss ADJECTIVE
uncertain

die **Ungewissheit** NOUN
uncertainty

ungewöhnlich ADJECTIVE
unusual

ungewohnt ADJECTIVE
unaccustomed

das **Ungeziefer** NOUN
vermin

ungezogen ADJECTIVE
rude

ungezwungen ADJECTIVE
natural

unglaublich ADJECTIVE
incredible

das **Unglück** (PL die **Unglücke**) NOUN
1 accident
□ Er ist bei einem Unglück ums Leben gekommen. He lost his life in an accident.
2 misfortune
□ Lass sie in ihrem Unglück nicht allein. Don't leave her alone in her misfortune.
3 bad luck
□ Eine schwarze Katze bringt Unglück. A black cat means bad luck.

unglücklich ADJECTIVE
1 unhappy
□ Sie ist furchtbar unglücklich. She's terribly unhappy.
2 unfortunate
□ ein unglücklicher Zufall an unfortunate coincidence □ eine unglückliche Formulierung an unfortunate choice of words
■ **Sie ist unglücklich gefallen.** She fell awkwardly.

ungültig ADJECTIVE
invalid

ungünstig ADJECTIVE
unfavourable

unheilbar ADJECTIVE
incurable

unheimlich ADJECTIVE, ADVERB
1 weird
□ Das war ein unheimliches Geräusch. That was a weird noise.
■ **Mir wird's etwas unheimlich.** I'm getting a bit scared.
2 incredibly
□ Das hat mich unheimlich gefreut. I was incredibly pleased about it.

unhöflich ADJECTIVE
impolite

die **Uni** (PL die **Unis**) NOUN
uni

die **Uniform** NOUN
uniform

uninteressant ADJECTIVE
uninteresting

die **Universität** NOUN
university

unklar ADJECTIVE
unclear
■ **über etwas im Unklaren sein** to be unclear about something □ Ich bin mir über mein Berufsziel noch im Unklaren. I'm still unclear about what I want to do.
■ **jemanden über etwas im Unklaren lassen** to leave somebody in the dark about something

unklug ADJECTIVE
unwise

die **Unkosten** PL NOUN
expenses

unlogisch ADJECTIVE
illogical

unlösbar ADJECTIVE
insoluble
□ ein unlösbares Problem an insoluble problem

unmissverständlich ADJECTIVE
unmistakeable

unmittelbar ADJECTIVE
immediate

unmöglich ADJECTIVE
impossible

die **Unmöglichkeit** NOUN
impossibility

unmoralisch ADJECTIVE
immoral

unnötig ADJECTIVE
unnecessary

unordentlich ADJECTIVE
untidy

die **Unordnung** NOUN
disorder

unparteiisch ADJECTIVE
impartial

unpassend ADJECTIVE
1 inappropriate
□ unpassende Kleidung inappropriate clothes
2 inopportune
□ zu einer unpassenden Zeit at an inopportune time

unpersönlich ADJECTIVE
impersonal
□ das unpersönliche Fürwort the impersonal pronoun

unpraktisch ADJECTIVE
unpractical

unpünktlich ADJECTIVE
■ **Sie ist immer unpünktlich.** She's always late.

das **Unrecht** NOUN
▷ *see also* **unrecht** ADJECTIVE
wrong
□ ein großes Unrecht a great wrong
■ **zu Unrecht** wrongly

unrecht ADJECTIVE
▷ *see also* **das Unrecht** NOUN
wrong
□ Du tust ihr unrecht. You are wronging her.
■ **unrecht haben** to be wrong

unregelmäßig ADJECTIVE
irregular
□ ein unregelmäßiges Verb an irregular verb

unreif ADJECTIVE
1 not ripe
□ Der Apfel ist noch unreif. The apple's not ripe yet.

2 immature
□ Elisabeth ist noch furchtbar unreif. Elisabeth's still terribly immature.

unrichtig ADJECTIVE
incorrect

die **Unruhe** NOUN
unrest

der **Unruhestifter** (PL die **Unruhestifter**) NOUN
troublemaker

unruhig ADJECTIVE
restless

uns PRONOUN

LANGUAGE TIP **uns** is the accusative and dative of **wir**.

1 us
□ Sie haben uns eingeladen. They've invited us.
2 to us
□ Sie haben es uns gegeben. They gave it to us.
3 ourselves
□ Wir fragen uns, ob das sein muss. We're asking ourselves whether that is necessary.
4 each other
□ Wir lieben uns. We love each other.

unschlagbar ADJECTIVE
invincible

die **Unschuld** NOUN
innocence

unschuldig ADJECTIVE
innocent

unselbstständig ADJECTIVE
dependent

unser ADJECTIVE
1 our
□ Unser Deutschlehrer ist nett. Our German teacher's nice. □ Unser Haus ist ganz in der Nähe der Schule. Our house is very near the school. □ Unsere Lehrer sind prima. Our teachers are great.
2 ours
□ Das ist nicht euer Lehrer, das ist unserer. He's not your teacher, he's ours. □ Seine Note war besser als unsere. His mark was better than ours. □ Deine Eltern sind netter als unsere. Your parents are nicer than ours.

unseretwegen ADVERB
1 for our sake
□ Ihr braucht unseretwegen nicht zu warten. You needn't wait for our sake.
2 on our account
□ Hat sie sich unseretwegen so aufgeregt? Did she get so upset on our account?
3 as far as we're concerned
□ Unseretwegen kann man das gern anders machen. As far as we're concerned you're welcome to do it differently.

unsicher ADJECTIVE
1 uncertain
□ Es ist unsicher, ob wir kommen können. It's uncertain whether we can come.
2 insecure
□ Elisabeth ist sehr unsicher. Elisabeth's very insecure.

unsichtbar ADJECTIVE
invisible

der **Unsinn** NOUN
nonsense
□ Unsinn erzählen to talk nonsense
■ **Unsinn machen** to do silly things

unsportlich ADJECTIVE
not sporty
□ Tobias ist ziemlich unsportlich. Tobias is not at all sporty.
■ **unsportliches Verhalten** unsportsmanlike behaviour

unsympathisch ADJECTIVE
unpleasant
□ ein unsympathischer Mensch an unpleasant person
■ **Er ist mir unsympathisch.** I don't like him.

unten ADVERB
1 at the bottom
□ Das beste Buch lag unten auf dem Stapel. The best book was at the bottom of the pile. □ Er stand unten an der Treppe. He was standing at the bottom of the stairs. □ unten am Berg at the bottom of the mountain
2 downstairs
□ Mutter ist unten in der Küche. Mother's downstairs in the kitchen.
■ **nach unten** down

unter PREPOSITION
1 under

LANGUAGE TIP Use the accusative to express movement or a change of place. Use the dative when there is no change of place.

□ Die Katze lag unter dem Tisch. The cat lay under the table. □ Der Ball rollte unter den Tisch. The ball rolled under the table. □ unter achtzehn Jahren under eighteen years of age
2 below
□ Temperaturen unter null below-zero temperatures
3 among
□ Unter den Büchern war auch ein Atlas. There was also an atlas among the books.
■ **Sie waren unter sich.** They were by themselves.
■ **einer unter ihnen** one of them
■ **unter anderem** among other things

das **Unterbewusstsein** NOUN
subconscious

unterbrechen (PRESENT **unterbricht**, IMPERFECT **unterbrach**, PERFECT **hat unterbrochen**) VERB [11]
to interrupt

die **Unterbrechung** NOUN
interruption

unterdrücken (PERFECT **hat unterdrückt**) VERB [7]
1 to suppress
□ Sie unterdrückte ein Lächeln. She suppressed a smile.
2 to oppress
□ Menschen unterdrücken to oppress people

untere ADJECTIVE
lower
□ die unteren Stockwerke the lower floors

untergehen (IMPERFECT **ging unter**, PERFECT **ist untergegangen**) VERB [29]
1 to sink
2 to set
□ sobald die Sonne untergegangen ist ... as soon as the sun has set ...
■ **Die Welt geht unter.** The world's coming to an end.
■ **Seine Rede ging im Lärm unter.** His speech was drowned out by the noise.

das **Untergeschoss** NOUN
basement

unterhalb PREPOSITION
LANGUAGE TIP The preposition **unterhalb** takes the genitive.
below
□ Ihr Haus befindet sich unterhalb der Kirche. Her house is below the church.

unterhalten (PRESENT **unterhält**, IMPERFECT **unterhielt**, PERFECT **hat unterhalten**) VERB [33]
1 to entertain
□ Sie hat uns den ganzen Abend mit lustigen Geschichten unterhalten. She entertained us with funny stories all evening.
2 to run
□ Das Schwimmbad wird von der Stadt unterhalten. The swimming pool is run by the town council.
■ **sich unterhalten** to talk □ Wir haben uns über dich unterhalten. We talked about you.

unterhaltsam ADJECTIVE
entertaining

die **Unterhaltung** NOUN
1 talk
□ Es war eine sehr aufschlussreiche Unterhaltung. It was a very informative talk.
2 entertainment
□ Zur Unterhaltung der Gäste spielt die örtliche Musikkapelle. Entertainment will be provided by the local brass band.

das **Unterhemd** (PL die **Unterhemden**) NOUN
vest

die **Unterhose** NOUN
underpants
□ eine Unterhose a pair of underpants

die **Unterkunft** (PL die **Unterkünfte**) NOUN
accommodation

der **Untermieter** (PL die **Untermieter**) NOUN
lodger

das **Unternehmen** (PL die **Unternehmen**) NOUN
▷ *see also* **unternehmen** VERB
enterprise

unternehmen (PRESENT **unternimmt**, IMPERFECT **unternahm**, PERFECT **hat unternommen**) VERB [52]
▷ *see also* **das Unternehmen** NOUN
■ **Was sollen wir heute unternehmen?** What shall we do today?

der **Unternehmer** (PL die **Unternehmer**) NOUN
entrepreneur

unternehmungslustig ADJECTIVE
enterprising

der **Unterricht** NOUN
lessons
□ Nachmittags haben wir selten Unterricht. We seldom have lessons in the afternoon.

unterrichten (PERFECT **hat unterrichtet**) VERB [2]
1 to teach
□ Sie unterrichtet Englisch und Französisch. She teaches English and French.
■ **Wer unterrichtet euch in Sport?** Who do you have for sport?
2 to inform
□ Wir müssen deine Eltern davon unterrichten. We'll have to inform your parents.

das **Unterrichtsfach** (PL die **Unterrichtsfächer**) NOUN
subject

der **Unterrock** (PL die **Unterröcke**) NOUN
underskirt

untersagt ADJECTIVE
forbidden

unterschätzen (PERFECT **hat unterschätzt**) VERB [36]
to underestimate

unterscheiden (IMPERFECT **unterschied**, PERFECT **hat unterschieden**) VERB [60]
to distinguish
□ Man muss zwischen Sachlichkeit und Unfreundlichkeit unterscheiden. You have to distinguish between objectivity and unfriendliness.
■ **sich unterscheiden** to differ

der **Unterschied** (PL die **Unterschiede**) NOUN
difference
■ **im Unterschied zu** as distinct from

unterschiedlich ADJECTIVE
different
□ Sie haben sehr unterschiedliche Begabungen. They have very different talents. □ Sie sind unterschiedlich groß. They're different sizes.
■ **Das Wetter war sehr unterschiedlich.** The weather was mixed.

unterschreiben (IMPERFECT **unterschrieb**, PERFECT **hat unterschrieben**) VERB [61]
to sign
□ Du musst das Zeugnis unterschreiben lassen. You have to have the report signed.

die **Unterschrift** NOUN
signature

unterste ADJECTIVE
bottom
□ Es ist im untersten Fach. It's on the bottom shelf.
■ **Sie ist in der untersten Klasse.** She's in the first form.

sich **unterstellen (1)** (PERFECT **hat sich untergestellt**) VERB [4]
LANGUAGE TIP Note that here the stress is on **unter**.
to take shelter
□ Es hat so stark geregnet, dass wir uns unterstellen mussten. It was raining so heavily that we had to take shelter.

unterstellen (2) (PERFECT **hat unterstellt**) VERB [18]
LANGUAGE TIP Note that here the stress is on **stellen**.
to imply
□ Willst du mir vielleicht unterstellen, dass ich das absichtlich getan habe? Are you perhaps implying that I did it on purpose?

unterstreichen (IMPERFECT **unterstrich**, PERFECT **hat unterstrichen**) VERB
to underline

die **Unterstufe** NOUN
lower school

unterstützen (PERFECT **hat unterstützt**) VERB [36]
to support

die **Unterstützung** NOUN
support

untersuchen (PERFECT **hat untersucht**) VERB [18]
to examine

die **Untersuchung** NOUN
examination

die **Untertasse** NOUN
saucer
□ eine fliegende Untertasse a flying saucer

unterteilen (PERFECT **hat unterteilt**) VERB [7]
to divide up

der **Untertitel** (PL die **Untertitel**) NOUN
subtitle

die **Unterwäsche** NOUN
underwear

unterwegs ADVERB
on the way

untreu ADJECTIVE
unfaithful
□ Ich hoffe, du warst mir nicht untreu. I hope you weren't unfaithful to me.

untröstlich ADJECTIVE
inconsolable

unübersichtlich ADJECTIVE
unclear
□ eine unübersichtliche Darstellung an unclear presentation
■ **eine unübersichtliche Kurve** a blind corner

ununterbrochen ADJECTIVE
uninterrupted

unveränderlich ADJECTIVE
unchangeable

unverantwortlich ADJECTIVE
irresponsible

unverbesserlich ADJECTIVE
incorrigible

unverbleit ADJECTIVE
unleaded
□ Ich fahre unverbleit. I use unleaded.

unvergesslich ADJECTIVE
unforgettable

unvermeidlich ADJECTIVE
unavoidable

unvernünftig ADJECTIVE
foolish

unverschämt ADJECTIVE
impudent

die **Unverschämtheit** NOUN
impudence

unverzeihlich ADJECTIVE
unpardonable

unvollständig ADJECTIVE
incomplete

unvorsichtig ADJECTIVE
careless

unvorstellbar ADJECTIVE
inconceivable

unwahr ADJECTIVE
untrue

unwahrscheinlich ADJECTIVE, ADVERB
1 unlikely
□ eine unwahrscheinliche Geschichte an unlikely story
2 incredibly
□ Ich habe mich unwahrscheinlich gefreut. I was incredibly pleased.

unwichtig ADJECTIVE
unimportant

unwirksam ADJECTIVE
ineffective

unzählig ADJECTIVE
countless

unzerbrechlich ADJECTIVE
unbreakable

unzertrennlich ADJECTIVE
inseparable

unzufrieden ADJECTIVE
dissatisfied

unzutreffend ADJECTIVE
incorrect

uralt ADJECTIVE
ancient

der **Ureinwohner** (PL die **Ureinwohner**) NOUN
original inhabitant

der **Urin** (PL die **Urine**) NOUN
urine

die **Urkunde** NOUN
certificate

der **Urlaub** (PL die **Urlaube**) NOUN
holiday
□ Wir fahren morgen in Urlaub. We're going on holiday tomorrow. □ Wo warst du im Urlaub? Where did you go on holiday?

die **Ursache** NOUN
cause
■ **Keine Ursache!** That's all right.

ursprünglich ADJECTIVE, ADVERB
1 original
□ Wir mussten unsere ursprünglichen Pläne aufgeben. We had to abandon our original plans.
2 originally
□ Ursprünglich wollten wir nach Griechenland fahren. We originally wanted to go to Greece.

das **Urteil** (PL die **Urteile**) NOUN
1 opinion
□ Wie lautet dein Urteil? What's your opinion?
2 sentence
□ Die Richter haben das Urteil noch nicht verkündet. The judges haven't passed sentence yet.

urteilen VERB [38]
to judge

der **Urwald** (PL die **Urwälder**) NOUN
jungle

die **USA** PL NOUN
USA
■ **aus den USA** from the USA
■ **in den USA** in the USA
■ **nach den USA** to the USA

usw. ABBREVIATION (= *und so weiter*)
etc

vage ADJECTIVE
vague

die **Vanille** NOUN
vanilla

die **Vase** NOUN
vase

der **Vater** (PL die Väter) NOUN
father

das **Vaterunser** (PL die Vaterunser) NOUN
Lord's prayer

der **Vati** (PL die Vatis) NOUN
daddy

der **Vegetarier** (PL die Vegetarier) NOUN
vegetarian

die **Vegetarierin** NOUN
vegetarian

vegetarisch ADJECTIVE
vegetarian

das **Veilchen** (PL die Veilchen) NOUN
violet

die **Vene** NOUN
vein

das **Ventil** (PL die Ventile) NOUN
valve

der **Ventilator** (PL die Ventilatoren) NOUN
fan

verabreden (PERFECT **hat verabredet**) VERB [54]
to arrange
□ Wir sollten Zeit und Ort des Treffens verabreden. We ought to arrange when and where to meet.
■ **sich mit jemandem verabreden** to arrange to meet somebody
■ **mit jemandem verabredet sein** to have arranged to meet somebody □ Ich bin mit meiner Mutter verabredet. I've arranged to meet my mother.

die **Verabredung** NOUN
date

verabschieden (PERFECT **hat verabschieden**) VERB [54]
to say goodbye to
□ Wir verabschiedeten unsere Gäste. We said goodbye to our guests.
■ **sich verabschieden** to take one's leave

verallgemeinern (PERFECT **hat verallgemeinert**) VERB [88]
to generalize

veralten (PERFECT **ist veraltet**) VERB [2]
to become obsolete

veränderlich ADJECTIVE
changeable

verändern (PERFECT **hat verändert**) VERB [88]
to change
■ **sich verändern** to change □ Sie hat sich in den letzten beiden Monaten verändert. She's changed in the last couple of months.

die **Veränderung** NOUN
change

die **Veranlagung** NOUN
disposition
□ eine nervöse Veranlagung a nervous disposition

veranlassen (PERFECT **hat veranlasst**) VERB [84]
■ **etwas veranlassen** to have something done
■ **sich veranlasst sehen, etwas zu tun** to be prompted to do something

veranschaulichen (PERFECT **hat veranschaulicht**) VERB [7]
to illustrate

veranstalten (PERFECT **hat veranstaltet**) VERB [2]
to organize

der **Veranstalter** (PL die Veranstalter) NOUN
organizer

die **Veranstaltung** NOUN
event

verantworten (PERFECT **hat verantwortet**) VERB [2]
to take responsibility for
□ Wenn das nicht klappt, hast du das zu verantworten. If it doesn't work, you'll have to take responsibility for it.
■ **Das kann ich nicht verantworten.** I couldn't possibly allow that.

verantwortlich ADJECTIVE
responsible

die **Verantwortung** NOUN
responsibility

verarbeiten (PERFECT **hat verarbeitet**) VERB [2]
1 to process
□ In diesem Werk wird Metall verarbeitet. Metal is processed in this factory.
■ **etwas zu etwas verarbeiten** to make something into something □ Der Plastikmüll

wird zu Parkbänken verarbeitet. Plastic waste is made into park benches.
2 to digest
□ Ich muss die Reiseeindrücke erst noch verarbeiten. I still have to digest my impressions from the journey.

verärgern (PERFECT **hat verärgert**) VERB [88]
to annoy

das **Verb** (PL die **Verben**) NOUN
verb

der **Verband** (PL die **Verbände**) NOUN
1 dressing
■ **Die Schwester hat ihm einen Verband angelegt.** The nurse dressed his wound.
2 association
□ Die Bauern haben sich zu einem Verband zusammengeschlossen. The farmers have formed an association.

der **Verbandskasten** (PL die **Verbandskästen**) NOUN
first-aid box

verbergen (PRESENT **verbirgt**, IMPERFECT **verbarg**, PERFECT **hat verborgen**) VERB
to hide
■ **sich vor jemandem verbergen** to hide from somebody

verbessern (PERFECT **hat verbessert**) VERB [88]
1 to improve
□ Ich konnte meine Noten verbessern. I was able to improve my marks.
2 to correct
□ Meine Mutter hat meine Hausaufgaben verbessert. My mother corrected my homework.
■ **sich verbessern** to improve □ In Mathe habe ich mich verbessert. I've improved in maths.

die **Verbesserung** NOUN
1 improvement
□ eine Verbesserung seiner Leistungen an improvement in his work
2 correction
□ Schreibt bitte die Verbesserung ins Heft. Please write the correction in your exercise book.

verbiegen (IMPERFECT **verbog**, PERFECT **hat verbogen**) VERB
to bend

verbieten (IMPERFECT **verbot**, PERFECT **hat verboten**) VERB [8]
to forbid
□ Meine Mutter hat mir verboten, mit Frank auszugehen. My mother forbade me to go out with Frank.

verbinden (IMPERFECT **verband**, PERFECT **hat verbunden**) VERB
1 to combine
□ Ich habe das Nützliche mit dem Angenehmen verbunden. I was able to combine business with pleasure.
2 to bandage
□ Die Wunde muss verbunden werden. The wound has to be bandaged.
■ **jemandem die Augen verbinden** to blindfold somebody
3 to connect
□ Ein Kanal verbindet die beiden Flüsse. A canal connects the two rivers.
4 to put through
□ Können Sie mich bitte mit Frau Karl verbinden? Can you put me through to Mrs Karl, please? □ Ich verbinde! I'm putting you through.
■ **Sie sind falsch verbunden.** You've got the wrong number.

die **Verbindung** (PL die **Verbindungen**) NOUN
1 connection
□ Es gibt eine direkte Verbindungen nach München. There is a direct connection to Munich.
2 communication
□ eine telefonische Verbindung a telephone communication
■ **eine chemische Verbindung** a compound

verbleit ADJECTIVE
leaded

verblüffen (PERFECT **hat verblüfft**) VERB [84]
to amaze

verbluten (PERFECT **ist verblutet**) VERB [2]
to bleed to death

verborgen ADJECTIVE
hidden

das **Verbot** (PL die **Verbote**) NOUN
ban
□ Die Regierung verhängte ein Verbot für Rindfleischimporte aus England. The government imposed a ban on beef imports from England.

verboten ADJECTIVE
forbidden
■ **Rauchen verboten!** No smoking

der **Verbrauch** NOUN
consumption

verbrauchen (PERFECT **hat verbraucht**) VERB [84]
to use up
□ Das Gerät verbraucht viel Strom. The machine uses up a lot of electricity.

der **Verbraucher** (PL die **Verbraucher**) NOUN
consumer

der **Verbrauchermarkt** (PL die **Verbrauchermärkte**) NOUN
hypermarket

das **Verbrechen** (PL die **Verbrechen**) NOUN
crime

der **Verbrecher** (PL die **Verbrecher**) NOUN
criminal

verbreiten (PERFECT **hat verbreitet**) VERB [2]
1 to spread
□ eine Krankheit verbreiten to spread a disease
2 to broadcast

□ eine Nachricht verbreiten to broadcast a message
■ **sich verbreiten** to spread □ Die Seuche hat sich inzwischen im ganzen Land verbreitet. The epidemic has since spread all over the country. □ Die Nachricht von seinem Tod hat sich schnell verbreitet. The news of his death spread quickly.

verbrennen (IMPERFECT **verbrannte**, PERFECT **hat verbrannt**) VERB [12]
1 to burn
□ In dieser Anlage wird Müll verbrannt. Waste is burnt in this plant.
2 to cremate
□ Sie möchte nach ihrem Tod verbrannt werden. She'd like to be cremated when she dies.

verbringen (IMPERFECT **verbrachte**, PERFECT **hat verbracht**) VERB [13]
to spend
□ Wir haben das Wochenende im Schwarzwald verbracht. We spent the weekend in the Black Forest.

verbrühen (PERFECT **hat verbrüht**) VERB [7]
to scald
□ Ich habe mir den Arm verbrüht. I've scalded my arm.
■ **sich verbrühen** to scald oneself □ Pass auf, dass du dich nicht verbrühst. Careful you don't scald yourself.

der **Verdacht** (PL die **Verdachte**) NOUN
suspicion

verdächtig ADJECTIVE
suspicious

verdächtigen (PERFECT **hat verdächtigt**) VERB [84]
to suspect

verdammt ADJECTIVE, ADVERB
damned
□ Diese verdammten Fliegen! These damned flies!
■ **Verdammt noch mal!** Damn it all!
■ **Verdammt!** Damn!

verdampfen (PERFECT **ist verdampft**) VERB [7]
to evaporate

verdanken (PERFECT **hat verdankt**) VERB [84]
■ **jemandem sein Leben verdanken** to owe one's life to somebody □ Sie verdankt ihm ihr Leben. She owes her life to him.

verdauen (PERFECT **hat verdaut**) VERB [84]
to digest

verdaulich ADJECTIVE
■ **Das ist schwer verdaulich.** That's hard to digest.

die **Verdauung** NOUN
digestion

verderben (PRESENT **verdirbt**, IMPERFECT **verdarb**, PERFECT **hat/ist verdorben**) VERB

LANGUAGE TIP Use **haben** to form the perfect tense. Use **sein** to form the perfect tense for 'to go bad'.

1 to ruin
□ Du verdirbst dir bei dem schlechten Licht die Augen. You'll ruin your eyes in this bad light. □ Er hat mir den Urlaub verdorben. He ruined my holiday.
2 to corrupt
□ Geld verdirbt den Menschen. Money corrupts people.
■ **es mit jemandem verderben** to get into somebody's bad books □ Sie will es mit keinem verderben. She doesn't want to get into anybody's bad books.
3 to go bad
□ Die Wurst ist verdorben. The sausage has gone bad.

verdienen (PERFECT **hat verdient**) VERB [84]
1 to earn
□ Wie viel verdient dein Vater? How much does your father earn?
2 to deserve
□ Du hast die Strafe verdient. You deserved the punishment.

verdreifachen (PERFECT **hat verdreifacht**) VERB [7]
to treble

verdünnen (PERFECT **hat verdünnt**) VERB [7]
to dilute

verdunsten (PERFECT **ist verdunstet**) VERB [2]
to evaporate

verdursten (PERFECT **ist verdurstet**) VERB [2]
to die of thirst

verdutzt ADJECTIVE
nonplussed

der **Verein** (PL die **Vereine**) NOUN
club
□ ein Sportverein a sports club

vereinbar ADJECTIVE
compatible
□ mit etwas vereinbar compatible with something

vereinbaren (PERFECT **hat vereinbart**) VERB [84]
to agree on

die **Vereinbarung** NOUN
agreement

vereinen (PERFECT **hat vereint**) VERB [84]
1 to unite
□ Das geteilte Land wurde wieder vereint. The divided country was reunited.
2 to reconcile
□ Ich kann das nicht mit meinem Gewissen vereinen. I can't reconcile that with my conscience.
■ **Mit vereinten Kräften schaffen wir das.** If we all pull together, we'll manage to do it.
■ **die Vereinten Nationen** the United Nations

vereinfachen (PERFECT **hat vereinfacht**) VERB [84]
to simplify

German-English

vereinigen (PERFECT **hat vereinigt**) VERB [84]
to unite

vereinzelt ADJECTIVE
isolated
□ vereinzelte Schauer isolated showers

vererben (PERFECT **hat vererbt**) VERB [18]
to leave
□ Meine Oma hat mir all ihre Bücher vererbt. My granny left me all her books.
■ **sich vererben** to be hereditary
□ Krampfadern vererben sich. Varicose veins are hereditary.

verfahren (PRESENT **verfährt**, IMPERFECT **verfuhr**, PERFECT **hat/ist verfahren**) VERB [21]
1 to proceed
□ Wie sollen wir verfahren? How shall we proceed?
2 to use up
□ Wir haben 50 Liter Benzin verfahren. We have used up 50 litres of petrol.
■ **Wir haben uns verfahren.** We have lost our way.

das **Verfahren** (PL die **Verfahren**) NOUN
1 process
□ Das ist ein neuartiges Verfahren zum Recyceln von Plastik. This is a new recycling process for plastic.
2 proceedings
□ ein Verfahren gegen jemanden einleiten to bring proceedings against somebody

die **Verfassung** NOUN
1 constitution
□ Die Opposition hat eine Änderung der Verfassung beantragt. The opposition's called for an amendment to the constitution.
2 state
□ Ich bin nicht in der Verfassung, da mitzumachen. I'm in no state to join in.

verfolgen (PERFECT **hat verfolgt**) VERB [84]
1 to pursue
□ Die Polizei verfolgte die Täter. The police pursued the culprits.
■ **Die Hunde verfolgten ihre Fährte.** The dogs tracked them.
2 to persecute
□ In vielen Ländern werden Minderheiten verfolgt. Minorities are persecuted in many countries.

die **Verfolgung** NOUN
1 hunt
□ Die Verfolgung der Täter war erfolgreich. The hunt for the culprits had a successful outcome.
2 persecution
□ die Verfolgung von Minderheiten the persecution of minorities

verfügbar ADJECTIVE
available

die **Verfügung** NOUN
■ **etwas zur Verfügung haben** to have something at one's disposal □ Nicht alle Schüler haben einen Computer zur Verfügung. Not all pupils have a computer at their disposal.
■ **allen zur Verfügung stehen** to be open to all
■ **Ich stehe Ihnen zur Verfügung.** I am at your service.

verführen (PERFECT **hat verführt**) VERB [84]
1 to tempt
□ Verführ mich nicht, ich habe schon zwei Stück Kuchen gegessen. Don't tempt me, I've already had two pieces of cake.
2 to seduce
□ Er hat versucht, sie zu verführen. He tried to seduce her.

die **Vergangenheit** NOUN
past
□ in der Vergangenheit in the past

der **Vergaser** (PL die **Vergaser**) NOUN
carburettor

vergaß VERB ▷ *see* **vergessen**

vergeben (PRESENT **vergibt**, IMPERFECT **vergab**, PERFECT **hat vergeben**) VERB [28]
to forgive
□ Kannst du mir noch einmal vergeben? Can you forgive me one more time?
□ Diese Lüge werde ich dir nie vergeben. I'll never forgive you for that lie.
■ **vergeben sein** to be taken □ Tut mir leid, die Stelle ist schon vergeben. Sorry, the job's already taken.
■ **Er ist schon vergeben.** He's already spoken for.

LANGUAGE TIP Word for word, **Er ist schon vergeben** means 'He is already given away'.

vergeblich ADVERB, ADJECTIVE
in vain
□ Wir haben uns vergeblich bemüht. We tried, but in vain. □ All mein Reden war vergeblich. All my words were in vain.

vergehen (IMPERFECT **verging**, PERFECT **ist vergangen**) VERB [29]
to pass
■ **Wie schnell die Zeit doch vergeht!** How time flies!
■ **Mir ist der Appetit vergangen.** I've lost my appetite.
■ **sich an jemandem vergehen** to indecently assault somebody □ Er soll sich an kleinen Mädchen vergangen haben. He's said to have indecently assaulted young girls.

vergessen (PRESENT **vergisst**, IMPERFECT **vergaß**, PERFECT **hat vergessen**) VERB [83]
to forget
□ Ich habe seinen Namen vergessen. I've forgotten his name.
■ **Vergiss nicht, die Blumen zu gießen.** Remember to water the flowers.

V

vergesslich ADJECTIVE
forgetful

vergeuden (PERFECT **hat vergeudet**) VERB [7]
to squander

vergewaltigen (PERFECT **hat vergewaltigt**) VERB [7]
to rape
□ Er hat eine Frau vergewaltigt. He raped a woman.

die **Vergewaltigung** NOUN
rape

sich **vergewissern** (PERFECT **hat sich vergewissert**) VERB [88]
to make sure

vergiften (PERFECT **hat vergiftet**) VERB [2]
to poison

die **Vergiftung** NOUN
poisoning

vergisst VERB ▷ *see* **vergessen**

der **Vergleich** (PL die **Vergleiche**) NOUN
comparison
■ **im Vergleich zu** compared with

vergleichen (IMPERFECT **verglich**, PERFECT **hat verglichen**) VERB
to compare
□ Er hat mein Wörterbuch mit seinem verglichen. He compared my dictionary with his. □ Man kann doch Äpfel und Birnen nicht vergleichen. You can't compare apples and pears.

das **Vergnügen** (PL die **Vergnügen**) NOUN
pleasure
■ **Viel Vergnügen!** Have fun!

vergnügt ADJECTIVE
cheerful

vergraben (PRESENT **vergräbt**, IMPERFECT **vergrub**, PERFECT **hat vergraben**) VERB
to bury

vergrößern (PERFECT **hat vergrößert**) VERB [88]
1 to enlarge
□ Ich habe das Foto vergrößern lassen. I had the photo enlarged.
2 to extend
□ Wir wollen das Haus vergrößern. We want to extend the house.
■ **sich vergrößern** to grow larger
□ Die Klasse hat sich stark vergrößert. The class has grown considerably larger.

verhaften (PERFECT **hat verhaftet**) VERB [2]
to arrest

das **Verhalten** NOUN
▷ *see also* **verhalten** VERB
behaviour

sich **verhalten** (PRESENT **verhält sich**, IMPERFECT **verhielt sich**, PERFECT **hat sich verhalten**) VERB [33]
▷ *see also* **das Verhalten** NOUN
to behave
□ Er hat sich uns gegenüber sehr fair verhalten. He behaved very fairly towards us.

das **Verhältnis** (GEN des **Verhältnisses**, PL die **Verhältnisse**) NOUN
1 affair
□ Er hat ein Verhältnis mit einer verheirateten Frau. He's having an affair with a married woman.
2 proportion
□ Unser Gehalt steht in keinem Verhältnis zu unserer Leistung. Our salary is not in proportion to our efforts.
■ **Verhältnisse 1** conditions □ Wenn die Verhältnisse anders wären, könnten wir die Arbeit schneller beenden. If conditions were different we could get the work finished sooner. **2** background □ Er kommt aus bescheidenen Verhältnissen. He comes from a modest background.
■ **über seine Verhältnisse leben** to live beyond one's means

verhältnismäßig ADVERB
relatively

verhandeln (PERFECT **hat verhandelt**) VERB [34]
to negotiate
□ Sie verhandeln einen Waffenstillstand. They're negotiating a ceasefire.
■ **Mein Fall wird nächste Woche vor dem Arbeitsgericht verhandelt.** My case is being heard by the industrial tribunal next week.

die **Verhandlung** NOUN
1 negotiation
□ die Friedensverhandlungen peace negotiations □ Wir sind mit der Firma noch in Verhandlung. We're still involved in negotiations with the company.
2 trial
□ Die Verhandlung gegen Klitt ist morgen. Klitt's trial is tomorrow.
3 hearing
□ die Verhandlung vor dem Arbeitsgericht the hearing before the industrial tribunal

verharmlosen (PERFECT **hat verharmlost**) VERB [7]
to play down

verhauen (PERFECT **hat verhauen**) VERB [7]
to beat up

verheerend ADJECTIVE
devastating

verheimlichen (PERFECT **hat verheimlicht**) VERB [7]
■ **jemandem etwas verheimlichen** to keep something secret from somebody

verheiratet ADJECTIVE
married

verhindern (PERFECT **hat verhindert**) VERB [88]
to prevent
■ **verhindert sein** to be unable to make it
□ Ich bin leider verhindert. I'm afraid I can't make it.

verhungern (PERFECT **ist verhungert**) VERB [88]
to starve to death

das **Verhütungsmittel** (PL die **Verhütungsmittel**) NOUN
contraceptive

sich **verirren** (PERFECT **hat sich verirrt**) VERB [84]
to get lost
□ Wir hatten uns im Nebel verirrt. We lost our way in the fog.

der **Verkauf** (PL die **Verkäufe**) NOUN
sale

verkaufen (PERFECT **hat verkauft**) VERB [84]
to sell

der **Verkäufer** (PL die **Verkäufer**) NOUN
shop assistant
□ Der Verkäufer hat uns sehr gut beraten. The shop assistant was extremely helpful.

die **Verkäuferin** NOUN
shop assistant
□ Sie ist Verkäuferin in einer Modeboutique. She's a shop assistant in a fashion boutique.

der **Verkehr** NOUN
1 traffic
□ Heute war viel Verkehr auf den Straßen. There was heavy traffic on the roads today.
2 intercourse
□ Haben Sie mit der Frau Verkehr gehabt? Did you have intercourse with this woman?

die **Verkehrsampel** NOUN
traffic lights

das **Verkehrsamt** (PL die **Verkehrsämter**) NOUN
tourist office

die **Verkehrsmeldung** NOUN
traffic announcement

das **Verkehrsmittel** (PL die **Verkehrsmittel**) NOUN
means of transport

das **Verkehrsschild** (PL die **Verkehrsschilder**) NOUN
road sign

der **Verkehrsunfall** (PL die **Verkehrsunfälle**) NOUN
traffic accident

das **Verkehrszeichen** (PL die **Verkehrszeichen**) NOUN
traffic sign

verkehrt ADJECTIVE
wrong
□ Das war die verkehrte Antwort. That was the wrong answer.
■ **verkehrt herum** back to front □ Du hast deinen Pulli verkehrt herum an. You've got your pullover on back to front.

sich **verkleiden** (PERFECT **hat sich verkleidet**) VERB [54]
to dress up
□ Sie verkleidete sich als Hexe. She dressed up as a witch.

verkleinern (PERFECT **hat verkleinert**) VERB [88]
to reduce
□ Wir sollten den Zeilenabstand verkleinern. We should reduce the line spacing.
■ **sich verkleinern** to grow smaller
□ Die Klasse hat sich stark verkleinert. The class has grown considerably smaller.

der **Verlag** (PL die **Verlage**) NOUN
publisher

verlangen (PERFECT **hat verlangt**) VERB [84]
to ask for
□ Ich verlange etwas mehr Verständnis. I'm asking for a bit more understanding.
□ Wie viel hat er dafür verlangt? How much did he ask for it?
■ **etwas von jemandem verlangen** to expect something of somebody □ Unser Chemielehrer verlangt zu viel von uns. Our chemistry teacher expects too much of us.

verlängern (PERFECT **hat verlängert**) VERB [88]
1 to extend
□ Wir haben die Ferien um eine Woche verlängert. We've extended our holiday by a week.
2 to lengthen
□ Wir müssen das Seil verlängern. We'll have to lengthen the rope.

verlassen (PRESENT **verlässt**, IMPERFECT **verließ**, PERFECT **hat verlassen**) VERB [42]
▷ *see also* **verlassen** ADJECTIVE
to leave
□ Er hat seine Frau und Kinder verlassen. He's left his wife and children.
■ **Verlassen Sie sofort das Gebäude!** Get out of the building immediately.
■ **sich verlassen auf** to depend on
□ Ich kann mich doch auf dich verlassen. I hope I can depend on you.

verlassen ADJECTIVE
▷ *see also* **verlassen** VERB
1 deserted
□ eine verlassene Gegend a deserted area
□ die verlassene Ehefrau the deserted wife
2 empty
□ ein verlassenes Haus an empty house

sich **verlaufen** (PRESENT **verläuft sich**, IMPERFECT **verlief sich**, PERFECT **hat sich verlaufen**) VERB [43]
1 to get lost
□ Wir haben uns im Wald verlaufen. We got lost in the forest.
2 to disperse
□ Nach Ende der Veranstaltung verlief sich die Menge. After the event the crowd dispersed.

verlegen ADJECTIVE
embarrassed
■ **nicht verlegen um** never at a loss for
□ Sie ist nie um eine Ausrede verlegen. She's never at a loss for an excuse.

verleihen (IMPERFECT **verlieh**, PERFECT **hat verliehen**) VERB
1 to lend
□ Ich habe mein Wörterbuch an sie verliehen.

I've lent her my dictionary.
2 to hire out
□ Ich suche jemanden, der Fahrräder verleiht. I'm looking for somebody who hires out bikes.
3 to award
□ Sie hat einen Preis verliehen bekommen. She was awarded a prize.

verleiten (PERFECT **hat verleitet**) VERB [2]
■ **jemanden dazu verleiten, etwas zu tun** to tempt somebody into doing something

verlernen (PERFECT **hat verlernt**) VERB [84]
to forget

verletzen (PERFECT **hat verletzt**) VERB [36]
1 to hurt
□ Deine Bemerkung hat mich verletzt. Your remark hurt me.
2 to injure
□ Sie ist schwer verletzt. She's seriously injured.
■ **ein Gesetz verletzen** to violate a law

der/die **Verletzte** (GEN des/der **Verletzten**, PL die **Verletzten**) NOUN
injured person
□ Auf der Straße lag ein Verletzter. An injured person was lying in the street.

die **Verletzung** NOUN
injury
■ **Er hatte schwere Verletzungen.** He was seriously injured.
■ **Das ist eine Verletzung der Spielregeln.** That's against the rules of the game.

sich **verlieben** (PERFECT **hat sich verliebt**) VERB [84]
■ **sich in jemanden verlieben** to fall in love with somebody

verliebt ADJECTIVE
in love
□ Ich bin in Anke verliebt. I'm in love with Anke.

verlieren (IMPERFECT **verlor**, PERFECT **hat verloren**) VERB [85]
to lose

der **Verlierer** (PL die **Verlierer**) NOUN
loser

sich **verloben** (PERFECT **hat sich verlobt**) VERB [84]
■ **sich mit jemandem verloben** to get engaged to somebody

der **Verlobte** (GEN des **Verlobten**, PL die **Verlobten**) NOUN
▷ *see also* **die Verlobte** NOUN
fiancé
□ Mathias ist mein Verlobter. Mathias is my fiancé.

die **Verlobte** (GEN der **Verlobten**, PL die **Verlobten**) NOUN
▷ *see also* **der Verlobte** NOUN
fiancée
□ Ingrid ist seine Verlobte. Ingrid's his fiancée.

die **Verlobung** NOUN
engagement

verlor, verloren VERB ▷ *see* **verlieren**

verloren ADJECTIVE
lost
□ die verlorene Zeit wieder einholen to make up for lost time
■ **verlorene Eier** poached eggs
■ **verloren gehen** to get lost

die **Verlosung** NOUN
raffle

der **Verlust** (PL die **Verluste**) NOUN
loss

vermehren (PERFECT **hat vermehrt**) VERB [7]
increase
□ Die Firma hat ihren Umsatz vermehrt. The company has increased its turnover.
■ **sich vermehren** to reproduce □ Wie vermehren sich Regenwürmer? How do earthworms reproduce?

vermeiden (IMPERFECT **vermied**, PERFECT **hat vermieden**) VERB
to avoid

vermieten (PERFECT **hat vermietet**) VERB [2]
1 to let
□ 'Zimmer zu vermieten' 'Rooms to let'
2 to rent
□ Sie vermietet Zimmer. She rents rooms.
3 to hire out
□ Wir vermieten Boote und Fahrräder. We hire out boats and bikes.

der **Vermieter** (PL die **Vermieter**) NOUN
landlord

die **Vermieterin** NOUN
landlady

vermissen (PERFECT **hat vermisst**) VERB [7]
to miss
□ Ich habe dich vermisst. I missed you.
■ **Ich vermisse eines meiner Bücher.** One of my books is missing.

das **Vermögen** (PL die **Vermögen**) NOUN
wealth
■ **ein Vermögen kosten** to cost a fortune

vermuten (PERFECT **hat vermutet**) VERB [2]
1 to guess
□ Ich kann nur vermuten, was er damit gemeint hat. I can only guess what he meant by that.
■ **Man vermutet, dass er im Ausland ist.** He is thought to be abroad.
2 to suspect
□ Die Polizei vermutet, dass er der Täter ist. The police suspect that he's the culprit.
3 to suppose
□ Ich vermute, dass er das noch nicht weiß. I don't suppose that he knows that yet.

vermutlich ADJECTIVE, ADVERB
1 probable
□ die vermutliche Ursache the probable cause
2 probably
□ Sie ist vermutlich schon gegangen. She has probably already left.

die **Vermutung** NOUN
1 supposition
□ Das legt die Vermutung nahe, dass sie schon gegangen ist. It seems a likely supposition that she's already gone.
2 suspicion
□ Die Polizei hat eine Vermutung, wer der Täter gewesen sein könnte. The police have a suspicion as to who the culprit could have been.

vernachlässigen (PERFECT **hat vernachlässigt**) VERB [84]
to neglect

vernichten (PERFECT **hat vernichtet**) VERB [2]
to destroy
■ **Insekten vernichten** to exterminate insects
■ **Unkraut vernichten** to eradicate weeds

die **Vernunft** NOUN
reason

vernünftig ADJECTIVE
reasonable
□ Sei doch vernünftig! Be reasonable!
□ ein vernünftiger Preis a reasonable price
■ **etwas Vernünftiges essen** to eat something decent

veröffentlichen (PERFECT **hat veröffentlicht**) VERB [84]
to publish

die **Verpackung** NOUN
packing

verpassen (PERFECT **hat verpasst**) VERB [7]
to miss
■ **jemandem eine Ohrfeige verpassen** to give somebody a clip round the ear

verpflegen (PERFECT **hat verpflegt**) VERB [7]
to cater for
□ Die Flüchtlinge wurden vom Roten Kreuz verpflegt. The Red Cross catered for the refugees.

die **Verpflegung** NOUN
food
□ Für Ihre Verpflegung wird gesorgt. Food will be laid on. □ Die Verpflegung im Schullandheim war gut. The food at the school camp was good.

verpflichten (PERFECT **hat verpflichtet**) VERB [2]
to sign
□ Der VfB will Köpke verpflichten. VfB want to sign Köpke.
■ **sich verpflichten, etwas zu tun** to promise to do something □ Du hast dich verpflichtet, für die Musik zu sorgen. You promised to organize the music.
■ **Sie haben sich verpflichtet, für Ersatz zu sorgen.** You undertook to find a replacement.
■ **verpflichtet sein, etwas zu tun** to be obliged to do something
■ **Er ist zum Stillschweigen verpflichtet.** He's sworn to silence.
■ **Das verpflichtet Sie zu nichts.** This doesn't commit you to anything.
■ **jemandem zu Dank verpflichtet sein** to be obliged to somebody

verprügeln (PERFECT **hat verprügelt**) VERB [7]
to beat up

verraten (PRESENT **verrät**, IMPERFECT **verriet**, PERFECT **hat verraten**) VERB
1 to betray
□ Er hat seine Mittäter verraten. He betrayed his accomplices.
2 to report
□ Fritz hat uns beim Lehrer verraten. Fritz reported us to the teacher.
3 to tell
□ Verrate mir doch, wer es war. Tell me who it was. □ Ich habe dieses Geheimnis niemandem verraten. I haven't told anyone the secret.
■ **sich verraten** to give oneself away

verregnet ADJECTIVE
rainy

verreisen (PERFECT **ist verreist**) VERB [84]
to go away
□ Ich möchte diesen Sommer verreisen. I'd like to go away this summer.
■ **Wir wollen nach Israel verreisen.** We intend to go to Israel.

verrenken (PERFECT **hat verrenkt**) VERB [7]
to sprain
□ Er hat sich den Knöchel verrenkt. He sprained his ankle.

verrosten (PERFECT **ist verrostet**) VERB [2]
to rust

verrückt ADJECTIVE
crazy

der/die **Verrückte** (GEN des/der **Verrückten**, PL die **Verrückten**) NOUN
maniac
□ Er ist gefahren wie ein Verrückter. He drove like a maniac.

die **Verrücktheit** NOUN
madness

verrufen ADJECTIVE
disreputable

der **Vers** (GEN des **Verses**, PL die **Verse**) NOUN
verse

der **Versager** (PL die **Versager**) NOUN
failure

versalzen (PERFECT **hat versalzen**) VERB
to put too much salt in
□ Sie hat die Suppe versalzen. She put too much salt in the soup.
■ **Die Suppe ist versalzen.** There's too much salt in the soup.

versammeln (PERFECT **hat versammelt**) VERB [34]
to assemble

die **Versammlung** NOUN
meeting

das **Versandhaus** (GEN des **Versandhauses**, PL die **Versandhäuser**) NOUN mail-order firm

versäumen (PERFECT **hat versäumt**) VERB [84]
to miss
□ Ich habe wegen Krankheit drei Stunden versäumt. I missed three lessons due to illness. □ Sie sollten nicht versäumen, sich die Kathedrale anzusehen. Don't miss a visit to the cathedral.
■ **es versäumen, etwas zu tun** to fail to do something □ Sie hat es versäumt, sich rechtzeitig anzumelden. She failed to register in time.

verschenken (PERFECT **hat verschenkt**) VERB [7]
to give away

verschicken (PERFECT **hat verschickt**) VERB [7]
to send away

verschieben (IMPERFECT **verschob**, PERFECT **hat verschoben**) VERB
to postpone
□ Wir müssen das Fest verschieben. We'll have to postpone the party.

verschieden ADJECTIVE
different
□ Die zwei Brüder sind sehr verschieden. The two brothers are very different. □ Sie sind verschieden groß. They are different sizes.
■ **verschiedene** various □ Wir haben verschiedene Sehenswürdigkeiten besichtigt. We've seen various sights.

verschlafen (PRESENT **verschläft**, IMPERFECT **verschlief**, PERFECT **hat verschlafen**) VERB [58]
▷ *see also* **verschlafen** ADJECTIVE
1 to sleep in
□ Tut mir leid, ich habe verschlafen. Sorry, I slept in.
2 to sleep through
□ Er hat den ganzen Vormittag verschlafen. He slept through the whole morning.
3 to forget
□ Ich habe deinen Geburtstag total verschlafen. I completely forgot your birthday.

verschlafen ADJECTIVE
▷ *see also* **verschlafen** VERB
sleepy
□ Sie sah mich mit einem verschlafenen Blick an. She gave me a sleepy look. □ ein verschlafenes kleines Dorf a sleepy little village

verschlechtern (PERFECT **hat verschlechtert**) VERB [88]
to make worse
□ Das verschlechtert die Lage. That makes the situation worse.
■ **sich verschlechtern 1** to get worse
□ Die Lage hat sich verschlechtert. The situation's got worse. □ In Englisch habe ich mich verschlechtert. My marks in English have got worse. **2** to deteriorate
□ Sein Gesundheitszustand hat sich noch weiter verschlechtert. His condition has deteriorated even further.

verschlimmern (PERFECT **hat verschlimmert**) VERB [88]
to make worse
□ Du verschlimmerst alles, wenn du weiter lügst. You'll make everything worse if you go on lying.
■ **sich verschlimmern** to get worse
□ Die Lage hat sich verschlimmert. The situation's got worse.

der **Verschluss** (GEN des **Verschlusses**, PL die **Verschlüsse**) NOUN
1 cap
□ Die Flasche hat einen kindersicheren Verschluss. The bottle has a childproof cap.
2 fastening
□ Kannst du mir den Verschluss an meinem Kleid aufmachen? Can you undo the fastening of my dress?
3 catch
□ der Verschluss der Tasche the catch of the bag □ der Verschluss an einer Halskette the catch of a necklace

verschmutzen (PERFECT **hat verschmutzt**) VERB [7]
1 to soil
■ **stark verschmutzt** very dirty
2 to pollute
□ die Umwelt verschmutzen to pollute the environment

verschneit ADJECTIVE
snow-covered
□ eine verschneite Straße a snow-covered road

verschonen (PERFECT **hat verschont**) VERB [84]
■ **jemanden mit etwas verschonen** to spare somebody something
□ Sie verschonte mich mit den ganzen Einzelheiten. She spared me all the details.

verschreiben (IMPERFECT **verschrieb**, PERFECT **hat verschrieben**) VERB [61]
to prescribe
□ Der Arzt hat mir Antibiotika verschrieben. The doctor prescribed me antibiotics.
■ **sich verschreiben** to make a spelling mistake

verschütten (PERFECT **hat verschüttet**) VERB [7]
to spill
□ Sie hat den Kaffee verschüttet. She spilt the coffee.
■ **verschüttet werden** to be buried
□ Bei dem Erdbeben wurden zahlreiche Menschen verschüttet. Many people were buried in the earthquake.

verschweigen (IMPERFECT **verschwieg**, PERFECT **hat verschwiegen**) VERB
■ **jemandem etwas verschweigen** to keep something from somebody

verschwenden (PERFECT **hat verschwendet**) VERB [7]
to waste

□ Zeit verschwenden to waste time

die **Verschwendung** NOUN
waste

verschwinden (IMPERFECT **verschwand**, PERFECT **ist verschwunden**) VERB [86]
to disappear

verschwitzt ADJECTIVE
sweaty

verschwommen ADJECTIVE
blurred

das **Versehen** (PL die **Versehen**) NOUN
oversight
□ Das war ein Versehen. It was an oversight.
■ **aus Versehen** by mistake

versehentlich ADVERB
by mistake

versenden (IMPERFECT **versendete** *or* **versandte**, PERFECT **hat versendet** *or* **versandt**) VERB
to dispatch

versessen ADJECTIVE
■ **auf etwas versessen sein** to be mad about something □ Sie ist ganz versessen auf ihn. She's mad about him.

versetzen (PERFECT **hat versetzt**) VERB [7]
to transfer
□ Mein Vater wird nach Berlin versetzt. My father's being transferred to Berlin.
■ **jemanden in die nächste Klasse versetzen** to move somebody up into the next class

> **DID YOU KNOW...?**
> In Germany, pupils do not automatically move up (**versetzt werden**) to the next class at the end of the school year. If their performance is not good enough, they have to repeat the school year. This is known as **sitzen bleiben.**

■ **jemanden versetzen** to stand somebody up □ Meine Freundin hat mich versetzt. My girlfriend stood me up.
■ **sich in jemandes Lage versetzen** to put oneself in somebody's shoes □ Wenn du dich einmal in meine Lage versetzt ... If you put yourself in my shoes ...
■ **jemandem einen Schlag versetzen** to hit somebody
■ **jemandem einen Tritt versetzen** to kick somebody
■ **jemanden in gute Laune versetzen** to put somebody in a good mood

verseuchen (PERFECT **hat verseucht**) VERB [7]
to contaminate

versichern (PERFECT **hat versichert**) VERB [88]
1 to assure
□ Er hat mir versichert, dass das stimmt. He assured me that this is correct.
2 to insure
□ Wir sind nicht gegen Diebstahl versichert. We are not insured against theft.

die **Versicherung** NOUN
insurance

sich **versöhnen** (PERFECT **hat sich versöhnt**) VERB [84]
to make up
□ Na, habt ihr euch wieder versöhnt? Well, have you two made up again?
■ **sich mit jemandem versöhnen** to make it up with somebody □ Ich habe mich wieder mit ihm versöhnt. I made it up with him again.

versorgen (PERFECT **hat versorgt**) VERB [7]
to supply
□ Von hier aus wird die Stadt mit Elektrizität versorgt. The town is supplied with electricity from here.
■ **einen Kranken versorgen** to look after a patient
■ **eine Familie versorgen** to support a family

sich **verspäten** (PERFECT **hat sich verspätet**) VERB [2]
to be late

verspätet ADJECTIVE
late
□ die verspätete Ankunft the late arrival
■ **der verspätete Flug** the delayed flight
■ **verspätete Glückwünsche** belated best wishes

die **Verspätung** NOUN
delay
■ **Verspätung haben** to be late

das **Versprechen** (PL die **Versprechen**) NOUN
▷ *see also* **versprechen** VERB
promise
□ Sie hat ihr Versprechen gehalten. She kept her promise.

versprechen (PRESENT **verspricht**, IMPERFECT **versprach**, PERFECT **hat versprochen**) VERB [70]
▷ *see also* **das Versprechen** NOUN
to promise
□ Du hast es versprochen. You promised.
■ **Ich habe mir von dem Kurs mehr versprochen.** I expected more from this course.

der **Verstand** NOUN
mind
□ den Verstand verlieren to go out of one's mind
■ **über jemandes Verstand gehen** to be beyond somebody

verständigen (PERFECT **hat verständigt**) VERB [7]
to inform
□ Wir müssen ihre Eltern verständigen. We must inform her parents.
■ **sich verständigen** to communicate
□ Wir konnten uns auf Englisch verständigen. We were able to communicate in English.

■ **sich auf etwas verständigen** to agree on something □ Wir haben uns auf folgendes Vorgehen verständigt. We've agreed on the following plan of action.

verständlich ADJECTIVE
understandable
■ **sich verständlich ausdrücken** to express oneself clearly

verständnisvoll ADJECTIVE
understanding
□ Meine Eltern sind sehr verständnisvoll. My parents are very understanding.

verstärken (PERFECT **hat verstärkt**) VERB [7]
1 to strengthen
□ Wir müssen den Karton verstärken. We'll have to strengthen the box. □ ein Team verstärken to strengthen a team
2 to amplify
□ den Ton verstärken to amplify the sound
■ **Das verstärkt die Schmerzen.** That makes the pain worse.

der **Verstärker** (PL die **Verstärker**) NOUN
amplifier

die **Verstärkung** NOUN
reinforcements
□ Wir brauchen Verstärkung. We need reinforcements.

verstauchen (PERFECT **hat verstaucht**) VERB [7]
to sprain
□ Ich habe mir den Knöchel verstaucht. I've sprained my ankle.

das **Versteck** (PL die **Verstecke**) NOUN
hiding place

verstecken (PERFECT **hat versteckt**) VERB [7]
to hide

verstehen (IMPERFECT **verstand**, PERFECT **hat verstanden**) VERB [72]
to understand
□ Ich habe die Frage nicht verstanden. I didn't understand the question.
□ Ich verstehe nicht. I don't understand.
■ **sich verstehen** to get on □ Die beiden verstehen sich blendend. The two of them get on marvellously.
■ **Das versteht sich von selbst.** That goes without saying.

verstopft ADJECTIVE
1 blocked
□ ein verstopfter Abfluss a blocked drain
2 constipated
□ Ich bin seit gestern verstopft. I've been constipated since yesterday.

verstreuen (PERFECT **hat verstreut**) VERB [7]
to scatter

der **Versuch** (PL die **Versuche**) NOUN
1 attempt
□ Ich habe den Versuch gemacht, Spanisch zu lernen. I made an attempt to learn Spanish.
□ Sie ist schon beim ersten Versuch gescheitert. She failed at the very first attempt.
2 experiment
□ Versuche mit Tieren lehnen wir ab. We disapprove of experiments with animals.

versuchen (PERFECT **hat versucht**) VERB [84]
to try
□ Ich versuche zu kommen. I'll try to come.
□ Willst du mal die Soße versuchen? Would you like to try the sauce?
■ **sich an etwas versuchen** to try one's hand at something □ Ich habe mich am Töpfern versucht. I tried my hand at pottery.

vertagen (PERFECT **hat vertagt**) VERB [7]
to adjourn

vertauschen (PERFECT **hat vertauscht**) VERB [7]
1 to mix up
□ Die Babys wurden im Krankenhaus vertauscht. They mixed the babies up at the hospital. □ Er hat offensichtlich seinen Mantel mit meinem vertauscht. He must have got his coat and mine mixed up.
2 to exchange
□ Er hat seinen Sportwagen mit einem Familienwagen vertauscht. He exchanged his sports car for a family car.

verteidigen (PERFECT **hat verteidigt**) VERB [84]
to defend

der **Verteidiger** (PL die **Verteidiger**) NOUN
1 defender
□ Der Verteidiger wurde gefoult. The defender was fouled.
2 defence counsel
□ Wer ist der Verteidiger des Angeklagten? Who's counsel for the defence?

verteilen (PERFECT **hat verteilt**) VERB [84]
1 to hand out
□ Sie verteilte die Hefte an die Schüler. She handed the exercise books out to the pupils.
2 to spread
□ Die Salbe sollte gleichmäßig auf der Haut verteilt werden. The ointment should be spread evenly over the skin.

der **Vertrag** (PL die **Verträge**) NOUN
1 contract
□ ein Arbeitsvertrag a contract of employment
2 treaty
□ ein Friedensvertrag a peace treaty

vertragen (PRESENT **verträgt**, IMPERFECT **vertrug**, PERFECT **hat vertragen**) VERB [77]
1 to be able to stand
□ Ich vertrage die Hitze nicht. I can't stand the heat.
2 to tolerate
□ Ich kann eine solche Behandlung nicht vertragen. I can't tolerate such treatment.
■ **sich vertragen** to get along □ Die beiden vertragen sich blendend. The two of them get along marvellously.
■ **sich wieder vertragen** to patch things up

□ Na, vertragt ihr euch wieder? Well, have you patched things up again?

verträglich ADJECTIVE

1 good-natured

□ ein verträglicher Mensch a good-natured person

2 easily digestible

□ Im Sommer sollte man nur leicht verträgliche Speisen zu sich nehmen. In summer, you should only eat easily digestible food.

■ **Das Medikament ist gut verträglich.** The drug has no side effects.

das **Vertrauen** NOUN

▷ *see also* **vertrauen** VERB

trust

□ Vertrauen zu jemandem haben to have trust in somebody

vertrauen (PERFECT **hat vertraut**) VERB [84]

▷ *see also* **das Vertrauen** NOUN

■ **jemandem vertrauen** to trust somebody

■ **vertrauen auf** to rely on □ Ich vertraue auf dich. I'm relying on you.

■ **Ich vertraue auf mein Glück.** I'm trusting my luck.

vertraulich ADJECTIVE

1 confidential

□ ein vertrauliches Gespräch a confidential talk

2 familiar

□ Ich verbiete mir diesen vertraulichen Ton. I'll not have you talking to me in such familiar way.

vertraut ADJECTIVE

familiar

□ vertraute Gesichter familiar faces

vertreiben (IMPERFECT **vertrieb**, PERFECT **hat vertrieben**) VERB

1 to drive

□ Er hat uns von seinem Grundstück vertrieben. He drove us off his land.

2 to sell

□ Wir vertreiben Hardware und Software. We sell hardware and software.

■ **sich die Zeit vertreiben** to pass the time

□ Ich habe mir die Zeit mit Kreuzworträtseln vertrieben. I passed the time doing crosswords.

vertreten (PRESENT **vertritt**, IMPERFECT **vertrat**, PERFECT **hat vertreten**) VERB [79]

1 to stand in for

□ Während ich in Urlaub bin, vertritt mich Frau Wengel. While I'm on holiday, Mrs Wengel's standing in for me.

2 to represent

□ Die Lobby vertritt die Interessen der Wirtschaft. The lobby represents business interests.

■ **eine Meinung vertreten** to hold an opinion

■ **sich den Fuß vertreten** to twist one's ankle □ Ich habe mir den Fuß vertreten. I've twisted my ankle.

■ **sich die Beine vertreten** to stretch one's legs □ Ich will mir nur etwas die Beine vertreten. I just want to stretch my legs a bit.

der **Vertreter** (PL die **Vertreter**) NOUN

sales representative

□ Er ist Vertreter für Collins. He's a sales representative for Collins.

der **Vertrieb** (PL die **Vertriebe**) NOUN

1 sale

□ Der Vertrieb von Raubkopien steht unter Strafe. The sale of pirate copies is punishable by law.

2 marketing department

□ Sie arbeitet im Vertrieb. She works in the marketing department.

sich **vertun** (IMPERFECT **vertat sich**, PERFECT **hat sich vertan**) VERB [81]

to make a mistake

verübeln (PERFECT **hat verübelt**) VERB [7]

■ **jemandem etwas verübeln** to be cross with somebody because of something

verüben (PERFECT **hat verübt**) VERB [7]

to commit

verunglücken (PERFECT **ist verunglückt**) VERB [84]

to have an accident

□ Sie sind mit dem Auto verunglückt. They've had a car accident.

verursachen (PERFECT **hat verursacht**) VERB [84]

to cause

verurteilen (PERFECT **hat verurteilt**) VERB [84]

to condemn

vervielfältigen (PERFECT **hat vervielfältigt**) VERB [84]

to copy

vervollständigen (PERFECT **hat vervollständigt**) VERB [7]

to complete

die **Verwaltung** NOUN

administration

□ Er arbeitet in der Verwaltung. He works in administration.

verwandt ADJECTIVE

■ **mit jemandem verwandt sein** to be related to somebody

der/die **Verwandte** (GEN des/der **Verwandten**, PL die **Verwandten**) NOUN

relative

□ Ein Verwandter von mir ist gestern gestorben. A relative of mine died yesterday.

die **Verwandtschaft** NOUN

relations

□ Die ganze Verwandtschaft war eingeladen. All my relations were invited.

verwechseln (PERFECT **hat verwechselt**) VERB [34]

1 to confuse

□ Du darfst die beiden Begriffe nicht

verwechseln. You mustn't confuse the two ideas.
2 to mix up
□ Sie haben offensichtlich die Mäntel verwechselt. They must have got their coats mixed up.
■ **verwechseln mit 1** to confuse with □ Ich verwechsle 'akut' immer mit 'aktuell'. I always confuse 'akut' with 'aktuell'. **2** to mistake for □ Ich habe dich mit deiner Schwester verwechselt. I mistook you for your sister.
■ **Sie sind zum Verwechseln ähnlich.** They're the spitting image of each other.

die **Verwechslung** NOUN
mix-up

verweigern (PERFECT **hat verweigert**) VERB [88]
■ **jemandem etwas verweigern** to refuse somebody something □ Sie verweigerte ihm das Besuchsrecht für die Kinder. She refused him access to the children.
■ **den Gehorsam verweigern** to refuse to obey
■ **die Aussage verweigern** to refuse to testify

der **Verweis** (GEN des **Verweises**, PL die **Verweise**) NOUN
reprimand
□ Er hat für sein Zuspätkommen einen schweren Verweis bekommen. He was given a severe reprimand for being late.

verwelken (PERFECT **ist verwelkt**) VERB [7]
to fade

verwenden (IMPERFECT **verwendete** *or* **verwandte**, PERFECT **hat verwendet** *or* **verwandt**) VERB
1 to use
□ Verwenden Sie einen Computer? Do you use a computer?
2 to spend *(effort, time, work)*
□ Ich habe auf diesen Aufsatz viel Zeit verwendet. I spent a lot of time on this essay.

verwerten (PERFECT **hat verwertet**) VERB [2]
to utilize

verwirren (PERFECT **hat verwirrt**) VERB [84]
1 to confuse
□ Jetzt hast du mich total verwirrt. Now you've completely confused me.
2 to tangle up *(thread)*
□ Die Katze hat die Wolle verwirrt. The cat's tangled the wool up.

verwöhnen (PERFECT **hat verwöhnt**) VERB [84]
to spoil

verwunden (PERFECT **hat verwundet**) VERB [7]
to wound

der/die **Verwundete** (GEN des/der **Verwundeten**, PL die **Verwundeten**) NOUN
injured person
□ Der Arzt versorgt gerade einen Verwundeten. The doctor is just attending to an injured person.

die **Verwundung** NOUN
injury

das **Verzeichnis** (GEN des **Verzeichnisses**, PL die **Verzeichnisse**) NOUN
list
□ Am Ende des Buches ist ein Verzeichnis aller Fachbegriffe. At the end of the book there's a list of all the technical terms.
■ **das Inhaltsverzeichnis** the table of contents

verzeihen (IMPERFECT **verzieh**, PERFECT **hat verziehen**) VERB
to forgive
□ jemandem etwas verzeihen to forgive somebody for something

die **Verzeihung** NOUN
forgiveness
■ **Verzeihung! 1** sorry □ Verzeihung, ich wollte Sie nicht treten. Sorry, I didn't mean to kick you. **2** excuse me □ Verzeihung, aber können Sie mir sagen, wie spät es ist? Excuse me, could you tell me what time it is?

verzichten (PERFECT **hat verzichtet**) VERB [2]
■ **auf etwas verzichten 1** to do without something □ Ich werde heute wohl auf meinen Mittagsschlaf verzichten müssen. It looks like I'll have to do without my afternoon nap today. □ Ich verzichte auf deine Hilfe. I can do without your help. **2** to forego something □ Er hat auf eine Bezahlung verzichtet. He forewent payment. □ Ich verzichte nicht auf meine Rechte. I won't forego my rights.

die **Verzierung** NOUN
decoration

verzögern (PERFECT **hat verzögert**) VERB [88]
to delay

verzollen (PERFECT **hat verzollt**) VERB [84]
to pay duty on
□ Den Whisky müssen Sie verzollen. You have to pay duty on that whisky.
■ **Haben Sie etwas zu verzollen?** Have you anything to declare?

die **Verzögerung** NOUN
delay

verzweifeln (PERFECT **ist verzweifelt**) VERB [7]
to despair

verzweifelt ADJECTIVE
desperate

die **Verzweiflung** NOUN
despair

der **Vetter** (PL die **Vettern**) NOUN
cousin

das **Videogerät** (PL die **Videogeräte**) NOUN
video recorder

der **Videorekorder** (PL die **Videorekorder**) NOUN
video recorder

das **Vieh** NOUN
cattle
□ Das Vieh ist auf der Weide. The cattle are out in the meadow.

viel ADJECTIVE, ADVERB
1 a lot of
□ Sie haben viel Arbeit. They've got a lot of work.
2 much
□ Wir haben nicht viel Geld. We haven't got much money. □ Wir haben nicht viel gelernt. We didn't learn much.
■ **Vielen Dank!** Thank you very much.
3 a lot
□ Wir haben viel gesehen. We saw a lot.
■ **viel zu wenig** far too little
■ **Viel Glück!** Good luck.
■ **so viel** so much □ Sie hat so viel gelernt. She's learned so much. □ Rede nicht so viel. Don't talk so much.
■ **so viel wie** as much as □ Sie hat so viel wie ich bekommen. She got as much as I did.
□ so viel wie möglich as much as possible
■ **wie viel?** how much?
■ **zu viel** too much

viele PL PRONOUN
1 a lot of
□ Sie hat viele Bücher. She's got a lot of books.
2 many
□ Er hat nicht viele Fehler gemacht. He didn't make many mistakes. □ Viele Schüler mögen Chemie nicht. Many pupils don't like chemistry.
■ **Viele wissen das nicht.** A lot of people don't know that.

vieles PRONOUN
many things
□ Vieles war neu für mich. Many things were new to me.

vielleicht ADVERB
perhaps

vielmals ADVERB
■ **Danke vielmals!** Many thanks!

vielseitig ADJECTIVE
many-sided

vielversprechend ADJECTIVE
promising

vier NUMBER
▷ *see also* **die Vier** NOUN
four

die **Vier** NOUN
▷ *see also* **vier** NUMBER
1 four
2 adequate

DID YOU KNOW...?
German marks range from one (**sehr gut**) to six (**ungenügend**).

das **Viereck** (PL die **Vierecke**) NOUN
1 rectangle
2 square

viereckig ADJECTIVE
1 rectangular
2 square

vierte ADJECTIVE
fourth
□ Sie hat erst beim vierten Klingeln abgenommen. She didn't answer until the fourth ring. □ Er kam als Vierter. He was the fourth to arrive.

das **Viertel** (PL die **Viertel**) NOUN
quarter
□ Viertel vor zwei quarter to two

das **Vierteljahr** (PL die **Vierteljahre**) NOUN
quarter

vierteljährlich ADJECTIVE
quarterly

vierteln VERB [88]
1 to divide by four
□ wenn man den Betrag viertelt ... if you divide the amount by four ...
2 to cut into quarters
□ Sie hat den Kuchen geviertelt. She cut the cake into quarters.

die **Viertelstunde** NOUN
quarter of an hour

vierzehn NUMBER
fourteen
■ **in vierzehn Tagen** in a fortnight

vierzig NUMBER
forty

die **Villa** (PL die **Villen**) NOUN
villa

virtuell ADJECTIVE
virtual
□ die virtuelle Realität virtual reality

die **Visen** PL NOUN ▷ *see* **Visum**

die **Visitenkarte** NOUN
business card

das **Visum** (PL die **Visen**) NOUN
visa

das **Vitamin** (PL die **Vitamine**) NOUN
vitamin

der **Vogel** (PL die **Vögel**) NOUN
bird
■ **einen Vogel haben** to have a screw loose
■ **jemandem den Vogel zeigen** to make a rude sign

LANGUAGE TIP Word for word, **jemandem den Vogel zeigen** means 'to show somebody the bird'.

DID YOU KNOW...?
In Germany you make a rude sign at somebody by tapping your forehead to show that you think they are stupid.

die **Vokabel** NOUN
word

das **Vokabular** (PL die **Vokabulare**) NOUN
vocabulary

der **Vokal** (PL die **Vokale**) NOUN
vowel

das Volk (PL die **Völker**) NOUN
1 people
□ das einfache Volk the simple people
2 nation
□ das deutsche Volk the German nation

das **Volksfest** (PL die **Volksfeste**) NOUN
fair

die **Volkshochschule** NOUN
adult education classes

die **Volkswirtschaft** NOUN
economics

voll ADJECTIVE
full
■ **voll und ganz** completely
■ **jemanden für voll nehmen** to take somebody seriously

völlig ADJECTIVE, ADVERB
1 complete
□ bis zur völligen Erschöpfung to the point of complete exhaustion
2 completely
□ Das ist völlig unmöglich. That's completely impossible. □ Ich bin völlig deiner Meinung. I completely agree with you.

volljährig ADJECTIVE
of age
□ volljährig werden to come of age

vollkommen ADJECTIVE
perfect
□ vollkommen richtig perfectly right
■ **vollkommen unmöglich** completely impossible

das **Vollkornbrot** (PL die **Vollkornbrote**) NOUN
wholemeal bread

vollmachen VERB [48]
to fill up

die **Vollmacht** NOUN
power of attorney

der **Vollmond** NOUN
full moon
□ bei Vollmond at full moon

die **Vollpension** NOUN
full board

vollständig ADJECTIVE
complete

volltanken VERB [4]
to fill up *(car)*

vom = von dem

von PREPOSITION

LANGUAGE TIP **von** takes the dative.

1 from
□ von Hamburg nach Kiel from Hamburg to Kiel
■ **von ... bis** from ... to □ von morgens bis abends from morning to night
■ **von ... an** from ... □ Von Mai an wohnen wir in Regensburg. We'll be living in Regensburg from May.
■ **von ... aus** from ... □ Ich habe es vom Fenster aus gesehen. I saw it from my window.
■ **etwas von sich aus tun** to do something of one's own accord □ Du solltest das von dir aus machen. You should do it of your own accord.
■ **von mir aus** I don't mind □ Von mir aus können wir gehen. I don't mind if we go.
■ **Von wo bist du?** Where are you from?
■ **Von wann ist der Brief?** When's the letter from?
2 by
□ Ich bin von einem Hund gebissen worden. I was bitten by a dog. □ ein Gedicht von Schiller a poem by Schiller
■ **von etwas kommen** to be caused by something □ Der Husten kommt vom Rauchen. The cough is caused by smoking.
3 of
□ ein Freund von mir a friend of mine □ Wie nett von dir! How nice of you!
■ **jeweils zwei von zehn** two out of every ten
4 about
□ Er erzählte vom Urlaub. He talked about his holiday.
■ **Von wegen!** No way!

voneinander ADVERB
from each other

vor PREPOSITION, ADVERB

LANGUAGE TIP Use the accusative to express movement or a change of place. Use the dative when there is no change of place.

1 in front of
□ Er stand vor dem Spiegel. He stood in front of the mirror. □ Stell den Stuhl vor das Fenster. Put the chair in front of the window.
2 before
□ Der Artikel steht vor dem Substantiv. The article goes before the noun. □ Vor der Kirche links abbiegen. Turn left just before you get to the church. □ Ich war vor ihm da. I was there before him.
3 ago
□ vor zwei Tagen two days ago □ vor einem Jahr a year ago
■ **Es ist fünf vor vier.** It's five to four.
■ **vor Kurzem** a little while ago
4 with
□ vor Wut with rage □ vor Liebe with love
■ **vor Hunger sterben** to die of hunger
■ **vor lauter Arbeit** because of work
■ **vor allem** above all
■ **vor und zurück** backwards and forwards

vorankommen (IMPERFECT **kam voran**, PERFECT **ist vorangekommen**) VERB [40]
to make progress

voraus ADVERB
ahead

□ Fahr du schon mal voraus. You go on ahead. □ Er war seiner Zeit voraus. He was ahead of his time.
■ **im Voraus** in advance

vorausgehen (IMPERFECT **ging voraus**, PERFECT **ist vorausgegangen**) VERB [29]
1 to go on ahead
□ Geht ihr voraus, ich komme nach. Go on ahead, I'll catch up with you.
2 to precede
□ Der Schlägerei ging ein Streit voraus. The fight was preceded by an argument.

voraussetzen (PERFECT **hat vorausgesetzt**) VERB [15]
to assume
□ Ich setze voraus, dass du auch kommst. I assume that you're coming too.
■ **vorausgesetzt, dass ...** provided that ...

die **Voraussetzung** NOUN
prerequisite
■ **unter der Voraussetzung, dass ...** provided that ...

voraussichtlich ADVERB
probably

vorbei ADVERB
past
□ Fahren Sie am Rathaus vorbei. Drive past the town hall.
■ **Ich sehe noch kurz bei ihr vorbei.** I'll just pop round to her place.
■ **vorbei sein** to be over □ Damit ist es nun vorbei. That's all over now.

vorbeigehen (IMPERFECT **ging vorbei**, PERFECT **ist vorbeigegangen**) VERB [29]
to go past
□ Er ging vorbei, ohne zu grüßen. He went past without saying hello.
■ **an etwas vorbeigehen** to go past something □ Sie ist am Schaufenster vorbeigegangen, ohne es zu beachten. She went past the shop window without looking at it.
■ **bei jemandem vorbeigehen** to call in at somebody's □ Kannst du beim Bäcker vorbeigehen? Can you call in at the baker's? □ Ich gehe noch schnell bei meiner Freundin vorbei. I'm just going to call in at my girlfriend's.

vorbeikommen (IMPERFECT **kam vorbei**, PERFECT **ist vorbeigekommen**) VERB [40]
■ **bei jemandem vorbeikommen** to drop in on somebody

vorbereiten (PERFECT **hat vorbereitet**) VERB [2]
to prepare

die **Vorbereitung** NOUN
preparation

vorbeugen (PERFECT **hat vorgebeugt**) VERB [4]
■ **sich vorbeugen** to lean forward
■ **einer Sache vorbeugen** to prevent something □ um einer Erkältung vorzubeugen to prevent a cold

die **Vorbeugung** NOUN
prevention
□ zur Vorbeugung gegen for the prevention of

das **Vorbild** (PL die **Vorbilder**) NOUN
role model
□ Er ist mein Vorbild. He's my role model.
■ **sich jemanden zum Vorbild nehmen** to follow somebody's example □ Du solltest dir deinen Bruder zum Vorbild nehmen. You ought to follow your brother's example.

vordere ADJECTIVE
front
□ Das Haus hat einen vorderen und einen hinteren Eingang. The house has a front door and a back door.

die **Vorderseite** NOUN
front

vorderste ADJECTIVE
front
□ die vorderste Reihe the front row

voreilig ADJECTIVE
hasty
□ Du solltest nicht voreilig urteilen. You shouldn't make hasty judgements.

voreingenommen ADJECTIVE
biased

vorenthalten (PRESENT **enthält vor**, IMPERFECT **enthielt vor**, PERFECT **hat vorenthalten**) VERB [33]
■ **jemandem etwas vorenthalten** to withhold something from somebody

vorerst ADVERB
for the moment

die **Vorfahrt** NOUN
right of way
■ **Vorfahrt achten!** Give way!

der **Vorfall** (PL die **Vorfälle**) NOUN
incident

vorführen (PERFECT **hat vorgeführt**) VERB [4]
to show

der **Vorgänger** (PL die **Vorgänger**) NOUN
predecessor

das **Vorgehen** NOUN
▷ *see also* **vorgehen** VERB
action

vorgehen (IMPERFECT **ging vor**, PERFECT **ist vorgegangen**) VERB [29]
▷ *see also* **das Vorgehen** NOUN
1 to go on ahead
□ Geht ihr vor, ich komme nach. Go on ahead, I'll catch up.
2 to go up to
□ Sie ging ans Rednerpult vor. She went up to the lectern.
3 to proceed
□ Ich weiß nicht, wie wir vorgehen sollen. I don't know how we should proceed.
■ **Die Uhr geht vor.** The clock is fast.
■ **Was geht hier vor?** What's going on here?

vorgestern ADVERB
the day before yesterday

vorhaben (PRESENT **hat vor**, IMPERFECT **hatte vor**, PERFECT **hat vorgehabt**) VERB [32]
to intend
□ Wir haben vor, nach Italien zu fahren. We intend to go to Italy. □ Was hast du vor? What do you intend to do?
■ **Ich habe heute viel vor.** I've got a lot planned for today.
■ **Hast du schon was vor?** Have you got anything on?
■ **Was hast du heute Abend vor?** What are you doing this evening?

der **Vorhang** (PL die **Vorhänge**) NOUN
curtain

vorher ADVERB
beforehand

die **Vorhersage** NOUN
forecast

vorhersehbar ADJECTIVE
predictable

vorhersehen (PRESENT **sieht vorher**, IMPERFECT **sah vorher**, PERFECT **hat vorhergesehen**) VERB [64]
to foresee

vorhin ADVERB
just now

vorig ADJECTIVE
previous

vorkommen (IMPERFECT **kam vor**, PERFECT **ist vorgekommen**) VERB [40]
1 to happen
□ So ein Fehler sollte nicht vorkommen. A mistake like that shouldn't happen.
■ **Es kommt vor, dass ich früh ins Bett gehe.** I sometimes go to bed early.
■ **jemandem vorkommen** to seem to somebody □ Er kam mir traurig vor. He seemed sad to me. □ Das kommt mir komisch vor. That seems funny to me.
■ **sich dumm vorkommen** to feel stupid
□ Ich kam mir dumm vor. I felt stupid.
2 to come out
□ Komm endlich hinter dem Schrank vor. Come out from behind that cupboard, will you?

vorläufig ADJECTIVE
provisional

vorlaut ADJECTIVE
impertinent

vorlesen (PRESENT **liest vor**, IMPERFECT **las vor**, PERFECT **hat vorgelesen**) VERB [45]
to read out

vorletzte ADJECTIVE
last but one
□ Ich wohne im vorletzten Haus. My house is the last but one.

die **Vorliebe** NOUN
partiality
■ **eine Vorliebe für etwas haben** to be partial to something □ Sie hat eine Vorliebe für Krimis. She's partial to detective stories.

der **Vormittag** (PL die **Vormittage**) NOUN
morning
□ am Vormittag in the morning

vormittags ADVERB
in the morning

vorn ADVERB
in front
□ Der deutsche Schwimmer liegt vorn. The German swimmer is in front.
■ **Er stand ganz vorn in der Schlange.** He was right at the front of the queue.
■ **nach vorn** to the front
■ **von vorn anfangen** to start at the beginning
■ **wieder von vorn anfangen** to start again from the beginning

der **Vorname** (GEN des **Vornamens**, PL die **Vornamen**) NOUN
first name

vornehm ADJECTIVE
1 distinguished
□ eine vornehme Familie a distinguished family
2 refined
□ sich vornehm ausdrücken to use refined language □ vornehme Manieren refined manners
3 posh
□ ein vornehmes Hotel a posh hotel
4 elegant
□ eine vornehme Dame an elegant lady
■ **Tu nicht so vornehm!** Don't put on airs and graces.

vornehmen (PRESENT **nimmt vor**, IMPERFECT **nahm vor**, PERFECT **hat vorgenommen**) VERB [52]
■ **sich etwas vornehmen** to resolve to do something □ Ich habe mir vorgenommen, das nie wieder zu tun. I've resolved never to do that again.

vornherein ADVERB
■ **von vornherein** from the start

der **Vorort** (PL die **Vororte**) NOUN
suburb

der **Vorrat** (PL die **Vorräte**) NOUN
stock
□ solange der Vorrat reicht while stocks last

vorrätig ADJECTIVE
in stock

der **Vorschlag** (PL die **Vorschläge**) NOUN
suggestion

vorschlagen (PRESENT **schlägt vor**, IMPERFECT **schlug vor**, PERFECT **hat vorgeschlagen**) VERB [59]
to suggest

die **Vorschrift** NOUN
rule

□ Das ist gegen die Vorschriften. It's against the rules.

die **Vorsicht** NOUN
caution
■ **Vorsicht!** 1 Look out! 2 Caution!
■ **Vorsicht, Stufe!** Mind the step!

vorsichtig ADJECTIVE
careful

die **Vorspeise** NOUN
starter

der **Vorsprung** (PL die **Vorsprünge**) NOUN
lead
□ Wir haben einen Vorsprung vor unseren Konkurrenten gewonnen. We have gained a lead over our competitors.

die **Vorstadt** (PL die **Vorstädte**) NOUN
suburbs

vorstellbar ADJECTIVE
conceivable

vorstellen (PERFECT **hat vorgestellt**) VERB [4]
■ **sich etwas vorstellen** to imagine something □ Stell dir mal vor, wir wären jetzt im Urlaub. Imagine we were on holiday right now.
■ **jemanden jemandem vorstellen** to introduce somebody to somebody
□ Darf ich Ihnen meinen Mann vorstellen? May I introduce my husband to you?

die **Vorstellung** NOUN
1 performance
□ Die Vorstellung endet gegen zehn Uhr. The performance ends at about ten.
2 idea
□ Hast du eine Vorstellung, wie wir das machen sollen? Have you got any idea how we should do that? □ Du hast ja keine Vorstellung, wie weh das tut. You've no idea how much it hurts.

das **Vorstellungsgespräch** (PL die **Vorstellungsgespräche**) NOUN
interview *(for job)*

der **Vorteil** (PL die **Vorteile**) NOUN
advantage
■ **im Vorteil sein** to have the advantage

der **Vortrag** (PL die **Vorträge**) NOUN
talk
□ einen Vortrag halten to give a talk

vorüber ADVERB
over

vorübergehend ADJECTIVE
1 passing
□ eine vorübergehende Phase a passing phase
2 temporarily
□ Das Geschäft ist vorübergehend geschlossen. The shop's temporarily closed.

das **Vorurteil** (PL die **Vorurteile**) NOUN
prejudice

der **Vorverkauf** (PL die **Vorverkäufe**) NOUN
advance booking

die **Vorwahl** NOUN
dialling code
□ Was ist die Vorwahl von Liverpool? What's the dialling code for Liverpool?

der **Vorwand** (PL die **Vorwände**) NOUN
pretext

vorwärts ADVERB
forward

vorwerfen (PRESENT **wirft vor**, IMPERFECT **warf vor**, PERFECT **hat vorgeworfen**) VERB [92]
■ **jemandem etwas vorwerfen** to accuse somebody of something □ Er hat mir mangelndes Interesse vorgeworfen. He accused me of lack of interest.
■ **sich nichts vorzuwerfen haben** to have nothing to reproach oneself for □ Ich habe mir nichts vorzuwerfen. I've nothing to reproach myself for.

vorwiegend ADVERB
predominantly

das **Vorwort** (PL die **Vorworte**) NOUN
preface

der **Vorwurf** (PL die **Vorwürfe**) NOUN
reproach
■ **jemandem Vorwürfe machen** to reproach somebody
■ **sich Vorwürfe machen** to reproach oneself

vorzeigen (PERFECT **hat vorgezeigt**) VERB [4]
to show

vorziehen (IMPERFECT **zog vor**, PERFECT **hat vorgezogen**) VERB [96]
1 to prefer
□ Was ziehst du vor: Kaffee oder Tee? Do you prefer coffee or tea?
2 to pull forward
□ Du solltest den Stuhl etwas vorziehen. You should pull your chair forward a bit.

vulgär ADJECTIVE
vulgar
□ sich vulgär ausdrücken to use vulgar language

der **Vulkan** (PL die **Vulkane**) NOUN
volcano

die **Waage** NOUN

1 scales

□ Die Waage stimmt nicht genau. The scales aren't accurate.

2 Libra

□ Ulla ist Waage. Ulla's Libra.

waagerecht ADJECTIVE

horizontal

wach ADJECTIVE

■ **wach sein** to be awake

die **Wache** NOUN

guard

□ Wache stehen to stand guard

das **Wachs** (GEN des **Wachses**, PL die **Wachse**) NOUN

wax

wachsen (PRESENT **wächst**, IMPERFECT **wuchs**, PERFECT **ist gewachsen**) VERB [87]

to grow

das **Wachstum** NOUN

growth

wackelig ADJECTIVE

wobbly

die **Wade** NOUN

calf

□ Ich habe mich an der Wade verletzt. I've hurt my calf.

die **Waffe** NOUN

weapon

die **Waffel** NOUN

1 waffle

□ Heute gab's zum Mittagessen Waffeln. We had waffles for lunch today.

2 wafer

□ Willst du eine Waffel zu deinem Eis? Would you like a wafer with your ice?

der **Wagen** (PL die **Wagen**) NOUN

▷ *see also* **wagen** VERB

1 car

□ Seid ihr mit dem Wagen da? Did you come by car?

2 carriage

□ ein Eisenbahnwagen a railway carriage

■ **ein Pferdewagen** a cart

wagen VERB [38]

▷ *see also* **der Wagen** NOUN

■ **es wagen, etwas zu tun** to dare to do something

■ **sich irgendwohin wagen** to dare to go somewhere

der **Wagenheber** (PL die **Wagenheber**) NOUN

jack *(for car)*

die **Wahl** (PL die **Wahlen**) NOUN

1 choice

□ Du hast die Wahl. It's your choice.

2 election

□ Wann sind die nächsten Wahlen? When are the next elections?

wählen VERB [38]

1 to choose

□ Du kannst wählen, entweder das rote oder das grüne. You can choose, either the red one or the green one.

2 to vote

□ Wer wurde zum Klassensprecher gewählt? Who was voted class representative?

■ **Wählt Kowalski!** Vote for Kowalski.

■ **Nächsten Sonntag wird gewählt.** There are elections next Sunday.

3 to dial

□ Sie wählte die Nummer ihrer Freundin. She dialled her friend's number.

wählerisch ADJECTIVE

particular

das **Wahlfach** (PL die **Wahlfächer**) NOUN

optional subject

der **Wahnsinn** NOUN

madness

wahnsinnig ADJECTIVE, ADVERB

1 mad

□ Wer hatte denn diese wahnsinnige Idee? Whose mad idea was it?

2 incredibly

□ Das Kleid war wahnsinnig schön. The dress was incredibly pretty. □ Das tut wahnsinnig weh. It's incredibly sore.

wahr ADJECTIVE

true

□ eine wahre Geschichte a true story

■ **Sie ist verheiratet, nicht wahr?** She's married, isn't she?

während PREPOSITION, CONJUNCTION

LANGUAGE TIP The preposition **während** takes the genitive.

1 during

□ Was hast du während der Ferien gemacht? What did you do during the holidays?

2 while

□ Sie sah fern, während sie ihre Hausaufgaben machte. She was watching TV while she was doing her homework.

3 whereas

□ Er ist ganz nett, während seine Frau unhöflich ist. He's quite nice, whereas his wife's impolite.

die **Wahrheit** NOUN
truth

wahrnehmen (PRESENT **nimmt wahr**, IMPERFECT **nahm wahr**, PERFECT **hat wahrgenommen**) VERB [52]
to perceive

der **Wahrsager** (PL die **Wahrsager**) NOUN
fortune teller

die **Wahrsagerin** NOUN
fortune teller

wahrscheinlich ADJECTIVE, ADVERB

1 likely

□ Das ist nicht sehr wahrscheinlich. That's not very likely.

2 probably

□ Er kommt wahrscheinlich nicht. He's probably not coming.

die **Währung** NOUN
currency

der **Wal** (PL die **Wale**) NOUN
whale

der **Wald** (PL die **Wälder**) NOUN

1 wood

□ Hinter unserem Haus ist ein Wald. There's a wood behind our house.

2 forest

□ die Wälder Kanadas the forests of Canada

Wales NEUT NOUN
Wales

■ **aus Wales** from Wales

■ **in Wales** in Wales

■ **nach Wales** to Wales

der **Walfisch** (PL die **Walfische**) NOUN
whale

der **Waliser** (PL die **Waliser**) NOUN
Welshman

■ **Er ist Waliser.** He's Welsh.

■ **die Waliser** the Welsh

die **Waliserin** NOUN
Welshwoman

■ **Sie ist Waliserin.** She's Welsh.

walisisch ADJECTIVE
Welsh

die **Walnuss** (PL die **Walnüsse**) NOUN
walnut

die **Wand** (PL die **Wände**) NOUN
wall

der **Wanderer** (PL die **Wanderer**) NOUN
rambler

die **Wanderin** NOUN
rambler

wandern (PERFECT **ist gewandert**) VERB [88]
to hike

□ Wir sind am Wochenende gewandert. We went hiking at the weekend.

die **Wanderung** NOUN
hike

der **Wandschrank** (PL die **Wandschränke**) NOUN
wall cupboard

wann ADVERB
when

war VERB ▷ *see* **sein**

die **Ware** NOUN
goods

das **Warenhaus** (GEN des **Warenhauses**, PL die **Warenhäuser**) NOUN
department store

warf VERB ▷ *see* **werfen**

warm ADJECTIVE
warm

□ Heute ist es wärmer als gestern. It's warmer today than yesterday.

■ **ein warmes Essen** a hot meal

■ **Mir ist warm.** I'm warm.

die **Wärme** NOUN
warmth

die **Wärmflasche** NOUN
hot-water bottle

warnen VERB [38]
to warn

□ jemanden vor etwas warnen to warn somebody of something

die **Warnung** NOUN
warning

warten VERB [2]
to wait

□ Ich habe eine Stunde gewartet. I waited an hour.

■ **warten auf** to wait for □ Ich warte draußen auf dich. I'll wait outside for you.

■ **auf sich warten lassen** to take a long time

der **Wartesaal** (PL die **Wartesäle**) NOUN
waiting room *(in station)*

das **Wartezimmer** (PL die **Wartezimmer**) NOUN
waiting room

warum ADVERB
why

was PRONOUN

1 what

□ Was hast du gesagt? What did you say?

□ Was für eine Enttäuschung! What a disappointment!

■ **Was für ein ...** What kind of ... □ Was für ein Fahrrad hast du? What kind of bike do you have?

2 something

□ Heute gibt's was Leckeres zum Mittagessen. We're having something delicious for lunch today.

waschbar ADJECTIVE
washable

das **Waschbecken** (PL die **Waschbecken**) NOUN
washbasin

die **Wäsche** NOUN
washing
□ Wäsche waschen to do the washing
■ **die Bettwäsche** bed linen
■ **die Unterwäsche** underwear

die **Wäscheklammer** NOUN
clothes peg

die **Wäscheleine** NOUN
washing line

waschen (PRESENT **wäscht**, IMPERFECT **wusch**, PERFECT **hat gewaschen**) VERB [89]
to wash
■ **sich waschen** to have a wash
■ **sich die Hände waschen** to wash one's hands □ Ich muss mir die Hände waschen. I'll have to wash my hands.

die **Waschmaschine** NOUN
washing machine

das **Waschmittel** (PL die **Waschmittel**) NOUN
detergent

das **Waschpulver** (PL die **Waschpulver**) NOUN
washing powder

der **Waschsalon** (PL die **Waschsalons**) NOUN
launderette

das **Wasser** (PL die **Wasser** *or* **Wässer**) NOUN
water

wasserdicht ADJECTIVE
waterproof

der **Wasserfall** (PL die **Wasserfälle**) NOUN
waterfall

die **Wasserfarbe** NOUN
watercolour

der **Wasserhahn** (PL die **Wasserhähne**) NOUN
tap

der **Wassermann** NOUN
Aquarius
□ Gerda ist Wassermann. Gerda's Aquarius.

die **Wassermelone** NOUN
water melon

der **Wasserstoff** NOUN
hydrogen

die **Watte** NOUN
cotton wool

das **WC** (PL die **WCs**) NOUN
WC

das **Web-Magazin** (PL die **Web-Magazine**) NOUN
webzine

die **Webseite** NOUN
web page

der **Wechsel** (GEN (PL die **Wechsel**) NOUN
change

der **Wechselkurs** (GEN des **Wechselkurses**, PL die **Wechselkurse**) NOUN
rate of exchange

wechseln VERB [34]
1 to change
□ Wir mussten einen Reifen wechseln. We had to change a tyre. □ Wie viel Geld wechselst du? How much money are you changing?
■ **Blicke wechseln** to exchange glances
2 to have change
□ Können Sie wechseln? Do you have any change? □ Kannst du mir zwanzig Euro in Münzen wechseln? Have you got change for twenty euros?

die **Wechselstube** NOUN
bureau de change

wecken VERB [38]
to wake up

der **Wecker** (PL die **Wecker**) NOUN
alarm clock

weder CONJUNCTION
neither
■ **weder ... noch ...** neither ... nor ...

der **Weg** (PL die **Wege**) NOUN
▷ *see also* **weg** ADVERB
1 way
□ Es gibt sicher einen Weg, das zu reparieren. There must be a way to repair it.
2 path
□ Ein Weg führte zur Kapelle hinauf. A path led up to the chapel.
3 route
□ Welchen Weg habt ihr genommen? Which route did you take?
■ **sich auf den Weg machen** to be on one's way
■ **jemandem aus dem Weg gehen** to keep out of somebody's way

weg ADVERB
▷ *see also* **der Weg** NOUN
away
□ Geh weg! Go away!
■ **Weg da!** Out of the way!
■ **Finger weg!** Hands off!
■ **Er war schon weg.** He'd already left.

wegen PREPOSITION
LANGUAGE TIP The preposition **wegen** takes the dative or sometimes the genitive.
because of
□ Wegen dir bin ich zu spät gekommen. Because of you I arrived late. □ Wegen des schlechten Wetters wurde die Veranstaltung abgesagt. The event was cancelled because of the bad weather.

weggehen (IMPERFECT **ging weg**, PERFECT **ist weggegangen**) VERB [29]
to go away

weglassen (PRESENT **lässt weg**, IMPERFECT **ließ weg**, PERFECT **hat weggelassen**) VERB [42]
to leave out

German-English

weglaufen (PRESENT **läuft weg**, IMPERFECT **lief weg**, PERFECT **ist weggelaufen**) VERB [43]
to run away

weglegen (PERFECT **hat weggelegt**) VERB [4]
to put aside

wegmachen (PERFECT **hat weggemacht**) VERB [48]
to get rid of
□ einen Fleck wegmachen to get rid of a stain

wegmüssen (PRESENT **muss weg**, IMPERFECT **musste weg**, PERFECT **hat weggemusst** *or* **wegmüssen**) VERB [51]
to have to go

wegnehmen (PRESENT **nimmt weg**, IMPERFECT **nahm weg**, PERFECT **hat weggenommen**) VERB [52]
to take away

wegtun (IMPERFECT **tat weg**, PERFECT **hat weggetan**) VERB [81]
to put away

der **Wegweiser** (PL die **Wegweiser**) NOUN
signpost

wegwerfen (PRESENT **wirft weg**, IMPERFECT **warf weg**, PERFECT **hat weggeworfen**) VERB [92]
to throw away

weh ADJECTIVE ▷ *see* **wehtun**

der **Wehrdienst** (PL die **Wehrdienste**) NOUN
military service

DID YOU KNOW...?
Young men are generally conscripted into the **Wehrdienst** when they leave school. The basic period of military service is 9 months.

der **Wehrdienstverweigerer** (PL die **Wehrdienstverweigerer**) NOUN
conscientious objector

sich **wehren** VERB [38]
to defend oneself

die **Wehrpflicht** NOUN
compulsory military service

wehtun (IMPERFECT **tat weh**, PERFECT **hat wehgetan**) VERB [81]
1 to hurt
□ Mein Bein tut weh. My leg hurts.
2 to be sore
□ Mein Hals tut weh. My throat's sore.
■ **sich wehtun** to hurt oneself □ Hast du dir wehgetan? Have you hurt yourself?
■ **jemandem wehtun** to hurt somebody
□ Ich möchte dir nicht wehtun, aber das war nicht sehr intelligent. I don't want to hurt you, but that really wasn't very clever.

das **Weibchen** (PL die **Weibchen**) NOUN
female

weiblich ADJECTIVE
feminine
□ ein weibliches Substantiv a feminine noun

weich ADJECTIVE
soft
□ ein weiches Bett a soft bed

sich **weigern** VERB [88]
to refuse

das **Weihnachten** (GEN des **Weihnachten**) NOUN
Christmas
□ an Weihnachten at Christmas
■ **Frohe Weihnachten!** Merry Christmas.

die **Weihnachtsferien** PL NOUN
Christmas holidays

das **Weihnachtslied** (PL die **Weihnachtslieder**) NOUN
Christmas carol

der **Weihnachtsmann** (PL die **Weihnachtsmänner**) NOUN
Father Christmas

der **Weihnachtsmarkt** (PL die **Weihnachtsmärkte**) NOUN
Christmas fair

der **Weihnachtstag** (PL die **Weihnachtstage**) NOUN
■ **der erste Weihnachtstag** Christmas Day

LANGUAGE TIP Word for word, **der erste Weihnachtstag** means 'the first day of Christmas'.

■ **der zweite Weihnachtstag** Boxing Day

LANGUAGE TIP Word for word, **der zweite Weihnachtstag** means 'the second day of Christmas'.

weil CONJUNCTION
because

die **Weile** NOUN
while
□ Es wird eine Weile dauern. It'll take a while.

der **Wein** (PL die **Weine**) NOUN
wine

der **Weinberg** (PL die **Weinberge**) NOUN
vineyard

LANGUAGE TIP Word for word, **Weinberg** means 'wine mountain'.

der **Weinbrand** (PL die **Weinbrände**) NOUN
brandy

weinen VERB [38]
to cry
■ **Das ist zum Weinen.** It's enough to make you cry.

das **Weinglas** (GEN des **Weinglases**, PL die **Weingläser**) NOUN
wine glass

die **Weinkarte** NOUN
wine list

der **Weinkeller** (PL die **Weinkeller**) NOUN
1 wine cellar
2 wine bar

die **Weinprobe** NOUN
wine tasting

die **Weinstube** NOUN
wine bar

die **Weintraube** NOUN
grape

W

die **Weise** NOUN
way
□ Die Art und Weise, wie er uns behandelt hat. The way he treated us.
■ **auf diese Weise** in this way

die **Weisheit** NOUN
wisdom

der **Weisheitszahn** (PL die **Weisheitszähne**) NOUN
wisdom tooth

weiß VERB ▷ *see* **wissen**

weiß ADJECTIVE
white

das **Weißbrot** (PL die **Weißbrote**) NOUN
white bread

der **Weißwein** (PL die **Weißweine**) NOUN
white wine

weit ADJECTIVE, ADVERB
1 long
□ Das ist eine weite Reise. That's a long journey. □ Das war sein weitester Wurf. That was his longest throw.
2 far
□ Wie weit ist es ...? How far is it ...?
□ Nach Berlin ist es weiter als nach München. It's further to Berlin than to Munich.
□ so weit wie möglich as far as possible
□ Das geht zu weit. That's going too far.
3 baggy
□ Sie hatte einen weiten Pulli an. She was wearing a baggy pullover.
■ **ein weiter Begriff** a broad idea
■ **so weit sein** to be ready □ Ich bin so weit. I'm ready.
■ **Ich bin so weit zufrieden.** By and large I'm quite satisfied.

weitaus ADVERB
by far

weiter ADJECTIVE, ADVERB
further
□ Wenn du noch weitere Fragen hast ... If you have any further questions ... □ Alles Weitere besprechen wir morgen. We can discuss any further details tomorrow.
■ **ohne weiteres** just like that □ Ich kann doch nicht so ohne weiteres gehen. I can't go just like that.
■ **weiter nichts** nothing else
■ **weiter niemand** nobody else

sich **weiterbilden** (PERFECT **hat sich weitergebildet**) VERB [4]
to continue one's education

die **Weiterbildung** NOUN
further education

die **Weiterfahrt** NOUN
continuation of the journey

weitergehen (IMPERFECT **ging weiter**, PERFECT **ist weitergegangen**) VERB [29]
to go on

weiterhin ADVERB
■ **etwas weiterhin tun** to go on doing something

weiterleiten (PERFECT **hat weitergeleitet**) VERB [4]
to pass on

weitermachen (PERFECT **hat weitergemacht**) VERB [48]
to continue

der **Weitsprung** NOUN
long jump

der **Weizen** NOUN
wheat

welche PRONOUN
1 which
□ Welcher Mann? Which man? □ Welche Frau? Which woman? □ Welches Mädchen? Which girl? □ Welcher von beiden? Which of the two? □ Welchen hast du genommen? Which one did you take?
2 what
□ Welch eine Überraschung! What a surprise!
■ **Welche Freude!** What joy!
3 some
□ Ich habe Kirschen, willst du welche? I have some cherries, would you like some?
□ Ich habe welche. I have some.
4 any
□ Ich brauche Briefmarken, hast du welche? I need stamps, have you got any?
□ Ich brauche Kleingeld, hast du welches? I need change, have you got any?

die **Welle** NOUN
wave

die **Wellenlänge** NOUN
wavelength

der **Wellensittich** (PL die **Wellensittiche**) NOUN
budgie

die **Welt** NOUN
world

das **Weltall** NOUN
universe

weltberühmt ADJECTIVE
world-famous

der **Weltkrieg** (PL die **Weltkriege**) NOUN
world war

der **Weltmeister** (PL die **Weltmeister**) NOUN
world champion

der **Weltraum** NOUN
space

wem PRONOUN
LANGUAGE TIP **wem** is the dative of **wer**.
to whom
■ **Mit wem bist du gekommen?** Who did you come with?

wen PRONOUN
LANGUAGE TIP **wen** is the accusative of **wer**.
whom

■ **Wen hast du gesehen?** Who did you see?

wenig ADJECTIVE, ADVERB
little
■ **so wenig wie** as little as □ Er macht so wenig wie möglich. He does as little as possible. □ Ich habe so wenig Geld wie du. I have as little money as you.
■ **zu wenig** too little

wenige PL PRONOUN
few
□ Das wissen nur wenige. Only a few people know that.

weniger ADJECTIVE, ADVERB
1 less
□ Ich habe weniger Geld als du. I have less money than you.
2 fewer
□ Ich habe weniger Fehler gemacht. I've made fewer mistakes.
3 minus
□ Zehn weniger drei ist sieben. Ten minus three is seven.

wenigste ADJECTIVE
least
□ Das ist das wenigste, was ich tun kann. That's the least I can do.
■ **am wenigsten** the least □ Die Clowns haben mir am wenigsten gefallen. I liked the clowns the least.

wenigstens ADVERB
at least

wenn CONJUNCTION
1 if
□ Wenn er anruft, sag mir Bescheid. If he calls, tell me.
■ **selbst wenn ...** even if ...
■ **wenn ich doch ...** if only I ...
2 when
□ Wenn ich nach Hause komme, dusche ich erst mal. When I get home, the first thing I'm going to do is have a shower.
■ **immer wenn** whenever □ Immer wenn ich frage, lacht er nur. Whenever I ask, he just laughs.

wer PRONOUN
who
LANGUAGE TIP Be careful! **wer** does not mean **where**.

die **Werbeagentur** NOUN
advertising agency

das **Werbefernsehen** NOUN
commercial television

werben (PRESENT **wirbt**, IMPERFECT **warb**, PERFECT **hat geworben**) VERB [90]
to advertise
□ Im Fernsehen wird zu viel geworben. There's too much advertising on TV.
■ **Mitglieder werben** to recruit members

der **Werbespot** (PL die **Werbespots**) NOUN
commercial

die **Werbung** NOUN
1 advert
□ Hast du die Werbung für den neuen Schokoriegel gesehen? Have you seen the advert for the new chocolate bar? □ Wenn Werbung kommt, schalte ich um. I switch over when the adverts come on.
2 advertising
□ Er arbeitet in der Werbung. He works in advertising.
■ **für etwas Werbung machen** to advertise something

werden (PRESENT **wird**, IMPERFECT **wurde**, PERFECT **ist geworden** *or* **worden**) VERB [91]
1 to become
□ Sie ist Lehrerin geworden. She became a teacher. □ Er ist reich geworden. He became rich. □ Was ist aus ihm geworden? What became of him?
■ **Erster werden** to come first
■ **Was willst du einmal werden?** What do you want to be?
■ **rot werden** to turn red
■ **Es ist gut geworden.** It turned out well.
■ **Die Fotos sind gut geworden.** The photos have come out well.
■ **Es ist nichts geworden.** It came to nothing.
■ **Es wird Tag.** It's getting light.
■ **Es wird Nacht.** It's getting dark.
■ **Mir wird kalt.** I'm getting cold.
■ **Mir wird schlecht.** I feel sick.
■ **Das muss anders werden.** That'll have to change.
2 will
LANGUAGE TIP **werden** is used to form the future tense.
□ Er wird es tun. He'll do it. □ Er wird das nicht tun. He won't do it. □ Sie wird in der Küche sein. She'll be in the kitchen.
■ **Es wird gleich regnen.** It's going to rain.
3 to be
LANGUAGE TIP **werden** is used to form the passive.
□ gebraucht werden to be needed □ Er ist erschossen worden. He's been shot.
□ Mir wurde gesagt, dass ... I was told that ...
LANGUAGE TIP **werden** is used to form the conditional tense.
■ **Ich würde ...** I would ...
■ **Er würde gern ...** He'd like to ...
■ **Ich würde lieber ...** I'd rather ...

werfen (PRESENT **wirft**, IMPERFECT **warf**, PERFECT **hat geworfen**) VERB [92]
to throw

das **Werken** NOUN
handicrafts

die **Werkstatt** (PL die **Werkstätten**) NOUN
1 workshop
□ eine Werkstatt für Behinderte a workshop for the handicapped

2 garage
□ Das Auto ist in der Werkstatt. The car's in the garage.

der **Werktag** (PL die **Werktage**) NOUN
working day

werktags ADVERB
on working days

das **Werkzeug** (PL die **Werkzeuge**) NOUN
tool

der **Wert** (PL die **Werte**) NOUN
▷ *see also* **wert** ADJECTIVE
value
■ **Wert legen auf** to attach importance to
□ Sie legt großen Wert auf rechtzeitiges Erscheinen. She attaches great importance to punctuality.
■ **Es hat doch keinen Wert.** There's no point.

wert ADJECTIVE
▷ *see also* **der Wert** NOUN
worth
□ Wie viel ist das Bild wert? How much is that picture worth? □ Das ist nichts wert. It's not worth anything. □ Das ist viel wert. It's worth a lot.

wertlos ADJECTIVE
worthless

wertvoll ADJECTIVE
valuable

das **Wesen** (PL die **Wesen**) NOUN
manner
□ Er hat ein freundliches Wesen. He has a friendly manner.

wesentlich ADJECTIVE
significant

weshalb ADVERB
why

die **Wespe** NOUN
wasp

wessen PRONOUN
LANGUAGE TIP **wessen** is the genitive of **wer**.
whose

die **Weste** NOUN
waistcoat

der **Westen** NOUN
west

westlich ADJECTIVE, PREPOSITION, ADVERB
westerly
□ in westlicher Richtung in a westerly direction
■ **westlich einer Sache** to the west of something □ Das Kraftwerk liegt westlich der Stadt. The power station's to the west of the city.
■ **westlich von** west of □ Essen liegt westlich von Bochum. Essen's west of Bochum.

weswegen ADVERB
why

der **Wettbewerb** (PL die **Wettbewerbe**) NOUN
competition

die **Wette** NOUN
bet

wetten VERB [2]
to bet
□ Ich wette, du fällst durchs Examen. I bet you fail the exam.

das **Wetter** NOUN
weather

der **Wetterbericht** (PL die **Wetterberichte**) NOUN
weather report

die **Wetterlage** (PL die **Wetterlagen**) NOUN
weather situation

die **Wettervorhersage** NOUN
weather forecast

der **Wettkampf** (PL die **Wettkämpfe**) NOUN
contest

der **Wettlauf** (PL die **Wettläufe**) NOUN
race

wichtig ADJECTIVE
important

der **Widder** (PL die **Widder**) NOUN
1 ram
2 Aries
□ Horst ist Widder. Horst's Aries.

widerlich ADJECTIVE
disgusting

widerspenstig ADJECTIVE
wilful

widersprechen (PRESENT **widerspricht**, IMPERFECT **widersprach**, PERFECT **hat widersprochen**) VERB [70]
■ **jemandem widersprechen** to contradict somebody

der **Widerspruch** (PL die **Widersprüche**) NOUN
contradiction

der **Widerstand** (PL die **Widerstände**) NOUN
resistance

widerwillig ADJECTIVE
unwilling

wie ADVERB
1 how
□ Wie groß? How big? □ Wie schnell? How fast? □ Wie schön! How lovely! □ Und wie! And how! □ Wie wär's? How about it? □ Wie geht's dir? How are you?
■ **Wie bitte? 1** Pardon? □ Wie bitte, was haben Sie gesagt? Pardon, what did you say? **2** What? □ Wie bitte, du willst zweitausend Euro von mir haben? What? You want me to give you two thousand euros?
■ **so schön wie ...** as beautiful as ...
■ **wie ich schon sagte** as I said
2 like
□ wie du like you □ singen wie ein ... to sing like a ...
■ **wie zum Beispiel** such as

wieder ADVERB
again
□ wieder da sein to be back again □ Gehst du schon wieder? Are you off again?
■ **wieder ein ...** another ... □ wenn du wieder einen Geldbeutel findest ... if you find another purse ...

wiederaufbereiten (PERFECT **hat wiederaufbereitet**) VERB [2]
to recycle

wiederbekommen (IMPERFECT **bekam wieder**, PERFECT **hat wiederbekommen**) VERB [40]
to get back

wiedererkennen (IMPERFECT **erkannte wieder**, PERFECT **hat wiedererkannt**) VERB [39]
to recognize

wiederholen (PERFECT **hat wiederholt**) VERB [4]
to repeat

die **Wiederholung** NOUN
1 repetition
□ Es darf keine Wiederholung dieses Vorfalls geben. There must be no repetition of this incident.
2 repeat
□ Im Fernsehen kommen zu viele Wiederholungen. There are too many repeats on TV.

das **Wiederhören** NOUN
■ **Auf Wiederhören!** Goodbye! *(on telephone, radio)*

wiedersehen (PRESENT **sieht wieder**, IMPERFECT **sah wieder**, PERFECT **hat wiedergesehen**) VERB [64]
to see again
■ **Auf Wiedersehen!** Goodbye.

wiederverwerten (PERFECT **hat wiederverwertet**) VERB [7]
to recycle

die **Wiege** NOUN
cradle

wiegen (IMPERFECT **wog**, PERFECT **hat gewogen**) VERB
to weigh
□ Ich habe mich heute früh gewogen. I weighed myself this morning.

Wien NEUT NOUN
Vienna

die **Wiese** NOUN
meadow

wieso ADVERB
why

wie viel ADJECTIVE
how much
□ Wie viel hat das gekostet? How much did it cost?
■ **wie viel Menschen** how many people

wievielte ADJECTIVE
■ **Zum wievielten Mal?** How many times?
■ **Den Wievielten haben wir?** What's the date?

wieweit CONJUNCTION
to what extent

wild ADJECTIVE
wild

wildfremd ADJECTIVE
■ **ein wildfremder Mensch** a complete stranger

will VERB ▷ *see* **wollen**

der **Wille** (GEN des **Willens**, PL die **Willen**) NOUN
will
□ Ich habe es aus freiem Willen getan. I did it of my own free will.

willkommen ADJECTIVE
welcome
□ Herzlich willkommen! Welcome!
■ **jemanden willkommen heißen** to welcome somebody

wimmeln VERB [88]
■ **Es wimmelt von ...** It's teeming with ...

die **Wimper** NOUN
eyelash

die **Wimperntusche** NOUN
mascara

der **Wind** (PL die **Winde**) NOUN
wind

die **Windel** NOUN
nappy
□ Kannst du dem Baby die Windeln wechseln? Can you change the baby's nappy?

die **Windenergie** NOUN
wind energy

windig ADJECTIVE
windy
□ Es ist windig. It's windy.

die **Windmühle** NOUN
windmill

die **Windpocken** PL NOUN
chickenpox
□ Windpocken sind ansteckend. Chickenpox is catching.

die **Windschutzscheibe** NOUN
windscreen

das **Windsurfen** NOUN
windsurfing

der **Winkel** (PL die **Winkel**) NOUN
1 angle
□ ein spitzer Winkel an acute angle
2 corner
□ Ich habe jeden Winkel des Zimmers durchsucht. I've searched every corner of the room.

winken VERB [38]
to wave
□ jemandem winken to wave to somebody

der **Winter** (PL die **Winter**) NOUN
winter
□ im Winter in winter

winzig ADJECTIVE
tiny
wir PRONOUN
we
□ Wir kommen. We're coming.
■ **wir alle** all of us
■ **Wir sind's.** It's us.
die **Wirbelsäule** NOUN
spine
wird VERB ▷ *see* **werden**
wirft VERB ▷ *see* **werfen**
wirken VERB [38]
1 to have an effect
□ Die Tablette wirkt schon. The pill's already having an effect.
2 to seem
□ Er wirkte traurig. He seemed sad.
wirklich ADJECTIVE, ADVERB
1 real
□ Er ist ein wirklicher Freund. He's a real friend.
2 really
□ Das ist wirklich passiert. That really happened. □ Ich weiß es wirklich nicht. I really don't know.
die **Wirklichkeit** NOUN
reality
wirksam ADJECTIVE
effective
die **Wirkung** NOUN
effect
□ Wirkung auf etwas haben to have an effect on something
wirr ADJECTIVE
confused
der **Wirsing** NOUN
savoy cabbage
wirst VERB ▷ *see* **werden**
der **Wirt** (PL die **Wirte**) NOUN
landlord
die **Wirtin** NOUN
landlady
die **Wirtschaft** NOUN
1 pub
□ Wir sind in einer Wirtschaft eingekehrt. We stopped at a pub.
2 economy
□ Die Wirtschaft leidet unter der Rezession. The economy's suffering because of the recession.
wirtschaftlich ADJECTIVE
1 economical
□ Die große Packung ist wirtschaftlicher. The large packet's more economical.
2 economic
□ ein wirtschaftlicher Aufschwung an economic upswing
die **Wirtschaftslehre** NOUN
economics
das **Wirtshaus** (GEN des **Wirtshauses**, PL die **Wirtshäuser**) NOUN
inn

wischen VERB [48]
to wipe
das **Wissen** NOUN
▷ *see also* **wissen** VERB
knowledge
wissen (PRESENT **weiß**, IMPERFECT **wusste**, PERFECT **hat gewusst**) VERB [93]
▷ *see also* **das Wissen** NOUN
to know
□ Sie weiß sehr viel. She knows a lot.
□ Weißt du, wie die Hauptstadt von Deutschland heißt? Do you know what the capital of Germany is called? □ Ich weiß es nicht. I don't know.
■ **Was weiß ich!** How should I know?
die **Wissenschaft** NOUN
science
der **Wissenschaftler** (PL die **Wissenschaftler**) NOUN
scientist
wissenschaftlich ADJECTIVE
scientific
die **Witwe** NOUN
widow
□ Sie ist Witwe. She's a widow.
der **Witwer** (PL die **Witwer**) NOUN
widower
□ Er ist Witwer. He's a widower.
der **Witz** (GEN des **Witzes**, PL die **Witze**) NOUN
joke
□ einen Witz erzählen to tell a joke
witzig ADJECTIVE
funny
wo ADVERB
where
□ Wo warst du? Where were you?
LANGUAGE TIP Be careful! **wo** does not mean **who**.
woanders ADVERB
elsewhere
die **Woche** NOUN
week
□ nächste Woche next week
das **Wochenende** (PL die **Wochenenden**) NOUN
weekend
□ am Wochenende at the weekend
wochenlang ADJECTIVE, ADVERB
for weeks
der **Wochentag** (PL die **Wochentage**) NOUN
weekday
wochentags ADVERB
on weekdays
wöchentlich ADJECTIVE, ADVERB
weekly
wofür ADVERB
what ... for
□ Wofür brauchst du das Geld? What do you need the money for?
wog VERB ▷ *see* **wiegen**

woher ADVERB
where ... from
□ Woher sind Sie? Where do you come from?

wohin ADVERB
1 where ... to
□ Wohin zieht ihr um? Where are you moving to?
2 where
□ Wohin gehst du? Where are you going?

das **Wohl** NOUN
▷ *see also* **wohl** ADVERB
benefit
□ zu eurem Wohl for your benefit
■ **Zum Wohl!** Cheers!

wohl ADVERB
▷ *see also* **das Wohl** NOUN
probably
□ Das hat er wohl vergessen. He's probably forgotten.
■ **Es ist wohl gestohlen worden.** It must have been stolen.
■ **Das ist doch wohl nicht dein Ernst!** Surely you're not being serious!
■ **Das mag wohl sein.** That may well be.
■ **Ob das wohl stimmt?** I wonder if that's true.
■ **Er weiß das sehr wohl.** He knows that perfectly well.
■ **Ich muss wohl oder übel hingehen.** I have to go whether I like it or not.

sich **wohlfühlen** VERB [4]
1 to be happy
□ Ich fühle mich in diesem Haus sehr wohl. I'm very happy in this house.
2 to feel well
□ Sie fühlte sich nicht wohl. She didn't feel well.

die **Wohltätigkeitsorganisation** NOUN
charitable organization

der **Wohnblock** (PL die **Wohnblocks**) NOUN
block of flats

wohnen VERB [38]
to live
□ Ich wohne in Bremen. I live in Bremen.

die **Wohngemeinschaft** NOUN
■ **Ich wohne in einer Wohngemeinschaft.** I share a flat.

das **Wohnheim** (PL die **Wohnheime**) NOUN
1 home
□ ein Wohnheim für ältere Menschen a home for senior citizens
■ **ein Studentenwohnheim** a hall of residence
2 hostel

der **Wohnort** (PL die **Wohnorte**) NOUN
place of residence

der **Wohnsitz** (GEN des **Wohnsitzes**, PL die **Wohnsitze**) NOUN
place of residence

die **Wohnung** NOUN
flat

der **Wohnwagen** (PL die **Wohnwagen**) NOUN
caravan

das **Wohnzimmer** (PL die **Wohnzimmer**) NOUN
living room

der **Wolf** (PL die **Wölfe**) NOUN
wolf

die **Wolke** NOUN
cloud

der **Wolkenkratzer** (PL die **Wolkenkratzer**) NOUN
skyscraper

wolkenlos ADJECTIVE
cloudless

wolkig ADJECTIVE
cloudy

die **Wolle** NOUN
wool

wollen (PRESENT **will**, IMPERFECT **wollte**, PERFECT **hat gewollt** *or* **wollen**) VERB [94]

> LANGUAGE TIP The past participle **wollen** is used when **wollen** is a modal auxiliary.

to want
□ Er hat nicht gewollt. He didn't want to.
□ Er wollte das nicht. He didn't want it.
□ Ich will nach Hause. I want to go home.
□ Ich will, dass du mir zuhörst. I want you to listen to me.
■ **Wenn du willst.** If you like.
■ **etwas tun wollen** to want to do something □ Er hat unbedingt gehen wollen. He really wanted to go. □ Er will ein Haus kaufen. He wants to buy a house.
■ **etwas gerade tun wollen** to be on the point of doing something □ Ich wollte gerade gehen. I was on the point of going.
■ **Ich wollte, ich wäre ...** I wish I were ...

womit ADVERB
1 with which
□ Das ist der Gegenstand, womit er erschlagen wurde. This is the instrument with which he was killed.
2 what ... with
□ Womit hast du das repariert? What did you repair it with?

wonach ADVERB
1 what ... for
□ Das war genau, wonach er gesucht hatte. That was just what he had been looking for.
2 what ... by
□ Wonach sollen wir die Uhr stellen? What shall we set the clock by?
■ **der Tag, wonach er verunglückte** the day before his accident

woran ADVERB
■ **das Paket, woran dieser Zettel hing** the parcel the note was attached to
■ **Woran war dieser Zettel befestigt?**

What was this note attached to?
■ **Woran ist er gestorben?** What did he die of?

worauf ADVERB
what ... on
□ Worauf soll ich den Computer stellen? What shall I put the computer on?
■ **der Tisch, worauf der Computer steht** the table the computer is on

woraus ADVERB
■ **das Material, woraus es hergestellt ist** the material it is made of
■ **das Leck, woraus Gas strömte** the hole gas was pouring out of

worin ADVERB
what ... in
□ Worin war das versteckt? What was it hidden in?
■ **die Schublade, worin der Schlüssel ist** the drawer the key is in
■ **Worin besteht der Unterschied?** What's the difference?

das **Wort** (PL die **Wörter** *or* **Worte**) NOUN
word
□ Sie sprach ein paar bewegende Worte. She said a few moving words. □ Manche Wörter werden wie im Französischen ausgesprochen. Some words are pronounced as in French.
■ **jemanden beim Wort nehmen** to take somebody at his word □ Ich nahm sie beim Wort. I took her at her word.
■ **mit anderen Worten** in other words

das **Wörterbuch** (PL die **Wörterbücher**) NOUN
dictionary

LANGUAGE TIP Word for word, **Wörterbuch** means 'word book'.

wörtlich ADJECTIVE
literal

der **Wortschatz** (GEN des **Wortschatzes**) NOUN
vocabulary

das **Wortspiel** (PL die **Wortspiele**) NOUN
pun

worüber ADVERB
■ **das Thema, worüber wir reden** the subject we're talking about
■ **der Tisch, worüber eine Lampe hing** the table a lamp was hanging over
■ **Worüber kann ich meinen Mantel legen?** Where can I put my coat?

worunter ADVERB
what ... under
□ Worunter hat sich die Katze verkrochen? What did the cat crawl under?
■ **der Tisch, worunter die Katze lag** the table the cat was lying under

wovon ADVERB
■ **Das war es, wovon wir sprachen.** That was what we were talking about.
■ **das Essen, wovon ihm schlecht wurde** the food which made him ill

wovor ADVERB
■ **das Haus, wovor du stehst** the house you're standing in front of
■ **die Arbeit, wovor sie am meisten Angst hat** the test which she's most afraid of

wozu ADVERB
1 why
□ Wozu willst du das wissen? Why do you want to know that?
2 what ... for
□ Wozu dient dieser Schalter? What's this switch for? □ Wozu brauchst du einen Computer? What do you need a computer for?

das **Wrack** (PL die **Wracks**) NOUN
wreck

der **Wucher** NOUN
■ **Das ist Wucher!** That's daylight robbery!

wund ADJECTIVE
sore
□ Ich habe mir die Füße beim Einkaufen wund gelaufen. My feet are sore from going round the shops.

die **Wunde** NOUN
wound

das **Wunder** (PL die **Wunder**) NOUN
miracle
■ **es ist kein Wunder** it's no wonder

wunderbar ADJECTIVE
wonderful

wundern VERB [88]
to surprise
□ Diese Frage hat mich sehr gewundert. This question really surprised me.
■ **sich wundern über** to be surprised at
□ Ich wundere mich immer wieder über ihr Wissen. I'm always surprised at how much she knows. □ Ich wundere mich, dass er noch nicht angerufen hat. I'm surprised that he hasn't phoned yet.
■ **Ich muss mich schon über dich wundern.** I must say you surprise me.
■ **Es wundert mich, dass du das fragst.** I'm surprised you ask.
■ **Er wird sich noch wundern!** He's in for a surprise!

wunderschön ADJECTIVE
beautiful

wundervoll ADJECTIVE
wonderful

der **Wunsch** (PL die **Wünsche**) NOUN
wish

wünschen VERB [48]
to wish
□ Ich wünsche dir viel Erfolg! I wish you every success.
■ **sich etwas wünschen** to want something
□ Ich wünsche mir zum Geburtstag Inline-Skates. I want in-line skates for my birthday.

wurde VERB ▷ *see* **werden**

der **Wurf** (PL die **Würfe**) NOUN
throw

der **Würfel** (PL die **Würfel**) NOUN
1 dice
□ zwei Würfel two dice □ Wir haben Würfel gespielt. We played dice.
2 cube
□ Ein Würfel hat sechs gleich große Flächen. A cube has six equal surfaces.

würfeln VERB [34]
1 to throw a dice
□ Ich bin dran mit Würfeln. It's my turn to throw the dice. □ Wir haben darum gewürfelt, wer abwaschen muss. We threw a dice to see who was going to wash up.
2 to dice
□ den Speck würfeln to dice the bacon

der **Würfelzucker** NOUN
lump sugar

der **Wurm** (PL die **Würmer**) NOUN
worm

die **Wurst** (PL die **Würste**) NOUN
1 sausage
□ Leberwurst liver sausage
2 cold meat
■ **eine Wurstplatte** a platter of cold meat
■ **Das ist mir Wurst.** I don't give a toss.

das **Würstchen** (PL die **Würstchen**) NOUN
sausage

die **Würze** NOUN
seasoning

die **Wurzel** NOUN
root

wusch VERB ▷ *see* **waschen**

wusste VERB ▷ *see* **wissen**

die **Wüste** NOUN
desert

die **Wut** NOUN
rage
■ **eine Wut haben** to be furious

der **Wutanfall** (PL die **Wutanfälle**) NOUN
fit of rage

wütend ADJECTIVE
furious
□ Ich bin wütend auf ihn. I'm furious with him.

x-beliebig ADJECTIVE
any ... whatever
□ Wähle eine x-beliebige Zahl. Choose any number whatever.

x-mal ADVERB
any number of times
□ Ich habe es ihm x-mal gesagt. I've told him any number of times.

das **Xylofon** (PL die **Xylofone**) NOUN
xylophone

Yy

das **Yoga** (GEN des **Yoga** *or* **Yogas**) NOUN
yoga

das **Ypsilon** (GEN des **Ypsilon** *or* **Ypsilons**, PL die **Ypsilons**) NOUN
the letter Y

Zz

zaghaft ADJECTIVE
timid

zäh ADJECTIVE
1 tough
□ Das Steak ist zäh. The steak's tough.
□ Ich bin zäh, ich halte es noch eine Weile aus. I'm tough, I can stand it for a bit yet.
2 slow-moving
□ Der Verkehr war zäh. Traffic was slow-moving.

die **Zahl** NOUN
number

zahlen VERB [38]
to pay
□ Wie viel hast du dafür gezahlt? How much did you pay for it?
■ **Zahlen bitte!** The bill, please!

zählen VERB [38]
to count
□ Ich zähle bis drei. I'll count to three.
□ Ich habe die Hefte gezählt. I've counted the exercise books.
■ **zählen auf** to count on □ Wir zählen auf dich. We're counting on you.
■ **zählen zu** to be one of □ Er zählt zu den besseren Schülern. He's one of the better pupils.

zahlreich ADJECTIVE
numerous

die **Zahlung** NOUN
payment

das **Zahlwort** (PL die **Zahlwörter**) NOUN
numeral

zahm ADJECTIVE
tame

der **Zahn** (PL die **Zähne**) NOUN
tooth

der **Zahnarzt** (GEN des **Zahnarztes**, PL die **Zahnärzte**) NOUN
dentist

die **Zahnbürste** NOUN
toothbrush

die **Zahncreme** (PL die **Zahncremes**) NOUN
toothpaste

das **Zahnfleisch** NOUN
gums
□ Mein Zahnfleisch blutet. My gums are bleeding.

die **Zahnpasta** (PL die **Zahnpasten**) NOUN
toothpaste

die **Zahnschmerzen** MASC PL NOUN
toothache
□ Zahnschmerzen sind sehr unangenehm. Toothache is very unpleasant.

der **Zahnstein** NOUN
tartar

der **Zahnstocher** (PL die **Zahnstocher**) NOUN
toothpick

die **Zange** NOUN
1 pliers
□ Ich brauche eine isolierte Zange. I need a pair of insulated pliers.
2 pincers
□ die Zangen eines Hummers a lobster's pincers

zappeln VERB [34]
1 to wriggle
□ Der Fisch zappelt noch. The fish is still wriggling.
2 to fidget
□ Hör auf zu zappeln. Stop fidgeting.

zart ADJECTIVE
1 soft
□ zarte Haut soft skin
2 gentle
□ eine zarte Berührung a gentle touch
3 delicate
□ zarte Farben delicate colours □ Sie ist ein sehr zartes Kind. She's a very delicate child.
■ **zartes Fleisch** tender meat

zärtlich ADJECTIVE
loving
□ Mein Freund ist sehr zärtlich. My boyfriend's very loving. □ ein zärtlicher Kuss a loving kiss □ eine zärtliche Berührung a loving touch

die **Zauberei** NOUN
magic

der **Zaun** (PL die **Zäune**) NOUN
fence

z. B. ABBREVIATION *(= zum Beispiel)*
e.g.

der **Zebrastreifen** (PL die **Zebrastreifen**) NOUN
zebra crossing

die **Zehe** NOUN
toe
□ die große Zehe the big toe
■ **eine Knoblauchzehe** a clove of garlic

zehn NUMBER
ten

zehnte ADJECTIVE
tenth

das **Zeichen** (PL die **Zeichen**) NOUN
sign

der **Zeichentrickfilm** (PL die **Zeichentrickfilme**) NOUN
animated cartoon

zeichnen VERB [53]
to draw
□ Marek kann gut zeichnen. Marek's good at drawing. □ Sie hat eine Maus gezeichnet. She's drawn a mouse.

die **Zeichnung** NOUN
drawing

der **Zeigefinger** (PL die **Zeigefinger**) NOUN
index finger

zeigen VERB [38]
1 to show
□ Sie hat mir ihre Fotos gezeigt. She showed me her photos. □ Zeig mal, was du da hast. Show us what you've got there.
2 to point
□ Sie zeigte an die Tafel. She pointed to the blackboard.
■ **zeigen auf** to point at □ Man zeigt nicht mit dem Finger auf Menschen. Don't point at people.
■ **es wird sich zeigen** time will tell □ Es wird sich zeigen, ob er das kann. Time will tell whether he can do it.
■ **Es zeigte sich, dass ...** It turned out that ...
□ Es zeigte sich, dass der Text zu schwierig war. It turned out that the text was too difficult.

der **Zeiger** (PL die **Zeiger**) NOUN
1 hand
□ der große und der kleine Zeiger der Uhr the big hand and the little hand of the clock
2 pointer
□ der Zeiger der Waage the pointer of the scales

die **Zeile** NOUN
line
□ Ich schreibe ihr ein paar Zeilen. I'm going to write her a few lines.

die **Zeit** NOUN
1 time
□ Wir haben keine Zeit mehr. We haven't got any more time. □ Um welche Zeit seid ihr nach Hause gekommen? What time did you get home?
2 tense
□ die Zeiten der Vergangenheit the past tenses
■ **sich Zeit lassen** to take one's time
□ Da hast du dir aber viel Zeit gelassen. You've been taking your time.
■ **von Zeit zu Zeit** from time to time
■ **Zeit raubend** ▷ *see* **zeitraubend**

zeitlich ADJECTIVE
chronological

die **Zeitlupe** NOUN
slow motion
□ in Zeitlupe in slow motion

zeitraubend ADJECTIVE
time-consuming

der **Zeitraum** (PL die **Zeiträume**) NOUN
period
□ innerhalb dieses Zeitraums within this period

die **Zeitschrift** NOUN
magazine

die **Zeitung** NOUN
newspaper

die **Zeitverschwendung** NOUN
waste of time
□ Das ist doch Zeitverschwendung! That's just a waste of time.

die **Zelle** NOUN
1 cell
□ Im Alter sterben die Zellen ab. Cells die off in old age.
2 call box
□ Ich rufe aus einer Zelle an. I'm phoning from a call box.

das **Zelt** (PL die **Zelte**) NOUN
tent

zelten VERB [2]
to camp

der **Zeltplatz** (GEN des **Zeltplatzes**, PL die **Zeltplätze**) NOUN
camp site

der **Zement** (PL die **Zemente**) NOUN
cement

zensieren (PERFECT **hat zensiert**) VERB [76]
1 to censor
□ Der Film wurde zensiert. The film was censored.
2 to give a mark
□ Wie hat deine Deutschlehrerin den Aufsatz zensiert? What mark did your German teacher give you for your essay?

die **Zensur** NOUN
mark
□ Ich habe durchweg gute Zensuren. I've got good marks in everything.

der **Zentimeter** (PL die **Zentimeter**) NOUN
centimetre

der **Zentner** (PL die **Zentner**) NOUN
hundredweight
□ drei Zentner three hundredweight

zentral ADJECTIVE
central

die **Zentrale** NOUN
1 head office

□ Das Gerät müssen wir in der Zentrale anfordern. We'll have to order the appliance from the head office.

2 switchboard

□ Du musst dich über die Zentrale verbinden lassen. You have to go through the switchboard.

die **Zentralheizung** NOUN
central heating

das **Zentrum** (PL die **Zentren**) NOUN
centre

zerbrechen (PRESENT **zerbricht**, IMPERFECT **zerbrach**, PERFECT **hat/ist zerbrochen**) VERB [11]

LANGUAGE TIP For the perfect tense use **haben** when the verb has an object and **sein** when there is no object.

to break

□ Sie hat den Teller zerbrochen. She's broken the plate. □ Der Teller ist zerbrochen. The plate broke.

zerbrechlich ADJECTIVE
fragile

zerreißen (IMPERFECT **zerriss**, PERFECT **hat/ist zerrissen**) VERB

LANGUAGE TIP For the perfect tense use **haben** when the verb has an object and **sein** when there is no object.

1 to tear to pieces

□ Sie hat seinen Brief zerrissen. She tore his letter to pieces.

2 to tear

□ Der Umschlag ist unterwegs zerrissen. The envelope got torn in the post.

zerren VERB [38]
to drag

□ Er zerrte sie in die Büsche. He dragged her into the bushes.

■ **zerren an** to tug at □ Der Hund zerrte an der Leine. The dog tugged at its leash.

zerrissen VERB ▷ *see* **zerreißen**

zerschlagen (PRESENT **zerschlägt**, IMPERFECT **zerschlug**, PERFECT **hat zerschlagen**) VERB [59]
to smash

□ Sie haben alles Porzellan zerschlagen. They smashed all the china.

■ **sich zerschlagen** to fall through

□ Unsere Ferienpläne haben sich zerschlagen. Our holiday plans have fallen through.

zerstören (PRESENT **hat zerstört**) VERB [95]
to destroy

die **Zerstörung** NOUN
destruction

zerstreuen (PERFECT **hat zerstreut**) VERB [95]

1 to entertain

□ Er hat uns mit lustigen Geschichten zerstreut. He entertained us with amusing stories.

2 to scatter

□ Warum hast du die Blätter im ganzen Zimmer zerstreut? Why have you scattered the papers all over the room? □ Unsere Familie ist über ganz Deutschland zerstreut. Our family's scattered all over Germany.

■ **jemandes Angst zerstreuen** to allay somebody's fears

zerstreut ADJECTIVE

1 absent-minded

□ Er ist furchtbar zerstreut. He's terribly absent-minded.

2 scattered

□ Sie sammelte die zerstreuten Seiten auf. She picked up the scattered pages.

der **Zettel** (PL die **Zettel**) NOUN

1 note

□ Auf dem Küchentisch liegt ein Zettel für dich. There's a note on the kitchen table for you.

2 piece of paper

□ Sie schrieb seine Telefonnummer auf einen Zettel. She wrote his telephone number on a piece of paper.

3 form

□ Wenn du dem Klub beitreten willst, musst du diesen Zettel ausfüllen. If you want to join the club you'll have to fill in this form.

das **Zeug** NOUN

1 stuff

□ Was ist das für ein Zeug? What's this stuff? □ mein Sportzeug my sports stuff

2 gear

□ mein Angelzeug my fishing gear

■ **dummes Zeug** nonsense □ Das ist doch dummes Zeug. That's just a lot of nonsense.

■ **das Zeug haben zu** to have the makings of □ Er hat das Zeug zum Lehrer. He has the makings of a teacher.

der **Zeuge** (GEN des **Zeugen**, PL die **Zeugen**) NOUN
witness

die **Zeugin** NOUN
witness

das **Zeugnis** (GEN des **Zeugnisses**, PL die **Zeugnisse**) NOUN
report

□ Oliver hat ein sehr gutes Zeugnis. Oliver's got a very good report.

die **Ziege** NOUN
goat

der **Ziegel** (PL die **Ziegel**) NOUN

1 brick

□ eine Mauer aus Ziegeln a brick wall

2 tile

□ Deutsche Dächer sind meist mit roten Ziegeln gedeckt. German roofs are usually covered with red tiles.

ziehen (IMPERFECT **zog**, PERFECT **hat/ist gezogen**) VERB [96]

LANGUAGE TIP Use **sein** to form the perfect tense for 'to move' (house) and 'to roam'. Use **haben** for 'to move' (in chess), 'to draw' and 'to pull'.

1 to draw

□ Er hat eine Niete gezogen. He drew a blank.

2 to pull

□ Sie zog mich am Ärmel. She pulled at my sleeve.

3 to move

□ Sie sind nach Wuppertal gezogen. They've moved to Wuppertal. □ Er zog mit seinem Turm. He moved his rook.

4 to roam

□ Früher zogen die Zigeuner durchs Land. In the old days, gypsies used to roam the countryside.

■ **Es zieht.** There's a draught.

■ **sich in die Länge ziehen** to be drawn out

das **Ziel** (PL die **Ziele**) NOUN

1 destination

□ Unser heutiges Ziel ist Bonn. Our destination today is Bonn.

2 finishing line

□ Er ging als Erster durchs Ziel. He was the first to cross the finishing line.

3 target

□ Ulm war das Ziel eines Bombenangriffs. Ulm was the target of an air raid.

4 goal

□ Es ist nicht mein Ziel im Leben, reich zu werden. Getting rich is not my goal in life.

zielen VERB [38]

to aim

□ Er hat auf seine Beine gezielt. He aimed at his legs.

die **Zielscheibe** NOUN

target

□ Er traf die Zielscheibe mit seinem ersten Schuss. He hit the target with his first shot.

ziemlich ADJECTIVE, ADVERB

1 quite

□ Das war eine ziemliche Katastrophe. That was quite a disaster.

2 fair

□ eine ziemliche Menge Fehler a fair number of mistakes

3 rather

□ Er war ziemlich sauer. He was rather cross.

■ **ziemlich viel** quite a bit □ Wir haben ziemlich viel erledigt. We've got through quite a bit.

sich **zieren** VERB [76]

to act coy

zierlich ADJECTIVE

dainty

die **Ziffer** NOUN

figure

zig ADJECTIVE

umpteen

die **Zigarette** NOUN

cigarette

die **Zigarettenschachtel** NOUN

cigarette packet

das **Zigarillo** (PL die **Zigarillos**) NOUN

LANGUAGE TIP You can also say **der Zigarillo.**

cigarillo

die **Zigarre** NOUN

cigar

der **Zigeuner** (PL die **Zigeuner**) NOUN

gypsy

die **Zigeunerin** NOUN

gypsy

das **Zimmer** (PL die **Zimmer**) NOUN

room

■ **'Zimmer frei'** 'Vacancies'

das **Zimmermädchen** (PL die **Zimmermädchen**) NOUN

chambermaid

der **Zimmernachweis** (GEN des **Zimmernachweises**, PL die **Zimmernachweise**) NOUN

accommodation office

der **Zimt** NOUN

cinnamon

das **Zinn** NOUN

1 tin

□ In Cornwall wurde früher Zinn abgebaut. They used to mine tin in Cornwall.

2 pewter

□ Mein Bruder sammelt Zinn. My brother collects pewter.

der **Zins** (GEN des **Zinses**, PL die **Zinsen**) NOUN

interest

□ acht Prozent Zinsen eight per cent interest

zirka ADVERB

approximately

der **Zirkus** (GEN des **Zirkus**, PL die **Zirkusse**) NOUN

circus

zischen VERB [48]

to hiss

das **Zitat** (PL die **Zitate**) NOUN

quotation

zitieren (PERFECT **hat zitiert**) VERB [76]

to quote

die **Zitrone** NOUN

lemon

die **Zitronenlimonade** NOUN

lemonade

der **Zitronensaft** (PL die **Zitronensäfte**) NOUN

lemon juice

zittern VERB [88]

to tremble

□ vor Angst zittern to tremble with fear

■ **Sie zitterte vor Kälte.** She was shivering.

der **Zivildienst** NOUN

community service

DID YOU KNOW...?
Instead of doing national service in the German armed forces, young men can opt to do community service as **Zivildienstleistende** or **Zivis**, for example with the Red Cross or in an old people's home.

die **Zivilisation** NOUN

civilization

zögern VERB [88]
to hesitate

der **Zoll** (PL die **Zölle**) NOUN
1 customs
□ Wir mussten am Zoll lange warten. We had to wait a long time at customs.
2 duty
□ Darauf musst du Zoll bezahlen. You have to pay duty on that.

der **Zollbeamte** (GEN des **Zollbeamten**, PL die **Zollbeamten**) NOUN
customs official
□ Ein Zollbeamter hat unser Auto durchsucht. A customs official searched our car.

zollfrei ADJECTIVE
duty-free

die **Zollkontrolle** NOUN
customs check

die **Zone** NOUN
zone

der **Zoo** (PL die **Zoos**) NOUN
zoo

zoologisch ADJECTIVE
zoological

der **Zopf** (PL die **Zöpfe**) NOUN
1 plait
□ zwei blonde Zöpfe two blonde plaits
2 pigtail
□ Sie hatte ihre Haare zu einem Zopf zusammengebunden. She had put her hair into a pigtail.

der **Zorn** NOUN
anger

zornig ADJECTIVE
angry

zu PREPOSITION, CONJUNCTION, ADVERB

LANGUAGE TIP The preposition **zu** takes the dative.

1 to
□ zum Bahnhof gehen to go to the station □ zum Arzt gehen to go to the doctor □ zur Schule gehen to go to school □ zur Kirche gehen to go to church □ Sollen wir zu euch gehen? Shall we go to your place?
■ **Sie sah zu ihm hin.** She looked towards him.
■ **zum Fenster herein** through the window
■ **zu meiner Linken** on my left

LANGUAGE TIP **zu** is used with the infinitive.

□ etwas zu essen something to eat □ um besser sehen zu können in order to see better □ ohne es zu wissen without knowing it
2 at
□ zu Ostern at Easter
■ **zu Hause** at home
■ **bis zum ersten Mai** 1 until the first of May □ Das Sonderangebot gilt bis zum ersten Mai. The special offer is valid until the first of May. 2 by the first of May □ Bis zum ersten Mai muss mein Referat fertig sein. My assignment has to be finished by the first of May.
■ **zu meinem Geburtstag** for my birthday
■ **zu meiner Zeit** in my time
3 with
□ Wein zum Essen trinken to drink wine with one's meal
■ **sich zu jemandem setzen** to sit down beside somebody
4 on
□ Anmerkungen zu etwas notes on something
5 for
□ Wasser zum Waschen water for washing
■ **Papier zum Schreiben** paper to write on
■ **zu etwas werden** to develop into something □ Sie ist zu einer hübschen jungen Dame geworden. She's developed into an attractive young lady.
■ **jemanden zu etwas machen** to make somebody something □ Sie haben mich zur Klassensprecherin gemacht. They made me class representative.
■ **drei zu zwei** three two □ Unsere Mannschaft hat drei zu zwei gewonnen. Our team won three two.
■ **das Stück zu drei Euro** at three euros each
■ **zum ersten Mal** for the first time
■ **zu meiner Freude** to my delight
■ **zum Scherz** as a joke
■ **zu Fuß** on foot
■ **Es ist zum Weinen.** It's enough to make you cry.
6 too
□ zu schnell too fast □ zu sehr too much
7 closed
□ Die Geschäfte haben zu. The shops are closed.
■ **zu sein** to be shut □ Das Fenster war zu. The window was shut.

das **Zubehör** (PL die **Zubehöre**) NOUN
accessories
□ Das Zubehör kostet extra. You pay extra for the accessories.

zubereiten (PERFECT **hat zubereitet**) VERB [2]
to prepare

zubinden (IMPERFECT **band zu**, PERFECT **hat zugebunden**) VERB
to tie up

zubringen (IMPERFECT **brachte zu**, PERFECT **hat zugebracht**) VERB [13]
to spend
□ Ich habe viel Zeit bei ihnen zugebracht. I spent a lot of time with them.

die **Zucchini** PL NOUN
courgette

züchten VERB [2]
1 to breed
□ Er züchtet Tauben. He breeds pigeons.

2 to grow
□ Mein Vater züchtet Rosen. My father grows roses.

zucken VERB [38]
1 to twitch
□ Seine Mundwinkel zuckten. The corners of his mouth twitched.
2 to flash
□ Ein Blitz zuckte durch die Nacht. Lightning flashed across the night sky.
■ **mit den Schultern zucken** to shrug one's shoulders

der **Zucker** NOUN
1 sugar
□ Ich nehme keinen Zucker in den Tee. I don't take sugar in my tea.
2 diabetes
□ Meine Tante hat Zucker. My aunt's got diabetes.

der **Zuckerguss** (GEN des **Zuckergusses**, PL die **Zuckergüsse**) NOUN
icing

zudecken (PERFECT **hat zugedeckt**) VERB [4]
1 to cover up
□ Man sollte das Loch zudecken. They ought to cover up the hole.
2 to tuck up
□ Sie deckte die Kinder zu. She tucked the children up.

zueinander ADVERB
1 to one another
□ Seid nett zueinander. Be nice to one another.
■ **Wir haben viel Vertrauen zueinander.** We trust each other.
2 together
□ Wir halten zueinander, egal, was kommt. Whatever happens, we'll stick together.

zuerst ADVERB
1 first
□ Was soll ich zuerst machen? What shall I do first? □ Er ist zuerst gekommen, dann kam seine Schwester. He arrived first, then his sister.
2 at first
□ Zuerst war sie noch etwas schüchtern. At first, she was still a bit shy.
■ **zuerst einmal** first of all □ Wir sollten zuerst einmal klären, was das kostet. First of all we ought to check how much it costs.

die **Zufahrt** NOUN
approach road
■ **'keine Zufahrt'** 'no access'

der **Zufall** (PL die **Zufälle**) NOUN
1 chance
□ Wie es der Zufall so wollte ... As chance would have it ...
■ **durch Zufall** by chance □ Ich habe es durch Zufall gefunden. I found it by chance.
2 coincidence
□ Es war schon ein Zufall, dass ich ihm in London begegnet bin. It was quite a coincidence that I met him in London.
□ Was für ein glücklicher Zufall! What a happy coincidence! □ So ein Zufall! What a coincidence!

zufällig ADJECTIVE, ADVERB
1 chance
□ eine zufällige Begegnung a chance meeting
2 by chance
□ Ich habe das Restaurant ganz zufällig gefunden. I found the restaurant quite by chance.
■ **Ich habe zufällig Zeit.** I happen to have time.
3 by any chance
□ Hast du zufällig mein Heft gesehen? Have you seen my exercise book by any chance?

zufrieden ADJECTIVE
satisfied
□ Ich bin mit deinen Leistungen nicht zufrieden. I'm not satisfied with your work.
□ Bist du jetzt zufrieden? Are you satisfied now? □ ein zufriedener Gesichtsausdruck a satisfied expression

zufrieren (IMPERFECT **fror zu**, PERFECT **ist zugefroren**) VERB
to freeze over
□ Der See ist zugefroren. The lake's frozen over.

der **Zug** (PL die **Züge**) NOUN
1 train
□ Wir sind mit dem Zug gefahren. We went by train.
2 draught
□ Hier ist ein furchtbarer Zug. There's a terrible draught in here.
3 move
□ Du bist am Zug. It's your move.
4 gulp
□ Er trank das Glas auf einen Zug leer. He emptied the glass in one gulp.
5 trait
□ Sein Geiz ist ein unangenehmer Zug an ihm. His meanness is an unpleasant trait.
■ **etwas in vollen Zügen genießen** to enjoy something to the full

die **Zugabe** NOUN
1 free gift
□ ein Handy als Zugabe. a mobile as a free gift
2 encore
□ Die Zuhörer brüllten: 'Zugabe, Zugabe'. The audience roared: 'encore, encore'.

zugeben (PRESENT **gibt zu**, IMPERFECT **gab zu**, PERFECT **hat zugegeben**) VERB [28]
to admit
□ Gib doch zu, dass du dich getäuscht hast. Admit you were wrong. □ Sie wollte ihren Irrtum nicht zugeben. She didn't want to admit her mistake.

zugehen (IMPERFECT **ging zu**, PERFECT **ist zugegangen**) VERB [29]
to shut
□ Die Tür geht nicht zu. The door won't shut.
■ **auf jemanden zugehen** to walk up to somebody □ Sie ging auf den Mann zu und fragte ihn nach dem Weg. She walked up to the man and asked him the way.
■ **auf etwas zugehen** to walk towards something □ Sie ging auf den Eingang zu, kehrte dann aber wieder um. She walked towards the entrance but then turned back again.
■ **Es geht dort seltsam zu.** There are strange goings-on there.
■ **dem Ende zugehen** to be nearing the end

der **Zugführer** (PL die **Zugführer**) NOUN
chief guard *(on train)*

zugig ADJECTIVE
draughty

zügig ADJECTIVE
swift
□ eine zügige Entscheidung a swift decision

zugreifen (IMPERFECT **griff zu**, PERFECT **hat zugegriffen**) VERB
1 to help oneself
□ Greift ungeniert zu, es ist genügend Kuchen da! Feel free to help yourselves, there's plenty of cake.
2 to seize
□ Er sah das Seil und griff zu. He saw the rope and seized it.
3 to lend a hand
□ Du könntest ruhig ein bisschen zugreifen und mich nicht alles allein machen lassen. You could at least lend a hand a bit instead of letting me do everything.

zugrunde ADVERB
■ **elend zugrunde gehen** to come to a wretched end □ Er fing an zu trinken und ging elend zugrunde. He took to drink and came to a wretched end.
■ **zugrunde richten** to destroy □ Alkohol und Drogen haben sie zugrunde gerichtet. Alcohol and drugs have destroyed her.
■ **einer Sache etwas zugrunde legen** to base something on something □ Diesem Film liegt ein Roman zugrunde. This film is based on a novel.

zugunsten PREPOSITION
LANGUAGE TIP The preposition **zugunsten** takes the dative or the genitive.
in favour of
□ Das Gericht entschied zugunsten des Angeklagten. The court decided in favour of the accused.

das **Zuhause** (GEN des **Zuhause**) NOUN
home

zuhören (PERFECT **hat zugehört**) VERB [4]
to listen
□ Du hörst mir ja gar nicht zu. You're not listening to me at all.

der **Zuhörer** (PL die **Zuhörer**) NOUN
listener

zukommen (IMPERFECT **kam zu**, PERFECT **ist zugekommen**) VERB [40]
■ **auf jemanden zukommen** to come up to somebody □ Er kam auf uns zu und fragte uns, wie spät es ist. He came up to us and asked what time it was.
■ **jemandem etwas zukommen lassen** to give somebody something □ Mein Onkel hat mir etwas Geld zukommen lassen. My uncle gave me some money.
■ **etwas auf sich zukommen lassen** to take something as it comes □ Warum lässt du diese Sache nicht einfach auf dich zukommen? Why don't you just take things as they come?

die **Zukunft** NOUN
future
□ in Zukunft in the future

die **Zukunftspläne** PL NOUN
plans for the future

zulassen (PRESENT **lässt zu**, IMPERFECT **ließ zu**, PERFECT **hat zugelassen**) VERB [42]
1 to allow
□ Ich kann es nicht zulassen, dass du so spät noch fernsiehst. I can't allow you to watch TV so late.
2 to register
□ Hast du dein Moped schon zugelassen? Have you registered your moped yet?
3 to leave closed
□ Bitte lass das Fenster zu. Please leave the window closed.

zulässig ADJECTIVE
permissible

zuleide ADVERB
■ **jemandem etwas zuleide tun** to hurt somebody □ Bitte tu ihr nichts zuleide. Please don't hurt her.

zuletzt ADVERB
1 last
□ Er wurde zuletzt in Begleitung einer Dame gesehen. He was last seen in the company of a lady. □ Wir sollten das zuletzt machen. We should do that last.
2 in the end
□ Zuletzt hat sie es dann doch verstanden. In the end she understood.

zuliebe ADVERB
■ **jemandem zuliebe** to please somebody
□ Er ist mir zuliebe zu Hause geblieben. He stayed at home to please me.

zum = **zu dem**

zumachen (PERFECT **hat zugemacht**) VERB [4]
1 to shut
□ Mach bitte die Tür zu. Please shut the door.
□ Wann machen die Geschäfte zu? When do

the shops shut?
2 to fasten
□ Kannst du mal bitte mein Kleid zumachen? Can you fasten my dress, please?

zumindest ADVERB
at least

zumute ADVERB
■ **Wie ist ihm zumute?** How does he feel?

zumuten (PERFECT **hat zugemutet**) VERB [2]
■ **jemandem etwas zumuten** to ask something of somebody □ Das kann ich ihm nicht zumuten. I can't ask that of him.

die **Zumutung** NOUN
■ **Das ist eine Zumutung!** That's asking too much.

zunächst ADVERB
first of all
□ Wir sollten zunächst diese Frage klären. We ought to clear this issue up first of all.
■ **zunächst einmal** to start with

zunehmen (PRESENT **nimmt zu**, IMPERFECT **nahm zu**, PERFECT **hat zugenommen**) VERB [52]
1 to increase
□ Der Lärm nahm zu. The noise increased.
2 to put on weight
□ Ich habe schon wieder zugenommen. I've put on weight yet again.
■ **Er hat fünf Kilo zugenommen.** He's put on five kilos.

die **Zuneigung** NOUN
affection

die **Zunge** NOUN
tongue

zur = **zu der**

sich **zurechtfinden** (IMPERFECT **fand sich zurecht**, PERFECT **hat sich zurechtgefunden**) VERB [24]
to find one's way

zurechtkommen (IMPERFECT **kam zurecht**, PERFECT **ist zurechtgekommen**) VERB [40]
to manage

zurechtlegen (PERFECT **hat zurechtgelegt**) VERB [4]
to sort out
□ Ich habe die Sachen für die Ferien schon zurechtgelegt. I've already sorted out my things for my holiday.
■ **sich eine Ausrede zurechtlegen** to think up an excuse □ Na, welche Ausrede hast du dir denn diesmal zurechtgelegt? Well, what excuse have you thought up this time?

zurück ADVERB
back

zurückbekommen (IMPERFECT **bekam zurück**, PERFECT **hat zurückbekommen**) VERB [40]
to get back

zurückbringen (IMPERFECT **brachte zurück**, PERFECT **hat zurückgebracht**) VERB [13]
to bring back

zurückerstatten (PERFECT **hat zurückerstattet**) VERB [2]
to refund

zurückfahren (PRESENT **fährt zurück**, IMPERFECT **fuhr zurück**, PERFECT **ist/hat zurückgefahren**) VERB [21]

LANGUAGE TIP For the perfect tense use **haben** when the verb has an object and **sein** when there is no object.

to return
□ Wann fahrt ihr zurück? When do you return?
■ **jemanden zurückfahren** to drive somebody back □ Sie hat mich nach Hause zurückgefahren. She drove me back home.

zurückgeben (PRESENT **gibt zurück**, IMPERFECT **gab zurück**, PERFECT **hat zurückgegeben**) VERB [28]
to give back
□ Gib mir bitte mein Buch zurück. Please give me my book back.

zurückgehen (IMPERFECT **ging zurück**, PERFECT **ist zurückgegangen**) VERB [29]
1 to go back
□ Wir sollten zurückgehen, bevor es zu spät wird. We should go back before it gets too late.
2 to recede
□ Das Hochwasser ist zurückgegangen. The floodwater receded.
3 to fall
□ Die Nachfrage geht zurück. Demand is falling.
■ **zurückgehen auf** to date back to □ Die Gründung der Stadt Aachen geht auf Karl den Großen zurück. The founding of the city of Aachen dates back to Charlemagne.

zurückhaltend ADJECTIVE
reserved
□ Er ist sehr zurückhaltend. He is very reserved.

zurückkehren (PERFECT **ist zurückgekehrt**) VERB [15]
to return

zurückkommen (IMPERFECT **kam zurück**, PERFECT **ist zurückgekommen**) VERB [40]
to come back
□ Er kam nach dem Film zurück. He came back after the film. □ Darf ich auf das zurückkommen, was Sie vorhin gesagt haben? May I come back to what you were saying earlier?
■ **Komm nicht zu spät zurück.** Don't be too late back.

zurücklegen (PERFECT **hat zurückgelegt**) VERB [15]
1 to put back
□ Leg das Buch bitte an seinen Platz zurück. Please put the book back in its place.
2 to put by

□ Wir haben für die Ferien etwas Geld zurückgelegt. We've put some money by for the holidays.

3 to put aside

□ Können Sie mir diesen Pulli bitte zurücklegen? Could you put this pullover aside for me, please?

4 to cover

□ Wir haben heute zweihundert Kilometer zurückgelegt. We've covered two hundred kilometres today.

zurücknehmen (PRESENT **nimmt zurück**, IMPERFECT **nahm zurück**, PERFECT **hat zurückgenommen**) VERB [52]

to take back

zurückrufen (PERFECT **hat zurückgerufen**) VERB [56]

to call back

□ Können Sie mich morgen zurückrufen? Can you call me back tomorrow?

zurücktreten (PRESENT **tritt zurück**, IMPERFECT **trat zurück**, PERFECT **ist zurückgetreten**) VERB [79]

1 to step back

□ Treten Sie etwas zurück bitte! Step back a bit, please.

2 to resign

□ Warum ist er zurückgetreten? Why did he resign?

zurückzahlen (PERFECT **hat zurückgezahlt**) VERB [15]

to repay

□ Du solltest endlich das geliehene Geld zurückzahlen. It's high time you repaid the money you borrowed.

zurückziehen (IMPERFECT **zog zurück**, PERFECT **hat zurückgezogen**) VERB [96]

1 to pull back

□ Sie zog die Hand zurück. She pulled her hand back.

2 to withdraw

□ ein Angebot zurückziehen to withdraw an offer

■ **sich zurückziehen** to retire □ Sie hat sich in ihr Zimmer zurückgezogen. She has retired to her room. □ Er hat sich aus dem öffentlichen Leben zurückgezogen. He has retired from public life.

zurzeit ADVERB

at the moment

zusagen (PERFECT **hat zugesagt**) VERB [4]

1 to promise

□ Er hat mir seine Hilfe zugesagt. He promised to help me.

2 to accept an invitation

□ Die meisten Gäste haben zugesagt. Most of the guests have accepted the invitation.

■ **jemandem zusagen** to appeal to somebody □ Das Konzert hat mir nicht zugesagt. The concert didn't appeal to me.

zusammen ADVERB

together

zusammenbleiben (IMPERFECT **blieb zusammen**, PERFECT **sind zusammengeblieben**) VERB [10]

to stay together

zusammenbrechen (PRESENT **bricht zusammen**, IMPERFECT **brach zusammen**, PERFECT **ist zusammengebrochen**) VERB [11]

1 to collapse

□ Das Gebäude ist zusammengebrochen. The building collapsed.

2 to break down

□ Als sie von seinem Tod erfuhr, ist sie zusammengebrochen. When she heard of his death she broke down.

zusammenfassen (PERFECT **hat zusammengefasst**) VERB [15]

to summarize

□ Sie fasste das Gesagte noch einmal kurz zusammen. She briefly summarized once again what had been said.

die **Zusammenfassung** NOUN

summary

der **Zusammenhang** (PL die **Zusammenhänge**) NOUN

connection

□ Gibt es einen Zusammenhang zwischen diesen Ereignissen? Is there a connection between these events?

■ **im Zusammenhang mit** in connection with

□ Zwei Männer wurden im Zusammenhang mit dem Mord verhört. Two men were questioned in connection with the murder.

■ **aus dem Zusammenhang** out of context

□ Du hast mich aus dem Zusammenhang zitiert. You've quoted me out of context.

zusammenhängen (IMPERFECT **hing zusammen**, PERFECT **hat zusammengehangen**) VERB [69]

to be connected

□ Die beiden Ereignisse hängen miteinander zusammen. The two events are connected.

zusammenkommen (IMPERFECT **kam zusammen**, PERFECT **ist zusammengekommen**) VERB [40]

1 to meet up

□ Früher sind wir öfter zusammengekommen. We used to meet up more often.

2 to come together

□ Es ist alles zusammengekommen. Everything came together.

zusammenlegen (PERFECT **hat zusammengelegt**) VERB [15]

1 to fold

□ Sie legte die Wäsche zusammen. She folded the washing.

2 to merge

□ Die beiden Klassen sollen zusammengelegt werden. The two classes are to be merged.

3 to combine
□ Wir können unsere Geburtstagspartys doch zusammenlegen. We can combine our birthday parties.
4 to club together
□ Wir haben zusammengelegt und ihr eine CD gekauft. We clubbed together and bought her a CD.

zusammennehmen (PRESENT **nimmt zusammen**, IMPERFECT **nahm zusammen**, PERFECT **hat zusammengenommen**) VERB [52]
to summon up
□ Ich musste meinen ganzen Mut zusammennehmen. I had to summon up all my courage.
■ **alles zusammengenommen** all in all
■ **sich zusammennehmen** to pull oneself together

zusammenpassen (PERFECT **hat zusammengepasst**) VERB [4]
1 to be well suited
□ Die beiden passen gut zusammen. The two are well suited.
2 to go together
□ Der Pulli und die Hose passen nicht zusammen. The pullover and the trousers don't go together.

das **Zusammensein** NOUN
get-together
□ ein gemütliches Zusammensein a cosy get-together

zusammenstellen (PERFECT **hat zusammengestellt**) VERB [15]
1 to put together
□ Stellt alle Stühle zusammen. Put all the chairs together.
2 to compile
□ Ich habe eine Wunschliste zusammengestellt. I've compiled a list of presents I'd like.

der **Zusammenstoß** (GEN des **Zusammenstoßes**, PL die **Zusammenstöße**) NOUN
collision

zusammenstoßen (PRESENT **stößt zusammen**, IMPERFECT **stieß zusammen**, PERFECT **sind zusammengestoßen**) VERB
to collide

zusammenzählen (PERFECT **hat zusammengezählt**) VERB [4]
to add up

zusätzlich ADJECTIVE, ADVERB
1 additional
□ Wir sollen eine zusätzliche Englischstunde bekommen. We're to get an additional English lesson.
2 in addition
□ Zusätzlich zu den Matheaufgaben muss ich noch Physik machen. I still have some physics to do in addition to my maths homework.

zuschauen (PERFECT **hat zugeschaut**) VERB [4]
to watch
□ Habt ihr beim Match zugeschaut? Did you watch the match?

die **Zuschauer** MASC PL NOUN
audience
□ Die Zuschauer haben geklatscht. The audience clapped.

der **Zuschlag** (PL die **Zuschläge**) NOUN
surcharge
□ Für den ICE brauchst du einen Zuschlag. You have to pay a surcharge if you go by Intercity Express.

zusehen (PRESENT **sieht zu**, IMPERFECT **sah zu**, PERFECT **hat zugesehen**) VERB [64]
to watch
□ Wir haben beim Match zugesehen. We watched the match. □ Er stand nur dabei und sah zu. He just stood there watching.
■ **jemandem zusehen** to watch somebody
□ Ich habe ihr dabei zugesehen, wie sie ihr Zimmer aufräumte. I watched her tidy up her room.
■ **zusehen, dass etwas gemacht wird** to make sure something is done □ Sieh zu, dass die Kinder früh ins Bett kommen. Make sure that the children go to bed early.

zusenden (IMPERFECT **sendete** *or* **sandte zu**, PERFECT **hat zugesendet** *or* **zugesandt**) VERB
to send
□ Wir werden Ihnen unseren Prospekt zusenden. We'll send you our brochure.

der **Zustand** (PL die **Zustände**) NOUN
1 state
□ Das Haus war in einem furchtbaren Zustand. The house was in an awful state.
□ Das sind hier ja schreckliche Zustände. This is a terrible state of affairs.
2 condition
□ Das Auto ist noch in gutem Zustand. The car's still in good condition.

zustande ADVERB
■ **zustande bringen** to bring about
■ **zustande kommen** to come about

zuständig ADJECTIVE
■ **Dafür bin ich nicht zuständig.** That's not my responsibility.
■ **der zuständige Beamte** the official in charge

zustimmen (PERFECT **hat zugestimmt**) VERB [4]
to agree
□ Ich stimme dir zu. I agree with you.

die **Zustimmung** NOUN
1 consent
□ Du brauchst die Zustimmung deiner Eltern. You need your parents' consent.
2 approval
□ wenn das deine Zustimmung findet if that meets with your approval

zustoßen (PRESENT **stößt zu**, IMPERFECT **stieß zu**, PERFECT **ist zugestoßen**) VERB
to happen
□ Ihm ist doch hoffentlich nichts zugestoßen. Let's hope nothing's happened to him.

die **Zutaten** FEM PL NOUN
ingredients

zutreffen (PRESENT **trifft zu**, IMPERFECT **traf zu**, PERFECT **hat zugetroffen**) VERB [78]
1 to be true
□ Es trifft nicht zu, dass ich das Buch mitgenommen habe. It's not true that I took the book with me.
2 to apply
□ Diese Beschreibung trifft nicht auf sie zu. This description doesn't apply to her.

zutreffend ADJECTIVE
■ **Zutreffendes bitte unterstreichen.** Please underline where applicable.

zuverlässig ADJECTIVE
reliable

zuversichtlich ADJECTIVE
confident

zuviel ADVERB ▷ *see* **viel**

zuvor ADVERB
before
□ der Tag zuvor the day before

zuwenig ADVERB ▷ *see* **wenig**

zuziehen (IMPERFECT **zog zu**, PERFECT **hat zugezogen**) VERB [96]
1 to draw
□ Es wird dunkel, zieh bitte die Vorhänge zu. It's getting dark, please draw the curtains.
2 to call in
□ Wir sollten einen Fachmann zuziehen. We should call in an expert.
■ **sich etwas zuziehen** to catch something
□ Ich habe mir eine Erkältung zugezogen. I've caught a cold.

zuzüglich PREPOSITION

LANGUAGE TIP The preposition **zuzüglich** takes the genitive.

plus
□ zweihundert Euro zuzüglich der Spesen two hundred euros plus expenses

der **Zwang** (PL die **Zwänge**) NOUN
compulsion

zwängen VERB [38]
to squeeze

zwanglos ADJECTIVE
informal
□ ein zwangloses Gespräch an informal talk

zwanzig NUMBER
twenty

zwar ADVERB
although
□ Ich habe das zwar gesagt, aber es war nicht so gemeint. Although I said it, it wasn't meant like that.
■ **das ist zwar ..., aber ...** that may be ... but ... □ Das ist zwar viel, aber mir reicht es nicht. That may be a lot, but it's not enough for me.
■ **und zwar 1** to be precise □ und zwar am Sonntag on Sunday to be precise **2** in fact □ und zwar so schnell, dass ... in fact, so quickly that ...

der **Zweck** (PL die **Zwecke**) NOUN
1 purpose
□ Was ist der Zweck Ihres Besuchs? What's the purpose of your visit?
2 point
□ Was ist der Zweck dieser Übung? What's the point of this exercise? □ Es hat keinen Zweck. There's no point.

zwecklos ADJECTIVE
pointless

zwei NUMBER
▷ *see also* **die Zwei** NOUN
two

die **Zwei** NOUN
▷ *see also* **zwei** NUMBER
1 two
2 good

DID YOU KNOW...? German marks range from one (**sehr gut**) to six (**ungenügend**).

zweideutig ADJECTIVE
1 ambiguous
□ Sie hat sich zweideutig ausgedrückt. She expressed herself very ambiguously.
2 suggestive
□ Er macht immer so zweideutige Witze. He's always making such suggestive jokes.

zweierlei ADJECTIVE
two different
□ zweierlei Stoff two different kinds of material □ Das sind doch zweierlei Dinge. They're two different things.
■ **zweierlei Meinung** of differing opinions

zweifach ADJECTIVE, ADVERB
1 double
□ die zweifache Menge double the quantity
2 twice
□ Der Brief war zweifach gefaltet. The letter had been folded twice.

der **Zweifel** (PL die **Zweifel**) NOUN
doubt
□ ohne Zweifel without doubt

zweifelhaft ADJECTIVE
1 doubtful
□ Es ist noch zweifelhaft, ob wir kommen. It's still doubtful whether we're coming.
2 dubious
□ eine zweifelhafte Lösung a dubious solution
■ **ein zweifelhaftes Kompliment** a backhanded compliment

zweifellos ADVERB
doubtless

■ **Sie hat sich zweifellos bemüht.** There's no doubt that she tried.

zweifeln VERB [34]
■ **an etwas zweifeln** to doubt something □ Ich zweifle an der Richtigkeit dieser Aussage. I doubt the truth of this statement.
■ **zweifeln, ob** to doubt whether □ Ich zweifle, ob wir das schaffen. I doubt whether we'll make it.

der **Zweig** (PL die **Zweige**) NOUN
branch

die **Zweigstelle** NOUN
branch
□ Die nächste Zweigstelle ist in Villach. The nearest branch is in Villach.

zweihundert NUMBER
two hundred

zweimal ADVERB
twice

zweisprachig ADJECTIVE
bilingual

zweispurig ADJECTIVE
two-lane

zweit ADVERB
■ **zu zweit 1** together □ Wir fahren zu zweit in die Ferien. We're going on holiday together. **2** in twos □ Stellt euch zu zweit auf. Line up in twos.

zweitbeste ADJECTIVE
second best

zweite ADJECTIVE
second
□ Er kam als Zweiter. He was the second to arrive.

zweitens ADVERB
secondly

zweitgrößte ADJECTIVE
second largest

zweitklassig ADJECTIVE
inferior

der **Zwerg** (PL die **Zwerge**) NOUN
dwarf

die **Zwetschge** NOUN
damson

der **Zwieback** (PL die **Zwiebacke**) NOUN
rusk

die **Zwiebel** NOUN
onion
□ Sebastian mag keine Zwiebeln. Sebastian doesn't like onions.

der **Zwilling** (PL die **Zwillinge**) NOUN
twin
□ Diese Zwillinge sehen sich zum Verwechseln ähnlich. The twins are the spitting image of each other.
■ **Zwillinge** Gemini □ Michael ist Zwilling. Michael's Gemini.

zwingen (IMPERFECT **zwang**, PERFECT **hat gezwungen**) VERB [97]
to force

zwinkern VERB [88]
to wink
□ Als sie das sagte, zwinkerte er wissend. When she said that he winked knowingly.

zwischen PREPOSITION

> LANGUAGE TIP Use the accusative to express movement or a change of place. Use the dative when there is no change of place.

between
□ Er stand zwischen den beiden Mädchen. He was standing between the two girls.
□ Stell deinen Stuhl zwischen unsere. Put your chair between ours.

das **Zwischending** NOUN
cross
□ Das ist ein Zwischending zwischen Schreibmaschine und Computer. It's a cross between a typewriter and a computer.

zwischendurch ADVERB
in between
□ Wir haben zwischendurch eine Pause gemacht. We had a break in between.

der **Zwischenfall** (PL die **Zwischenfälle**) NOUN
incident

die **Zwischenfrage** NOUN
question

zwölf NUMBER
twelve

Zypern NEUT NOUN
Cyprus
■ **aus Zypern** from Cyprus
■ **nach Zypern** to Cyprus

German in Action

Map of Germany

Map of Germany

- In area, Germany (357,045 km^2) is a third bigger than the UK (244,110 km^2).
- The population of Germany is about 82.5 million, a third more than that of the UK. The birth rate is low (1.4 children per woman).
- The German economy is the biggest in the EU and one of the biggest in the world.
- The Rhine, which rises in Switzerland and flows into the North Sea in Holland is 1,320 km long. Most of this great river is in Germany (865 km).

Some useful phrases

Das ist meine Schwester Christel.	This is my sister, Christel.
Sie heiratet im nächsten Sommer.	She's getting married next summer.
Ich habe einen Zwillingsbruder.	I have a twin brother.
Ich habe eine Zwillingsschwester.	I have a twin sister.
Ich habe einen Halbbruder.	I have a half-brother.
Ich bin ein Einzelkind.	I'm an only child.
Meine Eltern leben getrennt.	My parents are separated.
Meine Eltern sind geschieden.	My parents are divorced.
Mein Großvater ist letztes Jahr gestorben.	My grandfather died last year.
Meine Mutter hat wieder geheiratet.	My mother has got married again.

Beziehungen	**Relationships**
Ich vertrage mich gut mit meiner Schwester.	I get on well with my sister.
Ich vertrage mich überhaupt nicht mit meinem Bruder.	I don't get on at all with my brother.
Mein bester Freund heißt Max.	My best friend is called Max.
Ich habe drei beste Freundinnen.	I've got three best friends.
Wir sind immer zusammen.	We're always together.
Ich habe mich mit Michaela gestritten.	I've had a quarrel with Michaela.
Mit Katharina rede ich nicht mehr.	I'm not talking to Katharina any more.

Familienmitglieder	**Members of the family**
mein Vater	my father
meine Mutter	my mother
meine Eltern	my parents
mein Bruder	my brother
meine Schwester	my sister
mein Onkel	my uncle
meine Tante	my aunt
mein Cousin	my cousin (male)
meine Cousine	my cousin (female)
mein Großvater	my grandfather
meine Großmutter	my grandmother
mein Opa	my granddad
meine Oma	my gran
meine Großeltern	my grandparents
mein großer Bruder	my big brother
meine kleine Schwester	my little sister
der Freund meiner Schwester	my sister's boyfriend
die Freundin meines Bruders	my brother's girlfriend
der Verlobte meiner Schwester	my sister's fiancé
die Verlobte meines Bruders	my brother's fiancée

Gefühle	**Emotions**
Ich bin ...	**I am ...**
traurig	sad
erfreut	pleased
glücklich	happy
böse	angry
verliebt	in love
gekränkt	hurt
Ich bin verliebt in Angela.	I'm in love with Angela.
Bruno und ich haben uns getrennt.	Bruno and I have split up.
Ich freue mich, dass du kommst.	I'm pleased you're coming.
Ich bin traurig darüber, dass ich weggehe.	I'm sad to be leaving.
Ich hoffe, du bist nicht allzu böse.	I hope you're not too angry.
Sie war gekränkt, dass sie nicht eingeladen war.	She was hurt that she wasn't invited.

At home

At home

Wo wohnst du? / Where do you live?

Wo wohnst du?	Where do you live?
Ich wohne ...	**I live ...**
in einem Dorf	in a village
in einer Kleinstadt	in a small town
im Stadtzentrum	in the town centre
am Stadtrand von London	in the suburbs of London
auf dem Land	in the countryside
am Meer	at the seaside
an einem kleinen Fluss	beside a small river
100 km von Manchester entfernt	100 km from Manchester
nördlich von Birmingham	north of Birmingham
in einem Einzelhaus	in a detached house
in einem Doppelhaus	in a semi-detached house
in einem zweistöckigen Haus	in a two-storey house
in einem Wohnblock	in a block of flats
in einer Wohnung	in a flat
in einer Siedlung	on a housing estate
Ich wohne in einer Wohnung ...	**I live in a flat ...**
im Erdgeschoss	on the ground floor
im ersten Stock	on the first floor
im zweiten Stock	on the second floor
im obersten Stock	on the top floor
Ich wohne ...	**I live ...**
in einem modernen Haus	in a modern house
in einem Neubau	in a new house
in einem alten edwardianischen Haus	in an old Edwardian house

Von zu Hause zur Schule / From home to school

Von zu Hause zur Schule	From home to school
Die Schule ist ziemlich weit von meinem Haus entfernt.	School is quite a long way from my house.
Ich wohne fünf Minuten zu Fuß von der Schule entfernt.	I live five minutes' walk from school.
Mein Vater fährt mich im Auto zur Schule.	My father takes me to school in the car.
Ich fahre mit dem Bus zur Schule.	I go to school by bus.

Zu Hause / At home

Zu Hause	At home
Im Erdgeschoss ist ...	**On the ground floor there is ...**
die Küche	the kitchen
das Wohnzimmer	the living room
das Esszimmer	the dining room
der Salon	the lounge
Im Obergeschoss ist ...	**Upstairs there is ...**
mein Zimmer	my bedroom
das Zimmer meines Bruders	my brother's bedroom
das Zimmer meiner Eltern	my parents' room
das Gästezimmer	the spare bedroom
das Badezimmer	the bathroom
ein Arbeitszimmer	a study
ein Garten	a garden
ein Fußballplatz	a football pitch
ein Tennisplatz	a tennis court
ein Nachbar	a neighbour
die Leute gegenüber	the people opposite
die Nachbarn nebenan	the next-door neighbours

Some useful phrases

Mein Haus ist sehr klein.	My house is very small.
Mein Zimmer ist aufgeräumt.	My room is tidy.
Ich teile mein Zimmer mit meinem Bruder.	I share my bedroom with my brother.
Mein bester Freund wohnt in derselben Straße wie ich.	My best friend lives in the same street as me.
Neben meinem Haus ist ein Tennisplatz.	There's a tennis court next to my house.
Wir ziehen nächsten Monat um.	We're moving next month.

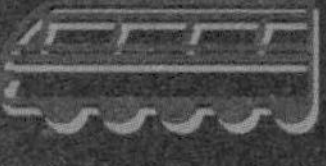

Einige Sehenswürdigkeiten	A few landmarks
ein Kino	a cinema
ein Theater	a theatre
ein Museum	a museum
ein Geldautomat	a cash dispenser
das Fremdenverkehrsbüro	the tourist office
eine Kathedrale	a cathedral
eine Kirche	a church
eine Moschee	a mosque
eine Fußgängerzone	a pedestrian precinct
eine Bank	a bank
das Schwimmbad	the swimming pool
die Eislaufbahn	the ice rink
die Stadtbücherei	the public library
das Rathaus	the town hall
ein Platz	a square
der Marktplatz	the market square

Verkehrsmittel	Means of transport
ein Bus	a bus
ein (Reise)bus	a coach
die U-Bahn	the underground
die Straßenbahn	the tram
der Zug	the train
der Bahnhof	the station
der Busbahnhof	the bus station
eine U-Bahn-Station	an underground station
Wann fährt der nächste Zug nach Köln?	What time is the next train to Cologne?
Eine einfache Karte nach Hamburg.	I'd like a single to Hamburg.
Eine Rückfahrkarte nach Berlin bitte.	A return to Berlin, please.
Wo ist Gleis 10?	Where is platform 10?
Wo ist die nächste U-Bahn-Station?	Where is the nearest underground station?

Richtungen	Directions
gegenüber	opposite
neben	next to
in der Nähe von	near
zwischen ... und ...	between ... and ...
Wo ist der Busbahnhof?	Where's the bus station?
Ich suche das Fremdenverkehrsbüro.	I'm looking for the tourist office.
Gehen Sie bis zum Ende der Straße.	Go right to the end of the street.
Biegen Sie rechts ab.	Turn right.
Überqueren Sie die Brücke.	Cross the bridge.
Nehmen Sie die erste Straße links.	Take the first street on the left.
Es ist auf der rechten Seite.	It's on your right.
Es ist gegenüber dem Kino.	It's opposite the cinema.
Es ist neben dem Postamt.	It's next to the post office.

My plans for the future

My plans for the future

Arbeit	Work
Ich möchte ... studieren	**I'd like to study ...**
Medizin	medicine
Maschinenbau	engineering
Jura	law
Soziologie	sociology
Psychologie	psychology
Sprachen	languages
Architektur	architecture
Ich möchte ...	**I'd like to ...**
viel Geld verdienen	earn lots of money
in einem Geschäft arbeiten	work in a shop
in einer Bank arbeiten	work in a bank
in der Tourismusbranche arbeiten	work in tourism
eine Lehre machen	do an apprenticeship
einen Abschluss machen	do a qualification
Ich möchte ... werden	**I'd like to be ...**
Rechtsanwalt/-anwältin	a solicitor
Lehrer(in)	a teacher
Zahnarzt/-ärztin	a dentist
Sänger(in)	a singer
Friseur/Friseuse	a hairdresser
Journalist(in)	a journalist
Schauspieler	an actor
Schauspielerin	an actress
Fußballprofi	a professional footballer
Musiker(in)	a musician
Politiker(in)	a politician
Ich glaube, dieser Beruf ist ...	**I think this job is ...**
interessant	interesting
anstrengend	tiring
langweilig	boring
stressig	stressful
gut bezahlt	well paid
schlecht bezahlt	badly paid

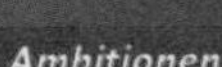

Ambitionen	Ambitions
Ich habe vor, zur Universität zu gehen.	I'm planning to go to university.
Danach möchte ich ins Ausland gehen.	Afterwards I'd like to go abroad.
Ich möchte heiraten und viele Kinder haben.	I'd like to get married and have lots of children.
Ich weiß noch nicht, was ich machen will.	I don't know yet what I want to do.

Prüfungen	Exams
eine Prüfung	an exam
eine schriftliche Prüfung	a written exam
eine mündliche Prüfung	an oral exam
das Ergebnis	the results
Ich mache dieses Jahr mein GCSE.	I'm doing my GCSEs this year.
Meine erste Prüfung ist nächsten Montag.	I'm going to do my first exam next Monday.
Ich hoffe, ich bestehe meine Prüfungen.	I hope I'll pass my exams.
Ich glaube, ich bin durch die Matheprüfung gefallen.	I think I've failed my maths exam.
Ich bekomme das Ergebnis im August.	I'll get the results in August.
Ich habe in meinen Prüfungen gut abgeschnitten.	I've done well in my exams.
Nächstes Jahr mache ich acht Prüfungen.	I'm going to do eight exams next year.

Jobs and hobbies

Sport	Sports
Ich spiele ...	**I play ...**
Fußball	football
Basketball	basketball
Rugby	rugby
Tennis	tennis
Tischtennis	table tennis
Ich ...	**I ...**
fahre Ski	ski
fahre Kanu	canoe
mache Gymnastik	do gymnastics
schwimme	swim
gehe Reiten	go horse riding
gehe Segeln	go sailing
Ich mache diesen Sommer einen Segelkurs.	I'm going to do a sailing course this summer.
Ich bin noch nie Ski gefahren.	I've never been skiing.
Ich will das Kanufahren lernen.	I'm going to learn how to canoe.

Arbeit	Jobs
ein Lebenslauf	a CV
ein Vorstellungsgespräch	an interview
Ich arbeite ...	**I work ...**
samstags in einer Apotheke	at a chemist's on Saturdays
in den Ferien im Supermarkt	at the supermarket in the holidays
am Wochenende in einem Bekleidungsgeschäft	in a clothes shop at the weekend
Ich babysitte.	I do baby-sitting.
Ich gehe für eine alte Frau einkaufen.	I do an old lady's shopping for her.
Ich trage Zeitungen aus.	I deliver papers.
Ich verdiene 8 Euro die Stunde.	I earn 8 euros an hour.
Ich hatte noch nie einen Job.	I've never had a job.
Ich suche mir in diesem Sommer einen Job.	I'm going to look for a job for this summer.

Musikinstrumente	Musical instruments
Ich spiele ...	**I play the ...**
Geige	violin
Klavier	piano
Gitarre	guitar
Querflöte	flute
Ich spiele Geige, seit ich acht bin.	I've been playing the violin since I was eight.
Ich spiele im Schulorchester.	I play in the school orchestra.
Ich möchte gern Gitarre lernen.	I'd like to learn to play the guitar.

Kochen zu Hause	Cooking at home
Ich koche gern.	I like cooking.
Ich kann nicht kochen.	I can't cook.
Ich kann sehr gut Kuchen backen.	I'm very good at making cakes.

Meine Lieblingshobbys	My favourite hobbies
Ich lese gern Romane.	I like reading novels.
Ich höre gern auf meinem Zimmer Musik.	I love listening to music in my room.
Ich gehe gern mit meinen Freunden in die Stadt.	I love going into town with my friends.
Am liebsten gehe ich Reiten.	My favourite hobby is riding.
Ich gehe lieber mit meinen Freunden aus.	I'd rather go out with my friends.

Describing someone

Persönlichkeit	Personality
Er/Sie ist ...	**He/She is ...**
lustig	funny
nett	nice
schüchtern	shy
still	quiet
lästig	annoying
großzügig	generous
gesprächig	talkative
intelligent	intelligent
dumm	stupid
geizig	stingy
seltsam	strange

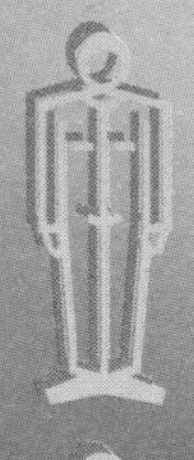

Farben	Colours
gelb	yellow
orange	orange
rot	red
rosa	pink
violett	purple
blau	blue
grün	green
braun	brown
grau	grey
schwarz	black
weiß	white
kastanienbraun	maroon
marineblau	navy (blue)
türkis	turquoise
beige	beige
cremefarben	cream
Für Augen:	**For eyes:**
haselnussbraun	hazel
Für Haare:	**For hair:**
rotbraun	auburn
blond	blonde, fair
hellblond	very fair
dunkelblond	light brown
brünett	brunette
kupferrot	ginger
grau meliert	greying
Ich habe haselnussbraune Augen.	I've got hazel eyes.
Er hat braunes Haar.	He's got brown hair.
Sie hat kurze graue Haare.	She's got short grey hair.
Sie hat rote Haare.	She's got red hair.
Er hat eine Glatze.	He's bald.
Sie hat lange lockige blonde Haare.	She's got long curly blonde hair.

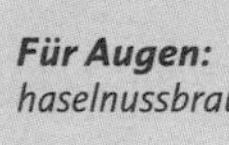

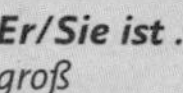

Merkmale	Characteristics
Er/Sie ist ...	**He/She is ...**
groß	tall
klein	small
schlank	slim
dick	fat
gutaussehend	good-looking
jung	young
alt	old
Er ist etwa dreißig.	He's about thirty.
Sie ist groß, schlank und sieht ziemlich gut aus.	She's tall, slim and quite nice-looking.
Er sieht aus wie Brad Pitt.	He looks like Brad Pitt.

Describing someone

Kleidung	Clothes
ein Pullover	a jumper
eine Hose	trousers
eine Bluse	a blouse
ein T-Shirt	a T-shirt
ein Mantel	a coat
eine Jacke	a jacket
eine Strickjacke	a cardigan
ein Kleid	a dress
ein Rock	a skirt
eine Krawatte	a tie
ein Jackett	a jacket
ein Hemd	a shirt
Schuhe	shoes
Turnschuhe	trainers
Stiefel	boots
Sie trägt ein hellblaues T-Shirt.	She's wearing a light blue T-shirt.
Er trägt einen dunkelgrauen Anzug.	He's wearing a dark grey suit.
Meine Uniform besteht aus einem marineblauen Rock, einer weißen Bluse, einer braun und grau gestreiften Krawatte, grauen Strümpfen, einem braunen Blazer und schwarzen Schuhen.	My uniform consists of a navy blue skirt, a white blouse, a tie with brown and grey stripes, grey socks, a brown blazer and black shoes.

Keeping fit and healthy

Mahlzeiten	Meals
das Frühstück	breakfast
das Mittagessen	lunch
das Abendessen	dinner
Ich liebe ...	**I love ...**
Schokolade	chocolate
Salat	salad
Fisch	fish
Limonade	lemonade
Gemüse	vegetables
Erdbeeren	strawberries
Ich mag kein ...	**I don't like ...**
Mineralwasser	mineral water
Ich mag keine ...	**I don't like ...**
Bananen	bananas
Ich mag keinen ...	**I don't like ...**
Orangensaft	orange juice
Ich esse kein Schweinefleisch.	I don't eat pork.
Ich esse viel Obst.	I eat a lot of fruit.
Ich esse kein Junkfood zwischen Mahlzeiten.	I don't eat junk food between meals.
Ich vermeide kohlensäurehaltige Getränke.	I avoid fizzy drinks.
Ich bin Vegetarier(in).	I'm a vegetarian.
Ich bin allergisch gegen Erdnüsse.	I'm allergic to peanuts.

Beschwerden	Ailments
Ich habe Schmerzen ...	**I have a sore ...**
im Magen	stomach
im Rücken	back
im Knie	knee
im Fuß	foot
im Nacken	neck
im Kopf	head
im Hals	throat
im Bein	leg
Ich habe Zahnschmerzen.	I've got toothache.
Mir tun die Ohren weh.	I've got earache.
Meine Augen tun weh.	My eyes are hurting.
Ich bin erkältet.	I've got a cold.
Ich habe Grippe.	I've got flu.
Mir ist schlecht.	I feel sick.
Ich bin müde.	I'm tired.
Ich bin krank.	I'm ill.
Mir ist ...	**I am ...**
kalt	cold
heiß	hot
Ich habe ...	**I am ...**
Angst	scared
Durst	thirsty
Hunger	hungry

Ich habe Angst davor, durch die Prüfung zu fallen.
I'm afraid that I'm going to fail the exam.

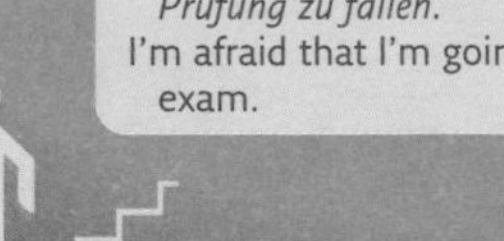

Fit bleiben	Keeping fit
Ich treibe viel Sport.	I do a lot of sport.
Ich rauche nicht.	I don't smoke.
Ich gehe früh schlafen.	I go to bed early.
Ich gehe zu Fuß zur Schule.	I walk to school.
Es ist gut für die Gesundheit.	It's good for your health.
Alkohol schadet der Gesundheit.	Alcohol is bad for your health.

When your number answers

Hallo! Kann ich bitte mit Valerie sprechen?	Hello! Could I speak to Valerie, please?
Könnten Sie ihn/sie bitten, mich zurückzurufen?	Would you ask him/her to call me back, please?
Ich rufe in einer halben Stunde wieder an.	I'll call back in half an hour.

Answering the telephone

Hallo! Hier spricht Mark.	Hello! It's Mark speaking.
Am Apparat.	Speaking.
Wer ist am Apparat?	Who's speaking?

When the switchboard answers

Wer spricht bitte?	Who shall I say is calling?
Ich stelle Sie durch.	I'm putting you through.
Bitte bleiben Sie am Apparat.	Please hold.
Möchten Sie eine Nachricht hinterlassen?	Would you like to leave a message?

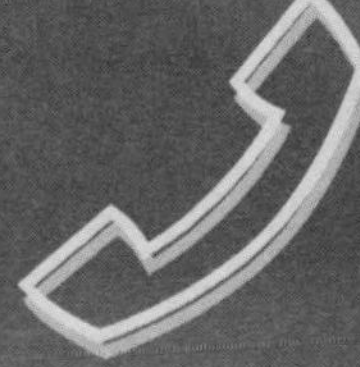

Difficulties

Ich komme nicht durch.	I can't get through.
Tut mir leid, ich habe mich verwählt.	I'm sorry, I dialled the wrong number.
Die Verbindung ist sehr schlecht.	This is a very bad line.
Ihr Telefon ist kaputt.	Their phone is out of order.
Ich kann Sie nicht verstehen!	You're breaking up!
Ich habe kein Gesprächsguthaben mehr.	I've no credit left on my phone

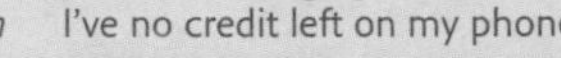

Letter

Writing a letter

Petra Hammann
Friedrichstraße 35
30169 Hannover

Hannover, 14. Februar 2008

Liebe Eltern,

vielen Dank für die CDs, die Ihr mir geschickt habt. Ihr habt gut ausgewählt – es sind meine beiden Lieblingsgruppen, die ich mir jetzt bestimmt pausenlos anhören werde!

Hier gibt es nicht viel Neues. Ich verbringe fast meine gesamte Zeit damit, mich auf meine Prüfungen vorzubereiten, die übernächste Woche beginnen. Ich hoffe natürlich, dass ich sie alle bestehen werde, aber die Matheprüfung macht mir etwas Sorgen: es ist das Fach, das ich am wenigsten mag.

Mutti sagte, dass Ihr nächste Woche nach Kreta fliegt. Ich wünsche Euch einen tollen Urlaub – sicher kommt ihr beide braungebrannt zurück.

Viele Grüße

Eure Petra

Alternatively
Herzliche Grüße
Alles Gute

Writing a personal letter
Your own name and address
Town/city you are writing from, and the date

Starting a personal letter

Vielen Dank für Deinen Brief.	Thank you for your letter.
Es war schön, von Dir zu hören.	It was lovely to hear from you.
Tut mir leid, dass ich nicht früher geschrieben habe.	I'm sorry I didn't write sooner.

Ending a personal letter

Schreib mir bald!	Write soon!
Viele Grüße auch an Gisela.	Give my love to Gisela.
Sebastian lässt herzlich grüßen.	Sebastian sends his best wishes.

Writing an email

Datei	Bearbeiten	Ansicht	Verfassen	Hilfe	Senden
			Nachricht erstellen		
			Antworten		
			Allen antworten		
			Weiterleiten		
			Anlage		

An: alice@xpnet.de
Cc: marion@festnet.com
Betreff: Konzert
Bcc:

Hallo!

Ich habe mir gerade die neue CD von Rockstar gekauft – fantastisch!

Ich habe drei Gratiskarten für das Rockstar-Konzert nächsten Samstag in Frankfurt und ich hoffe, dass Ihr beide mitkommen könnt.

Bis bald!

Saying your email address
To give your e-mail address to someone in German, say
"alice at x p net Punkt d e"

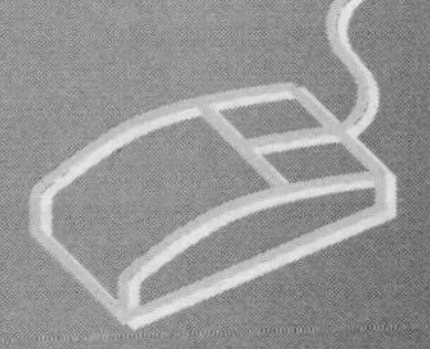

German	English
Neue Nachricht (f)	new message
An	to
Von	from
Betreff (m)	subject
Cc	cc (carbon copy)
Bcc	bcc
Anlage (f)	attachment
Senden	send
Datei (f)	file
Bearbeiten	edit
Ansicht (f)	view
Extras (pl)	tools
Verfassen	compose
Hilfe (f)	help
Antworten	reply (to sender)
Allen antworten	reply to all
Weiterleiten	forward
Datum (nt)	date

SMS-Kürzel	German	English
8ung	*Achtung*	look out
akla	*alles klar*	okay
bb	*bis bald*	see you soon
DaD	*denk an dich*	thinking of you
div	*danke im Voraus*	thanks in advance
GA	*Gruß an*	love/greetings to
GiE	*Ganz im Ernst*	seriously
GLG	*Ganz liebe Grüße*	love
gn8	*gute Nacht*	good night
GuK, G&K	*Gruß und Kuss*	love and kisses
ild	*Ich liebe dich*	I love you
mediwi	*melde dich wieder*	get in touch
mfg	*mit freundlichen Grüßen*	yours
rumian	*ruf mich an*	call me
sfh	*Schluss für heute*	enough for today
siw	*soweit ich weiß*	as far as I know
sTn	*schönen Tag noch*	have a nice day
sz	*schreib zurück*	write back
vlg	*viele Grüße*	love/greetings
vv	*viel Vergnügen*	have fun
wamadu-heu?	*was machst du heute?*	what are you up to today?

You will notice that just as the numbers 2, 4 and 8 are used in English in text messages (C U 2moro; R U coming 4 Xmas?; Gr8!), German texts also use 8 for all "acht" sounds.

Dates, festivals and holidays

Wochentage	**Days of the week**
Montag	Monday
Dienstag	Tuesday
Mittwoch	Wednesday
Donnerstag	Thursday
Freitag	Friday
Samstag	Saturday
Sonntag	Sunday
am Montag	on Monday
montags	on Mondays
jeden Montag	every Monday
letzten Dienstag	last Tuesday
nächsten Freitag	next Friday
Samstag in einer Woche	a week on Saturday
Samstag in zwei Wochen	two weeks on Saturday

Feiertage	**Festivals**
Weihnachten	Christmas
Heiligabend	Christmas Eve
der erste Weihnachtstag	Christmas Day
der zweite Weihnachtstag	Boxing Day
Silvester	New Year's Eve
der Neujahrstag	New Year's Day
der Valentinstag	Valentine's Day
der erste April	April Fool's Day
der Karfreitag	Good Friday
Ostern	Easter
Pfingsten	Whitsun
der Muttertag	Mother's Day
Allerheiligen	All Saints' Day
der Ramadan	Ramadan
Frohe Weihnachten!	Happy Christmas!
April, April!	April fool!
zu Ostern	at Easter
das neue Jahr feiern	to celebrate New Year
Was machst du zu Weihnachten?	What do you do at Christmas?
Wir verbringen den zweiten Weihnachtstag zu Hause.	We spend Boxing Day at home.
Zu Neujahr besuchen wir meinen Cousin.	We go to my cousins' for New Year.

Monate	**Months of the year**
Januar	January
Februar	February
März	March
April	April
Mai	May
Juni	June
Juli	July
August	August
September	September
Oktober	October
November	November
Dezember	December
Welches Datum ist heute?	What date is it today?
Es ist der 16. Juni.	It's the 16th of June.
Wann hast du Geburtstag?	What date is your birthday?
Am 22. Mai.	It's the 22nd of May.

Die Ferien	**Holidays**
die Sommerferien	the summer holidays
die Herbstferien	the autumn holidays
die Weihnachtsferien	the Christmas holidays
die Osterferien	the Easter holidays
der Strand	the seaside
die Berge	the mountains
Was machst du in den Ferien?	What are you going to do in the holidays?
Wir fahren diesen Sommer eine Woche nach Italien.	We're going to Italy for a week this summer.
Wir fahren dieses Jahr nicht in Urlaub.	We're not going on holiday this year.
Im Februar gehen wir immer Ski fahren.	We always go skiing in February.
Nächstes Jahr fahre ich für eine Woche zu meiner Brieffreundin in Frankreich.	I'm going to stay with my pen-friend in France for a week next year.
Im letzten Sommer war ich in den USA.	Last summer I went to the United States.

Wie spät ist es? Es ist...	**What time is it? It's...**

ein Uhr

zehn nach eins

Viertel nach eins

halb zwei

zwanzig vor zwei

Viertel vor zwei

Um wie viel Uhr?	**At what time?**

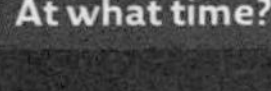

um Mitternacht

um Mittag

um ein Uhr (nachmittags)

um acht Uhr (abends)

um 11:15 Uhr or
elf Uhr fünfzehn

um 20:45 Uhr or
zwanzig Uhr fünfundvierzig

In German times are often given in the twenty-four hour clock.

Numbers

Numbers

0	*null*
1	*eins*
2	*zwei*
3	*drei*
4	*vier*
5	*fünf*
6	*sechs*
7	*sieben*
8	*acht*
9	*neun*
10	*zehn*
11	*elf*
12	*zwölf*
13	*dreizehn*
14	*vierzehn*
15	*fünfzehn*
16	*sechzehn*
17	*siebzehn*
18	*achtzehn*
19	*neunzehn*
20	*zwanzig*
21	*einundzwanzig*
22	*zweiundzwanzig*
30	*dreißig*
40	*vierzig*
50	*fünfzig*
60	*sechzig*
70	*siebzig*
80	*achtzig*
90	*neunzig*
100	*(ein)hundert*
101	*(ein)hundert-(und)eins*
200	*zweihundert*
300	*dreihundert*
301	*dreihundert(und)-eins*
1,000	*(ein)tausend*
2,000	*zweitausend*
1,000,000	*eine Million*

Examples
zehn Euro – ten euros
auf Seite neunzehn – on page nineteen
in Kapitel sieben – in chapter seven

Fractions etc

1/2	*ein halb*
1/3	*ein Drittel*
2/3	*zwei Drittel*
1/4	*ein Viertel*
3/4	*drei Viertel*
1/5	*ein Fünftel*
0.5	*null Komma fünf (0,5)*
3.4	*drei Komma vier (3,4)*
10%	*zehn Prozent*
100%	*hundert Prozent*
1st	*erste(r, s)*
2nd	*zweite(r, s)*
3rd	*dritte(r, s)*
4th	*vierte(r, s)*
5th	*fünfte(r, s)*
6th	*sechste(r, s)*
7th	*siebte(r, s)*
8th	*achte(r, s)*
9th	*neunte(r, s)*
10th	*zehnte(r, s)*
11th	*elfte(r, s)*
12th	*zwölfte(r, s)*
13th	*dreizehnte(r, s)*
14th	*vierzehnte(r, s)*
15th	*fünfzehnte(r, s)*
16th	*sechzehnte(r, s)*
17th	*siebzehnte(r, s)*
18th	*achtzehnte(r, s)*
19th	*neunzehnte(r, s)*
20th	*zwanzigste(r, s)*
21st	*einundzwanzigste(r, s)*
22nd	*zweiundzwanzigste(r, s)*
30th	*dreißigste(r, s)*
100th	*hundertste(r, s)*
101st	*hunderterste(r, s)*
1000th	*tausendste(r, s)*

Examples
er wohnt im fünften Stock – he lives on the fifth floor
es war das achte Mal – it was the eighth time
jeder zehnte Mann/jede zehnte Frau – one in ten men/women

Contents

German verb tables

This section is designed to help you find all the verb forms you need in German. From page 22 to 27 you will find a list of 97 regular and irregular verbs with a summary of their main forms, followed on pages 28 to 38 by some very common regular and irregular verbs shown in full, with example phrases.

How to find the verb forms you need

Most of the verbs on the **German-English** side of the dictionary are followed by a number in square brackets. Each of these numbers corresponds to a verb in this section.

lachen VERB [48]
to laugh

In this example, the number [48] after the verb **lachen** means that **lachen** follows the same pattern as verb number 48 in the list, which is **machen**. In this instance, **machen** is given in full on page 34.

diskutieren (PERFECT **hat diskutiert**) VERB [76]
to discuss

For other verbs, a summary of the main forms is given. In the example above, **diskutieren** follows the same pattern as verb number [76] in the list, which is **studieren**. On page 26 of this section, you can see that the main forms of **studieren** are given to show you how this verb (and others like it) works.

In the full verb tables, you will find examples of **weak**, **strong** and **mixed** verb forms. **Weak** verbs follow regular patterns, **strong** verbs follow irregular patterns and **mixed** verbs follow a mixture of regular and irregular patterns. In these tables, **machen** is an example of a **weak** verb, **wissen** is an example of a **mixed** verb and the rest are **strong** verbs.

Remember to visit **www.collinslanguage.com** for further help with verb tables.

Verb tables

The present tense

The present tense is used to talk about what is true at the moment, what happens regularly and what is happening now, for example, 'I'm a student'; 'She works as a consultant'; 'I'm studying German'.

There is more than one way to express the present tense in English. For example, you can either say 'I give', 'I am giving' or occasionally 'I do give'. In German, you use the same form **ich gebe** for all these.

In English you can also use the present tense to talk about something that is going to happen in the near future. You can do the same in German.

Morgen **spiele ich** Tennis.	**I'm going** to play tennis tomorrow.
Wir nehmen den Zug um zehn Uhr.	**We're getting** the 10 o'clock train.

The future tense

The future tense is used to talk about something that will happen or will be true. There are several ways to express the future tense in English: you can use the future tense ('I'll ask him on Tuesday'), the present tense ('I'm not working tomorrow'), or 'going to' followed by an infinitive ('She's going to study in Switzerland for a year'). In German you can also use the future tense (if you want to emphasize the future, express doubt or suppose something about the future) or the present tense. You cannot use the verb **gehen** (to go) followed by an infinitive.

Das **werde ich** erst nächstes Jahr **machen können**.	**I won't be able to do** that until next year.
Ich nehme den letzten Zug.	**I'm taking** the last train.
Das **wirst du bereuen**.	**You're going to** regret that.

The imperfect tense

The imperfect tense is one of the tenses used to talk about the past, especially in descriptions, and to say what used to happen, for example 'I used to work in Manchester'; 'It was sunny yesterday'.

Ich war ganz traurig, als sie wegging.	**I was** very sad when she left.
Es gab ein großes Problem mit Drogen.	**There was** a big problem with drugs.
Samstags **spielte ich** Tennis.	**I used to play** tennis on Saturdays.

The perfect tense

The perfect tense is made up of two parts: the present tense of **haben** or **sein**, and the German past participle (like 'given', 'finished' and 'done' in English).

Most verbs form the perfect tense with **haben**. There are two main groups of verbs which form their perfect tense with **sein** instead of **haben**: two verbs which mean 'to happen' (**geschehen** and **passieren**) and a group of verbs that are mainly used to talk about movement or a change of some kind, including:

gehen	to go
kommen	to come
ankommen	to arrive
abfahren	to leave
aussteigen	to get off
einsteigen	to get on
sterben	to die
sein	to be
werden	to become
bleiben	to remain
begegnen	to meet
gelingen	to succeed
aufstehen	to get up
fallen	to fall

Gestern **bin ich** ins Kino **gegangen**.	**I went** to the cinema yesterday.
Sie ist ganz früh **abgefahren**.	**She left** really early.

The imperative

The imperative is a form of the verb used when giving orders and instructions, for example, 'Be quiet!', 'Shut the door!', 'Don't go!'

In German, there are several forms of the imperative that are used to give instructions or orders to someone. These correspond to **du**, **ihr** and **Sie**. For the **du** form most verbs simply use the verb stem (an **-e** can be added to help pronunciation). The **ihr** form adds a **-t** to the stem and the **Sie** form adds **-en**.

Hol(e)!	**Fetch!**
Holt!	**Fetch!**
Holen Sie!	**Fetch!**

The subjunctive

The subjunctive is a verb form that is used in certain circumstances to express some sort of feeling, or to show there is doubt about whether something will happen or something is true. It is used much more frequently in German than in English, for example in indirect speech.

Direct Speech

Sie sagte: „Er **kennt** deine Schwester".	She said, "He **knows** your sister."

Indirect Speech

Sie sagte, er **kenne** meine Schwester.	She said he **knew** my sister.

The conditional

The conditional is a verb form used to talk about things that would happen or that would be true under certain conditions, for instance, 'I would help you if I could'. It is also used to say what you would like or need, for example, 'Could you give me the bill?'. The conditional tense in German is made up of two parts: the **würde** form – the imperfect subjunctive of the verb **werden** (*to become*) – and the infinitive of the main verb, which normally goes at the end of the sentence.

Was **würden** Sie an meiner Stelle **tun**?	What **would** you do in my position?
Das **würde** ich nie von dir **verlangen**.	I **would** never ask that of you.

German verb forms

INFINITIVE	PRESENT	PERFECT	IMPERFECT	FUTURE	PRESENT SUBJUNCTIVE
1 **annehmen** verb with a spelling change	ich nehme an du **nimmst** an er/sie/es **nimmt** an wir nehmen an	ich habe **angenommen** du **nahmst** an	ich **nahm** an du nehmest an er/sie/es **nahm** an wir **nahmen** an	ich werde annehmen	ich nehme an
2 **arbeiten**	ich arbeite	ich habe gearbeitet	ich arbeitete	ich werde arbeiten	ich arbeite
3 **atmen**	ich atme	ich habe geatmet	ich atmete	ich werde atmen	ich atme
4 **ausreichen**	ich reiche aus du reichst aus	ich habe ausgereicht	ich reichte aus	ich werde ausreichen	ich reiche aus du reichest aus
5 **beginnen** verb with a spelling change	ich beginne	ich habe **begonnen**	ich **begann** du **begannst** wir **begannen**	ich werde beginnen	ich beginne du beginnest
6 **beißen** verb with a spelling change	ich beiße du beißt	ich habe **gebissen**	ich **biss** du **bissest** er/sie/es **biss** wir **bissen** ihr **bisst** sie/Sie **bissen**	ich werde beißen	ich beiße du beißest
7 **bestellen**	ich bestelle du bestellst	ich habe **bestellt**	ich bestellte	ich werde bestellen	ich bestelle du bestellest
8 **bieten** verb with a spelling change	ich biete	ich habe **geboten**	ich **bot** du **bot(e)st** wir **boten**	ich werde bieten	ich biete
9 **bitten** verb with a spelling change	ich bitte	ich habe **gebeten** du **bat(e)st** wir **baten**	ich **bat**	ich werde bitten	ich bitte
10 **bleiben** verb with a spelling change	ich bleibe du bleibst	ich bin **geblieben** du **bliebst** wir **blieben**	ich **blieb**	ich werde bleiben	ich bleibe du bleibest
11 **brechen** verb with a spelling change	ich breche du br**i**chst er/sie/es br**i**cht wir brechen	ich habe/bin **gebrochen**	ich **brach** du **brachst** er/sie/es **brach** wir **brachen**	ich werde brechen	ich breche du brechest
12 **brennen** verb with a spelling change	ich brenne du brennst	ich habe gebr**a**nnt	ich br**a**nnte du br**a**nntest wir br**a**nnten	ich werde brennen	ich brenne du brennest
13 **bringen** verb with a spelling change	ich bringe du bringst	ich habe **gebracht**	ich **brachte** du **brachtest** wir **brachten**	ich werde bringen	ich bringe du bringest
14 **denken** verb with a spelling change	ich denke du denkst	ich habe **gedacht**	ich **dachte** du **dachtest** wir **dachten**	ich werde denken	ich denke du denkest
15 **durchsetzen**	ich setze durch du setzt durch	ich habe durchgesetzt	ich setzte durch	ich werde durchsetzen	ich setze durch du setzest durch

INFINITIVE	PRESENT	PERFECT	IMPERFECT	FUTURE	PRESENT SUBJUNCTIVE
16 **dürfen** verb with a spelling change	ich **darf** du **darfst** er/sie/es **darf** wir dürfen ihr dürft sie/Sie dürfen	ich habe ged**u**rft/ **dürfen**	ich d**u**rfte du d**u**rftest er/sie/es d**u**rfte	ich werde dürfen	ich dürfe du dürfest wir d**u**rften ihr d**u**rftet sie/Sie d**u**rften
17 **empfehlen** verb with a spelling change	ich empfehle du empf**ie**hlst er/sie/es empf**ie**hlt wir empfehlen	ich habe **empfohlen**	ich **empfahl** du **empfahlst** er/sie/es **empfahl** wir **empfahlen**	ich werde empfehlen	ich empfehle du empfehlest
18 **entdecken**	ich entdecke	ich habe **entdeckt**	ich entdeckte	ich werde entdecken	ich entdecke
19 **erzählen**	ich erzähle du erzählst	ich habe **erzählt**	ich erzählte	ich werde erzählen	ich erzähle du erzählest
20 **essen**	see full verb table page x				
21 **fahren**	see full verb table page x				
22 **fallen** verb with a spelling change	ich falle du f**ä**llst er/sie/es f**ä**llt wir fallen	ich bin **gefallen**	ich **fiel** du **fielst** er/sie/es **fiel** wir **fielen**	ich werde fallen	ich falle du fallest
23 **fangen** verb with a spelling change	ich fange du f**ä**ngst er/sie/es f**ä**ngt wir fangen	ich habe **gefangen**	ich **fing** du **fingst** er/sie/es **fing** wir **fingen**	ich werde fangen	ich fange du fangest
24 **finden** verb with a spelling change	ich finde du findest	ich habe **gefunden**	ich **fand** du **fand(e)st** wir **fanden**	ich werde finden	ich finde
25 **fliegen** verb with a spelling change	ich fliege du fliegst	ich habe/ bin **geflogen**	ich **flog** du **flogst** wir **flogen**	ich werde fliegen	ich fliege du fliegest
26 **fliehen** verb with a spelling change	ich fliehe du fliehst	ich bin/ habe **geflohen**	ich **floh** du **flohst** wir **flohen**	ich werde fliehen	ich fliehe du fliehest
27 **fließen** verb with a spelling change	ich fließe du fließt	ich bin **geflossen**	ich **floss** du **flossest** wir **flossen**	ich werde fließen	ich fließe du fließest
28 **geben** verb with a spelling change	ich gebe du g**i**bst er/sie/es g**i**bt wir geben	ich habe **gegeben**	ich **gab** du **gabst** er/sie/es **gab** wir **gaben**	ich werde geben	ich gebe du gebest
29 **gehen**	see full verb table page x				
30 **gewinnen** verb with a spelling change	ich gewinne du gewinnst	ich habe **gewonnen**	ich **gewann** du **gewannst** wir **gewannen**	ich werde gewinnen	ich gewinne du gewinnest
31 **grüßen**	ich grüße du grüßt	ich habe gegrüßt	ich grüßte	ich werde grüßen	ich grüße du grüßest
32 **haben**	see full verb table page x				
33 **halten** verb with a spelling change	ich halte du h**ä**ltst er/sie/es **hält** wir halten	ich habe **gehalten**	ich **hielt** du **hielt(e)st** er/sie/es **hielt** wir **hielten**	ich werde halten	ich halte du haltest

	INFINITIVE	PRESENT	PERFECT	IMPERFECT	FUTURE	PRESENT SUBJUNCTIVE
34	**handeln**	ich handle du handelst	ich habe gehandelt	ich handelte	ich werde handeln	ich handle du handlest
35	**hängen** verb with a spelling change	ich hänge du hängst	ich habe **gehangen**	ich **hing** du **hingst** wir **hingen**	ich werde hängen	ich hänge du hängest
36	**heizen**	ich heize du heizt	ich habe geheizt	ich heizte	ich werde heizen	ich heize du heizest
37	**helfen** verb with a spelling change	ich helfe du h**i**lfst er/sie/es h**i**lft wir helfen	ich habe **geholfen**	ich **half** du **halfst** er/sie/es **half** wir **halfen**	ich werde helfen	ich helfe du helfest
38	**holen**	ich hole du holst	ich habe geholt	ich holte	ich werde holten	ich hole du holest
39	**kennen** verb with a spelling change	ich kenne du kennst	ich habe gek**a**nnt	ich k**a**nnte du k**a**nntest wir k**a**nnten	ich werde kennen	ich kenne du kennest
40	**kommen**	see full verb table page x				
41	**können**	see full verb table page x				
42	**lassen** verb with a spelling change	ich lasse du l**ä**sst er/sie/es l**ä**sst wir lassen	ich habe **gelassen**	ich **ließ** du **ließest** er/sie/es **ließ** wir **ließen**	ich werde lassen	ich lasse du lassest
43	**laufen** verb with a spelling change	ich laufe du l**ä**ufst er/sie/es l**ä**uft wir laufen	ich bin **gelaufen**	ich **lief** du **liefst** er/sie/es **lief** wir **liefen**	ich werde laufen	ich laufe du laufest
44	**leiden** verb with a spelling change	ich leide	ich habe **gelitten**	ich **litt** du **litt(e)st** wir **litten**	ich werde leiden	ich leide
45	**lesen** verb with a spelling change	ich lese du l**ie**st er/sie/es l**ie**st wir lesen	ich habe **gelesen**	ich **las** du **lasest** er/sie/es **las** wir **lasen**	ich werde lesen	ich lese du lesest
46	**liegen** verb with a spelling change	ich liege du liegst	ich habe **gelegen**	ich **lag** du **lagst** wir **lagen**	ich werde legen	ich liege du liegest
47	**lügen** verb with a spelling change	ich lüge du lügst	ich habe **gelogen**	ich **log** du **logst** wir **logen**	ich werde lügen	ich lüge du lügest
48	**machen**	see full verb table page x				
49	**misstrauen**	ich misstraue du misstraust	ich habe **misstraut**	ich misstraute	ich werde misstrauen	ich misstraue du misstrauest
50	**mögen** verb with a spelling change	ich **mag** du m**a**gst er/sie/es **mag** wir mögen ihr mögt sie/Sie mögen	ich habe **gemocht/** **mögen**	ich **mochte** du **mochtest** er/sie/es **mochte** wir **mochten** ihr **mochtet** sie/Sie **mochten**	ich werde mögen	ich möge du mögest
51	**müssen**	see full verb table page x				

	INFINITIVE	PRESENT	PERFECT	IMPERFECT	FUTURE	PRESENT SUBJUNCTIVE
52	**nehmen** verb with a spelling change	ich nehme du **nimmst** er/sie/es **nimmt** wir nehmen	ich habe **genommen**	ich **nahm** du **nahmst** er/sie/es **nahm** wir **nahmen**	ich werde nehmen	ich nehme du nehmest
53	**rechnen**	ich rechne	ich habe gerechnet	ich rechnete	ich werde rechnen	ich rechne
54	**reden**	ich rede	ich habe geredet	ich redete	ich werde redden	ich rede
55	**rennen** verb with a spelling change	ich renne du rennst	ich bin ger**a**nnt	ich r**a**nnte du r**a**nntest wir r**a**nnten	ich werde rennen	ich renne du rennest
56	**rufen** verb with a spelling change	ich rufe du rufst	ich habe **gerufen**	ich **rief** du **riefst** wir **riefen**	ich werde rufen	ich rufe du rufest
57	**scheinen** verb with a spelling change	ich scheine du scheinst	ich habe **geschienen**	ich **schien** du **schienst** wir **schienen**	ich werde scheinen	ich scheine du scheinest
58	**schlafen** verb with a spelling change	ich schlafe du schl**ä**fst er/sie/es schl**ä**ft wir schlafen	ich habe **geschlafen**	ich **schlief** du **schliefst** er/sie/es **schlief** wir **schliefen**	ich werde schlafen	ich schlafe du schlafest
59	**schlagen** verb with a spelling change	ich schlage du schl**ä**gst er/sie/es schl**ä**gt wir schlagen	ich habe **geschlagen**	ich **schlug** du **schlugst** er/sie/es **schlug** wir **schlugen**	ich werde schlagen	ich schlage du schlagest
60	**schneiden** verb with a spelling change	ich schneide	ich habe **geschnitten**	ich **schnitt** du **schnittst** wir **schnitten**	ich werde schneiden	ich schneide
61	**schreiben** verb with a spelling change	ich schreibe du schreibst	ich habe **geschrieben**	ich **schrieb** du **schriebst** wir **schrieben**	ich werde schreiben	ich schreibe du schreibest
62	**schreien** verb with a spelling change	ich schreie du schreist	ich habe **geschrien**	ich **schrie** du **schriest** wir **schrien**	ich werde schreien	ich schreie du schreiest
63	**schwimmen** verb with a spelling change	ich schwimme du schwimmst	ich bin **gesch-wommen**	ich **schwamm** du **schwammst** wir **schwammen**	ich werde schwimmen	ich schwimme du schwimmest
64	**sehen** verb with a spelling change	ich sehe du s**ie**hst er/sie/es s**ie**ht wir sehen	ich habe **gesehen**	ich **sah** du **sahst** er/sie/es **sah** wir **sahen**	ich werde sehen	ich sehe du sehest
65	**sein**	see full verb table page x				
66	**singen** verb with a spelling change	ich singe du singst	ich habe **gesungen**	ich **sang** du **sangst** wir **sangen**	ich werde singen	ich singe du singest
67	**sinken** verb with a spelling change	ich sinke du sinkst	ich bin **gesunken**	ich **sank** du **sankst** wir **sanken**	ich werde sinken	ich sinke du sinkest
68	**sitzen** verb with a spelling change	ich sitze du sitzt	ich habe **gesessen**	ich **saß** du **saßest** wir **saßen**	ich werde sitzen	ich sitze du sitzest

INFINITIVE	PRESENT	PERFECT	IMPERFECT	FUTURE	PRESENT SUBJUNCTIVE
69 **sollen**	ich soll du sollst	ich habe gesollt/**sollen**	ich sollte	ich werde sollen	ich solle du sollest
70 **sprechen** verb with a spelling change	ich spreche du sprichst er/sie/es spricht wir sprechen	ich habe **gesprochen**	ich **sprach** du **sprachst** er/sie/es **sprach** wir **sprachen**	ich werde sprechen	ich spreche du sprechest
71 **springen** verb with a spelling change	ich springe du springst	ich bin **gesprungen**	ich **sprang** du **sprangst** wir **sprangen**	ich werde springen	ich springe du springest
72 **stehen** verb with a spelling change	ich stehe du stehst	ich habe **gestanden**	ich **stand** du **stand(e)st** wir **standen**	ich werde stehen	ich stehe du stehest
73 **stehle** verb with a spelling change	ich stehle du stiehlst er/sie/es stiehlt wir stehlen	ich habe **gestohlen**	ich **stahl** du **stahlst** er/sie/es **stahl** wir **stahlen**	ich werde stehlen	ich stehle du stehlest
74 **steigen** verb with a spelling change	ich steige du steigst	ich bin **gestiegen**	ich **stieg** du **stiegst** wir **stiegen**	ich werde steigen	ich steige du steigest
75 **sterben** verb with a spelling change	ich sterbe du stirbst er/sie/es stirbt wir sterben	ich bin **gestorben**	ich **starb** du **starbst** er/sie/es **starb** wir **starben**	ich werde sterben	ich sterbe du sterbest
76 **studieren**	ich studiere du studierst	ich habe **studiert**	ich studierte	ich werde studieren	ich studiere du studierest
77 **tragen** verb with a spelling change	ich trage du trägst er/sie/es trägt wir tragen	ich habe **getragen**	ich **trug** du **trugst** er/sie/es **trug** wir **trugen**	ich werde tragen	ich trage du tragest
78 **treffen** verb with a spelling change	ich treffe du triffst er/sie/es trifft wir treffen	ich habe **getroffen**	ich **traf** du **trafst** er/sie/es **traf** wir **trafen**	ich werde treffen	ich treffe du treffest
79 **treten** verb with a spelling change	ich trete du **trittst** er/sie/es **tritt** wir treten	ich habe/ bin **getreten**	ich **trat** du **trat(e)st** er/sie/es **trat** wir **traten**	ich werde treten	ich trete du tretest
80 **trinken** verb with a spelling change	ich trinke du trinkst	ich habe **getrunken**	ich **trank** du **trankst** wir **tranken**	ich werde trinken	ich trinke du trinkest
81 **tun** verb with a spelling change	ich tue du tust er/sie/es tut wir tun ihr tut sie/Sie tun	ich habe **getan**	ich **tat** du **tat(e)st** er/sie/es **tat** wir **taten** ihr **tatet** sie/Sie **taten**	ich werde tun	ich tue du tuest
82 **sich überlegen**	ich überlege mir du überlegst dir	ich habe mir **überlegt**	ich überlegte mir	ich werde mir überlegen	ich überlege mir du überlegest dir

INFINITIVE	PRESENT	PERFECT	IMPERFECT	FUTURE	PRESENT SUBJUNCTIVE
83 **vergessen** verb with a spelling change	ich vergesse du vergisst er/sie/es vergisst wir vergessen	ich habe **vergessen**	ich **vergaß** du **vergaßest** er/sie/es **vergaß** wir **vergaßen**	ich werde vergessen	ich vergesse du vergessest
84 **verlangen**	ich verlange du verlangst	ich habe **verlangt**	ich verlangte	ich werde verlangen	ich verlange du verlangest
85 **verlieren** verb with a spelling change	ich verliere du verlierst	ich habe **verloren**	ich **verlor** du **verlorst** wir **verloren**	ich werde verlieren	ich verliere du verlierest
86 **versch-winden** verb with a spelling change	ich verschwinde	ich bin **versch-wunden**	ich **verschwand** du **versch-wand(e)st** wir **versch-wanden**	ich werde verschwinden	ich verschwinde
87 **wachsen** verb with a spelling change	ich wachse du wächst er/sie/es wächst wir wachsen	ich bin **gewachsen**	ich **wuchs** du **wuchsest** er/sie/es **wuchs** wir **wuchsen**	ich werde wachsen	ich wachse du wachsest
88 **wandern**	ich wand(e)re du wanderst	ich bin gewandert	ich wanderte	ich werde wandern	ich wand(e)re du wandrest
89 **waschen** verb with a spelling change	ich wasche du wäschst er/sie/es wäscht wir waschen	ich habe **gewaschen**	ich **wusch** du **wuschest** er/sie/es **wusch** wir **wuschen**	ich werde waschen	ich wasche du waschest
90 **werben** verb with a spelling change	ich werbe du wirbst er/sie/es wirbt wir werben	ich habe **geworben**	ich **warb** du **warbst** er/sie/es **warb** wir **wurben**	ich werde werben	ich werbe du werbest
91 **werden**	see full verb table page x				
92 **werfen** verb with a spelling change	ich werfe du wirfst er/sie/es wirft wir werfen	ich habe **geworfen**	ich **warf** du **warfst** er/sie/es **warf** wir **warfen**	ich werde werfen	ich werfe du werfest
93 **wissen**	see full verb table page x				
94 **wollen** verb with a spelling change	ich **will** du willst er/sie/es **will** wir wollen ihr wollt sie/Sie wollen	ich habe gewollt/**wollen**	ich wollte	ich werde werfen	ich wolle du wollest
95 **zerstören**	ich zerstöre du zerstörst	ich habe zerstört	ich zerstörte	ich werde zerstören	ich zerstöre du zerstörest
96 **ziehen** verb with a spelling change	ich ziehe du ziehst	ich bin/habe **gezogen**	ich **zog** du **zogst** wir **zogen**	ich werde ziehen	ich ziehe du ziehest
97 **zwingen** verb with a spelling change	ich zwinge du zwingst	ich habe **gezwungen**	ich **zwang** du **zwangst** wir **zwangen**	ich werde zwingen	ich zwinge du zwingest

essen (to eat)

	PRESENT		PRESENT SUBJUNCTIVE
ich	**esse**	ich	**esse**
du	**isst**	du	**essest**
er/sie/es	**isst**	er/sie/es	**esse**
wir	**essen**	wir	**essen**
ihr	**esst**	ihr	**esset**
sie/Sie	**essen**	sie/Sie	**essen**

	PERFECT		IMPERFECT
ich	**habe gegessen**	ich	**aß**
du	**hast gegessen**	du	**aßest**
er/sie/es	**hat gegessen**	er/sie/es	**aß**
wir	**haben gegessen**	wir	**aßen**
ihr	**habt gegessen**	ihr	**aßt**
sie/Sie	**haben gegessen**	sie/Sie	**aßen**

	FUTURE		CONDITIONAL
ich	**werde essen**	ich	**würde essen**
du	**wirst essen**	du	**würdest essen**
er/sie/es	**wird essen**	er/sie/es	**würde essen**
wir	**werden essen**	wir	**würden essen**
ihr	**werdet essen**	ihr	**würdet essen**
sie/Sie	**werden essen**	sie/Sie	**würden essen**

PAST PARTICIPLE

gegessen

PRESENT PARTICIPLE

essend

IMPERATIVE

iss!/essen wir!/esst!/essen Sie!

EXAMPLE PHRASES

Ich **esse** kein Fleisch. I don't eat meat.
Wir **haben** nichts **gegessen**. We haven't had anything to eat.
Ich möchte etwas **essen**. I'd like something to eat.

ich = I **du** = you **er** = he/it **sie** = she/it **es** = it/he/she **wir** = we **ihr** = you **sie** = they **Sie** = you

fahren (to drive/to go)

	PRESENT		PRESENT SUBJUNCTIVE
ich	**fahre**	ich	**fahre**
du	**fährst**	du	**fahrest**
er/sie/es	**fährt**	er/sie/es	**fahre**
wir	**fahren**	wir	**fahren**
ihr	**fahrt**	ihr	**fahret**
sie/Sie	**fahren**	sie/Sie	**fahren**

	PERFECT		IMPERFECT
ich	**bin gefahren**	ich	**fuhr**
du	**bist gefahren**	du	**fuhrst**
er/sie/es	**ist gefahren**	er/sie/es	**fuhr**
wir	**sind gefahren**	wir	**fuhren**
ihr	**seid gefahren**	ihr	**fuhrt**
sie/Sie	**sind gefahren**	sie/Sie	**fuhren**

	FUTURE		CONDITIONAL
ich	**werde fahren**	ich	**würde fahren**
du	**wirst fahren**	du	**würdest fahren**
er/sie/es	**wird fahren**	er/sie/es	**würde fahren**
wir	**werden fahren**	wir	**würden fahren**
ihr	**werdet fahren**	ihr	**würdet fahren**
sie/Sie	**werden fahren**	sie/Sie	**würden fahren**

PAST PARTICIPLE

gefahren

PRESENT PARTICIPLE

fahrend

IMPERATIVE

fahr(e)!/fahren wir!/fahrt!/fahren Sie!

EXAMPLE PHRASES

Sie **fahren** mit dem Bus in die Schule. They go to school by bus.
Rechts **fahren**! Drive on the right!
Ich **bin** mit der Familie nach Spanien **gefahren**. I went to Spain with my family.
Sie **hat** das Auto **gefahren**. She drove the car.

ich = I **du** = you **er** = he/it **sie** = she/it **es** = it/he/she **wir** = we **ihr** = you **sie** = they **Sie** = you

gehen (to go)

	PRESENT		PRESENT SUBJUNCTIVE
ich	**gehe**	ich	**gehe**
du	**gehst**	du	**gehest**
er/sie/es	**geht**	er/sie/es	**gehe**
wir	**gehen**	wir	**gehen**
ihr	**geht**	ihr	**gehet**
sie/Sie	**gehen**	sie/Sie	**gehen**

	PERFECT		IMPERFECT
ich	**bin gegangen**	ich	**ging**
du	**bist gegangen**	du	**gingst**
er/sie/es	**ist gegangen**	er/sie/es	**ging**
wir	**sind gegangen**	wir	**gingen**
ihr	**seid gegangen**	ihr	**gingt**
sie/Sie	**sind gegangen**	sie/Sie	**gingen**

	FUTURE		CONDITIONAL
ich	**werde gehen**	ich	**würde gehen**
du	**wirst gehen**	du	**würdest gehen**
er/sie/es	**wird gehen**	er/sie/es	**würde gehen**
wir	**werden gehen**	wir	**würden gehen**
ihr	**werdet gehen**	ihr	**würdet gehen**
sie/Sie	**werden gehen**	sie/Sie	**würden gehen**

PAST PARTICIPLE

gegangen

PRESENT PARTICIPLE

gehend

IMPERATIVE

geh(e)!/gehen wir!/geht!/gehen Sie!

EXAMPLE PHRASES

Die Kinder **gingen** ins Haus. The children went into the house.
Wie **geht** es dir? How are you?
Wir **sind** gestern schwimmen **gegangen**. We went swimming yesterday.

ich = I **du** = you **er** = he/it **sie** = she/it **es** = it/he/she **wir** = we **ihr** = you **sie** = they **Sie** = you

haben (to have)

	PRESENT		PRESENT SUBJUNCTIVE
ich	**habe**	ich	**habe**
du	**hast**	du	**habest**
er/sie/es	**hat**	er/sie/es	**habe**
wir	**haben**	wir	**haben**
ihr	**habt**	ihr	**habet**
sie/Sie	**haben**	sie/Sie	**haben**

	PERFECT		IMPERFECT
ich	**habe gehabt**	ich	**hatte**
du	**hast gehabt**	du	**hattest**
er/sie/es	**hat gehabt**	er/sie/es	**hatte**
wir	**haben gehabt**	wir	**hatten**
ihr	**habt gehabt**	ihr	**hattet**
sie/Sie	**haben gehabt**	sie/Sie	**hatten**

	FUTURE		CONDITIONAL
ich	**werde haben**	ich	**würde haben**
du	**wirst haben**	du	**würdest haben**
er/sie/es	**wird haben**	er/sie/es	**würde haben**
wir	**werden haben**	wir	**würden haben**
ihr	**werdet haben**	ihr	**würdet haben**
sie/Sie	**werden haben**	sie/Sie	**würden haben**

PAST PARTICIPLE

gehabt

PRESENT PARTICIPLE

habend

IMPERATIVE

hab(e)!/haben wir!/habt!/haben Sie!

EXAMPLE PHRASES

Hast du eine Schwester? Have you got a sister?
Er **hatte** Hunger. He was hungry.
Sie **hat** heute Geburtstag. It's her birthday today.

ich = I **du** = you **er** = he/it **sie** = she/it **es** = it/he/she **wir** = we **ihr** = you **sie** = they **Sie** = you

kommen (to come)

	PRESENT		PRESENT SUBJUNCTIVE
ich	**komme**	ich	**komme**
du	**kommst**	du	**kommest**
er/sie/es	**kommt**	er/sie/es	**komme**
wir	**kommen**	wir	**kommen**
ihr	**kommt**	ihr	**kommet**
sie/Sie	**kommen**	sie/Sie	**kommen**

	PERFECT		IMPERFECT
ich	**bin gekommen**	ich	**kam**
du	**bist gekommen**	du	**kamst**
er/sie/es	**ist gekommen**	er/sie/es	**kam**
wir	**sind gekommen**	wir	**kamen**
ihr	**seid gekommen**	ihr	**kamt**
sie/Sie	**sind gekommen**	sie/Sie	**kamen**

	FUTURE		CONDITIONAL
ich	**werde kommen**	ich	**würde kommen**
du	**wirst kommen**	du	**würdest kommen**
er/sie/es	**wird kommen**	er/sie/es	**würde kommen**
wir	**werden kommen**	wir	**würden kommen**
ihr	**werdet kommen**	ihr	**würdet kommen**
sie/Sie	**werden kommen**	sie/Sie	**würden kommen**

PAST PARTICIPLE

gekommen

PRESENT PARTICIPLE

kommend

IMPERATIVE

komm(e)!/kommen wir!/kommt!/kommen Sie!

EXAMPLE PHRASES

Er **kam** die Straße entlang. He was coming along the street.
Ich **komme** zu deiner Party. I'm coming to your party.
Woher **kommst** du? Where do you come from?

ich = I **du** = you **er** = he/it **sie** = she/it **es** = it/he/she **wir** = we **ihr** = you **sie** = they **Sie** = you

können (to be able to)

	PRESENT		PRESENT SUBJUNCTIVE
ich	**kann**	ich	**könne**
du	**kannst**	du	**könnest**
er/sie/es	**kann**	er/sie/es	**könne**
wir	**können**	wir	**können**
ihr	**könnt**	ihr	**könnet**
sie/Sie	**können**	sie/Sie	**können**

	PERFECT		IMPERFECT
ich	**habe gekonnt/können**	ich	**konnte**
du	**hast gekonnt/können**	du	**konntest**
er/sie/es	**hat gekonnt/können**	er/sie/es	**konnte**
wir	**haben gekonnt/können**	wir	**konnten**
ihr	**habt gekonnt/können**	ihr	**konntet**
sie/Sie	**haben gekonnt/können**	sie/Sie	**konnten**

	FUTURE		CONDITIONAL
ich	**werde können**	ich	**würde können**
du	**wirst können**	du	**würdest können**
er/sie/es	**wird können**	er/sie/es	**würde können**
wir	**werden können**	wir	**würden können**
ihr	**werdet können**	ihr	**würdet können**
sie/Sie	**werden können**	sie/Sie	**würden können**

PAST PARTICIPLE

gekonnt/können*

PRESENT PARTICIPLE

könnend

*This form is used when combined with another infinitive.

EXAMPLE PHRASES

Er **kann** gut schwimmen. He can swim well.
Sie **konnte** kein Wort Deutsch. She couldn't speak a word of German.
Kann ich gehen? Can I go?

ich = I **du** = you **er** = he/it **sie** = she/it **es** = it/he/she **wir** = we **ihr** = you **sie** = they **Sie** = you

machen (to do *or* to make)

PRESENT		PRESENT SUBJUNCTIVE	
ich	**mache**	ich	**mache**
du	**machst**	du	**machest**
er/sie/es	**macht**	er/sie/es	**mache**
wir	**machen**	wir	**machen**
ihr	**macht**	ihr	**machet**
sie/Sie	**machen**	sie/Sie	**machen**

PERFECT		IMPERFECT	
ich	**habe gemacht**	ich	**machte**
du	**hast gemacht**	du	**machtest**
er/sie/es	**hat gemacht**	er/sie/es	**machte**
wir	**haben gemacht**	wir	**machten**
ihr	**habt gemacht**	ihr	**machtet**
sie/Sie	**haben gemacht**	sie/Sie	**machten**

FUTURE		CONDITIONAL	
ich	**werde machen**	ich	**würde machen**
du	**wirst machen**	du	**würdest machen**
er/sie/es	**wird machen**	er/sie/es	**würde machen**
wir	**werden machen**	wir	**würden machen**
ihr	**werdet machen**	ihr	**würdet machen**
sie/Sie	**werden machen**	sie/Sie	**würden machen**

PAST PARTICIPLE
gemacht

PRESENT PARTICIPLE
machend

IMPERATIVE
mach!/macht!/machen Sie!

EXAMPLE PHRASES

Was **machst** du? What are you doing?
Ich **habe** die Betten **gemacht**. I made the beds.
Ich **werde** es morgen **machen**. I'll do it tomorrow.

ich = I **du** = you **er** = he/it **sie** = she/it **es** = it/he/she **wir** = we **ihr** = you **sie** = they **Sie** = you

müssen (to have to)

	PRESENT		PRESENT SUBJUNCTIVE
ich	**muss**	ich	**müsse**
du	**musst**	du	**müssest**
er/sie/es	**muss**	er/sie/es	**müsse**
wir	**müssen**	wir	**müssen**
ihr	**müsst**	ihr	**müsset**
sie/Sie	**müssen**	sie/Sie	**müssen**

	PERFECT		IMPERFECT
ich	**habe gemusst/müssen**	ich	**musste**
du	**hast gemusst/müssen**	du	**musstest**
er/sie/es	**hat gemusst/müssen**	er/sie/es	**musste**
wir	**haben gemusst/müssen**	wir	**mussten**
ihr	**habt gemusst/müssen**	ihr	**musstet**
sie/Sie	**haben gemusst/müssen**	sie/Sie	**mussten**

	FUTURE		CONDITIONAL
ich	**werde müssen**	ich	**würde müssen**
du	**wirst müssen**	du	**würdest müssen**
er/sie/es	**wird müssen**	er/sie/es	**würde müssen**
wir	**werden müssen**	wir	**würden müssen**
ihr	**werdet müssen**	ihr	**würdet müssen**
sie/Sie	**werden müssen**	sie/Sie	**würden müssen**

PAST PARTICIPLE

gemusst/müssen*

PRESENT PARTICIPLE

müssend

*This form is used when combined with another infinitive.

EXAMPLE PHRASES

Ich **muss** auf die Toilette. I must go to the loo.
Wir **müssen** jeden Abend unsere Hausaufgaben machen. We have to do our homework every night.
Sie **hat** abwaschen **müssen**. She had to wash up.

ich = I **du** = you **er** = he/it **sie** = she/it **es** = it/he/she **wir** = we **ihr** = you **sie** = they **Sie** = you

sein (to be)

	PRESENT		PRESENT SUBJUNCTIVE
ich	**bin**	ich	**sei**
du	**bist**	du	**sei(e)st**
er/sie/es	**ist**	er/sie/es	**sei**
wir	**sind**	wir	**seien**
ihr	**seid**	ihr	**seiet**
sie/Sie	**sind**	sie/Sie	**seien**

	PERFECT		IMPERFECT
ich	**bin gewesen**	ich	**war**
du	**bist gewesen**	du	**warst**
er/sie/es	**ist gewesen**	er/sie/es	**war**
wir	**sind gewesen**	wir	**waren**
ihr	**seid gewesen**	ihr	**wart**
sie/Sie	**sind gewesen**	sie/Sie	**waren**

	FUTURE		CONDITIONAL
ich	**werde sein**	ich	**würde sein**
du	**wirst sein**	du	**würdest sein**
er/sie/es	**wird sein**	er/sie/es	**würde sein**
wir	**werden sein**	wir	**würden sein**
ihr	**werdet sein**	ihr	**würdet sein**
sie/Sie	**werden sein**	sie/Sie	**würden sein**

PAST PARTICIPLE

gewesen

PRESENT PARTICIPLE

seiend

IMPERATIVE

sei!/seien wir!/seid!/seien Sie!

EXAMPLE PHRASES

Er **ist** zehn Jahre alt. He is ten years old.
Wir **waren** gestern im Theater. We were at the theatre yesterday.
Mir **war** kalt. I was cold.

ich = I **du** = you **er** = he/it **sie** = she/it **es** = it/he/she **wir** = we **ihr** = you **sie** = they **Sie** = you

werden (to become)

	PRESENT		PRESENT SUBJUNCTIVE
ich	**werde**	ich	**werde**
du	**wirst**	du	**werdest**
er/sie/es	**wird**	er/sie/es	**werde**
wir	**werden**	wir	**werden**
ihr	**werdet**	ihr	**werdet**
sie/Sie	**werden**	sie/Sie	**werden**

	PERFECT		IMPERFECT
ich	**bin geworden**	ich	**wurde**
du	**bist geworden**	du	**wurdest**
er/sie/es	**ist geworden**	er/sie/es	**wurde**
wir	**sind geworden**	wir	**wurden**
ihr	**seid geworden**	ihr	**wurdet**
sie/Sie	**sind geworden**	sie/Sie	**wurden**

	FUTURE		CONDITIONAL
ich	**werde werden**	ich	**würde werden**
du	**wirst werden**	du	**würdest werden**
er/sie/es	**wird werden**	er/sie/es	**würde werden**
wir	**werden werden**	wir	**würden werden**
ihr	**werdet werden**	ihr	**würdet werden**
sie/Sie	**werden werden**	sie/Sie	**würden werden**

PAST PARTICIPLE

geworden

PRESENT PARTICIPLE

werdend

IMPERATIVE

werde!/werden wir!/werdet!/werden Sie!

EXAMPLE PHRASES

Mit **wird** schlecht. I feel ill.
Ich will Lehrerin **werden**. I want to be a teacher.
Der Kuchen **ist** gut **geworden**. The cake turned out well.

ich = I **du** = you **er** = he/it **sie** = she/it **es** = it/he/she **wir** = we **ihr** = you **sie** = they **Sie** = you

wissen (to know)

	PRESENT		PRESENT SUBJUNCTIVE
ich	**weiß**	ich	**wisse**
du	**weißt**	du	**wissest**
er/sie/es	**weiß**	er/sie/es	**wisse**
wir	**wissen**	wir	**wissen**
ihr	**wisst**	ihr	**wisset**
sie/Sie	**wissen**	sie/Sie	**wissen**

	PERFECT		IMPERFECT
ich	**habe gewusst**	ich	**wusste**
du	**hast gewusst**	du	**wusstest**
er/sie/es	**hat gewusst**	er/sie/es	**wusste**
wir	**haben gewusst**	wir	**wussten**
ihr	**habt gewusst**	ihr	**wusstet**
sie/Sie	**haben gewusst**	sie/Sie	**wussten**

	FUTURE		CONDITIONAL
ich	**werde wissen**	ich	**würde wissen**
du	**wirst wissen**	du	**würdest wissen**
er/sie/es	**wird wissen**	er/sie/es	**würde wissen**
wir	**werden wissen**	wir	**würden wissen**
ihr	**werdet wissen**	ihr	**würdet wissen**
sie/Sie	**werden wissen**	sie/Sie	**würden wissen**

PAST PARTICIPLE

gewusst

PRESENT PARTICIPLE

wissend

IMPERATIVE

wisse!/wissen wir!/wisset!/wissen Sie!

EXAMPLE PHRASES

Ich **weiß** nicht. I don't know.
Er **hat** nichts davon **gewusst**. He didn't know anything about it.
Sie **wussten**, wo das Kino war. They knew where the cinema was.

ich = I **du** = you **er** = he/it **sie** = she/it **es** = it/he/she **wir** = we **ihr** = you **sie** = they **Sie** = you

Aa

A NOUN
die Eins (PL die Einsen) *(school mark)*
□ I got an A for my essay. Ich habe für meinen Aufsatz eine Eins bekommen.

a ARTICLE

LANGUAGE TIP In the nominative use **ein** for masculine and neuter nouns, **eine** for feminine nouns.

1 ein
□ a man ein Mann □ I saw a man. Ich habe einen Mann gesehen. □ a child ein Kind □ an apple ein Apfel
2 eine
□ a woman eine Frau □ He gave it to a woman. Er hat es einer Frau gegeben.

LANGUAGE TIP You do not translate 'a' when you want to describe what somebody does for a living.

□ He's a butcher. Er ist Metzger. □ She's a doctor. Sie ist Ärztin.
■ **once a week** einmal pro Woche
■ **thirty kilometres an hour** dreißig Kilometer in der Stunde
■ **thirty pence a kilo** dreißig Pence das Kilo
■ **a hundred pounds** einhundert Pfund

AA NOUN *(= Automobile Association)*
der ADAC

to **abandon** VERB
1 verlassen (PRESENT verlässt, IMPERFECT verließ, PERFECT hat verlassen) *(place)*
2 aufgeben (PRESENT gibt auf, IMPERFECT gab auf, PERFECT hat aufgegeben) *(plan, idea)*

abbey NOUN
das Kloster (PL die Klöster)

abbreviation NOUN
die Abkürzung

ability NOUN
die Fähigkeit
■ **to have the ability to do something** fähig sein, etwas zu tun

able ADJECTIVE
■ **to be able to do something** etwas tun können

to **abolish** VERB
abschaffen (PERFECT hat abgeschafft)

abortion NOUN
die Abtreibung
■ **She had an abortion.** Sie hat abgetrieben.

about PREPOSITION, ADVERB
1 wegen *(concerning)*
□ I'm phoning about tomorrow's meeting. Ich rufe wegen des morgigen Treffens an.
2 etwa *(approximately)*
□ It takes about ten hours. Es dauert etwa zehn Stunden. □ about a hundred pounds etwa hundert Pfund □ at about eleven o'clock um etwa elf Uhr
3 in ... herum *(around)*
□ to walk about the town in der Stadt herumlaufen
4 über
□ a book about London ein Buch über London
■ **to be about to do something** gerade etwas tun wollen □ I was about to go out. Ich wollte gerade gehen.
■ **to talk about something** über etwas reden □ We talked about the weather. Wir haben über das Wetter geredet.
■ **What's the film about?** Wovon handelt der Film?
■ **How about going to the cinema?** Wie wär's, wenn wir ins Kino gingen?

above PREPOSITION, ADVERB
über
□ above forty degrees über vierzig Grad

LANGUAGE TIP Use the accusative to express movement or a change of place. Use the dative when there is no change of place.

□ He put his hands above his head. Er hielt die Hände über den Kopf. □ It's in the cupboard above the sink. Es ist im Schrank über der Spüle.
■ **the flat above** die Wohnung darüber
■ **mentioned above** oben erwähnt
■ **above all** vor allem

abroad ADVERB
1 im Ausland
□ She lives abroad. Sie lebt im Ausland.
2 ins Ausland
□ to go abroad ins Ausland gehen

abrupt ADJECTIVE
brüsk
□ He was a bit abrupt with me. Er war etwas brüsk zu mir.

abruptly ADVERB
plötzlich

□ He got up abruptly. Er stand plötzlich auf.

absence NOUN
die Abwesenheit

absent ADJECTIVE
abwesend

absent-minded ADJECTIVE
zerstreut
□ She's a bit absent-minded. Sie ist etwas zerstreut.

absolutely ADVERB
1 völlig *(completely)*
□ Beate's absolutely right. Beate hat völlig recht.
2 ganz sicher
□ Do you think it's a good idea? — Absolutely! Meinst du, das ist eine gute Idee? — Ganz sicher!

absurd ADJECTIVE
absurd
□ That's absurd! Das ist absurd!

abuse NOUN
▷ *see also* **abuse** VERB
der Missbrauch *(of power, drugs)*
■ **child abuse** die Kindesmisshandlung
■ **to shout abuse at somebody** jemanden beschimpfen

to **abuse** VERB
▷ *see also* **abuse** NOUN
missbrauchen (PERFECT hat missbraucht)
■ **to abuse drugs** Drogen missbrauchen
■ **abused children** misshandelte Kinder

abusive ADJECTIVE
beleidigend
□ He became abusive. Er wurde beleidigend.

academic ADJECTIVE
■ **the academic year** das Studienjahr

academy NOUN
die Akademie
□ a military academy eine Militärakademie

to **accelerate** VERB
beschleunigen (PERFECT hat beschleunigt)

accelerator NOUN
das Gaspedal (PL die Gaspedale)

accent NOUN
der Akzent (PL die Akzente)
□ He's got a German accent. Er hat einen deutschen Akzent.

to **accept** VERB
annehmen (PRESENT nimmt an, IMPERFECT nahm an, PERFECT hat angenommen)

acceptable ADJECTIVE
annehmbar

access NOUN
1 der Zugang
□ He has access to confidential information. Er hat Zugang zu vertraulichen Informationen.
2 das Besuchsrecht
□ The father has access to the children. Der Vater hat ein Besuchsrecht.

accessible ADJECTIVE
erreichbar
□ It's easily accessible. Es ist leicht erreichbar.

accessory NOUN
■ **fashion accessories** die Modeartikel *pl*

accident NOUN
der Unfall (PL die Unfälle)
□ to have an accident einen Unfall haben
■ **by accident 1** *(by mistake)* versehentlich
□ The burglar killed him by accident. Der Einbrecher hat ihn versehentlich getötet.
2 *(by chance)* zufällig □ She met him by accident. Sie ist ihm zufällig begegnet.

accidental ADJECTIVE
zufällig

to **accommodate** VERB
unterbringen (IMPERFECT brachte unter, PERFECT hat untergebracht)
■ **The hotel can accommodate fifty people.** Das Hotel hat Platz für fünfzig Gäste.

accommodation NOUN
die Unterkunft (PL die Unterkünfte)

to **accompany** VERB
begleiten (PERFECT hat begleitet)

accord NOUN
■ **of his own accord** aus eigenem Antrieb
□ He left of his own accord. Er ist aus eigenem Antrieb gegangen.

accordingly ADVERB
entsprechend

according to PREPOSITION
laut
□ According to him, everyone had gone. Laut ihm waren alle weggegangen.

accordion NOUN
das Akkordeon (PL die Akkordeons)

account NOUN
1 das Konto (PL die Konten)
□ a bank account ein Bankkonto
■ **to do the accounts** die Buchführung machen
2 der Bericht (PL die Berichte) *(report)*
■ **He gave a detailed account of what happened.** Er berichtete genau, was passiert war.
■ **to take something into account** etwas berücksichtigen
■ **on account of** wegen □ We couldn't go out on account of the rain. Wir konnten wegen des Regens nicht raus.
■ **to account for** erklären □ She was ill, which accounts for her poor results. Sie war krank, was ihre schlechten Resultate erklärte.

accountable ADJECTIVE
■ **to be accountable to someone** jemandem gegenüber verantwortlich sein

accountancy NOUN
die Buchführung

accountant NOUN
1 der Buchhalter (PL die Buchhalter)
die Buchhalterin *(bookkeeper)*
□ She's an accountant. Sie ist Buchhalterin.

2 der Steuerberater (PL die Steuerberater)
die Steuerberaterin *(tax consultant)*

accuracy NOUN
die Genauigkeit

accurate ADJECTIVE
genau
□ accurate information genaue Information

accurately ADVERB
genau

accusation NOUN
der Vorwurf (PL die Vorwürfe)

to **accuse** VERB
■ **to accuse somebody 1** jemanden beschuldigen □ She accused me of lying. Sie beschuldigte mich, ich würde lügen.
2 *(police)* jemanden anklagen □ The police are accusing her of murder. Die Polizei klagt sie wegen Mordes an.

ace NOUN
das Ass (GEN des Asses, PL die Asse)
□ the ace of hearts das Herzass

ache NOUN
▷ *see also* **ache** VERB
der Schmerz (GEN des Schmerzes, PL die Schmerzen)
□ I have an ache in my side. Ich habe Schmerzen in der Seite.

to **ache** VERB
▷ *see also* **ache** NOUN
wehtun (IMPERFECT tat weh, PERFECT hat wehgetan)
□ My leg's aching. Mein Bein tut weh.

to **achieve** VERB
1 erreichen (PERFECT hat erreicht) *(an aim)*
2 erringen (IMPERFECT errang, PERFECT hat errungen) *(victory)*

achievement NOUN
die Leistung
□ That was quite an achievement. Das war eine Leistung.

acid NOUN
die Säure

acid rain NOUN
der saure Regen

acne NOUN
die Akne
□ She's got acne. Sie hat Akne.

to **acquit** VERB
■ **to be acquitted** freigesprochen werden
□ He was acquitted of murder. Er wurde von der Mordanklage freigesprochen.

acre NOUN
der Morgen (PL die Morgen)

acrobat NOUN
der Akrobat (GEN des Akrobaten, PL die Akrobaten)
die Akrobatin
□ He's an acrobat. Er ist Akrobat.

across PREPOSITION, ADVERB
über

LANGUAGE TIP Use the accusative to express movement or a change of place. Use the dative when there is no change of place.

□ the shop across the road der Laden über der Straße □ to walk across the road über die Straße gehen
■ **across from** *(opposite)* gegenüber +*dat*
□ He sat down across from her. Er setzte sich ihr gegenüber.

to **act** VERB
▷ *see also* **act** NOUN
1 spielen *(in play, film)*
□ He acts well. Er spielt gut. □ She's acting the part of Juliet. Sie spielt die Rolle der Julia.
2 handeln *(take action)*
□ The police acted quickly. Die Polizei hat schnell gehandelt.
■ **She acts as his interpreter.** Sie übersetzt für ihn.

act NOUN
▷ *see also* **act** VERB
der Akt (PL die Akte) *(in play)*
□ in the first act im ersten Akt

action NOUN
die Handlung
■ **The film was full of action.** In dem Film gab es viel Action.
■ **to take firm action against somebody** hart gegen jemanden vorgehen

active ADJECTIVE
aktiv
□ He's a very active person. Er ist ein sehr aktiver Mensch. □ an active volcano ein aktiver Vulkan

activity NOUN
die Tätigkeit
■ **outdoor activities** die Betätigung im Freien *sing*

actor NOUN
der Schauspieler (PL die Schauspieler)
□ His father is a well-known actor. Sein Vater ist ein bekannter Schauspieler.

actress NOUN
die Schauspielerin
□ Her sister is a well-known actress. Ihre Schwester ist eine bekannte Schauspielerin.

actual ADJECTIVE
wirklich
□ The film is based on actual events. Der Film basiert auf wirklichen Begebenheiten.

LANGUAGE TIP Be careful not to translate **actual** by **aktuell**.

actually ADVERB
1 wirklich *(really)*
□ Did it actually happen? Ist das wirklich passiert?
2 eigentlich *(in fact)*
□ Actually, I don't know him at all. Eigentlich kenne ich ihn überhaupt nicht.

acupuncture NOUN
die Akupunktur

ad NOUN
1 die Anzeige *(in paper)*
2 die Werbung *(on TV, radio)*

AD ABBREVIATION
n. Chr. *(= nach Christus)*
□ in 800 AD im Jahre 800 n. Chr.

to **adapt** VERB
bearbeiten (PERFECT hat bearbeitet)
□ His novel was adapted for television. Sein Roman wurde fürs Fernsehen bearbeitet.
■ **to adapt to something** *(get used to)* sich in etwas eingewöhnen □ He has adapted to his new school. Er hat sich in seiner neuen Schule eingewöhnt.

adaptor NOUN
der Adapter (PL die Adapter)

to **add** VERB
hinzufügen (PERFECT hat hinzugefügt)
□ Add two eggs to the mixture. Fügen Sie dem Teig zwei Eier hinzu.
■ **to add up** zusammenzählen □ Add the figures up. Zähle die Zahlen zusammen.

addict NOUN
der Süchtige (PL des Süchtigen, PL die Süchtigen)
die Süchtige (PL der Süchtigen) *(drug addict)*
□ an addict *(man)* ein Süchtiger
■ **Martin's a football addict.** Martin ist ein Fußballnarr.

addicted ADJECTIVE
süchtig
□ She's addicted to heroin. Sie ist heroinsüchtig. □ She's addicted to soap operas. Sie ist süchtig nach Seifenopern.

addition NOUN
■ **in addition** außerdem □ He broke his leg and, in addition, caught a cold. Er hat sich das Bein gebrochen und außerdem einen Schnupfen bekommen.
■ **in addition to** zusätzlich zu □ In addition to the price of the CD, there's a charge for postage. Zusätzlich zum Preis der CD wird eine Versandgebühr berechnet.

address NOUN
▷ *see also* **address** VERB
die Adresse
□ What's your address? Wie ist Ihre Adresse?

to **address** VERB
▷ *see also* **address** NOUN
1 adressieren (PERFECT hat adressiert) *(envelope, letter)*
2 sprechen zu (PRESENT spricht, IMPERFECT sprach, PERFECT hat gesprochen) *(speak to)*
□ She addressed the audience. Sie sprach zum Publikum.

adjective NOUN
das Adjektiv (PL die Adjektive)

to **adjust** VERB
einstellen (PERFECT hat eingestellt)
□ He adjusted the seat to the right height. Er stellte den Stuhl auf die richtige Höhe ein.
■ **to adjust to something** *(get used to)* sich in etwas eingewöhnen □ He has adjusted to his new school. Er hat sich in seiner neuen Schule eingewöhnt.

adjustable ADJECTIVE
verstellbar

administration NOUN
die Verwaltung

admiral NOUN
der Admiral (PL die Admirale)

to **admire** VERB
bewundern (PERFECT hat bewundert)

admission NOUN
der Eintritt
□ 'admission free' 'Eintritt frei'

to **admit** VERB
zugeben (PRESENT gibt zu, IMPERFECT gab zu, PERFECT hat zugegeben)
□ I must admit that ... Ich muss zugeben, dass ... □ He admitted that he'd done it. Er gab zu, dass er es getan hat.

adolescence NOUN
die Pubertät

adolescent NOUN
der Jugendliche (PL des Jugendlichen, PL die Jugendlichen)
die Jugendliche (GEN der Jugendlichen)
□ an adolescent *(male)* ein Jugendlicher

to **adopt** VERB
1 adoptieren (PERFECT hat adoptiert) *(child)*
□ Phil was adopted. Phil wurde adoptiert.
2 annehmen (PRESENT nimmt an, IMPERFECT nahm an, PERFECT hat angenommen) *(idea)*
□ Her suggestion was adopted. Ihr Vorschlag wurde angenommen.

adopted ADJECTIVE
adoptiert
■ **an adopted son** ein Adoptivsohn

adoption NOUN
die Adoption

to **adore** VERB
bewundern (PERFECT hat bewundert)

Adriatic Sea NOUN
die Adria

adult NOUN
der Erwachsene (GEN des Erwachsenen, PL die Erwachsenen)
die Erwachsene (GEN der Erwachsenen)
□ an adult *(man)* ein Erwachsener
■ **adult education** die Erwachsenenbildung

to **advance** VERB
▷ *see also* **advance** NOUN
1 vorrücken (PERFECT ist vorgerückt) *(move forward)*
□ The troops are advancing. Die Truppen rücken vor.
2 Fortschritte machen *(progress)*
□ Technology has advanced a lot. Die Technik hat große Fortschritte gemacht.

advance NOUN
▷ *see also* **advance** VERB
■ **in advance** vorher □ They bought the tickets in advance. Sie haben die Karten vorher gekauft.

advance booking NOUN
die Vorbestellung
□ Reductions are offered for advance booking. Bei Vorbestellung gibt es Rabatt.
■ **Advance booking is essential.** Es ist wichtig vorzubestellen.

advanced ADJECTIVE
fortgeschritten

advantage NOUN
der Vorteil (PL die Vorteile)
□ Going to university has many advantages. Das Studium hat viele Vorteile.
■ **to take advantage of something** etwas ausnutzen □ Let's take advantage of the good weather. Wir sollten das schöne Wetter ausnutzen.
■ **to take advantage of somebody** jemanden ausnutzen □ The company was taking advantage of its employees. Die Firma nutzte ihre Angestellten aus.

adventure NOUN
das Abenteuer (PL die Abenteuer)

adverb NOUN
das Adverb (PL die Adverbien)

advert NOUN ▷ *see* **advertisement**

to **advertise** VERB
annoncieren (PERFECT hat annonciert)
□ Jobs are advertised in the paper. Stellenangebote werden in der Zeitung annonciert.

advertisement NOUN
1 die Anzeige *(in paper)*
2 die Werbung *(on TV, radio)*

advertising NOUN
die Werbung
□ She works in advertising. Sie ist in der Werbung tätig. □ They've increased spending on advertising. Sie geben mehr Geld für Werbung aus.

advice NOUN
der Rat
□ to give somebody advice jemandem einen Rat geben
■ **a piece of advice** ein Rat □ He gave me a good piece of advice. Er gab mir einen guten Rat.

to **advise** VERB
raten (PRESENT rät, IMPERFECT riet, PERFECT hat geraten)
□ He advised me to wait. Er riet mir zu warten. □ He advised me not to go. Er hat mir geraten, nicht zu gehen.

aerial NOUN
die Antenne

aerobics PL NOUN
das Aerobic
□ I'm going to aerobics tonight. Ich mache heute Abend Aerobic.

aeroplane NOUN
das Flugzeug (PL die Flugzeuge)

aerosol NOUN
der Spray (PL die Sprays)

affair NOUN
1 das Verhältnis (GEN des Verhältnisses, PL die Verhältnisse) *(romantic)*
□ to have an affair with somebody mit jemandem ein Verhältnis haben
2 die Angelegenheit *(event)*

to **affect** VERB
1 beeinflussen (PERFECT hat beeinflusst) *(influence)*
□ Does junk food affect children's behaviour? Beeinflusst Junkfood das Verhalten von Kindern?
2 beeinträchtigen (PERFECT hat beeinträchtigt) *(have effect on)*
□ The weather has affected sales. Das Wetter hat den Absatz beeinträchtigt.

affectionate ADJECTIVE
liebevoll

to **afford** VERB
sich leisten
□ I can't afford a new pair of jeans. Ich kann mir keine neue Jeans leisten. □ We can't afford to go on holiday. Wir können es uns nicht leisten, in Urlaub zu fahren.

afraid ADJECTIVE
■ **to be afraid of something** vor etwas Angst haben □ I'm afraid of spiders. Ich habe Angst vor Spinnen.
■ **I'm afraid I can't come.** ich kann leider nicht kommen.
■ **I'm afraid so.** Ja, leider.
■ **I'm afraid not.** Leider nicht.

Africa NOUN
Afrika *neut*
■ **from Africa** aus Afrika
■ **to Africa** nach Afrika

African ADJECTIVE
▷ *see also* **African** NOUN
afrikanisch

African NOUN
▷ *see also* **African** ADJECTIVE
der Afrikaner (PL die Afrikaner)
die Afrikanerin

after PREPOSITION, ADVERB, CONJUNCTION
nach +*dat*
□ after dinner nach dem Abendessen
□ He ran after me. Er rannte mir nach.
■ **soon after** kurz danach
■ **after I'd had a rest** nachdem ich mich ausgeruht hatte
■ **After eating I left.** Nachdem ich gegessen hatte, ging ich.
■ **after all** schließlich

afternoon NOUN
der Nachmittag (PL die Nachmittage)

English-German

a

□ three o'clock in the afternoon drei Uhr nachmittags □ this afternoon heute Nachmittag □ on Saturday afternoon Samstag Nachmittag

afters PL NOUN
der Nachtisch *sing* (PL die Nachtische)

aftershave NOUN
das Aftershave (PL die Aftershaves)

afterwards ADVERB
danach
□ She left not long afterwards. Sie ging kurz danach.

again ADVERB
1 wieder *(once more)*
□ They're friends again. Sie sind wieder Freunde.
2 noch einmal *(one more time)*
□ Can you tell me again? Kannst du mir das noch einmal sagen?
■ **not ... again** nie mehr □ I won't go there again. Dort gehe ich nie mehr hin.
■ **Do it again!** Mach's noch mal!
■ **Not again!** Nicht schon wieder!
■ **again and again** immer wieder

against PREPOSITION
gegen
□ He leant against the wall. Er lehnte gegen die Wand. □ I'm against animal testing. Ich bin gegen Tierversuche.

age NOUN
das Alter (PL die Alter)
□ an age limit eine Altersgrenze
■ **at the age of sixteen** mit sechzehn
■ **I haven't seen her for ages.** Ich habe sie schon ewig nicht mehr gesehen.

aged ADJECTIVE
■ **aged ten** zehn Jahre alt

agenda NOUN
die Tagesordnung

agent NOUN
der Agent (GEN des Agenten, PL die Agenten)
die Agentin
■ **an estate agent** ein Immobilienmakler
■ **a travel agent** ein Reisebüro

aggressive ADJECTIVE
aggressiv

ago ADVERB
■ **two days ago** vor zwei Tagen
■ **two years ago** vor zwei Jahren
■ **not long ago** vor Kurzem
■ **How long ago did it happen?** Wie lange ist das her?

agony NOUN
■ **He was in agony.** Er hatte furchtbare Schmerzen.

to **agree** VERB
■ **to agree with somebody** jemandem zustimmen □ I agree with your sister. Ich stimme deiner Schwester zu.
■ **to agree to do something** bereit sein, etwas zu tun □ He agreed to go and pick her up. Er war bereit, sie abzuholen.
■ **to agree that ...** *(admit)* zugeben, dass ...
□ I agree that it's difficult. Ich gebe zu, dass das schwierig ist.
■ **Garlic doesn't agree with me.** Ich vertrage Knoblauch nicht.

agreed ADJECTIVE
ausgemacht
□ at the agreed time zur ausgemachten Zeit

agreement NOUN
die Abmachung
■ **to be in agreement** übereinstimmen
□ Everybody was in agreement with Ray. Alle stimmten mit Ray überein.

agricultural ADJECTIVE
landwirtschaftlich

agriculture NOUN
die Landwirtschaft

ahead ADVERB
voraus
□ We sent him on ahead. Wir schickten ihn voraus.
■ **The Germans are five points ahead.** Die Deutschen führen mit fünf Punkten.
■ **She looked straight ahead.** Sie sah geradeaus.
■ **ahead of time** vorzeitig
■ **to plan ahead** vorausplanen
■ **Go ahead!** Ja bitte!

aid NOUN
■ **in aid of charity** für wohltätige Zwecke

AIDS NOUN
das Aids (GEN des Aids)
□ He died of AIDS. Er starb an Aids.

to **aim** VERB
▷ *see also* **aim** NOUN
■ **to aim at** zielen auf +*acc* □ He aimed a gun at me. Er zielte mit der Pistole auf mich.
■ **The film is aimed at children.** Der Film ist für Kinder gedacht.
■ **to aim to do something** beabsichtigen, etwas zu tun □ Janice aimed to leave at five o'clock. Janice beabsichtigte, um fünf Uhr zu gehen.

aim NOUN
▷ *see also* **aim** VERB
das Ziel (PL die Ziele)
□ The aim of the festival is to raise money. Ziel des Festivals ist, Geld aufzutreiben.

air NOUN
die Luft (PL die Lüfte)
■ **to get some fresh air** frische Luft schnappen
■ **by air** mit dem Flugzeug □ I prefer to travel by air. Ich reise lieber mit dem Flugzeug.

air-conditioned ADJECTIVE
mit Klimaanlage

air conditioning NOUN
die Klimaanlage

Air Force NOUN
die Luftwaffe

air hostess NOUN
die Stewardess (PL die Stewardessen)
□ She's an air hostess. Sie ist Stewardess.

airline NOUN
die Fluggesellschaft

airmail NOUN
■ **by airmail** mit Luftpost

airplane NOUN (US)
das Flugzeug (PL die Flugzeuge)

airport NOUN
der Flughafen (PL die Flughäfen)

aisle NOUN
1 der Mittelgang (PL die Mittelgänge) *(in church)*
2 der Gang (PL die Gänge) *(in plane)*
□ an aisle seat ein Platz am Gang

alarm NOUN
der Alarm (PL die Alarme) *(warning)*
■ **a fire alarm** ein Feueralarm

alarm clock NOUN
der Wecker (PL die Wecker)

album NOUN
das Album (PL die Alben)

alcohol NOUN
der Alkohol

alcoholic NOUN
▷ *see also* **alcoholic** ADJECTIVE
der Alkoholiker (PL die Alkoholiker)
die Akoholikerin
□ He's an alcoholic. Er ist Alkoholiker.

alcoholic ADJECTIVE
▷ *see also* **alcoholic** NOUN
alkoholisch
□ alcoholic drinks alkoholische Getränke

alert ADJECTIVE
1 aufgeweckt *(bright)*
□ He's a very alert baby. Er ist ein sehr aufgewecktes Baby.
2 wachsam *(paying attention)*
□ We must stay alert. Wir müssen wachsam bleiben.

A levels PL NOUN
das Abitur *sing*

> **DID YOU KNOW...?**
> Germans take their **Abitur** at the age of 19. The students sit examinations in a variety of subjects to attain an overall grade. If you pass, you have the right to a place at university.

alike ADVERB
■ **to look alike** sich ähnlich sehen □ The two sisters look alike. Die beiden Schwestern sehen sich ähnlich.

alive ADJECTIVE
am Leben

all ADJECTIVE, PRONOUN, ADVERB
1 alle
□ all the books alle Bücher
■ **all the time** die ganze Zeit
■ **all day** den ganzen Tag
2 alles
□ He ate it all. Er hat alles gegessen.
□ I ate all of it. Ich habe alles gegessen.
■ **All of us went.** Wir sind alle hingegangen.
■ **after all** schließlich □ After all, nobody can make us go. Schließlich kann uns niemand zwingen hinzugehen.
■ **all alone** ganz allein □ She's all alone. Sie ist ganz allein.
■ **not at all** überhaupt nicht □ I'm not tired at all. Ich bin überhaupt nicht müde.
■ **The score is five all.** Es steht fünf zu fünf.

allergic ADJECTIVE
allergisch
■ **to be allergic to something** allergisch gegen etwas sein □ I'm allergic to cats. Ich bin allergisch gegen Katzen.

allergy NOUN
die Allergie (PL die Allergien)
□ Have you got any allergies? Hast du Allergien?

alley NOUN
die Gasse

to **allow** VERB
■ **to be allowed to do something** etwas tun dürfen □ He's not allowed to go out at night. Er darf abends nicht ausgehen.
■ **to allow somebody to do something** jemandem erlauben, etwas zu tun
□ His mum allowed him to go out. Seine Mama hat ihm erlaubt auszugehen.

all right ADVERB
1 gut *(okay)*
□ Everything turned out all right. Alles ist gut gegangen.
■ **Are you all right?** Bist du in Ordnung?
2 okay *(not bad)*
□ The film was all right. Der Film war okay.
3 einverstanden *(when agreeing)*
□ We'll talk about it later. — All right. Wir reden später darüber. — Einverstanden.
■ **Is that all right with you?** Ist das okay?

almond NOUN
die Mandel (PL die Mandeln)

almost ADVERB
fast
□ I've almost finished. Ich bin fast fertig.

alone ADJECTIVE, ADVERB
allein
□ She lives alone. Sie lebt allein.
■ **to leave somebody alone** jemanden in Ruhe lassen □ Leave her alone! Lass sie in Ruhe!
■ **to leave something alone** etwas nicht anfassen □ Leave my things alone! Fass meine Sachen nicht an!

along PREPOSITION, ADVERB
entlang
□ Chris was walking along the beach. Chris ging am Strand entlang.

■ **all along** die ganze Zeit □ He was lying to me all along. Er hat mich die ganze Zeit belogen.

aloud ADVERB
laut
□ He read the poem aloud. Er las das Gedicht vor.

alphabet NOUN
das Alphabet (PL die Alphabete)

Alps PL NOUN
die Alpen *fem pl*

already ADVERB
schon
□ Liz had already gone. Liz war schon weg.

also ADVERB
auch

LANGUAGE TIP Be careful not to translate **also** by the German word **also**.

altar NOUN
der Altar (PL die Altare)

to **alter** VERB
verändern (PERFECT hat verändert)

alternate ADJECTIVE
■ **on alternate days** abwechselnd jeden zweiten Tag

alternative NOUN
▷ *see also* **alternative** ADJECTIVE
die Alternative
□ Fruit is a healthy alternative to chocolate. Obst ist eine gesunde Alternative zu Schokolade.
■ **You have no alternative.** Du hast keine andere Wahl.
■ **There are several alternatives.** Es gibt mehrere Möglichkeiten.

alternative ADJECTIVE
▷ *see also* **alternative** NOUN
andere
□ an alternative solution eine andere Lösung
□ an alternative suggestion ein anderer Vorschlag
■ **alternative medicine** die alternative Medizin

alternatively ADVERB
■ **Alternatively, we could just stay at home.** Wir könnten auch zu Hause bleiben.

although CONJUNCTION
obwohl
□ Although she was tired, she stayed up late. Obwohl sie müde war, blieb sie lange auf.

altogether ADVERB
1 insgesamt *(in total)*
□ You owe me twenty pounds altogether. Du schuldest mir insgesamt zwanzig Pfund.
2 ganz *(completely)*
□ I'm not altogether happy with your work. Ich bin mit Ihrer Arbeit nicht ganz zufrieden.

aluminium (US **aluminum**) NOUN
das Aluminium

always ADVERB
immer
□ He's always moaning. Er beklagt sich immer.

am VERB ▷ *see* **be**

a.m. ABBREVIATION
morgens
□ at four a.m. um vier Uhr morgens

amateur NOUN
der Amateur (PL die Amateure)
die Amateurin
□ He's an amateur. Er ist Amateur.

to **amaze** VERB
■ **to be amazed** erstaunt sein □ I was amazed that I managed to do it. Ich war erstaunt, dass ich es geschafft habe.

amazing ADJECTIVE
1 erstaunlich *(surprising)*
□ That's amazing news! Das sind erstaunliche Neuigkeiten!
2 ausgezeichnet *(excellent)*
□ Vivian's an amazing cook. Vivian ist eine ausgezeichnete Köchin.

ambassador NOUN
der Botschafter (PL die Botschafter)
die Botschafterin

amber ADJECTIVE
■ **an amber light** eine gelbe Ampel

ambition NOUN
der Ehrgeiz (GEN des Ehrgeizes)

ambitious ADJECTIVE
ehrgeizig
□ She's very ambitious. Sie ist sehr ehrgeizig.

ambulance NOUN
der Krankenwagen (PL die Krankenwagen)

amenities PL NOUN
■ **The hotel has very good amenities.** Das Hotel hat viel zu bieten.

America NOUN
Amerika *neut*
■ **from America** aus Amerika
■ **in America** in Amerika
■ **to America** nach Amerika

American ADJECTIVE
▷ *see also* **American** NOUN
amerikanisch
□ He's American. Er ist Amerikaner.
□ She's American. Sie ist Amerikanerin.

American NOUN
▷ *see also* **American** ADJECTIVE
der Amerikaner (PL die Amerikaner)
die Amerikanerin
■ **the Americans** die Amerikaner

among PREPOSITION
unter +*dat*
□ I was among friends. Ich war unter Freunden.
■ **among other things** unter anderem

amount NOUN
1 der Betrag (PL die Beträge)

□ a large amount of money ein großer Geldbetrag
2 die Menge
□ a huge amount of rice eine enorme Menge Reis

amp NOUN
1 das Ampere (GEN des Ampere, PL die Ampere) *(of electricity)*
2 der Verstärker (PL die Verstärker) *(for hi-fi)*

amplifier NOUN
der Verstärker (PL die Verstärker) *(for hi-fi)*

to **amuse** VERB
belustigen (PERFECT hat belustigt)
■ **He was most amused by the story.** Er fand die Geschichte sehr lustig.

amusement NOUN
das Vergnügen (PL die Vergnügen) *(enjoyment)*
■ **amusement arcade** die Spielhalle

an ARTICLE ▷ *see* **a**

to **analyse** VERB
analysieren (PERFECT hat analysiert)

analysis NOUN
die Analyse

to **analyze** VERB (US)
analysieren (PERFECT hat analysiert)

ancestor NOUN
der Vorfahr (GEN des Vorfahren, PL die Vorfahren)
die Vorfahrin

anchor NOUN
der Anker (PL die Anker)

ancient ADJECTIVE
alt
□ This is an ancient custom. Das ist ein alter Brauch.
■ **ancient Greece** das antike Griechenland
■ **an ancient monument** ein historisches Denkmal

and CONJUNCTION
und
□ you and me du und ich □ Two and two are four. Zwei und zwei gibt vier. □ He talked and talked. Er redete und redete.
■ **Please try and come!** Versuche bitte zu kommen!
■ **better and better** immer besser

angel NOUN
der Engel (PL die Engel)

LANGUAGE TIP Be careful not to translate **angel** by the German word **Angel**.

anger NOUN
die Wut

angle NOUN
der Winkel (PL die Winkel)

angler NOUN
der Angler (PL die Angler)
die Anglerin

angling NOUN
das Angeln
□ His favourite hobby is angling. Angeln ist sein Lieblingshobby.

angry ADJECTIVE
böse
□ Dad looks very angry. Papa sieht sehr böse aus.
■ **to be angry with somebody** mit jemandem böse sein □ Mum's really angry with you. Mama ist sehr böse mit dir.
■ **to get angry** wütend werden

animal NOUN
das Tier (PL die Tiere)

ankle NOUN
der Fußknöchel (PL die Fußknöchel)

anniversary NOUN
der Jahrestag (PL die Jahrestage)
■ **wedding anniversary** der Hochzeitstag

to **announce** VERB
ankündigen (PERFECT hat angekündigt)

announcement NOUN
die Ankündigung

to **annoy** VERB
ärgern
□ He's really annoying me. Er ärgert mich echt.
■ **to get annoyed** wütend werden □ I saw that he was getting annoyed. Ich sah, dass er wütend wurde.

annoying ADJECTIVE
ärgerlich
□ It's really annoying. Es ist wirklich ärgerlich.

annual ADJECTIVE
jährlich
□ an annual meeting ein jährliches Treffen

anonymous ADJECTIVE
anonym

anorak NOUN
der Anorak (PL die Anoraks)

another ADJECTIVE

LANGUAGE TIP Use **noch ein** for masculine and neuter nouns, **noch eine** for feminine nouns.

1 noch ein
□ I bought another hat. Ich habe noch einen Hut gekauft. □ Would you like another piece of cake? Möchtest du noch ein Stück Kuchen?
noch eine
□ Would you like another cup of tea? Möchten Sie noch eine Tasse Tee?

LANGUAGE TIP Use **ein anderer** for masculine, **eine andere** for feminine and **ein anderes** for neuter nouns.

2 ein anderer *(different)*
□ Could you show me another hat? Könnten Sie mir einen anderen Hut zeigen?
eine andere
□ My girlfriend goes to another school. Meine Freundin besucht eine andere Schule.
ein anderes
□ Have you got another shirt? Haben Sie noch ein anderes Hemd?
■ **another time** ein andermal

English-German

a

to **answer** VERB
▷ *see also* **answer** NOUN
beantworten (PERFECT hat beantwortet)
□ Can you answer my question? Kannst du meine Frage beantworten?
■ **to answer the phone** ans Telefon gehen
■ **to answer the door** aufmachen □ Can you answer the door, please? Kannst du bitte aufmachen?

answer NOUN
▷ *see also* **answer** VERB
1 die Antwort *(to question)*
2 die Lösung *(to problem)*

answering machine NOUN
der Anrufbeantworter (PL die Anrufbeantworter)

ant NOUN
die Ameise

to **antagonize** VERB
verärgern (PERFECT hat verärgert)
□ He didn't want to antagonize her. Er wollte sie nicht verärgern.

Antarctic NOUN
die Antarktis

anthem NOUN
■ **the national anthem** die Nationalhymne

antibiotic NOUN
das Antibiotikum (PL die Antibiotika)

antidepressant NOUN
das Antidepressivum (PL die Antidepressiva)

antique NOUN
die Antiquität *(furniture)*

antique shop NOUN
der Antiquitätenladen (PL die Antiquitätenläden)

antiseptic NOUN
das Antiseptikum (PL die Antiseptika)

any ADJECTIVE, PRONOUN, ADVERB
LANGUAGE TIP In most cases 'any' is not translated.
□ Would you like any bread? Möchten Sie Brot? □ Have you got any mineral water? Haben Sie Mineralwasser?
LANGUAGE TIP Use **kein** for 'not any'.
□ We haven't got any milk left. Wir haben keine Milch mehr. □ I haven't got any money. Ich habe kein Geld. □ I haven't got any books. Ich habe keine Bücher. □ Sorry, we haven't got any. Tut mir leid, wir haben keine.
■ **any more 1** *(additional)* noch etwas □ Would you like any more coffee? Möchten Sie noch etwas Kaffee? **2** *(no longer)* nicht mehr □ I don't love him any more. Ich liebe ihn nicht mehr.

anybody PRONOUN
1 jemand *(in question)*
□ Has anybody got a pen? Hat jemand etwas zum Schreiben?
2 jeder *(no matter who)*
□ Anybody can learn to swim. Jeder kann schwimmen lernen.
LANGUAGE TIP Use **niemand** for 'not ... anybody'.
□ I can't see anybody. Ich kann niemanden sehen.

anyhow ADVERB
sowieso
□ He doesn't want to go out and anyhow he's not allowed. Er will nicht ausgehen, und er darf es sowieso auch nicht.

anyone PRONOUN
1 jemand *(in question)*
□ Has anyone got a pen? Hat jemand etwas zum Schreiben?
2 jeder *(no matter who)*
□ Anyone can learn to swim. Jeder kann schwimmen lernen.
LANGUAGE TIP Use **niemand** for 'not ... anyone'.
□ I can't see anyone. Ich kann niemanden sehen.

anything PRONOUN
1 etwas *(in question)*
□ Would you like anything to eat? Möchtest du etwas zu essen?
2 alles *(no matter what)*
□ Anything could happen. Alles könnte passieren.
LANGUAGE TIP Use **nichts** for 'not ... anything'.
□ I can't hear anything. Ich kann nichts hören.

anyway ADVERB
sowieso
□ He doesn't want to go out and anyway he's not allowed. Er will nicht ausgehen, und er darf es sowieso auch nicht.

anywhere ADVERB
1 irgendwo *(in question)*
□ Have you seen my coat anywhere? Hast du irgendwo meinen Mantel gesehen?
2 überall
□ You can buy stamps almost anywhere. Man kann fast überall Briefmarken kaufen.
LANGUAGE TIP Use **nirgends** for 'not ... anywhere'.
3 nirgends
□ I can't find it anywhere. Ich kann es nirgends finden.

apart ADVERB
■ **The two towns are ten kilometres apart.** Die zwei Städte liegen zehn Kilometer voneinander entfernt.
■ **apart from** abgesehen von □ Apart from that, everything's fine. Davon abgesehen ist alles in Ordnung.

apartment NOUN
die Wohnung

to **apologize** VERB
sich entschuldigen (PERFECT hat sich entschuldigt)

□ He apologized for being late. Er entschuldigte sich für sein Zuspätkommen.
■ **I apologize!** Ich bitte um Entschuldigung!

apology NOUN
die Entschuldigung

apostrophe NOUN
der Apostroph (PL die Apostrophe)

apparatus NOUN
der Apparat (PL die Apparate)

apparent ADJECTIVE
offensichtlich

apparently ADVERB
offensichtlich

to **appeal** VERB
▷ *see also* **appeal** NOUN
bitten (IMPERFECT bat, PERFECT hat gebeten)
□ They appealed for help. Sie baten um Hilfe.
■ **to appeal to somebody** *(attract)* jemanden reizen □ Does that appeal to you? Reizt dich das?

appeal NOUN
▷ *see also* **appeal** VERB
der Aufruf (PL die Aufrufe)

to **appear** VERB
1 kommen (IMPERFECT kam, PERFECT ist gekommen) *(come into view)*
□ The bus appeared around the corner. Der Bus kam um die Ecke.
■ **to appear on TV** im Fernsehen auftreten
2 scheinen (IMPERFECT schien, PERFECT hat geschienen) *(seem)*
□ She appeared to be asleep. Sie schien zu schlafen.

appearance NOUN
das Äußere (GEN des Äußeren) *(looks)*
□ She takes great care over her appearance. Sie achtet sehr auf ihr Äußeres.

appendicitis NOUN
die Blinddarmentzündung

appetite NOUN
der Appetit

to **applaud** VERB
klatschen

applause NOUN
der Beifall

apple NOUN
der Apfel (PL die Äpfel)
■ **an apple tree** ein Apfelbaum *masc*

applicant NOUN
der Bewerber (PL die Bewerber)
die Bewerberin
□ There were a hundred applicants for the job. Es gab hundert Bewerber für die Stelle.

application NOUN
■ **a job application** eine Bewerbung

application form NOUN
1 das Bewerbungsformular (PL die Bewerbungsformulare) *(for job)*
2 das Anmeldeformular (PL die Anmeldeformulare) *(for university)*

to **apply** VERB
■ **to apply for a job** sich für eine Stelle bewerben □ She applied for the PA job. Sie bewarb sich für die Stelle als Chefsekretärin.
■ **to apply to** *(be relevant)* zutreffen auf
□ This rule doesn't apply to me. Diese Regel trifft auf mich nicht zu.

appointment NOUN
der Termin (PL die Termine)
□ I've got a dental appointment. Ich habe einen Zahnarzttermin.

to **appreciate** VERB
zu schätzen wissen (PRESENT weiß zu schätzen, IMPERFECT wusste zu schätzen, PERFECT hat zu schätzen gewusst)
□ I really appreciate your help. Ich weiß deine Hilfe wirklich zu schätzen.

apprentice NOUN
der Lehrling (PL die Lehrlinge)

LANGUAGE TIP **der Lehrling** is also used for women.

□ She is an apprentice. Sie ist Lehrling.

to **approach** VERB
1 sich nähern *(get nearer to)*
□ He approached the house. Er näherte sich dem Haus.
2 angehen (IMPERFECT ging an, PERFECT hat angegangen) *(tackle)*
□ to approach a problem ein Problem angehen

appropriate ADJECTIVE
passend
□ That dress isn't very appropriate for an interview. Dieses Kleid ist für ein Vorstellungsgespräch nicht sehr passend.

approval NOUN
die Zustimmung

to **approve** VERB
■ **to approve of** gutheißen □ I don't approve of his choice. Ich heiße seine Wahl nicht gut.
■ **They didn't approve of his girlfriend.** Sie hatten etwas gegen seine Freundin.

approximate ADJECTIVE
ungefähr

apricot NOUN
die Aprikose

April NOUN
der April
□ in April im April
■ **April Fool's Day** der erste April
■ **April Fool!** April, April!

apron NOUN
die Schürze

Aquarius NOUN
der Wassermann
□ I'm Aquarius. Ich bin Wassermann.

Arab ADJECTIVE
▷ *see also* **Arab** NOUN
arabisch
□ the Arab countries die arabischen Länder

Arab NOUN
▷ *see also* **Arab** ADJECTIVE
der Araber (PL die Araber)
die Araberin

Arabic ADJECTIVE
arabisch

arch NOUN
der Bogen (PL die Bögen)

archaeologist (US **archeologist**) NOUN
der Archäologe (GEN des Archäologen, PL die Archäologen)
die Archäologin
□ She's an archaeologist. Sie ist Archäologin.

archaeology NOUN
die Archäologie

archbishop NOUN
der Erzbischof (PL die Erzbischöfe)

archeologist NOUN (US)
der Archäologe (GEN des Archäologen, PL die Archäologen)
die Archäologin
□ She's an archaeologist. Sie ist Archäologin.

archeology NOUN (US)
die Archäologie

architect NOUN
der Architekt (GEN des Architekten, PL die Architekten)
die Architektin
□ She's an architect. Sie ist Architektin.

architecture NOUN
die Architektur

Arctic NOUN
die Arktis

are VERB ▷ *see* **be**

area NOUN
1 die Gegend
□ She lives in the London area. Sie lebt in der Gegend von London.
2 das Viertel (PL die Viertel)
□ my favourite area of London mein Lieblingsviertel von London
3 die Fläche
□ an area of one thousand square metres eine Fläche von eintausend Quadratmetern

Argentina NOUN
Argentinien *neut*
■ **from Argentina** aus Argentinien
■ **to Argentina** nach Argentinien

Argentinian ADJECTIVE
argentinisch

to **argue** VERB
streiten (IMPERFECT stritt, PERFECT hat gestritten)
□ They never stop arguing. Sie streiten dauernd.

argument NOUN
der Streit (PL die Streite)
■ **to have an argument** Streit haben
□ They had an argument. Sie hatten Streit.

Aries NOUN
der Widder
□ I'm Aries. Ich bin Widder.

arm NOUN
der Arm (PL die Arme)

armchair NOUN
der Sessel (PL die Sessel)

armour (US **armor**) NOUN
die Rüstung
■ **a suit of armour** eine Rüstung

army NOUN
die Armee (PL die Armeen)

around PREPOSITION, ADVERB
1 um
□ around the corner um die Ecke
2 etwa *(approximately)*
□ around a hundred pounds etwa einhundert Pfund
3 gegen *(date, time)*
□ around eight p.m. gegen acht Uhr abends.
■ **around here** 1 *(nearby)* hier in der Nähe □ Is there a chemist's around here? Gibt es hier in der Nähe eine Apotheke? 2 *(in this area)* hier in der Gegend □ He lives around here. Er wohnt hier in der Gegend.

to **arrange** VERB
■ **to arrange to do something** verabreden, etwas zu tun □ They arranged to go out together on Friday. Sie haben verabredet, am Freitag zusammen auszugehen.
■ **to arrange a meeting** ein Treffen ausmachen □ Can we arrange a meeting? Können wir ein Treffen ausmachen?
■ **to arrange a party** eine Party vorbereiten

arrangement NOUN
der Plan (PL die Pläne) *(plan)*
■ **They made arrangements to go out on Friday night.** Sie haben verabredet, am Freitagabend auszugehen.

to **arrest** VERB
▷ *see also* **arrest** NOUN
verhaften (PERFECT hat verhaftet)
□ The police have arrested five people. Die Polizei hat fünf Leute verhaftet.

arrest NOUN
▷ *see also* **arrest** VERB
die Verhaftung
■ **You're under arrest!** Sie sind verhaftet!

arrival NOUN
die Ankunft (PL die Ankünfte)

to **arrive** VERB
ankommen (IMPERFECT kam an, PERFECT ist angekommen)
□ I arrived at five o'clock. Ich bin um fünf Uhr angekommen.

arrogant ADJECTIVE
arrogant

arrow NOUN
der Pfeil (PL die Pfeile)

art NOUN
die Kunst (PL die Künste)

artery NOUN
die Arterie

art gallery NOUN
die Kunstgalerie

article NOUN
der Artikel (PL die Artikel)
□ a newspaper article ein Zeitungsartikel

artificial ADJECTIVE
künstlich

artist NOUN
der Künstler (PL die Künstler)
die Künstlerin
□ She's an artist. Sie ist Künstlerin.

artistic ADJECTIVE
künstlerisch

as CONJUNCTION, ADVERB
1 als *(while)*
□ He came in as I was leaving. Er kam herein, als ich gehen wollte.
■ **He works as a waiter in the holidays.** In den Ferien jobbt er als Kellner.
2 da *(since)*
□ As it's Sunday, you can have a lie-in. Da es Sonntag ist, kannst du ausschlafen.
■ **as ... as** so ... wie □ Peter's as tall as Michael. Peter ist so groß wie Michael. □ Her coat cost twice as much as mine. Ihr Mantel hat doppelt so viel wie meiner gekostet.
■ **as much ... as** so viel ... wie □ I haven't got as much money as you. Ich habe nicht so viel Geld wie du.
■ **as soon as possible** sobald wie möglich □ I'll do it as soon as possible. Ich tue es sobald wie möglich.
■ **as from tomorrow** ab morgen □ As from tomorrow, the shops will stay open until ten p.m. Ab morgen haben die Geschäfte bis zehn Uhr abends auf.
■ **as if** als ob
■ **as though** als ob
LANGUAGE TIP Note that **als ob** is followed by the subjunctive.
□ She acted as though she hadn't seen me. Sie tat so, als ob sie mich nicht sähe.

asap ABBREVIATION *(= as soon as possible)*
sobald wie möglich

ash NOUN
die Asche

ashamed ADJECTIVE
■ **to be ashamed** sich schämen
□ You should be ashamed of yourself! Du solltest dich schämen!

ashtray NOUN
der Aschenbecher (PL die Aschenbecher)

Asia NOUN
Asien *neut*
■ **from Asia** aus Asien
■ **to Asia** nach Asien

Asian ADJECTIVE
▷ *see also* **Asian** NOUN
asiatisch
□ He's Asian. Er ist Asiate. □ She's Asian. Sie ist Asiatin.

Asian NOUN
▷ *see also* **Asian** ADJECTIVE
der Asiate (GEN des Asiaten, PL die Asiaten)
die Asiatin

to **ask** VERB
1 fragen *(inquire, request)*
□ 'Have you finished?' she asked. 'Bist du fertig?' fragte sie.
■ **to ask somebody something** jemanden etwas fragen □ He asked her how old she was. Er fragte sie, wie alt sie ist.
■ **to ask for something** um etwas bitten □ He asked for a cup of tea. Er bat um eine Tasse Tee.
■ **to ask somebody to do something** jemanden bitten, etwas zu tun □ She asked him to do the shopping. Sie bat ihn einzukaufen.
■ **to ask about something** sich nach etwas erkundigen □ I asked about train times to Leeds. Ich habe mich nach Zugverbindungen nach Leeds erkundigt.
■ **to ask somebody a question** jemanden etwas fragen
2 einladen (PRESENT lädt ein, IMPERFECT lud ein, PERFECT hat eingeladen) *(invite)*
□ Have you asked Matthew to the party? Hast du Matthew zur Party eingeladen?
■ **He asked her out.** *(on a date)* Er hat sie um ein Rendezvous gebeten.

asleep ADJECTIVE
■ **to be asleep** schlafen □ He's asleep. Er schläft.
■ **to fall asleep** einschlafen □ I fell asleep in front of the TV. Ich bin beim Fernsehen eingeschlafen.

asparagus NOUN
der Spargel (PL die Spargel)

aspect NOUN
der Aspekt (PL die Aspekte)

aspirin NOUN
die Schmerztablette

asset NOUN
der Vorteil (PL die Vorteile)
□ Her experience will be an asset. Ihre Erfahrung wird von Vorteil sein.

assignment NOUN
das Referat (PL die Referate) *(in school)*

assistance NOUN
die Hilfe

assistant NOUN
1 der Verkäufer (PL die Verkäufer)
die Verkäuferin *(in shop)*
2 der Assistent (GEN des Assistenten, PL die Assistenten)
die Assistentin *(helper)*

association NOUN
der Verband (PL die Verbände)

assortment NOUN
1 die Auswahl *(choice)*

□ a large assortment of cheeses eine große Auswahl an Käse
2 die Mischung *(mixture)*
□ an assortment of biscuits eine Keksmischung

to **assume** VERB
annehmen (PRESENT nimmt an, IMPERFECT nahm an, PERFECT hat angenommen)
□ I assume she won't be coming. Ich nehme an, dass sie nicht kommt.

to **assure** VERB
versichern (PERFECT hat versichert)
□ He assured me he was coming. Er versicherte mir, dass er kommt.

asthma NOUN
das Asthma
□ I've got asthma. Ich habe Asthma.

to **astonish** VERB
erstaunen (PERFECT hat erstaunt)
□ She was astonished. Sie war erstaunt.

astonishing ADJECTIVE
erstaunlich

astrology NOUN
die Astrologie

astronaut NOUN
der Astronaut (GEN des Astronauten, PL die Astronauten)
die Astronautin

astronomy NOUN
die Astronomie

asylum NOUN
das Asyl
□ to ask for asylum um Asyl bitten

asylum-seeker NOUN
der Asylbewerber (PL die Asylbewerber)
die Asylbewerberin

at PREPOSITION
1 um
□ at four o'clock um vier Uhr
2 an
□ at Christmas an Weihnachten □ What are you doing at the weekend? Was machst du am Wochenende?
■ **at night** nachts
3 mit
□ at fifty kilometres per hour mit fünfzig Stundenkilometern
4 in
□ at school in der Schule □ at the office im Büro
■ **at home** zu Hause
■ **two at a time** jeweils zwei
■ **at the races** beim Pferderennen

at NOUN
das At-Zeichen (PL die At-Zeichen) *(@ symbol)*

ate VERB ▷ *see* **eat**

Athens NOUN
Athen *neut*
■ **from Athens** aus Athen

athlete NOUN
der Athlet (GEN des Athleten, PL die Athleten)
die Athletin

athletic ADJECTIVE
athletisch

athletics NOUN
die Leichtathletik
□ I like watching the athletics on TV. Ich sehe mir im Fernsehen gern Leichtathletik an.

Atlantic NOUN
der Atlantik

atlas NOUN
der Atlas (GEN des Atlasses, PL die Atlanten)

atmosphere NOUN
die Atmosphäre

atom NOUN
das Atom (PL die Atome)

atomic ADJECTIVE
■ **an atomic bomb** eine Atombombe

to **attach** VERB
festbinden (IMPERFECT band fest, PERFECT hat festgebunden)
□ They attached a rope to the car. Sie banden ein Seil am Auto fest.
■ **Please find attached ...** Anbei erhalten Sie ...

attached ADJECTIVE
■ **to be attached to somebody** an jemandem hängen □ He's very attached to his family. Er hängt sehr an seiner Familie.

to **attack** VERB
▷ *see also* **attack** NOUN
angreifen (IMPERFECT griff an, PERFECT hat angegriffen)
□ The dog attacked me. Der Hund hat mich angegriffen.

attack NOUN
▷ *see also* **attack** VERB
der Angriff (PL die Angriffe)

attempt NOUN
▷ *see also* **attempt** VERB
der Versuch (PL die Versuche)
□ She gave up after several attempts. Sie gab nach mehreren Versuchen auf.

to **attempt** VERB
▷ *see also* **attempt** NOUN
versuchen (PERFECT hat versucht)
■ **to attempt to do something** versuchen, etwas zu tun □ I attempted to write a song. Ich habe versucht, ein Lied zu schreiben.

to **attend** VERB
teilnehmen (PRESENT nimmt teil, IMPERFECT nahm teil, PERFECT hat teilgenommen)
□ to attend a meeting an einem Treffen teilnehmen

attention NOUN
die Aufmerksamkeit
■ **to pay attention to something** auf etwas achten □ He didn't pay attention to what I was saying. Er hat nicht darauf geachtet, was ich sagte.

attic NOUN
der Speicher (PL die Speicher)

attitude NOUN
die Einstellung
□ I really don't like your attitude! Mir gefällt deine Einstellung nicht!

attorney NOUN (US)
der Rechtsanwalt (PL die Rechtsanwälte)
die Rechtsanwältin
□ My mother's an attorney. Meine Mutter ist Rechtsanwältin.

to **attract** VERB
anziehen (IMPERFECT zog an, PERFECT hat angezogen)
□ The Lake District attracts lots of tourists. Der Lake District zieht viele Touristen an.

attraction NOUN
die Attraktion
□ a tourist attraction eine Touristenattraktion

attractive ADJECTIVE
attraktiv
□ She's very attractive. Sie ist sehr attraktiv.

aubergine NOUN
die Aubergine

auction NOUN
die Auktion

audience NOUN
die Zuschauer *masc pl (in theatre)*
□ The audience clapped. Die Zuschauer klatschten.

audition NOUN
1 die Vorsprechprobe *(of actor)*
2 das Vorspiel (PL die Vorspiele) *(of musician)*

August NOUN
der August
□ in August im August

aunt NOUN
die Tante
□ my aunt meine Tante

aunty NOUN
die Tante
□ my aunty meine Tante

au pair NOUN
das Au-pair-Mädchen (PL die Au-pair-Mädchen)
□ She's an au pair. Sie ist Au-pair-Mädchen.

Australia NOUN
Australien *neut*
■ **from Australia** aus Australien
■ **in Australia** in Australien
■ **to Australia** nach Australien

Australian ADJECTIVE
▷ *see also* **Australian** NOUN
australisch
□ He's Australian. Er ist Australier.
□ She's Australian. Sie ist Australierin.

Australian NOUN
▷ *see also* **Australian** ADJECTIVE
der Australier (PL die Australier)
die Australierin
■ **the Australians** die Australier

Austria NOUN
Österreich *neut*
■ **from Austria** aus Österreich
■ **in Austria** in Österreich
■ **to Austria** nach Österreich

Austrian ADJECTIVE
▷ *see also* **Austrian** NOUN
österreichisch
□ He's Austrian. Er ist Österreicher.
□ She's Austrian. Sie ist Österreicherin.

Austrian NOUN
▷ *see also* **Austrian** ADJECTIVE
der Österreicher (PL die Österreicher)
die Österreicherin
■ **the Austrians** die Österreicher

author NOUN
der Autor (PL die Autoren)
die Autorin
□ She's a famous author. Sie ist eine berühmte Autorin.

autobiography NOUN
die Autobiografie

autograph NOUN
das Autogramm (PL die Autogramme)
□ May I have your autograph? Kann ich Ihr Autogramm haben?

automatic ADJECTIVE
automatisch
□ an automatic door eine automatische Tür

automatically ADVERB
automatisch

autumn NOUN
der Herbst (PL die Herbste)
□ in autumn im Herbst

availability NOUN
die Erhältlichkeit *(of goods)*
■ **subject to availability** falls vorrätig

available ADJECTIVE
erhältlich
□ Brochures are available on request. Prospekte sind auf Anfrage erhältlich.
■ **Is Mr Cooke available today?** Ist Herr Cooke heute zu sprechen?

avalanche NOUN
die Lawine

avenue NOUN
die Allee

average NOUN
▷ *see also* **average** ADJECTIVE
der Durchschnitt (PL die Durchschnitte)
□ on average im Durchschnitt

average ADJECTIVE
▷ *see also* **average** NOUN
durchschnittlich
□ the average price der durchschnittliche Preis

avocado NOUN
die Avocado (PL die Avocados)

to **avoid** VERB
1 meiden (IMPERFECT mied, PERFECT hat gemieden)
□ He avoids her when she's in a bad mood. Er meidet sie, wenn sie schlechte Laune hat.

2 vermeiden
□ You should avoid going out on your own at night. Du solltest vermeiden, nachts allein auszugehen.

awake ADJECTIVE
■ **to be awake** wach sein □ Is she awake? Ist sie wach? □ He was still awake. Er war noch wach.

award NOUN
der Preis (PL die Preise)
□ He's won an award. Er hat einen Preis bekommen. □ the award for the best actor der Preis für den besten Schauspieler

aware ADJECTIVE
■ **to be aware that ...** sich bewusst sein, dass ...
■ **to be aware of something** etwas merken
□ We are aware of what is happening. Wir merken, was geschieht.
■ **not that I am aware of** nicht dass ich wüsste

away ADJECTIVE, ADVERB
weg *(not here)*
□ Felix is away today. Felix ist heute weg.
□ He's away for a week. Er ist eine Woche lang weg.
■ **The town's two kilometres away.** Die Stadt ist zwei Kilometer entfernt.
■ **The coast is two hours away by car.** Zur Küste sind es mit dem Auto zwei Stunden.
■ **Go away!** Geh weg!

away match NOUN
das Auswärtsspiel (PL die Auswärtsspiele)
□ Our team has an away match this week. Unsere Mannschaft hat diese Woche ein Auswärtsspiel.

awful ADJECTIVE
schrecklich
□ That's awful! Das ist schrecklich!
■ **an awful lot of ...** furchtbar viel ...
□ an awful lot of work furchtbar viel Arbeit
□ an awful lot of mistakes furchtbar viele Fehler

awfully ADVERB
furchtbar
□ I'm awfully sorry. Es tut mir furchtbar leid.

awkward ADJECTIVE
1 schwierig *(difficult)*
□ an awkward situation eine schwierige Situation □ It's a bit awkward for me to come and see you. Es ist für mich etwas schwierig, dich zu besuchen.
2 unangenehm *(embarrassing)*
□ an awkward question eine unangenehme Frage

axe NOUN
die Axt (PL die Äxte)

Bb

BA ABBREVIATION *(= Bachelor of Arts)*
der Magister (PL die Magister)
■ **She's got a BA in History.** Sie hat einen Magistertitel in Geschichte.

baby NOUN
das Baby (PL die Babys)

baby carriage NOUN (US)
der Buggy (PL die Buggys)

to **babysit** VERB
babysitten
□ Veronika is babysitting for her friend. Veronika babysittet bei ihrer Freundin.

babysitter NOUN
der Babysitter (PL die Babysitter)
die Babysitterin

babysitting NOUN
das Babysitten

bachelor NOUN
der Junggeselle (GEN des Junggesellen, PL die Junggesellen)
□ He's a bachelor. Er ist Junggeselle.

back NOUN
▷ *see also* **back** ADJECTIVE, VERB
1 der Rücken (PL die Rücken) *(of person, horse, book)*
2 die Rückseite *(of page, house)*
□ Write your name on the back. Schreiben Sie Ihren Namen auf die Rückseite.
■ **in the back of the car** hinten im Auto
■ **at the back** hinten □ He's sitting at the back. Er sitzt hinten.

back ADJECTIVE, ADVERB
▷ *see also* **back** NOUN, VERB
hintere
□ the back wheel of my bike das hintere Rad meines Fahrrads
■ **the back seat** der Rücksitz
■ **the back door** die Hintertür
■ **to get back** zurückkommen □ What time did you get back? Wann bist du zurückgekommen?
■ **We went there by bus and walked back.** Wir sind mit dem Bus hingefahren und zu Fuß zurückgegangen.
■ **He's not back yet.** Er ist noch nicht zurück.
■ **to call somebody back** jemanden zurückrufen □ I'll call back later. Ich rufe später zurück.

to **back** VERB
▷ *see also* **back** NOUN, ADJECTIVE
■ **to back somebody** für jemanden sein
□ I'm backing him. Ich bin für ihn.
■ **to back a horse** auf ein Pferd setzen
□ He backed the wrong horse. Er hat auf das falsche Pferd gesetzt.
■ **to back out** einen Rückzieher machen
□ They promised to help and then backed out. Sie haben versprochen zu helfen, haben dann aber einen Rückzieher gemacht.
■ **to back somebody up** jemanden unterstützen

backache NOUN
die Rückenschmerzen *masc pl*
□ to have backache Rückenschmerzen haben

backbone NOUN
das Rückgrat (PL die Rückgrate)

to **backfire** VERB
schiefgehen (IMPERFECT ging schief, PERFECT ist schiefgegangen) *(go wrong)*

background NOUN
der Hintergrund (PL die Hintergründe)
□ a house in the background ein Haus im Hintergrund □ his family background sein familiärer Hintergrund
■ **background noise** die Hintergrundgeräusche *neut pl*

backhand NOUN
die Rückhand (PL die Rückhände)

backing NOUN
die Unterstützung *(support)*

backpack NOUN
der Rucksack (PL die Rucksäcke)

backpacker NOUN
der Wanderer (PL die Wanderer)
die Wanderin

back pain NOUN
die Rückenschmerzen *masc pl*
□ to have back pain Rückenschmerzen haben

backside NOUN
der Hintern (GEN des Hintern, PL die Hintern)

backstroke NOUN
das Rückenschwimmen

backup NOUN
die Unterstützung *(support)*
■ **a backup file** eine Sicherungsdatei

backwards ADVERB
zurück
□ to take a step backwards einen Schritt zurück machen
■ **to fall backwards** nach hinten fallen

back yard NOUN
der Hinterhof (PL die Hinterhöfe)

bacon NOUN
der Speck
□ bacon and eggs Eier mit Speck

bad ADJECTIVE
1 schlecht
□ a bad film ein schlechter Film □ the bad weather das schlechte Wetter □ to be in a bad mood schlechte Laune haben □ not bad nicht schlecht □ That's not bad at all. Das ist gar nicht schlecht.

WORD POWER
You can use a number of other words instead of **bad** to mean 'terrible':
awful schrecklich
□ an awful journey eine schreckliche Reise
dreadful furchtbar
□ a dreadful mistake ein furchtbarer Fehler
hopeless hoffnungslos
□ a hopeless team eine hoffnungslose Mannschaft
terrible furchtbar
□ a terrible book ein furchtbares Buch

■ **to be bad at something** in etwas schlecht sein □ I'm really bad at maths. In Mathe bin ich wirklich schlecht.
2 schlimm *(serious)*
□ a bad accident ein schlimmer Unfall
3 böse *(naughty)*
□ You bad boy! Du böser Junge!
■ **to go bad** *(food)* schlecht werden
■ **I feel bad about it.** Das tut mir echt leid.

badge NOUN
1 der Button (PL die Buttons) *(metal)*
2 der Aufkleber (PL die Aufkleber) *(sticker)*

badly ADVERB
schlecht
□ badly paid schlecht bezahlt
■ **badly wounded** schwer verletzt
■ **He's badly in need of some money.** Er braucht dringend Geld.

badminton NOUN
das Badminton
□ to play badminton Badminton spielen

bad-tempered ADJECTIVE
■ **to be bad-tempered 1** *(by nature)* griesgrämig sein □ He's a really bad-tempered person. Er ist wirklich ein griesgrämiger Mensch. **2** *(temporarily)* schlechte Laune haben □ He was really bad-tempered yesterday. Er hatte gestern wirklich schlechte Laune.

to **baffle** VERB
verblüffen (PERFECT hat verblüfft)
□ She was baffled. Sie war verblüfft.

bag NOUN
die Tasche
■ **an old bag** *(person)* eine alte Schachtel

baggage NOUN
das Gepäck

baggage reclaim NOUN
die Gepäckausgabe

baggy ADJECTIVE
weit *(clothes)*

bagpipes PL NOUN
der Dudelsack (PL die Dudelsäcke)
□ Ed plays the bagpipes. Ed spielt Dudelsack.

to **bake** VERB
backen (PRESENT bäckt, IMPERFECT backte, PERFECT hat gebacken)
□ to bake a cake einen Kuchen backen

baked beans PL NOUN
die gebackenen Bohnen *pl*

baker NOUN
der Bäcker (PL die Bäcker)
die Bäckerin
□ He's a baker. Er ist Bäcker.

bakery NOUN
die Bäckerei

baking ADJECTIVE
■ **It's baking in here!** Hier ist es furchtbar heiß!

balance NOUN
▷ *see also* **balance** VERB
das Gleichgewicht
□ to lose one's balance das Gleichgewicht verlieren

to **balance** VERB
▷ *see also* **balance** NOUN
balancieren (PERFECT ist balanciert)
□ I balanced on the window ledge. Ich balancierte auf dem Fensterbrett.
■ **The boxes were carefully balanced.** Die Kartons befanden sich genau im Gleichgewicht.

balanced ADJECTIVE
ausgewogen
□ a balanced diet eine ausgewogene Ernährung

balcony NOUN
der Balkon (PL die Balkone)

bald ADJECTIVE
glatzköpfig
■ **to be bald** eine Glatze haben

ball NOUN
der Ball (PL die Bälle)

ballet NOUN
das Ballett (PL die Ballette)
LANGUAGE TIP Note that you pronounce the 'tt' in German.
□ We went to a ballet. Wir sind ins Ballett gegangen.
■ **ballet lessons** Ballettstunden

ballet dancer NOUN
der Balletttänzer (PL die Balletttänzer)
die Balletttänzerin

ballet shoes PL NOUN
die Ballettschuhe *masc pl*

balloon NOUN
der Luftballon (PL die Luftballone) *(at parties)*
■ **a hot-air balloon** ein Heißluftballon

ballpoint pen NOUN
der Kugelschreiber (PL die Kugelschreiber)

ban NOUN
▷ *see also* **ban** VERB
das Verbot (PL die Verbote)

to **ban** VERB
▷ *see also* **ban** NOUN
verbieten (IMPERFECT verbot, PERFECT hat verboten)
□ to ban somebody from doing something jemandem verbieten, etwas zu tun
■ **She was banned from driving.** Sie bekam Fahrverbot.

banana NOUN
die Banane
□ a banana skin eine Bananenschale

band NOUN
1 die Band (PL die Bands) *(rock band)*
2 die Kapelle *(brass band)*

bandage NOUN
▷ *see also* **bandage** VERB
der Verband (PL die Verbände)

to **bandage** VERB
▷ *see also* **bandage** NOUN
verbinden (IMPERFECT verband, PERFECT hat verbunden)
□ She bandaged his arm. Sie verband ihm den Arm.

Band-Aid® NOUN (US)
das Heftpflaster (PL die Heftpflaster)

bandit NOUN
der Bandit (GEN des Banditen, PL die Banditen)

bang NOUN
▷ *see also* **bang** VERB
1 der Knall (PL die Knalle)
□ I heard a loud bang. Ich habe einen lauten Knall gehört.
2 der Schlag (PL die Schläge)
□ a bang on the head ein Schlag auf den Kopf
■ **Bang!** Peng!

to **bang** VERB
▷ *see also* **bang** NOUN
anschlagen (PRESENT schlägt an, IMPERFECT schlug an, PERFECT hat angeschlagen) *(part of body)*
□ I banged my head. Ich habe mir den Kopf angeschlagen.
■ **to bang the door** die Tür zuknallen
■ **to bang on the door** gegen die Tür hämmern

banger NOUN
die Bratwurst (PL die Bratwürste)
□ bangers and mash Bratwürste mit Kartoffelbrei

bank NOUN
1 die Bank (PL die Banken) *(financial)*
2 das Ufer (PL die Ufer) *(of river, lake)*

to **bank on** VERB
sich verlassen auf (PRESENT verlässt, IMPERFECT verließ, PERFECT hat verlassen)
□ I'm banking on you coming. Ich verlasse mich darauf, dass du kommst. □ I wouldn't bank on it. Ich würde mich nicht darauf verlassen.

bank account NOUN
das Bankkonto (PL die Bankkonten)

banker NOUN
der Banker (PL die Banker)
die Bankerin

bank holiday NOUN
der Feiertag (PL die Feiertage)

banknote NOUN
die Banknote

bankrupt ADJECTIVE
bankrott

banned ADJECTIVE
verboten

bar NOUN
1 die Bar (PL die Bars) *(pub)*
2 die Theke *(counter)*
■ **a bar of chocolate** eine Tafel Schokolade
■ **a bar of soap** ein Stück Seife

barbaric ADJECTIVE
barbarisch

barbecue NOUN
das Barbecue (PL die Barbecues)
■ **We could have a barbecue this evening.** Wir könnten heute Abend grillen.

barber NOUN
der Herrenfriseur (PL die Herrenfriseure)

bare ADJECTIVE
nackt

barefoot ADJECTIVE, ADVERB
barfuß
□ They go around barefoot. Sie laufen barfuß herum. □ She was barefoot. Sie war barfuß.

barely ADVERB
kaum
□ I could barely hear her. Ich konnte sie kaum hören.

bargain NOUN
das Schnäppchen (PL die Schnäppchen)
□ It was a bargain! Das war ein Schnäppchen!

barge NOUN
der Kahn (PL die Kähne)

to **bark** VERB
bellen

barmaid NOUN
die Bardame
□ She's a barmaid. Sie ist Bardame.

barman NOUN
der Barkeeper (PL die Barkeeper)
□ He's a barman. Er ist Barkeeper.

English-German

b

barn NOUN
die Scheune

barrel NOUN
das Fass (GEN des Fasses, PL die Fässer)

barrier NOUN
die Schranke

bartender NOUN (US)
der Barkeeper (PL die Barkeeper)

base NOUN
1 die Basis (PL die Basen) *(basis)*
□ a good base for a successful career eine gute Basis für eine erfolgreiche Karriere
2 der Fuß (GEN des Fußes, PL die Füße) *(of lamp, mountain)*
3 der Boden (PL die Böden) *(of container)*
4 die Grundlage *(for paint, make-up)*
5 der Stützpunkt (PL die Stützpunkte) *(military)*

baseball NOUN
der Baseball
□ a baseball cap eine Baseballmütze

based ADJECTIVE
■ **based on** basierend auf +*dat*

basement NOUN
das Untergeschoss (GEN des Untergeschosses, PL die Untergeschosse)

to **bash** VERB
▷ *see also* **bash** NOUN
■ **to bash something in** etwas einschlagen
□ They bashed the door in. Sie schlugen die Tür ein.

bash NOUN
▷ *see also* **bash** VERB
■ **I'll have a bash.** Ich versuch's mal.

basic ADJECTIVE
1 elementar *(knowledge, education)*
■ **basic vocabulary** der Grundwortschatz
■ **It's a basic model.** Es ist ein Grundmodell.
2 einfach
□ The accommodation is pretty basic. Die Unterkunft ist sehr einfach.

basically ADVERB
eigentlich
□ Basically, I just don't like him. Eigentlich mag ich ihn nicht.

basics PL NOUN
die Grundlagen *fem pl*

basil NOUN
das Basilikum

basin NOUN
das Waschbecken (PL die Waschbecken) *(washbasin)*

basis NOUN
■ **on a daily basis** täglich
■ **on a regular basis** regelmäßig

basket NOUN
der Korb (PL die Körbe)

basketball NOUN
der Basketball

bass NOUN
der Bass (GEN des Basses, PL die Bässe)
□ He plays bass. Er spielt Bass. □ He's a bass. Er singt Bass.
■ **a bass drum** eine Basstrommel
■ **a bass guitar** eine Bassgitarre

bassoon NOUN
das Fagott (PL die Fagotte)
□ I play the bassoon. Ich spiele Fagott.

bastard NOUN
der Scheißkerl *(rude)* (PL die Scheißkerle)
□ You bastard! Du Scheißkerl!

bat NOUN
1 der Schläger (PL die Schläger) *(for cricket, rounders, table tennis)*
2 die Fledermaus (PL die Fledermäuse) *(animal)*

bath NOUN
1 das Bad (PL die Bäder)
□ a hot bath ein heißes Bad
■ **to have a bath** baden
2 die Badewanne *(bathtub)*
□ There's a spider in the bath. In der Badewanne ist eine Spinne.

to **bathe** VERB
baden

bathing suit NOUN (US)
der Badeanzug (PL die Badeanzüge)

bathroom NOUN
das Badezimmer (PL die Badezimmer)

baths PL NOUN
das Schwimmbad (PL die Schwimmbäder)

bath towel NOUN
das Badetuch (PL die Badetücher)

batter NOUN
der Pfannkuchenteig

battery NOUN
die Batterie

battle NOUN
die Schlacht
□ the Battle of Hastings die Schlacht von Hastings
■ **It was a battle, but we managed in the end.** Es war ein Kampf, aber wir haben es schließlich geschafft.

battleship NOUN
das Schlachtschiff (PL die Schlachtschiffe)

bay NOUN
die Bucht

BC ABBREVIATION *(= before Christ)*
v. Chr. *(= vor Christus)*
□ in 200 BC im Jahre 200 v. Chr.

to **be** VERB
sein (PRESENT ist, IMPERFECT war, PERFECT ist gewesen)
□ I'm tired. Ich bin müde. □ You're late. Du bist spät dran. □ She's English. Sie ist Engländerin. □ It's cold. Es ist kalt. □ It's a nice day. Es ist ein schöner Tag. □ It's four o'clock. Es ist vier Uhr. □ I'm fourteen. Ich bin vierzehn. □ We are all happy. Wir sind alle glücklich. □ I've been ill. Ich war krank. □ I've never been to Dresden. Ich war noch nie in Dresden.

■ **to be beaten** geschlagen werden

LANGUAGE TIP Questions like 'isn't it?' don't exist in German.

□ She's pretty, isn't she? Sie ist hübsch, nicht wahr? □ The film was good, wasn't it? Der Film war gut, nicht wahr?

LANGUAGE TIP You do not translate 'a' when you want to describe somebody's occupation.

□ She's a doctor. Sie ist Ärztin. □ He's a student. Er ist Student. □ He's a bachelor. Er ist Junggeselle.

■ **I'm cold.** Mir ist kalt.

■ **I'm hungry.** Ich habe Hunger.

beach NOUN
der Strand (PL die Strände)

bead NOUN
die Perle

beak NOUN
der Schnabel (PL die Schnäbel)

beam NOUN
der Strahl (PL die Strahlen)

beans PL NOUN
1 die Bohnen *fem pl*
2 die gebackenen Bohnen *fem pl (baked beans)*

DID YOU KNOW...?
Few Germans eat baked beans and not many shops sell them.

□ beans on toast gebackene Bohnen in Tomatensoße auf Toast

■ **broad beans** dicke Bohnen

■ **green beans** grüne Bohnen

■ **kidney beans** Kidneybohnen

bean sprouts PL NOUN
die Sojasprossen *pl*

bear NOUN
▷ *see also* **bear** VERB
der Bär (GEN des Bären, PL die Bären)

to **bear** VERB
▷ *see also* **bear** NOUN
ertragen (PRESENT erträgt, IMPERFECT ertrug, PERFECT hat ertragen) *(endure)*

□ I can't bear it. Ich kann es nicht ertragen.

■ **to bear up** sich halten

■ **Bear up!** Kopf hoch!

■ **If you would bear with me for a moment** ... Wenn Sie sich bitte einen Moment gedulden könnten ...

beard NOUN
der Bart (PL die Bärte)

□ He's got a beard. Er hat einen Bart.

■ **a man with a beard** ein bärtiger Mann

bearded ADJECTIVE
bärtig

beat NOUN
▷ *see also* **beat** VERB
der Rhythmus (GEN des Rhythmus, PL die Rhythmen)

to **beat** VERB
▷ *see also* **beat** NOUN
schlagen (PRESENT schlägt, IMPERFECT schlug, PERFECT hat geschlagen)

□ We beat them three nil. Wir haben sie drei zu null geschlagen.

■ **Beat it!** Hau ab! *(informal)*

■ **to beat somebody up** jemanden zusammenschlagen *(informal)*

beautiful ADJECTIVE
schön

beautifully ADVERB
schön

beauty NOUN
die Schönheit

beauty spot NOUN
das schöne Fleckchen (PL die schönen Fleckchen)

became VERB ▷ *see* **become**

because CONJUNCTION
weil

□ I did it because ... Ich habe es getan, weil ...

■ **because of** wegen □ because of the weather wegen des Wetters

to **become** VERB
werden (PRESENT wird, IMPERFECT wurde, PERFECT ist geworden)

□ He became famous. Er wurde berühmt.

LANGUAGE TIP Be careful not to translate **to become** by **bekommen**.

bed NOUN
das Bett (PL die Betten)

□ in bed im Bett

■ **to go to bed** ins Bett gehen □ to go to bed with somebody mit jemandem ins Bett gehen

bed and breakfast NOUN
das Zimmer mit Frühstück (PL die Zimmer mit Frühstück)

□ How much is it for bed and breakfast? Wie viel kostet das Zimmer mit Frühstück?

■ **We stayed in a bed and breakfast.** Wir waren in einer Frühstückspension.

bedclothes PL NOUN
die Bettwäsche *sing*

bedding NOUN
das Bettzeug

bedroom NOUN
das Schlafzimmer (PL die Schlafzimmer)

bedsit NOUN
das möblierte Zimmer (GEN des möblierten Zimmers, PL die möblierten Zimmer)

bedspread NOUN
die Tagesdecke

bedtime NOUN
■ **Ten o'clock is my usual bedtime.** Ich gehe normalerweise um zehn Uhr ins Bett.

■ **Bedtime!** Ab ins Bett!

bee NOUN
die Biene

beef NOUN
das Rindfleisch

■ **roast beef** das Roastbeef

beefburger NOUN
die Frikadelle

been VERB ▷ *see* **be**

beer NOUN
das Bier (PL die Biere *or* Bier)
LANGUAGE TIP When ordering more than one beer use the plural form **Bier**.
□ Two beers, please! Zwei Bier bitte!

beetle NOUN
der Käfer (PL die Käfer)

beetroot NOUN
die Rote Bete

before PREPOSITION, CONJUNCTION, ADVERB
1 vor
□ before Tuesday vor Dienstag
2 bevor
□ Wash your hands before eating. Wasch die Hände bevor du isst. □ I'll phone before I leave. Ich rufe an, bevor ich gehe.
3 schon *(already)*
□ I've seen this film before. Ich habe diesen Film schon gesehen. □ Have you been to Scotland before? Warst du schon einmal in Schottland?
■ **the day before** am Tag davor
■ **the week before** die Woche davor

beforehand ADVERB
vorher

to **beg** VERB
1 betteln *(for money)*
2 anflehen (PERFECT hat angefleht)
□ He begged me to stop. Er flehte mich an aufzuhören.

began VERB ▷ *see* **begin**

beggar NOUN
der Bettler (PL die Bettler)
die Bettlerin

to **begin** VERB
anfangen (PRESENT fängt an, IMPERFECT fing an, PERFECT hat angefangen)
■ **to begin doing something** anfangen, etwas zu tun

beginner NOUN
der Anfänger (PL die Anfänger)
die Anfängerin
□ I'm just a beginner. Ich bin noch Anfänger.

beginning NOUN
der Anfang (PL die Anfänge)
□ in the beginning am Anfang

begun VERB ▷ *see* **begin**

behalf NOUN
■ **on behalf of somebody** für jemanden
□ on her behalf für sie

to **behave** VERB
sich benehmen (PRESENT benimmt sich, IMPERFECT benahm sich, PERFECT hat sich benommen)
□ He behaved like an idiot. Er hat sich wie ein Idiot benommen. □ She behaved very badly. Sie hat sich sehr schlecht benommen.
■ **to behave oneself** sich anständig benehmen □ Did the children behave themselves? Haben sich die Kinder anständig benommen?
■ **Behave!** Sei brav!

behaviour (US **behavior**) NOUN
das Benehmen

behind PREPOSITION, ADVERB
▷ *see also* **behind** NOUN
hinter
LANGUAGE TIP Use the accusative to express movement or a change of place. Use the dative when there is no change of place.
□ the wall behind the television die Wand hinter dem Fernseher □ The book fell behind the television. Das Buch fiel hinter den Fernseher.
■ **to be behind** *(late)* im Rückstand sein
□ I'm behind with my revision. Ich bin mit dem Pauken im Rückstand.

behind NOUN
▷ *see also* **behind** PREPOSITION, ADVERB
der Hintern (GEN des Hintern, PL die Hintern)

beige ADJECTIVE
beige

Belgian ADJECTIVE
▷ *see also* **Belgian** NOUN
belgisch
■ **He's Belgian.** Er ist Belgier.
■ **She's Belgian.** Sie ist Belgierin.

Belgian NOUN
▷ *see also* **Belgian** ADJECTIVE
der Belgier (PL die Belgier)
die Belgierin
■ **the Belgians** die Belgier

Belgium NOUN
Belgien *neut*
■ **from Belgium** aus Belgien
■ **in Belgium** in Belgien
■ **to Belgium** nach Belgien

to **believe** VERB
glauben
□ I don't believe you. Ich glaube dir nicht.
■ **to believe in something** an etwas glauben
□ Do you believe in ghosts? Glaubst du an Gespenster? □ to believe in God an Gott glauben

bell NOUN
1 die Klingel *(doorbell, in school)*
■ **to ring the bell** klingeln
■ **When the bell rings the children go out into the playground.** Wenn es klingelt, gehen die Kinder auf den Schulhof.
2 die Glocke *(in church)*
3 das Glöckchen (PL die Glöckchen)
□ Our cat has a bell on its neck. Unsere Katze hat ein Glöckchen um den Hals.

belly NOUN
der Bauch (PL die Bäuche)

to belong VERB
gehören (PERFECT hat gehört)
■ **to belong to somebody** jemandem gehören
□ Who does it belong to? Wem gehört das?
□ That belongs to me. Das gehört mir.
■ **Do you belong to the club?** Bist du Mitglied im Klub?
■ **Where does this belong?** Wo gehört das hin?

belongings PL NOUN
die Sachen *fem pl*

below PREPOSITION, ADVERB
1 unterhalb
□ below the castle unterhalb der Burg
2 unter
LANGUAGE TIP Use the accusative to express movement or a change of place. Use the dative when there is no change of place.
□ The sun sank below the horizon. Die Sonne sank unter den Horizont. □ We were below the clouds. Wir waren unter den Wolken.
3 darunter
□ on the floor below im Stock darunter
■ **ten degrees below freezing** zehn Grad unter null

belt NOUN
der Gürtel (PL die Gürtel)

beltway NOUN (US)
die Umgehungsstraße

bench NOUN
1 die Bank (PL die Bänke) *(seat)*
2 die Werkbank (PL die Werkbänke) *(for woodwork)*

bend NOUN
▷ *see also* **bend** VERB
1 die Kurve *(in road)*
2 die Biegung *(in river)*

to bend VERB
▷ *see also* **bend** NOUN
1 beugen *(leg, arm)*
□ I can't bend my arm. Ich kann den Arm nicht beugen.
■ **to bend down** sich bücken
■ **to bend over** sich nach vorne beugen
2 verbiegen (IMPERFECT verbog, PERFECT hat verbogen) *(object)*
□ You've bent it. Du hast es verbogen.
■ **It bends easily.** Das lässt sich leicht biegen.
■ **'do not bend'** 'nicht knicken'

beneath PREPOSITION
unter
LANGUAGE TIP Use the accusative to express movement or a change of place. Use the dative when there is no change of place.
□ He placed his boots beneath the chair. Er stellte seine Stiefel unter den Stuhl.
□ She found his jumper beneath the bed. Sie fand seinen Pullover unter dem Bett.

benefit NOUN
▷ *see also* **benefit** VERB
der Vorteil (PL die Vorteile) *(advantage)*
■ **unemployment benefit** die Arbeitslosenunterstützung

to benefit VERB
▷ *see also* **benefit** NOUN
profitieren
□ You'll benefit from that experience. Du wirst von dieser Erfahrung profitieren.
■ **He benefited from the change.** Die Veränderung hat ihm gutgetan.

bent VERB ▷ *see* **bend**

bent ADJECTIVE
verbogen
□ a bent fork eine verbogene Gabel

berserk ADJECTIVE
■ **to go berserk** durchdrehen □ She went berserk. Sie hat durchgedreht.

berth NOUN
1 die Koje *(on ship)*
2 der Schlafwagenplatz (PL die Schlafwagenplätze) *(on train)*

beside PREPOSITION
neben
LANGUAGE TIP Use the accusative to express movement or a change of place. Use the dative when there is no change of place.
□ the lamp beside the television die Lampe neben dem Fernseher □ Put that chair beside the television. Stell den Stuhl neben den Fernseher.
■ **I was beside myself.** Ich war außer mir.
■ **That's beside the point.** Das tut hier nichts zur Sache.

besides ADVERB
außerdem
□ Besides, it's too expensive. Und außerdem ist es zu teuer.

best ADJECTIVE, ADVERB
1 beste
□ He's the best player in the team. Er ist der beste Spieler der Mannschaft. □ Janet's the best at maths. Janet ist in Mathe die Beste.
2 am besten
□ Emma sings best. Emma singt am besten.
■ **to do one's best** sein Bestes tun □ I did my best. Ich habe mein Bestes getan.
■ **to make the best of it** das Beste daraus machen □ We'll have to make the best of it. Wir müssen das Beste daraus machen.

best man NOUN
der Trauzeuge (GEN des Trauzeugen, PL die Trauzeugen)
DID YOU KNOW...?
There is no real equivalent in Germany to 'best man'. A **Trauzeuge** is merely an official witness to the wedding ceremony.

bet NOUN
▷ *see also* **bet** VERB
die Wette
□ to make a bet eine Wette machen

to **bet** VERB
▷ *see also* **bet** NOUN
wetten
■ **I bet you he won't come.** Wetten, dass er nicht kommt.
■ **I bet he forgot.** Wetten, dass er es vergessen hat.

to **betray** VERB
verraten (PRESENT verrät, IMPERFECT verriet, PERFECT hat verraten)

better ADJECTIVE, ADVERB
besser
□ This one's better than that one. Dieses hier ist besser als das da. □ a better way to do it eine bessere Methode □ You'd better do it straight away. Das machst du besser sofort. □ I'd better go home. Ich gehe besser nach Hause. □ That's better! Das ist schon besser!
■ **better still** noch besser □ Go tomorrow, or better still, today. Geh morgen, oder noch besser heute.
■ **to get better 1** *(improve)* besser werden □ I hope the weather gets better soon. Ich hoffe, das Wetter wird bald besser. □ My German is getting better. Mein Deutsch wird besser. **2** *(from illness)* sich erholen
■ **I hope you get better soon.** Gute Besserung!
■ **to feel better** sich besser fühlen □ Are you feeling better now? Fühlst du dich jetzt besser?

betting shop NOUN
das Wettbüro (PL die Wettbüros)

> DID YOU KNOW...?
> There are very few betting shops in Germany and betting is far less popular than in the UK.

between PREPOSITION
zwischen

> LANGUAGE TIP Use the accusative to express movement or a change of place. Use the dative when there is no change of place.

□ The cathedral is between the town hall and the river. Der Dom liegt zwischen dem Rathaus und dem Fluss. □ He sat down between the two girls. Er setzte sich zwischen die beiden Mädchen. □ between fifteen and twenty minutes zwischen fünfzehn und zwanzig Minuten

to **beware** VERB
■ **'Beware of the dog!'** 'Vorsicht bissiger Hund!'

to **bewilder** VERB
verwirren
□ She was bewildered. Sie war verwirrt.

beyond PREPOSITION
hinter
□ There was a lake beyond the mountain. Hinter dem Berg war ein See.
■ **beyond belief** nicht zu glauben
■ **beyond repair** nicht mehr zu reparieren

biased ADJECTIVE
voreingenommen

Bible NOUN
die Bibel

bicycle NOUN
das Fahrrad (PL die Fahrräder)

bifocals PL NOUN
die Bifokalbrille
□ a pair of bifocals eine Bifokalbrille

big ADJECTIVE
groß
□ a big house ein großes Haus □ a bigger house ein größeres Haus □ my big brother mein großer Bruder □ her big sister ihre große Schwester

> WORD POWER
> You can use a number of other words instead of **big** to mean 'large':
> **enormous** riesig
> □ an enormous cake ein riesiger Kuchen
> **gigantic** riesengroß
> □ gigantic rocks riesengroße Felsen
> **huge** riesig
> □ a huge garden ein riesiger Garten
> **massive** enorm groß
> □ a massive TV ein enorm großer Fernseher

■ **He's a big guy.** Er ist kräftig gebaut.

bigheaded ADJECTIVE
eingebildet

bike NOUN
das Fahrrad (PL die Fahrräder)
□ by bike mit dem Fahrrad

bikini NOUN
der Bikini (PL die Bikinis)

bilingual ADJECTIVE
zweisprachig

bill NOUN
1 die Rechnung
□ the gas bill die Gasrechnung
■ **Can we have the bill, please?** Können wir bitte zahlen?
2 der Geldschein (PL die Geldscheine) *(banknote)*
□ a dollar bill ein Dollarschein

billiards SING NOUN
das Billard
□ to play billiards Billard spielen

billion NOUN
die Milliarde

bin NOUN
1 der Abfalleimer (PL die Abfalleimer) *(indoors)*
2 der Mülleimer (PL die Mülleimer) *(outside)*

bingo NOUN

das Bingo

binoculars PL NOUN
das Fernglas (PL die Ferngläser)
▫ a pair of binoculars ein Fernglas

biochemistry NOUN
die Biochemie

biography NOUN
die Biografie

biology NOUN
die Biologie

bird NOUN
der Vogel (PL die Vögel)

bird-watching NOUN
■ **My hobby's bird-watching.** Mein Hobby ist das Beobachten von Vögeln.

Biro® NOUN
der Kuli (PL die Kulis)

birth NOUN
die Geburt
▫ date of birth das Geburtsdatum

birth certificate NOUN
die Geburtsurkunde

birth control NOUN
die Empfängnisverhütung

birthday NOUN
der Geburtstag (PL die Geburtstage)
▫ When's your birthday? Wann hast du Geburtstag? ▫ a birthday cake ein Geburtstagskuchen ▫ I'm going to have a birthday party. Ich gebe eine Geburtstagsparty.

biscuit NOUN
der Keks (PL die Kekse)

bishop NOUN
der Bischof (PL die Bischöfe)

bit VERB ▹ *see* **bite**

bit NOUN
das Stück (PL die Stücke) *(piece)*
▫ Would you like another bit? Möchtest du noch ein Stück? ▫ a bit of cake ein Stück Kuchen
■ **a bit 1** etwas ▫ He's a bit mad. Er ist etwas verrückt. ▫ a bit too hot etwas zu heiß
2 ein bisschen ▫ Wait a bit! Warte ein bisschen! ▫ Do you play football? — A bit. Spielst du Fußball? — Ein bisschen.
■ **a bit of** *(a little)* etwas ▫ a bit of music etwas Musik ▫ It's a bit of a nuisance. Das ist schon etwas ärgerlich.
■ **to fall to bits** kaputtgehen
■ **to take something to bits** etwas auseinandernehmen
■ **bit by bit** nach und nach

bitch NOUN
1 das Miststück (PL die Miststücke) *(rude: person)*
2 die Hündin *(female dog)*

to **bite** VERB
▹ *see also* **bite** NOUN
1 beißen (IMPERFECT biss, PERFECT hat gebissen) *(person, dog)*
2 stechen (PRESENT sticht, IMPERFECT stach, PERFECT hat gestochen) *(insect)*
▫ I got bitten by mosquitoes. Ich bin von Mücken gestochen worden.
■ **to bite one's nails** an den Nägeln kauen

bite NOUN
▹ *see also* **bite** VERB
1 der Stich (PL die Stiche) *(insect bite)*
2 der Biss (GEN des Bisses, PL die Bisse) *(animal bite)*
■ **to have a bite to eat** eine Kleinigkeit essen

bitter ADJECTIVE
▹ *see also* **bitter** NOUN
1 bitter
2 bitterkalt *(weather, wind)*
▫ It's bitter today. Heute ist es bitterkalt.

bitter NOUN
▹ *see also* **bitter** ADJECTIVE
das dunkle Bier (PL die dunklen Biere)

DID YOU KNOW...?
German beers are completely different from British ones. There is no real equivalent to 'bitter'.

black ADJECTIVE
schwarz
▫ a black jacket eine schwarze Jacke
■ **She's black.** Sie ist eine Schwarze.

blackberry NOUN
die Brombeere

blackbird NOUN
die Amsel

blackboard NOUN
die Tafel

black coffee NOUN
der schwarze Kaffee (PL die schwarzen Kaffees)

blackcurrant NOUN
die Schwarze Johannisbeere

blackmail NOUN
▹ *see also* **blackmail** VERB
die Erpressung
▫ That's blackmail! Das ist Erpressung!

to **blackmail** VERB
▹ *see also* **blackmail** NOUN
erpressen (PERFECT hat erpresst)
▫ He blackmailed her. Er erpresste sie.

blackout NOUN
der Stromausfall (PL die Stromausfälle) *(power cut)*
■ **to have a blackout** *(faint)* ohnmächtig werden

black pudding NOUN
die Blutwurst (PL die Blutwürste)

blacksmith NOUN
der Schmied
▫ He's a blacksmith. Er ist Schmied.

blade NOUN
die Klinge

to **blame** VERB
■ **Don't blame me!** Ich bin nicht schuld!

■ **I blame him.** Ich gebe ihm die Schuld.
■ **He blamed it on my sister.** Er gab meiner Schwester die Schuld.

blank ADJECTIVE
▷ *see also* **blank** NOUN
leer
■ **My mind went blank.** Ich hatte ein Brett vor dem Kopf.

blank NOUN
▷ *see also* **blank** ADJECTIVE
die Lücke
□ Fill in the blanks. Füllt die Lücken aus.

blank cheque NOUN
der Blankoscheck (PL die Blankoschecks)

blanket NOUN
die Decke

blast NOUN
■ **a bomb blast** eine Bombenexplosion

blatant ADJECTIVE
unverschämt
□ a blatant liar ein unverschämter Lügner

blaze NOUN
das Feuer (PL die Feuer)

blazer NOUN
der Blazer (PL die Blazer)

bleach NOUN
das Bleichmittel (PL die Bleichmittel)

bleached ADJECTIVE
gebleicht
□ bleached hair gebleichtes Haar

bleak ADJECTIVE
trostlos
□ The future looks bleak. Die Zukunft sieht trostlos aus.

to **bleed** VERB
bluten
□ My nose is bleeding. Ich blute aus der Nase.

bleeper NOUN
der Piepser (PL die Piepser)

blender NOUN
der Mixer (PL die Mixer)

to **bless** VERB
segnen *(religiously)*
■ **Bless you!** *(after sneezing)* Gesundheit!

blew VERB ▷ *see* **blow**

blind ADJECTIVE
▷ *see also* **blind** NOUN
blind

blind NOUN
▷ *see also* **blind** ADJECTIVE
das Rollo (PL die Rollos) *(fabric)*

blindfold NOUN
▷ *see also* **blindfold** VERB
die Augenbinde

to **blindfold** VERB
▷ *see also* **blindfold** NOUN
■ **to blindfold somebody** jemandem die Augen verbinden

to **blink** VERB
zwinkern

bliss NOUN
■ **It was bliss!** Es war eine Wonne!

blister NOUN
die Blase

blizzard NOUN
der Schneesturm (PL die Schneestürme)

blob NOUN
der Tropfen (PL die Tropfen)
□ a blob of glue ein Tropfen Klebstoff

block NOUN
▷ *see also* **block** VERB
der Block (PL die Blöcke)
□ He lives in our block. Er lebt in unserem Block.
■ **a block of flats** ein Wohnblock *masc*

to **block** VERB
▷ *see also* **block** NOUN
blockieren (PERFECT hat blockiert)

blockage NOUN
die Verstopfung *(in pipe or tube)*
□ The tea leaves created a blockage in the pipe. Die Teeblätter haben eine Verstopfung im Rohr verursacht.

blog NOUN
das Blog *(Internet)*

bloke NOUN
der Typ *(informal)* (PL die Typen)

blonde ADJECTIVE
blond
□ She's got blonde hair. Sie hat blondes Haar.

blood NOUN
das Blut

blood pressure NOUN
der Blutdruck
□ to have high blood pressure hohen Blutdruck haben

blood sports PL NOUN
der Blutsport

blood test NOUN
die Blutuntersuchung

bloody ADJECTIVE
■ **bloody difficult** verdammt schwer *(informal)*
■ **that bloody television** der Scheißfernseher *(informal)*
■ **Bloody hell!** Scheiße! *(informal)*

blouse NOUN
die Bluse

blow NOUN
▷ *see also* **blow** VERB
der Schlag (PL die Schläge)

to **blow** VERB
▷ *see also* **blow** NOUN
1 blasen (PRESENT bläst, IMPERFECT blies, PERFECT hat geblasen) *(person)*
2 wehen *(wind)*
■ **to blow one's nose** sich die Nase putzen
□ Blow your nose! Putz dir die Nase!
■ **to blow a whistle** pfeifen
■ **to blow out a candle** eine Kerze ausblasen

■ **to blow up** 1 in die Luft jagen □ The terrorists blew up a police station. Die Terroristen haben ein Polizeirevier in die Luft gejagt. 2 aufblasen □ to blow up a balloon einen Luftballon aufblasen

■ **The house blew up.** Das Haus flog in die Luft.

blow-dry NOUN
das Föhnen
□ A cut and blow-dry, please. Schneiden und Föhnen bitte.

blown VERB ▷ *see* **blow**

blue ADJECTIVE
blau
□ a blue dress ein blaues Kleid
■ **a blue film** ein Pornofilm *masc*
■ **It came out of the blue.** Das kam aus heiterem Himmel.

blues PL NOUN
der Blues *sing* (GEN des Blues) *(music)*

to **bluff** VERB
▷ *see also* **bluff** NOUN
bluffen

bluff NOUN
▷ *see also* **bluff** VERB
der Bluff (PL die Bluffs)
□ It's just a bluff. Das ist ein Bluff.

blunder NOUN
der Schnitzer (PL die Schnitzer)

blunt ADJECTIVE
1 unverblümt *(person)*
2 stumpf *(knife)*

to **blush** VERB
rot werden (PRESENT wird rot, IMPERFECT wurde rot, PERFECT ist rot geworden)

board NOUN
1 das Brett (PL die Bretter)
2 die Tafel *(blackboard)*
□ Write it on the board. Schreib es an die Tafel.
3 das Schwarze Brett (PL die Schwarzen Bretter) *(noticeboard)*
■ **on board** an Bord
■ **full board** die Vollpension

boarder NOUN
der Internatsschüler (PL die Internatsschüler)
die Internatsschülerin

board game NOUN
das Brettspiel (PL die Brettspiele)

boarding card NOUN
die Bordkarte

boarding school NOUN
das Internat (PL die Internate)
□ I go to boarding school. Ich gehe in ein Internat.

to **boast** VERB
prahlen
□ to boast about something mit etwas prahlen

boat NOUN
das Boot (PL die Boote)

body NOUN
der Körper (PL die Körper)

bodybuilding NOUN
das Bodybuilding
□ He does bodybuilding. Er macht Bodybuilding.

bodyguard NOUN
der Leibwächter (PL die Leibwächter)

bog NOUN
das Moor (PL die Moore) *(marsh)*

boil NOUN
▷ *see also* **boil** VERB
der Furunkel (PL die Furunkel)

to **boil** VERB
▷ *see also* **boil** NOUN
kochen
□ to boil some water Wasser kochen □ to boil an egg ein Ei kochen □ The water's boiling. Das Wasser kocht.
■ **to boil over** überkochen □ The milk boiled over. Die Milch ist übergekocht.

boiled ADJECTIVE
■ **a soft-boiled egg** ein weich gekochtes Ei *neut*
■ **boiled potatoes** Salzkartoffeln *fem pl*

boiling ADJECTIVE
■ **It's boiling in here!** Hier ist eine Bruthitze!
■ **boiling hot** brütend heiß □ a boiling hot day ein brütend heißer Tag

bolt NOUN
1 der Riegel (PL die Riegel) *(on door)*
2 der Bolzen (PL die Bolzen) *(with nut)*

bomb NOUN
▷ *see also* **bomb** VERB
die Bombe

LANGUAGE TIP Note that you pronounce the second 'b' in German.

to **bomb** VERB
▷ *see also* **bomb** NOUN
bombardieren (PERFECT hat bombardiert)

bomber NOUN
der Bomber (PL die Bomber)

LANGUAGE TIP Note that you pronounce the second 'b' in German.

bombing NOUN
der Bombenangriff (PL die Bombenangriffe)

bond NOUN
die Bindung *(between people)*
□ a strong bond eine enge Bindung

bone NOUN
1 der Knochen (PL die Knochen) *(of human, animal)*
2 die Gräte *(of fish)*

bone dry ADJECTIVE
knochentrocken

bonfire NOUN
das Feuer (PL die Feuer)

bonnet NOUN
die Motorhaube *(of car)*

bonus NOUN
1 der Bonus (PL die Bonusse) *(extra payment)*
2 der Vorteil *(added advantage)*

book NOUN
▷ *see also* **book** VERB
das Buch (PL die Bücher)

to **book** VERB
▷ *see also* **book** NOUN
buchen
□ We haven't booked. Wir haben nicht gebucht.

bookcase NOUN
1 das Bücherregal (PL die Bücherregale) *(open)*
2 der Bücherschrank (PL die Bücherschränke) *(with doors)*

booklet NOUN
die Broschüre

bookmark NOUN
das Lesezeichen (PL die Lesezeichen)

bookshelf NOUN
das Bücherbrett (PL die Bücherbretter)
■ **bookshelves** das Bücherregal *sing*

bookshop NOUN
die Buchhandlung

to **boost** VERB
Auftrieb geben (PRESENT gibt, IMPERFECT gab, PERFECT hat gegeben)
□ The win boosted our morale. Der Sieg gab uns moralischen Auftrieb.

boot NOUN
1 der Kofferraum (PL die Kofferräume) *(of car)*
2 der Stiefel (PL die Stiefel) *(footwear)*
■ **football boots** die Fußballschuhe *masc pl*

booze NOUN
der Alkohol

border NOUN
die Grenze

bore VERB ▷ *see* **bear**

bored ADJECTIVE
■ **to be bored** sich langweilen □ I'm bored. Ich langweile mich.
■ **She gets bored easily.** Ihr wird schnell langweilig.

boredom NOUN
die Langeweile (GEN der Langenweile)

boring ADJECTIVE
langweilig

born ADJECTIVE
■ **to be born** geboren werden □ I was born in 1982. Ich bin 1982 geboren.

borne VERB ▷ *see* **bear**

to **borrow** VERB
ausleihen (IMPERFECT lieh aus, PERFECT hat ausgeliehen)
□ Can I borrow your pen? Kann ich deinen Schreiber ausleihen?
■ **to borrow something from somebody** sich etwas von jemandem leihen
□ I borrowed some money from a friend. Ich habe mir von einem Freund Geld geliehen.

Bosnia NOUN
Bosnien *neut*
■ **from Bosnia** aus Bosnien
■ **to Bosnia** nach Bosnien

Bosnian ADJECTIVE
bosnisch

boss NOUN
der Chef (PL die Chefs)
die Chefin

to **boss around** VERB
■ **to boss somebody around** jemanden herumkommandieren

bossy ADJECTIVE
herrisch

both ADJECTIVE, PRONOUN
beide
□ We both went. Wir sind beide gegangen.
□ Emma and Jane both went. Emma und Jane sind beide gegangen. □ Both of your answers are wrong. Beide Antworten sind falsch.
□ Both of them have left. Beide sind gegangen. □ Both of us went. Wir sind beide gegangen.
■ **both ... and** sowohl ... als auch □ He speaks both French and Italian. Er spricht sowohl Französisch als auch Italienisch.

bother NOUN
▷ *see also* **bother** VERB
der Ärger
□ We had a spot of bother with the car. Wir hatten Ärger mit dem Auto.
■ **No bother!** Kein Problem!

to **bother** VERB
▷ *see also* **bother** NOUN
1 beunruhigen (PERFECT hat beunruhigt) *(worry)*
□ Is something bothering you? Beunruhigt dich etwas?
2 stören *(disturb)*
□ I'm sorry to bother you. Es tut mir leid, dass ich dich störe.
■ **no bother** kein Problem
■ **Don't bother!** Nicht nötig!
■ **to bother to do something** es für nötig finden, etwas zu tun □ He didn't bother to tell me about it. Er hat es nicht für nötig gefunden, es mir zu sagen.

bottle NOUN
die Flasche

bottle bank NOUN
der Altglascontainer (PL die Altglascontainer)

bottle-opener NOUN
der Flaschenöffner (PL die Flaschenöffner)

bottom NOUN
▷ *see also* **bottom** ADJECTIVE
1 der Boden (PL die Böden) *(of container, bag, sea)*
2 der Hintern (GEN des Hintern, PL die Hintern) *(buttocks)*
3 das Ende (PL die Enden) *(of list)*
■ **at the bottom of page two** unten auf Seite zwei

bottom ADJECTIVE
▷ *see also* **bottom** NOUN
unterste

□ the bottom shelf das unterste Regalbrett
■ **the bottom sheet** das Bettlaken

bought VERB ▷ *see* **buy**

to **bounce** VERB
hüpfen (PERFECT ist gehüpft)

bouncer NOUN
der Rausschmeißer (PL die Rausschmeißer)

bound ADJECTIVE
■ **He's bound to say that.** Er muss das ja sagen.
■ **She's bound to come.** Sie kommt sicher.

boundary NOUN
die Grenze

bow NOUN
▷ *see also* **bow** VERB
1 die Schleife *(knot)*
□ to tie a bow eine Schleife machen
2 der Bogen (PL die Bogen)
□ a bow and arrow ein Pfeil und Bogen

to **bow** VERB
▷ *see also* **bow** NOUN
sich verneigen (PERFECT hat sich verneigt)

bowels PL NOUN
die Eingeweide *neut pl*

bowl NOUN
▷ *see also* **bowl** VERB
die Schale *(for soup, cereal)*

to **bowl** VERB
▷ *see also* **bowl** NOUN
werfen (PRESENT wirft, IMPERFECT warf, PERFECT hat geworfen) *(in cricket)*

bowler NOUN
der Werfer (PL die Werfer)
die Werferin *(in cricket)*

bowling NOUN
das Bowling
■ **to go bowling** Bowling spielen
■ **a bowling alley** eine Bowlingbahn

bowls SING NOUN
das Boccia (GEN des Boccia)
LANGUAGE TIP The 'cc' in **Boccia** is pronounced like 'ch' in church.
□ to play bowls Boccia spielen

bow tie NOUN
die Fliege

box NOUN
die Schachtel
□ a box of matches eine Schachtel Streichhölzer
■ **a cardboard box** ein Karton *masc*

boxer NOUN
der Boxer (PL die Boxer)

boxer shorts PL NOUN
die Boxershorts *pl*
□ He was wearing a pair of boxer shorts. Er trug Boxershorts.

boxing NOUN
das Boxen

Boxing Day NOUN
der zweite Weihnachtsfeiertag

boy NOUN
der Junge (GEN des Jungen, PL die Jungen)

boyfriend NOUN
der Freund (PL die Freunde)
□ Have you got a boyfriend? Hast du einen Freund?

bra NOUN
der BH (PL die BHs)

brace NOUN
die Zahnspange *(on teeth)*
□ She wears a brace. Sie hat eine Zahnspange.

bracelet NOUN
das Armband (PL die Armbänder)

brackets PL NOUN
die Klammern *fem pl*
□ in brackets in Klammern

brain NOUN
das Gehirn (PL die Gehirne)

brainy ADJECTIVE
gescheit

brake NOUN
▷ *see also* **brake** VERB
die Bremse

to **brake** VERB
▷ *see also* **brake** NOUN
bremsen

branch NOUN
1 der Zweig (PL die Zweige) *(of tree)*
2 die Filiale *(of bank)*

brand NOUN
die Marke
□ a well-known brand of coffee eine bekannte Kaffeemarke

brand name NOUN
der Markenname (GEN des Markennamens, PL die Markennamen)

brand-new ADJECTIVE
brandneu

brandy NOUN
der Weinbrand (PL die Weinbrände)

brass NOUN
das Messing *(metal)*
■ **the brass section** die Blechbläser *masc pl*

brass band NOUN
die Blaskapelle

brat NOUN
■ **He's a spoiled brat.** Er ist ein verwöhnter Balg.

brave ADJECTIVE
mutig
LANGUAGE TIP Be careful not to translate **brave** by **brav**.

Brazil NOUN
Brasilien *neut*
■ **from Brazil** aus Brasilien
■ **to Brazil** nach Brasilien

bread NOUN
das Brot (PL die Brote)
□ bread and butter Brot mit Butter

■ **brown bread** das Graubrot
■ **white bread** das Weißbrot

DID YOU KNOW...?
There is a huge variety of types of bread in Germany which can't simply be divided into brown and white.

break NOUN
▷ *see also* **break** VERB
die Pause *(rest)*
□ to take a break eine Pause machen
□ during morning break während der Vormittagspause
■ **the Christmas break** die Weihnachtsfeiertage *masc pl*
■ **Give me a break!** Mach mal halblang!

to **break** VERB
▷ *see also* **break** NOUN
1 kaputt machen (PERFECT hat kaputt gemacht)
□ Careful, you'll break something! Vorsicht, du machst sonst was kaputt!
2 brechen (PRESENT bricht, IMPERFECT brach, PERFECT hat gebrochen) *(record, law)*
□ to break a promise sein Versprechen brechen
■ **to break one's leg** sich das Bein brechen
□ I broke my leg. Ich habe mir das Bein gebrochen.
■ **He broke his arm.** Er hat sich den Arm gebrochen.
3 brechen *(get broken)*
□ Careful, it'll break! Vorsicht, es bricht!

to **break down** VERB
eine Panne haben (PRESENT hat eine Panne, IMPERFECT hatte eine Panne, PERFECT hat eine Panne gehabt)
□ The car broke down. Das Auto hatte eine Panne.

to **break in** VERB
einbrechen (PRESENT bricht ein, IMPERFECT brach ein, PERFECT hat eingebrochen)

to **break into** VERB
einbrechen in (PRESENT bricht ein, IMPERFECT brach ein, PERFECT ist eingebrochen)
□ Thieves broke into the house. Diebe brachen in das Haus ein.

to **break off** VERB
abbrechen (PRESENT bricht ab, IMPERFECT brach ab, PERFECT hat abgebrochen)
□ I broke off a small piece. Ich habe ein kleines Stück abgebrochen.

to **break open** VERB
aufbrechen (PRESENT bricht auf, IMPERFECT brach auf, PERFECT hat aufgebrochen) *(door, cupboard)*

to **break out** VERB
ausbrechen (PRESENT bricht aus, IMPERFECT brach aus, PERFECT ist ausgebrochen)
■ **to break out in a rash** einen Ausschlag bekommen

to **break up** VERB
1 sich auflösen (PERFECT hat sich aufgelöst) *(crowd)*
2 zu Ende gehen (IMPERFECT ging zu Ende, PERFECT ist zu Ende gegangen) *(meeting, party)*
3 sich trennen *(couple)*
■ **to break up a fight** eine Schlägerei beenden
■ **We break up next Wednesday.** Nächsten Mittwoch ist der letzte Schultag.

breakdown NOUN
1 die Panne *(in vehicle)*
□ to have a breakdown eine Panne haben
2 der Nervenzusammenbruch (PL die Nervenzusammenbrüche) *(mental)*
□ to have a breakdown einen Nervenzusammenbruch haben

breakdown van NOUN
das Pannenfahrzeug (PL die Pannenfahrzeuge)

breakfast NOUN
das Frühstück (PL die Frühstücke)
□ What would you like for breakfast? Was möchtest du zum Frühstück?
■ **to have breakfast** frühstücken

break-in NOUN
der Einbruch (PL die Einbrüche)

breast NOUN
die Brust (PL die Brüste)
■ **chicken breast** die Hähnchenbrust

to **breast-feed** VERB
stillen

breaststroke NOUN
das Brustschwimmen

breath NOUN
der Atem
□ to be out of breath außer Atem sein
■ **to have bad breath** Mundgeruch haben
■ **to get one's breath back** verschnaufen

to **breathe** VERB
atmen
■ **to breathe in** einatmen
■ **to breathe out** ausatmen

to **breed** VERB
▷ *see also* **breed** NOUN
züchten
□ to breed dogs Hunde züchten

breed NOUN
▷ *see also* **breed** VERB
die Rasse

breeze NOUN
die Brise

brewery NOUN
die Brauerei

bribe NOUN
▷ *see also* **bribe** VERB
die Bestechung

to **bribe** VERB
▷ *see also* **bribe** NOUN
bestechen (PRESENT besticht, IMPERFECT bestach, PERFECT hat bestochen)

brick NOUN
der Backstein (PL die Backsteine)
□ a brick wall eine Backsteinmauer

bricklayer NOUN
der Maurer (PL die Maurer)
die Maurerin

bride NOUN
die Braut (PL die Bräute)

bridegroom NOUN
der Bräutigam (PL die Bräutigame)

bridesmaid NOUN
die Brautjungfer

bridge NOUN
1 die Brücke
□ a suspension bridge eine Hängebrücke
2 das Bridge (GEN des Bridge)
□ to play bridge Bridge spielen

brief ADJECTIVE
kurz

briefcase NOUN
die Aktentasche

briefly ADVERB
kurz

briefs PL NOUN
die Unterhose
□ a pair of briefs eine Unterhose

bright ADJECTIVE
1 hell *(light)*
2 leuchtend *(colour)*
□ a brighter colour eine leuchtendere Farbe
■ **bright blue** hellblau
3 intelligent
□ He's not very bright. Er ist nicht besonders intelligent.

brilliant ADJECTIVE
1 prima *(wonderful)*
□ Brilliant! Prima!
2 glänzend *(clever)*
□ a brilliant scientist ein glänzender Wissenschaftler

to **bring** VERB
1 bringen (IMPERFECT brachte, PERFECT hat gebracht)
□ Could you bring me my trainers? Könntest du mir meine Sportschuhe bringen?
2 mitbringen *(bring along)*
□ Bring warm clothes. Bringt warme Kleidung mit! □ Can I bring a friend? Darf ich einen Freund mitbringen?
■ **to bring about** herbeiführen
■ **to bring back** zurückbringen
■ **to bring forward** vorverlegen
□ The meeting was brought forward. Die Sitzung wurde vorverlegt.
■ **to bring up** aufziehen □ She brought up five children on her own. Sie hat fünf Kinder alleine aufgezogen.

Britain NOUN
Großbritannien *neut*
■ **from Britain** aus Großbritannien
■ **in Britain** in Großbritannien
■ **to Britain** nach Großbritannien
■ **Great Britain** Großbritannien

British ADJECTIVE
britisch
■ **He's British.** Er ist Brite.
■ **She's British.** Sie ist Britin.
■ **the British** die Briten *masc pl*
■ **the British Isles** die Britischen Inseln

Brittany NOUN
die Bretagne
■ **in Brittany** in der Bretagne

broad ADJECTIVE
breit *(wide)*
■ **in broad daylight** am helllichten Tag

broadcast NOUN
▷ *see also* **broadcast** VERB
die Sendung

to **broadcast** VERB
▷ *see also* **broadcast** NOUN
senden
□ The interview was broadcast all over the world. Das Interview wurde in der ganzen Welt gesendet.

broad-minded ADJECTIVE
tolerant

broccoli SING NOUN
die Brokkoli *masc pl*
□ Broccoli is her favourite vegetable. Ihr Lieblingsgemüse ist Brokkoli.

brochure NOUN
die Broschüre

to **broil** VERB (US)
grillen

broke VERB ▷ *see* **break**

broke ADJECTIVE
■ **to be broke** *(without money)* pleite sein

broken VERB ▷ *see* **break**

broken ADJECTIVE
1 kaputt
□ It's broken. Es ist kaputt.
2 gebrochen *(limb)*
□ He's got a broken arm. Er hat einen gebrochenen Arm.

bronchitis NOUN
die Bronchitis

bronze NOUN
die Bronze
□ the bronze medal die Bronzemedaille

brooch NOUN
die Brosche

broom NOUN
der Besen (PL die Besen)

brother NOUN
der Bruder (PL die Brüder)
□ my brother mein Bruder □ my big brother mein großer Bruder

brother-in-law NOUN
der Schwager (PL die Schwäger)

brought VERB ▷ *see* **bring**

brown ADJECTIVE
braun
■ **brown bread** das Graubrot

Brownie NOUN
der Wichtel (PL die Wichtel) *(Girl Guide)*

to **browse** VERB
browsen (PERFECT hat gebrowst) *(computer)*
■ **to browse in a shop** sich in einem Geschäft umsehen

browser NOUN
der Browser (PL die Browser) *(Internet)*

bruise NOUN
der blaue Fleck (PL die blauen Flecke)

brush NOUN
▷ *see also* **brush** VERB
1 die Bürste
2 der Pinsel (PL die Pinsel) *(paintbrush)*

to **brush** VERB
▷ *see also* **brush** NOUN
bürsten
■ **to brush one's hair** sich die Haare bürsten
□ I brushed my hair. Ich habe mir die Haare gebürstet.
■ **to brush one's teeth** die Zähne putzen
□ I've brushed my teeth. Ich habe die Zähne geputzt.

Brussels NOUN
Brüssel *neut*
□ to Brussels nach Brüssel

Brussels sprouts PL NOUN
der Rosenkohl *sing*
□ Do you like Brussels sprouts? Magst du Rosenkohl?

brutal ADJECTIVE
brutal

BSc ABBREVIATION *(= Bachelor of Science)*
der Magister (PL die Magister)
■ **She's got a BSc in Chemistry.** Sie hat einen Magistertitel in Chemie.

BSE NOUN *(= bovine spongiform encephalopathy)*
das BSE

bubble NOUN
die Blase

bubble bath NOUN
das Schaumbad (PL die Schaumbäder)

bubble gum NOUN
der Bubblegum (PL die Bubblegums)

bucket NOUN
der Eimer (PL die Eimer)

buckle NOUN
die Schnalle *(on belt, watch, shoe)*

Buddhism NOUN
der Buddhismus (GEN des Buddhismus)
□ Buddhism and Hinduism Buddhismus und Hinduismus

Buddhist ADJECTIVE
buddhistisch

buddy NOUN (US)
der Kumpel (PL die Kumpel)

budget NOUN
▷ *see also* **budget** VERB
das Budget (PL die Budgets)

to **budget** VERB
▷ *see also* **budget** NOUN
einplanen (PERFECT hat eingeplant)
□ They budgeted $10 million for advertising. Sie planten 10 Millionen Dollar für Werbung ein.

budgie NOUN
der Wellensittich (PL die Wellensittiche)

buffet NOUN
das Büfett (PL die Büfetts)

buffet car NOUN
der Speisewagen (PL die Speisewagen)

bug NOUN
1 die Wanze *(insect)*
■ **There are many bugs there.** Dort gibt es viel Ungeziefer.
■ **a stomach bug** eine Magen-Darm-Infektion
■ **There's a bug going round.** Da geht etwas herum.
2 der Programmfehler (PL die Programmfehler) *(in computer)*

bugged ADJECTIVE
verwanzt
□ The room was bugged. Das Zimmer war verwanzt.

buggy NOUN
der Kinderwagen (PL die Kinderwagen)

to **build** VERB
bauen
□ They're going to build houses here. Hier werden Häuser gebaut.
■ **to build up** *(increase)* zunehmen

builder NOUN
1 der Bauunternehmer (PL die Bauunternehmer)
die Bauunternehmerin *(owner of firm)*
2 der Bauarbeiter (PL die Bauarbeiter)
die Bauarbeiterin *(worker)*

building NOUN
das Gebäude (PL die Gebäude)

built VERB ▷ *see* **build**

bulb NOUN
die Glühbirne *(electric)*

Bulgaria NOUN
Bulgarien *neut*
■ **from Bulgaria** aus Bulgarien
■ **to Bulgaria** nach Bulgarien

bull NOUN
der Stier (PL die Stiere)

bullet NOUN
die Kugel

bulletin board NOUN
das Schwarze Brett (PL die Schwarzen Bretter) *(computer)*

bullfighting NOUN
der Stierkampf (PL die Stierkämpfe)

bully NOUN
▷ *see also* **bully** VERB
■ **He's a big bully.** Er tyrannisiert andere gern.

to **bully** VERB
▷ *see also* **bully** NOUN
tyrannisieren (PERFECT hat tyrannisiert)

bum NOUN
der Po (PL die Pos) *(informal: bottom)*

bum bag NOUN
die Gürteltasche

bump NOUN
▷ *see also* **bump** VERB
1 die Beule *(lump)*
2 der Zusammenstoß (GEN des Zusammenstoßes, PL die Zusammenstöße) *(minor accident)*
■ **We had a bump.** Es hat gebumst.

to **bump** VERB
▷ *see also* **bump** NOUN
■ **to bump into something** gegen etwas laufen □ She bumped into the wall. Sie ist gegen die Wand gelaufen.
■ **We bumped into his car.** Wir sind in sein Auto gefahren.
■ **I bumped into an old friend.** Ich bin zufällig einem alten Freund begegnet.

bumper NOUN
die Stoßstange

bumpy ADJECTIVE
holperig

bun NOUN
das Brötchen (PL die Brötchen)

bunch NOUN
■ **a bunch of flowers** ein Blumenstrauß *masc*
■ **a bunch of grapes** eine Traube
■ **a bunch of keys** ein Schlüsselbund *masc*

bunches PL NOUN
die Rattenschwänze *masc pl*
□ She has her hair in bunches. Sie hat Rattenschwänze.

bungalow NOUN
der Bungalow (PL die Bungalows)

bunk NOUN
1 das Bett (PL die Betten)
2 die Koje *(on ship)*

burger NOUN
der Hamburger (PL die Hamburger)

burglar NOUN
der Einbrecher (PL die Einbrecher)
die Einbrecherin

to **burglarize** VERB (US)
einbrechen in *+acc* (PRESENT bricht ein, IMPERFECT brach ein, PERFECT ist eingebrochen)
□ Her house was burglarized. Bei ihr wurde eingebrochen.

burglary NOUN
der Einbruch (PL die Einbrüche)

to **burgle** VERB
einbrechen in *+acc* (PRESENT bricht ein, IMPERFECT brach ein, PERFECT ist eingebrochen)
□ Her house was burgled. Bei ihr wurde eingebrochen.

burn NOUN
▷ *see also* **burn** VERB
die Verbrennung

to **burn** VERB
▷ *see also* **burn** NOUN
1 verbrennen (IMPERFECT verbrannte, PERFECT hat verbrannt) *(rubbish, documents)*
2 anbrennen lassen (PRESENT lässt anbrennen, IMPERFECT ließ anbrennen, PERFECT hat anbrennen lassen) *(food)*
□ I burned the cake. Ich habe den Kuchen anbrennen lassen.
3 brennen (IMPERFECT brannte, PERFECT hat gebrannt) *(CD, DVD)*
■ **to burn oneself** sich verbrennen
□ I burned myself on the oven door. Ich habe mich an der Ofentür verbrannt.
■ **I've burned my hand.** Ich habe mir die Hand verbrannt.
■ **to burn down** abbrennen □ The factory burned down. Die Fabrik ist abgebrannt.

to **burst** VERB
platzen (PERFECT ist geplatzt)
□ The balloon burst. Der Luftballon ist geplatzt.
■ **to burst a balloon** einen Luftballon platzen lassen
■ **to burst out laughing** laut loslachen
■ **to burst into flames** in Flammen aufgehen
■ **to burst into tears** in Tränen ausbrechen

to **bury** VERB
1 begraben (PRESENT begräbt, IMPERFECT begrub, PERFECT hat begraben) *(dead people, animals)*
□ We buried my guinea pig in the garden. Wir haben mein Meerschweinchen im Garten begraben.
2 vergraben *(things)*
□ My dog buries his bones. Mein Hund vergräbt seine Knochen.

bus NOUN
der Bus (GEN des Busses, PL die Busse)
□ the bus driver der Busfahrer □ the school bus der Schulbus
■ **a bus pass** *(monthly)* eine Monatskarte für den Bus

DID YOU KNOW...?
Almost all German cities operate an integrated public transport system; you can buy a weekly (**Wochenkarte**), monthly (**Monatskarte**) or yearly (**Jahreskarte**) pass which are valid for that period on all buses, trams and light railway vehicles in a particular zone.

■ **a bus station** ein Busbahnhof *masc*
■ **a bus ticket** eine Busfahrkarte

bush NOUN
der Busch (PL die Büsche)

business NOUN
1 die Firma (PL die Firmen) *(firm)*

□ He's got his own business. Er hat seine eigene Firma.
2 das Geschäft (PL die Geschäfte) *(commerce)*
□ a business trip eine Geschäftsreise
■ **He's away on business.** Er ist geschäftlich unterwegs.
■ **It's none of my business.** Das geht mich nichts an.

businessman NOUN
der Geschäftsmann (PL die Geschäftsleute)

businesswoman NOUN
die Geschäftsfrau

busker NOUN
der Straßenmusikant (GEN des Straßenmusikanten, PL die Straßenmusikanten)
die Straßenmusikantin

bus stop NOUN
die Bushaltestelle

bust NOUN
der Busen (PL die Busen) *(chest)*
■ **bust measurement** die Oberweite

busy ADJECTIVE
1 beschäftigt *(person)*
2 belebt *(shop, street)*
3 besetzt *(phone line)*
■ **It's been a busy day.** Es war viel los heute.

busy signal NOUN (US)
das Besetztzeichen (PL die Besetztzeichen)

but CONJUNCTION
aber
□ I'd like to come, but I'm busy. Ich würde gerne kommen, aber ich habe zu tun.

butcher NOUN
der Metzger (PL die Metzger)
die Metzgerin
□ He's a butcher. Er ist Metzger.

butcher's NOUN
die Metzgerei

butter NOUN
die Butter

butterfly NOUN
der Schmetterling (PL die Schmetterlinge)

buttocks PL NOUN
der Hintern *sing* (GEN des Hintern, PL die Hintern)

button NOUN
der Knopf (PL die Knöpfe)

to **buy** VERB
▹ *see also* **buy** NOUN
kaufen
□ He bought me an ice cream. Er hat mir ein Eis gekauft.
■ **to buy something from somebody** etwas von jemandem kaufen □ I bought a watch from him. Ich habe von ihm eine Uhr gekauft.

buy NOUN
▹ *see also* **buy** VERB
der Kauf (PL die Käufe)
□ It was a good buy. Es war ein guter Kauf.

by PREPOSITION
1 von
□ They were caught by the police. Sie wurden von der Polizei erwischt. □ a painting by Picasso ein Gemälde von Picasso
2 mit
□ by car mit dem Auto □ by train mit dem Zug □ by bus mit dem Bus
3 bei *(close to)*
□ Where's the bank? — It's by the post office. Wo ist die Bank? — Sie ist bei der Post.
■ **by day** bei Tag
■ **by night** bei Nacht
4 bis *(not later than)*
□ We have to be there by four o'clock. Wir müssen bis vier Uhr dort sein.
■ **by the time ...** bis ... □ By the time I got there it was too late. Bis ich dort war, war es zu spät.
■ **That's fine by me.** Ist in Ordnung!
■ **all by himself** ganz allein
■ **all by herself** ganz allein
■ **I did it all by myself.** Ich habe es ganz allein gemacht.
■ **by the way** übrigens

bye EXCLAMATION
tschüs!

bypass NOUN
die Umgehungsstraße *(road)*

Cc

cab NOUN
das Taxi (PL die Taxis)

cabbage NOUN
der Kohl

cabin NOUN
die Kabine *(on ship)*

cabinet NOUN
■ **a bathroom cabinet** ein Badezimmerschränkchen *neut*
■ **a drinks cabinet** eine Bar

cable NOUN
das Kabel (PL die Kabel)

cable car NOUN
die Drahtseilbahn

cable television NOUN
das Kabelfernsehen

cactus NOUN
der Kaktus (GEN des Kaktus, PL die Kakteen)

cadet NOUN
■ **a police cadet** ein Polizeischüler *masc*
■ **a cadet officer** ein Offiziersanwärter *masc*

café NOUN
die Imbissstube

cage NOUN
der Käfig (PL die Käfige)

cagoule NOUN
die Windjacke

cake NOUN
der Kuchen (PL die Kuchen)

to **calculate** VERB
rechnen

calculation NOUN
die Rechnung

calculator NOUN
der Taschenrechner (PL die Taschenrechner)

calendar NOUN
der Kalender (PL die Kalender)

calf NOUN
1 das Kalb (PL die Kälber) *(of cow)*
2 die Wade *(of leg)*

call NOUN
▷ *see also* **call** VERB
der Anruf (PL die Anrufe) *(by phone)*
□ Thanks for your call. Danke für Ihren Anruf.
■ **a phone call** ein Telefongespräch *neut*
■ **to be on call** *(doctor)* Bereitschaftsdienst haben □ He's on call this evening. Er hat heute Abend Bereitschaftsdienst.

to **call** VERB
▷ *see also* **call** NOUN
1 anrufen (IMPERFECT rief an, PERFECT hat angerufen) *(by phone)*
□ I'll tell him you called. Ich sage ihm, dass du angerufen hast. □ This is the number to call. Das ist die Nummer, die du anrufen musst.
■ **to call back** *(phone again)* zurückrufen
□ I'll call back at six o'clock. Ich rufe um sechs Uhr zurück.
2 rufen *(fetch)*
□ We called the police. Wir haben die Polizei gerufen.
3 nennen (IMPERFECT nannte, PERFECT hat genannt) *(by name)*
□ Everyone calls him Jimmy. Alle nennen ihn Jimmy.
■ **to be called** heißen □ He's called Fluffy. Er heißt Fluffy. □ What's she called? Wie heißt sie?
■ **to call somebody names** jemanden beschimpfen
■ **to call for** abholen □ I'll call for you at half past two. Ich hole dich um halb drei ab.
■ **to call off** absagen □ The match was called off. Das Spiel wurde abgesagt.

call box NOUN
die Telefonzelle

call centre NOUN
das Callcenter (PL die Callcenters)

calm ADJECTIVE
ruhig

to **calm down** VERB
sich beruhigen (PERFECT hat sich beruhigt)
□ Calm down! Beruhige dich!

Calor gas® NOUN
das Butangas

calorie NOUN
die Kalorie

calves PL NOUN ▷ *see* **calf**

camcorder NOUN
der Camcorder (PL die Camcorder)

came VERB ▷ *see* **come**

camel NOUN
das Kamel (PL die Kamele)

camera NOUN
1 der Fotoapparat (PL die Fotoapparate) *(for photos)*
2 die Kamera (PL die Kameras) *(for filming, TV)*

cameraman NOUN
der Kameramann (PL die Kameramänner)

cameraphone NOUN
das Fotohandy (PL die Fotohandys)

to **camp** VERB
▷ *see also* **camp** NOUN
zelten

camp NOUN
▷ *see also* **camp** VERB
das Lager (PL die Lager)
■ **a camp bed** eine Campingliege

campaign NOUN
▷ *see also* **campaign** VERB
die Kampagne

to **campaign** VERB
▷ *see also* **campaign** NOUN
sich einsetzen (PERFECT hat sich eingesetzt)
□ They are campaigning for a change in the law. Sie setzen sich für eine Gesetzesänderung ein.

camper NOUN
1 der Camper (PL die Camper)
die Camperin *(person)*
2 das Wohnmobil (PL die Wohnmobile) *(van)*

camping NOUN
das Camping
■ **to go camping** zelten □ We went camping in Cornwall. Wir waren in Cornwall zelten.

camping gas® NOUN
das Campinggas

campsite NOUN
der Zeltplatz (PL die Zeltplätze)

campus NOUN
das Universitätsgelände (PL die Universitätsgelände)

can NOUN
▷ *see also* **can** VERB
1 die Dose *(tin)*
□ a can of sweetcorn eine Dose Mais
□ a can of beer eine Dose Bier
2 der Kanister (PL die Kanister) *(jerry can)*
□ a can of petrol ein Benzinkanister

can VERB
▷ *see also* **can** NOUN
können (PRESENT kann, IMPERFECT konnte, PERFECT hat können)
□ I can't come. Ich kann nicht kommen.
□ Can I help you? Kann ich dir helfen?
□ You could hire a bike. Du könntest dir ein Fahrrad mieten. □ I couldn't sleep. Ich konnte nicht schlafen. □ I can swim. Ich kann schwimmen. □ He can't drive. Er kann nicht Auto fahren. □ Can you speak German? Können Sie Deutsch?
■ **That can't be true!** Das darf nicht wahr sein!
■ **You could be right.** Da könntest du recht haben.

Canada NOUN
Kanada *neut*
■ **from Canada** aus Kanada
■ **in Canada** in Kanada
■ **to Canada** nach Kanada

Canadian ADJECTIVE
▷ *see also* **Canadian** NOUN
kanadisch
□ He's Canadian. Er ist Kanadier.
□ She's Canadian. Sie ist Kanadierin.

Canadian NOUN
▷ *see also* **Canadian** ADJECTIVE
der Kanadier (PL die Kanadier)
die Kanadierin

canal NOUN
der Kanal (PL die Kanäle)

Canaries NOUN
■ **the Canaries** die Kanarischen Inseln *pl*

canary NOUN
der Kanarienvogel (PL die Kanarienvögel)

to **cancel** VERB
1 absagen (PERFECT hat abgesagt)
□ The match was cancelled. Das Spiel wurde abgesagt.
2 stornieren (PERFECT hat storniert) *(booking)*
□ He cancelled his hotel booking. Er hat seine Hotelreservierung storniert.

cancellation NOUN
die Absage

cancer NOUN
der Krebs (GEN des Krebses)
□ He's got cancer. Er hat Krebs.
■ **I'm Cancer.** Ich bin Krebs.

candidate NOUN
der Kandidat (GEN des Kandidaten, PL die Kandidaten)
die Kandidatin

candle NOUN
die Kerze

candy NOUN (US)
1 das Bonbon (PL die Bonbons) *(sweet)*
2 die Süßigkeit *(sweets)*

candyfloss NOUN
die Zuckerwatte

cannabis NOUN
das Cannabis (GEN des Cannabis)

canned ADJECTIVE
in Dosen *(food)*
□ canned soup Suppe in Dosen

cannot VERB ▷ *see* **can**

canoe NOUN
das Kanu (PL die Kanus)

canoeing NOUN
■ **to go canoeing** Kanu fahren □ We went canoeing. Wir gingen Kanu fahren.

can-opener NOUN
der Dosenöffner (PL die Dosenöffner)

can't VERB ▷ *see* **can**

canteen NOUN
die Kantine

canvas NOUN
die Leinwand (PL die Leinwände)

cap NOUN
1 die Mütze *(hat)*
2 der Verschluss (GEN des Verschlusses, PL die Verschlüsse) *(of bottle, tube)*

capable ADJECTIVE
fähig
■ **to be capable of doing something** etwas tun können □ She is capable of looking after herself. Sie kann auf sich selbst aufpassen.

capacity NOUN
1 die Fähigkeit
□ He has the capacity to succeed. Er hat die Fähigkeit, Erfolg zu haben.
2 das Fassungsvermögen *(quantity)*
□ a capacity of fifty litres ein Fassungsvermögen von fünfzig Litern

cape NOUN
das Kap (PL die Kaps)
□ Cape Horn Kap Hoorn

capital NOUN
1 die Hauptstadt (PL die Hauptstädte)
□ Cardiff is the capital of Wales. Cardiff ist die Hauptstadt von Wales.
2 der Großbuchstabe (GEN des Großbuchstaben, PL die Großbuchstaben) *(letter)*
□ Write your address in capitals. Schreib deine Adresse in Großbuchstaben.

capitalism NOUN
der Kapitalismus (GEN des Kapitalismus)

capital punishment NOUN
die Todesstrafe

Capricorn NOUN
der Steinbock
□ I'm Capricorn. Ich bin Steinbock.

to **capsize** VERB
kentern (PERFECT ist gekentert)

captain NOUN
der Kapitän (PL die Kapitäne)
die Kapitänin
□ She's captain of the hockey team. Sie ist die Kapitänin der Hockeymannschaft.

caption NOUN
die Bildunterschrift

to **capture** VERB
1 gefangen nehmen (PRESENT nimmt gefangen, IMPERFECT nahm gefangen, PERFECT hat gefangen genommen) *(person)*
□ He was captured by the enemy. Er wurde vom Feind gefangen genommen.
2 fangen (PRESENT fängt, IMPERFECT fing, PERFECT hat gefangen) *(animal)*
□ They managed to capture the lion. Sie konnten den Löwen fangen.

car NOUN
das Auto (PL die Autos)
■ **to go by car** mit dem Auto fahren
□ We went by car. Wir sind mit dem Auto gefahren.
■ **a car crash** ein Autounfall *masc*

caramel NOUN
das Karamellbonbon (PL die Karamellbonbons) *(sweet)*

caravan NOUN
der Wohnwagen (PL die Wohnwagen)
□ a caravan site ein Campingplatz für Wohnwagen

car boot sale NOUN
der Flohmarkt (PL die Flohmärkte)

card NOUN
die Karte
■ **a card game** ein Kartenspiel *neut*

cardboard NOUN
der Karton (PL die Kartons)

cardigan NOUN
die Strickjacke

card phone NOUN
das Kartentelefon (PL die Kartentelefone)

care NOUN
▷ *see also* **care** VERB
die Vorsicht
■ **with care** vorsichtig
■ **to take care of** aufpassen auf *+acc*
□ I take care of the children on Saturdays. Ich passe samstags auf die Kinder auf.
■ **Take care!** 1 *(Be careful!)* Sei vorsichtig!
2 *(Look after yourself!)* Pass auf dich auf!

to **care** VERB
▷ *see also* **care** NOUN
■ **to care about** achten auf *+acc* □ They care about their image. Sie achten auf ihr Image.
■ **I don't care!** Das ist mir egal!
□ She doesn't care. Das ist ihr egal.
■ **to care for somebody** *(patients, old people)* jemanden pflegen

career NOUN
die Karriere

careful ADJECTIVE
vorsichtig
□ Be careful! Sei vorsichtig!

carefully ADVERB
1 sorgsam
□ She carefully avoided the subject. Sie vermied das Thema sorgsam.
2 vorsichtig *(safely)*
□ Drive carefully! Fahr vorsichtig!
■ **Think carefully!** Denk gut nach!

careless ADJECTIVE
1 schluderig *(work)*
■ **a careless mistake** ein Flüchtigkeitsfehler *masc*
2 nachlässig *(person)*
□ She's very careless. Sie ist sehr nachlässig.
3 unvorsichtig
□ a careless driver ein unvorsichtiger Fahrer

caretaker NOUN
der Hausmeister (PL die Hausmeister)
die Hausmeisterin

car ferry NOUN
die Autofähre

cargo NOUN
die Fracht

car hire NOUN
der Autoverleih (PL die Autoverleihe)

Caribbean ADJECTIVE
▷ *see also* **Caribbean** NOUN
karibisch

Caribbean NOUN
▷ *see also* **Caribbean** ADJECTIVE
1 die Karibik *(islands)*
□ We're going to the Caribbean. Wir fahren in die Karibik. □ He's from the Caribbean. Er kommt aus der Karibik.
2 das Karibische Meer *(sea)*

caring ADJECTIVE
liebevoll
■ **the caring professions** die Pflegeberufe

carnation NOUN
die Nelke

carnival NOUN
der Karneval (PL die Karnevale)

carol NOUN
■ **a Christmas carol** ein Weihnachtslied *neut*

car park NOUN
der Parkplatz (PL die Parkplätze)

carpenter NOUN
der Schreiner (PL die Schreiner)
die Schreinerin
□ He's a carpenter. Er ist Schreiner.

carpentry NOUN
die Schreinerei

carpet NOUN
der Teppich (PL die Teppiche)
□ a Persian carpet ein Perserteppich

carriage NOUN
der Eisenbahnwagen (PL die Eisenbahnwagen)

carrier bag NOUN
die Tragetasche

carrot NOUN
die Karotte

to **carry** VERB
tragen (PRESENT trägt, IMPERFECT trug, PERFECT hat getragen)
□ He carried her bag. Er trug ihre Tasche.
■ **a plane carrying a hundred passengers** ein Flugzeug mit hundert Passagieren an Bord
■ **to carry on** weitermachen □ Carry on! Mach weiter!
■ **She carried on talking.** Sie redete weiter.
■ **to carry out** *(orders)* ausführen

carrycot NOUN
die Babytragetasche

cart NOUN
der Karren (PL die Karren)

carton NOUN
die Tüte *(of milk, juice)*

cartoon NOUN
1 der Zeichentrickfilm (PL die Zeichentrickfilme) *(film)*
2 der Cartoon (PL die Cartoons) *(in newspaper)*
■ **a strip cartoon** ein Comic *masc*

cartridge NOUN
die Patrone

to **carve** VERB
aufschneiden (IMPERFECT schnitt auf, PERFECT hat aufgeschnitten) *(meat)*

case NOUN
1 der Koffer (PL die Koffer)
□ I've packed my case. Ich habe meinen Koffer gepackt.
2 der Fall (PL die Fälle)
□ in some cases in manchen Fällen
□ Which case does 'außer' take? Welcher Fall steht nach 'außer'?
■ **in that case** in dem Fall □ I don't want it. — In that case, I'll take it. Ich will es nicht. — In dem Fall nehme ich es.
■ **in case** für den Fall □ in case it rains für den Fall, dass es regnet
■ **just in case** für alle Fälle □ Take some money, just in case. Nimm für alle Fälle Geld mit.

cash NOUN
das Bargeld
□ I desperately need some cash. Ich brauche dringend Bargeld.
■ **in cash** in bar □ two thousand pounds in cash zweitausend Pfund in bar
■ **to pay cash** bar bezahlen
■ **I'm a bit short of cash.** Ich bin etwas knapp bei Kasse.
■ **a cash card** eine Geldautomatenkarte
■ **the cash desk** die Kasse
■ **a cash dispenser** ein Geldautomat *masc*
■ **a cash register** eine Registrierkasse

cashew nut NOUN
die Cashewnuss (PL die Cashewnüsse)

cashier NOUN
der Kassierer (PL die Kassierer)
die Kassiererin

cashmere NOUN
der Kaschmir
□ a cashmere sweater ein Kaschmirpullover

casino NOUN
das Kasino (PL die Kasinos)

casserole NOUN
der Schmortopf (PL die Schmortöpfe)
■ **a casserole dish** eine Kasserolle

cassette NOUN
die Kassette
■ **cassette recorder** der Kassettenrekorder
■ **cassette player** der Kassettenspieler

cast NOUN
die Besetzung
□ After the play, we met the cast. Nach dem Stück haben wir die Besetzung kennengelernt.

castle NOUN
die Burg

casual ADJECTIVE
1 leger
□ casual clothes legere Kleidung
2 lässig
□ a casual attitude eine lässige Haltung
3 beiläufig
□ It was just a casual remark. Es war nur eine beiläufige Bemerkung.

casually ADVERB
■ **to dress casually** sich leger kleiden

casualty NOUN
die Unfallstation *(hospital department)*

cat NOUN
die Katze
□ Have you got a cat? Hast du eine Katze?

catalogue NOUN
der Katalog (PL die Kataloge)

catalytic converter NOUN
der Katalysator (PL die Katalysatoren)

catarrh NOUN
der Katarrh (PL die Katarrhe)

catastrophe NOUN
die Katastrophe

to **catch** VERB
1 fangen (PRESENT fängt, IMPERFECT fing, PERFECT hat gefangen)
□ My cat catches birds. Meine Katze fängt Vögel.
■ **to catch a thief** einen Dieb fassen
■ **to catch somebody doing something** jemanden dabei erwischen, wie er etwas tut
□ If they catch you smoking ... Wenn sie dich beim Rauchen erwischen ...
2 nehmen (PRESENT nimmt, IMPERFECT nahm, PERFECT hat genommen) *(bus, train)*
□ We caught the last bus. Wir haben den letzten Bus genommen.
3 mitbekommen (IMPERFECT bekam mit, PERFECT hat mitbekommen) *(hear)*
□ I didn't catch his name. Ich habe seinen Namen nicht mitbekommen.
■ **to catch up** aufholen □ I'm trying to catch up: I was away last week. Ich versuche aufzuholen: ich war letzte Woche weg.
■ **to catch a cold** einen Schnupfen bekommen

catching ADJECTIVE
ansteckend
□ It's not catching. Das ist nicht ansteckend.

catering NOUN
■ **Who did the catering?** Wer hat das Essen und die Getränke geliefert?

cathedral NOUN
die Kathedrale

Catholic ADJECTIVE
▷ *see also* **Catholic** NOUN
katholisch

Catholic NOUN
▷ *see also* **Catholic** ADJECTIVE
der Katholik (GEN des Katholiken, PL die Katholiken)
die Katholikin
■ **I'm a Catholic.** Ich bin katholisch.

cattle PL NOUN
das Vieh *sing*

caught VERB ▷ *see* **catch**

cauliflower NOUN
der Blumenkohl (PL die Blumenkohle)

cause NOUN
▷ *see also* **cause** VERB
die Ursache
□ the cause of the fire die Ursache des Feuers

to **cause** VERB
▷ *see also* **cause** NOUN
verursachen (PERFECT hat verursacht)
□ to cause an accident einen Unfall verursachen

cautious ADJECTIVE
vorsichtig

cautiously ADVERB
vorsichtig

cave NOUN
die Höhle

caviar NOUN
der Kaviar

CCTV ABBREVIATION *(= closed-circuit television)*
die Videoüberwachung

CD NOUN *(= compact disc)*
die CD (PL die CDs)

CD player NOUN
der CD-Spieler (PL die CD-Spieler)

CD-ROM NOUN
die CD-ROM (PL die CD-ROMs)

CDT NOUN *(= Craft, Design and Technology)*
die Arbeitslehre

ceasefire NOUN
der Waffenstillstand (PL die Waffenstillstände)

ceiling NOUN
die Decke

to **celebrate** VERB
feiern *(birthday)*

celebration NOUN
die Feier

celebrity NOUN
die Berühmtheit

celery NOUN
der Stangensellerie (GEN des Stangensellerie, PL die Stangenselleries)

cell NOUN
die Zelle

cellar NOUN
der Keller (PL die Keller)
□ a wine cellar ein Weinkeller

cello NOUN
das Cello (PL die Celli)
□ I play the cello. Ich spiele Cello.

cell phone NOUN (US)
das Handy (PL die Handys)

cement NOUN
der Zement

cemetery NOUN
der Friedhof (PL die Friedhöfe)

English-German

C

cent NOUN
der Cent (PL die Cents *or* Cent)

LANGUAGE TIP When talking about amounts of money use the plural form **Cent**.

□ twenty cents zwanzig Cent

centenary NOUN
das hundertjährige Jubiläum (PL die hundertjährigen Jubiläen)

center NOUN (US)
das Zentrum (PL die Zentren)
□ a sports center ein Sportzentrum

centigrade ADJECTIVE
■ **twenty degrees centigrade** zwanzig Grad Celsius

centimetre (US **centimeter**) NOUN
der Zentimeter (PL die Zentimeter)
□ twenty centimetres zwanzig Zentimeter

central ADJECTIVE
zentral

central heating NOUN
die Zentralheizung

centre NOUN
das Zentrum (PL die Zentren)
□ a sports centre ein Sportzentrum

century NOUN
das Jahrhundert (PL die Jahrhunderte)
□ the twentieth century das zwanzigste Jahrhundert □ the twenty-first century das einundzwanzigste Jahrhundert

cereal NOUN
die Getreideflocken *fem pl*
□ I have cereal for breakfast. Zum Frühstück esse ich Getreideflocken.

ceremony NOUN
die Zeremonie

certain ADJECTIVE
1 sicher
□ I'm absolutely certain it was him. Ich bin ganz sicher, dass er es war.
■ **I don't know for certain.** Ich bin mir nicht sicher.
■ **to make certain** sich vergewissern □ I made certain the door was locked. Ich habe mich vergewissert, dass die Tür abgeschlossen war.
2 bestimmt
□ a certain person eine bestimmte Person

certainly ADVERB
natürlich
□ I certainly expected something better. Ich habe natürlich etwas Besseres erwartet.
■ **Certainly not!** Sicher nicht!
■ **So it was a surprise? — It certainly was!** Also war's eine Überraschung? — Und ob!

certificate NOUN
die Urkunde

CFC NOUN (*= chlorofluorocarbon*)
der FCKW (*= Fluorchlorkohlenwasserstoff*)

chain NOUN
die Kette

chair NOUN
1 der Stuhl (PL die Stühle)
□ a table and four chairs ein Tisch und vier Stühle
2 der Sessel (PL die Sessel) *(armchair)*

chairlift NOUN
der Sessellift (PL die Sessellifte)

chairman NOUN
der Vorsitzende (GEN des Vorsitzenden, PL die Vorsitzenden)
□ a chairman ein Vorsitzender

chalet NOUN
das Ferienhaus (PL die Ferienhäuser)

chalk NOUN
die Kreide

challenge NOUN
▷ *see also* **challenge** VERB
die Herausforderung

to **challenge** VERB
▷ *see also* **challenge** NOUN
■ **She challenged me to a race.** Sie wollte mit mir um die Wette laufen.

challenging ADJECTIVE
anspruchsvoll
□ a challenging job eine anspruchsvolle Arbeit

chambermaid NOUN
das Zimmermädchen (PL die Zimmermädchen)

champagne NOUN
der Champagner (PL die Champagner)

champion NOUN
der Meister (PL die Meister)
die Meisterin

championship NOUN
die Meisterschaft

chance NOUN
1 die Chance
□ Do you think I've got any chance? Meinst du, ich habe eine Chance? □ Their chances of winning are very good. Ihre Gewinnchancen sind sehr gut.
2 die Möglichkeit
□ a chance to travel eine Möglichkeit, auf Reisen zu gehen
■ **I'll write when I get the chance.** Ich schreibe, sobald ich dazu komme.
■ **by chance** zufällig □ We met by chance. Wir haben uns zufällig kennengelernt.
■ **to take a chance** ein Risiko eingehen
□ I'm taking no chances! Ich gehe kein Risiko ein!
■ **No chance!** Denkste!

Chancellor of the Exchequer NOUN
der Schatzkanzler (PL die Schatzkanzler)

chandelier NOUN
der Kronleuchter (PL die Kronleuchter)

to **change** VERB
▷ *see also* **change** NOUN
1 sich verändern (PERFECT hat sich verändert)

□ The town has changed a lot. Die Stadt hat sich sehr verändert.

2 wechseln *(money, job)*

□ I'd like to change fifty pounds. Ich würde gern fünfzig Pfund wechseln. □ He wants to change his job. Er möchte den Job wechseln.

■ **You have to change trains in Stuttgart.** Sie müssen in Stuttgart umsteigen.

■ **I'm going to change my shoes.** Ich ziehe andere Schuhe an.

■ **to change one's mind** es sich anders überlegen □ I've changed my mind. Ich habe es mir anders überlegt.

■ **to change gear** schalten

3 sich umziehen (IMPERFECT zog sich um, PERFECT hat sich umgezogen)

□ She's changing to go out. Sie zieht sich zum Ausgehen um.

■ **to get changed** sich umziehen □ I'm going to get changed. Ich ziehe mich um.

4 umtauschen (PERFECT hat umgetauscht) *(swap)*

□ Can I change this sweater? It's too small. Kann ich diesen Pullover umtauschen? Er ist zu klein.

change NOUN

▷ *see also* **change** VERB

1 die Änderung

■ **There's been a change of plan.** Die Pläne haben sich geändert.

■ **a change of clothes** Kleidung zum Wechseln

■ **for a change** zur Abwechslung □ Let's play tennis for a change. Lass uns zur Abwechslung Tennis spielen.

2 das Kleingeld *(money)*

□ I haven't got any change. Ich habe kein Kleingeld.

changeable ADJECTIVE

wechselhaft

changing room NOUN

der Umkleideraum (PL die Umkleideräume)

channel NOUN

das Programm (PL die Programme) *(TV)*

□ There's football on the other channel. Im anderen Programm gibt es Fußball.

■ **the English Channel** der Ärmelkanal

■ **the Channel Islands** die Kanalinseln

■ **the Channel Tunnel** der Kanaltunnel

chaos NOUN

das Chaos (GEN des Chaos)

chap NOUN

der Kerl (PL die Kerle)

□ He's a nice chap. Er ist ein netter Kerl.

chapel NOUN

die Kapelle *(part of church)*

chapter NOUN

das Kapitel (PL die Kapitel)

character NOUN

1 der Charakter (PL die Charaktere)

□ Give me some idea of his character. Beschreiben Sie mir seinen Charakter.

■ **She's quite a character.** Sie ist ein Unikum.

2 die Figur *(in play, film)*

□ the character played by Tom Cruise die Figur, die Tom Cruise spielt

characteristic NOUN

das Merkmal (PL die Merkmale)

charcoal NOUN

die Holzkohle

charge NOUN

▷ *see also* **charge** VERB

die Gebühr

□ Is there a charge for delivery? Wird für die Zustellung eine Gebühr erhoben? □ an extra charge eine Extragebühr

■ **free of charge** kostenlos

■ **to reverse the charges** ein R-Gespräch führen □ I'd like to reverse the charges. Ich möchte gern ein R-Gespräch führen.

■ **to be on a charge** angeklagt sein □ He's on a charge of murder. Er ist des Mordes angeklagt.

■ **to be in charge** die Verantwortung haben □ Mrs Munday was in charge of the group. Mrs Munday hatte die Verantwortung für die Gruppe.

to **charge** VERB

▷ *see also* **charge** NOUN

1 verlangen (PERFECT hat verlangt) *(money)*

□ How much did he charge you? Wie viel hat er verlangt? □ They charge ten pounds an hour. Sie verlangen zehn Pfund die Stunde.

2 anklagen (PERFECT hat angeklagt) *(with crime)*

□ The police have charged him with murder. Die Polizei hat ihn des Mordes angeklagt.

charity NOUN

die Wohlfahrt

□ She does a lot of work for charity. Sie arbeitet viel für die Wohlfahrt.

■ **He gave the money to charity.** Er hat das Geld für wohltätige Zwecke gespendet.

charm NOUN

der Charme

LANGUAGE TIP Note that the 'e' in **Charme** is silent.

□ He's got a lot of charm. Er hat viel Charme.

charming ADJECTIVE

bezaubernd

chart NOUN

die Grafik

□ The chart shows the rise of unemployment. Die Grafik stellt den Anstieg der Arbeitslosigkeit dar.

■ **the charts** die Hitparade *sing* □ This album is number one in the charts. Dieses Album ist auf Platz eins der Hitparade.

charter flight NOUN

der Charterflug (PL die Charterflüge)

to chase VERB
▷ *see also* **chase** NOUN
verfolgen (PERFECT hat verfolgt)

chase NOUN
▷ *see also* **chase** VERB
die Verfolgung
■ **a car chase** eine Verfolgungsjagd im Auto

chat NOUN
das Schwätzchen (PL die Schwätzchen)
□ to have a chat ein Schwätzchen halten

chat room NOUN
der Chatroom (PL die Chatrooms)

chat show NOUN
die Talkshow (PL die Talkshows)

chauvinist NOUN
■ **male chauvinist** der Chauvi

cheap ADJECTIVE
billig
□ a cheap T-shirt ein billiges T-Shirt □ It's cheaper by bus. Mit dem Bus ist es billiger.

to cheat VERB
▷ *see also* **cheat** NOUN
betrügen (IMPERFECT betrog, PERFECT hat betrogen)
□ He cheated me. Er hat mich betrogen.
■ **You're cheating!** *(in games, at school)* Du schummelst!

cheat NOUN
▷ *see also* **cheat** VERB
der Betrüger (PL die Betrüger)
die Betrügerin

check NOUN
▷ *see also* **check** VERB
1 die Kontrolle
□ a security check eine Sicherheitskontrolle
2 die Rechnung *(US: bill)*
□ The waiter brought us the check. Der Kellner brachte uns die Rechnung.
3 der Scheck (PL die Schecks) (US)
□ to write a check einen Scheck ausstellen

to check VERB
▷ *see also* **check** NOUN
nachsehen (PRESENT sieht nach, IMPERFECT sah nach, PERFECT hat nachgesehen)
□ I'll check the time of the train. Ich sehe die Abfahrtszeiten des Zuges nach. □ Could you check the oil, please? Könnten Sie bitte das Öl nachsehen?
■ **to check in** einchecken □ What time do I have to check in? Wann muss ich einchecken?
■ **to check out** *(from hotel)* sich auschecken

checked ADJECTIVE
kariert
□ a checked shirt ein kariertes Hemd

checkers SING NOUN (US)
Dame *fem*
□ Checkers is her favourite game. Dame ist ihr Lieblingsspiel.

check-in NOUN
der Check-in (PL die Check-ins)

checking account NOUN (US)
das Girokonto (PL die Girokonten)

checkout NOUN
die Kasse

check-up NOUN
der Check-up (PL die Check-ups)

cheddar NOUN
der Cheddar (PL die Cheddars)

cheek NOUN
1 die Wange
□ He kissed her on the cheek. Er küsste sie auf die Wange.
2 die Frechheit
□ What a cheek! So eine Frechheit!

cheeky ADJECTIVE
frech
□ Don't be cheeky! Sei nicht so frech!
□ a cheeky smile ein freches Lächeln

cheer NOUN
▷ *see also* **cheer** VERB
der Hurraruf (PL die Hurrarufe)
■ **to give a cheer** Hurra rufen
■ **Cheers!** **1** *(good health)* Prost! **2** *(thanks)* Danke schön!

to cheer VERB
▷ *see also* **cheer** NOUN
1 anfeuern (PERFECT hat angefeuert) *(team)*
2 zujubeln (PERFECT hat zugejubelt) *(speaker)*
□ The speaker was cheered. Dem Redner wurde zugejubelt.
■ **to cheer somebody up** jemanden aufheitern □ I was trying to cheer him up. Ich habe versucht, ihn aufzuheitern.
■ **Cheer up!** Kopf hoch!

cheerful ADJECTIVE
fröhlich

cheerio EXCLAMATION
tschüs

cheese NOUN
der Käse (PL die Käse)

chef NOUN
der Küchenchef (PL die Küchenchefs)

chemical NOUN
die Chemikalie

chemist NOUN
1 der Apotheker (PL die Apotheker)
die Apothekerin *(pharmacist)*
2 die Apotheke *(pharmacy)*
□ You get it from the chemist. Du bekommst das in der Apotheke.
3 die Drogerie *(shop selling toiletries)*
4 der Chemiker (PL die Chemiker)
die Chemikerin *(scientist)*

chemistry NOUN
die Chemie
□ the chemistry lab das Chemielabor

cheque NOUN
der Scheck (PL die Schecks)
□ to write a cheque einen Scheck ausstellen
□ to pay by cheque mit Scheck bezahlen

chequebook NOUN
das Scheckheft (PL die Scheckhefte)

DID YOU KNOW...?
German banks provide customers with cheques in an envelope or wallet, usually ten at a time, rather than chequebooks.

cherry NOUN
die Kirsche

chess NOUN
das Schach
□ to play chess Schach spielen

chessboard NOUN
das Schachbrett (PL die Schachbretter)

chest NOUN
die Brust (PL die Brüste) *(of person)*
■ **his chest measurement** seine Oberweite
■ **a chest of drawers** eine Kommode

chestnut NOUN
die Kastanie

to **chew** VERB
kauen

chewing gum NOUN
der Kaugummi (PL die Kaugummis)

chick NOUN
das Küken (PL die Küken)
□ a hen and her chicks eine Henne mit ihren Küken

chicken NOUN
1 das Hähnchen (PL die Hähnchen) *(food)*
□ I bought a chicken in the supermarket. Ich habe im Supermarkt ein Hähnchen gekauft.
2 das Huhn (PL die Hühner) *(live)*
□ They keep chickens. Sie halten Hühner.

chickenpox SING NOUN
die Windpocken *pl*
□ My sister has chickenpox. Meine Schwester hat Windpocken.

chickpeas PL NOUN
die Kichererbsen *pl*

chief NOUN
▷ *see also* **chief** ADJECTIVE
der Chef (PL die Chefs)
□ the chief of security der Sicherheitschef

chief ADJECTIVE
▷ *see also* **chief** NOUN
hauptsächlich
□ the chief reason der hauptsächliche Grund

child NOUN
das Kind (PL die Kinder)
□ all the children alle Kinder

childish ADJECTIVE
kindisch

child minder NOUN
die Tagesmutter (PL die Tagesmütter)

children PL NOUN ▷ *see* **child**

Chile NOUN
Chile *neut*
■ **from Chile** aus Chile
■ **to Chile** nach Chile

to **chill** VERB
kalt stellen
□ Put the wine in the fridge to chill. Stell den Wein kalt.

chilli NOUN
der Chili (PL die Chilis)
■ **chilli peppers** die Peperoni *pl*

chilly ADJECTIVE
kühl

chimney NOUN
der Schornstein (PL die Schornsteine)

chin NOUN
das Kinn (PL die Kinne)

china NOUN
das Porzellan
□ a china plate ein Porzellanteller *masc*

China NOUN
China *neut*
■ **from China** aus China
■ **to China** nach China

Chinese ADJECTIVE
▷ *see also* **Chinese** NOUN
chinesisch
□ a Chinese restaurant ein chinesisches Restaurant
■ **a Chinese man** ein Chinese
■ **a Chinese woman** eine Chinesin

Chinese NOUN
▷ *see also* **Chinese** ADJECTIVE
das Chinesisch (GEN des Chinesischen) *(language)*
■ **the Chinese** *(people)* die Chinesen

chip NOUN
der Chip (PL die Chips) *(in computer)*

chips PL NOUN
1 die Pommes frites *fem pl (fried potatoes)*
□ We bought some chips. Wir haben Pommes frites gekauft.
2 die Kartoffelchips *masc pl (crisps)*

LANGUAGE TIP Be careful not to translate **chips** by the German word **Chips**.

chiropodist NOUN
der Fußpfleger (PL die Fußpfleger)
die Fußpflegerin
□ He's a chiropodist. Er ist Fußpfleger.

chives PL NOUN
der Schnittlauch

chocolate NOUN
die Schokolade
□ a chocolate cake ein Schokoladenkuchen
□ hot chocolate heiße Schokolade

choice NOUN
die Wahl
□ I had no choice. Ich hatte keine andere Wahl.

choir NOUN
der Chor (PL die Chöre)
□ I sing in the school choir. Ich singe im Schulchor.

to **choke** VERB
ersticken (PERFECT ist erstickt)
□ He's choking! Er erstickt!

to **choose** VERB
auswählen (PERFECT hat ausgewählt)
□ She chose the red shirt. Sie hat das rote Hemd ausgewählt.

to **chop** VERB
▷ *see also* **chop** NOUN
klein hacken (PERFECT hat klein gehackt)
□ She chopped the onions. Sie hackte die Zwiebeln klein.

chop NOUN
▷ *see also* **chop** VERB
das Kotelett (PL die Koteletts)
□ a pork chop ein Schweinekotelett

chopsticks PL NOUN
die Stäbchen *neut pl*

chose VERB ▷ *see* **choose**

chosen VERB ▷ *see* **choose**

Christ NOUN
Christus (GEN Christi)
□ the birth of Christ die Geburt Christi

christening NOUN
die Taufe

Christian NOUN
▷ *see also* **Christian** ADJECTIVE
der Christ (GEN des Christen, PL die Christen)
die Christin

Christian ADJECTIVE
▷ *see also* **Christian** NOUN
christlich

Christian name NOUN
der Vorname (GEN des Vornamens, PL die Vornamen)

Christmas NOUN
Weihnachten *neut*
□ Happy Christmas! Fröhliche Weihnachten!
■ **Christmas Day** der erste Weihnachtsfeiertag
■ **Christmas Eve** Heiligabend

DID YOU KNOW...?
Traditionally, in Germany gifts are exchanged on Christmas Eve.

□ on Christmas Eve an Heiligabend
■ **a Christmas tree** ein Weihnachtsbaum *masc*
■ **a Christmas card** eine Weihnachtskarte

DID YOU KNOW...?
Most Germans send very few Christmas cards.

■ **Christmas dinner** das Weihnachtsessen

DID YOU KNOW...?
Germans traditionally eat goose at Christmas rather than turkey.

■ **Christmas pudding**

DID YOU KNOW...?
Germans don't have any traditional dessert at Christmas. Most know what Christmas pudding is, but almost always refer to it as **Plumpudding**.

to **chuck out** VERB
rauswerfen (PRESENT wirft raus, IMPERFECT warf raus, PERFECT hat rausgeworfen)
□ Chuck out those old magazines. Werf diese alten Zeitschriften raus.

chunk NOUN
das Stück (PL die Stücke)
□ Cut the meat into chunks. Schneiden Sie das Fleisch in Stücke.

church NOUN
die Kirche
□ I don't go to church. Ich gehe nicht in die Kirche.
■ **the Church of England** die anglikanische Kirche

cider NOUN
der Apfelwein

cigar NOUN
die Zigarre

cigarette NOUN
die Zigarette

cigarette lighter NOUN
der Zigarettenanzünder (PL die Zigarettenanzünder)

cinema NOUN
das Kino (PL die Kinos)
□ I'm going to the cinema this evening. Ich gehe heute Abend ins Kino.

cinnamon NOUN
der Zimt

circle NOUN
der Kreis (PL die Kreise)

circular ADJECTIVE
rund

circulation NOUN
1 der Kreislauf *(of blood)*
2 die Auflage *(of newspaper)*

circumstances PL NOUN
die Umstände *masc pl*

circus NOUN
der Zirkus (GEN des Zirkus, PL die Zirkusse)

citizen NOUN
der Bürger (PL die Bürger)
die Bürgerin
■ **a German citizen** ein deutscher Staatsbürger

city NOUN
die Stadt (PL die Städte)
■ **the city centre** die Innenstadt □ It's in the city centre. Es liegt in der Innenstadt.
■ **the City** die Londoner City

city technology college NOUN
die technische Fachschule

civilization NOUN
die Zivilisation

civil servant NOUN
der Beamte (GEN des Beamten, PL die Beamten)
die Beamtin

DID YOU KNOW...?
In Germany most teachers are **Beamte**.

□ He's a civil servant. Er ist Beamter.

civil war NOUN
der Bürgerkrieg (PL die Bürgerkriege)

to **claim** VERB
▷ *see also* **claim** NOUN
1 behaupten (PERFECT hat behauptet)
□ He claims to have found the money. Er behauptet, er habe das Geld gefunden.
LANGUAGE TIP Note the use of the subjunctive.
2 bekommen (IMPERFECT bekam, PERFECT hat bekommen) *(receive)*
□ She's claiming unemployment benefit. Sie bekommt Arbeitslosenunterstützung.
■ **to claim on one's insurance** seine Versicherung in Anspruch nehmen
□ We claimed on our insurance. Wir haben unsere Versicherung in Anspruch genommen.

claim NOUN
▷ *see also* **claim** VERB
der Anspruch (PL die Ansprüche) *(on insurance policy)*
■ **to make a claim for damages** Schadenersatz beanspruchen

to **clap** VERB
klatschen *(applaud)*
□ The audience clapped. Das Publikum klatschte.
■ **to clap one's hands** klatschen

clarinet NOUN
die Klarinette
□ I play the clarinet. Ich spiele Klarinette.

to **clash** VERB
1 sich beißen (IMPERFECT bissen sich, PERFECT haben sich gebissen) *(colours)*
□ These colours clash. Diese Farben beißen sich.
2 sich überschneiden (IMPERFECT überschnitt sich, PERFECT hat sich überschnitten) *(events)*
□ The concert clashes with Ann's party. Das Konzert überschneidet sich mit Anns Party.

clasp NOUN
der Verschluss (GEN des Verschlusses, PL die Verschlüsse) *(of necklace)*

class NOUN
1 die Klasse *(group)*
□ We're in the same class. Wir sind in derselben Klasse.
2 die Stunde *(lesson)*
□ I go to dancing classes. Ich nehme Tanzstunden.

classic ADJECTIVE
▷ *see also* **classic** NOUN
klassisch
□ a classic example ein klassisches Beispiel

classic NOUN
▷ *see also* **classic** ADJECTIVE
der Klassiker (PL die Klassiker) *(book, film)*

classical ADJECTIVE
klassisch
□ I like classical music. Ich mag klassische Musik.

classmate NOUN
der Klassenkamerad (GEN des Klassenkameraden, PL die Klassenkameraden)
die Klassenkameradin

classroom NOUN
die Klassenzimmer (PL die Klassenzimmer)

classroom assistant NOUN
die Assistenzlehrkraft (PL die Assistenzlehrkräfte)

clause NOUN
1 die Klausel *(in legal document)*
2 der Satz (GEN des Satzes, PL die Sätze) *(in grammar)*

claw NOUN
1 die Kralle *(of cat, dog)*
2 die Klaue *(of bird)*
3 die Schere *(of crab, lobster)*

clean ADJECTIVE
▷ *see also* **clean** VERB
sauber
□ a clean shirt ein sauberes Hemd

to **clean** VERB
▷ *see also* **clean** ADJECTIVE
sauber machen (PERFECT hat sauber gemacht)

cleaner NOUN
der Putzmann (PL die Putzmänner)
die Putzfrau
□ She's a cleaner. Sie ist Putzfrau.

cleaner's NOUN
die Reinigung

cleaning lady NOUN
die Putzfrau

cleansing lotion NOUN
die Reinigungslotion

clear ADJECTIVE
▷ *see also* **clear** VERB
1 klar
□ It's clear you don't believe me. Es ist klar, dass du mir nicht glaubst.
2 frei *(road, way)*
□ The road's clear now. Die Straße ist jetzt frei.

to **clear** VERB
▷ *see also* **clear** ADJECTIVE
1 räumen
□ The police are clearing the road after the accident. Die Polizei räumt die Straße nach dem Unfall.
2 sich auflösen (PERFECT hat sich aufgelöst) *(fog, mist)*
□ The mist soon cleared. Der Nebel löste sich bald auf.
■ **to be cleared of a crime** von einem Verbrechen freigesprochen werden
□ She was cleared of murder. Sie wurde von der Mordanklage freigesprochen.
■ **to clear the table** den Tisch abräumen
□ I'll clear the table. Ich räume den Tisch ab.

■ **to clear up** aufräumen □ Who's going to clear all this up? Wer räumt das alles auf?
■ **I think it's going to clear up.** *(weather)* Ich glaube, es hellt sich auf.

clearly ADVERB
klar
□ She explained it very clearly. Sie hat es sehr klar erklärt. □ The English coast was clearly visible. Die englische Küste war klar zu sehen.
■ **to speak clearly** deutlich sprechen

clementine NOUN
die Klementine

to **clench** VERB
■ **She clenched her fists.** Sie ballte die Fäuste.

clerk NOUN
der Büroangestellte (GEN des Büroangestellten, PL die Büroangestellten)
die Büroangestellte (GEN der Büroangestellten)
□ She's a clerk. Sie ist Büroangestellte.

clever ADJECTIVE
1 klug
□ She's very clever. Sie ist sehr klug.
2 genial *(ingenious)*
□ a clever system ein geniales System
□ What a clever idea! Das ist eine geniale Idee!

to **click on** VERB
anklicken (PERFECT hat angeklickt) *(computer)*
□ to click on an icon ein Icon anklicken
■ **to click on the mouse** mit der Maus klicken

client NOUN
der Klient (GEN des Klienten, PL die Klienten)
die Klientin

cliff NOUN
die Klippe

climate NOUN
das Klima (PL die Klimas)

to **climb** VERB
1 steigen auf *+acc* (IMPERFECT stieg, PERFECT ist gestiegen)
□ We're going to climb Snowdon. Wir steigen auf den Snowdon.
2 hinaufgehen (IMPERFECT ging hinauf, PERFECT ist hinaufgegangen) *(stairs)*
□ I watched him climb the stairs. Ich sah ihn die Treppe hinaufgehen.
■ **She finds it difficult to climb the stairs.** Das Treppensteigen fällt ihr schwer.

climber NOUN
der Kletterer (PL die Kletterer)
die Kletterin

climbing NOUN
das Klettern
■ **to go climbing** klettern gehen
□ We're going climbing in Scotland. Wir gehen in Schottland klettern.

clingfilm NOUN
die Frischhaltefolie

clinic NOUN
die Klinik

cloakroom NOUN
1 die Garderobe *(for coats)*
2 die Toilette *(toilet)*

clock NOUN
die Uhr
■ **a grandfather clock** eine Standuhr
■ **an alarm clock** ein Wecker *masc*
■ **a clock radio** ein Radiowecker *masc*

clockwork NOUN
das Uhrwerk
■ **to go like clockwork** wie am Schnürchen gehen *(informal)*

clog NOUN
1 der Clog (PL die Clogs) *(modern)*
2 der Holzschuh (PL die Holzschuhe) *(traditional, made of wood)*

clone NOUN
▷ *see also* **clone** VERB
der Klon (PL die Klone)

to **clone** VERB
▷ *see also* **clone** NOUN
klonen
□ a cloned sheep ein geklontes Schaf

close ADJECTIVE, ADVERB
▷ *see also* **close** VERB
1 nahe *(near)*
□ close relations nahe Verwandte □ I'm very close to my sister. Ich stehe meiner Schwester sehr nahe.
■ **The shops are very close.** Die Geschäfte sind ganz in der Nähe.
■ **She's a close friend of mine.** Sie ist eine gute Freundin von mir.
■ **Come closer!** Komm näher!
■ **close to** in der Nähe *+gen* □ The youth hostel is close to the station. Die Jugendherberge ist in der Nähe des Bahnhofs.
2 knapp *(contest)*
□ It's going to be very close. Das wird sehr knapp.
3 schwül *(weather)*
□ It's close today. Es ist schwül heute.

to **close** VERB
▷ *see also* **close** ADJECTIVE
schließen (IMPERFECT schloss, PERFECT hat geschlossen)
□ What time does the pool close? Wann schließt das Schwimmbad?
□ The doors close automatically. Die Türen schließen automatisch.
■ **Please close the door.** Bitte mach die Tür zu.

closed ADJECTIVE
geschlossen
□ The bank's closed. Die Bank ist geschlossen.

closely ADVERB
genau *(look, examine)*

cloth NOUN
der Stoff (PL die Stoffe) *(material)*
■ **a cloth** ein Lappen *masc* □ Wipe it with a damp cloth. Wischen Sie es mit einem feuchten Lappen ab.

clothes PL NOUN
die Kleider *neut pl*
□ new clothes neue Kleider
■ **a clothes line** eine Wäscheleine
■ **a clothes peg** eine Wäscheklammer

cloud NOUN
die Wolke

cloudy ADJECTIVE
bewölkt

clove NOUN
■ **a clove of garlic** eine Knoblauchzehe

clown NOUN
der Clown (PL die Clowns)

club NOUN
der Klub (PL die Klubs)
□ a tennis club ein Tennisklub □ the youth club der Jugendklub
■ **clubs** *(in cards)* Kreuz *neut* □ the ace of clubs das Kreuzass

to **club together** VERB
zusammenlegen (PERFECT hat zusammengelegt)
□ We clubbed together to buy her a present. Wir haben zusammengelegt, um ein Geschenk für sie zu kaufen.

clubbing NOUN
■ **to go clubbing** in Klubs gehen

clue NOUN
der Hinweis (PL die Hinweise)
□ an important clue ein wichtiger Hinweis
■ **I haven't a clue.** Ich habe keine Ahnung.

clumsy ADJECTIVE
tollpatschig
□ Toby is even clumsier than his sister. Toby ist noch tollpatschiger als seine Schwester.

clutch NOUN
▷ *see also* **clutch** VERB
die Kupplung *(of car)*

to **clutch** VERB
▷ *see also* **clutch** NOUN
umklammern (PERFECT hat umklammert)
□ She clutched my arm. Sie umklammerte meinen Arm.

clutter NOUN
der Kram
□ There's so much clutter in here. Hier liegt so viel Kram herum.

coach NOUN
1 der Reisebus (GEN des Reisebusses, PL die Reisebusse)
■ **by coach** mit dem Bus □ We went there by coach. Wir sind mit dem Bus dorthin gefahren.
■ **the coach station** der Busbahnhof
■ **a coach trip** eine Busreise
2 der Trainer (PL die Trainer)
die Trainerin *(trainer)*
□ the German coach der deutsche Trainer

coal NOUN
die Kohle
□ a coal mine eine Kohlezeche
■ **a coal miner** ein Bergarbeiter *masc*

coarse ADJECTIVE
1 grob
□ coarse black cloth grober schwarzer Stoff
2 grobkörnig
□ The sand is very coarse on that beach. Der Sand an diesem Strand ist sehr grobkörnig.

coast NOUN
die Küste
□ It's on the west coast of Scotland. Es liegt an der Westküste Schottlands.

coastguard NOUN
die Küstenwache

coat NOUN
der Mantel (PL die Mäntel)
□ a warm coat ein warmer Mantel
■ **a coat of paint** ein Anstrich *masc*

coat hanger NOUN
der Kleiderbügel (PL die Kleiderbügel)

cobweb NOUN
das Spinnennetz

cocaine NOUN
das Kokain

cock NOUN
der Hahn (PL die Hähne) *(bird)*

cockerel NOUN
der Hahn (PL die Hähne)

cockney NOUN
der Cockney (PL die Cockneys)
□ I'm a cockney. Ich bin Cockney.

cocoa NOUN
der Kakao (PL die Kakaos *or* Kakao)
□ a cup of cocoa eine Tasse Kakao

LANGUAGE TIP When ordering more than one cup of cocoa use the plural form **Kakao**.

□ Two cocoas, please. Zwei Kakao bitte.

coconut NOUN
die Kokosnuss (PL die Kokosnüsse)

cod NOUN
der Kabeljau (PL die Kabeljaue)

code NOUN
der Code (PL die Codes)

coffee NOUN
der Kaffee (PL die Kaffees *or* Kaffee)
□ A cup of coffee, please. Eine Tasse Kaffee, bitte.

LANGUAGE TIP When ordering more than one coffee use the plural form **Kaffee**.

□ Two coffees, please. Zwei Kaffee bitte.

coffeepot NOUN
die Kaffeekanne

coffee table NOUN
der Couchtisch (PL die Couchtische)

coffin NOUN
der Sarg (PL die Särge)

coin NOUN
die Münze
■ **a five-mark coin** ein Fünfmarkstück *neut*

coincidence NOUN
der Zufall (PL die Zufälle)

coin phone NOUN
das Münztelefon

Coke® NOUN
die Cola (PL die Colas)
□ a can of Coke® eine Dose Cola

colander NOUN
der Seiher (PL die Seiher)

cold ADJECTIVE
▷ *see also* **cold** NOUN
kalt
□ The water's cold. Das Wasser ist kalt.
□ It's cold today. Heute ist es kalt.

LANGUAGE TIP When you talk about a person being 'cold', you use the impersonal construction.

□ I'm cold. Mir ist kalt. □ Are you cold? Ist dir kalt?

cold NOUN
▷ *see also* **cold** ADJECTIVE
1 die Kälte
□ I can't stand the cold. Ich kann Kälte nicht ausstehen.
2 der Schnupfen (PL die Schnupfen)
□ to catch a cold einen Schnupfen bekommen □ to have a cold einen Schnupfen haben □ I've got a bad cold. Ich habe einen üblen Schnupfen.
■ **a cold sore** ein Fieberbläschen *neut*

coleslaw NOUN
der Krautsalat (PL die Krautsalate)

to **collapse** VERB
zusammenbrechen (PRESENT bricht zusammen, IMPERFECT brach zusammen, PERFECT ist zusammengebrochen)
□ He collapsed. Er brach zusammen.

collar NOUN
1 der Kragen (PL die Kragen) *(of coat, shirt)*
2 das Halsband (PL die Halsbänder) *(for animal)*

collarbone NOUN
das Schlüsselbein (PL die Schlüsselbeine)
□ I broke my collarbone. Ich habe mir das Schlüsselbein gebrochen.

colleague NOUN
der Kollege (GEN des Kollegen, PL die Kollegen)
die Kollegin

to **collect** VERB
1 einsammeln (PERFECT hat eingesammelt)
□ The teacher collected the exercise books. Der Lehrer hat die Hefte eingesammelt.
2 sammeln
□ I collect stamps. Ich sammle Briefmarken.
□ They're collecting for charity. Sie sammeln für wohltätige Zwecke.
3 abholen (PERFECT hat abgeholt) *(come to fetch)*
□ Their mother collects them from school. Ihre Mutter holt sie von der Schule ab.
□ They collect the rubbish twice a week. Der Müll wird zweimal pro Woche abgeholt.

collect call NOUN (US)
das R-Gespräch (PL die R-Gespräche)

collection NOUN
die Sammlung
□ my CD collection meine CD-Sammlung □ a collection for charity eine Spendensammlung

collector NOUN
der Sammler (PL die Sammler)
die Sammlerin

college NOUN
die Fachhochschule

DID YOU KNOW...?
A **Fachhochschule** is an institute of higher education for pupils aged over 18, which combines academic studies with work experience. It is oriented towards the needs of industry and commerce.

to **collide** VERB
zusammenstoßen (PRESENT stößt zusammen, IMPERFECT stieß zusammen, PERFECT ist zusammengestoßen)

collie NOUN
der Collie (PL die Collies)

colliery NOUN
die Zeche

collision NOUN
der Zusammenstoß (GEN des Zusammenstoßes, PL die Zusammenstöße)

colon NOUN
der Doppelpunkt *(punctuation mark)*

colonel NOUN
der Oberst (GEN des Obersten, PL die Obersten)

colour (US **color**) NOUN
die Farbe
□ What colour is it? Welche Farbe hat es?
■ **a colour film** *(for camera)* ein Farbfilm *masc*

colourful (US **colorful**) ADJECTIVE
farbig

colouring (US **coloring**) NOUN
der Farbstoff (PL die Farbstoffe) *(for food)*

comb NOUN
▷ *see also* **comb** VERB
der Kamm (PL die Kämme)

to **comb** VERB
▷ *see also* **comb** NOUN
■ **to comb one's hair** sich kämmen
□ You haven't combed your hair. Du hast dich nicht gekämmt.

combination NOUN
die Kombination

to **combine** VERB
vereinen (PERFECT hat vereint)
□ The film combines humour with suspense. Der Film vereint Humor und Spannung.

to **come** VERB
kommen (IMPERFECT kam, PERFECT ist gekommen)
□ I'm coming! Ich komme! □ The letter came this morning. Der Brief kam heute früh. □ Can I come too? Kann ich mitkommen? □ Some friends came to see us. Einige Freunde sind zu Besuch gekommen. □ I'll come with you. Ich komme mit dir.
■ **to come across** zufällig finden □ I came across some old photos. Ich fand zufällig einige alte Fotos.
■ **She comes across as a nice girl.** Sie scheint ein nettes Mädchen zu sein.
■ **to come back** zurückkommen □ Come back! Komm zurück!
■ **to come down 1** *(person, lift)* herunterkommen **2** *(prices)* fallen
■ **to come from** kommen aus □ I come from Germany. Ich komme aus Deutschland. □ Where do you come from? Woher kommen Sie?
■ **to come in** hereinkommen □ Come in! Herein!
■ **Come on!** Na komm!
■ **to come out** herauskommen □ when we came out of the cinema als wir aus dem Kino kamen □ It's just come out on DVD. Es ist gerade als DVD herausgekommen.
■ **to come round** *(after faint, operation)* wieder zu sich kommen
■ **to come up** heraufkommen □ Come up here! Komm hier herauf!
■ **to come up to somebody** auf jemanden zukommen □ She came up to me and kissed me. Sie kam auf mich zu und küsste mich.

comedian NOUN
der Komiker (PL die Komiker)
die Komikerin

comedy NOUN
die Komödie

comfortable ADJECTIVE
bequem
■ **I'm very comfortable, thanks.** Danke, ich fühle mich sehr wohl.

comic NOUN
das Comicheft (PL die Comichefte) *(magazine)*

comic strip NOUN
der Comicstrip (PL die Comicstrips)

coming ADJECTIVE
kommend
□ in the coming months in den kommenden Monaten

comma NOUN
das Komma (PL die Kommas)

command NOUN
der Befehl (PL die Befehle)

comment NOUN
▷ *see also* **comment** VERB
der Kommentar (PL die Kommentare)
□ He made no comment. Er gab keinen Kommentar ab. □ No comment! Kein Kommentar!

to **comment** VERB
▷ *see also* **comment** NOUN
■ **to comment on something** eine Bemerkung zu etwas machen

commentary NOUN
der Kommentar (PL die Kommentare) *(on TV, radio)*

commentator NOUN
der Sportreporter (PL die Sportreporter)
die Sportreporterin *(sports)*

commercial NOUN
der Werbespot (PL die Werbespots)

commission NOUN
die Provision
□ Salesmen work on commission. Verkäufer arbeiten auf Provisionsbasis.

to **commit** VERB
■ **to commit a crime** ein Verbrechen begehen
■ **to commit oneself** sich festlegen □ I don't want to commit myself. Ich will mich nicht festlegen.
■ **to commit suicide** Selbstmord begehen □ He committed suicide. Er beging Selbstmord.

committee NOUN
der Ausschuss (GEN des Ausschusses, PL die Ausschüsse)

common ADJECTIVE
▷ *see also* **common** NOUN
gebräuchlich
□ 'Smith' is a very common surname. 'Smith' ist ein sehr gebräuchlicher Nachname.
■ **in common** gemein □ We've got a lot in common. Wir haben viel gemein.

common NOUN
▷ *see also* **common** ADJECTIVE
die Gemeindewiese
□ We went for a walk on the common. Wir sind auf der Gemeindewiese spazieren gegangen.

Commons PL NOUN
■ **the House of Commons** das britische Unterhaus

common sense NOUN
der gesunde Menschenverstand
□ Use your common sense! Benutze deinen gesunden Menschenverstand!

to **communicate** VERB
kommunizieren (PERFECT hat kommuniziert)

communication NOUN
die Kommunikation

communion NOUN
die Kommunion
□ my First Communion meine Erstkommunion

communism NOUN
der Kommunismus (GEN des Kommunismus)

English-German

C

communist NOUN
▷ *see also* **communist** ADJECTIVE
der Kommunist (GEN des Kommunisten, PL die Kommunisten)
die Kommunistin

communist ADJECTIVE
▷ *see also* **communist** NOUN
kommunistisch
■ **the Communist Party** die Kommunistische Partei

community NOUN
die Gemeinschaft
■ **the local community** die Gemeinde

to **commute** VERB
pendeln (PERFECT ist gependelt)
□ She commutes between Liss and London. Sie pendelt zwischen Liss und London.

compact disc NOUN
die Compact Disc (PL die Compact Discs)
■ **compact disc player** der CD-Spieler

companion NOUN
der Gefährte (GEN des Gefährten, PL die Gefährten)
die Gefährtin

company NOUN
1 das Unternehmen (PL die Unternehmen)
□ He works for a big company. Er arbeitet für ein großes Unternehmen.
2 die Gesellschaft
□ an insurance company eine Versicherungsgesellschaft
■ **a theatre company** ein Theaterensemble *neut*
■ **to keep somebody company** jemandem Gesellschaft leisten □ I'll keep you company. Ich leiste dir Gesellschaft.

comparatively ADVERB
relativ

to **compare** VERB
vergleichen (IMPERFECT verglich, PERFECT hat verglichen)
□ People always compare him with his brother. Die Leute vergleichen ihn immer mit seinem Bruder.
■ **compared with** im Vergleich zu
□ Oxford is small compared with London. Im Vergleich zu London ist Oxford klein.

comparison NOUN
der Vergleich (PL die Vergleiche)

compartment NOUN
das Abteil (PL die Abteile)

compass NOUN
der Kompass (GEN des Kompasses, PL die Kompasse)

compensation NOUN
der Schadenersatz
□ I got a thousand pounds compensation. Ich bekam tausend Pfund Schadenersatz.

compere NOUN
der Conférencier (PL die Conférenciers)

to **compete** VERB
teilnehmen (PRESENT nimmt teil, IMPERFECT nahm teil, PERFECT hat teilgenommen)
□ I'm competing in the marathon. Ich nehme am Marathon teil.
■ **to compete for something** um etwas kämpfen □ They are competing for a place in the UEFA cup. Sie kämpfen um einen Platz im UEFA-Pokal.
■ **There are fifty students competing for six places.** Fünfzig Studenten bewerben sich auf sechs Studienplätze.

competent ADJECTIVE
kompetent

competition NOUN
der Wettbewerb (PL die Wettbewerbe) *(organized event)*
□ a singing competition ein Gesangswettbewerb

competitive ADJECTIVE
■ **I'm a very competitive person.** Ich bin ein sehr ehrgeiziger Mensch.

competitor NOUN
der Teilnehmer (PL die Teilnehmer)
die Teilnehmerin *(participant)*

to **complain** VERB
sich beschweren (PERFECT hat sich beschwert)
□ I'm going to complain to the manager. Ich werde mich beim Geschäftsführer beschweren. □ We complained about the noise. Wir haben uns über den Lärm beschwert.

complaint NOUN
die Beschwerde
□ There were lots of complaints about the food. Es gab viele Beschwerden über das Essen.

complete ADJECTIVE
vollständig

completely ADVERB
völlig

complexion NOUN
der Teint (PL die Teints)

complicated ADJECTIVE
kompliziert

compliment NOUN
▷ *see also* **compliment** VERB
das Kompliment (PL die Komplimente)

to **compliment** VERB
▷ *see also* **compliment** NOUN
■ **They complimented me on my German.** Sie haben mir Komplimente zu meinem Deutsch gemacht.

complimentary ADJECTIVE
■ **complimentary ticket** der Freifahrschein

to **compose** VERB
komponieren (PERFECT hat komponiert) *(music)*
■ **to be composed of something** aus etwas bestehen □ The team is composed of two boys and three girls. Die Mannschaft besteht aus zwei Jungen und drei Mädchen.

composer NOUN
der Komponist (GEN des Komponisten, PL die Komponisten)
die Komponistin

comprehension NOUN
das Verständnis *(school exercise)*

comprehensive ADJECTIVE
umfassend
□ a comprehensive guide ein umfassender Reiseführer

comprehensive school NOUN
die Gesamtschule

DID YOU KNOW...?
Gesamtschulen are the exception rather than the rule in Germany.

compromise NOUN
▷ *see also* **compromise** VERB
der Kompromiss (GEN des Kompromisses, PL die Kompromisse)
□ We reached a compromise. Wir haben einen Kompromiss gefunden.

to **compromise** VERB
▷ *see also* **compromise** NOUN
einen Kompromiss schließen (IMPERFECT schloss, PERFECT hat geschlossen)

compulsory ADJECTIVE
obligatorisch

computer NOUN
der Computer (PL die Computer)

computer game NOUN
das Computerspiel (PL die Computerspiele)

computer programmer NOUN
der Programmierer (PL die Programmierer)
die Programmiererin
□ She's a computer programmer. Sie ist Programmiererin.

computer science NOUN
die Informatik

computing NOUN
die Informatik

to **concentrate** VERB
sich konzentrieren (PERFECT hat sich konzentriert)
□ I couldn't concentrate. Ich konnte mich nicht konzentrieren.

concentration NOUN
die Konzentration

concern NOUN
▷ *see also* **concern** VERB
die Sorge
□ to express concern about something Sorge über etwas ausdrücken

to **concern** VERB
▷ *see also* **concern** NOUN
betreffen (PRESENT betrifft, IMPERFECT betraf, PERFECT hat betroffen)
□ It concerns all of us. Es betrifft uns alle.

concerned ADJECTIVE
■ **to be concerned** sich Sorgen machen
□ I am concerned about him. Ich mache mir Sorgen um ihn.
■ **as far as I'm concerned** was mich betrifft

concerning NOUN
bezüglich
□ For further information concerning the job, contact Mr Ross. Für weitere Informationen bezüglich der Stelle wenden Sie sich an Herrn Ross.

concert NOUN
das Konzert (PL die Konzerte)

concrete NOUN
der Beton (PL die Betons)

to **condemn** VERB
verurteilen (PERFECT hat verurteilt)

condition NOUN
1 die Bedingung
□ I'll do it, on one condition ... Ich mache es unter einer Bedingung ...
2 der Zustand (PL die Zustände)
□ in good condition in gutem Zustand

conditional NOUN
der Konditional

conditioner NOUN
die Spülung *(for hair)*

condom NOUN
das Kondom (PL die Kondome)

to **conduct** VERB
dirigieren (PERFECT hat dirigiert) *(orchestra)*

conductor NOUN
der Dirigent (GEN des Dirigenten, PL die Dirigenten)
die Dirigentin

cone NOUN
1 die Eistüte
□ an ice-cream cone eine Eistüte
2 der Kegel (PL die Kegel) *(geometric shape)*
■ **a traffic cone** ein Pylon *masc*

conference NOUN
die Konferenz

to **confess** VERB
gestehen (IMPERFECT gestand, PERFECT hat gestanden)
□ He finally confessed. Er hat schließlich gestanden. □ He confessed to the murder. Er hat den Mord gestanden.

confession NOUN
1 das Geständnis (GEN des Geständnisses, PL die Geständnisse)
□ He signed a confession. Er unterschrieb ein Geständnis.
2 die Beichte *(in church)*
□ to go to confession zur Beichte gehen

confetti NOUN
das Konfetti

confidence NOUN
1 das Vertrauen
□ I've got confidence in you. Ich habe Vertrauen in dich.
2 das Selbstvertrauen
□ She lacks confidence. Sie hat zu wenig Selbstvertrauen.

confident ADJECTIVE
1 zuversichtlich *(sure of something)*
□ I'm confident everything will be okay. Ich bin zuversichtlich, dass alles gut gehen wird.
2 selbstbewusst *(self-assured)*
□ She's seems a confident person. Sie scheint eine selbstbewusste Frau zu sein.

confidential ADJECTIVE
vertraulich

to **confirm** VERB
bestätigen (PERFECT hat bestätigt) *(booking)*

confirmation NOUN
die Bestätigung

conflict NOUN
der Konflikt (PL die Konflikte)

to **confuse** VERB
durcheinanderbringen (IMPERFECT brachte durcheinander, PERFECT hat durcheinandergebracht)
□ Don't confuse me! Bring mich nicht durcheinander!

confused ADJECTIVE
durcheinander

confusing ADJECTIVE
verwirrend

confusion NOUN
das Durcheinander

to **congratulate** VERB
beglückwünschen (PERFECT hat beglückwünscht)
□ All my friends congratulated me. Alle meine Freunde haben mich beglückwünscht.

congratulations PL NOUN
der Glückwunsch (PL die Glückwünsche)
□ Congratulations on your new job! Herzlichen Glückwunsch zum neuen Job!

conjunction NOUN
die Konjunktion

conjurer NOUN
der Zauberkünstler (PL die Zauberkünstler)
die Zauberkünstlerin

connection NOUN
1 der Zusammenhang (PL die Zusammenhänge)
□ There's no connection between the two events. Es besteht kein Zusammenhang zwischen den beiden Ereignissen.
2 der Kontakt (PL die Kontakte) *(electrical)*
□ There's a loose connection. Da ist ein Wackelkontakt.
3 der Anschluss (GEN des Anschlusses, PL die Anschlüsse) *(of trains, planes)*
□ We missed our connection. Wir haben unseren Anschluss verpasst.

to **conquer** VERB
erobern (PERFECT hat erobert)

conscience NOUN
das Gewissen
□ I have a guilty conscience. Ich habe ein schlechtes Gewissen.

conscious ADJECTIVE
bewusst
□ politically conscious politisch bewusst □ a conscious effort eine bewusste Anstrengung
■ **to be conscious of something** **1** *(know)* sich einer Sache bewusst sein □ I was conscious of his disapproval. Ich war mir seiner Missbilligung bewusst. **2** *(notice)* etwas bemerken □ She was conscious of Max looking at her. Sie hatte bemerkt, dass Max sie ansah.

consciousness NOUN
das Bewusstsein
■ **to lose consciousness** bewusstlos werden
□ I lost consciousness. Ich wurde bewusstlos.

consequence NOUN
die Folge

consequently ADVERB
folglich

conservation NOUN
der Schutz
□ nature conservation der Naturschutz

conservative ADJECTIVE
▷ *see also* **conservative** NOUN
konservativ
■ **the Conservative Party** die Konservative Partei

Conservative NOUN
▷ *see also* **conservative** ADJECTIVE
der Konservative (GEN des Konservativen, PL die Konservativen)
die Konservative
□ a Conservative *(man)* ein Konservativer
■ **to vote Conservative** die Konservativen wählen
■ **the Conservatives** die Konservativen

conservatory NOUN
der Wintergarten (PL die Wintergärten)

to **consider** VERB
in Erwägung ziehen (IMPERFECT zog in Erwägung, PERFECT hat in Erwägung gezogen)
□ We considered cancelling our holiday. Wir zogen in Erwägung, den Urlaub abzusagen.
■ **I'm considering the idea.** Ich denke darüber nach.
■ **He considered it a waste of time.** Er hielt es für Zeitverschwendung.

considerate ADJECTIVE
aufmerksam
□ That was very considerate of you. Das war sehr aufmerksam von dir.
■ **not very considerate** nicht sehr rücksichtsvoll

considering PREPOSITION
1 dafür, dass
□ Considering we were there for a month ... Dafür, dass wir einen Monat da waren ...
2 unter den Umständen
□ I got a good mark, considering. Unter den Umständen bekam ich eine gute Note.

to **consist** VERB
■ **to consist of** bestehen aus □ The band consists of three guitarists and a drummer.

Die Band besteht aus drei Gitarristen und einem Schlagzeuger.

consistent ADJECTIVE
beständig
□ He's our most consistent player. Er ist unser beständigster Spieler.

consonant NOUN
der Konsonant (GEN des Konsonanten, PL die Konsonanten)

constant ADJECTIVE
beständig

constantly ADVERB
dauernd

constipated ADJECTIVE
verstopft

to **construct** VERB
bauen

construction NOUN
der Bau

to **consult** VERB
1 um Rat fragen *(solicitor, doctor)*
2 nachsehen in +*dat* (PRESENT sieht nach, IMPERFECT sah nach, PERFECT hat nachgesehen) *(book)*
□ Consult the dictionary! Sieh im Wörterbuch nach!

consumer NOUN
der Verbraucher (PL die Verbraucher)
die Verbraucherin

contact NOUN
▷ *see also* **contact** VERB
der Kontakt (PL die Kontakte)
□ I'm in contact with her. Ich bin in Kontakt mit ihr.

to **contact** VERB
▷ *see also* **contact** NOUN
sich in Verbindung setzen mit
□ Please contact us immediately. Bitte setzen Sie sich sofort mit uns in Verbindung.
■ **Where can we contact you?** Wo können wir Sie erreichen?

contact lenses PL NOUN
die Kontaktlinsen *fem pl*

to **contain** VERB
enthalten (PRESENT enthält, IMPERFECT enthielt, PERFECT hat enthalten)

container NOUN
der Behälter (PL die Behälter)

contempt NOUN
die Verachtung

contents PL NOUN
der Inhalt
■ **table of contents** das Inhaltsverzeichnis

contest NOUN
der Wettbewerb (PL die Wettbewerbe)

contestant NOUN
der Teilnehmer (PL die Teilnehmer)
die Teilnehmerin

context NOUN
der Zusammenhang (PL die Zusammenhänge)

continent NOUN
der Kontinent (PL die Kontinente)
□ How many continents are there? Wie viele Kontinente gibt es?
■ **the Continent** Kontinentaleuropa *neut*
□ on the Continent in Kontinentaleuropa
■ **I've never been to the Continent.** Ich war noch nie auf dem Kontinent.

continental breakfast NOUN
das kleine Frühstück

continental quilt NOUN
die Steppdecke

to **continue** VERB
weitermachen (PERFECT hat weitergemacht)
□ We'll continue tomorrow. Wir machen morgen weiter.
■ **Please continue!** Bitte fahren Sie fort!
■ **She continued talking to her friend.** Sie redete weiter mit ihrer Freundin.

continuous ADJECTIVE
laufend
■ **continuous assessment** laufende Leistungskontrolle

contraceptive NOUN
das Verhütungsmittel (PL die Verhütungsmittel)

contract NOUN
der Vertrag (PL die Verträge)

to **contradict** VERB
widersprechen (PRESENT widerspricht, IMPERFECT widersprach, PERFECT hat widersprochen)
□ Don't contradict me! Widersprich mir nicht!

contrary NOUN
das Gegenteil
■ **on the contrary** im Gegenteil

contrast NOUN
der Kontrast (PL die Kontraste)

to **contribute** VERB
1 beitragen (PRESENT trägt bei, IMPERFECT trug bei, PERFECT hat beigetragen)
□ The treaty will contribute to world peace. Der Vertrag wird zum Weltfrieden beitragen.
2 spenden *(donate)*
□ She contributed ten pounds. Sie hat zehn Pfund gespendet.

contribution NOUN
der Beitrag (PL die Beiträge)

control NOUN
▷ *see also* **control** VERB
die Kontrolle
■ **to lose control** *(of vehicle)* die Kontrolle verlieren □ He lost control of the car. Er hat die Kontrolle über das Auto verloren.
■ **the controls** *(of machine)* die Bedienelemente *neut pl*
■ **to be in control** das Sagen haben
■ **to keep control** *(of people)* Disziplin halten
□ He can't keep control of the class. Er kann in der Klasse keine Disziplin halten.

English-German

C

■ **out of control** *(child, class)* außer Rand und Band

to **control** VERB
▷ *see also* **control** NOUN
1 unter Kontrolle haben (PRESENT hat unter Kontrolle, IMPERFECT hatte unter Kontrolle, PERFECT hat unter Kontrolle gehabt) *(country, organization)*
2 Disziplin halten in +*dat* (PRESENT hält Disziplin in, IMPERFECT hielt Disziplin in, PERFECT hat Disziplin gehalten in)
□ He can't control the class. Er kann in der Klasse keine Disziplin halten.
3 unter Kontrolle halten
□ I couldn't control the horse. Ich konnte das Pferd nicht mehr unter Kontrolle halten.
4 regeln *(regulate)*
□ You can control the volume. Sie können die Lautstärke regeln.
■ **to control oneself** sich beherrschen

controversial ADJECTIVE
umstritten
□ a controversial book ein umstrittenes Buch

convenient ADJECTIVE
günstig *(place)*
□ The hotel's convenient for the airport. Das Hotel ist in günstiger Lage zum Flughafen. □ It's not convenient for me right now. Es ist gerade ungünstig.
■ **Would Monday be convenient for you?** Würde dir Montag passen?

conventional ADJECTIVE
konventionell

convent school NOUN
die Klosterschule

conversation NOUN
die Unterhaltung
■ **a German conversation class** deutsche Konversation

to **convert** VERB
umbauen (PERFECT hat umgebaut)
□ We've converted the loft into a spare room. Wir haben den Speicher zu einem Gästezimmer umgebaut.

convict NOUN
▷ *see also* **convict** VERB
der Häftling
□ an escaped convict ein entflohener Häftling

to **convict** VERB
▷ *see also* **convict** NOUN
überführen (PERFECT hat überführt)
□ He was convicted of the murder. Er wurde des Mordes überführt.

conviction NOUN
die Überzeugung
□ She spoke with great conviction. Sie sprach mit großer Überzeugung.
■ **He has three previous convictions for robbery.** Er ist bereits dreimal wegen Raubes vorbestraft.

to **convince** VERB
überzeugen (PERFECT hat überzeugt)
□ I'm not convinced. Ich bin nicht überzeugt.

to **cook** VERB
▷ *see also* **cook** NOUN
kochen
□ I can't cook. Ich kann nicht kochen. □ She's cooking lunch. Sie kocht das Mittagessen.
■ **to be cooked** fertig sein □ When the potatoes are cooked ... Wenn die Kartoffeln fertig sind ...

cook NOUN
▷ *see also* **cook** VERB
der Koch (PL die Köche)
die Köchin
□ Werner's an excellent cook. Werner ist ein ausgezeichneter Koch.

cookbook NOUN
das Kochbuch (PL die Kochbücher)

cooker NOUN
der Herd (PL die Herde)
□ a gas cooker ein Gasherd

cookery NOUN
das Kochen
■ **a cookery class** ein Kochkurs *masc*

cookie NOUN (US)
der Keks (GEN des Kekses, PL die Kekse)

cooking NOUN
das Kochen
■ **I like cooking.** Ich koche gern.

cool ADJECTIVE
▷ *see also* **cool** VERB
1 kühl
□ a cooler place ein kühlerer Ort
2 cool *(great)*
□ That,s really cool! Das ist echt cool!
■ **to stay cool** *(keep calm)* ruhig bleiben
□ He stayed cool. Er blieb ruhig.

to **cool** VERB
▷ *see also* **cool** ADJECTIVE
kühlen
■ **Just cool it!** Immer mit der Ruhe! *(informal)*

cooperation NOUN
die Zusammenarbeit

cop NOUN
der Polizist (GEN des Polizisten, PL die Polizisten)
die Polizistin

to **cope** VERB
es schaffen
□ It was hard, but we coped. Es war schwer, aber wir haben es geschafft.
■ **to cope with** bewältigen □ She's got a lot of problems to cope with. Sie hat eine Menge Probleme zu bewältigen.

copper NOUN
1 das Kupfer
□ a copper bracelet ein Kupferarmband
2 der Polizist (GEN des Polizisten, PL die Polizisten)

die Polizistin *(police officer)*

copy NOUN
▷ *see also* **copy** VERB
1 die Kopie *(of letter, document)*
2 das Exemplar (PL die Exemplare) *(of book)*

to **copy** VERB
▷ *see also* **copy** NOUN
1 abschreiben (IMPERFECT schrieb ab, PERFECT hat abgeschrieben) *(write down)*
□ She copied the sentence. Sie schrieb den Satz ab. □ The teacher accused him of copying. Der Lehrer warf ihm vor, abgeschrieben zu haben.
2 nachmachen (PERFECT hat nachgemacht) *(person)*
□ She always copies her sister. Sie macht ihrer Schwester alles nach.
3 kopieren (PERFECT hat kopiert) *(computer)*
□ to copy and paste kopieren und einfügen

core NOUN
der Stein *(of fruit)*

cork NOUN
1 der Korken (PL die Korken) *(of bottle)*
2 der Kork *(material)*
□ a cork table mat ein Korkuntersetzer *masc*

corkscrew NOUN
der Korkenzieher (PL die Korkenzieher)

corn NOUN
1 das Getreide (PL die Getreide) *(wheat)*
2 der Mais *(sweetcorn)*
■ **corn on the cob** der Maiskolben

corner NOUN
1 die Ecke
□ in a corner of the room in einer Ecke des Zimmers □ the shop on the corner das Geschäft an der Ecke □ He lives just round the corner. Er wohnt gleich um die Ecke.
2 der Eckball (PL die Eckbälle) *(in football)*

cornet NOUN
1 das Kornett (PL die Kornette)
□ He plays the cornet. Er spielt Kornett.
2 die Eistüte *(ice cream)*

cornflakes PL NOUN
die Cornflakes *pl*

cornstarch NOUN (US)
das Maismehl

Cornwall NOUN
Cornwall *neut*
■ **in Cornwall** in Cornwall

corporal NOUN
der Stabsunteroffizier (PL die Stabsunteroffiziere)

corporal punishment NOUN
die Prügelstrafe

corpse NOUN
die Leiche

correct ADJECTIVE
▷ *see also* **correct** VERB
richtig
□ That's correct. Das ist richtig. □ the correct answer die richtige Antwort

to **correct** VERB
▷ *see also* **correct** ADJECTIVE
korrigieren (PERFECT hat korrigiert)

correction NOUN
die Verbesserung

correctly ADVERB
richtig

correspondent NOUN
der Korrespondent (GEN des Korrespondenten, PL die Korrespondenten)
die Korrespondentin

corridor NOUN
der Korridor (PL die Korridore)

corruption NOUN
die Korruption

Corsica NOUN
Korsika *neut*
■ **from Corsica** aus Korsika
■ **to Corsica** nach Korsika

cosmetics PL NOUN
die Kosmetika *neut pl*

cosmetic surgery NOUN
die Schönheitschirurgie

to **cost** VERB
▷ *see also* **cost** NOUN
kosten
□ The meal cost seventy euros. Das Essen hat siebzig Euro gekostet. □ How much does it cost? Wie viel kostet das? □ It costs too much. Das kostet zu viel.

cost NOUN
▷ *see also* **cost** VERB
die Kosten *pl*
□ the cost of living die Lebenshaltungskosten
■ **at all costs** um jeden Preis

costume NOUN
das Kostüm (PL die Kostüme)

cosy ADJECTIVE
gemütlich

cot NOUN
1 das Kinderbett (PL die Kinderbetten) *(for children)*
2 die Campingliege *(camp bed)*

cottage NOUN
das kleine Haus (GEN des kleinen Hauses, PL die kleinen Häuser)
■ **a thatched cottage** ein Haus mit Strohdach

cottage cheese NOUN
der Hüttenkäse

cotton NOUN
die Baumwolle
□ a cotton shirt ein Baumwollhemd *neut*
■ **cotton candy** die Zuckerwatte
■ **cotton wool** die Watte

couch NOUN
die Couch (PL die Couchs)

couchette NOUN
der Platz im Liegewagen (PL die Plätze im Liegewagen)

to **cough** VERB
▹ see also **cough** NOUN
husten

cough NOUN
▹ see also **cough** VERB
der Husten
□ a bad cough ein schlimmer Husten
□ I've got a cough. Ich habe Husten.

could VERB ▹ see **can**

council NOUN
der Gemeinderat (PL die Gemeinderäte)
□ He's on the council. Er ist im Gemeinderat.
■ **a council estate** eine Siedlung des sozialen Wohnungsbaus
■ **a council house** eine Sozialwohnung

DID YOU KNOW...?
In Germany the council provides flats rather than houses.

councillor NOUN
der Gemeinderat (PL die Gemeinderäte)
die Gemeinderätin
□ She's a local councillor. Sie ist Gemeinderätin.

to **count** VERB
zählen
■ **to count on** zählen auf +*acc* □ You can count on me. Du kannst auf mich zählen.

counter NOUN
1 der Ladentisch (PL die Ladentische) *(in shop)*
2 der Schalter (PL die Schalter) *(in post office, bank)*
3 die Spielmarke *(in game)*

country NOUN
das Land (PL die Länder)
□ the border between the two countries die Grenze zwischen den beiden Ländern
■ **in the country** auf dem Land □ I live in the country. Ich wohne auf dem Land.
■ **country dancing** der Volkstanz

countryside NOUN
die Landschaft

county NOUN
die Grafschaft

DID YOU KNOW...?
The nearest German equivalent of a county would be a **Bundesland**.

■ **the county council** der Grafschaftsrat

DID YOU KNOW...?
The nearest German equivalent of a county council would be the **Landtag**.

couple NOUN
das Paar (PL die Paare)
□ the couple who live next door das Paar von nebenan
■ **a couple** ein paar

LANGUAGE TIP Note that in this sense **paar** is spelt with a small 'p'.

□ a couple of hours ein paar Stunden
□ Could you wait a couple of minutes? Könntest du ein paar Minuten warten?

courage NOUN
der Mut

courgette NOUN
die Zucchini (PL die Zucchini)

courier NOUN
1 der Reiseleiter (PL die Reiseleiter)
die Reiseleiterin *(for tourists)*
2 der Kurier (PL die Kuriere) *(delivery service)*
□ They sent it by courier. Sie haben es mit Kurier geschickt.

course NOUN
1 der Kurs (PL die Kurse)
□ a German course ein Deutschkurs
□ to go on a course einen Kurs machen
2 der Gang (PL die Gänge)
□ the first course der erste Gang
■ **the main course** das Hauptgericht
3 der Platz (PL die Plätze)
□ a golf course ein Golfplatz
■ **of course** natürlich □ Do you love me? — Of course I do! Liebst du mich? — Aber natürlich!

court NOUN
1 das Gericht (PL die Gerichte) *(of law)*
□ He was in court last week. Er war letzte Woche vor Gericht.
2 der Platz (PL die Plätze) *(tennis)*
□ There are tennis and squash courts. Es gibt Tennis- und Squashplätze.

courtyard NOUN
der Hof (PL die Höfe)

cousin NOUN
1 der Vetter (PL die Vettern) *(man)*
2 die Cousine *(woman)*

cover NOUN
▹ see also **cover** VERB
1 der Umschlag (PL die Umschläge) *(of book)*
2 der Bezug (PL die Bezüge) *(of duvet)*

to **cover** VERB
▹ see also **cover** NOUN
1 bedecken (PERFECT hat bedeckt)
□ Cover the dough with a cloth. Bedecke den Teig mit einem Tuch.
■ **My face was covered with mosquito bites.** Mein Gesicht war voller Mückenstiche.
2 decken
□ Our insurance didn't cover it. Unsere Versicherung hat das nicht gedeckt.
■ **to cover up a scandal** einen Skandal vertuschen

cow NOUN
die Kuh (PL die Kühe)

coward NOUN
der Feigling (PL die Feiglinge)

LANGUAGE TIP **der Feigling** is also used for women.

□ She's a coward. Sie ist ein Feigling.

cowardly ADJECTIVE
feige

cowboy NOUN
der Cowboy (PL die Cowboys)

crab NOUN
die Krabbe

crack NOUN
▷ *see also* **crack** VERB
1 der Riss (GEN des Risses, PL die Risse) *(in wall)*
2 der Sprung (PL die Sprünge) *(in cup, window)*
3 das Crack *(drug)*
■ **I'll have a crack at it.** Ich werd's mal versuchen.

to **crack** VERB
▷ *see also* **crack** NOUN
1 knacken *(nut)*
2 aufschlagen (PRESENT schlägt auf, IMPERFECT schlug auf, PERFECT hat aufgeschlagen) *(egg)*
■ **to crack a joke** einen Witz reißen
■ **to crack down on** hart durchgreifen gegen
□ The police are cracking down on graffiti. Die Polizei greift hart gegen Graffiti durch.

cracked ADJECTIVE
kaputt *(cup, window)*

cracker NOUN
1 der Cracker (PL die Cracker) *(biscuit)*
2 das Knallbonbon (PL die Knallbonbons) *(Christmas cracker)*

cradle NOUN
die Wiege

craft NOUN
das Werken
□ We do craft at school. Wir haben Werken in der Schule.
■ **a craft centre** ein Kunstgewerbezentrum *neut*

craftsman NOUN
der Kunsthandwerker (PL die Kunsthandwerker)

to **cram** VERB
1 stopfen
□ We crammed our stuff into the boot. Wir haben unsere Sachen in den Kofferraum gestopft.
2 pauken *(for exams)*

crane NOUN
der Kran *(machine)*

to **crash** VERB
▷ *see also* **crash** NOUN
kaputt fahren (PRESENT fährt kaputt, IMPERFECT fuhr kaputt, PERFECT hat kaputt gefahren)
□ He's crashed his car. Er hat sein Auto kaputt gefahren.
■ **The plane crashed.** Das Flugzeug stürzte ab.
■ **to crash into something** auf etwas fahren
□ My brother crashed into the back of a lorry. Mein Bruder ist hinten auf einen Lastwagen gefahren.

crash NOUN
▷ *see also* **crash** VERB
1 der Unfall (PL die Unfälle) *(of car)*
2 das Unglück (PL die Unglücke) *(of plane)*
■ **a crash helmet** ein Sturzhelm *masc*
■ **a crash course** ein Crashkurs *masc*

to **crawl** VERB
▷ *see also* **crawl** NOUN
krabbeln (PERFECT ist gekrabbelt) *(baby)*

crawl NOUN
▷ *see also* **crawl** VERB
das Kraulen
■ **to do the crawl** kraulen

crazy ADJECTIVE
verrückt

cream ADJECTIVE
▷ *see also* **cream** NOUN
cremefarben *(colour)*

cream NOUN
▷ *see also* **cream** ADJECTIVE
die Sahne
□ strawberries and cream Erdbeeren mit Sahne □ a cream cake eine Sahnetorte
■ **cream cheese** der Frischkäse
■ **sun cream** die Sonnencreme

crease NOUN
die Falte

creased ADJECTIVE
zerknittert

to **create** VERB
schaffen (IMPERFECT schuf, PERFECT hat geschaffen)

creation NOUN
die Schöpfung

creative ADJECTIVE
kreativ

creature NOUN
das Lebewesen (PL die Lebewesen)

crèche NOUN
die Kinderkrippe

credit NOUN
der Kredit (PL die Kredite)
□ on credit auf Kredit

credit card NOUN
die Kreditkarte

creep NOUN
▷ *see also* **creep** VERB
■ **It gives me the creeps.** Es ist mir nicht geheuer.

to **creep** VERB
▷ *see also* **creep** NOUN
kriechen (IMPERFECT kroch, PERFECT ist gekrochen)

cress NOUN
die Kresse

crew NOUN
die Mannschaft

crew cut NOUN
der Bürstenhaarschnitt (PL die Bürstenhaarschnitte)

cricket NOUN
1 das Cricket

> **DID YOU KNOW...?**
> Cricket is practically never played in Germany.

□ I play cricket. Ich spiele Cricket.
■ **a cricket bat** ein Cricketschläger *masc*
2 die Grille *(insect)*

crime NOUN
1 das Verbrechen (PL die Verbrechen)
□ Murder is a crime. Mord ist ein Verbrechen.
2 die Kriminalität *(lawlessness)*
□ Crime is rising. Die Kriminalität nimmt zu.

criminal NOUN
▷ *see also* **criminal** ADJECTIVE
der Verbrecher (PL die Verbrecher)
die Verbrecherin

criminal ADJECTIVE
▷ *see also* **criminal** NOUN
kriminell
□ It's criminal! Das ist kriminell!
■ **It's a criminal offence.** Das ist eine strafbare Handlung.
■ **to have a criminal record** vorbestraft sein

crippled ADJECTIVE
gelähmt
□ He was crippled in an accident. Er ist seit einem Unfall gelähmt.

crisis NOUN
die Krise

crisp ADJECTIVE
knusprig *(food)*

crisps PL NOUN
die Chips *masc pl*
□ a bag of crisps eine Tüte Chips

criterion NOUN
das Kriterium (PL die Kriterien)

critic NOUN
der Kritiker (PL die Kritiker)
die Kritikerin

critical ADJECTIVE
kritisch

criticism NOUN
die Kritik

to **criticize** VERB
kritisieren (PERFECT hat kritisiert)

Croatia NOUN
Kroatien *neut*
■ **from Croatia** aus Kroatien
■ **to Croatia** nach Kroatien

to **crochet** VERB
häkeln

crocodile NOUN
das Krokodil (PL die Krokodile)

crook NOUN
der Verbrecher (PL die Verbrecher) *(criminal)*

crop NOUN
die Ernte
□ a good crop of apples eine gute Apfelernte

cross NOUN
▷ *see also* **cross** ADJECTIVE, VERB
das Kreuz (PL die Kreuze)

cross ADJECTIVE
▷ *see also* **cross** NOUN, VERB
böse
□ to be cross about something wegen etwas böse sein

to **cross** VERB
▷ *see also* **cross** ADJECTIVE, NOUN
überqueren (PERFECT hat überquert) *(street, bridge)*
■ **to cross out** durchstreichen
■ **to cross over** hinübergehen

cross-country NOUN
das Querfeldeinrennen (PL die Querfeldeinrennen) *(race)*
■ **cross-country skiing** der Langlauf

crossing NOUN
1 die Überfahrt *(by boat)*
□ the crossing from Dover to Calais die Überfahrt von Dover nach Calais
2 der Fußgängerüberweg (PL die Fußgängerüberwege) *(for pedestrians)*

crossroads SING NOUN
die Kreuzung

crossword NOUN
das Kreuzworträtsel (PL die Kreuzworträtsel)
□ I like doing crosswords. Ich mache gern Kreuzworträtsel.

to **crouch down** VERB
sich niederkauern (PERFECT hat sich niedergekauert)

crow NOUN
die Krähe

crowd NOUN
▷ *see also* **crowd** VERB
die Menge
■ **the crowd** *(at sports match)* die Zuschauer *masc pl*

to **crowd** VERB
▷ *see also* **crowd** NOUN
sich drängen
□ The children crowded round the model. Die Kinder drängten sich um das Modell.

crowded ADJECTIVE
voll

crown NOUN
die Krone

crucifix NOUN
das Kruzifix (PL die Kruzifixe)

crude ADJECTIVE
ordinär *(vulgar)*

cruel ADJECTIVE
grausam

cruise NOUN
die Kreuzfahrt
□ to go on a cruise eine Kreuzfahrt machen

crumb NOUN
der Krümel (PL die Krümel)

to **crush** VERB
▷ *see also* **crush** NOUN
1 zerquetschen (PERFECT hat zerquetscht)
□ The tomatoes got crushed. Die Tomaten wurden zerquetscht.
2 quetschen *(finger)*
□ I crushed my finger in the car door. Ich habe mir den Finger in der Autotür gequetscht.

crush NOUN
▷ *see also* **crush** VERB
■ **to have a crush on somebody** für jemanden schwärmen

crutch NOUN
die Krücke

cry NOUN
▷ *see also* **cry** VERB
der Schrei
□ a cry of fear ein Angstschrei
■ **to have a good cry** sich ausweinen

to **cry** VERB
▷ *see also* **cry** NOUN
weinen
□ The baby's crying. Das Baby weint.

crystal NOUN
der Kristall (PL die Kristalle)

CTC NOUN *(= city technology college)*
die technische Fachschule

cub NOUN
1 das Junge (GEN des Jungen, PL die Jungen)
□ the lioness and her cub die Löwin und ihr Junges *(animal)*
2 der Wölfling (PL die Wölflinge) *(scout)*

cube NOUN
der Würfel (PL die Würfel)

cubic ADJECTIVE
■ **a cubic metre** ein Kubikmeter *masc*

cucumber NOUN
die Gurke

cuddle NOUN
▷ *see also* **cuddle** VERB
■ **Come and give me a cuddle.** Komm und nimm mich in den Arm.

to **cuddle** VERB
▷ *see also* **cuddle** NOUN
■ **to cuddle somebody** jemanden in den Arm nehmen

cue NOUN
das Queue (PL die Queues) *(for snooker, pool)*

LANGUAGE TIP **Queue** is pronounced as if spelt 'Kö'.

culottes PL NOUN
der Hosenrock (PL die Hosenröcke)
□ a pair of culottes ein Hosenrock

culture NOUN
die Kultur

cunning ADJECTIVE
schlau

cup NOUN
1 die Tasse
□ a china cup eine Porzellantasse □ a cup of coffee eine Tasse Kaffee
2 der Pokal (PL die Pokale) *(trophy)*

cupboard NOUN
der Schrank (PL die Schränke)

to **cure** VERB
▷ *see also* **cure** NOUN
heilen

cure NOUN
▷ *see also* **cure** VERB
das Mittel (PL die Mittel)
□ a cure for a cold ein Mittel gegen Schnupfen

curious ADJECTIVE
neugierig

curl NOUN
▷ *see also* **curl** VERB
die Locke

to **curl** VERB
▷ *see also* **curl** NOUN
in Locken legen *(hair)*

curly ADJECTIVE
lockig
□ When I was young my hair was curlier. Als ich jung war, waren meine Haare lockiger.

currant NOUN
die Korinthe *(dried fruit)*

currency NOUN
die Währung
□ foreign currency ausländische Währung

current NOUN
▷ *see also* **current** ADJECTIVE
die Strömung
□ The current is very strong. Die Strömung ist sehr stark.

current ADJECTIVE
▷ *see also* **current** NOUN
aktuell
□ the current situation die aktuelle Lage

current account NOUN
das Girokonto (PL die Girokonten)

current affairs PL NOUN
die Tagespolitik *sing*

curriculum NOUN
der Lehrplan (PL die Lehrpläne)

curriculum vitae NOUN
der Lebenslauf (PL die Lebensläufe)

curry NOUN
das Curry (PL die Currys)

curse NOUN
der Fluch (PL die Flüche) *(spell)*

curtain NOUN
der Vorhang (PL die Vorhänge)

cushion NOUN
das Kissen (PL die Kissen)

custard NOUN
die Vanillesoße *(for pouring)*

custody NOUN
das Sorgerecht *(of child)*
□ He got custody of his son. Er bekam das Sorgerecht für seinen Sohn.
■ **to be remanded in custody** inhaftiert werden

custom NOUN
der Brauch (PL die Bräuche)
□ It's an old custom. Es ist ein alter Brauch.

customer NOUN
der Kunde (GEN des Kunden, PL die Kunden)
die Kundin

customs PL NOUN
der Zoll (PL die Zölle)

customs officer NOUN
der Zollbeamte (GEN des Zollbeamten, PL die Zollbeamten)
die Zollbeamtin
□ a customs officer *(man)* ein Zollbeamter

cut NOUN
▷ *see also* **cut** VERB
1 die Schnittwunde
□ He's got a cut on his forehead. Er hat eine Schnittwunde an der Stirn.
2 die Senkung *(in price)*
3 die Kürzung *(in spending)*
■ **a cut and blow-dry** Schneiden und Föhnen

to **cut** VERB
▷ *see also* **cut** NOUN
1 schneiden (IMPERFECT schnitt, PERFECT hat geschnitten)
□ I'll cut some bread. Ich schneide Brot.
■ **I cut my foot on a piece of glass.** Ich habe mir den Fuß an einer Glasscherbe verletzt.
■ **to cut oneself** sich schneiden
□ Watch you don't cut yourself! Pass auf, dass du dich nicht schneidest!
2 senken *(price)*
3 kürzen *(spending)*
■ **to cut down** 1 *(tree)* fällen 2 einschränken
□ I'm cutting down on chocolate. Ich bin dabei, meinen Schokoladenkonsum einzuschränken.
■ **The electricity was cut off.** Der Strom wurde abgestellt.
■ **to cut up** *(vegetables, meat)* klein schneiden

cutback NOUN
die Kürzung
□ cutbacks in public services Kürzungen bei den öffentlichen Ausgaben

cute ADJECTIVE
niedlich

cutlery NOUN
das Besteck (PL die Bestecke)

CV NOUN *(= curriculum vitae)*
der Lebenslauf (PL die Lebensläufe)

cybercafé NOUN
das Internet-Café (PL die Internet-Cafés)

to **cycle** VERB
▷ *see also* **cycle** NOUN
Rad fahren (PRESENT fährt Rad, IMPERFECT fuhr Rad, PERFECT ist Rad gefahren)
□ I like cycling. Ich fahre gern Rad.
■ **I cycle to school.** Ich fahre mit dem Rad zur Schule.

cycle NOUN
▷ *see also* **cycle** VERB
das Fahrrad (PL die Fahrräder)
□ a cycle ride eine Fahrradfahrt

cycling NOUN
das Radfahren
□ My hobby is cycling. Radfahren ist mein Hobby.

cyclist NOUN
der Radfahrer (PL die Radfahrer)
die Radfahrerin

cylinder NOUN
der Zylinder (PL die Zylinder)

Cyprus NOUN
Zypern *neut*
■ **from Cyprus** aus Zypern
■ **in Cyprus** auf Zypern
■ **to Cyprus** nach Zypern

Czech ADJECTIVE
▷ *see also* **Czech** NOUN
tschechisch
■ **the Czech Republic** die Tschechische Republik

Czech NOUN
▷ *see also* **Czech** ADJECTIVE
1 der Tscheche (GEN des Tschechen, PL die Tschechen)
die Tschechin *(person)*
2 das Tschechisch (GEN des Tschechischen) *(language)*

Dd

dad NOUN
der Papa (PL die Papas)
□ his dad sein Papa □ I'll ask Dad. Ich werde Papa fragen.

daddy NOUN
der Papa (PL die Papas)
□ my daddy mein Papa

daffodil NOUN
die Osterglocke

daft ADJECTIVE
verrückt

daily ADJECTIVE, ADVERB
täglich
□ It's part of my daily routine. Es gehört zu meiner täglichen Routine. □ The pool is open daily from nine a.m. to six p.m. Das Schwimmbad ist täglich von neun bis achtzehn Uhr geöffnet.

dairy NOUN
die Molkerei *(company)*

dairy products PL NOUN
die Milchprodukte *neut pl*

daisy NOUN
das Gänseblümchen (PL die Gänseblümchen)

dam NOUN
der Damm (PL die Dämme)

damage NOUN
▷ *see also* **damage** VERB
der Schaden (PL die Schäden)
□ The storm did a lot of damage. Der Sturm hat viel Schaden angerichtet.

to **damage** VERB
▷ *see also* **damage** NOUN
beschädigen (PERFECT hat beschädigt)

damn NOUN
▷ *see also* **damn** ADJECTIVE
■ **I don't give a damn!** Das ist mir scheißegal! *(informal)*
■ **Damn!** Verdammt! *(informal)*

damn ADJECTIVE, ADVERB
▷ *see also* **damn** NOUN
■ **It's a damn nuisance!** Es ist verdammt ärgerlich! *(informal)*

damp ADJECTIVE
feucht

dance NOUN
▷ *see also* **dance** VERB
der Tanz (PL die Tänze)
□ The last dance was a waltz. Der letzte Tanz war ein Walzer. □ Are you going to the dance tonight? Gehst du heute Abend zum Tanz?

to **dance** VERB
▷ *see also* **dance** NOUN
tanzen

dancer NOUN
der Tänzer (PL die Tänzer)
die Tänzerin

dancing NOUN
das Tanzen
■ **to go dancing** tanzen gehen □ Let's go dancing! Lass uns tanzen gehen!

dandruff NOUN
die Schuppen *fem pl*

Dane NOUN
der Däne (GEN des Dänen, PL die Dänen)
die Dänin

danger NOUN
die Gefahr
■ **in danger** in Gefahr □ His life is in danger. Sein Leben ist in Gefahr.
■ **I'm in danger of failing maths.** Es könnte durchaus sein, dass ich in Mathe durchfalle.

dangerous ADJECTIVE
gefährlich

Danish ADJECTIVE
▷ *see also* **Danish** NOUN
dänisch

Danish NOUN
▷ *see also* **Danish** ADJECTIVE
das Dänisch (GEN des Dänischen) *(language)*

Danube NOUN
die Donau

to **dare** VERB
sich trauen
■ **to dare to do something** sich trauen, etwas zu tun □ I didn't dare to tell my parents. Ich habe mich nicht getraut, es meinen Eltern zu sagen.
■ **I dare say it'll be okay.** Ich denke, dass das in Ordnung ist.

daring ADJECTIVE
mutig

dark ADJECTIVE
▷ *see also* **dark** NOUN
dunkel
□ It's dark. Es ist dunkel. □ It's getting dark.

Es wird dunkel. □ She's got dark hair. Sie hat dunkle Haare. □ a dark green sweater ein dunkelgrüner Pullover

dark NOUN
▷ *see also* **dark** ADJECTIVE
die Dunkelheit
□ after dark nach Einbruch der Dunkelheit
■ **in the dark** im Dunkeln
■ **I'm afraid of the dark.** Ich habe Angst im Dunkeln.

darkness NOUN
die Dunkelheit
■ **The room was in darkness.** Das Zimmer war dunkel.

darling NOUN
der Liebling (PL die Lieblinge)
LANGUAGE TIP **der Liebling** is also used for women.
□ Thank you, darling! Danke, Liebling!

dart NOUN
der Pfeil (PL die Pfeile)
■ **to play darts** Darts spielen

dash NOUN
▷ *see also* **dash** VERB
der Bindestrich *(punctuation mark)*

to **dash** VERB
▷ *see also* **dash** NOUN
1 rennen (IMPERFECT rannte, PERFECT ist gerannt)
□ Everyone dashed to the window. Alle rannten zum Fenster.
2 sich beeilen (PERFECT hat sich beeilt)
□ I've got to dash! Ich muss mich beeilen!

dashboard NOUN
das Armaturenbrett (PL die Armaturenbretter)

data PL NOUN
die Daten *pl*

database NOUN
die Datenbank (PL die Datenbanken) *(on computer)*

date NOUN
1 das Datum (PL die Daten)
□ my date of birth mein Geburtsdatum
■ **What's the date today?** der Wievielte ist heute?
■ **to have a date with somebody** mit jemandem eine Verabredung haben
□ She's got a date with Ian tonight. Sie hat heute Abend eine Verabredung mit Ian.
■ **out of date 1** *(passport)* abgelaufen **2** *(technology)* veraltet **3** *(clothes)* altmodisch
2 die Dattel *(fruit)*

daughter NOUN
die Tochter (PL die Töchter)

daughter-in-law NOUN
die Schwiegertochter (PL die Schwiegertöchter)

dawn NOUN
das Morgengrauen
□ at dawn im Morgengrauen

day NOUN
der Tag (PL die Tage)
□ We stayed in Vienna for three days. Wir sind drei Tage in Wien geblieben. □ I stayed at home all day. Ich war den ganzen Tag zu Hause.
■ **every day** jeden Tag
■ **during the day** tagsüber
■ **the day before** der Tag davor
■ **the day before my birthday** der Tag vor meinem Geburtstag
■ **the day after** der Tag danach
■ **the day after my birthday** der Tag nach meinem Geburtstag
■ **the day before yesterday** vorgestern
□ He arrived the day before yesterday. Er ist vorgestern angekommen.
■ **the day after tomorrow** übermorgen
□ We're leaving the day after tomorrow. Wir fahren übermorgen ab.

dead ADJECTIVE, ADVERB
1 tot
□ He was already dead. Er war schon tot.
■ **He was shot dead.** Er wurde erschossen.
2 völlig *(totally)*
□ You're dead right! Du hast völlig recht!
■ **dead on time** ganz pünktlich □ The train arrived dead on time. Der Zug kam ganz pünktlich an.

dead end NOUN
die Sackgasse

deadline NOUN
der Termin (PL die Termine)
□ We'll never meet the deadline. Den Termin schaffen wir nie.

dead spot NOUN *(mobile)*
das Funkloch (PL die Funklöcher)

deaf ADJECTIVE
taub

deafening ADJECTIVE
ohrenbetäubend

deal NOUN
▷ *see also* **deal** VERB
das Geschäft (PL die Geschäfte)
■ **It's a deal!** Abgemacht!
■ **a great deal** viel □ a great deal of money viel Geld

to **deal** VERB
▷ *see also* **deal** NOUN
geben (PRESENT gibt, IMPERFECT gab, PERFECT hat gegeben) *(cards)*
□ It's your turn to deal. Du gibst!
■ **to deal with something** sich um etwas kümmern □ He promised to deal with it immediately. Er versprach, sich sofort darum zu kümmern.

dealer NOUN
der Händler (PL die Händler)
die Händlerin
□ a drug dealer ein Drogenhändler
□ an antique dealer ein Antiquitätenhändler

dear ADJECTIVE
1 lieb

■ **Dear Mrs Sinclair** 1 Liebe Frau Sinclair 2 *(more formal)* Sehr geehrte Frau Sinclair
■ **Dear Sir/Madam** *(in a circular)* Sehr geehrte Damen und Herren
2 teuer *(expensive)*

death NOUN
der Tod (PL die Tode)
□ after her death nach ihrem Tod
□ I was bored to death. Ich habe mich zu Tode gelangweilt.

debate NOUN
▹ *see also* **debate** VERB
die Debatte

to **debate** VERB
▹ *see also* **debate** NOUN
debattieren (PERFECT hat debattiert)
□ We debated the issue. Wir haben die Frage debattiert.

debt NOUN
die Schulden *fem pl*
□ He's got a lot of debts. Er hat viel Schulden.
■ **to be in debt** verschuldet sein

decade NOUN
das Jahrzehnt (PL die Jahrzehnte)

decaffeinated ADJECTIVE
entkoffeiniert

decay NOUN
■ **tooth decay** die Karies

to **deceive** VERB
täuschen

December NOUN
der Dezember
□ in December im Dezember

decent ADJECTIVE
ordentlich
□ a decent education eine ordentliche Ausbildung

to **decide** VERB
1 beschließen (IMPERFECT beschloss, PERFECT hat beschlossen)
□ I decided to write to her. Ich habe beschlossen, ihr zu schreiben. □ I decided not to go. Ich habe beschlossen, nicht hinzugehen.
2 sich entscheiden (IMPERFECT entschied sich, PERFECT hat sich entschieden)
□ I can't decide. Ich kann mich nicht entscheiden. □ Haven't you decided yet? Hast du dich noch nicht entschieden?
■ **to decide on something** über etwas entscheiden □ We haven't decided on the name yet. Wir haben noch nicht über den Namen entschieden.

decimal ADJECTIVE
dezimal
□ the decimal system das Dezimalsystem

decision NOUN
die Entscheidung
□ to make a decision eine Entscheidung treffen

decisive ADJECTIVE
entschlossen *(person)*

deck NOUN
1 das Deck (PL die Decks) *(of ship)*
□ on deck an Deck
2 das Spiel (PL die Spiele) *(of cards)*

deckchair NOUN
der Liegestuhl (PL die Liegestühle)

to **declare** VERB
erklären (PERFECT hat erklärt)

to **decline** VERB
1 ablehnen (PERFECT hat abgelehnt)
□ He declined to comment. Er lehnte einen Kommentar ab.
2 zurückgehen (IMPERFECT ging zurück, PERFECT ist zurückgegangen)
□ The birth rate is declining. Die Geburtenrate geht zurück.

to **decorate** VERB
1 dekorieren (PERFECT hat dekoriert)
□ I decorated the cake with glacé cherries. Ich habe den Kuchen mit glasierten Kirschen dekoriert.
2 streichen (IMPERFECT strich, PERFECT hat gestrichen) *(paint)*
3 tapezieren (PERFECT hat tapeziert) *(wallpaper)*

decorations PL NOUN
der Schmuck
□ Christmas decorations der Weihnachtsschmuck

decrease NOUN
▹ *see also* **decrease** VERB
die Abnahme
□ a decrease in the number of unemployed people eine Abnahme der Arbeitslosenzahl

to **decrease** VERB
▹ *see also* **decrease** NOUN
abnehmen (PRESENT nimmt ab, IMPERFECT nahm ab, PERFECT hat abgenommen)

dedicated ADJECTIVE
engagiert
□ a very dedicated teacher ein sehr engagierter Lehrer

to **deduct** VERB
abziehen (IMPERFECT zog ab, PERFECT hat abgezogen)

deep ADJECTIVE
tief *(water, hole, cut)*
□ How deep is the lake? Wie tief ist der See?
□ a hole four metres deep ein vier Meter tiefes Loch □ He's got a deep voice. Er hat eine tiefe Stimme.
■ **to take a deep breath** tief einatmen
■ **The snow was really deep.** Es lag sehr viel Schnee.

deeply ADVERB
zutiefst *(depressed)*

deer NOUN
das Reh (PL die Rehe)

defeat NOUN
▷ *see also* **defeat** VERB
die Niederlage

to **defeat** VERB
▷ *see also* **defeat** NOUN
besiegen (PERFECT hat besiegt)

defect NOUN
der Defekt (PL die Defekte)

defence NOUN
die Verteidigung

to **defend** VERB
verteidigen (PERFECT hat verteidigt)

defender NOUN
der Verteidiger (PL die Verteidiger)
die Verteidigerin

defense NOUN (US)
die Verteidigung

to **define** VERB
definieren (PERFECT hat definiert)

definite ADJECTIVE
1 genau
□ I haven't got any definite plans. Ich habe noch keine genauen Pläne.
2 eindeutig
□ It's a definite improvement. Es ist eine eindeutige Verbesserung.
3 sicher
□ Perhaps we'll go to Spain, but it's not definite. Vielleicht fahren wir nach Spanien, aber es ist noch nicht sicher.
■ **He was definite about it.** Er war sich sehr sicher.

definitely ADVERB
eindeutig
□ He's definitely the best. Er ist eindeutig der Beste.
■ **He's the best player. — Definitely!** Er ist der beste Spieler. — Absolut!
■ **I definitely think he'll come.** Ich bin sicher, dass er kommt.

definition NOUN
die Definition

degree NOUN
1 der Grad (PL die Grade)
□ a temperature of thirty degrees eine Temperatur von dreißig Grad
2 der Universitätsabschluss (GEN des Universitätsabschlusses, PL die Universitätsabschlüsse)
□ a degree in English ein Universitätsabschluss in Englisch

to **delay** VERB
▷ *see also* **delay** NOUN
verschieben (IMPERFECT verschob, PERFECT hat verschoben)
□ We delayed our departure. Wir haben unsere Abreise verschoben.
■ **to be delayed** Verspätung haben
□ Our flight was delayed. Unser Flug hatte Verspätung.

delay NOUN
▷ *see also* **delay** VERB
die Verzögerung
■ **without delay** unverzüglich

to **delete** VERB
löschen *(on computer, tape)*

deliberate ADJECTIVE
absichtlich

deliberately ADVERB
absichtlich
□ She did it deliberately. Sie hat es absichtlich getan.

delicate ADJECTIVE
1 zierlich
□ She has very delicate hands. Sie hat sehr zierliche Hände.
2 zerbrechlich *(object)*
□ That vase is very delicate. Die Vase ist sehr zerbrechlich.
3 anfällig *(often ill)*
□ a delicate child ein anfälliges Kind
4 heikel *(situation)*
□ The situation is rather delicate. Die Lage ist ziemlich heikel.

delicatessen SING NOUN
das Feinkostgeschäft (PL die Feinkostgeschäfte)

delicious ADJECTIVE
köstlich

delight NOUN
die Freude

delighted ADJECTIVE
hocherfreut
□ He'll be delighted. Er wird hocherfreut sein.

delightful ADJECTIVE
wunderbar *(meal, evening)*

to **deliver** VERB
1 austragen (PRESENT trägt aus, IMPERFECT trug aus, PERFECT hat ausgetragen)
□ I deliver newspapers. Ich trage Zeitungen aus.
2 ausliefern (PERFECT hat ausgeliefert) *(mail)*

delivery NOUN
die Lieferung

to **demand** VERB
▷ *see also* **demand** NOUN
fordern

demand NOUN
▷ *see also* **demand** VERB
die Nachfrage *(for product)*

demanding ADJECTIVE
anspruchsvoll
□ a demanding job eine anspruchsvolle Arbeit

demo NOUN
die Demo (PL die Demos) *(protest)*

democracy NOUN
die Demokratie

democratic ADJECTIVE
demokratisch

to **demolish** VERB
abreißen (IMPERFECT riss ab, PERFECT hat abgerissen) *(building)*

to **demonstrate** VERB
1 vorführen (PERFECT hat vorgeführt) *(show)*
□ She demonstrated the technique. Sie hat die Methode vorgeführt.
2 demonstrieren (PERFECT hat demonstriert) *(protest)*
□ to demonstrate against something gegen etwas demonstrieren

demonstration NOUN
1 die Vorführung *(of method, technique)*
2 die Demonstration *(protest)*

demonstrator NOUN
der Demonstrant (GEN des Demonstranten, PL die Demonstranten)
die Demonstrantin *(protester)*

denim NOUN
der Jeansstoff
■ **a denim jacket** eine Jeansjacke

denims PL NOUN
die Jeans *fem pl (jeans)*
□ a pair of denims eine Jeans

Denmark NOUN
Dänemark *neut*
■ **from Denmark** aus Dänemark
■ **to Denmark** nach Dänemark

dense ADJECTIVE
1 dicht *(crowd, fog)*
2 dick *(smoke)*
■ **He's so dense!** Er ist furchtbar blöd! *(informal)*

dent NOUN
▷ *see also* **dent** VERB
die Delle

to **dent** VERB
▷ *see also* **dent** NOUN
eindellen (PERFECT hat eingedellt)

dental ADJECTIVE
■ **dental treatment** die Zahnbehandlung
■ **dental floss** die Zahnseide
■ **dental surgeon** der Zahnarzt

dentist NOUN
der Zahnarzt (PL die Zahnärzte)
die Zahnärztin
□ Catherine is a dentist. Catherine ist Zahnärztin.

to **deny** VERB
leugnen
□ She denied everything. Sie hat alles geleugnet.

deodorant NOUN
das Deo (PL die Deos)

to **depart** VERB
1 abreisen (PERFECT ist abgereist) *(person)*
2 abfahren (PRESENT fährt ab, IMPERFECT fuhr ab, PERFECT ist abgefahren) *(train)*

department NOUN
1 die Abteilung *(in shop)*
□ the shoe department die Schuhabteilung
2 der Fachbereich (PL die Fachbereiche) *(university, school)*
□ the English department der Fachbereich Englisch

department store NOUN
das Kaufhaus (GEN des Kaufhauses, PL die Kaufhäuser)

departure NOUN
die Abfahrt

departure lounge NOUN
die Abflughalle

to **depend** VERB
■ **to depend on** abhängen von □ The price depends on the quality. Der Preis hängt von der Qualität ab.
■ **depending on the weather** je nach Wetterlage
■ **It depends.** Das kommt drauf an.

to **deport** VERB
abschieben (IMPERFECT schob ab, PERFECT hat abgeschoben)

deposit NOUN
1 die Anzahlung *(part payment)*
□ You have to pay a deposit when you book. Sie müssen eine Anzahlung leisten, wenn Sie buchen.
2 die Kaution *(when hiring something)*
□ You get the deposit back when you return the bike. Sie bekommen die Kaution zurück, wenn Sie das Fahrrad zurückbringen.
3 das Pfand (PL die Pfänder) *(on bottle)*

depressed ADJECTIVE
deprimiert
□ I'm feeling depressed. Ich bin deprimiert.

depressing ADJECTIVE
deprimierend

depth NOUN
die Tiefe

deputy head NOUN
der Konrektor (PL die Konrektoren)
die Konrektorin

to **descend** VERB
hinuntersteigen (IMPERFECT stieg hinunter, PERFECT ist hinuntergestiegen)

to **describe** VERB
beschreiben (IMPERFECT beschrieb, PERFECT hat beschrieben)

description NOUN
die Beschreibung

desert NOUN
die Wüste

desert island NOUN
die einsame Insel

to **deserve** VERB
verdienen (PERFECT hat verdient)
□ He deserves a holiday. Er hat einen Urlaub verdient.
■ **She deserves to be punished.** Sie gehört bestraft.

design NOUN
▷ *see also* **design** VERB

1 das Design (PL die Designs)
□ fashion design das Modedesign
■ **It's a completely new design.** Es ist eine völlig neue Konstruktion.
2 das Muster (PL die Muster) *(pattern)*
□ a geometric design ein geometrisches Muster

to **design** VERB
▷ *see also* **design** NOUN
entwerfen (PRESENT entwirft, IMPERFECT entwarf, PERFECT hat entworfen) *(clothes, furniture)*

designer NOUN
der Modeschöpfer (PL die Modeschöpfer)
die Modeschöpferin *(of clothes)*
■ **designer clothes** die Designerkleidung *sing*

desire NOUN
▷ *see also* **desire** VERB
das Verlangen (PL die Verlangen)

to **desire** VERB
▷ *see also* **desire** NOUN
wünschen
□ if desired falls gewünscht

desk NOUN
1 der Schreibtisch (PL die Schreibtische) *(in office)*
2 die Bank (PL die Bänke) *(in school)*
3 die Rezeption *(in hotel)*
4 der Schalter (PL die Schalter) *(at airport)*

despair NOUN
die Verzweiflung
■ **I was in despair.** Ich war verzweifelt.

desperate ADJECTIVE
verzweifelt
□ a desperate situation eine verzweifelte Lage
■ **to get desperate** fast verzweifeln □ I was getting desperate. Ich bin fast verzweifelt.
■ **I'm desperate for a drink.** Ich brauche dringend etwas zu trinken.

desperately ADVERB
1 äußerst
□ We're desperately worried. Wir sind äußerst besorgt.
2 verzweifelt
□ He was desperately trying to persuade her. Er versuchte verzweifelt, sie zu überzeugen.

to **despise** VERB
verachten (PERFECT hat verachtet)

despite PREPOSITION
trotz
□ despite the bad weather trotz des schlechten Wetters

dessert NOUN
der Nachtisch
□ for dessert zum Nachtisch

destination NOUN
das Ziel (PL die Ziele)

to **destroy** VERB
zerstören (PERFECT hat zerstört)

destruction NOUN
die Zerstörung

detached house NOUN
das Einzelhaus (GEN des Einzelhauses, PL die Einzelhäuser)

detail NOUN
das Detail (PL die Details)
■ **in detail** ganz genau

detailed ADJECTIVE
ausführlich

detective NOUN
der Detektiv (PL die Detektive)
die Detektivin
■ **a private detective** ein Privatdetektiv
■ **a detective story** eine Detektivgeschichte

detention NOUN
■ **to get a detention** nachsitzen müssen
□ He got a detention. Er musste nachsitzen.

detergent NOUN
das Waschmittel (PL die Waschmittel)

determined ADJECTIVE
entschlossen
■ **to be determined to do something** entschlossen sein, etwas zu tun
□ She's determined to marry him. Sie ist entschlossen, ihn zu heiraten.

detour NOUN
der Umweg (PL die Umwege)

devaluation NOUN
die Abwertung

devastated ADJECTIVE
am Boden zerstört
□ I was devastated. Ich war am Boden zerstört.

devastating ADJECTIVE
1 erschütternd *(upsetting)*
2 verheerend *(flood, storm)*

to **develop** VERB
1 entwickeln (PERFECT hat entwickelt)
□ to get a film developed einen Film entwickeln lassen
2 sich entwickeln (PERFECT hat sich entwickelt)
□ Girls develop faster. Mädchen entwickeln sich schneller. □ The argument developed into a fight. Der Streit entwickelte sich zu einer Schlägerei.
■ **a developing country** ein Entwicklungsland *neut*

development NOUN
die Entwicklung
□ the latest developments die neuesten Entwicklungen

device NOUN
das Gerät

devil NOUN
der Teufel (PL die Teufel)
□ Poor devil! Armer Teufel!

to **devise** VERB
sich ausdenken (IMPERFECT dachte sich aus, PERFECT hat sich ausgedacht)

□ We have devised a way to help him. Wir haben uns etwas ausgedacht, um ihm zu helfen.

devoted ADJECTIVE
■ **He's completely devoted to her.** Er liebt sie über alles.

diabetes NOUN
der Zucker
□ She's got diabetes. Sie hat Zucker.

diabetic NOUN
der Zuckerkranke (GEN des Zuckerkranken, PL die Zuckerkranken)
die Zuckerkranke (GEN der Zuckerkranken)
■ **I'm a diabetic.** Ich habe Zucker.

diagonal ADJECTIVE
diagonal

diagram NOUN
das Diagramm (PL die Diagramme)

to **dial** VERB
wählen *(number)*
■ **He dialled the wrong number.** Er hat sich verwählt.

dialling tone NOUN
das Amtszeichen (PL die Amtszeichen)

dialogue NOUN
der Dialog (PL die Dialoge)

diamond NOUN
der Diamant (GEN des Diamanten, PL die Diamanten)
□ a diamond ring ein Diamantring *masc*
■ **diamonds** *(in cards)* das Karo □ the ace of diamonds das Karoass

diaper NOUN (US)
die Windel

diarrhoea NOUN
der Durchfall (PL die Durchfälle)
□ I've got diarrhoea. Ich habe Durchfall.

diary NOUN
1 der Kalender (PL die Kalender)
□ I've got her address in my diary. Ich habe ihre Adresse in meinem Kalender.
2 das Tagebuch (PL die Tagebücher)
□ I keep a diary. Ich führe ein Tagebuch.

dice NOUN
der Würfel (PL die Würfel)

dictation NOUN
das Diktat (PL die Diktate)

dictator NOUN
der Diktator (PL die Diktatoren)

dictionary NOUN
das Wörterbuch (PL die Wörterbücher)

did VERB ▷ *see* **do**

to **die** VERB
sterben (PRESENT stirbt, IMPERFECT starb, PERFECT ist gestorben)
□ She's dying. Sie stirbt. □ He died last year. Er ist letztes Jahr gestorben.
■ **to be dying to do something** es kaum erwarten können, etwas zu tun □ I'm dying to see you. Ich kann es kaum erwarten, dich zu sehen.

to **die down** VERB
nachlassen (PRESENT lässt nach, IMPERFECT ließ nach, PERFECT hat nachgelassen)
□ The wind is dying down. Der Wind lässt nach.

diesel NOUN
1 der Diesel *(fuel)*
□ Thirty litres of diesel, please. Dreißig Liter Diesel, bitte.
2 der Diesel (PL die Diesel) *(car)*
□ Our car's a diesel. Unser Auto ist ein Diesel.

diet NOUN
▷ *see also* **diet** VERB
1 die Nahrung
□ a healthy diet gesunde Nahrung
2 die Diät *(for slimming)*
■ **I'm on a diet.** Ich mache eine Diät.

to **diet** VERB
▷ *see also* **diet** NOUN
eine Diät machen
□ I've been dieting for two months. Ich mache seit zwei Monaten eine Diät.

difference NOUN
der Unterschied (PL die Unterschiede)
□ There's not much difference in age between us. Es besteht kein großer Altersunterschied zwischen uns.
■ **It makes no difference.** Das ist egal.

different ADJECTIVE
verschieden
□ We are very different. Wir sind sehr verschieden.
■ **Berlin is different from London.** Berlin ist anders als London.

difficult ADJECTIVE
schwierig
□ It's difficult to choose. Es ist schwierig, sich zu entscheiden.

difficulty NOUN
die Schwierigkeit
□ to have difficulty doing something Schwierigkeiten haben, etwas zu tun
■ **without difficulty** problemlos

to **dig** VERB
1 graben (PRESENT gräbt, IMPERFECT grub, PERFECT hat gegraben) *(hole)*
2 umgraben (PERFECT hat umgegraben) *(garden)*
■ **to dig something up** etwas ausgraben

digestion NOUN
die Verdauung

digger NOUN
der Bagger (PL die Bagger)

digital ADJECTIVE
digital
□ the digital revolution die digitale Revolution
■ **a digital camera** eine Digitalkamera
■ **a digital radio** ein DAB-Radio *neut*
■ **a digital watch** eine Digitaluhr
■ **digital TV** das Digitalfernsehen

dim ADJECTIVE
1 schwach *(light)*
2 beschränkt *(stupid)*

dimension NOUN
das Maß (GEN des Maßes, PL die Maße) *(measurement)*

to **diminish** VERB
abnehmen (PRESENT nimmt ab, IMPERFECT nahm ab, PERFECT hat abgenommen)

din NOUN
der Krach (PL die Kräche)

diner NOUN (US)
die Gaststätte

dinghy NOUN
■ **a rubber dinghy** ein Gummiboot *neut*
■ **a sailing dinghy** ein Segelboot *neut*

dining car NOUN
der Speisewagen (PL die Speisewagen)

dining room NOUN
das Esszimmer (PL die Esszimmer)

dinner NOUN
1 das Mittagessen (PL die Mittagessen) *(at midday)*
2 das Abendessen (PL die Abendessen) *(in the evening)*

dinner jacket NOUN
die Smokingjacke

dinner party NOUN
die Abendgesellschaft
■ **We're having a dinner party on Saturday.** Wir haben am Samstag Leute zum Essen eingeladen.

dinner time NOUN
die Essenszeit

dinosaur NOUN
der Dinosaurier (PL die Dinosaurier)

dip NOUN
▷ *see also* **dip** VERB
der Dip (PL die Dips)
□ a spicy dip ein pikanter Dip
■ **to go for a dip** kurz mal ins Wasser gehen

to **dip** VERB
▷ *see also* **dip** NOUN
1 tauchen
□ She dipped her hand in the water. Sie tauchte ihre Hand ins Wasser.
2 tunken
□ He dipped a biscuit into his tea. Er tunkte einen Keks in seinen Tee.

diploma NOUN
das Diplom (PL die Diplome)
■ **She has a diploma in social work.** Sie hat Sozialarbeiterin gelernt.

diplomat NOUN
der Diplomat (GEN des Diplomaten, PL die Diplomaten)
die Diplomatin

diplomatic ADJECTIVE
diplomatisch

direct ADJECTIVE, ADVERB
▷ *see also* **direct** VERB
direkt
□ the most direct route der direkteste Weg
□ You can't fly to Stuttgart direct from Glasgow. Sie können von Glasgow nicht direkt nach Stuttgart fliegen.

to **direct** VERB
▷ *see also* **direct** ADJECTIVE
Regie führen bei *(film, play)*
□ Who directed the film? Wer hat bei dem Film Regie geführt?

direction NOUN
die Richtung
□ We're going in the wrong direction. Wir fahren in die falsche Richtung.
■ **to ask somebody for directions** jemanden nach dem Weg fragen

director NOUN
1 der Direktor (PL die Direktoren)
die Direktorin *(of company)*
2 der Regisseur (PL die Regisseure)
die Regisseurin *(of play, film)*
3 der Leiter (PL die Leiter)
die Leiterin *(of programme)*

directory NOUN
1 das Verzeichnis (GEN des Verzeichnisses, PL die Verzeichnisse)
□ file directory das Dateiverzeichnis
2 das Telefonbuch (PL die Telefonbücher) *(telephone book)*

dirt NOUN
der Schmutz

dirty ADJECTIVE
schmutzig
□ to get dirty sich schmutzig machen
□ to get something dirty etwas schmutzig machen □ a dirty joke ein schmutziger Witz

disabled ADJECTIVE
behindert
■ **the disabled** die Behinderten *masc pl*

disadvantage NOUN
der Nachteil (PL die Nachteile)

to **disagree** VERB
■ **We always disagree.** Wir sind nie einer Meinung.
■ **I disagree!** Ich bin anderer Meinung.
■ **He disagreed with me.** Er war anderer Meinung als ich.

disagreement NOUN
die Meinungsverschiedenheit

to **disappear** VERB
verschwinden (IMPERFECT verschwand, PERFECT ist verschwunden)

disappearance NOUN
das Verschwinden

disappointed ADJECTIVE
enttäuscht

disappointing ADJECTIVE
enttäuschend

disappointment NOUN
die Enttäuschung

disaster NOUN
die Katastrophe
disastrous ADJECTIVE
katastrophal
disc NOUN
die Platte
discipline NOUN
die Disziplin
disc jockey NOUN
der Diskjockey (PL die Diskjockeys)
disco NOUN
die Disco (PL die Discos)
□ There's a disco at the school tonight. Heute Abend gibt es in der Schule eine Disco.
to **disconnect** VERB
1 ausstecken (PERFECT hat ausgesteckt) *(electrical equipment)*
2 abstellen (PERFECT hat abgestellt) *(telephone, water supply)*
discount NOUN
der Rabatt (PL die Rabatte)
□ a discount of twenty per cent zwanzig Prozent Rabatt
■ **a discount for students** eine Studentenermäßigung
to **discourage** VERB
entmutigen (PERFECT hat entmutigt)
■ **to get discouraged** sich entmutigen lassen □ Don't get discouraged! Lass dich nicht entmutigen!
to **discover** VERB
entdecken (PERFECT hat entdeckt)
discovery NOUN
die Entdeckung
discrimination NOUN
die Diskriminierung
□ racial discrimination die Rassendiskriminierung
to **discuss** VERB
1 besprechen (PRESENT bespricht, IMPERFECT besprach, PERFECT hat besprochen)
□ I'll discuss it with my parents. Ich werde es mit meinen Eltern besprechen.
2 diskutieren über *+acc* (PERFECT hat diskutiert) *(topic)*
□ We discussed the problem. Wir haben über das Problem diskutiert.
discussion NOUN
die Diskussion
disease NOUN
die Krankheit
disgraceful ADJECTIVE
schändlich
to **disguise** VERB
verkleiden (PERFECT hat verkleidet)
□ He was disguised as a policeman. Er war als Polizist verkleidet.
disgusted ADJECTIVE
angewidert
□ I was absolutely disgusted. Ich war total angewidert.
disgusting ADJECTIVE
1 widerlich *(food, smell)*
□ It looks disgusting. Es sieht widerlich aus.
2 abscheulich *(disgraceful)*
□ That's disgusting! Das ist abscheulich!
dish NOUN
1 die Schüssel
□ a china dish eine Porzellanschüssel
■ **the dishes** das Geschirr *sing*
■ **to do the dishes** abwaschen □ He never does the dishes. Er wäscht nie ab.
2 das Gericht (PL die Gerichte) *(food)*
□ a vegetarian dish ein vegetarisches Gericht
dishonest ADJECTIVE
unehrlich
dish soap NOUN (US)
das Spülmittel (PL die Spülmittel)
dish towel NOUN (US)
das Geschirrtuch (PL die Geschirrtücher)
dishwasher NOUN
die Geschirrspülmaschine
disinfectant NOUN
das Desinfektionsmittel (PL die Desinfektionsmittel)
disk NOUN
die Platte
■ **the hard disk** die Festplatte
■ **a floppy disk** eine Diskette
diskette NOUN
die Diskette
to **dislike** VERB
▷ *see also* **dislike** NOUN
nicht mögen (PRESENT mag nicht, IMPERFECT mochte nicht, PERFECT hat nicht gemocht)
□ I've always disliked cabbage. Kohl habe ich noch nie gemocht.
dislike NOUN
▷ *see also* **dislike** VERB
■ **my likes and dislikes** was ich mag und nicht mag
dismal ADJECTIVE
kläglich
□ a dismal failure ein kläglicher Fehlschlag
to **dismiss** VERB
entlassen (PRESENT entlässt, IMPERFECT entließ, PERFECT hat entlassen) *(employee)*
disobedient ADJECTIVE
ungehorsam
display NOUN
▷ *see also* **display** VERB
die Auslage *(of goods)*
■ **to be on display** ausgestellt sein
□ Her best paintings were on display. Ihre besten Bilder waren ausgestellt.
■ **a firework display** ein Feuerwerk *neut*
to **display** VERB
▷ *see also* **display** NOUN
1 zeigen

English-German

d

□ She proudly displayed her medal. Sie zeigte stolz ihre Medaille.

2 ausstellen (PERFECT hat ausgestellt) *(in shop window)*

□ The fruit displayed in the shop window ... Das Obst, das im Schaufenster ausgestellt war ...

disposable ADJECTIVE

zum Wegwerfen

■ **disposable nappies** die Wegwerfwindeln *fem pl*

to **disqualify** VERB

disqualifizieren (PERFECT hat disqualifiziert)

■ **to be disqualified** disqualifiziert werden

□ He was disqualified. Er wurde disqualifiziert.

to **disrupt** VERB

1 stören

□ Protesters disrupted the meeting. Protestierende haben die Versammlung gestört.

2 unterbrechen (PRESENT unterbricht, IMPERFECT unterbrach, PERFECT hat unterbrochen) *(service)*

□ Train services were disrupted. Der Zugverkehr wurde unterbrochen.

dissatisfied ADJECTIVE

unzufrieden

□ We were dissatisfied with the service. Wir waren mit dem Service unzufrieden.

to **dissolve** VERB

1 auflösen (PERFECT hat aufgelöst)

□ Dissolve the crystals in water. Löse die Kristalle in Wasser auf.

2 sich auflösen

□ Sugar dissolves quickly in hot tea. Zucker löst sich in heißem Tee schnell auf.

distance NOUN

die Entfernung

□ a distance of forty kilometres eine Entfernung von vierzig Kilometern

■ **It's within walking distance.** Man kann zu Fuß hingehen.

■ **in the distance** in der Ferne

distant ADJECTIVE

weit

□ in the distant future in weiter Zukunft

distillery NOUN

die Brennerei

□ a whisky distillery eine Whiskybrennerei

distinction NOUN

1 die Unterscheidung

□ to make a distinction between ... unterscheiden zwischen ...

2 die Auszeichnung

□ I got a distinction in my piano exam. Ich habe meine Klavierprüfung mit Auszeichnung bestanden.

distinctive ADJECTIVE

auffällig

to **distract** VERB

ablenken (PERFECT hat abgelenkt)

to **distribute** VERB

verteilen (PERFECT hat verteilt)

district NOUN

1 das Viertel (PL die Viertel) *(of town)*

2 die Gegend *(of country)*

to **disturb** VERB

stören

■ **I'm sorry to disturb you.** Verzeihen Sie die Störung.

ditch NOUN

▷ *see also* **ditch** VERB

der Graben (PL die Gräben)

to **ditch** VERB

▷ *see also* **ditch** NOUN

Schluss machen mit *(informal)*

□ She's just ditched her boyfriend. Sie hat gerade mit ihrem Freund Schluss gemacht.

dive NOUN

▷ *see also* **dive** VERB

der Kopfsprung (PL die Kopfsprünge)

to **dive** VERB

▷ *see also* **dive** NOUN

1 tauchen *(under water)*

□ They are diving for pearls. Sie tauchen nach Perlen.

2 einen Kopfsprung machen *(into water)*

□ She dived into the water. Sie machte einen Kopfsprung ins Wasser.

diver NOUN

der Taucher (PL die Taucher)

die Taucherin *(with breathing apparatus)*

diversion NOUN

die Umleitung *(for traffic)*

to **divide** VERB

1 teilen

□ Divide the pastry in half. Teilen Sie den Teig in zwei Teile. □ Twelve divided by three is four. Zwölf geteilt durch drei macht vier.

2 sich aufteilen (PERFECT hat sich aufgeteilt)

□ We divided into two groups. Wir haben uns in zwei Gruppen aufgeteilt.

diving NOUN

1 das Tauchen *(under water)*

2 das Springen *(into water)*

■ **diving board** das Sprungbrett

division NOUN

1 die Division

□ division and multiplication Division und Multiplikation

■ **the division of labour** die Arbeitsteilung

2 die Liga (PL die Ligen) *(in football)*

divorce NOUN

die Scheidung

divorced ADJECTIVE

geschieden

□ My parents are divorced. Meine Eltern sind geschieden.

Diwali NOUN

das Diwali *neut*

DIY NOUN *(= do-it-yourself)*

das Heimwerken
■ **to do DIY** Heimwerker sein
■ **a DIY shop** ein Geschäft für Heimwerker
■ **DIY superstore** der Baumarkt

dizzy ADJECTIVE
■ **I feel dizzy.** Mir ist schwindlig.

DJ NOUN *(= disc jockey)*
der Diskjockey (PL die Diskjockeys)

to **do** VERB
1 machen
□ What are you doing this evening? Was macht ihr heute Abend? □ I haven't done my homework. Ich habe meine Hausaufgaben noch nicht gemacht. □ She did it by herself. Sie hat es allein gemacht.
2 tun (IMPERFECT tat, PERFECT hat getan)
□ What shall I do? Was soll ich tun?
□ I'll do my best. Ich werde mein Bestes tun.
□ I'll tell you what to do. Ich sage dir, was du tun sollst.
LANGUAGE TIP In combination with certain nouns and verbs 'do' is not translated.
□ I do a lot of cycling. Ich fahre viel Rad.
□ She was doing her knitting. Sie strickte.
□ to do the ironing bügeln
■ **to do well** erfolgreich sein □ The firm is doing well. Die Firma ist sehr erfolgreich.
■ **She's doing well at school.** Sie ist gut in der Schule.
3 reichen *(be enough)*
□ It's not very good, but it'll do. Es ist nicht besonders gut, aber es wird reichen. □ That'll do, thanks. Danke, das reicht.
LANGUAGE TIP In English 'do' is used to make questions. In German, questions are expressed by reversing the order of verb and subject.
□ Do you like German food? Magst du deutsches Essen? □ Where does he live? Wo wohnt er? □ Do you speak English? Sprechen Sie Englisch? □ What do you do in your spare time? Was machen Sie in Ihrer Freizeit?
□ Where did you go for your holidays? Wohin seid ihr in den Ferien gefahren?
LANGUAGE TIP Use **nicht** in negative sentences for 'don't'.
□ I don't understand. Ich verstehe nicht.
□ Why didn't you come? Warum bist du nicht gekommen?
LANGUAGE TIP 'do' is not translated when it is used in place of another verb.
□ I hate maths. — So do I. Ich hasse Mathe. — Ich auch. □ I didn't like the film. — Neither did I. Ich mochte den Film nicht. — Ich auch nicht. □ Do you like horses? — No, I don't. Magst du Pferde? — Nein.
LANGUAGE TIP Questions like 'doesn't it?' don't exist in German.
□ The bus stops at the youth hostel, doesn't it? Der Bus hält an der Jugendherberge, nicht wahr? □ You go swimming on Fridays, don't you? Du gehst freitags schwimmen, nicht wahr?
■ **How do you do?** Guten Tag!
■ **to do up 1** *(shoes, shirt, cardigan)* zumachen □ Do up your shoes! Mach deine Schuhe zu! **2** *(renovate)* renovieren
□ They're doing up an old cottage. Sie renovieren ein altes Haus.
■ **I could do with a holiday.** Ich könnte einen Urlaub gebrauchen.
■ **to do without** ohne etwas auskommen
□ I couldn't do without my computer. Ich käme nicht ohne meinen Computer aus.

dock NOUN
das Dock (PL die Docks) *(for ships)*

doctor NOUN
der Arzt (PL die Ärzte)
die Ärztin
□ She's a doctor. Sie ist Ärztin. □ She'd like to be a doctor. Sie möchte gerne Ärztin werden.

document NOUN
das Dokument (PL die Dokumente)

documentary NOUN
der Dokumentarfilm (PL die Dokumentarfilme)

to **dodge** VERB
ausweichen (IMPERFECT wich aus, PERFECT ist ausgewichen) *(attacker)*
□ to dodge something einer Sache ausweichen

Dodgems® PL NOUN
der Autoskooter *sing* (PL die Autoskooter)
□ to go on the Dodgems Autoskooter fahren

does VERB ▷ *see* **do**

doesn't = **does not**

dog NOUN
der Hund (PL die Hunde)
□ Have you got a dog? Hast du einen Hund?

do-it-yourself NOUN
das Heimwerken

dole NOUN
die Arbeitslosenunterstützung
■ **to be on the dole** stempeln gehen
□ A lot of people are on the dole. Viele Menschen gehen stempeln.
■ **to go on the dole** sich arbeitslos melden

doll NOUN
die Puppe

dollar NOUN
der Dollar (PL die Dollars *or* Dollar)
LANGUAGE TIP When talking about amounts of money use the plural form **Dollar**.
□ That costs fifty dollars. Das kostet fünfzig Dollar.

dolphin NOUN
der Delfin (PL die Delfine)

domestic ADJECTIVE
■ **a domestic flight** ein Inlandsflug *masc*

dominoes SING NOUN
■ **to have a game of dominoes**
Domino spielen

to **donate** VERB
spenden

done VERB ▷ *see* **do**

donkey NOUN
der Esel (PL die Esel)

donor NOUN
der Spender (PL die Spender)
die Spenderin

don't = **do not**

door NOUN
die Tür

doorbell NOUN
die Klingel
■ **to ring the doorbell** klingeln
■ **Suddenly the doorbell rang.** Es klingelte plötzlich.

doorman NOUN
der Portier (PL die Portiers)

doorstep NOUN
die Eingangsstufe

dormitory NOUN
der Schlafsaal (PL die Schlafsäle)

dose NOUN
die Dosis (PL die Dosen)

dosh NOUN
die Kohle *(informal: money)*

dot NOUN
der Punkt (PL die Punkte) *(on letter 'i', in E-mail address)*
■ **on the dot** genau □ He arrived at nine o'clock on the dot. Er kam genau um neun Uhr.

to **double** VERB
▷ *see also* **double** ADJECTIVE
sich verdoppeln (PERFECT hat sich verdoppelt)
□ The number of attacks has doubled.
Die Zahl der Überfälle hat sich verdoppelt.

double ADJECTIVE, ADVERB
▷ *see also* **double** VERB
doppelt
□ a double helping eine doppelte Portion
■ **to cost double** doppelt so viel kosten
□ First-class tickets cost double. Fahrscheine erster Klasse kosten doppelt so viel.
■ **a double bed** ein Doppelbett *neut*
■ **a double room** ein Doppelzimmer *neut*
■ **a double-decker bus** ein Doppeldeckerbus *masc*

double bass NOUN
der Kontrabass (GEN des Kontrabasses, PL die Kontrabässe)
□ I play the double bass. Ich spiele Kontrabass.

to **double-click** VERB
doppelklicken (PERFECT hat doppelgeklickt) *(computer)*

double glazing NOUN
das Doppelfenster (PL die Doppelfenster)

doubles PL NOUN
das Doppel (PL die Doppel) *(in tennis)*
□ to play mixed doubles gemischtes Doppel spielen

doubt NOUN
▷ *see also* **doubt** VERB
der Zweifel (PL die Zweifel)
□ I have my doubts. Ich habe meine Zweifel.

to **doubt** VERB
▷ *see also* **doubt** NOUN
bezweifeln (PERFECT hat bezweifelt)
□ I doubt it. Das bezweifle ich.
■ **to doubt that** bezweifeln, dass □ I doubt he'll agree. Ich bezweifle, dass er zustimmt.

doubtful ADJECTIVE
■ **to be doubtful about doing something** nicht wissen, ob man etwas tun soll
□ I'm doubtful about going by myself.
Ich weiß nicht, ob ich allein gehen soll.
■ **It's doubtful.** Es ist fraglich.
■ **You sound doubtful.** Du scheinst nicht sicher zu sein.

dough NOUN
der Teig (PL die Teige)

doughnut NOUN
der Berliner (PL die Berliner)
□ a jam doughnut ein gefüllter Berliner

Dover NOUN
Dover *neut*
□ We went from Dover to Boulogne.
Wir sind von Dover nach Boulogne gefahren.

down ADVERB, ADJECTIVE, PREPOSITION
1 unten *(below)*
□ down on the first floor unten im ersten Stock □ It's down there. Es ist da unten.
2 auf den Boden *(to the ground)*
□ He threw down his racket. Er warf seinen Schläger auf den Boden.
■ **They live just down the road.** Sie wohnen etwas weiter unten.
■ **to come down** herunterkommen
□ Come down here! Komm herunter!
■ **to go down** hinuntergehen □ They went down into the cellar. Sie gingen in den Keller hinunter.
■ **to sit down** sich hinsetzen □ Sit down! Setz dich hin!
■ **to feel down** niedergeschlagen sein
□ I'm feeling a bit down. Ich bin etwas niedergeschlagen.
■ **The computer's down.** Der Computer ist abgestürzt.

to **download** VERB
▷ *see also* **download** NOUN
runterladen (PRESENT lädt runter, IMPERFECT lud runter, PERFECT hat runtergeladen) *(computer)*
□ to download a file eine Datei runterladen

download NOUN
▷ *see also* **download** VERB
der Download (PL die Downloads)
□ a free download ein Gratis-Download

downpour NOUN
der Regenguss (GEN des Regengusses, PL die Regengüsse)
□ a sudden downpour ein plötzlicher Regenguss

downstairs ADVERB, ADJECTIVE
1 unten
□ The bathroom's downstairs. Das Badezimmer ist unten.
■ **the people downstairs** die Leute von unten
■ **to go downstairs** nach unten gehen
2 untere
□ the downstairs bathroom das untere Badezimmer

downtown ADVERB (US)
im Stadtzentrum

to **doze** VERB
dösen
■ **to doze off** einnicken

dozen NOUN
das Dutzend (PL die Dutzende *or* Dutzend)

LANGUAGE TIP When talking about more than one dozen use the plural form **Dutzend**.

□ two dozen zwei Dutzend □ a dozen eggs ein Dutzend Eier
■ **I've told you that dozens of times.** Ich habe dir das schon x-mal gesagt.

drab ADJECTIVE
trist *(clothes)*

draft NOUN (US)
der Luftzug (PL die Luftzüge)
■ **There's a draft!** Es zieht!

to **drag** VERB
▷ *see also* **drag** NOUN
schleppen *(thing, person)*

drag NOUN
▷ *see also* **drag** VERB
■ **It's a real drag!** Das ist echt öde! *(informal)*
■ **in drag** in Frauenkleidern □ He was in drag. Er hatte Frauenkleider an.

dragon NOUN
der Drache (GEN des Drachen, PL die Drachen)

drain NOUN
▷ *see also* **drain** VERB
der Abfluss (GEN des Abflusses, PL die Abflüsse)
□ The drains are blocked. Der Abfluss ist verstopft.

to **drain** VERB
▷ *see also* **drain** NOUN
abtropfen lassen (PRESENT lässt abtropfen, IMPERFECT ließ abtropfen, PERFECT hat abtropfen lassen) *(vegetables, pasta)*

draining board NOUN
das Ablaufbrett (PL die Ablaufbretter)

drainpipe NOUN
das Regenrohr (PL die Regenrohre)

drama NOUN
das Drama (PL die Dramen)
□ Drama is my favourite subject. Drama ist mein Lieblingsfach.
■ **drama school** die Schauspielschule
□ I'd like to go to drama school. Ich würde gerne auf die Schauspielschule gehen.

dramatic ADJECTIVE
dramatisch
□ It was really dramatic! Es war wirklich dramatisch! □ a dramatic improvement eine dramatische Besserung

drank VERB ▷ *see* **drink**

drapes PL NOUN (US)
die Vorhänge *masc pl*

drastic ADJECTIVE
drastisch *(change)*
□ to take drastic action drastische Maßnahmen ergreifen

draught NOUN
der Luftzug
■ **There's a draught!** Es zieht!

draughts SING NOUN
Dame *fem*
□ to play draughts Dame spielen

draw NOUN
▷ *see also* **draw** VERB
1 das Unentschieden (PL die Unentschieden) *(sport)*
□ The game ended in a draw. Das Spiel endete mit einem Unentschieden.
2 die Ziehung *(in lottery)*
□ The draw takes place on Saturday. Die Ziehung findet am Samstag statt.

to **draw** VERB
▷ *see also* **draw** NOUN
1 malen
□ He's good at drawing. Er kann gut malen.
□ to draw a picture ein Bild malen
■ **to draw a line** einen Strich machen
2 unentschieden spielen *(sport)*
□ We drew two all. Wir haben zwei zu zwei gespielt.
■ **to draw the curtains** die Vorhänge zuziehen
■ **to draw lots** losen

to **draw on** VERB
zurückgreifen auf (IMPERFECT griff zurück, PERFECT hat zurückgegriffen)
□ Draw on your own experience. Greife auf deine eigenen Erfahrungen zurück.

to **draw up** VERB
halten (PRESENT hält, IMPERFECT hielt, PERFECT hat gehalten)
□ The car drew up in front of the house. Das Auto hielt vor dem Haus.

drawback NOUN
der Nachteil (PL die Nachteile)

drawer NOUN
die Schublade

drawing NOUN
die Zeichnung

drawing pin NOUN
die Reißzwecke

drawn VERB ▷ *see* **draw**

dreadful ADJECTIVE
1 furchtbar
□ a dreadful mistake ein furchtbarer Fehler
□ You look dreadful. *(ill)* Du siehst furchtbar aus. □ I feel dreadful. Ich fühle mich furchtbar.
2 schrecklich
□ The weather was dreadful. Das Wetter war schrecklich.

to **dream** VERB
▷ *see also* **dream** NOUN
träumen
□ I dreamt I was in Belgium. Ich habe geträumt, ich sei in Belgien.
LANGUAGE TIP Note the use of the subjunctive.

dream NOUN
▷ *see also* **dream** VERB
der Traum (PL die Träume)
□ It was just a dream. Es war nur ein Traum.
□ a bad dream ein böser Traum

to **drench** VERB
■ **to get drenched** klatschnass werden
□ We got drenched. Wir wurden klatschnass.

dress NOUN
▷ *see also* **dress** VERB
das Kleid (PL die Kleider)

to **dress** VERB
▷ *see also* **dress** NOUN
sich anziehen (IMPERFECT zog sich an, PERFECT hat sich angezogen)
□ I got up, dressed, and went downstairs. Ich stand auf, zog mich an und ging hinunter.
■ **to dress somebody** jemanden anziehen
□ She dressed the children. Sie zog die Kinder an.
■ **to get dressed** sich anziehen □ I got dressed quickly. Ich habe mich schnell angezogen.
■ **to dress up** sich verkleiden □ I dressed up as a ghost. Ich habe mich als Gespenst verkleidet.

dressed ADJECTIVE
angezogen
□ I'm not dressed yet. Ich bin noch nicht angezogen. □ How was she dressed? Wie war sie angezogen?
■ **She was dressed in a green sweater and jeans.** Sie hatte einen grünen Pullover und Jeans an.

dresser NOUN
die Kommode *(furniture)*

dressing NOUN
das Dressing (PL die Dressings) *(for salad)*

dressing gown NOUN
der Morgenmantel (PL die Morgenmäntel)

dressing table NOUN
der Frisiertisch (PL die Frisiertische)

drew VERB ▷ *see* **draw**

drier NOUN
1 der Wäschetrockner (PL die Wäschetrockner) *(for washing)*
2 der Haartrockner (PL die Haartrockner) *(for hair)*

drift NOUN
▷ *see also* **drift** VERB
■ **a snow drift** eine Schneeverwehung

to **drift** VERB
▷ *see also* **drift** NOUN
treiben (IMPERFECT trieb, PERFECT ist getrieben) *(boat, snow)*

drill NOUN
▷ *see also* **drill** VERB
der Bohrer (PL die Bohrer)

to **drill** VERB
▷ *see also* **drill** NOUN
bohren

to **drink** VERB
▷ *see also* **drink** NOUN
trinken (IMPERFECT trank, PERFECT hat getrunken)
□ What would you like to drink? Was möchtest du trinken? □ She drank three cups of tea. Sie trank drei Tassen Tee.
□ He'd been drinking. Er hatte getrunken.
□ I don't drink. Ich trinke nicht.

drink NOUN
▷ *see also* **drink** VERB
1 das Getränk (PL die Getränke)
□ a cold drink ein kaltes Getränk □ a hot drink ein heißes Getränk
2 der Drink (PL die Drinks) *(alcoholic)*
■ **They've gone out for a drink.** Sie sind etwas trinken gegangen.
■ **to have a drink** etwas trinken

drinking water NOUN
das Trinkwasser

drive NOUN
▷ *see also* **drive** VERB
1 die Fahrt
□ It's a long drive. Es ist eine lange Fahrt.
■ **to go for a drive** fahren □ We went for a drive in the country. Wir sind aufs Land gefahren.
2 die Auffahrt *(of house)*
□ He parked his car in the drive. Er parkte sein Auto in der Auffahrt.

to **drive** VERB
▷ *see also* **drive** NOUN
1 fahren (PRESENT fährt, IMPERFECT fuhr, PERFECT ist/hat gefahren)
□ My mother drives me to school. Meine Mutter fährt mich in die Schule. □ I drove down to London. Ich bin nach London gefahren.

LANGUAGE TIP When **fahren** is used with an object it takes **haben** not **sein**.
□ He drove me home. Er hat mich nach Hause gefahren.

2 Auto fahren (PRESENT fährt Auto, IMPERFECT fuhr Auto, PERFECT ist Auto gefahren) *(operate a car)*
□ Can you drive? Kannst du Auto fahren?
■ **She's learning to drive.** Sie macht den Führerschein.

3 mit dem Auto fahren *(go by car)*
□ Did you go by train? — No, we drove. Seid ihr mit dem Zug gefahren? — Nein, wir sind mit dem Auto gefahren.
■ **to drive somebody mad** jemanden wahnsinnig machen □ He drives her mad. Er macht sie wahnsinnig.

driver NOUN
der Fahrer (PL die Fahrer)
die Fahrerin
□ She's an excellent driver. Sie ist eine ausgezeichnete Fahrerin. □ He's a bus driver. Er ist Busfahrer.

driver's license NOUN (US)
der Führerschein (PL die Führerscheine)

driving instructor NOUN
der Fahrlehrer (PL die Fahrlehrer)
die Fahrlehrerin
□ He's a driving instructor. Er ist Fahrlehrer.

driving lesson NOUN
die Fahrstunde

driving licence NOUN
der Führerschein (PL die Führerscheine)

driving test NOUN
die Fahrprüfung
■ **to take one's driving test** die Fahrprüfung machen □ He's taking his driving test tomorrow. Er macht morgen die Fahrprüfung.
■ **She's just passed her driving test.** Sie hat gerade ihren Führerschein gemacht.

drizzle NOUN
▷ *see also* **drizzle** VERB
der Nieselregen

to **drizzle** VERB
▷ *see also* **drizzle** NOUN
nieseln

drop NOUN
▷ *see also* **drop** VERB
der Tropfen (PL die Tropfen)
□ a drop of water ein Wassertropfen

to **drop** VERB
▷ *see also* **drop** NOUN

1 fallen lassen (PRESENT lässt fallen, IMPERFECT ließ fallen, PERFECT hat fallen lassen)
□ I dropped the glass. Ich habe das Glas fallen lassen.

2 aufgeben (PRESENT gibt auf, IMPERFECT gab auf, PERFECT hat aufgegeben) *(abandon)*
□ I'm going to drop chemistry. Ich gebe Chemie auf.

3 absetzen (PERFECT hat abgesetzt)
□ Could you drop me at the station? Könntest du mich am Bahnhof absetzen?

drought NOUN
die Dürre

drove VERB ▷ *see* **drive**

to **drown** VERB
ertrinken (IMPERFECT ertrank, PERFECT ist ertrunken)
□ A boy drowned here yesterday. Hier ist gestern ein Junge ertrunken.

drug NOUN

1 das Medikament (PL die Medikamente) *(medicine)*
□ They need food and drugs. Sie brauchen Nahrung und Medikamente.

2 die Droge *(illegal)*
□ hard drugs harte Drogen □ soft drugs weiche Drogen □ to take drugs Drogen nehmen
■ **a drug addict** *(man)* ein Drogensüchtiger
■ **She's a drug addict.** Sie ist drogensüchtig.
■ **a drug pusher** ein Dealer *masc*
■ **a drug smuggler** ein Drogenschmuggler *masc*
■ **the drugs squad** das Rauschgiftdezernat

drugstore NOUN (US)
der Drugstore (PL die Drugstores)

drum NOUN
die Trommel
□ an African drum eine afrikanische Trommel
■ **a drum kit** ein Schlagzeug *neut*
■ **drums** das Schlagzeug *sing* □ I play drums. Ich spiele Schlagzeug.

drummer NOUN
der Schlagzeuger (PL die Schlagzeuger)
die Schlagzeugerin *(in rock group)*

drunk VERB ▷ *see* **drink**

drunk ADJECTIVE
▷ *see also* **drunk** NOUN
betrunken
□ He was drunk. Er war betrunken.

drunk NOUN
▷ *see also* **drunk** ADJECTIVE
der Betrunkene (GEN des Betrunkenen, PL die Betrunkenen)
die Betrunkene (GEN der Betrunkenen)
□ a drunk *(man)* ein Betrunkener
□ The streets were full of drunks. Die Straßen waren voll von Betrunkenen.

dry ADJECTIVE
▷ *see also* **dry** VERB
trocken
□ The paint isn't dry yet. Die Farbe ist noch nicht trocken.
■ **a long dry period** eine lange Trockenzeit

to **dry** VERB
▷ *see also* **dry** ADJECTIVE

1 trocknen
□ The washing will dry quickly in the sun. Die Wäsche wird in der Sonne schnell trocknen.

□ some dried flowers getrocknete Blumen
■ **to dry one's hair** sich die Haare föhnen
□ I haven't dried my hair yet. Ich habe mir noch nicht die Haare geföhnt.
2 trocknen lassen (PRESENT lässt trocknen, IMPERFECT ließ trocknen, PERFECT hat trocknen lassen) *(clothes)*
□ There's nowhere to dry clothes here. Hier kann man nirgends Kleider trocknen lassen.
■ **to dry the dishes** das Geschirr abtrocknen

dry-cleaner's NOUN
die Reinigung

dryer NOUN
der Wäschetrockner (PL die Wäschetrockner) *(for clothes)*
■ **a tumble dryer** ein Wäschetrockner
■ **a hair dryer** ein Föhn *masc*

DTP ABBREVIATION *(= Desktop Publishing)*
DTP

dubbed ADJECTIVE
synchronisiert
□ The film was dubbed into German. Der Film war deutsch synchronisiert.

dubious ADJECTIVE
■ **My parents were a bit dubious about it.** Meine Eltern hatten ihre Zweifel.

duck NOUN
die Ente

due ADJECTIVE, ADVERB
■ **to be due to do something** etwas tun sollen □ He's due to arrive tomorrow. Er soll morgen ankommen.
■ **The plane's due in half an hour.** Das Flugzeug sollte in einer halben Stunde ankommen.
■ **When's the baby due?** Wann kommt das Baby?
■ **due to** wegen □ The trip was cancelled due to bad weather. Der Ausflug wurde wegen des schlechten Wetters abgesagt.

dug VERB ▷ *see* **dig**

dull ADJECTIVE
1 langweilig
□ He's nice, but a bit dull. Er ist nett, aber ein bisschen langweilig.
2 trüb *(weather, day)*

dumb ADJECTIVE
1 taub
■ **She's deaf and dumb.** Sie ist taubstumm.
2 blöd *(stupid)*
□ That was a really dumb thing I did! Da habe ich etwas echt Blödes gemacht!

dummy NOUN
der Schnuller (PL die Schnuller) *(for baby)*

dump NOUN
▷ *see also* **dump** VERB
■ **It's a real dump!** Das ist ein Dreckloch! *(informal)*
■ **a rubbish dump** eine Müllkippe

to **dump** VERB
▷ *see also* **dump** NOUN
1 abladen (PRESENT lädt ab, IMPERFECT lud ab, PERFECT hat abgeladen) *(waste)*
■ **'no dumping'** 'Schutt abladen verboten'
2 Schluss machen mit *(informal: get rid of)*
□ He's just dumped his girlfriend. Er hat gerade mit seiner Freundin Schluss gemacht.

dungarees PL NOUN
die Latzhose
□ a pair of dungarees eine Latzhose

dungeon NOUN
das Verlies (PL die Verliese)

duration NOUN
die Dauer

during PREPOSITION
während
□ during the holidays während der Ferien
■ **during the day** tagsüber

dusk NOUN
die Dämmerung
□ at dusk bei Dämmerung

dust NOUN
▷ *see also* **dust** VERB
der Staub

to **dust** VERB
▷ *see also* **dust** NOUN
abstauben (PERFECT hat abgestaubt)
□ I dusted the shelves. Ich habe das Regal abgestaubt.
■ **I hate dusting!** Ich hasse Staubwischen!

dustbin NOUN
der Mülleimer (PL die Mülleimer)

dustman NOUN
der Müllmann (PL die Müllmänner)
■ **He's a dustman.** Er arbeitet bei der Müllabfuhr.

dusty ADJECTIVE
staubig

Dutch ADJECTIVE
▷ *see also* **Dutch** NOUN
holländisch
□ She's Dutch. Sie ist Holländerin.

Dutch NOUN
▷ *see also* **Dutch** ADJECTIVE
das Holländisch (GEN des Holländischen) *(language)*
■ **the Dutch** die Holländer *masc pl*

Dutchman NOUN
der Holländer (PL die Holländer)

Dutchwoman NOUN
die Holländerin

duty NOUN
die Pflicht
□ It was his duty to tell the police. Es war seine Pflicht, die Polizei zu informieren.
■ **to be on duty** Dienst haben

duty-free ADJECTIVE
zollfrei
■ **the duty-free shop** der Duty-free-Laden

duvet NOUN
das Deckbett (PL die Deckbetten)

DVD NOUN *(= digital video disc)*
die DVD (PL die DVDs)

DVD player NOUN
der DVD-Player (PL die DVD-Player)

dwarf NOUN
der Zwerg (PL die Zwerge)
die Zwergin

dye NOUN
▷ *see also* **dye** VERB
der Farbstoff
■ **hair dye** das Haarfärbemittel

to **dye** VERB
▷ *see also* **dye** NOUN
färben
□ to dye something red etwas rot färben
□ She has dyed her hair blonde. Sie hat blond gefärbte Haare.

dynamic ADJECTIVE
dynamisch

dyslexia NOUN
die Legasthenie
■ **She has dyslexia.** Sie ist Legasthenikerin.

Ee

each ADJECTIVE, PRONOUN
jeder
□ Each person has their own desk. Jeder hat seinen eigenen Schreibtisch. □ They have ten points each. Jeder hat zehn Punkte. □ He gave each of us ten pounds. Er gab jedem von uns zehn Pfund. □ each day jeder Tag
jede
□ Each dancer wore a different costume. Jede Tänzerin trug ein anderes Kostüm. □ He gave each of the dancers a red rose. Er gab jeder Tänzerin eine rote Rose.
jedes
□ Each house has a garden. Jedes Haus hat einen Garten. □ The girls each have their own bedroom. Jedes der Mädchen hat sein eigenes Zimmer.
■ **each other** einander □ They hate each other. Sie hassen einander. □ We wrote to each other. Wir haben einander geschrieben.
■ **They don't know each other.** Sie kennen sich nicht.

eager ADJECTIVE
■ **He was eager to talk to us.** Er wollte unbedingt mit uns sprechen.

eagle NOUN
der Adler (PL die Adler)

ear NOUN
das Ohr (PL die Ohren)

earache NOUN
die Ohrenschmerzen *masc pl*
□ to have earache Ohrenschmerzen haben

earlier ADVERB
1 vorher
□ I saw him earlier. Ich habe ihn vorher gesehen.
2 früher *(in the morning)*
□ I ought to get up earlier. Ich sollte früher aufstehen.

early ADVERB, ADJECTIVE
früh
□ I have to get up early. Ich muss früh aufstehen. □ I came early to get a good seat. Ich bin früh gekommen, um einen guten Platz zu bekommen.
■ **to have an early night** früh ins Bett gehen

to **earn** VERB
verdienen (PERFECT hat verdient)
□ She earns five pounds an hour. Sie verdient fünf Pfund in der Stunde.

earnings PL NOUN
der Verdienst (PL die Verdienste)

earring NOUN
der Ohrring (PL die Ohrringe)

earth NOUN
die Erde

earthquake NOUN
das Erdbeben (PL die Erdbeben)

easily ADVERB
leicht

east ADJECTIVE, ADVERB
▷ *see also* **east** NOUN
nach Osten
□ We were travelling east. Wir sind nach Osten gefahren.
■ **the east coast** die Ostküste
■ **an east wind** ein Ostwind *masc*
■ **east of** östlich von □ It's east of London. Es liegt östlich von London.

east NOUN
▷ *see also* **east** ADJECTIVE
der Osten
□ in the east im Osten

Easter NOUN
Ostern *neut*
□ at Easter an Ostern □ We went to Spain for Easter. Wir waren über Ostern in Spanien.

Easter egg NOUN
das Osterei (PL die Ostereier)

eastern ADJECTIVE
östlich
□ the eastern part of the island der östliche Teil der Insel
■ **Eastern Europe** Osteuropa *neut*

easy ADJECTIVE
einfach

easy chair NOUN
der Sessel (PL die Sessel)

easy-going ADJECTIVE
locker
□ She's very easy-going. Sie ist echt locker.

to **eat** VERB
essen (PRESENT isst, IMPERFECT aß, PERFECT hat gegessen)
□ Would you like something to eat? Möchtest du etwas essen?

EC NOUN *(= European Community)*
die EG *(= Europäische Gemeinschaft)*

eccentric ADJECTIVE
exzentrisch

echo NOUN
das Echo (PL die Echos)

ecology NOUN
die Ökologie

e-commerce NOUN
der E-Commerce (GEN des E-Commerce)

economic ADJECTIVE
rentabel *(profitable)*

economical ADJECTIVE
sparsam

economics SING NOUN
die Volkswirtschaft
□ He's studying economics. Er studiert Volkswirtschaft.

to **economize** VERB
sparen
□ to economize on something mit etwas sparen

economy NOUN
die Wirtschaft
□ the German economy die deutsche Wirtschaft

ecstasy NOUN
das Ecstasy (GEN des Ecstasy) *(drug)*
■ **to be in ecstasy** entzückt sein

eczema NOUN
der Hautausschlag (PL die Hautausschläge)

edge NOUN
1 der Rand (PL die Ränder)
□ They live on the edge of the moors. Sie leben am Rand des Moors.
2 die Kante *(of table)*
3 das Ufer (PL die Ufer) *(of lake)*

edgy ADJECTIVE
nervös

Edinburgh NOUN
Edinburgh *neut*

editor NOUN
der Redakteur (PL die Redakteure)
die Redakteurin *(of newspaper)*

educated ADJECTIVE
gebildet

education NOUN
1 das Bildungswesen
□ There should be more investment in education. Es sollte mehr Geld ins Bildungswesen investiert werden.
2 das Lehramt *(teaching)*
□ She works in education. Sie ist im Lehramt tätig.

educational ADJECTIVE
lehrreich *(experience)*
□ It was very educational. Das was sehr lehrreich.

effect NOUN
der Effekt (PL die Effekte)
□ special effects Spezialeffekte

effective ADJECTIVE
effektiv

efficient ADJECTIVE
effizient

effort NOUN
die Bemühung
■ **to make an effort to do something** sich bemühen, etwas zu tun

e.g. ABBREVIATION
z. B. *(= zum Beispiel)*

egg NOUN
das Ei (PL die Eier)
□ a hard-boiled egg ein hart gekochtes Ei
□ a soft-boiled egg ein weich gekochtes Ei
■ **a fried egg** ein Spiegelei
■ **scrambled eggs** die Rühreier *neut pl*

egg cup NOUN
der Eierbecher (PL die Eierbecher)

eggplant NOUN (US)
die Aubergine

Egypt NOUN
Ägypten *neut*
□ to Egypt nach Ägypten

eight NUMBER
acht
□ She's eight. Sie ist acht.

eighteen NUMBER
achtzehn
□ She's eighteen. Sie ist achtzehn.

eighteenth ADJECTIVE
achtzehnte
■ **the eighteenth of August** der achtzehnte August

eighth ADJECTIVE
achte
□ the eighth floor der achte Stock
□ the eighth of August der achte August

eighty NUMBER
achtzig
□ She's eighty. Sie ist achtzig.

Eire NOUN
Irland *neut*
■ **from Eire** aus Irland
■ **in Eire** in Irland
■ **to Eire** nach Irland

either ADVERB, CONJUNCTION, PRONOUN
1 auch kein
□ I don't like milk, and I don't like eggs either. Ich mag keine Milch und ich mag auch keine Eier.
2 auch nicht
□ I've never been to Spain. — I haven't either. Ich war noch nie in Spanien. — Ich auch nicht.
■ **either ... or ...** entweder ... oder ...
□ You can have either ice cream or yoghurt. Du kannst entweder Eis oder Joghurt haben.
■ **either of them** einer von beiden □ Take either of them. Nimm einen von beiden.
■ **I don't like either of them.** Ich mag keinen von beiden.

elastic NOUN
das Gummiband (PL die Gummibänder)

elastic band NOUN
das Gummiband (PL die Gummibänder)

elbow NOUN
der Ellbogen (PL die Ellbogen)

elder ADJECTIVE
älter
□ my elder sister meine ältere Schwester

elderly ADJECTIVE
älter
□ an elderly lady eine ältere Dame
■ **the elderly** ältere Leute *pl*

eldest ADJECTIVE
älteste
□ my eldest brother mein ältester Bruder
□ my eldest sister meine älteste Schwester
□ He's the eldest. Er ist der Älteste.

to **elect** VERB
wählen

election NOUN
die Wahl

electric ADJECTIVE
elektrisch
□ an electric fire ein elektrischer Ofen
□ an electric guitar eine elektrische Gitarre
■ **an electric blanket** eine Heizdecke

electrical ADJECTIVE
elektrisch
■ **an electrical engineer**
ein Elektrotechniker

electrician NOUN
der Elektriker (PL die Elektriker)
die Elektrikerin
□ He's an electrician. Er ist Elektriker.

electricity NOUN
der Strom
□ They cut off our electricity. Sie haben den Strom abgestellt.

electronic ADJECTIVE
elektronisch

electronics SING NOUN
die Elektronik
□ My hobby is electronics. Elektronik ist mein Hobby.

elegant ADJECTIVE
elegant

elementary school NOUN (US)
die Grundschule

elephant NOUN
der Elefant (GEN des Elefanten, PL die Elefanten)

elevator NOUN (US)
der Aufzug (PL die Aufzüge)

eleven NUMBER
elf
□ She's eleven. Sie ist elf.

eleventh ADJECTIVE
elfte
□ the eleventh floor der elfte Stock
□ the eleventh of August der elfte August

else ADVERB
1 anders
□ somebody else jemand anders □ nobody else niemand anders □ somewhere else irgendwo anders □ anywhere else irgendwo anders
2 anderes
□ nothing else nichts anderes □ something else etwas anderes □ anything else etwas anderes
■ **Would you like anything else?** Möchtest du noch etwas?
■ **I don't want anything else.** Ich will nichts anderes.
■ **Give me the money, or else!** Gib mir das Geld, sonst gibt's was!

email NOUN
▷ *see also* **email** VERB
die E-Mail (PL die E-Mails)
□ My email address is ... Meine E-Mail-Adresse ist ...

to **email** VERB
▷ *see also* **email** NOUN
mailen (PERFECT hat gemailt)
□ Did you email it? Hast du es gemailt?
■ **to email somebody** jemandem eine E-Mail senden

embankment NOUN
die Böschung

embarrassed ADJECTIVE
verlegen
□ He seemed to be pretty embarrassed. Er schien sehr verlegen.
■ **I was really embarrassed.** Es war mir wirklich peinlich.

embarrassing ADJECTIVE
peinlich
□ It was so embarrassing. Es war so peinlich.

embassy NOUN
die Botschaft

to **embroider** VERB
besticken (PERFECT hat bestickt)

embroidery NOUN
die Stickerei
■ **I do embroidery.** Ich sticke.

emergency NOUN
der Notfall (PL die Notfälle)
□ This is an emergency! Dies ist ein Notfall!
□ in an emergency in einem Notfall
■ **an emergency exit** ein Notausgang *masc*
■ **an emergency landing** eine Notlandung
■ **the emergency services** die Rettungsdienste *masc pl*

to **emigrate** VERB
auswandern (PERFECT ist ausgewandert)

emotion NOUN
das Gefühl (PL die Gefühle)

emotional ADJECTIVE
emotional *(person)*

emperor NOUN

der Kaiser (PL die Kaiser)

to emphasize VERB
betonen (PERFECT hat betont)

empire NOUN
das Reich (PL die Reiche)

to employ VERB
beschäftigen (PERFECT hat beschäftigt)
□ The factory employs six hundred people. Die Fabrik beschäftigt sechshundert Leute.

employee NOUN
der Angestellte (GEN des Angestellten, PL die Angestellten)
die Angestellte (GEN der Angestellten)
□ He's an employee. Er ist Angestellter.

employer NOUN
der Arbeitgeber (PL die Arbeitgeber)
die Arbeitgeberin

employment NOUN
die Beschäftigung

empty ADJECTIVE
▷ *see also* **empty** VERB
leer

to empty VERB
▷ *see also* **empty** ADJECTIVE
leeren
■ **to empty something out** etwas ausleeren

to encourage VERB
ermutigen (PERFECT hat ermutigt)
■ **to encourage somebody to do something** jemanden ermutigen, etwas zu tun

encouragement NOUN
die Ermutigung

encyclopedia NOUN
das Lexikon (PL die Lexika)

end NOUN
▷ *see also* **end** VERB
das Ende (PL die Enden)
□ the end of the holidays das Ende der Ferien
□ at the end of the street am Ende der Straße
□ at the other end of the table am anderen Ende des Tisches
■ **the end of the film** der Schluss des Films
■ **in the end** schließlich □ In the end I decided to stay at home. Schließlich habe ich beschlossen, zu Hause zu bleiben. □ It turned out all right in the end. Schließlich ging alles gut.
■ **for hours on end** stundenlang

to end VERB
▷ *see also* **end** NOUN
zu Ende sein (PRESENT ist zu Ende, IMPERFECT war zu Ende, PERFECT ist zu Ende gewesen)
□ What time does the film end? Wann ist der Film zu Ende?
■ **to end up doing something** schließlich etwas tun □ I ended up walking home. Ich bin schließlich zu Fuß nach Hause gegangen.

ending NOUN
der Schluss (GEN des Schlusses, PL die Schlüsse)
□ It was an exciting film, especially the ending. Es war ein spannender Film, besonders am Schluss.

endless ADJECTIVE
endlos
□ The journey seemed endless. Die Reise erschien endlos.

enemy NOUN
der Feind (PL die Feinde)
die Feindin

energetic ADJECTIVE
voller Energie *(person)*

energy NOUN
die Energie

engaged ADJECTIVE
1 besetzt *(busy, in use)*
□ I phoned, but it was engaged. Ich habe angerufen, aber es war besetzt.
2 verlobt *(to be married)*
□ She's engaged to Brian. Sie ist mit Brian verlobt.
■ **to get engaged** sich verloben

engagement NOUN
die Verlobung
□ an engagement ring ein Verlobungsring *masc*

engine NOUN
der Motor (PL die Motoren)

engineer NOUN
1 der Ingenieur (PL die Ingenieure)
die Ingenieurin
□ He's an engineer. Er ist Ingenieur.
2 der Lokomotivführer (PL die Lokomotivführer) *(train driver)*

engineering NOUN
die Technik
□ genetic engineering die Gentechnik
■ **mechanical engineering** der Maschinenbau

England NOUN
England *neut*
■ **from England** aus England
■ **in England** in England
■ **to England** nach England

DID YOU KNOW...?
Germans frequently use **England** to mean Great Britain or the United Kingdom.

English ADJECTIVE
▷ *see also* **English** NOUN
englisch
■ **He's English.** Er ist Engländer.
■ **She's English.** Sie ist Engländerin.
■ **English people** die Engländer *masc pl*

English NOUN
▷ *see also* **English** ADJECTIVE
das Englisch (GEN des Englischen) *(language)*
□ Do you speak English? Sprechen Sie Englisch?
■ **the English** *(people)* die Engländer *masc pl*

Englishman NOUN
der Engländer (PL die Engländer)

Englishwoman NOUN
die Engländerin

to **enjoy** VERB
genießen (IMPERFECT genoss, PERFECT hat genossen)
□ I enjoyed my holiday. Ich habe meinen Urlaub genossen.
■ **Did you enjoy the film?** Hat dir der Film gefallen?
■ **Did you enjoy your meal?** Hat es Ihnen geschmeckt?
■ **to enjoy oneself** sich amüsieren □ I really enjoyed myself. Ich habe mich richtig amüsiert. □ Did you enjoy yourselves at the party? Habt ihr euch auf der Party amüsiert?

enjoyable ADJECTIVE
nett

enlargement NOUN
die Vergrößerung *(of photo)*

enormous ADJECTIVE
riesig

enough PRONOUN, ADJECTIVE
genug
□ enough time genug Zeit □ I didn't have enough money. Ich hatte nicht genug Geld. □ big enough groß genug □ warm enough warm genug
■ **Have you got enough?** Reicht dir das?
■ **I've had enough!** Mir reicht's!
■ **That's enough.** Das reicht.

to **enquire** VERB
sich erkundigen (PERFECT hat sich erkundigt)
■ **to enquire about something** sich nach etwas erkundigen □ I'm going to enquire about train times. Ich werde mich nach den Abfahrtszeiten der Züge erkundigen.

enquiry NOUN
die Untersuchung *(official investigation)*
■ **to make an enquiry** sich erkundigen □ I'd like to make an enquiry about hotels. Ich möchte mich über Hotels erkundigen.

to **enter** VERB
betreten (PRESENT betritt, IMPERFECT betrat, PERFECT hat betreten) *(room)*
■ **to enter a competition** an einem Wettbewerb teilnehmen

to **entertain** VERB
unterhalten (PRESENT unterhält, IMPERFECT unterhielt, PERFECT hat unterhalten) *(guests)*

entertainer NOUN
der Entertainer (PL die Entertainer)
die Entertainerin

entertaining ADJECTIVE
unterhaltsam

enthusiasm NOUN
die Begeisterung

enthusiast NOUN
■ **a railway enthusiast** ein Eisenbahnfan *masc*
■ **She's a DIY enthusiast.** Sie ist begeisterte Heimwerkerin.

enthusiastic ADJECTIVE
begeistert

entire ADJECTIVE
ganz
□ the entire world die ganze Welt

entirely ADVERB
ganz

entrance NOUN
der Eingang (PL die Eingänge)
■ **an entrance exam** eine Aufnahmeprüfung
■ **entrance fee** der Eintritt

entry NOUN
der Eingang (PL die Eingänge) *(way in)*
■ **'no entry'** **1** *(on door)* 'kein Zutritt' **2** *(on road sign)* 'Einfahrt verboten'
■ **an entry form** ein Teilnahmeformular *neut*

entry phone NOUN
die Gegensprechanlage

envelope NOUN
der Umschlag (PL die Umschläge)

envious ADJECTIVE
neidisch

environment NOUN
die Umwelt

environmental ADJECTIVE
■ **environmental pollution** die Umweltverschmutzung
■ **environmental protection** der Umweltschutz

environment-friendly ADJECTIVE
umweltfreundlich

envy NOUN
▷ *see also* **envy** VERB
der Neid

to **envy** VERB
▷ *see also* **envy** NOUN
beneiden (PERFECT hat beneidet)
□ I don't envy you! Ich beneide dich nicht!

epileptic NOUN
der Epileptiker (PL die Epileptiker)
die Epileptikerin

episode NOUN
die Folge *(of TV programme, story)*

equal ADJECTIVE
▷ *see also* **equal** VERB
gleich

to **equal** VERB
▷ *see also* **equal** ADJECTIVE
■ **Ten times two equals twenty.** Zehn mal zwei ist gleich zwanzig.

equality NOUN
die Gleichheit

to **equalize** VERB
ausgleichen (IMPERFECT glich aus, PERFECT hat ausgeglichen) *(in sport)*

equator NOUN
der Äquator

equipment NOUN
die Ausrüstung
□ fishing equipment die Anglerausrüstung
□ skiing equipment die Skiausrüstung

equipped ADJECTIVE
■ **equipped with** ausgerüstet mit
■ **to be well equipped** gut ausgestattet sein

equivalent NOUN
das Äquivalent (PL die Äquivalente)
■ **to be equivalent to something** einer Sache entsprechen □ Twenty-five per cent is equivalent to a quarter. Fünfundzwanzig Prozent entspricht einem Viertel.

error NOUN
der Fehler (PL die Fehler)

escalator NOUN
die Rolltreppe

escape NOUN
▷ *see also* **escape** VERB
der Ausbruch (PL die Ausbrüche) *(from prison)*

to **escape** VERB
▷ *see also* **escape** NOUN
ausbrechen (PRESENT bricht aus, IMPERFECT brach aus, PERFECT ist ausgebrochen)
□ A lion has escaped. Ein Löwe ist ausgebrochen. □ to escape from prison aus dem Gefängnis ausbrechen

escort NOUN
die Eskorte
□ a police escort eine Polizeieskorte

Eskimo NOUN
der Eskimo (PL die Eskimos)
die Eskimofrau

especially ADVERB
besonders
□ It's very hot there, especially in the summer. Dort ist es sehr heiß, besonders im Sommer.

essay NOUN
der Aufsatz (PL die Aufsätze)
□ a history essay ein Aufsatz in Geschichte

essential ADJECTIVE
wichtig
□ It's essential to bring warm clothes. Es ist ganz wichtig, warme Kleidung mitzubringen.

estate NOUN
die Siedlung *(housing estate)*
□ I live on an estate. Ich wohne in einer Siedlung.

estate agent NOUN
der Immobilienmakler (PL die Immobilienmakler)
die Immobilienmaklerin

estate car NOUN
der Kombiwagen (PL die Kombiwagen)

to **estimate** VERB
schätzen
□ They estimated it would take three weeks. Sie schätzten, dass es drei Wochen dauern würde.

etc ABBREVIATION *(= et cetera)*
usw. *(= und so weiter)*

Ethiopia NOUN
Äthiopien *neut*
■ **in Ethiopia** in Äthiopien

ethnic ADJECTIVE
1 ethnisch *(racial)*
□ an ethnic minority eine ethnische Minderheit
2 folkloristisch *(clothes, music)*

e-ticket NOUN
das E-Ticket (PL die E-Tickets)

EU NOUN *(= European Union)*
die EU *(= Europäische Union)*

euro NOUN
der Euro (PL die Euros)

Europe NOUN
Europa *neut*
■ **from Europe** aus Europa
■ **in Europe** in Europa
■ **to Europe** nach Europa

European ADJECTIVE
▷ *see also* **European** NOUN
europäisch
■ **He's European.** Er ist Europäer.

European NOUN
▷ *see also* **European** ADJECTIVE
der Europäer (PL die Europäer)
die Europäerin *(person)*

to **evacuate** VERB
evakuieren (PERFECT hat evakuiert)

eve NOUN
■ **Christmas Eve** der Heilige Abend
■ **New Year's Eve** Silvester *neut*

even ADVERB
▷ *see also* **even** ADJECTIVE
sogar
□ I like all animals, even snakes. Ich mag alle Tiere, sogar Schlangen.
■ **even if** selbst wenn □ I'd never do that, even if you asked me. Ich würde das nie tun, selbst wenn du mich darum bitten würdest.
■ **not even** nicht einmal □ He never stops working, not even at the weekend. Er hört nie auf zu arbeiten, nicht einmal am Wochenende.
■ **even though** obwohl □ He's never got any money, even though his parents are quite rich. Er hat nie Geld, obwohl seine Eltern ziemlich reich sind.
■ **I liked Hamburg even more than Munich.** Hamburg hat mir noch besser gefallen als München.

even ADJECTIVE
▷ *see also* **even** ADVERB
gleichmäßig
□ an even layer of snow eine gleichmäßige Schneeschicht
■ **an even number** eine gerade Zahl
■ **to get even with somebody** es jemandem heimzahlen

evening NOUN
der Abend (PL die Abende)
□ in the evening am Abend □ all evening den ganzen Abend □ yesterday evening gestern Abend □ tomorrow evening morgen Abend
■ **Good evening!** Guten Abend!

evening class NOUN
der Abendkurs (PL die Abendkurse)

event NOUN
das Ereignis (GEN des Ereignisses, PL die Ereignisse)
■ **a sporting event** eine Sportveranstaltung

eventful ADJECTIVE
ereignisreich

eventual ADJECTIVE
schließlich
■ **the eventual outcome** das Endergebnis
LANGUAGE TIP Be careful not to translate **eventual** by **eventuell**.

eventually ADVERB
schließlich

ever ADVERB
1 schon einmal
□ Have you ever been to America? Warst du schon einmal in Amerika? □ Have you ever seen her? Hast du sie schon einmal gesehen?
2 je
□ the best I've ever seen das Beste, was ich je gesehen habe
■ **for the first time ever** das allererste Mal
■ **ever since** seit □ ever since I met him seit ich ihn kenne
■ **ever since then** seither

every ADJECTIVE
jeder
□ every student jeder Student □ every day jeden Tag
jede
□ every mother jede Mutter □ every week jede Woche
jedes
□ every child jedes Kind □ every year jedes Jahr
■ **every time** jedes Mal □ Every time I see him, he's depressed. Jedes Mal, wenn ich ihn sehe, ist er deprimiert.
■ **every now and then** ab und zu

everybody PRONOUN
1 alle
□ Everybody had a good time. Alle hatten ihren Spaß.
2 jeder
□ Everybody makes mistakes. Jeder macht mal Fehler.

everyone PRONOUN
1 alle
□ Everyone opened their presents. Alle machten ihre Geschenke auf.
2 jeder
□ Everyone should have a hobby. Jeder sollte ein Hobby haben.

everything PRONOUN
alles
□ You've thought of everything! Du hast an alles gedacht! □ Money isn't everything. Geld ist nicht alles.

everywhere ADVERB
überall
□ I've looked everywhere. Ich habe überall gesucht. □ There were policemen everywhere. Überall waren Polizisten.

evil ADJECTIVE
böse

ex- PREFIX
Ex-
□ his ex-wife seine Ex-Frau

exact ADJECTIVE
genau

exactly ADVERB
genau
□ exactly the same genau das gleiche
□ It's exactly ten o'clock. Es ist genau zehn Uhr.

to **exaggerate** VERB
übertreiben (IMPERFECT übertrieb, PERFECT hat übertrieben)

exaggeration NOUN
die Übertreibung

exam NOUN
die Prüfung
□ a German exam eine Deutschprüfung
□ the exam results die Prüfungsergebnisse

examination NOUN
die Prüfung
■ **a medical examination** eine ärztliche Untersuchung

to **examine** VERB
untersuchen (PERFECT hat untersucht)
□ The doctor examined him. Der Arzt untersuchte ihn.
■ **He examined her passport.** Er prüfte ihren Pass.

examiner NOUN
der Prüfer (PL die Prüfer)
die Prüferin

example NOUN
das Beispiel (PL die Beispiele)
■ **for example** zum Beispiel

excellent ADJECTIVE
ausgezeichnet
□ Her results were excellent. Ihre Noten waren ausgezeichnet.

except PREPOSITION
außer
□ everyone except me alle außer mir
■ **except for** abgesehen von □ It was super except for the weather. Abgesehen vom Wetter war es super.
■ **except that** außer, dass □ The weather was great, except that it was a bit cold. Das Wetter war toll, außer dass es etwas kalt war.

exception NOUN
die Ausnahme
□ to make an exception eine Ausnahme machen

exceptional ADJECTIVE
außergewöhnlich

excess baggage NOUN
das Übergewicht (PL die Übergewichte)

to **exchange** VERB
tauschen
□ I exchanged the book for a DVD. Ich habe das Buch gegen eine DVD getauscht.

exchange rate NOUN
der Wechselkurs (PL die Wechselkurse)

excited ADJECTIVE
aufgeregt

exciting ADJECTIVE
aufregend

exclamation mark NOUN
das Ausrufezeichen (PL die Ausrufezeichen)

excuse NOUN
▷ *see also* **excuse** VERB
die Entschuldigung

to **excuse** VERB
▷ *see also* **excuse** NOUN
■ **Excuse me!** Entschuldigung!

ex-directory ADJECTIVE
■ **She's ex-directory.** Ihre Nummer steht nicht im Telefonbuch.

to **execute** VERB
1 hinrichten (PERFECT hat hingerichtet) *(kill)*
2 ausführen (PERFECT hat ausgeführt) *(plan)*

execution NOUN
die Hinrichtung *(punishment)*
□ His execution took place yesterday. Seine Hinrichtung fand gestern statt.

executive NOUN
der leitende Angestellte (GEN des leitenden Angestellten, PL die leitenden Angestellten)
die leitende Angestellte (GEN der leitenden Angestellten) *(in business)*
□ He's an executive. Er ist leitender Angestellter.

exercise NOUN
1 die Übung
□ an exercise book ein Übungsheft
2 die Bewegung
□ You need more exercise. Sie brauchen mehr Bewegung.
■ **an exercise bike** ein Heimtrainer *masc*
■ **She does her exercises every morning.** Sie macht jeden Morgen ihre Gymnastik.

exhaust NOUN
der Auspuff
■ **exhaust fumes** die Abgase *pl*

exhausted ADJECTIVE
erschöpft

exhaust pipe NOUN
das Auspuffrohr (PL die Auspuffrohre)

exhibition NOUN
die Ausstellung

to **exist** VERB
existieren (PERFECT hat existiert)
■ **It doesn't exist.** Das gibt es nicht.

exit NOUN
der Ausgang (PL die Ausgänge) *(way out)*

exotic ADJECTIVE
exotisch

to **expect** VERB
1 erwarten (PERFECT hat erwartet)
□ I'm expecting him for dinner. Ich erwarte ihn zum Abendessen. □ She's expecting a baby. Sie erwartet ein Kind. □ I didn't expect that from him. Das habe ich von ihm nicht erwartet.
2 annehmen (PRESENT nimmt an, IMPERFECT nahm an, PERFECT hat angenommen)
□ I expect he'll be late. Ich nehme an, dass er sich verspäten wird. □ I expect so. Das nehme ich mal an.

expedition NOUN
die Expedition

to **expel** VERB
■ **to get expelled** *(from school)* von der Schule verwiesen werden

expenses PL NOUN
die Kosten *pl*

expensive ADJECTIVE
teuer

experience NOUN
▷ *see also* **experience** VERB
die Erfahrung

to **experience** VERB
▷ *see also* **experience** NOUN
1 haben (PRESENT hat, IMPERFECT hatte, PERFECT hat gehabt)
□ They're experiencing some problems. Sie haben einige Probleme.
2 empfinden (IMPERFECT empfand, PERFECT hat empfunden) *(feel)*
□ He experienced fear and excitement. Er empfand Angst und Aufregung.

experienced ADJECTIVE
erfahren

experiment NOUN
das Experiment (PL die Experimente)

expert NOUN
der Fachmann (PL die Fachleute)
die Fachfrau
□ He's a computer expert. Er ist ein Computerfachmann.
■ **He's an expert cook.** Er kocht ausgezeichnet.

to **expire** VERB
ablaufen (PRESENT läuft ab, IMPERFECT lief ab, PERFECT ist abgelaufen) *(passport)*

to **explain** VERB
erklären (PERFECT hat erklärt)

explanation NOUN
die Erklärung

to **explode** VERB
explodieren (PERFECT ist explodiert)

to **exploit** VERB
ausbeuten (PERFECT hat ausgebeutet)
exploitation NOUN
die Ausbeutung
to **explore** VERB
erkunden (PERFECT hat erkundet) *(place)*
explorer NOUN
der Forscher (PL die Forscher)
die Forscherin
explosion NOUN
die Explosion
explosive ADJECTIVE
▷ *see also* **explosive** NOUN
explosiv
explosive NOUN
▷ *see also* **explosive** ADJECTIVE
der Sprengstoff (PL die Sprengstoffe)
to **export** VERB
exportieren (PERFECT hat exportiert)
to **express** VERB
ausdrücken (PERFECT hat ausgedrückt)
■ **to express oneself** sich ausdrücken
□ I can't express myself. Ich kann mich nicht ausdrücken.
expression NOUN
der Ausdruck (PL die Ausdrücke)
■ **It's an English expression.** Das ist eine englische Redewendung.
expressway NOUN (US)
die Schnellstraße
extension NOUN
1 der Anbau (PL die Anbauten) *(of building)*
2 der Apparat (PL die Apparate) *(telephone)*
■ **Extension 3137, please.** Apparat 3137, bitte.
extensive ADJECTIVE
1 ausgedehnt
□ The hotel is situated in extensive grounds. Das Hotel liegt auf einem ausgedehnten Gelände.
2 umfangreich
□ He has an extensive knowledge of the subject. Er hat ein umfangreiches Wissen auf diesem Gebiet.
■ **extensive damage** schwere Schäden *pl*
extensively ADVERB
viel
□ He has travelled extensively. Er ist viel gereist.
extent NOUN
■ **to some extent** in gewisser Weise
exterior ADJECTIVE
äußere
□ the exterior walls die äußeren Wände
extinct ADJECTIVE
■ **to become extinct** aussterben
■ **to be extinct** ausgestorben sein
□ The species is almost extinct. Diese Art ist fast ausgestorben.
extinguisher NOUN
der Feuerlöscher (PL die Feuerlöscher) *(fire extinguisher)*
extortionate ADJECTIVE
überzogen
extra ADJECTIVE, ADVERB
zusätzlich
□ an extra blanket eine zusätzliche Decke
■ **to pay extra** extra bezahlen
■ **Breakfast is extra.** Frühstück wird extra berechnet.
■ **It costs extra.** Das kostet extra.
extraordinary ADJECTIVE
außergewöhnlich
extravagant ADJECTIVE
verschwenderisch *(person)*
extreme ADJECTIVE
extrem
extremely ADVERB
äußerst
extremist NOUN
der Extremist (GEN des Extremisten, PL die Extremisten)
die Extremistin
eye NOUN
das Auge (PL die Augen)
□ I've got green eyes. Ich habe grüne Augen.
■ **to keep an eye on something** auf etwas aufpassen
eyebrow NOUN
die Augenbraue
eyelash NOUN
die Wimper
eyelid NOUN
das Augenlid (PL die Augenlider)
eyeliner NOUN
der Eyeliner (PL die Eyeliner)
eye shadow NOUN
der Lidschatten (PL die Lidschatten)
eyesight NOUN
das Sehvermögen
□ Her eyesight is deteriorating. Ihr Sehvermögen lässt nach.
■ **to have good eyesight** gute Augen haben

Ff

fabric NOUN
der Stoff (PL die Stoffe)
fabulous ADJECTIVE
traumhaft
□ The show was fabulous. Die Show war traumhaft.
face NOUN
▷ *see also* **face** VERB
1 das Gesicht (PL die Gesichter) *(of person)*
2 das Zifferblatt (PL die Zifferblätter) *(of clock)*
3 die Wand (PL die Wände) *(of cliff)*
■ **on the face of it** auf den ersten Blick
■ **in the face of these difficulties** angesichts dieser Schwierigkeiten
■ **face to face** Auge in Auge
■ **a face cloth** ein Waschlappen *masc*
to **face** VERB
▷ *see also* **face** NOUN
konfrontiert sein mit (PRESENT ist konfrontiert mit, IMPERFECT war konfrontiert mit, PERFECT ist konfrontiert gewesen mit) *(place, problem)*
■ **to face up to something** sich einer Sache stellen □ You must face up to your responsibilities. Sie müssen sich Ihrer Verantwortung stellen.
facilities PL NOUN
die Einrichtungen *fem pl*
■ **This school has excellent facilities.** Diese Schule ist ausgezeichnet ausgestattet.
■ **toilet facilities** Toiletten *fem pl*
■ **cooking facilities** die Kochgelegenheit *sing*
fact NOUN
die Tatsache
■ **in fact** tatsächlich
factory NOUN
die Fabrik
to **fade** VERB
1 verblassen (PERFECT ist verblasst) *(colour)*
□ The colour has faded. Die Farbe ist verblasst.
■ **My jeans have faded.** Meine Jeans sind verbleicht.
2 schwächer werden (PRESENT wird schwächer, IMPERFECT wurde schwächer, PERFECT ist schwächer geworden)
□ The light was fading fast. Das Licht wurde schnell schwächer.
3 abnehmen (PRESENT nimmt ab, IMPERFECT nahm ab, PERFECT hat abgenommen)
□ The noise gradually faded. Der Lärm nahm allmählich ab.
fag NOUN
die Kippe *(informal: cigarette)*
to **fail** VERB
▷ *see also* **fail** NOUN
1 durchfallen in +*dat* (PRESENT fällt durch, IMPERFECT fiel durch, PERFECT ist durchgefallen)
□ I failed the history exam. Ich bin in der Geschichtsprüfung durchgefallen.
2 durchfallen
□ In our class, no one failed. In unserer Klasse ist niemand durchgefallen.
3 versagen (PERFECT hat versagt)
□ My brakes failed. Meine Bremsen haben versagt.
■ **to fail to do something** etwas nicht tun
□ She failed to return her library books. Sie hat die Bücher aus der Bücherei nicht zurückgebracht.
fail NOUN
▷ *see also* **fail** VERB
■ **without fail** ganz bestimmt
failure NOUN
1 das Versagen
□ a mechanical failure ein mechanisches Versagen
■ **feelings of failure** das Gefühl zu versagen
2 der Versager (PL die Versager)
die Versagerin
□ He's a failure. Er ist ein Versager.
faint ADJECTIVE
▷ *see also* **faint** VERB
schwach
□ His voice was very faint. Seine Stimme war sehr schwach.
■ **I feel faint.** Mir ist schwindlig.
to **faint** VERB
▷ *see also* **faint** ADJECTIVE
ohnmächtig werden (PRESENT wird ohnmächtig, IMPERFECT wurde ohnmächtig, PERFECT ist ohnmächtig geworden)
□ All of a sudden she fainted. Plötzlich wurde sie ohnmächtig.
fair ADJECTIVE
▷ *see also* **fair** NOUN

1 fair
□ That's not fair. Das ist nicht fair.
2 blond *(hair)*
□ He's got fair hair. Er hat blonde Haare.
3 hell *(skin)*
□ people with fair skin Menschen mit heller Haut
4 schön *(weather)*
□ The weather was fair. Das Wetter war schön.
5 gut *(good enough)*
□ I have a fair chance of winning. Ich habe gute Gewinnchancen.
6 ordentlich *(sizeable)*
□ That's a fair distance. Das ist eine ordentliche Entfernung.

fair NOUN
▹ *see also* **fair** ADJECTIVE
das Volksfest (PL die Volksfeste)
□ They went to the fair. Sie sind aufs Volksfest gegangen.
■ **a trade fair** eine Handelsmesse

fairground NOUN
der Rummelplatz (PL die Rummelplätze)

fair-haired ADJECTIVE
blond

fairly ADVERB
1 gerecht
□ The cake was divided fairly. Der Kuchen wurde gerecht verteilt.
2 ziemlich *(quite)*
□ That's fairly good. Das ist ziemlich gut.

fairness NOUN
die Fairness

fairy NOUN
die Fee

fairy tale NOUN
das Märchen (PL die Märchen)

faith NOUN
1 der Glaube (GEN des Glaubens)
□ the Catholic faith der katholische Glaube
2 das Vertrauen
□ People have lost faith in the government. Die Menschen haben das Vertrauen in die Regierung verloren.

faithful ADJECTIVE
treu

faithfully ADVERB
■ **Yours faithfully ...** *(in letter)* Hochachtungsvoll ...

fake NOUN
▹ *see also* **fake** ADJECTIVE
die Fälschung
□ The painting was a fake. Das Gemälde war eine Fälschung.

fake ADJECTIVE
▹ *see also* **fake** NOUN
gefälscht
□ a fake certificate eine gefälschte Urkunde
■ **She wore fake fur.** Sie trug eine Pelzimitation.

fall NOUN
▹ *see also* **fall** VERB
1 der Sturz (GEN des Sturzes, PL die Stürze)
■ **She had a nasty fall.** Sie ist übel gestürzt.
■ **a fall of snow** ein Schneefall *masc*
■ **the Niagara Falls** die Niagarafälle
2 der Herbst (PL die Herbste) *(US: autumn)*
□ in fall im Herbst

to fall VERB
▹ *see also* **fall** NOUN
1 hinfallen (PRESENT fällt hin, IMPERFECT fiel hin, PERFECT ist hingefallen)
□ He tripped and fell. Er ist gestolpert und hingefallen.
2 fallen
□ Prices are falling. Die Preise fallen.
■ **to fall apart** auseinanderfallen □ The book fell apart when he opened it. Das Buch fiel auseinander, als er es öffnete.
■ **to fall down 1** *(person)* hinfallen □ She's fallen down. Sie ist hingefallen.
2 *(building)* einfallen □ The wall fell down. Die Mauer ist eingefallen.
■ **to fall for 1** hereinfallen auf *+acc* □ They fell for it. Sie sind darauf hereingefallen.
2 sich verlieben in *+acc* □ She's falling for him. Sie ist dabei, sich in ihn zu verlieben.
■ **to fall off** herunterfallen von □ The book fell off the shelf. Das Buch ist vom Regal heruntergefallen.
■ **to fall out** sich zerstreiten □ Sarah's fallen out with her boyfriend. Sarah hat sich mit ihrem Freund zerstritten.
■ **to fall through** ins Wasser fallen □ Our plans have fallen through. Unsere Pläne sind ins Wasser gefallen.

false ADJECTIVE
falsch
■ **a false alarm** falscher Alarm
■ **false teeth** das Gebiss

fame NOUN
der Ruhm

familiar ADJECTIVE
vertraut
□ a familiar face ein vertrautes Gesicht
■ **to be familiar with something** mit etwas vertraut sein □ I'm familiar with his work. Ich bin mit seiner Arbeit vertraut.

family NOUN
die Familie
□ the Airlie family die Familie Airlie

famine NOUN
die Hungersnot (PL die Hungersnöte)

famous ADJECTIVE
berühmt

fan NOUN
1 der Fächer (PL die Fächer) *(hand-held)*
2 der Ventilator (PL die Ventilatoren) *(electric)*
3 der Fan (PL die Fans) *(of person, band, sport)*

LANGUAGE TIP **der Fan** is also used for women.

◻ I'm a fan of theirs. Ich bin ein Fan von ihnen. ◻ football fans Fußballfans

fanatic NOUN
der Fanatiker (PL die Fanatiker)
die Fanatikerin

to **fancy** VERB
■ **to fancy something** Lust auf etwas haben
◻ I fancy an ice cream. Ich habe Lust auf ein Eis.
■ **to fancy doing something** Lust haben, etwas zu tun
■ **He fancies her.** Er steht auf sie.

fancy dress NOUN
das Kostüm (PL die Kostüme)
■ **He was wearing fancy dress.** Er war kostümiert.
■ **a fancy-dress ball** ein Kostümball *masc*

fantastic ADJECTIVE
fantastisch

far ADJECTIVE, ADVERB
weit
◻ Is it far? Ist es weit? ◻ How far is it? Wie weit ist es? ◻ How far is it to Geneva? Wie weit ist es nach Genf?
■ **far from 1** weit entfernt von ◻ It's not far from London. Es ist nicht weit von London entfernt. **2** überhaupt nicht ◻ It's far from easy. Es ist überhaupt nicht einfach.
■ **How far have you got?** *(with a task)* Wie weit bist du gekommen?
■ **at the far end** am anderen Ende ◻ at the far end of the room am anderen Ende des Zimmers
■ **far better** viel besser
■ **as far as I know** soviel ich weiß

fare NOUN
der Fahrpreis (PL die Fahrpreise)
■ **half fare** halber Preis
■ **full fare** voller Preis

Far East NOUN
der Ferne Osten
■ **in the Far East** im Fernen Osten

farm NOUN
der Bauernhof (PL die Bauernhöfe)

farmer NOUN
der Bauer (GEN des Bauern, PL die Bauern)
die Bäuerin
◻ He's a farmer. Er ist Bauer.
■ **a farmers' market** ein Bauernmarkt *masc*

farmhouse NOUN
das Bauernhaus (GEN des Bauernhauses, PL die Bauernhäuser)

farming NOUN
die Landwirtschaft
■ **dairy farming** die Milchwirtschaft

fascinating ADJECTIVE
faszinierend

fashion NOUN
die Mode
■ **in fashion** in Mode

fashionable ADJECTIVE
modisch
◻ Jane wears very fashionable clothes. Jane trägt sehr modische Kleidung.
■ **a fashionable restaurant** ein Restaurant, das in Mode ist

fast ADJECTIVE, ADVERB
schnell
◻ He can run fast. Er kann schnell laufen.
◻ a fast car ein schnelles Auto
■ **That clock's fast.** Die Uhr geht vor.
■ **He's fast asleep.** Er schläft fest.

LANGUAGE TIP Be careful not to translate **fast** by the German word **fast**.

fat ADJECTIVE
▷ *see also* **fat** NOUN
dick *(person)*

> **WORD POWER**
> You can use a number of other words instead of **fat**:
> **chubby** pummelig
> ◻ a chubby baby ein pummeliges Baby
> **overweight** übergewichtig
> ◻ an overweight man ein übergewichtiger Mann
> **plump** rundlich
> ◻ a plump woman eine rundliche Frau

fat NOUN
▷ *see also* **fat** ADJECTIVE
das Fett (PL die Fette)
■ **It's very high in fat.** Es ist sehr fett.

fatal ADJECTIVE
1 tödlich *(causing death)*
◻ a fatal accident ein tödlicher Unfall
2 fatal *(disastrous)*
◻ He made a fatal mistake. Er machte einen fatalen Fehler.

father NOUN
der Vater (PL die Väter)
◻ my father mein Vater
■ **Father Christmas** der Weihnachtsmann

father-in-law NOUN
der Schwiegervater (PL die Schwiegerväter)

faucet NOUN (US)
der Wasserhahn (PL die Wasserhähne)

fault NOUN
1 die Schuld *(mistake)*
◻ It's my fault. Es ist meine Schuld.
2 der Fehler (PL die Fehler) *(defect)*
◻ a mechanical fault ein mechanischer Fehler

faulty ADJECTIVE
defekt
◻ This machine is faulty. Die Maschine ist defekt.

favour (US **favor**) NOUN
der Gefallen (PL die Gefallen)
■ **to do somebody a favour** jemandem einen Gefallen tun ◻ Could you do me a favour? Könntest du mir einen Gefallen tun?

■ to be in favour of something für etwas sein □ I'm in favour of nuclear disarmament. Ich bin für nukleare Abrüstung.

favourite (US **favorite**) ADJECTIVE
▷ *see also* **favourite** NOUN
■ Blue's my favourite colour. Blau ist meine Lieblingsfarbe.

favourite (US **favorite**) NOUN
▷ *see also* **favourite** ADJECTIVE
1 der Liebling (PL die Lieblinge)
LANGUAGE TIP **der Liebling** is also used for women.
□ She's his favourite. Sie ist sein Liebling.
2 der Favorit (PL die Favoriten)
die Favoritin
□ Liverpool are favourites to win the Cup. Der FC Liverpool ist Favorit für den Pokal.

fax NOUN
▷ *see also* **fax** VERB
das Fax (GEN des Fax, PL die Faxe)

to **fax** VERB
▷ *see also* **fax** NOUN
faxen

fear NOUN
▷ *see also* **fear** VERB
die Furcht

to **fear** VERB
▷ *see also* **fear** NOUN
befürchten (PERFECT hat befürchtet)
□ You have nothing to fear. Sie haben nichts zu befürchten.

feather NOUN
die Feder

feature NOUN
die Eigenschaft *(of person, object)*
□ an important feature eine wichtige Eigenschaft

February NOUN
der Februar
■ in February im Februar

fed VERB ▷ *see* **feed**

fed up ADJECTIVE
■ to be fed up with something etwas satthaben □ I'm fed up with him. Ich habe ihn satt.

to **feed** VERB
füttern
□ Have you fed the cat? Hast du die Katze gefüttert?
■ He worked hard to feed his family. Er arbeitete hart, um seine Familie zu ernähren.

to **feel** VERB
1 sich fühlen
□ I don't feel well. Ich fühle mich nicht wohl.
□ I feel a bit lonely. Ich fühle mich etwas einsam.
2 spüren
□ I didn't feel much pain. Ich habe keine großen Schmerzen gespürt.
3 befühlen (PERFECT hat befühlt)
□ The doctor felt his forehead. Der Arzt hat ihm die Stirn befühlt.
■ I was feeling hungry. Ich hatte Hunger.
■ I felt very cold. Mir war sehr kalt.
■ I feel like ... *(want)* Ich habe Lust auf ...
□ Do you feel like an ice cream? Hast du Lust auf ein Eis?

feeling NOUN
das Gefühl (PL die Gefühle)
□ a feeling of satisfaction ein Gefühl der Befriedigung
■ an itchy feeling ein Jucken *neut*

feet PL NOUN ▷ *see* **foot**

fell VERB ▷ *see* **fall**

felt VERB ▷ *see* **feel**

felt-tip pen NOUN
der Filzschreiber (PL die Filzschreiber)

female ADJECTIVE
▷ *see also* **female** NOUN
weiblich
□ a female animal ein weibliches Tier
□ the female sex das weibliche Geschlecht
LANGUAGE TIP In many cases, the ending indicates clearly whether the noun refers to a man or a woman and there is therefore no need for the word 'female'.
□ male and female students Studenten und Studentinnen

female NOUN
▷ *see also* **female** ADJECTIVE
das Weibchen (PL die Weibchen) *(animal)*

feminine ADJECTIVE
feminin

feminist NOUN
der Feminist (GEN des Feministen, PL die Feministen)
die Feministin

fence NOUN
der Zaun (PL die Zäune)

fern NOUN
der Farn (PL die Farne)

ferocious ADJECTIVE
wild

ferry NOUN
die Fähre

fertile ADJECTIVE
fruchtbar

fertilizer NOUN
das Düngemittel (PL die Düngemittel)

festival NOUN
das Festival (PL die Festivals)
□ a jazz festival ein Jazzfestival

to **fetch** VERB
1 holen
□ Fetch the bucket. Hol den Eimer.
2 einbringen (IMPERFECT brachte ein, PERFECT hat eingebracht) *(sell for)*
□ His painting fetched five thousand pounds. Sein Bild hat fünftausend Pfund eingebracht.

fever NOUN
das Fieber *(temperature)*

few ADJECTIVE, PRONOUN
wenige *(not many)*
□ few books wenige Bücher
■ **a few** ein paar □ a few hours ein paar Stunden □ How many apples do you want? — A few. Wie viele Äpfel willst du? — Ein paar.
■ **quite a few people** einige Leute

fewer ADJECTIVE
weniger
□ There are fewer people than there were yesterday. Es sind weniger Leute da als gestern. □ There are fewer students in this class. In dieser Klasse sind weniger Schüler.

fiancé NOUN
der Verlobte (GEN des Verlobten, PL die Verlobten)
□ He's my fiancé. Er ist mein Verlobter.

fiancée NOUN
die Verlobte (GEN der Verlobten, PL die Verlobten)
□ She's my fiancée. Sie ist meine Verlobte.

fiction NOUN
die Romane *masc pl (novels)*

field NOUN
1 das Feld (PL die Felder) *(in countryside)*
□ a field of wheat ein Weizenfeld
2 der Platz (GEN des Platzes, PL die Plätze) *(for sport)*
□ a football field ein Fußballplatz
3 das Gebiet (PL die Gebiete) *(subject)*
□ He's an expert in his field. Er ist Fachmann auf seinem Gebiet.

fierce ADJECTIVE
1 gefährlich
□ The dog looked very fierce. Der Hund sah sehr gefährlich aus.
2 heftig
□ a fierce attack ein heftiger Angriff
■ **The wind was very fierce.** Es wehte ein sehr scharfer Wind.

fifteen NUMBER
fünfzehn
□ I'm fifteen. Ich bin fünfzehn.

fifteenth ADJECTIVE
fünfzehnte
□ the fifteenth of August der fünfzehnte August

fifth ADJECTIVE
fünfte
□ the fifth floor der fünfte Stock □ the fifth of August der fünfte August

fifty NUMBER
fünfzig
□ He's fifty. Er ist fünfzig.

fifty-fifty ADJECTIVE, ADVERB
halbe-halbe
□ They split the money fifty-fifty. Sie teilten das Geld halbe-halbe.
■ **a fifty-fifty chance** eine fünfzigprozentige Chance

fight NOUN
▷ *see also* **fight** VERB
1 die Schlägerei
□ There was a fight in the pub. In der Kneipe gab es eine Schlägerei.
2 der Kampf (PL die Kämpfe)
□ the fight against cancer der Kampf gegen Krebs

to **fight** VERB
▷ *see also* **fight** NOUN
1 sich prügeln *(physically)*
□ They were fighting. Sie haben sich geprügelt.
2 streiten (IMPERFECT stritt, PERFECT hat gestritten) *(quarrel)*
□ He's always fighting with his wife. Er streitet dauernd mit seiner Frau.
3 bekämpfen (PERFECT hat bekämpft) *(combat)*
□ Doctors fought the disease. Die Ärzte bekämpften die Krankheit.

to **fight back** VERB
sich wehren

fighting NOUN
die Schlägerei
□ Fighting broke out outside the pub. Vor der Kneipe kam es zu einer Schlägerei.

figure NOUN
1 die Zahl *(number)*
□ Can you give me the exact figures? Können Sie mir genaue Zahlen nennen?
2 die Gestalt *(outline of person)*
□ Mary saw the figure of a man on the bridge. Mary sah die Gestalt eines Mannes auf der Brücke.
3 die Figur *(shape)*
□ She's got a good figure. Sie hat eine gute Figur. □ I have to watch my figure. Ich muss auf meine Figur achten.
4 die Persönlichkeit *(personality)*
□ She's an important political figure. Sie ist eine wichtige politische Persönlichkeit.

to **figure out** VERB
1 ausrechnen (PERFECT hat ausgerechnet)
□ I'll figure out how much it'll cost. Ich werde ausrechnen, wie viel das kostet.
2 herausfinden (IMPERFECT fand heraus, PERFECT hat herausgefunden)
□ I couldn't figure out what it meant. Ich konnte nicht herausfinden, was das bedeutet.
3 schlau werden aus (PRESENT wird schlau, IMPERFECT wurde schlau, PERFECT ist schlau geworden)
□ I can't figure him out at all. Ich werde aus ihm überhaupt nicht schlau.

file NOUN
▷ *see also* **file** VERB
1 die Akte *(document)*
□ Have we got a file on the suspect? Haben wir über den Verdächtigen eine Akte?

English–German

f

2 die Aktenmappe *(folder)*
□ She keeps all her letters in a cardboard file. Sie bewahrt all ihre Briefe in einer Aktenmappe auf.
3 der Aktenordner (PL die Aktenordner) *(ring binder)*
4 die Datei *(on computer)*
5 die Feile *(for nails, metal)*

to file VERB
▷ *see also* **file** NOUN
1 abheften (PERFECT hat abgeheftet) *(papers)*
2 feilen *(nails, metal)*
□ I'll have to file my nails. Ich muss mir die Nägel feilen.

to fill VERB
füllen
□ She filled the glass with water. Sie füllte das Glas mit Wasser.
■ **to fill in 1** ausfüllen □ Can you fill this form in, please? Können Sie bitte dieses Formular ausfüllen? **2** auffüllen □ He filled the hole in with soil. Er füllte das Loch mit Erde auf.
■ **to fill up** vollmachen □ He filled the cup up to the brim. Er machte die Tasse bis zum Rand voll.
■ **Fill it up, please.** *(at petrol station)* Volltanken, bitte.

film NOUN
der Film (PL die Filme)

film star NOUN
der Filmstar (PL die Filmstars)
LANGUAGE TIP **der Filmstar** is also used for women.
□ She's a film star. Sie ist ein Filmstar.

filthy ADJECTIVE
schmutzig

final ADJECTIVE
▷ *see also* **final** NOUN
1 letzte *(last)*
□ our final match of the season unser letztes Spiel der Saison
2 endgültig *(definite)*
□ a final decision eine endgültige Entscheidung
■ **I'm not going and that's final.** Ich gehe nicht, und damit basta.

final NOUN
▷ *see also* **final** ADJECTIVE
das Finale (PL die Finale)
□ Murray is in the final. Murray ist im Finale.

finally ADVERB
1 schließlich *(lastly)*
□ Finally, I would like to say ... Und schließlich möchte ich sagen ...
2 letztendlich *(eventually)*
□ They finally decided to leave on Saturday. Sie haben letztendlich beschlossen, am Samstag zu fahren.

financial ADJECTIVE
finanziell

to find VERB
finden (IMPERFECT fand, PERFECT hat gefunden)
□ I can't find the exit. Ich kann den Ausgang nicht finden. □ Did you find your pen? Hast du deinen Schreiber gefunden?
■ **to find something out** etwas herausfinden □ I'm determined to find out the truth. Ich bin entschlossen, die Wahrheit herauszufinden.
■ **to find out about 1** *(make enquiries)* sich erkundigen nach □ Try to find out about the cost of a hotel. Versuche, dich nach dem Preis für ein Hotel zu erkundigen.
2 *(by chance)* erfahren □ I found out about their affair. Ich habe von ihrem Verhältnis erfahren.

fine ADJECTIVE, ADVERB
▷ *see also* **fine** NOUN
1 ausgezeichnet *(very good)*
□ He's a fine musician. Er ist ein ausgezeichneter Musiker.
■ **How are you? — I'm fine.** Wie geht's? — Gut!
■ **I feel fine.** Mir geht's gut.
■ **The weather is fine today.** Das Wetter ist heute schön.
2 fein *(not coarse)*
□ She's got very fine hair. Sie hat sehr feine Haare.

fine NOUN
▷ *see also* **fine** ADJECTIVE
1 die Geldbuße
□ She got a fine. Sie hat eine Geldbuße bekommen.
2 der Strafzettel (PL die Strafzettel) *(for traffic offence)*
□ I got a fine for speeding. Ich habe einen Strafzettel bekommen, weil ich zu schnell gefahren bin.

finger NOUN
der Finger (PL die Finger)
□ my little finger mein kleiner Finger

fingernail NOUN
der Fingernagel (PL die Fingernägel)

finish NOUN
▷ *see also* **finish** VERB
das Finish (PL die Finishs) *(of race)*
□ We saw the finish of the London Marathon. Wir sahen das Finish des Londoner Marathonlaufs.

to finish VERB
▷ *see also* **finish** NOUN
1 fertig sein (PRESENT ist fertig, IMPERFECT war fertig, PERFECT ist fertig gewesen)
□ I've finished! Ich bin fertig!
2 zu Ende sein (PRESENT ist zu Ende, IMPERFECT war zu Ende, PERFECT ist zu Ende gewesen)
□ The film has finished. Der Film ist zu Ende.
■ **I've finished the book.** Ich habe das Buch zu Ende gelesen.

■ **to finish doing something** etwas zu Ende machen ▫ Let me finish writing this letter. Lass mich den Brief zu Ende schreiben.

Finland NOUN
Finnland *neut*
■ **from Finland** aus Finnland
■ **to Finland** nach Finnland

Finn NOUN
der Finne (GEN des Finnen, PL die Finnen)
die Finnin

Finnish ADJECTIVE
▹ *see also* **Finnish** NOUN
finnisch
■ **She's Finnish.** Sie ist Finnin.

Finnish NOUN
▹ *see also* **Finnish** ADJECTIVE
das Finnisch (GEN des Finnischen) *(language)*

fir NOUN
die Tanne
■ **fir cone** der Tannenzapfen
■ **fir tree** der Tannenbaum

fire NOUN
▹ *see also* **fire** VERB
1 das Feuer (PL die Feuer)
▫ He made a fire to warm himself up. Er machte ein Feuer, um sich aufzuwärmen.
■ **to be on fire** brennen
2 der Brand (PL die Brände) *(accidental)*
■ **The house was destroyed by fire.** Das Haus ist abgebrannt.
3 die Heizung *(heater)*
▫ Turn the fire on. Mach die Heizung an.
■ **the fire brigade** die Feuerwehr
■ **a fire alarm** ein Feueralarm *masc*
■ **a fire engine** ein Feuerwehrauto *neut*
■ **a fire escape** *(stairs)* eine Feuertreppe
■ **a fire extinguisher** ein Feuerlöscher *masc*
■ **a fire station** eine Feuerwehrstation

to **fire** VERB
▹ *see also* **fire** NOUN
schießen (IMPERFECT schoss, PERFECT hat geschossen) *(shoot)*
▫ She fired twice. Sie hat zweimal geschossen.
■ **to fire at somebody** auf jemanden schießen ▫ The terrorist fired at the crowd. Der Terrorist hat in die Menge geschossen.
■ **to fire a gun** einen Schuss abgeben
■ **to fire somebody** jemanden feuern
▫ He was fired from his job. Er wurde aus seinem Job gefeuert.

fireman NOUN
der Feuerwehrmann (PL die Feuerwehrleute)
▫ He's a fireman. Er ist Feuerwehrmann.

fireplace NOUN
der offene Kamin (PL die offenen Kamine)

fireworks PL NOUN
das Feuerwerk (PL die Feuerwerke)
▫ Are you going to see the fireworks? Seht ihr euch das Feuerwerk an?

firm ADJECTIVE
▹ *see also* **firm** NOUN
streng
▫ to be firm with somebody streng mit jemandem sein

firm NOUN
▹ *see also* **firm** ADJECTIVE
die Firma (PL die Firmen)
▫ He works for a large firm in London. Er arbeitet für eine große Firma in London.

first ADJECTIVE, ADVERB
▹ *see also* **first** NOUN
1 erste
▫ my first boyfriend mein erster Freund
▫ the first time das erste Mal ▫ the first of August der erste August
■ **Rachel came first.** *(in exam, race)* Rachel war Erste.
■ **John came first.** *(in exam, race)* John war Erster.
2 zuerst
▫ I want to get a job, but first I have to pass my exams. Ich will mir einen Job suchen, aber zuerst muss ich meine Prüfung bestehen.
■ **first of all** zuallererst

first NOUN
▹ *see also* **first** ADJECTIVE
der Erste (GEN des Ersten, PL die Ersten)
die Erste (GEN der Ersten)
▫ She was the first to arrive. Sie ist als Erste angekommen.
■ **at first** zuerst

first aid NOUN
die Erste Hilfe
■ **a first aid kit** ein Verbandszeug *neut*

first-class ADJECTIVE
1 erster Klasse
▫ a first-class ticket ein Ticket erster Klasse
2 erstklassig
▫ a first-class meal ein erstklassiges Essen

DID YOU KNOW...?
In Germany there is no first-class or second-class post. However, letters cost more to send than postcards, so you have to remember to say what you are sending when buying stamps. There is also an express service.

firstly ADVERB
1 zuerst
▫ Firstly, let's see what the book is about. Wir wollen erst mal sehen, wovon das Buch handelt.
2 erstens
▫ firstly ... secondly ... erstens ... zweitens ...

fish NOUN
▹ *see also* **fish** VERB
der Fisch (PL die Fische)
▫ I caught three fish. Ich habe drei Fische gefangen. ▫ I don't like fish. Ich mag Fisch nicht.

to fish VERB
▷ *see also* **fish** NOUN
fischen
■ **to go fishing** fischen gehen □ We went fishing in the River Dee. Wir haben im Dee gefischt.

fisherman NOUN
der Fischer (PL die Fischer)
□ He's a fisherman. Er ist Fischer.

fish finger NOUN
das Fischstäbchen (PL die Fischstäbchen)

fishing NOUN
das Angeln
□ My hobby is fishing. Angeln ist mein Hobby.

fishing boat NOUN
das Fischerboot (PL die Fischerboote)

fishing rod NOUN
die Angel

fishing tackle NOUN
das Angelzeug

fishmonger's NOUN
der Fischladen (PL die Fischläden)

fish sticks PL NOUN (US)
die Fischstäbchen

fist NOUN
die Faust (PL die Fäuste)

to fit VERB
▷ *see also* **fit** ADJECTIVE, NOUN
1 passen (PERFECT hat gepasst) *(be the right size)*
□ Does it fit? Passt es? □ These trousers don't fit me. *(wrong size)* Diese Hose passt mir nicht.
2 einbauen (PERFECT hat eingebaut) *(fix up)*
□ He fitted an alarm in his car. Er hat eine Alarmanlage in sein Auto eingebaut.
3 anbringen (IMPERFECT brachte an, PERFECT hat angebracht) *(attach)*
□ She fitted a plug to the hair dryer. Sie brachte am Föhn einen Stecker an.
■ **to fit in 1** *(match up)* passen zu
□ That story doesn't fit in with what he told us. Diese Geschichte passt nicht zu dem, was er uns gesagt hat. **2** *(person)* sich einpassen
□ She fitted in well at her new school. Sie hat sich in ihrer neuen Schule gut eingepasst.

fit ADJECTIVE
▷ *see also* **fit** VERB, NOUN
fit *(healthy)*
□ He felt relaxed and fit after his holiday. Nach seinem Urlaub fühlte er sich entspannt und fit.

fit NOUN
▷ *see also* **fit** ADJECTIVE, VERB
■ **to have a fit 1** *(epileptic)* einen Anfall haben **2** *(be angry)* Zustände bekommen
□ My Mum will have a fit! Meine Mutter bekommt Zustände!

fitted carpet NOUN
der Teppichboden (PL die Teppichböden)

fitted kitchen NOUN
die Einbauküche

fitting room NOUN
die Umkleidekabine

five NUMBER
fünf
□ He's five. Er ist fünf.

to fix VERB
1 reparieren (PERFECT hat repariert) *(mend)*
□ Can you fix my bike? Kannst du mein Fahrrad reparieren?
2 festlegen (PERFECT hat festgelegt) *(decide)*
□ Let's fix a date for the party. Lass uns einen Tag für die Party festlegen. □ They fixed a price for the car. Sie haben einen Preis für das Auto festgelegt.
3 machen
□ Janice fixed some food for us. Janice hat uns etwas zum Essen gemacht.

fixed ADJECTIVE
festgesetzt
□ at a fixed price zu einem festgesetzten Preis
■ **at a fixed time** zu einer bestimmten Zeit
■ **My parents have very fixed ideas.** Meine Eltern haben ziemlich festgelegte Ansichten.

fizzy ADJECTIVE
mit Kohlensäure
□ I don't like fizzy drinks. Ich mag keine Getränke mit Kohlensäure.

flabby ADJECTIVE
wabbelig

flag NOUN
die Fahne

flame NOUN
die Flamme

flamingo NOUN
der Flamingo (PL die Flamingos)

flan NOUN
1 der Kuchen (PL die Kuchen) *(sweet)*
□ a raspberry flan ein Himbeerkuchen
2 die Quiche (PL die Quiches) *(savoury)*
□ a cheese and onion flan eine Käse-Zwiebel-Quiche

flannel NOUN
der Waschlappen (PL die Waschlappen) *(for face)*

to flap VERB
flattern mit
□ The bird flapped its wings. Der Vogel flatterte mit den Flügeln.

flash NOUN
▷ *see also* **flash** VERB
das Blitzlicht (PL die Blitzlichter)
□ Has your camera got a flash? Hat dein Fotoapparat ein Blitzlicht?
■ **a flash of lightning** ein Blitz *masc*
■ **in a flash** blitzschnell

to flash VERB
▷ *see also* **flash** NOUN
1 blinken
□ The police car's blue light was flashing. Das Blaulicht des Polizeiautos blinkte.

2 leuchten mit
□ They flashed a torch in his face. Sie leuchteten ihm mit einer Taschenlampe ins Gesicht.
■ **She flashed her headlights.** Sie betätigte die Lichthupe.

flask NOUN
die Thermosflasche®

flat ADJECTIVE
▷ *see also* **flat** NOUN
1 flach
□ flat shoes flache Schuhe
■ **a flat roof** ein Flachdach *neut*
2 platt *(tyre)*
□ I've got a flat tyre. Ich habe einen platten Reifen.

flat NOUN
▷ *see also* **flat** ADJECTIVE
die Wohnung
□ She lives in a flat. Sie wohnt in einer Wohnung.

flatscreen NOUN
der Flachbildschirm (PL die Flachbildschirme)
□ a flatscreen TV ein Flachbildschirm-Fernseher

to **flatter** VERB
schmeicheln
□ Are you trying to flatter me? Willst du mir schmeicheln? □ I feel flattered. Ich fühle mich geschmeichelt.

flavour NOUN
der Geschmack (PL die Geschmäcke)
□ This cheese has a very strong flavour. Dieser Käse hat einen sehr pikanten Geschmack.
■ **Which flavour of ice cream would you like?** Was für ein Eis möchtest du?

flavouring NOUN
das Aroma (PL die Aromen)

flea NOUN
der Floh (PL die Flöhe)

flew VERB ▷ *see* **fly**

flexible ADJECTIVE
flexibel
■ **flexible working hours** gleitende Arbeitszeit

to **flick** VERB
schnipsen
□ She flicked the ash off her jumper. Sie schnipste die Asche von ihrem Pullover.
■ **to flick through a book** ein Buch durchblättern

to **flicker** VERB
flackern
□ The light flickered. Das Licht flackerte.

flight NOUN
der Flug (PL die Flüge)
□ What time is the flight to Munich? Um wie viel Uhr geht der Flug nach München?
■ **a flight of stairs** eine Treppe

flight attendant NOUN
der Flugbegleiter (PL die Flugbegleiter)
die Flugbegleiterin

to **fling** VERB
schmeißen (IMPERFECT schmiss, PERFECT hat geschmissen)
□ He flung the dictionary onto the floor. Er schmiss das Wörterbuch auf den Boden.

to **float** VERB
schwimmen (IMPERFECT schwamm, PERFECT ist geschwommen)
□ A leaf was floating on the water. Auf dem Wasser schwamm ein Blatt.

flock NOUN
■ **a flock of sheep** eine Schafherde
■ **a flock of birds** ein Vogelschwarm *neut*

flood NOUN
▷ *see also* **flood** VERB
1 die Überschwemmung
□ The rain has caused many floods. Der Regen hat zu vielen Überschwemmungen geführt.
2 die Flut
□ He received a flood of letters. Er erhielt eine Flut von Briefen.

to **flood** VERB
▷ *see also* **flood** NOUN
überschwemmen (PERFECT hat überschwemmt)
□ The river has flooded the village. Der Fluss hat das Dorf überschwemmt.

flooding NOUN
die Überschwemmung

floor NOUN
1 der Fußboden (PL die Fußböden)
■ **a tiled floor** ein Fliesenboden
■ **on the floor** auf dem Boden
2 der Stock (PL die Stock) *(storey)*
■ **the first floor** der erste Stock □ on the first floor im ersten Stock
■ **the ground floor** das Erdgeschoss
LANGUAGE TIP Be careful not to translate **floor** by **Flur**.

flop NOUN
der Flop (PL die Flops)
□ The film was a flop. Der Film war ein Flop.

floppy disk NOUN
die Diskette

florist NOUN
der Florist (GEN des Floristen, PL die Floristen)
die Floristin

flour NOUN
das Mehl (PL die Mehle)

to **flow** VERB
fließen (IMPERFECT floss, PERFECT ist geflossen)
□ Water was flowing from the pipe. Aus dem Rohr floss Wasser.

flower NOUN
▷ *see also* **flower** VERB
die Blume

to flower VERB
▷ *see also* **flower** NOUN
blühen

flown VERB ▷ *see* **fly**

flu NOUN
die Grippe
□ She's got flu. Sie hat Grippe.

fluent ADJECTIVE
■ **He speaks fluent German.** Er spricht fließend Deutsch.

flung VERB ▷ *see* **fling**

flush NOUN
▷ *see also* **flush** VERB
die Spülung *(of toilet)*

to flush VERB
▷ *see also* **flush** NOUN
■ **to flush the toilet** spülen

flute NOUN
die Querflöte
□ I play the flute. Ich spiele Querflöte.

fly NOUN
▷ *see also* **fly** VERB
die Fliege *(insect)*

to fly VERB
▷ *see also* **fly** NOUN
fliegen (IMPERFECT flog, PERFECT ist geflogen)
□ He flew from Berlin to New York. Er flog von Berlin nach New York.
■ **to fly away** wegfliegen □ The bird flew away. Der Vogel flog weg.

foal NOUN
das Fohlen (PL die Fohlen)

focus NOUN
▷ *see also* **focus** VERB
■ **to be out of focus** unscharf sein
□ The house is out of focus in this photo. Das Haus ist auf diesem Foto unscharf.

to focus VERB
▷ *see also* **focus** NOUN
scharf einstellen (PERFECT hat scharf eingestellt)
□ Try to focus the binoculars. Versuch, das Fernglas scharf einzustellen.
■ **to focus on something 1** *(with camera)* die Kamera auf etwas einstellen
□ The cameraman focused on the bird. Der Kameramann stellte die Kamera auf den Vogel ein. **2** *(concentrate)* sich auf etwas konzentrieren □ Let's focus on the plot. Wir wollen uns auf die Handlung konzentrieren.

fog NOUN
der Nebel (PL die Nebel)

foggy ADJECTIVE
neblig
□ a foggy day ein nebliger Tag

foil NOUN
die Alufolie *(kitchen foil)*
□ She wrapped the meat in foil. Sie wickelte das Fleisch in Alufolie.

fold NOUN
▷ *see also* **fold** VERB
die Falte

to fold VERB
▷ *see also* **fold** NOUN
falten
□ He folded the newspaper in half. Er faltete die Zeitung in der Mitte zusammen.
■ **to fold up 1** zusammenfalten *(paper)*
2 zusammenklappen *(chair)*
■ **to fold one's arms** die Arme verschränken
□ She folded her arms. Sie verschränkte die Arme.

folder NOUN
1 die Mappe
□ She kept all her letters in a folder. Sie bewahrte all ihre Briefe in einer Mappe auf.
2 der Ordner (PL die Ordner) *(ring binder)*

folding ADJECTIVE
■ **a folding chair** ein Klappstuhl *masc*
■ **a folding bed** ein Klappbett *neut*

to follow VERB
folgen (PERFECT ist gefolgt)
□ She followed him. Sie folgte ihm.
■ **You go first and I'll follow.** Geh du vor, ich komme nach.

following ADJECTIVE
folgend
□ the following day am folgenden Tag

fond ADJECTIVE
■ **to be fond of somebody** jemanden gernhaben □ I'm very fond of her. Ich habe sie sehr gern.

food NOUN
die Nahrung
■ **We need to buy some food.** Wir müssen etwas zum Essen kaufen.
■ **cat food** das Katzenfutter
■ **dog food** das Hundefutter

food processor NOUN
die Küchenmaschine

fool NOUN
der Idiot (GEN des Idioten, PL die Idioten)
die Idiotin

foot NOUN
1 der Fuß (GEN des Fußes, PL die Füße) *(of person)*
□ My feet are aching. Mir tun die Füße weh.
■ **on foot** zu Fuß
2 der Fuß (PL die Fuß) *(12 inches)*

DID YOU KNOW...?
In Germany measurements are in metres and centimetres rather than feet and inches. A foot is about 30 centimetres.

□ Dave is six foot tall. Dave ist ein Meter achtzig groß. □ That mountain is five thousand feet high. Dieser Berg ist eintausendsechshundert Meter hoch.

football NOUN
der Fußball (PL die Fußbälle)
□ I like playing football. Ich spiele gern

Fußball. □ Paul threw the football over the fence. Paul warf den Fußball über den Zaun.

footballer NOUN
der Fußballer (PL die Fußballer)
die Fußballerin

football player NOUN
der Fußballspieler (PL die Fußballspieler)
die Fußballspielerin
□ He's a famous football player. Er ist ein bekannter Fußballspieler.

footpath NOUN
der Fußweg (PL die Fußwege)
□ the footpath through the forest der Fußweg durch den Wald

footprint NOUN
der Fußabdruck (PL die Fußabdrücke)
□ He saw footprints in the sand. Er sah Fußabdrücke im Sand.

footstep NOUN
der Schritt (PL die Schritte)
□ I can hear footsteps on the stairs. Ich höre Schritte auf der Treppe.

for PREPOSITION

LANGUAGE TIP There are several ways of translating 'for'. Scan the examples to find one that is similar to what you want to say.

1 für
□ a present for me ein Geschenk für mich □ He works for the government. Er arbeitet für die Regierung. □ I'll do it for you. Ich mache es für dich. □ Are you for or against the idea? Bist du für oder gegen die Idee? □ Oxford is famous for its university. Oxford ist für seine Universität berühmt. □ I sold it for five pounds. Ich habe es für fünf Pfund verkauft.
■ **What for?** Wofür? □ Give me some money! — What for? Gib mir Geld! — Wofür? □ What's it for? Wofür ist das?

LANGUAGE TIP When referring to periods of time, use **lang** for the future and completed action in the past, and **seit** (with the German verb in the present tense) for something that started in the past and is still going on.

2 lang
□ He worked in Germany for two years. Er hat zwei Jahre lang in Deutschland gearbeitet. □ She will be away for a month. Sie wird einen Monat lang weg sein.
■ **There are road works for three kilometres.** Es gibt dort über drei Kilometer Bauarbeiten.

3 seit
□ He's been learning German for two years. Er lernt seit zwei Jahren Deutsch. □ She's been away for a month. Sie ist seit einem Monat weg.
■ **What's the German for 'lion'?** Wie sagt man 'lion' auf Deutsch?
■ **It's time for lunch.** Es ist Zeit zum Mittagessen.
■ **the train for London** der Zug nach London
■ **for sale** zu verkaufen □ The factory's for sale. Die Fabrik ist zu verkaufen.

to **forbid** VERB
verbieten (IMPERFECT verbot, PERFECT hat verboten)
■ **to forbid somebody to do something** jemandem verbieten, etwas zu tun □ I forbid you to go out tonight! Ich verbiete dir, heute Abend auszugehen!

forbidden ADJECTIVE
verboten
□ Smoking is strictly forbidden. Rauchen ist streng verboten.

force NOUN
▷ *see also* **force** VERB
die Gewalt
□ the forces of nature die Naturgewalten
■ **The force of the explosion blew out all the windows.** Die Explosion war so stark, dass alle Fenster kaputtgingen.
■ **in force** in Kraft □ The new law has been in force since May. Das neue Gesetz ist seit Mai in Kraft.

to **force** VERB
▷ *see also* **force** NOUN
zwingen (IMPERFECT zwang, PERFECT hat gezwungen)
□ They forced him to open the safe. Sie zwangen ihn, den Safe aufzumachen.

forecast NOUN
■ **the weather forecast** die Wettervorhersage

foreground NOUN
der Vordergrund
□ in the foreground im Vordergrund

forehead NOUN
die Stirn

foreign ADJECTIVE
ausländisch

foreigner NOUN
der Ausländer (PL die Ausländer)
die Ausländerin

to **foresee** VERB
vorhersehen (PRESENT sieht vorher, IMPERFECT sah vorher, PERFECT hat vorhergesehen)
□ He had foreseen the problem. Er hatte das Problem vorhergesehen.

forest NOUN
der Wald (PL die Wälder)

forever ADVERB
1 für immer
□ He's gone forever. Er ist für immer weg.
2 dauernd *(always)*
□ She's forever complaining. Sie beklagt sich dauernd.

forgave VERB ▷ *see* **forgive**

English-German

f

to **forge** VERB
fälschen
▫ She tried to forge his signature. Sie versuchte, seine Unterschrift zu fälschen.

forged ADJECTIVE
gefälscht
▫ forged banknotes gefälschte Banknoten

to **forget** VERB
vergessen (PRESENT vergisst, IMPERFECT vergaß, PERFECT hat vergessen)
▫ I've forgotten his name. Ich habe seinen Namen vergessen. ▫ I'm sorry, I completely forgot! Tut mir leid, das habe ich total vergessen!

forgetful ADJECTIVE
vergesslich

to **forgive** VERB
▪ **to forgive somebody** jemandem verzeihen
▫ I forgive you. Ich verzeihe dir.
▪ **to forgive somebody for doing something** jemandem verzeihen, etwas getan zu haben
▫ She forgave him for forgetting her birthday. Sie verzieh ihm, dass er ihren Geburtstag vergessen hat.

forgot, forgotten VERB ▹*see* **forget**

fork NOUN
1 die Gabel *(for eating, gardening)*
▫ He ate his chips with a fork. Er aß seine Pommes frites mit einer Gabel.
2 die Gabelung *(in road)*
▪ **There was a fork in the road.** Die Straße gabelte sich.

form NOUN
1 das Formular (PL die Formulare) *(paper)*
▫ to fill in a form ein Formular ausfüllen
2 die Form *(type)*
▫ I'm against hunting in any form. Ich bin gegen die Jagd in jeglicher Form.
▪ **in top form** in Topform

formal ADJECTIVE
1 formell *(occasion)*
▫ a formal dinner ein formelles Abendessen
2 förmlich *(person)*
3 gehoben *(language)*
▫ a formal word ein gehobener Ausdruck
▪ **formal clothes** die Gesellschaftskleidung *sing*
▪ **He's got no formal qualifications.** Er hat keinen offiziellen Abschluss.

former ADJECTIVE
früher
▫ a former pupil ein früherer Schüler
▫ the former Prime Minister der frühere Premierminister

formerly ADVERB
früher

fort NOUN
das Fort (PL die Forts)

forth ADVERB
▪ **to go back and forth** hin- und hergehen
▪ **and so forth** und so weiter

forthcoming ADJECTIVE
kommend
▫ the forthcoming meeting die kommende Besprechung

fortnight NOUN
▪ **a fortnight** vierzehn Tage ▫ I'm going on holiday for a fortnight. Ich verreise für vierzehn Tage.

fortunate ADJECTIVE
▪ **to be fortunate** Glück haben ▫ He was extremely fortunate to survive. Es war Glück, dass er überlebt hat.
▪ **It's fortunate that I remembered the map.** Zum Glück habe ich an die Landkarte gedacht.

fortunately ADVERB
zum Glück
▫ Fortunately, it didn't rain. Zum Glück hat es nicht geregnet.

fortune NOUN
das Vermögen (PL die Vermögen)
▫ Kate earns a fortune! Kate verdient ein Vermögen!
▪ **to tell somebody's fortune** jemandem wahrsagen

forty NUMBER
vierzig
▫ He's forty. Er ist vierzig.

forward ADVERB
▹*see also* **forward** VERB
▪ **to move forward** sich vorwärtsbewegen

to **forward** VERB
▹*see also* **forward** ADVERB
nachsenden (IMPERFECT sandte nach, PERFECT hat nachgesandt)
▫ He forwarded all her letters. Er sandte alle ihre Briefe nach.

to **foster** VERB
in Pflege nehmen (PRESENT nimmt, IMPERFECT nahm, PERFECT hat genommen)
▫ She has fostered more than fifteen children. Sie hat mehr als fünfzehn Kinder in Pflege genommen.

foster child NOUN
das Pflegekind (PL die Pflegekinder)
▫ She's their foster child. Sie ist ihr Pflegekind.

fought VERB ▹*see* **fight**

foul ADJECTIVE
▹*see also* **foul** NOUN
furchtbar
▫ The weather was foul. Das Wetter war furchtbar. ▫ What a foul smell! Was für ein furchtbarer Gestank!

foul NOUN
▹*see also* **foul** ADJECTIVE
das Foul (PL die Fouls)
▫ Ferguson committed a foul. Ferguson hat ein Foul begangen.

found VERB ▷ *see* **find**

to **found** VERB
gründen
□ Baden-Powell founded the Scout Movement. Baden-Powell hat die Pfadfinderbewegung gegründet.

foundations PL NOUN
das Fundament (PL die Fundamente)

fountain NOUN
der Brunnen (PL die Brunnen)

fountain pen NOUN
der Füllfederhalter (PL die Füllfederhalter)

four NUMBER
vier
□ She's four. Sie ist vier.

fourteen NUMBER
vierzehn
□ I'm fourteen. Ich bin vierzehn.

fourteenth ADJECTIVE
vierzehnte
□ the fourteenth of August der vierzehnte August

fourth ADJECTIVE
vierte
□ the fourth floor der vierte Stock
□ the fourth of August der vierte August

fox NOUN
der Fuchs (GEN des Fuchses, PL die Füchse)

fragile ADJECTIVE
zerbrechlich

frame NOUN
der Rahmen (PL die Rahmen) *(for picture)*

France NOUN
Frankreich *neut*
■ **from France** aus Frankreich
■ **in France** in Frankreich
■ **to France** nach Frankreich

frantic ADJECTIVE
■ **I was going frantic.** Ich bin fast durchgedreht.
■ **I was frantic with worry.** Ich habe mir furchtbare Sorgen gemacht.

fraud NOUN
1 der Betrug *(crime)*
□ He was jailed for fraud. Er kam wegen Betrugs ins Gefängnis.
2 der Betrüger (PL die Betrüger)
die Betrügerin *(person)*
□ He's not a real doctor, he's a fraud. Er ist kein echter Arzt, er ist ein Betrüger.

freckles PL NOUN
die Sommersprossen *pl*

free ADJECTIVE
▷ *see also* **free** VERB
1 kostenlos *(free of charge)*
□ a free brochure eine kostenlose Broschüre
2 frei *(not busy, not taken)*
□ Is this seat free? Ist dieser Platz frei?
■ **'admission free'** 'Eintritt frei'
■ **Are you free after school?** Hast du nach der Schule Zeit?

to **free** VERB
▷ *see also* **free** ADJECTIVE
befreien (PERFECT hat befreit)

freedom NOUN
die Freiheit

freeway NOUN (US)
die Autobahn

to **freeze** VERB
1 gefrieren (IMPERFECT gefror, PERFECT ist gefroren)
□ The water had frozen. Das Wasser war gefroren.
2 einfrieren *(food)*
□ She froze the rest of the raspberries. Sie hat die restlichen Himbeeren eingefroren.

freezer NOUN
der Gefrierschrank (PL die Gefrierschränke)

freezing ADJECTIVE
■ **It's freezing!** Es ist eiskalt! *(informal)*
■ **I'm freezing!** Mir ist eiskalt! *(informal)*
■ **three degrees below freezing** drei Grad minus

freight NOUN
die Fracht *(goods)*
■ **a freight train** ein Güterzug *masc*

French ADJECTIVE
▷ *see also* **French** NOUN
französisch
□ He's French. Er ist Franzose.
□ She's French. Sie ist Französin.

French NOUN
▷ *see also* **French** ADJECTIVE
das Französisch (GEN des Französischen) *(language)*
□ Do you speak French? Sprechen Sie Französisch?
■ **the French** *(people)* die Franzosen *masc pl*

French beans PL NOUN
die grünen Bohnen *fem pl*
□ She's very fond of French beans. Sie mag grüne Bohnen besonders gern.

French fries PL NOUN
die Pommes frites *pl*

French horn NOUN
das Waldhorn (PL die Waldhörner)
□ I play the French horn. Ich spiele Waldhorn.

French kiss NOUN
der Zungenkuss (GEN des Zungenkusses, PL die Zungenküsse)

French loaf NOUN
das Stangenbrot (PL die Stangenbrote)

Frenchman NOUN
der Franzose (GEN des Franzosen, PL die Franzosen)

French windows PL NOUN
die Verandatür

Frenchwoman NOUN
die Französin

frequent ADJECTIVE
häufig

□ frequent showers häufige Niederschläge
■ **There are frequent buses to the town centre.** Es gehen häufig Busse ins Stadtzentrum.

fresh ADJECTIVE
frisch
□ I need some fresh air. Ich brauche frische Luft.

to **freshen up** VERB
sich frisch machen
□ I'd like to go and freshen up. Ich würde mich gerne frisch machen.

to **fret** VERB
sich verrückt machen
□ Don't fret about your exams. Mach dich wegen der Prüfung nicht verrückt.

Friday NOUN
der Freitag (PL die Freitage)
□ on Friday am Freitag □ every Friday jeden Freitag □ last Friday letzten Freitag □ next Friday nächsten Freitag
■ **on Fridays** freitags

fridge NOUN
der Kühlschrank (PL die Kühlschränke)

fried ADJECTIVE
gebraten
□ fried onions gebratene Zwiebeln
■ **a fried egg** ein Spiegelei *neut*

friend NOUN
der Freund (PL die Freunde)
die Freundin

friendly ADJECTIVE
freundlich
□ She's really friendly. Sie ist wirklich freundlich. □ Liverpool is a very friendly city. Liverpool ist eine sehr freundliche Stadt.

friendship NOUN
die Freundschaft

fright NOUN
der Schrecken (PL die Schrecken)
□ I got a terrible fright! Ich habe einen furchtbaren Schrecken bekommen!

to **frighten** VERB
Angst machen
□ Horror films frighten him. Horrorfilme machen ihm Angst.

frightened ADJECTIVE
■ **to be frightened** Angst haben
□ I'm frightened! Ich habe Angst!
■ **to be frightened of something** vor etwas Angst haben □ Anna's frightened of spiders. Anna hat Angst vor Spinnen.

frightening ADJECTIVE
beängstigend

fringe NOUN
der Pony (PL die Ponys) *(of hair)*
□ She's got a fringe. Sie hat einen Pony.

Frisbee® NOUN
das Frisbee® (PL die Frisbees)
□ to play Frisbee Frisbee spielen

fro ADVERB
■ **to and fro** hin und her

frog NOUN
der Frosch (PL die Frösche)

from PREPOSITION
1 aus *(from country, town)*
□ I'm from Yorkshire. Ich bin aus Yorkshire.
□ I come from Perth. Ich bin aus Perth.
■ **Where do you come from?** Woher sind Sie?
2 von *(from person)*
□ a letter from my sister ein Brief von meiner Schwester
■ **The hotel is one kilometre from the beach.** Das Hotel ist einen Kilometer vom Strand entfernt.
3 ab *(number)*
□ from ten pounds ab zehn Pfund □ from the age of fourteen ab vierzehn
■ **from ... to ...** 1 *(distance)* von ... nach ...
□ He flew from London to Paris. Er flog von London nach Paris. 2 *(time)* von ... bis ...
□ from one o'clock to two von eins bis zwei
■ **The price was reduced from ten pounds to five.** Der Preis war von zehn auf fünf Pfund herabgesetzt.
■ **from ... onwards** ab ... □ We'll be at home from seven o'clock onwards. Wir werden ab sieben Uhr zu Hause sein.

front NOUN
▷ *see also* **front** ADJECTIVE
die Vorderseite
□ the front of the house die Vorderseite des Hauses
■ **in front** davor □ a house with a car in front ein Haus mit einem Auto davor
■ **in front of** vor

> LANGUAGE TIP Use the accusative to express movement or a change of place. Use the dative when there is no change of place.

□ He stood in front of the house. Er stand vor dem Haus. □ He ran in front of a bus. Er lief vor einen Bus. □ the car in front of us das Auto vor uns
■ **in the front** *(of car)* vorn □ I was sitting in the front. Ich saß vorn.
■ **at the front of the train** vorn im Zug

front ADJECTIVE
▷ *see also* **front** NOUN
vordere
□ the front row die vordere Reihe □ the front seats of the car die vorderen Sitze des Autos
■ **the front door** die Haustür

frontier NOUN
die Grenze

frost NOUN
der Frost (PL die Fröste)

frosting NOUN (US)
der Zuckerguss (GEN des Zuckergusses)

frosty ADJECTIVE
frostig
□ It's frosty today. Heute ist es frostig.
to **frown** VERB
die Stirn runzeln
□ He frowned. Er runzelte die Stirn.
froze, frozen VERB ▷ *see* **freeze**
frozen ADJECTIVE
▷ *see also* **freeze**
tiefgefroren *(food)*
□ frozen chips tiefgefrorene Pommes frites
fruit NOUN
1 die Frucht (PL die Früchte)
□ an exotic fruit eine exotische Frucht
2 das Obst
□ Fruit is very healthy. Obst ist sehr gesund.
■ **fruit juice** der Fruchtsaft
■ **a fruit salad** ein Obstsalat *masc*
fruit machine NOUN
der Spielautomat (GEN des Spielautomaten, PL die Spielautomaten)
frustrated ADJECTIVE
frustriert
to **fry** VERB
braten (PRESENT brät, IMPERFECT briet, PERFECT hat gebraten)
□ Fry the onions for five minutes. Braten Sie die Zwiebeln fünf Minuten lang.
frying pan NOUN
die Bratpfanne
fuel NOUN
das Benzin (PL die Benzine) *(for car, aeroplane)*
□ to run out of fuel kein Benzin mehr haben
to **fulfil** VERB
erfüllen (PERFECT hat erfüllt)
□ Robert fulfilled his dream of becoming a pilot. Robert hat sich seinen Traum erfüllt und ist Pilot geworden.
full ADJECTIVE, ADVERB
1 voll
□ The tank's full. Der Tank ist voll.
2 ausführlich
□ He asked for full information on the job. Er bat um ausführliche Informationen über die Stelle.
■ **your full name** Name und Vornamen
■ **My full name is Ian John Marr.** Ich heiße Ian John Marr.
■ **I'm full.** *(after meal)* Ich bin satt.
■ **at full speed** mit Höchstgeschwindigkeit
□ He drove at full speed. Er fuhr Höchstgeschwindigkeit.
■ **There was a full moon.** Es war Vollmond.
full stop NOUN
der Punkt (PL die Punkte)
full-time ADJECTIVE, ADVERB
ganztags
□ She works full-time. Sie arbeitet ganztags.
■ **She's got a full-time job.** Sie hat einen Ganztagsjob.
fully ADVERB
ganz
□ He hasn't yet fully recovered. Er hat sich noch nicht ganz erholt.
fumes PL NOUN
die Abgase *neut pl*
□ dangerous fumes gefährliche Abgase
■ **exhaust fumes** Autoabgase
fun ADJECTIVE
▷ *see also* **fun** NOUN
lustig
□ She's a fun person. Sie ist ein lustiger Mensch.
fun NOUN
▷ *see also* **fun** ADJECTIVE
■ **to have fun** Spaß haben □ We had great fun playing in the snow. Wir hatten beim Spielen im Schnee unseren Spaß.
■ **for fun** zum Spaß □ He entered the competition just for fun. Er hat am Wettbewerb nur zum Spaß mitgemacht.
■ **to make fun of somebody** sich über jemanden lustig machen □ They made fun of him. Sie machten sich über ihn lustig.
■ **It's fun!** Das macht Spaß!
■ **Have fun!** Viel Spaß!
funds PL NOUN
■ **to raise funds** Spenden sammeln
funeral NOUN
die Beerdigung
funfair NOUN
das Volksfest (PL die Volksfeste)
funny ADJECTIVE
1 lustig *(amusing)*
□ It was really funny. Es war wirklich lustig.
2 komisch *(strange)*
□ There's something funny about him. Er hat etwas Komisches an sich.
fur NOUN
1 der Pelz (GEN des Pelzes, PL die Pelze)
□ a fur coat ein Pelzmantel *masc*
2 das Fell (PL die Felle)
□ the dog's fur das Fell des Hundes
furious ADJECTIVE
wütend
□ Dad was furious with me. Papa war wütend auf mich.
furniture NOUN
die Möbel *neut pl*
□ a piece of furniture ein Möbelstück *neut*
further ADVERB, ADJECTIVE
weiter entfernt
□ London is further from Manchester than Leeds is. London ist weiter von Manchester entfernt als Leeds.
■ **How much further is it?** Wie weit ist es noch?
further education NOUN
die Weiterbildung
fuse NOUN
die Sicherung

□ The fuse has blown. Die Sicherung ist durchgebrannt.

fuss NOUN
die Aufregung
□ What's all the fuss about? Was soll die ganze Aufregung?
■ **to make a fuss** Theater machen
□ He's always making a fuss about nothing. Er macht immer Theater wegen nichts.

fussy ADJECTIVE
pingelig
□ She is very fussy about her food. Sie ist mit dem Essen sehr pingelig.

future NOUN
1 die Zukunft
■ **in future** in Zukunft □ Be more careful in future. Sei in Zukunft vorsichtiger.
■ **What are your plans for the future?** Was für Zukunftspläne haben Sie?
2 das Futur *(in grammar)*
□ Put this sentence into the future. Setzt diesen Satz ins Futur.

Gg

to **gain** VERB
■ **to gain weight** zunehmen
■ **to gain speed** schneller werden
gallery NOUN
die Galerie
□ an art gallery eine Kunstgalerie
to **gamble** VERB
spielen
gambler NOUN
der Spieler (PL die Spieler)
die Spielerin
gambling NOUN
das Glücksspiel (PL die Glücksspiele)
■ **He likes gambling.** Er spielt gern.
game NOUN
das Spiel (PL die Spiele)
□ The children were playing a game. Die Kinder spielten ein Spiel. □ a game of football ein Fußballspiel □ a game of cards ein Kartenspiel
gang NOUN
die Gang (PL die Gangs)
gangster NOUN
der Gangster (PL die Gangster)
gap NOUN
1 die Lücke
□ There's a gap in the hedge. In der Hecke ist eine Lücke.
2 die Pause
□ a gap of four years eine Pause von vier Jahren
garage NOUN
1 die Garage *(for parking cars)*
2 die Werkstatt (PL die Werkstätten) *(for repairs)*
garbage NOUN
der Müll
□ the garbage can die Mülltonne
■ **That's garbage!** Das ist Blödsinn!
garden NOUN
der Garten (PL die Gärten)
garden centre NOUN
das Gartencenter (PL die Gartencenter)
gardener NOUN
der Gärtner (PL die Gärtner)
die Gärtnerin
□ He's a gardener. Er ist Gärtner.
gardening NOUN
die Gartenarbeit
□ Margaret loves gardening. Margaret liebt Gartenarbeit.
gardens PL NOUN
der Park *sing* (PL die Parks)
garlic NOUN
der Knoblauch
garment NOUN
das Kleidungsstück (PL die Kleidungsstücke)
gas NOUN
1 das Gas (PL die Gase)
■ **a gas cooker** ein Gasherd *masc*
■ **a gas cylinder** eine Gasflasche
■ **a gas fire** ein Gasofen *masc*
■ **a gas leak** eine undichte Stelle in der Gasleitung
2 das Benzin (US)
■ **a gas station** eine Tankstelle
gasoline NOUN (US)
das Benzin
gate NOUN
1 das Tor (PL die Tore) *(of garden)*
2 das Gatter (PL die Gatter) *(of field)*
3 der Flugsteig (PL die Flugsteige) *(at airport)*
gateau NOUN
die Torte
to **gather** VERB
sich versammeln (PERFECT haben sich versammelt) *(assemble)*
□ People gathered in front of the church. Menschen versammelten sich vor der Kirche.
■ **to gather speed** schneller werden □ The train gathered speed. Der Zug wurde schneller.
gave VERB ▷ *see* **give**
gay ADJECTIVE
schwul *(homosexual)*
to **gaze** VERB
■ **to gaze at something** etwas anstarren
□ He gazed at her. Er starrte sie an.
GCSE NOUN *(= General Certificate of Secondary Education)*
die mittlere Reife
gear NOUN
1 der Gang (PL die Gänge) *(in car)*
□ in first gear im ersten Gang
■ **to change gear** schalten
2 die Ausrüstung
□ camping gear die Campingausrüstung
■ **your sports gear** *(clothes)* dein Sportzeug *neut*

gear lever NOUN
der Schalthebel (PL die Schalthebel)

gearshift NOUN (US)
der Schaltknüppel (PL die Schaltknüppel)

geese PL NOUN ▷ *see* **goose**

gel NOUN
das Gel (PL die Gele)

LANGUAGE TIP Note that in German the 'g' in **Gel** is pronounced like the 'g' in girl.

□ hair gel das Haargel

gem NOUN
der Edelstein (PL die Edelsteine)

Gemini SING NOUN
die Zwillinge *masc pl*
□ I'm Gemini. Ich bin Zwilling.

gender NOUN
das Geschlecht (PL die Geschlechter)

general NOUN
▷ *see also* **general** ADJECTIVE
der General (PL die Generäle)

general ADJECTIVE
▷ *see also* **general** NOUN
allgemein
■ **in general** im Allgemeinen

general election NOUN
die allgemeinen Wahlen *fem pl*

general knowledge NOUN
die Allgemeinbildung

generally ADVERB
normalerweise
□ I generally go shopping on Saturday. Ich gehe normalerweise samstags einkaufen.

generation NOUN
die Generation
□ the younger generation die jüngere Generation

generator NOUN
der Generator (PL die Generatoren)

generous ADJECTIVE
großzügig
□ That's very generous of you. Das ist sehr großzügig von Ihnen.

genetic ADJECTIVE
genetisch

genetically ADVERB
genetisch
■ **genetically modified** genmanipuliert

Geneva NOUN
Genf *neut*
■ **to Geneva** nach Genf
■ **Lake Geneva** der Genfer See

genius NOUN
das Genie (PL die Genies)
□ She's a genius! Sie ist ein Genie!

gentle ADJECTIVE
sanft

gentleman NOUN
der Gentleman (PL die Gentlemen)
■ **Good morning, gentlemen.** Guten Morgen, meine Herren.

gently ADVERB
sanft

gents SING NOUN
die Herrentoilette
■ **'gents'** *(on sign)* 'Herren'

genuine ADJECTIVE
1 echt *(real)*
□ These are genuine diamonds. Das sind echte Diamanten.
2 geradlinig *(sincere)*
□ She's a very genuine person. Sie ist ein sehr geradliniger Mensch.

geography NOUN
die Geografie

gerbil NOUN
die Wüstenrennmaus (PL die Wüstenrennmäuse)

germ NOUN
die Bazille

German ADJECTIVE
▷ *see also* **German** NOUN
deutsch
□ He is German. Er ist Deutscher. □ She is German. Sie ist Deutsche.
■ **German shepherd** der Schäferhund

German NOUN
▷ *see also* **German** ADJECTIVE
1 der Deutsche (GEN des Deutschen, PL die Deutschen)
die Deutsche (GEN der Deutschen) *(person)*
□ a German *(man)* ein Deutscher
■ **the Germans** die Deutschen
2 das Deutsch (GEN des Deutschen) *(language)*
□ Do you speak German? Sprechen sie Deutsch?

German measles NOUN
die Röteln *pl*
□ to have German measles die Röteln haben

Germany NOUN
Deutschland *neut*
■ **from Germany** aus Deutschland
■ **in Germany** in Deutschland
■ **to Germany** nach Deutschland

gesture NOUN
die Geste

to **get** VERB
1 bekommen (IMPERFECT bekam, PERFECT hat bekommen) *(receive)*
□ I got lots of presents. Ich habe viele Geschenke bekommen. □ He got first prize. Er hat den ersten Preis bekommen.
□ Jackie got good exam results. Jackie hat gute Noten bekommen.
■ **have got** haben □ How many have you got? Wie viele hast du?
2 holen *(fetch)*
□ Get help! Hol Hilfe!
3 fassen *(catch)*
□ They've got the thief. Sie haben den Dieb gefasst.

4 nehmen (PRESENT nimmt, IMPERFECT nahm, PERFECT hat genommen) *(train, bus)*
□ I'm getting the bus into town. Ich nehme den Bus in die Stadt.
5 verstehen (IMPERFECT verstand, PERFECT hat verstanden) *(understand)*
□ I don't get the joke. Ich verstehe den Witz nicht.
6 kommen (IMPERFECT kam, PERFECT ist gekommen) *(go)*
□ How do you get to the castle? Wie kommt man zur Burg?
7 werden (PRESENT wird, IMPERFECT wurde, PERFECT ist geworden) *(become)*
□ to get old alt werden
■ **to get something done** etwas machen lassen □ to get something repaired etwas reparieren lassen □ to get one's hair cut sich die Haare schneiden lassen
■ **to get something for somebody** jemandem etwas holen □ She got the book for me. Sie holte mir das Buch.
■ **to have got to do something** etwas tun müssen □ I've got to tell him. Ich muss es ihm sagen.
■ **to get away** entkommen □ One of the burglars got away. Einer der Einbrecher ist entkommen.
■ **You'll never get away with it.** Das wird man dir niemals durchgehen lassen.
■ **to get back** **1** zurückkommen □ What time did you get back? Wann seid ihr zurückgekommen? **2** zurückbekommen □ He got his money back. Er hat sein Geld zurückbekommen.
■ **to get down** herunterkommen □ Get down from there! Komm da runter!
■ **to get in** heimkommen □ What time did you get in last night? Wann bist du heute Nacht nach Hause gekommen?
■ **to get into** einsteigen in *+acc* □ Sharon got into the car. Sharon stieg ins Auto ein.
■ **to get off** **1** *(vehicle)* aussteigen aus □ Isobel got off the train. Isobel stieg aus dem Zug aus. **2** *(bike)* absteigen von □ He got off his bike. Er stieg vom Fahrrad ab.
■ **to get on** **1** *(vehicle)* einsteigen in *+acc* □ Phyllis got on the bus. Phyllis stieg in den Bus ein. **2** *(bike)* steigen auf *+acc* □ Carol got on her bike. Carol stieg auf ihr Fahrrad.
■ **to get on with somebody** sich mit jemandem verstehen □ He doesn't get on with his parents. Er versteht sich nicht mit seinen Eltern. □ We got on really well. Wir haben uns wirklich gut verstanden.
■ **to get out** aussteigen aus □ Jason got out of the car. Jason stieg aus dem Auto aus.
■ **Get out!** Raus!
■ **to get something out** etwas hervorholen □ She got the map out. Sie holte die Karte hervor.
■ **to get over something** **1** sich von etwas erholen □ It took her a long time to get over the illness. Sie brauchte lange Zeit, um sich von der Krankheit zu erholen. **2** etwas überwinden □ He managed to get over the problem. Er konnte das Problem überwinden.
■ **to get round to something** zu etwas kommen □ I'll get round to it eventually. Ich werde schon noch dazu kommen.
■ **to get together** sich treffen □ Could we get together this evening? Könnten wir uns heute abend treffen?
■ **to get up** aufstehen □ What time do you get up? Wann stehst du auf?

ghetto blaster NOUN
das tragbare Kofferradio (PL die tragbaren Kofferradios)

ghost NOUN
das Gespenst (PL die Gespenster)

giant ADJECTIVE
▷ *see also* **giant** NOUN
riesig
□ They ate a giant meal. Sie haben ein riesiges Essen vertilgt.

giant NOUN
▷ *see also* **giant** ADJECTIVE
der Riese (GEN des Riesen, PL die Riesen)
die Riesin

gift NOUN
1 das Geschenk (PL die Geschenke) *(present)*
2 die Begabung *(talent)*
■ **to have a gift for something** für etwas begabt sein □ Dave has a gift for painting. Dave ist künstlerisch begabt.

LANGUAGE TIP Be careful not to translate **gift** by the German word **Gift**.

gifted ADJECTIVE
begabt
□ Janice is a gifted pianist. Janice ist eine begabte Pianistin.

gift shop NOUN
der Geschenkladen (PL die Geschenkläden)

gigantic ADJECTIVE
riesengroß

to **giggle** VERB
kichern

gin NOUN
der Gin (PL die Gins *or* Gin)

LANGUAGE TIP When ordering more than one gin use the plural form **Gin**.

□ Three gins, please. Drei Gin bitte.
■ **a gin and tonic** ein Gin Tonic

ginger NOUN
▷ *see also* **ginger** ADJECTIVE
der Ingwer
□ Add a teaspoon of ginger. Fügen Sie einen Teelöffel Ingwer zu.

ginger ADJECTIVE
▷ *see also* **ginger** NOUN
rot
□ David has ginger hair. David hat rote Haare.

gipsy NOUN
der Zigeuner (PL die Zigeuner)
die Zigeunerin

giraffe NOUN
die Giraffe

girl NOUN
das Mädchen (PL die Mädchen)
□ They've got a girl and two boys. Sie haben ein Mädchen und zwei Jungen. □ a five-year-old girl ein fünfjähriges Mädchen
■ **an English girl** eine junge Engländerin

girlfriend NOUN
die Freundin
□ Damon's girlfriend is called Justine. Damons Freundin heißt Justine. □ She often went out with her girlfriends. Sie ging oft mit ihren Freundinnen aus.

to **give** VERB
geben (PRESENT gibt, IMPERFECT gab, PERFECT hat gegeben)
■ **to give something to somebody** jemandem etwas geben □ He gave me ten pounds. Er gab mir zehn Pfund.
■ **to give something back to somebody** jemandem etwas zurückgeben □ I gave the book back to him. Ich habe ihm das Buch zurückgegeben.
■ **to give in** nachgeben □ His mum gave in and let him watch TV. Seine Mama hat nachgegeben und ihn fernsehen lassen.
■ **to give out** austeilen □ The teacher gave out the books. Der Lehrer hat die Bücher ausgeteilt.
■ **to give up** aufgeben □ I couldn't do it, so I gave up. Ich habe es nicht gekonnt, also habe ich aufgegeben.
■ **to give up doing something** etwas aufgeben □ He gave up smoking. Er hat das Rauchen aufgegeben.
■ **to give oneself up** sich ergeben □ He gave himself up. Er hat sich ergeben.
■ **to give way** *(in traffic)* die Vorfahrt achten

glad ADJECTIVE
froh
□ She's glad she's done it. Sie ist froh, dass sie es getan hat.

glamorous ADJECTIVE
glamourös *(person)*

to **glance** VERB
▷ *see also* **glance** NOUN
■ **to glance at something** einen Blick auf etwas werfen □ He glanced at his watch. Er warf einen Blick auf seine Uhr.

glance NOUN
▷ *see also* **glance** VERB
der Blick (PL die Blicke)
□ at first glance auf den ersten Blick

to **glare** VERB
■ **to glare at somebody** jemanden wütend ansehen □ He glared at me. Er sah mich wütend an.

glaring ADJECTIVE
■ **a glaring mistake** ein eklatanter Fehler

glass NOUN
das Glas (GEN des Glases, PL die Gläser)
□ a glass of milk ein Glas Milch

glasses PL NOUN
die Brille
□ Veronika wears glasses. Veronika trägt eine Brille.

to **gleam** VERB
funkeln
□ Her eyes gleamed with excitement. Ihre Augen funkelten vor Aufregung.

glider NOUN
das Segelflugzeug (PL die Segelflugzeuge)

gliding NOUN
das Segelfliegen
□ My hobby is gliding. Segelfliegen ist mein Hobby.

glimpse NOUN
■ **to catch a glimpse of somebody** jemanden kurz zu sehen bekommen

to **glitter** VERB
glitzern

global ADJECTIVE
weltweit
■ **on a global scale** weltweit

global warming NOUN
die Erwärmung der Erdatmosphäre

globe NOUN
der Globus (GEN des Globus, PL die Globen)

gloomy ADJECTIVE
1 düster
□ a small gloomy flat eine kleine, düstere Wohnung
2 niedergeschlagen
□ She's been feeling very gloomy recently. Sie fühlt sich in letzter Zeit sehr niedergeschlagen.

glorious ADJECTIVE
herrlich

glove NOUN
der Handschuh (PL die Handschuhe)

glove compartment NOUN
das Handschuhfach (PL die Handschuhfächer)

to **glow** VERB
leuchten
□ Her watch glows in the dark. Ihre Uhr leuchtet im Dunkeln.

glue NOUN
▷ *see also* **glue** VERB
der Klebstoff (PL die Klebstoffe)

to **glue** VERB
▷ *see also* **glue** NOUN
kleben
□ to glue something together etwas zusammenkleben

GM ABBREVIATION *(= genetically modified)*
genmanipuliert
◻ GM food genmanipulierte Lebensmittel *pl*

GMO NOUN *(= genetically modified organism)*
der genmanipulierte Organismus (GEN des genmanipulierten Organismus, PL die genmanipulierten Organismen)

go NOUN
▹ *see also* **go** VERB
■ **to have a go at doing something** etwas versuchen ◻ He had a go at making a cake. Er hat versucht, einen Kuchen zu backen.
■ **Whose go is it?** Wer ist dran?

to **go** VERB
▹ *see also* **go** NOUN
1 gehen (IMPERFECT ging, PERFECT ist gegangen)
◻ I'm going to the cinema tonight. Ich gehe heute Abend ins Kino. ◻ I'm going now. Ich gehe jetzt.
2 weggehen *(leave)*
◻ Where's Thomas? — He's gone. Wo ist Thomas? — Er ist weggegangen.
3 fahren (PRESENT fährt, IMPERFECT fuhr, PERFECT ist gefahren) *(vehicle)*
◻ My car won't go. Mein Auto fährt nicht.
■ **to go home** nach Hause gehen ◻ I go home at about four o'clock. Ich gehe um etwa vier Uhr nach Hause.
■ **to go for a walk** einen Spaziergang machen ◻ Shall we go for a walk? Sollen wir einen Spaziergang machen?
■ **How did it go?** Wie ist es gelaufen?
■ **I'm going to do it tomorrow.** Ich werde es morgen tun.
■ **It's going to be difficult.** Es wird schwierig werden.

to **go after** VERB
nachgehen *+dat* (IMPERFECT ging nach, PERFECT ist nachgegangen) *(follow)*
◻ I went after him. Ich ging ihm nach.
■ **Quick, go after them!** Schnell, ihnen nach!

to **go ahead** VERB
vorangehen (IMPERFECT ging voran, PERFECT ist vorangegangen)
■ **to go ahead with something** etwas durchführen

to **go around** VERB
herumgehen (IMPERFECT ging herum, PERFECT ist herumgegangen)
◻ There's a rumour going around that they're getting married. Es geht das Gerücht um, sie würden heiraten.

to **go away** VERB
weggehen (IMPERFECT ging weg, PERFECT ist weggegangen)
◻ Go away! Geh weg!

to **go back** VERB
zurückgehen (IMPERFECT ging zurück, PERFECT ist zurückgegangen)
◻ We went back to the same place. Wir sind an denselben Ort zurückgegangen.
■ **Is he still here? — No, he's gone back home.** Ist er noch hier? — Nein, er ist nach Hause gegangen.

to **go by** VERB
vorbeigehen (IMPERFECT ging vorbei, PERFECT ist vorbeigegangen)
◻ Two policemen went by. Zwei Polizisten gingen vorbei.

to **go down** VERB
1 hinuntergehen (IMPERFECT ging hinunter, PERFECT ist hinuntergegangen) *(person)*
◻ to go down the stairs die Treppe hinuntergehen
2 sinken (IMPERFECT sank, PERFECT ist gesunken) *(decrease)*
◻ The price of computers has gone down. Die Preise für Computer sind gesunken.
3 Luft verlieren (IMPERFECT verlor Luft, PERFECT hat Luft verloren) *(deflate)*
◻ My airbed kept going down. Meine Luftmatratze verlor dauernd Luft.
■ **My brother's gone down with flu.** Mein Bruder hat die Grippe bekommen.

to **go for** VERB
angreifen (IMPERFECT griff an, PERFECT hat angegriffen) *(attack)*
◻ The dog went for me. Der Hund griff mich an.
■ **Go for it!** *(go on!)* Na los!

to **go in** VERB
hineingehen (IMPERFECT ging hinein, PERFECT ist hineingegangen)
◻ He knocked and went in. Er klopfte und ging hinein.

to **go off** VERB
1 losgehen (IMPERFECT ging los, PERFECT ist losgegangen)
◻ The bomb went off. Die Bombe ging los.
◻ The fire alarm went off. Der Feueralarm ging los.
2 klingeln
◻ My alarm clock goes off at seven every morning. Mein Wecker klingelt jeden Morgen um sieben Uhr.
3 schlecht werden (PRESENT wird schlecht, IMPERFECT wurde schlecht, PERFECT ist schlecht geworden)
■ **The milk's gone off.** Die Milch ist sauer geworden.
4 weggehen *(go away)*
◻ He went off in a huff. Er ist beleidigt weggegangen.

to **go on** VERB
1 los sein (PRESENT ist los, IMPERFECT war los, PERFECT ist los gewesen) *(happen)*
◻ What's going on? Was ist los?
2 dauern *(carry on)*
◻ The concert went on until eleven o'clock at night. Das Konzert hat bis nach elf Uhr nachts gedauert.

■ **to go on doing something** etwas weiter tun □ He went on reading. Er las weiter.
■ **to go on at somebody** an jemandem herumkritisieren □ My parents always go on at me. Meine Eltern kritisieren dauernd an mir herum.
■ **Go on!** Na los! □ Go on, tell us! Na los, sag schon!

to **go out** VERB
ausgehen (IMPERFECT ging aus, PERFECT ist ausgegangen)
□ Are you going out tonight? Gehst du heute Abend aus? □ Suddenly the lights went out. Plötzlich ging das Licht aus.
■ **to go out with somebody** mit jemandem ausgehen □ Are you going out with him? Gehst du mit ihm aus?

to **go past** VERB
■ **to go past something** an etwas vorbeigehen □ He went past the shop. Er ging an dem Geschäft vorbei.

to **go round** VERB
■ **to go round a corner** um die Ecke biegen
■ **to go round to somebody's house** jemanden besuchen
■ **to go round a museum** sich ein Museum ansehen
■ **to go round the shops** einen Einkaufsbummel machen

to **go through** VERB
fahren durch (PRESENT fährt, IMPERFECT fuhr, PERFECT ist gefahren) *(by car)*
■ **We went through London to get to Birmingham.** Wir sind über London nach Birmingham gefahren.

to **go up** VERB
1 hinaufgehen (IMPERFECT ging hinauf, PERFECT ist hinaufgegangen) *(person)*
□ to go up the stairs die Treppe hinaufgehen
2 steigen (IMPERFECT stieg, PERFECT ist gestiegen) *(increase)*
□ The price has gone up. Der Preis ist gestiegen.
■ **to go up in flames** in Flammen aufgehen
□ The factory went up in flames. Die Fabrik ist in Flammen aufgegangen.

to **go with** VERB
passen zu
□ Does this blouse go with that skirt? Passt diese Bluse zu dem Rock?

goal NOUN
1 das Tor (PL die Tore) *(sport)*
□ to score a goal ein Tor schießen
2 das Ziel (PL die Ziele) *(aim)*
□ His goal is to become the world champion. Sein Ziel ist es, Weltmeister zu werden.

goalkeeper NOUN
der Torwart (PL die Torwarte)

goat NOUN
die Ziege
■ **goat's cheese** der Ziegenkäse

god NOUN
der Gott (PL die Götter)
□ I believe in God. Ich glaube an Gott.

goddaughter NOUN
die Patentochter (PL die Patentöchter)

godfather NOUN
der Patenonkel (PL die Patenonkel)
□ my godfather mein Patenonkel

godmother NOUN
die Patentante
□ my godmother meine Patentante

godson NOUN
der Patensohn (PL die Patensöhne)

goes VERB ▷ *see* **go**

goggles PL NOUN
die Schutzbrille

gold NOUN
das Gold
□ They found some gold. Sie haben Gold gefunden. □ a gold necklace eine goldene Halskette

goldfish NOUN
der Goldfisch (PL die Goldfische)
□ I've got five goldfish. Ich habe fünf Goldfische.

gold-plated ADJECTIVE
vergoldet

golf NOUN
das Golf
□ My dad plays golf. Mein Papa spielt Golf.
■ **a golf club** 1 *(stick)* ein Golfschläger *masc*
2 *(place)* ein Golfklub *masc*

golf course NOUN
der Golfplatz (GEN des Golfplatzes, PL die Golfplätze)

gone VERB ▷ *see* **go**

good ADJECTIVE
1 gut
□ It's a very good film. Das ist ein sehr guter Film.
■ **Vegetables are good for you.** Gemüse ist gesund.
■ **to be good at something** gut in etwas sein
□ Maree's very good at maths. Maree ist sehr gut in Mathe.

> **WORD POWER**
> You can use a number of other words instead of **good** to mean 'great':
> **excellent** ausgezeichnet
> □ an excellent book ein ausgezeichnetes Buch
> **fantastic** fantastisch
> □ fantastic weather fantastisches Wetter
> **great** toll
> □ a great film ein toller Film
> **fabulous** traumhaft
> □ a fabulous idea eine traumhafte Idee

2 freundlich *(kind)*
□ They were very good to me. Sie waren sehr freundlich zu mir. □ That's very good of you.

Das ist sehr freundlich von Ihnen.

3 artig *(not naughty)*

□ Be good! Sei artig!

■ **for good** für immer □ One day he left for good. Eines Tages ist er für immer weggegangen.

■ **Good morning!** Guten Morgen!

■ **Good afternoon!** Guten Tag!

■ **Good evening!** Guten Abend!

■ **Good night!** Gute Nacht!

■ **It's no good complaining.** Es hat keinen Wert, sich zu beklagen.

goodbye EXCLAMATION
auf Wiedersehen

Good Friday NOUN
der Karfreitag (PL die Karfreitage)

good-looking ADJECTIVE
gut aussehend

■ **Andrew's very good-looking.** Andrew sieht sehr gut aus.

good-natured ADJECTIVE
gutmütig

goods PL NOUN
die Ware *(in shop)*

■ **a goods train** ein Güterzug *masc*

to **Google**® VERB
googeln

goose NOUN
die Gans (PL die Gänse)

gooseberry NOUN
die Stachelbeere

gorgeous ADJECTIVE

1 hinreißend

□ She's gorgeous! Sie sieht hinreißend aus!

2 herrlich

□ The weather was gorgeous. Das Wetter war herrlich.

gorilla NOUN
der Gorilla (PL die Gorillas)

gospel NOUN
das Evangelium (PL die Evangelien)

gossip NOUN

▷ *see also* **gossip** VERB

1 der Tratsch *(rumours)*

□ Tell me the gossip! Erzähl mir den neuesten Tratsch!

2 die Klatschtante *(woman)*

□ She's such a gossip! Sie ist eine furchtbare Klatschtante!

3 das Klatschweib (PL die Klatschweiber) *(man)*

□ What a gossip! So ein Klatschweib!

to **gossip** VERB

▷ *see also* **gossip** NOUN

1 schwatzen *(chat)*

□ They were always gossiping. Sie haben dauernd geschwatzt.

2 tratschen *(about somebody)*

□ They gossiped about her. Sie haben über sie getratscht.

got VERB ▷ *see* **get**

gotten VERB ▷ *see* **get**

government NOUN
die Regierung

GP NOUN *(= General Practitioner)*
der praktische Arzt (PL die praktischen Ärzte)
die praktische Ärztin

GPS NOUN *(= global positioning system)*
das GPS (PL die GPS)

to **grab** VERB
packen

□ She grabbed her umbrella and ran out of the door. Sie packte ihren Schirm und lief zur Tür hinaus.

graceful ADJECTIVE
anmutig

grade NOUN

1 die Note *(mark)*

□ He got good grades. Er hat gute Noten bekommen.

2 die Klasse *(class)*

□ Which grade are you in? In welcher Klasse bist du?

grade school NOUN (US)
die Grundschule

gradual ADJECTIVE
allmählich

gradually ADVERB
allmählich

□ We gradually got used to it. Wir haben uns allmählich daran gewöhnt.

graduate NOUN

▷ *see also* **graduate** VERB

der Hochschulabsolvent (GEN des Hochschulabsolventen, PL die Hochschulabsolventen)
die Hochschulabsolventin

to **graduate** VERB

▷ *see also* **graduate** NOUN

das Examen machen

graffiti PL NOUN
die Graffiti *pl*

grain NOUN
das Korn (PL die Körner)

gram NOUN
das Gramm (PL die Gramme *or* Gramm)

> LANGUAGE TIP When specifying a quantity of something use the plural form **Gramm**.

□ five hundred grams of cheese fünfhundert Gramm Käse

grammar NOUN
die Grammatik

grammar school NOUN
das Gymnasium (PL die Gymnasien)

> DID YOU KNOW...?
> **Gymnasium** education begins after year 4 of the **Grundschule** and lasts until year 13 (however, pupils can leave after year 10). It mainly prepares children for university education.

grammatical ADJECTIVE
grammatisch

gramme NOUN
das Gramm (PL die Gramme *or* Gramm)

LANGUAGE TIP When specifying a quantity of something use the plural form **Gramm**.

□ five hundred grammes of cheese fünfhundert Gramm Käse

grand ADJECTIVE
prachtvoll
□ She lives in a very grand house. Sie wohnt in einem prachtvollen Haus.

grandchild NOUN
der Enkel (PL die Enkel)

granddad NOUN
der Opa (PL die Opas)
□ my granddad mein Opa

granddaughter NOUN
die Enkelin

grandfather NOUN
der Großvater (PL die Großväter)
□ my grandfather mein Großvater

grandma NOUN
die Oma (PL die Omas)
□ my grandma meine Oma

grandmother NOUN
die Großmutter (PL die Großmütter)
□ my grandmother meine Großmutter

grandpa NOUN
der Opa (PL die Opas)
□ my grandpa mein Opa

grandparents PL NOUN
die Großeltern *pl*
□ my grandparents meine Großeltern

grandson NOUN
der Enkel (PL die Enkel)

granny NOUN
die Oma (PL die Omas)
□ my granny meine Oma

grant NOUN
1 das Stipendium (PL die Stipendien) *(for study)*
2 die Unterstützung *(for industry, organization)*

grape NOUN
die Traube

grapefruit NOUN
die Grapefruit (PL die Grapefruits)

graph NOUN
die grafische Darstellung

graphics PL NOUN
die Grafik *sing*

to **grasp** VERB
1 packen *(with hand)*
2 verstehen (IMPERFECT verstand, PERFECT hat verstanden)
□ I couldn't grasp the difference. Ich habe den Unterschied nicht verstanden.

grass NOUN
das Gras (GEN des Grases)
□ The grass is long. Das Gras ist hoch.
■ **to cut the grass** den Rasen mähen

grasshopper NOUN
die Heuschrecke

to **grate** VERB
reiben (IMPERFECT rieb, PERFECT hat gerieben)
□ to grate some cheese Käse reiben

grateful ADJECTIVE
dankbar

grave NOUN
das Grab (PL die Gräber)

gravel NOUN
der Kies

graveyard NOUN
der Friedhof (PL die Friedhöfe)

gravy NOUN
die Bratensoße

grease NOUN
das Fett (PL die Fette)

greasy ADJECTIVE
fettig
□ He has greasy hair. Er hat fettige Haare.
■ **The food was very greasy.** Das Essen war sehr fett.

great ADJECTIVE
1 toll
□ That's great! Das ist toll!

> WORD POWER
> You can use a number of other words instead of **great** to mean 'good':
> **amazing** ausgezeichnet
> □ an amazing cook ein ausgezeichneter Koch
> **marvellous** wunderbar
> □ a marvellous idea eine wunderbare Idee
> **superb** großartig
> □ a superb meal ein großartiges Essen
> **wonderful** wunderbar
> □ a wonderful opportunity eine wunderbare Gelegenheit

2 groß *(big)*
□ a great mansion eine große Villa

Great Britain NOUN
Großbritannien *neut*
■ **from Great Britain** aus Großbritannien
■ **in Great Britain** in Großbritannien
■ **to Great Britain** nach Großbritannien

great-grandfather NOUN
der Urgroßvater (PL die Urgroßväter)

great-grandmother NOUN
die Urgroßmutter (PL die Urgroßmütter)

Greece NOUN
Griechenland *neut*
■ **from Greece** aus Griechenland
■ **to Greece** nach Griechenland

greedy ADJECTIVE
gierig
□ Don't be so greedy! Sei nicht so gierig!

Greek ADJECTIVE
▷ *see also* **Greek** NOUN

griechisch
□ I love Greek food. Ich mag griechisches Essen sehr gern. □ Dionysis is Greek. Dionysis ist Grieche. □ She's Greek. Sie ist Griechin.

Greek NOUN
▷ *see also* **Greek** ADJECTIVE
1 der Griechin (GEN des Griechen, PL die Griechen)
die Griechin *(person)*
2 das Griechisch (GEN des Griechischen) *(language)*

green ADJECTIVE
▷ *see also* **green** NOUN
grün
□ a green car ein grünes Auto □ a green salad ein grüner Salat
■ **the Green Party** die Grünen *masc pl*

green NOUN
▷ *see also* **green** ADJECTIVE
das Grün
□ a dark green ein dunkles Grün
■ **greens** *(vegetables)* das Grüngemüse *sing*
■ **the Greens** *(party)* die Grünen

greengrocer's NOUN
der Gemüsehändler (PL die Gemüsehändler)

greenhouse NOUN
das Treibhaus (GEN des Treibhauses, PL die Treibhäuser)
■ **the greenhouse effect** der Treibhauseffekt

Greenland NOUN
Grönland *neut*

to **greet** VERB
begrüßen (PERFECT hat begrüßt)
□ He greeted me with a kiss. Er begrüßte mich mit einem Kuss.

greeting NOUN
■ **Greetings from Bangor!** Grüße aus Bangor!
■ **'Season's Greetings'** 'fröhliche Weihnachten und ein glückliches neues Jahr'

greetings card NOUN
die Grußkarte

grew VERB ▷ *see* **grow**

grey ADJECTIVE
grau
□ She's got grey hair. Sie hat graue Haare.
□ He's going grey. Er wird grau.

grey-haired ADJECTIVE
grauhaarig

grid NOUN
1 das Gitter (PL die Gitter) *(on map)*
2 das Netz (GEN des Netzes, PL die Netze) *(of electricity)*

grief NOUN
der Kummer

grill NOUN
▷ *see also* **grill** VERB
der Grill (PL die Grills) *(of cooker)*
■ **a mixed grill** ein Grillteller *masc*

to **grill** VERB
▷ *see also* **grill** NOUN
grillen

grim ADJECTIVE
schlimm
□ Things look grim. Es sieht schlimm aus.

to **grin** VERB
▷ *see also* **grin** NOUN
grinsen
□ Dave grinned at me. Dave grinste mich an.

grin NOUN
▷ *see also* **grin** VERB
das Grinsen

to **grind** VERB
1 mahlen (PERFECT hat gemahlen) *(coffee, pepper)*
2 hacken *(meat)*

to **grip** VERB
packen
□ He gripped my arm tightly. Er packte mich fest am Arm.

gripping ADJECTIVE
spannend *(exciting)*

grit NOUN
der Splitt (PL die Splitte)

to **groan** VERB
▷ *see also* **groan** NOUN
stöhnen
□ He groaned with pain. Er stöhnte vor Schmerzen.

groan NOUN
▷ *see also* **groan** VERB
das Stöhnen *(of pain)*

grocer NOUN
der Lebensmittelhändler (PL die Lebensmittelhändler)
die Lebensmittelhändlerin
□ He's a grocer. Er ist Lebensmittelhändler.

groceries PL NOUN
die Einkäufe *masc pl*

grocer's (shop) NOUN
das Lebensmittelgeschäft (PL die Lebensmittelgeschäfte)

grocery store NOUN (US)
das Lebensmittelgeschäft (PL die Lebensmittelgeschäfte)

groom NOUN
der Bräutigam (PL die Bräutigame) *(bridegroom)*
□ the groom and his best man der Bräutigam und sein Trauzeuge

to **grope** VERB
■ **to grope for something** nach etwas tasten
□ He groped for the light switch. Er tastete nach dem Lichtschalter.

gross ADJECTIVE
abscheulich *(revolting)*
□ It was really gross! Es war wirklich abscheulich!

grossly ADVERB
total

□ We're grossly underpaid. Wir sind total unterbezahlt.

ground NOUN
▷ *see also* **ground** VERB
1 der Boden (PL die Böden) *(earth)*
□ The ground's wet. Der Boden ist nass.
2 der Platz (GEN des Platzes, PL die Plätze) *(for sport)*
□ a football ground ein Fußballplatz
3 der Grund (PL die Gründe) *(reason)*
□ We've got grounds for complaint. Wir haben Grund zur Klage.
■ **on the ground** auf dem Boden □ We sat on the ground. Wir saßen auf dem Boden.

ground VERB ▷ *see* **grind**
▷ *see also* **ground** NOUN
■ **ground coffee** gemahlener Kaffee

group NOUN
die Gruppe

to **grow** VERB
1 wachsen (PRESENT wächst, IMPERFECT wuchs, PERFECT ist gewachsen) *(plant, person, animal)*
□ Grass grows quickly. Gras wächst schnell.
□ Haven't you grown! Bist du aber gewachsen!
■ **to grow a beard** sich einen Bart wachsen lassen □ You should grow a beard. Du solltest dir einen Bart wachsen lassen.
■ **He's grown out of his jacket.** Er ist aus der Jacke herausgewachsen.
2 zunehmen (PRESENT nimmt zu, IMPERFECT nahm zu, PERFECT hat zugenommen) *(increase)*
□ The number of unemployed has grown. Die Zahl der Arbeitslosen hat zugenommen.
3 anbauen (PERFECT hat angebaut) *(cultivate)*
□ My Dad grows potatoes. Mein Papa baut Kartoffeln an.
■ **to grow up** erwachsen werden □ Oh, grow up! Werd endlich erwachsen!

to **growl** VERB
knurren

grown VERB ▷ *see* **grow**

growth NOUN
das Wachstum
□ economic growth das Wirtschaftswachstum

grub NOUN
die Fressalien *fem pl (informal)*

grudge NOUN
■ **to bear a grudge against somebody** einen Groll gegen jemanden haben □ He's always borne a grudge against me. Er hat schon immer einen Groll gegen mich gehabt.

gruesome ADJECTIVE
furchtbar

guarantee NOUN
▷ *see also* **guarantee** VERB
die Garantie
□ a five-year guarantee eine Garantie von fünf Jahren

to **guarantee** VERB
▷ *see also* **guarantee** NOUN
garantieren (PERFECT hat garantiert)
□ I can't guarantee he'll come. Ich kann nicht garantieren, dass er kommt.

to **guard** VERB
▷ *see also* **guard** NOUN
bewachen (PERFECT hat bewacht)
□ They guarded the palace. Sie bewachten den Palast.
■ **to guard against something** gegen etwas Vorsichtsmaßnahmen ergreifen

guard NOUN
▷ *see also* **guard** VERB
der Zugbegleiter (PL die Zugbegleiter)
die Zugbegleiterin *(of train)*
■ **a security guard** ein Wachtmann *masc*
■ **a guard dog** ein Wachhund *masc*

to **guess** VERB
▷ *see also* **guess** NOUN
raten (PRESENT rät, IMPERFECT riet, PERFECT hat geraten)
□ Can you guess what it is? Rate mal, was das ist. □ to guess wrong falsch raten

guess NOUN
▷ *see also* **guess** VERB
die Vermutung
□ It's just a guess. Es ist nur eine Vermutung.
■ **Have a guess!** Rate mal!

guest NOUN
der Gast (PL die Gäste)
LANGUAGE TIP **der Gast** is also used for women.
□ She is our guest. Sie ist unser Gast. □ We have guests staying with us. Wir haben Gäste.

guesthouse NOUN
die Pension
□ We stayed in a guesthouse. Wir haben in einer Pension gewohnt.

guide NOUN
1 der Führer (PL die Führer) *(book)*
□ We bought a guide to Cologne. Wir haben einen Führer von Köln gekauft.
2 der Führer (PL die Führer)
die Führerin *(person)*
□ The guide showed us round the castle. Unser Führer hat uns die Burg gezeigt.
3 die Pfadfinderin *(Girl Guide)*
■ **the Guides** die Pfadfinderinnen

guidebook NOUN
der Führer (PL die Führer)

guide dog NOUN
der Blindenhund (PL die Blindenhunde)

guilty ADJECTIVE
schuldig
□ to feel guilty sich schuldig fühlen □ She was found guilty. Sie wurde schuldig gesprochen.

guinea pig NOUN
das Meerschweinchen (PL die Meerschweinchen)

guitar NOUN
die Gitarre
□ I play the guitar. Ich spiele Gitarre.

gum NOUN
der Kaugummi (PL die Kaugummis) *(chewing gum)*
■ **gums** *(in mouth)* das Zahnfleisch *sing*

gun NOUN
1 die Pistole *(small)*
2 das Gewehr (PL die Gewehre) *(rifle)*

gunpoint NOUN
■ **at gunpoint** mit Waffengewalt

gust NOUN
■ **a gust of wind** ein Windstoß *masc*

guts PL NOUN
der Mumm *(informal: courage)*
□ He's certainly got guts. Er hat wirklich Mumm.
■ **I hate his guts.** Ich kann ihn nicht ausstehen.

guy NOUN
der Typ (PL die Typen)
□ Who's that guy? Wer ist der Typ?
■ **He's a nice guy.** Er ist ein netter Kerl.

gym NOUN
die Turnhalle
■ **gym classes** die Turnstunden

gymnast NOUN
der Turner (PL die Turner)
die Turnerin
□ She's a gymnast. Sie ist Turnerin.

gymnastics NOUN
das Turnen
■ **to do gymnastics** turnen

gypsy NOUN
der Zigeuner (PL die Zigeuner)
die Zigeunerin

English-German

g

Hh

habit NOUN
die Angewohnheit
□ a bad habit eine schlechte Angewohnheit
hacker NOUN
der Hacker (PL die Hacker)
die Hackerin
had VERB ▷ *see* **have**
haddock NOUN
der Schellfisch
hadn't = **had not**
hail NOUN
▷ *see also* **hail** VERB
der Hagel
to **hail** VERB
▷ *see also* **hail** NOUN
hageln
□ It's hailing. Es hagelt.
hair NOUN
die Haare *neut pl*
□ She's got long hair. Sie hat lange Haare.
□ He's got black hair. Er hat schwarze Haare.
□ He's losing his hair. Ihm gehen die Haare aus.
■ **to brush one's hair** sich die Haare bürsten
□ I brush my hair every morning. Ich bürste mir jeden Morgen die Haare.
■ **to wash one's hair** sich die Haare waschen
□ I need to wash my hair. Ich muss mir die Haare waschen.
■ **to have one's hair cut** sich die Haare schneiden lassen □ I've just had my hair cut. Ich habe mir gerade die Haare schneiden lassen.
■ **a hair** ein Haar *neut*
hairbrush NOUN
die Haarbürste
hair clip NOUN
die Haarspange
haircut NOUN
der Haarschnitt (PL die Haarschnitte)
■ **to have a haircut** sich die Haare schneiden lassen □ I've just had a haircut. Ich habe mir gerade die Haare schneiden lassen.
hairdresser NOUN
der Friseur (PL die Friseure)
die Friseuse
□ He's a hairdresser. Er ist Friseur.
hairdresser's NOUN
der Friseur (PL die Friseure)
□ at the hairdresser's beim Friseur
hair dryer NOUN
der Haartrockner (PL die Haartrockner)
hair gel NOUN
das Haargel (PL die Haargele)

LANGUAGE TIP In German the 'g' in **Haargel** is pronounced like the 'g' in girl.

hairgrip NOUN
die Haarklemme
hair spray NOUN
der Haarspray (PL die Haarsprays)
hairstyle NOUN
die Frisur
hairy ADJECTIVE
haarig
□ He's got hairy legs. Er hat die haarige Beine.
half NOUN
▷ *see also* **half** ADJECTIVE
1 die Hälfte
□ half of the cake die Hälfte des Kuchens
2 die Kinderfahrkarte *(ticket)*
□ A half to York, please. Ein Kinderfahrkarte nach York bitte.
■ **two and a half** zweieinhalb
■ **half an hour** eine halbe Stunde
■ **half past ten** halb elf
■ **half a kilo** ein halbes Kilo
■ **to cut something in half** etwas in zwei Teile schneiden
half ADJECTIVE, ADVERB
▷ *see also* **half** NOUN
1 halb
□ a half chicken ein halbes Hähnchen
2 fast
□ He was half asleep. Er schlief fast.
half-hour NOUN
die halbe Stunde
half-price ADJECTIVE, ADVERB
■ **at half-price** zum halben Preis
half-term NOUN
die kleinen Ferien *pl*
half-time NOUN
die Halbzeit
halfway ADVERB
1 auf halber Strecke
□ halfway between Oxford and London auf halber Strecke zwischen Oxford und London
2 in der Mitte

□ halfway through the chapter in der Mitte des Kapitels

hall NOUN
1 der Flur (PL die Flure) *(in house)*
2 der Saal (PL die Säle)
□ the village hall der Gemeindesaal
■ **hall of residence** das Wohnheim

Hallowe'en NOUN
der Abend vor Allerheiligen

hallway NOUN
der Flur (PL die Flure)

halt NOUN
■ **to come to a halt** zum Stehen kommen

ham NOUN
der Schinken (PL die Schinken)
□ a ham sandwich ein Schinkensandwich *neut*

hamburger NOUN
der Hamburger (PL die Hamburger)

hammer NOUN
der Hammer (PL die Hämmer)

hamster NOUN
der Hamster (PL die Hamster)

hand NOUN
▷ *see also* **hand** VERB
1 die Hand (PL die Hände) *(of person)*
■ **to give somebody a hand** jemandem helfen □ Can you give me a hand? Kannst du mir mal helfen?
■ **on the one hand ..., on the other hand ...** einerseits ..., anderseits ...
2 der Zeiger (PL die Zeiger) *(of clock)*

to **hand** VERB
▷ *see also* **hand** NOUN
reichen
□ He handed me the book. Er reichte mir das Buch.
■ **to hand something in** etwas abgeben
□ Martin handed his exam paper in. Martin gab seine Prüfungsarbeit ab.
■ **to hand something out** etwas austeilen
□ The teacher handed out the books. Der Lehrer teilte die Bücher aus.
■ **to hand something over** etwas übergeben
□ She handed the keys over to me. Sie übergab mir die Schlüssel.

handbag NOUN
die Handtasche

handball NOUN
1 der Handball *(sport)*
2 das Handspiel *(foul)*

handbook NOUN
das Handbuch (PL die Handbücher)

handcuffs PL NOUN
die Handschellen *fem pl*

handkerchief NOUN
das Taschentuch (PL die Taschentücher)

handle NOUN
▷ *see also* **handle** VERB
1 die Klinke *(of door)*
2 der Henkel (PL die Henkel) *(of cup)*
3 der Griff (PL die Griffe) *(of knife)*
4 der Stiel (PL die Stiele) *(of saucepan)*

to **handle** VERB
▷ *see also* **handle** NOUN
■ **He handled it well.** Er hat das gut gemacht.
■ **Kath handled the travel arrangements.** Kath hat sich um die Reisevorbereitungen gekümmert.
■ **She's good at handling children.** Sie kann gut mit Kindern umgehen.

handlebars PL NOUN
die Lenkstange *sing*

handmade ADJECTIVE
handgemacht

handsome ADJECTIVE
gut aussehend
□ a handsome man ein gut aussehender Mann
■ **He's very handsome.** Er sieht sehr gut aus.

handwriting NOUN
die Handschrift

handy ADJECTIVE
1 praktisch
□ This knife's very handy. Dieses Messer ist sehr praktisch.
2 zur Hand
□ Have you got a pen handy? Hast du einen Schreiber zur Hand?

to **hang** VERB
1 aufhängen (PERFECT hat aufgehängt)
□ Mike hung the painting on the wall. Mike hängte das Bild an der Wand auf.
2 hängen
□ They hanged the criminal. Sie hängten den Verbrecher.
■ **to hang around** rumhängen □ On Saturdays we hang around in the park. Samstags hängen wir im Park rum.
■ **to hang on** warten □ Hang on a minute, please. Bitte warte einen Moment.
■ **to hang up 1** *(clothes)* aufhängen □ Hang your jacket up on the hook. Häng deine Jacke am Haken auf. **2** *(phone)* auflegen □ I tried to phone him but he hung up on me. Ich habe versucht, mit ihm zu telefonieren, aber er hat einfach aufgelegt.

hanger NOUN
der Bügel (PL die Bügel) *(for clothes)*

hang-gliding NOUN
das Drachenfliegen
■ **to go hang-gliding** Drachen fliegen gehen

hangover NOUN
der Kater (PL die Kater)
□ to have a hangover einen Kater haben

to **happen** VERB
passieren (PERFECT ist passiert)
□ What's happened? Was ist passiert?

■ **as it happens** zufälligerweise □ As it happens I saw him yesterday. Zufälligerweise habe ich ihn gestern gesehen.

happily ADVERB

1 fröhlich

□ 'Don't worry!' he said happily. 'Mach dir keine Sorgen!' sagte er fröhlich.

2 zum Glück *(fortunately)*

□ Happily, everything went well. Zum Glück ging alles gut.

happiness NOUN

das Glück

happy ADJECTIVE

glücklich

□ Janet looks happy. Janet sieht glücklich aus.

■ **I'm very happy with your work.** Ich bin sehr zufrieden mit Ihrer Arbeit.

■ **Happy birthday!** Herzlichen Glückwunsch zum Geburtstag!

> **WORD POWER**
> You can use a number of other words instead of **happy** to mean 'glad':
> **cheerful** fröhlich
> □ a cheerful little boy ein fröhlicher kleiner Junge
> **delighted** erfreut
> □ a delighted smile ein erfreutes Lächeln
> **glad** froh
> □ to be glad froh sein
> **satisfied** zufrieden
> □ a satisfied customer ein zufriedener Kunde

harbour NOUN

der Hafen (PL die Häfen)

hard ADJECTIVE, ADVERB

1 hart

□ This cheese is very hard. Dieser Käse ist sehr hart. □ He's worked very hard. Er hat sehr hart gearbeitet.

2 schwierig

□ This question's too hard for me. Diese Frage ist für mich zu schwierig.

hard disk NOUN

die Festplatte *(of computer)*

hardly ADVERB

kaum

□ I've hardly got any money. Ich habe kaum Geld. □ I hardly know you. Ich kenne Sie kaum.

■ **hardly ever** fast nie

hard up ADJECTIVE

pleite

hardware NOUN

die Hardware

hare NOUN

der Feldhase (GEN des Feldhasen, PL die Feldhasen)

to **harm** VERB

■ **to harm somebody** jemandem wehtun

□ I didn't mean to harm you. Ich wollte Ihnen nicht wehtun.

■ **to harm something** einer Sache schaden

□ Chemicals harm the environment. Chemikalien schaden der Umwelt.

harmful ADJECTIVE

schädlich

□ harmful chemicals schädliche Chemikalien

harmless ADJECTIVE

harmlos

□ Most spiders are harmless. Die meisten Spinnen sind harmlos.

harsh ADJECTIVE

1 hart

□ He deserves a harsh punishment. Er verdient es, hart bestraft zu werden.

2 rau

□ She's got a very harsh voice. Sie hat eine sehr raue Stimme.

harvest NOUN

die Ernte

has VERB ▷ *see* **have**

hasn't = **has not**

hat NOUN

der Hut (PL die Hüte)

to **hate** VERB

hassen

□ I hate maths. Ich hasse Mathe.

hatred NOUN

der Hass (GEN des Hasses)

haunted ADJECTIVE

verwunschen

□ a haunted house ein verwunschenes Haus

to **have** VERB

1 haben (PRESENT hat, IMPERFECT hatte, PERFECT hat gehabt)

□ Have you got a sister? Hast du eine Schwester? □ He's got blue eyes. Er hat blaue Augen. □ I've got a cold. Ich habe eine Erkältung.

> **LANGUAGE TIP** The perfect tense of most verbs is formed with **haben**.

□ They have eaten. Sie haben gegessen.

□ Have you done your homework? Hast du deine Hausaufgaben gemacht?

> **LANGUAGE TIP** Questions like 'hasn't he?' don't exist in German.

□ He's done it, hasn't he? Er hat es getan, nicht wahr?

> **LANGUAGE TIP** 'have' is not translated when it is used in place of another verb.

□ Have you got any money? — No, I haven't. Hast du Geld? — Nein. □ Does she have any pets? — Yes, she has. Hat sie Haustiere? — Ja. □ He hasn't done his homework. — Yes, he has. Er hat seine Hausaufgaben nicht gemacht. — Doch.

2 sein (PRESENT ist, IMPERFECT war, PERFECT ist gewesen)

> **LANGUAGE TIP** The perfect tense of some verbs is formed with **sein**.

□ They have arrived. Sie sind angekommen.
□ Has he gone? Ist er gegangen?

LANGUAGE TIP 'have' plus noun is sometimes translated by a German verb.

□ He had his breakfast. Er hat gefrühstückt.
□ to have a shower duschen □ to have a bath baden
■ **to have got to do something** etwas tun müssen □ She's got to do it. Sie muss es tun.
■ **to have a party** eine Party machen
■ **I had my hair cut yesterday.** Ich habe mir gestern die Haare schneiden lassen.

haven't = **have not**

hay NOUN
das Heu

hay fever NOUN
der Heuschnupfen
□ Do you get hay fever? Hast du manchmal Heuschnupfen?

hazelnut NOUN
die Haselnuss (PL die Haselnüsse)

he PRONOUN
er
□ He loves dogs. Er liebt Hunde.

head NOUN
▷ *see also* **head** VERB
1 der Kopf (PL die Köpfe) *(of person)*
□ The wine went to my head. Der Wein ist mir in den Kopf gestiegen.
2 der Rektor (PL die Rektoren)
die Rektorin *(of private or primary school)*
3 der Direktor (PL die Direktoren)
die Direktorin *(of state secondary school)*
4 das Oberhaupt (PL die Oberhäupten) *(leader)*
□ a head of state ein Staatsoberhaupt
■ **to have a head for figures** gut mit Zahlen umgehen können
■ **Heads or tails? — Heads.** Kopf oder Zahl? — Kopf.

to **head** VERB
▷ *see also* **head** NOUN
■ **to head for something** auf etwas zugehen
□ He headed straight for the bar. Er ging direkt auf die Theke zu.

headache NOUN
die Kopfschmerzen *masc pl*
□ I've got a headache. Ich habe Kopfschmerzen.

headlight NOUN
der Scheinwerfer (PL die Scheinwerfer)

headline NOUN
die Schlagzeile

headmaster NOUN
1 der Rektor (PL die Rektoren) *(of private or primary school)*
2 der Direktor (PL die Direktoren) *(of state secondary school)*

headmistress NOUN
1 die Rektorin *(of private or primary school)*
2 die Direktorin *(of state secondary school)*

headphones PL NOUN
der Kopfhörer (PL die Kopfhören)
□ a set of headphones ein Kopfhörer

headquarters PL NOUN
das Hauptquartier
□ The bank's headquarters are in London. Das Hauptquartier der Bank ist in London.

headteacher NOUN
1 der Rektor (PL die Rektoren)
die Rektorin *(of private or primary school)*
2 der Direktor (PL die Direktoren)
die Direktorin *(of state secondary school)*

to **heal** VERB
heilen

health NOUN
die Gesundheit

healthy ADJECTIVE
gesund
□ She's a healthy person. Sie ist gesund.
□ a healthy diet eine gesunde Ernährung

heap NOUN
der Haufen (PL die Haufen)
□ a rubbish heap ein Müllhaufen

to **hear** VERB
hören
□ He heard the dog bark. Er hörte den Hund bellen. □ She can't hear very well. Sie hört nicht gut. □ I heard that she was ill. Ich habe gehört, dass sie krank war. □ Did you hear the good news? Hast du die gute Nachricht gehört?
■ **to hear about something** von etwas hören
■ **to hear from somebody** von jemandem hören □ I haven't heard from him recently. Ich habe in letzter Zeit nichts von ihm gehört.

heart NOUN
das Herz (GEN des Herzens, PL die Herzen)
■ **to learn something by heart** etwas auswendig lernen
■ **the ace of hearts** das Herzass

heart attack NOUN
der Herzinfarkt (PL die Herzinfarkte)

heartbroken ADJECTIVE
zutiefst betrübt

heat NOUN
▷ *see also* **heat** VERB
die Hitze

to **heat** VERB
▷ *see also* **heat** NOUN
erhitzen (PERFECT hat erhitzt)
□ Heat gently for five minutes. Erhitzen Sie es bei schwacher Hitze fünf Minuten lang.
■ **to heat up 1** *(cooked food)* aufwärmen
□ He heated the soup up. Er hat die Suppe aufgewärmt. **2** *(water, oven)* heiß werden
□ The water is heating up. Das Wasser wird heiß.

heater NOUN
der Heizofen (PL die Heizöfen)
□ an electric heater ein elektrischer Heizofen

heather NOUN
das Heidekraut (PL die Heidekräuter)

heating NOUN
die Heizung

heaven NOUN
der Himmel (PL die Himmel)

heavily ADVERB
schwer
□ The car was heavily loaded. Das Auto war schwer beladen.
■ **He drinks heavily.** Er trinkt viel.
■ **It was raining heavily.** Es regnete stark.

heavy ADJECTIVE
1 schwer
□ This bag's very heavy. Diese Tasche ist sehr schwer.
■ **heavy rain** starker Regen
2 anstrengend *(busy)*
□ I've got a very heavy week ahead. Ich habe eine anstrengende Woche vor mir.
■ **to be a heavy drinker** viel trinken

he'd = **he would, he had**

hedge NOUN
die Hecke

hedgehog NOUN
der Igel (PL die Igel)

heel NOUN
der Absatz (GEN des Absatzes, PL die Absätze)

height NOUN
1 die Größe *(of person)*
2 die Höhe *(of object, mountain)*

heir NOUN
der Erbe (GEN des Erben, PL die Erben)

heiress NOUN
die Erbin

held VERB ▷ *see* **hold**

helicopter NOUN
der Hubschrauber (PL die Hubschrauber)

hell NOUN
die Hölle
■ **Hell!** Mist! *(informal)*

he'll = **he will, he shall**

hello EXCLAMATION
hallo

helmet NOUN
der Helm (PL die Helme)

to **help** VERB
▷ *see also* **help** NOUN
helfen (PRESENT hilft, IMPERFECT half, PERFECT hat geholfen)
■ **to help somebody** jemandem helfen
□ Can you help me? Kannst du mir helfen?
■ **Help!** Hilfe!
■ **Help yourself!** Bedienen Sie sich!
■ **He can't help it.** Er kann nichts dafür.

help NOUN
▷ *see also* **help** VERB
die Hilfe
□ Do you need any help? Brauchst du Hilfe?

helpful ADJECTIVE
hilfreich
□ a helpful suggestion ein hilfreicher Vorschlag
■ **He was very helpful.** Er war eine große Hilfe.

help menu NOUN
das Hilfemenü (PL die Hilfemenüs)

hen NOUN
die Henne

her ADJECTIVE
▷ *see also* **her** PRONOUN
ihr
□ her father ihr Vater □ her mother ihre Mutter □ her child ihr Kind □ her parents ihre Eltern

LANGUAGE TIP Do not use **ihr** with parts of the body.

□ She's going to wash her hair. Sie wäscht sich die Haare. □ She's cleaning her teeth. Sie putzt sich die Zähne. □ She's hurt her foot. Sie hat sich am Fuß verletzt.

her PRONOUN
▷ *see also* **her** ADJECTIVE
1 sie
□ I can see her. Ich kann sie sehen. □ Look at her! Sieh sie an! □ It's her again. Sie ist es schon wieder. □ I'm older than her. Ich bin älter als sie.

LANGUAGE TIP Use **sie** after prepositions which take the accusative.

□ I was thinking of her. Ich habe an sie gedacht.
2 ihr

LANGUAGE TIP Use **ihr** after prepositions which take the dative.

□ I'm going with her. Ich gehe mit ihr mit.
□ He sat next to her. Er saß neben ihr.

LANGUAGE TIP Use **ihr** when 'her' means 'to her'.

□ I gave her a book. Ich gab ihr ein Buch. □ I told her the truth. Ich habe ihr die Wahrheit gesagt.

herb NOUN
das Kraut (PL die Kräuter)

here ADVERB
hier
□ I live here. Ich wohne hier. □ Here's Helen. Hier ist Helen. □ Here are the books. Hier sind die Bücher. □ Here he is! Da ist er ja!

hero NOUN
der Held (GEN des Helden, PL die Helden)
□ He's a real hero! Er ist ein echter Held!

heroin NOUN
das Heroin
□ Heroin is a hard drug. Heroin ist eine harte Droge.
■ **a heroin addict** *(man)* ein Heroinsüchtiger
■ **She's a heroin addict.** Sie ist heroinsüchtig.

heroine NOUN
die Heldin
□ **the heroine of the novel** die Heldin des Romans

hers PRONOUN
1 ihrer
□ **Is this her coat? — No, hers is black.** Ist das ihr Mantel? — Nein, ihrer ist schwarz.
ihre
□ **Is this her cup? — No, hers is red.** Ist das ihre Tasse? — Nein, ihre ist rot.
ihres
□ **Is this her car? — No, hers is white.** Ist das ihr Auto? — Nein, ihres ist weiß.
2 ihre
□ **my parents and hers** meine Eltern und ihre
□ **I have my reasons and she has hers.** Ich habe meine Gründe und sie hat ihre.
■ **Is this hers?** Gehört das ihr? □ **This book is hers.** Dieses Buch gehört ihr. □ **Whose is this? — It's hers.** Wem gehört das? — Es gehört ihr.

herself PRONOUN
1 sich
□ **She's hurt herself.** Sie hat sich verletzt.
□ **She talked mainly about herself.** Sie redete hauptsächlich über sich selbst.
2 selbst
□ **She did it herself.** Sie hat es selbst gemacht.
■ **by herself** allein □ **She doesn't like travelling by herself.** Sie verreist nicht gern allein.

he's = **he is, he has**

to **hesitate** VERB
zögern

heterosexual ADJECTIVE
heterosexuell

hi EXCLAMATION
hallo

hiccups PL NOUN
der Schluckauf *sing*
□ **He had the hiccups.** Er hatte einen Schluckauf.

to **hide** VERB
sich verstecken (PERFECT hat sich versteckt)
□ **He hid behind a bush.** Er versteckte sich hinter einem Busch.
■ **to hide something** etwas verstecken
□ **Paula hid the present.** Paula hat das Geschenk versteckt.

hide-and-seek NOUN
■ **to play hide-and-seek** Verstecken spielen

hideous ADJECTIVE
scheußlich

hi-fi NOUN
die Hi-Fi-Anlage

high ADJECTIVE, ADVERB
hoch
□ **It's too high.** Es ist zu hoch. □ **How high is the wall?** Wie hoch ist die Mauer? □ **The wall's two metres high.** Die Mauer ist zwei Meter hoch.

LANGUAGE TIP Before a noun or after an article, use **hohe**.

□ **She's got a very high voice.** Sie hat eine sehr hohe Stimme. □ **a high price** ein hoher Preis
□ **a high temperature** eine hohe Temperatur
□ **at high speed** mit hoher Geschwindigkeit
■ **It's very high in fat.** Es ist sehr fetthaltig.
■ **to be high** *(on drugs)* high sein *(informal)*
■ **to get high** *(on drugs)* high werden *(informal)*
□ **to get high on crack** von Crack high werden

higher education NOUN
die Hochschulbildung

high-heeled ADJECTIVE
■ **high-heeled shoes** hochhackige Schuhe

high jump NOUN
der Hochsprung (PL die Hochsprünge) *(sport)*

highlight NOUN
▷ *see also* **highlight** VERB
der Höhepunkt (PL die Höhepunkte)
□ **the highlight of the evening** der Höhepunkt des Abends

to **highlight** VERB
▷ *see also* **highlight** NOUN
markieren (PERFECT hat markiert)
□ **She highlighted the word in yellow.** Sie markierte das Wort in Gelb.

highlighter NOUN
der Textmarker (PL die Textmarker)

high-rise NOUN
das Hochhaus (GEN des Hochhauses, PL die Hochhäuser)
□ **I live in a high-rise.** Ich wohne in einem Hochhaus.

high school NOUN
das Gymnasium (PL die Gymnasien)

to **hijack** VERB
entführen (PERFECT hat entführt)

hijacker NOUN
der Entführer (PL die Entführer)
die Entführerin

hike NOUN
die Wanderung

hiking NOUN
■ **to go hiking** wandern gehen

hilarious ADJECTIVE
urkomisch
□ **It was hilarious!** Es war urkomisch!

hill NOUN
der Hügel (PL die Hügel)
□ **She walked up the hill.** Sie ging den Hügel hinauf.

hill-walking NOUN
das Bergwandern
■ **to go hill-walking** Bergwanderungen machen

him PRONOUN
1 ihn
□ **I can see him.** Ich kann ihn sehen. □ **Look at him!** Sieh ihn an!

LANGUAGE TIP Use **ihn** after prepositions which take the accusative.

□ I did it for him. Ich habe es für ihn getan.

2 ihm

LANGUAGE TIP Use **ihm** after prepositions which take the dative.

□ I travelled with him. Ich bin mit ihm gereist.
□ I haven't heard from him. Ich habe nichts von ihm gehört.

LANGUAGE TIP Use **ihm** when 'him' means 'to him'.

□ I gave him a book. Ich gab ihm ein Buch.
□ I told him the truth. Ich habe ihm die Wahrheit gesagt.

3 er

□ It's him again. Er ist es schon wieder.
□ I'm older than him. Ich bin älter als er.

himself PRONOUN

1 sich

□ He's hurt himself. Er hat sich verletzt.
□ He talked mainly about himself. Er redete hauptsächlich über sich selbst.

2 selbst

□ He did it himself. Er hat es selbst gemacht.
■ **by himself** allein □ He was travelling by himself. Er reiste allein.

Hindu ADJECTIVE

hinduistisch

■ **a Hindu temple** ein Hindutempel *masc*

hint NOUN

▷ *see also* **hint** VERB

die Andeutung

□ to drop a hint eine Andeutung machen
■ **I can take a hint.** Ich verstehe schon.

to **hint** VERB

▷ *see also* **hint** NOUN

andeuten (PERFECT hat angedeutet)

□ He hinted that I'd get the job. Er deutete an, dass ich die Stelle bekommen würde.

hip NOUN

die Hüfte

hippie NOUN

der Hippie (PL die Hippies)

LANGUAGE TIP **der Hippie** is also used for women.

□ She was a hippie. Sie war ein Hippie.

hippo NOUN

das Nilpferd (PL die Nilpferde)

to **hire** VERB

▷ *see also* **hire** NOUN

1 mieten

□ to hire a car ein Auto mieten

2 anstellen (PERFECT hat angestellt) *(person)*

□ They hired a cleaner. Sie haben eine Putzfrau angestellt.

hire NOUN

▷ *see also* **hire** VERB

der Verleih (PL die Verleihe)

■ **car hire** der Autoverleih
■ **for hire** zu vermieten

hire car NOUN

der Mietwagen (PL die Mietwagen)

his ADJECTIVE

▷ *see also* **his** PRONOUN

sein

□ his father sein Vater □ his mother seine Mutter □ his child sein Kind □ his parents seine Eltern

LANGUAGE TIP Do not use **sein** with parts of the body.

□ He's going to wash his hair. Er wäscht sich die Haare. □ He's cleaning his teeth. Er putzt sich die Zähne. □ He's hurt his foot. Er hat sich am Fuß verletzt.

his PRONOUN

▷ *see also* **his** ADJECTIVE

1 seiner

□ Is this his coat? — No, his is black. Ist das sein Mantel? — Nein, seiner ist schwarz.

seine

□ Is this his cup? — No, his is red. Ist das seine Tasse? — Nein, seine ist rot.

seines

□ Is this his car? — No, his is white. Ist das sein Auto? — Nein, seines ist weiß.

2 seine

□ my parents and his meine Eltern und seine
□ I have my reasons and he has his. Ich habe meine Gründe und er hat seine.
■ **Is this his?** Gehört das ihm? □ This book is his. Dieses Buch gehört ihm. □ Whose is this? — It's his. Wem gehört das? — Das gehört ihm.

history NOUN

die Geschichte

to **hit** VERB

▷ *see also* **hit** NOUN

1 schlagen (PRESENT schlägt, IMPERFECT schlug, PERFECT hat geschlagen)

□ Andrew hit him. Andrew hat ihn geschlagen.

2 anfahren (PRESENT fährt an, IMPERFECT fuhr an, PERFECT hat angefahren)

□ He was hit by a car. Er wurde von einem Auto angefahren.

3 treffen (PRESENT trifft, IMPERFECT traf, PERFECT hat getroffen)

□ The arrow hit the target. Der Pfeil traf sein Ziel.
■ **to hit it off with somebody** sich gut mit jemandem verstehen □ She hit it off with his parents. Sie hat sich mit seinen Eltern gut verstanden.

hit NOUN

▷ *see also* **hit** VERB

1 der Hit (PL die Hits) *(song)*

□ their latest hit ihr neuester Hit.

2 der Erfolg (PL die Erfolge) *(success)*

□ The film was a massive hit. Der Film war ein enormer Erfolg.

hitch NOUN
das Problem (PL die Probleme)
□ a slight hitch ein kleines Problem

to **hitchhike** VERB
per Anhalter fahren (PRESENT fährt, IMPERFECT fuhr, PERFECT ist gefahren)

hitchhiker NOUN
der Anhalter (PL die Anhalter)
die Anhalterin

hitchhiking NOUN
das Trampen
□ Hitchhiking is dangerous. Trampen ist gefährlich.

hit man NOUN
der Killer (PL die Killer)

HIV-negative ADJECTIVE
HIV-negativ

HIV-positive ADJECTIVE
HIV-positiv

hobby NOUN
das Hobby (PL die Hobbys)
□ What are your hobbies? Welche Hobbys haben Sie?

hockey NOUN
das Hockey
□ I play hockey. Ich spiele Hockey.

to **hold** VERB
1 halten (PRESENT hält, IMPERFECT hielt, PERFECT hat gehalten) *(hold on to)*
□ Hold this end of the rope, please. Halt bitte dieses Ende des Seils.
■ **She held a bottle in her hand.** Sie hatte eine Flasche in der Hand.
2 fassen *(contain)*
□ This bottle holds two litres. Diese Flasche fasst zwei Liter.
■ **to hold a meeting** eine Versammlung abhalten
■ **Hold the line!** *(on telephone)* Bleiben Sie am Apparat!
■ **Hold it!** *(wait)* Sekunde!
■ **to get hold of something** *(obtain)* etwas bekommen □ I couldn't get hold of it. Ich habe es nicht bekommen.

to **hold on** VERB
1 sich festhalten (PRESENT hält sich fest, IMPERFECT hielt sich fest, PERFECT hat sich festgehalten) *(keep hold)*
□ The cliff was slippery, but he managed to hold on. Die Klippe war rutschig, aber er konnte sich festhalten.
■ **to hold on to something 1** sich an etwas klammern □ He held on to the railing. Er klammerte sich an das Geländer. **2** etwas behalten □ He held on to the book, just in case. Er hat das Buch vorsichtshalber behalten.
2 warten *(wait)*
□ Hold on, I'm coming! Warte, ich komme!
■ **Hold on!** *(on telephone)* Bleiben Sie am Apparat!

to **hold up** VERB
■ **to hold up one's hand** die Hand heben
□ I held up my hand. Ich hob die Hand.
■ **to hold somebody up** *(delay)* jemanden aufhalten □ I was held up at the office. Ich wurde im Büro aufgehalten.
■ **to hold up a bank** *(rob)* eine Bank überfallen

hold-up NOUN
1 der Überfall (PL die Überfälle) *(at bank)*
2 die Verzögerung *(delay)*
3 der Stau (PL die Staus) *(traffic jam)*

hole NOUN
das Loch (PL die Löcher)

holiday NOUN
1 die Ferien *pl (from school)*
□ Did you have a good holiday? Hattet ihr schöne Ferien?
■ **on holiday** in den Ferien □ to go on holiday in die Ferien fahren □ We are on holiday. Wir haben Ferien.
■ **the school holidays** die Schulferien
2 der Urlaub (PL die Urlaube) *(from work)*
□ Did you have a good holiday? Hattet ihr einen schönen Urlaub?
■ **on holiday** im Urlaub □ to go on holiday in Urlaub fahren □ We are on holiday. Wir sind im Urlaub.
3 der Feiertag (PL die Feiertage) *(public holiday)*
□ Next Wednesday is a holiday. Nächsten Mittwoch ist ein Feiertag.
4 der freie Tag (PL die freien Tage) *(day off)*
■ **He took a day's holiday.** Er nahm einen Tag frei.
■ **a holiday camp** ein Ferienlager *neut*
■ **a holiday home** eine Ferienwohnung *fem*

Holland NOUN
Holland *neut*
■ **from Holland** aus Holland
■ **in Holland** in Holland
■ **to Holland** nach Holland

hollow ADJECTIVE
hohl

holly NOUN
die Stechpalme

holy ADJECTIVE
heilig

home NOUN
▷ *see also* **home** ADVERB
das Zuhause (GEN des Zuhause)
■ **at home** zu Hause
■ **Make yourself at home.** Machen Sie es sich bequem.

home ADVERB
▷ *see also* **home** NOUN
1 zu Hause
□ to be at home zu Hause sein
2 nach Hause
□ to go home nach Hause gehen
■ **to get home** nach Hause kommen □ What

time did he get home? Wann ist er nach Hause gekommen?

home address NOUN
die Adresse
□ What's your home address? Wie ist Ihre Adresse?

homeland NOUN
das Heimatland (PL die Heimatländer)

homeless ADJECTIVE
obdachlos
■ **the homeless** die Obdachlosen *masc pl*

home match NOUN
das Heimspiel (PL die Heimspiele)

homeopathy NOUN
die Homöopathie

home page NOUN
die Homepage (PL die Homepages) *(Internet)*

homesick ADJECTIVE
■ **to be homesick** Heimweh haben

homework NOUN
die Hausaufgaben *fem pl*
□ Have you done your homework? Hast du deine Hausaufgaben gemacht? □ my geography homework meine Erdkundeaufgaben

homosexual ADJECTIVE
▷ *see also* **homosexual** NOUN
homosexuell

homosexual NOUN
▷ *see also* **homosexual** ADJECTIVE
der Homosexuelle (GEN des Homosexuellen, PL die Homosexuellen)
□ a homosexual *(man)* ein Homosexueller

honest ADJECTIVE
ehrlich
□ She's an honest person. Sie ist ein ehrlicher Mensch. □ He was honest with her. Er war ehrlich zu ihr.

honestly ADVERB
ehrlich
□ I honestly don't know. Ich weiß es ehrlich nicht.

honesty NOUN
die Ehrlichkeit

honey NOUN
der Honig

honeymoon NOUN
die Flitterwochen *fem pl*

honour NOUN
die Ehre

hood NOUN
1 die Kapuze
□ a coat with a hood ein Mantel mit Kapuze
2 die Motorhaube *(of car)*

hook NOUN
der Haken (PL die Haken)
□ He hung the painting on the hook. Er hängte das Bild an den Haken.
■ **to take the phone off the hook** das Telefon aushängen
■ **a fish-hook** ein Angelhaken

hooligan NOUN
der Rowdy (PL die Rowdys)

hooray EXCLAMATION
hurra

Hoover® NOUN
der Staubsauger (PL die Staubsauger)

to **hoover** VERB
staubsaugen
□ She hoovered the lounge. Sie hat im Wohnzimmer gestaubsaugt.

to **hop** VERB
hüpfen (PERFECT ist gehüpft)

to **hope** VERB
▷ *see also* **hope** NOUN
hoffen
□ I hope he comes. Ich hoffe, er kommt.
□ I'm hoping for good results. Ich hoffe, dass ich gute Noten bekomme.
■ **I hope so.** Hoffentlich.
■ **I hope not.** Hoffentlich nicht.

hope NOUN
▷ *see also* **hope** VERB
die Hoffnung
■ **to give up hope** die Hoffnung aufgeben
□ Don't give up hope! Gib die Hoffnung nicht auf!

hopeful ADJECTIVE
1 zuversichtlich
□ I'm hopeful. Ich bin zuversichtlich.
■ **He's hopeful of winning.** Er rechnet sich Gewinnchancen aus.
2 aussichtsreich *(situation)*
■ **The prospects look hopeful.** Die Aussichten sind gut.

hopefully ADVERB
hoffentlich
□ Hopefully he'll make it in time. Hoffentlich schafft er es noch.

hopeless ADJECTIVE
hoffnungslos
□ I'm hopeless at maths. In Mathe bin ich ein hoffnungsloser Fall.

horizon NOUN
der Horizont (PL die Horizonte)

horizontal ADJECTIVE
horizontal

horn NOUN
1 die Hupe *(of car)*
■ **He sounded his horn.** Er hat gehupt.
2 das Horn (PL die Hörner)
□ I play the horn. Ich spiele Horn.

horoscope NOUN
das Horoskop (PL die Horoskope)

horrible ADJECTIVE
furchtbar
□ What a horrible dress! Was für ein furchtbares Kleid!

to **horrify** VERB
entsetzen
□ I was horrified by the news. Ich war über die

Neuigkeiten entsetzt.

horrifying ADJECTIVE
schrecklich
□ a horrifying accident ein schrecklicher Unfall

horror NOUN
der Horror

horror film NOUN
der Horrorfilm (PL die Horrorfilme)

horse NOUN
das Pferd (PL die Pferde)

horse-racing NOUN
das Pferderennen (PL die Pferderennen)

horseshoe NOUN
das Hufeisen (PL die Hufeisen)

hose NOUN
der Schlauch (PL die Schläuche)
□ a garden hose ein Gartenschlauch

LANGUAGE TIP Be careful not to translate **hose** by the German word **Hose**.

hosepipe NOUN
der Schlauch (PL die Schläuche)

hospital NOUN
das Krankenhaus (GEN des Krankenhauses, PL die Krankenhäuser)
□ Take me to the hospital! Bringen Sie mich ins Krankenhaus! □ in hospital im Krankenhaus

hospitality NOUN
die Gastfreundschaft

host NOUN
1 der Gastgeber (PL die Gastgeber)
die Gastgeberin
2 der Moderator (PL die Moderatoren)
die Moderatorin *(television)*

hostage NOUN
die Geisel
□ to take somebody hostage jemanden als Geisel nehmen

hostel NOUN
die Herberge

hostile ADJECTIVE
feindlich

hot ADJECTIVE
1 heiß *(warm)*
□ a hot bath ein heißes Bad □ a hot country ein heißes Land □ It's hot. Es ist heiß. □ It's very hot today. Heute ist es sehr heiß.

LANGUAGE TIP When you talk about a person being 'hot', you use the impersonal construction.

□ I'm hot. Mir ist heiß. □ I'm too hot. Mir ist es zu heiß.
2 scharf *(spicy)*
□ a very hot curry ein sehr scharfes Curry

hot dog NOUN
der Hotdog (PL die Hotdogs)

hotel NOUN
das Hotel (PL die Hotels)
□ We stayed in a hotel. Wir haben in einem Hotel übernachtet.

hour NOUN
die Stunde
□ She always takes hours to get ready. Sie braucht immer Stunden, bis sie fertig ist.
■ **a quarter of an hour** eine Viertelstunde
■ **half an hour** eine halbe Stunde
■ **two and a half hours** zweieinhalb Stunden

hourly ADJECTIVE, ADVERB
stündlich
□ There are hourly buses. Der Bus verkehrt stündlich.
■ **to be paid hourly** stundenweise bezahlt werden

house NOUN
das Haus (GEN des Hauses, PL die Häuser)
■ **at his house** bei ihm zu Hause
■ **We stayed at their house.** Wir haben bei ihnen übernachtet.

housewife NOUN
die Hausfrau
□ She's a housewife. Sie ist Hausfrau.

housework NOUN
die Hausarbeit
□ to do the housework die Hausarbeit machen

hovercraft NOUN
das Luftkissenfahrzeug (PL die Luftkissenfahrzeuge)

how ADVERB
wie
□ How old are you? Wie alt bist du? □ How far is it to Edinburgh? Wie weit ist es nach Edinburgh? □ How long have you been here? Wie lange sind Sie schon hier? □ How are you? Wie geht's?
■ **How much?** Wie viel? □ How much sugar do you want? Wie viel Zucker willst du?
■ **How many?** Wie viele? □ How many girls are there in the class? Wie viele Mädchen sind in der Klasse?

however CONJUNCTION
aber
□ This, however, isn't true. Das ist aber nicht wahr.

to **howl** VERB
heulen

HTML ABBREVIATION *(= hypertext markup language)*
HTML

to **hug** VERB
▷ *see also* **hug** NOUN
umarmen (PERFECT hat umarmt)
□ He hugged her. Er umarmte sie.

hug NOUN
▷ *see also* **hug** VERB
■ **to give somebody a hug** jemanden umarmen □ She gave them a hug. Sie umarmte sie.

huge ADJECTIVE
riesig

to **hum** VERB
summen
□ She hummed to herself. Sie summte vor sich hin.

human ADJECTIVE
menschlich
□ the human body der menschliche Körper

human being NOUN
der Mensch (GEN des Menschen, PL die Menschen)

humble ADJECTIVE
bescheiden

humour NOUN
der Humor
■ **to have a sense of humour** Humor haben

hundred NUMBER
■ **a hundred** einhundert □ a hundred euros einhundert Euro
■ **five hundred** fünfhundert
■ **five hundred and one** fünfhundertundeins
■ **hundreds of people** Hunderte von Menschen

hung VERB ▷ *see* **hang**

Hungarian ADJECTIVE
ungarisch

Hungary NOUN
Ungarn *neut*
■ **from Hungary** aus Ungarn
■ **to Hungary** nach Ungarn

hunger NOUN
der Hunger

hungry ADJECTIVE
■ **to be hungry** Hunger haben □ I'm hungry. Ich habe Hunger.

to **hunt** VERB
jagen
□ People used to hunt wild boar. Menschen haben früher Wildschweine gejagt.
■ **to go hunting** auf die Jagd gehen
■ **The police are hunting the killer.** Die Polizei sucht den Mörder.
■ **to hunt for something** *(search)* nach etwas suchen □ I hunted everywhere for that DVD. Ich habe überall nach dieser DVD gesucht.

hunting NOUN
das Jagen
□ I'm against hunting. Ich bin gegen Jagen.
■ **fox-hunting** die Fuchsjagd

hurdle NOUN
die Hürde
□ the 100 metres hurdles die 100 Meter Hürden

hurricane NOUN
der Orkan (PL die Orkane)

to **hurry** VERB
▷ *see also* **hurry** NOUN
eilen (PERFECT ist geeilt)
□ Sharon hurried back home. Sharon eilte nach Hause.
■ **Hurry up!** Beeil dich!

hurry NOUN
▷ *see also* **hurry** VERB
■ **to be in a hurry** in Eile sein
■ **to do something in a hurry** etwas auf die Schnelle machen
■ **There's no hurry.** Das eilt nicht.

to **hurt** VERB
▷ *see also* **hurt** ADJECTIVE
wehtun (IMPERFECT tat weh, PERFECT hat wehgetan)
□ That hurts. Das tut weh. □ My leg hurts. Mein Bein tut weh. □ It hurts to have a tooth out. Es tut weh, wenn einem ein Zahn gezogen wird.
■ **to hurt somebody 1** jemandem wehtun □ You're hurting me! Du tust mir weh! **2** *(offend)* jemanden verletzen □ His remarks hurt me. Seine Bemerkungen haben mich verletzt.
■ **to hurt oneself** sich wehtun □ I fell over and hurt myself. Ich bin hingefallen und habe mir wehgetan.

hurt ADJECTIVE
▷ *see also* **hurt** VERB
verletzt
□ Is he badly hurt? Ist er schlimm verletzt? □ He was hurt in the leg. Er hatte ein verletztes Bein. □ Luckily, nobody got hurt. Zum Glück wurde niemand verletzt. □ I was hurt by what he said. Was er sagte hat mich verletzt.

husband NOUN
der Ehemann (PL die Ehemänner)

hut NOUN
die Hütte

hymn NOUN
das Kirchenlied (PL die Kirchenlieder)

hypermarket NOUN
der Verbrauchermarkt (PL die Verbrauchermärkte)

hyphen NOUN
der Bindestrich (PL die Bindestriche)

Ii

I PRONOUN
ich
□ I speak German. Ich spreche Deutsch.
□ Ann and I Ann und ich

ice NOUN
1 das Eis
■ **There was ice on the lake.** Der See war gefroren.
2 das Glatteis *(on road)*

iceberg NOUN
der Eisberg (PL die Eisberge)

icebox NOUN (US)
der Kühlschrank (PL die Kühlschränke)

ice cream NOUN
das Eis (PL die Eis)
□ vanilla ice cream das Vanilleeis

ice cube NOUN
der Eiswürfel (PL die Eiswürfel)

ice hockey NOUN
das Eishockey

Iceland NOUN
Island *neut*
■ **from Iceland** aus Island
■ **to Iceland** nach Island

ice lolly NOUN
das Eis am Stiel

ice rink NOUN
die Eisbahn

ice-skating NOUN
das Schlittschuhlaufen
■ **I like ice-skating.** Ich laufe gern Schlittschuh.
■ **to go ice-skating** Schlittschuh laufen gehen

icing NOUN
der Zuckerguss (GEN des Zuckergusses) *(on cake)*
■ **icing sugar** der Puderzucker

icon NOUN
das Icon (PL die Icons) *(computer)*
□ to click on an icon ein Icon anklicken

ICT NOUN *(= Information and Communications Technology)*
die IuK *(= Informations- und Kommunikationstechnik)*

icy ADJECTIVE
eiskalt
□ There was an icy wind. Es wehte ein eiskalter Wind.
■ **The roads are icy.** Die Straßen sind vereist.

I'd = I had, I would

idea NOUN
die Idee
□ Good idea! Gute Idee!

ideal ADJECTIVE
ideal

identical ADJECTIVE
identisch
□ identical to identisch mit

identification NOUN
die Identifikation
■ **Have you got any identification?** Können Sie sich ausweisen?

to **identify** VERB
identifizieren (PERFECT hat identifiziert)

identity card NOUN
der Personalausweis (PL die Personalausweise)

idiom NOUN
die Redewendung

idiot NOUN
der Idiot (GEN des Idioten, PL die Idioten)
die Idiotin

idiotic ADJECTIVE
idiotisch

idle ADJECTIVE
faul *(lazy)*
□ to be idle faul sein
■ **idle gossip.** sinnloses Geschwätz
■ **I asked out of idle curiosity.** Ich habe aus reiner Neugier gefragt.

i.e. ABBREVIATION
d. h. *(= das heißt)*

if CONJUNCTION
1 wenn
□ You can have it if you like. Wenn du willst, kannst du es haben.
2 ob *(whether)*
□ Do you know if he's there? Weißt du, ob er da ist?
■ **if only** wenn doch nur □ If only I had more money! Wenn ich doch nur mehr Geld hätte!
■ **if not** falls nicht □ Are you coming? If not, I'll go with Mark. Kommst du? Falls nicht, gehe ich mit Mark.

ignorant ADJECTIVE
unwissend

to **ignore** VERB
1 nicht beachten (PERFECT hat nicht beachtet)

□ She ignored my advice. Sie hat meinen Rat nicht beachtet.

2 ignorieren (PERFECT hat ignoriert)

□ She saw me, but she ignored me. Sie sah mich, hat mich aber ignoriert.

■ **Just ignore him!** Beachte ihn einfach nicht!

ill ADJECTIVE
krank *(sick)*

■ **to be taken ill** krank werden □ She was taken ill while on holiday. Sie wurde im Urlaub krank.

I'll = I will

illegal ADJECTIVE
illegal

illegible ADJECTIVE
unleserlich

illness NOUN
die Krankheit

to **ill-treat** VERB
misshandeln (PERFECT hat misshandelt)

illusion NOUN
die Illusion

illustration NOUN
die Illustration

I'm = I am

image NOUN
das Image (GEN des Image, PL die Images) *(public image)*

□ the company's image das Image der Firma

imagination NOUN
die Fantasie

□ You need a lot of imagination to be a writer. Als Schriftsteller braucht man viel Fantasie.

■ **It's just your imagination!** Das bildest du dir nur ein!

to **imagine** VERB
sich vorstellen (PERFECT hat sich vorgestellt)

□ Imagine how I felt! Stell dir vor, wie mir zumute war!

■ **Is he angry? — I imagine so.** Ist er böse? — Ich denke schon.

to **imitate** VERB
nachmachen (PERFECT hat nachgemacht)

imitation NOUN
die Imitation

immediate ADJECTIVE
sofortig

□ We need an immediate answer. Wir brauchen eine sofortige Antwort.

■ **in the immediate future** in unmittelbarer Zukunft

immediately ADVERB
sofort

□ I'll do it immediately. Ich mache es sofort.

immigrant NOUN
der Einwanderer (PL die Einwanderer)
die Einwanderin

immigration NOUN
die Einwanderung

immoral ADJECTIVE
unmoralisch

immune ADJECTIVE

■ **to be immune to something** gegen etwas immun sein □ She is immune to measles. Sie ist gegen Masern immun.

impartial ADJECTIVE
unparteiisch

impatience NOUN
die Ungeduld

impatient ADJECTIVE
ungeduldig

□ People are getting impatient. Die Leute werden ungeduldig.

impersonal ADJECTIVE
unpersönlich

to **implement** VERB
ausführen (PERFECT hat ausgeführt)

□ Chris will implement the plan. Chris wird den Plan ausführen.

to **imply** VERB
andeuten (PERFECT hat angedeutet)

□ Are you implying I stole it? Wollen Sie andeuten, ich hätte es gestohlen?

to **import** VERB
importieren (PERFECT hat importiert)

importance NOUN
die Wichtigkeit

□ the importance of a good knowledge of German die Wichtigkeit guter Deutschkenntnisse

important ADJECTIVE
wichtig

to **impose** VERB
auferlegen (PERFECT hat auferlegt)

□ to impose a penalty eine Strafe auferlegen

impossible ADJECTIVE
unmöglich

to **impress** VERB
beeindrucken (PERFECT hat beeindruckt)

□ She's trying to impress you. Sie will dich beeindrucken.

impressed ADJECTIVE
beeindruckt

□ I'm very impressed! Ich bin sehr beeindruckt!

impression NOUN
der Eindruck (PL die Eindrücke)

□ I was under the impression that ... Ich hatte den Eindruck, dass ...

impressive ADJECTIVE
beeindruckend

to **improve** VERB

1 verbessern (PERFECT hat verbessert) *(make better)*

□ The hotel has improved its service. Das Hotel hat den Service verbessert.

2 besser werden (PRESENT wird besser, IMPERFECT wurde besser, PERFECT ist besser geworden) *(get better)*

□ The weather is improving. Das Wetter wird besser. □ My German has improved. Mein Deutsch ist besser geworden.

improvement NOUN
1 die Verbesserung *(of condition)*
□ It's a great improvement. Das ist eine gewaltige Verbesserung.
2 der Fortschritt (PL die Fortschritte) *(of learner)*
□ There's been an improvement in his German. Er hat in Deutsch Fortschritte gemacht.

in PREPOSITION, ADVERB

LANGUAGE TIP Use the accusative to express movement or a change of place. Use the dative when there is no change of place.

1 in
□ It's in my bag. Es ist in meiner Tasche.
□ Put it in my bag. Tu es in meine Tasche.
□ I read it in this book. Ich habe es in diesem Buch gelesen. □ Write it in your address book. Schreib es in dein Adressbuch. □ in hospital im Krankenhaus □ in school in der Schule □ in London in London □ in Germany in Deutschland □ in Switzerland in der Schweiz □ in May im Mai □ in spring im Frühling □ in the rain im Regen □ I'll see you in three weeks. Ich sehe dich in drei Wochen.

LANGUAGE TIP Sometimes 'in' is not translated.

□ It happened in 1996. Es geschah 1996.
□ in the morning morgens □ in the afternoon nachmittags □ at six in the evening um sechs Uhr abends
2 mit
□ the boy in the blue shirt der Junge mit dem blauen Hemd □ It was written in pencil. Es war mit Bleistift geschrieben. □ in a loud voice mit lauter Stimme □ She paid in dollars. Sie hat mit Dollar bezahlt.
3 auf
□ in German auf Deutsch □ in English auf Englisch

LANGUAGE TIP 'in' is sometimes translated using the genitive.

□ the best pupil in the class der beste Schüler der Klasse □ the tallest person in the family der Größte der Familie
■ **in the beginning** am Anfang
■ **in the country** auf dem Land
■ **in time** rechtzeitig □ We arrived in time for dinner. Wir kamen rechtzeitig zum Abendessen.
■ **in here** hier drin □ It's hot in here. Hier drin ist es heiß.
■ **one person in ten** einer von zehn
■ **to be in** *(at home, work)* da sein
□ He wasn't in. Er war nicht da.
■ **to ask somebody in** jemanden hereinbitten

inaccurate ADJECTIVE
1 ungenau *(not precise)*
□ an inaccurate translation eine ungenaue Übersetzung
2 unrichtig *(not correct)*
□ What he said was inaccurate. Was er sagte war unrichtig.

inadequate ADJECTIVE
unzulänglich

incentive NOUN
die Motivation
□ There is no incentive to work. Es gibt keine Motivation zu arbeiten.

inch NOUN
der Zoll (PL die Zoll)

DID YOU KNOW...?
In Germany measurements are given in metres and centimetres rather than feet and inches. An inch is about 2.5 centimetres.

■ **six inches** fünfzehn Zentimeter

incident NOUN
der Vorfall (PL die Vorfälle)

inclined ADJECTIVE
■ **to be inclined to do something** dazu tendieren, etwas zu tun □ He's inclined to arrive late. Er tendiert dazu, zu spät zu kommen.

to **include** VERB
einschließen (IMPERFECT schloss ein, PERFECT hat eingeschlossen)
□ Service is not included. Bedienung ist nicht eingeschlossen.

including PREPOSITION
inklusive
□ That will be two hundred euros, including VAT. Das macht zweihundert Euro, inklusive Mehrwertsteuer.

inclusive ADJECTIVE
■ **The inclusive price is two hundred euros.** Das kostet alles in allem zweihundert Euro.
■ **inclusive of VAT** inklusive Mehrwertsteuer

income NOUN
das Einkommen (PL die Einkommen)

income tax NOUN
die Einkommensteuer

incompetent ADJECTIVE
inkompetent

incomplete ADJECTIVE
unvollständig

inconsistent ADJECTIVE
1 widersprüchlich
■ **to be inconsistent with ...** im Widerspruch stehen zu ...
2 unbeständig
□ Your work is very inconsistent. Die Qualität deiner Arbeit ist sehr unbeständig.

inconvenience NOUN
■ **I don't want to cause any inconvenience.** Ich möchte keine Umstände machen.

inconvenient ADJECTIVE
■ **That's very inconvenient for me.** Das passt mir gar nicht.

incorrect ADJECTIVE
unrichtig

English–German

i

increase NOUN
▷ *see also* **increase** VERB
die Zunahme
□ an increase in road accidents eine Zunahme an Verkehrsunfällen

to **increase** VERB
▷ *see also* **increase** NOUN
1 zunehmen (PRESENT nimmt zu, IMPERFECT nahm zu, PERFECT hat zugenommen) *(traffic, number)*
□ Traffic on motorways has increased. Der Verkehr auf den Autobahnen hat zugenommen.
2 steigen (IMPERFECT stieg, PERFECT ist gestiegen) *(price, demand)*
□ with increasing demand bei steigender Nachfrage
3 stärker werden (PRESENT wird stärker, IMPERFECT wurde stärker, PERFECT ist stärker geworden) *(pain, wind)*
■ **to increase in size** größer werden
■ **to increase something** etwas erhöhen
□ They have increased the price. Sie haben den Preis erhöht.
■ **increased cost of living** höhere Lebenshaltungskosten

incredible ADJECTIVE
unglaublich

indecisive ADJECTIVE
unentschlossen *(person)*

indeed ADVERB
wirklich
□ It's very hard indeed. Es ist wirklich schwer.
■ **Know what I mean? — Indeed I do.** Weißt du, was ich meine? — Ja, ganz genau.
■ **Thank you very much indeed!** Ganz herzlichen Dank!

independence NOUN
die Unabhängigkeit

independent ADJECTIVE
unabhängig
■ **an independent school** eine Privatschule

index NOUN
das Verzeichnis (GEN des Verzeichnisses, PL die Verzeichnisse) *(in book)*

India NOUN
Indien *neut*
■ **from India** aus Indien
■ **to India** nach Indien

Indian ADJECTIVE
▷ *see also* **Indian** NOUN
1 indisch
2 indianisch *(American Indian)*

Indian NOUN
▷ *see also* **Indian** ADJECTIVE
der Inder (PL die Inder)
die Inderin *(person)*
■ **an American Indian** ein Indianer *masc*

to **indicate** VERB
1 zeigen
□ His reaction indicates how he feels about it. Seine Reaktion zeigt, was er davon hält.
2 andeuten (PERFECT hat angedeutet) *(make known)*
□ He indicated that he may resign. Er hat angedeutet, dass er vielleicht zurücktritt.
3 anzeigen (PERFECT hat angezeigt) *(technical device)*
□ The gauge indicated a very high temperature. Das Messgerät zeigte eine sehr hohe Temperatur an.
■ **to indicate left** links blinken

indicator NOUN
der Blinker (PL die Blinker) *(in car)*

indigestion NOUN
die Magenverstimmung
■ **I've got indigestion.** Ich habe eine Magenverstimmung.

individual NOUN
▷ *see also* **individual** ADJECTIVE
das Individuum (PL die Individuen)

individual ADJECTIVE
▷ *see also* **individual** NOUN
individuell

indoor ADJECTIVE
■ **an indoor swimming pool** ein Hallenbad

indoors ADVERB
im Haus
□ They're indoors. Sie sind im Haus.
■ **to go indoors** hineingehen □ We'd better go indoors. Wir gehen besser hinein.

industrial ADJECTIVE
industriell

industrial estate NOUN
das Industriegebiet (PL die Industriegebiete)

industry NOUN
die Industrie
□ the tourist industry die Tourismusindustrie
□ the oil industry die Erdölindustrie
■ **I'd like to work in industry.** Ich würde gern in der freien Wirtschaft arbeiten.

inefficient ADJECTIVE
ineffizient

inevitable ADJECTIVE
unvermeidlich

inexpensive ADJECTIVE
preiswert
□ an inexpensive hotel ein preiswertes Hotel
■ **inexpensive holidays** günstige Ferien

inexperienced ADJECTIVE
unerfahren

infant school NOUN
die Grundschule

DID YOU KNOW...?
The **Grundschule** is a primary school which children attend from the age of 6 to 10. Many children attend **Kindergarten** before going to the **Grundschule**.

infection NOUN
die Entzündung
□ an ear infection eine Ohrenentzündung
□ a throat infection eine Halsentzündung

infectious ADJECTIVE
ansteckend
□ It's not infectious. Es ist nicht ansteckend.

infinitive NOUN
der Infinitiv (PL die Infinitive)

infirmary NOUN
das Krankenhaus (GEN des Krankenhauses, PL die Krankenhäuser)

inflatable ADJECTIVE
■ **an inflatable mattress** eine Luftmatratze
■ **an inflatable dinghy** ein Gummiboot *neut*

inflation NOUN
die Inflation

influence NOUN
▷ *see also* **influence** VERB
der Einfluss (GEN des Einflusses, PL die Einflüsse)
□ He's a bad influence on her. Er hat einen schlechten Einfluss auf sie.

to **influence** VERB
▷ *see also* **influence** NOUN
beeinflussen (PERFECT hat beeinflusst)

influenza NOUN
die Grippe

to **inform** VERB
informieren (PERFECT hat informiert)
■ **to inform somebody of something** jemanden über etwas informieren □ Nobody informed me of the new plan. Niemand hat mich über den neuen Plan informiert.

informal ADJECTIVE
1 locker *(person)*
2 zwanglos *(party)*
□ 'informal dress' 'zwanglose Kleidung'
3 umgangssprachlich *(colloquial)*
■ **informal language** die Umgangssprache
■ **an informal visit** ein inoffizieller Besuch

information NOUN
die Information
□ important information wichtige Informationen
■ **a piece of information** eine Information
■ **Could you give me some information about Berlin?** Können Sie mir einige Informationen über Berlin geben?

information office NOUN
die Auskunft (PL die Auskünfte)

information technology NOUN
die Informationstechnik

infuriating ADJECTIVE
äußerst ärgerlich

ingenious ADJECTIVE
genial

ingredient NOUN
die Zutat

inhabitant NOUN
der Einwohner (PL die Einwohner)
die Einwohnerin *(of country, town)*

inhaler NOUN
der Inhalator (PL die Inhalatoren)

to **inherit** VERB
erben
□ She inherited her father's house. Sie erbte das Haus ihres Vaters.

initials PL NOUN
die Initialen *fem pl*
□ Her initials are CDT. Ihre Initialen sind CDT.

initiative NOUN
die Initiative

to **inject** VERB
spritzen *(drug)*
□ He injected himself with heroin. Er hat sich Heroin gespritzt.

injection NOUN
die Spritze

to **injure** VERB
verletzen (PERFECT hat verletzt)

injured ADJECTIVE
verletzt

injury NOUN
die Verletzung

injury time NOUN
■ **to play injury time** nachspielen

injustice NOUN
die Ungerechtigkeit

ink NOUN
die Tinte

in-laws PL NOUN
die Schwiegereltern *pl*

inn NOUN
das Gasthaus (GEN des Gasthauses, PL die Gasthäuser)

inner ADJECTIVE
■ **the inner city** die Innenstadt

inner tube NOUN
der Schlauch (PL die Schläuche)

innocent ADJECTIVE
unschuldig

inquest NOUN
die gerichtliche Untersuchung

to **inquire** VERB
■ **to inquire about something** sich nach etwas erkundigen

inquiries office NOUN
die Auskunft (PL die Auskünfte)

inquiry NOUN
die Untersuchung *(official investigation)*

inquisitive ADJECTIVE
neugierig

insane ADJECTIVE
wahnsinnig

inscription NOUN
die Inschrift

insect NOUN
das Insekt (PL die Insekten)

insect repellent NOUN
das Insektenschutzmittel (PL die Insektenschutzmittel)

insensitive ADJECTIVE
gefühllos

to **insert** VERB
einwerfen (PRESENT wirft ein, IMPERFECT warf ein, PERFECT hat eingeworfen)
□ I inserted a coin. Ich warf eine Münze ein.

inside NOUN
▷ *see also* **inside** ADVERB
das Innere (GEN des Inneren)

inside ADVERB, PREPOSITION
▷ *see also* **inside** NOUN
innen
□ inside and outside innen und außen
■ **They're inside.** Sie sind drinnen.
■ **to go inside** hineingehen
■ **Come inside!** Kommt herein!

LANGUAGE TIP Use the accusative to express movement or a change of place. Use the dative when there is no change of place.

■ **inside the house 1** im Haus □ She was inside the house. Sie war im Haus. **2** ins Haus □ She went inside the house. Sie ging ins Haus.

insincere ADJECTIVE
unaufrichtig

to **insist** VERB
darauf bestehen (IMPERFECT bestand darauf, PERFECT hat darauf bestanden)
□ I didn't want to, but he insisted. Ich wollte nicht, aber er hat darauf bestanden.
■ **to insist on doing something** darauf bestehen, etwas zu tun □ She insisted on paying. Sie hat darauf bestanden zu bezahlen.
■ **He insisted he was innocent.** Er beteuerte seine Unschuld.

to **inspect** VERB
kontrollieren (PERFECT hat kontrolliert)

inspector NOUN
der Kommissar (PL die Kommissare)
die Kommissarin *(police)*
□ Inspector Jill Brown Kommissarin Jill Brown

to **install** VERB
installieren (PERFECT hat installiert)

instalment (US **installment**) NOUN
1 die Rate
□ to pay in instalments in Raten zahlen
2 die Folge *(of TV, radio serial)*
3 der Teil *(of publication)*

instance NOUN
■ **for instance** zum Beispiel

instant ADJECTIVE
sofortig
□ It was an instant success. Es war ein sofortiger Erfolg.
■ **instant coffee** der Pulverkaffee

instantly ADVERB
sofort

instead ADVERB
■ **instead of 1** *(followed by noun)* anstelle von □ Use honey instead of sugar. Nehmen Sie Honig anstelle von Zucker. **2** *(followed by verb)* statt □ We played tennis instead of going swimming. Wir spielten Tennis statt schwimmen zu gehen.
■ **The pool was closed, so we played tennis instead.** Das Schwimmbad war zu, also spielten wir stattdessen Tennis.

instinct NOUN
der Instinkt (PL die Instinkte)

institute NOUN
das Institut

institution NOUN
die Institution

to **instruct** VERB
anweisen (IMPERFECT wies an, PERFECT hat angewiesen)
■ **to instruct somebody to do something** jemanden anweisen, etwas zu tun
□ She instructed us to wait outside. Sie wies uns an, draußen zu warten.

instructions PL NOUN
1 die Anweisungen *fem pl*
□ Follow the instructions carefully. Befolgen Sie die Anweisungen genau.
2 die Gebrauchsanweisung *(manual)*
□ Where are the instructions? Wo ist die Gebrauchsanweisung?

instructor NOUN
der Lehrer (PL die Lehrer)
die Lehrerin
□ a skiing instructor ein Skilehrer
□ a driving instructor ein Fahrlehrer

instrument NOUN
das Instrument (PL die Instrumente)
□ Do you play an instrument? Spielst du ein Instrument?

insufficient ADJECTIVE
unzureichend

insulin NOUN
das Insulin

insult NOUN
▷ *see also* **insult** VERB
die Beleidigung

to **insult** VERB
▷ *see also* **insult** NOUN
beleidigen (PERFECT hat beleidigt)

insurance NOUN
die Versicherung
□ his car insurance seine Kraftfahrzeugversicherung
■ **an insurance policy** eine Versicherungspolice

intelligent ADJECTIVE
intelligent

to **intend** VERB
■ **to intend to do something** beabsichtigen, etwas zu tun □ I intend to do German at university. Ich beabsichtige, Deutsch zu studieren.

intense ADJECTIVE
stark

intensive ADJECTIVE
intensiv

intention NOUN
die Absicht

intercom NOUN
die Sprechanlage

interest NOUN
▷ *see also* **interest** VERB
das Interesse (PL die Interessen)
□ to show an interest in something Interesse an etwas zeigen □ What interests do you have? Welche Interessen hast du?
■ **My main interest is music.** Ich interessiere mich hauptsächlich für Musik.

to **interest** VERB
▷ *see also* **interest** NOUN
interessieren (PERFECT hat interessiert)
□ It doesn't interest me. Das interessiert mich nicht.
■ **to be interested in something** sich für etwas interessieren □ I'm not interested in politics. Ich interessiere mich nicht für Politik.

interesting ADJECTIVE
interessant

interior NOUN
das Innere (GEN des Inneren)

interior designer NOUN
der Innenarchitekt (GEN des Innenarchitekten, PL die Innenarchitekten)
die Innenarchitektin

intermediate ADJECTIVE
■ **an intermediate course** ein Kurs für fortgeschrittene Anfänger

internal ADJECTIVE
innere
□ the internal organs die inneren Organe

international ADJECTIVE
international

internet NOUN
das Internet
□ on the internet im Internet

internet café NOUN
das Internet-Café (PL die Internet-Cafés)

internet user NOUN
der Internetbenutzer (PL die Internetbenutzer)
die Internetbenutzerin

to **interpret** VERB
übersetzen (PERFECT hat übersetzt)
□ Steve couldn't speak German, so his friend interpreted. Steve konnte kein Deutsch, also übersetzte sein Freund.

interpreter NOUN
der Dolmetscher (PL die Dolmetscher)
die Dolmetscherin

to **interrupt** VERB
unterbrechen (PRESENT unterbricht, IMPERFECT unterbrach, PERFECT hat unterbrochen)

interruption NOUN
die Unterbrechung

interval NOUN
die Pause *(in play, concert)*

interview NOUN
▷ *see also* **interview** VERB
1 das Interview (PL die Interviews) *(on TV, radio)*
2 das Vorstellungsgespräch (PL die Vorstellungsgespräche) *(for job)*

to **interview** VERB
▷ *see also* **interview** NOUN
interviewen (PERFECT hat interviewt) *(on TV, radio)*
□ I was interviewed on the radio. Ich wurde im Radio interviewt.

interviewer NOUN
der Moderator (PL die Moderatoren)
die Moderatorin *(on TV, radio)*

intimate ADJECTIVE
eng
□ an intimate friendship eine enge Freundschaft
■ **my intimate feelings** meine innersten Gefühle

into PREPOSITION
in

LANGUAGE TIP In this sense **in** is followed by the accusative.

□ He got into the car. Er stieg ins Auto.
□ I'm going into town. Ich gehe in die Stadt.
□ Translate it into German. Übersetze das ins Deutsche. □ Divide into two groups. Teilt euch in zwei Gruppen.

intranet NOUN
das Intranet (PL die Intranets)

to **introduce** VERB
vorstellen (PERFECT hat vorgestellt)
□ He introduced me to his parents. Er stellte mich seinen Eltern vor.

introduction NOUN
die Einleitung *(in book)*

intruder NOUN
der Eindringling (PL die Eindringlinge)

LANGUAGE TIP **der Eindringling** is also used for women.

intuition NOUN
die Intuition

to **invade** VERB
eindringen in *+acc* (IMPERFECT drang ein, PERFECT ist eingedrungen)
□ to invade a country in ein Land eindringen

invalid NOUN
der Kranke (GEN des Kranken, PL die Kranken)
die Kranke (GEN der Kranken)
□ an invalid *(man)* ein Kranker

to **invent** VERB
erfinden (IMPERFECT erfand, PERFECT hat erfunden)

invention NOUN
die Erfindung

inventor NOUN
der Erfinder (PL die Erfinder)
die Erfinderin

to **invest** VERB
investieren (PERFECT hat investiert)

investigation NOUN
die Untersuchung *(police)*

investment NOUN
die Investition

invigilator NOUN
die Aufsicht

LANGUAGE TIP **die Aufsicht** is also used for men.

□ You have to ask the invigilator. Du musst die Aufsicht fragen.

invisible ADJECTIVE
unsichtbar

invitation NOUN
die Einladung

to **invite** VERB
einladen (PRESENT lädt ein, IMPERFECT lud ein, PERFECT hat eingeladen)

□ He's not invited. Er ist nicht eingeladen.

■ **to invite somebody to a party** jemanden zu einer Party einladen

to **involve** VERB
mit sich bringen (IMPERFECT brachte mit sich, PERFECT hat mit sich gebracht)

□ This will involve a lot of work. Das wird viel Arbeit mit sich bringen.

■ **His job involves a lot of travelling.** Er muss in seinem Job viel reisen.

■ **to be involved in something** *(crime, drugs)* in etwas verwickelt sein □ He was involved in the murder. Er war in den Mord verwickelt.

■ **to be involved with somebody** *(in relationship)* mit jemandem eine Beziehung haben

■ **I don't want to get involved.** Ich will damit nichts zu tun haben.

iPod® NOUN
der iPod® (PL die iPods)

IQ NOUN *(= intelligence quotient)*
der IQ (GEN des IQ, PL die IQ)
(= Intelligenzquotient)

Iran NOUN
der Iran

LANGUAGE TIP Note that the definite article is used in German for countries which are masculine.

■ **from Iran** aus dem Iran

■ **in Iran** im Iran

■ **to Iran** in den Iran

Iraq NOUN
der Irak

LANGUAGE TIP Note that the definite article is used in German for countries which are masculine.

■ **from Iraq** aus dem Irak

■ **in Iraq** im Irak

■ **to Iraq** in den Irak

Iraqi NOUN
▷ *see also* **Iraqi** ADJECTIVE
der Iraker (PL die Iraker)
die Irakerin

Iraqi ADJECTIVE
▷ *see also* **Iraqi** NOUN
irakisch

Ireland NOUN
Irland *neut*

■ **from Ireland** aus Irland

■ **in Ireland** in Irland

■ **to Ireland** nach Irland

Irish ADJECTIVE
▷ *see also* **Irish** NOUN
irisch

□ Irish music irische Musik

■ **He's Irish.** Er ist Ire.

■ **She's Irish.** Sie ist Irin.

Irish NOUN
▷ *see also* **Irish** ADJECTIVE
das Irisch (GEN des Irischen) *(language)*

■ **the Irish** *(people)* die Iren *masc pl*

Irishman NOUN
der Ire (GEN des Iren, PL die Iren)

Irishwoman NOUN
die Irin

iron NOUN
▷ *see also* **iron** VERB

1 das Eisen *(metal)*

2 das Bügeleisen (PL die Bügeleisen) *(for clothes)*

to **iron** VERB
▷ *see also* **iron** NOUN
bügeln

ironic ADJECTIVE
ironisch

ironing NOUN
das Bügeln

■ **to do the ironing** bügeln

ironing board NOUN
das Bügelbrett (PL die Bügelbretter)

ironmonger's (shop) NOUN
die Eisenwarenhandlung

irrelevant ADJECTIVE
irrelevant

□ That's irrelevant. Das ist irrelevant.

irresponsible ADJECTIVE
verantwortungslos *(person)*

■ **That was irresponsible of him.** Das war unverantwortlich von ihm.

irritating ADJECTIVE
nervend

is VERB ▷ *see* **be**

Islam NOUN
der Islam

LANGUAGE TIP Note that the definite article is used in German.

Islamic ADJECTIVE
islamisch

□ Islamic fundamentalists islamische Fundamentalisten

■ **Islamic law** das Recht des Islams

island NOUN
die Insel

isle NOUN
■ **the Isle of Man** die Insel Man
■ **the Isle of Wight** die Insel Wight

isolated ADJECTIVE
abgelegen *(place)*
■ **She feels very isolated.** Sie fühlt sich sehr isoliert.
■ **an isolated case** ein Einzelfall *masc*

ISP ABBREVIATION *(= Internet Service Provider)*
der Internet-Anbieter (PL die Internet-Anbieter)

Israel NOUN
Israel *neut*
■ **from Israel** aus Israel
■ **to Israel** nach Israel

Israeli NOUN
▷ *see also* **Israeli** ADJECTIVE
der Israeli (GEN des Israeli, PL die Israeli)
die Israeli (GEN der Israeli)

Israeli ADJECTIVE
▷ *see also* **Israeli** NOUN
israelisch
■ **He's Israeli.** Er ist Israeli.

issue NOUN
▷ *see also* **issue** VERB
1 die Frage *(matter)*
□ a controversial issue eine umstrittene Frage
2 die Ausgabe *(of magazine)*

to **issue** VERB
▷ *see also* **issue** NOUN
ausgeben (PRESENT gibt aus, IMPERFECT gab aus, PERFECT hat ausgegeben) *(equipment, supplies)*

it PRONOUN

LANGUAGE TIP Remember to check if 'it' stands for a masculine, feminine or neuter noun, and use the appropriate gender and case.

1 er
□ Your hat? — It's on the table. Dein Hut? — Er ist auf dem Tisch.
sie
□ Where's your watch? — It's broken. Wo ist deine Uhr? — Sie ist kaputt.
es
□ Have you seen her new dress, it's very pretty. Hast du ihr neues Kleid gesehen, es ist sehr hübsch.
2 ihn
□ Where's my hat? — I haven't seen it. Wo ist mein Hut? — Ich habe ihn nicht gesehen.
sie
□ Where's your jacket? — I've lost it. Wo ist deine Jacke? — Ich habe sie verloren.
es
□ Take my ruler, I don't need it. Nimm mein Lineal, ich brauche es nicht.
■ **It's raining.** Es regnet.
■ **It's six o'clock.** Es ist sechs Uhr.
■ **It's Friday tomorrow.** Morgen ist Freitag.
■ **Who is it? — It's me.** Wer ist's? — Ich bin's.
■ **It's expensive.** Das ist teuer.

Italian ADJECTIVE
▷ *see also* **Italian** NOUN
italienisch
■ **She's Italian.** Sie ist Italienerin.

Italian NOUN
▷ *see also* **Italian** ADJECTIVE
1 der Italiener (PL die Italiener)
die Italienerin *(person)*
2 das Italienisch (GEN des Italienischen) *(language)*

italics PL NOUN
die Kursivschrift
■ **in italics** kursiv

Italy NOUN
Italien *neut*
■ **from Italy** aus Italien
■ **in Italy** in Italien
■ **to Italy** nach Italien

to **itch** VERB
jucken
□ It itches. Es juckt. □ My head's itching. Mein Kopf juckt.

itchy ADJECTIVE
■ **My arm is itchy.** Mein Arm juckt.

it'd = **it had, it would**

item NOUN
der Artikel (PL die Artikel) *(object)*

itinerary NOUN
die Reiseroute

it'll = **it will**

its ADJECTIVE

LANGUAGE TIP Remember to check if 'its' refers back to a masculine, feminine or neuter noun, and use the appropriate gender and case.

sein
□ The dog is in its kennel. Der Hund ist in seiner Hütte.
ihr
□ The cup is in its usual place. Die Tasse ist an ihrem üblichen Platz.
sein
□ The baby is in its cot. Das Baby ist in seinem Bett.

it's = **it is, it has**

itself PRONOUN
1 sich
□ The dog scratched itself. Der Hund kratzte sich.
2 selbst
□ The heating switches itself off. Die Heizung schaltet von selbst aus.

I've = **I have**

Jj

jab NOUN
die Spritze *(injection)*

jack NOUN
1 der Wagenheber (PL die Wagenheber) *(for car)*
2 der Bube (GEN des Buben, PL die Buben) *(playing card)*

jacket NOUN
die Jacke
■ **jacket potatoes** gebackene Kartoffeln

jackpot NOUN
der Jackpot (PL die Jackpots)
□ to win the jackpot den Jackpot gewinnen

jail NOUN
▷ *see also* **jail** VERB
das Gefängnis (GEN des Gefängnisses, PL die Gefängnisse)
■ **She was sent to jail.** Sie musste ins Gefängnis.

to **jail** VERB
▷ *see also* **jail** NOUN
einsperren (PERFECT hat eingesperrt)
■ **He was jailed for ten years.** Er hat zehn Jahre Gefängnis bekommen.

jam NOUN
die Marmelade
□ strawberry jam Erdbeermarmelade
■ **a traffic jam** ein Verkehrsstau *masc*

jam jar NOUN
das Marmeladenglas (GEN des Marmeladenglases, PL die Marmeladengläser)

jammed ADJECTIVE
■ **The window's jammed.** Das Fenster klemmt.

jam-packed ADJECTIVE
brechend voll
□ The room was jam-packed. Der Raum war brechend voll.

janitor NOUN
der Hausmeister (PL die Hausmeister)
die Hausmeisterin
□ He's a janitor. Er ist Hausmeister.

January NOUN
der Januar
■ **in January** im Januar

Japan NOUN
Japan *neut*
■ **from Japan** aus Japan
■ **to Japan** nach Japan

Japanese ADJECTIVE
▷ *see also* **Japanese** NOUN
japanisch

Japanese NOUN
▷ *see also* **Japanese** ADJECTIVE
1 der Japaner (PL die Japaner)
die Japanerin *(person)*
■ **the Japanese** die Japaner *masc pl*
2 das Japanisch (GEN des Japanischen) *(language)*

jar NOUN
das Glas (GEN des Glases, PL die Gläser)
□ an empty jar ein leeres Glas □ a jar of honey ein Glas Honig

jaundice NOUN
die Gelbsucht
□ She's suffering from jaundice. Sie hat Gelbsucht.

javelin NOUN
der Speer (PL die Speere)

jaw NOUN
der Kiefer (PL die Kiefer)

jazz NOUN
der Jazz (GEN des Jazz)

jealous ADJECTIVE
eifersüchtig

jeans PL NOUN
die Jeans *fem pl*
□ a pair of jeans eine Jeans

Jehovah's Witness NOUN
der Zeuge Jehovas (GEN des Zeugen Jehovas, PL die Zeugen Jehovas)
die Zeugin Jehovas
□ She's a Jehovah's Witness. Sie ist Zeugin Jehovas.

Jello® NOUN (US)
der Wackelpudding

jelly NOUN
1 der Wackelpudding *(dessert)*
2 die Marmelade *(jam)*

jellyfish NOUN
die Qualle

jersey NOUN
der Pullover (PL die Pullover)

Jesus NOUN
Jesus *masc* (GEN des Jesus)

jet NOUN
das Düsenflugzeug (PL die Düsenflugzeuge) *(plane)*

jetlag NOUN
■ **to be suffering from jetlag** unter der Zeitverschiebung leiden

jetty NOUN
die Mole

Jew NOUN
der Jude (GEN des Juden, PL die Juden)
die Jüdin

jewel NOUN
der Edelstein (PL die Edelsteine) *(stone)*

jeweller NOUN
der Juwelier (PL die Juweliere)
die Juwelierin
□ He's a jeweller. Er ist Juwelier.

jeweller's shop NOUN
das Juweliergeschäft (PL die Juweliergeschäfte)

jewellery NOUN
der Schmuck

Jewish ADJECTIVE
jüdisch

jigsaw NOUN
das Puzzle (PL die Puzzles)

job NOUN
1 der Job (PL die Jobs)
□ He's lost his job. Er hat seinen Job verloren.
□ I've got a Saturday job. Ich habe einen Samstagsjob.
2 die Arbeit *(chore, task)*
□ That was a difficult job. Das war eine schwierige Arbeit.

job centre NOUN
das Arbeitsamt (PL die Arbeitsämter)

jobless ADJECTIVE
arbeitslos

jockey NOUN
der Jockey (PL die Jockeys)

to **jog** VERB
joggen

jogging NOUN
das Jogging
□ I like jogging. Ich mag Jogging.
■ **to go jogging** joggen

john NOUN (US)
das Klo (PL die Klos) *(informal)*

to **join** VERB
1 beitreten (PRESENT tritt bei, IMPERFECT trat bei, PERFECT ist beigetreten) *(become member of)*
□ I'm going to join the tennis club. Ich trete dem Tennisklub bei.
2 sich anschließen (IMPERFECT schloss sich an, PERFECT hat sich angeschlossen) *(accompany)*
□ Do you mind if I join you? Macht es dir etwas aus, wenn ich mich dir anschließe?

to **join in** VERB
1 mitmachen (PERFECT hat mitgemacht)
□ He doesn't join in with what we do. Er macht nicht mit bei den Dingen, die wir tun.
2 einstimmen (PERFECT hat eingestimmt)
□ She started singing, and the audience joined in. Sie begann zu singen, und das Publikum stimmte mit ein.

joiner NOUN
der Schreiner (PL die Schreiner)
die Schreinerin
□ She's a joiner. Sie ist Schreinerin.

joint NOUN
1 das Gelenk (PL die Gelenke) *(in body)*
2 der Braten (PL die Braten) *(of meat)*
3 der Joint (PL die Joints) *(drugs)*

joke NOUN
▷ *see also* **joke** VERB
der Witz (GEN des Witzes, PL die Witze)
□ to tell a joke einen Witz erzählen

to **joke** VERB
▷ *see also* **joke** NOUN
Spaß machen
□ I'm only joking. Ich mache nur Spaß.

jolly ADJECTIVE
fröhlich

Jordan NOUN
Jordanien *neut (country)*
■ **from Jordan** aus Jordanien
■ **to Jordan** nach Jordanien

to **jot down** VERB
notieren (PERFECT hat notiert)

jotter NOUN
der Notizblock (PL die Notizblöcke) *(pad)*

journalism NOUN
der Journalismus (GEN des Journalismus)

journalist NOUN
der Journalist (GEN des Journalisten, PL die Journalisten)
die Journalistin
□ She's a journalist. Sie ist Journalistin.

journey NOUN
1 die Reise
□ I don't like long journeys. Ich mag lange Reisen nicht.
■ **to go on a journey** eine Reise machen
2 die Fahrt *(to school, work)*
□ the journey to school die Fahrt zur Schule
■ **a bus journey** eine Busfahrt

joy NOUN
die Freude

joystick NOUN
der Joystick (PL die Joysticks) *(for computer game)*

judge NOUN
▷ *see also* **judge** VERB
der Richter (PL die Richter)
die Richterin
□ She's a judge. Sie ist Richterin.

to **judge** VERB
▷ *see also* **judge** NOUN
beurteilen (PERFECT hat beurteilt) *(assess)*
□ You can judge for yourself which is better. Du kannst das selbst beurteilen, welches besser ist.

judo NOUN
das Judo (GEN des Judo)
□ My hobby is judo. Judo ist mein Hobby.

jug NOUN
der Krug (PL die Krüge)

juggler NOUN
der Jongleur
die Jongleurin

juice NOUN
der Saft (PL die Säfte)
□ orange juice der Orangensaft

July NOUN
der Juli
■ **in July** im Juli

jumble sale NOUN
der Flohmarkt (PL die Flohmärkte)

to **jump** VERB
springen (IMPERFECT sprang, PERFECT ist gesprungen)
□ to jump out of the window aus dem Fenster springen □ to jump off the roof vom Dach springen
■ **to jump over something** über etwas springen □ He jumped over the fence. Er sprang über den Zaun.

jumper NOUN
1 der Pullover (PL die Pullover)
2 das Trägerkleid (PL die Trägerkleider) *(dress)*

junction NOUN
1 die Kreuzung *(of roads)*
2 die Ausfahrt *(motorway exit)*

June NOUN
der Juni
■ **in June** im Juni

jungle NOUN
der Dschungel (PL die Dschungel)

junior NOUN
■ **the juniors** die Grundschüler *masc pl*

junior school NOUN
die Grundschule

DID YOU KNOW...?
The **Grundschule** is a primary school which children attend from the age of 6 to 10.

junk NOUN
der Krempel *(old things)*
□ The attic's full of junk. Der Speicher ist voller Krempel.
■ **to eat junk food** Junkfood essen
■ **a junk shop** ein Trödelladen *masc*

jury NOUN
die Geschworenen *masc pl (in court)*

just ADVERB
1 gerade *(barely)*
□ We had just enough money. Wir hatten gerade genug Geld. □ just in time gerade noch rechtzeitig
2 kurz *(shortly)*
□ just after Christmas kurz nach Weihnachten
3 genau *(exactly)*
□ just here genau hier
4 eben *(this minute)*
□ I did it just now. Ich habe es eben gemacht.
□ He's just arrived. Er ist eben angekommen.
■ **I'm rather busy just now.** Ich bin gerade ziemlich beschäftigt.
■ **I'm just coming!** Ich komme schon!
5 nur *(only)*
□ It's just a suggestion. Es ist nur ein Vorschlag.

justice NOUN
die Gerechtigkeit

to **justify** VERB
rechtfertigen

kangaroo NOUN
das Känguru (PL die Kängurus)

karate NOUN
das Karate (GEN des Karate)
□ I like karate. Ich mag Karate.

kebab NOUN
der Kebab (PL die Kebabs)

keen ADJECTIVE
1 begeistert *(enthusiastic)*
□ He doesn't seem very keen. Er scheint nicht gerade begeistert.
2 eifrig *(hardworking)*
□ She's a keen student. Sie ist eine eifrige Studentin.
■ **to be keen on something** etwas mögen
□ I'm keen on maths. Ich mag Mathe.
□ I'm not very keen on maths. Ich mag Mathe nicht besonders.
■ **to be keen on somebody** *(fancy them)* auf jemanden stehen □ He's keen on her. Er steht auf sie.
■ **to be keen on doing something** Lust haben, etwas zu tun □ I'm not very keen on going. Ich habe keine große Lust zu gehen.

to **keep** VERB
1 behalten (PRESENT behält, IMPERFECT behielt, PERFECT hat behalten) *(retain)*
□ You can keep it. Das kannst du behalten.
2 sein (PRESENT ist, IMPERFECT war, PERFECT ist gewesen) *(remain)*
□ Keep quiet! Sei still!
■ **Keep still!** Halt still!
■ **I keep forgetting my keys.** Ich vergesse dauernd meine Schlüssel.
■ **to keep on doing something 1** *(continue)* etwas weiter tun □ He kept on reading. Er las weiter. **2** *(repeatedly)* etwas dauernd tun
□ The car keeps on breaking down. Das Auto ist dauernd kaputt.
■ **'keep out'** 'Kein Zutritt'
■ **to keep up** mithalten □ Matthew walks so fast I can't keep up. Matthew geht so schnell, da kann ich nicht mithalten.

keep-fit NOUN
die Gymnastik
□ I like keep-fit. Ich mache gern Gymnastik.
■ **I go to keep-fit classes.** Ich gehe zur Gymnastik.

kennel NOUN
die Hundehütte

kept VERB ▷ *see* **keep**

kerosene NOUN (US)
das Petroleum

kettle NOUN
der Wasserkessel (PL die Wasserkessel)

key NOUN
der Schlüssel (PL die Schlüssel)

keyboard NOUN
1 die Tastatur *(of piano, computer)*
2 das Keyboard (PL die Keyboards) *(of electric organ)*
□ ... with Mike Moran on keyboards ... mit Mike Moran am Keyboard

keyring NOUN
der Schlüsselring (PL die Schlüsselringe)

kick NOUN
▷ *see also* **kick** VERB
der Tritt (PL die Tritte)

to **kick** VERB
▷ *see also* **kick** NOUN
treten (PRESENT tritt, IMPERFECT trat, PERFECT hat getreten)
□ He kicked me. Er hat mich getreten.
□ He kicked the ball hard. Er trat kräftig gegen den Ball.
■ **to kick off** *(in football)* anfangen

kick-off NOUN
der Anstoß (GEN des Anstoßes, PL die Anstöße)
□ Kick-off is at ten o'clock. Um zehn Uhr ist Anstoß.

kid NOUN
▷ *see also* **kid** VERB
das Kind (PL die Kinder) *(child)*

to **kid** VERB
▷ *see also* **kid** NOUN
Spaß machen
□ I'm just kidding. Ich mache nur Spaß.

to **kidnap** VERB
entführen (PERFECT hat entführt)

kidney NOUN
die Niere
□ He's got kidney trouble. Er hat Nierenprobleme. □ I don't like kidneys. Ich mag Nieren nicht.

to **kill** VERB
töten

■ **to be killed** umkommen ◻ He was killed in a car accident. Er kam bei einem Unfall um. ◻ Luckily, nobody was killed. Zum Glück ist niemand dabei umgekommen.
■ **to kill oneself** sich umbringen ◻ He killed himself. Er hat sich umgebracht.

killer NOUN
1 der Mörder (PL die Mörder)
die Mörderin *(murderer)*
◻ The police are searching for the killer. Die Polizei sucht nach dem Mörder.
2 der Killer (PL die Killer) *(hitman)*
◻ a hired killer ein Auftragskiller
■ **Meningitis can be a killer.** Hirnhautentzündung kann tödlich sein.

kilo NOUN
das Kilo (PL die Kilos *or* Kilo)
LANGUAGE TIP When specifying a quantity of something use the plural form **Kilo**.
◻ twenty euros a kilo zwanzig Euro das Kilo
◻ three kilos of tomatoes drei Kilo Tomaten

kilometre NOUN
der Kilometer (PL die Kilometer)
◻ a hundred kilometres hundert Kilometer

kilt NOUN
der Kilt (PL die Kilts)

kind ADJECTIVE
▷ *see also* **kind** NOUN
nett
■ **to be kind to somebody** zu jemandem nett sein
■ **Thank you for being so kind.** Vielen Dank, dass Sie so nett waren.

kind NOUN
▷ *see also* **kind** ADJECTIVE
die Art
◻ It's a kind of sausage. Es ist eine Art Wurst.
■ **a new kind of dictionary** ein neuartiges Wörterbuch

kindergarten NOUN
der Kindergarten (PL die Kindergärten)
DID YOU KNOW...?
Many German children go to **Kindergarten** from the age of 3 to 6.

kindly ADVERB
freundlicherweise

kindness NOUN
die Freundlichkeit

king NOUN
der König (PL die Könige)

kingdom NOUN
das Königreich (PL die Königreiche)

kiosk NOUN
1 die Telefonzelle *(phone box)*
2 der Kiosk (PL die Kioske)
◻ a newspaper kiosk ein Zeitungskiosk

kipper NOUN
der Räucherhering (PL die Räucherheringe)

kiss NOUN
▷ *see also* **kiss** VERB
der Kuss (GEN des Kusses, PL die Küsse)
◻ a passionate kiss ein leidenschaftlicher Kuss

to **kiss** VERB
▷ *see also* **kiss** NOUN
1 küssen
◻ He kissed me. Er küsste mich.
2 sich küssen
◻ They kissed. Sie küssten sich.

kit NOUN
1 das Zeug *(clothes for sport)*
◻ I've forgotten my gym kit. Ich habe mein Sportzeug vergessen.
2 der Kasten (PL die Kästen)
◻ a tool kit ein Werkzeugkasten ◻ a first-aid kit ein Erste-Hilfe-Kasten
■ **puncture repair kit** das Flickzeug
■ **sewing kit** das Nähzeug

kitchen NOUN
die Küche
◻ a fitted kitchen eine Einbauküche
■ **the kitchen units** die Küchenschränke
■ **a kitchen knife** ein Küchenmesser *neut*

kite NOUN
der Drachen (PL die Drachen)

kitten NOUN
das Kätzchen (PL die Kätzchen)

knee NOUN
das Knie (PL die Knie)
◻ He was on his knees. Er lag auf den Knien.

to **kneel (down)** VERB
sich hinknien (PERFECT hat sich hingekniet)

knew VERB ▷ *see* **know**

knickers PL NOUN
die Unterhose
◻ a pair of knickers eine Unterhose

knife NOUN
das Messer (PL die Messer)
■ **a sheath knife** ein Fahrtenmesser
■ **a penknife** ein Taschenmesser

to **knit** VERB
stricken

knitting NOUN
das Stricken
■ **I like knitting.** Ich stricke gern.

knives PL NOUN ▷ *see* **knife**

knob NOUN
1 der Griff *(on door)*
2 der Knopf (PL die Knöpfe) *(on radio, TV)*

to **knock** VERB
▷ *see also* **knock** NOUN
klopfen
◻ to knock on the door an die Tür klopfen
■ **Someone's knocking at the door.** Es klopft.
■ **She was knocked down by a car.** Ein Auto hat sie umgefahren.
■ **He was knocked out.** *(stunned)* Er wurde bewusstlos geschlagen.
■ **to knock somebody out** *(defeat)* jemanden schlagen ◻ Liverpool knocked Aston Villa out

of the cup. Der FC Liverpool hat Aston Villa im Pokalspiel geschlagen.

■ **They were knocked out early in the tournament.** Sie schieden beim Turnier früh aus.

■ **to knock something over** etwas umstoßen □ I accidentally knocked the milk over. Ich habe aus Versehen die Milch umgestoßen.

knock NOUN

▷ *see also* **knock** VERB

■ **There was a knock on the door.** Es hat geklopft.

knot NOUN

der Knoten (PL die Knoten)

to **know** VERB

LANGUAGE TIP Use **wissen** for knowing facts, **kennen** for knowing people and places.

1 wissen (PRESENT weiß, IMPERFECT wusste, PERFECT hat gewusst)

□ It's a long way. — Yes, I know. Es ist weit. — Ja, ich weiß. □ I don't know. Ich weiß nicht. □ I don't know what to do. Ich weiß nicht, was ich tun soll. □ I don't know how to do it. Ich weiß nicht, wie ich es machen soll.

2 kennen (IMPERFECT kannte, PERFECT hat gekannt)

□ I know her. Ich kenne sie. □ I know Berlin well. Ich kenne Berlin gut.

■ **I don't know any French.** Ich kann kein Französisch.

■ **to know that ...** wissen, dass ... □ I know that you like chocolate. Ich weiß, dass du Schokolade magst. □ I didn't know that your dad was a policeman. Ich wusste nicht, dass dein Vater Polizist ist.

■ **to know about something 1** *(be aware of)* von etwas wissen □ Do you know about the meeting this afternoon? Weißt du von dem Treffen heute Nachmittag? **2** *(be knowledgeable about)* sich mit etwas auskennen □ He knows a lot about cars. Er kennt sich mit Autos aus. □ I don't know much about computers. Mit Computern kenne ich mich nicht besonders aus.

■ **to get to know somebody** jemanden kennenlernen

■ **How should I know?** *(I don't know!)* Wie soll ich das wissen?

■ **You never know!** Man kann nie wissen!

know-all NOUN

der Besserwisser (PL die Besserwisser)

die Besserwisserin

□ He's such a know-all! So ein Besserwisser!

know-how NOUN

das Know-how (GEN des Know-how)

knowledge NOUN

1 das Wissen *(general knowledge)*

□ Our knowledge of the universe is limited. Unser Wissen über das Universum ist begrenzt.

2 die Kenntnisse *fem pl (things learnt)*

□ my knowledge of German meine Deutschkenntnisse

knowledgeable ADJECTIVE

■ **to be knowledgeable about something** viel über etwas wissen □ She is very knowledgeable about physics. Sie weiß viel über Physik.

■ **She's very knowledgeable about computers.** Sie kennt sich mit Computern gut aus.

known VERB ▷ *see* **know**

Koran NOUN

der Koran

Korea NOUN

Korea *neut*

■ **from Korea** aus Korea

■ **to Korea** nach Korea

kosher ADJECTIVE

koscher

lab NOUN *(= laboratory)*
das Labor (PL die Labors)
■ **a lab technician** ein Laborant *masc*

label NOUN
1 der Aufkleber (PL die Aufkleber) *(sticker)*
2 das Etikett (PL die Etiketts) *(on clothes)*
3 der Anhänger (PL die Anhänger) *(for luggage)*

laboratory NOUN
das Labor (PL die Labors)

labor union NOUN (US)
die Gewerkschaft

Labour NOUN
die Labour-Party
□ My parents vote Labour. Meine Eltern wählen die Labour-Party.
■ **the Labour Party** die Labour-Party

labourer NOUN
der Arbeiter (PL die Arbeiter)
die Arbeiterin
■ **a farm labourer** ein Landarbeiter

lace NOUN
1 der Schnürsenkel (PL die Schnürsenkel) *(of shoe)*
2 die Spitze
□ a lace collar ein Spitzenkragen

lack NOUN
der Mangel (PL die Mängel)
□ his lack of experience sein Mangel an Erfahrung

lacquer NOUN
der Lack (PL die Lacke)

lad NOUN
der Junge (GEN des Jungen, PL die Jungen)

ladder NOUN
1 die Leiter
2 die Laufmasche *(in tights)*

lady NOUN
die Dame
□ a young lady eine junge Dame
■ **Ladies and gentlemen ...** Meine Damen und Herren ...
■ **the ladies'** die Damentoilette

ladybird NOUN
der Marienkäfer (PL die Marienkäfer)

to **lag behind** VERB
hinterherhinken (PERFECT ist hinterhergehinkt)

lager NOUN
das helle Bier (PL die hellen Biere)

DID YOU KNOW...?
German beers are completely different from British ones. There is no real equivalent to 'lager'.

laid VERB ▷ *see* **lay**

laid-back ADJECTIVE
locker

lain VERB ▷ *see* **lie**

lake NOUN
der See (PL die Seen)
■ **Lake Geneva** der Genfer See
■ **Lake Constance** der Bodensee

lamb NOUN
das Lamm (PL die Lämmer)
■ **a lamb chop** ein Lammkotelett *neut*

lame ADJECTIVE
lahm
■ **My pony is lame.** Mein Pony lahmt.

lamp NOUN
die Lampe

lamppost NOUN
der Laternenpfahl (PL die Laternenpfähle)

lampshade NOUN
der Lampenschirm

land NOUN
▷ *see also* **land** VERB
das Land (PL die Länder)
□ a piece of land ein Stück Land

to **land** VERB
▷ *see also* **land** NOUN
landen (PERFECT ist gelandet) *(plane, passenger)*

landing NOUN
1 die Landung *(of plane)*
2 der Treppenabsatz (GEN des Treppenabsatzes, PL die Treppenabsätze) *(of staircase)*

landlady NOUN
die Vermieterin

landlord NOUN
der Vermieter (PL die Vermieter)

landmark NOUN
das Wahrzeichen (PL die Wahrzeichen)
□ Big Ben is a London landmark. Big Ben ist ein Londoner Wahrzeichen.

landowner NOUN
der Grundbesitzer (PL die Grundbesitzer)
die Grundbesitzerin

landscape NOUN
die Landschaft

lane NOUN
1 das Sträßchen (PL die Sträßchen) *(in country)*
2 die Spur *(on motorway)*

language NOUN
die Sprache
□ a difficult language eine schwierige Sprache
■ **to use bad language** Kraftausdrücke benutzen

language laboratory NOUN
das Sprachlabor (PL die Sprachlabors)

lap NOUN
die Runde *(sport)*
□ I ran ten laps. Ich bin zehn Runden gelaufen.
■ **on my lap** auf meinem Schoß

laptop NOUN
der Laptop (PL die Laptops) *(computer)*

larder NOUN
die Speisekammer

large ADJECTIVE
groß
□ a large house ein großes Haus □ a large dog ein großer Hund

largely ADVERB
größtenteils

laser NOUN
der Laser (PL die Laser)

lass NOUN
das Mädchen (PL die Mädchen)

last ADJECTIVE, ADVERB
▷ *see also* **last** VERB
1 letzte
□ one last time ein letztes Mal □ the last question die letzte Frage □ last Friday letzten Freitag □ last week letzte Woche
2 als Letzte
□ He arrived last. Er kam als Letzter an.
3 zuletzt
□ I've lost my bag. — When did you see it last? Ich habe meine Tasche verloren. — Wann hast du sie zuletzt gesehen?
■ **When I last saw him, he was okay.** Als ich ihn das letzte Mal sah, war er in Ordnung.
■ **the last time** das letzte Mal □ the last time I saw her als ich sie das letzte Mal sah
□ That's the last time I take your advice! Das ist das letzte Mal, dass ich auf deinen Rat höre!
■ **last night 1** *(evening)* gestern Abend
□ I got home at midnight last night. Ich bin gestern Abend um Mitternacht nach Hause gekommen. **2** *(sleeping hours)* heute Nacht
□ I couldn't sleep last night. Ich konnte heute Nacht nicht schlafen.
■ **at last** endlich

to **last** VERB
▷ *see also* **last** ADJECTIVE
dauern
□ The concert lasts two hours. Das Konzert dauert zwei Stunden.

lastly ADVERB
schließlich
□ Lastly I'd like to mention that ... Und schließlich möchte ich erwähnen, dass ...

late ADJECTIVE, ADVERB
1 zu spät
□ Hurry up or you'll be late! Beeil dich, du kommst sonst zu spät! □ I'm often late for school. Ich komme oft zu spät zur Schule.
■ **to arrive late** zu spät kommen
□ She arrived late. Sie kam zu spät.
2 spät
□ I went to bed late. Ich bin spät ins Bett gegangen. □ in the late afternoon am späten Nachmittag
■ **in late May** Ende Mai

lately ADVERB
in letzter Zeit
□ I haven't seen him lately. Ich habe ihn in letzter Zeit nicht gesehen.

later ADVERB
später
□ I'll do it later. Ich mache es später.
■ **See you later!** Bis später!

latest ADJECTIVE
neueste
□ the latest news die neuesten Nachrichten
□ their latest album ihr neuestes Album
■ **at the latest** spätestens □ by ten o'clock at the latest bis spätestens zehn Uhr

Latin NOUN
das Latein
□ I do Latin. Ich lerne Latein.

Latin America NOUN
Lateinamerika *neut*
■ **from Latin America** aus Lateinamerika
■ **to Latin America** nach Lateinamerika

Latin American ADJECTIVE
lateinamerikanisch

laugh NOUN
▷ *see also* **laugh** VERB
das Lachen
■ **It was a good laugh.** *(it was fun)* Es war lustig.

to **laugh** VERB
▷ *see also* **laugh** NOUN
lachen
■ **to laugh at something** über etwas lachen
□ She didn't laugh at my joke. Sie hat über meinen Witz nicht gelacht.
■ **to laugh at somebody** jemanden auslachen □ They laughed at her. Sie lachten sie aus.

to **launch** VERB
1 auf den Markt bringen (IMPERFECT brachte, PERFECT hat gebracht) *(product)*
2 abschießen (IMPERFECT schoss ab, PERFECT hat abgeschossen) *(rocket)*

Launderette® NOUN
der Waschsalon (PL die Waschsalons)

Laundromat® NOUN (US)
der Waschsalon (PL die Waschsalons)

laundry NOUN
die Wäsche *(clothes)*

lavatory NOUN
die Toilette

lavender NOUN
der Lavendel

law NOUN
1 das Gesetz (GEN des Gesetzes, PL die Gesetze)
□ It's against the law. Das ist gegen das Gesetz.
2 Jura *(subject)*
□ She's studying law. Sie studiert Jura.

lawn NOUN
der Rasen (PL die Rasen)

lawnmower NOUN
der Rasenmäher (PL die Rasenmäher)

law school NOUN (US)
die juristische Fakultät

lawyer NOUN
der Rechtsanwalt (PL die Rechtsanwälte)
die Rechtsanwältin
□ My mother's a lawyer. Meine Mutter ist Rechtsanwältin.

to **lay** VERB

LANGUAGE TIP 'lay' is also a form of 'lie (2)' VERB

legen
□ She laid the baby in her cot. Sie legte das Baby ins Bettchen.
■ **to lay the table** den Tisch decken
■ **to lay something on** 1 *(provide)* etwas bereitstellen □ They laid on extra buses. Sie stellten zusätzliche Busse bereit.
2 *(prepare)* etwas vorbereiten □ They had laid on a special meal. Sie hatten ein besonderes Essen vorbereitet.
■ **to lay off** entlassen □ My father's been laid off. Mein Vater ist entlassen worden.

lay-by NOUN
der Rastplatz (GEN des Rastplatzes, PL die Rastplätze)

layer NOUN
die Schicht

layout NOUN
das Design (PL die Designs) *(of house, garden)*

lazy ADJECTIVE
faul

lb. ABBREVIATION *(= pound)*
Pfund

to **lead** VERB
▷ *see also* **lead (1)** NOUN *and* **lead (2)** NOUN
führen
□ the street that leads to the station die Straße, die zum Bahnhof führt
■ **to lead the way** vorangehen □ She led the way. Sie ist vorangegangen.
■ **to lead somebody away** jemanden abführen □ The police led the man away. Die Polizei führte den Mann ab.

lead (1) NOUN
▷ *see also* **lead** VERB *and* **lead (2)** NOUN
1 das Kabel (PL die Kabel) *(cable)*
2 die Hundeleine *(for dog)*
■ **to be in the lead** in Führung sein □ Our team is in the lead. Unsere Mannschaft ist in Führung.

lead (2) NOUN
▷ *see also* **lead** VERB *and* **lead (1)** NOUN
das Blei *(metal)*

leader NOUN
1 der Führer (PL die Führer)
die Führerin *(of expedition, gang)*
2 der Anführer (PL die Anführer)
die Anführerin *(of political party)*

lead-free ADJECTIVE
■ **lead-free petrol** das bleifreie Benzin

lead singer NOUN
der Leadsinger (PL die Leadsinger)
die Leadsingerin

leaf NOUN
das Blatt (PL die Blätter)

leaflet NOUN
der Prospekt (PL die Prospekte) *(advertising)*
□ a leaflet about their products einen Prospekt über ihre Produkte

league NOUN
die Liga (GEN der Liga, PL die Ligen)
□ the Premier League die erste Liga

DID YOU KNOW...?
The 'Premier League' is similar to the German **Bundesliga**.

■ **They are at the top of the league.** Sie sind Tabellenführer.

leak NOUN
▷ *see also* **leak** VERB
die undichte Stelle
□ a gas leak eine undichte Stelle in der Gasleitung

to **leak** VERB
▷ *see also* **leak** NOUN
1 undicht sein (PRESENT ist undicht, IMPERFECT war undicht, PERFECT ist undicht gewesen) *(pipe)*
2 auslaufen (PRESENT läuft aus, IMPERFECT lief aus, PERFECT ist ausgelaufen) *(water)*
3 austreten (PRESENT tritt aus, IMPERFECT trat aus, PERFECT ist ausgetreten) *(gas)*

to **lean** VERB
sich lehnen
□ Don't lean over too far. Lehn dich nicht zu weit vor. □ She leant out of the window. Sie lehnte sich zum Fenster hinaus.
■ **to lean forward** sich nach vorn beugen
■ **to lean on something** sich auf etwas stützen □ He leant on the wall. Er stützte sich auf die Mauer.
■ **to be leaning against something** gegen etwas gelehnt sein □ The ladder was leaning against the wall. Die Leiter war gegen die Wand gelehnt.

■ **to lean something against a wall** etwas an einer Mauer anlehnen □ He leant his bike against the wall. Er lehnte sein Fahrrad an der Mauer an.

to leap VERB
springen (IMPERFECT sprang, PERFECT ist gesprungen)
□ He leapt out of his chair when his team scored. Er sprang vom Stuhl auf, als seine Mannschaft ein Tor schoss.

leap year NOUN
das Schaltjahr (PL die Schaltjahre)

to learn VERB
lernen
□ I'm learning to ski. Ich lerne Ski fahren.

learner NOUN
■ **She's a quick learner.** Sie lernt schnell.
■ **German learners** *(people learning German)* Deutschschüler *masc pl*

learner driver NOUN
der Fahrschüler (PL die Fahrschüler)
die Fahrschülerin

learnt VERB ▷ *see* **learn**

least ADVERB, ADJECTIVE, PRONOUN
■ **the least 1** *(followed by noun)* wenigste □ the least time die wenigste Zeit □ She has the least money. Sie hat das wenigste Geld. **2** *(followed by adjective)* am wenigsten ... □ the least intelligent pupil der am wenigsten intelligente Schüler □ the least attractive woman die am wenigsten attraktive Frau □ the least interesting book das am wenigsten interessante Buch **3** *(after a verb)* am wenigsten □ Maths is the subject I like the least. Mathe ist das Fach, das ich am wenigsten mag.
■ **It's the least I can do.** Das ist das wenigste, was ich tun kann.
■ **at least 1** mindestens □ It'll cost at least two hundred pounds. Das kostet mindestens zweihundert Pfund. **2** wenigstens □ ... but at least nobody was hurt. ... aber wenigstens wurde niemand verletzt.
■ **It's totally unfair – at least, that's my opinion.** Das ist total ungerecht – zumindest meiner Meinung nach.

leather NOUN
das Leder (PL die Leder)
□ a black leather jacket eine schwarze Lederjacke

to leave VERB
▷ *see also* **leave** NOUN
1 lassen (PRESENT lässt, IMPERFECT ließ, PERFECT hat gelassen) *(deliberately)*
□ He always leaves his camera in the car. Er lässt immer seinen Fotoapparat im Auto.
2 vergessen (PRESENT vergisst, IMPERFECT vergaß, PERFECT hat vergessen) *(by mistake)*
□ I've left my book at home. Ich habe mein Buch zu Hause vergessen.
■ **Don't leave anything behind.** Lassen Sie nichts liegen.
3 abfahren (PRESENT fährt ab, IMPERFECT fuhr ab, PERFECT ist abgefahren) *(bus, train)*
□ The bus leaves at eight. Der Bus fährt um acht ab.
4 abfliegen (IMPERFECT flog ab, PERFECT ist abgeflogen) *(plane)*
□ The plane leaves at six. Das Flugzeug fliegt um sechs ab.
5 weggehen (IMPERFECT ging weg, PERFECT ist weggegangen) *(person)*
□ She's just left. Sie ist eben weggegangen.
■ **She left home last year.** Sie ist letztes Jahr von zu Hause weggezogen.
6 verlassen (PRESENT verlässt, IMPERFECT verließ, PERFECT hat verlassen) *(abandon)*
□ She left her husband. Sie hat ihren Mann verlassen.
■ **to leave somebody alone** jemanden in Ruhe lassen □ Leave me alone! Lass mich in Ruhe!
■ **to leave out** auslassen □ You've left out a comma. Du hast ein Komma ausgelassen.
■ **I felt really left out.** Ich fühlte mich richtig ausgeschlossen.

leave NOUN
▷ *see also* **leave** VERB
der Urlaub (PL die Urlaube) *(from job, army)*
□ a week's leave eine Woche Urlaub

leaves PL NOUN ▷ *see* **leaf**

Lebanon NOUN
der Libanon

LANGUAGE TIP Note that the definite article is used in German for countries which are masculine.

■ **from Lebanon** aus dem Libanon
■ **in Lebanon** im Libanon
■ **to Lebanon** in den Libanon

lecture NOUN
▷ *see also* **lecture** VERB
1 der Vortrag (PL die Vorträge) *(public)*
2 die Vorlesung *(at university)*

LANGUAGE TIP Be careful not to translate **lecture** by **Lektüre**.

to lecture VERB
▷ *see also* **lecture** NOUN
1 unterrichten (PERFECT hat unterrichtet)
□ She lectures at the technical college. Sie unterrichtet an der Fachschule.
2 belehren (PERFECT hat belehrt) *(tell off)*
□ He's always lecturing us. Er belehrt uns andauernd.

lecturer NOUN
der Dozent (GEN des Dozenten, PL die Dozenten)
die Dozentin
□ She's a lecturer. Sie ist Dozentin.

led VERB ▷ *see* **lead**

leek NOUN
der Lauch (PL die Lauche)

left VERB ▹ *see* **leave**

left ADJECTIVE, ADVERB
▹ *see also* **left** NOUN
1 linke
▫ the left foot der linke Fuß ▫ my left arm mein linker Arm ▫ your left hand deine linke Hand ▫ her left eye ihr linkes Auge
2 links
▫ Turn left at the traffic lights. Biegen Sie an der Ampel links ab.
■ **Look left!** Sehen Sie nach links!
■ **I haven't got any money left.** Ich habe kein Geld mehr.

left NOUN
▹ *see also* **left** ADJECTIVE
die linke Seite
■ **on the left** links ▫ Remember to drive on the left. Vergiss nicht, links zu fahren.

left-hand ADJECTIVE
■ **the left-hand side** die linke Seite
■ **It's on the left-hand side.** Es liegt links.

left-handed ADJECTIVE
linkshändig

left-luggage office NOUN
die Gepäckaufbewahrung

leg NOUN
das Bein (PL die Beine)
▫ I've broken my leg. Ich habe mir das Bein gebrochen.
■ **a chicken leg** eine Hähnchenkeule
■ **a leg of lamb** eine Lammkeule

legal ADJECTIVE
legal

leggings PL NOUN
die Leggings *pl*

leisure NOUN
die Freizeit
▫ What do you do in your leisure time? Was machen Sie in Ihrer Freizeit?

leisure centre NOUN
das Freizeitzentrum (PL die Freizeitzentren)

lemon NOUN
die Zitrone

lemonade NOUN
die Limonade

to **lend** VERB
leihen (IMPERFECT lieh, PERFECT hat geliehen)
▫ I can lend you some money. Ich kann dir Geld leihen.

length NOUN
die Länge
■ **It's about a metre in length.** Es ist etwa einen Meter lang.

lens NOUN
1 die Kontaktlinse *(contact lens)*
2 das Glas (GEN des Glases, PL die Gläser) *(of spectacles)*
3 das Objektiv (PL die Objektive) *(of camera)*

Lent NOUN
die Fastenzeit
▫ during Lent während der Fastenzeit

lent VERB ▹ *see* **lend**

lentil NOUN
die Linse

Leo NOUN
der Löwe (GEN des Löwen)
▫ I'm Leo. Ich bin Löwe.

leotard NOUN
der Gymnastikanzug (PL die Gymnastikanzüge)

lesbian NOUN
die Lesbierin
■ **She's a lesbian.** Sie ist lesbisch.

less PRONOUN, ADVERB, ADJECTIVE
weniger
▫ A bit less, please. Etwas weniger, bitte.
▫ I've got less time for hobbies now. Ich habe jetzt weniger Zeit für Hobbys.
■ **He's less intelligent than his brother.** Er ist nicht so intelligent wie sein Bruder.
■ **less than** weniger als ▫ It costs less than a hundred euros. Es kostet weniger als hundert Euro. ▫ less than half weniger als die Hälfte ▫ He spent less than me. Er hat weniger als ich ausgegeben. ▫ I've got less than you. Ich habe weniger als du.

lesson NOUN
1 die Lektion
▫ 'Lesson Sixteen' *(in textbook)* 'Lektion sechzehn'
2 die Stunde *(class)*
▫ A lesson lasts forty minutes. Eine Stunde dauert vierzig Minuten.

to **let** VERB
1 lassen (PRESENT lässt, IMPERFECT ließ, PERFECT hat gelassen) *(allow)*
■ **to let somebody do something** jemanden etwas tun lassen ▫ Let me have a look. Lass mich mal sehen. ▫ My mother won't let me go out tonight. Meine Mutter lässt mich heute Abend nicht ausgehen.
■ **to let somebody down** jemanden enttäuschen ▫ I won't let you down. Ich werde dich nicht enttäuschen.
■ **to let somebody know** jemandem Bescheid sagen ▫ I'll let you know as soon as possible. Ich sage Ihnen sobald wie möglich Bescheid.
■ **to let go** *(release)* loslassen ▫ Let me go! Lass mich los!
■ **to let in** hineinlassen ▫ They wouldn't let me in. Sie wollten mich nicht hineinlassen.
■ **Let's go to the cinema!** Lass uns ins Kino gehen!
■ **Let's go!** Gehen wir!
2 vermieten (PERFECT hat vermietet) *(hire out)*
■ **'to let'** 'zu vermieten'

letter NOUN
1 der Brief (PL die Briefe)
▫ She wrote me a long letter. Sie hat mir einen langen Brief geschrieben.

2 der Buchstabe (GEN des Buchstaben, PL die Buchstaben) *(of alphabet)*
□ the letters of the alphabet die Buchstaben des Alphabets

letterbox NOUN
der Briefkasten (PL die Briefkästen)

lettuce NOUN
der Kopfsalat (PL die Kopfsalate)

leukaemia NOUN
die Leukämie
□ He suffers from leukaemia. Er leidet an Leukämie.

level ADJECTIVE
▷ *see also* **level** NOUN
eben
□ A snooker table must be perfectly level. Ein Snookertisch muss ganz eben sein.

level NOUN
▷ *see also* **level** ADJECTIVE
1 der Wasserstand (PL die Wasserstände) *(of river, lake)*
□ The level of the river is rising. Der Wasserstand des Flusses steigt.
2 die Höhe *(height)*
□ at eye level in Augenhöhe
■ **A levels** das Abitur

DID YOU KNOW...?
Germans take their **Abitur** at the age of 19. The students sit examinations in a variety of subjects to attain an overall grade. If you pass, you have the right to a place at university.

level crossing NOUN
der Bahnübergang (PL die Bahnübergänge)

lever NOUN
der Hebel (PL die Hebel)

liable ADJECTIVE
■ **He's liable to lose his temper.** Er wird leicht wütend.

liar NOUN
der Lügner (PL die Lügner)
die Lügnerin

liberal ADJECTIVE
liberal *(opinions)*
■ **the Liberal Democrats** die Liberaldemokraten

liberation NOUN
die Befreiung

Libra NOUN
die Waage
□ I'm Libra. Ich bin Waage.

librarian NOUN
der Bibliothekar (PL die Bibliothekare)
die Bibliothekarin
□ She's a librarian. Sie ist Bibliothekarin.

library NOUN
1 die Bücherei *(public lending library)*
2 die Bibliothek *(of school, university)*

Libya NOUN
Libyen *neut*
■ **from Libya** aus Libyen
■ **to Libya** nach Libyen

licence NOUN
der Schein (PL die Scheine)
■ **a driving licence** ein Führerschein

to **lick** VERB
lecken

lid NOUN
der Deckel (PL die Deckel)

lie NOUN
▷ *see also* **lie (1)** VERB *and* **lie (2)** VERB
die Lüge
□ That's a lie! Das ist eine Lüge!
■ **to tell a lie** lügen

to **lie (1)** VERB
▷ *see also* **lie** NOUN *and* **lie (2)** VERB
lügen (IMPERFECT log, PERFECT hat gelogen) *(not tell the truth)*
□ I know she's lying. Ich weiß, dass sie lügt.

to **lie (2)** VERB
▷ *see also* **lie** NOUN *and* **lie (1)** VERB
liegen (IMPERFECT lag, PERFECT hat gelegen)
□ He was lying on the sofa. Er lag auf dem Sofa.
□ When I'm on holiday I lie on the beach all day. In den Ferien liege ich den ganzen Tag am Strand.
■ **to lie down** sich hinlegen
■ **to be lying down** liegen

lie-in NOUN
■ **to have a lie-in** ausschlafen □ She has a lie-in on Sundays. Sonntags schläft sie aus.

lieutenant NOUN
der Leutnant (PL die Leutnants)

life NOUN
das Leben (PL die Leben)

lifebelt NOUN
der Rettungsring (PL die Rettungsringe)

lifeboat NOUN
das Rettungsboot (PL die Rettungsboote)

lifeguard NOUN
1 der Rettungsschwimmer (PL die Rettungsschwimmer)
die Rettungsschwimmerin *(at beach)*
2 der Bademeister (PL die Bademeister)
die Bademeisterin *(at swimming pool)*

life jacket NOUN
die Schwimmweste

life-saving NOUN
das Rettungsschwimmen
□ I've done a course in life-saving. Ich habe einen Kurs im Rettungsschwimmen gemacht.

lifestyle NOUN
der Lebensstil (PL die Lebensstile)

to **lift** VERB
▷ *see also* **lift** NOUN
hochheben (IMPERFECT hob hoch, PERFECT hat hochgehoben)
□ I can't lift it. Ich kann es nicht hochheben.

lift NOUN
▷ *see also* **lift** VERB
der Aufzug (PL die Aufzüge)

□ The lift isn't working. Der Aufzug geht nicht.
■ **He gave me a lift to the cinema.** Er hat mich zum Kino gefahren.
■ **Would you like a lift?** Wollen Sie mitfahren?

light ADJECTIVE
▷ *see also* **light** NOUN, VERB
1 leicht *(not heavy)*
□ a light jacket eine leichte Jacke □ a light meal ein leichtes Essen
2 hell *(colour)*
□ a light blue sweater ein hellblauer Pullover

light NOUN
▷ *see also* **light** ADJECTIVE, VERB
1 das Licht (PL die Lichter)
□ to switch on the light das Licht anmachen
□ to switch off the light das Licht ausmachen
2 die Lampe
□ There's a light by my bed. Ich habe am Bett eine Lampe.
■ **the traffic lights** die Ampel *sing*
■ **Have you got a light?** *(for cigarette)* Haben Sie Feuer?

to **light** VERB
▷ *see also* **light** ADJECTIVE, NOUN
anzünden (PERFECT hat angezündet) *(candle, cigarette, fire)*

light bulb NOUN
die Glühbirne

lighter NOUN
das Feuerzeug (PL die Feuerzeuge) *(for cigarettes)*

lighthouse NOUN
der Leuchtturm (PL die Leuchttürme)

lightning NOUN
der Blitz (GEN des Blitzes, PL die Blitze)
■ **a flash of lightning** ein Blitz
■ **There was a flash of lightning.** Es hat geblitzt.

to **like** VERB
▷ *see also* **like** PREPOSITION
mögen (PRESENT mag, IMPERFECT mochte, PERFECT hat gemocht)
□ I don't like mustard. Ich mag Senf nicht.
□ I like Paul, but I don't want to go out with him. Ich mag Paul, aber ich will nicht mit ihm ausgehen.
■ **I like riding.** Ich reite gern.
■ **Would you like ...?** Möchtest du ...?
□ Would you like some coffee? Möchtest du Kaffee? □ Would you like to go for a walk? Möchtest du einen Spaziergang machen?
■ **I'd like ...** Ich hätte gern ... □ I'd like an orange juice, please. Ich hätte gern einen Orangensaft, bitte.
■ **I'd like to ...** Ich würde gern ... □ I'd like to go to Russia one day. Eines Tages würde ich gern nach Russland fahren. □ I'd like to wash my hands. Ich würde mir gern die Hände waschen.
■ **... if you like** ... wenn du möchtest

like PREPOSITION
▷ *see also* **like** VERB
1 so *(this way)*
□ It's fine like that. So ist es gut. □ Do it like this. Mach das so.
2 wie *(similar to)*
□ a city like Munich eine Stadt wie München
□ It's a bit like salmon. Es ist ein bisschen wie Lachs.
■ **What's the weather like?** Wie ist das Wetter?
■ **to look like somebody** jemandem ähnlich sehen □ You look like my brother. Du siehst meinem Bruder ähnlich.

likely ADJECTIVE
wahrscheinlich
□ That's not very likely. Das ist nicht sehr wahrscheinlich.
■ **She's likely to come.** Sie kommt wahrscheinlich.
■ **She's not likely to come.** Sie kommt wahrscheinlich nicht.

Lilo® NOUN
die Luftmatratze

lime NOUN
die Limone *(fruit)*

limit NOUN
die Grenze
■ **the speed limit** die Geschwindigkeitsbegrenzung

limousine NOUN
die Limousine

to **limp** VERB
hinken

line NOUN
1 die Linie
□ a straight line eine gerade Linie
2 der Strich (PL die Striche) *(to divide, cancel)*
□ Draw a line under each answer. Machen Sie unter jede Antwort einen Strich.
3 das Gleis (GEN des Gleises, PL die Gleise) *(railway track)*
4 die Schlange
□ to stand in line Schlange stehen
■ **Hold the line, please.** *(on telephone)* Bleiben Sie bitte am Apparat.
■ **It's a very bad line.** *(on telephone)* Die Verbindung ist sehr schlecht.

linen NOUN
das Leinen
□ a linen jacket eine Leinenjacke

liner NOUN
der Überseedampfer (PL die Überseedampfer) *(ship)*

linguist NOUN
■ **to be a good linguist** sprachbegabt sein
□ She's a good linguist. Sie ist sehr sprachbegabt.

lining NOUN
das Futter (PL die Futter) *(of clothes)*

link NOUN
▷ *see also* **link** VERB

1 der Zusammenhang (PL die Zusammenhänge)
□ the link between smoking and cancer der Zusammenhang zwischen Rauchen und Krebs
2 der Link (PL die Links) *(computer)*

to **link** VERB
▷ *see also* **link** NOUN
verbinden (IMPERFECT verband, PERFECT hat verbunden)

lino NOUN
das Linoleum

lion NOUN
der Löwe (GEN des Löwen, PL die Löwen)

lioness NOUN
die Löwin

lip NOUN
die Lippe

to **lip-read** VERB
von den Lippen ablesen (PRESENT liest von den Lippen ab, IMPERFECT las von den Lippen ab, PERFECT hat von den Lippen abgelesen)
■ **I'm learning to lip-read.** Ich lerne gerade Lippenlesen.

lip salve NOUN
der Lippenpflegestift (PL die Lippenpflegestifte)

lipstick NOUN
der Lippenstift (PL die Lippenstifte)

liqueur NOUN
der Likör (PL die Liköre)

liquid NOUN
die Flüssigkeit

liquidizer NOUN
der Mixer (PL die Mixer)

list NOUN
▷ *see also* **list** VERB
die Liste

to **list** VERB
▷ *see also* **list** NOUN
aufzählen (PERFECT hat aufgezählt)
□ List your hobbies. Zählen Sie Ihre Hobbys auf.

to **listen** VERB
zuhören (PERFECT hat zugehört)
□ Listen to me! Hör mir zu!
■ **Listen to this!** Hör dir das an!

listener NOUN
der Zuhörer (PL die Zuhörer)
die Zuhörerin

lit VERB ▷ *see* **light**

liter NOUN (US)
der Liter (PL die Liter)

literally ADVERB
buchstäblich *(completely)*
□ It was literally impossible to find a seat. Es war buchstäblich unmöglich, einen Platz zu finden.
■ **to translate literally** wörtlich übersetzen

literature NOUN
die Literatur
□ I'm studying English Literature. Ich studiere englische Literatur.

litre NOUN
der Liter (PL die Liter)
□ three litres drei Liter

litter NOUN
der Abfall (PL die Abfälle)

litter bin NOUN
der Abfallkorb (PL die Abfallkörbe)

little ADJECTIVE
klein
□ a little girl ein kleines Mädchen

WORD POWER
You can use a number of other words instead of **little** to mean 'small':
miniature Miniatur-
□ a miniature version eine Miniaturversion
minute winzig
□ a minute flat eine winzige Wohnung
tiny winzig
□ a tiny garden ein winziger Garten

■ **a little** ein bisschen □ How much would you like? — Just a little. Wie viel möchtest du? — Nur ein bisschen.
■ **very little** sehr wenig □ We've got very little time. Wir haben sehr wenig Zeit.
■ **little by little** nach und nach

live ADJECTIVE
▷ *see also* **live** VERB
1 lebendig *(animal)*
2 live *(broadcast)*
■ **There's live music on Fridays.** Freitags gibt es Livemusik.

to **live** VERB
▷ *see also* **live** ADJECTIVE
1 leben
□ I live with my grandmother. Ich lebe bei meiner Großmutter. □ They're living together. Sie leben zusammen.
■ **to live on something** von etwas leben
□ He lived on bread and water. Er lebte von Brot und Wasser. □ He lives on benefit. Er lebt von der Unterstützung.
2 wohnen *(in house, town)*
□ Where do you live? Wo wohnst du?
□ I live in Edinburgh. Ich wohne in Edinburgh.

lively ADJECTIVE
lebhaft
□ She's got a lively personality. Sie ist ein lebhafter Typ.

liver NOUN
die Leber
■ **liver sausage** die Leberwurst

lives PL NOUN ▷ *see* **life**

living NOUN
■ **to make a living** sich seinen Lebensunterhalt verdienen □ How do you make your living? Wie verdienst du dir deinen Lebensunterhalt?
■ **What does she do for a living?** Was macht sie beruflich?

living room NOUN
das Wohnzimmer (PL die Wohnzimmer)

lizard NOUN
die Echse

load NOUN
▷ *see also* **load** VERB
■ **loads of** eine Menge □ loads of people eine Menge Leute □ loads of money eine Menge Geld
■ **You're talking a load of rubbish!** Du redest vielleicht einen Unsinn!

to **load** VERB
▷ *see also* **load** NOUN
beladen (PRESENT belädt, IMPERFECT belud, PERFECT hat beladen)
□ He's loading the van right now. Er belädt gerade den Lieferwagen.

loaf NOUN
der Laib (PL die Laibe)
■ **a loaf of bread** ein Brot *neut*

loan NOUN
▷ *see also* **loan** VERB
das Darlehen (PL die Darlehen) *(money)*

to **loan** VERB
▷ *see also* **loan** NOUN
ausleihen (IMPERFECT lieh aus, PERFECT hat ausgeliehen)

to **loathe** VERB
verabscheuen (PERFECT hat verabscheut)
□ I loathe her. Ich verabscheue sie.

loaves PL NOUN ▷ *see* **loaf**

lobster NOUN
der Hummer (PL die Hummer)

local ADJECTIVE
örtlich
□ the local police die örtliche Polizei
■ **the local paper** das Lokalblatt
■ **a local call** ein Ortsgespräch *neut*

loch NOUN
der See (PL die Seen)

lock NOUN
▷ *see also* **lock** VERB
das Schloss (GEN des Schlosses, PL die Schlösser)
□ The lock is broken. Das Schloss ist kaputt.

to **lock** VERB
▷ *see also* **lock** NOUN
abschließen (IMPERFECT schloss ab, PERFECT hat abgeschlossen)
□ Make sure you lock your door. Schließen Sie die Tür ab.
■ **to be locked out** ausgesperrt sein
□ The door slammed and I was locked out. Die Tür schlug zu und ich war ausgesperrt.

locker NOUN
das Schließfach (PL die Schließfächer)
■ **the locker room** der Umkleideraum
■ **the left-luggage lockers** die Gepäckschließfächer

locket NOUN
das Medaillon (PL die Medaillons)

lodger NOUN
der Untermieter (PL die Untermieter)
die Untermieterin

loft NOUN
der Speicher (PL die Speicher)

log NOUN
das Scheit (PL die Scheite) *(of wood)*

logical ADJECTIVE
logisch

to **log in** VERB
einloggen (PERFECT hat eingeloggt) *(computer)*

to **log off** VERB
ausloggen (PERFECT hat ausgeloggt) *(computer)*

to **log on** VERB
einloggen (PERFECT hat eingeloggt) *(computer)*

to **log out** VERB
ausloggen (PERFECT hat ausgeloggt) *(computer)*

lollipop NOUN
der Lutscher (PL die Lutscher)

lolly NOUN
das Eis am Stiel *(ice lolly)*

London NOUN
London *neut*
■ **from London** aus London
■ **to London** nach London

Londoner NOUN
der Londoner (PL die Londoner)
die Londonerin

loneliness NOUN
die Einsamkeit

lonely ADJECTIVE
einsam
■ **to feel lonely** sich einsam fühlen
□ She feels lonely. Sie fühlt sich einsam.

long ADJECTIVE, ADVERB
▷ *see also* **long** VERB
lang
□ She's got long hair. Sie hat lange Haare.
□ The room is six metres long. Das Zimmer ist sechs Meter lang.
■ **how long?** *(time)* wie lange? □ How long did you stay there? Wie lange bist du dortgeblieben? □ How long is the flight? Wie lange dauert der Flug?

> LANGUAGE TIP When you want to say how long you 'have been' doing something, use the present tense in German.

□ How long have you been here? Wie lange bist du schon da? □ I've been waiting a long time. Ich warte schon lange.
■ **It takes a long time.** Das dauert lange.
■ **as long as** solange □ I'll come as long as it's not too expensive. Ich komme mit, solange es nicht zu teuer ist.

to **long** VERB
▷ *see also* **long** ADJECTIVE
■ **to long to do something** es kaum erwarten können, etwas zu tun □ I'm longing to see my boyfriend again. Ich kann es kaum erwarten, bis ich meinen Freund wiedersehe.

long-distance ADJECTIVE
■ **a long-distance call** ein Ferngespräch *neut*

longer ADVERB
▷ *see also* **long** ADJECTIVE
■ **They're no longer going out together.** Sie gehen nicht mehr miteinander.
■ **I can't stand it any longer.** Ich halte das nicht länger aus.

long jump NOUN
der Weitsprung (PL die Weitsprünge)

loo NOUN
das Klo (PL die Klos) *(informal)*
□ Where's the loo? Wo ist das Klo?
■ **I need the loo.** Ich muss mal. *(informal)*

look NOUN
▷ *see also* **look** VERB
■ **to have a look** ansehen □ Have a look at this! Sieh dir das mal an!
■ **I don't like the look of it.** Das gefällt mir nicht.

to **look** VERB
▷ *see also* **look** NOUN
1 sehen (PRESENT sieht, IMPERFECT sah, PERFECT hat gesehen)
■ **Look!** Sieh mal!
■ **to look at something** etwas ansehen
□ Look at the picture. Sieh dir das Bild an.
2 aussehen (PERFECT hat ausgesehen) *(seem)*
□ She looks surprised. Sie sieht überrascht aus. □ That cake looks nice. Der Kuchen sieht gut aus. □ It looks fine. Es sieht gut aus.
■ **to look like somebody** jemandem ähnlich sehen □ He looks like his brother. Er sieht seinem Bruder ähnlich.
■ **What does she look like?** Wie sieht sie aus?
■ **Look out!** Pass auf!
■ **to look after** sich kümmern um □ I look after my little sister. Ich kümmere mich um meine kleine Schwester.
■ **to look for** suchen □ I'm looking for my passport. Ich suche meinen Pass.
■ **to look forward to something** sich auf etwas freuen □ I'm looking forward to the holidays. Ich freue mich auf die Ferien.
■ **Looking forward to hearing from you ...** In der Hoffnung, bald etwas von dir zu hören, ...
■ **to look round** sich umsehen □ I shouted and he looked round. Ich habe gerufen, und er sah sich um. □ I'm just looking round. Ich sehe mich nur um. □ I like looking round the shops. Ich sehe mich gern in den Geschäften um.
■ **to look round a museum** ein Museum ansehen
■ **to look up** *(word, name)* nachschlagen
□ If you don't know a word, look it up in the dictionary. Wenn du ein Wort nicht weißt, schlage es im Wörterbuch nach.

loose ADJECTIVE
weit *(clothes)*
■ **loose change** das Kleingeld

lord NOUN
der Lord (PL die Lords) *(feudal)*
■ **the House of Lords** das Oberhaus
■ **the Lord** *(god)* Gott
■ **Good Lord!** Großer Gott!

lorry NOUN
der Lastwagen (PL die Lastwagen)

lorry driver NOUN
der Lastwagenfahrer (PL die Lastwagenfahrer)
die Lastwagenfahrerin
□ He's a lorry driver. Er ist Lastwagenfahrer.

to **lose** VERB
verlieren (IMPERFECT verlor, PERFECT hat verloren)
□ I've lost my purse. Ich habe meinen Geldbeutel verloren.
■ **to get lost** sich verlaufen □ I was afraid I'd get lost. Ich hatte Angst, mich zu verlaufen.

loss NOUN
der Verlust (PL die Verluste)

lost VERB ▷ *see* **lose**

lost ADJECTIVE
verloren

lost-and-found NOUN (US)
das Fundbüro (PL die Fundbüros)

lost property office NOUN
das Fundbüro (PL die Fundbüros)

lot NOUN
■ **a lot** viel
■ **a lot of 1** viel □ He earns a lot of money. Er verdient viel Geld. **2** viele □ We saw a lot of interesting things. Wir haben viele interessante Dinge gesehen.
■ **lots of** eine Menge □ lots of money eine Menge Geld □ lots of friends eine Menge Freunde
■ **What did you do at the weekend? — Not a lot.** Was hast du am Wochenende gemacht? — Nicht viel.
■ **Do you like football? — Not a lot.** Magst du Fußball? — Nicht besonders.
■ **That's the lot.** Das ist alles.

lottery NOUN
das Lotto
■ **to win the lottery** im Lotto gewinnen

loud ADJECTIVE
laut
□ The television is too loud. Der Fernseher ist zu laut.

loudly ADVERB
laut

loudspeaker NOUN
der Lautsprecher (PL die Lautsprecher)

lounge NOUN
das Wohnzimmer (PL die Wohnzimmer)

lousy ADJECTIVE
lausig schlecht *(informal)*
□ The food in the canteen is lousy. Das Essen in der Kantine ist lausig schlecht.
■ **I feel lousy.** Mir geht's lausig schlecht.

love NOUN
▷ *see also* **love** VERB
die Liebe

■ **to be in love** verliebt sein □ She's in love with Paul. Sie ist in Paul verliebt.
■ **to make love** sich lieben
■ **Give Heike my love.** Grüß Heike von mir.
■ **Love, Rosemary.** Alles Liebe, Rosemary.

to love VERB
▷ *see also* **love** NOUN
1 lieben *(person, thing)*
□ I love you. Ich liebe dich. □ I love chocolate. Ich liebe Schokolade.
2 mögen (PRESENT mag, IMPERFECT mochte, PERFECT hat gemocht) *(like a lot)*
□ Everybody loves her. Alle mögen sie.
■ **I'd love to come.** Ich würde liebend gern kommen.
■ **I love skiing.** Ich fahre unheimlich gern Ski.

lovely ADJECTIVE
1 wunderbar
□ What a lovely surprise! Was für eine wunderbare Überraschung!
2 schön *(pretty)*
□ They've got a lovely house. Sie haben ein schönes Haus.
■ **It's a lovely day.** Es ist ein herrlicher Tag.
■ **She's a lovely person.** Sie ist ein sehr netter Mensch.
■ **Is your meal OK? — Yes, it's lovely.** Schmeckt dein Essen? — Ja, prima.
■ **Have a lovely time!** Viel Spaß!

lover NOUN
der Liebhaber (PL die Liebhaber)
die Liebhaberin

low ADJECTIVE, ADVERB
niedrig
□ low prices niedrige Preise
■ **That plane is flying very low.** Das Flugzeug fliegt sehr tief.
■ **the low season** die Nebensaison □ in the low season in der Nebensaison

lower sixth NOUN
die zwölfte Klasse
□ He's in the lower sixth. Er ist in der zwölften Klasse.

low-fat ADJECTIVE
mager
■ **a low-fat yoghurt** ein Magerjoghurt *masc*

loyalty NOUN
die Treue

loyalty card NOUN
die Kundenkarte

L-plates PL NOUN
das L-Schild (PL die L-Schilder)

luck NOUN
das Glück
□ She hasn't had much luck. Sie hat nicht viel Glück gehabt.
■ **Good luck!** Viel Glück!
■ **Bad luck!** So ein Pech!

luckily ADVERB
zum Glück

lucky ADJECTIVE
■ **to be lucky 1** *(be fortunate)* Glück haben
□ He's lucky, he's got a job. Er hat Glück, er hat Arbeit.
■ **He wasn't hurt. — That was lucky!** Er wurde nicht verletzt. — Das war Glück!
2 *(bring luck)* Glück bringen □ Black cats are lucky. Schwarze Katzen bringen Glück.
■ **a lucky horseshoe** ein Glückshufeisen *neut*

luggage NOUN
das Gepäck

lukewarm ADJECTIVE
lauwarm

lump NOUN
1 das Stück (PL die Stücke)
□ a lump of coal ein Stück Kohle
2 die Beule *(swelling)*
□ He's got a lump on his forehead. Er hat eine Beule an der Stirn.

lunatic NOUN
der Verrückte (GEN des Verrückten, PL die Verrückten)
die Verrückte (GEN der Verrückten)
□ a lunatic *(man)* ein Verrückter
■ **He's an absolute lunatic.** Er ist total verrückt.

lunch NOUN
das Mittagessen (PL die Mittagessen)
■ **to have lunch** zu Mittag essen □ We have lunch at twelve o'clock. Wir essen um zwölf Uhr zu Mittag.

luncheon voucher NOUN
die Essensmarke

lung NOUN
die Lunge
□ lung cancer der Lungenkrebs

luscious ADJECTIVE
köstlich

lush ADJECTIVE
üppig

lust NOUN
das Verlangen

Luxembourg NOUN
Luxemburg *neut (country, city)*
■ **from Luxembourg** aus Luxemburg
■ **to Luxembourg** nach Luxemburg

luxurious ADJECTIVE
luxuriös

luxury NOUN
der Luxus (GEN des Luxus)
□ It was luxury! Das war wirklich ein Luxus!
■ **a luxury hotel** ein Luxushotel *neut*

lying VERB ▷ *see* **lie**

lyrics PL NOUN
der Text *sing* (PL die Texte) *(of song)*

Mm

mac NOUN
der Regenmantel (PL die Regenmäntel)

macaroni SING NOUN
die Makkaroni *pl*

machine NOUN
die Maschine

machine gun NOUN
das Maschinengewehr

machinery NOUN
die Maschinen *fem pl*

mackerel NOUN
die Makrele

mad ADJECTIVE
1 verrückt *(insane)*
□ You're mad! Du bist verrückt!
■ **to be mad about** verrückt sein nach
□ Ann is mad about John. Ann ist verrückt nach John. □ He's mad about football. Er ist verrückt nach Fußball.
2 wütend *(angry)*
□ She'll be mad when she finds out. Wenn sie das erfährt, wird sie wütend sein.
■ **to be mad at somebody** wütend auf jemanden sein □ She was mad at me. Sie war wütend auf mich.

madam NOUN
LANGUAGE TIP In German no form of address is normally used apart from **Sie**.
□ Would you like to order, Madam? Möchten Sie bestellen?

made VERB ▷ *see* **make**

madly ADVERB
■ **They're madly in love.** Sie sind wahnsinnig verliebt.

madman NOUN
der Verrückte (GEN des Verrückten, PL die Verrückten)
□ a madman ein Verrückter

madness NOUN
der Wahnsinn
□ It's absolute madness. Das ist totaler Wahnsinn.

magazine NOUN
die Zeitschrift

maggot NOUN
die Made

magic ADJECTIVE
▷ *see also* **magic** NOUN
1 magisch *(magical)*
□ magic powers magische Kräfte
■ **a magic trick** ein Zaubertrick *masc*
■ **a magic wand** ein Zauberstab *masc*
2 echt toll *(brilliant)*
□ It was magic! Es war echt toll!

magic NOUN
▷ *see also* **magic** ADJECTIVE
das Zaubern
□ My hobby is magic. Zaubern ist mein Hobby.

magician NOUN
der Zauberkünstler (PL die Zauberkünstler)
die Zauberkünstlerin *(conjurer)*

magnet NOUN
der Magnet

magnificent ADJECTIVE
1 wundervoll *(beautiful)*
□ a magnificent view eine wundervolle Aussicht
2 ausgezeichnet *(outstanding)*
□ It was a magnificent film. Es war ein ausgezeichneter Film.

magnifying glass NOUN
die Lupe

maid NOUN
die Hausangestellte (GEN der Hausangestellten) *(servant)*
■ **an old maid** *(spinster)* eine alte Jungfer

maiden name NOUN
der Mädchenname (GEN des Mädchennamens, PL die Mädchennamen)

mail NOUN
die Post
□ Here's your mail. Hier ist deine Post.
■ **by mail** per Post
■ **e-mail** *(electronic mail)* die E-Mail

mailbox NOUN (US)
der Briefkasten (PL die Briefkästen)

mailing list NOUN
die Mailingliste

mailman NOUN (US)
der Briefträger (PL die Briefträger)

main ADJECTIVE
■ **the main problem** das Hauptproblem
■ **the main thing** die Hauptsache

mainly ADVERB
hauptsächlich

main road NOUN
die Hauptstraße

□ I don't like cycling on main roads. Ich fahre nicht gern auf Hauptstraßen Rad.

to **maintain** VERB
instand halten (PRESENT hält instand, IMPERFECT hielt instand, PERFECT hat instand gehalten) *(machine, building)*

maintenance NOUN
die Instandhaltung *(of machine, building)*

maize NOUN
der Mais

majesty NOUN
die Majestät
■ **Your Majesty** Eure Majestät

major ADJECTIVE
groß
□ a major problem ein großes Problem
■ **in C major** in C-Dur

Majorca NOUN
Mallorca *neut*
■ **to Majorca** nach Mallorca

majority NOUN
die Mehrheit

make NOUN
▷ *see also* **make** VERB
die Marke
□ What make is that car? Welche Marke ist das Auto?

to **make** VERB
▷ *see also* **make** NOUN
1 machen
□ He made it himself. Er hat es selbst gemacht. □ I make my bed every morning. Ich mache jeden Morgen mein Bett. □ two and two make four. zwei und zwei macht vier.
■ **to make lunch** das Mittagessen machen
□ She's making lunch. Sie macht das Mittagessen.
■ **I'm going to make a cake.** Ich werde einen Kuchen backen.
2 herstellen (PERFECT hat hergestellt) *(manufacture)*
□ made in Germany in Deutschland hergestellt
3 verdienen (PERFECT hat verdient) *(earn)*
□ He makes a lot of money. Er verdient viel Geld.
■ **to make somebody do something** jemanden zwingen, etwas zu tun
□ My mother makes me do my homework. Meine Mutter zwingt mich, meine Hausaufgaben zu machen.
■ **to make a phone call** telefonieren
□ I'd like to make a phone call. Ich würde gern telefonieren.
■ **to make fun of somebody** sich über jemanden lustig machen □ They made fun of him. Sie haben sich über ihn lustig gemacht.
■ **What time do you make it?** Wie viel Uhr hast du?

to **make out** VERB
1 entziffern (PERFECT hat entziffert)
□ I can't make out the address. Ich kann die Adresse nicht entziffern.
2 verstehen (IMPERFECT verstand, PERFECT hat verstanden)
□ I can't make her out at all. Ich kann sie überhaupt nicht verstehen.
3 behaupten (PERFECT hat behauptet)
□ They're making out it was my fault. Sie behaupten, es wäre meine Schuld gewesen.
■ **to make a cheque out to somebody** jemandem einen Scheck ausstellen

to **make up** VERB
1 erfinden (IMPERFECT erfand, PERFECT hat erfunden) *(invent)*
□ He made up the whole story. Er hat die ganze Geschichte erfunden.
2 sich versöhnen (PERFECT haben sich versöhnt) *(after argument)*
□ They soon made up. Sie haben sich bald wieder versöhnt.
■ **to make oneself up** sich schminken
□ She spends hours making herself up. Sie schminkt sich immer stundenlang.

maker NOUN
der Hersteller (PL die Hersteller)
□ Germany's biggest car maker Deutschlands größter Autohersteller

make-up NOUN
das Make-up (PL die Make-ups)

Malaysia NOUN
Malaysia *neut*
■ **to Malaysia** nach Malaysia

male ADJECTIVE
männlich
□ a male kitten ein männliches Katzenjunges
□ Sex: male. Geschlecht: männlich

LANGUAGE TIP In many cases, the ending in German indicates clearly whether the noun refers to a man or a woman and there is therefore no need for the word 'male'.

□ male and female students Studenten und Studentinnen
■ **a male chauvinist** ein Macho *masc*
■ **a male nurse** ein Krankenpfleger *masc*

mall NOUN
das Einkaufszentrum (PL die Einkaufszentren)

Malta NOUN
Malta *neut*
■ **from Malta** aus Malta
■ **to Malta** nach Malta

mammoth ADJECTIVE
monumental
□ a mammoth task eine monumentale Aufgabe

man NOUN
der Mann (PL die Männer)
□ an old man ein alter Mann

to **manage** VERB
1 leiten *(be in charge of)*
□ She manages a big store. Sie leitet ein großes Geschäft.

2 managen *(band, football team)*
□ He manages the team. Er managt die Mannschaft.
3 klarkommen (IMPERFECT kam klar, PERFECT ist klargekommen) *(get by)*
□ We haven't got much money, but we manage. Wir haben nicht viel Geld, aber wir kommen klar. □ It's okay, I can manage. Das ist okay, ich komme klar.
4 schaffen
□ Can you manage okay? Schaffst du es?
□ I can't manage all that. *(food)* Das schaffe ich nicht alles.
■ **to manage to do something** es schaffen, etwas zu tun □ I managed to pass the exam. Ich habe die Prüfung geschafft.

manageable ADJECTIVE
machbar *(task)*

management NOUN
die Leitung *(organization)*
□ the management of the company die Leitung des Unternehmens □ 'under new management' 'unter neuer Leitung'

manager NOUN
1 der Geschäftsführer (PL die Geschäftsführer)
die Geschäftsführerin *(of company, shop, restaurant)*
2 der Manager (PL die Manager)
die Managerin *(of performer, football team)*

manageress NOUN
die Geschäftsführerin

mandarin NOUN
die Mandarine *(fruit)*

mango NOUN
die Mango (PL die Mangos)

mania NOUN
die Manie

maniac NOUN
der Verrückte (GEN des Verrückten, PL die Verrückten)
die Verrückte (GEN der Verrückten)
□ He drives like a maniac. Er fährt wie ein Verrückter.

to **manipulate** VERB
manipulieren (PERFECT hat manipuliert)

mankind NOUN
die Menschheit

man-made ADJECTIVE
synthetisch *(fibre)*

manner NOUN
die Art und Weise
□ in this manner auf diese Art und Weise
■ **She behaves in an odd manner.** Sie benimmt sich eigenartig.
■ **He has a confident manner.** Er wirkt selbstsicher.

manners PL NOUN
das Benehmen *sing*
□ good manners gutes Benehmen
■ **Her manners are appalling.** Sie benimmt sich schrecklich.
■ **It's bad manners to speak with your mouth full.** Es gehört sich nicht, mit vollem Mund zu sprechen.

manpower NOUN
die Arbeitskräfte *fem pl*

mansion NOUN
die Villa (PL die Villen)

mantelpiece NOUN
der Kaminsims (GEN des Kaminsimses, PL die Kaminsimse)

manual NOUN
das Handbuch (PL die Handbücher)

to **manufacture** VERB
herstellen (PERFECT hat hergestellt)

manufacturer NOUN
der Hersteller (PL die Hersteller)

manure NOUN
der Mist

manuscript NOUN
das Manuskript (PL die Manuskripte)

many ADJECTIVE, PRONOUN
viele
□ The film has many special effects. In dem Film gibt es viele Spezialeffekte. □ He hasn't got many friends. Er hat nicht viele Freunde.
□ Were there many people at the concert? Waren viele Leute in dem Konzert?
■ **very many** sehr viele □ I haven't got very many CDs. Ich habe nicht sehr viele CDs.
■ **Not many.** Nicht viele.
■ **How many?** Wie viele? □ How many do you want? Wie viele möchten Sie?
■ **How many euros do you get for one pound?** Wie viel Euro bekommt man für ein Pfund?
■ **too many** zu viele □ That's too many. Das sind zu viele. □ She makes too many mistakes. Sie macht zu viele Fehler.
■ **so many** so viele □ I didn't know that so many would come. Ich wusste nicht, dass so viele kommen würden. □ I've never seen so many policemen. Ich habe noch nie so viele Polizisten gesehen.

map NOUN
1 die Landkarte *(of country, area)*
2 der Stadtplan (PL die Stadtpläne) *(of town)*
LANGUAGE TIP Be careful not to translate **map** by **Mappe**.

marathon NOUN
der Marathonlauf (PL die Marathonläufe)
□ the London marathon der Londoner Marathonlauf

marble NOUN
der Marmor
□ a marble statue eine Marmorstatue
■ **to play marbles** Murmeln spielen

March NOUN
der März
□ in March im März

English-German

m

march NOUN
▷ *see also* **march** VERB
der Protestmarsch (GEN des Protestmarsches, PL die Protestmärsche) *(demonstration)*

to **march** VERB
▷ *see also* **march** NOUN
1 marschieren (PERFECT ist marschiert) *(soldiers)*
2 aufmarschieren (PERFECT ist aufmarschiert) *(protesters)*

mare NOUN
die Stute

margarine NOUN
die Margarine

margin NOUN
der Rand (PL die Ränder)
□ I wrote notes in the margin. Ich schrieb Notizen an den Rand.

marijuana NOUN
das Marihuana

marital status NOUN
der Familienstand

mark NOUN
▷ *see also* **mark** VERB
1 die Note *(in school)*
□ I get good marks for German. Ich habe in Deutsch gute Noten.
2 der Fleck (PL die Flecken) *(stain)*
□ You've got a mark on your shirt. Du hast einen Fleck auf dem Hemd.
3 die Mark (PL die Mark) *(old German currency)*

to **mark** VERB
▷ *see also* **mark** NOUN
korrigieren (PERFECT hat korrigiert)
□ The teacher hasn't marked my homework yet. Der Lehrer hat meine Hausarbeit noch nicht korrigiert.

market NOUN
der Markt (PL die Märkte)

marketing NOUN
das Marketing (GEN des Marketing)

marketplace NOUN
der Marktplatz (GEN des Marktplatzes, PL die Marktplätze)

marmalade NOUN
die Orangenmarmelade

maroon ADJECTIVE
burgunderrot *(colour)*

marriage NOUN
die Ehe

married ADJECTIVE
verheiratet
□ They are not married. Sie sind nicht verheiratet. □ They have been married for fifteen years. Sie sind seit fünfzehn Jahren verheiratet.
■ **a married couple** ein Ehepaar *neut*

marrow NOUN
der Kürbis (GEN des Kürbisses, PL die Kürbisse) *(vegetable)*

to **marry** VERB
heiraten
□ He wants to marry her. Er will sie heiraten.
■ **to get married** heiraten □ My sister's getting married in June. Meine Schwester heiratet im Juni.

marvellous ADJECTIVE
wunderbar
□ She's a marvellous cook. Sie ist eine wunderbare Köchin. □ The weather was marvellous. Das Wetter war wunderbar.

marzipan NOUN
der Marzipan (PL die Marzipane)

mascara NOUN
die Wimperntusche

masculine ADJECTIVE
männlich

mashed potatoes PL NOUN
der Kartoffelbrei
□ sausages and mashed potatoes Würstchen mit Kartoffelbrei

mask NOUN
die Maske

masked ADJECTIVE
maskiert
□ a masked man ein maskierter Mann

mass NOUN
1 der Haufen (PL die Haufen)
□ a mass of books and papers ein Haufen Bücher und Papiere
2 die Messe *(in church)*
□ We go to mass on Sunday. Wir gehen am Sonntag zur Messe.
■ **the mass media** die Massenmedien

massage NOUN
die Massage

massive ADJECTIVE
enorm

to **master** VERB
beherrschen (PERFECT hat beherrscht)
□ to master a language eine Sprache beherrschen

masterpiece NOUN
das Meisterstück (PL die Meisterstücke)

mat NOUN
der Vorleger (PL die Vorleger) *(doormat)*
■ **a table mat** ein Untersetzer *masc*
■ **a place mat** ein Set *neut*

match NOUN
▷ *see also* **match** VERB
1 das Streichholz (GEN des Streichholzes, PL die Streichhölzer)
□ a box of matches eine Schachtel Streichhölzer
2 das Spiel (PL die Spiele) *(sport)*
□ a football match ein Fußballspiel

to **match** VERB
▷ *see also* **match** NOUN
passen zu
□ The jacket matches the trousers. Die Jacke passt zu der Hose. □ These colours don't match. Diese Farben passen nicht zueinander.

matching ADJECTIVE
farblich abgestimmt
□ matching wallpaper and curtains farblich abgestimmte Tapeten und Vorhänge

mate NOUN
der Kumpel (PL die Kumpel) *(informal)*
LANGUAGE TIP **der Kumpel** is also used for women.
□ On Friday night I go out with my mates. Freitag Abend gehe ich mit meinen Kumpels aus.

material NOUN
1 der Stoff (PL die Stoffe) *(cloth)*
2 das Material (PL die Materialien) *(information, data)*
□ I'm collecting material for my project. Ich sammle Material für mein Referat.
■ **raw materials** die Rohstoffe

mathematics SING NOUN
die Mathematik

maths SING NOUN
die Mathe

matron NOUN
die Oberschwester *(in hospital)*

matter NOUN
▹ *see also* **matter** VERB
die Angelegenheit
□ It's a serious matter. Das ist eine ernste Angelegenheit.
■ **It's a matter of life and death.** Es geht um Leben und Tod.
■ **What's the matter?** Was ist los?
■ **as a matter of fact** tatsächlich

to **matter** VERB
▹ *see also* **matter** NOUN
■ **it doesn't matter 1** *(I don't mind)* das macht nichts □ I can't give you the money today. — It doesn't matter. Ich kann dir das Geld heute nicht geben. — Das macht nichts.
2 *(makes no difference)* das ist egal □ Shall I phone today or tomorrow? — Whenever, it doesn't matter. Soll ich heute oder morgen anrufen? — Wann du willst, das ist egal.
■ **It matters a lot to me.** Das ist mir sehr wichtig.

mattress NOUN
die Matratze

mature ADJECTIVE
reif
□ She's very mature for her age. Sie ist sehr reif für ihr Alter.

maximum NOUN
▹ *see also* **maximum** ADJECTIVE
das Maximum (PL die Maxima)

maximum ADJECTIVE
▹ *see also* **maximum** NOUN
■ **the maximum speed** die Höchstgeschwindigkeit
■ **the maximum amount** der Höchstbetrag

May NOUN
der Mai
■ **in May** im Mai
■ **May Day** der Erste Mai

may VERB
■ **He may come.** Er kommt vielleicht.
□ It may rain. Es regnet vielleicht.
■ **Are you going to the party? — I don't know, I may.** Gehst du zur Party? — Ich weiß nicht, vielleicht.
■ **May I smoke?** Darf ich rauchen?

maybe ADVERB
vielleicht
□ maybe not vielleicht nicht □ a bit boring, maybe vielleicht etwas langweilig □ Maybe she's at home. Vielleicht ist sie zu Hause.
□ Maybe he'll change his mind. Vielleicht überlegt er es sich anders.

mayonnaise NOUN
die Mayonnaise

mayor NOUN
der Bürgermeister (PL die Bürgermeister)
die Bürgermeisterin

maze NOUN
der Irrgarten (PL die Irrgärten)

me PRONOUN
1 mich
□ Can you hear me? Kannst du mich hören?
□ Look at me! Sieh mich an!
LANGUAGE TIP Use **mich** after prepositions which take the accusative.
□ Is this present for me? Ist das Geschenk für mich? □ Wait for me! Warte auf mich!
2 mir
LANGUAGE TIP Use **mir** after prepositions which take the dative.
□ Will you come with me? Kommst du mit mir mit? □ He sat next to me. Er saß neben mir.
LANGUAGE TIP Use **mir** when 'me' means 'to me'.
□ Give me the book, please! Gib mir bitte das Buch! □ She told me the truth. Sie hat mir die Wahrheit erzählt.
3 ich
□ It's me! Ich bin's! □ Me too! Ich auch!
□ She's older than me. Sie ist älter als ich.

meal NOUN
das Essen (PL die Essen)

mealtime NOUN
■ **at mealtimes** zur Essenszeit

to **mean** VERB
▹ *see also* **mean** ADJECTIVE *and* **means** NOUN
1 bedeuten (PERFECT hat bedeutet) *(signify)*
□ What does 'besetzt' mean? Was bedeutet 'besetzt'? □ I don't know what it means. Ich weiß nicht, was es bedeutet.
2 meinen *(mean to say)*
□ What do you mean? Was meinst du damit?
□ That's not what I meant. Das habe ich nicht gemeint. □ Which one do you mean? Welchen meinst du? □ Do you really mean it? Meinst du das wirklich?

English-German

m

■ **to mean to do something** etwas tun wollen □ I didn't mean to offend you. Ich wollte dich nicht kränken.

mean ADJECTIVE
▷ *see also* **mean** VERB *and* **means** NOUN
1 geizig *(with money)*
□ He's too mean to buy Christmas presents. Er ist zu geizig, um Weihnachtsgeschenke zu kaufen.
2 gemein *(unkind)*
□ You're being mean to me. Du bist gemein zu mir. □ That's a really mean thing to say! Das ist gemein, so etwas zu sagen!

meaning NOUN
die Bedeutung
LANGUAGE TIP Be careful not to translate **meaning** by **Meinung**.

means NOUN
▷ *see also* **mean** VERB *and* **adjective**
die Möglichkeit
□ a means of storing power eine Möglichkeit, Energie zu speichern □ We have the means to do that. Wir haben die Möglichkeit, das zu tun.
■ **a means of transport** ein Transportmittel *neut*
■ **He'll do it by any possible means.** Er wird es tun, egal wie.
■ **by means of** mit □ He got in by means of a stolen key. Er kam mit einem gestohlenen Schlüssel hinein.
■ **by all means** selbstverständlich □ Can I come? — By all means! Kann ich kommen? — Selbstverständlich!
■ **by no means** keineswegs □ That was by no means the end of the matter. Damit war die Sache keineswegs erledigt.

meant VERB ▷ *see* **mean**

meanwhile ADVERB
inzwischen

measles SING NOUN
die Masern *pl*
□ She's got measles. Sie hat Masern.

to **measure** VERB
1 ausmessen (PRESENT misst aus, IMPERFECT maß aus, PERFECT hat ausgemessen)
□ I measured the page. Ich habe die Seite ausgemessen.
2 messen
□ The room measures three metres by four. Das Zimmer misst drei auf vier Meter.

measurement NOUN
das Maß (PL die Maße) *(of object)*
□ What are the measurements of the room? Wie sind die Maße des Zimmers? □ What are your measurements? Was sind Ihre Maße?
■ **my waist measurement** meine Taillenweite
■ **What's your neck measurement?** Welche Kragenweite haben Sie?

meat NOUN
das Fleisch
□ I don't eat meat. Ich esse kein Fleisch.

Mecca NOUN
Mekka *neut*

mechanic NOUN
der Mechaniker (PL die Mechaniker)
die Mechanikerin
□ He's a mechanic. Er ist Mechaniker.

mechanical ADJECTIVE
mechanisch

medal NOUN
die Medaille
■ **the gold medal** die Goldmedaille

media PL NOUN
die Medien *neut pl*

median strip NOUN (US)
der Mittelstreifen (PL die Mittelstreifen)

medical ADJECTIVE
▷ *see also* **medical** NOUN
medizinisch
□ medical treatment die medizinische Behandlung
■ **medical insurance** die Krankenversicherung
■ **to have medical problems** gesundheitliche Probleme haben
■ **She's a medical student.** Sie ist Medizinstudentin.

medical NOUN
▷ *see also* **medical** ADJECTIVE
■ **to have a medical** sich ärztlich untersuchen lassen

medicine NOUN
die Medizin
□ I want to study medicine. Ich möchte Medizin studieren. □ I need some medicine. Ich brauche Medizin.
■ **alternative medicine** die alternative Medizin

Mediterranean ADJECTIVE
südländisch *(person, character, scenery)*
■ **the Mediterranean** das Mittelmeer

medium ADJECTIVE
mittlere
□ a man of medium height ein Mann von mittlerer Größe

medium-sized ADJECTIVE
mittelgroß
□ a medium-sized town eine mittelgroße Stadt

to **meet** VERB
1 treffen (PRESENT trifft, IMPERFECT traf, PERFECT hat getroffen) *(by chance)*
□ I met Paul when I was walking the dog. Ich habe Paul getroffen, als ich mit dem Hund spazieren war.
2 sich treffen *(by arrangement)*
□ Let's meet in front of the tourist office. Treffen wir uns doch vor dem Verkehrsbüro. □ I'm going to meet my friends. Ich treffe mich mit meinen Freunden.
3 kennenlernen (PERFECT hat kennengelernt) *(get to know)*

□ I like meeting new people. Ich lerne gerne neue Leute kennen.
■ **Have you met him before?** Kennen Sie ihn?
4 abholen (PERFECT hat abgeholt) *(pick up)*
□ I'll meet you at the station. Ich hole dich am Bahnhof ab.

meeting NOUN
1 die Besprechung *(for work)*
□ a business meeting eine geschäftliche Besprechung
2 das Treffen (PL die Treffen) *(socially)*
□ their first meeting ihr erstes Treffen

mega ADJECTIVE
■ **He's mega rich.** Er ist superreich. *(informal)*

melody NOUN
die Melodie

melon NOUN
die Melone

to **melt** VERB
schmelzen (PRESENT schmilzt, IMPERFECT schmolz, PERFECT ist geschmolzen)
□ The snow is melting. Der Schnee schmilzt.

member NOUN
das Mitglied (PL die Mitglieder)
■ **a Member of Parliament** 1 *(man)* ein Abgeordneter 2 *(woman)* eine Abgeordnete

membership NOUN
die Mitgliedschaft *(of party, union)*
□ I'm going to apply for membership. Ich werde mich um Mitgliedschaft bewerben.

membership card NOUN
der Mitgliedsausweis (PL die Mitgliedsausweise)

memento NOUN
das Andenken (PL die Andenken)

memorial NOUN
das Denkmal (PL die Denkmäler)
■ **a war memorial** ein Kriegerdenkmal

to **memorize** VERB
auswendig lernen

memory NOUN
1 das Gedächtnis (GEN des Gedächtnisses)
□ I haven't got a good memory. Ich habe kein gutes Gedächtnis.
2 die Erinnerung *(recollection)*
□ to bring back memories Erinnerungen wachrufen
3 der Speicher (GEN die Speicher) *(computer)*

men PL NOUN ▷ *see* **man**

to **mend** VERB
flicken

meningitis NOUN
die Hirnhautentzündung

mental ADJECTIVE
1 geistig
■ **a mental illness** eine Geisteskrankheit
2 wahnsinnig *(mad)*
□ You're mental! Du bist wahnsinnig!
■ **a mental hospital** eine psychiatrische Klinik

to **mention** VERB
erwähnen (PERFECT hat erwähnt)
■ **Thank you! — Don't mention it!** Danke! — Bitte!

menu NOUN
1 die Speisekarte
□ Could I have the menu please? Könnte ich bitte die Speisekarte haben?
2 das Menü (PL die Menüs) *(on computer)*

merchant NOUN
der Händler (PL die Händler)
die Händlerin
□ a wine merchant ein Weinhändler

mercy NOUN
die Gnade

mere ADJECTIVE
bloß
□ It's a mere formality. Das ist eine bloße Formalität.
■ **a mere five percent** ganze fünf Prozent

meringue NOUN
die Meringe

merry ADJECTIVE
■ **Merry Christmas!** Fröhliche Weihnachten!

merry-go-round NOUN
das Karussell (PL die Karussells)

mess NOUN
die Unordnung
□ His bedroom's always in a mess. In seinem Schlafzimmer herrscht ständig Unordnung.

to **mess about** VERB
■ **to mess about with something** *(interfere with)* an etwas herumfummeln □ Stop messing about with my computer! Hör auf, an meinem Computer herumzufummeln!
■ **Don't mess about with my things!** Lass meine Sachen in Ruhe!

to **mess up** VERB
■ **to mess something up** etwas durcheinanderbringen □ My little brother has messed up my room. Mein kleiner Bruder hat mein Zimmer durcheinandergebracht.

message NOUN
die Nachricht

messenger NOUN
der Bote (GEN des Boten, PL die Boten)
die Botin

messy ADJECTIVE
1 schmutzig *(dirty)*
□ a messy job eine schmutzige Arbeit
2 unordentlich *(untidy)*
□ Your room's really messy. Dein Zimmer ist wirklich unordentlich. □ She's so messy! Sie ist so unordentlich!
■ **My writing is terribly messy.** Ich habe eine schreckliche Schrift.

met VERB ▷ *see* **meet**

metal NOUN
das Metall (PL die Metalle)

meter NOUN
1 der Zähler (PL die Zähler) *(for gas, electricity, taxi)*
2 die Parkuhr *(parking meter)*

method NOUN
die Methode

Methodist NOUN
der Methodist (GEN des Methodisten, PL die Methodisten)
die Methodistin
□ She's a Methodist. Sie ist Methodistin.

metre NOUN
der Meter (PL die Meter)

metric ADJECTIVE
metrisch

Mexico NOUN
Mexiko *neut*
■ **from Mexico** aus Mexiko
■ **to Mexico** nach Mexiko

to **miaow** VERB
miauen (PERFECT hat miaut)

mice PL NOUN ▷ *see* **mouse**

microchip NOUN
der Mikrochip (PL die Mikrochips)

microphone NOUN
das Mikrofon (PL die Mikrofone)

microscope NOUN
das Mikroskop (PL die Mikroskope)

microwave NOUN
die Mikrowelle

microwave oven NOUN
der Mikrowellenherd (PL die Mikrowellenherde)

mid ADJECTIVE
■ **in mid May** Mitte Mai

midday NOUN
der Mittag (PL die Mittage)
■ **at midday** um zwölf Uhr mittags

middle NOUN
die Mitte
■ **in the middle of the road** mitten auf der Straße
■ **in the middle of the night** mitten in der Nacht
■ **the middle seat** der mittlere Sitz

middle-aged ADJECTIVE
mittleren Alters
□ a middle-aged man ein Mann mittleren Alters □ She's middle-aged. Sie ist mittleren Alters.

Middle Ages PL NOUN
■ **the Middle Ages** das Mittelalter

middle-class ADJECTIVE
■ **a middle-class family** eine Familie der Mittelschicht

Middle East NOUN
der Nahe Osten
□ in the Middle East im Nahen Osten

middle name NOUN
der zweite Vorname (GEN des zweiten Vornamens, PL die zweiten Vornamen)

midge NOUN
die Mücke

midnight NOUN
die Mitternacht
■ **at midnight** um Mitternacht

midwife NOUN
die Hebamme
□ She's a midwife. Sie ist Hebamme.

might VERB

LANGUAGE TIP Use **vielleicht** to express possibility.

□ He might come later. Er kommt vielleicht später. □ We might go to Spain next year. Wir fahren nächstes Jahr vielleicht nach Spanien. □ She might not have understood. Sie hat es vielleicht nicht verstanden.

migraine NOUN
die Migräne
□ I've got a migraine. Ich habe Migräne.

mike NOUN
das Mikro (PL die Mikros)

mild ADJECTIVE
mild
□ The winters are quite mild. Die Winter sind ziemlich mild.

mile NOUN
die Meile

DID YOU KNOW...?
In Germany distances and speeds are expressed in kilometres. A mile is about 1.6 kilometres.

□ It's five miles from here. Es ist acht Kilometer von hier. □ at fifty miles per hour mit achtzig Kilometern pro Stunde
■ **We walked miles!** Wir sind meilenweit gegangen!

military ADJECTIVE
militärisch

milk NOUN
▷ *see also* **milk** VERB
die Milch
□ tea with milk der Tee mit Milch

to **milk** VERB
▷ *see also* **milk** NOUN
melken (PERFECT hat gemolken)

milk chocolate NOUN
die Milchschokolade

milkman NOUN
der Milchmann (PL die Milchmänner)
□ He's a milkman. Er ist Milchmann.

milk shake NOUN
der Milchshake (PL die Milchshakes)

mill NOUN
die Mühle *(for grain)*

millennium NOUN
das Jahrtausend

millimetre NOUN
der Millimeter (PL die Millimeter)

million NOUN
die Million

millionaire NOUN
der Millionär (PL die Millionäre)
die Millionärin

to **mimic** VERB
nachmachen (PERFECT hat nachgemacht)

mince NOUN
das Hackfleisch

to **mind** VERB
▷ *see also* **mind** NOUN
aufpassen auf +*acc* (PERFECT hat aufgepasst)
□ Could you mind the baby this afternoon? Kannst du heute Nachmittag auf das Baby aufpassen? □ Could you mind my bags? Können Sie auf mein Gepäck aufpassen?
■ **Do you mind if I open the window?** Macht es Ihnen etwas aus, wenn ich das Fenster aufmache?
■ **I don't mind.** Es macht mir nichts aus. □ I don't mind the noise. Der Lärm macht mir nichts aus.
■ **Never mind!** Macht nichts!
■ **Mind that bike!** Pass auf das Fahrrad auf!
■ **Mind the step!** Vorsicht Stufe!

mind NOUN
▷ *see also* **mind** VERB
■ **to make up one's mind** sich entscheiden □ I haven't made up my mind yet. Ich habe mich noch nicht entschieden.
■ **to change one's mind** es sich anders überlegen □ I've changed my mind. Ich habe es mir anders überlegt.
■ **Are you out of your mind?** Bist du wahnsinnig?

mine PRONOUN
▷ *see also* **mine** NOUN
1 meiner
□ Is this your coat? — No, mine's black. Ist das dein Mantel? — Nein, meiner ist schwarz.
meine
□ Is this your cup? — No, mine's red. Ist das deine Tasse? — Nein, meine ist rot.
meines
□ Is this your car? — No, mine's green. Ist das dein Auto? — Nein, meines ist grün.
2 meine
□ her parents and mine ihre Eltern und meine □ Your hands are dirty, mine are clean. Deine Hände sind schmutzig, meine sind sauber.
■ **It's mine.** Das gehört mir. □ This book is mine. Dieses Buch gehört mir. □ Whose is this? — It's mine. Wem gehört das? — Es gehört mir.

mine NOUN
▷ *see also* **mine** PRONOUN
die Mine
■ **a land mine** eine Landmine
■ **a coal mine** ein Kohlebergwerk *neut*

miner NOUN
der Bergarbeiter (PL die Bergarbeiter)

mineral water NOUN
das Mineralwasser (PL die Mineralwasser)

miniature NOUN
die Miniatur

minibus NOUN
der Minibus (GEN des Minibusses, PL die Minibusse)

minicab NOUN
das Kleintaxi (PL die Kleintaxis)

Minidisc® NOUN
die Minidisc® (PL die Minidiscs)

minimum NOUN
▷ *see also* **minimum** ADJECTIVE
das Mininum (PL die Minima)

minimum ADJECTIVE
▷ *see also* **minimum** NOUN
■ **minimum age** das Mindestalter
■ **minimum amount** der Mindestbetrag
■ **minimum wage** der Mindestlohn

miniskirt NOUN
der Minirock (PL die Miniröcke)

minister NOUN
1 der Minister (PL die Minister)
die Ministerin *(in government)*
2 der Pfarrer (PL die Pfarrer)
die Pfarrerin *(of church)*

ministry NOUN
das Ministerium (PL die Ministerien) *(in politics)*

mink NOUN
der Nerz
□ a mink coat ein Nerzmantel *masc*

minor ADJECTIVE
kleiner
□ a minor problem ein kleineres Problem
□ a minor operation eine kleinere Operation
■ **in D minor** in d-Moll

minority NOUN
die Minderheit

mint NOUN
1 die Pfefferminze *(plant)*
■ **mint sauce** die Pfefferminzsoße
2 das Pfefferminzbonbon (PL die Pfefferminzbonbons) *(sweet)*

minus PREPOSITION
minus
□ sixteen minus three is thirteen. Sechzehn minus drei ist dreizehn. □ It's minus two degrees outside. Draußen hat es zwei Grad minus. □ I got a B minus. Ich habe eine Zwei minus bekommen.

DID YOU KNOW...?
In Germany, grades are given from 1 to 6, with 1 being the best.

minute NOUN
▷ *see also* **minute** ADJECTIVE
die Minute
■ **Wait a minute!** Einen Augenblick!

minute ADJECTIVE
▷ *see also* **minute** NOUN
winzig
□ Her flat is minute. Ihre Wohnung ist winzig.

miracle NOUN
das Wunder (PL die Wunder)

mirror NOUN
der Spiegel (PL die Spiegel)

to **misbehave** VERB
sich schlecht benehmen (PRESENT benimmt sich schlecht, IMPERFECT benahm sich schlecht, PERFECT hat sich schlecht benommen)

miscellaneous ADJECTIVE
verschieden
□ miscellaneous items verschiedene Artikel

mischief NOUN
die Dummheiten *fem pl*
□ She's always up to mischief. Sie macht dauernd Dummheiten.

mischievous ADJECTIVE
verschmitzt

miser NOUN
der Geizhals (GEN des Geizhalses, PL die Geizhälse)

miserable ADJECTIVE
1 unglücklich *(person)*
□ You're looking miserable. Du siehst richtig unglücklich aus.
2 schrecklich *(weather)*
□ The weather was miserable. Das Wetter war schrecklich.
■ **to feel miserable** sich miserabel fühlen
□ I'm feeling miserable. Ich fühle mich miserabel.

misery NOUN
1 das Elend
□ All that money brought nothing but misery. All das Geld hat nichts als Elend gebracht.
2 der Miesepeter *(informal)* (PL die Miesepeter)
□ She's a real misery. Sie ist ein richtiger Miesepeter.

misfortune NOUN
das Unglück (PL die Unglücke)

mishap NOUN
das Missgeschick (PL die Missgeschicke)

to **misjudge** VERB
falsch einschätzen (PERFECT hat falsch eingeschätzt) *(person)*
□ I've misjudged her. Ich habe sie falsch eingeschätzt.
■ **He misjudged the bend.** Er hat sich in der Kurve verschätzt.

to **mislay** VERB
verlegen (PERFECT hat verlegt)
□ I've mislaid my passport. Ich habe meinen Pass verlegt.

to **mislead** VERB
irreführen (PERFECT hat irregeführt)

misleading ADJECTIVE
irreführend

misprint NOUN
der Druckfehler (PL die Druckfehler)

Miss NOUN
das Fräulein

DID YOU KNOW...?
Nowadays it is regarded as old-fashioned to call somebody **Fräulein** and **Frau** is used instead.

□ Miss Jones Frau Jones

to **miss** VERB
verpassen (PERFECT hat verpasst)
□ Hurry or you'll miss the bus. Beeil dich, sonst verpasst du den Bus! □ to miss an opportunity eine Gelegenheit verpassen
■ **I miss you.** Du fehlst mir. □ I'm missing my family. Meine Familie fehlt mir.
■ **He missed the target.** Er hat nicht getroffen.

missing ADJECTIVE
fehlend
□ the missing part das fehlende Teil
■ **to be missing** fehlen □ My rucksack is missing. Mein Rucksack fehlt.
□ Two members of the group are missing. Zwei Mitglieder der Gruppe fehlen.

missionary NOUN
der Missionar (PL die Missionare)
die Missionarin

mist NOUN
der Nebel (PL die Nebel)

LANGUAGE TIP Be careful not to translate **mist** by the German word **Mist**.

mistake NOUN
▷ *see also* **mistake** VERB
der Fehler (PL die Fehler)
□ It was a mistake to buy those yellow shoes. Es war ein Fehler, diese gelben Schuhe zu kaufen.
■ **a spelling mistake** ein Rechtschreibfehler
■ **to make a mistake** **1** *(in writing, speaking)* einen Fehler machen **2** *(get mixed up)* sich vertun □ I'm sorry, I made a mistake. Tut mir leid, ich habe mich vertan.
■ **by mistake** aus Versehen □ I took his bag by mistake. Ich habe aus Versehen seine Tasche genommen.

to **mistake** VERB
▷ *see also* **mistake** NOUN
■ **He mistook me for my sister.** Er hat mich mit meiner Schwester verwechselt.

mistaken ADJECTIVE
■ **to be mistaken** sich irren □ If you think I'm going to get up at six o'clock, you're mistaken. Wenn du meinst, ich würde um sechs Uhr aufstehen, dann irrst du dich.

mistakenly ADVERB
irrtümlicherweise

mistletoe NOUN
die Mistel

mistook VERB ▷ *see* **mistake**

mistress NOUN
1 die Lehrerin *(teacher)*
□ our German mistress unsere Deutschlehrerin

2 die Geliebte (GEN der Geliebten) *(lover)*
□ He's got a mistress. Er hat eine Geliebte.

to **mistrust** VERB
misstrauen (PERFECT hat misstraut)
□ I mistrust her. Ich misstraue ihr.

misty ADJECTIVE
neblig
□ a misty morning ein nebliger Morgen

to **misunderstand** VERB
missverstehen (IMPERFECT missverstand, PERFECT hat missverstanden)
□ Sorry, I misunderstood you. Entschuldigung, ich habe Sie missverstanden.

misunderstanding NOUN
das Missverständnis (GEN des Missverständnisses, PL die Missverständnisse)

misunderstood VERB ▷ *see* **misunderstand**

mix NOUN
▷ *see also* **mix** VERB
die Mischung
□ It's a mix of science fiction and comedy. Es ist eine Mischung aus Science-Fiction und Komödie.
■ **a cake mix** eine Backmischung

to **mix** VERB
▷ *see also* **mix** NOUN
1 vermischen (PERFECT hat vermischt)
□ Mix the flour with the sugar. Vermischen Sie das Mehl mit dem Zucker.
2 verbinden (IMPERFECT verband, PERFECT hat verbunden)
□ He's mixing business with pleasure. Er verbindet das Geschäftliche mit dem Vergnügen.
■ **to mix with somebody** *(associate)* mit jemandem verkehren
■ **He doesn't mix much.** Er geht nicht viel unter Menschen.
■ **to mix up** verwechseln □ He always mixes me up with my sister. Er verwechselt mich immer mit meiner Schwester. □ The travel agent mixed up the bookings. Das Reisebüro hat die Buchungen verwechselt.
■ **I'm getting mixed up.** Ich werde ganz konfus.

mixed ADJECTIVE
gemischt
□ a mixed salad ein gemischter Salat
□ a mixed school eine gemischte Schule
■ **a mixed grill** ein Grillteller *masc*

mixer NOUN
der Mixer (PL die Mixer) *(for food)*

mixture NOUN
die Mischung
□ a mixture of spices eine Gewürzmischung
■ **cough mixture** der Hustensaft

mix-up NOUN
die Verwechslung

MMS NOUN *(= multimedia messaging service)*
der MMS®

to **moan** VERB
sich beklagen (PERFECT hat sich beklagt)
□ She's always moaning. Sie beklagt sich dauernd.

mobile NOUN
das Handy (PL die Handys) *(phone)*

mobile home NOUN
das Wohnmobil (PL die Wohnmobile)

mobile phone NOUN
das Handy (PL die Handys)

to **mock** VERB
▷ *see also* **mock** ADJECTIVE
sich lustig machen über *+acc*
□ Stop mocking him! Mach dich nicht über ihn lustig!

mock ADJECTIVE
▷ *see also* **mock** VERB
■ **a mock exam** eine Übungsprüfung

mod cons PL NOUN
■ **with all mod cons** mit allem Komfort

model NOUN
▷ *see also* **model** ADJECTIVE, VERB
1 das Modell (PL die Modelle)
□ the latest model das neueste Modell
□ a model of the castle ein Modell der Burg
2 das Mannequin (PL die Mannequins) *(fashion)*
□ She's a famous model. Sie ist ein berühmtes Mannequin.

model ADJECTIVE
▷ *see also* **model** NOUN, VERB
■ **a model plane** ein Modellflugzeug *neut*
■ **a model railway** eine Modelleisenbahn
■ **He's a model pupil.** Er ist ein vorbildlicher Schüler.

to **model** VERB
▷ *see also* **model** NOUN, ADJECTIVE
als Model arbeiten
□ She was modelling in New York. Sie arbeitete in New York als Model.
■ **She was modelling a Paul Costello outfit.** Sie führte ein Outfit von Paul Costello vor.

modem NOUN
das Modem (PL die Modems)

moderate ADJECTIVE
gemäßigt
□ His views are quite moderate. Er hat sehr gemäßigte Ansichten.
■ **a moderate amount of alcohol** wenig Alkohol
■ **a moderate price** ein annehmbarer Preis

modern ADJECTIVE
modern

to **modernize** VERB
modernisieren (PERFECT hat modernisiert)

modest ADJECTIVE
bescheiden

to **modify** VERB
ändern

moist ADJECTIVE
feucht

□ This cake is very moist. Dieser Kuchen ist sehr feucht. □ Sow the seeds in moist compost. Säen Sie den Samen in feuchten Kompost.

moisture NOUN
die Feuchtigkeit

moisturizer NOUN
1 die Feuchtigkeitscreme (PL die Feuchtigkeitscremes) *(cream)*
2 die Feuchtigkeitslotion *(lotion)*

moldy ADJECTIVE (US)
schimmlig

mole NOUN
1 der Maulwurf (PL die Maulwürfe) *(animal)*
2 der Leberfleck (PL die Leberflecke) *(on skin)*

moment NOUN
der Augenblick (PL die Augenblicke)
□ Could you wait a moment? Können Sie einen Augenblick warten? □ in a moment in einem Augenblick □ Just a moment! Einen Augenblick!
■ **at the moment** momentan
■ **any moment now** jeden Moment
□ They'll be arriving any moment now. Sie können jeden Moment kommen.

momentous ADJECTIVE
bedeutsam

monarch NOUN
der Monarch (GEN des Monarchen, PL die Monarchen)
die Monarchin

monarchy NOUN
die Monarchie

monastery NOUN
das Kloster (PL die Klöster)

Monday NOUN
der Montag (PL die Montage)
□ on Monday am Montag □ every Monday jeden Montag □ last Monday letzten Montag □ next Monday nächsten Montag
■ **on Mondays** montags

money NOUN
das Geld (PL die Gelder)
□ I need to change some money. Ich muss Geld wechseln.
■ **to make money** Geld verdienen

mongrel NOUN
die Promenadenmischung
□ My dog's a mongrel. Mein Hund ist eine Promenadenmischung.

monitor NOUN
der Monitor (PL die Monitore) *(of computer)*

monk NOUN
der Mönch (PL die Mönche)

monkey NOUN
der Affe (GEN des Affen, PL die Affen)

monopoly NOUN
das Monopol
■ **to play Monopoly®** Monopoly spielen

monotonous ADJECTIVE
monoton

monster NOUN
das Monster (PL die Monster)

month NOUN
der Monat (PL die Monate)
□ this month diesen Monat □ next month nächsten Monat □ last month letzten Monat □ every month jeden Monat □ at the end of the month Ende des Monats

monthly ADJECTIVE
monatlich

monument NOUN
das Denkmal (PL die Denkmäler)

mood NOUN
die Laune
□ to be in a bad mood schlechte Laune haben □ to be in a good mood gute Laune haben

moody ADJECTIVE
1 launisch *(temperamental)*
2 schlecht gelaunt *(in a bad mood)*

moon NOUN
der Mond (PL die Monde)
■ **There's a full moon tonight.** Heute ist Vollmond.
■ **to be over the moon** *(happy)* überglücklich sein

moor NOUN
▷ *see also* **moor** VERB
das Moor (PL die Moore)

to **moor** VERB
▷ *see also* **moor** NOUN
festmachen (PERFECT hat festgemacht) *(boat)*

mop NOUN
der Mopp (PL die Mopps) *(for floor)*

moped NOUN
das Moped (PL die Mopeds)

moral ADJECTIVE
▷ *see also* **moral** NOUN
moralisch

moral NOUN
▷ *see also* **moral** ADJECTIVE
die Moral
□ the moral of the story die Moral der Geschichte
■ **morals** die Moral *sing*

morale NOUN
die Stimmung
□ Their morale is very low. Ihre Stimmung ist sehr schlecht.

more ADJECTIVE, PRONOUN, ADVERB
mehr
□ a bit more etwas mehr □ There are more girls in the class. In der Klasse sind mehr Mädchen.
■ **more than** mehr als □ She practises more than I do. Sie übt mehr als ich. □ I spent more than two hundred euros. Ich habe mehr als zweihundert Euro ausgegeben. □ More girls than boys do German. Mehr Mädchen als Jungen lernen Deutsch.

LANGUAGE TIP In comparisons you usually add **-er** to the adjective.

□ Could you speak more slowly? Könnten Sie langsamer sprechen? □ He's more intelligent than me. Er ist intelligenter als ich. □ Beer is more expensive in Britain. Bier ist in Großbritannien teurer.

LANGUAGE TIP When referring to an additional amount, over and above what there already is, you usually use **noch**.

□ Is there any more? Gibt es noch mehr? □ Would you like some more? Möchten Sie noch etwas? □ It'll take a few more days. Es braucht noch ein paar Tage. □ Could I have some more chips? Kann ich noch Pommes frites haben? □ Do you want some more tea? Möchten sie noch Tee?

■ **There isn't any more.** Es ist nichts mehr da.

■ **more or less** mehr oder weniger

■ **more than ever** mehr denn je

moreover ADVERB
außerdem

morning NOUN
der Morgen (PL die Morgen)

□ every morning jeden Morgen

■ **this morning** heute Morgen

■ **tomorrow morning** morgen früh □ I have to get up at six tomorrow morning. Ich muss morgen früh um sechs aufstehen.

■ **in the morning** morgens □ at seven o'clock in the morning um sieben Uhr morgens

■ **a morning paper** eine Morgenzeitung

Morocco NOUN
Marokko *neut*

■ **from Morocco** auf Marokko

■ **to Morocco** nach Marokko

mortgage NOUN
die Hypothek (PL die Hypotheken)

Moscow NOUN
Moskau *neut*

■ **to Moscow** nach Moskau

Moslem NOUN
der Moslem (PL die Moslems)
die Moslime

□ He's a Moslem. Er ist Moslem.

mosque NOUN
die Moschee

mosquito NOUN
die Stechmücke

■ **a mosquito bite** ein Mückenstich *masc*

most ADVERB, ADJECTIVE, PRONOUN

1 die meisten

□ most of my friends die meisten meiner Freunde □ most of them die meisten von ihnen □ most people die meisten Menschen

□ Most cats are affectionate. Die meisten Katzen sind anhänglich.

2 am meisten

□ what I hate most was ich am meisten hasse

■ **most of the time** meist

■ **most of the evening** fast den ganzen Abend

■ **most of the money** fast das ganze Geld

■ **the most** am meisten □ He's the one who talks the most. Er ist derjenige, der am meisten redet.

■ **to make the most of something** das Beste aus etwas machen

■ **at the most** höchstens □ Two hours at the most. Höchstens zwei Stunden.

LANGUAGE TIP For the superlative you usually add **-ste** to the adjective.

□ the most expensive seat der teuerste Platz

□ the most boring work die langweiligste Arbeit □ the most expensive restaurant das teuerste Restaurant

mostly ADVERB

■ **The teachers are mostly quite nice.** Die meisten unserer Lehrer sind ganz nett.

MOT NOUN
der TÜV *(= Technischer Überwachungsverein)*

□ My car failed its MOT. Mein Auto ist nicht durch den TÜV gekommen.

motel NOUN
das Motel (PL die Motels)

moth NOUN
die Motte

mother NOUN
die Mutter (PL die Mütter)

□ my mother meine Mutter

■ **mother tongue** die Muttersprache

mother-in-law NOUN
die Schwiegermutter (PL die Schwiegermütter)

Mother's Day NOUN
der Muttertag (PL die Muttertage)

DID YOU KNOW...?
In Germany **Muttertag** is on the second Sunday in May.

motionless ADJECTIVE
bewegungslos

motivated ADJECTIVE
motiviert

□ He is highly motivated. Er ist höchst motiviert.

motivation NOUN
die Motivation

motive NOUN
das Motiv (PL die Motive)

□ the motive for the killing das Motiv für den Mord

motor NOUN
der Motor (PL die Motoren)

□ The boat has a motor. Das Boot hat einen Motor.

motorbike NOUN
das Motorrad (PL die Motorräder)

motorboat NOUN
das Motorboot (PL die Motorboote)

motorcycle NOUN
das Motorrad (PL die Motorräder)

motorcyclist NOUN
der Motorradfahrer (PL die Motorradfahrer)
die Motorradfahrerin

motorist NOUN
der Autofahrer (PL die Autofahrer)
die Autofahrerin

motor mechanic NOUN
der Automechaniker (PL die Automechaniker)
die Automechanikerin

motor racing NOUN
das Autorennen (PL die Autorennen)

motorway NOUN
die Autobahn
□ on the motorway auf der Autobahn

mouldy ADJECTIVE
schimmlig

mountain NOUN
der Berg (PL die Berge)
■ **a mountain bike** ein Mountainbike *neut*

mountaineer NOUN
der Bergsteiger (PL die Bergsteiger)
die Bergsteigerin

mountaineering NOUN
das Bergsteigen
■ **I go mountaineering.** Ich gehe bergsteigen.

mountainous ADJECTIVE
bergig

mouse NOUN
die Maus (PL die Mäuse) *(also for computer)*
□ white mice weiße Mäuse

mouse mat NOUN
das Mousepad (PL die Mousepads) *(computer)*

mousse NOUN
1 die Creme (PL die Cremes) *(food)*
■ **chocolate mousse** die Schokoladencreme
2 der Schaumfestiger (PL die Schaumfestiger) *(for hair)*

moustache NOUN
der Schnurrbart (PL die Schnurrbärte)
□ He's got a moustache. Er hat einen Schnurrbart.

mouth NOUN
der Mund (PL die Münder)

mouthful NOUN
der Bissen (PL die Bissen)

mouth organ NOUN
die Mundharmonika (PL die Mundharmonikas)
□ I play the mouth organ. Ich spiele Mundharmonika.

mouthwash NOUN
das Mundwasser (PL die Mundwasser)

move NOUN
▹ *see also* **move** VERB
1 der Zug (PL die Züge)
□ That was a good move. Das war ein guter Zug.
■ **It's your move.** Du bist dran.
2 der Umzug (PL die Umzüge)
□ our move from Oxford to Luton unser Umzug von Oxford nach Luton
■ **to get a move on** schneller machen
■ **Get a move on!** Nun mach schon!

to **move** VERB
▹ *see also* **move** NOUN
1 bewegen (PERFECT hat bewegt)
□ I can't move my arm. Ich kann den Arm nicht bewegen. □ I was very moved by the film. Der Film hat mich sehr bewegt.
■ **Could you move your stuff?** Könntest du dein Zeug wegtun?
■ **Could you move your car?** Könnten Sie Ihr Auto wegfahren?
2 sich bewegen
□ Try not to move. Versuche, dich nicht zu bewegen.
■ **Don't move!** Keine Bewegung!
3 fahren (PRESENT fährt, IMPERFECT fuhr, PERFECT ist gefahren) *(vehicle)*
□ The car was moving very slowly. Das Auto fuhr sehr langsam.
■ **to move house** umziehen □ She's moving house in July. Sie zieht im Juli um.
■ **to move forward** sich vorwärtsbewegen
■ **to move in** einziehen □ They're moving in next week. Sie ziehen nächste Woche ein.
■ **to move over** rücken □ Could you move over a bit? Könnten Sie ein Stückchen rücken?

movement NOUN
die Bewegung

movie NOUN
der Film (PL die Filme)
■ **the movies** das Kino *sing* □ Let's go to the movies! Lass uns ins Kino gehen!

moving ADJECTIVE
1 fahrend *(not stationary)*
□ a moving bus ein fahrender Bus
2 ergreifend *(touching)*
□ a moving story eine ergreifende Geschichte

to **mow** VERB
mähen
□ to mow the lawn den Rasen mähen

mower NOUN
der Rasenmäher (PL die Rasenmäher)

mown VERB ▹ *see* **mow**

MP NOUN *(= Member of Parliament)*
der Abgeordnete (GEN des Abgeordneten, PL die Abgeordneten)
die Abgeordnete (GEN der Abgeordneten)
□ an MP *(man)* ein Abgeordneter □ She's an MP. Sie ist Abgeordnete.

MP3 player NOUN
der MP3-Spieler (PL die MP3-Spieler)

mph ABBREVIATION *(= miles per hour)*
Meilen pro Stunde

Mr NOUN *(= Mister)*
Herr

Mrs NOUN
Frau

MS NOUN *(= multiple sclerosis)*
MS
□ She's got MS. Sie hat MS.

Ms NOUN
Frau

DID YOU KNOW...?
Generally **Frau** is used to address all women whether married or not.

much ADJECTIVE, ADVERB, PRONOUN
1 viel
□ I haven't got much money. Ich habe nicht viel Geld. □ I haven't got very much money. Ich habe nicht sehr viel Geld. □ This is much better. Das ist viel besser. □ I feel much better now. Ich fühle mich jetzt viel besser.
2 sehr
LANGUAGE TIP Use **sehr** with most verbs.
□ I didn't like it much. Es hat mir nicht sehr gefallen. □ I enjoyed the film very much. Der Film hat mir sehr gefallen.
3 viel
LANGUAGE TIP Use **viel** with verbs implying physical activity.
□ She doesn't travel much. Sie reist nicht viel. □ We didn't laugh much. Wir haben nicht viel gelacht.
■ **Do you go out much?** Gehst du oft aus?
■ **Thank you very much.** Vielen Dank!
■ **not much** nicht viel □ What's on TV? — Not much. Was kommt im Fernsehen? — Nicht viel. □ What do you think of it? — Not much. Was hältst du davon? — Nicht viel.
■ **How much?** Wie viel? □ How much do you want? Wie viel möchtest du? □ How much time have you got? Wie viel Zeit hast du? □ How much is it? *(cost)* Wie viel kostet das?
■ **too much** zu viel □ That's too much! Das ist zu viel! □ It costs too much. Das kostet zu viel. □ They gave us too much homework. Sie haben uns zu viele Hausaufgaben aufgegeben.
■ **so much** so viel □ I didn't think it would cost so much. Ich hatte nicht gedacht, dass es so viel kosten würde. □ I've never seen so much traffic. Ich habe noch nie so viel Verkehr erlebt.

mud NOUN
der Schlamm

muddle NOUN
das Durcheinander
■ **to be in a muddle** durcheinander sein

to **muddle up** VERB
verwechseln (PERFECT hat verwechselt) *(people)*
□ He muddles me up with my sister. Er verwechselt mich mit meiner Schwester.
■ **to get muddled up** durcheinanderkommen □ I'm getting muddled up. Ich komme durcheinander.

muddy ADJECTIVE
schlammig

muesli NOUN
das Müsli (PL die Müsli)

muffler NOUN (US)
der Schalldämpfer (PL die Schalldämpfer)

mug NOUN
▷ *see also* **mug** VERB
der Becher (PL die Becher)
□ Do you want a cup or a mug? Möchtest du eine Tasse oder einen Becher?
■ **a beer mug** ein Bierkrug *masc*

to **mug** VERB
▷ *see also* **mug** NOUN
überfallen (PRESENT überfällt, IMPERFECT überfiel, PERFECT hat überfallen)
□ He was mugged in the city centre. Er wurde in der Innenstadt überfallen.

mugger NOUN
der Straßenräuber (PL die Straßenräuber)
die Straßenräuberin

mugging NOUN
der Überfall (PL die Überfälle)
□ Mugging has increased in recent years. Die Zahl der Überfälle hat in den letzten Jahren zugenommen.

muggy ADJECTIVE
schwül
□ It's muggy today. Es ist schwül heute.

multiple choice test NOUN
der Multiple-Choice-Test (PL die Multiple-Choice-Tests)

multiple sclerosis NOUN
die multiple Sklerose
□ She's got multiple sclerosis. Sie hat multiple Sklerose.

multiplication NOUN
die Multiplikation

to **multiply** VERB
multiplizieren (PERFECT hat multipliziert)
□ to multiply six by three sechs mit drei multiplizieren

multi-storey car park NOUN
das Parkhaus (GEN des Parkhauses, PL die Parkhäuser)

mum NOUN
die Mama (PL die Mamas)
□ my mum meine Mama □ I'll ask Mum. Ich frage Mama.

mummy NOUN
1 die Mutti (PL die Muttis) *(mum)*
□ Mummy says I can go. Mutti sagt, ich kann gehen.
2 die Mumie *(Egyptian)*

mumps SING NOUN
der Mumps
□ My brother's got mumps. Mein Bruder hat Mumps.

Munich NOUN
München *neut*
■ **to Munich** nach München

murder NOUN
▷ *see also* **murder** VERB
der Mord (PL die Morde)
LANGUAGE TIP Be careful not to translate **murder** by **Mörder**.

to **murder** VERB
▷ *see also* **murder** NOUN
ermorden (PERFECT hat ermordet)
□ He was murdered. Er wurde ermordet.

murderer NOUN
der Mörder (PL die Mörder)
die Mörderin

muscle NOUN
der Muskel (PL die Muskeln)

muscular ADJECTIVE
muskulös

museum NOUN
das Museum (PL die Museen)

mushroom NOUN
1 der Pilz (PL die Pilze)
2 der Champignon (PL die Champignons) *(button mushroom)*
□ mushroom omelette
das Champignonomelett

music NOUN
die Musik

musical ADJECTIVE
▷ *see also* **musical** NOUN
musikalisch
□ I'm not musical. Ich bin nicht musikalisch.
■ **a musical instrument** ein Musikinstrument *neut*

musical NOUN
▷ *see also* **musical** ADJECTIVE
das Musical (PL die Musicals)

music centre NOUN
die Stereoanlage

musician NOUN
der Musiker (PL die Musiker)
die Musikerin

Muslim NOUN
der Moslem (PL die Moslems)
die Moslime
□ He's a Muslim. Er ist Moslem.

mussel NOUN
die Miesmuschel

must VERB
1 müssen (PRESENT muss, IMPERFECT musste, PERFECT hat gemusst)
□ I must buy some presents. Ich muss Geschenke kaufen. □ I really must go now. Ich muss jetzt wirklich gehen. □ You must be tired. Du musst müde sein. □ They must have plenty of money. Sie müssen viel Geld haben. □ You must come and see us. Sie müssen uns besuchen.
2 dürfen (PRESENT darf, IMPERFECT durfte, PERFECT hat gedurft)
LANGUAGE TIP Use **dürfen** in negative sentences.
□ You mustn't say things like that. So was darfst du nicht sagen.
■ **You mustn't forget to send her a card.** Vergiss nicht, ihr eine Karte zu schicken.

mustard NOUN
der Senf (PL die Senfe)

to **mutter** VERB
murmeln

mutton NOUN
das Hammelfleisch

mutual ADJECTIVE
gegenseitig
□ The feeling was mutual. Das Gefühl war gegenseitig.
■ **a mutual friend** ein gemeinsamer Freund

my ADJECTIVE
mein
□ my father mein Vater □ my aunt meine Tante □ my car mein Auto □ my parents meine Eltern
■ **my friend** 1 *(male)* mein Freund 2 *(female)* meine Freundin
LANGUAGE TIP Do not use **mein** with parts of the body.
□ I want to wash my hair. Ich will mir die Haare waschen. □ I'm going to clean my teeth. Ich putze mir die Zähne. □ I've hurt my foot. Ich habe mich am Fuß verletzt.

myself PRONOUN
1 mich
□ I've hurt myself. Ich habe mich verletzt. □ When I look at myself in the mirror ... Wenn ich mich im Spiegel ansehe ... □ I don't like talking about myself. Ich rede nicht gern über mich selbst.
2 mir
□ I said to myself ... Ich sagte mir ... □ I am not very pleased with myself. Ich bin mit mir selbst nicht sehr zufrieden.
3 selbst
□ I made it myself. Ich habe es selbst gemacht.
■ **by myself** allein □ I don't like travelling by myself. Ich verreise nicht gern allein.

mysterious ADJECTIVE
rätselhaft

mystery NOUN
das Rätsel (PL die Rätsel)
■ **a murder mystery** *(novel)* ein Krimi *masc*

myth NOUN
1 der Mythos (GEN des Mythos, PL die Mythen) *(legend)*
□ a Greek myth ein griechischer Mythos
2 das Märchen (PL die Märchen) *(untrue idea)*
□ That's a myth. Das ist ein Märchen.

mythology NOUN
die Mythologie

Nn

naff ADJECTIVE
ätzend *(informal)*

to **nag** VERB
herumnörgeln an (PERFECT hat herumgenörgelt) *(scold)*
□ She's always nagging me. Sie nörgelt dauernd an mir herum.

nail NOUN
der Nagel (PL die Nägel)
□ Don't bite your nails! Kau nicht an den Nägeln!

nailbrush NOUN
die Nagelbürste

nailfile NOUN
die Nagelfeile

nail scissors PL NOUN
die Nagelschere
□ a pair of nail scissors eine Nagelschere

nail varnish NOUN
der Nagellack (PL die Nagellacke)
■ **nail varnish remover** der Nagellackentferner

naked ADJECTIVE
nackt

name NOUN
der Name (GEN des Namens, PL die Namen)
■ **What's your name?** Wie heißt du?

nanny NOUN
das Kindermädchen (PL die Kindermädchen)
□ She's a nanny. Sie ist Kindermädchen.

nap NOUN
das Nickerchen (PL die Nickerchen)
■ **to have a nap** ein Nickerchen machen

napkin NOUN
die Serviette

nappy NOUN
die Windel

narrow ADJECTIVE
eng

narrow-minded ADJECTIVE
engstirnig

nasty ADJECTIVE
1 übel *(bad)*
□ a nasty cold eine üble Erkältung □ a nasty smell ein übler Geruch
2 böse *(unfriendly)*
□ He gave me a nasty look. Er warf mir einen bösen Blick zu.

nation NOUN
die Nation

national ADJECTIVE
national
■ **a national newspaper** eine überregionale Zeitung
■ **the national elections** die Parlamentswahlen

DID YOU KNOW...?
In Germany the national elections are called **Bundestagswahlen**.

national anthem NOUN
die Nationalhymne

National Health Service NOUN
der staatliche Gesundheitsdienst

DID YOU KNOW...?
In Germany there are a large number of health schemes, not just a single service.

nationalism NOUN
der Nationalismus (GEN des Nationalismus)
□ Scottish Nationalism der schottische Nationalismus

nationalist NOUN
der Nationalist (GEN des Nationalisten, PL die Nationalisten)

nationality NOUN
die Staatsangehörigkeit

National Lottery NOUN
das Lotto

national park NOUN
der Nationalpark (PL die Nationalparks)

native ADJECTIVE
■ **my native country** mein Heimatland *neut*
■ **native language** die Muttersprache
□ English is not their native language. Englisch ist nicht ihre Muttersprache.
■ **a Native American** ein Indianer *masc*

natural ADJECTIVE
natürlich

naturalist NOUN
der Naturforscher (PL die Naturforscher)
die Naturforscherin

naturally ADVERB
natürlich
□ Naturally, we were very disappointed. Natürlich waren wir sehr enttäuscht.

nature NOUN
die Natur

English-German

naughty ADJECTIVE
böse
□ Naughty girl! Böses Mädchen!
■ **Don't be naughty!** Sei nicht ungezogen!

navy NOUN
die Marine
□ He's in the navy. Er ist bei der Marine.

navy-blue ADJECTIVE
marineblau
□ a navy-blue shirt ein marineblaues Hemd

Nazi NOUN
der Nazi (PL die Nazis)
□ the Nazis die Nazis
LANGUAGE TIP **der Nazi** is also used for women.
□ She was a Nazi. Sie war ein Nazi.

near ADJECTIVE
▷ *see also* **near** PREPOSITION
nah
□ It's fairly near. Es ist ziemlich nah.
□ It's near enough to walk. Es ist nah genug, um zu Fuß zu gehen.
■ **nearest** nächste □ Where's the nearest service station? Wo ist die nächste Tankstelle? □ the nearest shops die nächsten Geschäfte

near PREPOSITION, ADVERB
▷ *see also* **near** ADJECTIVE
in der Nähe von
□ I live near Liverpool. Ich wohne in der Nähe von Liverpool. □ near my house in der Nähe meines Hauses
■ **near here** hier in der Nähe □ Is there a bank near here? Ist hier in der Nähe eine Bank?
■ **near to** in der Nähe *+gen* □ It's very near to the school. Es ist ganz in der Nähe der Schule.

nearby ADVERB, ADJECTIVE
1 in der Nähe
□ There's a supermarket nearby. Es gibt einen Supermarkt in der Nähe.
2 nahe gelegen *(close)*
□ a nearby garage eine nahe gelegene Tankstelle

nearly ADVERB
fast
□ Dinner's nearly ready. Das Essen ist fast fertig. □ I'm nearly fifteen. Ich bin fast fünfzehn. □ I nearly missed the train. Ich habe fast meinen Zug verpasst.

neat ADJECTIVE
ordentlich
□ She has very neat writing. Sie hat eine sehr ordentliche Schrift.
■ **a neat whisky** ein Whisky pur

neatly ADVERB
ordentlich
□ neatly folded ordentlich gefaltet
□ neatly dressed ordentlich gekleidet

necessarily ADVERB
■ **not necessarily** nicht unbedingt

necessary ADJECTIVE
nötig

necessity NOUN
die Notwendigkeit
□ A car is a necessity, not a luxury. Ein Auto ist eine Notwendigkeit und kein Luxus.

neck NOUN
1 der Hals (GEN des Halses, PL die Hälse) *(of body)*
2 der Ausschnitt (PL die Ausschnitte) *(of garment)*
□ a V-neck sweater ein Pullover mit V-Ausschnitt

necklace NOUN
die Halskette

to **need** VERB
▷ *see also* **need** NOUN
brauchen
□ I need a bigger size. Ich brauche eine größere Größe.
■ **to need to do something** etwas tun müssen □ I need to change some money. Ich muss Geld wechseln.

need NOUN
▷ *see also* **need** VERB
■ **There's no need to book.** Man braucht nicht zu buchen.

needle NOUN
die Nadel

needlework NOUN
die Handarbeit
□ We have needlework lessons at school. Wir haben Handarbeitsunterricht an der Schule.

negative NOUN
▷ *see also* **negative** ADJECTIVE
das Negativ (PL die Negative) *(photo)*

negative ADJECTIVE
▷ *see also* **negative** NOUN
negativ
□ He's got a very negative attitude. Er hat eine sehr negative Einstellung.

neglected ADJECTIVE
ungepflegt *(untidy)*
□ The garden is neglected. Der Garten ist ungepflegt.

negligee NOUN
das Negligé (PL die Negligés)

to **negotiate** VERB
verhandeln

negotiations PL NOUN
die Verhandlungen *pl*

neighbour NOUN
der Nachbar (GEN des Nachbarn, PL die Nachbarn)
die Nachbarin
□ the neighbours' garden der Garten der Nachbarn

neighbourhood NOUN
die Nachbarschaft

neither PRONOUN, CONJUNCTION, ADVERB
weder noch

n

□ Carrots or peas? — Neither, thanks. Karotten oder Erbsen? — Weder noch, danke.
■ **Neither of them is coming.** Keiner von beiden kommt.
■ **neither ... nor ...** weder ... noch ...
□ Neither Sarah nor Tamsin is coming to the party. Weder Sarah noch Tamsin kommen zur Party.
■ **Neither do I.** Ich auch nicht. □ I don't like him. — Neither do I! Ich mag ihn nicht. — Ich auch nicht!
■ **Neither have I.** Ich auch nicht. □ I've never been to Spain. — Neither have I. Ich war noch nie in Spanien. — Ich auch nicht.

neon NOUN
das Neon
■ **a neon light** eine Neonlampe

nephew NOUN
der Neffe (GEN des Neffen, PL die Neffen)
□ my nephew mein Neffe

nerve NOUN
der Nerv (PL die Nerven)
□ She gets on my nerves. Sie geht mir auf die Nerven.
■ **He's got a nerve!** Der hat vielleicht Nerven!

nerve-racking ADJECTIVE
nervenaufreibend

nervous ADJECTIVE
nervös *(tense)*
□ I bite my nails when I'm nervous. Wenn ich nervös bin, kaue ich an den Nägeln.
■ **to be nervous about something** vor etwas Angst haben □ I'm a bit nervous about flying to Paris by myself. Ich habe etwas Angst, allein nach Paris zu fliegen.

nest NOUN
das Nest (PL die Nester)

net NOUN
das Netz (GEN des Netzes, PL die Netze)
□ a fishing net ein Fischnetz

Net NOUN
■ **the Net** das Internet

netball NOUN
der Netzball

Netherlands PL NOUN
die Niederlande *pl*

LANGUAGE TIP Note that the definite article is used in German for countries which are plural.

■ **from the Netherlands** aus den Niederlanden
■ **in the Netherlands** in den Niederlanden
■ **to the Netherlands** in die Niederlande

network NOUN
1 das Netz (GEN des Netzes, PL die Netze)
2 das Netzwerk (PL die Netzwerke) *(for computers)*

neurotic ADJECTIVE
neurotisch

never ADVERB
nie
□ Have you ever been to Germany? — No, never. Waren Sie schon mal in Deutschland? — Nein, nie. □ I never write letters. Ich schreibe nie Briefe. □ Never again! Nie wieder!
■ **Never mind.** Macht nichts!

new ADJECTIVE
neu
□ her new boyfriend ihr neuer Freund □ I need a new dress. Ich brauche ein neues Kleid.

newborn ADJECTIVE
■ **a newborn baby** ein neugeborenes Kind

newcomer NOUN
der Neuling (PL die Neulinge)

LANGUAGE TIP **der Neuling** is also used for women.

news SING NOUN

LANGUAGE TIP **Nachricht** is a piece of news; **Nachrichten** is the news, for example on TV.

1 die Nachrichten *fem pl*
□ good news gute Nachrichten □ I've had some bad news. Ich habe schlechte Nachrichten bekommen. □ I watch the news every evening. Ich sehe mir jeden Abend die Nachrichten an. □ I listen to the news every morning. Ich höre jeden Morgen die Nachrichten.
2 die Nachricht
□ That's wonderful news! Das ist eine wunderbare Nachricht!

newsagent NOUN
der Zeitungshändler (PL die Zeitungshändler)
die Zeitungshändlerin

news dealer NOUN (US)
der Zeitungshändler (PL die Zeitungshändler)
die Zeitungshändlerin

newspaper NOUN
die Zeitung
□ I deliver newspapers. Ich trage Zeitungen aus.

newsreader NOUN
der Nachrichtensprecher (PL die Nachrichtensprecher)
die Nachrichtensprecherin

New Year NOUN
das Neujahr
□ to celebrate New Year Neujahr feiern
■ **Happy New Year!** Ein gutes neues Jahr!
■ **New Year's Day** der Neujahrstag
■ **New Year's Eve** das Silvester
□ a New Year's Eve party eine Silvesterparty

New Zealand NOUN
Neuseeland *neut*
■ **from New Zealand** aus Neuseeland
■ **in New Zealand** in Neuseeland
■ **to New Zealand** nach Neuseeland

New Zealander NOUN
der Neuseeländer (PL die Neuseeländer)
die Neuseeländerin

English-German

next ADJECTIVE, ADVERB, PREPOSITION
1 nächste
□ next Saturday nächsten Samstag □ next week nächste Woche □ next year nächstes Jahr □ the next train der nächste Zug
■ **Next please!** der Nächste, bitte!
2 danach *(afterwards)*
□ What happened next? Was ist danach passiert?
■ **What shall I do next?** Was soll ich als Nächstes machen?
■ **next to** neben

LANGUAGE TIP Use the accusative to express movement or a change of place. Use the dative when there is no change of place.

□ I sat down next to my sister. Ich setzte mich neben meine Schwester. □ The post office is next to the bank. Die Post ist neben der Bank.
■ **the next day** am nächsten Tag □ The next day we visited Heidelberg. Am nächsten Tag haben wir Heidelberg besucht.
■ **the next time** das nächste Mal □ the next time you see her wenn du sie das nächste Mal siehst
■ **next door** nebenan □ They live next door. Sie wohnen nebenan. □ the people next door die Leute von nebenan
■ **the next room** das Nebenzimmer

NHS NOUN *(= National Health Service)*
der staatliche Gesundheitsdienst

DID YOU KNOW...?
In Germany there are a large number of health schemes, not just a single service.

n

nice ADJECTIVE
1 nett *(kind)*
□ Your parents are nice. Deine Eltern sind nett. □ It was nice of you to remember my birthday. Es war nett, dass du an meinen Geburtstag gedacht hast. □ to be nice to somebody nett zu jemandem sein
2 hübsch *(pretty)*
□ That's a nice dress! Das ist ein hübsches Kleid! □ Ulm is a nice town. Ulm ist eine hübsche Stadt.
3 schön
□ nice weather schönes Wetter □ It's a nice day. Es ist ein schöner Tag.
4 lecker *(food)*
□ This pizza's very nice. Diese Pizza ist sehr lecker.
■ **Have a nice time!** Viel Spaß!

WORD POWER
You can use a number of other words instead of **nice** to mean 'pretty':
attractive attraktiv
□ an attractive woman eine attraktive Frau
beautiful schön
□ a beautiful painting ein schönes Bild
lovely wunderbar
□ a lovely surprise eine wunderbare Überraschung
pretty hübsch
□ a pretty girl ein hübsches Mädchen

nickname NOUN
der Spitzname (GEN des Spitznamens, PL die Spitznamen)

niece NOUN
die Nichte
□ my niece meine Nichte

Nigeria NOUN
Nigeria *neut*
□ in Nigeria in Nigeria

night NOUN
1 die Nacht (PL die Nächte)
□ I want a single room for two nights. Ich möchte ein Einzelzimmer für zwei Nächte.
■ **at night** nachts
■ **Good night!** Gute Nacht!
■ **a night club** ein Nachtklub *masc*
2 der Abend (PL die Abende) *(evening)*
□ last night gestern Abend

nightdress NOUN
das Nachthemd (PL die Nachthemden)

nightie NOUN
das Nachthemd (PL die Nachthemden)

nightlife NOUN
das Nachtleben
□ There's plenty of nightlife. Dort gibt es ein reges Nachtleben.

nightmare NOUN
der Albtraum (PL die Albträume)
□ I had a nightmare. Ich hatte einen Albtraum.
□ It was a real nightmare! Es war ein Albtraum!

nightshirt NOUN
das Nachthemd (PL die Nachthemden)

nil NOUN
null
□ We won one nil. Wir haben eins zu null gewonnen.

nine NUMBER
neun
□ She's nine. Sie ist neun.

nineteen NUMBER
neunzehn
□ She's nineteen. Sie ist neunzehn.

nineteenth ADJECTIVE
neunzehnte
□ the nineteenth of August der neunzehnte August

ninety NUMBER
neunzig
□ She's ninety. Sie ist neunzig.

ninth ADJECTIVE
neunte
□ the ninth floor der neunte Stock
□ the ninth of August der neunte August

no ADVERB, ADJECTIVE
1 nein
□ Are you coming? — No. Kommst du? — Nein.
□ Would you like some more? — No thank you. Möchten Sie noch etwas? — Nein danke.
2 kein *(not any)*
□ There's no hot water. Es gibt kein heißes Wasser. □ There are no trains on Sundays. Sonntags verkehren keine Züge. □ No problem. Kein Problem. □ I've got no idea. Ich habe keine Ahnung.
■ **No way!** Auf keinen Fall!
■ **'no smoking'** 'Rauchen verboten'

nobody PRONOUN
niemand
□ Who's going with you? — Nobody. Wer geht mit dir mit? — Niemand.
□ There was nobody in the office. Es war niemand im Büro.

to **nod** VERB
nicken

noise NOUN
der Lärm
□ Please make less noise. Macht bitte weniger Lärm.

noisy ADJECTIVE
laut
□ It's too noisy here. Hier ist es zu laut.

to **nominate** VERB
nominieren (PERFECT hat nominiert)
□ She was nominated for an Oscar. Sie war für einen Oscar nominiert.

none PRONOUN
keiner
□ None of my friends wanted to come. Keiner meiner Freunde wollte kommen.
□ How many brothers have you got? — None. Wie viele Brüder hast du? — Keinen.
keine
□ Milk? There's none left. Milch? Es ist keine mehr da.
keines
□ Which of the books have you read? — None. Welches der Bücher hast du gelesen? — Keines.
■ **There are none left.** Es sind keine mehr da.

nonsense NOUN
der Unsinn
□ She talks a lot of nonsense. Sie redet viel Unsinn. □ Nonsense! Unsinn!

nonsmoker NOUN
der Nichtraucher (PL die Nichtraucher)
die Nichtraucherin
□ She's a nonsmoker. Sie ist Nichtraucherin.

nonsmoking ADJECTIVE
■ **a nonsmoking area** ein Nichtraucherbereich *masc*

nonstop ADJECTIVE, ADVERB
1 nonstop
□ We flew nonstop. Wir sind nonstop geflogen.
■ **a nonstop flight** ein Nonstop-Flug *masc*
2 ununterbrochen
□ Liz talks nonstop. Liz redet ununterbrochen.

noodles PL NOUN
die Nudeln *fem pl*

noon NOUN
der Mittag (PL die Mittage)
■ **at noon** um zwölf Uhr mittags

no one PRONOUN
niemand
□ Who's going with you? — No one. Wer geht mit dir mit? — Niemand. □ There was no one in the office. Es war niemand im Büro.

nor CONJUNCTION
■ **neither ... nor** weder ... noch □ neither the cinema nor the swimming pool weder das Kino noch das Schwimmbad
■ **Nor do I.** Ich auch nicht. □ I didn't like the film. — Nor did I. Der Film hat mir nicht gefallen. — Mir auch nicht.
■ **Nor have I.** Ich auch nicht. □ I haven't seen him. — Nor have I. Ich habe ihn nicht gesehen. — Ich auch nicht.

normal ADJECTIVE
normal
□ at the normal time zur normalen Zeit
□ a normal car ein normales Auto

normally ADVERB
1 normalerweise *(usually)*
□ I normally arrive at nine o'clock. Normalerweise komme ich um neun Uhr.
2 normal *(as normal)*
□ In spite of the strike, the airports are working normally. Trotz des Streiks arbeiten die Flughäfen normal.

Normandy NOUN
die Normandie
■ **in Normandy** in der Normandie

north ADJECTIVE, ADVERB
▷ *see also* **north** NOUN
nach Norden
□ We were travelling north. Wir sind nach Norden gefahren.
■ **the north coast** die Nordküste
■ **a north wind** ein Nordwind *masc*
■ **north of** nördlich von □ It's north of London. Es liegt nördlich von London.

north NOUN
▷ *see also* **north** ADJECTIVE
der Norden
□ in the north im Norden

North America NOUN
Nordamerika *neut*
■ **from North America** aus Nordamerika
■ **to North America** nach Nordamerika

northbound ADJECTIVE
in Richtung Norden
□ northbound traffic der Verkehr in Richtung Norden

northeast NOUN
der Nordosten
□ in the northeast im Nordosten

northern ADJECTIVE
nördlich
□ the northern part of the island der nördliche Teil der Insel
■ **Northern Europe** Nordeuropa *neut*

Northern Ireland NOUN
Nordirland *neut*
■ **from Northern Ireland** aus Nordirland
■ **in Northern Ireland** in Nordirland
■ **to Northern Ireland** nach Nordirland

North Pole NOUN
der Nordpol

North Sea NOUN
die Nordsee

northwest NOUN
der Nordwesten
□ in the northwest im Nordwesten

Norway NOUN
Norwegen *neut*
■ **from Norway** aus Norwegen
■ **to Norway** nach Norwegen

Norwegian ADJECTIVE
▷ *see also* **Norwegian** NOUN
norwegisch
■ **He's Norwegian.** Er ist Norweger.

Norwegian NOUN
▷ *see also* **Norwegian** ADJECTIVE
1 der Norweger (PL die Norweger)
die Norwegerin *(person)*
2 das Norwegisch (GEN des Norwegischen) *(language)*

nose NOUN
die Nase

nosebleed NOUN
das Nasenbluten
□ I often get nosebleeds. Ich habe oft Nasenbluten.

nosey ADJECTIVE
neugierig
□ She's very nosey. Sie ist sehr neugierig.

not ADVERB
1 nicht
□ Are you coming or not? Kommst du oder nicht? □ I'm not sure. Ich bin nicht sicher.
□ It's not raining. Es regnet nicht.
■ **not really** eigentlich nicht
■ **not at all** überhaupt nicht
■ **not yet** noch nicht □ Have you finished? — Not yet. Bist du fertig? — Noch nicht.
□ They haven't arrived yet. Sie sind noch nicht angekommen.
2 nein
□ Can you lend me ten pounds? — I'm afraid not. Können Sie mir zehn Pfund leihen? — Leider nein.

note NOUN
1 die Notiz
■ **to take notes** sich Notizen machen
□ You should take notes. Du solltest dir Notizen machen.
2 der Brief (PL die Briefe) *(letter)*
■ **I'll write her a note.** Ich werde ihr schreiben.
3 der Schein (PL die Scheine) *(banknote)*
□ a five-pound note ein Fünfpfundschein

to **note down** VERB
aufschreiben (IMPERFECT schrieb auf, PERFECT hat aufgeschrieben)

notebook NOUN
1 das Notizbuch (PL die Notizbücher)
2 der Notebookcomputer (PL die Notebookcomputer) *(computer)*

notepad NOUN
der Notizblock (PL die Notizblöcke)

notepaper NOUN
das Briefpapier

nothing NOUN
nichts
□ What's wrong? — Nothing. Was ist los? — Nichts. □ nothing special nichts Besonderes
□ He does nothing. Er tut nichts. □ He ate nothing for breakfast. Er hat nichts zum Frühstück gegessen.

notice NOUN
▷ *see also* **notice** VERB
die Notiz *(sign)*
□ to put up a notice eine Notiz aushängen
□ Don't take any notice of him! Nimm keine Notiz von ihm!
■ **a warning notice** ein Warnschild *neut*

to **notice** VERB
▷ *see also* **notice** NOUN
bemerken (PERFECT hat bemerkt)

notice board NOUN
das Anschlagbrett (PL die Anschlagbretter)

nought NOUN
die Null

noun NOUN
das Substantiv (PL die Substantive)

novel NOUN
der Roman (PL die Romane)

novelist NOUN
der Romanautor (PL die Romanautoren)
die Romanautorin

November NOUN
der November
□ in November im November

now ADVERB, CONJUNCTION
jetzt
□ What are you doing now? Was tust du jetzt?
■ **just now** gerade □ I'm rather busy just now. Ich bin gerade ziemlich beschäftigt.
□ I did it just now. Ich habe es gerade getan.
■ **by now** inzwischen □ He should be there by now. Er müsste inzwischen dort sein.
□ It should be ready by now. Es müsste inzwischen fertig sein.
■ **now and then** ab und zu

nowhere ADVERB
nirgends
□ nowhere else sonst nirgends

nuclear ADJECTIVE
nuklear
■ **nuclear power** die Kernkraft
■ **a nuclear power station** ein Kernkraftwerk *neut*

nude ADJECTIVE
▷ *see also* **nude** NOUN
nackt
□ to sunbathe nude nackt sonnenbaden

nude NOUN
▷ *see also* **nude** ADJECTIVE
■ **in the nude** nackt

nudist NOUN
der Nudist (GEN des Nudisten, PL die Nudisten)
die Nudistin

nuisance NOUN
■ **It's a nuisance.** Es ist sehr lästig.
■ **Sorry to be a nuisance.** Tut mir leid, dass ich schon wieder ankomme.

numb ADJECTIVE
taub
□ numb with cold taub vor Kälte

number NOUN
1 die Anzahl *(total amount)*
□ a large number of people eine große Anzahl von Menschen
2 die Nummer *(of house, telephone, bank account)*
□ They live at number five. Sie wohnen in der Nummer fünf. □ What's your phone number? Wie ist Ihre Telefonnummer?
■ **You've got the wrong number.** Sie sind falsch verbunden.
3 die Zahl *(figure, digit)*
□ I can't read the second number. Ich kann die zweite Zahl nicht lesen.

number plate NOUN
das Nummernschild (PL die Nummernschilder)

DID YOU KNOW...?
The first letters of a German number plate allow you to tell where the car's owner lives. Thus L stands for Leipzig, LB for Ludwigsburg, LU for Ludwigshafen, etc.

nun NOUN
die Nonne
□ She's a nun. Sie ist Nonne.

nurse NOUN
die Krankenschwester
□ She's a nurse. Sie ist Krankenschwester.
der Krankenpfleger
□ He's a nurse. Er ist Krankenpfleger.

nursery NOUN
1 die Kindergarten (PL die Kindergärten) *(for children)*
2 die Baumschule *(for plants)*

nursery school NOUN
der Kindergarten (PL die Kindergärten)

DID YOU KNOW...?
German children go to **Kindergarten** from the age of 3 to 6.

nursery slope NOUN
der Idiotenhügel (PL die Idiotenhügel)

nut NOUN
1 die Nuss (PL die Nüsse)
2 die Mutter *(made of metal)*

nutmeg NOUN
der Muskat

nutritious ADJECTIVE
nahrhaft

nuts ADJECTIVE
■ **He's nuts.** Er spinnt. *(informal)*

nutter NOUN
■ **He's a nutter.** Er ist völlig durchgeknallt. *(informal)*

nylon NOUN
das Nylon

Oo

oak NOUN
die Eiche
□ an oak table ein Eichentisch *masc*

oar NOUN
das Ruder (PL die Ruder)

oats PL NOUN
der Hafer

obedient ADJECTIVE
gehorsam

to **obey** VERB
gehorchen (PERFECT hat gehorcht)
□ She didn't obey her mother. Sie hat ihrer Mutter nicht gehorcht.
■ **to obey the rules** die Regeln befolgen

object NOUN
der Gegenstand (PL die Gegenstände)
□ a familiar object ein vertrauter Gegenstand

objection NOUN
der Einspruch (PL die Einsprüche)

objective NOUN
das Ziel (PL die Ziele)

oblong ADJECTIVE
länglich

oboe NOUN
die Oboe
□ I play the oboe. Ich spiele Oboe.

obscene ADJECTIVE
obszön

observant ADJECTIVE
aufmerksam

to **observe** VERB
beobachten (PERFECT hat beobachtet)

obsessed ADJECTIVE
besessen
□ He's completely obsessed with trains. Er ist von Zügen ganz besessen.

obsession NOUN
die Leidenschaft
□ Football's an obsession of mine. Fußball ist meine Leidenschaft.

obsolete ADJECTIVE
veraltet

obstacle NOUN
das Hindernis (GEN des Hindernisses, PL die Hindernisse)

obstinate ADJECTIVE
stur

to **obstruct** VERB
behindern (PERFECT hat behindert)
□ A lorry was obstructing the traffic. Ein Lastwagen hat den Verkehr behindert.

to **obtain** VERB
erhalten (IMPERFECT erhielt, PERFECT hat erhalten)

obvious ADJECTIVE
offensichtlich

obviously ADVERB
1 natürlich *(of course)*
□ Do you want to pass the exam? — Obviously! Willst du die Prüfung bestehen? — Natürlich! □ Obviously not! Natürlich nicht!
2 offensichtlich *(visibly)*
□ She was obviously exhausted. Sie war offensichtlich erschöpft.

occasion NOUN
die Gelegenheit
□ a special occasion eine besondere Gelegenheit
■ **on several occasions** mehrmals

occasionally ADVERB
ab und zu

occupation NOUN
die Beschäftigung

to **occupy** VERB
besetzen (PERFECT hat besetzt)
□ That seat is occupied. Der Platz ist besetzt.

to **occur** VERB
passieren (PERFECT ist passiert) *(happen)*
□ The accident occurred yesterday. Der Unfall ist gestern passiert.
■ **It suddenly occurred to me that ...** Plötzlich ist mir eingefallen, dass ...

ocean NOUN
der Ozean (PL die Ozeane)

o'clock ADVERB
■ **at four o'clock** um vier Uhr
■ **It's five o'clock.** Es ist fünf Uhr.

October NOUN
der Oktober
□ in October im Oktober

octopus NOUN
der Tintenfisch (PL die Tintenfische)

odd ADJECTIVE
1 eigenartig
□ That's odd! Das ist eigenartig!

2 ungerade
□ an odd number eine ungerade Zahl

of PREPOSITION
von
□ some photos of my holiday Fotos von meinen Ferien □ three of us drei von uns □ a friend of mine ein Freund von mir □ That's very kind of you. Das ist sehr nett von Ihnen. □ Can I have half of that? Kann ich die Hälfte davon haben?

LANGUAGE TIP 'of' is not translated when specifying a quantity of something.

□ a kilo of oranges ein Kilo Orangen

LANGUAGE TIP 'of' is often expressed by using the genitive.

□ the end of the film das Ende des Films □ the top of the stairs das obere Ende der Treppe □ the front of the house die Vorderseite des Hauses
■ **a boy of ten** ein zehnjähriger Junge
■ **the fourteenth of September** der vierzehnte September
■ **It's made of wood.** Es ist aus Holz.

off ADVERB, PREPOSITION, ADJECTIVE

LANGUAGE TIP For other expressions with 'off', see the verbs 'get', 'take', 'turn' etc.

1 aus *(heater, light, TV)*
□ All the lights are off. Alle Lichter sind aus.
2 zu *(tap, gas)*
□ Are you sure the tap is off? Bist du sicher, dass der Hahn zu ist?
3 abgesagt *(cancelled)*
□ The match is off. Das Spiel wurde abgesagt.
■ **to be off sick** krank sein
■ **a day off** ein freier Tag
■ **to take a day off work** sich einen Tag freinehmen □ I'm taking a day off work tomorrow. Ich werde mir morgen einen Tag freinehmen.
■ **She's off school today.** Sie ist heute nicht in der Schule.
■ **I must be off now.** Ich muss jetzt gehen.
■ **I'm off.** Ich gehe jetzt.

offence NOUN
das Vergehen (PL die Vergehen) *(crime)*

offensive ADJECTIVE
anstößig

offer NOUN
▷ *see also* **offer** VERB
das Angebot (PL die Angebote)
□ a good offer ein günstiges Angebot
■ **'on special offer'** 'im Sonderangebot'

to **offer** VERB
▷ *see also* **offer** NOUN
anbieten (IMPERFECT bot an, PERFECT hat angeboten)
□ He offered to help me. Er bot mir seine Hilfe an. □ I offered to go with them. Ich habe ihnen angeboten mitzugehen.

office NOUN
das Büro (PL die Büros)
□ She works in an office. Sie arbeitet in einem Büro.
■ **doctor's office** die Arztpraxis

officer NOUN
der Offizier (PL die Offiziere) *(in army)*
■ **a police officer** *(man)* ein Polizeibeamter

official ADJECTIVE
offiziell

off-licence NOUN
die Wein- und Spirituosenhandlung

off-peak ADJECTIVE
außerhalb der Stoßzeiten
□ It's cheaper to travel off-peak. Es ist billiger, außerhalb der Stoßzeiten zu fahren.
■ **off-peak calls** Gespräche zum Billigtarif

offside ADJECTIVE
im Abseits *(in football)*

often ADVERB
oft
□ It often rains. Es regnet oft. □ How often do you go to church? Wie oft gehst du in die Kirche? □ I'd like to go skiing more often. Ich würde gern öfter Ski fahren.

oil NOUN
▷ *see also* **oil** VERB
1 das Öl (PL die Öle) *(for lubrication, cooking)*
■ **an oil painting** ein Ölgemälde *neut*
2 das Erdöl *(petroleum)*
□ North Sea oil Erdöl aus der Nordsee

to **oil** VERB
▷ *see also* **oil** NOUN
ölen

oil rig NOUN
die Bohrinsel
□ He works on an oil rig. Er arbeitet auf einer Bohrinsel.

oil slick NOUN
der Ölteppich (PL die Ölteppiche)

oil well NOUN
die Ölquelle

ointment NOUN
die Salbe

okay EXCLAMATION, ADJECTIVE
okay
□ Could you call back later? — Okay! Kannst du später anrufen? — Okay! □ I'll meet you at six o'clock, okay? Ich treffe dich um sechs Uhr, okay? □ Is that okay? Ist das okay? □ How was your holiday? — It was okay. Wie waren die Ferien? — Okay.
■ **I'll do it tomorrow, if that's okay with you.** Ich mache das morgen, wenn du einverstanden bist.
■ **Are you okay?** Bist du in Ordnung?

old ADJECTIVE
alt
□ an old dog ein alter Hund □ old people alte Menschen □ my old English teacher mein

alter Englischlehrer □ How old are you? Wie alt bist du? □ He's ten years old. Er ist zehn Jahre alt. □ my older brother mein älterer Bruder □ my older sister meine ältere Schwester □ She's two years older than me. Sie ist zwei Jahre älter als ich. □ He's the oldest in the family. Er ist der Älteste der Familie.

old age pensioner NOUN
der Rentner (PL die Rentner)
die Rentnerin
□ She's an old age pensioner. Sie ist Rentnerin.

old-fashioned ADJECTIVE
altmodisch
□ She wears old-fashioned clothes. Sie trägt altmodische Kleidung. □ My parents are rather old-fashioned. Meine Eltern sind ziemlich altmodisch.

olive NOUN
die Olive

olive oil NOUN
das Olivenöl (PL die Olivenöle)

Olympic ADJECTIVE
olympisch
■ **the Olympics** die Olympischen Spiele

omelette NOUN
das Omelett (PL die Omeletts)

on PREPOSITION, ADVERB
▷ *see also* **on** ADJECTIVE

LANGUAGE TIP There are several ways of translating 'on'. Scan the examples to find one that is similar to what you want to say. For other expressions with 'on' see the verbs 'go', 'put', 'turn' etc.

1 auf

LANGUAGE TIP Use the accusative to express movement or a change of place. Use the dative when there is no change of place.

□ It's on the table. Es ist auf dem Tisch. □ Please, put it on the table. Stell es bitte auf den Tisch. □ on an island auf einer Insel □ on the left auf der linken Seite

2 an
□ on Friday am Freitag □ on Christmas Day am ersten Weihnachtsfeiertag □ on the twentieth of June am zwanzigsten Juni □ on my birthday an meinem Geburtstag
■ **on Fridays** freitags

LANGUAGE TIP Use the accusative to express movement or a change of place. Use the dative when there is no change of place.

□ There was not a single picture on the wall. An der Wand hing kein einziges Bild. □ She hung a picture up on the wall. Sie hängte ein Bild an die Wand.

3 in
□ on the second floor im zweiten Stock □ on TV im Fernsehen □ What's on TV? Was kommt im Fernsehen? □ I heard it on the radio. Ich habe es im Radio gehört.
■ **on the bus** **1** *(by bus)* mit dem Bus □ I go into town on the bus. Ich fahre mit dem Bus in die Stadt. **2** *(inside)* im Bus □ There were no empty seats on the bus. Es gab keinen freien Platz im Bus.
■ **I go to school on my bike.** Ich fahre mit dem Fahrrad zur Schule.
■ **on holiday** in den Ferien □ They're on holiday. Sie sind in den Ferien.
■ **They are on strike.** Sie streiken.

on ADJECTIVE
▷ *see also* **on** PREPOSITION

1 an *(heater, light, TV)*
□ I left the light on. Ich habe das Licht angelassen. □ Is the dishwasher on? Ist die Spülmaschine an?

2 auf *(tap, gas)*
□ Leave the tap on. Lass den Hahn auf.
■ **What's on at the cinema?** Was gibt's im Kino?

once ADVERB
einmal
□ once a week einmal pro Woche □ once more noch einmal □ I've been to Germany once before. Ich war schon einmal in Deutschland.
■ **Once upon a time ...** Es war einmal ...
■ **at once** sofort
■ **once in a while** ab und zu

one NUMBER, PRONOUN

LANGUAGE TIP Use **ein** for masculine and neuter nouns, **eine** for feminine nouns.

1 ein
□ one man ein Mann □ one child ein Kind □ We stayed there for one day. Wir sind einen Tag dortgeblieben.

2 eine
□ one minute eine Minute □ Do you need a stamp? — No thanks, I've got one. Brauchst du eine Briefmarke? — Nein danke, ich habe eine. □ I've got one brother and one sister. Ich habe einen Bruder und eine Schwester.

3 eins

LANGUAGE TIP Use **eins** when counting.

□ one, two, three eins, zwei, drei

4 man *(impersonal)*
□ One never knows. Man kann nie wissen.
■ **this one** **1** *(masculine)* dieser □ Which foot hurts? — This one. Welcher Fuß tut weh? — Dieser. **2** *(feminine)* diese □ Which is your cup? — This one. Welche ist deine Tasse? — Diese. **3** *(neuter)* dieses □ Which is the best photo? — This one. Welches ist das beste Foto? — Dieses.
■ **that one** **1** *(masculine)* der da □ Which pen did you use? — That one. Welchen Schreiber hast du benützt? — Den da. **2** *(feminine)* die da □ Which bag is yours? — That one. Welche ist deine Tasche? — Die da. **3** *(neuter)*

das da □ Which is your car? — That one. Welches ist Ihr Auto? — Das da.

oneself PRONOUN

1 sich
□ to hurt oneself sich wehtun

2 selbst
□ It's quicker to do it oneself. Es geht schneller, wenn man es selbst macht.

one-way ADJECTIVE
■ **a one-way street** eine Einbahnstraße

onion NOUN
die Zwiebel
□ onion soup die Zwiebelsuppe

on-line ADJECTIVE
online

only ADVERB, ADJECTIVE, CONJUNCTION

1 einzig
□ Monday is the only day I'm free. Montag ist mein einziger freier Tag. □ German is the only subject I like. Deutsch ist das einzige Fach, das ich mag.

2 nur
□ How much was it? — Only twenty euros. Wie viel hat es gekostet? — Nur zwanzig Euro. □ We only want to stay for one night. Wir wollen nur eine Nacht bleiben. □ the same sweater, only in black der gleiche Pullover, nur in Schwarz
■ **an only child** ein Einzelkind *neut*

onwards ADVERB
ab
□ from July onwards ab Juli

open ADJECTIVE
▷ *see also* **open** VERB
offen
□ The window was open. Das Fenster war offen.
■ **The baker's is open on Sunday morning.** Die Bäckerei hat am Sonntagmorgen auf.
■ **in the open air** im Freien

to **open** VERB
▷ *see also* **open** ADJECTIVE

1 aufmachen (PERFECT hat aufgemacht)
□ Can I open the window? Kann ich das Fenster aufmachen? □ What time do the shops open? Um wie viel Uhr machen die Geschäfte auf?

2 aufgehen (IMPERFECT ging auf, PERFECT ist aufgegangen)
□ The door opens automatically. Die Tür geht automatisch auf. □ The door opened and in came Jim. Die Tür ging auf und Jim kam herein.

opening hours PL NOUN
die Öffnungszeiten *fem pl*

opera NOUN
die Oper

to **operate** VERB
bedienen (PERFECT hat bedient) *(machine)*
■ **to operate on someone** jemanden operieren

operation NOUN
die Operation
□ a major operation eine größere Operation
■ **to have an operation** operiert werden
□ I have never had an operation. Ich bin noch nie operiert worden.

operator NOUN
der Telefonist (GEN des Telefonisten, PL die Telefonisten)
die Telefonistin *(on telephone)*

opinion NOUN
die Meinung
□ He asked me my opinion. Er fragte mich nach meiner Meinung. □ What's your opinion? Was ist deine Meinung?
■ **in my opinion** meiner Meinung nach

opinion poll NOUN
die Meinungsumfrage

opponent NOUN
der Gegner (PL die Gegner)
die Gegnerin

opportunity NOUN
die Gelegenheit
■ **to have the opportunity to do something** die Gelegenheit haben, etwas zu tun
□ I've never had the opportunity to go to Germany. Ich hatte noch nie die Gelegenheit, nach Deutschland zu fahren.

opposed ADJECTIVE
■ **to be opposed to something** gegen etwas sein □ I'm opposed to violence. Ich bin gegen Gewalt.

opposing ADJECTIVE
gegnerisch *(team)*

opposite ADJECTIVE, ADVERB, PREPOSITION

1 entgegengesetzt
□ It's in the opposite direction. Es ist in der entgegengesetzten Richtung.

2 gegenüber
□ They live opposite. Sie wohnen gegenüber.
□ the girl sitting opposite me das Mädchen, das mir gegenüber saß
■ **the opposite sex** das andere Geschlecht

opposition NOUN
die Opposition

optician NOUN
der Optiker (PL die Optiker)
die Optikerin
□ She's an optician. Sie ist Optikerin.

optimist NOUN
der Optimist (GEN des Optimisten, PL die Optimisten)
die Optimistin
□ She's an optimist. Sie ist Optimistin.

optimistic ADJECTIVE
optimistisch

option NOUN

1 die Wahl *(choice)*
□ I've got no option. Ich habe keine andere Wahl.

2 das Wahlfach (PL die Wahlfächer) *(optional subject)*
□ I'm doing geology as my option. Ich habe Geologie als Wahlfach.

optional ADJECTIVE
fakultativ

or CONJUNCTION
1 oder
□ Tea or coffee? Tee oder Kaffee?
LANGUAGE TIP Use **weder ... noch** in negative sentences.
□ I don't eat meat or fish. Ich esse weder Fleisch noch Fisch.
2 sonst *(otherwise)*
□ Hurry up or you'll miss the bus. Beeil dich, sonst verpasst du den Bus.
■ **Give me the money, or else!** Gib mir das Geld, sonst gibt's was!

oral ADJECTIVE
▷ *see also* **oral** NOUN
mündlich
□ an oral exam eine mündliche Prüfung

oral NOUN
▷ *see also* **oral** ADJECTIVE
die mündliche Prüfung
□ I've got my German oral soon. Ich habe bald meine mündliche Prüfung in Deutsch.

orange NOUN
▷ *see also* **orange** ADJECTIVE
die Orange
■ **an orange juice** ein Orangensaft *masc*

orange ADJECTIVE
▷ *see also* **orange** NOUN
orangerot *(colour)*

orchard NOUN
der Obstgarten (PL die Obstgärten)

orchestra NOUN
1 das Orchester (PL die Orchester)
□ I play in the school orchestra. Ich spiele im Schulorchester.
2 das Parkett *(stalls)*
□ We sat in the orchestra. Wir saßen im Parkett.

order NOUN
▷ *see also* **order** VERB
1 die Reihenfolge *(sequence)*
□ in alphabetical order in alphabetischer Reihenfolge
2 die Bestellung *(at restaurant, in shop)*
□ The waiter took our order. Der Ober nahm unsere Bestellung auf.
3 der Befehl (PL die Befehle) *(instruction)*
□ That's an order. Das ist ein Befehl.
■ **in order to** um zu □ He does it in order to earn money. Er tut es, um Geld zu verdienen.
■ **'out of order'** 'außer Betrieb'

to **order** VERB
▷ *see also* **order** NOUN
bestellen (PERFECT hat bestellt)
□ We ordered steak and chips. Wir haben Steak mit Pommes frites bestellt. □ Are you ready to order? Möchten Sie bestellen?

to **order about** VERB
herumkommandieren (PERFECT hat herumkommandiert)
□ She was fed up with being ordered about. Sie hatte es satt, herumkommandiert zu werden.

ordinary ADJECTIVE
1 gewöhnlich
□ an ordinary day ein gewöhnlicher Tag
2 normal *(people)*
□ an ordinary family eine normale Familie
□ He's just an ordinary guy. Er ist ein ganz normaler Mensch.

organ NOUN
die Orgel *(instrument)*
□ I play the organ. Ich spiele Orgel.

organic ADJECTIVE
biologisch angebaut *(fruit)*
■ **organic vegetables** das Biogemüse *sing*

organization NOUN
die Organisation

to **organize** VERB
organisieren (PERFECT hat organisiert)

origin NOUN
der Ursprung (PL die Ursprünge)

original ADJECTIVE
originell
□ It's a very original idea. Das ist eine sehr originelle Idee.
■ **Our original plan was to go camping.** Ursprünglich wollten wir zelten.

originally ADVERB
ursprünglich

Orkney NOUN
die Orkneyinseln *fem pl*
■ **in Orkney** auf den Orkneyinseln

ornament NOUN
die Verzierung

orphan NOUN
das Waisenkind (PL die Waisenkinder)
□ She's an orphan. Sie ist ein Waisenkind.

ostrich NOUN
der Strauß (GEN des Straußes, PL die Strauße)

other ADJECTIVE, PRONOUN
andere
□ Have you got these jeans in other colours? Haben Sie diese Jeans in anderen Farben?
□ on the other side of the street auf der anderen Straßenseite
■ **the other day** neulich
■ **the other one** 1 *(masculine)* der andere □ This hat? — No, the other one. Dieser Hut? — Nein, der andere. 2 *(feminine)* die andere □ This cup? — No, the other one. Diese Tasse? — Nein, die andere. 3 *(neuter)* das andere □ This photo? — No, the other one. Dieses Foto? — Nein, das andere.
■ **the others** die anderen □ The others are

going but I'm not. Die anderen gehen, ich nicht.

otherwise ADVERB, CONJUNCTION

sonst

□ Note down the number, otherwise you'll forget it. Schreib dir die Nummer auf, sonst vergisst du sie. □ Put some sunscreen on, you'll get burned otherwise. Creme dich ein, sonst bekommst du einen Sonnenbrand. □ I'm tired, but otherwise I'm fine. Ich bin müde, aber sonst geht's mir gut.

ought VERB

LANGUAGE TIP If you want to say that you feel obliged to do something, use the conditional tense of **sollen**.

□ I ought to phone my parents. Ich sollte meine Eltern anrufen. □ You ought not to do that. Du solltest das nicht tun.

LANGUAGE TIP If you want to say that something is likely, use the conditional tense of **müssen**.

□ He ought to win. Er müsste gewinnen.

ounce NOUN

die Unze

our ADJECTIVE

unser

□ Our boss is quite nice. Unser Chef ist ganz nett. □ Our company is going to expand. Unsere Firma wird expandieren. □ Our house is quite big. Unser Haus ist ziemlich groß. □ Our neighbours are very nice. Unsere Nachbarn sind sehr nett.

LANGUAGE TIP Do not use **unser** with parts of the body.

□ We had to shut our eyes. Wir mussten die Augen zumachen.

ours PRONOUN

1 unserer

□ Your garden is very big, ours is much smaller. Euer Garten ist sehr groß, unserer ist viel kleiner.

unsere

□ Your school is very different from ours. Eure Schule ist ganz anderes als unsere.

unseres

□ Your house is bigger than ours. Euer Haus ist größer als unseres.

2 unsere

□ Our teachers are strict. — Ours are too. Unsere Lehrer sind streng. — Unsere auch.

■ **Is this ours?** Gehört das uns? □ This car is ours. Das Auto gehört uns. □ Whose is this? — It's ours. Wem gehört das? — Uns.

ourselves PRONOUN

1 uns

□ We really enjoyed ourselves. Wir haben uns wirklich amüsiert.

2 selbst

□ We built our garage ourselves. Wir haben die Garage selbst gebaut.

out ADVERB

LANGUAGE TIP There are several ways of translating 'out'. Scan the examples to find one that is similar to what you want to say. For other expressions with 'out', see the verbs 'go', 'put', 'turn' etc.

1 draußen *(outside)*

□ It's cold out. Es ist kalt draußen.

2 aus *(light, fire)*

□ All the lights are out. Alle Lichter sind aus.

■ **She's out.** Sie ist weg. □ She's out for the afternoon. Sie ist den ganzen Nachmittag weg.

■ **She's out shopping.** Sie ist zum Einkaufen.

■ **out there** da draußen □ It's cold out there. Es ist kalt da draußen.

■ **to go out** ausgehen □ I'm going out tonight. Ich gehe heute Abend aus.

■ **to go out with somebody** mit jemandem gehen □ I've been going out with him for two months. Ich gehe seit zwei Monaten mit ihm.

■ **out of 1** aus □ to drink out of a glass aus einem Glas trinken **2** von □ in nine cases out of ten in neun von zehn Fällen **3** außerhalb □ He lives out of town. Er wohnt außerhalb der Stadt. □ three kilometres out of town drei Kilometer außerhalb der Stadt

■ **out of curiosity** aus Neugier

■ **out of work** arbeitslos

■ **That is out of the question.** Das kommt nicht infrage.

■ **You're out!** *(in game)* Du bist draußen!

■ **'way out'** 'Ausgang'

outbreak NOUN

der Ausbruch (PL die Ausbrüche)

□ a salmonella outbreak ein Ausbruch von Salmonellenvergiftung □ the outbreak of war der Kriegsausbruch

outcome NOUN

das Ergebnis (PL die Ergebnisse)

outdoor ADJECTIVE

im Freien

□ outdoor activities Aktivitäten im Freien

■ **an outdoor swimming pool** ein Freibad *neut*

outdoors ADVERB

im Freien

outfit NOUN

das Outfit (PL die Outfits)

□ a cowboy outfit ein Cowboyoutfit

outgoing ADJECTIVE

aufgeschlossen

□ She's very outgoing. Sie ist sehr aufgeschlossen.

outing NOUN

der Ausflug (PL die Ausflüge)

□ to go on an outing einen Ausflug machen

outline NOUN

1 der Grundriss (GEN des Grundrisses, PL die Grundrisse) *(summary)*

□ This is an outline of the plan. Das ist der Grundriss des Plans.

2 der Umriss (GEN des Umrisses, PL die Umrisse) *(shape)*
□ We could see the outline of the mountain. Wir konnten den Umriss des Berges erkennen.

outlook NOUN
1 die Einstellung *(attitude)*
□ my outlook on life meine Einstellung zum Leben
2 die Aussichten *pl (prospects)*

outrageous ADJECTIVE
1 unerhört *(behaviour)*
2 unverschämt *(price)*

outset NOUN
der Anfang (PL die Anfänge)
□ at the outset am Anfang

outside NOUN
▷ *see also* **outside** ADJECTIVE
die Außenseite

outside ADJECTIVE, ADVERB, PREPOSITION
▷ *see also* **outside** NOUN
1 äußere
□ the outside walls die äußeren Mauern
2 draußen
□ It's very cold outside. Draußen ist es sehr kalt.
3 außerhalb
□ outside the school außerhalb der Schule
□ outside school hours außerhalb der Schulzeit

outsize ADJECTIVE
übergroß

outskirts PL NOUN
der Stadtrand *sing*
□ on the outskirts of the town am Stadtrand

outstanding ADJECTIVE
bemerkenswert

oval ADJECTIVE
oval

oven NOUN
der Backofen (PL die Backöfen)

over PREPOSITION, ADVERB, ADJECTIVE
1 über

LANGUAGE TIP Use the accusative to express movement or a change of place. Use the dative when there is no change of place.

□ The ball went over the wall. Der Ball flog über die Mauer. □ There's a mirror over the washbasin. Über dem Becken ist ein Spiegel.
2 über *+acc (more than)*
□ It's over twenty kilos. Es ist über zwanzig Kilo schwer. □ The temperature was over thirty degrees. Die Temperatur lag über dreißig Grad.
3 vorbei *(finished)*
□ I'll be happy when the exams are over. Ich bin froh, wenn die Prüfungen vorbei sind.
■ **over the holidays** die Ferien über
■ **over Christmas** über Weihnachten
■ **over here** hier
■ **over there** dort
■ **all over Scotland** in ganz Schottland

overall ADVERB
insgesamt *(generally)*
□ My results were quite good overall. Insgesamt hatte ich ganz gute Noten.

overalls PL NOUN
der Overall *sing* (PL die Overalls)

overcast ADJECTIVE
bedeckt
□ The sky was overcast. Der Himmel war bedeckt.

to **overcharge** VERB
zu viel berechnen (PERFECT hat zu viel berechnet)
□ He overcharged me. Er hat mir zu viel berechnet. □ They overcharged us for the meal. Sie haben uns für das Essen zu viel berechnet.

overcoat NOUN
der Mantel (PL die Mäntel)

overdone ADJECTIVE
verkocht *(food)*

overdose NOUN
die Überdosis (PL die Überdosen) *(of drugs)*
□ to take an overdose eine Überdosis nehmen

overdraft NOUN
der Überziehungskredit

to **overestimate** VERB
überschätzen (PERFECT hat überschätzt)

overhead projector NOUN
der Tageslichtprojektor (PL die Tageslichtprojektoren)

to **overlook** VERB
1 einen Blick haben auf *+acc* (PRESENT hat einen Blick auf, IMPERFECT hatte einen Blick auf, PERFECT hat einen Blick auf gehabt) *(have view of)*
□ The hotel overlooked the beach. Vom Hotel hat man einen Blick auf den Strand.
2 übersehen (PRESENT übersieht, IMPERFECT übersah, PERFECT hat übersehen) *(forget about)*
□ He had overlooked one important problem. Er hatte ein wichtiges Problem übersehen.

overseas ADVERB
1 im Ausland
□ I'd like to work overseas. Ich würde gern im Ausland arbeiten.
2 ins Ausland
□ His company has sent him overseas. Seine Firma hat ihn ins Ausland geschickt.

oversight NOUN
das Versehen (PL die Versehen)

to **oversleep** VERB
verschlafen (PRESENT verschläft, IMPERFECT verschlief, PERFECT hat verschlafen)
□ I overslept this morning. Ich habe heute morgen verschlafen.

to **overtake** VERB
überholen (PERFECT hat überholt)
□ He overtook me. Er hat mich überholt.

overtime NOUN
die Überstunden *fem pl*
□ to work overtime Überstunden machen

overtook VERB ▷ *see* **overtake**

overweight ADJECTIVE
■ **to be overweight** Übergewicht haben

to **owe** VERB
schulden
■ **to owe somebody something** jemandem etwas schulden □ You owe me five pounds. Du schuldest mir fünf Pfund.

owing to PREPOSITION
wegen
□ owing to bad weather wegen des schlechten Wetters

owl NOUN
die Eule

own ADJECTIVE
▷ *see also* **own** VERB
eigen
□ I've got my own bathroom. Ich habe mein eigenes Badezimmer.
■ **I'd like a room of my own.** Ich hätte gern ein eigenes Zimmer.
■ **on one's own** allein □ on her own allein □ on our own allein

to **own** VERB
▷ *see also* **own** ADJECTIVE
besitzen (IMPERFECT besaß, PERFECT hat besessen)
□ My father owns a small business. Mein Vater besitzt ein kleines Geschäft.

to **own up** VERB
zugeben (PRESENT gibt zu, IMPERFECT gab zu, PERFECT hat zugegeben)
□ to own up to something etwas zugeben

owner NOUN
der Besitzer (PL die Besitzer)
die Besitzerin

oxygen NOUN
der Sauerstoff

oyster NOUN
die Auster

ozone layer NOUN
die Ozonschicht

Pp

PA NOUN *(= personal assistant)*
der Chefsekretär (PL die Chefsekretäre)
die Chefsekretärin
□ She's a PA. Sie ist Chefsekretärin.
■ **the PA system** *(public address)* die Lautsprecheranlage

pace NOUN
das Tempo *(speed)*
□ Technology is developing at a rapid pace. Die Technologie entwickelt sich in schnellem Tempo.
■ **He was walking at a brisk pace.** Er ging mit schnellen Schritten.

Pacific NOUN
der Pazifik

pacifier NOUN (US)
der Schnuller (PL die Schnuller)

to **pack** VERB
▷ *see also* **pack** NOUN
packen
□ I'll help you pack. Ich helfe dir packen.
□ I've packed my case. Ich habe meinen Koffer gepackt.
■ **Pack it in!** *(stop it)* Lass es!

pack NOUN
▷ *see also* **pack** VERB
1 die Packung *(packet)*
□ a pack of cigarettes eine Packung Zigaretten
2 der Pack (PL die Packs) *(of yoghurts, cans)*
□ a six-pack ein Sechserpack
■ **a pack of cards** ein Spiel Karten *neut*

package NOUN
das Paket (PL die Pakete)
■ **a package holiday** eine Pauschalreise

packed ADJECTIVE
gerammelt voll
□ The cinema was packed. Das Kino war gerammelt voll.

packed lunch NOUN
das Lunchpaket (PL die Lunchpakete)
■ **I take a packed lunch to school.** Ich nehme für mittags etwas zum Essen in die Schule mit.

packet NOUN
die Packung
□ a packet of cigarettes eine Packung Zigaretten

pad NOUN
der Notizblock (PL die Notizblöcke) *(notepad)*

to **paddle** VERB
▷ *see also* **paddle** NOUN
1 paddeln *(canoe)*
2 planschen *(in water)*

paddle NOUN
▷ *see also* **paddle** VERB
das Paddel (PL die Paddel) *(for canoe)*
■ **to go for a paddle** planschen gehen

padlock NOUN
das Vorhängeschloss (GEN des Vorhängeschlosses, PL die Vorhängeschlösser)

page NOUN
▷ *see also* **page** VERB
die Seite *(of book)*

to **page** VERB
▷ *see also* **page** NOUN
■ **to page somebody** jemanden per Pager benachrichtigen

pager NOUN
der Pager (PL die Pager)

paid VERB ▷ *see* **pay**

paid ADJECTIVE
bezahlt
□ three weeks' paid holiday drei Wochen bezahlter Urlaub

pail NOUN
der Eimer (PL die Eimer)

pain NOUN
der Schmerz (GEN des Schmerzes, PL die Schmerzen)
□ a terrible pain ein furchtbarer Schmerz
■ **I've got pains in my stomach.** Ich habe Bauchschmerzen.
■ **to be in pain** Schmerzen haben □ She's in a lot of pain. Sie hat starke Schmerzen.
■ **He's a real pain.** Er geht einem echt auf die Nerven. *(informal)*

painful ADJECTIVE
schmerzhaft
■ **to suffer from painful periods** starke Periodenschmerzen haben
■ **to be painful** wehtun □ Is it painful? Tut es weh?

painkiller NOUN
das Schmerzmittel (PL die Schmerzmittel)

paint NOUN
▷ *see also* **paint** VERB
die Farbe

to paint VERB
▷ *see also* **paint** NOUN
1 streichen (IMPERFECT strich, PERFECT hat gestrichen)
□ to paint something green etwas grün streichen
2 malen *(pictures)*
□ She painted a picture of the house. Sie hat von dem Haus ein Bild gemalt.

paintbrush NOUN
der Pinsel (PL die Pinsel)

painter NOUN
der Maler (PL die Maler)
die Malerin
■ **a painter and decorator** ein Anstreicher

painting NOUN
1 das Malen
□ My hobby is painting. Malen ist mein Hobby.
2 das Bild (PL die Bilder) *(picture)*
□ a painting by Picasso ein Bild von Picasso

pair NOUN
das Paar (PL die Paare)
□ a pair of shoes ein Paar Schuhe
■ **a pair of scissors** eine Schere
■ **a pair of trousers** eine Hose
■ **a pair of jeans** eine Jeans
■ **in pairs** paarweise □ We work in pairs. Wir arbeiten paarweise.

pajamas PL NOUN (US)
der Schlafanzug (PL die Schlafanzüge)
□ my pajamas mein Schlafanzug
■ **a pair of pajamas** ein Schlafanzug

Pakistan NOUN
Pakistan *neut*
■ **from Pakistan** aus Pakistan
■ **to Pakistan** nach Pakistan

Pakistani NOUN
▷ *see also* **Pakistani** ADJECTIVE
der Pakistani (PL die Pakistani)
die Pakistani

Pakistani ADJECTIVE
▷ *see also* **Pakistani** NOUN
pakistanisch
■ **He's Pakistani.** Er ist Pakistani.

pal NOUN
der Kumpel (PL die Kumpel) *(informal)*
LANGUAGE TIP **der Kumpel** is also used for women.

palace NOUN
der Palast (PL die Paläste)

pale ADJECTIVE
blass
□ You're very pale. Du bist sehr blass.
■ **a pale blue shirt** ein hellblaues Hemd

Palestine NOUN
Palästina *neut*
■ **from Palestine** aus Palästina
■ **to Palestine** nach Palästina

Palestinian ADJECTIVE
▷ *see also* **Palestinian** NOUN
palästinensisch
■ **He's Palestinian.** Er ist Palästinenser.

Palestinian NOUN
▷ *see also* **Palestinian** ADJECTIVE
der Palästinenser (PL die Palästinenser)
die Palästinenserin

palm NOUN
der Handteller (PL die Handteller) *(of hand)*
■ **a palm tree** eine Palme

pamphlet NOUN
die Broschüre

pan NOUN
1 der Topf (PL die Töpfe) *(saucepan)*
2 die Pfanne *(frying pan)*

pancake NOUN
der Pfannkuchen (PL die Pfannkuchen)

panic NOUN
▷ *see also* **panic** VERB
die Panik

to panic VERB
▷ *see also* **panic** NOUN
in Panik geraten (PRESENT gerät in Panik, IMPERFECT geriet in Panik, PERFECT ist in Panik geraten)
□ She panicked. Sie geriet in Panik.
■ **Don't panic!** Nur keine Panik!

panther NOUN
der Panther (PL die Panther)

panties PL NOUN
der Slip (PL die Slips)
□ a pair of panties ein Slip

pantomime NOUN
das Weihnachtsmärchen (PL die Weihnachtsmärchen)

pants PL NOUN
1 die Unterhose *(underwear)*
□ a pair of pants eine Unterhose
2 die Hose *(trousers)*
□ a pair of pants eine Hose

pantyhose PL NOUN (US)
die Strumpfhose

paper NOUN
1 das Papier (PL die Papiere)
□ a piece of paper ein Stück Papier
□ a paper towel ein Papierhandtuch
2 die Zeitung *(newspaper)*
□ an advert in the paper eine Anzeige in der Zeitung
■ **an exam paper** eine Klausur

paperback NOUN
das Taschenbuch (PL die Taschenbücher)

paper boy NOUN
der Zeitungsjunge (GEN des Zeitungsjungen, PL die Zeitungsjungen)

paper clip NOUN
die Büroklammer

paper girl NOUN
das Zeitungsmädchen (PL die Zeitungsmädchen)

paper round NOUN
■ **to do a paper round** Zeitungen austragen

paperweight NOUN
der Briefbeschwerer (PL die Briefbeschwerer)
paperwork NOUN
die Schreibarbeit
□ I've got a lot of paperwork to do. Ich habe eine Menge Schreibarbeit zu erledigen.
parachute NOUN
der Fallschirm (PL die Fallschirme)
parade NOUN
die Parade
paradise NOUN
das Paradies (GEN des Paradieses, PL die Paradiese)
paraffin NOUN
das Petroleum
□ a paraffin lamp eine Petroleumlampe
paragraph NOUN
der Paragraf (GEN des Paragrafen, PL die Paragrafen)
parallel ADJECTIVE
parallel
paralyzed ADJECTIVE
gelähmt
paramedic NOUN
der Sanitäter (PL die Sanitäter)
die Sanitäterin
parcel NOUN
das Paket (PL die Pakete)
pardon NOUN
■ **Pardon?** Wie bitte?
parent NOUN
1 der Vater *(father)*
2 die Mutter *(mother)*
■ **my parents** meine Eltern
Paris NOUN
Paris *neut*
park NOUN
▷ *see also* **park** VERB
der Park (PL die Parks)
■ **a national park** ein Nationalpark
■ **a theme park** ein Themenpark
■ **a car park** ein Parkplatz *masc*
to **park** VERB
▷ *see also* **park** NOUN
parken
□ Where can I park my car? Wo kann ich mein Auto parken?
■ **We couldn't find anywhere to park.** Wir haben nirgends einen Parkplatz gefunden.
parking NOUN
das Parken
□ 'no parking' 'Parken verboten'
parking lot NOUN (US)
der Parkplatz (GEN des Parkplatzes, PL die Parkplätze)
parking meter NOUN
die Parkuhr
parking ticket NOUN
der Strafzettel (PL die Strafzettel)
parliament NOUN
das Parlament (PL die Parlamente)
parole NOUN
■ **on parole** auf Bewährung
parrot NOUN
der Papagei (PL die Papageien)
parsley NOUN
die Petersilie
part NOUN
1 der Teil (PL die Teile) *(section)*
□ The first part of the film was boring. Der erste Teil des Films war langweilig.
2 das Teil (PL die Teile) *(component)*
□ spare parts Ersatzteile
3 die Rolle *(in play, film)*
■ **to take part in something** an etwas teilnehmen □ A lot of people took part in the demonstration. An der Demonstration haben viele Menschen teilgenommen.
particular ADJECTIVE
bestimmt
□ I am looking for a particular book. Ich suche ein bestimmtes Buch. □ Are you looking for anything particular? Suchen Sie nach etwas Bestimmtem?
■ **nothing in particular** nichts Bestimmtes
particularly ADVERB
besonders
parting NOUN
der Scheitel (PL die Scheitel) *(in hair)*
partly ADVERB
zum Teil
partner NOUN
der Partner (PL die Partner)
die Partnerin
part-time ADJECTIVE, ADVERB
Teilzeit
□ a part-time job eine Teilzeitarbeit
□ She works part-time. Sie arbeitet Teilzeit.
party NOUN
1 die Party (PL die Partys)
□ a birthday party eine Geburtstagsparty
□ a Christmas party eine Weihnachtsparty
□ a New Year party eine Silvesterparty
2 die Partei *(political)*
□ the Conservative Party die Konservative Partei
3 die Gruppe *(group)*
□ a party of tourists eine Gruppe Touristen
pass NOUN
▷ *see also* **pass** VERB
der Pass (GEN des Passes, PL die Pässe)
□ The pass was blocked with snow. Der Pass war zugeschneit. □ That was a good pass by Ferguson. Das war ein guter Pass von Ferguson.
■ **to get a pass** *(in exam)* bestehen □ She got a pass in her piano exam. Sie hat ihre Klavierprüfung bestanden. □ I got six passes. Ich habe in sechs Fächern bestanden.
■ **a bus pass 1** *(monthly)* eine Monatskarte für den Bus **2** *(for old-age pensioners)* eine Seniorenkarte für den Bus

DID YOU KNOW...?
Almost all German cities operate an integrated public transport system; you can buy a weekly (**Wochenkarte**), monthly (**Monatskarte**) or yearly (**Jahreskarte**) pass which are valid for that period on all buses, trams and light railway vehicles in a particular zone.

to **pass** VERB
▷ *see also* **pass** NOUN
1 geben (PRESENT gibt, IMPERFECT gab, PERFECT hat gegeben) *(give)*
□ Could you pass me the salt? Könntest du mir das Salz geben?
2 vergehen (IMPERFECT verging, PERFECT ist vergangen) *(go by)*
□ The time has passed quickly. Die Zeit ist schnell vergangen.
3 vorbeigehen an *+dat* (IMPERFECT ging vorbei, PERFECT ist vorbeigegangen) *(on foot)*
□ I pass his house on my way to school. Auf dem Weg zur Schule gehe ich an seinem Haus vorbei.
4 vorbeifahren an *+dat* (PRESENT fährt vorbei, IMPERFECT fuhr vorbei, PERFECT ist vorbeigefahren) *(in vehicle)*
□ We passed the post office. Wir sind an der Post vorbeigefahren.
5 bestehen (IMPERFECT bestand, PERFECT hat bestanden) *(exam)*
□ Did you pass? Hast du bestanden?
■ **to pass an exam** eine Prüfung bestehen
□ I hope I'll pass the exam. Ich hoffe, dass ich die Prüfung bestehe.

to **pass out** VERB
ohnmächtig werden (PRESENT wird ohnmächtig, IMPERFECT wurde ohnmächtig, PERFECT ist ohnmächtig geworden) *(faint)*

passage NOUN
1 der Abschnitt (PL die Abschnitte) *(piece of writing)*
□ Read the passage carefully. Lest den Abschnitt sorgfältig durch.
2 der Gang (PL die Gänge) *(corridor)*

passenger NOUN
der Passagier (PL die Passagiere)
die Passagierin

passion NOUN
die Leidenschaft

passive ADJECTIVE
passiv
■ **passive smoking** das Passivrauchen

Passover NOUN
das Passahfest

passport NOUN
der Pass (GEN des Passes, PL die Pässe)
■ **passport control** die Passkontrolle

password NOUN
das Passwort (PL die Passwörter)

past ADVERB, PREPOSITION
▷ *see also* **past** NOUN
nach *(beyond)*
□ It's on the right, just past the station. Es ist auf der rechten Seite, gleich nach dem Bahnhof.
□ It's quarter past nine. Es ist Viertel nach neun.
□ It's past midnight. Es ist nach Mitternacht.
■ **It's half past ten.** Es ist halb elf.
■ **to go past 1** *(vehicle)* vorbeifahren
□ The bus went past without stopping. Der Bus ist vorbeigefahren, ohne anzuhalten.
□ The bus goes past our house. Der Bus fährt an unserem Haus vorbei. **2** *(on foot)* vorbeigehen □ He went past without saying hello. Er ging vorbei, ohne Hallo zu sagen.
□ I went past your house yesterday. Ich bin gestern an eurem Haus vorbeigegangen.

past NOUN
▷ *see also* **past** ADVERB
die Vergangenheit
□ She lives in the past. Sie lebt in der Vergangenheit.
■ **in the past** *(previously)* früher □ That was common in the past. Das war früher üblich.

pasta NOUN
die Teigwaren *fem pl*
□ Pasta is easy to cook. Teigwaren sind leicht zu kochen.

paste NOUN
der Leim (PL die Leime) *(glue)*

pasteurized ADJECTIVE
pasteurisiert

pastime NOUN
der Zeitvertreib (PL die Zeitvertreibe)
□ a popular pastime ein beliebter Zeitvertreib
■ **Her favourite pastime is knitting.** Stricken ist ihre Lieblingsbeschäftigung.

pastry NOUN
der Teig
■ **pastries** *(cakes)* das Gebäck *sing*

to **pat** VERB
streicheln (PERFECT hat gestreichelt) *(dog, cat)*

patch NOUN
1 das Stück (PL die Stücke)
□ a patch of material ein Stück Stoff
2 der Flicken (PL die Flicken) *(for flat tyre)*
■ **He's got a bald patch.** Er hat eine kahle Stelle.

patched ADJECTIVE
geflickt
□ a pair of patched jeans eine geflickte Jeans

pâté NOUN
die Fleischpastete
■ **liver pâté** die Leberwurst

path NOUN
der Weg (PL die Wege)

pathetic ADJECTIVE
schrecklich schlecht
□ Our team was pathetic. Unsere Mannschaft war schrecklich schlecht.

patience NOUN
1 die Geduld
□ He hasn't got much patience. Er hat nicht viel Geduld.
2 die Patience *(card game)*
□ to play patience Patience spielen

patient NOUN
▷ *see also* **patient** ADJECTIVE
der Patient (GEN des Patienten, PL die Patienten)
die Patientin

patient ADJECTIVE
▷ *see also* **patient** NOUN
geduldig

patio NOUN
die Terrasse

patriotic ADJECTIVE
patriotisch

patrol NOUN
1 die Patrouille *(military)*
2 die Streife *(of police)*

patrol car NOUN
der Streifenwagen (PL die Streifenwagen)

pattern NOUN
das Muster (PL die Muster)
□ a geometric pattern ein geometrisches Muster □ a sewing pattern ein Nähmuster

pause NOUN
die Pause

pavement NOUN
der Bürgersteig (PL die Bürgersteige)

pavilion NOUN
der Pavillon (PL die Pavillons)

paw NOUN
die Pfote

pay NOUN
▷ *see also* **pay** VERB
die Bezahlung

to **pay** VERB
▷ *see also* **pay** NOUN
bezahlen (PERFECT hat bezahlt)
□ They pay me more on Sundays. Sie bezahlen mir sonntags mehr. □ to pay by cheque mit Scheck bezahlen □ to pay by credit card mit Kreditkarte bezahlen
■ **to pay for something** für etwas bezahlen
□ I paid fifty euros for it. Ich habe fünfzig Euro dafür bezahlt. □ I paid for my ticket. Ich habe meine Fahrkarte bezahlt.
■ **to pay extra for something** für etwas extra bezahlen □ You have to pay extra for parking. Fürs Parken müssen Sie extra bezahlen.
■ **to pay attention** aufpassen □ You should pay more attention. Du solltest besser aufpassen.
■ **Don't pay any attention to him.** Beachte ihn einfach nicht.
■ **to pay somebody a visit** jemanden besuchen □ Paul paid us a visit last night. Paul hat uns gestern Abend besucht.
■ **to pay somebody back** *(money)* es jemandem zurückzahlen □ I'll pay you back tomorrow. Ich zahle es dir morgen zurück.

payment NOUN
die Bezahlung

payphone NOUN
der Münzfernsprecher (PL die Münzfernsprecher)

PC NOUN *(= personal computer)*
der PC (PL die PCs)
□ She typed the report on her PC. Sie hat den Bericht am PC erfasst.

PE NOUN *(= physical education)*
der Sportunterricht

pea NOUN
die Erbse

peace NOUN
1 der Frieden *(after war)*
2 die Stille *(quietness)*

peaceful ADJECTIVE
1 ruhig *(calm)*
□ a peaceful afternoon ein ruhiger Nachmittag
2 friedlich *(not violent)*
□ a peaceful protest ein friedlicher Protest

peach NOUN
der Pfirsich (PL die Pfirsiche)

peacock NOUN
der Pfau (PL die Pfauen)

peak NOUN
der Gipfel (PL die Gipfel) *(of mountain)*
■ **the peak rate** der Spitzentarif □ You pay the peak rate for calls at this time of day. Um diese Tageszeit zahlt man fürs Telefonieren den Spitzentarif.
■ **in peak season** in der Hochsaison

peanut NOUN
die Erdnuss (PL die Erdnüsse)
□ a packet of peanuts eine Packung Erdnüsse

peanut butter NOUN
die Erdnussbutter
□ a peanut-butter sandwich ein Brot mit Erdnussbutter

pear NOUN
die Birne

pearl NOUN
die Perle

pebble NOUN
der Kieselstein (PL die Kieselsteine)
■ **a pebble beach** ein Kieselstrand *masc*

peckish ADJECTIVE
■ **to feel a bit peckish** ein bisschen Hunger haben

peculiar ADJECTIVE
eigenartig
□ He's a peculiar person. Er ist ein eigenartiger Mensch. □ It tastes peculiar. Es schmeckt eigenartig.

pedal NOUN
das Pedal (PL die Pedale)

pedestrian NOUN
der Fußgänger (PL die Fußgänger)
die Fußgängerin

pedestrian crossing NOUN
der Fußgängerüberweg
(PL die Fußgängerüberwege)

pedestrianized ADJECTIVE
■ **a pedestrianized street** eine Fußgängerzone

pedigree ADJECTIVE
reinrassig *(animal)*
□ a pedigree labrador ein reinrassiger Labrador

pee NOUN
■ **to have a pee** pinkeln *(informal)*

peek NOUN
■ **to have a peek at something** einen kurzen Blick auf etwas werfen □ I had a peek at the baby. Ich habe einen kurzen Blick auf das Baby geworfen.

peel NOUN
▷ *see also* **peel** VERB
die Schale *(of orange)*

to **peel** VERB
▷ *see also* **peel** NOUN
1 schälen
□ Shall I peel the potatoes? Soll ich die Kartoffeln schälen?
2 sich schälen
□ My nose is peeling. Meine Nase schält sich.

peg NOUN
1 der Haken (PL die Haken) *(for coats)*
2 die Wäscheklammer *(clothes peg)*
3 der Hering (PL die Heringe) *(tent peg)*

Pekinese NOUN
der Pekinese (GEN des Pekinesen, PL die Pekinesen)

pelican crossing NOUN
die Fußgängerampel

pellet NOUN
die Schrotkugel *(for gun)*

pelvis NOUN
das Becken (PL die Becken)

pen NOUN
der Schreiber (PL die Schreiber)

to **penalize** VERB
bestrafen (PERFECT hat bestraft)

penalty NOUN
1 die Strafe *(punishment)*
□ the death penalty die Todesstrafe
2 der Elfmeter (PL die Elfmeter) *(in football)*
3 der Strafstoß (GEN des Strafstoßes, PL die Strafstöße) *(in rugby)*
■ **a penalty shoot-out** ein Elfmeterschießen *neut*

pence PL NOUN
die Pence *masc pl*

pencil NOUN
der Bleistift (PL die Bleistifte)
■ **in pencil** mit Bleistift

pencil case NOUN
das Federmäppchen
(PL die Federmäppchen)

pencil sharpener NOUN
der Bleistiftspitzer (PL die Bleistiftspitzer)

pendant NOUN
der Anhänger (PL die Anhänger)

pen friend NOUN
der Brieffreund (PL die Brieffreunde)
die Brieffreundin

penguin NOUN
der Pinguin (PL die Pinguine)

penicillin NOUN
das Penizillin

penis NOUN
der Penis (GEN des Penis, PL die Penisse)

penitentiary NOUN (US)
das Gefängnis (GEN des Gefängnisses, PL die Gefängnisse)

penknife NOUN
das Taschenmesser (PL die Taschenmesser)

penny NOUN
der Penny (PL die Pennys *or* Pence)

pension NOUN
die Rente

pensioner NOUN
der Rentner (PL die Rentner)
die Rentnerin

pentathlon NOUN
der Fünfkampf (PL die Fünfkämpfe)

people PL NOUN
1 die Leute *pl*
□ The people were nice. Die Leute waren nett. □ a lot of people viele Leute
2 die Menschen *masc pl (individuals)*
□ six people sechs Menschen □ several people mehrere Menschen
■ **German people** die Deutschen
■ **black people** die Schwarzen
■ **People say that ...** Man sagt, dass ...

pepper NOUN
1 der Pfeffer *(spice)*
□ Pass the pepper, please. Gib mir mal bitte den Pfeffer.
2 die Paprikaschote *(vegetable)*
□ a green pepper eine grüne Paprikaschote

peppermill NOUN
die Pfeffermühle

peppermint NOUN
das Pfefferminzbonbon
(PL die Pfefferminzbonbons) *(sweet)*
■ **peppermint chewing gum** der Kaugummi mit Pfefferminzgeschmack

per PREPOSITION
pro
□ per day pro Tag □ per week pro Woche
■ **thirty miles per hour** dreißig Meilen in der Stunde

per cent ADVERB
das Prozent
□ fifty per cent fünfzig Prozent

percentage NOUN
der Prozentsatz (GEN des Prozentsatzes, PL die Prozentsätze)

English-German

P

percussion NOUN
das Schlagzeug (PL die Schlagzeuge)
□ I play percussion. Ich spiele Schlagzeug.

perfect ADJECTIVE
perfekt
□ He speaks perfect English. Er spricht perfekt Englisch.

perfectly ADVERB
1 ganz
□ You know perfectly well what happened. Du weißt ganz genau, was passiert ist.
2 perfekt *(very well)*
□ The system worked perfectly. Das System hat perfekt funktioniert.

to **perform** VERB
spielen *(act, play)*

performance NOUN
1 die Vorstellung *(show)*
□ The performance lasts two hours. Die Vorstellung dauert zwei Stunden.
2 die Darstellung *(acting)*
□ his performance as Hamlet seine Darstellung des Hamlet
3 die Leistung *(results)*
□ the team's poor performance die schwache Leistung der Mannschaft

perfume NOUN
das Parfüm (PL die Parfüme)

perhaps ADVERB
vielleicht
□ a bit boring, perhaps etwas langweilig vielleicht □ Perhaps he's ill. Vielleicht ist er krank. □ perhaps not vielleicht nicht

period NOUN
1 die Zeit
□ for a limited period für eine begrenzte Zeit
2 die Epoche *(in history)*
□ the Victorian period die viktorianische Epoche
3 die Periode *(menstruation)*
□ I'm having my period. Ich habe meine Periode.
4 die Stunde *(lesson time)*
□ Each period lasts forty minutes. Jede Stunde dauert vierzig Minuten.

perm NOUN
die Dauerwelle
□ She's got a perm. Sie hat eine Dauerwelle.
■ **to have a perm** sich eine Dauerwelle machen lassen □ I'm going to have a perm. Ich lasse mir eine Dauerwelle machen.

permanent ADJECTIVE
1 dauerhaft *(damage, solution, relationship)*
□ a permanent solution eine dauerhafte Lösung
2 dauernd *(difficulties, tension)*
□ a permanent headache dauernde Kopfschmerzen
3 fest *(job, address)*
□ a permanent job eine feste Arbeit

permission NOUN
die Erlaubnis (PL die Erlaubnisse)
□ to ask somebody's permission jemanden um Erlaubnis bitten
■ **Could I have permission to leave early?** Darf ich früher gehen?

permit NOUN
der Schein (PL die Scheine)
□ a fishing permit ein Angelschein

to **persecute** VERB
verfolgen (PERFECT hat verfolgt)

Persian ADJECTIVE
■ **a Persian cat** eine Perserkatze

persistent ADJECTIVE
hartnäckig *(person)*

person NOUN
1 der Mensch (GEN des Menschen, PL die Menschen)
□ She's a very nice person. Sie ist ein netter Mensch.
2 die Person *(in grammar)*
□ first person singular erste Person Singular
■ **in person** persönlich

personal ADJECTIVE
persönlich

personality NOUN
die Persönlichkeit

personally ADVERB
persönlich
□ I don't know him personally. Ich kenne ihn nicht persönlich. □ Personally I don't agree. Ich persönlich bin nicht einverstanden.

personal stereo NOUN
der Walkman® (PL die Walkmans)

personnel NOUN
das Personal

perspiration NOUN
der Schweiß

to **persuade** VERB
überreden (PERFECT hat überredet)
■ **to persuade somebody to do something** jemanden überreden, etwas zu tun
□ She persuaded me to go with her. Sie hat mich überredet mitzukommen.

Peru NOUN
Peru *neut*

Peruvian ADJECTIVE
peruanisch

pessimist NOUN
der Pessimist (GEN des Pessimisten, PL die Pessimisten)
die Pessimistin
□ I'm a pessimist. Ich bin Pessimist.

pessimistic ADJECTIVE
pessimistisch

pest NOUN
die Nervensäge *(person)*
□ He's a real pest! Er ist eine echte Nervensäge!

to **pester** VERB
belästigen (PERFECT hat belästigt)
□ Stop pestering me! Hör auf, mich zu belästigen!

■ **The children pestered her to take them to the zoo.** Die Kinder ließen ihr keine Ruhe, mit ihnen in den Zoo zu gehen.

pesticide NOUN
das Pestizid

pet NOUN
das Haustier (PL die Haustiere)
□ Have you got a pet? Hast du ein Haustier?
■ **She's the teacher's pet.** Sie ist das Schätzchen der Lehrerin.

petition NOUN
die Petition

petrified ADJECTIVE
■ **to be petrified of something** panische Angst vor etwas haben □ She's petrified of spiders. Sie hat panische Angst vor Spinnen.

petrol NOUN
das Benzin (PL die Benzine)
■ **unleaded petrol** bleifreies Benzin

petrol station NOUN
die Tankstelle

petrol tank NOUN
der Benzintank (PL die Benzintanks)

phantom NOUN
der Geist (PL die Geister)

pharmacy NOUN
die Apotheke

pheasant NOUN
der Fasan (PL die Fasane)

philosophy NOUN
die Philosophie

phobia NOUN
die Phobie

phone NOUN
▷ *see also* **phone** VERB
1 das Telefon (PL die Telefone)
□ Where's the phone? Wo ist das Telefon?
□ Is there a phone here? Gibt es hier ein Telefon?
■ **by phone** telefonisch
2 das Handy (PL die Handys) *(mobile)*
□ I've got a new phone. Ich habe ein neues Handy.
■ **to be on the phone** *(speaking)* telefonieren
□ She's on the phone at the moment. Sie telefoniert gerade.
■ **Can I use the phone, please?** Kann ich mal bitte telefonieren?

to **phone** VERB
▷ *see also* **phone** NOUN
anrufen (IMPERFECT rief an, PERFECT hat angerufen)
□ I tried to phone you yesterday. Ich habe gestern versucht, dich anzurufen.

phone bill NOUN
die Telefonrechnung

phone book NOUN
das Telefonbuch (PL die Telefonbücher)

phone box NOUN
die Telefonzelle

phone call NOUN
der Anruf (PL die Anrufe)
□ There's a phone call for you. Da ist ein Anruf für Sie.
■ **to make a phone call** telefonieren
□ Can I make a phone call? Kann ich telefonieren?

phonecard NOUN
die Telefonkarte

phone number NOUN
die Telefonnummer

photo NOUN
das Foto (PL die Fotos)
□ to take a photo ein Foto machen □ to take a photo of somebody ein Foto von jemandem machen

photocopier NOUN
der Fotokopierer (PL die Fotokopierer)

photocopy NOUN
▷ *see also* **photocopy** VERB
die Fotokopie

to **photocopy** VERB
▷ *see also* **photocopy** NOUN
fotokopieren (PERFECT hat fotokopiert)

photograph NOUN
▷ *see also* **photograph** VERB
das Foto (PL die Fotos)
□ to take a photograph ein Foto machen
□ to take a photograph of somebody ein Foto von jemandem machen

LANGUAGE TIP Be careful not to translate **photograph** by **Fotograf**.

to **photograph** VERB
▷ *see also* **photograph** NOUN
fotografieren (PERFECT hat fotografiert)

photographer NOUN
der Fotograf (GEN des Fotografen, PL die Fotografen)
die Fotografin
□ She's a photographer. Sie ist Fotografin.

photography NOUN
die Fotografie
□ My hobby is photography. Mein Hobby ist die Fotografie.

phrase NOUN
die Wendung

phrase book NOUN
der Sprachführer (PL die Sprachführer)

physical ADJECTIVE
▷ *see also* **physical** NOUN
körperlich *(of the body)*
□ physical exercise körperliche Bewegung
■ **physical education** der Sportunterricht
■ **physical therapist** *(man)* der Krankengymnast

physical NOUN (US)
▷ *see also* **physical** ADJECTIVE
die ärztliche Untersuchung

physicist NOUN
der Physiker (PL die Physiker)
die Physikerin
□ He's a physicist. Er ist Physiker.

physics NOUN
die Physik
□ She teaches physics. Sie unterrichtet Physik.

physiotherapist NOUN
der Krankengymnast (GEN des Krankengymnasten, PL die Krankengymnasten)
die Krankengymnastin

physiotherapy NOUN
die Krankengymnastik

pianist NOUN
der Pianist (GEN des Pianisten, PL die Pianisten)
die Pianistin

piano NOUN
das Klavier (PL die Klaviere)
□ I play the piano. Ich spiele Klavier. □ I have piano lessons. Ich nehme Klavierstunden.

pick NOUN
▷ *see also* **pick** VERB
■ **Take your pick!** Du hast die Wahl!

to **pick** VERB
▷ *see also* **pick** NOUN
1 auswählen (PERFECT hat ausgewählt) *(choose)*
□ I picked the biggest piece. Ich habe das größte Stück ausgewählt.
2 pflücken *(fruit, flowers)*
■ **to pick on somebody** auf jemandem herumhacken □ She's always picking on me. Sie hackt dauernd auf mir herum.
■ **to pick out** auswählen □ I like them all – it's difficult to pick one out. Sie gefallen mir alle – es ist schwierig, eins auszuwählen.
■ **to pick up** **1** *(collect)* abholen □ We'll come to the airport to pick you up. Wir holen dich am Flughafen ab. **2** *(from floor)* aufheben □ Could you help me pick up the toys? Kannst du mir helfen, die Spielsachen aufzuheben? **3** *(learn)* aufschnappen *(informal)* □ I picked up some Spanish during my holiday. Ich habe während der Ferien etwas Spanisch aufgeschnappt.

pickpocket NOUN
der Taschendieb (PL die Taschendiebe)
die Taschendiebin

picnic NOUN
das Picknick (PL die Picknicke)
■ **to have a picnic** picknicken □ We had a picnic on the beach. Wir haben am Strand gepicknickt.

picture NOUN
1 das Bild (PL die Bilder)
□ The books has lots of pictures. Das Buch ist voller Bilder.
■ **to draw a picture of something** etwas zeichnen
2 das Foto (PL die Fotos)
□ My picture was in the paper. Mein Foto war in der Zeitung.
3 das Gemälde (PL die Gemälde) *(painting)*
□ a famous picture ein berühmtes Gemälde
■ **to paint a picture of something** etwas malen
■ **the pictures** *(cinema)* das Kino □ Shall we go to the pictures? Sollen wir ins Kino gehen?

picture messaging NOUN
das Picture Messaging

picturesque ADJECTIVE
malerisch

pie NOUN
1 die Pastete *(savoury)*
2 der Obstkuchen (PL die Obstkuchen) *(sweet)*
■ **an apple pie** ein gedeckter Apfelkuchen

piece NOUN
das Stück (PL die Stücke)
□ A small piece, please. Ein kleines Stück, bitte.
■ **a piece of furniture** ein Möbelstück *neut*
■ **a piece of advice** ein Ratschlag *masc*

pier NOUN
der Pier (PL die Piere)

pierced ADJECTIVE
1 durchstochen
□ I've got pierced ears. Ich habe durchstochene Ohrläppchen.
2 gepierct
□ She's got a pierced nose. Sie hat eine gepiercte Nase.

piercing ADJECTIVE
durchdringend *(cry)*

pig NOUN
das Schwein (PL die Schweine)

pigeon NOUN
die Taube

piggyback NOUN
■ **to give somebody a piggyback** jemanden huckepack nehmen

piggy bank NOUN
das Sparschwein (PL die Sparschweine)

pigtail NOUN
der Zopf (PL die Zöpfe)

pile NOUN
1 der Stapel (PL die Stapel) *(tidy)*
2 der Haufen (PL die Haufen) *(untidy)*

piles PL NOUN
die Hämorriden *pl*

pile-up NOUN
der Auffahrunfall (PL die Auffahrunfälle)

pill NOUN
die Pille
■ **to be on the pill** die Pille nehmen

pillar NOUN
die Säule

pillar box NOUN
der Briefkasten (PL die Briefkästen)

pillow NOUN
das Kopfkissen (PL die Kopfkissen)

pilot NOUN
der Pilot (GEN des Piloten, PL die Piloten)
die Pilotin
□ He's a pilot. Er ist Pilot.

pimple NOUN
der Pickel (PL die Pickel)

pin NOUN
die Stecknadel
■ **I've got pins and needles in my foot.** Mein Fuß ist eingeschlafen.

PIN NOUN *(= personal identification number)*
die PIN-Nummer

pinafore NOUN
die Schürze

pinball NOUN
der Flipper (PL die Flipper)
■ **to play pinball** flippern
■ **a pinball machine** ein Flipper

to **pinch** VERB
1 kneifen (IMPERFECT kniff, PERFECT hat gekniffen)
□ He pinched me! Er hat mich gekniffen!
2 klauen *(informal: steal)*
□ Who's pinched my pen? Wer hat meinen Schreiber geklaut?

pine NOUN
die Kiefer
□ a pine table ein Kieferntisch *masc*

pineapple NOUN
die Ananas (PL die Ananas)

pink ADJECTIVE
rosa
LANGUAGE TIP **rosa** is invariable.
□ a pink shirt ein rosa Hemd

pint NOUN
das Pint (PL die Pints)

DID YOU KNOW...?
In Germany measurements are in litres and centilitres. A pint is about 0.6 litres. German people don't drink pints of beer, they are more likely to order **ein großes Bier**.

■ **to have a pint** ein Bier trinken □ He's gone out for a pint. Er ist ein Bier trinken gegangen.

pipe NOUN
1 das Rohr (PL die Rohre) *(for water, gas)*
□ The pipes froze. Die Rohre sind eingefroren.
2 die Pfeife *(for smoking)*
□ He smokes a pipe. Er raucht Pfeife.
■ **the pipes** *(bagpipes)* der Dudelsack *sing*
□ He plays the pipes. Er spielt Dudelsack.

pirate NOUN
der Pirat (GEN des Piraten, PL die Piraten)

pirated ADJECTIVE
■ **a pirated video** ein Raubvideo *neut*

Pisces SING NOUN
die Fische *masc pl*
□ I'm Pisces. Ich bin Fisch.

pissed ADJECTIVE
besoffen *(informal)*

pissed off ADJECTIVE
■ **I'm pissed off with him.** Ich hab die Schnauze voll von ihm. *(rude)*

pistol NOUN
die Pistole

pitch NOUN
▷ *see also* **pitch** VERB
der Platz (GEN des Platzes, PL die Plätze)
□ a football pitch ein Fußballplatz

to **pitch** VERB
▷ *see also* **pitch** NOUN
aufschlagen (PRESENT schlägt auf, IMPERFECT schlug auf, PERFECT hat aufgeschlagen) *(tent)*
□ We pitched our tent near the beach. Wir haben unser Zelt in der Nähe des Strandes aufgeschlagen.

pity NOUN
▷ *see also* **pity** VERB
das Mitleid
■ **What a pity!** Wie schade!

to **pity** VERB
▷ *see also* **pity** NOUN
bemitleiden (PERFECT hat bemitleidet)

pizza NOUN
die Pizza (PL die Pizzas)

place NOUN
▷ *see also* **place** VERB
1 der Ort (PL die Orte) *(location)*
□ It's a quiet place. Es ist ein ruhiger Ort.
□ interesting places interessante Orte
2 der Platz (GEN des Platzes, PL die Plätze) *(space)*
□ a parking place ein Parkplatz □ a university place ein Studienplatz
■ **to change places** die Plätze tauschen
□ Tamsin, change places with Christine! Tamsin, tausch die Plätze mit Christine!
■ **to take place** stattfinden
■ **at your place** bei dir □ Shall we meet at your place? Sollen wir uns bei dir treffen?
■ **to my place** zu mir □ Do you want to come round to my place? Willst du noch zu mir mitkommen?

to **place** VERB
▷ *see also* **place** NOUN
legen
□ He placed his hand on hers. Er legte seine Hand auf ihre.
■ **He was placed third.** Er wurde Dritter.

plaid ADJECTIVE
kariert
□ a plaid shirt ein kariertes Hemd

plain NOUN
▷ *see also* **plain** ADJECTIVE
die Ebene

plain ADJECTIVE, ADVERB
▷ *see also* **plain** NOUN
1 einfarbig *(self-coloured)*
□ a plain carpet ein einfarbiger Teppich
2 einfach *(not fancy)*
□ a plain white blouse eine einfache weiße Bluse

plain chocolate NOUN
die bittere Schokolade

plait NOUN
der Zopf (PL die Zöpfe)
□ She wears her hair in a plait. Sie trägt einen Zopf.

plan NOUN
▷ *see also* **plan** VERB
der Plan (PL die Pläne)
□ What are your plans for the holidays? Welche Ferienpläne habt ihr? □ to make plans Pläne machen □ a plan of the campsite ein Plan des Zeltplatzes
■ **Everything went according to plan.** Alles lief nach Plan.
■ **my essay plan** das Konzept für meinen Aufsatz

to **plan** VERB
▷ *see also* **plan** NOUN
planen
□ We're planning a trip to Germany. Wir planen eine Reise nach Deutschland. □ Plan your revision carefully. Plant eure Stoffwiederholung sorgfältig.
■ **to plan to do something** vorhaben, etwas zu tun □ I'm planning to get a job in the holidays. Ich habe vor, mir einen Ferienjob zu suchen.

plane NOUN
das Flugzeug (PL die Flugzeuge)
□ by plane mit dem Flugzeug

planet NOUN
der Planet (GEN des Planeten, PL die Planeten)

planning NOUN
die Planung
■ **family planning** die Familienplanung
■ **The trip needs careful planning.** Die Reise muss sorgfältig geplant werden.

plant NOUN
▷ *see also* **plant** VERB
1 die Pflanze
□ to water the plants die Pflanzen gießen
2 die Fabrik *(factory)*

to **plant** VERB
▷ *see also* **plant** NOUN
pflanzen

plant pot NOUN
der Blumentopf (PL die Blumentöpfe)

plaque NOUN
1 die Gedenktafel *(to famous person, event)*
2 der Zahnbelag *(on teeth)*

plaster NOUN
1 das Pflaster (PL die Pflaster) *(sticking plaster)*
□ Have you got a plaster? Hast du ein Pflaster?
2 der Gips (GEN des Gipses, PL die Gipse) *(for fracture)*
□ Her leg's in plaster. Sie hat das Bein in Gips.

plastic NOUN
▷ *see also* **plastic** ADJECTIVE
das Plastik
□ It's made of plastic. Es ist aus Plastik.

plastic ADJECTIVE
▷ *see also* **plastic** NOUN
aus Plastik
□ a plastic mac ein Regenmantel aus Plastik
■ **a plastic bag** eine Plastiktüte

plate NOUN
der Teller (PL die Teller) *(for food)*

platform NOUN
1 der Bahnsteig (PL die Bahnsteige) *(at station)*
□ on platform seven auf Bahnsteig sieben
2 das Podium (PL die Podien) *(for performers)*

play NOUN
▷ *see also* **play** VERB
das Stück (PL die Stücke)
□ a play by Shakespeare ein Stück von Shakespeare □ to put on a play ein Stück aufführen

to **play** VERB
▷ *see also* **play** NOUN
1 spielen
□ He's playing with his friends. Er spielt mit seinen Freunden. □ What sort of music do they play? Welche Art von Musik spielen sie? □ I play hockey. Ich spiele Hockey. □ I play the guitar. Ich spiele Gitarre. □ She's always playing that record. Sie spielt dauernd diese Platte.
2 spielen gegen *(against person, team)*
□ Germany are playing Scotland. Deutschland spielt gegen Schottland.

to **play down** VERB
herunterspielen (PERFECT hat heruntergespielt)
□ He tried to play down his illness. Er versuchte, die Schwere seiner Krankheit herunterzuspielen.

player NOUN
der Spieler (PL die Spieler)
die Spielerin
□ a football player ein Fußballspieler

playful ADJECTIVE
verspielt

playground NOUN
1 der Schulhof (PL die Schulhöfe) *(at school)*
2 der Spielplatz (GEN des Spielplatzes, PL die Spielplätze) *(in park)*

playgroup NOUN
die Spielgruppe

playing card NOUN
die Spielkarte

playing field NOUN
der Sportplatz (GEN des Sportplatzes, PL die Sportplätze)

playtime NOUN
die Pause

to **play up** VERB
■ **The engine's playing up.** Der Motor macht Schwierigkeiten.

playwright NOUN
der Dramatiker (PL die Dramatiker)
die Dramatikerin

pleasant ADJECTIVE
angenehm

please EXCLAMATION
bitte
□ Two coffees, please. Zwei Kaffee bitte.

pleased ADJECTIVE
1 erfreut *(happy)*

□ My mother's not going to be very pleased. Meine Mutter wird nicht sehr erfreut sein.

2 zufrieden *(satisfied)*

□ It's beautiful, she'll be pleased with it. Es ist wunderschön, sie wird damit sehr zufrieden sein.

■ **to be pleased about something** sich über etwas freuen □ Are you pleased about the exam results? Freust du dich über die Prüfungsergebnisse?

■ **Pleased to meet you!** Angenehm!

pleasure NOUN

das Vergnügen (PL die Vergnügen)

□ I read for pleasure. Ich lese zum Vergnügen.

plenty NOUN

mehr als genug

□ I've got plenty. Ich habe mehr als genug.

□ That's plenty, thanks. Danke, das ist mehr als genug.

■ **I've got plenty to do.** Ich habe viel zu tun.

■ **plenty of** 1 viele □ plenty of opportunities viele Möglichkeiten 2 *(more than enough)* genügend □ I've got plenty of money. Ich habe genügend Geld. □ We've got plenty of time. Wir haben genügend Zeit.

pliers PL NOUN

die Zange *sing*

■ **a pair of pliers** eine Zange

plot NOUN

▷ *see also* **plot** VERB

1 die Handlung *(of story, play)*

2 die Verschwörung *(against somebody)*

□ a plot against the president eine Verschwörung gegen den Präsidenten

■ **a plot of land** ein Stück Land *neut*

■ **a vegetable plot** ein Gemüsebeet *neut*

to **plot** VERB

▷ *see also* **plot** NOUN

planen

□ They were plotting to kill him. Sie planten, ihn zu töten.

plough NOUN

▷ *see also* **plough** VERB

der Pflug (PL die Pflüge)

to **plough** VERB

▷ *see also* **plough** NOUN

pflügen

plug NOUN

1 der Stecker (PL die Stecker) *(electrical)*

□ The plug is faulty. Der Stecker ist kaputt.

2 der Stöpsel (PL die Stöpsel) *(for sink)*

to **plug in** VERB

einstecken (PERFECT hat eingesteckt)

□ Is it plugged in? Ist es eingesteckt?

plum NOUN

die Pflaume

□ plum jam die Pflaumenmarmelade

plumber NOUN

der Klempner (PL die Klempner)

die Klempnerin

□ He's a plumber. Er ist Klempner.

plump ADJECTIVE

rundlich

to **plunge** VERB

tauchen

plural NOUN

der Plural (PL die Plurale)

plus PREPOSITION, ADJECTIVE

plus

□ four plus three equals seven. Vier plus drei macht sieben. □ I got a B plus. Ich habe eine Zwei plus bekommen.

> **DID YOU KNOW...?**
> In Germany, grades are given from 1 to 6, with 1 being the best.

■ **three children plus a dog** drei Kinder und ein Hund

p.m. ABBREVIATION

■ **at eight p.m.** um acht Uhr abends

> **DID YOU KNOW...?**
> In Germany times are often given using the 24-hour clock.

□ at two p.m. um vierzehn Uhr

pneumonia NOUN

die Lungenentzündung

poached ADJECTIVE

■ **a poached egg** ein verlorenes Ei *neut*

pocket NOUN

die Tasche

■ **pocket money** das Taschengeld

□ eight pounds a week pocket money acht Pfund Taschengeld pro Woche

pocket calculator NOUN

der Taschenrechner (PL die Taschenrechner)

podcast NOUN

der Podcast (PL die Podcasts)

□ to download a podcast einen Podcast herunterladen

poem NOUN

das Gedicht (PL die Gedichte)

poet NOUN

der Dichter (PL die Dichter)

die Dichterin

poetry NOUN

die Gedichte *neut pl*

□ to write poetry Gedichte schreiben

point NOUN

▷ *see also* **point** VERB

1 der Punkt (PL die Punkte) *(spot, score)*

□ a point on the horizon ein Punkt am Horizont □ They scored five points. Sie machten fünf Punkte.

2 die Bemerkung *(comment)*

□ He made some interesting points. Er machte ein paar interessante Bemerkungen.

3 die Spitze *(tip)*

□ a pencil with a sharp point ein Bleistift mit einer scharfen Spitze

4 der Zeitpunkt *(in time)*

□ At that point, we were three one up. Zu dem Zeitpunkt lagen wir mit drei zu eins in Führung.
■ **a point of view** ein Gesichtspunkt *masc*
■ **to get the point** begreifen □ I don't get the point. Ich begreife das nicht.
■ **That's a good point!** Da hast du recht.
■ **There's no point.** Das hat keinen Wert.
□ There's no point in waiting. Es hat keinen Wert zu warten.
■ **What's the point?** Wozu? □ What's the point of leaving so early? Wozu so früh gehen?
■ **Punctuality isn't my strong point.** Pünktlichkeit ist nicht meine Stärke.
■ **two point five (2.5)** zwei Komma fünf (2,5)

to **point** VERB
▷ *see also* **point** NOUN
mit dem Finger zeigen
□ Don't point! Man zeigt nicht mit dem Finger!
■ **to point at somebody** auf jemanden zeigen □ She pointed at Anne. Sie zeigte auf Anne.
■ **to point a gun at somebody** auf jemanden mit der Waffe zielen
■ **to point something out 1** *(show)* auf etwas zeigen □ The guide pointed out Big Ben. Unser Führer zeigte auf Big Ben. **2** *(mention)* auf etwas hinweisen □ I should point out that ... Ich möchte darauf hinweisen, dass ...

pointless ADJECTIVE
nutzlos
□ It's pointless to argue. Es ist nutzlos zu streiten.

poison NOUN
▷ *see also* **poison** VERB
das Gift (PL die Gifte)

to **poison** VERB
▷ *see also* **poison** NOUN
vergiften (PERFECT hat vergiftet)

poisonous ADJECTIVE
giftig

to **poke** VERB
■ **He poked me in the eye.** Er stieß mir ins Auge.

poker NOUN
das Poker
□ I play poker. Ich spiele Poker.

Poland NOUN
Polen *neut*
■ **from Poland** aus Polen
■ **to Poland** nach Polen

polar bear NOUN
der Eisbär (GEN des Eisbären, PL die Eisbären)

Pole NOUN
der Pole (GEN des Polen, PL die Polen)
die Polin *(Polish person)*

pole NOUN
der Mast (PL die Masten)
□ a telegraph pole ein Telegrafenmast
■ **a tent pole** eine Zeltstange
■ **a ski pole** ein Skistock *masc*
■ **the North Pole** der Nordpol
■ **the South Pole** der Südpol

pole vault NOUN
das Stabhochspringen

police PL NOUN
die Polizei
□ We called the police. Wir haben die Polizei gerufen.

LANGUAGE TIP Note that 'police' is used with a plural verb and **Polizei** with a singular verb.

□ The police haven't arrived yet. Die Polizei ist noch nicht da.
■ **a police car** ein Polizeiwagen *masc*
■ **a police station** ein Polizeirevier *neut*

policeman NOUN
der Polizist (GEN des Polizisten, PL die Polizisten)
□ He's a policeman. Er ist Polizist.

policewoman NOUN
die Polizistin
□ She's a policewoman. Sie ist Polizistin.

polio NOUN
die Kinderlähmung

Polish ADJECTIVE
▷ *see also* **Polish** NOUN
polnisch
■ **He's Polish.** Er ist Pole.
■ **She's Polish.** Sie ist Polin.

Polish NOUN
▷ *see also* **Polish** ADJECTIVE
das Polnisch (GEN des Polnischen) *(language)*

polish NOUN
▷ *see also* **polish** VERB
1 die Schuhcreme (PL die Schuhcremes) *(for shoes)*
2 die Politur *(for furniture)*

to **polish** VERB
▷ *see also* **polish** NOUN
1 eincremen (PERFECT hat eingecremt) *(shoes)*
2 polieren (PERFECT hat poliert) *(glass, furniture)*

polite ADJECTIVE
höflich

politely ADVERB
höflich

politeness NOUN
die Höflichkeit

political ADJECTIVE
politisch

politician NOUN
der Politiker (PL die Politiker)
die Politikerin

politics PL NOUN
die Politik
□ I'm not interested in politics. Ich interessiere mich nicht für Politik.

poll NOUN
die Umfrage
□ The poll revealed that ... Die Umfrage ergab, dass ...

pollen NOUN
der Pollen (PL die Pollen)
to **pollute** VERB
verschmutzen (PERFECT hat verschmutzt)
polluted ADJECTIVE
verschmutzt
pollution NOUN
die Umweltverschmutzung
■ **air pollution** die Luftverschmutzung
polo-necked sweater NOUN
der Rollkragenpullover
(PL die Rollkragenpullover)
polo shirt NOUN
das Polohemd (PL die Polohemden)
polythene bag NOUN
die Plastiktüte
pond NOUN
der Teich (PL die Teiche)
□ We've got a pond in our garden. Wir haben einen Teich im Garten.
pony NOUN
das Pony (PL die Ponys)
ponytail NOUN
der Pferdeschwanz (GEN des Pferdeschwanzes, PL die Pferdeschwänze)
□ He's got a ponytail. Er hat einen Pferdeschwanz.
pony trekking NOUN
■ **to go pony trekking** Pony reiten gehen
poodle NOUN
der Pudel (PL die Pudel)
pool NOUN
1 die Pfütze *(puddle)*
2 der Teich (PL die Teiche) *(pond)*
3 das Schwimmbecken (PL die Schwimmbecken) *(for swimming)*
4 das Poolbillard *(game)*
□ Shall we have a game of pool? Sollen wir eine Partie Poolbillard spielen?
■ **the pools** *(football)* das Toto □ to do the pools Toto spielen
poor ADJECTIVE
1 arm
□ a poor family eine arme Familie □ They are poorer than we are. Sie sind ärmer als wir.
□ Poor David! Der arme David!
■ **the poor** die Armen *masc pl*
2 schlecht *(bad)*
□ a poor mark eine schlechte Note
poorly ADJECTIVE
■ **She's poorly.** Es geht ihr schlecht.
pop ADJECTIVE
■ **pop music** die Popmusik
■ **a pop star** ein Popstar *masc*
■ **a pop group** eine Popgruppe
■ **a pop song** ein Popsong *masc*
to **pop in** VERB
vorbeikommen (IMPERFECT kam vorbei, PERFECT ist vorbeigekommen)
to **pop out** VERB
kurz weggehen (IMPERFECT ging weg, PERFECT ist weggegangen)
□ I'm just popping out for an hour. Ich gehe nur mal kurz für eine Stunde weg.
to **pop round** VERB
■ **I'm just popping round to John's.** Ich gehe nur mal kurz zu John.
popcorn NOUN
das Popcorn
pope NOUN
der Papst (PL die Päpste)
poppy NOUN
der Mohn
Popsicle® NOUN (US)
das Eis am Stiel (GEN des Eises am Stiel, PL die Eis am Stiel)
popular ADJECTIVE
beliebt
□ She's a very popular girl. Sie ist sehr beliebt.
population NOUN
die Bevölkerung
porch NOUN
die Veranda (PL die Veranden)
pork NOUN
das Schweinefleisch
□ I don't eat pork. Ich esse kein Schweinefleisch.
■ **a pork chop** ein Schweinekotelett *neut*
porn NOUN
▷ *see also* **porn** ADJECTIVE
die Pornografie
porn ADJECTIVE
▷ *see also* **porn** NOUN
■ **a porn film** ein Pornofilm *masc*
■ **a porn mag** ein Pornoheft *neut*
pornographic ADJECTIVE
pornografisch
□ a pornographic magazine eine pornografische Zeitschrift
pornography NOUN
die Pornografie
porridge NOUN
der Haferbrei
port NOUN
1 der Hafen (PL die Häfen) *(harbour)*
2 der Portwein *(wine)*
□ a glass of port ein Glas Portwein
portable ADJECTIVE
tragbar
□ a portable TV ein tragbarer Fernseher
porter NOUN
1 der Portier (PL die Portiers) *(in hotel)*
2 der Gepäckträger (PL die Gepäckträger) *(at station)*
portion NOUN
die Portion
□ a large portion of chips eine große Portion Pommes frites
portrait NOUN
das Porträt (PL die Porträts)

Portugal NOUN
Portugal *neut*
■ **from Portugal** aus Portugal
■ **to Portugal** nach Portugal

Portuguese ADJECTIVE
▷ *see also* **Portuguese** NOUN
portugiesisch
■ **She's Portuguese.** Sie ist Portugiesin.

Portuguese NOUN
▷ *see also* **Portuguese** ADJECTIVE
1 der Portugiese (GEN des Portugiesen, PL die Portugiesen)
die Portugiesin *(person)*
2 das Portugiesisch (GEN des Portugiesischen) *(language)*

posh ADJECTIVE
vornehm
□ a posh hotel ein vornehmes Hotel

position NOUN
die Stellung
□ an uncomfortable position eine unbequeme Stellung

positive ADJECTIVE
1 positiv *(good)*
□ a positive attitude eine positive Einstellung
2 ganz sicher *(sure)*
□ I'm positive. Ich bin ganz sicher.

to **possess** VERB
besitzen (IMPERFECT besaß, PERFECT hat besessen)

possession NOUN
■ **Have you got all your possessions?** Hast du all deine Sachen?

possibility NOUN
die Möglichkeit
□ It's a possibility. Das ist eine Möglichkeit.

possible ADJECTIVE
möglich
□ as soon as possible sobald wie möglich

possibly ADVERB
vielleicht *(perhaps)*
□ Are you coming to the party? — Possibly. Kommst du zur Party? — Vielleicht.
■ **... if you possibly can.** ... wenn du irgend kannst.
■ **I can't possibly come.** Ich kann unmöglich kommen.

post NOUN
▷ *see also* **post** VERB
1 die Post *(letters)*
□ Is there any post for me? Ist Post für mich da?
2 der Pfosten (PL die Pfosten) *(pole)*
□ The ball hit the post. Der Ball traf den Pfosten.

to **post** VERB
▷ *see also* **post** NOUN
aufgeben (PRESENT gibt auf, IMPERFECT gab auf, PERFECT hat aufgegeben)
□ I've got some cards to post. Ich muss ein paar Karten aufgeben.

postage NOUN
das Porto (PL die Portos)

postbox NOUN
der Briefkasten (PL die Briefkästen)

postcard NOUN
die Postkarte

postcode NOUN
die Postleitzahl

DID YOU KNOW...?
German postcodes consist of a 5-figure number which precedes the name of the city.

poster NOUN
1 das Poster (PL die Poster)
□ I've got posters on my bedroom walls. Ich habe in meinem Zimmer Poster an den Wänden.
2 das Plakat (PL die Plakate) *(advertising)*
□ There are posters all over town. In der ganzen Stadt hängen Plakate.

postman NOUN
der Briefträger (PL die Briefträger)
□ He's a postman. Er ist Briefträger.

postmark NOUN
der Stempel (PL die Stempel)

post office NOUN
das Postamt (PL die Postämter)
□ Where's the post office, please? Wo ist das Postamt, bitte?
■ **She works for the post office.** Sie arbeitet bei der Post.

to **postpone** VERB
verschieben (IMPERFECT verschob, PERFECT hat verschoben)
□ The match has been postponed. Das Spiel wurde verschoben.

postwoman NOUN
die Briefträgerin
□ She's a postwoman. Sie ist Briefträgerin.

pot NOUN
1 der Topf (PL die Töpfe)
□ a pot of jam ein Marmeladentopf
2 die Kanne *(for hot drinks)*
3 das Gras *(marijuana)*
□ to smoke pot Gras rauchen
■ **pots and pans** Töpfe und Pfannen

potato NOUN
die Kartoffel
□ a baked potato eine gebackene Kartoffel
□ potato salad der Kartoffelsalat
■ **mashed potatoes** der Kartoffelbrei
■ **potato chips** die Kartoffelchips *masc pl*

potential NOUN
▷ *see also* **potential** ADJECTIVE
■ **He has great potential.** Er ist sehr vielversprechend.

potential ADJECTIVE
▷ *see also* **potential** NOUN
möglich
□ a potential problem ein mögliches Problem

pothole NOUN
das Schlagloch (PL die Schlaglöcher) *(in road)*

pot plant NOUN
die Topfpflanze

pottery NOUN
die Keramik

pound NOUN
▷ *see also* **pound** VERB
das Pfund (PL die Pfunde *or* Pfund) *(weight, money)*

LANGUAGE TIP When talking about an amount of money or specifying a quantity of something use the plural form **Pfund**.

□ two pounds of carrots zwei Pfund Karotten □ How many euros do you get for a pound? Wie viel Euro bekommt man für ein Pfund? □ a pound coin eine Pfundmünze

to **pound** VERB
▷ *see also* **pound** NOUN
pochen
□ My heart was pounding. Mein Herz hat gepocht.

to **pour** VERB
gießen (IMPERFECT goss, PERFECT hat gegossen) *(liquid)*
□ She poured some water into the pan. Sie goss etwas Wasser in den Topf.
□ It's pouring. Es gießt.
■ **She poured him a drink.** Sie goss ihm einen Drink ein.
■ **Shall I pour you a cup of tea?** Soll ich Ihnen eine Tasse Tee einschenken?
■ **in the pouring rain** im strömenden Regen

poverty NOUN
die Armut

powder NOUN
1 das Pulver
2 der Puder (PL die Puder) *(face powder)*

power NOUN
1 der Strom *(electricity)*
□ The power's off. Es gibt keinen Strom.
■ **a power cut** ein Stromausfall *masc*
■ **a power point** eine Steckdose
■ **a power station** ein Kraftwerk *neut*
2 die Energie *(energy)*
□ nuclear power die Kernenergie
□ solar power die Sonnenenergie
3 die Macht (PL die Mächte) *(authority)*
□ to be in power an der Macht sein

powerful ADJECTIVE
1 mächtig
□ a powerful man ein mächtiger Mann
2 kräftig *(physically)*
3 leistungsstark *(machine)*

practical ADJECTIVE
praktisch
□ a practical suggestion ein praktischer Vorschlag □ She's very practical. Sie ist sehr praktisch.

practically ADVERB
praktisch
□ It's practically impossible. Es ist praktisch unmöglich.

practice NOUN
1 das Training *(for sport)*
□ football practice das Fußballtraining
2 die Übung
□ You need more practice. Du brauchst mehr Übung.
■ **I've got to do my piano practice.** Ich muss Klavier üben.
■ **It's normal practice in our school.** Das ist in unserer Schule so üblich.
■ **in practice** in der Praxis
■ **a medical practice** eine Arztpraxis

to **practise** VERB
1 üben *(music, hobby, language)*
□ I ought to practise more. Ich sollte mehr üben. □ I practise the flute every evening. Ich übe jeden Abend Flöte. □ I practised my German when we were on holiday. Ich habe in den Ferien mein Deutsch geübt.
2 trainieren (PERFECT hat trainiert) *(sport)*
□ The team practises on Thursdays. Die Mannschaft trainiert donnerstags. □ I don't practise enough. Ich trainiere nicht genug.

practising ADJECTIVE
praktizierend
□ She's a practising Catholic. Sie ist praktizierende Katholikin.

to **praise** VERB
loben
□ The teacher praised her work. Der Lehrer lobte ihre Arbeit.

pram NOUN
der Kinderwagen (PL die Kinderwagen)

prawn NOUN
die Garnele

prawn cocktail NOUN
der Krabbencocktail (PL die Krabbencocktails)

to **pray** VERB
beten
□ to pray for something für etwas beten

prayer NOUN
das Gebet (PL die Gebete)

precaution NOUN
die Vorsichtsmaßnahme
□ to take precautions Vorsichtsmaßnahmen treffen

preceding ADJECTIVE
vorherig

precinct NOUN
■ **a shopping precinct** ein Einkaufsviertel *neut*
■ **a pedestrian precinct** eine Fußgängerzone

precious ADJECTIVE
kostbar

precise ADJECTIVE
genau

□ at that precise moment genau in diesem Augenblick

precisely ADVERB
genau
□ Precisely! Genau!
■ **at ten o'clock precisely** um Punkt zehn Uhr

to **predict** VERB
vorhersagen (PERFECT hat vorhergesagt)

predictable ADJECTIVE
vorhersehbar

prefect NOUN
DID YOU KNOW...?
German schools do not have prefects.
■ **My sister's a prefect.** Meine Schwester ist im letzten Schuljahr und führt die Aufsicht bei den Jüngeren.

to **prefer** VERB
lieber mögen (PRESENT mag lieber, IMPERFECT mochte lieber, PERFECT hat lieber gemocht)
□ Which would you prefer? Was magst du lieber? □ I prefer German to chemistry. Ich mag Deutsch lieber als Chemie.
■ **I preferred the first version.** Die erste Version hat mir besser gefallen.

preference NOUN
die Vorliebe
□ his preference for detective stories seine Vorliebe für Kriminalromane

pregnant ADJECTIVE
schwanger
□ She's six months pregnant. Sie ist im siebten Monat schwanger.

prehistoric ADJECTIVE
prähistorisch

prejudice NOUN
1 das Vorurteil (PL die Vorurteile)
□ That's just a prejudice. Das ist ein Vorurteil.
2 die Vorurteile *neut pl*
□ There's a lot of racial prejudice. Es gibt viele Rassenvorurteile.

prejudiced ADJECTIVE
voreingenommen
■ **to be prejudiced against somebody** gegen jemanden voreingenommen sein

premature ADJECTIVE
verfrüht
■ **a premature baby** eine Frühgeburt

Premier League NOUN
die erste Liga
□ in the Premier League in der ersten Liga
DID YOU KNOW...?
The 'Premier League' is similar to the German **Bundesliga**.

premises PL NOUN
die Geschäftsräume *masc pl*
□ They're moving to new premises. Sie ziehen in neue Geschäftsräume um.

premonition NOUN
die Vorahnung

preoccupied ADJECTIVE
■ **He's preoccupied with his exams.** Er denkt nur an seine Prüfungen.

prep NOUN
die Hausaufgaben *fem pl (homework)*
□ history prep die Hausaufgaben in Geschichte

preparation NOUN
die Vorbereitung

to **prepare** VERB
vorbereiten (PERFECT hat vorbereitet)
□ She prepares lessons in the evening. Abends bereitet sie Stunden vor.
■ **to prepare for something** Vorbereitungen für etwas treffen □ We're preparing for our holiday. Wir treffen Vorbereitungen für unseren Urlaub.

prepared ADJECTIVE
■ **to be prepared to do something** bereit sein, etwas zu tun □ I'm prepared to help you. Ich bin bereit, dir zu helfen.

prep school NOUN
die private Grundschule

Presbyterian NOUN
▷ *see also* **Presbyterian** ADJECTIVE
der Presbyterianer (PL die Presbyterianer)
die Presbyterianerin
□ She is a Presbyterian. Sie ist Presbyterianerin.

Presbyterian ADJECTIVE
▷ *see also* **Presbyterian** NOUN
presbyterianisch

to **prescribe** VERB
verschreiben (IMPERFECT verschrieb, PERFECT hat verschrieben) *(medicine)*
□ He prescribed me a course of antibiotics. Er hat mir eine Antibiotikakur verschrieben.

prescription NOUN
das Rezept (PL die Rezepte)
□ You can't get it without a prescription. Das bekommt man nicht ohne Rezept.

presence NOUN
die Anwesenheit
■ **presence of mind** die Geistesgegenwart

present ADJECTIVE
▷ *see also* **present** NOUN, VERB
1 anwesend *(in attendance)*
□ He wasn't present at the meeting. Er war bei der Besprechung nicht anwesend.
2 gegenwärtig *(current)*
□ the present situation die gegenwärtige Situation
■ **the present tense** die Gegenwart

present NOUN
▷ *see also* **present** ADJECTIVE, VERB
1 das Geschenk (PL die Geschenke) *(gift)*
□ I'm going to buy presents. Ich kaufe Geschenke.
■ **to give somebody a present** jemandem etwas schenken

2 die Gegenwart *(time)*
□ She was living in the past not the present. Sie lebte in der Vergangenheit, nicht in der Gegenwart.
■ **up to the present** bis heute
■ **for the present** momentan
■ **at present** im Augenblick
■ **the present tense** das Präsens

to **present** VERB
▷ *see also* **present** ADJECTIVE, NOUN
■ **to present somebody with something** *(prize, medal)* jemandem etwas verleihen

presenter NOUN
der Moderator (PL die Moderatoren)
die Moderatorin *(on TV)*

presently ADVERB
1 sofort *(soon)*
□ You'll feel better presently. Sie werden sich sofort besser fühlen.
2 im Moment *(at present)*
□ They're presently on tour. Sie sind im Moment auf Tournee.

president NOUN
der Präsident (GEN des Präsidenten, PL die Präsidenten)
die Präsidentin

press NOUN
▷ *see also* **press** VERB
die Presse
■ **a press conference** eine Pressekonferenz

to **press** VERB
▷ *see also* **press** NOUN
1 drücken
□ Don't press too hard! Nicht zu fest drücken!
2 treten auf *+acc* (PRESENT tritt auf, IMPERFECT trat, PERFECT hat getreten)
□ He pressed the accelerator. Er trat aufs Gaspedal.

pressed ADJECTIVE
■ **We are pressed for time.** Wir haben wenig Zeit.

press-up NOUN
der Liegestütz (GEN des Liegestützes, PL die Liegestütze)
□ I do twenty press-ups every morning. Ich mache jeden Morgen zwanzig Liegestütze.

pressure NOUN
▷ *see also* **pressure** VERB
der Druck
□ He's under a lot of pressure. Er steht unter viel Druck.
■ **a pressure group 1** *(small-scale, local)* eine Bürgerinitiative **2** *(large-scale, more political)* eine Pressure-Group

to **pressure** VERB
▷ *see also* **pressure** NOUN
Druck ausüben auf *+acc* (PERFECT hat Druck ausgeübt)
□ They are pressuring me. Sie üben Druck auf mich aus.

prestige NOUN
das Ansehen

prestigious ADJECTIVE
angesehen

presumably ADVERB
vermutlich

to **presume** VERB
annehmen (PRESENT nimmt an, IMPERFECT nahm an, PERFECT hat angenommen)
□ I presume so. Das nehme ich an.

to **pretend** VERB
■ **to pretend to do something** so tun, als ob man etwas täte

LANGUAGE TIP Note that **als ob** is followed by the subjunctive.

□ He pretended to be asleep. Er tat so, als ob er schliefe.

pretty ADJECTIVE, ADVERB
1 hübsch
□ She's very pretty. Sie ist sehr hübsch.
2 ziemlich *(rather)*
□ That film was pretty bad. Der Film war ziemlich schlecht.
■ **It's pretty much the same.** Das ist mehr oder weniger dasselbe.

to **prevent** VERB
verhindern (PERFECT hat verhindert)
■ **to prevent somebody from doing something** jemanden davon abhalten, etwas zu tun □ They tried to prevent us from smoking. Sie haben versucht, uns vom Rauchen abzuhalten.

previous ADJECTIVE
vorherig

previously ADVERB
früher

prey NOUN
die Beute
■ **a bird of prey** ein Raubvogel *masc*

price NOUN
der Preis (GEN des Preises, PL die Preise)

price list NOUN
die Preisliste

to **prick** VERB
stechen (PRESENT sticht, IMPERFECT stach, PERFECT hat gestochen)
□ I've pricked my finger. Ich habe mir in den Finger gestochen.

pride NOUN
der Stolz (GEN des Stolzes)

priest NOUN
der Priester (PL die Priester)
□ He's a priest. Er ist Priester.

primarily ADVERB
vor allem

primary ADJECTIVE
hauptsächlich

primary school NOUN
die Grundschule

English-German

DID YOU KNOW...?
Children in Germany begin **Grundschule** at the age of 6. The **Grundschule** provides primary education in school years 1 to 4.

□ She's still at primary school. Sie ist noch in der Grundschule.

prime minister NOUN
der Premierminister (PL die Premierminister)
die Premierministerin

primitive ADJECTIVE
primitiv

prince NOUN
der Prinz (GEN des Prinzen, PL die Prinzen)
□ the Prince of Wales der Prinz von Wales

princess NOUN
die Prinzessin
□ Princess Anne Prinzessin Anne

principal ADJECTIVE
▷ *see also* **principal** NOUN
■ **the principal reason** der Hauptgrund
■ **my principal concern** mein Hauptanliegen *neut*

principal NOUN
▷ *see also* **principal** ADJECTIVE
der Direktor (PL die Direktoren)
die Direktorin *(of college)*

principle NOUN
das Prinzip (PL die Prinzipien)
■ **on principle** aus Prinzip

print NOUN
1 der Abzug (PL die Abzüge) *(photo)*
□ colour prints Farbabzüge
2 die Schrift *(letters)*
■ **in small print** klein gedruckt
3 der Fingerabdruck (PL die Fingerabdrücke) *(fingerprint)*
4 der Kunstdruck (PL die Kunstdrucke) *(picture)*
□ a framed print ein gerahmter Kunstdruck

printer NOUN
der Drucker (PL die Drucker) *(machine)*

printout NOUN
der Ausdruck (PL die Ausdrucke)

priority NOUN
die Priorität

prison NOUN
das Gefängnis (GEN des Gefängnisses, PL die Gefängnisse)
■ **in prison** im Gefängnis

prisoner NOUN
der Gefangene (GEN des Gefangenen, PL die Gefangenen)
die Gefangene (GEN der Gefangenen)
□ a prisoner *(man)* ein Gefangener

prison officer NOUN
der Gefängniswärter (PL die Gefängniswärter)
die Gefängniswärterin

privacy NOUN
das Privatleben
□ an invasion of my privacy ein Eingriff in mein Privatleben

private ADJECTIVE
privat
■ **a private school** eine Privatschule
■ **private property** das Privateigentum
■ **'private'** *(on envelope)* 'persönlich'
■ **a private bathroom** ein eigenes Badezimmer
■ **I have private lessons.** Ich bekomme Nachhilfestunden.

to **privatize** VERB
privatisieren (PERFECT hat privatisiert)

privilege NOUN
das Privileg (PL die Privilegien)

prize NOUN
der Preis (GEN des Preises, PL die Preise)
□ to win a prize einen Preis gewinnen

prize-giving NOUN
die Preisverleihung

prizewinner NOUN
der Preisträger (PL die Preisträger)
die Preisträgerin

pro NOUN
der Profi (PL die Profis)

LANGUAGE TIP **der Profi** is also used for women.

□ This was her first year as a pro. Dies war ihr erstes Jahr als Profi.
■ **the pros and cons** das Für und Wider
□ We weighed up the pros and cons. Wir haben das Für und Wider abgewogen.

probability NOUN
die Wahrscheinlichkeit

probable ADJECTIVE
wahrscheinlich

probably ADVERB
wahrscheinlich
□ probably not wahrscheinlich nicht

problem NOUN
das Problem (PL die Probleme)
□ No problem! Kein Problem!

proceeds PL NOUN
der Erlös *sing* (GEN des Erlöses, PL die Erlöse)

process NOUN
der Prozess (GEN des Prozesses, PL die Prozesse)
□ the peace process der Friedensprozess
■ **to be in the process of doing something** gerade dabei sein, etwas zu tun □ We're in the process of painting the kitchen. Wir sind gerade dabei, die Küche zu streichen.

procession NOUN
die Prozession *(religious)*

to **produce** VERB
1 herstellen (PERFECT hat hergestellt) *(manufacture)*
2 inszenieren (PERFECT hat inszeniert) *(play, show)*
3 produzieren (PERFECT hat produziert) *(film)*

producer NOUN
1 der Regisseur (PL die Regisseure)
die Regisseurin *(of play, show)*
2 der Produzent (GEN des Produzenten, PL die Produzenten)

P

die Produzentin *(of film)*

product NOUN
das Produkt (PL die Produkte)

production NOUN
1 die Produktion
□ They're increasing production. Sie erhöhen die Produktion.
2 die Inszenierung *(play, show)*
□ a production of 'Hamlet' eine Hamletinszenierung

profession NOUN
der Beruf (PL die Berufe)

professional NOUN
▷ *see also* **professional** ADJECTIVE
der Profi (PL die Profis)
LANGUAGE TIP **der Profi** is also used for women.
□ She now plays as a professional. Sie spielt jetzt als Profi.

professional ADJECTIVE
▷ *see also* **professional** NOUN
professionell *(player)*
□ a very professional piece of work eine sehr professionelle Arbeit
■ **a professional musician** ein Berufsmusiker *masc*

professionally ADVERB
■ **She sings professionally.** Sie ist Sängerin von Beruf.

professor NOUN
der Professor (PL die Professoren)
die Professorin
■ **He's the German professor.** Er hat den Lehrstuhl für Deutsch inne.

profit NOUN
der Gewinn (PL die Gewinne)

profitable ADJECTIVE
gewinnbringend

program NOUN
▷ *see also* **program** VERB
das Programm (PL die Programme)
□ a computer program ein Computerprogramm

to **program** VERB
▷ *see also* **program** NOUN
programmieren (PERFECT hat programmiert)
□ to program a computer einen Computer programmieren

programme NOUN
das Programm (PL die Programme)

programmer NOUN
der Programmierer (PL die Programmierer)
die Programmiererin
□ She's a programmer. Sie ist Programmiererin.

programming NOUN
das Programmieren

progress NOUN
der Fortschritt (PL die Fortschritte)
□ You're making progress! Du machst Fortschritte!

to **prohibit** VERB
verbieten (IMPERFECT verbat, PERFECT hat verboten)
□ Smoking is prohibited. Das Rauchen ist verboten.

project NOUN
1 das Projekt (PL die Projekte) *(plan)*
2 das Referat (PL die Referate) *(at school)*
□ I'm doing a project on Berlin. Ich schreibe ein Referat über Berlin.

projector NOUN
der Projektor (PL die Projektoren)

promenade NOUN
die Strandpromenade

promise NOUN
▷ *see also* **promise** VERB
das Versprechen (PL die Versprechen)
□ You didn't keep your promise. Du hast dein Versprechen nicht gehalten.
■ **That's a promise!** Versprochen!

to **promise** VERB
▷ *see also* **promise** NOUN
versprechen (PRESENT verspricht, IMPERFECT versprach, PERFECT hat versprochen)
□ She promised to write. Sie hat versprochen zu schreiben. □ I'll write, I promise! Ich schreibe, das verspreche ich!

promising ADJECTIVE
vielversprechend

to **promote** VERB
■ **to be promoted** befördert werden
□ She was promoted after six months. Sie wurde nach sechs Monaten befördert.

promotion NOUN
1 die Beförderung *(in job)*
2 die Werbung *(advertising)*

prompt ADJECTIVE, ADVERB
schnell
□ a prompt reply eine schnelle Antwort
■ **at eight o'clock prompt** genau um acht Uhr

promptly ADVERB
pünktlich
□ We left promptly at seven. Wir sind pünktlich um sieben gegangen.

pronoun NOUN
das Pronomen (PL die Pronomen)

to **pronounce** VERB
aussprechen (PRESENT spricht aus, IMPERFECT sprach aus, PERFECT hat ausgesprochen)
□ How do you pronounce that word? Wie spricht man das Wort aus?

pronunciation NOUN
die Aussprache

proof NOUN
der Beweis (GEN des Beweises, PL die Beweise)

proper ADJECTIVE
1 echt *(genuine)*
□ proper German bread echtes deutsches Brot

2 ordentlich *(decent)*
□ We didn't have a proper lunch. Wir hatten kein ordentliches Mittagessen. □ It's difficult to get a proper job. Es ist schwierig, einen ordentlichen Job zu bekommen. □ We need proper training. Wir brauchen eine ordentliche Ausbildung.
3 richtig *(appropriate)*
□ You have to have the proper equipment. Sie brauchen die richtige Ausrüstung.
■ **If you had come at the proper time ...** Wenn du zur rechten Zeit gekommen wärst ...

properly ADVERB
1 richtig *(correctly)*
□ You're not doing it properly. Du machst das nicht richtig.
2 anständig *(appropriately)*
□ Dress properly for your interview. Zieh dich zum Vorstellungsgespräch anständig an.

property NOUN
das Eigentum
■ **'private property'** 'Privateigentum'
■ **stolen property** das Diebesgut

proportional ADJECTIVE
■ **proportional representation** das Verhältniswahlrecht

proposal NOUN
der Vorschlag (PL die Vorschläge) *(suggestion)*

to **propose** VERB
vorschlagen (PRESENT schlägt vor, IMPERFECT schlug vor, PERFECT hat vorgeschlagen)
□ I propose a new plan. Ich schlage einen neuen Plan vor.
■ **to propose to do something** vorhaben, etwas zu tun □ What do you propose to do? Was haben Sie zu tun vor?
■ **to propose to somebody** *(for marriage)* jemandem einen Heiratsantrag machen
□ He's proposed to her. Er hat ihr einen Heiratsantrag gemacht.

to **prosecute** VERB
strafrechtlich verfolgen (PERFECT hat verfolgt)
□ They were prosecuted for murder. Sie wurden wegen Mordes strafrechtlich verfolgt.
■ **'Shoplifters will be prosecuted'** 'Jeder Diebstahl wird zur Anzeige gebracht'

prospect NOUN
die Aussicht
□ It'll improve my career prospects. Das wird meine Berufsaussichten verbessern.

LANGUAGE TIP Be careful not to translate **prospect** by **Prospekt**.

prospectus NOUN
das Lehrprogramm (PL die Lehrprogramme) *(for school, university)*

prostitute NOUN
die Prostituierte (GEN der Prostituierten)
■ **a male prostitute** ein Prostituierter

to **protect** VERB
schützen

protection NOUN
der Schutz (GEN des Schutzes)

protein NOUN
das Protein (PL die Proteine)

protest NOUN
▷ *see also* **protest** VERB
der Protest (PL die Proteste)
□ He ignored their protests. Er hat ihre Proteste ignoriert.
■ **a protest march** ein Protestmarsch *masc*

to **protest** VERB
▷ *see also* **protest** NOUN
protestieren (PERFECT hat protestiert)

Protestant NOUN
▷ *see also* **Protestant** ADJECTIVE
der Protestant (GEN des Protestanten, PL die Protestanten)
die Protestantin
□ She's a Protestant. Sie ist Protestantin.

Protestant ADJECTIVE
▷ *see also* **Protestant** NOUN
protestantisch
□ a Protestant church eine protestantische Kirche

protester NOUN
der Demonstrant (GEN des Demonstranten, PL die Demonstranten)
die Demonstrantin

proud ADJECTIVE
stolz
□ Her parents are proud of her. Ihre Eltern sind stolz auf sie.

to **prove** VERB
beweisen (IMPERFECT bewies, PERFECT hat bewiesen)
□ The police couldn't prove it. Die Polizei konnte es nicht beweisen.

proverb NOUN
das Sprichwort (PL die Sprichwörter)

to **provide** VERB
stellen
□ We'll provide the food. Wir stellen das Essen.
■ **to provide somebody with something** jemandem etwas zur Verfügung stellen
□ They provided us with maps. Sie haben uns Karten zur Verfügung gestellt.

to **provide for** VERB
versorgen (PERFECT hat versorgt)
□ He can't provide for his family any more. Er kann seine Familie nicht mehr versorgen.

provided CONJUNCTION
vorausgesetzt, dass
□ He'll play provided he's fit. Er spielt, vorausgesetzt, dass er fit ist.

provisional ADJECTIVE
vorläufig

prowler NOUN
der Herumtreiber (PL die Herumtreiber)
die Herumtreiberin

prune NOUN
die Backpflaume

pseudonym NOUN
das Pseudonym (PL die Pseudonyme)

psychiatrist NOUN
der Psychiater (PL die Psychiater)
die Psychiaterin
□ She's a psychiatrist. Sie ist Psychiaterin.

psychoanalyst NOUN
der Psychoanalytiker (PL die Psychoanalytiker)
die Psychoanalytikerin

psychological ADJECTIVE
psychologisch

psychologist NOUN
der Psychologe (GEN des Psychologen, PL die Psychologen)
die Psychologin
□ He's a psychologist. Er ist Psychologe.

psychology NOUN
die Psychologie

PTO ABBREVIATION *(= please turn over)*
b. w. *(= bitte wenden)*

pub NOUN
die Kneipe

public NOUN
▷ *see also* **public** ADJECTIVE
die Öffentlichkeit
□ open to the public der Öffentlichkeit zugänglich
■ **in public** in der Öffentlichkeit

public ADJECTIVE
▷ *see also* **public** NOUN
öffentlich
□ public opinion die öffentliche Meinung
■ **a public holiday** ein gesetzlicher Feiertag
■ **the public address system** die Lautsprecheranlage

publican NOUN
der Gastwirt
die Gastwirtin
□ He's a publican. Er ist Gastwirt.

publicity NOUN
die Publicity

public school NOUN
die Privatschule

public transport NOUN
die öffentlichen Verkehrsmittel *neut pl*

> **DID YOU KNOW...?**
> Almost all German cities operate an integrated public transport system; you buy a single ticket which is valid on all buses, trams and light railway vehicles in a particular zone. You can buy a weekly **Wochenkarte**, monthly **Monatskarte** or yearly **Jahreskarte**.

to **publish** VERB
veröffentlichen (PERFECT hat veröffentlicht)

publisher NOUN
der Verlag (PL die Verlage) *(company)*

pudding NOUN
der Nachtisch
□ What's for pudding? Was gibt's zum Nachtisch?
■ **rice pudding** der Milchreis
■ **black pudding** die Blutwurst

puddle NOUN
die Pfütze

puff pastry NOUN
der Blätterteig

to **pull** VERB
ziehen (IMPERFECT zog, PERFECT hat gezogen)
□ Pull! Zieh!
■ **He pulled the trigger.** Er drückte ab.
■ **to pull a muscle** sich einen Muskel zerren
□ I've pulled a muscle. Ich habe mir einen Muskel gezerrt.
■ **You're pulling my leg!** Du willst mich wohl auf den Arm nehmen! *(informal)*
■ **to pull down** abreißen
■ **to pull out** **1** *(tooth, weed)* herausziehen **2** *(car)* ausscheren □ The car pulled out to overtake. Das Auto scherte aus, um zu überholen. **3** *(withdraw)* aussteigen
□ She pulled out of the tournament. Sie ist aus dem Turnier ausgestiegen.
■ **to pull through** *(survive)* durchkommen
□ They think he'll pull through. Sie meinen, er kommt durch.
■ **to pull up** anhalten *(car)*
□ A car pulled up beside me. Ein Auto hielt neben mir an.

pullover NOUN
der Pullover (PL die Pullover)

pulse NOUN
der Puls (GEN des Pulses, PL die Pulse)
□ The nurse felt his pulse. Die Schwester fühlte ihm den Puls.

pulses PL NOUN
die Hülsenfrüchte *fem pl*

pump NOUN
▷ *see also* **pump** VERB
1 die Pumpe
□ a bicycle pump eine Fahrradpumpe
■ **a petrol pump** eine Zapfsäule
2 der Sportschuh (PL die Sportschuhe) *(shoe)*

to **pump** VERB
▷ *see also* **pump** NOUN
pumpen
■ **to pump up** *(tyre)* aufpumpen

pumpkin NOUN
der Kürbis (GEN des Kürbisses, PL die Kürbisse)

punch NOUN
▷ *see also* **punch** VERB
1 der Schlag (PL die Schläge) *(blow)*
□ a violent punch ein heftiger Schlag
2 der Punsch *(drink)*

to **punch** VERB
▷ *see also* **punch** NOUN
1 schlagen (PRESENT schlägt, IMPERFECT schlug, PERFECT hat geschlagen) *(hit)*

□ He punched me! Er hat mich geschlagen!
2 entwerten (PERFECT hat entwertet) *(in ticket machine)*
□ Punch your ticket before you get on the train. Entwerten Sie Ihre Fahrkarte, bevor Sie in den Zug steigen.
3 knipsen *(by ticket inspector)*
□ He forgot to punch my ticket. Er hat vergessen, meine Fahrkarte zu knipsen.

punch-up NOUN
die Schlägerei *(informal)*

punctual ADJECTIVE
pünktlich

punctuation NOUN
die Zeichensetzung

puncture NOUN
die Reifenpanne
□ to have a puncture eine Reifenpanne haben

to **punish** VERB
bestrafen (PERFECT hat bestraft)
□ The teacher punished him. Der Lehrer bestrafte ihn.

punishment NOUN
die Strafe

punk NOUN
der Punker (PL die Punker)
die Punkerin *(person)*
■ **a punk rock band** eine Punkband

pupil NOUN
der Schüler (PL die Schüler)
die Schülerin

puppet NOUN
die Marionette

puppy NOUN
der junge Hund (PL die jungen Hunde)

to **purchase** VERB
erwerben (PRESENT erwirbt, IMPERFECT erwarb, PERFECT hat erworben)

pure ADJECTIVE
rein
□ pure orange juice reiner Orangensaft
■ **He's doing pure maths.** Er macht rein theoretische Mathematik.

purple ADJECTIVE
violett

purpose NOUN
der Zweck (PL die Zwecke)
□ What is the purpose of these changes? Welchen Zweck haben diese Veränderungen?
■ **his purpose in life** sein Lebensinhalt
■ **on purpose** absichtlich □ He did it on purpose. Er hat es absichtlich getan.

to **purr** VERB
schnurren

purse NOUN
1 der Geldbeutel (PL die Geldbeutel) *(for money)*
2 die Handtasche *(handbag)*

to **pursue** VERB
verfolgen (PERFECT hat verfolgt)

pursuit NOUN
die Aktivität
□ outdoor pursuits Aktivitäten im Freien

push NOUN
▷ *see also* **push** VERB
■ **to give somebody a push** jemanden stoßen
□ He gave me a push. Er hat mich gestoßen.

to **push** VERB
▷ *see also* **push** NOUN
1 drücken *(button)*
2 drängeln
□ Don't push! Nicht drängeln!
■ **to push somebody to do something** jemanden drängen, etwas zu tun
□ They're pushing me to go to university. Sie drängen mich zu studieren.
■ **to push drugs** mit Drogen handeln
■ **to push around** herumkommandieren
□ He likes pushing people around. Er kommandiert die Leute gern herum.
■ **Push off!** Hau ab! *(informal)*
■ **I pushed my way through.** Ich drängelte mich durch.

pushchair NOUN
der Sportwagen (PL die Sportwagen)

pusher NOUN
der Drogenhändler (PL die Drogenhändler)
die Drogenhändlerin *(of drugs)*

push-up NOUN
der Liegestütz (GEN des Liegestützes, PL die Liegestütze)
□ I do twenty push-ups every morning. Ich mache jeden Morgen zwanzig Liegestütze.

to **put** VERB

LANGUAGE TIP Use **legen** when you're putting something down flat, use **stellen** when you're standing something upright.

1 legen
□ Where shall I put my things? Wohin soll ich meine Sachen legen? □ She's putting the baby to bed. Sie legt das Baby ins Bett.
2 stellen
□ Put the vase on the table. Stell die Vase auf den Tisch.
■ **Don't forget to put your name on the paper.** Vergiss nicht, deinen Namen auf das Papier zu schreiben.

to **put aside** VERB
zurücklegen (PERFECT hat zurückgelegt)
□ Can you put this aside for me till tomorrow? Können Sie mir das bis morgen zurücklegen?

to **put away** VERB
wegräumen (PERFECT hat weggeräumt)
□ Can you put away the dishes, please? Kannst du bitte das Geschirr wegräumen?

to **put back** VERB
1 zurücklegen (PERFECT hat zurückgelegt)
□ Put it back when you've finished with it. Leg es zurück, wenn du es nicht mehr brauchst.

2 zurückstellen (PERFECT hat zurückgestellt)
□ to put the clock back die Uhr zurückstellen
□ Put the milk back in the fridge. Stell die Milch in den Kühlschrank zurück.

to **put down** VERB

1 abstellen (PERFECT hat abgestellt)
□ I'll put these bags down for a minute. Ich stelle diese Taschen für eine Minute ab.

2 aufschreiben (IMPERFECT schrieb auf, PERFECT hat aufgeschrieben) *(in writing)*
□ I've put down a few ideas. Ich habe ein paar Ideen aufgeschrieben.
■ **to have an animal put down** ein Tier einschläfern lassen □ We had to have our old dog put down. Wir mussten unseren alten Hund einschläfern lassen.

to **put forward** VERB

vorstellen (PERFECT hat vorgestellt)
□ to put the clock forward die Uhr vorstellen

to **put in** VERB

einbauen (PERFECT hat eingebaut) *(install)*
□ We've put in central heating. Wir haben eine Zentralheizung einbauen lassen.
■ **He has put in a lot of work on this project.** Er hat viel Arbeit in dieses Projekt gesteckt.

to **put off** VERB

1 ausmachen (PERFECT hat ausgemacht) *(switch off)*
□ Shall I put the light off? Soll ich das Licht ausmachen?

2 verschieben (IMPERFECT verschob, PERFECT hat verschoben) *(postpone)*
□ I keep putting it off. Ich verschiebe es dauernd.

3 stören *(distract)*
□ Stop putting me off! Hör auf, mich zu stören!

4 entmutigen (PERFECT hat entmutigt) *(discourage)*
□ He's not easily put off. Er lässt sich nicht so schnell entmutigen.

to **put on** VERB

1 anziehen (IMPERFECT zog an, PERFECT hat angezogen) *(clothes)*
□ I'll put my coat on. Ich ziehe mir den Mantel an.

2 auftragen (PRESENT trägt auf, IMPERFECT trug auf, PERFECT hat aufgetragen) *(lipstick)*

3 auflegen (PERFECT hat aufgelegt) *(record)*

4 anmachen (PERFECT hat angemacht) *(light, heater, TV)*
□ Shall I put the heater on? Soll ich den Heizofen anmachen?

5 aufführen (PERFECT hat aufgeführt) *(play, show)*
□ We're putting on 'Bugsy Malone'. Wir führen 'Bugsy Malone' auf.

6 aufstellen (PERFECT hat aufgestellt)
□ I'll put the potatoes on. Ich stelle die Kartoffeln auf.
■ **to put on weight** zunehmen □ He's put on a lot of weight. Er hat viel zugenommen.

to **put out** VERB

1 ausmachen (PERFECT hat ausgemacht) *(light, cigarette)*
□ Put the light out. Mach das Licht aus.

2 löschen *(fire)*
□ It took them five hours to put out the fire. Sie haben fünf Stunden gebraucht, um das Feuer zu löschen.

to **put through** VERB

verbinden (IMPERFECT verband, PERFECT hat verbunden)
□ Can you put me through to him? Können Sie mich mit ihm verbinden?
■ **I'm putting you through.** Ich verbinde.

to **put up** VERB

1 aufhängen (PERFECT hat aufgehängt) *(pin up)*
□ I'll put the poster up in my room. Ich hänge das Poster in meinem Zimmer auf.

2 aufschlagen (PRESENT schlägt auf, IMPERFECT schlug auf, PERFECT hat aufgeschlagen) *(tent)*
□ We put up our tent in a field. Wir haben unser Zelt auf einem Feld aufgeschlagen.

3 erhöhen (PERFECT hat erhöht) *(price)*
□ They've put up the price. Sie haben den Preis erhöht.

4 übernachten lassen (PRESENT lässt übernachten, IMPERFECT ließ übernachten, PERFECT hat übernachten lassen) *(accommodate)*
□ My friend will put me up for the night. Mein Freund lässt mich bei sich übernachten.
■ **to put one's hand up** sich melden □ If you have any questions, put up your hands. Wenn ihr Fragen habt, dann meldet euch.
■ **to put up with something** sich etwas gefallen lassen □ I'm not going to put up with it. Ich lasse mir das nicht gefallen.

puzzle NOUN

das Puzzle (PL die Puzzles) *(jigsaw)*

puzzled ADJECTIVE

verdutzt
□ You look puzzled! Du siehst verdutzt aus!

puzzling ADJECTIVE

rätselhaft

pyjamas PL NOUN

der Schlafanzug (PL die Schlafanzüge)
□ my pyjamas mein Schlafanzug
■ **a pair of pyjamas** ein Schlafanzug
■ **a pyjama top** ein Schlafanzugoberteil *neut*

pyramid NOUN

die Pyramide

Pyrenees PL NOUN

■ **the Pyrenees** die Pyrenäen *pl*

Qq

quad bike NOUN
das Quad (PL die Quads)

quaint ADJECTIVE
malerisch *(house, village)*

qualification NOUN
die Qualifikation
□ vocational qualifications die beruflichen Qualifikationen
■ **to leave school without any qualifications** die Schule ohne einen Abschluss verlassen

qualified ADJECTIVE
ausgebildet
□ a qualified driving instructor ein ausgebildeter Fahrlehrer □ a qualified nurse eine ausgebildete Krankenschwester

to **qualify** VERB
1 seinen Abschluss machen *(for job)*
□ She qualified as a teacher last year. Sie hat letztes Jahr ihren Abschluss als Lehrerin gemacht.
2 sich qualifizieren (PERFECT hat sich qualifiziert) *(in competition)*
□ Our team didn't qualify. Unsere Mannschaft konnte sich nicht qualifizieren.

quality NOUN
1 die Qualität
□ a good quality of life eine gute Lebensqualität
■ **good-quality ingredients** qualitativ hochwertige Zutaten
2 die Eigenschaft *(of person)*
□ good qualities gute Eigenschaften

quantity NOUN
die Menge

quarantine NOUN
die Quarantäne
□ in quarantine in Quarantäne

quarrel NOUN
▷ *see also* **quarrel** VERB
der Streit (PL die Streite)

to **quarrel** VERB
▷ *see also* **quarrel** NOUN
sich streiten (IMPERFECT stritt sich, PERFECT hat sich gestritten)

quarry NOUN
der Steinbruch (PL die Steinbrüche) *(for stone)*

quarter NOUN
das Viertel (PL die Viertel)
□ three quarters drei Viertel □ a quarter of an hour eine viertel Stunde
■ **three quarters of an hour** eine Dreiviertelstunde
■ **a quarter past ten** Viertel nach zehn
■ **a quarter to eleven** Viertel vor elf

quarter final NOUN
das Viertelfinale (PL die Viertelfinale)

quartet NOUN
das Quartett (PL die Quartette)
□ a string quartet ein Streichquartett

quay NOUN
der Kai (PL die Kais)

queasy ADJECTIVE
■ **I'm feeling queasy.** Mir ist schlecht.

queen NOUN
1 die Königin
□ Queen Elizabeth Königin Elisabeth
2 die Dame *(playing card)*
□ the queen of hearts die Herzdame

query NOUN
▷ *see also* **query** VERB
die Frage

to **query** VERB
▷ *see also* **query** NOUN
infrage stellen
□ No one queried my decision. Niemand hat meine Entscheidung infrage gestellt.
■ **They queried the bill.** Sie reklamierten die Rechnung.

question NOUN
▷ *see also* **question** VERB
die Frage
□ That's a difficult question. Das ist eine schwierige Frage.
■ **Can I ask a question?** Kann ich etwas fragen?
■ **It's out of the question.** Das kommt nicht infrage.

to **question** VERB
▷ *see also* **question** NOUN
befragen (PERFECT hat befragt)
■ **He was questioned by the police.** Die Polizei hat ihn vernommen.

question mark NOUN
das Fragezeichen (PL die Fragezeichen)

questionnaire NOUN
der Fragebogen (PL die Fragebögen)

queue NOUN
▷ *see also* **queue** VERB
die Schlange

to **queue** VERB
▷ *see also* **queue** NOUN
Schlange stehen (IMPERFECT stand Schlange, PERFECT hat Schlange gestanden)
□ We queued for an hour. Wir haben eine Stunde lang Schlange gestanden.
■ **to queue for something** für etwas anstehen □ We had to queue for tickets. Wir mussten für Karten anstehen.

quick ADJECTIVE, ADVERB
schnell
□ a quick lunch ein schnelles Mittagessen
□ Quick, phone the police! Schnell, rufen Sie die Polizei! □ It's quicker by train. Mit dem Zug geht es schneller.
■ **Be quick!** Beeil dich!
■ **She's a quick learner.** Sie lernt schnell.

quickly ADVERB
schnell
□ It was all over very quickly. Es war alles sehr schnell vorbei.

quiet ADJECTIVE
1 ruhig *(not talkative, peaceful)*
□ You're very quiet today. Du bist heute sehr ruhig. □ a quiet little town eine ruhige, kleine Stadt
2 leise *(not noisy)*
□ The engine's very quiet. Der Motor ist sehr leise.
■ **Be quiet!** Sei still!
■ **Quiet!** Ruhe!

quietly ADVERB
leise
□ He quietly opened the door. Er öffnete leise die Tür.

quilt NOUN
die Steppdecke *(duvet)*

to **quit** VERB
1 aufgeben (PRESENT gibt auf, IMPERFECT gab auf, PERFECT hat aufgegeben)
□ I quit my job last week. Ich habe meine Stelle letzte Woche aufgegeben.
2 aufhören
□ I quit smoking. Ich habe mit dem Rauchen aufgehört.

quite ADVERB
1 ziemlich *(rather)*
□ It's quite warm today. Heute ist es ziemlich warm. □ I've been there quite a lot. Ich war schon ziemlich oft da. □ quite a lot of money ziemlich viel Geld □ quite a few people ziemlich viele Leute □ It costs quite a lot. Es ist ziemlich teuer. □ It's quite a long way. Es ist ziemlich weit. □ It was quite a shock. Es war ein ziemlicher Schock.
■ **I quite liked the film, but ...** Der Film hat mir ganz gut gefallen, aber ...
2 ganz *(entirely)*
□ I'm not quite sure. Ich bin mir nicht ganz sicher. □ It's not quite the same. Das ist nicht ganz das Gleiche.
■ **quite good** ganz gut

quiz NOUN
das Quiz (GEN des Quiz, PL die Quiz)

quota NOUN
die Quote

quotation NOUN
das Zitat (PL die Zitate)
□ a quotation from Shakespeare ein Shakespearezitat

quotation marks PL NOUN
die Anführungszeichen *pl*

quote NOUN
▷ *see also* **quote** VERB
das Zitat (PL die Zitate)
□ a Shakespeare quote ein Shakespearezitat
■ **quotes** *(quotation marks)* die Anführungszeichen □ in quotes in Anführungszeichen

to **quote** VERB
▷ *see also* **quote** NOUN
zitieren (PERFECT hat zitiert)

Rr

rabbi NOUN
der Rabbiner (PL die Rabbiner)

rabbit NOUN
das Kaninchen (PL die Kaninchen)
■ **a rabbit hutch** ein Kaninchenstall *masc*

rabies SING NOUN
die Tollwut
■ **a dog with rabies** ein tollwütiger Hund

race NOUN
▷ *see also* **race** VERB
1 das Rennen (PL die Rennen) *(sport)*
□ a cycle race ein Radrennen
2 die Rasse *(species)*
□ the human race die Menschheit
■ **race relations** Rassenbeziehungen *fem pl*

to **race** VERB
▷ *see also* **race** NOUN
1 rennen (IMPERFECT rannte, PERFECT ist gerannt)
□ We raced to catch the bus. Wir sind gerannt, um den Bus zu erreichen.
2 um die Wette laufen mit (PRESENT läuft um die Wette, IMPERFECT lief um die Wette, PERFECT ist um die Wette gelaufen) *(have a race)*
□ I'll race you! Ich laufe mit dir um die Wette!

racecourse NOUN
die Pferderennbahn

racehorse NOUN
das Rennpferd (PL die Rennpferde)

racer NOUN
das Rennrad (PL die Rennräder) *(bike)*

racetrack NOUN
die Rennbahn

racial ADJECTIVE
■ **racial discrimination** die Rassendiskriminierung

racing car NOUN
der Rennwagen (PL die Rennwagen)

racing driver NOUN
der Rennfahrer (PL die Rennfahrer)
die Rennfahrerin

racism NOUN
der Rassismus (GEN des Rassismus)

racist ADJECTIVE
▷ *see also* **racist** NOUN
rassistisch
■ **He's racist.** Er ist ein Rassist.

racist NOUN
▷ *see also* **racist** ADJECTIVE
der Rassist (GEN des Rassisten, PL die Rassisten)
die Rassistin

rack NOUN
der Gepäckträger (PL die Gepäckträger)
(for luggage)

racket NOUN
1 der Schläger (PL die Schläger) *(for sport)*
□ my tennis racket mein Tennisschläger
2 der Krach *(noise)*
□ a terrible racket ein furchtbarer Krach

racquet NOUN
der Schläger (PL die Schläger)

radar NOUN
das Radar

radiation NOUN
die Strahlung

radiator NOUN
der Heizkörper (PL die Heizkörper)

radio NOUN
das Radio (PL die Radios)
■ **on the radio** im Radio
■ **a radio station** ein Rundfunksender *masc*

radioactive ADJECTIVE
radioaktiv

radio-controlled ADJECTIVE
ferngesteuert *(model plane, car)*

radish NOUN
1 das Radieschen (PL die Radieschen) *(small red)*
2 der Rettich (PL die Rettiche) *(long white)*

RAF NOUN (= *Royal Air Force*)
die britische Luftwaffe
□ He's in the RAF. Er ist bei der britischen Luftwaffe.

raffle NOUN
die Tombola (PL die Tombolas)
□ a raffle ticket ein Tombolalos *neut*

raft NOUN
das Floß (GEN des Floßes, PL die Flöße)

rag NOUN
der Lumpen (PL die Lumpen)
□ dressed in rags in Lumpen gekleidet
■ **a piece of rag** ein Lappen *masc*

rage NOUN
die Wut
□ mad with rage wild vor Wut
■ **to be in a rage** wütend sein □ She was in a rage. Sie war wütend.
■ **It's all the rage.** Es ist große Mode.

raid NOUN
▷ *see also* **raid** VERB
1 der Überfall (PL die Überfälle) *(burglary)*
□ There was a bank raid near my house. Es gab einen Banküberfall in der Nähe meines Hauses.
2 die Razzia (PL die Razzien)
□ a police raid eine Polizeirazzia

to **raid** VERB
▷ *see also* **raid** NOUN
eine Razzia machen in *+dat (police)*
□ The police raided the club. Die Polizei machte eine Razzia in dem Klub.

rail NOUN
1 das Geländer (PL die Geländer) *(on stairs, bridge, balcony)*
2 die Schiene *(on railway line)*
■ **by rail** mit dem Zug

railcard NOUN
die Bahncard® (PL die Bahncards)

railroad NOUN (US)
die Eisenbahn
■ **a railroad station** ein Bahnhof *masc*

railway NOUN
die Eisenbahn
□ the privatization of the railways die Privatisierung der Eisenbahn
■ **a railway line** eine Eisenbahnlinie
■ **a railway station** ein Bahnhof *masc*

rain NOUN
▷ *see also* **rain** VERB
der Regen
□ in the rain im Regen

to **rain** VERB
▷ *see also* **rain** NOUN
regnen
□ It rains a lot here. Hier regnet es viel.
■ **It's raining.** Es regnet.

rainbow NOUN
der Regenbogen (PL die Regenbogen)

raincoat NOUN
der Regenmantel (PL die Regenmäntel)

rainfall NOUN
der Niederschlag (PL die Niederschläge)

rainforest NOUN
der Regenwald (PL die Regenwälder)

rainy ADJECTIVE
regnerisch

to **raise** VERB
1 hochheben (IMPERFECT hob hoch, PERFECT hat hochgehoben) *(lift)*
□ He raised his hand. Er hob die Hand hoch.
2 heben (IMPERFECT hob, PERFECT hat gehoben) *(improve)*
□ They want to raise standards in schools. Sie wollen das Niveau in den Schulen heben.
■ **to raise money** Spenden sammeln
□ We're raising money for a new gym. Wir sammeln Spenden für eine neue Turnhalle.

raisin NOUN
die Rosine

rake NOUN
der Rechen (PL die Rechen)

rally NOUN
1 die Kundgebung *(of people)*
2 die Rallye (PL die Rallyes) *(sport)*
□ a rally driver ein Rallyefahrer *masc*
3 der Ballwechsel (PL die Ballwechsel) *(in tennis)*

Ramadan NOUN
der Ramadan

ramble NOUN
die Wanderung
□ to go for a ramble eine Wanderung machen

rambler NOUN
der Wanderer (PL die Wanderer)
die Wanderin

ramp NOUN
die Rampe *(for wheelchairs)*

ran VERB ▷ *see* **run**

ranch NOUN
die Ranch (PL die Ranches)

random ADJECTIVE
■ **a random selection** eine Zufallsauswahl
■ **at random** aufs Geratewohl □ We picked the number at random. Wir haben die Nummer aufs Geratewohl ausgewählt.

rang VERB ▷ *see* **ring**

range NOUN
▷ *see also* **range** VERB
die Auswahl
□ a wide range of colours eine große Auswahl an Farben
■ **a range of subjects** verschiedene Themen
□ We study a range of subjects. Wir studieren verschiedene Themen.
■ **a mountain range** eine Bergkette

to **range** VERB
▷ *see also* **range** NOUN
■ **to range from ... to** gehen von ... bis
□ Temperatures in summer range from twenty to thirty-five degrees. Die Temperaturen im Sommer gehen von zwanzig bis fünfunddreißig Grad.
■ **Tickets range from two to twenty pounds.** Karten kosten von zwei bis zwanzig Pfund.

rank NOUN
▷ *see also* **rank** VERB
■ **a taxi rank** ein Taxistand *masc*

to **rank** VERB
▷ *see also* **rank** NOUN
rangieren (PERFECT hat rangiert)
□ He's ranked third in the United States. Er rangiert in den Vereinigten Staaten an dritter Stelle.

ransom NOUN
das Lösegeld (PL die Lösegelder)

rap NOUN
der Rap *(music)*

rape NOUN
▷ *see also* **rape** VERB
die Vergewaltigung

English-German

r

to **rape** VERB
▷ *see also* **rape** NOUN
vergewaltigen (PERFECT hat vergewaltigt)

rapids PL NOUN
die Stromschnellen *fem pl*

rapist NOUN
der Vergewaltiger (PL die Vergewaltiger)

rare ADJECTIVE
1 selten *(unusual)*
□ a rare plant eine seltene Pflanze
2 blutig *(steak)*

rash NOUN
der Ausschlag (PL die Ausschläge)
□ I've got a rash. Ich habe einen Ausschlag.

rasher NOUN
■ **an egg and two rashers of bacon**
ein Ei und zwei Streifen Speck

raspberry NOUN
die Himbeere
□ raspberry jam die Himbeermarmelade

rat NOUN
die Ratte

rate NOUN
▷ *see also* **rate** VERB
1 der Preis (GEN des Preises, PL die Preise) *(price)*
□ There are reduced rates for students. Studenten bekommen ermäßigte Preise.
2 die Rate *(level)*
□ the divorce rate die Scheidungsrate
■ **a high rate of interest** ein hoher Zinssatz

to **rate** VERB
▷ *see also* **rate** NOUN
einschätzen (PERFECT hat eingeschätzt)
□ He was rated the best. Man schätzte ihn als den Besten ein.

rather ADVERB
ziemlich
□ I was rather disappointed. Ich war ziemlich enttäuscht. □ Twenty pounds! That's rather a lot! Zwanzig Pfund! Das ist aber ziemlich viel!
■ **rather a lot of** ziemlich viel □ rather a lot of work ziemlich viel Arbeit
■ **rather than** statt □ We decided to camp, rather than stay at a hotel. Wir haben beschlossen zu zelten statt im Hotel zu übernachten.
■ **I'd rather ...** Ich würde lieber ... □ I'd rather stay in tonight. Ich würde heute Abend lieber zu Hause bleiben. □ Would you like a sweet? — I'd rather have an apple. Möchtest du ein Bonbon? — Ich hätte lieber einen Apfel.

rattle NOUN
die Rassel *(for baby)*

rattlesnake NOUN
die Klapperschlange

to **rave** VERB
▷ *see also* **rave** NOUN
schwärmen
□ They raved about the film. Sie schwärmten von dem Film.

rave NOUN
▷ *see also* **rave** VERB
die Raveparty (PL die Ravepartys) *(party)*
■ **rave music** die Ravemusik

raven NOUN
der Rabe (GEN des Raben, PL die Raben)

ravenous ADJECTIVE
■ **to be ravenous** einen Riesenhunger haben
□ I'm ravenous! Ich habe einen Riesenhunger!

raving ADVERB
■ **raving mad** total verrückt *(informal)*

raw ADJECTIVE
roh *(food)*
■ **raw materials** die Rohstoffe *masc pl*

razor NOUN
der Rasierapparat (PL die Rasierapparate)
■ **a razor blade** eine Rasierklinge

RE NOUN *(= religious education)*
der Religionsunterricht

reach NOUN
▷ *see also* **reach** VERB
■ **out of reach** außer Reichweite □ The light switch was out of reach. Der Lichtschalter war außer Reichweite.
■ **within easy reach of** leicht zu erreichen
□ The hotel is within easy reach of the town centre. Das Hotel ist vom Stadtzentrum leicht zu erreichen.

to **reach** VERB
▷ *see also* **reach** NOUN
1 ankommen in *+dat* (IMPERFECT kam an, PERFECT ist angekommen)
□ We reached the hotel at ten o'clock. Wir sind um zehn Uhr im Hotel angekommen.
■ **We hope to reach the final.** Wir wollen ins Endspiel kommen.
2 treffen (PRESENT trifft, IMPERFECT traf, PERFECT hat getroffen) *(decision)*
□ Eventually they reached a decision. Sie haben schließlich eine Entscheidung getroffen.
■ **He reached for his gun.** Er griff nach seiner Pistole.

to **react** VERB
reagieren (PERFECT hat reagiert)

reaction NOUN
die Reaktion

reactor NOUN
der Reaktor (PL die Reaktoren)
□ a nuclear reactor ein Kernreaktor

to **read** VERB
lesen (PRESENT liest, IMPERFECT las, PERFECT hat gelesen)
□ I don't read much. Ich lese nicht viel.
□ Have you read it? Hast du es gelesen?
□ Read the text out loud. Lies den Text laut.

reader NOUN
der Leser (PL die Leser)
die Leserin *(person)*

readily ADVERB
bereitwillig
□ She readily agreed. Sie stimmte bereitwillig zu.

reading NOUN
das Lesen
□ Reading is one of my hobbies. Lesen ist eines meiner Hobbies.

ready ADJECTIVE
fertig
□ She's nearly ready. Sie ist fast fertig.
■ **He's always ready to help.** Er ist immer bereit zu helfen.
■ **a ready meal** ein Fertiggericht *neut*
■ **to get ready** sich fertig machen
□ She's getting ready to go out. Sie macht sich zum Ausgehen fertig.
■ **to get something ready** etwas machen

real ADJECTIVE
1 echt *(not fake)*
□ He wasn't a real policeman. Er war kein echter Polizist. □ It's real leather. Es ist echtes Leder.
2 wirklich
□ Her real name is Cordelia. Ihr wirklicher Name ist Cordelia. □ in real life im wirklichen Leben
■ **It was a real nightmare.** Es war wirklich ein Albtraum.

realistic ADJECTIVE
realistisch

reality NOUN
die Wirklichkeit

reality TV NOUN
das Reality TV

to **realize** VERB
■ **to realize that ...** bemerken, dass ...
□ We realized that something was wrong. Wir bemerkten, dass irgendetwas nicht stimmte.

really ADVERB
wirklich
□ She's really nice. Sie ist wirklich nett.
□ I'm learning Italian. — Really? Ich lerne Italienisch. — Wirklich? □ Do you really think so? Meinst du wirklich?
■ **Do you want to go? — Not really.** Willst du gehen? — Eigentlich nicht.

realtor NOUN (US)
der Immobilienhändler (PL die Immobilienhändler)
die Immobilienhändlerin

rear ADJECTIVE
▷ *see also* **rear** NOUN
hintere
□ the rear windows die hinteren Fenster
■ **the rear wheel** das Hinterrad

rear NOUN
▷ *see also* **rear** ADJECTIVE
das hintere Ende (PL die hinteren Enden)
□ at the rear of the train am hinteren Ende des Zuges

reason NOUN
der Grund (PL die Gründe)
□ There's no reason to think that ... Es gibt keinen Grund zu meinen, dass ...
■ **for security reasons** aus Sicherheitsgründen
■ **That was the main reason I went.** Das war der Hauptgrund, warum ich gegangen bin.

reasonable ADJECTIVE
1 vernünftig *(sensible)*
□ Be reasonable! Sei vernünftig!
2 ganz ordentlich *(not bad)*
□ He wrote a reasonable essay. Er hat einen ganz ordentlichen Aufsatz geschrieben.

reasonably ADVERB
ziemlich
□ reasonably well ziemlich gut
■ **reasonably priced accommodation** preiswerte Unterbringung

to **reassure** VERB
beruhigen (PERFECT hat beruhigt)

reassuring ADJECTIVE
beruhigend

rebel NOUN
▷ *see also* **rebel** VERB
der Rebell (PL die Rebellen)
die Rebellin

to **rebel** VERB
▷ *see also* **rebel** NOUN
rebellieren (PERFECT hat rebelliert)

rebellious ADJECTIVE
aufmüpfig

receipt NOUN
die Quittung

to **receive** VERB
erhalten (PRESENT erhält, IMPERFECT erhielt, PERFECT hat erhalten)

receiver NOUN
der Hörer (PL die Hörer) *(of phone)*
□ to pick up the receiver den Hörer abnehmen

recent ADJECTIVE
neueste
□ the recent developments in ... die neuesten Entwicklungen in ...
■ **in recent years** in den letzten Jahren

recently ADVERB
in letzter Zeit
□ I've been doing a lot of training recently. Ich habe in letzter Zeit viel trainiert.

reception NOUN
1 die Rezeption *(in hotel)*
□ Please leave your key at reception. Bitte geben Sie Ihren Schlüssel an der Rezeption ab.
2 der Empfang (PL die Empfänge) *(party)*
□ The reception will be at a hotel. Der Empfang findet in einem Hotel statt.

receptionist NOUN
der Empfangschef (PL die Empfangschefs)
die Empfangsdame

recession NOUN
die Rezession

recipe NOUN
das Rezept (PL die Rezepte)

to **reckon** VERB
meinen
□ What do you reckon? Was meinst du?

reclining ADJECTIVE
■ **a reclining seat** ein Liegesitz *masc*

recognizable ADJECTIVE
wiederzuerkennen
□ He was scarcely recognizable after the accident. Er war nach dem Unfall kaum wiederzuerkennen.

to **recognize** VERB
erkennen (IMPERFECT erkannte, PERFECT hat erkannt)
□ You'll recognize me by my red hair. Du wirst mich an meinen roten Haaren erkennen.

to **recommend** VERB
empfehlen (PRESENT empfiehlt, IMPERFECT empfahl, PERFECT hat empfohlen)
□ What do you recommend? Was können Sie empfehlen?

to **reconsider** VERB
■ **to reconsider something** sich etwas noch einmal überlegen □ I think you should reconsider your decision. Ich denke, du solltest dir die Entscheidung noch einmal überlegen.

record NOUN
▷ *see also* **record** VERB
1 die Schallplatte *(recording)*
□ my favourite record meine Lieblingsschallplatte
2 der Rekord (PL die Rekorde) *(sport)*
□ the world record der Weltrekord
■ **in record time** in Rekordzeit
□ She finished the job in record time. Sie war in Rekordzeit mit der Arbeit fertig.
■ **He's got a criminal record.** Er ist vorbestraft.
■ **records** *(of police, hospital)* die Akten
□ I'll check in the records. Ich sehe in den Akten nach.
■ **There is no record of your booking.** Ihre Buchung ist nirgends belegt.

to **record** VERB
▷ *see also* **record** NOUN
aufnehmen (PRESENT nimmt auf, IMPERFECT nahm auf, PERFECT hat aufgenommen) *(on film, tape)*
□ They've just recorded their new album. Sie haben eben ihr neues Album aufgenommen.

recorded delivery NOUN
■ **to send something recorded delivery** etwas per Einschreiben senden

recorder NOUN
die Blockflöte *(instrument)*
□ She plays the recorder. Sie spielt Blockflöte.
■ **a cassette recorder** ein Kassettenrekorder *masc*
■ **a video recorder** ein Videorekorder *masc*

recording NOUN
die Aufnahme

record player NOUN
der Plattenspieler (PL die Plattenspieler)

to **recover** VERB
sich erholen (PERFECT hat sich erholt)
□ He's recovering from a knee injury. Er erholt sich von einer Knieverletzung.

recovery NOUN
die Erholung
■ **Best wishes for a speedy recovery!** Gute Besserung!

rectangle NOUN
das Rechteck (PL die Rechtecke)

rectangular ADJECTIVE
rechteckig

to **recycle** VERB
wiederverwerten (PERFECT hat wiederverwertet)

recycling NOUN
das Recycling

red ADJECTIVE
rot
□ a red rose eine rote Rose □ red meat rotes Fleisch □ Peter's got red hair. Peter hat rote Haare.
■ **to go through a red light** bei Rot über die Ampel fahren

Red Cross NOUN
das Rote Kreuz

redcurrant NOUN
die Rote Johannisbeere

to **redecorate** VERB
renovieren (PERFECT hat renoviert)

red-haired ADJECTIVE
rothaarig

red-handed ADJECTIVE
■ **to catch somebody red-handed** jemanden auf frischer Tat ertappen □ He was caught red-handed. Er wurde auf frischer Tat ertappt.

redhead NOUN
der Rothaarige (GEN des Rothaarigen, PL die Rothaarigen)
die Rothaarige (GEN der Rothaarigen)
□ a redhead *(man)* ein Rothaariger

to **redo** VERB
noch einmal machen

to **reduce** VERB
ermäßigen (PERFECT hat ermäßigt)
□ at a reduced price zu ermäßigtem Preis
■ **'reduce speed now'** 'Geschwindigkeit verringern'

reduction NOUN
der Nachlass (GEN des Nachlasses, PL die Nachlässe)
□ a five per cent reduction ein Nachlass von fünf Prozent

■ **'Huge reductions!'** 'Stark reduzierte Preise!'

redundancy NOUN
die Entlassung
□ There were fifty redundancies. Es gab fünfzig Entlassungen.
■ **his redundancy payment** seine Abfindung

redundant ADJECTIVE
■ **to be made redundant** entlassen werden
□ He was made redundant yesterday. Er wurde gestern entlassen.

reed NOUN
das Schilf *(plant)*

reel NOUN
die Spule *(of thread)*

to **refer** VERB
■ **to refer to** anspielen auf *+acc* □ What are you referring to? Auf was spielst du an?

referee NOUN
der Schiedsrichter (PL die Schiedsrichter)
die Schiedsrichterin

reference NOUN
das Arbeitszeugnis (GEN des Arbeitszeugnisses, PL die Arbeitszeugnisse) *(for job application)*
□ Would you please give me a reference? Können Sie mir bitte ein Arbeitszeugnis geben?
■ **With reference to your letter of ...** Mit Bezug auf Ihren Brief vom ...
■ **a reference book** ein Nachschlagewerk *neut*

to **refill** VERB
nachfüllen (PERFECT hat nachgefüllt)
□ He refilled my glass. Er füllte mein Glas nach.

refinery NOUN
die Raffinerie

to **reflect** VERB
reflektieren (PERFECT hat reflektiert) *(light, image)*

reflection NOUN
das Spiegelbild (PL die Spiegelbilder) *(in mirror)*

reflex NOUN
der Reflex (GEN des Reflexes, PL die Reflexe)

reflexive ADJECTIVE
reflexiv
□ a reflexive verb ein reflexives Verb

refresher course NOUN
der Wiederholungskurs (GEN des Wiederholungskurses, PL die Wiederholungskurse)

refreshing ADJECTIVE
erfrischend

refreshments PL NOUN
die Erfrischungen *fem pl*

refrigerator NOUN
der Kühlschrank (PL die Kühlschränke)

to **refuel** VERB
auftanken (PERFECT hat aufgetankt)
□ Our plane refuelled in Boston. Unser Flugzeug hat in Boston aufgetankt.

refuge NOUN
die Zuflucht

refugee NOUN
der Flüchtling (PL die Flüchtlinge)
LANGUAGE TIP **der Flüchtling** is also used for women.

refund NOUN
▷ *see also* **refund** VERB
die Rückvergütung

to **refund** VERB
▷ *see also* **refund** NOUN
zurückerstatten (PERFECT hat zurückerstattet)

refusal NOUN
die Weigerung

to **refuse** VERB
▷ *see also* **refuse** NOUN
sich weigern

refuse NOUN
▷ *see also* **refuse** VERB
der Müll
■ **refuse collection** die Müllabfuhr

to **regain** VERB
■ **to regain consciousness** wieder zu Bewusstsein kommen

regard NOUN
▷ *see also* **regard** VERB
■ **Give my regards to Alice.** Grüße an Alice.
■ **Martin sends his regards.** Martin lässt grüßen.
■ **'with kind regards'** 'mit freundlichen Grüßen'

to **regard** VERB
▷ *see also* **regard** NOUN
■ **to regard something as** etwas betrachten als
■ **as regards ...** was ... betrifft □ As regards offensive weapons ... Was Angriffswaffen betrifft, ...

regarding PREPOSITION
betreffend
□ the laws regarding the export of animals die Gesetze den Export von Tieren betreffend
■ **Regarding John, ...** Was John betrifft, ...

regardless ADVERB
trotzdem
□ to carry on regardless trotzdem weitermachen

regiment NOUN
das Regiment (PL die Regimenter)

region NOUN
die Gegend

regional ADJECTIVE
regional

register NOUN
▷ *see also* **register** VERB
das Klassenbuch (PL die Klassenbücher) *(in school)*

to **register** VERB
▷ *see also* **register** NOUN

sich einschreiben (IMPERFECT schrieb sich ein, PERFECT hat sich eingeschrieben) *(at school, college)*

registered ADJECTIVE

■ **a registered letter** ein eingeschriebener Brief

registration NOUN

1 der Namensaufruf (PL die Namensaufrufe) *(in school)*

2 das polizeiliche Kennzeichen (PL die polizeilichen Kennzeichen) *(of car)*

regret NOUN

▷ *see also* **regret** VERB

das Bedauern

■ **I've got no regrets.** Ich bedaure nichts.

to **regret** VERB

▷ *see also* **regret** NOUN

bedauern (PERFECT hat bedauert)

□ You'll regret it! Du wirst es bedauern!

■ **to regret doing something** es bedauern, etwas getan zu haben □ I regretted I said that. Ich habe bedauert, dass ich das gesagt habe.

regular ADJECTIVE

1 regelmäßig

□ at regular intervals in regelmäßigen Abständen □ a regular verb ein regelmäßiges Verb

■ **to take regular exercise** regelmäßig Sport machen

2 normal *(average)*

□ a regular portion of fries eine normale Portion Pommes frites

regularly ADVERB

regelmäßig

regulation NOUN

die Bestimmung

rehearsal NOUN

die Probe

to **rehearse** VERB

proben

rein NOUN

der Zügel (PL die Zügel)

□ the reins die Zügel

reindeer NOUN

das Rentier (PL die Rentiere)

to **reject** VERB

verwerfen (PRESENT verwirft, IMPERFECT verwarf, PERFECT hat verworfen) *(idea, suggestion)*

□ We rejected the idea. Wir haben die Idee verworfen.

■ **I applied but they rejected me.** Ich habe mich beworben, wurde aber abgelehnt.

relapse NOUN

der Rückfall (PL die Rückfälle)

□ to have a relapse einen Rückfall haben

related ADJECTIVE

verwandt *(people)*

□ Are you related to her? Bist du mit ihr verwandt? □ We're related. Wir sind miteinander verwandt.

■ **The two events were not related.** Es bestand kein Zusammenhang zwischen den beiden Ereignissen.

relation NOUN

1 der Verwandte (GEN des Verwandten, PL die Verwandten)

die Verwandte (GEN der Verwandten) *(person)*

□ He's a distant relation. Er ist ein entfernter Verwandter. □ I've got relations in London. Ich habe Verwandte in London. □ my close relations meine engsten Verwandten

2 der Bezug (PL die Bezüge) *(connection)*

□ It has no relation to reality. Es hat keinen Bezug zur Wirklichkeit.

■ **in relation to** verglichen mit

relationship NOUN

die Beziehung

□ We have a good relationship. Wir haben eine gute Beziehung. □ I'm not in a relationship at the moment. Ich habe im Moment keine Beziehung.

relative NOUN

der Verwandte (GEN des Verwandten, PL die Verwandten)

die Verwandte (GEN der Verwandten)

□ a relative *(man)* ein Verwandter □ my close relatives meine engsten Verwandten

■ **all her relatives** ihre ganze Verwandtschaft

relatively ADVERB

relativ

to **relax** VERB

sich entspannen (PERFECT hat sich entspannt)

□ I relax listening to music. Ich entspanne mich beim Musikhören.

■ **Relax! Everything's fine.** Immer mit der Ruhe! Alles ist in Ordnung.

relaxation NOUN

die Entspannung

□ I don't have much time for relaxation. Ich habe nicht viel Zeit für Entspannung.

relaxed ADJECTIVE

entspannt

relaxing ADJECTIVE

entspannend

□ I find cooking relaxing. Ich finde Kochen entspannend.

relay NOUN

■ **a relay race** ein Staffellauf *masc*

to **release** VERB

▷ *see also* **release** NOUN

1 freilassen (PRESENT lässt frei, IMPERFECT ließ frei, PERFECT hat freigelassen) *(prisoner)*

2 veröffentlichen (PERFECT hat veröffentlicht) *(report, news)*

3 herausbringen (IMPERFECT brachte heraus, PERFECT hat herausgebracht) *(record, video)*

release NOUN

▷ *see also* **release** VERB

die Freilassung *(from prison)*

□ the release of Nelson Mandela die Freilassung Nelson Mandelas

■ **the band's latest release** die neueste Platte der Band

relegated ADJECTIVE
abgestiegen *(sport)*
□ We were relegated. Wir sind abgestiegen.

relevant ADJECTIVE
entsprechend *(documents)*
■ **That's not relevant.** Das ist nicht relevant.
■ **to be relevant to something** einen Bezug zu etwas haben □ Education should be relevant to real life. Die Ausbildung sollte einen Bezug zum wirklichen Leben haben.

reliable ADJECTIVE
zuverlässig
□ a reliable car ein zuverlässiges Auto □ He's not very reliable. Er ist nicht sehr zuverlässig.

relief NOUN
die Erleichterung
□ That's a relief! Das ist eine Erleichterung!

to **relieve** VERB
lindern
□ This injection will relieve the pain. Diese Spritze wird den Schmerz lindern.

relieved ADJECTIVE
erleichtert
□ I was relieved to hear ... Ich war erleichtert zu hören ...

religion NOUN
die Religion
□ What religion are you? Welche Religion hast du?

religious ADJECTIVE
religiös
□ I'm not religious. Ich bin nicht religiös.
■ **my religious beliefs** mein Glaube *masc*

reluctant ADJECTIVE
■ **to be reluctant to do something** etwas nur ungern tun □ They were reluctant to help us. Sie haben uns nur ungern geholfen.

reluctantly ADVERB
ungern
□ She reluctantly accepted. Sie hat ungern angenommen.

to **rely on** VERB
sich verlassen auf +*acc* (PRESENT verlässt sich, IMPERFECT verließ sich, PERFECT hat sich verlassen)
□ I'm relying on you. Ich verlasse mich auf dich.

to **remain** VERB
bleiben (IMPERFECT blieb, PERFECT ist geblieben)
■ **to remain silent** schweigen

remaining ADJECTIVE
restlich
□ the remaining ingredients die restlichen Zutaten

remains PL NOUN
die Reste *masc pl*
□ the remains of the picnic die Reste des Picknicks
■ **human remains** die menschlichen Überreste
■ **Roman remains** römische Ruinen

remake NOUN
das Remake (PL die Remakes) *(of film)*

remark NOUN
die Bemerkung

remarkable ADJECTIVE
bemerkenswert

remarkably ADVERB
bemerkenswert

to **remarry** VERB
wieder heiraten
□ She remarried three years ago. Sie hat vor drei Jahren wieder geheiratet.

remedy NOUN
das Mittel (PL die Mittel)
□ a good remedy for a sore throat ein gutes Mittel gegen Halsschmerzen

to **remember** VERB
sich erinnern (PERFECT hat sich erinnert)
□ I can't remember his name. Ich kann mich nicht an seinen Namen erinnern. □ I don't remember. Ich erinnere mich nicht.

> LANGUAGE TIP In German you often say 'don't forget' rather than 'remember' when reminding somebody about something.

□ Remember your passport! Vergiss deinen Pass nicht! □ Remember to write your name on the form. Vergiss nicht, deinen Namen auf das Formular zu schreiben.

Remembrance Day NOUN
der Volkstrauertag
□ on Remembrance Day am Volkstrauertag

to **remind** VERB
erinnern (PERFECT hat erinnert)
□ It reminds me of Scotland. Es erinnert mich an Schottland. □ I'll remind you tomorrow. Ich werde dich morgen daran erinnern.
□ Remind me to speak to Daniel. Erinnere mich, dass ich mit Daniel sprechen will.

remorse NOUN
die Reue
□ He showed no remorse. Er zeigte keine Reue.

remote ADJECTIVE
abgelegen
□ a remote village ein abgelegenes Dorf

remote control NOUN
die Fernbedienung

remotely ADVERB
entfernt
□ There was nobody remotely resembling this description. Niemand sah dieser Beschreibung auch nur entfernt ähnlich.
■ **It's remotely possible that ...** Es ist gerade eben noch möglich, dass ...

removable ADJECTIVE
abnehmbar

removal NOUN
der Umzug (PL die Umzüge) *(from house)*
■ **a removal van** ein Möbelwagen *masc*

to **remove** VERB
entfernen (PERFECT hat entfernt)
□ Did you remove the stain? Hast du den Fleck entfernt?

rendezvous NOUN
das Treffen (PL die Treffen)

to **renew** VERB
verlängern lassen (PRESENT lässt verlängern, IMPERFECT ließ verlängern, PERFECT hat verlängern lassen) *(passport, licence)*
□ You'll need to renew your passport. Du musst deinen Pass verlängern lassen.
■ **to renew a contract** einen Vertrag verlängern

renewable ADJECTIVE
erneuerbar *(energy, resource, passport)*

to **renovate** VERB
renovieren (PERFECT hat renoviert)
□ The building's been renovated. Das Gebäude ist renoviert worden.

renowned ADJECTIVE
berühmt

rent NOUN
▷ *see also* **rent** VERB
die Miete

LANGUAGE TIP Be careful not to translate **rent** by **Rente**.

to **rent** VERB
▷ *see also* **rent** NOUN
mieten
□ We rented a car. Wir haben ein Auto gemietet.

rental NOUN
die Miete
□ Car rental is included in the price. Die Automiete ist im Preis inbegriffen.

rental car NOUN (US)
der Mietwagen (PL die Mietwagen)

to **reorganize** VERB
umorganisieren (PERFECT hat umorganisiert)

rep NOUN *(= representative)*
der Vertreter (PL die Vertreter)
die Vertreterin

repaid VERB ▷ *see* **repay**

to **repair** VERB
▷ *see also* **repair** NOUN
reparieren (PERFECT hat repariert)
■ **to get something repaired** etwas reparieren lassen □ I got the washing machine repaired. Ich habe die Waschmaschine reparieren lassen.

repair NOUN
▷ *see also* **repair** VERB
die Reparatur

to **repay** VERB
zurückzahlen (PERFECT hat zurückgezahlt) *(money)*

repayment NOUN
die Rückzahlung

to **repeat** VERB
▷ *see also* **repeat** NOUN
wiederholen (PERFECT hat wiederholt)

repeat NOUN
▷ *see also* **repeat** VERB
die Wiederholung
□ There are too many repeats on TV. Es gibt zu viele Wiederholungen im Fernsehen.

repeatedly ADVERB
wiederholt

repellent NOUN
■ **insect repellent** das Insektenschutzmittel

repetitive ADJECTIVE
monoton *(movement, work)*

to **replace** VERB
ersetzen (PERFECT hat ersetzt)

replay NOUN
▷ *see also* **replay** VERB
■ **There will be a replay on Friday.** Das Spiel wird am Freitag wiederholt.

to **replay** VERB
▷ *see also* **replay** NOUN
wiederholen (PERFECT hat wiederholt) *(match)*

replica NOUN
die Kopie

reply NOUN
▷ *see also* **reply** VERB
die Antwort

to **reply** VERB
▷ *see also* **reply** NOUN
antworten

report NOUN
▷ *see also* **report** VERB
1 der Bericht (PL die Berichte) *(of event)*
□ a report in the paper ein Zeitungsbericht
2 das Zeugnis (GEN des Zeugnisses, PL die Zeugnisse) *(at school)*
□ I got a good report. Ich habe ein gutes Zeugnis bekommen.
■ **report card** das Zeugnis

to **report** VERB
▷ *see also* **report** NOUN
1 melden
□ I've reported the theft. Ich habe den Diebstahl gemeldet.
2 sich melden
□ Report to reception when you arrive. Melden Sie sich bei Ihrer Ankunft am Empfang.

reporter NOUN
der Reporter (PL die Reporter)
die Reporterin
□ She'd like to be a reporter. Sie möchte gern Reporterin werden.

to **represent** VERB
vertreten (PRESENT vertritt, IMPERFECT vertrat, PERFECT hat vertreten) *(person)*
□ My lawyer represented me in court.

Mein Anwalt hat mich vor Gericht vertreten.

representative ADJECTIVE
repräsentativ

reproduction NOUN
die Reproduktion

reptile NOUN
das Reptil (PL die Reptilien)

republic NOUN
die Republik

repulsive ADJECTIVE
abstoßend

reputable ADJECTIVE
angesehen

reputation NOUN
der Ruf

request NOUN
▷ *see also* **request** VERB
die Bitte

to **request** VERB
▷ *see also* **request** NOUN
bitten um (IMPERFECT bat, PERFECT hat gebeten)
□ He requested information. Er bat um Informationen.

to **require** VERB
erfordern (PERFECT hat erfordert)
□ Her job requires a lot of patience. Ihre Arbeit erfordert viel Geduld.

requirement NOUN
die Voraussetzung
□ What are the requirements for the job? Was sind die Voraussetzungen für diese Arbeit?
■ **entry requirements** *(for university)* die Aufnahmebedingungen

resat VERB ▷ *see* **resit**

to **rescue** VERB
▷ *see also* **rescue** NOUN
retten

rescue NOUN
▷ *see also* **rescue** VERB
die Rettung
□ a rescue operation eine Rettungsaktion
■ **a mountain rescue team** ein Team der Bergwacht
■ **the rescue services** der Rettungsdienst *sing*
■ **to come to somebody's rescue** jemandem zu Hilfe kommen □ He came to my rescue. Er kam mir zu Hilfe.

research NOUN
die Forschung *(experimental)*
□ He's doing research. Er ist in der Forschung tätig.
■ **Research has shown that ...** Forschungen haben ergeben, dass ...
■ **She's doing some research in the library.** Sie sammelt in der Bibliothek Material.

resemblance NOUN
die Ähnlichkeit

to **resent** VERB
übel nehmen (PRESENT nimmt übel, IMPERFECT nahm übel, PERFECT hat übel genommen)
□ I really resent your criticism. Ich nehme Ihnen Ihre Kritik wirklich übel.
■ **I resent being dependent on her.** Ich ärgere mich darüber, von ihr abhängig zu sein.

resentful ADJECTIVE
verärgert
□ He was resentful about the way they were treated. Er war verärgert darüber, wie sie behandelt wurden.

reservation NOUN
1 die Reservierung *(at restaurant)*
■ **I'd like to make a reservation for this evening.** Ich möchte für heute Abend einen Tisch reservieren.
2 die Buchung *(for journey, at hotel)*
■ **I've got a reservation for two nights.** Ich habe für zwei Nächte gebucht.

reserve NOUN
▷ *see also* **reserve** VERB
1 das Schutzgebiet (PL die Schutzgebiete) *(place)*
□ a nature reserve ein Naturschutzgebiet
2 der Reservespieler (PL die Reservespieler) die Reservespielerin *(person)*
□ She was reserve in the game last Saturday. Sie war beim Spiel letzten Samstag Reservespielerin.

to **reserve** VERB
▷ *see also* **reserve** NOUN
reservieren (PERFECT hat reserviert)
□ I'd like to reserve a table for tomorrow evening. Ich möchte für morgen Abend einen Tisch reservieren.

reserved ADJECTIVE
reserviert
□ a reserved seat ein reservierter Platz
□ He's quite reserved. Er ist ziemlich reserviert.

reservoir NOUN
das Reservoir (PL die Reservoire)

resident NOUN
der Bewohner (PL die Bewohner)
die Bewohnerin

residential ADJECTIVE
■ **a residential area** ein Wohngebiet *neut*

to **resign** VERB
1 zurücktreten (PRESENT tritt zurück, IMPERFECT trat zurück, PERFECT ist zurückgetreten)
□ The minister resigned. Der Minister ist zurückgetreten.
2 kündigen *(employee)*
□ She resigned to take up a post abroad. Sie kündigte, um einen Posten im Ausland zu übernehmen.

resistance NOUN
der Widerstand (PL die Widerstände)

to **resit** VERB
wiederholen (PERFECT hat wiederholt)
□ I'm resitting the exam in May. Ich wiederhole die Prüfung im Mai.

resolution NOUN
der Beschluss (GEN des Beschlusses, PL die Beschlüsse) *(decision)*

■ Have you made any New Year's resolutions? Hast du zum neuen Jahr gute Vorsätze gefasst?

resort NOUN
der Badeort (PL die Badeorte) *(at seaside)*
□ It's a resort on the Costa del Sol. Es ist ein Badeort an der Costa del Sol.
■ a ski resort ein Skiort
■ as a last resort als letzter Ausweg

resources PL NOUN
die Mittel *neut pl (financial)*
□ We haven't the resources to build a swimming pool. Wir haben nicht die Mittel, um ein Schwimmbad zu bauen.
■ natural resources Bodenschätze *masc pl*

respect NOUN
▷ *see also* **respect** VERB
der Respekt

to **respect** VERB
▷ *see also* **respect** NOUN
respektieren (PERFECT hat respektiert)

respectable ADJECTIVE
1 anständig
□ respectable people anständige Leute *pl*
2 ordentlich *(standard, marks)*

respectively ADVERB
beziehungsweise
□ Britain and Germany were third and fourth respectively. Großbritannien und Deutschland belegten den dritten beziehungsweise vierten Platz.

responsibility NOUN
die Verantwortung

responsible ADJECTIVE
1 verantwortlich
□ to be responsible for something für etwas verantwortlich sein
■ It's a responsible job. Es ist ein verantwortungsvoller Posten.
2 verantwortungsbewusst *(mature)*
□ You should be more responsible. Du solltest verantwortungsbewusster sein.

rest NOUN
▷ *see also* **rest** VERB
1 die Pause *(relaxation)*
□ five minutes' rest eine fünfminütige Pause
■ to have a rest sich ausruhen
□ We stopped to have a rest. Wir haben Halt gemacht, um uns auszuruhen.
2 der Rest (PL die Reste) *(remainder)*
□ I'll do the rest. Ich mache den Rest.
□ the rest of the money der Rest des Geldes
■ the rest of them die anderen □ The rest of them went swimming. Die anderen sind schwimmen gegangen.

to **rest** VERB
▷ *see also* **rest** NOUN
1 sich ausruhen (PERFECT hat sich ausgeruht) *(relax)*
□ She's resting in her room. Sie ruht sich in ihrem Zimmer aus.
2 schonen *(not overstrain)*
■ He has to rest his knee. Er muss sein Knie schonen.
3 lehnen *(lean)*
□ I rested my bike against the window. Ich habe mein Fahrrad ans Fenster gelehnt.

restaurant NOUN
das Restaurant (PL die Restaurants)
□ We don't often go to restaurants. Wir gehen nicht oft ins Restaurant.
■ a restaurant car ein Speisewagen *masc*

restful ADJECTIVE
ruhig

restless ADJECTIVE
unruhig

restoration NOUN
die Restauration

to **restore** VERB
restaurieren (PERFECT hat restauriert) *(building, picture)*

to **restrict** VERB
beschränken (PERFECT hat beschränkt)

rest room NOUN (US)
die Toilette

result NOUN
das Ergebnis (GEN des Ergebnisses, PL die Ergebnisse)
□ my exam results meine Prüfungsergebnisse
■ What was the result? — One nil. Wie ist das Spiel ausgegangen? — Eins zu null.

résumé NOUN (US)
1 die Zusammenfassung
□ a résumé of her speech eine Zusammenfassung ihrer Rede
2 der Lebenslauf (PL die Lebensläufe) *(CV)*

to **retire** VERB
in Rente gehen (IMPERFECT ging in Rente, PERFECT ist in Rente gegangen)
□ He retired last year. Er ist letztes Jahr in Rente gegangen.

retired ADJECTIVE
im Ruhestand
□ She's retired. Sie ist im Ruhestand.
□ a retired teacher ein Lehrer im Ruhestand

retirement NOUN
der Ruhestand

to **retrace** VERB
■ to retrace one's steps zurückgehen
□ I retraced my steps. Ich bin zurückgegangen.

return NOUN
▷ *see also* **return** VERB
1 die Rückkehr
□ after our return nach unserer Rückkehr
■ the return journey die Rückfahrt
■ a return match ein Rückspiel *neut*
2 die Rückfahrkarte *(ticket)*
□ A return to Freiburg, please. Eine Rückfahrkarte nach Freiburg, bitte.
■ in return dafür □ ... and I help her in return ... und dafür helfe ich ihr

■ **in return for** für
■ **Many happy returns!** Herzlichen Glückwunsch zum Geburtstag!

to **return** VERB
▷ *see also* **return** NOUN
1 zurückkommen (IMPERFECT kam zurück, PERFECT ist zurückgekommen) *(come back)*
□ I've just returned from holiday. Ich bin gerade aus den Ferien zurückgekommen.
■ **to return home** wieder nach Hause kommen
2 zurückkehren (PERFECT ist zurückgekehrt) *(go back)*
□ He returned to Germany the following year. Er ist im Jahr danach nach Deutschland zurückgekehrt.
3 zurückgeben (PRESENT gibt zurück, IMPERFECT gab zurück, PERFECT hat zurückgegeben) *(give back)*
□ She borrows my things and doesn't return them. Sie leiht sich meine Sachen aus und gibt sie dann nicht zurück.

reunion NOUN
das Treffen (PL die Treffen)

to **reuse** VERB
wiederverwenden (PERFECT hat wiederverwendet)

to **reveal** VERB
ans Licht bringen (IMPERFECT brachte ans Licht, PERFECT hat ans Licht gebracht) *(truth, facts)*
□ The survey reveals that many people are overweight. Die Untersuchung bringt ans Licht, dass viele Menschen Übergewicht haben.
■ **She refused to reveal the whereabouts of her daughter.** Sie weigerte sich, den Aufenthaltsort ihrer Tochter preiszugeben.
■ **It was revealed that ...** Es wurde bekannt gegeben, dass ...

revenge NOUN
die Rache
□ in revenge aus Rache
■ **to take revenge** sich rächen
□ They planned to take revenge on him. Sie haben geplant, sich an ihm zu rächen.

to **reverse** VERB
▷ *see also* **reverse** ADJECTIVE
rückwärtsfahren (PRESENT fährt rückwärts, IMPERFECT fuhr rückwärts, PERFECT ist rückwärtsgefahren) *(car)*
□ He reversed without looking. Er fuhr rückwärts ohne zu sehen.
■ **to reverse the charges** *(telephone)* ein R-Gespräch führen □ I'd like to make a reverse charge call. Ich möchte gern ein R-Gespräch führen.

reverse ADJECTIVE
▷ *see also* **reverse** VERB
umgekehrt
□ in reverse order in umgekehrter Reihenfolge
■ **in reverse gear** im Rückwärtsgang

review NOUN
1 die Überprüfung *(of policy, salary)*
2 die Prüfung *(of subject)*
■ **to be under review** überprüft werden

to **revise** VERB
den Stoff wiederholen
□ I haven't started revising yet. Ich habe noch nicht angefangen, den Stoff zu wiederholen.
■ **I've revised my opinion.** Ich habe meine Meinung geändert.

revision NOUN
die Wiederholung des Stoffes
■ **Have you done a lot of revision?** Hast du schon viel Stoff wiederholt?

to **revive** VERB
wiederbeleben (PERFECT hat wiederbelebt)
□ They tried to revive him. Sie versuchten, ihn wiederzubeleben.

revolting ADJECTIVE
ekelhaft

revolution NOUN
die Revolution
□ the French Revolution die Französische Revolution

revolutionary ADJECTIVE
revolutionär

revolver NOUN
der Revolver (PL die Revolver)

reward NOUN
die Belohnung

rewarding ADJECTIVE
dankbar
□ a rewarding job eine dankbare Arbeit

to **rewind** VERB
zurückspulen (PERFECT hat zurückgespult)
□ to rewind a cassette eine Kassette zurückspulen

rheumatism NOUN
das Rheuma

Rhine NOUN
der Rhein

rhinoceros NOUN
das Nashorn (PL die Nashörner)

rhubarb NOUN
der Rhabarber
□ a rhubarb tart ein Rhabarberkuchen

rhythm NOUN
der Rhythmus (GEN des Rhythmus, PL die Rhythmen)

rib NOUN
die Rippe

ribbon NOUN
das Band (PL die Bänder)

rice NOUN
der Reis
■ **rice pudding** der Milchreis

rich ADJECTIVE
reich
■ **the rich** die Reichen *masc pl*

to rid VERB

■ **to get rid of** loswerden □ I want to get rid of some old clothes. Ich will ein paar alte Kleider loswerden.

ride NOUN

▷ *see also* **ride** VERB

■ **to go for a ride 1** *(on horse)* reiten gehen **2** *(on bike)* mit dem Fahrrad fahren

■ **We went for a bike ride.** Wir haben eine Fahrt mit dem Fahrrad gemacht.

■ **It's a short bus ride to the town centre.** Die Stadtmitte ist nur eine kurze Busfahrt entfernt.

to ride VERB

▷ *see also* **ride** NOUN

reiten (IMPERFECT ritt, PERFECT ist geritten) *(on horse)*

□ I'm learning to ride. Ich lerne reiten.

■ **to ride a bike** Fahrrad fahren □ Can you ride a bike? Kannst du Fahrrad fahren?

rider NOUN

1 der Reiter (PL die Reiter)
die Reiterin *(on horse)*

□ She's a good rider. Sie ist eine gute Reiterin.

2 der Fahrradfahrer (PL die Fahrradfahrer)
die Fahrradfahrerin *(on bike)*

ridiculous ADJECTIVE

lächerlich

□ Don't be ridiculous! Mach dich nicht lächerlich!

riding NOUN

das Reiten

■ **to go riding** reiten gehen

■ **a riding school** eine Reitschule

rifle NOUN

das Gewehr (PL die Gewehre)

□ a hunting rifle ein Jagdgewehr

rig NOUN

■ **an oil rig** eine Bohrinsel

right ADJECTIVE, ADVERB

▷ *see also* **right** NOUN

LANGUAGE TIP There are several ways of translating 'right'. Scan the examples to find one that is similar to what you want to say.

1 richtig *(correct, suitable)*

□ the right answer die richtige Antwort □ Am I pronouncing it right? Spreche ich das richtig aus? □ It isn't the right size. Es ist nicht die richtige Größe. □ We're on the right train. Wir sind im richtigen Zug. □ It's not right to behave like that. Es ist nicht richtig, sich so zu benehmen.

■ **Is this the right road for Hamburg?** Sind wir hier richtig nach Hamburg?

■ **I think you did the right thing.** Ich glaube, du hast das Richtige getan.

■ **to be right 1** *(person)* recht haben □ You were right! Du hattest recht! **2** *(statement, opinion)* richtig sein □ That's right! Das ist richtig!

2 genau *(accurate)*

□ Do you have the right time? Haben Sie die genaue Zeit?

3 rechte *(not left)*

□ the right foot der rechte Fuß □ my right arm mein rechter Arm □ your right hand deine rechte Hand □ her right eye ihr rechtes Auge

4 rechts *(turn)*

□ Turn right at the lights. Biegen Sie an der Ampel rechts ab.

■ **Look right!** Sehen Sie nach rechts!

■ **Right! Let's get started.** Okay! Fangen wir an.

■ **right away** sofort □ I'll do it right away. Ich mache es sofort.

right NOUN

▷ *see also* **right** ADJECTIVE

1 das Recht (PL die Rechte)

□ You've got no right to do that. Du hast kein Recht, das zu tun.

2 die rechte Seite *(not left)*

■ **on the right** rechts □ Remember to drive on the right. Vergiss nicht, rechts zu fahren.

■ **right of way** die Vorfahrt □ We had right of way. Wir hatten Vorfahrt.

right-hand ADJECTIVE

■ **the right-hand side** die rechte Seite

■ **It's on the right-hand side.** Es liegt rechts.

right-handed ADJECTIVE

rechtshändig

rightly ADVERB

richtig

□ If I remember rightly ... Wenn ich mich richtig erinnere, ... □ She rightly decided that he was lying. Sie kam zu dem richtigen Schluss, dass er log.

rim NOUN

der Rand (PL die Ränder)

□ glasses with wire rims eine Brille mit Metallrand

ring NOUN

▷ *see also* **ring** VERB

1 der Ring (PL die Ringe)

□ a gold ring ein goldener Ring □ a diamond ring ein Diamantring

■ **a wedding ring** ein Ehering

2 der Kreis (GEN des Kreises, PL die Kreise) *(circle)*

□ to stand in a ring im Kreis stehen

3 das Klingeln *(of bell)*

■ **There was a ring at the door.** Es klingelt.

■ **to give somebody a ring** jemanden anrufen □ I'll give you a ring this evening. Ich rufe dich heute Abend an.

to ring VERB

▷ *see also* **ring** NOUN

1 anrufen (IMPERFECT rief an, PERFECT hat angerufen)

□ Your mother rang. Deine Mutter hat heute früh angerufen.

■ **to ring somebody** jemanden anrufen
□ I'll ring you tomorrow morning. Ich rufe dich morgen früh an.
■ **to ring somebody up** jemanden anrufen
2 klingeln
□ The phone's ringing. Das Telefon klingelt.
■ **to ring the bell** *(doorbell)* klingeln □ I rang the bell three times. Ich habe dreimal geklingelt.
■ **to ring back** zurückrufen □ I'll ring back later. Ich rufe später zurück.

ring binder NOUN
das Ringheft (PL die Ringhefte)

ring road NOUN
die Ringstraße

ringtone NOUN
der Klingelton (PL die Klingeltöne)

rink NOUN
1 die Eisbahn *(for ice-skating)*
2 die Rollschuhbahn *(for roller-skating)*

to **rinse** VERB
spülen

riot NOUN
▷ *see also* **riot** VERB
die Krawalle *masc pl*

to **riot** VERB
▷ *see also* **riot** NOUN
randalieren (PERFECT hat randaliert)

to **rip** VERB
zerreißen (IMPERFECT zerriss, PERFECT hat zerrissen)
□ I've ripped my jeans. Ich habe meine Jeans zerrissen. □ My skirt's ripped. Mein Rock ist zerrissen.

to **rip off** VERB
ausnehmen *(informal)* (PRESENT nimmt aus, IMPERFECT nahm aus, PERFECT hat ausgenommen)
□ The hotel ripped us off. Das Hotel hat uns ausgenommen.

to **rip up** VERB
zerreißen (IMPERFECT zerriss, PERFECT hat zerrissen)

ripe ADJECTIVE
reif

rip-off NOUN
■ **It's a rip-off!** Das ist Nepp! *(informal)*

rise NOUN
▷ *see also* **rise** VERB
1 der Anstieg (PL die Anstiege) *(in prices, temperature)*
□ a sudden rise in temperature ein plötzlicher Temperaturanstieg
2 die Gehaltserhöhung *(pay rise)*

to **rise** VERB
▷ *see also* **rise** NOUN
1 steigen (IMPERFECT stieg, PERFECT ist gestiegen) *(increase)*
□ Prices are rising. Die Preise steigen.
2 aufgehen (IMPERFECT ging auf, PERFECT ist aufgegangen)
□ The sun rises early in June. Die Sonne geht im Juni früh auf.

riser NOUN
■ **to be an early riser** ein Frühaufsteher sein

risk NOUN
▷ *see also* **risk** VERB
das Risiko (PL die Risiken)
■ **to take risks** Risiken eingehen □ I don't want to take risks. Ich möchte kein Risiko eingehen.
■ **It's at your own risk.** Auf eigene Gefahr.

to **risk** VERB
▷ *see also* **risk** NOUN
riskieren (PERFECT hat riskiert)
□ You risk getting a fine. Du riskierst einen Strafzettel. □ I wouldn't risk it. Das würde ich an deiner Stelle nicht riskieren.

risky ADJECTIVE
gefährlich

rival NOUN
▷ *see also* **rival** ADJECTIVE
der Rivale (GEN des Rivalen, PL die Rivalen)
die Rivalin

rival ADJECTIVE
▷ *see also* **rival** NOUN
rivalisierend
□ a rival gang eine rivalisierende Bande
■ **a rival company** ein Konkurrenzunternehmen *neut*

rivalry NOUN
die Rivalität *(between towns, schools)*

river NOUN
der Fluss (GEN des Flusses, PL die Flüsse)
■ **the river Rhine** der Rhein

Riviera NOUN
die Riviera
□ the Italian Riviera die italienische Riviera
■ **the French Riviera** die Côte d'Azur

road NOUN
die Straße
□ There's a lot of traffic on the roads. Es herrscht viel Verkehr auf den Straßen.
■ **They live across the road.** Sie wohnen gegenüber.

road map NOUN
die Straßenkarte

road rage NOUN
die Aggressivität im Straßenverkehr

road sign NOUN
das Verkehrsschild (PL die Verkehrsschilder)

roadworks PL NOUN
die Bauarbeiten *fem pl*

roast ADJECTIVE
■ **roast chicken** das Brathähnchen
■ **roast potatoes** die Bratkartoffeln
■ **roast pork** der Schweinebraten
■ **roast beef** der Rindsbraten

to **rob** VERB
■ **to rob somebody** jemanden berauben
□ I've been robbed. Ich bin beraubt worden.

■ **to rob a bank** eine Bank ausrauben
■ **to rob somebody of something** jemandem etwas rauben □ He was robbed of his wallet. Man hat ihm seine Brieftasche geraubt.

robber NOUN
der Räuber (PL die Räuber)
die Räuberin
■ **a bank robber** ein Bankräuber

robbery NOUN
der Raub (PL die Raube)
■ **a bank robbery** ein Bankraub
■ **armed robbery** der bewaffnete Raubüberfall

robin NOUN
das Rotkehlchen (PL die Rotkehlchen)

robot NOUN
der Roboter (PL die Roboter)

rock NOUN
▷ *see also* **rock** VERB
1 der Fels (GEN des Fels) *(substance)*
□ They tunnelled through the rock. Sie gruben einen Tunnel durch den Fels.
2 der Felsbrocken (PL die Felsbrocken) *(boulder)*
□ I sat on a rock. Ich saß auf einem Felsbrocken.
3 der Stein (PL die Steine) *(stone)*
□ The crowd threw rocks. Die Menge fing an, Steine zu werfen.
4 der Rock *(music)*
□ a rock concert ein Rockkonzert
□ He's a rock star. Er ist ein Rockstar.
5 die Zuckerstange *(sweet)*
□ a stick of rock eine Zuckerstange
■ **rock and roll** der Rock 'n' Roll

to **rock** VERB
▷ *see also* **rock** NOUN
erschüttern (PERFECT hat erschüttert)
□ The explosion rocked the building. Die Explosion erschütterte das Gebäude.

rockery NOUN
der Steingarten (PL die Steingärten)

rocket NOUN
die Rakete *(firework, spacecraft)*

rocking chair NOUN
der Schaukelstuhl (PL die Schaukelstühle)

rocking horse NOUN
das Schaukelpferd (PL die Schaukelpferde)

rod NOUN
die Angel *(for fishing)*

rode VERB ▷ *see* **ride**

role NOUN
die Rolle

role play NOUN
das Rollenspiel (PL die Rollenspiele)
□ to do a role play ein Rollenspiel machen

roll NOUN
▷ *see also* **roll** VERB
1 die Rolle
□ a roll of tape eine Rolle Klebstreifen
□ a toilet roll eine Rolle Toilettenpapier
2 das Brötchen (PL die Brötchen) *(bread)*

to **roll** VERB
▷ *see also* **roll** NOUN
rollen
■ **to roll out the pastry** den Teig ausrollen

roll call NOUN
der Namensaufruf (PL die Namensaufrufe)

roller NOUN
die Walze

Rollerblade® NOUN
der Rollerblade® (PL die Rollerblades)

roller coaster NOUN
die Achterbahn

roller skates PL NOUN
die Rollschuhe *masc pl*

roller-skating NOUN
das Rollschuhlaufen
■ **to go roller-skating** Rollschuh laufen

rolling pin NOUN
das Nudelholz (PL die Nudelhölzer)

Roman ADJECTIVE, NOUN
römisch *(ancient)*
□ a Roman villa eine römische Villa
□ the Roman empire das Römische Reich
■ **the Romans** die Römer *masc pl*

Roman Catholic NOUN
der Katholik (GEN des Katholiken, PL die Katholiken)
die Katholikin
□ He's a Roman Catholic. Er ist Katholik.

romance NOUN
1 der Liebesroman (PL die Liebesromane) *(novels)*
□ I read a lot of romances. Ich lese viele Liebesromane.
2 der romantische Zauber *(glamour)*
□ the romance of Venice der romantische Zauber von Venedig
■ **a holiday romance** ein Ferienflirt *masc*

Romania NOUN
Rumänien *neut*
■ **from Romania** aus Rumänien
■ **to Romania** nach Rumänien

Romanian ADJECTIVE
rumänisch

romantic ADJECTIVE
romantisch

roof NOUN
das Dach (PL die Dächer)

roof rack NOUN
der Dachträger (PL die Dachträger)

room NOUN
1 das Zimmer (PL die Zimmer)
□ the biggest room in the house das größte Zimmer des Hauses □ She's in her room. Sie ist in ihrem Zimmer. □ the music room das Musikzimmer
■ **a single room** ein Einzelzimmer
■ **a double room** ein Doppelzimmer
2 der Platz (GEN des Platzes) *(space)*
□ There's no room for that box. Es ist kein Platz für diese Schachtel.

roommate NOUN
der Zimmergenosse (GEN des Zimmergenossen, PL die Zimmergenossen)
die Zimmergenossin

root NOUN
die Wurzel

rope NOUN
das Seil (PL die Seile)

rose VERB ▷ *see* **rise**

rose NOUN
die Rose *(flower)*

to **rot** VERB
verfaulen (PERFECT ist verfault)

rotten ADJECTIVE
faulig *(decayed)*
□ a rotten apple ein fauliger Apfel
■ **rotten weather** das Mistwetter *(informal)*
■ **That's a rotten thing to do.** Das ist gemein.
■ **to feel rotten** sich mies fühlen *(informal)*

rough ADJECTIVE
1 rau
□ My hands are rough. Meine Hände sind rau.
□ It's a rough area. Das ist eine raue Gegend.
2 hart *(game)*
□ Rugby's a rough sport. Rugby ist ein harter Sport.
3 stürmisch *(water)*
□ The sea was rough. Das Meer war stürmisch.
4 ungefähr
□ I've got a rough idea. Ich habe eine ungefähre Vorstellung.
■ **to feel rough** sich nicht wohlfühlen
□ I feel rough. Ich fühle mich nicht wohl.

roughly ADVERB
ungefähr
□ It weighs roughly twenty kilos. Es wiegt ungefähr zwanzig Kilo.

round ADJECTIVE, ADVERB, PREPOSITION
▷ *see also* **round** NOUN
1 rund
□ a round table ein runder Tisch
2 um *(around)*
□ We were sitting round the table. Wir saßen um den Tisch herum. □ She wore a scarf round her neck. Sie trug einen Schal um den Hals.
■ **It's just round the corner.** *(very near)* Es ist gleich um die Ecke.
■ **to go round to somebody's house** bei jemandem vorbeigehen □ I went round to my friend's house. Ich bin bei meiner Freundin vorbeigegangen.
■ **to have a look round** sich umsehen
□ We're going to have a look round. Wir möchten uns umsehen.
■ **to go round a museum** sich ein Museum ansehen □ I went round the local museum. Ich habe mir das örtliche Museum angesehen.
■ **round here** hier in der Gegend □ Is there a chemist's round here? Gibt es hier in der Gegend eine Apotheke? □ He lives round here. Er wohnt hier in der Gegend.
■ **all round** ringsherum □ There were vineyards all round. Ringsherum waren Weinberge.
■ **all year round** das ganze Jahr über
■ **round about** *(roughly)* etwa □ It costs round about a hundred pounds. Es kostet etwa hundert Pfund. □ round about eight o'clock etwa um acht Uhr

round NOUN
▷ *see also* **round** ADJECTIVE
die Runde *(of tournament, boxing match)*
□ a round of golf eine Runde Golf
■ **a round of drinks** eine Runde □ He bought a round of drinks. Er hat eine Runde ausgegeben.

roundabout NOUN
1 der Kreisverkehr (PL die Kreisverkehre) *(at junction)*
2 das Karussell (PL die Karussells) *(at funfair)*

rounders SING NOUN
der Schlagball

round trip NOUN (US)
die Hin- und Rückfahrt
■ **a round-trip ticket** eine Rückfahrkarte

route NOUN
die Route
□ We're planning our route. Wir planen unsere Route.

route planner NOUN
der Routenplaner (PL die Routenplaner)

routine NOUN
die Routine

row (1) NOUN
▷ *see also* **row** VERB *and* **row (2)** NOUN
die Reihe
□ a row of houses eine Reihe Häuser
□ Our seats are in the front row. Unsere Plätze sind in der ersten Reihe.
■ **five times in a row** fünfmal hintereinander

row (2) NOUN
▷ *see also* **row** VERB *and* **row (1)** NOUN
1 der Krach *(noise)*
□ What's that terrible row? Was ist das für ein furchtbarer Krach?
2 der Streit (PL die Streite) *(quarrel)*
■ **to have a row** Streit haben □ They've had a row. Sie haben Streit gehabt.

to **row** VERB
▷ *see also* **row (1)** NOUN *and* **row (2)** NOUN
rudern
□ We took turns to row. Wir haben abwechselnd gerudert.

rowboat NOUN (US)
das Ruderboot (PL die Ruderboote)

rowing NOUN
das Rudern *(sport)*
□ My hobby is rowing. Rudern ist mein Hobby.
■ **a rowing boat** ein Ruderboot *neut*

royal ADJECTIVE
königlich
▫ the royal family die königliche Familie

to **rub** VERB
1 reiben (IMPERFECT rieb, PERFECT hat gerieben) *(stain)*
2 sich reiben *(part of body)*
▫ Don't rub your eyes! Reib dir nicht die Augen!
▪ **I rubbed myself dry with a towel.** Ich rieb mich mit einem Handtuch trocken.
▪ **to rub something out** etwas ausradieren

rubber NOUN
1 der Gummi (PL die Gummis)
▫ rubber soles die Gummisohlen
2 der Radiergummi (PL die Radiergummis) *(eraser)*
▫ Can I borrow your rubber? Kann ich deinen Radiergummi ausleihen?
▪ **a rubber band** ein Gummiband *neut*

rubbish NOUN
▹ *see also* **rubbish** ADJECTIVE
1 der Müll *(refuse)*
▫ When do they collect the rubbish? Wann wird der Müll abgeholt?
2 der Krempel *(junk)*
▫ They sell a lot of rubbish at the market. Sie verkaufen eine Menge Krempel auf dem Markt.
3 der Unsinn *(nonsense)*
▫ Don't talk rubbish! Red keinen Unsinn!
▪ **That's a load of rubbish!** Das ist doch Unsinn! *(informal)*
▪ **This magazine is rubbish!** Die Zeitschrift ist Schrott! *(informal)*
▪ **a rubbish bin** ein Mülleimer *masc*
▪ **a rubbish dump** eine Müllkippe

rubbish ADJECTIVE
▹ *see also* **rubbish** NOUN
miserabel *(informal)*
▫ They're a rubbish team! Sie sind eine miserable Mannschaft!

rucksack NOUN
der Rucksack (PL die Rucksäcke)

rude ADJECTIVE
1 unhöflich *(impolite)*
▫ It's rude to interrupt. Es ist unhöflich dazwischenzureden. ▫ He was very rude to me. Er war sehr unhöflich zu mir.
2 unanständig *(offensive)*
▫ a rude joke ein unanständiger Witz
▪ **a rude word** ein Schimpfwort *neut*

rug NOUN
1 der Teppich (PL die Teppiche)
▫ a Persian rug ein Perserteppich
2 die Decke *(blanket)*
▫ a tartan rug eine karierte Decke

rugby NOUN
das Rugby
▫ I play rugby. Ich spiele Rugby.

ruin NOUN
▹ *see also* **ruin** VERB
die Ruine
▫ the ruins of the castle die Ruine der Burg
▪ **My life is in ruins.** Mein Leben ist ruiniert.

to **ruin** VERB
▹ *see also* **ruin** NOUN
ruinieren (PERFECT hat ruiniert)
▫ You'll ruin your shoes. Du ruinierst dir deine Schuhe. ▫ That's far too expensive. You are ruining me! Das ist viel zu teuer. Du ruinierst mich noch!
▪ **It ruined our holiday.** Es hat uns den Urlaub verdorben.

rule NOUN
▹ *see also* **rule** VERB
1 die Regel
▫ the rules of grammar die Grammatikregeln
▪ **as a rule** in der Regel
2 die Vorschrift *(regulation)*
▫ It's against the rules. Das ist gegen die Vorschriften.

to **rule** VERB
▹ *see also* **rule** NOUN
regieren (PERFECT hat regiert)

to **rule out** VERB
ausschließen (IMPERFECT schloss aus, PERFECT hat ausgeschlossen) *(possibility)*

ruler NOUN
das Lineal (PL die Lineale)
▫ Can I borrow your ruler? Kann ich dein Lineal ausleihen?

rum NOUN
der Rum

rumour NOUN
das Gerücht (PL die Gerüchte)
▫ It's just a rumour. Es ist nur ein Gerücht.

rump steak NOUN
das Rumpsteak (PL die Rumpsteaks)

run NOUN
▹ *see also* **run** VERB
der Lauf (PL die Läufe) *(in cricket)*
▫ to score a run einen Lauf machen
▪ **to go for a run** einen Dauerlauf machen
▫ I go for a run every morning. Ich mache jeden Morgen einen Dauerlauf.
▪ **I did a ten-kilometre run.** Ich bin zehn Kilometer gelaufen.
▪ **on the run** auf der Flucht ▫ The criminals are still on the run. Die Verbrecher sind noch auf der Flucht.
▪ **in the long run** auf Dauer

to **run** VERB
▹ *see also* **run** NOUN
1 laufen (PRESENT läuft, IMPERFECT lief, PERFECT ist gelaufen)
▫ I ran five kilometres. Ich bin fünf Kilometer gelaufen.
▪ **to run a marathon** an einem Marathonlauf teilnehmen

2 leiten *(manage)*
□ He runs a large company. Er leitet ein großes Unternehmen.
3 veranstalten (PERFECT hat veranstaltet) *(organize)*
□ They run music courses in the holidays. Sie veranstalten Musikkurse während der Ferien.
4 laufen *(water)*
□ Don't leave the tap running. Lass das Wasser nicht laufen.
■ **to run a bath** ein Bad einlaufen lassen
5 fahren (PRESENT fährt, IMPERFECT fuhr, PERFECT hat gefahren) *(by car)*
□ I can run you to the station. Ich kann dich zum Bahnhof fahren.
■ **to run away** weglaufen □ They ran away before the police came. Sie sind weggelaufen, bevor die Polizei kam.
■ **Time is running out.** Die Zeit wird knapp.
■ **We ran out of money.** Uns ist das Geld ausgegangen.
■ **to run somebody over** jemanden überfahren
■ **to get run over** überfahren werden
□ Be careful, or you'll get run over! Pass auf, sonst wirst du überfahren!

rung VERB ▷ *see* **ring**

runner NOUN
der Läufer (PL die Läufer)
die Läuferin

runner beans PL NOUN
die Stangenbohnen *fem pl*

runner-up NOUN
der Zweite (GEN des Zweiten, PL die Zweiten)
die Zweite (GEN der Zweiten)

running NOUN
das Laufen
□ Running is my favourite sport. Laufen ist mein Lieblingssport.

run-up NOUN
■ **in the run-up to Christmas** in der Zeit vor Weihnachten

runway NOUN
die Startbahn

rural ADJECTIVE
ländlich

rush NOUN
▷ *see also* **rush** VERB
die Eile
■ **in a rush** in Eile

to **rush** VERB
▷ *see also* **rush** NOUN
1 rennen (IMPERFECT rannte, PERFECT ist gerannt) *(run)*
□ Everyone rushed outside. Alle rannten hinaus.
2 sich beeilen (PERFECT hat sich beeilt) *(hurry)*
□ There's no need to rush. Wir brauchen uns nicht zu beeilen.

rush hour NOUN
die Hauptverkehrszeit
□ in the rush hour in der Hauptverkehrszeit

rusk NOUN
der Zwieback (PL die Zwiebacke)

Russia NOUN
Russland *neut*
■ **from Russia** aus Russland
■ **to Russia** nach Russland

Russian ADJECTIVE
▷ *see also* **Russian** NOUN
russisch
■ **He's Russian.** Er ist Russe.
■ **She's Russian.** Sie ist Russin.

Russian NOUN
▷ *see also* **Russian** ADJECTIVE
1 der Russe (GEN des Russen, PL die Russen)
die Russin *(person)*
2 das Russisch (GEN des Russischen) *(language)*

rust NOUN
der Rost

rusty ADJECTIVE
rostig
□ a rusty bike ein rostiges Fahrrad
■ **My German is very rusty.** Mein Deutsch ist ziemlich eingerostet.

ruthless ADJECTIVE
rücksichtslos

rye NOUN
der Roggen
■ **rye bread** das Roggenbrot

Ss

Sabbath NOUN
1 der Sonntag (PL die Sonntage) *(Christian)*
2 der Sabbat (PL die Sabbate) *(Jewish)*

sack NOUN
▷ *see also* **sack** VERB
der Sack (PL die Säcke)
■ **to get the sack** gefeuert werden

to **sack** VERB
▷ *see also* **sack** NOUN
■ **to sack somebody** jemanden feuern
□ He was sacked. Er wurde gefeuert.

sacred ADJECTIVE
heilig

sacrifice NOUN
das Opfer (PL die Opfer)

sad ADJECTIVE
traurig

saddle NOUN
der Sattel (PL die Sättel)

saddlebag NOUN
die Satteltasche

sadly ADVERB
1 traurig
□ 'She's gone,' he said sadly. 'Sie ist weg', sagte er traurig.
2 leider *(unfortunately)*
□ Sadly, it was too late. Leider war es zu spät.

safe NOUN
▷ *see also* **safe** ADJECTIVE
der Safe (PL die Safes)
□ She put the money in the safe. Sie tat das Geld in den Safe.

safe ADJECTIVE
▷ *see also* **safe** NOUN
1 sicher
□ It's perfectly safe. Es ist völlig sicher.
□ This car isn't safe. Das Auto ist nicht sicher.
2 in Sicherheit *(out of danger)*
□ You're safe now. Sie sind jetzt in Sicherheit.
■ **to feel safe** sich sicher fühlen
■ **safe sex** Safer Sex

safety NOUN
die Sicherheit
■ **a safety belt** ein Sicherheitsgurt *masc*
■ **a safety pin** eine Sicherheitsnadel

Sagittarius NOUN
der Schütze (GEN des Schützen)
□ I'm Sagittarius. Ich bin Schütze.

Sahara NOUN
■ **the Sahara Desert** die Wüste Sahara

said VERB ▷ *see* **say**

sail NOUN
▷ *see also* **sail** VERB
das Segel (PL die Segel)

to **sail** VERB
▷ *see also* **sail** NOUN
1 segeln (PERFECT ist gesegelt) *(travel)*
2 abfahren (PRESENT fährt ab, IMPERFECT fuhr ab, PERFECT ist abgefahren) *(set off)*
□ The boat sails at eight o'clock. Das Schiff fährt um acht Uhr ab.

sailing NOUN
das Segeln
□ His hobby is sailing. Segeln ist sein Hobby.
■ **to go sailing** segeln gehen
■ **a sailing boat** ein Segelboot *neut*
■ **a sailing ship** ein Segelschiff *neut*

sailor NOUN
der Matrose (GEN des Matrosen, PL die Matrosen)
die Matrosin
□ He's a sailor. Er ist Matrose.

saint NOUN
der Heilige (GEN des Heiligen, PL die Heiligen)
die Heilige (GEN der Heiligen)
□ a saint *(man)* ein Heiliger

sake NOUN
■ **for the sake of** um ... willen □ for the sake of your parents um deiner Eltern willen

salad NOUN
der Salat (PL die Salate)
■ **salad cream** die Salatmayonnaise
■ **salad dressing** die Salatsoße

salami NOUN
die Salami (GEN der Salami, PL die Salamis)

salary NOUN
das Gehalt (PL die Gehälter)

sale NOUN
der Schlussverkauf (PL die Schlussverkäufe) *(end of season reductions)*
□ There's a sale on at Harrods. Bei Harrods ist Schlussverkauf.
■ **on sale** erhältlich
■ **'for sale'** 'zu verkaufen'

sales assistant NOUN
der Verkäufer (PL die Verkäufer)
die Verkäuferin

□ She's a sales assistant. Sie ist Verkäuferin.

salesman NOUN
1 der Vertreter (PL die Vertreter) *(sales rep)*
□ He's a salesman. Er ist Vertreter.
■ **a double-glazing salesman** ein Vertreter für Doppelfenster
2 der Verkäufer (PL die Verkäufer) *(sales assistant)*

sales rep NOUN
der Vertreter (PL die Vertreter)
die Vertreterin

saleswoman NOUN
1 die Vertreterin *(sales rep)*
□ She's a saleswoman. Sie ist Vertreterin.
2 die Verkäuferin *(sales assistant)*

salmon NOUN
der Lachs (GEN des Lachses, PL die Lachse)

salon NOUN
der Salon (PL die Salons)
□ a hair salon ein Friseursalon
□ a beauty salon ein Kosmetiksalon

saloon car NOUN
die Limousine

salt NOUN
das Salz (GEN des Salzes, PL die Salze)

salty ADJECTIVE
salzig

to **salute** VERB
grüßen

Salvation Army NOUN
die Heilsarmee

same ADJECTIVE
gleiche
□ The same coat is cheaper elsewhere. Der gleiche Mantel ist anderswo billiger.
□ He asked me the same question. Er hat mir die gleiche Frage gestellt. □ I have the same car. Ich habe das gleiche Auto.
□ We obviously have the same problems. Wir haben offensichtlich die gleichen Probleme.
■ **at the same time** zur gleichen Zeit
■ **It's not the same.** Das ist nicht das Gleiche.
■ **They're exactly the same.** Sie sind genau gleich.

sample NOUN
die Probe
□ a free sample of perfume eine kostenlose Parfümprobe

sand NOUN
der Sand

sandal NOUN
die Sandale
□ a pair of sandals ein Paar Sandalen

sand castle NOUN
die Sandburg

sandwich NOUN
das belegte Brot (PL die belegten Brote)
■ **a cheese sandwich** ein Käsebrot

sang VERB ▷ *see* **sing**

sanitary napkin NOUN (US)
die Damenbinde

sanitary towel NOUN
die Damenbinde

sank VERB ▷ *see* **sink**

Santa Claus NOUN
der Weihnachtsmann
(PL die Weihnachtsmänner)

sarcastic ADJECTIVE
sarkastisch

sardine NOUN
die Sardine

sat VERB ▷ *see* **sit**

satchel NOUN
der Schulranzen (PL die Schulranzen)

satellite NOUN
der Satellit (GEN des Satelliten, PL die Satelliten)
■ **a satellite dish** eine Satellitenschüssel
■ **satellite television** das Satellitenfernsehen

satisfactory ADJECTIVE
befriedigend

satisfied ADJECTIVE
zufrieden

sat nav NOUN
das GPS (PL die GPS)

Saturday NOUN
der Samstag (PL die Samstage)
□ on Saturday am Samstag □ every Saturday jeden Samstag □ last Saturday letzten Samstag □ next Saturday nächsten Samstag
■ **on Saturdays** samstags
■ **a Saturday job** ein Samstagsjob

sauce NOUN
die Soße

saucepan NOUN
der Kochtopf (PL die Kochtöpfe)

saucer NOUN
die Untertasse

Saudi Arabia NOUN
Saudi-Arabien *neut*
■ **to Saudi Arabia** nach Saudi-Arabien

sauna NOUN
die Sauna (PL die Saunas)

sausage NOUN
die Wurst (PL die Würste)
■ **a sausage roll** eine Wurst im Blätterteig

to **save** VERB
1 sparen *(money, time)*
□ I've saved fifty pounds. Ich habe fünfzig Pfund gespart. □ I saved money by waiting for the sales. Ich habe Geld gespart, weil ich bis zum Schlussverkauf gewartet habe.
□ We took a taxi to save time. Wir haben ein Taxi genommen, um Zeit zu sparen.
2 retten *(rescue)*
□ Luckily, all the passengers were saved. Zum Glück wurden alle Passagiere gerettet.
3 sichern *(on computer)*

□ I saved the file onto a diskette. Ich habe die Datei auf Diskette gesichert.
■ **to save up** sparen □ I'm saving up for a bike. Ich spare für ein Fahrrad.

savings PL NOUN
die Ersparnisse *fem pl*
□ She spent all her savings on a computer. Sie gab all ihre Ersparnisse für einen Computer aus.

savoury ADJECTIVE
pikant *(spicy)*

saw VERB ▷ *see* **see**

saw NOUN
die Säge

sax NOUN
das Saxofon (PL die Saxofone)
□ I play the sax. Ich spiele Saxofon.

saxophone NOUN
das Saxofon (PL die Saxofone)
□ I play the saxophone. Ich spiele Saxofon.

to **say** VERB
sagen
□ What did he say? Was hat er gesagt? □ Did you hear what she said? Hast du gehört, was sie gesagt hat? □ Could you say that again? Können Sie das noch einmal sagen?
■ **That goes without saying.** Das ist selbstverständlich.

saying NOUN
die Redensart
□ It's just a saying. Das ist so eine Redensart.

scale NOUN
1 der Maßstab (PL die Maßstäbe) *(of map)*
□ a large-scale map eine Karte großen Maßstabs
2 das Ausmaß (GEN des Ausmaßes, PL die Ausmaße) *(size, extent)*
□ a disaster on a massive scale eine Katastrophe von riesigem Ausmaß
3 die Tonleiter *(in music)*

scales PL NOUN
die Waage *sing (in kitchen, shop)*
■ **bathroom scales** die Personenwaage

scampi PL NOUN
die Scampi *pl*

scandal NOUN
1 der Skandal (PL die Skandale) *(outrage)*
□ It caused a scandal. Es hat einen Skandal verursacht.
2 der Tratsch *(gossip)*
□ It's just scandal. Das ist nur Tratsch.

Scandinavia NOUN
Skandinavien *neut*
■ **from Scandinavia** aus Skandinavien
■ **to Scandinavia** nach Skandinavien

Scandinavian ADJECTIVE
skandinavisch
■ **He's Scandinavian.** Er ist Skandinavier.

scar NOUN
die Narbe

scarce ADJECTIVE
1 knapp
□ scarce resources knappe Geldmittel
2 rar
□ Jobs are scarce. Jobs sind rar.

scarcely ADVERB
kaum
□ I scarcely knew him. Ich kannte ihn kaum.

scare NOUN
▷ *see also* **scare** VERB
der Schrecken (PL die Schrecken)
■ **a bomb scare** ein Bombenalarm *masc*

to **scare** VERB
▷ *see also* **scare** NOUN
■ **to scare somebody** jemandem Angst machen □ He scares me. Er macht mir Angst.

scarecrow NOUN
die Vogelscheuche

scared ADJECTIVE
■ **to be scared** Angst haben □ I was scared stiff. Ich hatte furchtbar Angst.
■ **to be scared of** Angst haben vor □ Are you scared of him? Hast du vor ihm Angst?

scarf NOUN
1 der Schal (PL die Schals) *(long)*
2 das Halstuch (PL die Halstücher) *(square)*

scary ADJECTIVE
furchterregend
□ It was really scary. Es war wirklich furchterregend.

scene NOUN
1 der Ort (PL die Orte) *(place)*
□ The police were soon on the scene. Die Polizei war schnell vor Ort. □ the scene of the crime der Ort des Verbrechens
2 das Spektakel (PL die Spektakel) *(event, sight)*
□ It was an amazing scene. Es war ein erstaunliches Spektakel.
■ **to make a scene** eine Szene machen

scenery NOUN
die Landschaft *(landscape)*

scent NOUN
der Duft (PL die Düfte) *(perfume)*

schedule NOUN
das Programm (PL die Programme)
□ a busy schedule ein volles Programm
■ **on schedule** planmäßig
■ **to be behind schedule** Verspätung haben

scheduled flight NOUN
der Linienflug (PL die Linienflüge)

scheme NOUN
1 der Plan (PL die Pläne) *(idea)*
□ a crazy scheme ein verrückter Plan
2 das Projekt (PL die Projekte) *(project)*
□ a council road-widening scheme ein Straßenverbreiterungsprojekt der Gemeinde

scholarship NOUN
das Stipendium (PL die Stipendien)

school NOUN
die Schule

■ **to go to school** in die Schule gehen

schoolbook NOUN
das Schulbuch (PL die Schulbücher)

schoolboy NOUN
der Schuljunge (GEN des Schuljungen, PL die Schuljungen)

schoolchildren NOUN
die Schulkinder *neut pl*

schoolgirl NOUN
das Schulmädchen (PL die Schulmädchen)

science NOUN
die Wissenschaft

science fiction NOUN
die Science-Fiction

scientific ADJECTIVE
wissenschaftlich

scientist NOUN
der Wissenschaftler (PL die Wissenschaftler)
die Wissenschaftlerin *(doing research)*
□ She's a scientist. Sie ist Wissenschaftlerin.
■ **He trained as a scientist.** Er hat eine wissenschaftliche Ausbildung.

scissors PL NOUN
die Schere
□ a pair of scissors eine Schere

to **scoff** VERB
futtern *(informal: eat)*
□ Mark scoffed all the sandwiches. Mark hat alle Brote gefuttert.

scooter NOUN
1 der Motorroller (PL die Motorroller)
2 der Roller (PL die Roller) *(child's toy)*

score NOUN
▷ *see also* **score** VERB
der Spielstand (PL die Spielstände)
■ **What's the score?** Wie steht das Spiel?
■ **The score was three nil.** Es stand drei zu null.

to **score** VERB
▷ *see also* **score** NOUN
1 schießen (IMPERFECT schoss, PERFECT hat geschossen) *(goal)*
□ to score a goal ein Tor schießen
2 machen *(point)*
□ to score six out of ten sechs von zehn Punkten machen
3 zählen *(keep score)*
□ Who's going to score? Wer zählt?

Scorpio NOUN
der Skorpion
□ I'm Scorpio. Ich bin Skorpion.

Scot NOUN
der Schotte (GEN des Schotten, PL die Schotten)
die Schottin

Scotch tape® NOUN (US)
der Tesafilm®

Scotland NOUN
Schottland *neut*
■ **from Scotland** aus Schottland
■ **in Scotland** in Schottland
■ **to Scotland** nach Schottland

Scots ADJECTIVE
schottisch
□ a Scots accent ein schottischer Akzent

Scotsman NOUN
der Schotte (GEN des Schotten, PL die Schotten)

Scotswoman NOUN
die Schottin

Scottish ADJECTIVE
schottisch
□ a Scottish accent ein schottischer Akzent
■ **He's Scottish.** Er ist Schotte.
■ **She's Scottish.** Sie ist Schottin.

scout NOUN
der Pfadfinder (PL die Pfadfinder)
□ I'm in the Scouts. Ich bin bei den Pfadfindern.
■ **girl scout** die Pfadfinderin

scrambled eggs PL NOUN
die Rühreier *neut pl*

scrap NOUN
▷ *see also* **scrap** VERB
1 das Stück (PL die Stücke)
□ a scrap of paper ein Stück Papier
2 die Schlägerei *(fight)*
■ **scrap iron** das Alteisen

to **scrap** VERB
▷ *see also* **scrap** NOUN
verwerfen (PRESENT verwirft, IMPERFECT verwarf, PERFECT hat verworfen) *(plan, idea)*
□ The plan was scrapped. Der Plan wurde verworfen.

scrapbook NOUN
das Album (PL die Alben)

to **scratch** VERB
▷ *see also* **scratch** NOUN
kratzen
□ Stop scratching! Hör auf zu kratzen!

scratch NOUN
▷ *see also* **scratch** VERB
der Kratzer (PL die Kratzer) *(on skin)*
■ **to start from scratch** von vorn anfangen

scream NOUN
▷ *see also* **scream** VERB
der Schrei (PL die Schreie)

to **scream** VERB
▷ *see also* **scream** NOUN
schreien (IMPERFECT schrie, PERFECT hat geschrien)

screen NOUN
1 die Leinwand (PL die Leinwände) *(cinema)*
2 der Bildschirm (PL die Bildschirme) *(television, computer)*
□ An error message appeared on the screen. Auf dem Bildschirm erschien eine Fehlermeldung.

screen saver NOUN
der Bildschirmschoner (PL die Bildschirmschoner) *(computer)*

English-German

S

screw NOUN
die Schraube

screwdriver NOUN
der Schraubenzieher
(PL die Schraubenzieher)

to **scribble** VERB
kritzeln

to **scrub** VERB
schrubben
□ He scrubbed the floor. Er schrubbte den Boden.

sculpture NOUN
die Skulptur

sea NOUN
das Meer (PL die Meere)

seafood NOUN
die Meeresfrüchte *fem pl*
□ I don't like seafood. Ich mag Meeresfrüchte nicht.

seagull NOUN
die Möwe

seal NOUN
▷ *see also* **seal** VERB
1 der Seehund (PL die Seehunde) *(animal)*
2 das Siegel (PL die Siegel) *(on container)*

to **seal** VERB
▷ *see also* **seal** NOUN
1 versiegeln (PERFECT hat versiegelt) *(container)*
2 zukleben (PERFECT hat zugeklebt) *(letter)*

seaman NOUN
der Seemann (PL die Seeleute)

to **search** VERB
▷ *see also* **search** NOUN
durchsuchen (PERFECT hat durchsucht)
□ They searched the woods for her. Sie haben den Wald nach ihr durchsucht.
■ **to search for something** nach etwas suchen □ He was searching for gold. Er suchte nach Gold.

search NOUN
▷ *see also* **search** VERB
die Suche

search engine NOUN
die Suchmaschine *(Internet)*

search party NOUN
der Suchtrupp (PL die Suchtrupps)

seashore NOUN
der Strand (PL die Strände)
□ on the seashore am Strand

seasick ADJECTIVE
seekrank
□ to be seasick seekrank sein

seaside NOUN
■ **at the seaside** am Meer
■ **We're going to the seaside.** Wir fahren ans Meer.

season NOUN
die Jahreszeit
□ What's your favourite season? Welche Jahreszeit hast du am liebsten?
■ **out of season** außerhalb der Saison
□ We went there out of season. Wir sind außerhalb der Saison dorthin gefahren.
■ **during the holiday season** während der Ferienzeit
■ **a season ticket** eine Dauerkarte

seat NOUN
der Platz (GEN des Platzes, PL die Plätze)

seat belt NOUN
der Sicherheitsgurt (PL die Sicherheitsgurte)
■ **Fasten your seat belt!** Schnalle dich an!

sea water NOUN
das Meerwasser

seaweed NOUN
die Alge

second ADJECTIVE
▷ *see also* **second** NOUN
zweite
□ the second man from the right der zweite Mann von rechts □ her second husband ihr zweiter Mann □ on the second page auf der zweiten Seite □ my second child mein zweites Kind
■ **to come second** *(in race)* Zweiter werden
□ She came second. Sie wurde Zweite.
■ **the second of August** der zweite August

second NOUN
▷ *see also* **second** ADJECTIVE
die Sekunde
□ It'll only take a second. Es dauert nur eine Sekunde.

secondary school NOUN
1 das Gymnasium (PL die Gymnasien)
2 die Realschule

DID YOU KNOW...?
Germans always specify the type of secondary school. **Gymnasium** takes nine years and leads to **Abitur**, **Realschule** takes six years and leads to **mittlere Reife**.

second-class ADJECTIVE, ADVERB
1 zweiter Klasse *(ticket, compartment)*
□ to travel second-class zweiter Klasse fahren
2 normal *(stamp, letter)*

DID YOU KNOW...?
In Germany there is no first-class or second-class post. However, letters cost more to send than postcards, so you have to remember to say what you are sending when buying stamps. There is also an express service.

□ to send something second-class etwas mit normaler Post schicken

second-hand ADJECTIVE
gebraucht
■ **a second-hand car** ein Gebrauchtwagen *masc*

secondly ADVERB
zweitens
□ firstly ... secondly ... erstens ... zweitens ...

secret ADJECTIVE
▷ *see also* **secret** NOUN
geheim
□ a secret mission eine geheime Mission

secret NOUN
▷ *see also* **secret** ADJECTIVE
das Geheimnis (GEN des Geheimnisses, PL die Geheimnisse)
□ It's a secret. Es ist ein Geheimnis.
□ Can you keep a secret? Kannst du ein Geheimnis für dich behalten?
■ **in secret** heimlich

secretary NOUN
der Sekretär (PL die Sekretäre)
die Sekretärin
□ She's a secretary. Sie ist Sekretärin.

secretly ADVERB
heimlich

section NOUN
1 der Teil (PL die Teile)
□ I passed the written section of the exam. Ich habe den schriftlichen Teil der Prüfung bestanden.
2 die Abteilung *(in shop)*
□ the food section die Lebensmittelabteilung

security NOUN
die Sicherheit
□ airport security die Sicherheit auf den Flughäfen
■ **to have no job security** keinen sicheren Job haben
■ **a security guard** ein Sicherheitsbeamter

security guard NOUN
der Wächter (PL die Wächter)
die Wächterin
■ **She's a security guard.** Sie ist beim Sicherheitsdienst.

sedan NOUN (US)
die Limousine

to **see** VERB
sehen (PRESENT sieht, IMPERFECT sah, PERFECT hat gesehen)
□ I can't see. Ich kann nichts sehen. □ I saw him yesterday. Ich habe ihn gestern gesehen.
□ Have you seen him? Hast du ihn gesehen?
■ **See you!** Tschüs! *(informal)*
■ **See you soon!** Bis bald!
■ **to see to something** sich um etwas kümmern □ The window's stuck. Can you see to it please? Das Fenster klemmt. Kannst du dich bitte darum kümmern?

seed NOUN
der Samen (PL die Samen)
■ **sunflower seeds** die Sonnenblumenkerne *masc pl*

to **seem** VERB
scheinen (IMPERFECT schien, PERFECT hat geschienen)
□ The shop seemed to be closed. Das Geschäft schien geschlossen zu haben.
□ That seems like a good idea. Das scheint eine gute Idee zu sein.
■ **She seems tired.** Sie wirkt müde.
■ **It seems that ...** Es sieht so aus, dass ...
□ It seems she's getting married. Es sieht so aus, dass sie heiratet.
■ **There seems to be a problem.** Anscheinend gibt's ein Problem.

seen VERB ▷ *see* **see**

seesaw NOUN
die Wippe

see-through ADJECTIVE
durchsichtig

seldom ADVERB
selten

to **select** VERB
auswählen (PERFECT hat ausgewählt)

selection NOUN
die Auswahl

self-assured ADJECTIVE
selbstsicher
□ He's very self-assured. Er ist sehr selbstsicher.

self-catering ADJECTIVE
■ **a self-catering apartment** eine Wohnung für Selbstversorger

self-centred ADJECTIVE
egozentrisch

self-confidence NOUN
das Selbstvertrauen
□ He hasn't got much self-confidence. Er hat nicht viel Selbstvertrauen.

self-conscious ADJECTIVE
gehemmt

self-contained ADJECTIVE
■ **a self-contained flat** eine separate Wohnung

self-control NOUN
die Selbstbeherrschung

self-defence NOUN
die Selbstverteidigung
□ self-defence classes der Selbstverteidigungskurs
■ **She killed him in self-defence.** Sie hat ihn in Notwehr getötet.

self-discipline NOUN
die Selbstdisziplin

self-employed ADJECTIVE
■ **to be self-employed** selbstständig sein
□ He's self-employed. Er ist selbstständig.
■ **the self-employed** die Selbstständigen *masc pl*

selfish ADJECTIVE
egoistisch
□ Don't be so selfish. Sei nicht so egoistisch.

self-respect NOUN
die Selbstachtung

self-service ADJECTIVE
■ **It's self-service.** *(café, shop)* Da ist Selbstbedienung.

■ **a self-service restaurant** ein Selbstbedienungsrestaurant *neut*

to **sell** VERB
verkaufen (PERFECT hat verkauft)
□ He sold it to me. Er hat es mir verkauft.
■ **to sell off** verkaufen
■ **The tickets are all sold out.** Alle Karten sind ausverkauft.
■ **The tickets sold out in three hours.** Die Karten waren in drei Stunden ausverkauft.

sell-by date NOUN
das Verfallsdatum (PL die Verfallsdaten)

selling price NOUN
der Verkaufspreis (GEN des Verkaufspreises, PL die Verkaufspreise)

Sellotape® NOUN
der Tesafilm®

semi NOUN
die Doppelhaushälfte
□ We live in a semi. Wir wohnen in einer Doppelhaushälfte.

semicircle NOUN
der Halbkreis (GEN des Halbkreises, PL die Halbkreise)

semicolon NOUN
der Strichpunkt (PL die Strichpunkte)

semi-detached house NOUN
die Doppelhaushälfte
□ We live in a semi-detached house. Wir wohnen in einer Doppelhaushälfte.

semi-final NOUN
das Halbfinale (PL die Halbfinale)

semi-skimmed milk NOUN
die fettarme Milch

to **send** VERB
schicken
□ She sent me money. Sie hat mir Geld geschickt.
■ **to send back** zurückschicken
■ **to send off 1** *(goods, letter)* abschicken **2** *(in sports match)* vom Platz schicken
□ He was sent off. Er wurde vom Platz geschickt.
■ **to send off for something 1** *(free)* etwas kommen lassen □ I've sent off for a brochure. Ich habe mir eine Broschüre kommen lassen. **2** *(paid for)* etwas bestellen □ She sent off for a DVD. Sie hat eine DVD bestellt.
■ **to send out** verschicken

sender NOUN
der Absender (PL die Absender)
die Absenderin

senior ADJECTIVE
leitend
□ senior management die leitenden Angestellten
■ **senior school** die weiterführende Schule
■ **senior pupils** die Oberstufenschüler

senior citizen NOUN
der Senior (PL die Senioren)
die Seniorin

sensational ADJECTIVE
sensationell

sense NOUN
1 der Sinn (PL die Sinne) *(faculty)*
□ the five senses die fünf Sinne □ the sixth sense der sechste Sinn
■ **the sense of touch** der Tastsinn
■ **the sense of smell** der Geschmacksinn
■ **sense of humour** der Sinn für Humor
□ He's got no sense of humour. Er hat keinen Sinn für Humor.
2 der Verstand *(wisdom)*
■ **Use your common sense!** Benutze deinen gesunden Menschenverstand!
■ **It makes sense.** Das macht Sinn.
■ **It doesn't make sense.** Das macht keinen Sinn.

senseless ADJECTIVE
sinnlos

sensible ADJECTIVE
vernünftig
□ Be sensible! Sei vernünftig! □ It would be sensible to check first. Es wäre vernünftig, zuerst nachzusehen.

LANGUAGE TIP Be careful not to translate **sensible** by **sensibel**.

sensitive ADJECTIVE
sensibel
□ She's very sensitive. Sie ist sehr sensibel.

sensuous ADJECTIVE
sinnlich

sent VERB ▷ *see* **send**

sentence NOUN
▷ *see also* **sentence** VERB
1 der Satz (GEN des Satzes, PL die Sätze)
□ What does this sentence mean? Was bedeutet dieser Satz?
2 das Urteil (PL die Urteile) *(judgment)*
□ The court will pass sentence tomorrow. Das Gericht wird morgen das Urteil verkünden.
3 die Strafe *(punishment)*
□ the death sentence die Todesstrafe
■ **He got a life sentence.** Er hat lebenslänglich bekommen.

to **sentence** VERB
▷ *see also* **sentence** NOUN
verurteilen (PERFECT hat verurteilt)
□ to sentence somebody to life imprisonment jemanden zu einer lebenslangen Gefängnisstrafe verurteilen □ to sentence somebody to death jemanden zum Tode verurteilen

sentimental ADJECTIVE
sentimental

separate ADJECTIVE
▷ *see also* **separate** VERB
getrennt
□ separate rooms getrennte Zimmer
■ **I wrote it on a separate sheet.** Ich habe es auf ein extra Blatt geschrieben.

■ **on separate occasions** bei verschiedenen Gelegenheiten

■ **on two separate occasions** zweimal

to **separate** VERB

▷ *see also* **separate** ADJECTIVE

1 trennen

2 sich trennen *(married couple)*

separately ADVERB

extra

separation NOUN

die Trennung

September NOUN

der September

□ in September im September

sequel NOUN

die Fortsetzung *(book, film)*

sequence NOUN

1 die Reihenfolge

□ in the correct sequence in der richtigen Reihenfolge

■ **in sequence** der Reihenfolge nach

■ **a sequence of events** eine Folge von Ereignissen

2 die Sequenz *(in film)*

sergeant NOUN

1 der Feldwebel (PL die Feldwebel)

die Feldwebelin *(army)*

2 der Polizeimeister (PL die Polizeimeister)

die Polizeimeisterin *(police)*

serial NOUN

die Fernsehserie

series SING NOUN

1 die Sendereihe

□ a TV series eine Sendereihe im Fernsehen

2 die Reihe *(of numbers)*

serious ADJECTIVE

1 ernst

□ You look very serious. Du siehst sehr ernst aus.

■ **Are you serious?** Ist das dein Ernst?

2 schwer *(illness, mistake)*

LANGUAGE TIP Be careful not to translate **serious** by **seriös**.

seriously ADVERB

im Ernst

□ No, but seriously ... Nein, aber im Ernst ...

■ **to take somebody seriously** jemanden ernst nehmen

■ **seriously injured** schwer verletzt

■ **Seriously?** Im Ernst?

sermon NOUN

die Predigt

servant NOUN

der Diener (PL die Diener)

die Dienerin

to **serve** VERB

▷ *see also* **serve** NOUN

1 servieren (PERFECT hat serviert)

□ Dinner is served. Das Essen ist serviert.

2 aufschlagen (PRESENT schlägt auf, IMPERFECT schlug auf, PERFECT hat aufgeschlagen)

□ It's Murray's turn to serve. Murray schlägt auf.

3 absitzen (IMPERFECT saß ab, PERFECT hat abgesessen) *(prison sentence)*

■ **to serve time** im Gefängnis sein

■ **It serves you right.** Das geschieht dir recht.

serve NOUN

▷ *see also* **serve** VERB

der Aufschlag (PL die Aufschläge) *(tennis)*

■ **It's your serve.** Du hast Aufschlag.

server NOUN

der Server (PL die Server) *(computer)*

to **service** VERB

▷ *see also* **service** NOUN

überholen (PERFECT hat überholt) *(car, washing machine)*

service NOUN

▷ *see also* **service** VERB

1 die Bedienung

□ Service is included. Die Bedienung ist inklusive.

2 die Inspektion *(of car)*

3 der Gottesdienst (PL die Gottesdienste) *(church service)*

■ **the Fire Service** die Feuerwehr

■ **the armed services** die Streitkräfte

service area NOUN

die Raststätte

service charge NOUN

die Bedienung

□ There's no service charge. Die Bedienung wird nicht extra berechnet.

serviceman NOUN

der Militärangehörige (GEN des Militärangehörigen, PL die Militärangehörigen)

□ a serviceman ein Militärangehöriger

■ **He's a serviceman.** Er ist beim Militär.

service station NOUN

die Tankstelle

serviette NOUN

die Serviette

session NOUN

die Sitzung

set NOUN

▷ *see also* **set** VERB

der Satz (GEN des Satzes, PL die Sätze)

□ a set of keys ein Satz Schlüssel

□ Williams won the set. *(tennis)* Williams hat den Satz gewonnen.

■ **a chess set** ein Schachspiel *neut*

■ **a train set** eine Spielzeugeisenbahn

to **set** VERB

▷ *see also* **set** NOUN

1 stellen *(alarm clock)*

□ I set the alarm for seven o'clock. Ich habe den Wecker auf sieben Uhr gestellt.

2 aufstellen (PERFECT hat aufgestellt) *(record)*

□ The world record was set last year. Der Weltrekord wurde letztes Jahr aufgestellt.

3 untergehen (IMPERFECT ging unter, PERFECT ist untergegangen) *(sun)*
□ The sun was setting. Die Sonne ging unter.
■ **The film is set in Morocco.** Der Film spielt in Marokko.
■ **to set off** aufbrechen □ We set off for London at nine o'clock. Wir sind um neun Uhr nach London aufgebrochen.
■ **to set out** aufbrechen □ We set out for London at nine o'clock. Wir sind um neun Uhr nach London aufgebrochen.
■ **to set the table** den Tisch decken

settee NOUN
das Sofa (PL die Sofas)

to **settle** VERB
1 lösen *(problem)*
2 beilegen (PERFECT hat beigelegt) *(argument)*
■ **to settle an account** eine Rechnung begleichen
■ **to settle down** *(calm down)* ruhiger werden
■ **Settle down!** Beruhige dich!
■ **to settle in** sich einleben
■ **to settle on something** sich für etwas entscheiden □ I finally settled on Crete for my holidays. Ich habe mich endlich dafür entschieden, nach Kreta in Urlaub zu fahren.

seven NUMBER
sieben
□ She's seven. Sie ist sieben.

seventeen NUMBER
siebzehn
□ He's seventeen. Er ist siebzehn.

seventeenth ADJECTIVE
siebzehnte
□ the seventeenth of August der siebzehnte August

seventh ADJECTIVE
siebte
□ the seventh floor der siebte Stock
□ the seventh of August der siebte August

seventy NUMBER
siebzig
□ She's seventy. Sie ist siebzig.

several ADJECTIVE, PRONOUN
einige
□ several schools einige Schulen
□ several of them einige von ihnen

to **sew** VERB
nähen
■ **to sew up** *(tear)* flicken

sewing NOUN
das Nähen
■ **I like sewing.** Ich nähe gern.
■ **a sewing machine** eine Nähmaschine

sewn VERB ▷ *see* **sew**

sex NOUN
das Geschlecht (PL die Geschlechter)
■ **to have sex with somebody** mit jemandem Verkehr haben
■ **sex education** der Aufklärungsunterricht

sexism NOUN
der Sexismus (GEN des Sexismus)

sexist ADJECTIVE
sexistisch

sexual ADJECTIVE
sexuell
□ sexual harassment die sexuelle Belästigung
■ **sexual discrimination** die Diskriminierung aufgrund des Geschlechts

sexuality NOUN
die Sexualität

sexy ADJECTIVE
sexy

shabby ADJECTIVE
schäbig

shade NOUN
1 der Schatten (PL die Schatten)
□ in the shade im Schatten
2 der Ton (PL die Töne) *(colour)*
□ a shade of blue ein Blauton

shadow NOUN
der Schatten (PL die Schatten)

to **shake** VERB
1 ausschütteln (PERFECT hat ausgeschüttelt)
□ She shook the rug. Sie hat den Teppich ausgeschüttelt.
2 schütteln
□ She shook the bottle. Sie hat die Flasche geschüttelt.
3 zittern *(tremble)*
□ He was shaking with fear. Er zitterte vor Angst.
■ **to shake one's head** *(in refusal)* den Kopf schütteln
■ **to shake hands with somebody** jemandem die Hand geben □ They shook hands. Sie gaben sich die Hand.

shaken ADJECTIVE
mitgenommen
□ I was feeling a bit shaken. Ich war etwas mitgenommen.

shaky ADJECTIVE
zittrig *(hand, voice)*

shall VERB
■ **Shall I shut the window?** Soll ich das Fenster zumachen?
■ **Shall we ask him to come with us?** Sollen wir ihn fragen, ob er mitkommt?

shallow ADJECTIVE
flach *(water, pool)*

shambles SING NOUN
das Chaos (GEN des Chaos)
□ It's a complete shambles. Es ist ein völliges Chaos.

shame NOUN
die Schande
□ The shame of it! Diese Schande!
■ **What a shame!** Wie schade!
■ **It's a shame that ...** Es ist schade, dass ...
□ It's a shame he isn't here. Es ist schade, dass er nicht da ist.

shampoo NOUN
das Shampoo (PL die Shampoos)
□ a bottle of shampoo eine Flasche Shampoo
shandy NOUN
das Bier mit Limonade

DID YOU KNOW...?
shandy is also called **das Alsterwasser** in North Germany and **der Radler** in South Germany.

shan't = **shall not**
shape NOUN
die Form
share NOUN
▷ *see also* **share** VERB
1 die Aktie *(in company)*
□ They've got shares in BT. Sie haben Aktien von BT.
2 der Anteil (PL die Anteile) *(portion)*
to **share** VERB
▷ *see also* **share** NOUN
teilen
□ to share a room with somebody ein Zimmer mit jemandem teilen
■ **to share out** verteilen □ They shared out the sweets. Sie haben die Bonbons verteilt.
shark NOUN
der Hai (PL die Haie)
sharp ADJECTIVE
1 scharf *(razor, knife)*
□ I need a sharper knife. Ich brauche ein schärferes Messer.
2 spitz *(spike, point)*
3 gescheit *(clever)*
□ She's very sharp. Sie ist sehr gescheit.
■ **at two o'clock sharp** Punkt zwei Uhr
to **shave** VERB
sich rasieren (PERFECT hat sich rasiert) *(have a shave)*
■ **to shave one's legs** sich die Beine rasieren
□ I don't shave my legs. Ich rasiere mir die Beine nicht.
shaver NOUN
■ **an electric shaver** ein Elektrorasierer *masc*
shaving cream NOUN
die Rasiercreme (PL die Rasiercremes)
shaving foam NOUN
der Rasierschaum
she PRONOUN
sie
□ She's very nice. Sie ist sehr nett.
shed NOUN
der Schuppen (PL die Schuppen)
she'd = **she had, she would**
sheep NOUN
das Schaf (PL die Schafe)
□ dozens of sheep Dutzende von Schafen
sheepdog NOUN
der Schäferhund (PL die Schäferhunde)
sheer ADJECTIVE
rein
□ It's sheer greed. Das ist die reine Gier.
sheet NOUN
das Leintuch (PL die Leintücher) *(on bed)*
■ **a sheet of paper** ein Blatt Papier *neut*
shelf NOUN
das Regal (PL die Regale)
shell NOUN
1 die Muschel *(on beach)*
2 die Schale *(of egg, nut)*
3 die Granate *(explosive)*
she'll = **she will**
shellfish NOUN
das Schalentier (PL die Schalentiere)
shell suit NOUN
der Jogginganzug (PL die Jogginganzüge)
shelter NOUN
■ **to take shelter** sich unterstellen
□ They took shelter beneath a bridge. Sie stellten sich unter einer Brücke unter.
■ **a bus shelter** eine überdachte Bushaltestelle
shelves PL NOUN ▷ *see* **shelf**
shepherd NOUN
der Schäfer (PL die Schäfer)
die Schäferin
sheriff NOUN
der Sheriff (PL die Sheriffs)
sherry NOUN
der Sherry (PL die Sherrys)
she's = **she is, she has**
Shetland Islands PL NOUN
die Shetlandinseln *fem pl*
shield NOUN
der Schild (PL die Schilde)
shift NOUN
▷ *see also* **shift** VERB
die Schicht
□ His shift starts at eight o'clock. Seine Schicht fängt um acht Uhr an.
□ the night shift die Nachtschicht
■ **to do shift work** Schicht arbeiten
to **shift** VERB
▷ *see also* **shift** NOUN
verschieben (IMPERFECT verschob, PERFECT hat verschoben) *(move)*
□ I couldn't shift the wardrobe. Ich konnte den Schrank nicht verschieben.
■ **Shift yourself!** jetzt aber los! *(informal)*
shifty ADJECTIVE
1 zwielichtig *(person)*
□ He looked shifty. Er sah zwielichtig aus.
2 unstet *(eyes)*
shin NOUN
das Schienbein (PL die Schienbeine)
to **shine** VERB
scheinen (IMPERFECT schien, PERFECT hat geschienen)
□ The sun was shining. Die Sonne schien.
shiny ADJECTIVE
glänzend

ship NOUN
das Schiff (PL die Schiffe)
shipbuilding NOUN
der Schiffbau
shipwreck NOUN
der Schiffbruch (PL die Schiffbrüche) *(accident)*
shipwrecked ADJECTIVE
■ **to be shipwrecked** Schiffbruch erleiden
shipyard NOUN
die Werft
shirt NOUN
1 das Hemd (PL die Hemden) *(man's)*
2 die Bluse *(woman's)*
shit EXCLAMATION
Scheiße! *(rude)*
to **shiver** VERB
zittern
shock NOUN
▷ *see also* **shock** VERB
der Schock (PL die Schocks)
■ **to get a shock** 1 *(surprise)* einen Schock bekommen 2 *(electric)* einen Schlag bekommen
■ **an electric shock** ein elektrischer Schlag
to **shock** VERB
▷ *see also* **shock** NOUN
schockieren (PERFECT hat schockiert) *(upset)*
□ I was shocked by the tragedy. Ich war über die Tragödie schockiert. □ Nothing shocks me any more. Mich schockiert nichts mehr.
shocked ADJECTIVE
schockiert
□ He'll be shocked if you say that. Wenn du das sagst, wird er schockiert sein.
shocking ADJECTIVE
schockierend
□ It's shocking! Es ist schockierend!
□ a shocking waste eine schockierende Verschwendung
shoe NOUN
der Schuh (PL die Schuhe)
shoelace NOUN
der Schnürsenkel (PL die Schnürsenkel)
shoe polish NOUN
die Schuhcreme (PL die Schuhcremes)
shoe shop NOUN
das Schuhgeschäft (PL die Schuhgeschäfte)
shone VERB ▷ *see* **shine**
shook VERB ▷ *see* **shake**
to **shoot** VERB
1 schießen (IMPERFECT schoss, PERFECT hat geschossen) *(gun, in football)*
□ Don't shoot! Nicht schießen!
■ **to shoot at somebody** auf jemanden schießen
■ **He was shot in the leg.** *(wounded)* Er wurde ins Bein getroffen.
■ **to shoot an arrow** einen Pfeil abschießen
2 erschießen (IMPERFECT erschoss, PERFECT hat erschossen) *(kill)*
□ He was shot by a sniper. Er wurde von einem Heckenschützen erschossen.
■ **to shoot oneself** *(dead)* sich erschießen
□ He shot himself with a revolver. Er erschoss sich mit einem Revolver.
3 drehen *(film)*
□ The film was shot in Prague. Der Film wurde in Prag gedreht.
shooting NOUN
1 die Schüsse *masc pl*
□ They heard shooting. Sie hörten Schüsse.
■ **a shooting** eine Schießerei
2 die Jagd *(hunting)*
□ to go shooting auf die Jagd gehen
shop NOUN
das Geschäft (PL die Geschäfte)
□ a sports shop ein Sportgeschäft
shop assistant NOUN
der Verkäufer (PL die Verkäufer)
die Verkäuferin
□ She's a shop assistant. Sie ist Verkäuferin.
shopkeeper NOUN
der Ladenbesitzer (PL die Ladenbesitzer)
die Ladenbesitzerin
□ He's a shopkeeper. Er ist Ladenbesitzer.
shoplifting NOUN
der Ladendiebstahl (PL die Ladendiebstähle)
shopping NOUN
die Einkäufe *masc pl (purchases)*
□ Can you get the shopping from the car? Kannst du die Einkäufe aus dem Auto holen?
■ **I love shopping.** Ich gehe gern einkaufen.
■ **to go shopping** einkaufen gehen
■ **a shopping bag** eine Einkaufstasche
■ **a shopping centre** ein Einkaufszentrum *neut*
shop window NOUN
das Schaufenster (PL die Schaufenster)
shore NOUN
die Küste
■ **on shore** an Land
short ADJECTIVE
1 kurz
□ a short skirt ein kurzer Rock □ short hair kurze Haare □ a short break eine kurze Pause
□ a short walk ein kurzer Spaziergang
■ **too short** zu kurz □ Our holiday was too short. Unser Urlaub war zu kurz.
2 klein *(person)*
□ She's quite short. Sie ist ziemlich klein.
■ **to be short of something** knapp an etwas sein □ I'm short of money. Ich bin knapp an Geld.
■ **In short, the answer's no.** Kurz, die Antwort ist nein.
■ **at short notice** kurzfristig
shortage NOUN
der Mangel
□ a water shortage ein Wassermangel
short cut NOUN
die Abkürzung

◻ I took a short cut. Ich habe eine Abkürzung genommen.

shorthand NOUN
das Steno

shortly ADVERB
1 bald
◻ He'll be arriving shortly. Er kommt bald.
2 kurz
◻ shortly after the accident kurz nach dem Unfall

shorts PL NOUN
die Shorts *pl*
◻ a pair of shorts ein Paar Shorts

short-sighted ADJECTIVE
kurzsichtig

short story NOUN
die Kurzgeschichte

shot VERB ▷ *see* **shoot**

shot NOUN
1 der Schuss (GEN des Schusses, PL die Schüsse) *(gunshot)*
2 das Foto (PL die Fotos) *(photo)*
◻ a shot of the church ein Foto der Kirche
3 die Spritze *(injection)*

shotgun NOUN
die Flinte

should VERB
sollen
◻ You should take more exercise. Du solltest mehr Sport machen.
■ **He should be there by now.** Er müsste jetzt da sein.
■ **That shouldn't be too hard.** Das dürfte nicht zu schwer sein.
■ **I should have told you before.** Ich hätte es dir vorher sagen sollen.
LANGUAGE TIP When 'should' means 'would' use **würde**.
◻ I should go if I were you. Ich würde gehen, wenn ich du wäre.
■ **I should be so lucky!** Das wäre zu schön!

shoulder NOUN
die Schulter
■ **a shoulder bag** eine Umhängetasche

shouldn't = **should not**

to **shout** VERB
▷ *see also* **shout** NOUN
schreien (IMPERFECT schrie, PERFECT hat geschrien)
◻ Don't shout! Schrei doch nicht so!
◻ 'Go away!' he shouted. 'Geh weg!' schrie er.

shout NOUN
▷ *see also* **shout** VERB
der Schrei (PL die Schreie)

shovel NOUN
die Schaufel

show NOUN
▷ *see also* **show** VERB
1 die Show (PL die Shows) *(performance)*
2 die Sendung *(programme)*
3 die Ausstellung *(exhibition)*

to **show** VERB
▷ *see also* **show** NOUN
1 zeigen
■ **to show somebody something** jemandem etwas zeigen ◻ Have I shown you my new trainers? Habe ich dir meine neuen Turnschuhe schon gezeigt?
2 beweisen (IMPERFECT bewies, PERFECT hat bewiesen)
◻ She showed great courage. Sie hat großen Mut bewiesen.
■ **It shows.** Das sieht man. ◻ I've never been riding before. — It shows. Ich bin noch nie geritten. — Das sieht man.
■ **to show off** angeben *(informal)*
■ **to show up** *(turn up)* aufkreuzen
◻ He showed up late. Er kreuzte zu spät auf.

shower NOUN
1 die Dusche
■ **to have a shower** duschen
2 der Schauer (PL die Schauer) *(of rain)*

showerproof ADJECTIVE
regendicht

showing NOUN
die Vorführung *(of film)*

shown VERB ▷ *see* **show**

show-off NOUN
der Angeber (PL die Angeber)
die Angeberin

shrank VERB ▷ *see* **shrink**

to **shriek** VERB
kreischen

shrimps PL NOUN
die Krabben *fem pl*

to **shrink** VERB
einlaufen (PRESENT läuft ein, IMPERFECT lief ein, PERFECT ist eingelaufen) *(clothes, fabric)*

Shrove Tuesday NOUN
der Fastnachtsdienstag

to **shrug** VERB
■ **He shrugged his shoulders.** Er zuckte mit den Schultern.

shrunk VERB ▷ *see* **shrink**

to **shudder** VERB
sich schütteln

to **shuffle** VERB
■ **to shuffle the cards** die Karten mischen

to **shut** VERB
zumachen (PERFECT hat zugemacht)
◻ What time do you shut? Wann machen Sie zu? ◻ What time do the shops shut? Wann machen die Geschäfte zu?
■ **to shut down** schließen ◻ The cinema shut down last year. Das Kino hat letztes Jahr geschlossen.
■ **to shut up 1** *(close)* verschließen
2 *(be quiet)* den Mund halten ◻ Shut up! Halt den Mund!

shutters PL NOUN
die Fensterläden *masc pl*

shuttle NOUN
1 das Pendelflugzeug (PL die Pendelflugzeuge) *(plane)*
2 der Pendelzug (PL die Pendelzüge) *(train)*
3 der Pendelbus (GEN des Pendelbusses, PL die Pendelbusse) *(bus)*

shuttlecock NOUN
der Federball (PL die Federbälle) *(badminton)*

shy ADJECTIVE
schüchtern

Sicily NOUN
Sizilien *neut*
■ **from Sicily** aus Sizilien
■ **to Sicily** nach Sizilien

sick ADJECTIVE
1 krank *(ill)*
□ He was sick for four days. Er war vier Tage krank.
2 übel *(joke, humour)*
□ That's really sick! Das war wirklich übel!
■ **to be sick** *(vomit)* sich übergeben
■ **I feel sick.** Mir ist schlecht.
■ **to be sick of something** etwas leid sein
□ I'm sick of your jokes. Ich bin deine Witze leid.

sickening ADJECTIVE
ekelhaft

sick leave NOUN
■ **to be on sick leave** krankgeschrieben sein
□ Rudi's on sick leave. Rudi ist krankgeschrieben.

sickness NOUN
die Krankheit

sick note NOUN
1 die Entschuldigung *(from parents)*
2 das ärztliche Attest (PL die ärztlichen Atteste) *(from doctor)*

sick pay NOUN
die Bezahlung im Krankheitsfall

side NOUN
1 die Seite
□ He was driving on the wrong side of the road. Er fuhr auf der falschen Straßenseite.
□ He's on my side. Er ist auf meiner Seite.
■ **side by side** nebeneinander
■ **the side entrance** der Seiteneingang
■ **to take sides** Partei ergreifen □ She always takes your side. Sie ergreift immer für dich Partei.
2 der Rand (PL die Ränder) *(edge)*
□ by the side of the road am Straßenrand
3 das Ufer (PL die Ufer) *(of pool, river)*
□ by the side of the lake am Ufer des Sees

sideboard NOUN
die Anrichte

side effect NOUN
der Nebeneffekt (PL die Nebeneffekte)

side street NOUN
die Seitenstraße

sidewalk NOUN (US)
der Bürgersteig (PL die Bürgersteige)

sideways ADVERB
1 von der Seite *(look)*
2 zur Seite *(move, be facing)*
■ **sideways on** von der Seite

sieve NOUN
das Sieb (PL die Siebe)

sigh NOUN
▷ *see also* **sigh** VERB
der Seufzer (PL die Seufzer)

to **sigh** VERB
▷ *see also* **sigh** NOUN
seufzen

sight NOUN
der Anblick
□ an amazing sight ein irrer Anblick
■ **in sight** in Sicht
■ **out of sight** nicht zu sehen
■ **to have poor sight** schlechte Augen haben
■ **to know somebody by sight** jemanden vom Sehen kennen
■ **the sights** *(tourist spots)* die Sehenswürdigkeiten □ to see the sights sich die Sehenswürdigkeiten ansehen

sightseeing NOUN
das Sightseeing
■ **to go sightseeing** Sightseeing machen

sign NOUN
▷ *see also* **sign** VERB
1 das Schild (PL die Schilder) *(notice)*
□ There was a big sign saying 'private'. Da war ein großes Schild, auf dem 'privat' stand.
■ **a road sign** ein Verkehrsschild
2 das Zeichen (PL die Zeichen) *(gesture, indication)*
□ There's no sign of improvement. Es gibt kein Zeichen einer Besserung.
■ **What sign are you?** *(star sign)* Was für ein Sternzeichen sind Sie?

to **sign** VERB
▷ *see also* **sign** NOUN
unterschreiben (IMPERFECT unterschrieb, PERFECT hat unterschrieben)
■ **to sign on 1** *(as unemployed)* sich arbeitslos melden **2** *(for course)* sich einschreiben

signal NOUN
▷ *see also* **signal** VERB
das Signal (PL die Signale)

to **signal** VERB
▷ *see also* **signal** NOUN
■ **to signal to somebody** jemandem ein Zeichen geben

signalman NOUN
der Stellwerkswärter (PL die Stellwerkswärter)
die Stellwerkswärterin

signature NOUN
die Unterschrift

significance NOUN
die Bedeutung

significant ADJECTIVE
bedeutend

sign language NOUN
die Zeichensprache

signpost NOUN
der Wegweiser (PL die Wegweiser)

silence NOUN
die Stille
□ There was absolute silence. Es herrschte absolute Stille.

silent ADJECTIVE
still

silicon chip NOUN
der Siliciumchip (PL die Siliciumchips)

silk NOUN
▷ *see also* **silk** ADJECTIVE
die Seide

silk ADJECTIVE
▷ *see also* **silk** NOUN
seiden
□ a silk scarf ein seidener Schal

silky ADJECTIVE
seidig

silly ADJECTIVE
dumm
□ That's the silliest excuse I've ever heard. Das ist die dümmste Ausrede, die ich je gehört habe.

silver NOUN
das Silber
□ a silver medal eine Silbermedaille

similar ADJECTIVE
ähnlich
□ My sister is very similar to me. Meine Schwester ist mir sehr ähnlich.

simple ADJECTIVE
1 einfach
□ It's very simple. Das ist sehr einfach.
2 einfältig *(simple-minded)*
□ He's a bit simple. Er ist etwas einfältig.

simply ADVERB
einfach
□ It's simply not possible. Es ist einfach nicht möglich.

simultaneous ADJECTIVE
gleichzeitig

sin NOUN
▷ *see also* **sin** VERB
die Sünde

to **sin** VERB
▷ *see also* **sin** NOUN
sündigen

since PREPOSITION, ADVERB, CONJUNCTION
1 seit
□ since Christmas seit Weihnachten
□ I haven't seen her since she left. Ich habe sie nicht gesehen, seit sie weggezogen ist.
■ **since then** seither □ I haven't seen him since then. Ich habe ihn seither nicht gesehen.
■ **ever since** seitdem
2 da *(because)*
□ Since you're tired, let's stay at home. Da du müde bist, bleiben wir doch zu Hause.

sincere ADJECTIVE
aufrichtig

sincerely ADVERB
■ **Yours sincerely ...** Mit freundlichen Grüßen ...

to **sing** VERB
singen (IMPERFECT sang, PERFECT hat gesungen)
□ He sang out of tune. Er hat falsch gesungen. □ Have you ever sung this tune before? Hast du die Melodie schon mal gesungen?

singer NOUN
der Sänger (PL die Sänger)
die Sängerin

singing NOUN
das Singen

single ADJECTIVE
▷ *see also* **single** NOUN
alleinstehend *(unmarried)*
■ **a single room** ein Einzelzimmer *neut*
■ **not a single thing** absolut nichts

single NOUN
▷ *see also* **single** ADJECTIVE
1 die einfache Fahrkarte *(ticket)*
□ A single to Bonn, please. Eine einfache Fahrkarte nach Bonn, bitte.
2 die Single (PL die Singles) *(record)*
■ **a CD single** eine CD-Single

single parent NOUN
■ **She's a single parent.** Sie ist alleinerziehende Mutter.
■ **a single parent family** eine Einelternteilfamilie

singles PL NOUN
das Einzel *sing* (PL die Einzel) *(in tennis)*
□ the women's singles das Dameneinzel

singular NOUN
der Singular (PL die Singulare)
□ in the singular im Singular

sinister ADJECTIVE
unheimlich

sink NOUN
▷ *see also* **sink** VERB
die Spüle

to **sink** VERB
▷ *see also* **sink** NOUN
sinken (IMPERFECT sank, PERFECT ist gesunken)

sir NOUN
LANGUAGE TIP In German no form of address is normally used apart from **Sie**.
□ Would you like to order, Sir? Möchten Sie bestellen?
■ **Yes sir.** Ja.

siren NOUN
die Sirene

sister NOUN
die Schwester
□ my little sister meine kleine Schwester

□ I wanted to speak to the sister on the ward. Ich wollte die Stationsschwester sprechen.

sister-in-law NOUN
die Schwägerin

to **sit** VERB
1 sitzen (IMPERFECT saß, PERFECT hat gesessen) *(be sitting)*
□ She was sitting on the floor. Sie saß auf dem Boden.
2 sich setzen *(sit down)*
□ Sit on that chair. Setz dich auf den Stuhl.
■ **to sit down** sich setzen
■ **to be sitting** sitzen
■ **to sit an exam** eine Prüfung machen

sitcom NOUN
die Situationskomödie

site NOUN
1 die Stätte
□ an archaeological site eine archäologische Stätte
■ **the site of the accident** der Unfallort
2 der Campingplatz (GEN des Campingplatzes, PL die Campingplätze) *(campsite)*
■ **a building site** eine Baustelle

sitting room NOUN
das Wohnzimmer (PL die Wohnzimmer)

situated ADJECTIVE
■ **to be situated** liegen □ The village is situated on the side of the hill. Das Dorf liegt am Berghang.

situation NOUN
die Situation

six NUMBER
sechs
□ He's six. Er ist sechs.

sixteen NUMBER
sechzehn
□ He's sixteen. Er ist sechzehn.

sixteenth ADJECTIVE
sechzehnte
□ the sixteenth of August der sechzehnte August

sixth ADJECTIVE
sechste
□ the sixth floor der sechste Stock
□ the sixth of August der sechste August

sixty NUMBER
sechzig
□ She's sixty. Sie ist sechzig.

size NOUN

DID YOU KNOW...?
Germany uses the European system for clothing and shoe sizes.

1 die Größe *(of object, clothing)*
□ What size do you take? Welche Größe haben Sie?
■ **I'm a size ten.** Ich habe Größe achtunddreißig.
2 die Schuhgröße *(of shoes)*
□ I take size six. Ich habe Schuhgröße neununddreißig.

to **skate** VERB
1 Schlittschuh laufen (PRESENT läuft Schlittschuh, IMPERFECT lief Schlittschuh, PERFECT ist Schlittschuh gelaufen) *(ice-skate)*
2 Rollschuh laufen (PRESENT läuft Rollschuh, IMPERFECT lief Rollschuh, PERFECT ist Rollschuh gelaufen) *(roller-skate)*

skateboard NOUN
das Skateboard (PL die Skateboards)

skateboarding NOUN
das Skateboardfahren
■ **to go skateboarding** Skateboard fahren

skates PL NOUN
1 die Schlittschuhe *masc pl*
2 die Rollschuhe *masc pl (roller skates)*

skating NOUN
1 das Schlittschuhlaufen
■ **to go skating** Schlittschuh laufen
■ **a skating rink** eine Eisbahn
2 das Rollschuhlaufen *(roller-skating)*
■ **to go skating** Rollschuh laufen
■ **a skating rink** eine Rollschuhbahn

skeleton NOUN
das Skelett (PL die Skelette)

sketch NOUN
▷ *see also* **sketch** VERB
die Skizze *(drawing)*

to **sketch** VERB
▷ *see also* **sketch** NOUN
skizzieren (PERFECT hat skizziert)

to **ski** VERB
▷ *see also* **ski** NOUN
Ski fahren (PRESENT fährt Ski, IMPERFECT fuhr Ski, PERFECT ist Ski gefahren)
□ Can you ski? Kannst du Ski fahren?

ski NOUN
▷ *see also* **ski** VERB
der Ski (PL die Skier)
■ **ski boots** die Skistiefel
■ **a ski lift** ein Skilift *masc*
■ **ski pants** die Skihose *sing*
■ **a ski pole** ein Skistock *masc*
■ **a ski slope** eine Skipiste
■ **a ski suit** ein Skianzug *masc*

to **skid** VERB
schleudern (PERFECT ist geschleudert)

skier NOUN
der Skifahrer (PL die Skifahrer)
die Skifahrerin

skiing NOUN
das Skifahren
■ **to go skiing** Ski fahren
■ **to go on a skiing holiday** in den Skiurlaub fahren

skilful ADJECTIVE
geschickt

skill NOUN
das Können
□ a lot of skill viel Können

skilled ADJECTIVE
■ **a skilled worker** ein Facharbeiter *masc*
skimmed milk NOUN
die Magermilch
skimpy ADJECTIVE
knapp *(clothes)*
skin NOUN
die Haut (PL die Häute)
■ **skin cancer** der Hautkrebs
skinhead NOUN
der Skinhead (PL die Skinheads)
LANGUAGE TIP **der Skinhead** is also used for women.
skinny ADJECTIVE
mager
skin-tight ADJECTIVE
hauteng
skip NOUN
▷ *see also* **skip** VERB
der Container (PL die Container) *(container)*
to **skip** VERB
▷ *see also* **skip** NOUN
1 seilspringen (PERFECT ist seilgesprungen) *(with rope)*
2 auslassen (PRESENT lässt aus, IMPERFECT ließ aus, PERFECT hat ausgelassen)
□ to skip a meal eine Mahlzeit auslassen
■ **I skipped the maths lesson.** Ich habe die Mathestunde geschwänzt.
skirt NOUN
der Rock (PL die Röcke)
skittles SING NOUN
das Kegeln
■ **to play skittles** kegeln
to **skive** VERB
faulenzen *(be lazy)*
■ **to skive off** schwänzen *(informal)*
□ to skive off school die Schule schwänzen
skull NOUN
der Schädel (PL die Schädel)
sky NOUN
der Himmel (PL die Himmel)
skyscraper NOUN
der Wolkenkratzer (PL die Wolkenkratzer)
slack ADJECTIVE
1 locker *(rope)*
2 nachlässig *(person)*
to **slag off** VERB
■ **to slag somebody off** über jemanden herziehen *(informal)*
□ She's always slagging me off. Sie zieht dauernd über mich her.
to **slam** VERB
zuknallen (PERFECT hat/ist zugeknallt)
LANGUAGE TIP For the perfect tense use **haben** when the verb has an object and **sein** when there is no object.
□ The door slammed. Die Tür ist zugeknallt.
□ She slammed the door. Sie hat die Tür zugeknallt.

slang NOUN
der Slang (PL die Slangs)
slap NOUN
▷ *see also* **slap** VERB
die Ohrfeige
to **slap** VERB
▷ *see also* **slap** NOUN
■ **to slap somebody** jemandem einen Klaps geben □ She slapped him. Sie gab ihm einen Klaps.
slate NOUN
1 der Schiefer (PL die Schiefer)
2 der Schieferziegel (PL die Schieferziegel) *(for roof)*
sledge NOUN
der Schlitten (PL die Schlitten)
sledging NOUN
■ **to go sledging** Schlitten fahren
sleep NOUN
▷ *see also* **sleep** VERB
der Schlaf
□ I need some sleep. Ich brauche Schlaf.
■ **to go to sleep** einschlafen
to **sleep** VERB
▷ *see also* **sleep** NOUN
schlafen (PRESENT schläft, IMPERFECT schlief, PERFECT hat geschlafen)
□ I couldn't sleep. Ich konnte nicht schlafen.
■ **to sleep with somebody** mit jemandem schlafen
■ **to sleep together** miteinander schlafen
■ **to sleep around** mit jedem schlafen
■ **to sleep in** verschlafen
sleeping bag NOUN
der Schlafsack (PL die Schlafsäcke)
sleeping car NOUN
der Schlafwagen (PL die Schlafwagen)
sleeping pill NOUN
die Schlaftablette
sleepover NOUN
die Übernachtung
■ **to have a sleepover** bei Freunden übernachten
sleepy ADJECTIVE
schläfrig
■ **to feel sleepy** schläfrig sein □ I was feeling sleepy. Ich war schläfrig.
■ **a sleepy little village** ein verschlafenes kleines Dorf
sleet NOUN
▷ *see also* **sleet** VERB
der Schneeregen
to **sleet** VERB
▷ *see also* **sleet** NOUN
■ **It's sleeting.** Es fällt Schneeregen.
sleeve NOUN
1 der Ärmel (PL die Ärmel)
□ long sleeves lange Ärmel □ short sleeves kurze Ärmel
2 die Hülle *(record sleeve)*

sleigh NOUN
der Pferdeschlitten (PL die Pferdeschlitten)

slept VERB ▷ *see* **sleep**

slice NOUN
▷ *see also* **slice** VERB
die Scheibe

to **slice** VERB
▷ *see also* **slice** NOUN
aufschneiden (IMPERFECT schnitt auf, PERFECT hat aufgeschnitten)

slick NOUN
■ **an oil slick** ein Ölteppich *masc*

slide NOUN
▷ *see also* **slide** VERB
1 die Rutschbahn *(in playground)*
2 das Dia (PL die Dias) *(photo)*
3 die Klemme *(hair slide)*

to **slide** VERB
▷ *see also* **slide** NOUN
rutschen (PERFECT ist gerutscht)

slight ADJECTIVE
klein
□ a slight problem ein kleines Problem □ a slight improvement eine kleine Verbesserung

slightly ADVERB
etwas

slim ADJECTIVE
▷ *see also* **slim** VERB
schlank

to **slim** VERB
▷ *see also* **slim** ADJECTIVE
abnehmen (PRESENT nimmt ab, IMPERFECT nahm ab, PERFECT hat abgenommen) *(be on a diet)*
□ I'm slimming. Ich nehme gerade ab.

sling NOUN
die Schlinge
□ She had her arm in a sling. Sie hatte den Arm in der Schlinge.

slip NOUN
▷ *see also* **slip** VERB
1 der Schnitzer (PL die Schnitzer) *(mistake)*
2 der Unterrock (PL die Unterröcke) *(underskirt)*
■ **a slip of paper** ein Zettel *masc*
■ **a slip of the tongue** ein Versprecher *masc*

to **slip** VERB
▷ *see also* **slip** NOUN
ausrutschen (PERFECT ist ausgerutscht)
□ He slipped on the ice. Er ist auf dem Eis ausgerutscht.
■ **to slip up** *(make a mistake)* einen Fehler machen

slipper NOUN
der Hausschuh (PL die Hausschuhe)
□ a pair of slippers ein Paar Hausschuhe

slippery ADJECTIVE
glatt

slip-up NOUN
der Schnitzer (PL die Schnitzer)
■ **There's been a slip-up.** Da ist etwas schiefgelaufen.

slope NOUN
der Abhang (PL die Abhänge)

sloppy ADJECTIVE
schlampig

slot NOUN
der Schlitz (GEN des Schlitzes, PL die Schlitze)

slot machine NOUN
1 der Geldspielautomat (GEN des Geldspielautomaten, PL die Geldspielautomaten) *(for gambling)*
2 der Automat (GEN des Automaten, PL die Automaten) *(vending machine)*

slow ADJECTIVE, ADVERB
langsam
□ He's a bit slow. Er ist etwas langsam.
■ **to go slow 1** *(person)* langsam gehen
2 *(car)* langsam fahren □ Drive slower! Fahr langsamer!
■ **My watch is slow.** Meine Uhr geht nach.

to **slow down** VERB
verlangsamen (PERFECT hat verlangsamt)

slowly ADVERB
langsam

slug NOUN
die Nacktschnecke *(animal)*

slum NOUN
der Slum (PL die Slums)

slush NOUN
der Matsch

sly ADJECTIVE
gerissen *(person)*
■ **a sly smile** ein verschmitztes Lächeln

smack NOUN
▷ *see also* **smack** VERB
der Klaps (GEN des Klapses, PL die Klapse) *(slap)*

to **smack** VERB
▷ *see also* **smack** NOUN
■ **to smack somebody** jemandem einen Klaps geben □ She smacked him. Sie gab ihm einen Klaps.

small ADJECTIVE
klein
■ **small change** das Kleingeld

LANGUAGE TIP Be careful not to translate **small** by **schmal**.

> WORD POWER
> You can use a number of other words instead of **small** to mean 'little':
> **miniature** Miniatur-
> □ a miniature version eine Miniaturversion
> **minute** winzig
> □ a minute flat eine winzige Wohnung
> **tiny** winzig
> □ a tiny garden ein winziger Garten

smart ADJECTIVE
1 schick *(elegant)*
2 intelligent *(clever)*
□ a smart idea eine intelligente Idee

smart phone NOUN
das Smartphone (PL die Smartphones)

smash NOUN
▷ *see also* **smash** VERB
der Zusammenstoß (GEN des Zusammenstoßes, PL die Zusammenstöße)

to **smash** VERB
▷ *see also* **smash** NOUN
1 kaputt machen (PERFECT hat kaputt gemacht) *(break)*
□ I've smashed my watch. Ich habe meine Uhr kaputt gemacht.
2 zerbrechen (PRESENT zerbricht, IMPERFECT zerbrach, PERFECT ist zerbrochen) *(get broken)*
□ The glass smashed into tiny pieces. Das Glas zerbrach in winzige Scherben.

smashing ADJECTIVE
klasse *(informal)*
□ I think he's smashing. Ich finde, er ist klasse.
LANGUAGE TIP **klasse** is invariable.
□ a smashing film ein klasse Film

smell NOUN
▷ *see also* **smell** VERB
der Geruch (PL die Gerüche)
■ **the sense of smell** der Geruchsinn

to **smell** VERB
▷ *see also* **smell** NOUN
1 stinken (IMPERFECT stank, PERFECT hat gestunken)
□ That old dog really smells! Der alte Hund stinkt!
■ **to smell of something** nach etwas riechen
□ It smells of petrol. Es riecht nach Benzin.
2 riechen (IMPERFECT roch, PERFECT hat gerochen) *(detect)*
□ I can't smell anything. Ich kann nichts riechen.

smelly ADJECTIVE
stinkend
■ **He's got smelly feet.** Seine Füße stinken.

smelt VERB ▷ *see* **smell**

smile NOUN
▷ *see also* **smile** VERB
das Lächeln

to **smile** VERB
▷ *see also* **smile** NOUN
lächeln

smiley NOUN
das Smiley (PL die Smileys)

smoke NOUN
▷ *see also* **smoke** VERB
der Rauch

to **smoke** VERB
▷ *see also* **smoke** NOUN
rauchen
□ I don't smoke. Ich rauche nicht.
□ He smokes cigars. Er raucht Zigarren.

smoker NOUN
der Raucher (PL die Raucher)
die Raucherin

smoking NOUN
das Rauchen
□ to give up smoking mit dem Rauchen aufhören □ Smoking is bad for you. Rauchen schadet der Gesundheit.
■ **'no smoking'** 'Rauchen verboten'

smooth ADJECTIVE
1 glatt *(surface)*
2 aalglatt *(person)*

smoothie NOUN
der Smoothie (PL die Smoothies)

SMS NOUN *(= short message service)*
die SMS

smudge NOUN
der Dreck

smug ADJECTIVE
selbstgefällig
□ He's looking smug. Er wirkt selbstgefällig.

to **smuggle** VERB
schmuggeln

smuggler NOUN
der Schmuggler (PL die Schmuggler)
die Schmugglerin

smuggling NOUN
das Schmuggeln

smutty ADJECTIVE
schmutzig
□ a smutty story eine schmutzige Geschichte

snack NOUN
der Snack (PL die Snacks)
□ to have a snack einen Snack zu sich nehmen

snack bar NOUN
die Imbissstube

snail NOUN
die Schnecke

snake NOUN
die Schlange

to **snap** VERB
brechen (PRESENT bricht, IMPERFECT brach, PERFECT ist gebrochen) *(break)*
□ The branch snapped. Der Zweig brach.
■ **to snap one's fingers** mit dem Finger schnipsen

snapshot NOUN
das Foto (PL die Fotos)

to **snarl** VERB
knurren *(animal)*

to **snatch** VERB
■ **to snatch something from somebody** jemandem etwas entreißen □ He snatched the keys from me. Er entriss mir die Schlüssel.
■ **My bag was snatched.** Man hat mir meine Handtasche entrissen.

to **sneak** VERB
■ **to sneak in** sich hineinschleichen
■ **to sneak out** sich hinausschleichen
■ **to sneak up on somebody** an jemanden heranschleichen

to **sneeze** VERB
niesen
to **sniff** VERB
1 schniefen
□ Stop sniffing! Hör auf zu schniefen!
2 schnüffeln an *+dat*
□ The dog sniffed my hand. Der Hund schnüffelte an meiner Hand.
■ **to sniff glue** schnüffeln
snob NOUN
der Snob (PL die Snobs)
LANGUAGE TIP **der Snob** is also used for women.
□ She is such a snob. Sie ist ein furchtbarer Snob.
snooker NOUN
das Snooker
□ to play snooker Snooker spielen
snooze NOUN
das Nickerchen (PL die Nickerchen)
□ to have a snooze ein Nickerchen machen
to **snore** VERB
schnarchen
snow NOUN
▷ *see also* **snow** VERB
der Schnee
to **snow** VERB
▷ *see also* **snow** NOUN
schneien
□ It's snowing. Es schneit.
snowball NOUN
der Schneeball (PL die Schneebälle)
snowboarding NOUN
das Snowboarding *neut*
snowflake NOUN
die Schneeflocke
snowman NOUN
der Schneemann (PL die Schneemänner)
□ to build a snowman einen Schneemann machen
so CONJUNCTION, ADVERB
1 also
□ The shop was closed, so I went home. Das Geschäft war zu, also ging ich nach Hause. □ It rained, so I got wet. Es hat geregnet, also bin ich nass geworden.
□ So, have you always lived in London? Also, hast du schon immer in London gewohnt?
■ **So what?** Na und?
2 so
□ It was so heavy! Es war so schwer! □ It's not so heavy! Es ist nicht so schwer! □ He was talking so fast I couldn't understand. Er hat so schnell geredet, dass ich nichts verstanden habe. □ How's your father? — Not so good. Wie geht's deinem Vater? — Nicht so gut.
□ He's like his sister but not so clever. Er ist wie seine Schwester, aber nicht so klug.
■ **so much** *(a lot)* so sehr □ I love you so much. Ich liebe dich so sehr!
■ **so much ...** so viel ... □ I've got so much work. Ich habe so viel Arbeit.
■ **so many ...** so viele ... □ I've got so many things to do today. Ich muss heute so viele Dinge erledigen.
■ **so do I** ich auch □ I love horses. — So do I. Ich mag Pferde. — Ich auch.
■ **so have we** wir auch □ I've been to Hamburg. — So have we. Ich war schon einmal in Hamburg. — Wir auch.
■ **I think so.** Ich glaube schon.
■ **I hope so.** Hoffentlich.
■ **That's not so.** Das ist nicht so.
■ **so far** bis jetzt □ It's been easy so far. Bis jetzt war es einfach.
■ **so far so good** so weit, so gut
■ **ten or so people** so etwa zehn Leute
■ **at five o'clock or so** so gegen fünf Uhr
to **soak** VERB
einweichen (PERFECT hat eingeweicht)
soaked ADJECTIVE
völlig durchnässt
□ We were soaked. Wir waren völlig durchnässt.
soaking ADJECTIVE
völlig durchnässt
□ We were soaking. Wir waren völlig durchnässt.
■ **soaking wet** patschnass □ Your shoes are soaking wet. Deine Schuhe sind patschnass.
soap NOUN
die Seife
soap opera NOUN
die Seifenoper
soap powder NOUN
das Waschpulver (PL die Waschpulver)
to **sob** VERB
schluchzen
□ She was sobbing. Sie schluchzte.
sober ADJECTIVE
nüchtern
to **sober up** VERB
nüchtern werden (PRESENT wird nüchtern, IMPERFECT wurde nüchtern, PERFECT ist nüchtern geworden)
soccer NOUN
der Fußball
□ to play soccer Fußball spielen
■ **a soccer player** ein Fußballspieler *masc*
social ADJECTIVE
sozial
□ social problems soziale Probleme
■ **a social class** eine gesellschaftliche Schicht
■ **I have a good social life.** Ich komme viel unter Leute.
socialism NOUN
der Sozialismus (GEN des Sozialismus)
socialist ADJECTIVE
▷ *see also* **socialist** NOUN
sozialistisch

socialist NOUN
▷ *see also* **socialist** ADJECTIVE
der Sozialist (GEN des Sozialisten, PL die Sozialisten)
die Sozialistin
□ She's a Socialist. Sie ist Sozialistin.

social security NOUN
1 die Sozialhilfe *(money)*
■ **to be on social security** Sozialhilfe bekommen
2 die Sozialversicherung *(organization)*

social worker NOUN
der Sozialarbeiter (PL die Sozialarbeiter)
die Sozialarbeiterin
□ She's a social worker. Sie ist Sozialarbeiterin.

society NOUN
1 die Gesellschaft
□ We live in a multicultural society. Wir leben in einer multikulturellen Gesellschaft.
2 der Verein (PL die Vereine)
□ the Royal Society for the Prevention of Cruelty to Animals der Tierschutzverein
■ **a drama society** eine Theatergruppe

sociology NOUN
die Soziologie

sock NOUN
die Socke

socket NOUN
die Steckdose

soda NOUN
das Sodawasser (PL die Sodawasser) *(soda water)*

soda pop NOUN (US)
die Limo (PL die Limos)

sofa NOUN
das Sofa (PL die Sofas)

soft ADJECTIVE
weich
■ **soft cheese** der Weichkäse
■ **to be soft on somebody** *(be kind to)* nachsichtig mit jemandem sein
■ **a soft drink** ein alkoholfreies Getränk
■ **soft drugs** weiche Drogen
■ **a soft option** eine bequeme Lösung

software NOUN
die Software

soggy ADJECTIVE
1 nass *(soaked)*
□ a soggy tissue ein nasses Taschentuch
2 weich *(not crisp)*
□ soggy chips weiche Pommes frites

soil NOUN
der Boden (PL die Böden)

solar ADJECTIVE
■ **solar eclipse** die Sonnenfinsternis

solar power NOUN
die Sonnenenergie

sold VERB ▷ *see* **sell**

soldier NOUN
der Soldat (GEN des Soldaten, PL die Soldaten)
die Soldatin
□ He's a soldier. Er ist Soldat.

solicitor NOUN
1 der Rechtsanwalt (PL die Rechtsanwälte)
die Rechtsanwältin *(for lawsuits)*
□ He's a solicitor. Er ist Rechtsanwalt.
2 der Notar (PL die Notare)
die Notarin *(for property, wills)*
□ She's a solicitor. Sie ist Notarin.

solid ADJECTIVE
1 stabil
□ a solid wall eine stabile Wand
2 massiv
□ solid gold massives Gold
■ **for three hours solid** drei geschlagene Stunden lang

solo NOUN
das Solo (PL die Soli)
□ a guitar solo ein Gitarrensolo

solution NOUN
die Lösung

to **solve** VERB
lösen

some ADJECTIVE, PRONOUN
1 ein paar
LANGUAGE TIP Use **ein paar** with plural nouns.
□ some nice pictures ein paar nette Bilder
□ I only sold some of them. Ich habe nur ein paar verkauft.
■ **Some people say that ...** Manche Leute sagen, dass ...
■ **some day** eines Tages
■ **some day next week** irgendwann nächste Woche
2 einige *(some but not all)*
□ Are these mushrooms poisonous? — Only some. Sind diese Pilze giftig? — Nur einige.
■ **I only took some of it.** Ich habe nur etwas davon genommen.
■ **I'm going to buy some stamps. Do you want some too?** Ich kaufe Briefmarken. Willst du auch welche?
■ **Would you like some coffee? — No thanks, I've got some.** Möchten Sie Kaffee? — Nein danke, ich habe schon welchen.
LANGUAGE TIP 'some' is frequently not translated.
□ Would you like some bread? Möchtest du Brot? □ Have you got some mineral water? Haben Sie Mineralwasser?

somebody PRONOUN
jemand
□ Somebody stole my bag. Jemand hat meine Tasche gestohlen.

somehow ADVERB
irgendwie
□ I'll do it somehow. Ich mache es irgendwie.
□ Somehow I don't think he believed me. Irgendwie hat er mir anscheinend nicht geglaubt.

someone PRONOUN
jemand
□ Someone stole my bag. Jemand hat meine Tasche gestohlen.

something PRONOUN
etwas
□ something special etwas Besonderes
□ Wear something warm. Zieh etwas Warmes an.
■ **That's really something!** Das ist echt toll!
■ **It cost a hundred pounds, or something like that.** Es kostet hundert Pfund, oder so in der Gegend.
■ **His name is Phil or something.** Er heißt Phil oder so ähnlich.

sometime ADVERB
mal
□ You must come and see us sometime. Du musst uns mal besuchen.
■ **sometime last month** irgendwann letzten Monat

sometimes ADVERB
manchmal
□ Sometimes I think she hates me. Manchmal denke ich, sie hasst mich.

somewhere ADVERB
irgendwo
□ I've left my keys somewhere. Ich habe irgendwo meine Schlüssel liegen lassen.
□ I'd like to live somewhere sunny. Ich würde gern irgendwo leben, wo es sonnig ist.

son NOUN
der Sohn (PL die Söhne)

song NOUN
das Lied (PL die Lieder)

son-in-law NOUN
der Schwiegersohn (PL die Schwiegersöhne)

soon ADVERB
bald
□ very soon sehr bald
■ **soon afterwards** kurz danach
■ **as soon as possible** sobald wie möglich

sooner ADVERB
früher
□ a bit sooner etwas früher □ sooner or later früher oder später

soot NOUN
der Ruß

soppy ADJECTIVE
sentimental

soprano NOUN
der Sopran (PL die Soprane)

sorcerer NOUN
der böse Zauberer (PL die bösen Zauberer)

sore ADJECTIVE
▷ *see also* **sore** NOUN
■ **It's sore.** Es tut weh.
■ **That's a sore point.** Das ist ein wunder Punkt.

sore NOUN
▷ *see also* **sore** ADJECTIVE
die Wunde

sorry ADJECTIVE
■ **I'm really sorry.** Es tut mir wirklich leid.
□ I'm sorry, I haven't got any change. Es tut mir leid, aber ich habe kein Kleingeld.
□ I'm sorry I'm late. Es tut mir leid, dass ich zu spät komme. □ I'm sorry about the noise. Es tut mir leid wegen des Lärms. □ You'll be sorry! Das wird dir leidtun!
■ **Sorry!** Entschuldigung!
■ **Sorry?** Wie bitte?
■ **I feel sorry for her.** Sie tut mir leid.

sort NOUN
die Art
□ There are different sorts of mushrooms. Es gibt verschiedene Arten von Pilzen.
■ ***what sort of ...*** **1** was für ein ...
□ What sort of cake is that? Was für ein Kuchen ist das? □ What sort of bike have you got? Was für ein Fahrrad hast du? **2** was für eine ... □ What sort of school do you go to? In was für eine Schule gehst du?

to **sort out** VERB
1 sortieren (PERFECT hat sortiert) *(objects)*
2 lösen *(problems)*

so-so ADVERB
so lala *(informal)*
□ How are you feeling? — So-so. Wie geht's dir? — So lala.

soul NOUN
1 die Seele *(spirit)*
2 der Soul *(music)*

sound NOUN
▷ *see also* **sound** VERB, ADJECTIVE
1 das Geräusch (PL die Geräusche) *(noise)*
■ **Don't make a sound!** Still!
■ **I heard the sound of footsteps.** Ich hörte Schritte.
2 die Lautstärke
□ Can I turn the sound down? Kann ich die Lautstärke runterdrehen?

to **sound** VERB
▷ *see also* **sound** NOUN, ADJECTIVE
klingen (IMPERFECT klang, PERFECT hat geklungen)
□ That sounds interesting. Das klingt interessant.
■ **It sounds as if she's doing well at school.** Allem Anschein nach ist sie gut in der Schule.
■ **That sounds like a good idea.** Das scheint eine gute Idee zu sein.

sound ADJECTIVE, ADVERB
▷ *see also* **sound** NOUN, VERB
gut
□ That's sound advice. Das ist ein guter Rat.
■ **to be sound asleep** fest schlafen

soundtrack NOUN
der Soundtrack (PL die Soundtracks)

soup NOUN
die Suppe

□ vegetable soup die Gemüsesuppe

sour ADJECTIVE
sauer

south ADJECTIVE, ADVERB
▷ *see also* **south** NOUN
nach Süden
□ We were travelling south. Wir sind nach Süden gefahren.
■ **the south coast** die Südküste
■ **a south wind** ein Südwind *masc*
■ **south of** südlich von □ It's south of London. Es liegt südlich von London.

south NOUN
▷ *see also* **south** ADJECTIVE
der Süden
□ in the south im Süden
■ **in the South of Germany** in Süddeutschland

South Africa NOUN
Südafrika *neut*
■ **from South Africa** aus Südafrika
■ **to South Africa** nach Südafrika

South America NOUN
Südamerika *neut*
■ **from South America** aus Südamerika
■ **to South America** nach Südamerika

South American NOUN
▷ *see also* **South American** ADJECTIVE
der Südamerikaner (PL die Südamerikaner)
die Südamerikanerin

South American ADJECTIVE
▷ *see also* **South American** NOUN
südamerikanisch

southbound ADJECTIVE
in Richtung Süden
□ southbound traffic der Verkehr in Richtung Süden

southeast NOUN
der Südosten
■ **southeast England** Südostengland *neut*

southern ADJECTIVE
südlich
□ the southern part of the island der südliche Teil der Insel
■ **Southern England** Südengland *neut*

South Pole NOUN
der Südpol

South Wales NOUN
Südwales *neut*
■ **to South Wales** nach Südwales

southwest NOUN
der Südwesten
■ **southwest Germany** Südwestdeutschland *neut*

souvenir NOUN
das Souvenir (PL die Souvenirs)
□ a souvenir shop ein Souvenirgeschäft

soya NOUN
die Soja

soy sauce NOUN
die Sojasoße

space NOUN
1 der Platz (GEN des Platzes)
□ There's enough space. Es ist genug Platz da.
■ **a parking space** ein Parkplatz
2 der Raum *(outer space)*

spacecraft NOUN
das Raumschiff (PL die Raumschiffe)

spade NOUN
der Spaten (PL die Spaten)
■ **spades** *(in cards)* das Pik □ the ace of spades das Pikass

Spain NOUN
Spanien *neut*
■ **from Spain** aus Spanien
■ **in Spain** in Spanien
■ **to Spain** nach Spanien

Spaniard NOUN
der Spanier (PL die Spanier)
die Spanierin

spaniel NOUN
der Spaniel (PL die Spaniel)

Spanish ADJECTIVE
▷ *see also* **Spanish** NOUN
spanisch
■ **He's Spanish.** Er ist Spanier.
■ **She's Spanish.** Sie ist Spanierin.

Spanish NOUN
▷ *see also* **Spanish** ADJECTIVE
das Spanisch (GEN des Spanischen) *(language)*
■ **the Spanish** die Spanier *masc pl*

to **spank** VERB
■ **to spank somebody** jemandem den Hintern versohlen

spanner NOUN
der Schraubenschlüssel (PL die Schraubenschlüssel)

to **spare** VERB
▷ *see also* **spare** ADJECTIVE, NOUN
■ **Can you spare a moment?** Hast du mal einen Moment Zeit?
■ **I can't spare the time.** Ich habe die Zeit nicht.
■ **There's no room to spare.** Es ist kein Platz übrig.
■ **We arrived with time to spare.** Wir waren zu früh da.

LANGUAGE TIP Be careful not to translate **to spare** by **sparen**.

spare NOUN
▷ *see also* **spare** ADJECTIVE, VERB
das Ersatzteil (PL die Ersatzteile)
■ **I've lost my key. — Have you got a spare?** Ich habe meinen Schlüssel verloren. — Hast du einen Ersatzschlüssel?

spare ADJECTIVE
▷ *see also* **spare** VERB, NOUN
■ **spare batteries** die Ersatzbatterien *fem pl*
■ **a spare part** ein Ersatzteil *neut*
■ **a spare room** ein Gästezimmer *neut*

■ **spare time** die Freizeit □ What do you do in your spare time? Was machen Sie in Ihrer Freizeit?
■ **spare wheel** das Reserverad

sparkling ADJECTIVE
mit Kohlensäure *(water)*
■ **sparkling wine** der Sekt

sparrow NOUN
der Spatz (GEN des Spatzen, PL die Spatzen)

spat VERB ▷ *see* **spit**

to **speak** VERB
sprechen (PRESENT spricht, IMPERFECT sprach, PERFECT hat gesprochen)
□ Do you speak English? Sprechen Sie Englisch?
■ **to speak to somebody** mit jemandem reden □ Have you spoken to him? Hast du mit ihm geredet? □ She spoke to him about it. Sie hat mit ihm darüber geredet.
■ **spoken German** gesprochenes Deutsch

to **speak up** VERB
lauter sprechen (PRESENT spricht, IMPERFECT sprach, PERFECT hat gesprochen)
□ Speak up, we can't hear you. Sprechen Sie lauter, wir können Sie nicht hören.

speaker NOUN
1 der Lautsprecher (PL die Lautsprecher) *(loudspeaker)*
2 der Redner (PL die Redner)
die Rednerin *(in debate)*

special ADJECTIVE
besondere
□ a special occasion ein besonderer Anlass

specialist NOUN
der Fachmann (PL die Fachleute)
die Fachfrau

speciality NOUN
die Spezialität

to **specialize** VERB
sich spezialisieren (PERFECT hat sich spezialisiert)
□ We specialize in skiing equipment. Wir haben uns auf Skiausrüstung spezialisiert.

specially ADVERB
1 besonders
□ It can be very cold here, specially in winter. Es kann hier sehr kalt werden, besonders im Winter.
2 speziell
□ It's specially designed for teenagers. Das ist speziell für Teenager gedacht.
■ **not specially** nicht besonders □ Do you like opera? — Not specially. Magst du Opern? — Nicht besonders.

species SING NOUN
die Art

specific ADJECTIVE
1 speziell *(particular)*
□ certain specific issues gewisse spezielle Fragen
2 genau *(precise)*
□ Could you be more specific? Könnten Sie sich etwas genauer ausdrücken?

specifically ADVERB
1 extra
□ It's specifically designed for teenagers. Es ist extra für Teenager gedacht.
2 genau
□ in Britain, or more specifically in England in Großbritannien, oder genauer gesagt in England □ I specifically said that ... Ich habe ganz genau gesagt, dass ...

specs PL NOUN
die Brille *sing*
□ a pair of specs eine Brille

spectacles PL NOUN
die Brille *sing*
□ a pair of spectacles eine Brille

spectacular ADJECTIVE
spektakulär

spectator NOUN
der Zuschauer (PL die Zuschauer)
die Zuschauerin

speech NOUN
die Rede
□ to make a speech eine Rede halten

speechless ADJECTIVE
sprachlos
□ speechless with admiration sprachlos vor Bewunderung □ I was speechless. Ich war sprachlos.

speed NOUN
1 der Gang (PL die Gänge)
■ **a three-speed bike** ein Dreigangrad *neut*
2 die Geschwindigkeit
□ at top speed mit Höchstgeschwindigkeit
■ **to speed up** schneller werden

speedboat NOUN
das Schnellboot (PL die Schnellboote)

speeding NOUN
das zu schnelle Fahren
□ He was fined for speeding. Er hat wegen zu schnellen Fahrens einen Strafzettel bekommen.

speed limit NOUN
die Geschwindigkeitsbegrenzung
□ to break the speed limit die Geschwindigkeitsbegrenzung überschreiten

speedometer NOUN
der Tachometer (PL die Tachometer)

to **spell** VERB
▷ *see also* **spell** NOUN
1 schreiben (IMPERFECT schrieb, PERFECT hat geschrieben) *(in writing)*
□ How do you spell that? Wie schreibt man das?
2 buchstabieren (PERFECT hat buchstabiert) *(out loud)*
□ Can you spell that please? Können Sie das bitte buchstabieren?

■ **I can't spell.** Ich kann keine Rechtschreibung.

spell NOUN
▷ *see also* **spell** VERB
■ **to cast a spell on somebody** jemanden verhexen
■ **to be under somebody's spell** von jemandem wie verzaubert sein

spelling NOUN
die Rechtschreibung
□ My spelling is terrible. Meine Rechtschreibung ist furchtbar.
■ **a spelling mistake** ein Rechtschreibfehler *masc*

spelt VERB ▷ *see* **spell**

to **spend** VERB
1 ausgeben (PRESENT gibt aus, IMPERFECT gab aus, PERFECT hat ausgegeben) *(money)*
2 verbringen (IMPERFECT verbrachte, PERFECT hat verbracht) *(time)*
□ He spent a month in Italy. Er verbrachte einen Monat in Italien.

LANGUAGE TIP Be careful not to translate **to spend** by **spenden**.

spice NOUN
das Gewürz (GEN des Gewürzes, PL die Gewürze)

spicy ADJECTIVE
scharf
□ Indian food's much spicier than German food. Indisches Essen ist viel schärfer als deutsches.

spider NOUN
die Spinne

to **spill** VERB
verschütten (PERFECT hat verschüttet) *(tip over)*
□ He spilled his coffee. Er hat seinen Kaffee verschüttet.
■ **to get spilt** verschüttet werden

spinach NOUN
der Spinat

spin drier NOUN
die Schleuder

spine NOUN
das Rückgrat (PL die Rückgrate)

spinster NOUN
die unverheiratete Frau

spire NOUN
der Kirchturm (PL die Kirchtürme)

spirit NOUN
1 der Mut *(courage)*
2 die Energie *(energy)*
■ **to be in good spirits** gut gelaunt sein

spirits PL NOUN
die Spirituosen *pl*

spiritual ADJECTIVE
geistlich
□ the spiritual leader of Tibet der geistliche Führer Tibets

to **spit** VERB
spucken
■ **to spit something out** etwas ausspucken
■ **It's spitting.** Es tröpfelt.

spite NOUN
▷ *see also* **spite** VERB
■ **in spite of** trotz □ in spite of the bad weather trotz des schlechten Wetters
■ **out of spite** aus Gehässigkeit

to **spite** VERB
▷ *see also* **spite** NOUN
ärgern
□ He just did it to spite me. Er tat es nur, um mich zu ärgern.

spiteful ADJECTIVE
1 gemein *(action)*
2 gehässig *(person)*

to **splash** VERB
▷ *see also* **splash** NOUN
bespritzen (PERFECT hat bespritzt)
□ Don't splash me! Bespritz mich nicht!

splash NOUN
▷ *see also* **splash** VERB
der Platsch
□ I heard a splash. Ich hörte einen Platsch.
■ **a splash of colour** ein Farbfleck *masc*

splendid ADJECTIVE
wunderbar

splint NOUN
die Schiene

splinter NOUN
der Splitter (PL die Splitter)

to **split** VERB
1 zerteilen (PERFECT hat zerteilt)
□ He split the wood with an axe. Er zerteilte das Holz mit einer Axt.
2 zerbrechen (PRESENT zerbricht, IMPERFECT zerbrach, PERFECT ist zerbrochen)
□ The ship hit a rock and split in two. Das Schiff lief auf einen Fels auf und zerbrach in zwei Teile.
3 teilen *(divide up)*
□ They split the profits. Sie teilten den Gewinn.
■ **to split up 1** *(couple)* sich trennen **2** *(group)* sich auflösen

to **spoil** VERB
1 verderben (PRESENT verdirbt, IMPERFECT verdarb, PERFECT hat verdorben)
□ It spoiled our evening. Es hat uns den Abend verdorben.
2 verwöhnen (PERFECT hat verwöhnt) *(child)*

spoiled ADJECTIVE
verwöhnt
□ a spoiled child ein verwöhntes Kind

spoilsport NOUN
der Spielverderber (PL die Spielverderber)
die Spielverderberin

spoilt ADJECTIVE
verwöhnt
□ a spoilt child ein verwöhntes Kind

spoilt VERB ▷ *see* **spoil**

spoke VERB ▷ *see* **speak**

spoke NOUN
die Speiche *(of wheel)*

spoken VERB ▷ *see* **speak**

spokesman NOUN
der Sprecher (PL die Sprecher)

spokeswoman NOUN
die Sprecherin

sponge NOUN
der Schwamm (PL die Schwämme)
■ **a sponge bag** ein Kulturbeutel *masc*
■ **a sponge cake** ein Rührkuchen *masc*

sponsor NOUN
▷ *see also* **sponsor** VERB
der Sponsor (PL die Sponsoren)
die Sponsorin

to **sponsor** VERB
▷ *see also* **sponsor** NOUN
sponsern
□ The festival was sponsored by ... Das Festival wurde gesponsert von ...

spontaneous ADJECTIVE
spontan

spooky ADJECTIVE
1 gruselig *(eerie)*
□ a spooky story eine gruselige Geschichte
2 komisch *(strange)*
□ a spooky coincidence ein komischer Zufall

spoon NOUN
der Löffel (PL die Löffel)
□ a spoon of sugar ein Löffel Zucker

spoonful NOUN
■ **a spoonful of soup** ein Löffel Suppe

sport NOUN
der Sport
□ What's your favourite sport? Was ist dein Lieblingssport?
■ **a sports bag** eine Sporttasche
■ **a sports car** ein Sportwagen *masc*
■ **a sports jacket** eine Sportjacke
■ **Go on, be a sport!** Nun komm schon, sei kein Frosch!

sportsman NOUN
der Sportler (PL die Sportler)

sportswear NOUN
die Sportkleidung

sportswoman NOUN
die Sportlerin

sporty ADJECTIVE
sportlich
□ I'm not very sporty. Ich bin nicht besonders sportlich.

spot NOUN
▷ *see also* **spot** VERB
1 der Fleck (PL die Flecke) *(mark)*
□ There's a spot of blood on your shirt. Du hast einen Blutfleck auf dem Hemd.
2 der Punkt (PL die Punkte) *(in pattern)*
□ a red dress with white spots ein rotes Kleid mit weißen Punkten
3 der Pickel (PL die Pickel) *(pimple)*
□ I've got a big spot on my chin. Ich habe einen großen Pickel am Kinn.
4 der Platz (GEN des Platzes, PL die Plätze) *(place)*
□ It's a lovely spot for a picnic. Es ist ein herrlicher Platz für ein Picknick.
■ **on the spot** 1 *(immediately)* sofort
□ They gave her the job on the spot. Sie haben ihr den Job sofort gegeben. 2 *(at the same place)* an Ort und Stelle □ They were able to mend the car on the spot. Sie konnten das Auto an Ort und Stelle reparieren.

to **spot** VERB
▷ *see also* **spot** NOUN
entdecken (PERFECT hat entdeckt)
□ I spotted Jack. Ich habe Jack entdeckt.

spotless ADJECTIVE
makellos

spotlight NOUN
das Scheinwerferlicht

spotty ADJECTIVE
pickelig *(pimply)*

spouse NOUN
der Ehemann (PL die Ehemänner)
die Ehefrau

to **sprain** VERB
▷ *see also* **sprain** NOUN
■ **I've sprained my ankle.** Ich habe mir den Fuß verstaucht.

sprain NOUN
▷ *see also* **sprain** VERB
die Verstauchung
□ It's just a sprain. Es ist nur eine Verstauchung.

spray NOUN
▷ *see also* **spray** VERB
das Spray (PL die Sprays)
□ hair spray das Haarspray

to **spray** VERB
▷ *see also* **spray** NOUN
sprühen
□ to spray perfume on one's hand sich Parfüm auf die Hand sprühen □ Somebody had sprayed graffiti on the wall. Irgendjemand hatte Graffiti auf die Wand gesprüht.

spread NOUN
▷ *see also* **spread** VERB
■ **cheese spread** der Streichkäse
■ **chocolate spread** der Schokoladenaufstrich

to **spread** VERB
▷ *see also* **spread** NOUN
1 streichen (IMPERFECT strich, PERFECT hat gestrichen)
□ to spread butter on a cracker Butter auf einen Cracker streichen
2 sich verbreiten (PERFECT hat sich verbreitet) *(disease, news)*
□ The news spread rapidly. Die Nachricht verbreitete sich schnell.
■ **to spread out** *(people)* sich verteilen
□ They spread out across the field.

Sie verteilten sich über das Feld.

spreadsheet NOUN
die Tabellenkalkulation *(computer program)*

spring NOUN
1 der Frühling (PL die Frühlinge) *(season)*
□ in spring im Frühling
2 die Feder *(metal coil)*
3 die Quelle *(water hole)*

spring-cleaning NOUN
der Frühjahrsputz (GEN des Frühjahrsputzes)

springtime NOUN
das Frühjahr (PL die Frühjahre)
□ in springtime im Frühjahr

sprinkler NOUN
der Rasensprenger (PL die Rasensprenger) *(for lawn)*

sprint NOUN
▷ *see also* **sprint** VERB
der Sprint (PL die Sprints)
■ **a hundred-metre sprint** ein Einhundertmeterlauf *masc*

to **sprint** VERB
▷ *see also* **sprint** NOUN
rennen (IMPERFECT rannte, PERFECT ist gerannt)
□ She sprinted for the bus. Sie rannte, um den Bus zu erreichen.

sprinter NOUN
der Sprinter (PL die Sprinter)
die Sprinterin

sprouts PL NOUN
■ **Brussels sprouts** der Rosenkohl *sing*

spy NOUN
▷ *see also* **spy** VERB
der Spion (PL die Spione)
die Spionin

to **spy** VERB
▷ *see also* **spy** NOUN
■ **to spy on somebody** jemandem nachspionieren □ She's spying on me. Sie spioniert mir nach.

spying NOUN
die Spionage

to **squabble** VERB
sich kabbeln
□ Stop squabbling! Hört auf, euch zu kabbeln!

square NOUN
▷ *see also* **square** ADJECTIVE
1 das Quadrat (PL die Quadrate)
□ a square and a triangle ein Quadrat und ein Dreieck
2 der Platz (GEN des Platzes, PL die Plätze)
□ the town square der Rathausplatz

square ADJECTIVE
▷ *see also* **square** NOUN
■ **two square metres** zwei Quadratmeter
■ **It's two metres square.** Es misst zwei mal zwei Meter.

squash NOUN
▷ *see also* **squash** VERB
das Squash *(sport)*
□ I play squash. Ich spiele Squash.
■ **a squash court** ein Squashcourt *masc*
■ **a squash racket** ein Squashschläger *masc*
■ **orange squash** der Orangensaft

to **squash** VERB
▷ *see also* **squash** NOUN
zerdrücken (PERFECT hat zerdrückt)
□ You're squashing me. Du zerdrückst mich.

to **squeak** VERB
1 quieksen *(mouse, child)*
2 quietschen *(creak)*

to **squeeze** VERB
1 pressen *(fruit, toothpaste)*
2 drücken *(hand, arm)*
□ to squeeze somebody's arm jemandem den Arm drücken
■ **to squeeze into tight jeans** sich in enge Jeans quetschen

to **squint** VERB
▷ *see also* **squint** NOUN
schielen

squint NOUN
▷ *see also* **squint** VERB
■ **He has a squint.** Er schielt.

squirrel NOUN
das Eichhörnchen (PL die Eichhörnchen)

to **stab** VERB
■ **to stab somebody** **1** *(wound)* jemanden mit dem Messer verletzen **2** *(kill)* jemanden erstechen

stable NOUN
▷ *see also* **stable** ADJECTIVE
der Stall (PL die Ställe)

stable ADJECTIVE
▷ *see also* **stable** NOUN
stabil
□ a stable relationship eine stabile Beziehung

stack NOUN
der Stapel (PL die Stapel)
□ a stack of books ein Stapel Bücher

stadium NOUN
das Stadion (PL die Stadien)

staff NOUN
1 die Belegschaft *(in company)*
2 die Lehrerschaft *(in school)*

stage NOUN
1 die Bühne *(in plays)*
2 das Podium (PL die Podien) *(for speeches, lectures)*
■ **at this stage** **1** an diesem Punkt □ at this stage in the negotiations an diesem Punkt der Verhandlungen **2** im Augenblick □ At this stage, one can't tell. Im Augenblick kann man das noch nicht sagen.
■ **to do something in stages** etwas in Etappen machen

to **stagger** VERB
taumeln (PERFECT ist getaumelt)

stain NOUN
▷ *see also* **stain** VERB
der Fleck (PL die Flecke)

to stain VERB
▷ *see also* **stain** NOUN
beflecken (PERFECT hat befleckt)

stainless steel NOUN
der Edelstahl

stain remover NOUN
der Fleckenentferner (PL die Fleckenentferner)

stair NOUN
die Stufe *(step)*

staircase NOUN
die Treppe

stairs PL NOUN
die Treppe *sing*

stale ADJECTIVE
altbacken *(bread)*

stalemate NOUN
das Patt (PL die Patts) *(in chess)*

stall NOUN
der Stand (PL die Stände)
□ He's got a market stall. Er hat einen Marktstand.
■ **the stalls** *(in cinema, theatre)* das Parkett *sing*

stamina NOUN
das Durchhaltevermögen

stammer NOUN
das Stottern
■ **He's got a stammer.** Er stottert.

to stamp VERB
▷ *see also* **stamp** NOUN
abstempeln (PERFECT hat abgestempelt) *(passport)*
■ **to stamp one's foot** mit dem Fuß aufstampfen

stamp NOUN
▷ *see also* **stamp** VERB
1 die Briefmarke
□ I need a stamp. Ich brauche eine Briefmarke. □ a stamp album ein Briefmarkenalbum □ a stamp collection eine Briefmarkensammlung
2 der Stempel (PL die Stempel) *(rubber stamp)*

stamped ADJECTIVE
■ **a stamped addressed envelope** ein frankierter und adressierter Rückumschlag

to stand VERB
1 stehen (IMPERFECT stand, PERFECT hat gestanden) *(be standing)*
□ He was standing by the door. Er stand an der Tür.
2 aufstehen (PERFECT ist aufgestanden) *(stand up)*
3 aushalten (PRESENT hält aus, IMPERFECT hielt aus, PERFECT hat ausgehalten) *(tolerate, withstand)*
□ I can't stand all this noise. Ich halte diesen Lärm nicht aus.
■ **to stand for** 1 *(be short for)* stehen für
□ 'BT' stands for 'British Telecom'. 'BT' steht für 'British Telecom'. **2** *(tolerate)* dulden
□ I won't stand for it! Ich dulde das nicht!
■ **to stand in for somebody** jemanden vertreten
■ **to stand out** herausragen
■ **to stand up** *(get up)* aufstehen
■ **to stand up for** eintreten für □ Stand up for your rights! Tretet für eure Rechte ein!

standard ADJECTIVE
▷ *see also* **standard** NOUN
normal
□ the standard procedure die normale Vorgehensweise
■ **standard German** das Hochdeutsch
■ **standard equipment** die Standardausrüstung

standard NOUN
▷ *see also* **standard** ADJECTIVE
das Niveau (PL die Niveaus)
□ The standard is very high. Das Niveau ist sehr hoch.
■ **the standard of living** der Lebensstandard
■ **She's got high standards.** Sie hat hohe Ansprüche.

stand-by ticket NOUN
das Stand-by-Ticket (PL die Stand-by-Tickets)

standpoint NOUN
der Standpunkt (PL die Standpunkte)

stands PL NOUN
die Tribüne *sing (at sports ground)*

stank VERB ▷ *see* **stink**

staple NOUN
▷ *see also* **staple** VERB
die Heftklammer

to staple VERB
▷ *see also* **staple** NOUN
zusammenheften (PERFECT hat zusammengeheftet)

stapler NOUN
die Heftmaschine

star NOUN
▷ *see also* **star** VERB
1 der Stern (PL die Sterne) *(in sky)*
2 der Star (PL die Stars) *(celebrity)*
LANGUAGE TIP **der Star** is also used for women.
□ She's a TV star. Sie ist ein Fernsehstar.
■ **the stars** *(horoscope)* die Sterne

to star VERB
▷ *see also* **star** NOUN
die Hauptrolle spielen
□ The film stars Nicole Kidman. Nicole Kidman spielt in dem Film die Hauptrolle.
■ **... starring Johnny Depp** ... mit Johnny Depp in der Hauptrolle

to stare VERB
■ **to stare at something** etwas anstarren

stark ADVERB
■ **stark naked** splitternackt

start NOUN
▷ *see also* **start** VERB

1 der Anfang (PL die Anfänge)
□ It's not much, but it's a start. Es ist nicht viel, aber es ist immerhin ein Anfang.
■ **Shall we make a start on the washing-up?** Sollen wir den Abwasch in Angriff nehmen?
2 der Start (PL die Starts) *(of race)*

to **start** VERB
▷ *see also* **start** NOUN
1 anfangen (PRESENT fängt an, IMPERFECT fing an, PERFECT hat angefangen)
□ What time does it start? Wann fängt es an?
■ **to start doing something** anfangen, etwas zu tun □ I started learning German three years ago. Ich habe vor drei Jahren angefangen, Deutsch zu lernen.
2 gründen *(organization)*
□ He wants to start his own business. Er möchte ein eigenes Geschäft gründen.
3 ins Leben rufen (IMPERFECT rief ins Leben, PERFECT hat ins Leben gerufen) *(campaign)*
□ She started the campaign. Sie hat die Kampagne ins Leben gerufen.
4 anlassen (PRESENT lässt an, IMPERFECT ließ an, PERFECT hat angelassen) *(car)*
□ He couldn't start the car. Er konnte das Auto nicht anlassen.
■ **The car wouldn't start.** Das Auto ist nicht angesprungen.
■ **to start off** *(leave)* aufbrechen
□ We started off first thing in the morning. Wir sind frühmorgens aufgebrochen.

starter NOUN
die Vorspeise *(first course)*

to **starve** VERB
verhungern (PERFECT ist verhungert) *(die)*
□ People were literally starving. Die Menschen sind förmlich verhungert.
■ **I'm starving!** Ich bin am Verhungern!
■ **They starved us in prison.** Sie ließen uns im Gefängnis hungern.

state NOUN
▷ *see also* **state** VERB
1 der Zustand (PL die Zustände)
■ **He was in a real state.** *(upset)* Er ist fast durchgedreht.
2 der Staat *(government)*
■ **the States** *(USA)* die Staaten
□ in the States in den Staaten

to **state** VERB
▷ *see also* **state** NOUN
1 erklären (PERFECT hat erklärt) *(say)*
□ He stated his intention to resign. Er erklärte seine Absicht zurückzutreten.
2 angeben (PRESENT gibt an, IMPERFECT gab an, PERFECT hat angegeben) *(give)*
□ Please state your name and address. Geben Sie bitte Ihren Namen und Ihre Adresse an.

stately home NOUN
das Schloss (GEN des Schlosses, PL die Schlössen)

statement NOUN
die Erklärung

station NOUN
der Bahnhof (PL die Bahnhöfe) *(railway)*
■ **the bus station** der Busbahnhof
■ **a police station** eine Polizeiwache
■ **a radio station** ein Rundfunksender *masc*

stationer's NOUN
das Schreibwarengeschäft (PL die Schreibwarengeschäfte)

station wagon NOUN (US)
der Kombiwagen (PL die Kombiwagen)

statue NOUN
die Statue

to **stay** VERB
▷ *see also* **stay** NOUN
1 bleiben (IMPERFECT blieb, PERFECT ist geblieben) *(remain)*
□ Stay here! Bleiben Sie hier!
■ **to stay in** *(not go out)* zu Hause bleiben
■ **to stay up** aufbleiben □ We stayed up till midnight. Wir sind bis um Mitternacht aufgeblieben.
2 übernachten (PERFECT hat übernachtet) *(spend the night)*
□ to stay with friends bei Freunden übernachten
■ **Where are you staying?** Wo wohnen Sie?
■ **to stay the night** über Nacht bleiben
■ **We stayed in Belgium for a few days.** Wir waren ein paar Tage in Belgien.

stay NOUN
▷ *see also* **stay** VERB
der Aufenthalt (PL die Aufenthalte)
□ my stay in Bonn mein Aufenthalt in Bonn

steady ADJECTIVE
1 stetig
□ steady progress stetiger Fortschritt
2 fest
□ a steady job eine feste Arbeit
3 ruhig *(voice, hand)*
4 solide *(person)*
■ **a steady boyfriend** ein fester Freund
■ **a steady girlfriend** eine feste Freundin
■ **Steady on!** Immer mit der Ruhe!

steak NOUN
das Steak (PL die Steaks) *(beef)*
□ steak and chips Steak mit Pommes frites

to **steal** VERB
stehlen (PRESENT stiehlt, IMPERFECT stahl, PERFECT hat gestohlen)

steam NOUN
der Dampf (PL die Dämpfe)
□ a steam engine eine Dampflokomotive

steel NOUN
der Stahl
□ a steel door eine Stahltür

steep ADJECTIVE
steil *(slope)*

steeple NOUN
der Kirchturm (PL die Kirchtürme)

steering wheel NOUN
das Lenkrad (PL die Lenkräder)

step NOUN
▷ *see also* **step** VERB
1 der Schritt (PL die Schritte) *(pace)*
□ He took a step forward. Er machte einen Schritt nach vorn.
2 die Stufe *(stair)*
□ She tripped over the step. Sie stolperte über die Stufe.

to **step** VERB
▷ *see also* **step** NOUN
■ **to step aside** zur Seite treten
□ She stepped aside to let him pass. Sie trat zur Seite, um ihn vorbeizulassen.
■ **to step back** zurücktreten

stepbrother NOUN
der Stiefbruder (PL die Stiefbrüder)

stepdaughter NOUN
die Stieftochter (PL die Stieftöchter)

stepfather NOUN
der Stiefvater (PL die Stiefväter)

stepladder NOUN
die Trittleiter

stepmother NOUN
die Stiefmutter (PL die Stiefmütter)

stepsister NOUN
die Stiefschwester

stepson NOUN
der Stiefsohn (PL die Stiefsöhne)

stereo NOUN
die Stereoanlage

sterling ADJECTIVE
■ **five pounds sterling** fünf britische Pfund

stew NOUN
der Eintopf (PL die Eintöpfe)

steward NOUN
der Steward (PL die Stewards)

stewardess NOUN
die Stewardess (PL die Stewardessen)

stick NOUN
▷ *see also* **stick** VERB
der Stock (PL die Stöcke)

to **stick** VERB
▷ *see also* **stick** NOUN
kleben *(with adhesive)*
■ **I can't stick it any longer.** Ich halte das nicht mehr aus.

to **stick out** VERB
herausstrecken (PERFECT hat herausgestreckt)
□ Lucy stuck out her tongue. Lucy streckte ihre Zunge heraus.

sticker NOUN
der Aufkleber (PL die Aufkleber)

stick insect NOUN
die Gespenstheuschrecke (PL die Gespenstheuschrecken)

sticky ADJECTIVE
klebrig
□ to have sticky hands klebrige Hände haben
■ **a sticky label** ein Aufkleber *masc*

stiff ADJECTIVE, ADVERB
steif *(rigid)*
■ **to have a stiff neck** einen steifen Hals haben
■ **to feel stiff** 1 steif sein □ I feel stiff after the long journey. Ich bin nach der langen Reise ganz steif. 2 Muskelkater haben □ I feel stiff after playing football yesterday. Ich habe gestern Fußball gespielt und habe jetzt Muskelkater.
■ **to be bored stiff** sich zu Tode langweilen
■ **to be frozen stiff** total durchgefroren sein
■ **to be scared stiff** furchtbare Angst haben

still ADVERB
▷ *see also* **still** ADJECTIVE
1 immer noch
□ I still haven't finished. Ich bin immer noch nicht fertig. □ Are you still in bed? Bist du immer noch im Bett?
■ **better still** noch besser
2 trotzdem *(even so)*
□ She knows I don't like it, but she still does it. Sie weiß, dass ich das nicht mag, sie macht es aber trotzdem.
3 immerhin *(after all)*
□ Still, it's the thought that counts. Es war immerhin gut gemeint.

still ADJECTIVE
▷ *see also* **still** ADVERB
still
□ Keep still! Halt still! □ Sit still! Sitz still!

sting NOUN
▷ *see also* **sting** VERB
der Stich (PL die Stiche)
□ a wasp sting ein Wespenstich

to **sting** VERB
▷ *see also* **sting** NOUN
stechen (PRESENT sticht, IMPERFECT stach, PERFECT hat gestochen)
□ I've been stung. Ich bin gestochen worden.

stingy ADJECTIVE
geizig

to **stink** VERB
▷ *see also* **stink** NOUN
stinken (IMPERFECT stank, PERFECT hat gestunken)
□ It stinks! Es stinkt!

stink NOUN
▷ *see also* **stink** VERB
der Gestank

to **stir** VERB
umrühren (PERFECT hat umgerührt)

to **stitch** VERB
▷ *see also* **stitch** NOUN
nähen *(cloth)*

stitch NOUN
▷ *see also* **stitch** VERB
der Stich (PL die Stiche)
□ I had five stitches. Ich wurde mit fünf Stichen genäht.

stock NOUN
▷ *see also* **stock** VERB
1 der Vorrat (PL die Vorräte) *(supply)*
2 das Lager (PL die Lager) *(in shop)*
□ in stock auf Lager
■ **out of stock** ausverkauft
3 die Brühe
□ chicken stock die Hühnerbrühe

to **stock** VERB
▷ *see also* **stock** NOUN
führen *(have in stock)*
□ Do you stock camping stoves? Führen Sie Campingkocher?
■ **to stock up** sich eindecken □ We stocked up with food. Wir deckten uns mit Lebensmitteln ein.

stock cube NOUN
der Brühwürfel (PL die Brühwürfel)

stocking NOUN
der Strumpf (PL die Strümpfe)

stole, stolen VERB ▷ *see* **steal**

stomach NOUN
1 der Magen (PL die Mägen)
□ on a full stomach mit vollem Magen
2 der Bauch (PL die Bäuche)
□ to lie on one's stomach auf dem Bauch liegen

stomachache NOUN
■ **to have a stomachache** Bauchschmerzen haben

stone NOUN
der Stein (PL die Steine) *(rock)*
□ a stone wall eine Steinmauer
□ a peach stone ein Pfirsichstein

DID YOU KNOW...?
In Germany weight is expressed in kilos. A stone is about 6.3 kg.

□ I weigh eight stone. Ich wiege fünfzig Kilo.

stood VERB ▷ *see* **stand**

stool NOUN
der Hocker (PL die Hocker)

to **stop** VERB
▷ *see also* **stop** NOUN
1 aufhören (PERFECT hat aufgehört)
□ He stopped crying. Er hörte auf zu weinen.
□ I think the rain's going to stop. Ich glaube, es hört auf zu regnen. □ You should stop smoking. Du solltest aufhören zu rauchen.
■ **to stop somebody doing something** jemanden daran hindern, etwas zu tun
■ **Stop it!** Hör auf!
2 halten (PRESENT hält, IMPERFECT hielt, PERFECT hat gehalten) *(bus, train, car)*
□ The bus doesn't stop here. Der Bus hält hier nicht.
3 stoppen
□ a campaign to stop whaling eine Kampagne, um den Walfang zu stoppen
■ **Stop!** Halt!

stop NOUN
▷ *see also* **stop** VERB
die Haltestelle
□ a bus stop eine Bushaltestelle
■ **This is my stop.** Ich muss jetzt aussteigen.

stopwatch NOUN
die Stoppuhr

store NOUN
▷ *see also* **store** VERB
1 das Geschäft (PL die Geschäfte) *(shop)*
□ a furniture store ein Möbelgeschäft
2 das Lager (PL die Lager) *(stock, storeroom)*

to **store** VERB
▷ *see also* **store** NOUN
1 lagern
□ They store potatoes in the cellar. Sie lagern Kartoffeln im Keller.
2 speichern *(information)*

storey NOUN
der Stock (PL die Stock)
□ the first storey der erste Stock
■ **a three-storey building** ein dreistöckiges Gebäude

storm NOUN
1 der Sturm (PL die Stürme) *(gale)*
2 das Gewitter (PL die Gewitter) *(thunderstorm)*

stormy ADJECTIVE
stürmisch

story NOUN
die Geschichte

stove NOUN
1 der Herd (PL die Herde) *(in kitchen)*
2 der Kocher (PL die Kocher) *(camping stove)*

straight ADJECTIVE
1 gerade
□ a straight line eine gerade Linie
2 glatt
□ straight hair glatte Haare
3 hetero *(heterosexual)*
■ **straight away** sofort
■ **straight on** geradeaus

straightforward ADJECTIVE
einfach

strain NOUN
▷ *see also* **strain** VERB
die Anstrengung *(stress)*
■ **It was a strain.** Es war anstrengend.

to **strain** VERB
▷ *see also* **strain** NOUN
sich verrenken (PERFECT hat sich verrenkt)
□ I strained my back. Ich habe mir den Rücken verrenkt.
■ **I strained a muscle.** Ich habe mir einen Muskel gezerrt.

strained ADJECTIVE
■ **a strained muscle** eine Muskelzerrung

stranded ADJECTIVE
■ **We were stranded.** Wir saßen fest.

strange ADJECTIVE
sonderbar

S

□ That's strange! Das ist sonderbar!

stranger NOUN
der Fremde (GEN des Fremden, PL die Fremden)
die Fremde (GEN der Fremden)
□ a stranger *(man)* ein Fremder
■ **Don't talk to strangers.** Sprich nicht mit fremden Menschen.
■ **I'm a stranger here.** Ich bin hier fremd.

to **strangle** VERB
erwürgen (PERFECT hat erwürgt)

strap NOUN
1 der Riemen (PL die Riemen) *(of bag, camera, shoe, suitcase)*
2 der Träger (PL die Träger) *(of bra, dress)*
3 das Armband (PL die Armbänder) *(of watch)*

straw NOUN
das Stroh
■ **That's the last straw!** Jetzt reicht's aber!

strawberry NOUN
die Erdbeere
□ strawberry jam die Erdbeermarmelade
□ a strawberry ice cream ein Erdbeereis

stray NOUN
■ **a stray cat** eine streunende Katze

stream NOUN
der Bach (PL die Bäche)

street NOUN
die Straße
□ in the street auf der Straße

streetcar NOUN (US)
die Straßenbahn

streetlamp NOUN
die Straßenlampe

street plan NOUN
der Stadtplan (PL die Stadtpläne)

streetwise ADJECTIVE
gewieft *(informal)*

strength NOUN
die Kraft (PL die Kräfte)

to **stress** VERB
▷ *see also* **stress** NOUN
betonen (PERFECT hat betont)
□ I would like to stress that ... Ich möchte betonen, dass ...

stress NOUN
▷ *see also* **stress** VERB
der Stress (GEN des Stresses)

to **stretch** VERB
1 sich strecken *(person, animal)*
□ The dog woke up and stretched. Der Hund wachte auf und streckte sich.
2 ausleiern (PERFECT ist ausgeleiert) *(get bigger)*
□ My sweater stretched when I washed it. Mein Pullover ist in der Wäsche ausgeleiert.
3 spannen *(stretch out)*
□ They stretched a rope between the trees. Sie spannten ein Seil zwischen den Bäumen.
■ **to stretch out one's arms** die Arme ausbreiten

stretcher NOUN
die Trage

stretchy ADJECTIVE
elastisch

strict ADJECTIVE
streng

strike NOUN
▷ *see also* **strike** VERB
der Streik (PL die Streiks)
■ **to be on strike** streiken
■ **to go on strike** in den Streik treten

to **strike** VERB
▷ *see also* **strike** NOUN
1 schlagen (PRESENT schlägt, IMPERFECT schlug, PERFECT hat geschlagen)
□ The clock struck three. Die Uhr schlug drei.
□ She struck him across the mouth. Sie schlug ihm auf den Mund.
2 streiken *(go on strike)*
■ **to strike a match** ein Streichholz anzünden

striker NOUN
1 der Streikende (GEN des Streikenden, PL die Streikenden)
die Streikende (GEN der Streikenden) *(person on strike)*
□ a striker *(man)* ein Streikender
2 der Torschütze (GEN des Torschützen, PL die Torschützen) *(footballer)*

striking ADJECTIVE
1 streikend *(on strike)*
□ striking bus drivers die streikenden Busfahrer
2 auffällig *(noticeable)*
□ a striking difference ein auffälliger Unterschied

string NOUN
1 die Schnur (PL die Schnüre)
□ a piece of string eine Schnur
2 die Saite *(of violin, guitar)*

to **strip** VERB
▷ *see also* **strip** NOUN
sich ausziehen (IMPERFECT zog sich aus, PERFECT hat sich ausgezogen) *(get undressed)*

strip NOUN
▷ *see also* **strip** VERB
der Streifen (PL die Streifen)
■ **a strip cartoon** ein Comicstrip *masc*

stripe NOUN
der Streifen (PL die Streifen)

striped ADJECTIVE
gestreift
□ a striped skirt ein gestreifter Rock

stripper NOUN
der Stripper (PL die Stripper)
die Stripperin

stripy ADJECTIVE
gestreift
□ a stripy shirt ein gestreiftes Hemd

to **stroke** VERB
▷ *see also* **stroke** NOUN
streicheln

stroke NOUN
▷ *see also* **stroke** VERB
der Schlag (PL die Schläge)
□ to have a stroke einen Schlag bekommen

stroll NOUN
■ **to go for a stroll** einen Spaziergang machen

stroller NOUN (US)
der Sportwagen (PL die Sportwagen) *(for child)*

strong ADJECTIVE
stark
□ She's very strong. Sie ist sehr stark.
□ Gerry is stronger than Robert. Gerry ist stärker als Robert.

strongly ADVERB
dringend
□ We strongly recommend that ... Wir empfehlen dringend, dass ...
■ **He smelt strongly of tobacco.** Er roch stark nach Tabak.
■ **strongly built** solide gebaut
■ **I don't feel strongly about it.** Das ist mir ziemlich egal.

struck VERB ▷ *see* **strike**

to **struggle** VERB
▷ *see also* **struggle** NOUN
sich wehren *(physically)*
□ He struggled, but he couldn't escape. Er wehrte sich, aber er konnte sich nicht befreien.
■ **to struggle to do something** 1 *(fight)* kämpfen, um etwas zu tun □ He struggled to get custody of his daughter. Er kämpfte, um das Sorgerecht für seine Tochter zu bekommen. 2 *(have difficulty)* Mühe haben, etwas zu tun □ She struggled to pay the bill. Sie hatte Mühe, die Rechnung zu bezahlen.

struggle NOUN
▷ *see also* **struggle** VERB
der Kampf (PL die Kämpfe) *(for independence, equality)*
□ It was a struggle. Es war ein Kampf.

stub NOUN
die Kippe *(of cigarette)*

stubborn ADJECTIVE
stur

to **stub out** VERB
ausdrücken (PERFECT hat ausgedrückt)
□ He stubbed out the cigarette. Er drückte die Zigarette aus.

stuck VERB ▷ *see* **stick**

stuck ADJECTIVE
■ **It's stuck.** Es klemmt.
■ **to get stuck** stecken bleiben □ We got stuck in a traffic jam. Wir sind im Stau stecken geblieben.

stuck-up ADJECTIVE
hochnäsig *(informal)*

stud NOUN
1 der Ohrstecker (PL die Ohrstecker) *(earring)*
2 der Stollen (PL die Stollen) *(on football boots)*

student NOUN
der Student (GEN des Studenten, PL die Studenten)
die Studentin

studio NOUN
das Studio (PL die Studios)
□ a TV studio ein Fernsehstudio
■ **a studio flat** eine Einzimmerwohnung

to **study** VERB
1 studieren (PERFECT hat studiert) *(at university)*
□ I plan to study biology. Ich habe vor, Biologie zu studieren.
2 lernen *(do homework)*
□ I've got to study tonight. Ich muss heute Abend lernen.

stuff NOUN
1 die Sachen *fem pl (things)*
□ There's some stuff on the table for you. Auf dem Tisch stehen Sachen für dich.
2 das Zeug *(possessions)*
□ Have you got all your stuff? Hast du all dein Zeug?

stuffy ADJECTIVE
stickig *(room)*
□ It's really stuffy in here. Hier drin ist es wirklich stickig.

to **stumble** VERB
stolpern (PERFECT ist gestolpert)

stung VERB ▷ *see* **sting**

stunk VERB ▷ *see* **stink**

stunned ADJECTIVE
sprachlos *(amazed)*
□ I was stunned. Ich war sprachlos.

stunning ADJECTIVE
umwerfend

stunt NOUN
der Stunt (PL die Stunts) *(in film)*

stuntman NOUN
der Stuntman (PL die Stuntmen)

stupid ADJECTIVE
blöd
□ a stupid joke ein blöder Witz
■ **Me, go jogging? Don't be stupid!** Ich und joggen? Du spinnst wohl!

to **stutter** VERB
▷ *see also* **stutter** NOUN
stottern

stutter NOUN
▷ *see also* **stutter** VERB
■ **He's got a stutter.** Er stottert.

style NOUN
der Stil (PL die Stile)
□ That's not his style. Das ist nicht sein Stil.

subject NOUN
1 das Thema (PL die Themen)
□ The subject of my project was the Internet. Das Thema meines Referats war das Internet.
2 das Fach (PL die Fächer) *(at school)*
□ What's your favourite subject? Was ist dein Lieblingsfach?

subjunctive NOUN
der Konjunktiv
submarine NOUN
das U-Boot (PL die U-Boote)
subscription NOUN
das Abonnement (PL die Abonnements) *(to paper, magazine)*
■ **to take out a subscription to something** etwas abonnieren
subsequently ADVERB
später
to **subsidize** VERB
subventionieren (PERFECT hat subventioniert)
subsidy NOUN
die Subvention
substance NOUN
die Substanz
substitute NOUN
▷ *see also* **substitute** VERB
der Ersatzspieler (PL die Ersatzspieler)
die Ersatzspielerin *(player)*
to **substitute** VERB
▷ *see also* **substitute** NOUN
ersetzen (PERFECT hat ersetzt)
□ to substitute wine for beer Bier durch Wein ersetzen
subtitled ADJECTIVE
mit Untertiteln
subtitles PL NOUN
die Untertitel *masc pl*
□ an English film with German subtitles ein englischer Film mit deutschen Untertiteln
subtle ADJECTIVE
fein
□ a subtle difference ein feiner Unterschied
to **subtract** VERB
abziehen (IMPERFECT zog ab, PERFECT hat abgezogen)
□ to subtract three from five drei von fünf abziehen
suburb NOUN
die Vorstadt (PL die Vorstädte)
□ a suburb of Berlin eine Vorstadt von Berlin
□ They live in the suburbs. Sie wohnen in der Vorstadt.
suburban ADJECTIVE
■ **a suburban train** eine S-Bahn
subway NOUN
1 die Unterführung *(underpass)*
2 die U-Bahn *(underground)*
to **succeed** VERB
Erfolg haben (PRESENT hat Erfolg, IMPERFECT hatte Erfolg, PERFECT hat Erfolg gehabt)
□ He succeeded in his plan. Er hatte mit seinem Plan Erfolg.
■ **I succeeded in convincing him.** Es ist mir gelungen, ihn zu überzeugen.
success NOUN
der Erfolg (PL die Erfolge)
□ The play was a great success. Das Stück war ein großer Erfolg.
successful ADJECTIVE
erfolgreich
□ a successful attempt ein erfolgreicher Versuch □ He's a successful businessman. Er ist ein erfolgreicher Geschäftsmann.
■ **to be successful in doing something** etwas mit Erfolg tun
successfully ADVERB
mit Erfolg
successive ADJECTIVE
■ **on four successive occasions** viermal hintereinander
such ADJECTIVE, ADVERB
so
□ such nice people so nette Leute
□ such a long journey eine so lange Reise
■ **such a lot of** 1 *(so much)* so viel □ such a lot of work so viel Arbeit 2 *(so many)* so viele
□ such a lot of mistakes so viele Fehler
■ **such as** *(like)* wie zum Beispiel
□ hot countries, such as India heiße Länder, wie zum Beispiel Indien
■ **not as such** nicht eigentlich □ He's not an expert as such, but ... Er ist nicht eigentlich ein Experte, aber ...
■ **There's no such thing.** So was gibt es nicht. □ There's no such thing as the yeti. So was wie den Yeti gibt es nicht.
such-and-such ADJECTIVE
der und der
□ such-and-such a place der und der Ort
die und die
□ such-and-such a time die und die Zeit
das und das
□ such-and-such a problem das und das Problem
to **suck** VERB
lutschen *(sweets)*
□ to suck one's thumb am Daumen lutschen
sudden ADJECTIVE
plötzlich
□ a sudden change eine plötzliche Änderung
■ **all of a sudden** plötzlich
suddenly ADVERB
plötzlich
□ Suddenly, the door opened. Plötzlich ging die Tür auf.
suede NOUN
das Wildleder
□ a suede jacket eine Wildlederjacke
to **suffer** VERB
leiden (IMPERFECT litt, PERFECT hat gelitten)
□ She was really suffering. Sie hat wirklich gelitten.
■ **to suffer from a disease** an einer Krankheit leiden
to **suffocate** VERB
ersticken (PERFECT ist erstickt)

sugar NOUN
der Zucker (PL die Zucker)

to **suggest** VERB
vorschlagen (PRESENT schlägt vor, IMPERFECT schlug vor, PERFECT hat vorgeschlagen)
□ I suggested they set off early. Ich habe vorgeschlagen, dass sie früh aufbrechen sollen.

suggestion NOUN
der Vorschlag (PL die Vorschläge)

suicide NOUN
der Selbstmord (PL die Selbstmorde)
□ to commit suicide Selbstmord begehen

suicide bomber NOUN
der Selbstmordattentäter (PL die Selbstmordattentäter)
die Selbstmordattentäterin

suicide bombing NOUN
das Selbstmordattentat (PL die Selbstmordattentate)

suit NOUN
▷ *see also* **suit** VERB
1 der Anzug (PL die Anzüge) *(man's)*
2 das Kostüm (PL die Kostüme) *(woman's)*

to **suit** VERB
▷ *see also* **suit** NOUN
1 passen *(be convenient for)*
□ What time would suit you? Welche Zeit würde Ihnen passen? □ That suits me fine. Das passt mir gut.
■ **Suit yourself!** Wie du willst!
2 stehen (IMPERFECT stand, PERFECT hat gestanden) *(look good on)*
□ That dress really suits you. Das Kleid steht dir wirklich.

suitable ADJECTIVE
1 passend
□ a suitable time eine passende Zeit
2 angemessen *(clothes)*
□ suitable clothing angemessene Kleidung

suitcase NOUN
der Koffer (PL die Koffer)

suite NOUN
die Suite *(of rooms)*
■ **a bedroom suite** eine Schlafzimmereinrichtung

to **sulk** VERB
schmollen

sulky ADJECTIVE
beleidigt

sultana NOUN
die Sultanine

sum NOUN
1 das Rechnen *(calculation)*
■ **She's good at sums.** Sie kann gut rechnen.
2 die Summe *(amount)*
□ a sum of money eine Geldsumme

to **sum up** VERB
zusammenfassen (PERFECT hat zusammengefasst)

to **summarize** VERB
zusammenfassen
(PERFECT hat zusammengefasst)

summary NOUN
die Zusammenfassung

summer NOUN
der Sommer (PL die Sommer)
□ in summer im Sommer
■ **summer clothes** die Sommerkleidung *sing*
■ **the summer holidays** die Sommerferien

summertime NOUN
der Sommer (PL die Sommer)
□ in summertime im Sommer

summit NOUN
der Gipfel (PL die Gipfel)

sun NOUN
die Sonne
□ in the sun in der Sonne

to **sunbathe** VERB
sonnenbaden (PERFECT hat sonnengebadet)

sunblock NOUN
das Sonnenschutzmittel
(PL die Sonnenschutzmittel)

sunburn NOUN
der Sonnenbrand (PL die Sonnenbrände)

sunburnt ADJECTIVE
■ **I got sunburnt.** Ich habe einen Sonnenbrand bekommen.

Sunday NOUN
der Sonntag (PL die Sonntage)
□ every Sunday jeden Sonntag □ last Sunday letzten Sonntag □ next Sunday nächsten Sonntag □ on Sunday am Sonntag
■ **on Sundays** sonntags

Sunday school NOUN
die Sonntagsschule

sunflower NOUN
die Sonnenblume

sung VERB ▷ *see* **sing**

sunglasses PL NOUN
die Sonnenbrille *sing*
□ a pair of sunglasses eine Sonnenbrille

sunk VERB ▷ *see* **sink**

sunlight NOUN
das Sonnenlicht

sunny ADJECTIVE
sonnig
□ a sunny morning ein sonniger Morgen
■ **It's sunny.** Die Sonne scheint.

sunrise NOUN
der Sonnenaufgang (PL die Sonnenaufgänge)

sunroof NOUN
das Schiebedach (PL die Schiebedächer)

sunscreen NOUN
die Sonnenschutzcreme
(PL die Sonnenschutzcremes)

sunset NOUN
der Sonnenuntergang
(PL die Sonnenuntergänge)

sunshine NOUN
der Sonnenschein

sunstroke NOUN
der Hitzschlag (PL die Hitzschläge)
□ to get sunstroke einen Hitzschlag bekommen

suntan NOUN
■ **to have a suntan** braun sein
■ **suntan lotion** die Sonnenmilch
■ **suntan oil** das Sonnenöl

super ADJECTIVE
klasse
LANGUAGE TIP **klasse** is invariable.
□ a super film ein klasse Film

superb ADJECTIVE
großartig

supermarket NOUN
der Supermarkt (PL die Supermärkte)

supernatural ADJECTIVE
übernatürlich

superstitious ADJECTIVE
abergläubisch

to **supervise** VERB
beaufsichtigen (PERFECT hat beaufsichtigt)

supervisor NOUN
1 der Vorarbeiter (PL die Vorarbeiter)
die Vorarbeiterin *(in factory)*
2 der Abteilungsleiter (PL die Abteilungsleiter)
die Abteilungsleiterin *(in department store)*

supper NOUN
das Abendessen (PL die Abendessen)

supplement NOUN
1 die Beilage *(of newspaper, magazine)*
2 der Zuschlag (PL die Zuschläge) *(money)*

supplies PL NOUN
die Vorräte *masc pl (food)*

to **supply** VERB
▷ *see also* **supply** NOUN
1 liefern *(goods, material)*
□ The farm supplied us with food.
Der Bauernhof lieferte uns die Lebensmittel.
2 stellen *(put at somebody's disposal)*
□ The centre supplied all the necessary equipment. Das Zentrum hat die ganze notwendige Ausrüstung gestellt.

supply NOUN
▷ *see also* **supply** VERB
der Vorrat (PL die Vorräte)
□ a supply of paper ein Papiervorrat
■ **the water supply** *(to town)*
die Wasserversorgung

supply teacher NOUN
der Aushilfslehrer (PL die Aushilfslehrer)
die Aushilfslehrerin

to **support** VERB
▷ *see also* **support** NOUN
1 unterstützen (PERFECT hat unterstützt)
□ My mum has always supported me.
Meine Mutti hat mich immer unterstützt.
■ **What team do you support?** Für welche Mannschaft bist du?
2 sorgen für *(financially)*
□ She had to support five children on her own.
Sie musste allein für ihre fünf Kinder sorgen.

support NOUN
▷ *see also* **support** VERB
die Unterstützung *(backing)*

supporter NOUN
1 der Fan (PL die Fans)
LANGUAGE TIP **der Fan** is also used for women.
□ a Liverpool supporter ein Liverpool-Fan
2 der Anhänger (PL die Anhänger)
die Anhängerin
□ She's a supporter of the Labour Party.
Sie ist Anhängerin der Labour-Party.

to **suppose** VERB
annehmen (PRESENT nimmt an, IMPERFECT nahm an, PERFECT hat angenommen)
□ I suppose he's late. Ich nehme an, er kommt zu spät. □ Suppose you won the lottery. Nimm mal an, du gewinnst im Lotto.
□ I suppose so. Das nehme ich an.
■ **to be supposed to do something** etwas tun sollen □ You're supposed to go straight home. Du solltest sofort nach Hause gehen.
■ **You're supposed to show your passport.**
Sie müssen Ihren Pass zeigen.

supposing CONJUNCTION
angenommen
□ Supposing you won the lottery ...
Angenommen, du gewinnst im Lotto ...

surcharge NOUN
der Zuschlag (PL die Zuschläge)

sure ADJECTIVE
sicher
□ Are you sure? Bist du sicher?
■ **Sure!** Klar!
■ **to make sure that ...** sich vergewissern, dass ... □ I'm going to make sure the door's locked. Ich werde mich vergewissern, dass die Tür abgeschlossen ist.

surely ADVERB
sicherlich
□ Surely you've been to London? Du warst doch sicherlich schon in London? □ The church is open on Sundays, surely? Die Kirche ist sonntags doch sicherlich geöffnet?

surf NOUN
▷ *see also* **surf** VERB
die Brandung

to **surf** VERB
▷ *see also* **surf** NOUN
surfen (PERFECT hat gesurft)
■ **to surf the Net** im Internet surfen

surface NOUN
die Oberfläche

surfboard NOUN
das Surfbrett (PL die Surfbretter)

surfing NOUN
das Surfen

■ **to go surfing** surfen gehen

surgeon NOUN
der Chirurg (GEN des Chirurgen, PL die Chirurgen)
die Chirurgin
□ She's a surgeon. Sie ist Chirurgin.

surgery NOUN
die Arztpraxis (PL die Arztpraxen) *(doctor's surgery)*
■ **surgery hours** die Sprechstunden

surname NOUN
der Nachname (GEN des Nachnamens, PL die Nachnamen)

surprise NOUN
die Überraschung

surprised ADJECTIVE
überrascht
□ I was surprised to see him. Ich war überrascht, ihn zu sehen.

surprising ADJECTIVE
überraschend

to **surrender** VERB
sich ergeben (PRESENT ergibt sich, IMPERFECT ergab sich, PERFECT hat sich ergeben)

surrogate mother NOUN
die Leihmutter (PL die Leihmütter)

to **surround** VERB
umstellen (PERFECT hat umstellt)
□ The police surrounded the house. Die Polizei hat das Haus umstellt.
□ You're surrounded! Sie sind umstellt!
■ **surrounded by** umgeben von □ The house is surrounded by trees. Das Haus ist von Bäumen umgeben.

surroundings PL NOUN
die Umgebung *sing*
□ a hotel in beautiful surroundings ein Hotel in wunderschöner Umgebung

survey NOUN
die Umfrage *(research)*

surveyor NOUN
1 der Gebäudesachverständige (GEN des Gebäudesachverständigen, PL die Gebäudesachverständigen)
die Gebäudesachverständige (GEN der Gebäudesachverständigen) *(of buildings)*
□ a surveyor *(man)* ein Gebäudesachverständiger
2 der Landvermesser (PL die Landvermesser)
die Landvermesserin *(of land)*

to **survive** VERB
überleben (PERFECT hat überlebt)

survivor NOUN
der Überlebende (GEN des Überlebenden, PL die Überlebenden)
die Überlebende (GEN der Überlebenden)
□ There were no survivors. Es gab keine Überlebenden.

to **suspect** VERB
▷ *see also* **suspect** NOUN
verdächtigen (PERFECT hat verdächtigt)

suspect NOUN
▷ *see also* **suspect** VERB
der Verdächtige (GEN des Verdächtigen, PL die Verdächtigen)
die Verdächtige (GEN der Verdächtigen)
□ a suspect *(man)* ein Verdächtiger

to **suspend** VERB
1 verweisen (IMPERFECT verwies, PERFECT hat verwiesen) *(from school)*
□ He was suspended. Er wurde von der Schule verwiesen.
2 sperren *(from team)*
3 suspendieren (PERFECT hat suspendiert) *(from job)*

suspender NOUN (US)
der Strumpfhalter (PL die Strumpfhalter) *(for stockings)*
■ **suspenders** *(US: braces)* die Hosenträger *masc pl*

suspense NOUN
1 die Ungewissheit *(waiting)*
□ The suspense was terrible. Die Ungewissheit war furchtbar.
2 die Spannung *(in story)*
■ **a film with lots of suspense** ein sehr spannender Film

suspension NOUN
1 der Ausschluss (GEN des Ausschlusses, PL die Ausschlüsse) *(from school)*
2 die Sperre *(from team)*
3 die Suspendierung *(from job)*

suspicious ADJECTIVE
1 argwöhnisch
□ He was suspicious at first. Zuerst war er argwöhnisch.
2 verdächtig *(suspicious-looking)*
□ a suspicious person eine verdächtige Person

to **swallow** VERB
schlucken

swam VERB ▷ *see* **swim**

swan NOUN
der Schwan (PL die Schwäne)

to **swap** VERB
tauschen
□ Do you want to swap? Willst du tauschen?
■ **to swap an apple for a sweet** einen Apfel für ein Bonbon eintauschen

to **swat** VERB
totschlagen (PRESENT schlägt tot, IMPERFECT schlug tot, PERFECT hat totgeschlagen)

to **sway** VERB
schwanken

to **swear** VERB
1 schwören (IMPERFECT schwor, PERFECT hat geschworen) *(make an oath)*
2 fluchen *(curse)*

swearword NOUN
der Kraftausdruck (PL die Kraftausdrücke)

sweat NOUN
▷ *see also* **sweat** VERB
der Schweiß (GEN des Schweißes)

to **sweat** VERB
▷ *see also* **sweat** NOUN
schwitzen

sweater NOUN
der Pullover (PL die Pullover)

sweaty ADJECTIVE
1 verschwitzt *(person, face)*
□ I'm all sweaty. Ich bin ganz verschwitzt.
2 feucht *(hands)*

Swede NOUN
der Schwede (GEN des Schweden, PL die Schweden)
die Schwedin *(person)*

swede NOUN
die Steckrübe *(vegetable)*

Sweden NOUN
Schweden *neut*
■ **from Sweden** aus Schweden
■ **to Sweden** nach Schweden

Swedish ADJECTIVE
▷ *see also* **Swedish** NOUN
schwedisch
■ **He's Swedish.** Er ist Schwede.
■ **She's Swedish.** Sie ist Schwedin.

Swedish NOUN
▷ *see also* **Swedish** ADJECTIVE
das Schwedisch (GEN des Schwedischen) *(language)*

to **sweep** VERB
fegen
□ to sweep the floor den Boden fegen

sweet NOUN
▷ *see also* **sweet** ADJECTIVE
1 das Bonbon (PL die Bonbons) *(candy)*
□ a bag of sweets eine Tüte Bonbons
2 der Nachtisch *(pudding)*
□ What sweet did you have? Was für einen Nachtisch hattest du?

sweet ADJECTIVE
▷ *see also* **sweet** NOUN
1 süß
□ Isn't she sweet? Ist sie nicht süß?
2 nett *(kind)*
□ That was really sweet of you. Das war wirklich nett von dir.
■ **sweet and sour pork** Schweinefleisch süß-sauer

sweetcorn NOUN
der Mais

sweltering ADJECTIVE
■ **It was sweltering.** Es war eine Bruthitze.

swept VERB ▷ *see* **sweep**

to **swerve** VERB
ausscheren (PERFECT ist ausgeschert)
□ He swerved to avoid the cyclist. Er scherte aus, um dem Fahrradfahrer auszuweichen.

swim NOUN
▷ *see also* **swim** VERB
■ **to go for a swim** schwimmen gehen

to **swim** VERB
▷ *see also* **swim** NOUN
schwimmen (IMPERFECT schwamm, PERFECT ist geschwommen)
□ Can you swim? Kannst du schwimmen?
□ She swam across the river. Sie schwamm über den Fluss.

swimmer NOUN
der Schwimmer (PL die Schwimmer)
die Schwimmerin
□ She's a good swimmer. Sie ist eine gute Schwimmerin.

swimming NOUN
das Schwimmen
■ **to go swimming** schwimmen gehen
■ **Do you like swimming?** Schwimmst du gern?
■ **a swimming cap** eine Bademütze
■ **a swimming costume** ein Badeanzug *masc*
■ **a swimming pool** ein Schwimmbad *neut*
■ **swimming trunks** die Badehose *sing*
□ a pair of swimming trunks eine Badehose

swimsuit NOUN
der Badeanzug (PL die Badeanzüge)

swing NOUN
▷ *see also* **swing** VERB
die Schaukel *(in playground, garden)*

to **swing** VERB
▷ *see also* **swing** NOUN
schaukeln

Swiss ADJECTIVE
▷ *see also* **Swiss** NOUN
Schweizer
□ I like Swiss cheese. Ich mag Schweizer Käse.
■ **Andreas is Swiss.** Andreas ist Schweizer.
■ **Claudie is Swiss.** Claudie ist Schweizerin.

Swiss NOUN
▷ *see also* **Swiss** ADJECTIVE
der Schweizer (PL die Schweizer)
die Schweizerin *(person)*
■ **the Swiss** die Schweizer

switch NOUN
▷ *see also* **switch** VERB
der Schalter (PL die Schalter) *(for light, radio etc)*

to **switch** VERB
▷ *see also* **switch** NOUN
tauschen
□ to switch A for B A gegen B tauschen

to **switch off** VERB
ausschalten (PERFECT hat ausgeschaltet)

to **switch on** VERB
anschalten (PERFECT hat angeschaltet)

Switzerland NOUN
die Schweiz (GEN der Schweiz)

LANGUAGE TIP Note that the definite article is used in German for countries which are feminine.

■ **from Switzerland** aus der Schweiz
■ **in Switzerland** in der Schweiz
■ **to Switzerland** in die Schweiz

swollen ADJECTIVE
geschwollen *(arm, leg)*

to **swop** VERB
tauschen
□ Do you want to swop? Willst du tauschen?
■ **to swop an apple for a sweet** eine Briefmarke für eine Münze eintauschen

sword NOUN
das Schwert (PL die Schwerter)

swore VERB ▷ *see* **swear**

sworn VERB ▷ *see* **swear**

to **swot** VERB
▷ *see also* **swot** NOUN
pauken *(informal)*
□ I'll have to swot for the maths exam. Ich muss für die Matheprüfung pauken.

swot NOUN
▷ *see also* **swot** VERB
der Streber (PL die Streber)
die Streberin *(informal)*

swum VERB ▷ *see* **swim**

swung VERB ▷ *see* **swing**

syllabus NOUN
der Lehrplan (PL die Lehrpläne)
□ on the syllabus auf dem Lehrplan

symbol NOUN
das Symbol (PL die Symbole)

sympathetic ADJECTIVE
verständnisvoll

LANGUAGE TIP Be careful not to translate **sympathetic** by **sympathisch**.

to **sympathize** VERB
■ **to sympathize with somebody** *(pity)* Mitgefühl mit jemandem haben

sympathy NOUN
das Mitleid

symptom NOUN
das Symptom

syringe NOUN
die Spritze

system NOUN
das System (PL die Systeme)

English-German

S

Tt

table NOUN
der Tisch (PL die Tische)
▫ to lay the table den Tisch decken
tablecloth NOUN
die Tischdecke
tablespoon NOUN
der Esslöffel (PL die Esslöffel)
▫ a tablespoon of sugar ein Esslöffel Zucker
tablespoonful NOUN
■ **a tablespoonful of sugar** ein Esslöffel Zucker
tablet NOUN
die Tablette
table tennis NOUN
das Tischtennis (GEN des Tischtennis)
▫ to play table tennis Tischtennis spielen
tabloid NOUN
das Boulevardblatt (PL die Boulevardblätter)
tackle NOUN
▷ *see also* **tackle** VERB
der Angriff (PL die Angriffe) *(in sport)*
■ **fishing tackle** das Angelzeug
to **tackle** VERB
▷ *see also* **tackle** NOUN
angreifen (IMPERFECT griff an, PERFECT hat angegriffen) *(in sport)*
■ **to tackle a problem** ein Problem angehen
tact NOUN
der Takt
tactful ADJECTIVE
taktvoll
tactics PL NOUN
die Taktik *sing*
tactless ADJECTIVE
taktlos
tadpole NOUN
die Kaulquappe
tag NOUN
das Etikett (PL die Etiketts) *(label)*
tail NOUN
der Schwanz (GEN des Schwanzes, PL die Schwänze)
■ **Heads or tails?** Kopf oder Zahl?
tailor NOUN
der Schneider (PL die Schneider)
die Schneiderin
▫ He's a tailor. Er ist Schneider.
to **take** VERB
1 nehmen (PRESENT nimmt, IMPERFECT nahm, PERFECT hat genommen)
▫ He took a plate from the cupboard. Er nahm einen Teller aus dem Schrank. ▫ We took a taxi. Wir haben ein Taxi genommen.
2 mitnehmen (PRESENT nimmt mit, IMPERFECT nahm mit, PERFECT hat mitgenommen) *(take along)*
▫ Are you taking your camera? Nimmst du deine Kamera mit? ▫ Don't take anything valuable with you. Nehmen Sie nichts Wertvolles mit. ▫ He goes to London every week, but he never takes me. Er fährt jede Woche nach London, aber er nimmt mich nie mit. ▫ Do you take your exercise books home? Nehmt ihr eure Hefte mit nach Hause?
3 bringen (IMPERFECT brachte, PERFECT hat gebracht) *(to a certain place)*
▫ She always takes him to school. Sie bringt ihn immer zur Schule. ▫ I'm taking my coat to the cleaner's. Ich bringe meinen Mantel in die Reinigung.
4 brauchen *(require)*
▫ She always takes hours to get ready. Sie braucht immer Stunden, bis sie fertig ist. ▫ It takes five people to do this job. Für diese Arbeit braucht man fünf Leute. ▫ That takes a lot of courage. Dazu braucht man viel Mut.
■ **It takes a lot of money to do that.** Das kostet viel Geld.
5 dauern *(last)*
▫ The journey took three hours. Die Fahrt dauerte drei Stunden. ▫ It won't take long. Das dauert nicht lange.
6 ertragen (PRESENT erträgt, IMPERFECT ertrug, PERFECT hat ertragen) *(tolerate)*
▫ He can't take being criticized. Er kann es nicht ertragen, kritisiert zu werden.
7 machen *(exam, test, subject)*
▫ Have you taken your driving test yet? Hast du deine Fahrprüfung schon gemacht? ▫ I'm taking German instead of French. Ich mache Deutsch statt Französisch.
to **take after** VERB
nachschlagen (PRESENT schlägt nach, IMPERFECT schlug nach, PERFECT hat nachgeschlagen)
▫ She takes after her mother. Sie schlägt ihrer Mutter nach.

to **take apart** VERB
■ **to take something apart** etwas auseinandernehmen

to **take away** VERB
1 wegnehmen (PRESENT nimmt weg, IMPERFECT nahm weg, PERFECT hat weggenommen) *(object)*
2 wegbringen (IMPERFECT brachte weg, PERFECT hat weggebracht) *(person)*
■ **hot meals to take away** warme Mahlzeiten zum Mitnehmen

to **take back** VERB
zurückbringen (IMPERFECT brachte zurück, PERFECT hat zurückgebracht)
□ I took it back to the shop. Ich habe es in den Laden zurückgebracht.
■ **I take it all back!** Ich nehme alles zurück!

to **take down** VERB
herunternehmen (PRESENT nimmt herunter, IMPERFECT nahm herunter, PERFECT hat heruntergenommen)
□ She took down the painting. Sie nahm das Gemälde herunter.

to **take in** VERB
verstehen (IMPERFECT verstand, PERFECT hat verstanden) *(understand)*
□ I didn't really take it in. Ich habe das nicht richtig verstanden.

to **take off** VERB
1 abfliegen (IMPERFECT flog ab, PERFECT ist abgeflogen) *(plane)*
□ The plane took off twenty minutes late. Das Flugzeug ist mit zwanzig Minuten Verspätung abgeflogen.
2 ausziehen (IMPERFECT zog aus, PERFECT hat ausgezogen) *(clothes)*
□ Take your coat off. Zieh den Mantel aus.

to **take out** VERB
herausnehmen (PRESENT nimmt heraus, IMPERFECT nahm heraus, PERFECT hat herausgenommen) *(from container, pocket)*
■ **He took her out to the theatre.** Er führte sie ins Theater aus.

to **take over** VERB
übernehmen (PRESENT übernimmt, IMPERFECT übernahm, PERFECT hat übernommen)
□ I'll take over now. Ich übernehme jetzt.
■ **to take over from somebody** jemanden ablösen □ Mr Jones has taken over from Mr Smith. Herr Jones hat Herrn Smith abgelöst.

takeaway NOUN
1 das Essen zum Mitnehmen (PL die Essen zum Mitnehmen) *(meal)*
2 die Imbissstube *(shop)*
□ a Chinese takeaway eine chinesische Imbissstube

takeoff NOUN
der Abflug (PL die Abflüge) *(of plane)*

talcum powder NOUN
der Puder (PL die Puder)

tale NOUN
die Geschichte *(story)*

talent NOUN
das Talent (PL die Talente)
□ She's got lots of talent. Sie hat sehr viel Talent.
■ **to have a talent for something** eine Begabung für etwas haben
■ **He's got a real talent for languages.** Er ist wirklich sprachbegabt.

talented ADJECTIVE
begabt

talk NOUN
▷ *see also* **talk** VERB
1 der Vortrag (PL die Vorträge) *(speech)*
□ She gave a talk on rock climbing. Sie hielt einen Vortrag über das Klettern.
2 das Gespräch (PL die Gespräche) *(conversation)*
□ We had a talk about her problems. Wir hatten ein Gespräch über ihre Probleme.
■ **I had a talk with my Mum about it.** Ich habe mit meiner Mutti darüber gesprochen.
3 das Gerede *(gossip)*
□ It's just talk. Das ist nur Gerede.

to **talk** VERB
▷ *see also* **talk** NOUN
reden
□ We talked about the weather. Wir haben über das Wetter geredet.
■ **to talk something over with somebody** etwas mit jemandem besprechen

talkative ADJECTIVE
redselig

tall ADJECTIVE
1 groß *(person, tree)*
□ They've cut down the tallest tree in the park. Sie haben den größten Baum im Park gefällt.
□ He's two metres tall. Er ist zwei Meter groß.
2 hoch *(building)*
LANGUAGE TIP Before a noun or after an article, use **hohe**.
□ a tall building ein hohes Gebäude

tame ADJECTIVE
zahm *(animal)*

tampon NOUN
der Tampon (PL die Tampons)

tan NOUN
■ **She's got a lovely tan.** Sie ist schön braun.

tangerine NOUN
die Mandarine

tank NOUN
1 der Tank (PL die Tanks) *(for water, petrol)*
2 der Panzer (PL die Panzer) *(military)*
■ **a fish tank** ein Aquarium *neut*

tanker NOUN
1 der Tanker (PL die Tanker) *(ship)*
□ an oil tanker ein Öltanker
2 der Tankwagen (PL die Tankwagen) *(truck)*
□ a petrol tanker ein Benzintankwagen

tap NOUN
1 der Wasserhahn (PL die Wasserhähne) *(water tap)*
2 der Klaps (PL die Klapse) *(gentle blow)*

tap-dancing NOUN
das Stepptanzen
■ **I do tap-dancing.** Ich mache Stepptanz.

to **tape** VERB
▷ *see also* **tape** NOUN
aufnehmen (PRESENT nimmt auf, IMPERFECT nahm auf, PERFECT hat aufgenommen) *(record)*
□ Did you tape that film last night? Hast du den Film gestern Abend aufgenommen?

tape NOUN
▷ *see also* **tape** VERB
1 die Kassette
□ a tape of Tom Jones eine Kassette von Tom Jones
2 der Klebstreifen (PL die Klebstreifen) *(sticky tape)*

tape deck NOUN
das Kassettendeck (PL die Kassettendecks)

tape measure NOUN
das Maßband (PL die Maßbänder)

tape recorder NOUN
der Kassettenrekorder (PL die Kassettenrekorder)

target NOUN
das Ziel (PL die Ziele)

tarmac NOUN
der Asphalt *(on road)*

tart NOUN
der Kuchen (PL die Kuchen)
□ an apple tart ein Apfelkuchen

tartan ADJECTIVE
im Schottenkaro
□ a tartan scarf ein Schal im Schottenkaro

task NOUN
die Aufgabe

taste NOUN
▷ *see also* **taste** VERB
der Geschmack (PL die Geschmäcke)
□ It's got a really strange taste. Es hat einen sehr eigenartigen Geschmack. □ She has good taste. Sie hat einen guten Geschmack.
■ **a joke in bad taste** ein geschmackloser Witz
■ **Would you like a taste?** Möchtest du mal probieren?

to **taste** VERB
▷ *see also* **taste** NOUN
1 probieren (PERFECT hat probiert)
□ Would you like to taste it? Möchtest du mal probieren?
2 schmecken
□ You can taste the garlic in it. Man kann den Knoblauch schmecken.
■ **to taste of something** nach etwas schmecken □ It tastes of fish. Es schmeckt nach Fisch.

tasteful ADJECTIVE
geschmackvoll

tasteless ADJECTIVE
1 fade *(food)*
2 geschmacklos *(in bad taste)*
□ a tasteless remark eine geschmacklose Bemerkung

tasty ADJECTIVE
schmackhaft

tattoo NOUN
die Tätowierung

taught VERB ▷ *see* **teach**

Taurus NOUN
der Stier
□ I'm Taurus. Ich bin Stier.

tax NOUN
die Steuer *(on goods, income)*

taxi NOUN
das Taxi (PL die Taxis)
□ a taxi driver ein Taxifahrer

taxi rank NOUN
der Taxistand (PL die Taxistände)

TB NOUN *(= tuberculosis)*
die TB *(= Tuberkulose)*

tea NOUN
1 der Tee (PL die Tees)
□ a cup of tea eine Tasse Tee

DID YOU KNOW...?
Usually, tea is not drunk with milk and sugar in Germany, but is served with lemon, and is referred to as **Schwarztee**. Fruit teas and herbal teas are also very widespread.

■ **a tea bag** ein Teebeutel *masc*
2 das Abendessen (PL die Abendessen) *(evening meal)*
□ We were having tea. Wir saßen beim Abendessen.

to **teach** VERB
1 beibringen (IMPERFECT brachte bei, PERFECT hat beigebracht)
□ My sister taught me to swim. Meine Schwester hat mir das Schwimmen beigebracht.
■ **That'll teach you!** Das wird dir eine Lehre sein!
2 unterrichten (PERFECT hat unterrichtet) *(in school)*
□ She teaches physics. Sie unterrichtet Physik.

teacher NOUN
der Lehrer (PL die Lehrer)
die Lehrerin
□ a maths teacher ein Mathelehrer □ She's a teacher. Sie ist Lehrerin. □ He's a primary school teacher. Er ist Grundschullehrer.

teacher's pet NOUN
Lehrers Schätzchen *neut*
□ She's teacher's pet. Sie ist Lehrers Schätzchen.

tea cloth NOUN
das Geschirrtuch (PL die Geschirrtücher)

team NOUN
die Mannschaft
□ a football team eine Fußballmannschaft
□ She was in my team. Sie war in meiner Mannschaft.

teapot NOUN
die Teekanne

tear NOUN
▷ *see also* **tear** VERB
die Träne
□ She was in tears. Sie war in Tränen aufgelöst.

to **tear** VERB
▷ *see also* **tear** NOUN
zerreißen (IMPERFECT zerriss, PERFECT hat/ist zerrissen)
□ Mind you don't tear the page. Pass auf, dass du die Seite nicht zerreißt.

LANGUAGE TIP For the perfect tense use **haben** when the verb has an object and **sein** when there is no object.

□ You've torn your shirt. Du hast dein Hemd zerrissen. □ Your shirt is torn. Dein Hemd ist zerrissen. □ It won't tear, it's very strong. Es zerreißt nicht, es ist sehr stark.
■ **to tear up** zerreißen □ He tore up the letter. Er zerriss den Brief.

tear gas NOUN
das Tränengas (GEN des Tränengases)

to **tease** VERB
1 quälen *(unkindly)*
□ Stop teasing that poor animal! Hör auf, das arme Tier zu quälen!
2 necken *(jokingly)*
□ He's teasing you. Er neckt dich nur.
■ **I was only teasing.** Ich habe nur einen Scherz gemacht.

teaspoon NOUN
der Teelöffel (PL die Teelöffel)
□ a teaspoon of sugar ein Teelöffel Zucker

teaspoonful NOUN
■ **a teaspoonful of sugar** ein Teelöffel Zucker

teatime NOUN
die Abendessenszeit *(in evening)*
□ It was nearly teatime. Es war fast Abendessenszeit.
■ **Teatime!** Abendessen!

tea towel NOUN
das Geschirrtuch (PL die Geschirrtücher)

technical ADJECTIVE
technisch
■ **a technical college** eine Fachhochschule

technician NOUN
der Techniker (PL die Techniker)
die Technikerin

technique NOUN
die Technik

techno NOUN
der Techno *(music)*

technological ADJECTIVE
technologisch

technology NOUN
die Technologie

teddy bear NOUN
der Teddybär (GEN des Teddybären, PL die Teddybären)

teenage ADJECTIVE
1 für Teenager
□ a teenage magazine eine Zeitschrift für Teenager
2 heranwachsend *(boys, girls)*
□ She has two teenage daughters. Sie hat zwei heranwachsende Töchter.

teenager NOUN
der Teenager (PL die Teenager)

LANGUAGE TIP **der Teenager** is also used for girls.

teens PL NOUN
■ **She's in her teens.** Sie ist ein Teenager.

tee-shirt NOUN
das T-Shirt (PL die T-Shirts)

teeth PL NOUN ▷ *see* **tooth**

to **teethe** VERB
zahnen

teetotal ADJECTIVE
■ **I'm teetotal.** Ich trinke keinen Alkohol.

telecommunications PL NOUN
die Nachrichtentechnik *sing*

teleconferencing NOUN
die Telekonferenzen *pl*

telephone NOUN
das Telefon (PL die Telefone)
□ on the telephone am Telefon
■ **a telephone box** eine Telefonzelle
■ **a telephone call** ein Anruf *masc*
■ **the telephone directory** das Telefonbuch
■ **a telephone number** eine Telefonnummer

telesales SING NOUN
der Telefonverkauf (PL die Telefonverkäufe)

telescope NOUN
das Teleskop (PL die Teleskope)

television NOUN
das Fernsehen
■ **on television** im Fernsehen
■ **a television programme** eine Fernsehsendung

to **tell** VERB
sagen
■ **to tell somebody something** jemandem etwas sagen □ Did you tell your mother? Hast du es deiner Mutter gesagt? □ I told him that I was going on holiday. Ich habe ihm gesagt, dass ich in Urlaub fahre.
■ **to tell somebody to do something** jemandem sagen, er solle etwas tun
□ He told me to wait a moment. Er sagte mir, ich solle einen Moment warten.
■ **to tell lies** lügen
■ **to tell a story** eine Geschichte erzählen
■ **I can't tell the difference between them.** Ich kann sie nicht unterscheiden.

to **tell off** VERB
schimpfen

telly NOUN
der Fernseher (PL die Fernseher)
■ **to watch telly** fernsehen
■ **on telly** im Fernsehen

temper NOUN
■ **to be in a temper** wütend sein
■ **to lose one's temper** wütend werden
□ I lost my temper. Ich bin wütend geworden.
■ **He's got a terrible temper.** Er ist furchtbar jähzornig.

temperature NOUN
die Temperatur *(of oven, water, person)*
■ **The temperature was thirty degrees.** Es waren dreißig Grad.
■ **to have a temperature** Fieber haben

temple NOUN
der Tempel (PL die Tempel)

temporary ADJECTIVE
vorläufig

to **tempt** VERB
in Versuchung führen
□ to tempt somebody to do something jemanden in Versuchung führen, etwas zu tun
■ **I'm very tempted!** Das reizt mich sehr!

temptation NOUN
die Versuchung

tempting ADJECTIVE
verlockend

ten NUMBER
zehn
□ She's ten. Sie ist zehn.

tenant NOUN
der Mieter (PL die Mieter)
die Mieterin

tender ADJECTIVE
1 zärtlich *(loving)*
2 empfindlich
□ My neck is still tender. Mein Hals ist noch immer empfindlich.

to **tend to** VERB
■ **to tend to do something** dazu neigen, etwas zu tun □ He tends to arrive late. Er neigt dazu, zu spät zu kommen.

tennis NOUN
das Tennis (GEN des Tennis)
□ Do you play tennis? Spielst du Tennis?
■ **a tennis ball** ein Tennisball *masc*
■ **a tennis court** ein Tennisplatz *masc*

tennis player NOUN
der Tennisspieler (PL die Tennisspieler)
die Tennisspielerin
□ He's a tennis player. Er ist Tennisspieler.

tenor NOUN
der Tenor (PL die Tenöre)

tenpin bowling NOUN
das Bowling
■ **to go tenpin bowling** Bowling spielen

tense ADJECTIVE
▹ *see also* **tense** NOUN
angespannt
□ a tense situation eine angespannte Situation

tense NOUN
▹ *see also* **tense** ADJECTIVE
■ **the present tense** das Präsens
■ **the future tense** das Futur

tension NOUN
die Spannung

tent NOUN
das Zelt (PL die Zelte)

tenth ADJECTIVE
zehnte
□ the tenth floor der zehnte Stock
□ the tenth of August der zehnte August

term NOUN
das Trimester (PL die Trimester) *(at school)*

DID YOU KNOW...?
In Germany the school and university year is divided into two semesters rather than three terms.

■ **to come to terms with something** sich mit etwas abfinden

terminal ADJECTIVE
▹ *see also* **terminal** NOUN
unheilbar *(illness, patient)*

terminal NOUN
▹ *see also* **terminal** ADJECTIVE
das Terminal (PL die Terminals) *(of computer)*
■ **an oil terminal** ein Ölterminal *masc*
■ **an air terminal** ein Terminal *masc*

terminally ADVERB
■ **to be terminally ill** unheilbar krank sein

terrace NOUN
1 die Terrasse *(patio)*
2 die Häuserreihe *(row of houses)*
■ **the terraces** *(at stadium)* die Ränge

terraced ADJECTIVE
■ **a terraced house** ein Reihenhaus *neut*

terrible ADJECTIVE
furchtbar
□ My German is terrible. Mein Deutsch ist furchtbar.

terribly ADVERB
furchtbar
□ He suffered terribly. Er litt furchtbar.
□ I'm terribly sorry. Es tut mir furchtbar leid.

terrier NOUN
der Terrier (PL die Terrier)

terrific ADJECTIVE
super *(wonderful)*
LANGUAGE TIP **super** is invariable.
□ That's terrific! Das ist super! □ You look terrific! Du siehst super aus!

terrified ADJECTIVE
■ **I was terrified!** Ich hatte furchtbare Angst!

terrorism NOUN
der Terrorismus (GEN des Terrorismus)

terrorist NOUN
der Terrorist (GEN des Terroristen, PL die Terroristen)
die Terroristin
■ **a terrorist attack** ein Terrorangriff *masc*

test NOUN
▹ *see also* **test** VERB
1 die Arbeit *(at school)*

□ I've got a test tomorrow. Ich schreibe morgen eine Arbeit.

2 der Test (PL die Tests) *(trial, check)*

□ nuclear tests Atomtests

3 die Untersuchung *(medical)*

□ a blood test eine Blutuntersuchung

□ They're going to do some more tests tomorrow. Sie machen morgen noch weitere Untersuchungen.

■ **driving test** die Fahrprüfung □ He's got his driving test tomorrow. Er hat morgen seine Fahrprüfung.

to test VERB

▷ *see also* **test** NOUN

1 probieren (PERFECT hat probiert)

■ **to test something out** etwas ausprobieren

2 abfragen (PERFECT hat abgefragt) *(class)*

□ He tested us on the new vocabulary. Er hat uns die neuen Wörter abgefragt.

■ **She was tested for drugs.** Man hat bei ihr ein Drogentest gemacht.

test match NOUN

das Länderspiel (PL die Länderspiele)

test tube NOUN

das Reagenzglas (GEN des Reagenzglases, PL die Reagenzgläser)

tetanus NOUN

der Tetanus (GEN des Tetanus)

□ a tetanus injection eine Tetanusspritze

text NOUN

▷ *see also* **text** VERB

die SMS (PL die SMS) *(text message)*

text VERB

▷ *see also* **text** NOUN

eine SMS schicken

□ I'll text you. Ich schicke dir eine SMS.

textbook NOUN

das Lehrbuch (PL die Lehrbücher)

■ **a German textbook** ein Deutschbuch

text message NOUN

die SMS (PL die SMS)

text messaging NOUN

das Versenden von SMS

textiles PL NOUN

die Textilien *fem pl*

■ **a textiles factory** eine Textilfabrik

Thames NOUN

die Themse

than CONJUNCTION

als

□ She's taller than me. Sie ist größer als ich.

□ I've got more books than him. Ich habe mehr Bücher als er. □ more than ten years mehr als zehn Jahre □ more than once mehr als einmal

to thank VERB

sich bedanken bei (PERFECT hat sich bedankt)

□ Don't forget to write and thank them. Vergiss nicht, ihnen zu schreiben und dich bei ihnen zu bedanken.

■ **thank you** danke

■ **thank you very much** vielen Dank

thanks EXCLAMATION

danke

■ **thanks to** dank □ Thanks to him, everything went OK. Dank ihm ging alles gut.

that ADJECTIVE, PRONOUN, CONJUNCTION

1 dieser

□ that man dieser Mann

diese

□ that woman diese Frau

dieses

□ that book dieses Buch

■ **that one 1** *(masculine)* der da □ This man? — No, that one. Dieser Mann? — Nein, der da. **2** *(feminine)* die da □ This woman? — No, that one. Diese Frau? — Nein, die da. **3** *(neuter)* das da □ Do you like this photo? — No, I prefer that one. Gefällt dir dieses Foto? — Nein, das da gefällt mir besser.

2 das

□ Did you see that? Hast du das gesehen?

□ What's that? Was ist das? □ Who's that? Wer ist das? □ Is that you? Bist du das?

■ **That's ...** Das ist ... □ That's my German teacher. Das ist meine Deutschlehrerin.

■ **That's what he said.** Das hat er gesagt.

LANGUAGE TIP In relative clauses use **der**, **die** or **das**, depending on the gender of the noun 'that' refers to.

3 der

□ the man that saw us der Mann, der uns sah

die

□ the woman that saw us die Frau, die uns sah

das

□ the child that saw us das Kind, das uns sah

die

□ the people that helped us die Leute, die uns geholfen haben

4 dass

□ He thought that Henry was ill. Er dachte, dass Henry krank war. □ I know that she likes chocolate. Ich weiß, dass sie Schokolade mag.

5 so

□ It was that big. Es war so groß. □ It's about that high. Es ist etwa so hoch. □ It's not that difficult. Es ist nicht so schwierig.

thatched ADJECTIVE

strohgedeckt

the ARTICLE

LANGUAGE TIP Use **der** with a masculine noun, **die** with a feminine noun, and **das** with a neuter noun. For plural nouns always use **die**.

1 der

□ the boy der Junge

die

□ the orange die Orange

das

□ the girl das Mädchen

2 die
□ the children die Kinder

theatre NOUN
das Theater (PL die Theater)

theft NOUN
der Diebstahl (PL die Diebstähle)

their ADJECTIVE
ihr
□ their father ihr Vater □ their mother ihre Mutter □ their child ihr Kind
□ their parents ihre Eltern

LANGUAGE TIP Do not use **ihr** with parts of the body.

□ They can't bend their arms. Sie können die Arme nicht bewegen.

theirs PRONOUN
1 ihrer
□ This is our computer, not theirs. Das ist unser Computer, nicht ihrer.
ihre
□ It's not our garage, it's theirs. Das ist nicht unsere Garage, sondern ihre.
ihres
□ It's not our car, it's theirs. Das ist nicht unser Auto, sondern ihres.
2 ihre
□ These are not our ideas, they're theirs. Das sind nicht unsere Ideen, sondern ihre.
■ **Is this theirs?** Gehört das ihnen? □ This car is theirs. Das Auto gehört ihnen. □ Whose is this? — It's theirs. Wem gehört das? — Ihnen.

them PRONOUN
1 sie
□ I didn't see them. Ich habe sie nicht gesehen.

LANGUAGE TIP Use **sie** after prepositions which take the accusative.

□ It's for them. Es ist für sie.
2 ihnen

LANGUAGE TIP Use **ihnen** when 'them' means 'to them'.

□ I gave them some brochures. Ich habe ihnen ein paar Broschüren gegeben. □ I told them the truth. Ich habe ihnen die Wahrheit gesagt.

LANGUAGE TIP Use **ihnen** after prepositions which take the dative.

□ Ann and Sophie came. Graham was with them. Ann und Sophie sind gekommen. Graham war bei ihnen.

theme NOUN
das Thema (PL die Themen)

themselves PRONOUN
1 sich
□ Did they hurt themselves? Haben sie sich verletzt?
2 selbst
□ They did it themselves. Sie haben es selbst gemacht.

then ADVERB, CONJUNCTION
1 dann
□ I get dressed. Then I have breakfast. Ich ziehe mich an. Dann frühstücke ich. □ My pen's run out. — Use a pencil then! Mein Kugelschreiber ist leer. — Dann nimm einen Bleistift!
2 damals *(at that time)*
□ There was no electricity then. Damals gab es keinen Strom.
■ **now and then** ab und zu □ Do you play chess? — Now and then. Spielst du Schach? — Ab und zu.
■ **By then it was too late.** Da war es schon zu spät.

therapy NOUN
die Therapie

there ADVERB

LANGUAGE TIP Use **dort** when something is in a fixed position, **dorthin** when there is movement involved.

1 dort
□ Can you see that house there? Siehst du das Haus dort? □ Berlin? I've never been there. Berlin? Ich war noch nie dort.
■ **over there** dort drüben
■ **in there** dort drin
■ **on there** darauf
■ **up there** dort oben
■ **down there** dort unten
2 dorthin
□ Put it there. Stell es dorthin. □ He went there on Friday. Er ging am Freitag dorthin.
■ **There he is!** Da ist er ja!
■ **There is ...** **1** Es ist ... □ There's a factory near my house. In der Nähe von meinem Haus ist eine Fabrik. **2** Es gibt ... □ There is a lot of poverty in the world. Es gibt viel Armut auf der Welt.
■ **There are ...** **1** Es sind ... □ There are five people in my family. In meiner Familie sind fünf Leute. **2** Es gibt ... □ There are many schools in this city. In dieser Stadt gibt es viele Schulen.
■ **There has been an accident.** Es hat einen Unfall gegeben.

therefore ADVERB
deshalb

there's = **there is, there has**

thermometer NOUN
das Thermometer (PL die Thermometer)

Thermos® NOUN
die Thermosflasche®

these ADJECTIVE, PRONOUN
1 die
□ these shoes die Schuhe
■ **THESE shoes** diese Schuhe hier
2 die hier
□ I want these! Ich möchte die hier!
□ I'm looking for some sandals. Can I try these? Ich suche Sandalen. Kann ich die hier anprobieren?

they PRONOUN
sie
□ Are there any tickets left? — No, they're all

sold. Gibt es noch Karten? — Nein, sie sind schon alle verkauft. □ Do you like those shoes? — No, they're horrible. Gefallen dir die Schuhe? — Nein, sie sind furchtbar.

■ **They say that ...** Man sagt, dass ...

they'd = **they had, they would**

they'll = **they will**

they're = **they are**

they've = **they have**

thick ADJECTIVE

1 dick *(not thin)*

□ one metre thick einen Meter dick

2 dumm *(stupid)*

thief NOUN

der Dieb (PL die Diebe)

die Diebin

thigh NOUN

der Schenkel

thin ADJECTIVE

dünn

> **WORD POWER**
> You can use a number of other words instead of **thin** to mean 'skinny':
> **lanky** schlaksig
> □ a lanky boy ein schlaksiger Junge
> **skinny** mager
> □ a skinny model ein mageres Modell
> **slim** schlank
> □ a slim girl ein schlankes Mädchen

thing NOUN

das Ding (PL die Dinge)

□ beautiful things schöne Dinge □ What's that thing called? Wie heißt das Ding da?

■ **my things** *(belongings)* meine Sachen

■ **You poor thing!** **1** *(man)* Du Armer! **2** *(woman)* Du Arme!

to **think** VERB

1 denken (IMPERFECT dachte, PERFECT hat gedacht)

□ I think you're wrong. Ich denke, du hast unrecht. □ What are you thinking about? Woran denkst du?

■ **What do you think about the suggestion?** Was halten Sie von dem Vorschlag?

2 glauben

□ I don't think I can come. Ich glaube nicht, dass ich kommen kann.

■ **I think so.** Ich glaube schon.

■ **I don't think so.** Ich glaube nicht.

3 nachdenken (PERFECT hat nachgedacht) *(spend time thinking)*

□ Think carefully before you reply. Denk gut nach, bevor du antwortest. □ I'll think about it. Ich denke darüber nach.

4 sich vorstellen (PERFECT hat sich vorgestellt) *(imagine)*

□ Think what life would be like without cars. Stell dir vor, wie es wäre, wenn es keine Autos gäbe.

■ **I'll think it over.** Ich werde es mir überlegen.

third ADJECTIVE

▷ *see also* **third** NOUN

dritte

□ the third day der dritte Tag □ the third time das dritte Mal □ the third of August der dritte August

■ **He came third.** Er wurde Dritter.

third NOUN

▷ *see also* **third** ADJECTIVE

das Drittel (PL die Drittel)

□ a third of the population ein Drittel der Bevölkerung

thirdly ADVERB

drittens

Third World NOUN

die Dritte Welt

thirst NOUN

der Durst

thirsty ADJECTIVE

■ **to be thirsty** Durst haben □ Are you thirsty? Hast du Durst?

thirteen NUMBER

dreizehn

□ I'm thirteen. Ich bin dreizehn.

thirteenth ADJECTIVE

dreizehnte

□ the thirteenth of August der dreizehnte August

thirty NUMBER

dreißig

□ She's thirty. Sie ist dreißig.

this ADJECTIVE, PRONOUN

1 dieser

□ this man dieser Mann

diese

□ this woman diese Frau

dieses

□ this child dieses Kind

■ **this one** **1** *(masculine)* der hier □ That man over there? — No, this one. Der Mann dort? — Nein, der hier. **2** *(feminine)* die hier □ That woman over there? — No, this one. Die Frau dort? — Nein, die hier. **3** *(neuter)* das hier □ I don't like that picture over there, I prefer this one. Das Bild dort gefällt mir nicht, das hier gefällt mir besser.

2 das

□ You see this? Siehst du das? □ What's this? Was ist das? □ This is my mother. *(introduction)* Das ist meine Mutter.

■ **This is Gavin speaking.** *(on the phone)* Hier spricht Gavin.

thistle NOUN

die Distel

thorough ADJECTIVE

gründlich

□ She's very thorough. Sie ist sehr gründlich.

thoroughly ADVERB

gründlich *(examine)*

those ADJECTIVE, PRONOUN
1 diese
□ those shoes diese Schuhe
■ **THOSE shoes** diese Schuhe dort
2 die da
□ I want those! Ich möchte die da! □ I'm looking for some sandals. Can I try those? Ich suche Sandalen. Kann ich die da anprobieren?

though CONJUNCTION, ADVERB
obwohl
□ It's warm, though it's raining. Es ist warm, obwohl es regnet.
■ **He's nice, though not very clever.** Er ist nett, aber nicht besonders klug.

thought VERB ▷ *see* **think**

thought NOUN
der Gedanke (GEN des Gedankens, PL die Gedanken) *(idea)*
□ I've just had a thought. Mir ist eben ein Gedanke gekommen.
■ **It was a nice thought, thank you.** Das war nett, vielen Dank.
■ **It's the thought that counts.** Es war gut gemeint.

thoughtful ADJECTIVE
1 nachdenklich *(deep in thought)*
□ You look thoughtful. Du siehst nachdenklich aus.
2 aufmerksam *(considerate)*
□ She's very thoughtful. Sie ist sehr aufmerksam.

thoughtless ADJECTIVE
gedankenlos

thousand NUMBER
■ **a thousand** eintausend □ a thousand euros eintausend Euro
■ **two thousand pounds** zweitausend Pfund
■ **thousands of people** Tausende von Menschen

thousandth ADJECTIVE
tausendste

thread NOUN
der Faden (PL die Fäden)

threat NOUN
die Drohung

to **threaten** VERB
drohen
□ He threatened me. Er hat mir gedroht. □ to threaten to do something drohen, etwas zu tun

three NUMBER
drei
□ She's three. Sie ist drei.

three-dimensional ADJECTIVE
dreidimensional

three-piece suite NOUN
die dreiteilige Polstergarnitur

threw VERB ▷ *see* **throw**

thrifty ADJECTIVE
sparsam

thrill NOUN
der Reiz (GEN des Reizes, PL die Reize) *(excitement)*
■ **It was a great thrill.** Es war sehr aufregend.

thrilled ADJECTIVE
■ **I was thrilled.** *(pleased)* Ich habe mich unheimlich gefreut.

thriller NOUN
der Thriller (PL die Thriller)

thrilling ADJECTIVE
spannend

throat NOUN
der Hals (GEN des Halses, PL die Hälse)
■ **to have a sore throat** Halsweh haben

to **throb** VERB
■ **a throbbing pain** ein pochender Schmerz
■ **My arm's throbbing.** Mir pocht es im Arm.

throne NOUN
der Thron (PL die Throne)

through PREPOSITION, ADJECTIVE, ADVERB
durch
□ through the window durch das Fenster
□ to go through Leeds durch Leeds fahren
□ to go through a tunnel durch einen Tunnel fahren
■ **I know her through my sister.** Ich kenne sie über meine Schwester.
■ **The window was dirty and I couldn't see through.** Das Fenster war schmutzig, und ich konnte nicht durchsehen.
■ **a through train** ein durchgehender Zug
■ **'no through road'** 'keine Durchfahrt'

throughout PREPOSITION
■ **throughout Britain** in ganz Großbritannien
■ **throughout the year** das ganze Jahr über

to **throw** VERB
werfen (PRESENT wirft, IMPERFECT warf, PERFECT hat geworfen)
□ He threw the ball to me. Er warf mir den Ball zu.
■ **to throw a party** eine Party machen
■ **That really threw him.** Das hat ihn aus der Fassung gebracht.
■ **to throw away 1** *(rubbish)* wegwerfen **2** *(chance)* vergeben
■ **to throw out 1** *(throw away)* wegwerfen **2** *(person)* rauswerfen □ I threw him out. Ich habe ihn rausgeworfen.
■ **to throw up** sich übergeben

thug NOUN
der Schlägertyp (PL die Schlägertypen)

thumb NOUN
der Daumen (PL die Daumen)

thumb tack NOUN (US)
die Reißzwecke

to **thump** VERB
■ **to thump somebody** jemandem eine verpassen *(informal)*
□ I thumped him. Ich habe ihm eine verpasst.

thunder NOUN
der Donner (PL die Donner)

thunderstorm NOUN
das Gewitter (PL die Gewitter)

thundery ADJECTIVE
gewitterig

Thursday NOUN
der Donnerstag (PL die Donnerstage)
□ on Thursday am Donnerstag □ every Thursday jeden Donnerstag □ last Thursday letzten Donnerstag □ next Thursday nächsten Donnerstag
■ **on Thursdays** donnerstags

thyme NOUN
der Thymian (PL die Thymiane)

tick NOUN
▹ *see also* **tick** VERB
1 das Häkchen (PL die Häkchen) *(mark)*
2 das Ticken *(of clock)*
■ **in a tick** in einer Sekunde

to **tick** VERB
▹ *see also* **tick** NOUN
1 ankreuzen (PERFECT hat angekreuzt)
□ Tick the appropriate box. Kreuzen Sie das entsprechende Kästchen an.
2 ticken *(clock)*
■ **to tick off** 1 *(on list)* abhaken 2 *(scold)* ausschimpfen

ticket NOUN
1 die Fahrkarte *(for bus, tube, train)*
□ an underground ticket eine Fahrkarte für die U-Bahn
2 das Ticket (PL die Tickets) *(for plane)*
3 die Eintrittskarte *(for theatre, concert, cinema, museum)*
■ **a parking ticket** ein Strafzettel *masc*

ticket inspector NOUN
der Fahrscheinkontrolleur (PL die Fahrscheinkontrolleure)
die Fahrscheinkontrolleurin

ticket office NOUN
1 der Fahrkartenschalter (PL die Fahrkartenschalter) *(for travel)*
2 die Kasse *(for theatre, cinema)*

to **tickle** VERB
kitzeln

ticklish ADJECTIVE
kitzlig
□ Are you ticklish? Bist du kitzlig?

tide NOUN
■ **high tide** die Flut
■ **low tide** die Ebbe

tidy ADJECTIVE
▹ *see also* **tidy** VERB
ordentlich
□ Your room is very tidy. Dein Zimmer ist sehr ordentlich. □ She's very tidy. Sie ist sehr ordentlich.

to **tidy** VERB
▹ *see also* **tidy** ADJECTIVE
aufräumen (PERFECT hat aufgeräumt)
□ Go and tidy your room. Geh und räum dein Zimmer auf.
■ **to tidy up** aufräumen □ Don't forget to tidy up afterwards. Vergesst nicht, nachher aufzuräumen.

tie NOUN
▹ *see also* **tie** VERB
die Krawatte *(necktie)*
■ **It was a tie.** *(in sport)* Es gab ein Unentschieden.

to **tie** VERB
▹ *see also* **tie** NOUN
1 zubinden (IMPERFECT band zu, PERFECT hat zugebunden) *(ribbon, shoelaces)*
■ **I tied a knot in the rope.** Ich machte einen Knoten in das Seil.
2 unentschieden spielen *(in sport)*
■ **They tied three all.** Sie haben drei zu drei gespielt.
■ **to tie up** 1 *(parcel)* zuschnüren 2 *(dog, boat)* anbinden 3 *(prisoner)* fesseln

tiger NOUN
der Tiger (PL die Tiger)

tight ADJECTIVE
1 eng *(tight-fitting)*
□ tight jeans enge Jeans
2 zu eng *(too tight)*
□ This dress is a bit tight. Das Kleid ist etwas zu eng.

to **tighten** VERB
1 spannen *(rope)*
2 anziehen (IMPERFECT zog an, PERFECT hat angezogen) *(screw)*

tightly ADVERB
fest *(hold)*

tights PL NOUN
die Strumpfhose *sing*
□ a pair of tights eine Strumpfhose

tile NOUN
1 der Dachziegel (PL die Dachziegel) *(on roof)*
2 die Fliese *(on wall, floor)*

tiled ADJECTIVE
1 gekachelt *(wall)*
2 mit Fliesen ausgelegt *(floor, room)*
■ **a tiled roof** ein Ziegeldach *neut*

till NOUN
▹ *see also* **till** PREPOSITION
die Kasse

till PREPOSITION, CONJUNCTION
▹ *see also* **till** NOUN
1 bis
□ I waited till ten o'clock. Ich habe bis zehn Uhr gewartet.
■ **till now** bis jetzt
■ **till then** bis dann
2 vor

LANGUAGE TIP Use **vor** if the sentence you want to translate contains a negative such as 'not' or 'never'.

□ It won't be ready till next week. Vor nächster Woche wird es nicht fertig.

English

t

◻ Till last year I'd never been to Germany. Vor letztem Jahr war ich nie in Deutschland.

time NOUN
1 die Zeit
◻ It's time to get up. Es ist Zeit zum Aufstehen. ◻ It was two o'clock, German time. Es war zwei Uhr, deutsche Zeit. ◻ I'm sorry, I haven't got time. Ich habe leider keine Zeit.
■ **What time is it?** Wie viel Uhr ist es?
■ **What time do you get up?** Um wie viel Uhr stehst du auf?
■ **on time** pünktlich ◻ He never arrives on time. Er kommt nie pünktlich.
■ **from time to time** von Zeit zu Zeit
■ **in time** rechtzeitig ◻ We arrived in time for lunch. Wir kamen rechtzeitig zum Mittagessen.
■ **just in time** gerade noch rechtzeitig
■ **in no time** im Nu ◻ It was ready in no time. Es war im Nu fertig.
2 der Moment (PL die Momente) *(moment)*
◻ This isn't a good time to ask him. Das ist kein guter Moment, um ihn zu fragen.
■ **for the time being** momentan
3 das Mal (PL die Male) *(occasion)*
◻ next time nächstes Mal
■ **this time** diesmal
■ **two at a time** jeweils zwei
■ **How many times?** Wie oft?
■ **at times** manchmal
■ **a long time** lange ◻ Have you lived here a long time? Wohnst du schon lange hier?
■ **in a week's time** in einer Woche
◻ I'll come back in a month's time. Ich komme in einem Monat wieder.
■ **Come and see us any time.** Besuchen sie uns, wann Sie wollen.
■ **to have a good time** sich amüsieren ◻ Did you have a good time? Habt ihr euch amüsiert?
■ **two times two** zwei mal zwei

time bomb NOUN
die Zeitbombe

time off NOUN
die Freizeit

timer NOUN
1 die Schaltuhr *(time switch)*
2 der Kurzzeitmesser (PL die Kurzzeitmesser) *(for cooking)*
■ **an egg timer** eine Eieruhr

time-share NOUN
das Timesharing-Appartement (PL die Timesharing-Appartements)

timetable NOUN
1 der Fahrplan (PL die Fahrpläne) *(for train, bus)*
2 der Stundenplan (PL die Stundenpläne) *(at school)*

time zone NOUN
die Zeitzone

tin NOUN
1 die Dose
◻ a tin of beans eine Dose Bohnen
◻ a biscuit tin eine Keksdose
2 das Zinn *(type of metal)*

tinned ADJECTIVE
in Dosen *(food)*
◻ tinned peaches Pfirsiche in Dosen

tin opener NOUN
der Dosenöffner (PL die Dosenöffner)

tinsel NOUN
die Rauschgoldgirlande

tinted ADJECTIVE
getönt *(spectacles, glass)*

tiny ADJECTIVE
winzig

tip NOUN
▷ *see also* **tip** VERB
1 das Trinkgeld (PL die Trinkgelder) *(money)*
◻ Shall I give him a tip? Soll ich ihm ein Trinkgeld geben?
2 der Tipp (PL die Tipps) *(advice)*
◻ a useful tip ein guter Tipp
3 die Spitze *(end)*
■ **It's on the tip of my tongue.** Es liegt mir auf der Zunge.
■ **a rubbish tip** eine Müllkippe
■ **This place is a complete tip!** Was für ein Saustall! *(informal)*

to **tip** VERB
▷ *see also* **tip** NOUN
■ **to tip somebody** jemandem ein Trinkgeld geben ◻ He tipped the taxi driver generously. Er gab dem Taxifahrer ein großzügiges Trinkgeld.

tipsy ADJECTIVE
beschwipst
◻ I'm feeling a bit tipsy. Ich bin etwas beschwipst.

tiptoe NOUN
■ **on tiptoe** auf Zehenspitzen

tired ADJECTIVE
müde
◻ I'm tired. Ich bin müde.
■ **to be tired of something** etwas leid sein

tiring ADJECTIVE
ermüdend

tissue NOUN
das Papiertaschentuch (PL die Papiertaschentücher)
◻ Have you got a tissue? Hast du ein Papiertaschentuch?

title NOUN
der Titel (PL die Titel)

title role NOUN
die Titelrolle

to PREPOSITION
1 nach
◻ to go to Munich nach München fahren
◻ We went to Italy. Wir sind nach Italien gefahren. ◻ the train to London der Zug nach London ◻ the road to Edinburgh die Straße nach Edinburgh ◻ to the left nach links
■ **I've never been to Munich.** Ich war noch nie in München.

2 in
□ to go to school in die Schule gehen
□ to go to the theatre ins Theater gehen
3 zu

LANGUAGE TIP Use **zu** when you talk about going to a particular place or person.

□ We drove to the station. Wir fuhren zum Bahnhof. □ to go to the doctor's zum Arzt gehen □ to go to the baker's zum Bäcker gehen □ Let's go to Anne's house. Lass uns zu Anne nach Hause gehen.
■ **a letter to his mother** ein Brief an seine Mutter
■ **It's hard to say.** Es ist schwer zu sagen.
■ **It's easy to criticize.** Es ist leicht zu kritisieren.
■ **something to drink** etwas zu trinken
4 bis *(as far as, until)*
□ to count to ten bis zehn zählen
□ It's ninety kilometres to the border. Es sind neunzig Kilometer bis zur Grenze.
■ **from ... to** von ... bis □ from nine o'clock to half past three von neun bis halb vier
■ **ten to nine** zehn vor neun

LANGUAGE TIP Use the dative when you say or give something to somebody.

□ Give it to me! Gib es mir! □ That's what he said to me. Das ist, was er zu mir gesagt hat.
□ We said goodbye to the neighbours. Wir sagten den Nachbarn Auf Wiedersehen.
□ I sold it to a friend. Ich habe es einem Freund verkauft.
■ **to talk to somebody** mit jemandem reden

LANGUAGE TIP When 'to' is used with the infinitive, it is often not translated.

□ I'd like to go. Ich würde gern gehen. □ I don't want to see him. Ich möchte ihn nicht sehen.
5 um ... zu *(in order to)*

LANGUAGE TIP **um ... zu** is used with the infinitive.

□ I did it to help you. Ich tat es, um dir zu helfen. □ She's too young to go to school. Sie ist noch zu jung, um in die Schule zu gehen.
■ **the key to the front door** der Schlüssel für die Haustür
■ **the answer to the question** die Antwort auf die Frage

toad NOUN
die Kröte

toadstool NOUN
der Giftpilz (GEN des Giftpilzes, PL die Giftpilze)

toast NOUN
1 der Toast (PL die Toasts)
□ a piece of toast eine Scheibe Toast
2 der Trinkspruch (PL die Trinksprüche) *(speech)*
□ to drink a toast to somebody einen Trinkspruch auf jemanden ausbringen

toaster NOUN
der Toaster (PL die Toaster)

toastie NOUN
der Toast (PL die Toasts)
□ a cheese toastie ein Käsetoast

tobacco NOUN
der Tabak

tobacconist's NOUN
der Tabakladen (PL die Tabakläden)

toboggan NOUN
der Schlitten (PL die Schlitten)

tobogganing NOUN
■ **to go tobogganing** Schlitten fahren

today ADVERB
heute
□ What did you do today? Was hast du heute gemacht?

toddler NOUN
das Kleinkind (PL die Kleinkinder)

toe NOUN
der Zeh (PL die Zehen)
□ my big toe mein großer Zeh

toffee NOUN
der Karamell

together ADVERB
1 zusammen
□ Are they still together? Sind sie noch zusammen?
2 gleichzeitig *(at the same time)*
□ Don't all speak together! Redet nicht alle gleichzeitig!
■ **together with** *(with person)* zusammen mit

toilet NOUN
die Toilette

toilet paper NOUN
das Toilettenpapier

toiletries PL NOUN
die Toilettenartikel *masc pl*

toilet roll NOUN
die Rolle Toilettenpapier

token NOUN
■ **a gift token** ein Geschenkgutschein *masc*

told VERB ▷ *see* **tell**

tolerant ADJECTIVE
tolerant

toll NOUN
die Benutzungsgebühr *(on bridge, motorway)*

tomato NOUN
die Tomate
□ tomato soup die Tomatensuppe

tomboy NOUN
der Wildfang
□ She's a real tomboy. Sie ist ein echter Wildfang.

tomorrow ADVERB
morgen
□ tomorrow morning morgen früh
□ tomorrow night morgen Abend
■ **the day after tomorrow** übermorgen

ton NOUN
die Tonne

□ That old bike weighs a ton. Das alte Fahrrad wiegt ja eine Tonne.

tongue NOUN
die Zunge
■ **to say something tongue in cheek** etwas nicht so ernst meinen

tonic NOUN
das Tonic (PL die Tonics) *(tonic water)*
■ **a gin and tonic** ein Gin Tonic

tonight ADVERB
1 heute Abend *(this evening)*
□ Are you going out tonight? Gehst du heute Abend aus?
2 heute Nacht *(during the night)*
□ I'll sleep well tonight. Ich werde heute Nacht gut schlafen.

tonsillitis NOUN
die Mandelentzündung
□ She's got tonsillitis. Sie hat eine Mandelentzündung.

tonsils PL NOUN
die Mandeln *fem pl*

too ADVERB, ADJECTIVE
1 auch *(as well)*
□ My sister came too. Meine Schwester ist auch mitgekommen.
2 zu *(excessively)*
□ The water's too hot. Das Wasser ist zu heiß.
□ We arrived too late. Wir sind zu spät gekommen.
■ **too much** zu viel □ too much noise zu viel Lärm □ At Christmas we always eat too much. Zu Weihnachten essen wir immer zu viel. □ Seventy euros? That's too much. Siebzig Euro? Das ist zu viel.
■ **too many** zu viele □ too many hamburgers zu viele Hamburger
■ **Too bad!** Da kann man nichts machen!

took VERB ▷ *see* **take**

tool NOUN
das Werkzeug (PL die Werkzeuge)
■ **a tool box** ein Werkzeugkasten *masc*

tooth NOUN
der Zahn (PL die Zähne)

toothache NOUN
die Zahnschmerzen *masc pl*
□ to have toothache Zahnschmerzen haben

toothbrush NOUN
die Zahnbürste

toothpaste NOUN
die Zahnpasta (PL die Zahnpasten)

top NOUN
▷ *see also* **top** ADJECTIVE
1 die Spitze *(of tree)*
2 der Gipfel (PL die Gipfel) *(of mountain)*
3 das Oberteil (PL die Oberteile) *(of garment)*
□ a bikini top ein Bikinioberteil
4 das Kopfende (PL die Kopfenden) *(of table)*
5 der Deckel (PL die Deckel) *(of box, jar)*
6 der Verschluss (GEN des Verschlusses, PL die Verschlüsse) *(of bottle)*
■ **at the top of the page** oben auf der Seite
■ **to reach the top of the ladder** oben auf der Leiter ankommen
■ **on top of** *(on)* oben auf □ on top of the cupboard oben auf dem Schrank
■ **There's a surcharge on top of that.** Es kommt noch ein Zuschlag dazu.
■ **from top to bottom** von oben bis unten
□ I searched the house from top to bottom. Ich habe das Haus von oben bis unten durchsucht.

top ADJECTIVE
▷ *see also* **top** NOUN
erstklassig *(first-class)*
□ a top hotel ein erstklassiges Hotel
■ **a top surgeon** ein Spitzenchirurg *masc*
■ **a top model** *(fashion)* ein Topmodel *neut*
■ **He always gets top marks.** Er bekommt immer Spitzennoten.
■ **the top floor** der oberste Stock
□ on the top floor im obersten Stock

topic NOUN
das Thema (PL die Themen)
□ The essay can be on any topic. Der Aufsatz kann über ein beliebiges Thema sein.

topical ADJECTIVE
aktuell
□ a topical issue ein aktuelles Problem

topless ADJECTIVE, ADVERB
oben ohne
□ to go topless oben ohne gehen

top-secret ADJECTIVE
streng geheim
□ top-secret documents streng geheime Dokumente

torch NOUN
die Taschenlampe

tore, torn VERB ▷ *see* **tear**

tortoise NOUN
die Schildkröte

torture NOUN
▷ *see also* **torture** VERB
die Folter
■ **It was pure torture.** Es war die Hölle. *(informal)*

to **torture** VERB
▷ *see also* **torture** NOUN
quälen
□ Stop torturing that poor animal! Hör auf, das arme Tier zu quälen!

Tory ADJECTIVE
▷ *see also* **Tory** NOUN
konservativ
□ the Tory government die konservative Regierung

Tory NOUN
▷ *see also* **Tory** ADJECTIVE
der Konservative (GEN des Konservativen, PL die Konservativen)
die Konservative (GEN der Konservativen)

□ a Tory *(man)* ein Konservativer
■ **the Tories** die Konservativen

to **toss** VERB
■ **to toss pancakes** Pfannkuchen in der Luft wenden
■ **Shall we toss for it?** Sollen wir eine Münze werfen?

total ADJECTIVE
▷ *see also* **total** NOUN
gesamt
□ the total amount der gesamte Betrag

total NOUN
▷ *see also* **total** ADJECTIVE
1 die Gesamtmenge *(amount)*
2 die Endsumme *(money, figures)*
■ **the grand total** die Gesamtsumme

totally ADVERB
völlig
□ He's totally useless. Er ist völlig unfähig.

touch NOUN
▷ *see also* **touch** VERB
■ **to get in touch with somebody** sich mit jemandem in Verbindung setzen
■ **to keep in touch with somebody** mit jemandem in Verbindung bleiben
■ **Keep in touch!** Lass von dir hören!
■ **to lose touch** sich aus den Augen verlieren
■ **to lose touch with somebody** jemanden aus den Augen verlieren

to **touch** VERB
▷ *see also* **touch** NOUN
berühren (PERFECT hat berührt)
■ **'Do not touch'** 'Nicht berühren'
■ **Don't touch that!** Fass das nicht an!

touchdown NOUN
die Landung

touched ADJECTIVE
gerührt
□ I was really touched. Ich war wirklich gerührt.

touching ADJECTIVE
rührend

touchline NOUN
die Seitenlinie

touchy ADJECTIVE
empfindlich
□ She's a bit touchy. Sie ist etwas empfindlich.

tough ADJECTIVE
1 hart
□ It was tough, but I managed OK. Es war hart, aber ich habe es geschafft. □ It's a tough job. Das ist eine harte Arbeit. □ He thinks he's a tough guy. Er meint, er sei ein harter Bursche.
2 zäh *(meat)*
□ The meat's tough. Das Fleisch ist zäh.
3 fest *(strong)*
□ tough leather gloves feste Lederhandschuhe
■ **Tough luck!** Das ist Pech!

toupee NOUN
das Toupet (PL die Toupets)

tour NOUN
▷ *see also* **tour** VERB
1 die Besichtigung *(of town, museum)*
■ **We went on a tour of the city.** Wir haben die Stadt besichtigt.
■ **a guided tour** eine Führung
■ **a package tour** eine Pauschalreise
2 die Tournee *(by singer, group)*
□ on tour auf Tournee □ to go on tour auf Tournee gehen

to **tour** VERB
▷ *see also* **tour** NOUN
■ **Sting's touring Europe.** *(singer, artiste)* Sting ist auf Europatournee.

tour guide NOUN
der Reiseleiter (PL die Reiseleiten)
die Reiseleiterin

tourism NOUN
der Tourismus (GEN des Tourismus)

tourist NOUN
der Tourist (GEN des Touristen, PL die Touristen)
die Touristin
■ **tourist information office** das Verkehrsbüro

tournament NOUN
das Turnier (PL die Turniere)

tour operator NOUN
der Reiseveranstalter (PL die Reiseveranstalter)

towards PREPOSITION
1 auf ... zu *(in the direction of)*
□ He came towards me. Er kam auf mich zu.
2 gegenüber *(of attitude)*
□ my feelings towards him meine Empfindungen ihm gegenüber

towel NOUN
das Handtuch (PL die Handtüchen)

tower NOUN
der Turm (PL die Türme)
■ **a tower block** ein Hochhaus *neut*

town NOUN
die Stadt (PL die Städte)
■ **a town plan** ein Stadtplan *masc*
■ **the town centre** die Stadtmitte
■ **the town hall** das Rathaus

tow truck NOUN (US)
der Abschleppwagen (PL die Abschleppwagen)

toy NOUN
das Spielzeug (PL die Spielzeuge)
■ **a toy shop** ein Spielwarengeschäft *neut*
■ **a toy car** ein Spielzeugauto *neut*

trace NOUN
▷ *see also* **trace** VERB
die Spur
□ There was no trace of him. Von ihm fehlte jede Spur.

to **trace** VERB
▷ *see also* **trace** NOUN
nachziehen (IMPERFECT zog nach, PERFECT hat nachgezogen) *(draw)*

tracing paper NOUN
das Pauspapier
track NOUN
1 der Pfad (PL die Pfade) *(dirt road)*
2 das Gleis (GEN des Gleises, PL die Gleise) *(railway line)*
3 die Rennbahn *(in sport)*
□ two laps of the track zwei Runden der Rennbahn
4 das Stück (PL die Stücke) *(song)*
□ This is my favourite track. Das ist mein Lieblingsstück.
5 die Spur *(trail)*
□ They followed the tracks for miles. Sie folgten der Spur meilenweit.
to **track down** VERB
■ **to track somebody down** jemanden finden □ The police never tracked down the killer. Die Polizei hat den Mörder nie gefunden.
tracksuit NOUN
der Jogginganzug (PL die Jogginganzüge)
tractor NOUN
der Traktor (PL die Traktoren)
trade NOUN
das Handwerk *(skill, job)*
□ to learn a trade ein Handwerk erlernen
trade union NOUN
die Gewerkschaft

DID YOU KNOW...?
Unions in Germany are organized within the **Deutscher Gewerkschaftsbund (DGB)**.

trade unionist NOUN
der Gewerkschafter (PL die Gewerkschafter)
die Gewerkschafterin
tradition NOUN
die Tradition
traditional ADJECTIVE
traditionell
traffic NOUN
der Verkehr
□ The traffic was terrible. Es war furchtbar viel Verkehr.
traffic circle NOUN (US)
der Kreisverkehr (PL die Kreisverkehre)
traffic jam NOUN
der Stau (PL die Staus)
traffic lights PL NOUN
die Ampel *sing*
traffic warden NOUN
1 der Hilfspolizist (GEN des Hilfspolizisten, PL die Hilfspolizisten) *(man)*
2 die Politesse *(woman)*
tragedy NOUN
die Tragödie
tragic ADJECTIVE
tragisch
trailer NOUN
1 der Anhänger (PL die Anhänger) *(vehicle)*
2 der Wohnwagen (PL die Wohnwagen) *(caravan)*
3 die Vorschau *(advert for film)*
train NOUN
▷ *see also* **train** VERB
der Zug (PL die Züge)
to **train** VERB
▷ *see also* **train** NOUN
trainieren (PERFECT hat trainiert) *(sport)*
□ to train for a race für ein Rennen trainieren
■ **to train as a teacher** eine Lehrerausbildung machen
■ **to train an animal to do something** ein Tier dressieren, etwas zu tun
trained ADJECTIVE
gelernt
□ She's a trained nurse. Sie ist gelernte Krankenschwester.
trainee NOUN
1 der Praktikant (GEN des Praktikanten, PL die Praktikanten)
die Praktikantin *(in profession)*
□ She's a trainee. Sie ist Praktikantin.
2 der Lehrling (PL die Lehrlinge) *(apprentice)*

LANGUAGE TIP **der Lehrling** is also used for women.

□ She's a trainee plumber. Sie ist Klempnerlehrling.
trainer NOUN
1 der Trainer (PL die Trainer)
die Trainerin *(sports coach)*
2 der Dresseur (PL die Dresseure)
die Dresseuse *(of animals)*
trainers PL NOUN
die Turnschuhe *masc pl*
□ a pair of trainers ein Paar Turnschuhe
training NOUN
1 die Ausbildung
□ a training course ein Ausbildungskurs *masc*
2 das Training (PL die Trainings) *(sport)*
tram NOUN
die Straßenbahn
tramp NOUN
der Landstreicher (PL die Landstreicher)
die Landstreicherin
trampoline NOUN
das Trampolin (PL die Trampoline)
tranquillizer NOUN
das Beruhigungsmittel (PL die Beruhigungsmittel)
□ She's on tranquillizers. Sie nimmt Beruhigungsmittel.
transfer NOUN
das Abziehbild (PL die Abziehbilder) *(sticker)*
transfusion NOUN
die Transfusion
transistor NOUN
der Transistor (PL die Transistoren)
transit lounge NOUN
die Transithalle

to **translate** VERB
übersetzen (PERFECT hat übersetzt)
□ to translate something into English etwas ins Englische übersetzen

translation NOUN
die Übersetzung

translator NOUN
der Übersetzer (PL die Übersetzer)
die Übersetzerin
□ Anita's a translator. Anita ist Übersetzerin.

transparent ADJECTIVE
durchsichtig

transplant NOUN
die Transplantation
□ a heart transplant eine Herztransplantation

transport NOUN
▷ *see also* **transport** VERB
der Transport (PL die Transporte)
□ the transport of goods der Warentransport

to **transport** VERB
▷ *see also* **transport** NOUN
transportieren (PERFECT hat transportiert)

trap NOUN
die Falle

trash NOUN (US)
der Müll

trash can NOUN (US)
der Mülleimer (PL die Mülleimer)

trashy ADJECTIVE
schlecht
□ a really trashy film ein wirklich schlechter Film

traumatic ADJECTIVE
traumatisch
□ a traumatic experience ein traumatisches Erlebnis

travel NOUN
▷ *see also* **travel** VERB
das Reisen

to **travel** VERB
▷ *see also* **travel** NOUN
reisen (PERFECT ist gereist)
□ I prefer to travel by train. Ich reise lieber mit dem Zug.
■ **I'd like to travel round the world.** Ich würde gern eine Weltreise machen.
■ **We travelled over eight hundred kilometres.** Wir haben über achthundert Kilometer zurückgelegt.
■ **News travels fast!** Neuigkeiten sprechen sich schnell herum!

travel agency NOUN
das Reisebüro (PL die Reisebüros)

travel agent NOUN
der Reisebürokaufmann (PL die Reisebürokaufleute)
die Reisebürokauffrau
□ She's a travel agent. Sie ist Reisebürokauffrau.
■ **at the travel agent's** im Reisebüro

traveller NOUN
1 der Fahrgast (PL die Fahrgäste) *(on bus, train)*
LANGUAGE TIP **der Fahrgast** is also used for women.
2 der Passagier (PL die Passagiere)
die Passagierin *(on plane)*

traveller's cheque NOUN
der Reisescheck (PL die Reiseschecks)

travelling NOUN
■ **I love travelling.** Ich reise sehr gern.

travel sickness NOUN
die Reisekrankheit

tray NOUN
das Tablett (PL die Tabletts)

to **tread** VERB
treten (PRESENT tritt, IMPERFECT trat, PERFECT ist getreten)
□ to tread on something auf etwas treten
□ He trod on her foot. Er ist ihr auf den Fuß getreten.

treasure NOUN
der Schatz (GEN des Schatzes, PL die Schätze)

treat NOUN
▷ *see also* **treat** VERB
1 das Geschenk (PL die Geschenke) *(present)*
2 der Leckerbissen (PL die Leckerbissen) *(food)*
■ **to give somebody a treat** jemandem eine besondere Freude machen

to **treat** VERB
▷ *see also* **treat** NOUN
behandeln (PERFECT hat behandelt) *(well, badly)*
■ **to treat somebody to something** jemandem etwas spendieren □ He treated us to an ice cream. Er hat uns ein Eis spendiert.

treatment NOUN
die Behandlung

to **treble** VERB
sich verdreifachen (PERFECT hat sich verdreifacht)
□ The price has trebled. Der Preis hat sich verdreifacht.

tree NOUN
der Baum (PL die Bäume)

to **tremble** VERB
zittern

tremendous ADJECTIVE
1 fantastisch
□ Gordon is a tremendous person. Gordon ist fantastisch.
2 gewaltig
□ a tremendous success ein gewaltiger Erfolg

trend NOUN
der Trend (PL die Trends) *(fashion)*

trendy ADJECTIVE
modisch

trial NOUN
der Prozess (GEN des Prozesses, PL die Prozesse) *(in court)*

triangle NOUN
das Dreieck (PL die Dreiecke)

tribe NOUN
der Stamm (PL die Stämme)

trick NOUN
▷ *see also* **trick** VERB
1 der Streich (PL die Streiche)
□ to play a trick on somebody jemandem einen Streich spielen
2 der Trick (PL die Tricks) *(knack)*
□ It's not easy: there's a trick to it. Das ist nicht leicht: Da ist ein Trick dabei.

to **trick** VERB
▷ *see also* **trick** NOUN
■ **to trick somebody** jemanden reinlegen

tricky ADJECTIVE
knifflig

tricycle NOUN
das Dreirad (PL die Dreiräder)

trifle NOUN
das Trifle (PL die Trifles) *(dessert)*

to **trim** VERB
▷ *see also* **trim** NOUN
1 schneiden (IMPERFECT schnitt, PERFECT hat geschnitten) *(hair)*
2 stutzen
□ He trimmed his moustache. Er stutzte seinen Schnurrbart.
3 mähen *(grass)*

trim NOUN
▷ *see also* **trim** VERB
■ **to have a trim** sich die Haare schneiden lassen □ You need a trim. Du solltest dir die Haare schneiden lassen.

trip NOUN
▷ *see also* **trip** VERB
die Reise
□ to go on a trip eine Reise machen
□ Have a good trip! Gute Reise!
■ **a day trip** ein Tagesausflug *masc*

to **trip** VERB
▷ *see also* **trip** NOUN
stolpern (PERFECT ist gestolpert) *(stumble)*

triple ADJECTIVE
dreifach

triplets PL NOUN
die Drillinge *masc pl*

trivial ADJECTIVE
trivial

trod, trodden VERB ▷ *see* **tread**

trolley NOUN
1 der Einkaufswagen (PL die Einkaufswagen) *(for shopping)*
2 der Kofferkuli (PL die Kofferkulis) *(for luggage)*

trombone NOUN
die Posaune
□ I play the trombone. Ich spiele Posaune.

troops PL NOUN
die Truppen *fem pl*
□ British troops die britischen Truppen

trophy NOUN
die Trophäe
□ to win a trophy eine Trophäe gewinnen

tropical ADJECTIVE
tropisch
□ tropical plants tropische Pflanzen
■ **The weather was tropical.** Es war tropisch heiß.

to **trot** VERB
traben (PERFECT ist getrabt)

trouble NOUN
das Problem (PL die Probleme)
□ The trouble is ... Das Problem ist ...
■ **What's the trouble?** Was ist das Problem?
■ **to be in trouble** in Schwierigkeiten sein
■ **stomach trouble** die Magenbeschwerden *fem pl*
■ **to take a lot of trouble over something** sich mit etwas viel Mühe geben □ I took a lot of trouble over that project. Ich habe mir mit dem Referat viel Mühe gegeben.
■ **Don't worry, it's no trouble.** Keine Sorge, das macht keine Mühe.

troublemaker NOUN
der Unruhestifter (PL die Unruhestifter)
die Unruhestifterin

trousers PL NOUN
die Hose *sing*
□ a pair of trousers eine Hose

trout NOUN
die Forelle

truant NOUN
■ **to play truant** die Schule schwänzen

truck NOUN
der Lastwagen (PL die Lastwagen)
■ **He's a truck driver.** Er ist Lastwagenfahrer.

trucker NOUN (US)
der Lastwagenfahrer (PL die Lastwagenfahrer) *(driver)*

true ADJECTIVE
wahr
□ true love wahre Liebe □ That's true. Das ist wahr.
■ **to come true** wahr werden □ I hope my dream will come true. Ich hoffe, mein Traum wird wahr.

trumpet NOUN
die Trompete
□ She plays the trumpet. Sie spielt Trompete.

trunk NOUN
1 der Stamm (PL die Stämme) *(of tree)*
2 der Rüssel (PL die Rüssel) *(of elephant)*
3 der Schrankkoffer (PL die Schrankkoffer) *(luggage)*
4 der Kofferraum (PL die Kofferräume) *(boot of car)*

trunks PL NOUN
■ **swimming trunks** die Badehose *sing*
□ a pair of trunks eine Badehose

trust NOUN
▷ *see also* **trust** VERB
das Vertrauen

□ to have trust in somebody Vertrauen zu jemandem haben

to **trust** VERB

▷ *see also* **trust** NOUN

■ **to trust somebody** jemandem vertrauen
□ Don't you trust me? Vertraust du mir nicht?
■ **Trust me!** Glaub mir!

trusting ADJECTIVE
vertrauensvoll

truth NOUN
die Wahrheit

truthful ADJECTIVE
ehrlich

try NOUN

▷ *see also* **try** VERB

der Versuch (PL die Versuche)
□ his third try sein dritter Versuch
■ **to have a try** es versuchen □ I'll have a try. Ich werd's versuchen.
■ **It's worth a try.** Der Versuch lohnt sich.
■ **to give something a try** etwas versuchen

to **try** VERB

▷ *see also* **try** NOUN

1 versuchen (PERFECT hat versucht) *(attempt)*
□ to try to do something versuchen, etwas zu tun
■ **to try again** es noch einmal versuchen
2 probieren (PERFECT hat probiert) *(taste)*
□ Would you like to try some? Möchtest du etwas probieren?
■ **to try on** *(clothes)* anprobieren
■ **to try something out** etwas ausprobieren

T-shirt NOUN
das T-Shirt (PL die T-Shirts)

tube NOUN
die Tube
■ **the Tube** *(underground)* die U-Bahn

tuberculosis NOUN
die Tuberkulose

Tuesday NOUN
der Dienstag (PL die Dienstage)
□ on Tuesday am Dienstag □ every Tuesday jeden Dienstag □ last Tuesday letzten Dienstag □ next Tuesday nächsten Dienstag
■ **on Tuesdays** dienstags

tug of war NOUN
das Tauziehen

tuition NOUN
1 der Unterricht
■ **extra tuition** die Nachhilfestunden *fem pl*
□ She receives extra tuition. Sie bekommt Nachhilfestunden.
2 die Studiengebühren *fem pl (tuition fees)*

tulip NOUN
die Tulpe

tumble dryer NOUN
der Wäschetrockner (PL die Wäschetrockner)

tummy NOUN
der Bauch (PL die Bäuche)
□ I've got a sore tummy. Ich habe Bauchschmerzen.

tuna NOUN
der Thunfisch (PL die Thunfische)

tune NOUN
die Melodie *(melody)*
■ **to play in tune** richtig spielen
■ **to sing out of tune** falsch singen

Tunisia NOUN
Tunesien *neut*
■ **in Tunisia** in Tunesien

tunnel NOUN
der Tunnel (PL die Tunnel)
■ **the Tunnel** *(Chunnel)* der Kanaltunnel

Turk NOUN
der Türke (GEN des Türken, PL die Türken)
die Türkin

Turkey NOUN
die Türkei

LANGUAGE TIP Note that the definite article is used in German for countries which are feminine.

■ **from Turkey** aus der Türkei
■ **in Turkey** in der Türkei
■ **to Turkey** in die Türkei

turkey NOUN
der Truthahn (PL die Truthähne)

Turkish ADJECTIVE

▷ *see also* **Turkish** NOUN

türkisch

Turkish NOUN

▷ *see also* **Turkish** ADJECTIVE

das Türkische (GEN des Türkischen) *(language)*

turn NOUN

▷ *see also* **turn** VERB

die Abbiegung *(in road)*
■ **'no left turn'** 'links abbiegen verboten'
■ **Whose turn is it?** Wer ist an der Reihe?
■ **It's my turn!** Ich bin an der Reihe!

to **turn** VERB

▷ *see also* **turn** NOUN

1 abbiegen (IMPERFECT bog ab, PERFECT ist abgebogen)
□ Turn right at the lights. Biegen Sie an der Ampel rechts ab.
2 werden (PRESENT wird, IMPERFECT wurde, PERFECT ist geworden) *(become)*
□ to turn red rot werden
■ **to turn into something** sich in etwas verwandeln □ The frog turned into a prince. Der Frosch verwandelte sich in einen Prinzen.

to **turn back** VERB
umkehren (PERFECT ist umgekehrt)
□ We turned back. Wir sind umgekehrt.

to **turn down** VERB
1 ablehnen (PERFECT hat abgelehnt) *(offer)*
2 leiser stellen *(radio, TV)*
3 herunterdrehen (PERFECT hat heruntergedreht) *(heating)*

to **turn off** VERB
1 ausmachen (PERFECT hat ausgemacht) *(light, radio)*
2 zudrehen (PERFECT hat zugedreht) *(tap)*
3 ausschalten (PERFECT hat ausgeschaltet) *(engine)*

to **turn on** VERB
1 anmachen (PERFECT hat angemacht) *(light, radio)*
2 aufdrehen (PERFECT hat aufgedreht) *(tap)*
3 anlassen (PRESENT lässt an, IMPERFECT ließ an, PERFECT hat angelassen) *(engine)*

to **turn out** VERB
■ **It turned out to be a mistake.** Es stellte sich heraus, dass das ein Fehler war.
■ **It turned out that she was right.** Es stellte sich heraus, dass sie recht hatte.

to **turn round** VERB
1 umkehren (PERFECT ist umgekehrt) *(car)*
□ At the end of the street we turned round. Am Ende der Straße kehrten wir um.
2 sich umdrehen (PERFECT hat sich umgedreht) *(person)*
□ I turned round. Ich drehte mich um.

to **turn up** VERB
1 aufkreuzen (PERFECT ist aufgekreuzt) *(arrive)*
2 höherstellen *(heater)*
3 lauter machen *(radio, TV)*

turning NOUN
■ **It's the third turning on the left.** Es ist die dritte Straße links.
■ **We took the wrong turning.** Wir sind falsch abgebogen.

turnip NOUN
die Steckrübe

turquoise ADJECTIVE
türkis *(colour)*

turtle NOUN
die Meeresschildkröte

tutor NOUN
der Lehrer (PL die Lehrer)
die Lehrerin *(private teacher)*

tuxedo NOUN (US)
der Smoking (PL die Smokings)

TV NOUN
das Fernsehen

tweezers PL NOUN
die Pinzette *sing*
□ a pair of tweezers eine Pinzette

twelfth ADJECTIVE
zwölfte
□ the twelfth floor der zwölfte Stock
□ the twelfth of August der zwölfte August

twelve NUMBER
zwölf
□ She's twelve. Sie ist zwölf. □ at twelve o'clock um zwölf Uhr

twentieth ADJECTIVE
zwanzigste
□ the twentieth of August der zwanzigste August

twenty NUMBER
zwanzig
□ He's twenty. Er ist zwanzig.

twice ADVERB
zweimal
■ **twice as much** doppelt so viel □ He gets twice as much pocket money as me. Er bekommt doppelt so viel Taschengeld wie ich.

twin NOUN
der Zwilling (PL die Zwillinge)
LANGUAGE TIP **der Zwilling** is also used for women.
■ **my twin brother** mein Zwillingsbruder *masc*
■ **her twin sister** ihre Zwillingsschwester
■ **identical twins** eineiige Zwillinge
■ **a twin room** ein Doppelzimmer mit zwei Betten

twinned ADJECTIVE
■ **Oxford is twinned with Bonn.** Oxford und Bonn sind Partnerstädte.

to **twist** VERB
1 biegen (IMPERFECT bog, PERFECT hat gebogen) *(bend)*
■ **I've twisted my ankle.** Ich habe mir den Fuß vertreten.
2 verdrehen (PERFECT hat verdreht) *(distort)*
□ You're twisting my words. Sie verdrehen meine Worte.

twit NOUN
der Trottel (PL die Trottel) *(informal)*
LANGUAGE TIP **der Trottel** is also used for women.

two NUMBER
zwei
□ She's two. Sie ist zwei.

type NOUN
▷ *see also* **type** VERB
die Art
□ What type of camera have you got? Welche Art von Fotoapparat hast du?

to **type** VERB
▷ *see also* **type** NOUN
Schreibmaschine schreiben (IMPERFECT schrieb Schreibmaschine, PERFECT hat Schreibmaschine geschrieben)
□ Can you type? Kannst du Schreibmaschine schreiben?
■ **to type a letter** einen Brief tippen

typewriter NOUN
die Schreibmaschine

typical ADJECTIVE
typisch
□ That's just typical! Das ist typisch!

tyre NOUN
der Reifen (PL die Reifen)
□ the tyre pressure der Reifendruck

Uu

UFO NOUN *(= unidentified flying object)*
das UFO (PL die UFOs) *(= unbekanntes Flugobjekt)*

ugh EXCLAMATION
igitt

ugly ADJECTIVE
hässlich

UK NOUN *(= United Kingdom)*
das Vereinigte Königreich
▪ **from the UK** aus dem Vereinigten Königreich
▪ **in the UK** im Vereinigten Königreich
▪ **to the UK** in das Vereinigte Königreich

ulcer NOUN
das Geschwür (PL die Geschwüre)

Ulster NOUN
Ulster *neut*
▪ **from Ulster** aus Ulster
▪ **in Ulster** in Ulster
▪ **to Ulster** nach Ulster

ultimate ADJECTIVE
äußerste
□ the ultimate challenge die äußerste Herausforderung
▪ **It was the ultimate adventure.** Das war das große Abenteuer.

ultimately ADVERB
schließlich
□ Ultimately, it's your decision. Schließlich ist es deine Entscheidung.

umbrella NOUN
1 der Regenschirm (PL die Regenschirme)
2 der Sonnenschirm (PL die Sonnenschirme) *(for sun)*

umlaut NOUN
der Umlaut
□ The plural of 'Haus' is written with an umlaut. Der Plural von 'Haus' wird mit Umlaut gebildet.
▪ **a umlaut** ä
▪ **o umlaut** ö
▪ **u umlaut** ü

umpire NOUN
der Schiedsrichter (PL die Schiedsrichter)
die Schiedsrichterin

UN NOUN *(= United Nations)*
die UN *pl*

unable ADJECTIVE
▪ **to be unable to do something** etwas nicht tun können □ I was unable to come. Ich konnte nicht kommen.

unacceptable ADJECTIVE
unannehmbar

unanimous ADJECTIVE
einstimmig
□ a unanimous decision ein einstimmiger Beschluss

unavoidable ADJECTIVE
umvermeidlich

unaware ADJECTIVE
▪ **to be unaware 1** *(not know about)* nichts wissen □ I was unaware of the regulations. Ich wusste nichts von den Bestimmungen.
2 *(not notice)* nicht merken □ She was unaware that she was being filmed. Sie merkte nicht, dass sie gefilmt wurde.

unbearable ADJECTIVE
unerträglich

unbeatable ADJECTIVE
unschlagbar

unbelievable ADJECTIVE
unglaublich

unborn ADJECTIVE
ungeboren
□ the unborn child das ungeborene Kind

unbreakable ADJECTIVE
unzerbrechlich

uncanny ADJECTIVE
unheimlich
□ That's uncanny! Das ist unheimlich!
▪ **an uncanny resemblance to** eine verblüffende Ähnlichkeit mit

uncertain ADJECTIVE
ungewiss
□ The future is uncertain. Die Zukunft ist ungewiss.
▪ **to be uncertain about something** sich über etwas nicht im Klaren sein □ I'm uncertain about her plans. Ich bin mir über ihre Pläne nicht im Klaren.

uncivilized ADJECTIVE
unzivilisiert

uncle NOUN
der Onkel (PL die Onkel)
□ my uncle mein Onkel

uncomfortable ADJECTIVE
unbequem

□ The seats are rather uncomfortable. Die Sitze sind ziemlich unbequem.

unconscious ADJECTIVE
bewusstlos

uncontrollable ADJECTIVE
unkontrollierbar

unconventional ADJECTIVE
unkonventionell

under PREPOSITION
unter

LANGUAGE TIP Use the accusative to express movement or a change of place. Use the dative when there is no change of place.

□ The ball rolled under the table. Der Ball rollte unter den Tisch. □ The cat's under the table. Die Katze ist unter dem Tisch. □ children under ten Kinder unter zehn
■ **under there** da drunter □ What's under there? Was ist da drunter?
■ **under twenty people** weniger als zwanzig Leute

underage ADJECTIVE
minderjährig

undercover ADJECTIVE, ADVERB
■ **an undercover agent** *(secret agent)* ein Geheimagent *masc*
■ **She was working undercover.** Sie führte verdeckte Ermittlungen durch.

underdog NOUN
der Underdog (PL die Underdogs)
□ We were the underdogs on this occasion. Wir waren diesmal die Underdogs.

to **underestimate** VERB
unterschätzen (PERFECT hat unterschätzt)
□ I underestimated her. Ich habe sie unterschätzt.

to **undergo** VERB
sich unterziehen (IMPERFECT unterzog sich, PERFECT hat sich unterzogen) *(operation)*

underground ADJECTIVE, ADVERB
▷ *see also* **underground** NOUN
1 unterirdisch
□ underground water pipes unterirdische Wasserrohre
■ **an underground car park** eine Tiefgarage
2 unter der Erde
□ Moles live underground. Maulwürfe leben unter der Erde.

underground NOUN
▷ *see also* **underground** ADJECTIVE
die U-Bahn
□ Is there an underground in Bonn? Gibt es in Bonn eine U-Bahn?

to **underline** VERB
unterstreichen (IMPERFECT unterstrich, PERFECT hat unterstrichen)

underneath PREPOSITION, ADVERB
1 unter

LANGUAGE TIP Use the accusative to express movement or a change of place. Use the dative when there is no change of place.

□ I put it underneath that pile. Ich habe es unter diesen Stapel gelegt. □ It was hidden underneath the carpet. Es war unter dem Teppich versteckt.
2 darunter
□ I got out of the car and looked underneath. Ich stieg aus dem Auto aus und sah darunter.

underpaid ADJECTIVE
unterbezahlt
□ I'm underpaid. Ich bin unterbezahlt.

underpants PL NOUN
die Unterhose *sing*
□ a pair of underpants eine Unterhose

underpass NOUN
die Unterführung

undershirt NOUN (US)
das Unterhemd (PL die Unterhemden)

underskirt NOUN
der Unterrock (PL die Unterröcke)

to **understand** VERB
verstehen (IMPERFECT verstand, PERFECT hat verstanden)
□ Do you understand? Verstehst du? □ I don't understand this word. Ich verstehe dieses Wort nicht. □ Is that understood? Ist das verstanden?

understanding ADJECTIVE
verständnisvoll
□ She's very understanding. Sie ist sehr verständnisvoll.

understood VERB ▷ *see* **understand**

undertaker NOUN
der Beerdigungsunternehmer (PL die Beerdigungsunternehmer)
die Beerdigungsunternehmerin

underwater ADJECTIVE, ADVERB
unter Wasser
□ It was filmed underwater. Es wurde unter Wasser gefilmt.
■ **an underwater camera** eine Unterwasserkamera

underwear NOUN
die Unterwäsche

underwent VERB ▷ *see* **undergo**

to **undo** VERB
aufmachen (PERFECT hat aufgemacht)

to **undress** VERB
sich ausziehen (IMPERFECT zog sich aus, PERFECT hat sich ausgezogen) *(get undressed)*
□ The doctor told me to get undressed. Der Arzt bat mich, mich auszuziehen.

uneconomic ADJECTIVE
unrentabel

unemployed ADJECTIVE
arbeitslos
□ He's unemployed. Er ist arbeitslos.

□ He's been unemployed for a year. Er ist seit einem Jahr arbeitslos.

■ **the unemployed** die Arbeitslosen *masc pl*

unemployment NOUN
die Arbeitslosigkeit

unexpected ADJECTIVE
unerwartet
□ an unexpected visitor ein unerwarteter Gast

unexpectedly ADVERB
überraschend
□ They arrived unexpectedly. Sie sind überraschend gekommen.

unfair ADJECTIVE
unfair
□ It's unfair to girls. Es ist Mädchen gegenüber unfair.

unfamiliar ADJECTIVE
unbekannt
□ I heard an unfamiliar voice. Ich hörte eine unbekannte Stimme.

unfashionable ADJECTIVE
unmodern

unfit ADJECTIVE
nicht fit
□ I'm rather unfit at the moment. Ich bin im Moment nicht sehr fit.

to **unfold** VERB
auseinanderfalten (PERFECT hat auseinandergefaltet)
□ She unfolded the map. Sie faltete die Karte auseinander.

unforgettable ADJECTIVE
unvergesslich

unfortunately ADVERB
leider
□ Unfortunately, I arrived late. Ich bin leider zu spät gekommen.

unfriendly ADJECTIVE
unfreundlich
□ They're a bit unfriendly. Sie sind etwas unfreundlich.

ungrateful ADJECTIVE
undankbar

unhappy ADJECTIVE
unglücklich
□ He was very unhappy as a child. Er war als Kind sehr unglücklich. □ to look unhappy unglücklich aussehen

unhealthy ADJECTIVE
ungesund

uni NOUN
die Uni (PL die Unis)
□ to go to uni zur Uni gehen

uniform NOUN
die Uniform
□ the school uniform die Schuluniform

> **DID YOU KNOW...?**
> School uniforms are virtually nonexistent in Germany.

uninhabited ADJECTIVE
unbewohnt

union NOUN
die Gewerkschaft *(trade union)*

Union Jack NOUN
die britische Flagge

unique ADJECTIVE
einzigartig

unit NOUN
die Einheit
□ a unit of measurement eine Maßeinheit

■ **a kitchen unit** ein Kücheneinbauschrank *masc*

United Kingdom NOUN
das Vereinigte Königreich

■ **from the United Kingdom** aus dem Vereinigten Königreich

■ **in the United Kingdom** im Vereinigten Königreich

■ **to the United Kingdom** in das Vereinigte Königreich

United Nations PL NOUN
die Vereinten Nationen *fem pl*

United States NOUN
die Vereinigten Staaten *masc pl*

■ **from the United States** aus den Vereinigten Staaten

■ **in the United States** in den Vereinigten Staaten

■ **to the United States** in die Vereinigten Staaten

universe NOUN
das Universum

university NOUN
die Universität
□ Do you want to go to university? Möchtest du auf die Universität gehen? □ Lancaster University die Universität von Lancaster

■ **She's at university.** Sie studiert.

unleaded petrol NOUN
das bleifreie Benzin

unless CONJUNCTION
es sei denn
□ unless he leaves es sei denn, er geht
□ I won't come unless you phone me. Ich komme nicht, es sei denn, du rufst an.

unlike PREPOSITION
im Gegensatz zu
□ Unlike him, I really enjoy flying. Im Gegensatz zu ihm fliege ich wirklich gern.

unlikely ADJECTIVE
unwahrscheinlich
□ It's possible, but unlikely. Es ist möglich, aber unwahrscheinlich.

unlisted ADJECTIVE (US)

■ **to have an unlisted number** nicht im Telefonbuch stehen

to **unload** VERB
ausladen (PRESENT lädt aus, IMPERFECT lud aus, PERFECT hat ausgeladen)

□ We unloaded the car. Wir haben das Auto ausgeladen.

■ **The lorries go there to unload.** Die Lastwagen fahren dorthin um abzuladen.

to **unlock** VERB
aufschließen (IMPERFECT schloss auf, PERFECT hat aufgeschlossen)
□ He unlocked the door. Er schloss die Tür auf.

unlucky ADJECTIVE
■ **to be unlucky** **1** *(number, object)* Unglück bringen □ They say thirteen is an unlucky number. Es heißt, dass die Zahl dreizehn Unglück bringt. **2** *(person)* kein Glück haben □ Did you win? — No, I was unlucky. Hast du gewonnen? — Nein, ich habe kein Glück gehabt.

unmarried ADJECTIVE
unverheiratet *(person)*
□ an unmarried couple ein unverheiratetes Paar
■ **an unmarried mother** eine ledige Mutter

unnatural ADJECTIVE
unnatürlich

unnecessary ADJECTIVE
unnötig

unofficial ADJECTIVE
1 inoffiziell *(meeting, leader)*
2 wild *(strike)*

to **unpack** VERB
auspacken (PERFECT hat ausgepackt) *(clothes, case)*
□ I went to my room to unpack. Ich ging auf mein Zimmer, um auszupacken.

unpleasant ADJECTIVE
unangenehm

to **unplug** VERB
ausstecken (PERFECT hat ausgesteckt)
□ She unplugged the TV. Sie hat den Fernseher ausgesteckt.

unpopular ADJECTIVE
unbeliebt

unpredictable ADJECTIVE
unvorhersehbar *(event)*

unreal ADJECTIVE
unglaublich *(incredible)*
□ It was unreal! Es war unglaublich!

unrealistic ADJECTIVE
unrealistisch

unreasonable ADJECTIVE
unmöglich
□ Her attitude was completely unreasonable. Ihre Haltung war völlig unmöglich.

unreliable ADJECTIVE
unzuverlässig
□ He's completely unreliable. Er ist total unzuverlässig.

to **unroll** VERB
aufrollen (PERFECT hat aufgerollt)

unsatisfactory ADJECTIVE
unbefriedigend

to **unscrew** VERB
aufschrauben (PERFECT hat aufgeschraubt)
□ She unscrewed the top of the bottle. Sie schraubte den Flaschenverschluss auf.

unshaven ADJECTIVE
unrasiert

unskilled ADJECTIVE
ungelernt
□ an unskilled worker ein ungelernter Arbeiter

unstable ADJECTIVE
1 nicht stabil *(object)*
2 labil *(person)*

unsteady ADJECTIVE
unsicher *(walk, voice)*
■ **He was unsteady on his feet.** Er war wackelig auf den Beinen.

unsuccessful ADJECTIVE
erfolglos *(attempt)*
□ an unsuccessful artist ein erfolgloser Künstler
■ **to be unsuccessful in doing something** keinen Erfolg bei etwas haben □ He was unsuccessful in getting a job. Er hatte bei der Arbeitssuche keinen Erfolg.

unsuitable ADJECTIVE
ungeeignet *(clothes, equipment)*

untidy ADJECTIVE
unordentlich

to **untie** VERB
1 aufmachen (PERFECT hat aufgemacht) *(knot, parcel)*
2 losbinden (IMPERFECT band los, PERFECT hat losgebunden) *(animal)*

until PREPOSITION, CONJUNCTION
1 bis
□ I waited until ten o'clock. Ich habe bis zehn Uhr gewartet.
■ **until now** bis jetzt □ It's never been a problem until now. Es war bis jetzt nie ein Problem.
■ **until then** bis dahin □ Until then I'd never been to Germany. Bis dahin war ich noch nie in Deutschland gewesen.
2 vor

LANGUAGE TIP Use **vor** if the sentence you want to translate contains a negative, such as 'not' or 'never'.

□ It won't be ready until next week. Es wird nicht vor nächster Woche fertig sein. □ Until last year I'd never been to Germany. Vor letztem Jahr war ich noch nie in Deutschland.

unusual ADJECTIVE
ungewöhnlich
□ an unusual shape eine ungewöhnliche Form □ It's unusual to get snow at this time of year. Es ist ungewöhnlich, dass es um diese Jahreszeit schneit.

unwilling ADJECTIVE
■ **to be unwilling to do something** nicht

gewillt sein, etwas zu tun □ He was unwilling to help me. Er war nicht gewillt, mir zu helfen.

to **unwind** VERB
sich entspannen (PERFECT hat sich entspannt) *(relax)*

unwise ADJECTIVE
unklug *(person)*
□ That was unwise of you. Das war unklug von dir.

unwound VERB ▷ *see* **unwind**

to **unwrap** VERB
auspacken (PERFECT hat ausgepackt)
□ Let's unwrap the presents. Packen wir die Geschenke aus.

up PREPOSITION, ADVERB
auf

LANGUAGE TIP Use the accusative to express movement or a change of place. Use the dative when there is no change of place.

□ He drove me up the hill. Er hat mich den Berg hinaufgefahren. □ the chapel up on the hill die Kapelle auf dem Berg
■ **up here** hier oben
■ **up there** dort oben
■ **up north** oben im Norden
■ **to be up** *(out of bed)* auf sein □ We were up at six. Wir waren um sechs Uhr auf.
□ He's not up yet. Er ist noch nicht auf.
■ **What's up?** Was gibt's?
■ **What's up with her?** Was ist los mit ihr?
■ **to get up** *(in the morning)* aufstehen
□ What time do you get up? Um wie viel Uhr stehst du auf?
■ **to go up 1** hinauffahren □ The bus went up the hill. Der Bus ist den Berg hinaufgefahren. **2** *(on foot)* hinaufgehen
□ We went up the hill. Wir sind den Berg hinaufgegangen.
■ **to go up to somebody** auf jemanden zugehen
■ **She came up to me.** Sie kam auf mich zu.
■ **up to** *(as far as)* bis □ to count up to fifty bis fünfzig zählen □ up to three hours bis zu drei Stunden □ up to now bis jetzt
■ **It's up to you.** Das ist dir überlassen.

LANGUAGE TIP For other expressions with 'up', see the verbs 'go', 'come', 'put', 'turn' etc.

upbringing NOUN
die Erziehung

uphill ADVERB
bergauf

upper sixth NOUN
■ **the upper sixth** die dreizehnte Klasse
□ She's in the upper sixth. Sie ist in der dreizehnten Klasse.

upright ADJECTIVE
■ **to stand upright** aufrecht stehen

upset NOUN
▷ *see also* **upset** ADJECTIVE, VERB
■ **a stomach upset** eine Magenverstimmung

upset ADJECTIVE
▷ *see also* **upset** NOUN, VERB
1 gekränkt *(hurt)*
□ She was upset when he said that. Sie fühlte sich gekränkt, als er das sagte.
2 betrübt *(sad)*
□ I was very upset when my father died. Ich war sehr betrübt, als mein Vater starb.
■ **an upset stomach** eine Magenverstimmung

to **upset** VERB
▷ *see also* **upset** NOUN, ADJECTIVE
aufregen (PERFECT hat aufgeregt)
□ Don't say anything to upset her! Sag nichts, was sie aufregen könnte.

upside down ADVERB
verkehrt herum
□ It's upside down. Es ist verkehrt herum.

upstairs ADVERB
oben
□ Where's your coat? — It's upstairs. Wo ist dein Mantel? — Er ist oben.
■ **the people upstairs** die Leute von oben
■ **to go upstairs** hinaufgehen

uptight ADJECTIVE
nervös *(nervous)*
□ She's really uptight. Sie ist echt nervös.

up-to-date ADJECTIVE
1 modern *(car, stereo)*
2 aktuell *(information)*
□ an up-to-date timetable ein aktueller Fahrplan
■ **to bring something up to date** etwas auf den neuesten Stand bringen
■ **to keep somebody up to date** jemanden auf dem Laufenden halten

upwards ADVERB
hinauf
□ to look upwards hinaufsehen

urgent ADJECTIVE
dringend
□ Is it urgent? Ist es dringend?

urine NOUN
der Urin

US SING NOUN
die USA *pl*
■ **from the US** aus den USA
■ **in the US** in den USA
■ **to the US** in die USA

us PRONOUN
uns
□ They saw us. Sie haben uns gesehen.
□ They gave us a map. Sie gaben uns eine Karte.
■ **Who is it? — It's us!** Wer ist da? — Wir sind's!

USA NOUN
die USA *pl*

■ **from the USA** aus den USA
■ **in the USA** in den USA
■ **to the USA** in die USA

use NOUN
▷ *see also* **use** VERB
■ **It's no use.** Es hat keinen Zweck. ☐ It's no use shouting, she's deaf. Es hat keinen Zweck zu brüllen, sie ist taub. ☐ It's no use, I can't do it. Es hat keinen Zweck, ich kann's nicht.
■ **to make use of something** etwas benützen

to **use** VERB
▷ *see also* **use** NOUN
benützen (PERFECT hat benützt)
☐ Can we use a dictionary in the exam? Können wir in der Prüfung ein Wörterbuch benützen?
■ **Can I use your phone?** Kann ich mal telefonieren?
■ **to use the toilet** auf die Toilette gehen
■ **to use up** aufbrauchen ☐ We've used up all the paint. Ich habe die ganze Farbe aufgebraucht.
■ **I used to live in London.** Ich habe früher mal in London gelebt.
■ **I used not to like maths, but now ...** Früher habe ich Mathe nicht gemocht, aber jetzt ...
■ **to be used to something** an etwas gewöhnt sein ☐ He wasn't used to driving on the right. Er war nicht daran gewöhnt, rechts zu fahren. ☐ Don't worry, I'm used to it. Keine Sorge, ich bin daran gewöhnt.
■ **a used car** ein Gebrauchtwagen *masc*

useful ADJECTIVE
nützlich

useless ADJECTIVE
nutzlos
☐ This map is just useless. Diese Karte ist echt nutzlos.
■ **You're useless!** Du bist zu nichts zu gebrauchen!
■ **It's useless asking her!** Es ist zwecklos, sie zu fragen!

user NOUN
der Benutzer (PL die Benutzer)
die Benutzerin

user-friendly ADJECTIVE
benutzerfreundlich

usual ADJECTIVE
üblich
☐ as usual wie üblich

usually ADVERB
normalerweise
☐ I usually get to school at half past eight. Ich bin normalerweise um halb neun in der Schule.

utility room NOUN
der Abstellraum (PL die Abstellräume)

U-turn NOUN
die Wende
■ **to do a U-turn** wenden
■ **'No U-turns'** 'Wenden verboten'

Vv

vacancy NOUN
1 die freie Stelle *(job)*
2 das freie Zimmer (PL die freien Zimmer) *(room in hotel)*
■ **'Vacancies'** 'Zimmer frei'
■ **'No vacancies'** 'Belegt'

vacant ADJECTIVE
1 frei *(seat, job)*
2 leer stehend *(building)*
3 leer *(look)*
□ a vacant look ein leerer Blick

vacation NOUN (US)
1 die Ferien *pl (from school)*
□ They went on vacation to Mexico. Sie haben in Mexiko Ferien gemacht.
2 der Urlaub (PL die Urlaube) *(from work)*
□ I have thirty days' vacation a year. Ich habe dreißig Tage Urlaub im Jahr.

to **vaccinate** VERB
impfen

to **vacuum** VERB
staubsaugen (IMPERFECT staubsaugte, PERFECT hat gestaubsaugt)
□ to vacuum the hall den Flur staubsaugen

vacuum cleaner NOUN
der Staubsauger (PL die Staubsauger)

vagina NOUN
die Vagina (PL die Vaginen)

vague ADJECTIVE
vage

vain ADJECTIVE
eitel
□ He's so vain! Er ist so eitel!
■ **in vain** umsonst

Valentine card NOUN
die Valentinskarte

DID YOU KNOW...?
Germans celebrate Valentine's Day by giving flowers rather than sending cards.

Valentine's Day NOUN
der Valentinstag (PL die Valentinstage)

valid ADJECTIVE
gültig
□ This ticket is valid for three months. Dieser Fahrschein ist drei Monate lang gültig.

valley NOUN
das Tal (PL die Täler)

valuable ADJECTIVE
wertvoll
□ a valuable picture ein wertvolles Bild
□ valuable help wertvolle Hilfe

valuables PL NOUN
die Wertsachen *fem pl*
□ Don't take any valuables with you. Nehmen Sie keine Wertsachen mit.

value NOUN
der Wert (PL die Werte)

van NOUN
der Lieferwagen (PL die Lieferwagen)

vandal NOUN
der Vandale (GEN des Vandalen, PL die Vandalen)
die Vandalin

vandalism NOUN
der Vandalismus (GEN des Vandalismus)

to **vandalize** VERB
mutwillig zerstören (PERFECT hat mutwillig zerstört)

vanilla NOUN
die Vanille
■ **vanilla ice cream** das Vanilleeis

to **vanish** VERB
verschwinden (IMPERFECT verschwand, PERFECT ist verschwunden)

variable ADJECTIVE
wechselhaft *(mood, weather)*

varied ADJECTIVE
abwechslungsreich
□ a varied diet eine abwechslungsreiche Kost
□ a varied life ein abwechslungsreiches Leben
■ **a varied selection** eine reichhaltige Auswahl

variety NOUN
1 die Abwechslung
□ She likes variety in her life. Sie hat gern Abwechslung im Leben.
2 die Sorte *(kind)*
□ a new variety of rose eine neue Rosensorte
■ **a variety of CDs** eine Vielzahl von CDs

various ADJECTIVE
verschieden
□ We visited various villages. Wir haben verschiedene Dörfer besucht.

to **vary** VERB
schwanken
□ It varies between two and four per cent. Es schwankt zwischen zwei und vier Prozent.

■ **It varies.** Das ist unterschiedlich.

vase NOUN
die Vase

VAT NOUN *(= value added tax)*
die Mehrwertsteuer

VCR NOUN *(= video cassette recorder)*
der Videorekorder (PL die Videorekorder)

VDU NOUN *(= visual display unit)*
der Bildschirm (PL die Bildschirme)

veal NOUN
das Kalbfleisch

vegan NOUN
der Veganer (PL die Veganer)
die Veganerin
□ I'm a vegan. Ich bin Veganerin.

vegetable NOUN
die Gemüsesorte
■ **vegetables** das Gemüse *sing*
■ **vegetable soup** die Gemüsesuppe

vegetarian ADJECTIVE
▷ *see also* **vegetarian** NOUN
vegetarisch
□ vegetarian lasagne die vegetarische Lasagne
■ **He's vegetarian.** Er ist Vegetarier.

vegetarian NOUN
▷ *see also* **vegetarian** ADJECTIVE
der Vegetarier (PL die Vegetarier)
die Vegetarierin
□ She's a vegetarian. Sie ist Vegetarierin.

vehicle NOUN
das Fahrzeug (PL die Fahrzeuge)

vein NOUN
die Vene

velvet NOUN
der Samt

vending machine NOUN
der Automat (GEN des Automaten, PL die Automaten)

Venetian blind NOUN
die Jalousie

verb NOUN
das Verb (PL die Verben)

verdict NOUN
das Urteil (PL die Urteile)

vertical ADJECTIVE
senkrecht

vertigo NOUN
das Schwindelgefühl
■ **He had an attack of vertigo.** Ihm wurde schwindlig.

very ADVERB
sehr
□ very tall sehr groß □ not very interesting nicht sehr interessant
■ **very much 1** sehr viel □ He didn't eat very much. Er hat nicht sehr viel gegessen.
2 *(like, love, respect)* sehr □ I love her very much. Ich liebe sie sehr.
■ **Thank you very much.** Vielen Dank.

vest NOUN
1 das Unterhemd (PL die Unterhemden)
2 die Weste *(waistcoat)*

vet NOUN
der Tierarzt (GEN des Tierarztes, PL die Tierärzte)
die Tierärztin
□ She's a vet. Sie ist Tierärztin.

via PREPOSITION
über
□ We went to Munich via Ulm. Wir sind über Ulm nach München gefahren.

vicar NOUN
der Pastor (PL die Pastoren)
die Pastorin
□ He's a vicar. Er ist Pastor.

vice NOUN
der Schraubstock (PL die Schraubstöcke) *(for holding things)*

vice versa ADVERB
umgekehrt

vicious ADJECTIVE
1 brutal
□ a vicious attack ein brutaler Überfall
2 bissig *(dog)*
3 bösartig *(person)*
■ **a vicious circle** ein Teufelskreis *masc*

victim NOUN
das Opfer (PL die Opfer)
□ He was the victim of a mugging. Er wurde das Opfer eines Straßenüberfalls.

victory NOUN
der Sieg (PL die Siege)

to video VERB
▷ *see also* **video** NOUN
auf Video aufnehmen (PRESENT nimmt auf Video auf, IMPERFECT nahm auf Video auf, PERFECT hat auf Video aufgenommen)

video NOUN
▷ *see also* **video** VERB
1 das Video (PL die Videos) *(film)*
□ to watch a video ein Video ansehen
□ a video of my family on holiday ein Video von meiner Familie in den Ferien
2 der Videorekorder (PL die Videorekorder) *(video recorder)*
□ Have you got a video? Habt ihr einen Videorekorder?
■ **a video camera** eine Videokamera
■ **a video cassette** eine Videokassette
■ **a video game** ein Videospiel *neut* □ He likes playing video games. Er spielt gern Videospiele.
■ **a video recorder** ein Videorekorder
■ **a video shop** eine Videothek

Vienna NOUN
Wien *neut*
■ **to Vienna** nach Wien

Vietnamese NOUN
▷ *see also* **Vietnamese** ADJECTIVE
der Vietnamese (PL die Vietnamesen)
die Vietnamesin

Vietnamese ADJECTIVE
▷ *see also* **Vietnamese** NOUN
vietnamesisch

view NOUN
1 die Aussicht
□ There's an amazing view. Man hat dort eine tolle Aussicht.
2 die Meinung *(opinion)*
□ in my view meiner Meinung nach

viewer NOUN
der Fernsehzuschauer (PL die Fernsehzuschauer)
die Fernsehzuschauerin

viewpoint NOUN
der Standpunkt (PL die Standpunkte)

vile ADJECTIVE
ekelhaft *(smell, food)*

villa NOUN
die Villa (PL die Villen)

village NOUN
das Dorf (PL die Dörfer)

villain NOUN
1 der Verbrecher (PL die Verbrecher)
die Verbrecherin *(criminal)*
2 der Bösewicht (PL die Bösewichte) *(in film)*

vine NOUN
die Weinrebe

vinegar NOUN
der Essig

vineyard NOUN
der Weinberg (PL die Weinberge)

viola NOUN
die Bratsche
□ I play the viola. Ich spiele Bratsche.

violence NOUN
die Gewalt

violent ADJECTIVE
1 gewalttätig *(person, film)*
■ **a violent crime** ein Gewaltverbrechen *neut*
2 gewaltig *(explosion)*

violin NOUN
die Geige
□ I play the violin. Ich spiele Geige.

violinist NOUN
der Geigenspieler (PL die Geigenspieler)
die Geigenspielerin

virgin NOUN
die Jungfrau
□ to be a virgin Jungfrau sein

Virgo NOUN
die Jungfrau
□ I'm Virgo. Ich bin Jungfrau.

virtual reality NOUN
die virtuelle Realität

virus NOUN
das Virus (GEN des Virus, PL die Viren)

visa NOUN
das Visum (PL die Visa)

visible ADJECTIVE
sichtbar

visit NOUN
▷ *see also* **visit** VERB
1 der Besuch (PL die Besuche)
□ my last visit to her mein letzter Besuch bei ihr
2 der Aufenthalt (PL die Aufenthalte) *(to country)*
□ Did you enjoy your visit to Germany? Hat euer Deutschlandaufenthalt Spaß gemacht?

to **visit** VERB
▷ *see also* **visit** NOUN
1 besuchen (PERFECT hat besucht) *(person)*
2 besichtigen (PERFECT hat besichtigt) *(place)*
□ We'd like to visit the castle. Wir würden gern die Burg besichtigen.

visitor NOUN
der Besucher (PL die Besucher)
die Besucherin
■ **to have a visitor** Besuch haben

visual ADJECTIVE
visuell

to **visualize** VERB
sich vorstellen (PERFECT hat sich vorgestellt)
□ I tried to visualize his face. Ich versuchte, mir sein Gesicht vorzustellen.

vital ADJECTIVE
äußerst wichtig
□ It's vital for you to take these tablets. Es ist äußerst wichtig, dass du diese Tabletten nimmst.
■ **of vital importance** äußerst wichtig

vitamin NOUN
das Vitamin (PL die Vitamine)

vivid ADJECTIVE
lebhaft
□ to have a vivid imagination eine lebhafte Fantasie haben

vocabulary NOUN
der Wortschatz (GEN des Wortschatzes, PL die Wortschätze)

vocational ADJECTIVE
beruflich
□ vocational training die berufliche Ausbildung
■ **a vocational college** eine Berufsschule

vodka NOUN
der Wodka (PL die Wodkas)

voice NOUN
die Stimme

voice mail NOUN
die Voicemail

volcano NOUN
der Vulkan (PL die Vulkane)

volleyball NOUN
der Volleyball
□ to play volleyball Volleyball spielen

volt NOUN
das Volt (GEN des Volt, PL die Volt)

voltage NOUN
die Spannung

voluntary ADJECTIVE
freiwillig *(contribution, statement)*

■ **to do voluntary work** ehrenamtlich tätig sein

volunteer NOUN
▷ *see also* **volunteer** VERB
der Freiwillige (GEN des Freiwilligen, PL die Freiwilligen)
die Freiwillige (GEN der Freiwilligen)
□ a volunteer *(man)* ein Freiwilliger

to **volunteer** VERB
▷ *see also* **volunteer** NOUN
■ **to volunteer to do something** sich freiwillig melden, etwas zu tun

to **vomit** VERB
sich übergeben (PRESENT übergibt sich, IMPERFECT übergab sich, PERFECT hat sich übergeben)

vote NOUN
▷ *see also* **vote** VERB
die Stimme

to **vote** VERB
▷ *see also* **vote** NOUN
wählen
□ to vote Labour Labour wählen
■ **to vote for somebody** für jemanden stimmen □ I voted for him. Ich habe für ihn gestimmt.

voucher NOUN
der Gutschein (PL die Gutscheine)
□ a gift voucher ein Geschenkgutschein

vowel NOUN
der Vokal (PL die Vokale)

vulgar ADJECTIVE
vulgär

wafer NOUN
die Waffel

wage NOUN
der Lohn (PL die Löhne)
□ He collected his wages. Er hat seinen Lohn abgeholt.

waist NOUN
die Taille

waistcoat NOUN
die Weste

to **wait** VERB
warten
■ **to wait for something** auf etwas warten
□ We were waiting for the bus. Wir haben auf den Bus gewartet.
■ **to wait for somebody** auf jemanden warten □ I'll wait for you. Ich warte auf dich.
□ Wait for me! Warte auf mich!
■ **Wait a minute!** Einen Augenblick!
■ **to keep somebody waiting** jemanden warten lassen □ They kept us waiting for hours. Sie haben uns stundenlang warten lassen.
■ **I can't wait for the holidays.** Ich kann die Ferien kaum erwarten.
■ **I can't wait to see him again.** Ich kann's kaum erwarten, bis ich ihn wiedersehe.

to **wait up** VERB
aufbleiben (IMPERFECT blieb auf, PERFECT ist aufgeblieben)
□ My mum always waits up till I get in. Meine Mutti bleibt immer auf, bis ich nach Hause komme.

waiter NOUN
der Kellner (PL die Kellner)

waiting list NOUN
die Warteliste

waiting room NOUN
das Wartezimmer (PL die Wartezimmer)

waitress NOUN
die Kellnerin

to **wake up** VERB
aufwachen (PERFECT ist aufgewacht)
□ I woke up at six o'clock. Ich bin um sechs Uhr aufgewacht.
■ **to wake somebody up** jemanden wecken
□ Would you wake me up at seven o'clock? Könntest du mich um sieben Uhr wecken?

Wales NOUN
Wales *neut*
□ the Prince of Wales der Prinz von Wales
■ **from Wales** aus Wales
■ **in Wales** in Wales
■ **to Wales** nach Wales

to **walk** VERB
▷ *see also* **walk** NOUN
1 gehen (IMPERFECT ging, PERFECT ist gegangen)
□ He walks fast. Er geht schnell.
2 zu Fuß gehen *(go on foot)*
□ Are you walking or going by bus? Geht ihr zu Fuß oder nehmt ihr den Bus? □ We walked ten kilometres. Wir sind zehn Kilometer zu Fuß gegangen.
■ **to walk the dog** mit dem Hund spazieren gehen

walk NOUN
▷ *see also* **walk** VERB
der Spaziergang (PL die Spaziergänge)
□ to go for a walk einen Spaziergang machen
■ **It's ten minutes' walk from here.** Von hier ist es zehn Minuten zu Fuß.

walkie-talkie NOUN
das Walkie-Talkie (PL die Walkie-Talkies)

walking NOUN
das Wandern
■ **I did some walking in the Alps last summer.** Ich bin letzten Sommer in den Alpen gewandert.

walking stick NOUN
der Spazierstock (PL die Spazierstöcke)

Walkman® NOUN
der Walkman® (PL die Walkmen)

wall NOUN
1 die Mauer
□ There's a wall round the garden. Um den Garten ist eine Mauer.
2 die Wand (PL die Wände)
□ They have lots of pictures on the wall. Sie haben viele Bilder an der Wand.

wallet NOUN
die Brieftasche

wallpaper NOUN
die Tapete

walnut NOUN
die Walnuss (PL die Walnüsse)

to **wander** VERB
■ **to wander around** herumlaufen

□ I just wandered around for a while. Ich bin einfach eine Zeit lang herumgelaufen.

to **want** VERB
möchten (PRESENT mag, IMPERFECT mochte, PERFECT hat gemocht)
□ Do you want some cake? Möchtest du Kuchen?
■ **to want to do something** etwas tun wollen □ I want to go to the cinema. Ich will ins Kino gehen. □ What do you want to do? Was willst du machen?

war NOUN
der Krieg (PL die Kriege)

ward NOUN
der Krankensaal (PL die Krankensäle) *(room in hospital)*

warden NOUN *(of youth hostel)*
der Herbergsvater (PL die Herbergsväter) *(man)*
die Herbergsmutter (PL die Herbergsmütter) *(woman)*

wardrobe NOUN
der Kleiderschrank (PL die Kleiderschränke) *(piece of furniture)*

warehouse NOUN
das Lagerhaus (GEN des Lagerhauses, PL die Lagerhäuser)

warm ADJECTIVE
1 warm
□ warm water warmes Wasser □ It's warm in here. Hier drin ist es warm. □ It's warmer in the kitchen. In der Küche ist es wärmer.

LANGUAGE TIP When you talk about a person being 'warm', you use the impersonal construction.

□ I'm warm. Mir ist warm. □ I'm too warm. Mir ist zu warm.
2 herzlich
□ a warm welcome ein herzlicher Empfang
■ **to warm up** 1 *(for sport)* sich aufwärmen 2 *(food)* aufwärmen □ I'll warm up some lasagne for you. Ich wärme dir etwas Lasagne auf.
■ **to warm over** aufwärmen

to **warn** VERB
warnen
□ Well, I warned you! Ich habe dich ja gewarnt.
■ **to warn somebody not to do something** jemanden davor warnen, etwas zu tun
□ He warned me not to go there. Er warnte mich davor, dort hinzugehen.

warning NOUN
die Warnung

Warsaw NOUN
Warschau *neut*
■ **to Warsaw** nach Warschau

wart NOUN
die Warze

was VERB ▷ *see* **be**

wash NOUN
▷ *see also* **wash** VERB
■ **to have a wash** sich waschen
□ I had a wash. Ich habe mich gewaschen.
■ **to give something a wash** etwas waschen
□ He gave the car a wash. Er hat das Auto gewaschen.

to **wash** VERB
▷ *see also* **wash** NOUN
1 waschen (PRESENT wäscht, IMPERFECT wusch, PERFECT hat gewaschen)
□ to wash something etwas waschen
2 sich waschen *(have a wash)*
□ Every morning I get up, wash and get dressed. Jeden Morgen stehe ich auf, wasche mich und ziehe mich an.
■ **to wash one's hands** sich die Hände waschen □ Where can I wash my hands? Wo kann ich mir die Hände waschen?
■ **to wash one's hair** sich die Haare waschen
□ You should wash your hair. Du solltest dir die Haare waschen.
■ **to wash up** abwaschen

washbasin NOUN
das Waschbecken (PL die Waschbecken)

washcloth NOUN (US)
der Waschlappen (PL die Waschlappen)

washing NOUN
die Wäsche *(clothes)*
■ **Have you got any washing?** Hast du etwas zu waschen?
■ **to do the washing** Wäsche waschen

washing machine NOUN
die Waschmaschine

washing powder NOUN
das Waschpulver (PL die Waschpulver)

washing-up NOUN
der Abwasch
□ to do the washing-up den Abwasch machen

washing-up liquid NOUN
das Spülmittel (PL die Spülmittel)

wasn't = **was not**

wasp NOUN
die Wespe

waste NOUN
▷ *see also* **waste** VERB
1 die Verschwendung
□ It's such a waste! Es ist so eine Verschwendung! □ It's a waste of time. Es ist Zeitverschwendung!
2 der Müll *(rubbish)*
□ nuclear waste der Atommüll

to **waste** VERB
▷ *see also* **waste** NOUN
verschwenden (PERFECT hat verschwendet)
□ I don't like wasting money. Ich verschwende nicht gerne Geld. □ There's no time to waste. Wir haben keine Zeit zu verschwenden.

wastepaper basket NOUN
der Papierkorb (PL die Papierkörbe)

watch NOUN
▷ *see also* **watch** VERB
die Uhr

to **watch** VERB
▷ *see also* **watch** NOUN
1 ansehen (PRESENT sieht an, IMPERFECT sah an, PERFECT hat angesehen) *(film, video)*
□ Did you watch that film last night? Hast du dir gestern Abend den Film angesehen?
■ **to watch television** fernsehen
2 zusehen (PRESENT sieht zu, IMPERFECT sah zu, PERFECT hat zugesehen)
□ Watch me! Sieh mir zu!
3 beobachten (PERFECT hat beobachtet) *(keep a watch on)*
□ The police were watching the house. Die Polizei beobachtete das Haus.
■ **to watch out** aufpassen
■ **Watch out!** Pass auf!

water NOUN
▷ *see also* **water** VERB
das Wasser (PL die Wasser)

to **water** VERB
▷ *see also* **water** NOUN
1 gießen (IMPERFECT goss, PERFECT hat gegossen) *(plant)*
□ He was watering his tulips. Er goss seine Tulpen.
2 sprengen *(garden)*
□ We should water the lawn. Wir sollten den Rasen sprengen.

waterfall NOUN
der Wasserfall (PL die Wasserfälle)

watering can NOUN
die Gießkanne

watermelon NOUN
die Wassermelone

waterproof ADJECTIVE
wasserdicht
□ Is this jacket waterproof? Ist die Jacke wasserdicht?

water-skiing NOUN
das Wasserskifahren
■ **to go water-skiing** Wasserski fahren

wave NOUN
▷ *see also* **wave** VERB
die Welle *(in water)*
■ **We gave him a wave.** Wir haben ihm zugewinkt.

to **wave** VERB
▷ *see also* **wave** NOUN
winken
■ **to wave at somebody** jemandem zuwinken □ I waved at my friend. Ich winkte meinem Freund zu.
■ **to wave goodbye** zum Abschied winken □ I waved her goodbye. Ich habe ihr zum Abschied gewinkt.

wavy ADJECTIVE
wellig
□ wavy hair welliges Haar

wax NOUN
das Wachs (GEN des Wachses)

way NOUN
1 die Art und Weise *(manner)*
□ That's no way to talk to your mother! Das ist keine Art und Weise, mit deiner Mutter zu reden!
■ **She looked at me in a strange way.** Sie sah mich sonderbar an.
■ **This book tells you the right way to do it.** Dieses Buch erklärt, wie man es machen muss.
■ **You're doing it the wrong way.** Du machst das falsch.
■ **In a way you're right.** In gewisser Weise hast du recht.
■ **a way of life** eine Art zu leben
2 der Weg *(route)*
□ I don't know the way. Ich kenne den Weg nicht.
■ **on the way** unterwegs □ We stopped for lunch on the way. Wir haben unterwegs angehalten und zu Mittag gegessen.
□ He's on his way. Er ist unterwegs.
■ **It's a long way.** Es ist weit. □ Berlin is a long way from London. Berlin ist weit von London entfernt.
■ **Which way is it?** In welcher Richtung ist es?
■ **The supermarket is this way.** Zum Supermarkt geht es in diese Richtung.
■ **Do you know the way to the hotel?** Wissen Sie, wie man zum Hotel kommt?
■ **'way in'** 'Eingang'
■ **'way out'** 'Ausgang'
■ **by the way ...** übrigens ...

we PRONOUN
wir
□ We're staying here for a week. Wir sind eine Woche lang hier.

weak ADJECTIVE
schwach
□ Maths is my weakest subject. In Mathe bin ich am schwächsten.

wealthy ADJECTIVE
reich

weapon NOUN
die Waffe

to **wear** VERB
tragen (PRESENT trägt, IMPERFECT trug, PERFECT hat getragen) *(clothes)*
□ She was wearing a hat. Sie trug einen Hut.
□ She was wearing black. Sie trug Schwarz.

weather NOUN
das Wetter
□ What was the weather like? Wie war das Wetter? □ The weather was lovely. Das Wetter war herrlich.

English-German

weather forecast NOUN
die Wettervorhersage

Web NOUN
■ **the Web** das Web

web address NOUN
die Internetadresse

webcam NOUN
die Webcam (PL die Webcams)

webmaster NOUN
der Webmaster (PL die Webmaster)
die Webmasterin

web page NOUN
die Webseite

website NOUN
die Website (PL die Websites)

webzine NOUN
das Web-Magazin (PL die Web-Magazine)

we'd = **we had, we would**

wedding NOUN
die Hochzeit
■ **wedding anniversary** der Hochzeitstag
■ **wedding dress** das Brautkleid
■ **wedding ring** der Ehering

Wednesday NOUN
der Mittwoch (PL die Mittwoche)
□ on Wednesday am Mittwoch
□ every Wednesday jeden Mittwoch
□ last Wednesday letzten Mittwoch
□ next Wednesday nächsten Mittwoch
■ **on Wednesdays** mittwochs

weed NOUN
das Unkraut
□ The garden's full of weeds. Der Garten ist voller Unkraut.

week NOUN
die Woche
□ last week letzte Woche □ every week jede Woche □ next week nächste Woche
□ in a week's time in einer Woche
■ **a week on Friday** Freitag in einer Woche

weekday NOUN
■ **on weekdays** werktags

weekend NOUN
das Wochenende (PL die Wochenenden)
□ at the weekend am Wochenende
□ at weekends am Wochenende
□ last weekend letztes Wochenende
□ next weekend nächstes Wochenende

to **weigh** VERB
wiegen (IMPERFECT wog, PERFECT hat gewogen)
□ How much do you weigh? Wie viel wiegst du? □ First, weigh the flour. Wiegen Sie zuerst das Mehl.
■ **to weigh oneself** sich wiegen

weight NOUN
das Gewicht (PL die Gewichte)
■ **to lose weight** abnehmen
■ **to put on weight** zunehmen

weightlifter NOUN
der Gewichtheber (PL die Gewichtheber)

weightlifting NOUN
das Gewichtheben

weird ADJECTIVE
sonderbar

welcome NOUN
▷ *see also* **welcome** VERB
■ **They gave her a warm welcome.** Sie haben sie herzlich empfangen.
■ **Welcome!** Herzlich willkommen!
□ Welcome to Germany! Herzlich willkommen in Deutschland!

to **welcome** VERB
▷ *see also* **welcome** NOUN
■ **to welcome somebody** jemanden begrüßen
■ **Thank you! — You're welcome!** Danke! — Bitte!

well ADJECTIVE, ADVERB
▷ *see also* **well** NOUN
1 gut
□ You did that really well. Das hast du wirklich gut gemacht.
■ **to do well** gut sein □ She's doing well at school. Sie ist gut in der Schule.
■ **to be well** *(in good health)* gesund sein
□ I'm not very well at the moment. Ich bin im Moment nicht gesund.
■ **Get well soon!** Gute Besserung!
■ **Well done!** Gut gemacht!
2 na ja
□ It's enormous! Well, quite big anyway. Es ist riesig! Na ja, jedenfalls ziemlich groß.
■ **as well** auch □ We worked hard, but we had some fun as well. Wir haben hart gearbeitet, aber auch Spaß gehabt.

well NOUN
▷ *see also* **well** ADJECTIVE
der Brunnen (PL die Brunnen)

we'll = **we will**

well-behaved ADJECTIVE
artig

well-dressed ADJECTIVE
gut angezogen

wellingtons PL NOUN
die Gummistiefel *masc pl*

well-known ADJECTIVE
bekannt
□ a well-known film star ein bekannter Filmstar

well-off ADJECTIVE
gut situiert

Welsh ADJECTIVE
▷ *see also* **Welsh** NOUN
walisisch
■ **He's Welsh.** Er ist Waliser.
■ **She's Welsh.** Sie ist Waliserin.
■ **Welsh people** die Waliser *masc pl*

Welsh NOUN
▷ *see also* **Welsh** ADJECTIVE
das Walisisch (GEN des Walisischen) *(language)*

Welshman NOUN
der Waliser (PL die Waliser)

Welshwoman NOUN
die Waliserin

went VERB ▷ *see* **go**

were VERB ▷ *see* **be**

we're = **we are**

weren't = **were not**

west NOUN
▷ *see also* **west** ADJECTIVE
der Westen
□ in the west im Westen

west ADJECTIVE, ADVERB
▷ *see also* **west** NOUN
nach Westen
□ We were travelling west. Wir fuhren nach Westen.
■ **the west coast** die Westküste
■ **a west wind** ein Westwind *masc*
■ **west of** westlich von □ Stroud is west of Oxford. Stroud liegt westlich von Oxford.
■ **the West Country** der Südwesten Englands

western NOUN
▷ *see also* **western** ADJECTIVE
der Western (GEN des Western, PL die Western) *(film)*

western ADJECTIVE
▷ *see also* **western** NOUN
westlich
■ **the western part of the island** der westliche Teil der Insel
■ **Western Europe** Westeuropa *neut*

West Indian ADJECTIVE
▷ *see also* **West Indian** NOUN
westindisch
■ **He's West Indian.** Er ist aus Westindien.

West Indian NOUN
▷ *see also* **West Indian** ADJECTIVE
der Westinder (PL die Westinder)
die Westinderin *(person)*

West Indies PL NOUN
die Westindischen Inseln *fem pl*
■ **in the West Indies** auf den Westindischen Inseln

wet ADJECTIVE
nass
□ wet clothes nasse Kleider □ to get wet nass werden
■ **wet weather** regnerisches Wetter
■ **dripping wet** klatschnass
■ **It was wet all week.** Es hat die ganze Woche geregnet.

wet suit NOUN
der Neoprenanzug (PL die Neoprenanzüge)

we've = **we have**

whale NOUN
der Wal (PL die Wale)

what ADJECTIVE, PRONOUN
1 was
□ What are you doing? Was tust du? □ What did you say? Was hast du gesagt? □ What is it? Was ist das? □ What's the matter? Was ist los? □ What happened? Was ist passiert? □ I saw what happened. Ich habe gesehen, was passiert ist. □ I heard what he said. Ich habe gehört, was er gesagt hat.
■ **What?** Was?
2 welcher
□ What name? Welcher Name?
welche
□ What colour is it? Welche Farbe hat es?
welches
□ What book do you want? Welches Buch möchten Sie?
welche
□ What subjects are you studying? Welche Fächer studierst du?
■ **What's the capital of Finland?** Wie heißt die Hauptstadt von Finnland?
■ **What a mess!** So ein Chaos!

wheat NOUN
der Weizen

wheel NOUN
das Rad (PL die Räder)
■ **the steering wheel** das Lenkrad

wheelchair NOUN
der Rollstuhl (PL die Rollstühle)

when ADVERB, CONJUNCTION
1 wann
□ When did he go? Wann ist er gegangen?
2 als
□ She was reading when I came in. Sie las, als ich hereinkam.

where ADVERB, CONJUNCTION
wo
□ Where's Emma today? Wo ist Emma heute? □ Where do you live? Wo wohnst du? □ a shop where you can buy gardening tools ein Geschäft, wo man Gartengeräte kaufen kann
■ **Where are you from?** Woher sind Sie?
■ **Where are you going?** Wohin gehst du?

LANGUAGE TIP Be careful not to translate **where** by **wer**.

whether CONJUNCTION
ob
□ I don't know whether to go or not. Ich weiß nicht, ob ich gehen soll oder nicht.

which ADJECTIVE, PRONOUN
1 welcher
□ Which coat is yours? Welcher Mantel ist deiner?
welche
□ Which CD did you buy? Welche CD hast du gekauft?
welches
□ Which book do you want? Welches Buch willst du?
welche
□ Which shoes should I wear? Welche Schuhe soll ich anziehen?

LANGUAGE TIP When asking 'which one' use **welcher** or **welche** or **welches**, depending on whether the noun is masculine, feminine or neuter.

■ **I know his brother. — Which one?** Ich kenne seinen Bruder. — Welchen?

■ **I know his sister. — Which one?** Ich kenne seine Schwester. — Welche?

■ **I took one of your books. — Which one?** Ich habe eines deiner Bücher genommen. — Welches?

■ **Which would you like?** Welches möchtest du?

■ **Which of these are yours?** Welche davon gehören dir?

LANGUAGE TIP In relative clauses use **der**, **die** or **das**, depending on the gender of the noun 'which' refers to.

2 der

□ the film which is on now der Film, der gerade läuft

die

□ the CD which is playing now die CD, die gerade läuft

das

□ the book which I am reading das Buch, das ich lese

die

□ the sweets which I ate die Süßigkeiten, die ich gegessen habe

while CONJUNCTION

▷ *see also* **while** NOUN

während

□ You hold the torch while I look inside. Halt du die Taschenlampe, während ich hineinsehe. □ She's dynamic, while he's more laid-back. Sie ist dynamisch, während er eher lässig ist.

while NOUN

▷ *see also* **while** CONJUNCTION

die Weile

□ after a while nach einer Weile

■ **a while ago** vor einer Weile □ He was here a while ago. Er war vor einer Weile hier.

■ **for a while** eine Zeit lang □ I lived in London for a while. Ich habe eine Zeit lang in London gelebt.

■ **quite a while** ziemlich lange

□ That happened quite a while ago. Das ist schon ziemlich lange her. □ I haven't seen him for quite a while. Ich habe ihn schon ziemlich lange nicht mehr gesehen.

whip NOUN

▷ *see also* **whip** VERB

die Peitsche

to **whip** VERB

▷ *see also* **whip** NOUN

1 peitschen

□ She whipped her horse. Sie peitschte ihr Pferd.

2 schlagen (PRESENT schlägt, IMPERFECT schlug, PERFECT hat geschlagen) *(eggs)*

whipped cream NOUN

die Schlagsahne

whisk NOUN

der Schneebesen (PL die Schneebesen)

whiskers PL NOUN

die Schnurrhaare *neut pl*

whisky NOUN

der Whisky (PL die Whiskys)

to **whisper** VERB

flüstern

whistle NOUN

▷ *see also* **whistle** VERB

die Pfeife

■ **The referee blew his whistle.** Der Schiedsrichter hat gepfiffen.

to **whistle** VERB

▷ *see also* **whistle** NOUN

pfeifen (IMPERFECT pfiff, PERFECT hat gepfiffen)

white ADJECTIVE

weiß

□ He's got white hair. Er hat weiße Haare.

■ **white wine** der Weißwein

■ **white bread** das Weißbrot

■ **white coffee** der Kaffee mit Milch

■ **a white man** ein Weißer

■ **a white woman** eine Weiße

■ **white people** die Weißen *masc pl*

whiteboard NOUN

die Weißwandtafel

□ an interactive whiteboard eine interaktive Weißwandtafel

Whitsun NOUN

das Pfingsten (GEN des Pfingsten, PL die Pfingsten)

who PRONOUN

1 wer

□ Who said that? Wer hat das gesagt?

□ Who's he? Wer ist er?

LANGUAGE TIP In relative clauses use **der**, **die** or **das**, depending on the gender of the noun 'who' refers to.

2 der

□ the man who saw us der Mann, der uns gesehen hat □ the man who we saw der Mann, den wir gesehen haben

die

□ the woman who saw us die Frau, die uns gesehen hat □ the woman who we saw die Frau, die wir gesehen haben

das

□ the child who saw us das Kind, das uns gesehen hat □ the child who we saw das Kind, das wir gesehen haben

die

□ the people who saw us die Leute, die uns gesehen haben

LANGUAGE TIP Be careful not to translate **who** by **wo**.

whole ADJECTIVE
▷ *see also* **whole** NOUN
ganz
□ the whole class die ganze Klasse
□ the whole day den ganzen Tag □ the whole world die ganze Welt

whole NOUN
▷ *see also* **whole** ADJECTIVE
■ **The whole of Wales was affected.** Ganz Wales war davon betroffen.
■ **on the whole** im Großen und Ganzen

wholemeal ADJECTIVE
■ **wholemeal bread** das Vollkornbrot
■ **wholemeal flour** das Vollkornmehl

wholewheat ADJECTIVE (US)
■ **wholewheat bread** das Vollkornbrot

whom PRONOUN
wen
□ Whom did you see? Wen hast du gesehen?
■ **the man to whom I spoke** der Mann, mit dem ich gesprochen habe
■ **the woman to whom I spoke** die Frau, mit der ich gesprochen habe

whose PRONOUN, ADJECTIVE
wessen
□ Whose book is this? Wessen Buch ist das?
■ **Whose is this?** Wem gehört das?
■ **I know whose it is.** Ich weiß, wem das gehört.
■ **the man whose picture was in the paper** der Mann, dessen Bild in der Zeitung war
■ **the woman whose picture was in the paper** die Frau, deren Bild in der Zeitung war
■ **the girl whose picture was in the paper** das Mädchen, dessen Bild in der Zeitung war

why ADVERB
warum
□ Why did you do that? Warum hast du das getan? □ Tell me why. Sag mir warum.
□ Why not? Warum nicht? □ All right, why not? Also gut, warum auch nicht?
■ **That's why he did it.** Deshalb hat er es getan.

wicked ADJECTIVE
1 böse *(evil)*
2 geil *(informal: really great)*

wicket NOUN
das Mal (PL die Male) *(stumps)*

wide ADJECTIVE, ADVERB
breit
□ a wide road eine breite Straße
■ **wide open** weit offen □ The door was wide open. Die Tür stand weit offen. □ The windows were wide open. Die Fenster waren weit offen.
■ **wide awake** hellwach

widow NOUN
die Witwe
□ She's a widow. Sie ist Witwe.

widower NOUN
der Witwer (PL die Witwen)
□ He's a widower. Er ist Witwer.

width NOUN
die Breite

wife NOUN
die Frau
□ his wife seine Frau

wig NOUN
die Perücke

wild ADJECTIVE
1 wild
□ a wild animal ein wildes Tier
2 verrückt *(crazy)*
□ She's a bit wild. Sie ist ein bisschen verrückt.

wild card NOUN
die Wildcard (PL die Wildcards)

wildlife NOUN
die Tierwelt
□ I'm interested in wildlife. Ich interessiere mich für die Tierwelt.

will NOUN
▷ *see also* **will** VERB
das Testament (PL die Testamente)
□ He left me some money in his will. Er hat mir in seinem Testament Geld vermacht.
■ **He came of his own free will.** Er ist freiwillig gekommen.

will VERB
▷ *see also* **will** NOUN

LANGUAGE TIP In German the present tense is often used to express somebody's intention to do something.

□ I'll show you your room. Ich zeige Ihnen Ihr Zimmer. □ I'll give you a hand. Ich helfe dir.
■ **Will you help me?** Hilfst du mir?
■ **Will you wash up? — No, I won't.** Wäschst du ab? — Nein.

LANGUAGE TIP Use the German future tense when referring to the more distant future.

□ I will come back one day. Ich werde eines Tages zurückkommen. □ It won't take long. Es wird nicht lange dauern.
■ **That'll be Dave.** Das wird Dave sein.
■ **Will you be quiet!** Werdet ihr wohl still sein!

willing ADJECTIVE
■ **to be willing to do something** bereit sein, etwas zu tun

to win VERB
▷ *see also* **win** NOUN
gewinnen (IMPERFECT gewann, PERFECT hat gewonnen)
□ Did you win? Hast du gewonnen?
■ **to win a prize** einen Preis bekommen

win NOUN
▷ *see also* **win** VERB
der Sieg (PL die Siege)

to wind VERB
▷ *see also* **wind** NOUN
1 wickeln *(rope, wool, wire)*

□ He wound the rope round the tree. Er wickelte das Seil um den Baum.

2 sich schlängeln *(river, path)*

□ The road winds through the valley. Die Straße schlängelt sich durch das Tal.

wind NOUN

▷ *see also* **wind** VERB

der Wind (PL die Winde)

□ a strong wind ein starker Wind

■ **a wind instrument** ein Blasinstrument *neut*

■ **wind power** die Windkraft

windmill NOUN

die Windmühle

window NOUN

das Fenster (PL die Fenster)

□ to break a window ein Fenster kaputt machen □ a broken window ein kaputtes Fenster

■ **a shop window** ein Schaufenster

windscreen NOUN

die Windschutzscheibe

windscreen wiper NOUN

der Scheibenwischer (PL die Scheibenwischer)

windshield NOUN (US)

die Windschutzscheibe

windshield wiper NOUN (US)

der Scheibenwischer (PL die Scheibenwischer)

windy ADJECTIVE

windig *(place)*

□ It's windy. Es ist windig.

wine NOUN

der Wein (PL die Weine)

□ a bottle of wine eine Flasche Wein

□ a glass of wine ein Glas Wein

■ **white wine** der Weißwein

■ **red wine** der Rotwein

■ **a wine bar** eine Weinstube

■ **a wine glass** ein Weinglas *neut*

■ **the wine list** die Getränkekarte

wing NOUN

der Flügel (PL die Flügel)

to **wink** VERB

■ **to wink at somebody** jemandem zublinzeln □ He winked at me. Er hat mir zugeblinzelt.

winner NOUN

der Sieger (PL die Sieger)

die Siegerin

winning ADJECTIVE

■ **the winning team** die Siegermannschaft

■ **the winning goal** das entscheidende Tor

winter NOUN

der Winter (PL die Winter)

□ in winter im Winter

winter sports PL NOUN

der Wintersport *sing*

to **wipe** VERB

abwischen (PERFECT hat abgewischt)

■ **to wipe one's feet** sich die Füße abstreifen

□ Wipe your feet! Streif dir die Füße ab!

■ **to wipe up** aufwischen

wire NOUN

der Draht (PL die Drähte)

wisdom tooth NOUN

der Weisheitszahn (PL die Weisheitszähne)

wise ADJECTIVE

weise

to **wish** VERB

▷ *see also* **wish** NOUN

■ **to wish for something** sich etwas wünschen □ What more could I wish for? Was mehr könnte ich mir wünschen?

■ **to wish to do something** etwas tun möchten □ I wish to make a complaint. Ich möchte mich beschweren.

■ **I wish you were here!** Ich wünschte, du wärst da!

■ **I wish you'd told me!** Wenn du mir das doch nur gesagt hättest!

wish NOUN

▷ *see also* **wish** VERB

der Wunsch (PL die Wünsche)

■ **to make a wish** sich etwas wünschen

□ You can make a wish. Du darfst dir etwas wünschen.

■ **'best wishes'** *(on greetings card)* 'Alles Gute'

■ **'with best wishes, Jo'** 'alles Liebe, Jo'

wit NOUN

der geistreiche Humor *(humour)*

with PREPOSITION

1 mit

□ Come with me. Komm mit mir. □ a woman with blue eyes eine Frau mit blauen Augen

■ **Fill the jug with water.** Tu Wasser in den Krug.

■ **He walks with a stick.** Er geht am Stock.

2 bei *(at the home of)*

□ We stayed with friends. Wir haben bei Freunden übernachtet.

3 vor

□ green with envy grün vor Neid □ to shake with fear vor Angst zittern

within PREPOSITION

■ **The shops are within easy reach.** Die Geschäfte sind schnell zu erreichen.

■ **within the week** innerhalb dieser Woche

without PREPOSITION

ohne

□ without a coat ohne einen Mantel

□ without speaking ohne etwas zu sagen

witness NOUN

der Zeuge (GEN des Zeugen, PL die Zeugen)

die Zeugin

□ There were no witnesses. Es gab keine Zeugen.

■ **witness box** der Zeugenstand

■ **witness stand** der Zeugenstand

witty ADJECTIVE

geistreich

wives PL NOUN ▷ *see* **wife**

woke up VERB ▷ *see* **wake up**
woken up VERB ▷ *see* **wake up**
wolf NOUN
der Wolf (PL die Wölfe)
woman NOUN
die Frau
■ **a woman doctor** eine Ärztin
won VERB ▷ *see* **win**
to **wonder** VERB
sich fragen
□ I wonder why she said that. Ich frage mich, warum sie das gesagt hat. □ I wonder what that means. Ich frage mich, was das bedeutet.
■ **I wonder where Caroline is.** Wo Caroline wohl ist?
wonderful ADJECTIVE
wunderbar
won't = **will not**
wood NOUN
1 das Holz (PL die Hölzer) *(timber)*
□ It's made of wood. Es ist aus Holz.
2 der Wald (PL die Wälder) *(forest)*
□ We went for a walk in the wood. Wir sind im Wald spazieren gegangen.
wooden ADJECTIVE
hölzern
■ **a wooden chair** ein Holzstuhl *masc*
woodwork NOUN
das Schreinern
□ Dieter's hobby is woodwork. Schreinern ist Dieters Hobby.
wool NOUN
die Wolle
□ It's made of wool. Es ist aus Wolle.
word NOUN
das Wort (PL die Wörter)
□ a difficult word ein schwieriges Wort
■ **What's the word for 'shop' in German?** Wie heißt 'shop' auf Deutsch?
■ **in other words** in anderen Worten
■ **to have a word with somebody** mit jemandem reden
■ **the words** *(lyrics)* der Text *sing* □ I really like the words of this song. Der Text dieses Liedes gefällt mir wirklich gut.
word processing NOUN
die Textverarbeitung
word processor NOUN
das Textverarbeitungssystem (PL die Textverarbeitungssysteme)
wore VERB ▷ *see* **wear**
work NOUN
▷ *see also* **work** VERB
die Arbeit
□ She's looking for work. Sie sucht Arbeit. □ He's at work at the moment. Er ist zurzeit bei der Arbeit. □ It's hard work. Das ist harte Arbeit.
■ **to be off work** *(sick)* krank sein
■ **He's out of work.** Er ist arbeitslos.

to **work** VERB
▷ *see also* **work** NOUN
1 arbeiten *(person)*
□ She works in a shop. Sie arbeitet in einem Laden. □ to work hard hart arbeiten
2 funktionieren (PERFECT hat funktioniert) *(machine, plan)*
□ The heating isn't working. Die Heizung funktioniert nicht. □ My plan worked perfectly. Mein Plan hat prima funktioniert.
■ **to work out 1** *(exercise)* trainieren □ I work out twice a week. Ich trainiere zweimal pro Woche. **2** *(turn out)* klappen □ In the end it worked out really well. Am Ende hat es richtig gut geklappt.
■ **to work something out** *(figure out)* auf etwas kommen □ I just couldn't work it out. Ich bin einfach nicht darauf gekommen.
■ **It works out at ten pounds each.** Das macht für jeden zehn Pfund.
worker NOUN
der Arbeiter (PL die Arbeiter)
die Arbeiterin
□ He's a factory worker. Er ist Fabrikarbeiter.
■ **She's a good worker.** Sie macht gute Arbeit.
work experience NOUN
das Praktikum (PL die Praktika)
□ work experience in a factory ein Praktikum in einer Fabrik
working-class ADJECTIVE
der Arbeiterklasse
□ a working-class family eine Familie der Arbeiterklasse
workman NOUN
der Arbeiter (PL die Arbeiter)
works NOUN
das Werk (PL die Werke) *(factory)*
worksheet NOUN
das Arbeitsblatt (PL die Arbeitsblätter)
workshop NOUN
die Werkstatt (PL die Werkstätten)
■ **a drama workshop** ein Theaterworkshop *masc*
workspace NOUN
der Arbeitsplatz (GEN des Arbeitsplatzes, PL die Arbeitsplätze)
workstation NOUN
der Arbeitsplatzcomputer (PL die Arbeitsplatzcomputer)
world NOUN
die Welt
■ **He's the world champion.** Er ist der Weltmeister.
World Wide Web NOUN
■ **the World Wide Web** das World Wide Web
worm NOUN
der Wurm (PL die Würmer)
worn VERB ▷ *see* **wear**
worn ADJECTIVE
abgenutzt

□ The carpet is a bit worn. Der Teppich ist etwas abgenutzt.

■ **worn out** *(tired)* erschöpft

worried ADJECTIVE
besorgt

□ She's very worried. Sie ist sehr besorgt.

■ **to be worried about something** sich wegen etwas Sorgen machen □ I'm worried about the exam. Ich mache mir wegen der Prüfung Sorgen.

■ **to look worried** besorgt aussehen

□ She looks worried. Sie sieht besorgt aus.

to **worry** VERB
sich Sorgen machen

□ You worry too much. Du machst dir zu viele Sorgen.

■ **Don't worry!** Keine Sorge!

worse ADJECTIVE, ADVERB
schlechter

□ My results were bad, but his were even worse. Meine Noten waren schlecht, aber seine waren noch schlechter. □ I'm feeling worse. Mir geht es schlechter.

■ **It was even worse than that.** Es war sogar noch schlimmer.

to **worship** VERB
anbeten (PERFECT hat angebetet)

□ He worships Lucy. Er betet Lucy an.

worst ADJECTIVE
▷ *see also* **worst** NOUN

■ **the worst 1** der schlechteste □ the worst student in the class der schlechteste Schüler der Klasse **2** die schlechteste □ He got the worst mark in the whole class. Er hat von der ganzen Klasse die schlechteste Note bekommen. **3** das schlechteste □ the worst report I've ever had das schlechteste Zeugnis, das ich je hatte

■ **my worst enemy** mein schlimmster Feind

■ **Maths is my worst subject.** In Mathe bin ich am schlechtesten.

worst NOUN
▷ *see also* **worst** ADJECTIVE
das Schlimmste (GEN des Schlimmsten)

□ The worst of it is that ... Das Schlimmste daran ist, dass ...

■ **at worst** schlimmstenfalls

■ **if the worst comes to the worst** schlimmstenfalls

worth ADJECTIVE

■ **to be worth** wert sein □ It's worth a lot of money. Es ist sehr viel Geld wert.

□ How much is it worth? Wie viel ist das wert?

■ **It's worth it.** Das lohnt sich. □ Is it worth it? Lohnt es sich? □ It's not worth it. Das lohnt sich nicht.

would VERB

■ **Would you like ...?** Möchtest du ...?

□ Would you like a biscuit? Möchtest du einen Keks? □ Would you like to go and see a film? Möchtest du ins Kino gehen?

■ **Would you close the door please?** Würden Sie bitte die Tür zumachen?

■ **I'd like ...** Ich würde gern ... □ I'd like to go to America. Ich würde gern nach Amerika fahren.

■ **Shall we go and see a film? — Yes, I'd like that.** Sollen wir ins Kino gehen? — Au ja!

■ **I said I'd do it.** Ich sagte, ich würde es tun.

■ **If you asked him he'd do it.** Wenn du ihn fragen würdest, würde er es tun.

■ **If you had asked him he would have done it.** Wenn du ihn gefragt hättest, hätte er es getan.

wouldn't = **would not**

wound VERB ▷ *see* **wind**

to **wound** VERB
▷ *see also* **wound** NOUN
verwunden (PERFECT hat verwundet)

□ He was wounded. Er wurde verwundet.

wound NOUN
▷ *see also* **wound** VERB
die Wunde

to **wrap** VERB
einpacken (PERFECT hat eingepackt)

□ She's wrapping the present. Sie packt das Geschenk ein.

■ **Can you wrap it for me please?** *(in shop)* Können Sie es mir bitte in Geschenkpapier einpacken?

■ **to wrap up** einpacken

wrapping paper NOUN
das Geschenkpapier

wreck NOUN
▷ *see also* **wreck** VERB
das Wrack (PL die Wracks)

□ That car is a wreck! Das Auto ist ein Wrack.
□ After the exam I was a complete wreck. Nach der Prüfung war ich ein totales Wrack.

to **wreck** VERB
▷ *see also* **wreck** NOUN

1 zerstören (PERFECT hat zerstört) *(building)*

□ The explosion wrecked the whole house. Die Explosion hat das ganze Haus zerstört.

2 kaputt fahren (PRESENT fährt kaputt, IMPERFECT fuhr kaputt, PERFECT hat kaputt gefahren) *(car)*

□ He's wrecked his car. Er hat sein Auto kaputt gefahren.

3 verderben (PRESENT verdirbt, IMPERFECT verdarb, PERFECT hat verdorben) *(plan, holiday)*

□ Our trip was wrecked by bad weather. Das schlechte Wetter hat uns den Ausflug verdorben.

wreckage NOUN
1 das Wrack (PL die Wracks) *(of vehicle)*
2 die Trümmer *pl (of building)*

wrestler NOUN
der Ringer (PL die Ringer)
die Ringerin

wrestling NOUN
das Ringen

□ His hobby is wrestling. Ringen ist sein Hobby.

wrinkled ADJECTIVE
faltig

wrist NOUN
das Handgelenk (PL die Handgelenke)

to **write** VERB
schreiben (IMPERFECT schrieb, PERFECT hat geschrieben)
□ to write a letter einen Brief schreiben
■ **to write to somebody** jemandem schreiben □ I'm going to write to her. Ich werde ihr schreiben.
■ **to write down** aufschreiben
□ I wrote down the address. Ich habe die Adresse aufgeschrieben. □ Can you write it down for me, please? Können Sie es mir bitte aufschreiben?

writer NOUN
der Schriftsteller (PL die Schriftsteller)
die Schriftstellerin
□ She's a writer. Sie ist Schriftstellerin.

writing NOUN
die Schrift
□ I can't read your writing. Ich kann deine Schrift nicht lesen.
■ **in writing** schriftlich

written VERB ▷ *see* **write**

wrong ADJECTIVE, ADVERB
1 falsch *(incorrect)*
□ The information was wrong. Die Information war falsch. □ the wrong answer die falsche Antwort
■ **You've got the wrong number.** Sie haben sich verwählt.
2 unrecht *(morally bad)*
□ I think fox hunting is wrong. Ich meine, dass Fuchsjagden unrecht sind.
■ **to be wrong** *(mistaken)* unrecht haben
□ You're wrong about that. Sie haben da unrecht.
■ **to do something wrong** etwas falsch machen □ You've done it wrong. Du hast das falsch gemacht. □ Have I done something wrong? Habe ich etwas falsch gemacht?
■ **to go wrong** *(plan)* schiefgehen
□ The robbery went wrong. Der Überfall ist schiefgegangen.
■ **What's wrong?** Was ist los?
■ **What's wrong with her?** Was ist mit ihr los?

wrote VERB ▷ *see* **write**

WWW ABBREVIATION *(= World Wide Web)*
■ **the WWW** das WWW

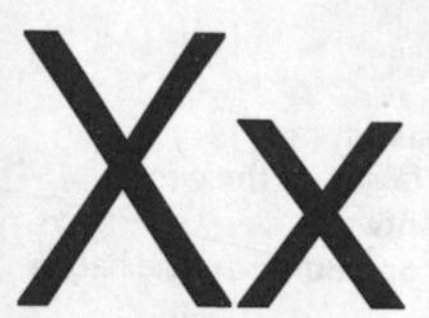

Xmas NOUN *(= Christmas)*
Weihnachten *neut*

to **X-ray** VERB
▷ *see also* **X-ray** NOUN
röntgen
□ They X-rayed my arm. Sie haben meinen Arm geröntgt.

X-ray NOUN
▷ *see also* **X-ray** VERB
die Röntgenaufnahme
■ **to have an X-ray** geröntgt werden

Yy

yacht NOUN
1 das Segelboot (PL die Segelboote) *(sailing boat)*
2 die Jacht *(luxury motorboat)*

yard NOUN
der Hof (PL die Höfe) *(of building)*
□ in the yard auf dem Hof

to **yawn** VERB
gähnen

year NOUN
das Jahr (PL die Jahre)
□ last year letztes Jahr □ next year nächstes Jahr □ to be fifteen years old fünfzehn Jahre alt sein
■ **an eight-year-old child** ein achtjähriges Kind

DID YOU KNOW...?
In Germany secondary schools, years are counted from the **fünfte Klasse** (youngest) to the **dreizehnte Klasse** (oldest).

□ year seven die fünfte Klasse □ year eight die sechste Klasse □ She's in year eleven. Sie ist in der neunten Klasse.
■ **He's a first-year.** Er ist in der fünften Klasse.

to **yell** VERB
schreien (IMPERFECT schrie, PERFECT hat geschrien)

yellow ADJECTIVE
gelb

yes ADVERB
1 ja
□ Do you like it? — Yes. Gefällt es dir? — Ja.
□ Yes please. Ja bitte.
2 doch

LANGUAGE TIP Use **doch** to contradict a negative statement or question.

□ Don't you like it? — Yes! Gefällt es dir nicht? — Doch! □ You're not Swiss, are you? — Yes I am! Sie sind nicht Schweizer, oder? — Doch, ich bin Schweizer. □ That's not true. — Yes it is! Das ist nicht wahr. — Doch!

yesterday ADVERB
gestern
□ yesterday morning gestern früh
□ yesterday afternoon gestern Nachmittag
□ yesterday evening gestern Abend
□ all day yesterday gestern den ganzen Tag
■ **the day before yesterday** vorgestern

yet ADVERB
1 noch
□ It has yet to be proved that ... Es muss noch bewiesen werden, dass ...
2 schon *(in questions)*
□ Has the murderer been caught yet? Ist der Mörder schon gefasst worden?
■ **not yet** noch nicht □ It's not finished yet. Es ist noch nicht fertig.
■ **not as yet** noch nicht □ There's no news as yet. Es gibt noch keine Nachricht.
■ **Have you finished yet?** Bist du fertig?

yield EXCLAMATION (US)
Vorfahrt achten *(on road sign)*

yob NOUN
der Rowdy (PL die Rowdys)

yoga NOUN
das Yoga *neut*

yoghurt NOUN
der Joghurt (PL die Joghurts)

yolk NOUN
das Eigelb (PL die Eigelbe)

you PRONOUN

LANGUAGE TIP Only use **du** when speaking to one person, and when the person is your own age or younger. Use **ihr** for several people of your own age or younger. If in doubt use the polite form **Sie**.

1 Sie *(polite form, singular and plural)*
□ Do you like football? Mögen Sie Fußball?
□ Can I help you? Kann ich Ihnen behilflich sein? □ I saw you yesterday. Ich habe Sie gestern gesehen. □ It's for you. Das ist für Sie.
2 du *(familiar singular)*
□ Do you like football? Magst du Fußball?
□ She's younger than you. Sie ist jünger als du. □ I know you. Ich kenne dich. □ I gave it you. Ich habe es dir gegeben. □ It's for you. Es ist für dich. □ I'll come with you. Ich komme mit dir mit.
3 ihr *(familiar plural)*
□ Do you two like football? Mögt ihr beiden Fußball? □ I told you to be quiet. Ich habe euch gesagt, ihr sollt still sein. □ This is for you two. Es ist für euch beide. □ Can I come with you? Kann ich mit euch mitkommen?

young ADJECTIVE
jung
□ young people junge Leute

younger ADJECTIVE
jünger
□ He's younger than me. Er ist jünger als ich.
□ my younger brother mein jüngerer Bruder
□ my younger sister meine jüngere Schwester

youngest ADJECTIVE
jüngste
□ his youngest brother sein jüngster Bruder
□ She's the youngest. Sie ist die Jüngste.

your ADJECTIVE

LANGUAGE TIP Only use **dein** when speaking to one person, and when the person is your own age or younger. For several people of your own age or younger use **euer**. If in doubt use the polite form **Ihr**.

1 Ihr *(polite form, singular and plural)*
□ your father Ihr Vater □ your mother Ihre Mutter □ your house Ihr Haus □ your seats Ihre Plätze
2 dein *(familiar singular)*
□ your brother dein Bruder □ your sister deine Schwester □ your book dein Buch □ your parents deine Eltern
3 euer *(familiar plural)*
□ your father euer Vater □ your mother eure Mutter □ your car euer Auto □ your teachers eure Lehrer

LANGUAGE TIP Do not use **Ihr, dein** or **euer** with parts of the body.

□ Would you like to wash your hands? Möchten Sie sich die Hände waschen?
□ Do you want to wash your hair? Möchtest du dir die Haare waschen? □ You two, go upstairs and brush your teeth. Ihr beide geht nach oben und putzt euch die Zähne.

yours PRONOUN

LANGUAGE TIP Only use **deiner/deine/deines** when talking to one person of your own age or younger. Use **euer/eure/eures** when talking to several people of your own age or younger. If in doubt use the polite form **Ihrer/Ihre/Ihres**.

1 Ihrer *(polite form, singular and plural)*
□ That's a nice coat. Is it yours? Das ist ein hübscher Mantel. Ist es Ihrer?
Ihre
□ What a pretty jacket. Is it yours? Was für eine hübsche Jacke. Ist das Ihre?
Ihres
□ I like that car. Is it yours? Das Auto gefällt mir. Ist es Ihres?
Ihre
□ my parents and yours meine Eltern und Ihre
■ **Is this yours?** Gehört das Ihnen?
□ This book is yours. Das Buch gehört Ihnen.
■ **Yours sincerely, ...** Mit freundlichen Grüßen ...
2 deiner *(familiar singular)*
□ I've lost my pen. Can I use yours? Ich habe meinen Schreiber verlegt. Kann ich deinen benützen?
deine
□ Nice jacket. Is it yours? Hübsche Jacke. Ist das deine?
deines
□ I like that car. Is it yours? Das Auto gefällt mir. Ist das deines?
deine
□ my parents and yours meine Eltern und deine
□ My hands are dirty, yours are clean. Meine Hände sind schmutzig, deine sind sauber.
■ **Is this yours?** Gehört das dir? □ This book is yours. Das Buch gehört dir. □ Whose is this? — It's yours. Wem gehört das? — Es gehört dir.
3 euer *(familiar plural)*
□ My computer is broken. Can I use yours? Mein Computer ist kaputt. Kann ich euren benutzen?
eure
□ I haven't got a torch. Can I use yours? Ich habe keine Taschenlampe. Kann ich eure benutzen?
eures
□ Our house is bigger than yours. Unser Haus ist größer als eures.
eure
□ our parents and yours unsere Eltern und eure
■ **Is this yours?** Gehört das euch? □ These books are yours. Diese Bücher gehören euch.
□ Whose is it? — It's yours. Wem gehört das? — Es gehört euch.

yourself PRONOUN

LANGUAGE TIP Only use **dich/dir** when talking to one person of your own age or younger. If in doubt use the polite form **sich**.

1 sich *(polite form)*
□ Have you hurt yourself? Haben Sie sich verletzt? □ Tell me about yourself! Erzählen Sie etwas von sich!
2 dich *(familiar form)*
□ Have you hurt yourself? Hast du dich verletzt?
3 dir *(familiar form)*
□ Tell me about yourself! Erzähl mir etwas von dir! □ If you are not happy with yourself ... Wenn du mit dir selbst nicht zufrieden bist ...
4 selbst
■ **Do it yourself!** **1** Machen Sie es selbst! **2** Mach's selbst!

yourselves PRONOUN

LANGUAGE TIP Only use **euch** when talking to people of your own age or younger. If in doubt use the polite form **sich**.

1 sich *(polite form)*
□ Did you enjoy yourselves? Haben Sie sich amüsiert?
2 euch *(familiar form)*
□ Did you enjoy yourselves? Habt ihr euch amüsiert?

3 selbst

■ **Did you make it yourselves?** **1** Haben Sie es selbst gemacht? **2** Habt ihr es selbst gemacht?

youth club NOUN

das Jugendzentrum (PL die Jugendzentren)

youth hostel NOUN

die Jugendherberge

Yugoslavia NOUN

Jugoslawien *neut*

■ **in the former Yugoslavia** im ehemaligen Jugoslawien

Zz

zany ADJECTIVE
irre komisch
□ a zany film ein irre komischer Film

zebra NOUN
das Zebra (PL die Zebras)

zebra crossing NOUN
der Zebrastreifen (PL die Zebrastreifen)

zero NOUN
die Null

Zimbabwe NOUN
Simbabwe *neut*
□ in Zimbabwe in Simbabwe

Zimmer frame® NOUN
der Gehapparat (PL die Gehapparate)

zip NOUN
der Reißverschluss (GEN des Reißverschlusses, PL die Reißverschlüsse)

zip code NOUN (US)
die Postleitzahl

zip drive NOUN
das Zip-Laufwerk (PL die Zip-Laufwerke)

zipper NOUN (US)
der Reißverschluss
(GEN des Reißverschlusses, PL die Reißverschlüsse)

zit NOUN
der Pickel (PL die Pickel)

zodiac NOUN
der Tierkreis (GEN des Tierkreises)
■ **the signs of the zodiac** die Sternzeichen

zone NOUN
die Zone

zoo NOUN
der Zoo (PL die Zoos)

zoom lens NOUN
das Zoomobjektiv (PL die Zoomobjektive)

zucchini PL NOUN (US)
die Zucchini *pl*